FLORIDA PROBATE CODE AND RELATED PROVISIONS

ASPEN PUBLISHERS

FLORIDA PROBATE CODE AND RELATED PROVISIONS

With Commentary

2007–2008

D. Kelly Weisberg
Professor of Law
Hastings College of the Law
University of California

Wolters Kluwer
Law & Business

AUSTIN BOSTON CHICAGO NEW YORK THE NETHERLANDS

http://lawschool.aspenpublishers.com

To contact Customer Care, e-mail customer.care@aspenpublishers.com, call 1-800-234-1660, fax 1-800-901-9075, or mail correspondence to:

Aspen Publishers
Attn: Order Department
PO Box 990
Frederick, MD 21705

Printed in the United States of America.

1 2 3 4 5 6 7 8 9 0

ISBN: 978-0-7355-6993-5

About Wolters Kluwer Law & Business

Wolters Kluwer Law & Business is a leading provider of research information and workflow solutions in key specialty areas. The strengths of the individual brands of Aspen Publishers, CCH, Kluwer Law International and Loislaw are aligned within Wolters Kluwer Law & Business to provide comprehensive, in-depth solutions and expert-authored content for the legal, professional and education markets.

CCH was founded in 1913 and has served more than four generations of business professionals and their clients. The CCH products in the Wolters Kluwer Law & Business group are highly regarded electronic and print resources for legal, securities, antitrust and trade regulation, government contracting, banking, pension, payroll, employment and labor, and healthcare reimbursement and compliance professionals.

Aspen Publishers is a leading information provider for attorneys, business professionals and law students. Written by preeminent authorities, Aspen products offer analytical and practical information in a range of specialty practice areas from securities law and intellectual property to mergers and acquisitions and pension/benefits. Aspen's trusted legal education resources provide professors and students with high-quality, up-to-date and effective resources for successful instruction and study in all areas of the law.

Kluwer Law International supplies the global business community with comprehensive English-language international legal information. Legal practitioners, corporate counsel and business executives around the world rely on the Kluwer Law International journals, loose-leafs, books and electronic products for authoritative information in many areas of international legal practice.

Loislaw is a premier provider of digitized legal content to small law firm practitioners of various specializations. Loislaw provides attorneys with the ability to quickly and efficiently find the necessary legal information they need, when and where they need it, by facilitating access to primary law as well as state-specific law, records, forms and treatises.

Wolters Kluwer Law & Business, a unit of Wolters Kluwer, is headquartered in New York and Riverwoods, Illinois. Wolters Kluwer is a leading multinational publisher and information services company.

SUMMARY OF CONTENTS

CONTENTS

PREFACE AND ACKNOWLEDGMENTS

Florida Probate Code and Related Provisions, with Commentary, provides an authoritative guide to Florida probate law tailored to the unique needs of the law student. It furnishes explanations of fundamental legal principles, background on statutes (current as well as repealed), commentary on selected statutes, notations on important case law developments, citations to recent law review articles, and a glossary explaining key terminology. It also elucidates current legal developments in the cutting-edge areas of advance health care directives. The book is designed primarily for use in courses in Wills and Trusts.

This book, however, goes far beyond the study of state law by illuminating important legislation on many tangential areas that are relevant to probate law and also by including pertinent model legislation. Part I includes a selective presentation of statutes from a variety of Florida codes and the state constitution. Parts II and III explore relevant provisions of the Restatement (Third) of Property: Wills and Other Donative Transfers, vol. 1 (1999) and vol. 2 (2003), as well as the Restatement of Trusts, vols. 1 and 2 (2003). The Restatements of the Law are drafted by the American Law Institute, an influential group of lawyers, law professors and judges, and constitute a law reform project to clarify underlying principles and make policy recommendations.

The remaining Parts cover various uniform acts, including the Uniform Principal and Income Act, Uniform Probate Code (Article II), Uniform Prudent Investor Act, and Uniform Trust Code. Three new uniform acts were approved in 2006 and are included herein: the revised Uniform Anatomical gift Act, Uniform Power of Attorney Act, and the Uniform Prudent Management of Institutional Funds Act.

In 2006, the Florida legislature substantially revised state law relating to trusts. The legislature adopted a significant portion of the Uniform Trust Code (UTC), thereby creating the Florida Trust Code (effective July 1, 2007). The new Florida Trust Code is also included herein.

This book is intended to be especially "user-friendly." Unlike traditional codes, which are targeted to practitioners with some knowledge of the underlying substantive law and its statutory provisions, this Code is written for students. It assumes that the readers have little or no prior knowledge of the field and therefore provides essential explanations, commentary, and definitions.

In addition, it is organized topically, rather than chronologically, enabling readers to find a given statute easily. All statutes addressing a given topic—probate code provisions as well as family law provisions, for example—are included in one location. Thus, if a reader is interested is learning about the legal regulation of adoption, he or she will quickly locate pertinent statutory provisions from different Florida Codes—set forth in the same place. New headings to the statutes distill the content of the provisions, and legislative histories include essential information. A Table of Cases, a Table of Statutes, and a detailed Index also help students navigate the material.

Equally important, the substantive material is presented in a logical progression. That is, the framework of this Code reflects the same theoretical structure as the basic Wills and Trusts law course. Thus, the coverage of the Florida Probate Code explores intestate succession, family protection, the formalities of will execution, testamentary capacity, will doctrines (integration, incorporation by reference, republication by codicil, acts of independent significance, extrinsic evidence and mistake), revocation of wills, will contracts and will substitutes. Then the book turns its attention to trusts, including discussion of trust creation and validity, modification and termination of trusts, trustees, beneficiaries, charitable trusts, and fiduciary administration. Finally, it addresses problems of construction (classification of testamentary gifts, ademption, satisfaction, abatement, exoneration, lapse and class gifts), and health care decisionmaking (planning for disability and death).

In the preparation of this book, I would like to acknowledge the invaluable assistance of Professor Ed Halbach, University of California at Berkeley, Boalt Hall School of Law, for his advice regarding the selection of relevant provisions and commentary from the Restatements and the Uniform Trust Code. Also appreciated is the research assistance of Irene Pertsovsky, Sirena Roberts, and Michael Shemtoub, students at Hastings College of the Law.

For permission to reprint from other works, I would like to thank the publishers:

I invite you to contact me with any comments, criticisms, and suggestions.

D. Kelly Weisberg
Professor of Law, Hastings College of the Law
200 McAllister Street, San Francisco, CA 94102
weisberg@uchastings.edu

PART I

~

FLORIDA PROBATE CODE

I
INTESTATE SUCCESSION

This chapter explores the inheritance laws that apply when a person dies without a will (or without a valid will that affects all of the person's property). First, the chapter explains key definitions and terminology, jurisdictional issues, and issues regarding the disposition of the decedent's remains and personal effects. Second, the chapter explores patterns of estate distribution for the surviving spouse, children, and other relatives. Third, it focuses on questions of status (posthumous children, aliens, adoptees, nonmarital children, and disqualification for misconduct). Finally, it addresses problems of simultaneous death and prior transactions of the decedent (advancements, releases, and assignments).

I. Introduction

A. Definitions and Terminology

This section provides an explanation of essential terminology and also sets forth the definitions of key terms that appear in the Florida Probate Act.

The term "probate" has multiple meanings. The term refers to a process, procedure, and court. First, "probate" refers to the process of administration of an estate. It also signifies the procedure of proving that a will is valid (i.e., admitting the will to probate). Finally, it refers to the court that both admits the will to probate and supervises the administration of the estate.

The probate estate is the estate that is subject to administration. Note that property that passes outside of probate (i.e., "nonprobate property" such as joint tenancy property, life insurance, payable on death accounts at financial institutions) is not considered part of the probate estate.

"Administration" is the process of collecting and managing the decedent's property, paying creditors' claims and, finally, distributing the remaining property to the heirs or beneficiaries.

At common law, "descent" referred to the passage of real property to the heirs of a person who died intestate. "Distribution" referred to the passage of personal property to the intestate's next of kin. In modern usage, the rules regarding both types of property (real and personal) are the same.

At common law, the term "heir" referred to those who took the intestate's realty, whereas those who inherited the intestate's personal property were "next of kin." Today, the term refers to persons who take real and/or personal property of the intestate. (A person who dies without a will is an intestate; one who dies with a will dies testate.) At common law, the surviving spouse of an intestate decedent was not considered an heir (i.e., the surviving spouse could not inherit the decedent's real property). Today, the term "heirs" include spouses because modern intestacy statutes give spouses a share of the intestate estate. William M. McGovern, Jr. & Sheldon F. Kurtz, Wills, Trusts and Estates Including Taxation and Future Interests §2.4 at 64-65 (3d ed. 2004) [hereinafter McGovern & Kurtz].

According to the Restatement (Third) of Property: Wills and Other Donative Transfers §2.1(b) (1999) [hereinafter Restatement (Third) of Property], the decedent's intestate estate "consisting of that part of the decedent's net probate estate that is not disposed of by a valid will, passes at the decedent's death to the decedent's heirs as provided by statute." (The Restatements are a product of the American Law Institute, an organization of lawyers, law professors, and judges involved in codifying and explaining the interrelationship between statutory and decisional law.)

The Uniform Probate Code (UPC), promulgated by the National Conference of Commissioners on Uniform State Laws (NCCUSL), has had a significant influence on the law of succession. (Specific provisions are discussed throughout this Code.) The UPC is model legislation that was completed by the NCCUSL in 1969, and substantially revised in 1990. The UPC was the product of a collaboration between the NCCUSL and the Real Property, Probate and Trust Law Section of the American Bar Association.

NCCUSL is an organization of lawyers, judges, and law professors, appointed by the states to draft proposals for uniform and model laws and to work toward their enactment. The original version of the UPC was enacted in 18 states but was enacted in part in many additional states. In 1990, NCCUSL reformulated Article II of the UPC to respond to developments in the law of gratuitous transfers. According to a Prefatory Note to those revisions, these developments consisted of:

> (1) the decline of formalism in favor of intent-serving policies; (2) the recognition that will substitutes and other inter vivos transfers have so proliferated that they now constitute a major, if not the major, form of wealth transmission; (3)

the advent of the multiple-marriage society, resulting in a significant fraction of the population being married more than once and having step-children and children by previous marriages and in the acceptance of a partnership or marital-sharing theory of marriage.

Unif. Prob. Code art. II, Prefatory Note (1990, amended 1993).

The Florida legislature enacted the Florida Probate Act in 1933 and revised it in 1945. The legislature subsequently adopted new probate legislation in 1976 that incorporated various provisions of the Uniform Probate Code. In 1997, the state legislature removed gender-specific language (Laws 1997, ch. 97-102). The Florida legislature again revised the probate code in 2001. See Henry P. Trawick, Jr., Redfearn Wills & Administration in Florida §1-2 (2006) [hereinafter Trawick]. In 2006, the Florida legislature adopted the Uniform Trust Code (effective July 1, 2007), pertaining to trusts and trust administration. That legislation is discussed infra in Chapters IX through XIII.

FLORIDA STATUTES

§731.005. Title

Chapters 731-735 shall be known and may be cited as the Florida Probate Code and referred to as the "code."

(Laws 1974, ch. 74-106, §1; Laws 1975, ch. 75-220, §1. Amended by Laws 2001, ch. 2001-226, §4, effective January 1, 2002.)

§731.103. Establishment of death

. . . (3) A person who is absent from the place of his or her last known domicile for a continuous period of 5 years and whose absence is not satisfactorily explained after diligent search and inquiry is presumed to be dead. The person's death is presumed to have occurred at the end of the period unless there is evidence establishing that death occurred earlier. Evidence showing that the absent person was exposed to a specific peril of death may be a sufficient basis for the court determining at any time after such exposure that he or she died less than 5 years after the date on which his or her absence commenced. A petition for this determination shall be filed in the county in Florida where the decedent maintained his or her domicile or in any county of this state if the decedent was not a resident of Florida at the time his or her absence commenced.

(Laws 1974, ch. 74-106, §1; Laws 1975, ch. 75-220, §2. Amended by Laws 1997, ch. 97-102, §946, effective July 1, 1997; Laws 2003, ch. 2003-154, §1, effective June 12, 2003.)

§731.201. General definitions

Subject to additional definitions in subsequent chapters that are applicable to specific chapters or parts, and unless the context otherwise requires, in this code, in §409.9101, and in chapters 737, 738, 739, and 744, the term:

(1) "Authenticated," when referring to copies of documents or judicial proceedings required to be filed with the court under this code, means a certified copy or a copy authenticated according to the Federal Rules of Civil Procedure.

(2) "Beneficiary" means heir at law in an intestate estate and devisee in a testate estate. The term "beneficiary" does not apply to an heir at law or a devisee after that person's interest in the estate has been satisfied. In the case of a devise to an existing trust or trustee, or to a trust or trustee described by will, the trustee is a beneficiary of the estate. Except as otherwise provided in this subsection, the beneficiary of the trust is not a beneficiary of the estate of which that trust or the trustee of that trust is a beneficiary. However, if each trustee is also a personal representative of the estate, the beneficiary or beneficiaries of the trust as defined in §737.303(4)(b) shall be regarded as a beneficiary of the estate.

(3) "Child" includes a person entitled to take as a child under this code by intestate succession from the parent whose relationship is involved, and excludes any person who is only a stepchild, a foster child, a grandchild, or a more remote descendant.

(4) "Claim" means a liability of the decedent, whether arising in contract, tort, or otherwise, and funeral expense. The term does not include an expense of administration or estate, inheritance, succession, or other death taxes.

(5) "Clerk" means the clerk or deputy clerk of the court.

(6) "Court" means the circuit court.

(7) "Curator" means a person appointed by the court to take charge of the estate of a decedent until letters are issued.

(8) "Devise," when used as a noun, means a testamentary disposition of real or personal property and, when used as a verb, means to dispose of real or personal property by will or trust. The term includes "gift," "give," "bequeath," "bequest," and "legacy." A devise is subject to charges for debts, expenses, and taxes as provided in this code, the will, or the trust.

(9) "Devisee" means a person designated in a will or trust to receive a devise. Except as otherwise provided in this subsection, in the case of a devise to an existing trust or trustee, or to a trust or trustee of a trust described by will, the trust or trustee, rather than the beneficiaries of the trust, is the devisee. However, if each trustee is also a personal representative of the estate, the beneficiary or beneficiaries of the trust as defined in §737.303(4)(b) shall be regarded as a devisee.

(10) "Distributee" means a person who has received estate property from a personal representative or other fiduciary other than as a creditor or purchaser. A testamentary trustee is a distributee only to the extent of distributed assets or increments to them remaining in the trustee's hands. A beneficiary of a testamentary trust to whom the trustee has distributed property received from a personal representative is a distributee. For purposes of this provision, "testamentary trustee" includes a trustee to whom assets are transferred by will, to the extent of the devised assets.

(11) "Domicile" means a person's usual place of dwelling and shall be synonymous with residence.

(12) "Estate" means the property of a decedent that is the subject of administration.

(13) "Exempt property" means the property of a decedent's estate which is described in §732.402.

(14) "File" means to file with the court or clerk.

(15) "Foreign personal representative" means a personal representative of another state or a foreign country.

(16) "Formal notice" means formal notice under the Florida Probate Rules.

(17) "Grantor" means one who creates or adds to a trust and includes "settlor" or "trustor" and a testator who creates or adds to a trust.

(18) "Heirs" or "heirs at law" means those persons, including the surviving spouse, who are entitled under the statutes of intestate succession to the property of a decedent.

(19) "Incompetent" means a minor or a person adjudicated incompetent.

(20) "Informal notice" or "notice" means informal notice under the Florida Probate Rules.

(21) "Interested person" means any person who may reasonably be expected to be affected by the outcome of the particular proceeding involved. In any proceeding affecting the estate or the rights of a beneficiary in the estate, the personal representative of the estate shall be deemed to be an interested person. In any proceeding affecting the expenses of the administration and obligations of a decedent's estate, or any claims described in §733.702(1), the trustee of a trust described in §733.707(3) is an interested person in the administration of the grantor's estate. The term does not include a beneficiary who has received complete distribution. The meaning, as it relates to particular persons, may vary from time to time and must be determined according to the particular purpose of, and matter involved in, any proceedings.

(22) "Letters" means authority granted by the court to the personal representative to act on behalf of the estate of the decedent and refers to what has been known as letters testamentary and letters of administration. All letters shall be designated "letters of administration."

(23) "Other state" means any state of the United States other than Florida and includes the District of Columbia, the Commonwealth of Puerto Rico, and any territory or possession subject to the legislative authority of the United States.

(24) "Parent" excludes any person who is only a stepparent, foster parent, or grandparent.

(25) "Personal representative" means the fiduciary appointed by the court to administer the estate and refers to what has been known as an administrator, administrator cum testamento annexo, administrator de bonis non, ancillary administrator, ancillary executor, or executor.

(26) "Petition" means a written request to the court for an order.

(27) "Probate of will" means all steps necessary to establish the validity of a will and to admit a will to probate.

(28) "Property" means both real and personal property or any interest in it and anything that may be the subject of ownership.

(29) "Protected homestead" means the property described in §4(a)(1), Art. X of the State Constitution on which at the death of the owner the exemption inures to the owner's surviving spouse or heirs under §4(b), Art. X of the State Constitution. For purposes of the code, real property owned as tenants by the entirety is not protected homestead.

(30) "Residence" means a person's place of dwelling.

(31) "Residuary devise" means a devise of the assets of the estate which remain after the provision for any devise which is to be satisfied by reference to a specific property or type of property, fund, sum, or statutory amount. If the will contains no devise which is to be satisfied by reference to a specific property or type of property, fund, sum, or stat utory amount, "residuary devise" or "residue" means a devise of all assets remaining after satisfying the obligations of the estate.

(32) "Security" means a security as defined in §517.021.

(33) "Security interest" means a security interest as defined in §671.201..

(34) "Trust" means an express trust, private or charitable, with additions to it, wherever and however created. It also includes a trust created or determined by a judgment or decree under which the trust is to be administered in the manner of an express trust. "Trust" excludes other constructive trusts, and it excludes resulting trusts; conservatorships; custodial arrangements pursuant to the Florida Uniform Transfers to Minors Act; business trusts providing for certificates to be issued to beneficiaries; common trust funds; land trusts under §689.05;trusts created by the form of the account or by the deposit agreement at a financial institution; voting trusts; security arrangements; liquidation trusts; trusts for the primary purpose of paying debts, dividends,

interest, salaries, wages, profits, pensions, or employee benefits of any kind; and any arrangement under which a person is nominee or escrowee for another.

(35) "Trustee" includes an original, additional, surviving, or successor trustee, whether or not appointed or confirmed by court.

(36) "Will" means an instrument, including a codicil, executed by a person in the manner prescribed by this code, which disposes of the person's property on or after his or her death and includes an instrument which merely appoints a personal representative or revokes or revises another will.

(Laws 1974, ch. 74-106, §1; Laws 1975, ch. 75-220, §4; Laws 1977, ch. 77-174, §1; Laws 1985, ch. 85-79, §2; Laws 1987, ch. 87-226, §66; Laws 1988, ch. 88-340, §1; Laws 1993, ch. 93-257, §7. Amended by Laws 1995, ch. 95- 401, §6, effective July 1, 1995; Laws 1997, ch. 97-102, §949, effective. July 1, 1997; Laws 1998, ch. 98-421, §52, effective July 1, 1998; Laws 2001, ch. 2001-226, §11, effective January 1, 2002; Laws 2002, ch. 2002-1, §106, effective May 21, 2002; Laws 2003, ch. 2003-154, §2, effective June 12, 2003; Laws 2005, ch. 2005-108, §2, effective July 1, 2005.)

B. Jurisdiction and Venue

A person who desires to prove a will or to probate an estate must bring the action in the proper court, i.e., the court that has jurisdiction over such matters. The court that performs the functions of proving a will to be valid (i.e., "admitting the will to probate") and supervising the administration of the estate is called the "probate court."

In Florida, the circuit courts have probate jurisdiction based on legislation (that is, Florida Statutes §26.012) implementing the provisions of Article V of the Florida Constitution. The Florida Probate Act is supplemented by Florida Probate Rules that were adopted by the Florida Supreme Court. In cases of conflict between a statute and the rules on a procedural point, the rules have more weight. Trawick, supra, at §2-6. For discussion of jurisdiction and venue regarding trust proceedings, see Chapter IX, Part II C infra.

An action must be brought in a court that has venue over the matter. Generally, for purposes of administration of an estate, venue is based on the decedent's domicile at the time of death (Fla. Stat. §733.101(a)).

§26.012. Circuit courts have jurisdiction regarding decedents' estates

(1) Circuit courts shall have jurisdiction of appeals from county courts except appeals of county court orders or judgments declaring invalid a state statute or a provision of the State Constitution and except orders or judgments of a county court which are certified by the county court to the district court of appeal to be of great public importance and which are accepted by the district court of appeal for review. Circuit courts shall have jurisdiction of appeals from final administrative orders of local government code enforcement boards.

(2) They shall have exclusive original jurisdiction:

(a) In all actions at law not cognizable by the county courts;

(b) Of proceedings relating to the settlement of the estates of decedents and minors, the granting of letters testamentary, guardianship, involuntary hospitalization, the determination of incompetency, and other jurisdiction usually pertaining to courts of probate;

(c) In all cases in equity including all cases relating to juveniles except traffic offenses as provided in chapters 316 and 985;

(d) Of all felonies and of all misdemeanors arising out of the same circumstances as a felony which is also charged;

(e) In all cases involving legality of any tax assessment or toll or denial of refund, except as provided in §72.011;

(f) In actions of ejectment; and

(g) In all actions involving the title and boundaries of real property.

(3) The circuit court may issue injunctions.

(4) The chief judge of a circuit may authorize a county court judge to order emergency hospitalizations pursuant to part I of chapter 394 in the absence from the county of the circuit judge; and the county court judge shall have the power to issue all temporary orders and temporary injunctions necessary or proper to the complete exercise of such jurisdiction.

(5) A circuit court is a trial court.

(Laws 1972, ch. 72-404, §3; Laws 1974, ch. 74-209, §1; Laws 1977, ch. 77-119, §1; Laws 1980, ch. 80-399, §1; Laws 1981, ch. 81-178, §1; Laws 1981, ch. 81-259, §22; Laws 1982, ch. 82-37, §12; Laws 1984, ch. 84-303, §2; Laws 1991, ch. 91-112, §5; Laws 1994, ch. 94-353, §27; Laws 1995, ch. 95-280, §52. Amended by Laws 1998, ch. 98-280, §3, effective June 30, 1998; Laws 2004, ch. 2004-11, §1, effective October 1, 2004.)

§731.105. Probate is in rem proceeding

Probate proceedings are in rem proceedings.

(Laws 1975, ch. 75-220, §3.)

§733.101. Venue for probate matters

(1) The venue for probate of wills and granting letters shall be:

(a) In the county in this state where the decedent was domiciled.

(b) If the decedent had no domicile in this state, then in any county where the decedent's property is located.

(c) If the decedent had no domicile in this state and possessed no property in this state, then in the county where any debtor of the decedent resides.

(2) For the purpose of this section, a married woman whose husband is an alien or a nonresident of Florida may establish or designate a separate domicile in this state.

(3) Whenever a proceeding is filed laying venue in an improper county, the court may transfer the action in the same manner as provided in the Florida Rules of Civil Procedure. Any action taken by the court or the parties before the transfer is not affected by the improper venue.

(Laws 1974, ch. 74-106, §1; Laws 1975, ch. 75-220, §46. Amended by Laws 1997, ch. 97-102, §981, effective July 1, 1997; Laws 2001, ch. 2001-226, §78, effective January 1, 2002.)

FLORIDA CONSTITUTION

Article 5, §5(b)

The circuit courts shall have original jurisdiction not vested in the county courts, and jurisdiction of appeals when provided by generals law. They shall have the power to issue writs of mandamus, quo warranto, certiorari, prohibition and habeas corpus, and all writs necessary or proper to the complete exercise of their jurisdiction. Jurisdiction of the circuit court shall be uniform throughout the state. They shall have the power of direct review of administrative action prescribed by general law.

Article 5, §20(c) (3)

Circuit courts shall have jurisdiction of appeals from county courts and municipal courts, except those appeals which may be taken directly to the supreme court; and they shall have exclusive original jurisdiction in all actions at law not cognizable by the county courts; or proceedings relating to the settlement of the estate of decedents and minors, the granting of letters testamentary, guardianship, involuntary hospitalization, the determination of incompetency, and other jurisdiction usually pertaining to courts of probate; in all cases in equity including all cases relating to juveniles; of all felonies and of all misdemeanors arising out of the same circumstances as a felony which is also charged; in all cases involving legality of any tax assessment or toll; in the action of ejectment; and in all actions involving the titles or boundaries or right of possession of real property. The circuit court may issue injunctions. There shall be judicial circuits which shall be the judicial circuits in existence on the date of adoption of this article. The chief judge of a circuit may authorize a county court judge to order emergency hospitalizations pursuant to Chapter 71-131, Laws of Florida, in the absence from the county of the circuit judge and the county court judge shall have the power to issue all temporary orders and temporary injunctions necessary or proper to the complete exercise of such jurisdiction.

C. Disposition of Decedent's Remains

According to the weight of authority in this country, a person possesses a sufficient proprietary interest in his or her body to make a valid direction as to the place and manner of burial. Such directions, provided that they are reasonable, may be judicially enforced.

Early British common law recognized a property interest in dead bodies. Remigius N. Nwabueze, Biotechnology and the New Property Regime in Human Bodies and Body Parts, 24 Loy. L.A. Int'l & Comp. L. Rev. 19, 22 (2002). Thus, before the nineteenth century, creditors could seize the body of a deceased debtor for debts owed.

By the mid-nineteenth century, public sentiment had changed sufficiently that a new rule developed. Blackstone enunciated this rule (called "a no-property rule in dead bodies") by stating:

> **[t]hough the heir has a property interest in the monuments and escutcheons of his ancestors, he has none in their bodies or ashes; nor can he bring any civil action . . . against their bodies or ashes or violate their remains.**

Cited in *id.* at 23.
American courts rejected the British no-property-in-dead-bodies rule. One court denounced the rule as follows:

> **The dogma of the English ecclesiastical law, that a child has no such claim, no such exclusive power, no peculiar interest in the dead body of its parent, is so utterly inconsistent with every enlightened perception of personal right, so inexpressibly repulsive to every proper moral sense, that its adoption would be an eternal disgrace to American jurisprudence.**

Ritter v. Couch, 76 S.E. 428, 430 (W. Va. 1912) (cited in Nwabueze, supra, at 28).

Prior to the 1970s, few states had statutes providing that a person could direct the manner of disposal of his or her body. Frank D. Wagner, Annot., Enforcement of Preference

Expressed by Decedent as to Disposition of His Body After Death, 54 A.L.R.3d 1037 §2(a)(1973). Many states now do so.

In Florida, "any" person may follow the decedent's written instructions about either the disposition of the decedent's body or funeral (Fla. Stat. §732.804). Absent a testamentary disposition of the remains, however, Florida case law recognizes the right of the surviving spouse or (if there is no surviving spouse) the next of kin to dispose of the deceased's body. Crocker v. Pleasant, 778 So. 2d 978, 987 (Fla. 2001) (recognizing the constitutionally protected right of parents to the possession of their son's body for burial). See also Susan L. Thomas, Cemeteries and Dead Bodies, 9 Fla. Jur. 2d §79 (2007).

Further, according to Florida statute (Fla. Stat. §406.50(4)), if more than one legally authorized person claims a body for interment, the person (or persons) having priority pursuant to the state intestate succession law (Fla. Stat. §732.103) will prevail.

Florida courts have addressed the issue of whether a decedent's testamentary directions concerning his funeral arrangements would be binding if family members subsequently object. In Cohen v. Guardianship of Cohen, 896 So. 2d 950 (Fla. Dist. Ct. App. 2005), an appellate court ruled that the trial court did not abuse its discretion by adhering to the testator's oral wishes that he be buried with his wife in Florida in contravention of his earlier testamentary directions that he be buried in New York. The court held that a testamentary disposition of the testator's body is not conclusive evidence of intent if it can be shown by clear and convincing evidence that he or she intended a different disposition.

A conflict about the disposition of a family member's remains occurred in the much publicized Florida case of Terri Schiavo, a woman who was in a persistent vegetative state. Following a lengthy legal battle between her husband and her parents, her life support system was disconnected. Her husband and her parents continued to disagree—this time about the disposition of her body. The husband chose to have her remains cremated whereas the parents preferred burial. The husband prevailed when, based on state law, he was given possession of her remains. Mitch Stacy, Shiavo Kin: Marker Not Meant to Anger Her Parents, Intelligencer, June 22, 2005, at 7B.

Florida law also provides for anatomical gifts. Pursuant to Florida Statutes §§765.510 to 765.519, a person may dispose of his or her body by gift or by will.

§406.50. Disposition of dead bodies

All public officers, agents, or employees of every county, city, village, town, or municipality and every person in charge of any prison, morgue, hospital, funeral parlor, or mortuary and all other persons coming into possession, charge, or control of any dead human body or remains which are unclaimed or which are required to be buried or cremated at public expense are hereby required to notify, immediately, the anatomical board, whenever any such body, bodies, or remains come into its possession, charge, or control. Notification of the anatomical board is not required if the death was caused by crushing injury, the deceased had a contagious disease, an autopsy was required to determine cause of death, the body was in a state of severe decomposition, or a family member objects to use of the body for medical education and research.

(1) The person or entity in charge or control of the dead body or human remains shall make a reasonable effort to determine:

(a) The identity of the deceased person and shall further make a reasonable effort to contact any relatives of such deceased person.

(b) Whether or not the deceased person is entitled to burial in a national cemetery as a veteran of the armed forces and, if so, shall make arrangements for such burial services in accordance with the provisions of 38 C.F.R. For purposes of this subsection, "a reasonable effort" includes contacting the county veterans service office or regional office of the United States Department of Veterans Affairs.

(2) Such dead human bodies as described in this chapter shall be delivered to the anatomical board as soon as possible after death.

(3) Nothing herein shall affect the right of a medical examiner to hold such dead body or remains for the purpose of investigating the cause of death, nor shall this chapter affect the right of any court of competent jurisdiction to enter an order affecting the disposition of such body or remains.

(4) In the event more than one legally authorized person claims a body for interment, the requests shall be prioritized in accordance with s. 732.103.

For purposes of this chapter, the term "anatomical board" means the anatomical board of this state located at the University of Florida Health Science Center, and the term "unclaimed" means a dead body or human remains that is not claimed by a legally authorized person, as defined in §497.005, interment at that person's expense.

(Laws 1953, ch. 28163, §6; Laws 1969, ch. 69-106, §§15, 35; Laws 1973, ch. 73-334, §22. Amended by Laws 1991, ch. 91-168, §1, effective October 1, 1991; Laws 1996, ch. 96-251, §1, effective October 1, 1996; Laws 2002, ch. 2002-204, §1. Renumbered from 245.06 in Fla. St. 2002, Supp. Amended by Laws 2004, ch. 2004-301, §141, effective October 1, 2005.)

§732.804. Decedent's written instructions regarding disposition of the body

Before issuance of letters, any person may carry out written instructions of the decedent relating to the decedent's body and funeral and burial arrangements. The fact that cremation occurred pursuant to a written direction signed by the decedent that the body be cremated is a complete defense to a cause of action against any person acting or relying on that direction.

(Laws 1974, ch. 74-106, §1; Laws 1975, ch. 75-220, §43. Amended by Laws 1997, ch. 97-102, §971, effective July 1, 1997; Laws 2001, ch. 2001-226, §58, effective January 1, 2002.).

§765.510. Policy: encouragement of anatomical gifts

Because of the rapid medical progress in the fields of tissue and organ preservation, transplantation of tissue, and tissue culture, and because it is in the public interest to aid the medical developments in these fields, the Legislature in enacting this part intends to encourage and aid the development of reconstructive medicine and surgery and the development of medical research by facilitating premortem and postmortem authorizations for donations of tissue and organs. It is the purpose of this part to regulate the gift of a body or parts of a body, the gift to be made after the death of a donor.

(Laws 1974, ch. 74-106, §1; Laws 1975, ch. 75-220, §45; Laws 1984, ch. 84-264, §3. Renumbered from §732.910, by Laws 2001, ch. 2001-226, §60, effective January 1, 2002.)

§765.511. Relevant definitions

As used in this part, the term:

(1) "Bank" or "storage facility" means a facility licensed, accredited, or approved under the laws of any state for storage of human bodies or parts thereof.

(2) "Death" means the absence of life as determined, in accordance with currently accepted medical standards, by the irreversible cessation of all respiration and circulatory function, or as determined, in accordance with §382.009, by the irreversible cessation of the functions of the entire brain, including the brain stem.

(3) "Donor" means an individual who makes a gift of all or part of his or her body.

(4) "Hospital" means a hospital licensed, accredited, or approved under the laws of any state and includes a hospital operated by the United States Government or a state, or a subdivision thereof, although not required to be licensed under state laws.

(5) "Physician" or "surgeon" means a physician or surgeon licensed to practice under chapter 458 or chapter 459 or similar laws of any state. "Surgeon" includes dental or oral surgeon.

(Laws 1974, ch. 74-106, §1; Laws 1975, ch. 75-220, §45; Laws 1997, ch. 97-102, §973; Laws 1998, ch. 98-68, §5. Renumbered from §732.911, by Laws 2001, ch. 2001-226, §61, effective January 1, 2002.)

§765.512. Eligibility of donors of anatomical gifts

(1) Any person who may make a will may give all or part of his or her body for any purpose specified in §765.510, the gift to take effect upon death. An anatomical gift made by an adult donor and not revoked by the donor as provided in §765.516 is irrevocable after the donor's death. A family member, guardian, representative ad litem, or health care surrogate of an adult donor who has made an anatomical gift pursuant to subsection (2) may not modify, deny, or prevent a donor's wish or intent to make an anatomical gift from being made after the donor's death.

(2) If the decedent has executed an agreement concerning an anatomical gift, by signing an organ and tissue donor card, by expressing his or her wish to donate in a living will or advance directive, or by signifying his or her intent to donate on his or her driver's license or in some other written form has indicated his or her wish to make an anatomical gift, and in the absence of actual notice of contrary indications by the decedent, the document is evidence of legally sufficient informed consent to donate an anatomical gift and is legally binding. Any surrogate designated by the decedent pursuant to part II of this chapter may give all or any part of the decedent's body for any purpose specified in §765.510.

(3) If the decedent has not executed an agreement concerning an anatomical gift or designated a surrogate pursuant to part II of this chapter to make an anatomical gift pursuant to the conditions of subsection (2), a member of one of the classes of persons listed below, in the order of priority stated and in the absence of actual notice of contrary indications by the decedent or actual notice of opposition by a member of the same or a prior class, may give all or any part of the decedent's body for any purpose specified in §765.510:

(a) The spouse of the decedent;

(b) An adult son or daughter of the decedent;

(c) Either parent of the decedent;

(d) An adult brother or sister of the decedent;

(e) A grandparent of the decedent;

(f) A guardian of the person of the decedent at the time of his or her death; or

(g) A representative ad litem who shall be appointed by a court of competent jurisdiction forthwith upon a petition heard ex parte filed by any person, which representative ad litem shall ascertain that no person of higher priority exists who objects to the gift of all or any part of the decedent's body and that no evidence exists of the decedent's having made a communication expressing a desire that his or her body or body parts not be donated upon death; but no gift shall be made by the spouse if any adult son or daughter objects, and provided that those of higher priority, if they are reasonably available, have been contacted and made aware of the proposed gift, and further provided that a reasonable search is made to show that there would have been no objection on religious grounds by the decedent.

(4) If the donee has actual notice of contrary indications by the decedent or, in the case of a spouse making the gift, an objection of an adult son or daughter or actual notice that a gift by a member of a class is opposed by a member of the same or a prior class, the donee shall not accept the gift.

(5) The person authorized by subsection (3) may make the gift after the decedent's death or immediately before the decedent's death.

(6) A gift of all or part of a body authorizes:

(a) Any examination necessary to assure medical acceptability of the gift for the purposes intended.

(b) The decedent's medical provider, family, or a third party to furnish medical records requested concerning the decedent's medical and social history.

(7) Once the gift has been made, the rights of the donee are paramount to the rights of others, except as provided by §765.517.

(Laws 1974, ch. 74-106, §1; Laws 1975, ch. 75-220, §45; Laws 1984, ch. 84-264, §4; Laws 1985, ch. 85-62, §62; Laws 1995, ch. 95-423, §5; Laws 1997, ch. 97-102, §974; Laws 1998, ch. 98-68, §6; Laws 1999, ch. 99-331, §12. Renumbered from §732.912, and amended by Laws 2001, ch. 2001-226, §62, effective January 1, 2002. Amended by Laws 2003, ch. 2003-46, §2, effective July 1, 2003.)

§765.513. Donees of body parts and purposes of anatomical gifts

The following persons or entities may become donees of gifts of bodies or parts of them for the purposes stated:

(1) Any hospital, surgeon, or physician for medical or dental education or research, advancement of medical or dental science, therapy, or transplantation.

(2) Any accredited medical or dental school, college, or university for education, research, advancement of medical or dental science, or therapy.

(3) Any bank or storage facility for medical or dental education, research, advancement of medical or dental science, therapy, or transplantation.

(4) Any individual specified by name for therapy or transplantation needed by him or her.

However, the Legislature declares that the public policy of this state prohibits restrictions on the possible recipients of an anatomical gift on the basis of race, color, religion, sex, national origin, age, physical handicap, health status, marital status, or economic status, and such restrictions are hereby declared void and unenforceable.

(Laws 1974, ch. 74-106, §1; Laws 1975, ch. 75-220, §45; Laws 1994, ch. 94-305, §1; Laws 1997, ch. 97-102, §975; Laws 1998, ch. 98-68, §7. Renumbered from §732.913 by Laws 2001, ch. 2001-226, §63, effective January 1,2002.)

§765.514. Manner of executing anatomical gifts

(1) A gift of all or part of the body under §765.512(1) may be made by will. The gift becomes effective upon the death of the testator without waiting for probate. If the will is not probated or if it is declared invalid for testamentary purposes, the gift is nevertheless valid to the extent that it has been acted upon in good faith.

(2)(a) A gift of all or part of the body under §765.512(1) may also be made by a document other than a will. The gift becomes effective upon the death of the donor. The document must be signed by the donor in the presence of two witnesses who shall sign the document in the donor's presence. If the donor cannot sign, the document may be signed for him or her at the donor's direction and in his or her presence and the presence of two witnesses who must sign the document in the donor's presence. Delivery of the document of gift during the donor's lifetime is not necessary to make the gift valid.

(b) The following form of written instrument shall be sufficient for any person to give all or part of his or her body for the purposes of this part:

UNIFORM DONOR CARD

The undersigned hereby makes this anatomical gift, if medically acceptable, to take effect on death. The words and marks below indicate my desires:

I give:

(a) ___ any needed organs or parts;

(b) ___ only the following organs or parts

[Specify the organ(s) or part(s)]

for the purpose of transplantation, therapy, medical research, or education;

(c) ___ my body for anatomical study if needed. Limitations or special wishes, if any:

(If applicable, list specific donee)

Signed by the donor and the following witnesses in the presence of each other:

(Signature of donor) (Date of birth of donor)

(Date signed) (City and State)

(Witness) (Witness)

(Address) (Address)

(3) The gift may be made to a donee specified by name. If the donee is not specified by name, the gift may be accepted by the attending physician as donee upon or following the donor's death. If the gift is made to a specified donee who is not available at the time and place of death, the attending physician may accept the gift as donee upon or following death in the absence of any expressed indication that the donor desired otherwise. However, the Legislature declares that the public policy of this state prohibits restrictions on the possible recipients of an anatomical gift on the basis of race, color, religion, sex, national origin, age, physical handicap, health status, marital status, or economic status, and such restrictions are hereby declared void and unenforceable. The physician who becomes a donee under this subsection shall not participate in the procedures for removing or transplanting a part.

(4) Notwithstanding §765.517(2), the donor may designate in his or her will or other document of gift the surgeon or physician to carry out the appropriate procedures. In the absence of a designation or if the designee is not available, the donee or other person authorized to accept the gift may employ or authorize any surgeon or physician for the purpose.

(5) Any gift by a member of a class designated in §765.512(3) must be made by a document signed by that person or made by that person's witnessed telephonic discussion, telegraphic message, or other recorded message.

(Laws 1974, ch. 74-106, §1; Laws 1975, ch. 75-220, §45; Laws 1983, ch. 83-171, §1; Laws 1994, ch. 94-305, §2; Laws 1995, ch. 95-423, §6; Laws 1997, ch. 97-102, §976; Laws 1998, c.. 98-68, §8; Laws 1999, ch. 99-331, §13. Renumbered from §732.914 and amended by Laws 2001, ch. 2001-226, §64, effective January 1, 2002.)

§765.515. Donor cards and registry

(1) If a gift is made through the program established by the Agency for Health Care Administration and the Department of Highway Safety and Motor Vehicles under the authority of §765.521, the completed donor registration card shall be delivered to the Department of Highway Safety and Motor Vehicles and processed in a manner specified in subsection (4), but delivery is not necessary to the validity of the gift. If the donor withdraws the gift, the records of the Department of Highway Safety and Motor Vehicles shall be updated to reflect such withdrawal.

(2) If a gift is not made through the program established by the Agency for Health Care Administration and the Department of Highway Safety and Motor Vehicles under the authority of §765.521 and is made by the donor to a specified donee, the document, other than a will, may be delivered to the donee to expedite the appropriate procedures immediately after death, but delivery is not necessary to the validity of the gift. Such document may be deposited in any hospital, bank, storage facility, or registry office that accepts such documents for safekeeping or for facilitation of procedures after death.

(3) On the request of any interested party upon or after the donor's death, the person in possession shall produce the document for examination.

(4) The Agency for Health Care Administration and the Department of Highway Safety and Motor Vehicles shall develop and implement an organ and tissue donor registry which shall record, through electronic means, organ and tissue donation documents submitted through the driver license identification program or by other sources. The registry shall be maintained in a manner which will allow, through electronic and telephonic methods, immediate access to organ and tissue donation documents 24 hours a day, 7 days a week. Hospitals, organ and tissue procurement agencies, and other parties identified by the agency by rule shall be allowed access through coded means to the information stored in the registry. Costs for the organ and tissue donor registry shall be paid from the Florida Organ and Tissue Donor Education and Procurement Trust Fund created by §765.52155. Funds deposited into the Florida Organ and Tissue Donor Education and Procurement Trust Fund shall be utilized by the Agency for Health Care Administration for maintaining the organ and tissue donor registry and for organ and tissue donor education.

(Laws 1974, ch. 74-106, §1; Laws 1975, ch. 75-220, § 45; Laws 1983, ch. 83-171, §2; Laws 1987, ch. 87-372, §1; Laws 1995, ch. 95-423, §7; Laws 1996, ch. 96-418, §33; Laws 1998, ch. 98-68, §9; Fla. St. 2000, Renumbered from §732.915, and amended by Laws 2001, ch. 2001-226, §65, effective January 1, 2002.)

§765.516. Amendment of terms of, or revocation of, anatomical gifts

(1) A donor may amend the terms of or revoke an anatomical gift by:

(a) The execution and delivery to the donee of a signed statement.

(b) An oral statement that is made in the presence of two persons, one of whom must not be a family member, and communicated to the donor's family or attorney or to the donee.

(c) A statement during a terminal illness or injury addressed to an attending physician, who must communicate the revocation of the gift to the procurement organization that is certified by the state.

(d) A signed document found on or about the donor's person.

(2) Any gift made by a will may also be amended or revoked in the manner provided for amendment or revocation of wills or as provided in subsection (1).

(Laws 1974, ch. 74-106, §1; Laws 1975, ch. 75-220, §45; Laws 1983, ch. 83-171, §3; Laws 1995, ch. 95-423, §8; Laws 1997, ch. 97-102, §977; Laws 1998, ch. 98-68, §10. Renumbered from §732.916, by Laws 2001, ch. 2001-226, §66, effective January 1, 2002. Amended by Laws 2003, ch. 2003-46, §3, effective July 1, 2003.)

§765.517. Rights and duties at death

(1) The donee, as specified under the provisions of §765.515(2), may accept or reject the gift. If the donee accepts a gift of the entire body or a part of the body to be used for scientific purposes other than a transplant, the donee may authorize embalming and the use of the body in funeral services, subject to the terms of the gift. If the gift is of a part of the body, the donee shall cause the part to be removed without unnecessary mutilation upon the death of the donor and before or after embalming. After removal of the part, custody of the remainder of the body vests in the surviving spouse, next of kin, or other persons under obligation to dispose of the body.

(2) The time of death shall be determined by a physician who attends the donor at the donor's death or, if there is no such physician, the physician who certifies the death. After death and in the absence of other qualified personnel, this physician may participate in, but shall not obstruct, the procedures to preserve the donor's organs or tissues and shall not be paid or reimbursed by, nor be associated with or employed by, an organ procurement organization, tissue bank, or eye bank. This physician shall not participate in the procedures for removing or transplanting a part.

(3) The organ procurement organization, tissue bank, or eye bank, or hospital medical professionals under the direction thereof, may perform any and all tests to evaluate the deceased as a potential donor and any invasive procedures on the deceased body in order to preserve the potential donor's organs. These procedures do not include the surgical removal of an organ or penetrating any body cavity, specifically for the purpose of donation, until a properly executed donor card or document is located or, if a properly executed donor card or document cannot be located, a person specified in §765.512(3) has been located, has been notified of the death, and has granted legal permission for the donation.

(4) All reasonable additional expenses incurred in the procedures to preserve the donor's organs or tissues shall be reimbursed by the organ procurement organization, tissue bank, or eye bank.

(5) A person who acts in good faith and without negligence in accord with the terms of this part or under the anatomical gift laws of another state or a foreign country is not liable for damages in any civil action or subject to prosecution for his or her acts in any criminal proceeding.

(6) The provisions of this part are subject to the laws of this state prescribing powers and duties with respect to autopsies.

(Laws 1974, ch. 74-106, §1; Laws 1975, ch. 75-220, §45; Laws 1983, ch. 83-171, §4; Laws 1995, ch. 95-423, §9; Laws 1997, ch. 97-102, §978; Laws 1999, ch. 99-331, §14. Renumbered from §732.917 and amended by Laws 2001, ch. 2001-226, §67, effective January 1, 2002.)

§765.518. Anatomical gifts and eye banks

(1) Any state, county, district, or other public hospital may purchase and provide the necessary facilities and equipment to establish and maintain an eye bank for restoration of sight purposes.

(2) The Department of Education may have prepared, printed, and distributed:

(a) A form document of gift for a gift of the eyes.

(b) An eye bank register consisting of the names of persons who have executed documents for the gift of their eyes.

(c) Wallet cards reciting the document of gift.

(Laws 1974, ch 74-106, §1; Laws 1975, ch 75-220, §45; Laws 1977, ch 77-147, §462. Renumbered from §732.918, by Laws 2001, ch. 2001-226, §68, effective January 1, 2002.)

§765.5185. Corneal removal by medical examiners

(1) In any case in which a patient is in need of corneal tissue for a transplant, a district medical examiner or an appropriately qualified designee with training in ophthalmologic techniques may, upon request of any eye bank authorized under §765.518, provide the cornea of a decedent whenever all of the following conditions are met:

(a) A decedent who may provide a suitable cornea for the transplant is under the jurisdiction of the medical examiner and an autopsy is required in accordance with §406.11.

(b) No objection by the next of kin of the decedent is known by the medical examiner.

(c) The removal of the cornea will not interfere with the subsequent course of an investigation or autopsy.

(2) Neither the district medical examiner nor the medical examiner's appropriately qualified designee nor any eye bank authorized under §765.518 may be held liable in any civil or criminal action for failure to obtain consent of the next of kin.

(Laws 1977, ch. 77-172, §1; Laws 1978, ch. 78-191, §1; Laws 1997, ch. 97-102, §979; Fla. St. 2000, §732.9185. Renumbered from §32.9185 by Laws 2001, ch. 2001-226, §69, effective January 1, 2002. Amended by Laws 2002, ch. 2002-1, §111, effective May 21, 2002.)

§765.519. Anatomical gifts of eyes by licensed funeral directors

With respect to a gift of an eye as provided for in this part, a licensed funeral director as defined in chapter 497 who has completed a course in eye enucleation and has received a certificate of competence from the Department of Ophthalmology of the University of Florida School of Medicine, the University of South Florida School of Medicine, or the University of Miami School of Medicine may enucleate eyes for gift after proper certification of death by a physician and in compliance with the intent of the gift as defined in this chapter. No properly certified funeral director acting in accordance with the terms of this part shall have any civil or criminal liability for eye enucleation.

(Laws 1974, ch. 74-106, §1; Laws 1975, ch. 75-220, §45; Laws 1980, ch. 80-157, §1. Renumbered from §732.919, by Laws 2001, ch. 2001-226, §70, effective January 1, 2002. Amended by Laws 2004, ch. 2004-301, §148, effective October 1, 2005.)

II. Intestacy

A. Share of Surviving Spouse and Issue

The term "testate succession" refers to the passage of property under a decedent's will. "Intestate succession" refers to the passage of property of a decedent who dies without a valid will.

At common law, the distribution of personal property and the descent of land were handled differently. The bulk of wealth consisted of real property. Land could not be devised by will until the Statute of Wills in 1540. However, a widow had a right to a portion of her husband's real property in the form of "dower." The husband's correlative right in his deceased wife's estate was termed "curtesy." The common law rights of surviving spouses are explained further in Chapter II, Section IIA infra.

In regard to personal property, at common law a husband acquired title to the wife's personal property upon marriage. Therefore, upon the wife's death, the law had no need to provide for the husband's inheritance of the wife's personal property. At the husband's death, ecclesiastical courts distributed his personal property to his widow and children. McGovern & Kurtz, supra, §3.2 at 121.

According to the Statute of Distribution of 1670, a widow inherited one-third of her husband's personal property if he left surviving issue but one-half if he did not. Id., §2.1 at 43.

Most jurisdictions today have abolished dower and curtesy. See, e.g., Fla. Stat. §732.111 (abolishing dower and curtesy in Florida). The few jurisdictions that retain these marital estates make no distinction between the rights of a surviving wife or husband in recognition of equal protection issues. Most jurisdictions have replaced dower with the forced share. For further discussion of forced share, see Chapter II, Section II(B) infra.

Jurisdictions utilize various approaches today to compute the intestate share of a surviving spouse. According to the Restatement (Third) of Property §2.2, "An intestate decedent's surviving spouse takes a share of the intestate estate as provided by statute. The exact share differs among the states. . . ."

Statutes generally take into consideration the existence and number of surviving children and (if no children or their descendants survive), the existence of other close relatives. In addition, many jurisdictions reflect the influence of the Uniform Probate Code by taking into consideration whether the decedent or the surviving spouse had children from prior relationships or whether all the decedent's surviving descendants are also descendants of the surviving spouse.

According to the basic intestacy scheme in all jurisdictions, a decedent's intestate estate passes first to the surviving spouse. If the decedent dies without leaving a spouse surviving (e.g., if the decedent dies as a single person or if the decedent's spouse predeceases), then the decedent's entire intestate estate passes to his or her descendants. If the decedent dies without having either a surviving spouse or surviving descendants, then the decedent's ancestors and collateral relatives take the decedent's estate.

1. Intestate Share of Surviving Spouse

The intestate share of the surviving spouse, according to Florida law, is set forth

below. Pursuant to Florida Statutes §§732.102 and 732.103, the surviving spouse takes all of the intestate's property if the decedent had no surviving issue. The term "issue" is synonymous with the term "descendants."

If the decedent had surviving issue who are also issue of the surviving spouse, then the surviving spouse takes $60,000 of the intestate estate plus one-half of the balance of the estate (Fla. Stat. §732.102(2)). (The remainder of the balance of the intestate estate descends to their issue.)

On the other hand, if the decedent dies leaving issue who are not issue of the surviving spouse, then the surviving spouse receives one half of the intestate estate (Fla. Stat. §732.102(3)). (The decedent's issue receive the balance of the estate (Fla. Stat. §732.103).

The Uniform Probate Code operates somewhat differently, although the goal of providing adequately for the surviving spouse is the same. The UPC provides that the intestate share of a decedent's surviving spouse is the entire intestate estate if the decedent leaves no descendant or parent surviving or if all of the decedent's surviving descendants are also descendants of the surviving spouse (and there are no other descendants of the surviving spouse who survive the decedent) (UPC §2-102(1)(i), (ii)).

However, if the decedent is survived by a spouse and their issue, plus the surviving spouse also has descendants who are not descendants of the decedent (such as children from a prior marriage of the surviving spouse), then the surviving spouse takes the first $150,000, plus one-half the balance of the estate. (The $150,000 figure is a suggested amount and may be modified by jurisdictions adopting the UPC.) If the decedent leaves surviving issue who are not descendants of the surviving spouse (such as children from a decedent's prior marriage), then the surviving spouse takes $100,000 plus one-half the balance. In this manner, the UPC takes into account the modern reconstituted family. (Article II of the UPC is set forth in Part V of this Code.)

§732.101. Intestate estate

(1) Any part of the estate of a decedent not effectively disposed of by will passes to the decedent's heirs as prescribed in the following sections of this code.

(2) The decedent's death is the event that vests the heirs' right to the decedent's intestate property.
(Laws 1974, ch. 74-106, §1; Laws 1975, ch. 75-220, §8. Amended by Laws 2001, ch. 2001-226, §14, effective January 1, 2002.)

§732.102. Surviving spouse's share of intestate estate

The intestate share of the surviving spouse is:

(1) If there is no surviving lineal descendant of the decedent, the entire intestate estate.

(2) If there are surviving lineal descendants of the decedent, all of whom are also lineal descendants of the surviving spouse, the first $60,000 of the intestate estate, plus one-half of the balance of the intestate estate. Property allocated to the surviving spouse to satisfy the $60,000 shall be valued at the fair market value on the date of distribution.

(3) If there are surviving lineal descendants, one or more of whom are not lineal descendants of the surviving spouse, one-half of the intestate estate.
(Laws 1974, ch. 74-106, §1; Laws 1975, ch. 75-220, §8. Amended by Laws 2001, ch. 2001-226, §15, effective January. 1, 2002.)

§732.103. Share of other heirs

The part of the intestate estate not passing to the surviving spouse under §732.102, or the entire intestate estate if there is no surviving spouse, descends as follows:

(1) To the lineal descendants of the decedent.

(2) If there is no lineal descendant, to the decedent's father and mother equally, or to the survivor of them.

(3) If there is none of the foregoing, to the decedent's brothers and sisters and the descendants of deceased brothers and sisters.

(4) If there is none of the foregoing, the estate shall be divided, one-half of which shall go to the decedent's paternal, and the other half to the decedent's maternal, kindred in the following order:

(a) To the grandfather and grandmother equally, or to the survivor of them.

(b) If there is no grandfather or grandmother, to uncles and aunts and descendants of deceased uncles and aunts of the decedent.

(c) If there is either no paternal kindred or no maternal kindred, the estate shall go to the other kindred who survive, in the order stated above.

(5) If there is no kindred of either part, the whole of the property shall go to the kindred of the last deceased spouse of the decedent as if the deceased spouse had survived the decedent and then died intestate entitled to the estate.

(6) If none of the foregoing, and if any of the descendants of the decedent's great-grandparents were Holocaust victims as defined in §626.9543(3)(b), including such victims in countries cooperating with the discriminatory policies of Nazi Germany, then to the lineal descendants of the great-grandparents. The court shall allow any such descendant to meet a reasonable, not unduly restrictive, standard of

proof to substantiate his or her lineage. This subsection only applies to escheated property and shall cease to be effective for proceedings filed after December 31, 2004.

(Laws 1974, ch. 74-106, §1; L. 1975, ch. 75-220, §8; L. 1977, ch. 77-174, §1. Amended by Laws 2001, ch. 2001-226, §16, effective January 1, 2002; Laws 2004, ch. 2004-390, §145, effective July 1, 2004; Laws 2006, ch. 2006-1, §102, effective July 4, 2006.)

§732.104. Inheritance per stirpes

Descent shall be per stirpes, whether to lineal descendants or to collateral heirs.

(Laws 1974, ch. 74-106, §1; Laws 1975, ch. 75-220, §9.)

2. Intestate Share of Surviving Issue

Intestacy schemes generally provide that descendants take the portion of a decedent's intestate estate that does not pass to the surviving spouse (or all of the intestate estate if the decedent is single at the time of death).

However, if more than one descendant survives, a determination must be made regarding the applicable method of dividing the decedent's property. If all of the decedent's children are alive, the decedent's property generally passes to them in equal shares (a per capita distribution). But, if some (or all) of the decedent's children predecease the intestate and those dead children leave issue surviving the decedent, then jurisdictions apply one of three different methods of property division:

- per stirpes,
- per capita with representation, or
- per capita at each generation.

The common law adopted a method of division called per stirpes. McGovern & Kurtz, supra, at §2.2. In this system, the ultimate takers of the intestate's estate are determined by roots or stocks. Under the principle of "representation," a descendant takes the share (or stands in the shoes) of his or her immediate, predeceased ancestor. Note that this method is subject to two principles: (1) a descendant who is related to the decedent more remotely than his or her immediate ancestor cannot inherit intestate if that immediate ancestor is still alive; and (2) many states (but not Florida) provide by statute that if all the issue are of the same degree of kinship to the decedent, then these issue share equally.

To illustrate, suppose the decedent had two children (A and B). One of those children (B) predeceased the decedent, leaving two children (C and D). When the decedent's intestate estate is divided according to a traditional per stirpes distribution, A would take one-half of the estate, but C and D would each take one-fourth (because they would share their dead parent B's share). This is the approach followed by Florida (discussed below).

Now suppose that the decedent leaves no child surviving. Rather, the decedent is survived only by grandchildren and great-grandchildren. The central question becomes: Which generation shall be the "root generation," i.e., the generation at which the estate is first divided? Under the minority approach (followed by Florida), the root generation is the generation nearest to the decedent, even if there are no members of that nearest generation who are alive at the decedent's death.

Florida follows a per stirpes approach to distribution. See, e.g., Fla. Stat. §732.104 (descent shall be per stirpes among lineal descendents as well as collateral heirs); Fla. Stat. §732.611 (devises shall be per stirpes among descendants, issue, and multi-generational classes, unless the will provides for a different method of distribution). See also In re Davol's Estate, 100 So. 2d 188 (Fla. Dist. Ct. App. 1958) (construing former Florida statute to mean that the estate is always divided at the generation closest to decedent and thereby dividing decedent's estate to the children of her three deceased siblings in stirpital shares—each child taking a fractional share of the one-third share that his or her parent would have taken).

In 2006, by a statutory amendment, the Florida legislature clarified that a per stirpes rule was to apply to all devises, even those to multi-generation classes by inserting the words "to descendants, issue, and other multi-generation classes" following "all devises" in Florida Statutes §732.611.

§732.103. Share of other heirs

The part of the intestate estate not passing to the surviving spouse under §732.102 or the entire intestate estate if there is no surviving spouse, descends as follows:

(1) To the lineal descendants of the decedent.

(2) If there is no lineal descendant, to the decedent's father and mother equally, or to the survivor of them.

(3) If there is none of the foregoing, to the decedent's brothers and sisters and the descendants of deceased brothers and sisters.

(4) If there is none of the foregoing, the estate shall be divided, one-half of which shall go to the decedent's paternal, and the other half to the decedent's maternal, kindred in the following order:

(a) To the grandfather and grandmother equally, or to the survivor of them.

(b) If there is no grandfather or grandmother, to uncles and aunts and descendants of deceased uncles and aunts of the decedent.

(c) If there is either no paternal kindred or no maternal kindred, the estate shall go to the other kindred who survive, in the order stated above.

(5) If there is no kindred of either part, the whole of the property shall go to the kindred of the last deceased spouse of the decedent as if the deceased spouse had survived the decedent and then died intestate entitled to the estate.

(6) If none of the foregoing, and if any of the descendants of the decedent's great-grandparents were Holocaust victims as defined in §626.9543(3)(b), [FN1] including such victims in countries cooperating with the discriminatory policies of Nazi Germany, then to the lineal descendants of the great-grandparents. The court shall allow any such descendant to meet a reasonable, not unduly restrictive, standard of proof to substantiate his or her lineage. This subsection only applies to escheated property and shall cease to be effective for proceedings filed after December 31, 2004.

[FN1] Redesignated as §626.9543(3)(a) by Laws 2004, ch. 2004-390, §76.

(Laws 1974, ch. 74-106, §1; Laws 1975, ch. 75-220, §8; Laws 1977, ch. 77-174, §1. Amended by Laws 2001, ch. 2001-226, §16, effective January 1, 2002; Laws 2004, ch. 2004-390, §145, effective July 1, 2004; L. 2006, ch. 2006-1, §102, effective July 4, 2006.)

§732.104. Descent shall be per stirpes

Descent shall be per stirpes, whether to lineal descendants or to collateral heirs.

(Laws 1974, ch. 74-106, §1; Laws 1975, ch. 75-220, §9.)

§732.611. All devises shall be per stirpes, even to multi-generational issue

Unless the will provides otherwise, all devises to descendants, issue, and other multigeneration classes shall be per stirpes.

(Laws 1974, ch. 74-106, §1; Laws 1975, ch. 75-220, §38. Amended by Laws 2006, ch. 2006-217, §35, effective July 1, 2007.)

B. Shares of Ascendants and Collateral Relatives

In the event that the intestate dies without leaving any surviving spouse or descendants, then the decedent's ancestors and collateral relatives succeed to the intestate's estate. Ascendants (or ancestors) are those persons who are related to the intestate in the ascending line (e.g., the decedent's parents or grandparents). Collateral relatives are those who are related to the decedent through an ancestor such as a parent or grandparent. Collateral relatives would include the decedent's brothers, sisters, nieces, nephews, cousins, etc. Under the intestacy scheme of all states, descendants (those related in a descending line or issue) are preferred to ascendants and collateral relatives.

According to the general intestate scheme, the parent or parents of an intestate take the portion of the intestate's estate that does not pass to the surviving spouse, provided that the decedent died without surviving issue. If the decedent left no spouse, issue or parent surviving, then the intestate's estate passes to the issue of the decedent's parents.

In Florida, as in other states, the general intestate scheme for the shares of ascendants and collateral relatives is set forth by statute. As explained above, Florida law first makes provision for the share of the surviving spouse of the intestate who takes the entire estate if there are no surviving issue. If there is no surviving spouse, then the entire intestate estate descends to the decedent's issue.

If the decedent died without leaving a spouse or issue surviving, then the intestate estate passes to the decedent's parents equally, or the survivor of them. If neither of the decedent's parents survives the decedent, then the decedent's intestate estate passes to the decedent's siblings and the descendants of any deceased sibling. If none of the foregoing persons survive, then the decedent's intestate estate is divided in half: one-half passes to the decedent's paternal kindred and the other half to the decedent's maternal kindred in the order specified by statute.

If no maternal or no paternal kindred of the decedent survive, then the decedent's intestate property passes to the "kindred of the last deceased spouse of the decedent" (Fla. Stat. §732.103(5)).

Florida law (Fla. Stat. §732.103) reflects a parentelic approach in terms of its distribution to relatives as distantly related as grandparents or the issue of grandparents (Fla. Stat. §§732.103(4)(a),(b) and (c)). The parentelic system dispenses with the necessity for counting degrees of kinship. Rather, the intestate estate is divided into two shares. One portion passes to the maternal grandparents and their kindred and the other portion to the paternal grandparents and their kindred.

Florida law also takes into consideration affinal relationships. (Affinity refers to relationships by marriage; consanguinity refers to relationships by blood.) Specifically,

if the decedent is not survived by a surviving spouse, issue, a parent (or issue of a parent), a grandparent (or issue of a grandparent), or other maternal or paternal kindred, but is survived by the kindred of the decedent's last predeceased spouse, then the remainder of the decedent's intestate estate passes to the kindred of that predeceased spouse (Fla. Stat. §732.103(5)).

For proceedings filed prior to December 31, 2004, Florida law permitted property that would have escheated to the state to pass to lineal descendants of the great-grandparents who happened to be Holocaust victims if the decedent was not survived by any other aforementioned kindred (Fla. Stat. §732.103(6)). Florida law liberalized the standard of proof to enable them to establish their degree of relationship to the decedent. This provision was necessary because many Holocaust survivors do not have the necessary birth records to prove their lineage. The statute (Fla. Stat. §732.103(6)) permitted any such descendant to meet a "reasonable, not unduly restrictive, standard of proof to substantiate his or her lineage." For a discussion of escheat, see infra Part II C.

Florida's parentelic approach was influenced by the UPC (§2-103). However, the UPC disallows inheritance by any persons more remote than grandparents and their issue. In addition, the UPC makes no provision for those issue or parents of a predeceased spouse.

Recall that Florida law follows a per stirpes approach for distribution among lineal descendants as well as collateral heirs. See, e.g., Fla. Stat. §§732.104, §732.611; In re Davol's Estate, 100 So. 2d 188 (Fla. Dist. Ct. App. 1958) (approving per stirpes distribution among decedent's nieces and nephews).

§732.103. Shares of other heirs

The part of the intestate estate not passing to the surviving spouse under §732.102, or the entire intestate estate if there is no surviving spouse, descends as follows

(1) To the lineal descendants of the decedent

(2) If there is no lineal descendant, to the decedent's father and mother equally, or to the survivor of them

(3) If there is none of the foregoing, to the decedent's brothers and sisters and the descendants of deceased brothers and sisters

(4) If there is none of the foregoing, the estate shall be divided, one-half of which shall go to the decedent's paternal, and the other half to the decedent's maternal, kindred in the following order

(a) To the grandfather and grandmother equally, or to the survivor of them

(b) If there is no grandfather or grandmother, to uncles and aunts and descendants of deceased uncles and aunts of the decedent

(c) If there is either no paternal kindred or no maternal kindred, the estate shall go to the other kindred who survive, in the order stated above

(5) If there is no kindred of either part, the whole of the property shall go to the kindred of the last deceased spouse of the decedent as if the deceased spouse had survived the decedent and then died intestate entitled to the estate

(6) If none of the foregoing, and if any of the descendants of the decedent's great-grandparents were Holocaust victims as defined in §626.9543(3)(b), [FN1] including such victims in countries cooperating with the discriminatory policies of Nazi Germany, then to the lineal descendants of the great-grandparents. The court shall allow any such descendant to meet a reasonable, not unduly restrictive, standard of proof to substantiate his or her lineage. This subsection only applies to escheated property and shall cease to be effective for proceedings filed after December 31, 2004.

[FN1] Redesignated as §626.9543(3)(a) by Laws 2004, ch. 2004-390, §76.

(Laws 1974, ch. 74-106, §1; Laws 1975, ch. 75-220, §8; Laws 1977, ch. 77-174, §1. Amended by Laws 2001, ch. 2001-226, §16, effective January 1, 2002; Laws 2004, ch. 2004-390, §145, effective July 1, 2004; L. 2006, ch. 2006-1, §102, effective July 4, 2006.)

§732.104. Inheritance per stirpes

Descent shall be per stirpes, whether to lineal descendants or to collateral heirs.

(Laws 1974, ch. 74-106, §1; Laws 1975, ch. 75-220, §9.

§732.105. Determination of shares of beneficiaries

(1) When property passes by intestate succession or the will is unclear and there is doubt about:

(a) Who is entitled to receive any part of the property, or

(b) The shares and amounts that any person is entitled to receive, any interested person may petition the court to determine beneficiaries or their shares.

(2) Any personal representative who makes distribution or takes any other action pursuant to an order determining beneficiaries shall be fully protected

(3) A separate civil action to determine beneficiaries may be brought when an estate has not been administered.

(Laws 1974, ch. 74-106, §1; Laws 1975, ch. 75-220, §48; L. 1977, ch. 77-104, §226; Laws 1977, ch. 77-174, §1. Amended by Laws 1997, ch. 97-

102, §983, effective July 1, 1997; Laws 2001, ch. 2001-226, §81, effective January 1, 2002.)

C. Escheat

Escheat applies if there is no taker of the decedent's intestate estate. If the decedent leaves no heirs to take his or her estate (or any portion of it), then the unclaimed property goes to the state. According to Florida law, when the probate court makes an order for final distribution of the decedent's estate, any balance that is not distributed to known heirs or beneficiaries is distributed to the state (Fla. Stat. §732.107). If the property remains unclaimed subsequently for a designated period of time, the title vests ("escheats") in the state.

Most states allow inheritance by very remote relatives (known as "laughing heirs" because they are so distantly related as to feel no sorrow at the decedent's death). Most jurisdictions prefer inheritance by such relatives rather than having the property escheat to the state. McGovern & Kurtz, supra, §2.2 at 54.

Florida law provides generally for the escheat of unclaimed and abandoned property (Fla. Stat. §§716.01-716.07). In addition, Florida law authorizes the procedure for escheat of property specifically of persons who die without leaving any statutorily designated persons surviving (Fla. Stat. §732.107). According to Probate Rule 5.486, a personal representative has the responsibility of initiating a proceeding (within one year after issuance of letters of administration) whenever it appears that escheated property may exist. If the personal representative fails to act, the responsibility falls to the Department of Legal Affairs. A person who wishes to challenge the escheat of a decedent's property may initiate a proceeding within ten years after issuance of letters of administration. Following a judicial hearing, if a claimant is successful, the court will order the state to repay the escheated property.

The state has the burden of proof that it has made a diligent search and inquiry that an intestate died without leaving any heirs. See In re Estate of Faskowitz, 941 So.2d 390 (Fla. Dist. Ct. App. 2006) (holding that the paternal relatives of an intestate had no burden to show that there were no additional lawful maternal heirs).

§716.01. Policy regarding unclaimed and abandoned property

It is hereby declared to be the policy of the state, while protecting the interests of the owners thereof, to possess all unclaimed and abandoned money and property for the benefit of all the people of the state, and this law shall be liberally construed to accomplish such purpose.
(Laws 1947, ch. 24333, §1.)

§716.02. Escheat of funds that are in the possession of federal agencies

All property within the provisions of subsections (1), (2), (3), (4) and (5), are declared to have escheated, or to escheat, including all principal and interest accruing thereon, and to have become the property of the state.

(1) All money or other property which has remained in, or has been deposited in the custody of, or under the control of, any court of the United States, in and for any district within this state, or which has been deposited with and is in the custody of any depository, registry, clerk or other officer of such court, or the United States treasury, which money or other property the rightful owner or owners thereof, either:

(a) Has been unknown for a period of 5 or more consecutive years; or,

(b) Has died, without having disposed thereof, and without having left heirs, next of kin or distributees, or

(c) Has made no demand for such money or other property for 5 years;

are declared to have escheated, or to escheat, together with all interest accrued thereon, and to have become the property of the state.

(2) After June 16, 1947, all money or other property which has remained in, or has been deposited in the custody of, or under the control of, any court of the United States, in and for any district within this state, for a period of 4 years, the rightful owner or owners of which, either:

(a) Shall have been unknown for a period of 4 years; or,

(b) Shall have died without having disposed thereof, and without having left or without leaving heirs, next of kin or distributees; or,

(c) Shall have failed within 4 years to demand the payment or delivery of such funds or other property;

is hereby declared to have escheated, or to escheat, together with all interest accrued thereon, and to have become the property of the state.

(3) All money or other property which has remained in, or has been deposited in the custody of, or under the control of any officer, department or agency of the United States for 5 or more consecutive years, which money or other property had its situs or source in this state, except as hereinafter provided in subsection (4), the sender of which is unknown, or who sent the money or other property for an unknown purpose, or money which is credited as "unknown," and which said governmental agency is unable to credit to any particular account, or the sender of which has been unknown for a period of 5 or more consecutive

years; or when known, has died without having disposed thereof, and without leaving heirs, next of kin or distributees, or for any reason is unclaimed from such governmental agency.

(4) In the event any money is due to any resident of this state as a refund, rebate or tax rebate from the United States Commissioner of Internal Revenue, the United States Treasurer, or other governmental agency or department, which said resident will, or is likely to have her or his rights to apply for and secure such refund or rebate barred by any statute of limitations or, in any event, has failed for a period of 1 year after said resident could have filed a claim for said refund or rebate, the Department of Financial Services is appointed agent of such resident to demand, file and apply for said refund or rebate, and is appointed to do any act which a natural person could do to recover such money, and it is hereby declared that when the department files such application or any other proceeding to secure such refund or rebate, its agency is coupled with an interest in the money sought and money recovered.

(5) It is the purpose of this chapter to include all funds or other property in the possession of the government of the United States, and of its departments, officers, and agencies, which property has its situs in this state or belonged to a resident thereof, and not to limit the application of this chapter by the naming of any particular agency. This chapter shall include all funds held in the United States Department of Veterans Affairs, Comptroller of Currency, United States Treasury, Department of Internal Revenue, federal courts, registry of federal courts, and such evidences of indebtedness as adjusted service bonds, old matured debts issued prior to 1917, unclaimed and interest thereon, postal savings bonds, liberty bonds, victory notes, treasury bonds, treasury notes, certificates of indebtedness, treasury bills, treasurer's savings certificates, bonuses and adjusted compensation, allotments, and all unclaimed refunds or rebates of whatever kind or nature, which are subjects of escheat, under the terms of this chapter. Provided, however, that nothing in this chapter shall be construed to mean that any refunds due ratepayers under order of any court of the United States shall become the property of the state.

(Laws 1947, ch. 24333, §2; Laws 1949, ch. 25035, §11; Laws 1969, ch. 69-106, §§12, 35; Laws 1970, ch. 70-405, §1. Amended by Laws 1993, ch. 93-268, §36, effective June 3, 1993; Laws 1997, ch. 97-102, §847, effective July 1, 1997; Laws 2003, ch. 2003-261, §1881, effective June 26, 2003.)

§716.03. Department of Financial Services is authorized to recover escheated property

When there exists, or may exist, escheated funds or property under this chapter, the Department of Financial Services shall demand or institute proceedings in the name of the state for an adjudication that an escheat to the state of such funds or property has occurred; and shall take appropriate action to recover such funds or property

(Laws 1947, ch. 24333, §3; Laws 1949, ch. 25035, §11; Laws 1969, ch. 69-106, §§12, 35. Amended by L. 2003, ch. 2003-261, §1882, effective June 26, 2003.)

§716.04. Determination of whether escheat has occurred

Whenever the Department of Financial Services is of the opinion an escheat has occurred, or shall occur, of any money or other property deposited in the custody of, or under the control of, any court of the United States, in and for any district within the state, or in the custody of any depository, registry or clerk or other officer of such court, or the treasury of the United States, it shall cause to be filed a complaint in the Circuit Court of Leon County, or in any other court of competent jurisdiction, to ascertain if any escheat has occurred, and to cause said court to enter a judgment or decree of escheat in favor of the state, with costs, disbursements, and attorney fee.

(Laws 1947, ch. 24333, §4; Laws 1969, ch. 69-106, §§12, 35. Amended by Laws 2003, ch. 2003-261, §1883, effective June 26, 2003.)

§716.05. Costs of recovering escheated property

When any funds or property which has escheated within the meaning of this chapter has been recovered by the Department of Financial Services, the department shall first pay all costs incident to the collection and recovery of such funds or property and shall promptly deposit the remaining balance of such funds or property with the Chief Financial Officer, to be distributed in accordance with law.

(Laws 1947, ch. 24333, §5; Laws 1969, ch. 69-106, §§12, 35; Laws 1983, ch. 83- 216, §153. Amended by Laws 2003, ch. 2003-261, §1884, effective June 26, 2003.)

§716.06 All records shall be public

All records in the office of the Chief Financial Officer or the Department of Financial Services relating to federal funds, pursuant to this chapter, shall be public records.

(Laws 1947, ch. 24333, §6; Laws 1969, ch. 69-106, §§12, 35. Amended by Laws 2003, ch. 2003-261, §1885, effective June 26, 2003.)

§716.07. Claimant may recover escheated property within 5 years

(1) Any person who claims any property, funds, or money delivered to the Treasurer or Chief Financial Officer under this chapter, shall, within 5 years from the date of receipt of such property, funds, or money, file a verified claim with the Chief Financial Officer, setting forth the facts upon which such party claims to be entitled to recover such money or property. All claims made for recovery of property, funds, or money, not filed within 5 years from the date that such property, funds, or money is received by the Chief Financial Officer, shall be forever barred, and the Chief Financial Officer shall be without power to consider or determine any claims so made by any claimant after 5 years from the date that the property, funds, or money was received by the Chief Financial Officer.

(2) The Chief Financial Officer shall approve or disapprove the claim. If the claim is approved, the funds, money, or property of the claimant, less any expenses and costs which shall have been incurred by the state in securing the possession of said property, as provided by this chapter, shall be delivered to the claimant by the Chief Financial Officer upon warrant issued according to law and her or his receipt taken therefor. If the court finds, upon any judicial review, that the claimant is entitled to the property, money, or funds claimed, and shall render judgment in her or his or its favor, declaring that the claimant is entitled to such property, funds, or money, then upon presentation of said judgment or a certified copy thereof to the Chief Financial Officer, the Chief Financial Officer shall draw her or his warrant for the amount of money stated in such judgment, without interest or cost to the state, less any sum paid by the state as costs or expenses in securing possession of such property, funds, or money. When payment has been made to any claimant, no action thereafter shall be maintained by any other claimant against the state or any officer thereof, for or on account of such money, property, or funds.
(Laws 1947, ch. 24333, §7; Laws 1963, ch. 63-559, §30; Laws 1969, ch. 69-106, §§12, 35; Laws 1978, ch. 78-95, §7. Amended by Laws 1997, ch. 97-102, §848, effective July 1, 1997; Laws 2003, ch. 2003-261, §1886, effective June 26, 2003.)

§732.107. Escheat for decedents' property

(1) When a person dies leaving an estate without being survived by any person entitled to a part of it, that part shall escheat to the state.

(2) Property that escheats shall be sold as provided in the Florida Probate Rules and the proceeds paid to the Chief Financial Officer of the state and deposited in the State School Fund.

(3) At any time within 10 years after the payment to the Chief Financial Officer, a person claiming to be entitled to the proceeds may reopen the administration to assert entitlement to the proceeds. If no claim is timely asserted, the state's rights to the proceeds shall become absolute.

(4) The Department of Legal Affairs shall represent the state in all proceedings concerning escheated estates.

(5)(a) If a person entitled to the proceeds assigns the rights to receive payment to an attorney, Florida-certified public accountant, or private investigative agency which is duly licensed to do business in this state pursuant to a written agreement with that person, the Department of Financial Services is authorized to make distribution in accordance with the assignment.

(b) Payments made to an attorney, Florida-certified public accountant, or private investigative agency shall be promptly deposited into a trust or escrow account which is regularly maintained by the attorney, Florida-certified public accountant, or private investigative agency in a financial institution authorized to accept such deposits and located in this state.

(c) Distribution by the attorney, Florida-certified public accountant, or private investigative agency to the person entitled to the proceeds shall be made within 10 days following final credit of the deposit into the trust or escrow account at the financial institution, unless a party to the agreement protests the distribution in writing before it is made.

(d) The department shall not be civilly or criminally liable for any proceeds distributed pursuant to this subsection, provided such distribution is made in good faith
(Laws 1974, ch. 74-106, §1; Laws 1975, ch. 75-220, § 10; Laws 1989, ch. 89- 291, §4; Laws 1989, ch. 89-299, §9. Amended by Laws 1997, ch. 97-102, §953, effective July 1, 1997; Laws 2001, ch. 2001-36, §32, effective October 1, 2001; Laws 2001, ch. 2001-226, §17, effective January 1, 2002; L. 2003, ch. 2003-261, §1896, effective June 26, 2003.)

§733.816. Disposition of unclaimed property held by personal representatives

(1) In all cases in which there is unclaimed property in the hands of a personal representative that cannot be distributed or paid because of the inability to find the lawful owner or because no lawful owner is known or because the lawful owner refuses to accept the property after a reasonable attempt to distribute it and after notice to that lawful owner, the court shall order the personal representative to sell the property and deposit the proceeds and cash already in hand, after retaining those amounts provided for in subsection (4), with

the clerk and receive a receipt, and the clerk shall deposit the funds in the registry of the court to be disposed of as follows:

(a) If the value of the funds is $500 or less, the clerk shall post a notice for 30 days at the courthouse door giving the amount involved, the name of the personal representative, and the other pertinent information that will put interested persons on notice.

(b) If the value of the funds is over $500, the clerk shall publish the notice once a month for 2 consecutive months in a newspaper of general circulation in the county.

After the expiration of 6 months from the posting or first publication, the clerk shall deposit the funds with the Chief Financial Officer after deducting the clerk's fees and the costs of publication.

(2) Upon receipt of the funds, the Chief Financial Officer shall deposit them to the credit of the State School Fund, to become a part of the school fund. All interest and all income that may accrue from the money while so deposited shall belong to the fund. The funds so deposited shall constitute and be a permanent appropriation for payments by the Chief Financial Officer in obedience to court orders entered as provided by subsection (3).

(3) Within 10 years from the date of deposit with the Chief Financial Officer, on written petition to the court that directed the deposit of the funds and informal notice to the Department of Legal Affairs, and after proof of entitlement, any person entitled to the funds before or after payment to the Chief Financial Officer and deposit as provided by subsection (1) may obtain a court order directing the payment of the funds to that person. All funds deposited with the Chief Financial Officer and not claimed within 10 years from the date of deposit shall escheat to the state for the benefit of the State School Fund.

(4) The personal representative depositing assets with the clerk is permitted to retain from the funds a sufficient amount to pay final costs of administration chargeable to the assets accruing between the deposit of the funds with the clerk of the court and the order of discharge. Any funds so retained which are surplus shall be deposited with the clerk prior to discharge of the personal representative

(5)(a) If a person entitled to the funds assigns the right to receive payment or part payment to an attorney or private investigative agency which is duly licensed to do business in this state pursuant to a written agreement with that person, the Department of Financial Services is authorized to make distribution in accordance with the assignment.

(b) Payments made to an attorney or private investigative agency shall be promptly deposited into a trust or escrow account which is regularly maintained by the attorney or private investigative agency in a financial institution located in this state and authorized to accept these deposits.

(c) Distribution by the attorney or private investigative agency to the person entitled to the funds shall be made within 10 days following final credit of the deposit into the trust or escrow account at the financial institution, unless a party to the agreement protests the distribution in writing before it is made.

(d) The department shall not be civilly or criminally liable for any funds distributed pursuant to this subsection, provided the distribution is made in good faith.

(Laws 1974, ch. 74-106, §1; Laws 1975, ch. 75-220, §95; Laws 1985, ch. 85-79, §6; L. 1989, ch. 89-291, §5; Laws 1989, ch. 89-299, §10. Amended by Laws 1995, ch. 95-401, §21, effective July 1, 1995; Laws 1997, ch. 97-102, §1025, effective July 1, 1997; Laws 2001, ch. 2001-226, §166, effective January 1, 2002; Laws 2003, ch. 2003-261, §1897, effective June 26, 2003.)

FLORIDA PROBATE RULES

5.386 Escheat

(a) Escheat Proceeding. If it appears to the personal representative that an estate may escheat or there is doubt about the existence of any person entitled to the estate, the personal representative shall institute a proceeding to determine beneficiaries within 1 year after letters have been issued to the personal representative, and notice shall be served on the Department of Legal Affairs. If the personal representative fails to institute the proceeding within the time fixed, it may be instituted by the Department of Legal Affairs.

(b) Court's Report. On or before January 15 of each year, each court shall furnish to the Department of Legal Affairs a list of all estates being administered in which no person appears to be entitled to the property and the personal representative has not instituted a proceeding for the determination of beneficiaries.

(c) Administration. Except as herein provided, escheated estates shall be administered as other estates.

(Added September 29, 1988, effective January 1, 1989 (537 So.2d 500). Amended September 24, 1992, effective January 1, 1993 (607 So.2d 1306).)

D. Other

1. Share of Half-Blood Relatives

Half-blood relatives are those persons who are related to an individual through one common ancestor (such as through the same mother or the same father). In contrast, persons related by whole blood share the

same common ancestors (i.e., share the same mother and father).

Most modern intestacy statutes do not make any distinctions between the inheritance rights of relatives of the whole blood and those of the half blood. See, e.g., UPC §2-107.

A few states, however, "postpone" half-blood relatives. That is, they specify that a half-blood relative is entitled to a smaller share of the decedent's intestate estate than a relative of the whole blood. Florida follows this approach. See Florida Statutes §732.105, providing that half-blood relatives inherit only half as much as relatives of the whole blood. This rule is subject to an exception: if all takers are half blood relatives, then they share equally.

For a proposal suggesting reforms to half blood statutes, see Ralph C. Brashier, Consanguinity, Sibling Relationships, and the Default Rules of Inheritance Law: Reshaping Half-Blood Statutes to Reflect the Evolving Family, 58 SMU L. Rev.137 (2005) (suggesting that states should invest probate courts with discretion in determining the intestate shares of half-blood relatives).

§732.105. Share of half-blood relatives

When property descends to the collateral kindred of the intestate and part of the collateral kindred are of the whole blood to the intestate and the other part of the half blood, those of the half blood shall inherit only half as much as those of the whole blood; but if all are of the half blood they shall have whole parts

(Laws 1974, ch. 74-106, §1; Laws 1975, ch. 75-220, § 10.)

2. Share of Foster Child or Stepchild

A stepparent-child relationship arises when a child's biological parent remarries. The new spouse of the child's biological parent becomes the child's stepparent. Under the general rule in most jurisdictions, only a stepchild who is adopted by the new spouse may inherit from or through the stepparent.

Florida statute excludes a stepchild or foster child (Fla. Stat. §732.201)(3)) from inheriting from an intestate, as well as prohibiting a stepparent or foster parent (Fla. Stat. §732.201(24)) from inheriting from an intestate stepchild or foster child.

Florida case law, similarly, excludes a stepchild and foster child from inheriting from a decedent who dies intestate unless the child qualifies as an heir based on the doctrine of equitable (also called "virtual") adoption. See, e.g., Houston v. McKinney, 45 So. 480 (Fla. 1907) (holding that an unadopted stepdaughter was not entitled to inherit real property of her intestate stepfather because the term "child" in the state intestacy statute signifies only biological offspring); Urick v. McFarland, 625 So.2d 1253 (Fla. Dist. Ct. App. 1993) (holding that an unadopted stepson was not entitled to an intestate share of his stepfather's estate under the doctrine of virtual adoption, absent proof of an agreement between stepparents and biological parents to adopt him). On the equitable adoption doctrine, see infra Part III C4.

Note also that stepchildren and foster children of a testator are not considered lineal descendants of a testator's grandparent, pursuant to the Florida antilapse statute, for purposes of saving a testator's gift to them from lapsing. See Romualdo P. Eclavea & Stephen Lease, Testate Succession, Death of Devisee Before Testator—Where Devisee is Grandparent, or Lineal Descendant of Grandparent, of Testator—Where Devisee is Adopted or Foster Child, 18 Fla. Jur. 2d Decedents' Property §411 (2007) (citing Tubbs v. Teeple, 388 So. 2d 239 (Fla. Dist. Ct. App. 1980)(stepdaughter); In re Skinner's Estate, 397 So. 2d 1193 (Fla. Dist. Ct. App. 1981)(foster son)). On the lapse doctrine, see infra Chapter XV, Part III.

Regarding stepchildren, the UPC creates an exception to the general rule that for purposes of inheritance by, from, or through the child, an adopted child is the child of the adopting parents and not of the child's biological parents. According to UPC §2-114(b)(ii), a stepparent adoption does not preclude the adopted stepchild's right to inherit from and through the child's noncustodial biological parent. However, that subsection does not permit correlative inheritance: it does not establish the right of the noncustodial biological parent (and that parent's relatives) to inherit from and through the adopted stepchild. For a discussion of Adoption, see Section IIIC infra.

For a discussion of the need for law reform, see Kim A. Feigenbaum, Note, The Changing Family Structure: Challenging Stepchildren's Lack of Inheritance Rights, 66 Brook. L. Rev. 167 (2000).

§732.201. General definitions

Subject to additional definitions in subsequent chapters that are applicable to specific chapters or parts, and unless the context otherwise requires, in this code, in §409.9101 and in chapters 737, 738, 739, and 744, the term:

...

(3) "Child" includes a person entitled to take as a child under this code by intestate succession from the parent whose relationship is involved, and excludes any person who is only a stepchild, a foster child, a grandchild, or a more remote descendant.

....

(24) "Parent" excludes any person who is only a stepparent, foster parent, or grandparent.

....

(Laws 1974, ch. 74-106, §1; Laws 1975, ch. 75-220, §4; Laws 1977, ch. 77-174, §1; Laws 1985, ch. 85-79, §2; Laws 1987, ch. 87-226, §66; Laws 1988, ch. 88-340, §1; Laws 1993, ch. 93-257, §7. Amended by Laws 1995, ch. 95- 401, §6, effective July 1, 1995; Laws 1997, ch. 97-102, §949, effective. July 1, 1997; Laws 1998, ch. 98-421, §52, effective July 1, 1998; Laws 2001, ch. 2001-226, §11, effective January 1, 2002; Laws 2002, ch. 2002-1, §106, effective May 21, 2002; Laws 2003, ch. 2003-154, §2, effective June 12, 2003; Laws 2005, ch. 2005-108, §2, effective July 1, 2005.)

[The remainder of the above statute is reprinted *supra* in Section IA.]

§732.103. Share of other heirs

The part of the intestate estate not passing to the surviving spouse under §732.102, or the entire intestate estate if there is no surviving spouse, descends as follows:

(1) To the lineal descendants of the decedent.

(2) If there is no lineal descendant, to the decedent's father and mother equally, or to the survivor of them.

(3) If there is none of the foregoing, to the decedent's brothers and sisters and the descendants of deceased brothers and sisters.

(4) If there is none of the foregoing, the estate shall be divided, one-half of which shall go to the decedent's paternal, and the other half to the decedent's maternal, kindred in the following order:

(a) To the grandfather and grandmother equally, or to the survivor of them.

(b) If there is no grandfather or grandmother, to uncles and aunts and descendants of deceased uncles and aunts of the decedent.

(c) If there is either no paternal kindred or no maternal kindred, the estate shall go to the other kindred who survive, in the order stated above.

(5) If there is no kindred of either part, the whole of the property shall go to the kindred of the last deceased spouse of the decedent as if the deceased spouse had survived the decedent and then died intestate entitled to the estate.

(6) If none of the foregoing, and if any of the descendants of the decedent's great-grandparents were Holocaust victims as defined in §626.9543(3)(b) [FN1] including such victims in countries cooperating with the discriminatory policies of Nazi Germany, then to the lineal descendants of the great-grandparents. The court shall allow any such descendant to meet a reasonable, not unduly restrictive, standard of proof to substantiate his or her lineage. This subsection only applies to escheated property and shall cease to be effective for proceedings filed after December 31, 2004.

[FN1] Redesignated as §626.9543(3)(a) by Laws 2004, ch. 2004-390, §76.

(Laws 1974, ch. 74-106, §1; Laws 1975, ch. 75-220, §8; Laws 1977, ch. 77-174, §1. Amended by Laws 2001, ch. 2001-226, §16, effective January 1, 2002; Laws 2004, ch. 2004-390, §145, effective July 1, 2004; Laws 2006, ch. 2006-1, §102, effective July 4, 2006.)

III. Questions of Status

A. Posthumous Children

State intestacy statutes generally make provisions for posthumous heirs. A posthumous heir is an heir who was conceived while the intestate was alive but born after the intestate's death. At common law, such heirs inherit as if they had been born during the decedent's lifetime.

Florida law (Fla. Stat. §732.106) follows the common law rule. In 1977, the Florida legislature revised the applicable statute by substituting the word "heirs" for the previous term "issue" in the definition of eligible persons who may inherit if born posthumously. The legislature thereby broadened the definition, stemming from the influence of UPC §2-108. However, one difference remains between Florida law and the UPC. The UPC (but not Florida) requires that a posthumous heir must survive at least 120 hours after birth in order to inherit from an intestate decedent (UPC §2-108).

Case law and legislation are beginning to address the issue of posthumously conceived children. The issue of posthumously conceived children first arose in California in Hecht v. Superior Court, 20 Cal. Rptr.2d 275 (Cal. Ct. App. 1993), in which the appellate court considered whether a decedent's sperm (15 vials of which he had deposited at a sperm bank prior to committing suicide) should be considered as "property" that was subject to probate court jurisdiction. The decedent's female partner sought to vacate an order directing the personal representative of decedent's estate to destroy all of decedent's sperm in the custody of the sperm bank. The Court of Appeal held that the decedent's interest in frozen sperm was "property" over which the probate court had jurisdiction. In ordering the release of the sperm to the partner, the court also ruled that artificial insemination to an unmarried woman does not violate public policy. The court based its decision on the decedent's intent to give the

frozen sperm to the partner (e.g., his will authorized release of the sperm to the partner). The court did not address the inheritance rights of any ensuing children but noted, in dicta, that, under the provisions of California law regulating inheritance by posthumous relatives of the decedent (Cal. Prob. Code §6407), "it is unlikely that the estate would be subject to claims with respect to any such children" resulting from the insemination. Hecht, 20 Cal. Rptr.2d at 290.

The California legislature subsequently enacted legislation (Cal. Prob. Code §§249.5, 249.6, 249.7, and 249.8, effective January 1, 2006) to provide inheritance rights for posthumously conceived children if the decedent provides written consent to the posthumous use of his genetic material, designates a person to control the use of his/her genetic material, and the child was in utero within two years of the decedent's death.

Case law also focuses on the right of posthumously conceived children to government benefits. In the most recent case involving Social Security benefits, Gillett-Netting v. Barnhart, 371 F.3d 593 ((9th Cir. 2004), a widow sought review of the denial of her claim for Social Security survivors' benefits that she filed on behalf of twins conceived by in vitro fertilization after her husband's death. The district court granted summary judgment for the Commissioner of Social Security, and the widow appealed. The Ninth Circuit Court of Appeals held that the posthumously conceived twins were "children" within the definition of the Social Security Act, and that the children were presumed dependent for purposes of entitlement to survivors' benefits because they were legitimate under applicable state law.

See also In Woodward v. Commissioner of Social Services, 760 N.E.2d 257 (Mass. 2002)(holding that posthumously conceived children had the right to Social Security survivor benefits if the wife established their genetic relationship with the decedent and that the decedent consented both to reproduce posthumously and to support any resulting child); In re Estate of Kolacy, 753 A.2d 1257 (N.J. Super. Ch. 2000) (holding that posthumously conceived children could inherit under state intestacy law, and thereby be eligible for federal benefits, if an adjudication of parentage did not unfairly intrude on the rights of others or cause "serious problems" with the orderly administration of estates).

To date, only a few states address the issue of the inheritance rights of posthumously conceived children. Some states grant rights to such children if the deceased parent gave written consent to the posthumous use of his sperm. See Ronald J. Scalise, Jr., New Developments in United States Succession Law, 54 Am. J. Comp. Law 103, 108 (2006) (citing statutes in Colorado, Delaware, Texas, Washington, and Wyoming). Other states specify limitations on post-mortem conception, requiring that the birth occur within periods ranging from 10 months to 3 years after the date of death of the decedent. See id. at 109. Still other states refuse to extend inheritance rights to posthumously conceived children. Id.

Florida law (Fla. Stat. §742.17(4)) provides that posthumously conceived children "shall not be eligible for a claim against the decedent's estate unless the child has been provided for by the decedent's will." The Florida statute was enacted in 1993 as part of comprehensive legislation that addressed various aspects of reproductive technology (e.g., provisions regarding the status of children born from donated genetic material, restrictions on the compensation for gamete donation, provisions for the relinquishment of the rights of gamete donors, requirements for the execution of a contract prior to engaging in gestational surrogacy, etc.). See 1993 Fla. Sess. Law Serv. Ch. 93-237 (C.S.H.B. 703).

The recently revised Uniform Parentage Act requires that, for a posthumously conceived child to have inheritance rights, the deceased spouse must have provided written consent that, if assisted reproduction were to occur after death, the deceased spouse would be a parent of the child. Uniform Parentage Act §707, 9B U.L.A. 43 (Supp. 2005). See also Human Fertilisation and Embryology (Deceased Fathers) Act 2003, Ch. 24 s.1 (Eng.) (recognizing decedent as father if he previously consented in writing, the woman elects within 42 days of the birth for the decedent to be treated as the father, and no other person is to be treated as the father).

See generally Michael E. Eisenberg, What's Mine is Mine and What's Yours is Mine—Examining Inheritance Rights by Intestate Succession from Children Conceived through Assisted Reproduction Under Florida Law, 3 Barry L. Rev. 127 (2002).

§732.106. Posthumous heirs

Heirs of the decedent conceived before his or her death, but born thereafter, inherit intestate property as if they had been born in the decedent's lifetime.

(Laws 1974, ch. 74-106, §1; Laws 1975, ch. 75-220, §10; Laws 1977, ch. 77-87, §6. Amended by Laws 1997, ch. 97-102, §952, effective July 1, 1997.)

§742.17. Posthumously-conceived heirs

A commissioning couple and the treating physician shall enter into a written agreement that provides for the disposition of the commissioning couple's eggs, sperm, and preembryos in the event of a divorce, the death of a spouse, or any other unforeseen circumstance.

(1) Absent a written agreement, any remaining eggs or sperm shall remain under the control of the party that provides the eggs or sperm.

(2) Absent a written agreement, decisionmaking authority regarding the disposition of preembryos shall reside jointly with the commissioning couple.

(3) Absent a written agreement, in the case of the death of one member of the commissioning couple, any eggs, sperm, or preembryos shall remain under the control of the surviving member of the commissioning couple.

(4) A child conceived from the eggs or sperm of a person or persons who died before the transfer of their eggs, sperm, or preembryos to a woman's body shall not be eligible for a claim against the decedent's estate unless the child has been provided for by the decedent's will.

(Laws 1993, ch. 93-237, §2.)

B. Aliens

At common law, an alien could not inherit real property in England. (An alien is a citizen of a foreign country.) According to the modern trend, however, noncitizens generally are able to inherit property unless a statute provides otherwise. McGovern & Kurtz, supra, §2.2 at 54-55.

At one time, many states had "reciprocity statutes," providing that an alien could not inherit from a United States citizen unless the alien's nation granted reciprocal rights to American citizens. In Zschernig v. Miller, 389 U.S. 429 (1968), the United States Supreme Court analyzed the constitutionality of an Oregon statute that stated conditions under which an alien not residing in the United States or its territories could take property in Oregon through testate or intestate succession. Zschernig involved proceedings by East German next-of-kin of an Oregon intestate against the administrator and Oregon officials for determination of heirship. The Oregon State Land Board argued that the property should escheat to the state. Invalidating the statute, Justice Douglas held that the statute constituted an intrusion by the state into the field of foreign affairs which the Constitution entrusts to the President and Congress. A few states (Nebraska, North Carolina, Oklahoma, Virginia, and Wyoming) still have reciprocity statutes. Restatement (Third) of Property, supra, §1.3, Statutory Note 2.

In contrast, some states have "retention" statutes that "require or permit retention by the state of the inheritance if it appears unlikely that the beneficiary will be able to enjoy that property." Id., §1.3, Statutory Note 3 (citing Connecticut, Maryland, Massachusetts, Nebraska, New Jersey, and New York). Still other states have prohibitions or restrictions on ownership of real property by nonresident aliens. Id., §1.3, Statutory Note 4 (citing Alaska, District of Columbia, Indiana, Iowa, Kentucky, Mississippi, Missouri, Oklahoma, Pennsylvania, South Carolina, and South Dakota).

The Florida Constitution permits state regulation of the rights of aliens to inherit real property (Fla. Const., Art I, §2). Florida formerly followed the Uniform Probate Code (UPC §2-111) in eliminating the bar on inheritance by aliens. However, in 2001, the Florida legislature amended the alienage statute (and thereby revised the UPC language) which formerly read: "No person is disqualified to take as an heir because he or she, or a person through whom he or she claims, is, or has been, an alien." (Laws 2001, ch. 2001-226, §18, effective Jan. 1, 2002). The current statute simply states that aliens shall have the same rights of inheritance as citizens (Fla. Stat. §732.1101). See also Restatement (Third) of Property, supra, at §1.3.

FLORIDA CONSTITUTION
§2. Basic rights

All natural persons, female and male alike, are equal before the law and have inalienable rights, among which are the right to enjoy and defend life and liberty, to pursue happiness, to be rewarded for industry, and to acquire, possess and protect property; except that the ownership, inheritance, disposition and possession of real property by aliens ineligible for citizenship may be regulated or prohibited by law. No person shall be deprived of any right because of race, religion, national origin, or physical disability.

(Amended, general election, Nov. 5, 1974; general election, Nov. 3, 1998.)

FLORIDA STATUTES
§732.1101. Aliens

Aliens shall have the same rights of inheritance as citizens.

(Laws 1974, ch. 74-106, §1; Laws 1975, ch. 75-220, §12. Amended by Laws 1997, ch. 97-102, §955, effective July 1, 1997; Laws 2001, ch. 2001-226, §18, effective January 1, 2002.)

C. Adoption

The common law did not recognize adoption which originated in the Roman and civil law systems. As a result, adoption in the United States is entirely a creation of statutory law. Massachusetts adopted the first comprehensive adoption statute in 1851. McGovern & Kurtz, supra, §2.10 at 92.

The inheritance rights of adopted children focus on four issues: (1) the right of adopted children to inherit by, from, and through their adoptive parents; (2) the right of biological parents to inherit by, from, and through their

adopted-away child; (3) adult adoption; and (4) equitable adoption.

1. Inheritance By, From, and Through Adoptive Parents

Today, the general rule is that adopted children inherit from their adoptive parents but not from their biological parents. This result follows because adoption severs all legal ties of the adopted child to the biological family. Thus, an adopted child inherits by, from, or through the adoptive parents. See, e.g., UPC §2-114 ("for purposes of intestate succession by, through, or from a person . . . an adopted individual is the child or his or her adopting parents"). See also McGovern & Kurtz, supra, §2.10 at 92-93.

The last area to be liberalized was the right of adopted children to inherit through their adoptive parents. Thus, if an adoptive parent's parent dies, the adopted child might not be considered as "issue" of a predeceased parent because a third party (such as a grandparent) is sometimes considered "a stranger to the adoption" (i.e., not a party to the adoption contract). The policy rationale is that the grandparent would not want an adopted child "foisted on" the grandparent. The same problem exists in terms of a will or trust leaving a class gift to "grandchildren." Traditionally, an adopted grandchild did not inherit because of similar "stranger to the adoption" reasoning. See McGovern & Kurtz, supra, §2.10 at 94-95.

A famous Florida case, In re Hewett's Estate, 13 So. 2d 904 (Fla. 1943), addressed the question whether an adoptee had the right to inherit through his or her adopting parents (i.e., to inherit from other members of the adoptive family). **When William B. Hewett died, his nearest relatives were two first cousins and the adopted daughter of a deceased first cousin. The relevant statute provided that an adopted child "shall be an heir at law and for the purpose of inheritance be regarded as a lineal descendant of its adopting parents." The adopted daughter of Hewett's deceased first cousin claimed that she was entitled to the same interest of Hewett's estate that her adoptive father would have been entitled to had he been living at the time of Hewett's death. Rejecting her argument, the court held that the statute should be strictly construed and that the legislature did not intent to "put property into the hands of unheard of adopted children, contrary to the wishes and expectations of such ancestors." Id. at 907.**

However, the modern trend, recognizing the increased acceptance of adoption, is to treat adopted children the same as their biological counterparts and to include inheritance "though" as well as "from" the adoptive parents. See Fla. Stat. §732.108(1).

2. Inheritance By, From, and Through Biological Parents

The corollary to the general rule that adoptees can inherit by, from, and through their adoptive parents is that adoptees' inheritance rights are cut off by, from, and through the biological parents. This result flows from the fact that adoption severs legal ties to the biological parents. Restatement (Third) of Property, supra, at §2.5, cmt. e.

The rule that adoptees cannot inherit from their biological parents is subject to exceptions. The most common exception occurs with a stepparent adoption in which a child is adopted by the spouse of a biological parent. Many jurisdictions provide that in such a case, the child does not lose the right to inherit from the noncustodial biological parent. See UPC §2-114(b). For example, Florida law provides that an adopted child does not lose the right to inherit from or through his or her biological parent in the following situations: if the adoption was by the spouse of a natural parent (Fla. Stat. §732.108(a),(b)), or if the adoption was by a close relative (Fla. Stat. §732.108(c)). See also In re Estate of Kanevsky, 506 So.2d 1101 (Fla. Dist. Ct. App. 1987) (holding that the adopted son of the intestate's predeceased niece was entitled to inherit from the intestate's estate, notwithstanding the fact that the niece's husband remarried after the niece's death and his second wife adopted the niece's son). For discussion of the inheritance rights of stepchildren, see Section III, D3 supra.

Florida law also provides that adoptees may be included in class gift terminology. The inclusion of adoptees as lineal descendants of adoptive parents in class gift language (i.e., as members of a class under a will or trust) depends on whether adoptees are entitled to inherit under state laws of intestate succession (Fla. Stat. §732.608). See also Eclavea & Lease, Testate Succession, "Child" or "Children"; Adopted Children, 18 Fla. Jur. 2d Decedents' Property §349.

§732.108. Inheritance rights of adopted persons

(1) For the purpose of intestate succession by or from an adopted person, the adopted person is a lineal descendant of the adopting parent and is one of the natural kindred of all members of the adopting parent's family, and is not a lineal descendant of his or her natural parents, nor is he or she one of the kindred of any member of the natural parent's family or any prior adoptive parent's family, except that:

(a) Adoption of a child by the spouse of a natural parent has no effect on the relationship between the child and the natural parent or the natural parent's family.

(b) Adoption of a child by a natural parent's spouse who married the natural parent after the death of the other natural parent has no effect on the relationship between the child and the family of the deceased natural parent.

(c) Adoption of a child by a close relative, as defined in §63.172(2), has no effect on the relationship between the child and the families of the deceased natural parents.

(Laws 1974, ch. 74-106, §1; Laws 1975, ch 75-220, §11; Laws 1977, ch. 77-87, §7; Laws 1977, ch. 77-174, § 1; Laws 1987, ch. 87-27, §2. Amended by Laws 1997, ch. 97-102, §954, effective July 1, 1997.)

§732.608. Class gifts: inclusion of adoptees

Adopted persons and persons born out of wedlock are included in class gift terminology and terms of relationship, in accordance with rules for determining relationships for purposes of intestate succession.

(Laws 1974, ch. 74-106, §1; Laws 1975, ch. 75-220, §38.)

§63.172. Effect of judgment of adoption on rights of birth parents

(1) A judgment of adoption, whether entered by a court of this state, another state, or of any other place, has the following effect:

(a) It relieves the birth parents of the adopted person, except a birth parent who is a petitioner or who is married to a petitioner, of all parental rights and responsibilities.

(b) It terminates all legal relationships between the adopted person and the adopted person's relatives, including the birth parents, except a birth parent who is a petitioner or who is married to a petitioner, so that the adopted person thereafter is a stranger to his or her former relatives for all purposes, including the interpretation or construction of documents, statutes, and instruments, whether executed before or after entry of the adoption judgment, that do not expressly include the adopted person by name or by some designation not based on a parent and child or blood relationship, except that rights of inheritance shall be as provided in the Florida Probate Code.

(c) Except for rights of inheritance, it creates the relationship between the adopted person and the petitioner and all relatives of the petitioner that would have existed if the adopted person were a blood descendant of the petitioner born within wedlock. This relationship shall be created for all purposes, including applicability of statutes, documents, and instruments, whether executed before or after entry of the adoption judgment, that do not expressly exclude an adopted person from their operation or effect.

(2) If one or both parents of a child die without the relationship of parent and child having been previously terminated and a spouse of the living parent or a close relative of the child thereafter adopts the child, the child's right of inheritance from or through the deceased parent is unaffected by the adoption and, unless the court orders otherwise, the adoption will not terminate any grandparental rights delineated under chapter 752. For purposes of this subsection, a close relative of a child is the child's brother, sister, grandparent, aunt, or uncle.

(Laws 1973, ch. 73-159, §17; Laws 1975, ch. 75-226, §11; Laws 1979, ch. 79-369, §1; Laws 1987, ch. 87-27, §1; Laws 1990, ch. 90-139, §1; Laws 1992, ch. 92-96, §18; Laws 1993, ch. 93-192, §1; Laws 1995, ch. 95-147, §342. Amended by Laws 2001, ch. 2001-226, §1, effective January 1, 2002.)

3. Adult Adoption

Adult adoption enables one adult to adopt another adult and thereby to create a legally recognized family relationship. Persons may resort to adult adoption not only to create inheritance rights, but also for the following reasons: to obtain decision-making authority regarding a partner in cases of emergency or incapacity; secure visitation rights upon hospitalization or imprisonment; and permit recovery in tort actions and beneficiary privileges under insurance policies, retirement funds, and employee benefit packages. Angie Smokla, Note, That's the Ticket: A New Way of Defining Family, 10 Cornell J.L. & Pub. Pol'y 629, 638 (2001). The practice does have some disadvantages: The adoption is irrevocable and destroys the adoptee's legal relationship with the natural parents (thereby terminating inheritance rights vis a vis the natural parent). Id. at 639.

All states except Alabama and Nebraska permit adult adoption, although some states restrict the practice. Id. at 638-639. For example, some states require that the adoptee be younger than the adopter (or a certain number of years younger), the adoptee be a specified relative, the adoptee lived with the adopter a specified number of years during the adoptee's minority or had a filial relationship with the adopter during minority, or that the adoptee must be disabled or mentally retarded. Id.

Florida and a few other states expressly restrict adoption by same-sex couples. Such bans apply to adult adoptions as well as adoption of minors. (However, Florida does permit same-sex couples to serve as foster parents.) Florida was the first state to ban adoptions by homosexuals in 1977 (Fla. Stat. §63.042(3)). See also Conn. Gen. Stat. §45a-726a (2004) (sexual orientation may be considered and nothing shall require

placement with a prospective adoptive or foster parent who is homosexual or bisexual); Miss. Ann. Code §93-17-3(2) (2004)(adoption by couples of the same gender is prohibited). New Hampshire formerly banned homosexual adoption, but lifted that ban in 2001. Martin R. Gardner, Adoption by Homosexuals in the Wake of Lawrence v. Texas, 6 J. L. Fam. Stud. 19, 30 (2004). Further, Utah bans adoption by unmarried, cohabiting couples (Utah Ann. Code §78-30-1(3)(b)(2002)), which by definition includes all same-sex couples.

In practice, even in states without a statutory ban, many state courts do not allow adoption by homosexuals or same-sex couples, either because courts maintain that such adoptions would be contrary to the best interests of the child, or because parental termination statutes prevent the practice. Gardner, supra, at 23.

The Florida ban has been challenged on the federal and state levels. In Lofton v. Secretary of the Department of Children and Family Services, 358 F.3d 804 (11th Cir. 2004), cert. denied, 543 U.S. 1081 (2005), gay and lesbian foster parents and guardians challenged the constitutionality of Florida's prohibition against adoption by gays and lesbians. The federal district court granted summary judgment for the state. The Eleventh Circuit affirmed, holding that relationships involving foster and legal guardian families did not create a protected liberty interest in family integrity under the Due Process Clause of the Fourteenth Amendment and also that the statute did not violate the Equal Protection Clause. See also Cox v. Florida Department of Health and Rehabilitative Services, 656 So. 2d 902 (Fla. 1995) (holding that the Florida ban on gay adoptions did not violate state constitutional rights to privacy or due process and was not unconstitutionally vague, but failing to reach the equal protection issue because of an insufficient record).

§63.042. Who may adopt

(1) Any person, a minor or an adult, may be adopted.

(2) The following persons may adopt:

(a) A husband and wife jointly;

(b) An unmarried adult; or

(c) A married person without the other spouse joining as a petitioner, if the person to be adopted is not his or her spouse, and if:

1. The other spouse is a parent of the person to be adopted and consents to the adoption; or

2. The failure of the other spouse to join in the petition or to consent to the adoption is excused by the court for good cause shown or in the best interest of the child.

(3) No person eligible to adopt under this statute may adopt if that person is a homosexual.

(4) No person eligible under this section shall be prohibited from adopting solely because such person possesses a physical disability or handicap, unless it is determined by the court or adoption entity that such disability or handicap renders such person incapable of serving as an effective parent.

(Laws 1973, ch. 73-159, §4; Laws 1977, ch. 77-140, §1; L. 1980, ch. 80-194, §1; Laws 1992, ch. 92-96, §4; Laws 1995, ch. 95-147, §336. Amended by Laws 2003, ch. 2003-58, §4, effective May 30, 2003.)

4. Equitable Adoption

Equitable adoption (also called "virtual adoption," "de facto adoption," or "adoption by estoppel") is a judicially created equitable remedy that protects the interests of a child whose foster parents or stepparents agree to adopt the child but never finalize the adoption. Florida recognizes equitable adoption and calls it "virtual adoption."

The issue of equitable adoption arises most often when the foster parent or stepparent dies intestate without legally adopting the child. Application of the doctrine results in enabling the child to inherit an intestate share of the deceased parent's estate.

Case law reflects two theoretical bases for the doctrine: (1) contract theory, and (2) estoppel theory. According to the contract theory, courts "presuppose that the foster parent as promisor has contracted to effect a legal adoption and that by granting relief the court is specifically enforcing that contract." Jan Ellen Rein, Relatives by Blood, Adoption, and Association: Who Should Get What and Why (The Impact of Adoptions, Adult Adoptions, and Equitable Adoptions on Intestate Succession and Class Gifts), 37 Vand. L. Rev. 711, 770 (1984).

On the other hand, courts using the estoppel theory "stress the child's performance of filial services for the foster parent and purport to protect the child 'against the fraud of the adoptive parents' neglect or design in failing to do that which he in equity was obligated to do.'" Id. at 771. Under the latter theory, courts emphasize that the parent (or his or her heirs) is estopped from asserting the invalidity of the adoption proceeding when the child "performed" filial responsibilities and the adoptive parents received all the benefits and, in fact, induced the child's performance based on representations as to the existence of the adoption. Rein criticizes that case law often fails to distinguish between the contract or estoppel analysis (id. at 771), and that the facts of most cases do not fit either of these legal theories well (id. at 772).

Most jurisdictions apply the doctrine in limited situations. In most states, the doctrine does not extend beyond the child. For

example, a foster parent may not inherit from an equitably adopted child. Rebecca C. Bell, Comment, Virtual Adoption: The Difficulty of Creating an Exception to the Statutory Scheme, 29 Stetson L. Rev. 415, 416 (1999). See also Jolley v. Seamco Laboratories, Inc., 828 So. 2d 1050 (Fla. Dist. Ct. App. 2002) (holding that an equitably adopted child was not a "survivor" for purposes of eligibility to sue for wrongful death of father).

Florida law has adhered strictly to the requirement that there must be an agreement to adopt between the biological parents and the foster parents. For example, in Green v. Boyd, 794 So. 2d 668 (Fla. Dist. Ct. App. 2001), the appellate court reversed a trial court ruling that plaintiff was equitably adopted by her stepfather who died intestate, absent clear and convincing evidence that there was an agreement to adopt her between her natural parents and alleged adoptive parents. However, in Matter of Heirs of Hodge, 470 So. 2d 740 (Fla. 1985), the appellate court found that there was sufficient evidence to conclude that the alleged adoptive parents agreed to adopt the daughter when her biological father gave her to the decedents when she was three years old and she lived with them as their daughter.

See also Restatement (Third) of Property, supra, at §2.5 cmt. k (discussing equitable adoption); Tracey Bateman Farrell, Annot., Modern Status of Law as to Equitable Adoption or Adoption by Estoppel, 122 A.L.R. 5th 205 (2004).

D. Nonmarital Children

Historically, children born out of wedlock (now termed "nonmarital children") were considered illegitimate and ineligible to inherit under intestacy laws. Gradually, the law permitted nonmarital children to inherit from their mother. McGovern & Kurtz, supra, §2.9 at 85 (pointing out that several American statutes so provided by the early nineteenth century). However, the nonmarital child's right to inherit by, from, and through the biological father has been more problematic because of problems of proof. Many states impose a higher standard of proof (or require particular kinds of proof) for nonmarital children to inherit from their biological fathers. Id. at 85-86. The United States Supreme Court held that, in order for a nonmarital child to inherit from a noncustodial biological father, a state may require a higher level of proof in the form of a judicial declaration of paternity (Lalli v. Lalli, 439 U.S. 259 (1978)), but may not require that the child's parents subsequently marry after the child's birth (Trimble v. Gordon, 430 U.S. 762 (1977)). As explained infra, this area of the law since has been liberalized.

Another area of inheritance law concerns the rights of parents of nonmarital children to inherit by, from, and through the child. Most states today allow parents of a nonmarital child, and their relatives, to inherit from the child. McGovern & Kurtz, supra, §2.9 at 89. The UPC, however, imposes limitations on the parents' ability to inherit from and through a nonmarital child. Specifically, UPC §2-114(c) provides that the parent of a nonmarital child and that parent's kin do not inherit from and through the nonmarital child unless that natural parent openly treated the child as his or her child, and provided child support during the child's minority. According to the Restatement (Third) of Property §2.5, "An individual is the child of his or her genetic parents, whether or not they are married to each other. . . ." Exceptions to this rule are if: the child has been adopted out, is born via assisted reproductive technology, or the parent has been disqualified from inheritance for certain acts of misconduct. See also McGovern & Kurtz, supra, §2.9 at 89.

Today, an increasing number of jurisdictions recognize the inheritance rights of nonmarital children to inherit from their mothers as well as their fathers. Many states have done so by adopting the Uniform Parentage Act (UPA), approved by NCCUSL in 1973. The UPA was the most important of the various uniform laws adopted by NCCUSL that addressed the rights of illegitimates. (Other uniform acts included: the Uniform Illegitimacy Act in 1922, the Uniform Blood Tests To Determine Paternity Act in 1952, and the Uniform Paternity Act in 1960, the Uniform Putative and Unknown Fathers Act in 1988, and the Uniform Status of Children of Assisted Conception Act in 1988.)

As of December 2000, the original version of the UPA was in effect in 19 states, and several additional states had enacted significant portions of it. The original UPA declared that all children should be treated equally without regard to the marital status of their parents, and established a set of rules for presumptions of parentage. When the UPC underwent substantial revision in 1990, it conferred additional importance on the Uniform Parentage Act by adopting similar language, providing that children have the right to inherit from their biological parents "without regard to the parents' marital status" (UPC §2-114(a)), and also providing that the parent and child relationship will be determined under the state's Parentage Act or other appropriate legislation.

NCCUSL promulgated a revised UPA in 2000 and amended it in 2002. The revised UPA replaces all earlier uniform acts dealing with parentage. As explained above, the original UPA established several presumptions to facilitate the determination of paternity. The revised and amended UPA retains these presumptions of paternity with minor modifications. Thus, a man is presumed to be the father of a child if: (1) the child was born during the father's marriage to the child's mother; (2) the child was conceived during the marriage but born within 300 days after its termination (by death, annulment, declaration of invalidity, or divorce); (3) the child was conceived or born during an invalid marriage or within 300 days after its termination by the aforementioned methods; (4) the child was born before a valid or invalid marriage accompanied by other facts indicating that the husband is the father (i.e., he voluntarily acknowledged paternity in state birth records, agreed to be and is named on the child's birth certificate, or promised in a writing to support the child); or (5) for the first 2 years of the child's life, the father resided in the same household with the child and openly held out the child as his own. UPA §204(a).

The revised Act makes two changes to the earlier presumptions of the former Act. New subsection (5) changes former UPA §4(4) that created a presumption of paternity by "holding out" (if a man "receives the child into his home and openly holds out the child as his natural child"). The lack of a time period in the earlier Act led to uncertainty about whether the presumption could arise if the child's residence in the home occurred for a brief time or took place long after the child's birth. See revised UPA §204(a) cmt. The revised Act now includes an explicit requirement that the man reside with the child for the first 2 years of the child's life. In addition, the revised UPA eliminates a presumption in the earlier Act that created a presumption of paternity if the man "acknowledges his paternity of the child in a writing filed with [named agency] [and] the mother does not dispute the acknowledgment within a reasonable time." UPA §4(5)(1973)). This presumption was eliminated because it conflicted with a new provision on voluntary acknowledgment of paternity which now establishes actual paternity rather than merely a presumption of paternity.

Increasing recognition of the rights of nonmarital children has led to a more favorable attitude by courts and legislatures toward inclusion of such children in wills. McGovern & Kurtz, supra, §2.9 at 90 (citing UPC §2-705 to the effect that unless a will provides otherwise "individuals born out of wedlock and their respective descendants [are] are included in class gifts. . . .").

See generally Ralph Brashier, Disinheritance and the Modern Family, 45 Case W. Res. L. Rev. 84 (1994); Karen A. Hauser, Inheritance Rights for Extramarital Children: New Science Plus Old Intermediate Scrutiny Add Up to the Need for Change, 65 U. Cin. L. Rev. 891 (1997).

Florida law formerly required that a nonmarital child could inherit from his or her father under intestate succession laws only if the father executed a written acknowledgment of paternity in the presence of a competent witness (Fla. Stat. §731.29(1), repealed). Case law established that the writing could be informal and that the witnesses did not need to subscribe to the acknowledgment. Wall v. Altobello, 49 So.2d 532 (Fla. 1950); In re Horne's Estate, 7 So.2d 13 (Fla. 1942). However, in In re Burris Estate, 361 So.2d 152 (Fla. 1978), the Florida Supreme Court held that such a requirement violates the nonmarital child's right to equal protection.

Currently, Florida law provides that a nonmarital child is a lineal descendant of his or her mother (and also kindred of all members of the mother's family) for purposes of intestate succession (Fla. Stat. §732.108(2)). However, a nonmarital child is a lineal descendant or his or her father (and kindred of all members of the father's family) only in the following situations: (1) the natural parents participated in a marriage ceremony before or after the child's birth, even though the attempted marriage was void (Fla. Stat. §732.108(2)(a)); (2) the paternity of the father was established by an adjudication before or after the father's death (Fla. Stat. §732.108(2)(b)); or (3) the father acknowledged his paternity in writing (Fla. Stat. §732.108(2)(c)).

Florida law also provides that nonmarital children will be included in class gift terminology in accordance with the rules for determining relationships for the purposes of intestate succession (Fla. Stat. §732.608).

§732.108. Nonmarital child's right to inherit by intestate succession

(1) For the purpose of intestate succession by or from an adopted person, the adopted person is a lineal descendant of the adopting parent and is one of the natural kindred of all members of the adopting parent's family, and is not a lineal descendant of his or her natural parents, nor is he or she one of the kindred of any member of the natural parent's family or any prior adoptive parent's family, except that:

(a) Adoption of a child by the spouse of a natural parent has no effect on the relationship between the child and the natural parent or the natural parent's family.

(b) Adoption of a child by a natural parent's spouse who married the natural parent after the death of the other natural parent has no effect on the relationship between the child and the family of the deceased natural parent.

(c) Adoption of a child by a close relative, as defined in s 63.172(2), has no effect on the relationship between the child and the families of the deceased natural parents.

(2) For the purpose of intestate succession in cases not covered by subsection (1), a person born out of wedlock is a lineal descendant of his or her mother and is one of the natural kindred of all members of the mother's family. The person is also a lineal descendant of his or her father and is one of the natural kindred of all members of the father's family, if:

(a) The natural parents participated in a marriage ceremony before or after the birth of the person born out of wedlock, even though the attempted marriage is void.

(b) The paternity of the father is established by an adjudication before or after the death of the father.

(c) The paternity of the father is acknowledged in writing by the father.

(Laws 1974, ch. 74-106, §1; Laws 1975, ch 75-220, §11; Laws 1977, ch. 77-87, §7; Laws 1977, ch. 77-174, §1; Laws 1987, ch. 87-27, §2. Amended by Laws 1997, ch. 97-102, §954, effective July 1, 1997.)

§732.608. Nonmarital child's right to inherit a class gift

Adopted persons and persons born out of wedlock are included in class gift terminology and terms of relationship, in accordance with rules for determining relationships for purposes of intestate succession.

(Laws 1974, ch. 74-106, §1; Laws 1975, ch. 75-220, §38.)

§731.29. Nonmarital child's right to inherit by intestate succession [repealed]

(1) Every illegitimate child is an heir of his mother, and also of the person who, in writing, signed in the presence of a competent witness, acknowledges himself to be the father. Such illegitimate child shall inherit from his mother and also, when so recognized, from his father, in the same manner as if the child had been born in lawful wedlock. However, such illegitimate child does not represent his father or mother by inheriting any part of the estate of the parents' kindred, either lineal or collateral, unless his parents have intermarried, in which event such illegitimate child shall be deemed legitimate for all purposes.

(2) If any illegitimate child dies intestate, without lawful issue or spouse, his estate shall descend to his mother, or, in case of her decease, to her heirs at law.

[Repealed by Laws 1974, ch. 74-106, §3.]

E. Disqualification for Misconduct

1. Slayer Disqualification

A person can lose the right to inherit under the intestacy statutes because of misconduct. The most common form of misconduct that serves as a bar to inheritance is the murder of the decedent (known as the "slayer disqualification").

The common law had no slayer disqualification because felons normally forfeited all their property. Thus, many American jurisdictions permitted slayers to inherit from their victims until legislatures remedied the gap by enacting statutory bars to inheritance. Most states now have statutes that prevent a murderer from inheriting from the victim. McGovern & Kurtz, supra, §2.7 at 68. These statutes developed in a piecemeal fashion; therefore, many statutes initially failed to address inheritance involving insurance policies or joint tenancy property. In such cases, courts sometimes used principles of constructive trust (an equitable remedy to prevent unjust enrichment) to preclude the slayer from inheriting. The policy justification is that a wrongdoer should not benefit from his or her wrong.

Many state statutes require that the slayer must have been "convicted" of murder in order to be barred from inheritance. Problems arise if the slayer has not been tried, or has been acquitted (or convicted of a lesser offense). Some courts conclude that the absence of a conviction does not prevent them from precluding the slayer from inheriting. In cases where a slayer has been acquitted (or convicted of a lesser offense), some courts justify the preclusion on the ground that the standard in a civil proceeding is lower than the reasonable doubt standard required for a criminal conviction. McGovern & Kurtz, supra, §2.7 at 70-71.

The Uniform Probate Code bars inheritance by an individual who "feloniously and intentionally kills the decedent" (UPC §2-803). The UPC extends the slayer disqualification to beneficiaries of many types of property (including joint tenancies and life insurance) (id.). In terms of joint tenancy property, the UPC terminates the right of survivorship but permits the slayer to retain his or her half-interest in the property (id. at §2-803(c)(2)). Moreover, the UPC also provides that the policy of preclusion can apply even if a particular property interest is not explicitly specified by statute (id. at §2-803(f)).

If the slayer is disqualified, the property is distributed as if the slayer predeceased the victim. McGovern & Kurtz, supra, §2.7 at 73; Restatement (Second) of Property, Donative Transfers, §34.8, cmt. b (1992); UPC §2-803 (property is distributed as if the killer

disclaimed). As a result, the children of the slayer may inherit the property, either by representation in the intestacy situation or under an anti-lapse statute in the testate situation.

Like the UPC, Florida law precludes a person who "unlawfully and intentionally" kills or participates in procuring the death of the decedent from inheriting by intestate succession or by the decedent's will or trust (Fla. Stat. §732.802(1)). All aforementioned property interests pass as if the slayer predeceased the decedent. Id.

Under the Florida slayer statute, the children of a slayer can take under the will or any other instrument of the decedent. See In re Estate of Benson, 548 So.2d 775 (Fla. Dist. Ct. 1989)(allowing murderer-brother's minor children to inherit their parent's share of his testate mother's estate).

The Florida slayer statute also precludes the slayer from taking the decedent's share of any joint tenancy interest in real or personal property or interest in multiple-party accounts in financial institutions (Fla. Stat. §732.802(2)). The slayer retains his or her interest but takes no rights by survivorship. In addition, the homicide results in a severance of the tenancy. The decedent's share passes to the decedent's heirs or beneficiaries (Fla. Stat. §732.802(2)). For discussion of joint tenancy, see Chapter VIII infra.

Similarly, the beneficiaries of life insurance policies, other contractual arrangement, or bonds, are precluded from taking any benefit by virtue of a slaying and the property is treated as if the killer had predeceased the decedent (Fla. Stat. §732.802(3)).

Like the UPC, Florida law has a "catch-all" provision that specifies that any acquisition of property or interest by the slayer that is not previously mentioned shall be treated "in accordance with the principles of this section" (Fla. Stat. §732.803)(4)). A recently adopted statute precludes the slayer from taking as a beneficiary of a trust (Fla. Stat. §736.1104).

For purposes of determining whether a killing was "unlawful and intentional," the Florida statute specifies that a final judgment of conviction of murder is conclusive. However, absent such a determination, the court may determine by "the greater weight of the evidence" whether the killing was unlawful and intentional (Fla. Stat. §732.802(5)).

Finally, Florida law addresses the rights of a bona fide purchaser who purchases property for value and without notice from the slayer prior to the homicide. By statute, a bona fide purchaser's rights shall not be affected if he or she purchased property from the killer which the slayer would have acquired except for the statute; however, the slayer is liable for the amount of the proceeds or the value of the property (Fla. Stat. §732.802(6)).

For classic articles on the slayer disqualification, see Mary Louise Fellows, The Slayer Rule: Not Solely a Matter of Equity, 71 Iowa L. Rev. 489 (1986); William M. McGovern, Jr., Homicide and Succession to Property, 68 Mich. L. Rev. 65 (1969); Jeffrey G. Sherman, Mercy Killing and the Right to Inherit, 61 U. Cin. L. Rev. 803 (1993).

§732.802. Slayer disqualification: generally

(1) A surviving person who unlawfully and intentionally kills or participates in procuring the death of the decedent is not entitled to any benefits under the will or under the Florida Probate Code, and the estate of the decedent passes as if the killer had predeceased the decedent. Property appointed by the will of the decedent to or for the benefit of the killer passes as if the killer had predeceased the decedent.

(2) Any joint tenant who unlawfully and intentionally kills another joint tenant thereby effects a severance of the interest of the decedent so that the share of the decedent passes as the decedent's property and the killer has no rights by survivorship. This provision applies to joint tenancies with right of survivorship and tenancies by the entirety in real and personal property; joint and multiple-party accounts in banks, savings and loan associations, credit unions, and other institutions; and any other form of coownership with survivorship incidents.

(3) A named beneficiary of a bond, life insurance policy, or other contractual arrangement who unlawfully and intentionally kills the principal obligee or the person upon whose life the policy is issued is not entitled to any benefit under the bond, policy, or other contractual arrangement; and it becomes payable as though the killer had predeceased the decedent.

(4) Any other acquisition of property or interest by the killer, including a life estate in homestead property, shall be treated in accordance with the principles of this section.

(5) A final judgment of conviction of murder in any degree is conclusive for purposes of this section. In the absence of a conviction of murder in any degree, the court may determine by the greater weight of the evidence whether the killing was unlawful and intentional for purposes of this section.

(6) This section does not affect the rights of any person who, before rights under this section have been adjudicated, purchases from the killer for value and without notice property which the killer would have acquired except for this section, but the killer is liable for the amount of the proceeds or the value of the property. Any insurance company, bank, or other obligor making payment according to the terms of its policy or obligation is not liable by reason of this section unless prior to payment it

has received at its home office or principal address written notice of a claim under this section.
(Laws 1974, ch. 74-106, §1; Laws 1975, ch. 75-220, §41; Laws 1982, ch. 82-71, §1.)

§736.1104. Slayer disqualification applicable to trust beneficiaries

(1) A beneficiary of a trust who unlawfully and intentionally kills or unlawfully and intentionally participates in procuring the death of the settlor or another person on whose death such beneficiary's interest depends, is not entitled to any trust interest, including homestead, dependent on the victim's death, and such interest shall devolve as though the killer had predeceased the victim.

(2) A final judgment of conviction of murder in any degree is conclusive for the purposes of this section. In the absence of a murder conviction in any degree, the court may determine by the greater weight of the evidence whether the killing was unlawful and intentional for purposes of this section.
(Laws 2006, ch. 2006-217, §11, effective July 1, 2007.)

2. Other Unworthy Heir Statutes

States have a variety of other "unworthy heir" statutes. Professor Frances Foster points out that many jurisdictions disqualify spouses who abandon the decedent, or disqualify parents who abandon or refuse to support their children. Frances H. Foster, The Family Paradigm of Inheritance Law, 80 N.C. L. Rev. 199, 207 n. 38 (2001). See also UPC §2-114(c) (permitting inheritance only if the parent has openly treated the child as belonging to the parent, and has not refused to support the child); Restatement (Third) of Property, supra, at §2.5(5) (barring a parent from inheriting from or through a child, if the parent "has refused to acknowledge or has abandoned his or her child, or a person whose parental rights have been terminated"). The common law barred an adulterous wife from claiming dower. McGovern & Kurtz, supra, §2.11 at 104.

An interesting case involving an unworthy heir statute is In re Estate of Lunsford, 547 S.E.2d 483 (N.C. Ct. App. 2001), vacated and remanded, 556 S.E.2d 292 (N.C. 2001). A mother obtained a wrongful death award on behalf of the estate of her 17-year-old daughter who was killed in an automobile accident. Because wrongful death proceeds in North Carolina are paid to surviving family members in accordance with intestate succession law (which bars a parent who abandons a child from inheriting), the court prevented the father from inheriting half of the proceeds. (The father had paid only $100 in child support and had visited the daughter rarely in 15 years.) The case was remanded for a determination of whether the father was eligible under one of two statutory exceptions (where the abandoning parent resumes care and maintenance at least one year prior to the child's death or where the parent was deprived of the custody under a court order but substantially complied with all court orders for child support). See generally Heyward D. Armstrong, Comment, In re Estate of Lunsford and Statutory Ambiguity: Trying to Reconcile Child Abandonment and the Intestate Succession Act, 81 N.C. L. Rev. 1149 (2003).

To date, California is the only state to disqualify an heir from inheritance through intestate succession, elective share, homestead allowance, or any other statutory allowances for manifesting a pattern of physical violence directed toward the decedent. Thomas H. Shepherd, Comment, It's the 21st Century . . . Time for Probate Codes to Address Family Violence: A Proposal that Deals with the Realities of the Problem, 20 St. Louis U. Pub. L. Rev. 449, 450 (2001). Specifically, California law precludes persons from exercising their inheritance rights if they physically abuse or neglect an elder or dependent adult. In such cases, the abuser is considered to have predeceased the decedent in the determination of shares of the estate (Cal. Prob. Code §259). Abuse is broadly defined to include physical abuse and neglect, false imprisonment, and fiduciary abuse. See generally Kymberleigh N. Korpus, Note, Extinguishing Inheritance Rights: California Breaks New Ground in the Fight Against Elder Abuse But Fails to Build an Effective Foundation, 52 Hastings L.J. 537 (2001); Robin L. Preble, Family Violence and Family Property: A Proposal For Reform, 13 Law & Ineq. 401 (1995).

Florida also has protective legislation for elderly persons, but the law does not disqualify abusers from inheriting. The Adult Protective Servives Act (Fla. Stat. §§415.101 to 415.113), enacted in 1973, requires mandatory reporting of abuse of elderly persons and disabled adults, provides protective services investigations of abuse, creates a private cause of action, and specifies penalties for abusers.

Florida case law disqualifies spouses for inheritance purposes because of designated "immoral" conduct (i.e., seeking a legal separation, bigamy, etc). For example, in In re Van Meter's Estate, 214 So. 2d 639 (Fla. Dist. Ct. App. 1968), the appellate court held that a wife, who procured a decree of separate maintenance, was not entitled to inherit the homestead of decedent. And, in Doherty v. Traxler, 66 So. 2d 274 (Fla. 1974), the Florida Supreme Court ruled that a man who married plaintiff and then 24 hours later left her, and subsequently had a bigamous marriage with another woman for 20 years, was disqualified from serving as administrator of the former's estate or inheriting her estate. See also In re Estate of Butler, 444 So. 2d 477 (Fla. Dist. Ct. App. 1984) (holding that decedent's first wife was estopped from asserting her rights as the decedent's widow because she knew that they had never been divorced when she married another person). See generally Theresa L. Leming, Descent and Distribution, Bigamous Marriage of the Surviving Spouse, 23 Am. Jur. 2d, §128 (2007).

Several commentators advocate law reform that would deny intestate shares to persons who abandon, fail to support, or maltreat a decedent. See Frances H. Foster, Towards a Behavior-Based Model of Inheritance?: The Chinese Experiment, 32 U.C. Davis L. Rev. 77 (1998); Paula A. Monopoli, "Deadbeat Dads": Should Support and Inheritance Be Linked?, 49 U. Miami L. Rev. 257 (1994); Preble, supra; Anne-Marie E. Rhodes, Abandoning Parents Under Intestacy: Where We Are, Where We Need to Go, 27 Ind. L. Rev. 517 (1994).

IV. Simultaneous Death

A basic tenet of inheritance law is that an heir must outlive the intestate (or a beneficiary must outlive a testator) in order to inherit from the decedent. The issue of survival of family members is cast into doubt when persons die simultaneously (technically, nearly simultaneously). This event occurs with increasing frequency because of the death of multiple family members in airplane crashes and automobile accidents. Simultaneous death poses a problem not merely for intestate succession but also for testate succession. Provisions in trusts also may lead to questions regarding the order of death.

The common law required survival only for an instant for inheritance purposes. That standard led to considerable litigation involving family members who attempted to prove that one family member had outlived another by manifesting even the slightest signs of life.

The original version of the Uniform Simultaneous Death Act first addressed the issue in 1940. That widely adopted Act required "sufficient evidence" to prove that two persons died otherwise than simultaneously. Uniform Simultaneous Death Act §2 (1940). The UPC now also requires survival for 120 hours and mandates a clear and convincing burden of proof. UPC §2-702(b). A beneficiary who fails to survive for the requisite period is deemed to have predeceased the decedent. A subsequent version of the Uniform Simultaneous Death Act followed the UPC by also requiring that a person survive by 120 hours in order to inherit from the decedent. Uniform Simultaneous Death Act §4 (1993).

Florida law provides rules for determining the sequence of deaths (Fla. Stat. §732.601). Florida has adopted the original version of USDA. According to Florida Statutes §732.601(1), when title to property or its devolution depends on priority of death and there is insufficient evidence that the persons have died otherwise than simultaneously, the property of each person shall be disposed of as if that person survived. On the other hand, if sufficient evidence as to the order of death does exist or a contrary intention does exist in the governing instrument, then the statute is not applicable.

Evidence that is sufficient to determine whether one person has survived the other is an evidentiary issue. For example, in Rimmer v. Tesla, 201 So. 2d 573 (Fla. Dist. Ct. App. 1967), the appellate court held that the testimony of a doctor, who arrived at the scene of the accident within minutes of the car accident and determined that husband had no carotid pulse in neck but that wife continued to breathe for 15 minutes before dying, was sufficient to support a finding that the deaths of husband and wife occurred otherwise than simultaneously, in an action instituted by wife's administratrix to establish the right to administer real property formerly held by both spouses.

Florida law (Fla. Stat. §732.601(3)) also applies in cases of joint tenancy. When there is insufficient evidence that two joint tenants or tenants by the entirety died otherwise than simultaneously, the property so held is to be distributed one-half as if one had survived and one-half as if the other had survived, unless a contrary intention appears in the governing instrument.

In addition, Florida law (Fla. Stat. §732.601) also applies in situations where the insured and the beneficiary in the insurance context have both died simultaneously. When the insured and the beneficiary in a policy of life or accident insurance have died and there is insufficient evidence that they died otherwise than simultaneously, the proceeds of the policy shall be distributed as if the insured had survived the beneficiary.

§732.601. Simultaneous Death Law

Unless a contrary intention appears in the governing instrument:

(1) When title to property or its devolution depends on priority of death and there is insufficient evidence that the persons have died otherwise than simultaneously, the property of each person shall be disposed of as if that person survived.

(2) When two or more beneficiaries are designated to take successively by reason of survivorship under another person's disposition of property and there is insufficient evidence that the

beneficiaries died otherwise than simultaneously, the property thus disposed of shall be divided into as many equal parts as there are successive beneficiaries and the parts shall be distributed to those who would have taken if each designated beneficiary had survived.

(3) When there is insufficient evidence that two joint tenants or tenants by the entirety died otherwise than simultaneously, the property so held shall be distributed one-half as if one had survived and one-half as if the other had survived. If there are more than two joint tenants and all of them so died, the property thus distributed shall be in the proportion that one bears to the number of joint tenants.

(4) When the insured and the beneficiary in a policy of life or accident insurance have died and there is insufficient evidence that they died otherwise than simultaneously, the proceeds of the policy shall be distributed as if the insured had survived the beneficiary.

(Laws 1974, ch. 74-106, §1; Laws 1975, ch. 75-220, §34. Amended by Laws 1997, ch. 97-102, §966, effective July 1, 1997; Laws 2001, ch. 2001-226, §50, effective January 1, 2002.)

V. Advancements, Releases, and Assignments

Some transactions by the decedent prior to death may affect the share of an heir to the decedent's intestate estate. An advancement is an inter vivos gift of real or personal property that anticipates the recipient's inheritance. If the gift is considered an advancement, then the donee's share of the donor's estate is reduced to compensate for the advancement. The process of equalization is referred to as "hotchpot."

Whether or not a gift is considered an advancement on an inheritance depends on the intent of the donor. McGovern & Kurtz, supra, at §2.6 at 63-65. The common law assumed a gift was an advancement, presuming that a decedent would wish to deal with all children equally. Florida, similar to the UPC (§2-109(a)), reverses this presumption, and thereby requires a writing to evidence the donor's intent to treat a gift as an advancement on a recipient's inheritance. Specifically, a gift will be treated as an advancement only if (1) the decedent declares in a contemporaneous writing that the gift is an advancement, or (2) if the heir acknowledges in writing that the gift is an advancement (Fla. Stat. §733.806; UPC §2-109(a)).

At common law, the doctrine applied only to children. In some states today, advancements affect descendants of the donor. McGovern & Kurtz, supra, §2.6 at 65. In Florida, and under the UPC, the doctrine applies to "heirs" (Fla. Stat. §733.806; UPC §2-109(a)).

Valuation of the advanced property occurs at the time the heir came into possession or enjoyment of the property or at the time of death of the decedent, whichever occurs first (Fla. Stat. §733.806, UPC §2-109(b)).

The valuation of an advancement arose in Livingstone v. Crickenberger, 141 So. 2d 794 (Fla. Dist. Ct. App. 1962). In a partition suit to divide the decedent's property, an appellate court held that the valuation of an advancement should not be based on the appraisal report of the commissioners that was made years after the heir acquired the property.

According to Florida law and the UPC, if the recipient of the property does not survive the decedent, the property shall not be taken into account in computing the intestate share to be received by the recipient's descendants unless the declaration or acknowledgment provides otherwise (Fla. Stat. §733.806, UPC §2-109(c)).

The Restatement (Third) of Property §2.6 also follows the UPC rule on advancements. Restatement (Third) of Property, supra, §2.6 cmt. b.

Note that the advancement doctrine operates in the intestate situation. A comparable rule as to gifts in the testate situation (i.e., a gift by a testator to a potential beneficiary after execution of a will) is referred to as the "satisfaction" doctrine, or "ademption by satisfaction" (Fla. Stat. §732.609). On the satisfaction doctrine, see Chapter XV infra.

Other transactions prior to the decedent's death that affect inheritance rights of the heirs are assignments of an expectancy interest and releases. An assignment occurs when a potential heir assigns his or her expectancy interest in the decedent's estate to someone other than the intestate for fair and adequate consideration. The term "expectancy interest" means that the assignor is giving away something he or she does not yet have. Therefore, because the interest is an expectancy and not a vested right, an assignment is not binding on the assignor's issue.

A release is similar to an assignment, except that, in exchange for consideration, the potential heir transfers his or her interest in certain property owned by the intestate to the intestate. For example, a parent quitclaims a deed for Blackacre to a child in exchange for a release of the child's share of the parent's estate. The effect of a release differs from that of an assignment. In the release situation, the child's issue (such as a grandchild) are bound by the release and will not share in the parent's estate. The policy rationale is that, unlike in the assignment situation, the parent

is on notice that the release has occurred and can take steps to bring the grandchild into the estate plan.

Under Florida law, an expectancy interest in property may be assigned. However, a mere quitclaim deed that contains no expression of an intent to convey an expectancy does not convey property that the grantor might inherit in the future. In re Rosin, 248 B.R. 625 (Bkrtcy, M.D. Fla. 1998). See also Diaz v. Rood, 851 So. 2d 843 (Fla. Dist. Ct. App. 2003) (holding that an expectancy may be the subject of an assignment but the trial court applied an incorrect standard to determine whether sufficient consideration existed to support a former husband's pre-divorce assignment of an inheritance in his father's estate to his separated wife).

On releases and assignments, see generally Katheleen R. Guzman, Releasing the Expectancy, 34 Ariz. St. L.J. 775 (2002) (examining the differences between releases and assignments within traditional succession doctrine and proposing reform in release law).

§732.609. Ademption by satisfaction

Property that a testator gave to a person in the testator's lifetime is treated as a satisfaction of a devise to that person, in whole or in part, only if the will provides for deduction of the lifetime gift, the testator declares in a contemporaneous writing that the gift is to be deducted from the devise or is in satisfaction of the devise, or the devisee acknowledges in writing that the gift is in satisfaction. For purposes of part satisfaction, property given during the testator's lifetime is valued at the time the devisee came into possession or enjoyment of the property or at the time of the death of the testator, whichever occurs first.

(Laws 1974, ch. 74-106, §1; Laws 1975, ch. 75-220, §38.)

§733.806. Advancement

If a person dies intestate, property that the decedent gave during lifetime to an heir is treated as an advancement against the heir's share of the estate only if declared in a contemporaneous writing by the decedent or acknowledged in writing by the heir. The property advanced shall be valued at the time the heir came into possession or enjoyment of the property or at the time of the death of the decedent, whichever first occurs. If the recipient of the property does not survive the decedent, the property shall not be taken into account in computing the intestate share to be received by the recipient's descendants unless the declaration or acknowledgment provides otherwise.

(Laws 1974, ch. 74-106, §1; Laws 1975, ch. 75-220, §89. Amended by Laws 1997, ch. 97-102, §1021, effective July 1, 1997; Laws 2001, ch. 2001-226, §157, effective January 1, 2002.)

II
FAMILY PROTECTION: POLICY LIMITATIONS ON FREEDOM OF TESTATION

This chapter focuses on policy limitations on the freedom of testation. One of the foremost considerations for limiting the power of testamentary disposition is family protection, i.e., the protection of the surviving spouse and children of the decedent. Protection of these family members takes the form of (1) allowances and exemptions, and (2) additional common law and statutory rights.

I. Allowances and Exemptions

Administration of an estate (whether testate or intestate) often is lengthy and costly. As a result, most jurisdictions provide certain minimal statutory rights for the surviving spouse (and often children) during the period of estate administration.

State statutes provide protection for family members in the form of: (1) family allowances, (2) homestead exemptions, and (3) personal property exemptions. These exemptions sometimes are referred to as "set-asides" because, upon granting of a petition, the court sets aside certain assets that are then unavailable for distribution to the heirs or beneficiaries. These statutory rights serve several purposes: to provide the spouse, minor, and dependent children of the decedent with a roof over their heads; provide these persons money with which to live while the estate is in administration (although sometimes for a shorter period); and give the dependents designated tangible property owned by the decedent.

The Florida family protection statutes are set forth in Florida Statutes §732.403 (family allowances), and §732.401 et seq. (homestead and exempt property).

A. Family Allowance

Many jurisdictions permit the court to grant an allowance for the support of the surviving spouse and children for the period during which the estate is in administration. A family allowance often is necessary because the decedent's assets are frozen during probate administration and also because death deprives dependent family members of the decedent's support. The policy is sometimes conceptualized as an extension of the husband's or father's duty of support. See, e.g., Anderson's Estate, 149 So. 2d 65, 67 (Fla. Dist. Ct. App. 1963) (explaining that the nature of the family allowance is analogous to a "temporary alimony award").

According to Florida law, persons who are entitled to the allowance include the surviving spouse, and "lineal heirs" whom the decedent was obligated to support and those whom he was actually supporting (discussed *infra*). For purposes of the statute, the term "lineal heir" means a lineal ascendant and lineal descendant of the decedent. The term has been construed to include adopted children. See Valdes v. Estate of Valdes, 913 So. 2d 1229 (Fla. Dist. Ct. App. 2005) (permitting the decedent's adopted child to receive a family allowance). Note that a family allowance is authorized for dependents of decedents who were *domiciled* in Florida at the time of death (Fla. Stat. §732.403).

Many state statutes, modeled after the UPC, provide support only for minor children. However, some states permit support for adult children in limited circumstances. For example, California law authorizes an allowance for "adult children of the decedent who are physically or mentally incapacitated from earning a living and were actually dependent in whole or in part upon the decedent for support" (Cal. Prob. Code §6540(a)), and gives the court discretion to award an allowance to other adult dependent children (Cal. Prob. Code §6540(b)(1)). The UPC protects "minor children whom the decedent was obligated to support and children who were in fact being supported by him" (UPC §2-404)." (As explained above, Florida Statutes §732.403 provides for an allowance to "lineal heirs.")

The family allowance is a cash allotment payable from the decedent's estate. According to the Florida statute, the allowance must be "reasonable" and cannot exceed $18,000 (Fla. Stat. §732.403). Formerly, the amount was set at $6,000 until a statutory amendment in 2001 (Laws 2001, ch. 2001-226, §40, effective January 1, 2002). The current amount was influenced by the UPC. Revisions to the UPC in 1990 set a ceiling, permitting the family allowance not to exceed $18,000, or $1500 per month for a period not to exceed one year (UPC §2-405 cmt.).

The factor of the recipient's need is no longer a condition for eligibility for the allowance in Florida. Before the 1973 revisions to the Florida Probate Code, the statute (Fla. Stat. §733.20(1)(d), now repealed)) provided for a "reasonable family allowance if necessary for support." That language was removed in 1973.

See DeSmidt v. DeSmidt, 563 So. 2d 193 (Fla. Dist. Ct. App. 1990) (explaining history of prior statute). In *DeSmidt*, the court of appeals held that an 80-year-old surviving spouse was "entitled" to a family allowance pursuant to the statutory language without being required to prove a need for support. However, a surviving spouse's needs are relevant in the determination of the "reasonableness" of the allowance. *Id.* at 194. See also *Valdes, supra*, at 1231 (the probate court retains the authority "to re-examine and modify an award, either upward or downward, as circumstances may require").

Generally, nonprobate assets are not reachable to satisfy the family allowance. Florida law, like that of many states, authorizes the payment of the family allowance "*out of the estate* . . . during administration of the estate" (Fla. Stat. §732.403 (emphasis added). The UPC permits some nonprobate assets to be reached if the estate is insolvent (UPC §6-102).

Payments cease upon the recipient's death. See Fla. Stat. §732.403 ("The death of any person entitled to a family allowance terminates the right to that part of the allowance not paid.") However, note that in some states, any unpaid family allowance passes to the recipient's estate. McGovern & Kurtz, *supra*, §3.4 at 137.

The amount of the allowance varies from jurisdiction to jurisdiction. Some statutes fix the amount, whereas other states leave the amount to judicial discretion. Many jurisdictions, like Florida, follow the UPC (2-404) and provide for "a *reasonable allowance* in money out of the estate for their maintenance during the period of administration" (emphasis added).

The purpose of the family allowance is to place the welfare of the decedent's family above the interests of creditors, heirs, legatees, and devisees. As a result, payment of the allowance generally is given priority in the payment of the decedent's debts. In Florida, the family allowance is paid only *after* payment of the expenses of administration, fees for the personal representative and attorneys, funeral expenses, federal and state claims/taxes, and medical expenses of the decedent's last illness (Fla. Stat. §733.707(e)).

The recipient of a family allowance receives the allowance *in addition to* other statutory benefits (e.g., homestead, exempt property, elective share) unless the will provides that the amount of the family allowance should be subtracted from those entitlements. See Fla. Stat. §732.403 ("The family allowance is not chargeable against any benefit or share otherwise passing to the surviving spouse or to the dependent lineal heirs, unless the will otherwise provides").

Family members may claim a family allowance in either the testate or intestate situations. In the testate situation, family members generally may claim both the family allowance as well as their share under the decedent's will (unless the will specifies otherwise). They may claim the allowance even if the decedent disinherits them. McGovern & Kurtz, *supra*, §3.4 at 138.

§ 732.403. "Family allowance," defined

In addition to protected homestead and statutory entitlements, if the decedent was domiciled in Florida at the time of death, the surviving spouse and the decedent's lineal heirs the decedent was supporting or was obligated to support are entitled to a reasonable allowance in money out of the estate for their maintenance during administration. The court may order this allowance to be paid as a lump sum or in periodic installments. The allowance shall not exceed a total of $18,000. It shall be paid to the surviving spouse, if living, for the use of the spouse and dependent lineal heirs. If the surviving spouse is not living, it shall be paid to the lineal heirs or to the persons having their care and custody. If any lineal heir is not living with the surviving spouse, the allowance may be made partly to the lineal heir or guardian or other person having the heir's care and custody and partly to the surviving spouse, as the needs of the dependent heir and the surviving spouse appear. The family allowance is not chargeable against any benefit or share otherwise passing to the surviving spouse or to the dependent lineal heirs, unless the will otherwise provides. The death of any person entitled to a family allowance terminates the right to that part of the allowance not paid. For purposes of this section, the term "lineal heir" or "lineal heirs" means lineal ascendants and lineal descendants of the decedent.

(Laws 1974, ch. 74-106, §1; Laws 1975, ch. 75-220, §19. Amended by Laws 1997, ch. 97-102, §960, effective July 1, 1997; Laws 2001, ch. 2001-226, §40, effective January 1, 2002.)

§ 732.707. Priority of expenses

(1) The personal representative shall pay the expenses of the administration and obligations of the decedent's estate in the following order:

(a) *Class 1.*--Costs, expenses of administration, and compensation of personal representatives and their attorneys fees and attorneys fees awarded under §733.106(3).

(b) *Class 2.*--Reasonable funeral, interment, and grave marker expenses, whether paid by a guardian, the personal representative, or any other person, not to exceed the aggregate of $6,000.

(c) *Class 3.*--Debts and taxes with preference under federal law, and claims pursuant to §§409.9101 and 414.28.

(d) *Class 4.*--Reasonable and necessary medical and hospital expenses of the last 60 days of the last illness of the decedent, including compensation of persons attending the decedent.

(e) *Class 5.*--Family allowance.

(f) *Class 6.*--Arrearage from court-ordered child support.

(g) *Class 7.*--Debts acquired after death by the continuation of the decedent's business, in accordance with §733.612(22), but only to the extent of the assets of that business.

(h) *Class 8.*--All other claims, including those founded on judgments or decrees rendered against the decedent during the decedent's lifetime, and any excess over the sums allowed in paragraphs (b) and (d).

(2) After paying any preceding class, if the estate is insufficient to pay all of the next succeeding class, the creditors of the latter class shall be paid ratably in proportion to their respective claims.

(3) Any portion of a trust with respect to which a decedent who is the grantor has at the decedent's death a right of revocation, as defined in paragraph (e), either alone or in conjunction with any other person, is liable for the expenses of the administration and obligations of the decedent's estate to the extent the decedent's estate is insufficient to pay them as provided in §733.607(2).

(a) For purposes of this subsection, any trusts established as part of, and all payments from, either an employee annuity described in §403 of the Internal Revenue Code of 1986, [FN1] as amended, an Individual Retirement Account, as described in § 408 of the Internal Revenue Code of 1986, [FN2] as amended, a Keogh (HR-10) Plan, or a retirement or other plan established by a corporation which is qualified under §401 of the Internal Revenue Code of 1986, [FN3] as amended, shall not be considered a trust over which the decedent has a right of revocation.

(b) For purposes of this subsection, any trust described in §664 of the Internal Revenue Code of 1986, [FN 4] as amended, shall not be considered a trust over which the decedent has a right of revocation.

(c) This subsection shall not impair any rights an individual has under a qualified domestic relations order as that term is defined in §414(p) of the Internal Revenue Code of 1986, [FN5] as amended.

(d) For purposes of this subsection, property held or received by a trust to the extent that the property would not have been subject to claims against the decedent's estate if it had been paid directly to a trust created under the decedent's will or other than to the decedent's estate, or assets received from any trust other than a trust described in this subsection, shall not be deemed assets of the trust available to the decedent's estate.

(e) For purposes of this subsection, a "right of revocation" is a power retained by the decedent, held in any capacity, to:

1. Amend or revoke the trust and revest the principal of the trust in the decedent; or

2. Withdraw or appoint the principal of the trust to or for the decedent's benefit.

[FN1] 26 U.S.C.A. §403
[FN2] 26 U.S.C.A. §408
[FN3] 26 U.S.C.A. §401
[FN4] 26 U.S.C.A. §664
[FN5] 26 U.S.C.A. §414(p)

(Laws 1974, ch. 74-106, §1; Laws 1975, ch. 75-220, §86; Laws 1977, ch. 77-87, §35; Laws 1985, ch. 85-79, §7; Laws 1987, ch. 87-226, §69; Laws 1993, ch. 93-208, §20; Laws 1993, ch. 93-257, §11. Amended by Laws 1995, ch. 95-401, §10, effective July 1, 1995; Laws 1997, ch. 97-102, §1018, effective July 1, 1997; Laws 1997, ch. 97-240, §3, effective May 30, 1997; Laws 2001, ch. 2001- 226, §150, effective January 1, 2002.)

Rule 5.407. Procedure for obtaining the family allowance

(a) Petition. An interested person may file a petition to determine family allowance.

(b) Contents. The petition shall be verified by the petitioner and shall:

(1) state the names and addresses of the decedent's surviving spouse and the decedent's lineal heirs who were being supported by the decedent or who were entitled to be supported by the decedent at the time of his death, stating the dates of birth of those who are minors; and

(2) for each person for whom an allowance is sought, state the person's name and relationship to the decedent, the basis on which the allowance is claimed, and the amount sought.

(c) Order. The order shall identify the persons entitled to the allowance, the amount to which each is entitled, the method of payment, and to whom payment should be made.

(Added June 19, 2003, effective January 1, 2004 (848 So.2d 1069).)

B. Homestead Exemption

Many jurisdictions provide for a homestead exemption to surviving dependent family members. The homestead exemption generally protects the principal family residence or a percentage of the equity in the residence (dependent on statute) from attachment by creditors. Protection for the homestead rights of a surviving spouse and children stems from the surviving spouse's common law right to a dower or curtesy interest in the decedent's real property. Gregory J. Duncan, Home Sweet Home? Litigation Aspects to Minnesota's Descent of Homestead, 29 Wm. Mitchell L. Rev. 185, 188 (2002).

States take four approaches to the homestead allowance:

- some follow the UPC approach;
- some have constitutional or statutory descent homesteads;
- others permit residency during probate proceedings or at the discretion of the court; and
- still others follow miscellaneous approaches.

Id., at 196-198. These approaches are explored below.

First, some states follow the UPC approach. The UPC provides a homestead allowance in the amount of $15,000 that is protected from creditors' claims. If the decedent left no surviving spouse, then each minor child and dependent child is entitled to an equal share of the $15,000 allowance (UPC §2-402). Under the UPC, the homestead allowance is exempt from creditors' claims against the estate and is added to any share passing by will, intestate succession, or elective share. Among states that follow the UPC by providing a fixed amount, those amounts range from $7500 to $27,000. Duncan, *supra*, at 195 n.57.

Second, some states provide, either by statute or state constitution, that the surviving spouse and children shall have a life estate or fee simple right in the homestead. Other states following this approach provide that close family members have a superior right to occupy the homestead (rather than vest in them a life estate). In the latter case specifying a right to occupancy, when the surviving spouse ceases to occupy the homestead, the survivor's rights terminate and the property descends according to the laws of descent. *Id.* at 196 n. 69.

Third, still other states permit a surviving spouse to possess and occupy the homestead during probate administration or for an indefinite period of time at the court's discretion. *Id.* at 197.

Finally, a few states take a combination of the aforementioned approaches. That is, some permit a cash award but, depending on the value of the property, may set off the homestead to the persons entitled to it. *Id.* at 197-198.

The Florida homestead protection provides for a constitutional descent homestead, having its basis in the 1868 state constitution. "It was conceived as a way to prevent wholesale loss of farms and homes after the conclusion of the Civil War." Brian V. McAvoy et al., Homestead, 12 Fla. Prac., Estate Planning §19:4 (2007). Constitutional amendments in 1995 abrogated the prohibition against devising the homestead and instead permitted disposition by will in limited circumstances (discussed *infra*).

For an interesting debate on whether property owned in a revocable trust is entitled to the constitutional homestead exemption and deemed to be owned by a "natural person," compare Engelke v. Estate of Engelke, 921 So. 2d 693 (Fla. Dist. Ct. App. 2006) (holding that the owner retained an ownership interest in the residence because he retained the right of revocation, even though the revocable trust held title to the property) with In re Bosonetto, 271 B.R. 403 (Bankr. M.D. Fla. 2001) (holding that the homestead exemption does not inure if the homestead is owned in a revocable trust by a grantor/trustee/beneficiary).

The Florida Constitution provides that the probate homestead shall be exempt from forced sale with certain exceptions (e.g., liens for the payment of taxes and assessments, contracts for purchase or repairs, etc.). The homestead shall be set apart for the use of the "surviving spouse or heirs of the owner" (Fla. Const. Art. X, §4(b)). The constitution defines the extent of the protected property by reference to its location outside a municipality (160 acres) or inside a municipality (one-half acre) and, in both cases, limited to the *residence* of the owner (decedent) and his or her family. On the method of determining the half-acre limitation, see Braswell v. Braswell, 890 So. 2d 379 (Fla. Dist. Ct. App. 2004) (holding that the trial court improperly added the square footage of certain structures (e.g., pool, garages, hallways, rooftops, etc.) to the square footage of the land under the condominium as the basis of the trial court's conclusion that the property exceeded the size of the homestead limitation).

After the definitional section, the Florida constitutional provision sets forth a limitation on the decedent's right to devise the homestead. If the deceased owner is survived by a spouse or minor child, the owner is prohibited from devising the homestead. If the deceased owner has no minor child, the owner may devise the homestead but only to a spouse (Fla. Const. Art. X,§4(c)).

If the decedent dies leaving neither a spouse nor a minor child surviving, then the testator may devise the homestead to anyone. In Harrell v. Snyder, 913 So. 2d 749 (Fla. Dist. Ct. App. 2005), a father died survived by three adult daughters. His will provided that his spouse would inherit his real and personal property. However, because he was divorced at the time of his death, his spouse was treated as if she had predeceased him. As a result, his real property passed by virtue of the residuary clause to a trust with the decedent's three daughters as beneficiaries. When one of the beneficiaries challenged the sale of the home by the personal representative, the court ruled that the home was protected homestead property and that, pursuant to Florida Statutes §733.608, the personal representative had the authority "to take possession of protected homestead property" to protect it for the heirs but not to sell it.

Property that is eligible for the homestead set-aside includes only property that is subject to probate administration (i.e., not property that passes outside the estate). McAvoy et al., 12 Fla. Prac., Estate Planning §19:12. According to statute, eligible property may not be property that is owned by the spouses as tenants by the entireties. ("For purposes of the code, real property owned as tenants by the entirety is not protected homestead.") (Fla. Stat. §731.201(29)). Such property vests automatically in the surviving spouse.

Homestead property has priority over many other claims. See, e.g., In re Estate of Mahaney, 903 So. 2d 234 (Fla. Dist. Ct. App. 2005) (holding that if a decedent who is not survived by a spouse or minor child devises a homestead to an heir, the homestead property cannot be sold in order to satisfy the general devises of the estate, even if such property passes via the residuary clause of the will). On abatement of legacies to satisfy debts generally, see Chapter XIV *infra*.

Florida law specifies the extent of the homestead right. Except as to homestead property when the decedent is survived by both a spouse and lineal descendants, an heir generally takes title in fee simple. Eclavea & Lease, Nature and Extent of Heir's Title, 17 Fla. Jur. 2d Decedents' Property §77. Thus, based on the Florida constitutional homestead protection, a testator may not devise less than a fee simple interest in homestead property to a spouse if there are no minor children. Kimberly C. Simmons, Devise of Homestead Property, 28A Fla. Jur. 2d Homesteads §78 (2006) (citing In re Mueller's Estate, 419 So. 2d 784 (Fla. Dist. Ct. App. 1982) (holding that testator's devise of only a life estate in the homestead property to his spouse was void)). If the decedent is survived by both a spouse and lineal descendants, the surviving spouse takes a life estate in the homestead. The lineal descendants, defined as those who were in being at the time of the decedent's death, take a vested remainder per stirpes (Fla. Stat. §732.401).

FLORIDA CONSTITUTION
Article 10, §4
Homestead and exemptions

(a) There shall be exempt from forced sale under process of any court, and no judgment, decree or execution shall be a lien thereon, except for the payment of taxes and assessments thereon, obligations contracted for the purchase, improvement or repair thereof, or obligations contracted for house, field or other labor performed on the realty, the following property owned by a natural person:

(1) a homestead, if located outside a municipality, to the extent of one hundred sixty acres of contiguous land and improvements thereon, which shall not be reduced without the owner's consent by reason of subsequent inclusion in a municipality; or if located within a municipality, to the extent of one-half acre of contiguous land, upon which the exemption shall be limited to the residence of the owner or the owner's family;

(2) personal property to the value of one thousand dollars.

(b) These exemptions shall inure to the surviving spouse or heirs of the owner.

(c) The homestead shall not be subject to devise if the owner is survived by spouse or minor child, except the homestead may be devised to the owner's

spouse if there be no minor child. The owner of homestead real estate, joined by the spouse if married, may alienate the homestead by mortgage, sale or gift and, if married, may by deed transfer the title to an estate by the entirety with the spouse. If the owner or spouse is incompetent, the method of alienation or encumbrance shall be as provided by law.
(Amended, general election, November 7, 1972; general election, November 6, 1984; general election, November 3, 1998.)

§222.08. Jurisdiction to order homestead

The circuit courts have equity jurisdiction to order and decree the setting apart of homesteads and of exemptions of personal property from forced sales.
(Laws 1881, ch. 3246, §2; Rev. St. 1892, §2005; Gen. St. 1906, §2527; Rev. Gen. St. 1920, §3882; Comp. Gen. Laws 1927, §5789.)

§731.201. Definitions: "protected homestead"

...

(29) "Protected homestead" means the property described in §4(a)(1), Art. X of the State Constitution on which at the death of the owner the exemption inures to the owner's surviving spouse or heirs under §4(b), Art. X of the State Constitution. For purposes of the code, real property owned as tenants by the entirety is not protected homestead....
(Laws 1974, ch. 74-106, §1; Laws 1975, ch. 75-220, §4; Laws 1977, ch. 77-174, §1; Laws 1985, ch. 85-79, §2; Laws 1987, ch. 87-226, §66; Laws 1988, ch. 88-340, §1; Laws 1993, ch. 93-257, §7. Amended by Laws 1995, ch. 95-401, §6, effective July 1, 1995; Laws 1997, ch. 97-102, §949, effective July 1, 1997; Laws 1998, ch. 98-421, §52, effective July 1, 1998; Laws 2001, ch. 2001-226, §11, effective January 1, 2002; Laws 2002, ch. 2002-1, §106, effective May 21, 2002; Laws 2003, ch. 2003-154, §2, effective June 12, 2003; Laws 2005, ch. 2005-108, §2, effective July 1, 2005; Laws 2006, ch. 2006-217, §29, effective July 1, 2007.)

§732.227. Definitions: homestead

For purposes of §§732.216-732.228, the term "homestead" refers only to property the descent and devise of which is restricted by §4(c), Art. X of the State Constitution.
(Laws 1992, ch. 92-200, §14.)

§732.401. Manner of descent of homestead: to whom and how

(1) If not devised as permitted by law and the Florida Constitution, the homestead shall descend in the same manner as other intestate property; but if the decedent is survived by a spouse and lineal descendants, the surviving spouse shall take a life estate in the homestead, with a vested remainder to the lineal descendants in being at the time of the decedent's death per stirpes.

(2) Subsection (1) shall not apply to property that the decedent and the surviving spouse owned as tenants by the entirety.
(Laws 1974, ch. 74-106, §1; Laws 1975, ch. 75-220, §17. Amended by Laws 2001, ch. 2001-226, §37, effective January 1, 2002.)

§732.4015. Devise of homestead

(1) As provided by the Florida Constitution, the homestead shall not be subject to devise if the owner is survived by a spouse or minor child, except that the homestead may be devised to the owner's spouse if there is no minor child.

(2) For the purposes of subsection (1), the term:

(a) "Owner" includes the grantor of a trust described in §733.707(3) that is evidenced by a written instrument which is in existence at the time of the grantor's death as if the interest held in trust was owned by the grantor.

(b) "Devise" includes a disposition by trust of that portion of the trust estate which, if titled in the name of the grantor of the trust, would be the grantor's homestead.
(Laws 1974, ch. 74-106, §1; Fla. St. 1974, Supp. §732.516; Laws 1975, ch. 75- 220, §§18, 30; Laws 1992, ch. 92-200, §16. Amended by Laws 1997, ch. 97-102, § 959, effective July 1, 1997; Laws 2001, ch. 2001-226, §38, effective January 1, 2002.)

§732.405. Devise of homestead

(1) As provided by the Florida Constitution, the homestead shall not be subject to devise if the owner is survived by a spouse or minor child, except that the homestead may be devised to the owner's spouse if there is no minor child.

(2) For the purposes of subsection (1), the term:

(a) "Owner" includes the grantor of a trust described in § 733.707(3) that is evidenced by a written instrument which is in existence at the time of the grantor's death as if the interest held in trust was owned by the grantor.

(b) "Devise" includes a disposition by trust of that portion of the trust estate which, if titled in the name of the grantor of the trust, would be the grantor's homestead.

(Laws 1974, ch. 74-106, §1; Fla. St. 1974, Supp. §732.516; Laws 1975, ch. 75- 220, §§18, 30; Laws 1992, ch. 92-200, §16. Amended by Laws 1997, ch. 97-102, §959, effective July 1, 1997; Laws 2001, ch. 2001-226, §38, effective January 1, 2002.)

Rule 5.406. Procedure to determine exempt property

(a) Petition. An interested person may file a petition to determine exempt property within the time allowed by law.

(b) Contents. The petition shall be verified by the petitioner and shall:

(1) describe the property and the basis on which it is claimed as exempt property; and

(2) state the name and address of the decedent's surviving spouse or, if none, the names and addresses of decedent's children entitled by law to the exempt property and the dates of birth of those who are minors.

(c) Order. The court shall determine each item of exempt property and its value and order the surrender of that property to the persons entitled to it.

(Added September 13, 1984, effective January 1, 1985 (458 So.2d 1079). Amended September 29, 1988, effective January 1, 1989 (537 So.2d 500); October 3, 1996, effective January 1, 1997 (683 So.2d 78).)

§733.608. Power of personal representative generally and regarding homestead

(1) All real and personal property of the decedent, except the protected homestead, within this state and the rents, income, issues, and profits from it shall be assets in the hands of the personal representative:

(a) For the payment of devises, family allowance, elective share, estate and inheritance taxes, claims, charges, and expenses of the administration and obligations of the decedent's estate.

(b) To enforce contribution and equalize advancement.

(c) For distribution.

(2) If property that reasonably appears to the personal representative to be protected homestead is not occupied by a person who appears to have an interest in the property, the personal representative is authorized, but not required, to take possession of that property for the limited purpose of preserving, insuring, and protecting it for the person having an interest in the property, pending a determination of its homestead status. If the personal representative takes possession of that property, any rents and revenues may be collected by the personal representative for the account of the heir or devisee, but the personal representative shall have no duty to rent or otherwise make the property productive.

(3) If the personal representative expends funds or incurs obligations to preserve, maintain, insure, or protect the property referenced in subsection (2), the personal representative shall be entitled to a lien on that property and its revenues to secure repayment of those expenditures and obligations incurred. These expenditures and obligations incurred, including, but not limited to, fees and costs, shall constitute a debt owed to the personal representative that is charged against and which may be secured by a lien on the protected homestead, as provided in this section. The debt shall include any amounts paid for these purposes after the decedent's death and prior to the personal representative's appointment to the extent later ratified by the personal representative in the court proceeding provided for in this section.

(a) On the petition of the personal representative or any interested person, the court having jurisdiction of the administration of the decedent's estate shall adjudicate the amount of the debt after formal notice to the persons appearing to have an interest in the property.

(b) The persons having an interest in the protected homestead shall have no personal liability for the repayment of the above noted debt. The personal representative may enforce payment of the debt through any of the following methods:

1. By foreclosure of the lien as provided in this section;

2. By offset of the debt against any other property in the personal representative's possession that otherwise would be distributable to any person having an interest in the protected homestead, but only to the extent of the fraction of the total debt owed to the personal representative the numerator of which is the value of that person's interest in the protected homestead and the denominator of which is the total value of the protected homestead; or

3. By offset of the debt against the revenues from the protected homestead received by the personal representative.

(4) The personal representative's lien shall attach to the property and take priority as of the date and time a notice of that lien is recorded in the official records of the county where that property is located, and the lien may secure expenditures and obligations

incurred, including, but not limited to, fees and costs made before or after recording the notice. The notice of lien may be recorded prior to the adjudication of the amount of the debt. The notice of lien also shall be filed in the probate proceeding, but failure to do so shall not affect the validity of the lien. A copy of the notice of lien shall be served by formal notice upon each person appearing to have an interest in the property. The notice of lien shall state:

(a) The name and address of the personal representative and the personal representative's attorney;

(b) The legal description of the property;

(c) The name of the decedent and also, to the extent known to the personal representative, the name and address of each person appearing to have an interest in the property; and

(d) That the personal representative has expended or is obligated to expend funds to preserve, maintain, insure, and protect the property and that the lien stands as security for recovery of those expenditures and obligations incurred, including, but not limited to, fees and costs.

Substantial compliance with the foregoing provisions shall render the notice in comportment with this section.

(5) The lien shall terminate upon the earliest of:

(a) Recording a satisfaction or release signed by the personal representative in the official records of the county where the property is located;

(b) The discharge of the personal representative when the estate administration is complete;

(c) One year from the recording of the lien in the official records unless a proceeding to determine the debt or enforce the lien has been filed; or

(d) The entry of an order releasing the lien.

(6) Within 14 days after receipt of the written request of any interested person, the personal representative shall deliver to the requesting person at a place designated in the written request an estoppel letter setting forth the unpaid balance of the debt secured by the lien referred to in this section. After complete satisfaction of the debt secured by the lien, the personal representative shall record within 30 days after complete payment, a satisfaction of the lien in the official records of the county where the property is located. If a judicial proceeding is necessary to compel compliance with the provisions of this subsection, the prevailing party shall be entitled to an award of attorney's fees and costs.

(7) The lien created by this section may be foreclosed in the manner of foreclosing a mortgage under the provisions of chapter 702.

(8) In any action for enforcement of the debt described in this section, the court shall award taxable costs as in chancery actions, including reasonable attorney's fees.

(9) A personal representative entitled to recover a debt for expenditures and obligations incurred, including, but not limited to, fees and costs, under this section may be relieved of the duty to enforce collection by an order of the court finding:

(a) That the estimated court costs and attorney's fees in collecting the debt will approximate or exceed the amount of the recovery; or

(b) That it is impracticable to enforce collection in view of the improbability of collection.

(10) A personal representative shall not be liable for failure to attempt to enforce collection of the debt if the personal representative reasonably believes it would have been economically impracticable.

(11) The personal representative shall not be liable for failure to take possession of the protected homestead or to expend funds on its behalf. In the event that the property is determined by the court not to be protected homestead, subsections (2)-(10) shall not apply and any liens previously filed shall be deemed released upon recording of the order in the official records of the county where the property is located.

(12) Upon the petition of an interested party to accommodate a sale or the encumbrance of the protected homestead, the court may transfer the lien provided for in this section from the property to the proceeds of the sale or encumbrance by requiring the deposit of the proceeds into a restricted account subject to the lien. The court shall have continuing jurisdiction over the funds deposited. The transferred lien shall attach only to the amount asserted by the personal representative, and any proceeds in excess of that amount shall not be subject to the lien or otherwise restricted under this section. Alternatively, the personal representative and the apparent owners of the protected homestead may agree to retain in escrow the amount demanded as reimbursement by the personal representative, to be held there under the continuing jurisdiction of the court pending a final determination of the amount properly reimbursable to the personal representative under this section.

(13) This act shall apply to estates of decedents dying after the date on which this act becomes a law.

(Laws 1974, ch. 74-106, §1; Laws 1975, ch. 75-220, §77; Laws 1977, ch. 77-87, §29. Amended by Laws 2001, ch. 2001-226, §131, effective January 1, 2002; Laws 2003, ch. 2003-154, §10, effective June 12, 2003.)

[Rules regarding the personal representative's duty to record liens on protected homesteads are included in Chapter XIV *infra*.]

Rule 5.405. Procedure to set aside homestead

(a) Petition. An interested person may file a petition to determine protected homestead real property owned by the decedent.

(b) Contents. The petition shall be verified by the petitioner and shall state:

(1) the date of the decedent's death;

(2) the county of the decedent's domicile at the time of death;

(3) the name of the decedent's surviving spouse and the names and dates of birth of the decedent's surviving lineal descendants;

(4) a legal description of the property owned by the decedent on which the decedent resided; and

(5) any other facts in support of the petition.

(c) Order. The court's order on the petition shall describe the real property and determine whether any of the real property constituted the protected homestead of the decedent. If the court determines that any of the real property was the protected homestead of the decedent, the order shall identify the person or persons entitled to the protected homestead real property and define the interest of each.

(Added September 13, 1984, effective January 1, 1985 (458 So.2d 1079). Amended September 29, 1988, effective January 1, 1989 (537 So.2d 500); September 24, 1992, effective January 1, 1993 (607 So.2d 1306); October 3, 1996, effective January 1, 1997 (683 So.2d 78); May 2, 2002 (824 So.2d 849).)

C. Personal Property Exemption

Many jurisdictions provide for a modest amount of exempt property (sometimes called "personal property set-asides") to pass to the decedent's surviving spouse and/or surviving children. Exempt personal property generally consists of such items as home furnishings, food, clothes, jewelry, firearms, sporting equipment, cars not used for income, certain quantities of farm animals, and household pets. Gerry W. Beyer, Wills, Trusts and Estates 263 (4th ed. 2007). This property is exempt from distribution to heirs and beneficiaries, as well as from sale by creditors. It is available in both testate and intestate situations.

Personal property exemptions (like homestead exemptions and family allowances) generally take precedence over creditors' claims and the decedent's will. McGovern & Kurtz, *supra*, §3.4 at 138.

Under the UPC, exempt property passes to the surviving spouse. Only in the event that no spouse survives do the decedent's children take the property. Florida also follows this rule (Fla. Stat. §732.402(1)).

UPC §2-403 imposes a limit of $10,000 as the maximum value of the exemption (which is in addition to the homestead allowance and the family allowance). Florida similarly follows these rules. See Fla. Stat. §732.402(2) (ceiling of $10,000); Fla. Stat. §732.402(4) ("Exempt property shall be in addition to protected homestead, statutory entitlements, and property passing under the decedent's will or by intestate succession").

In Florida, exempt property is protected by the state constitution and state statute. The Florida constitution provides for statutory protection from execution for debts of personal property up to $1000 (Fla. Const. Art. X, §4(a(2)). This provision benefits a decedent's spouse and intestate heirs but does not apply to beneficiaries of wills. Trawick, *supra*, at §4-3.

Additional statutory protection exists pursuant to Florida Statutes §732.402. That statute specifies that exempt property shall include: household furniture, furnishings and appliances in the decedent's residence (subject to a ceiling of $10,000, and valued as of the date of death), as well as automobiles. However, the automobiles have to be those that are held in the decedent's name and regularly used by the decedent or members of decedent's immediate family as their personal automobiles. For the definition of qualifying "automobiles," see Estate of Corbin v. Sherman, 645 So. 2d 39 (Fla. Dist. Ct. App. 1994) (holding that a motor home and a travel trailer do not qualify as exempt property).

Exempt personal property in Florida is subject to security interests ("perfected security interests thereon") (Fla. Stat. §732.402(3)). And, although in some states exempt personal property is not subject to devise, this is not the case in Florida. In Florida, a testator may devise such property, although the property will be exempt from creditors' claims if the devisee is a spouse or child. Trawick, *supra*, at §4-3 (citing Fla. Stat. §732.402(5)).

In Florida, the surviving spouse (or if there is no surviving spouse, then the children) must file a petition in a timely manner to claim the exempt property (Fla. Stat. §732.402(6)).

FLORIDA CONSTITUTION
Article 10, §4
Exempt personal property

(a) There shall be exempt from forced sale under process of any court, and no judgment, decree or execution shall be a lien thereon, except for the payment of taxes and assessments thereon, obligations contracted for the purchase, improvement or repair thereof, or obligations contracted for house, field or other labor performed on the realty, the following property owned by a natural person:

(1) [homestead provision, supra]

(2) personal property to the value of one thousand dollars.

(b) These exemptions shall inure to the surviving spouse or heirs of the owner....

(Amended, general election, November 7, 1972; general election, November 6, 1984; general election, November 3, 1998.)

FLORIDA STATUTES
§731.201. Definition: exempt property

...

(13) **"Exempt property"** means the property of a decedent's estate which is described in §732.402.

...

(Laws 1974, ch. 74-106, §1; Laws 1975, ch. 75-220, §4; Laws 1977, ch. 77-174, §1; Laws 1985, ch. 85-79, §2; Laws 1987, ch. 87-226, §66; Laws 1988, ch. 88-340, §1; Laws 1993, ch. 93-257, §7. Amended by Laws 1995, ch. 95-401, §6, effective July 1, 1995; Laws 1997, ch. 97-102, §949, effective July 1, 1997; Laws 1998, ch. 98-421, §52, effective July 1, 1998; Laws 2001, ch. 2001-226, §11, effective January 1, 2002; Laws 2002, ch. 2002-1, §106, effective May 21, 2002; Laws 2003, ch. 2003-154, §2, effective June 12, 2003; Laws 2005, ch. 2005-108, §2, effective July 1, 2005; Laws 2006, ch. 2006-217, §29, effective July 1, 2007.)

§732.402. Exempt property: share, definition, priority

(1) If a decedent was domiciled in this state at the time of death, the surviving spouse, or, if there is no surviving spouse, the children of the decedent shall have the right to a share of the estate of the decedent as provided in this section, to be designated "exempt property."

(2) Exempt property shall consist of:

(a) Household furniture, furnishings, and appliances in the decedent's usual place of abode up to a net value of $10,000 as of the date of death.

(b) All automobiles held in the decedent's name and regularly used by the decedent or members of the decedent's immediate family as their personal automobiles.

(c) Stanley G. Tate Florida Prepaid College Program contracts purchased and Florida College Savings agreements established under part IV of chapter 1009.

(d) All benefits paid pursuant to §112.1915. [death benefits for teachers and school administrators].

(3) Exempt property shall be exempt from all claims against the estate except perfected security interests thereon.

(4) Exempt property shall be in addition to protected homestead, statutory entitlements, and property passing under the decedent's will or by intestate succession.

(5) Property specifically or demonstratively devised by the decedent's will to any devisee shall not be included in exempt property. However, persons to whom property has been specifically or demonstratively devised and who would otherwise be entitled to it as exempt property under this section may have the court determine the property to be exempt from claims, except for perfected security interests thereon, after complying with the provisions of subsection (6).

(6) Persons entitled to exempt property shall be deemed to have waived their rights under this section unless a petition for determination of exempt property is filed by or on behalf of the persons entitled to the exempt property on or before the later of the date that is 4 months after the date of service of the notice of administration or the date that is 40 days after the date of termination of any proceeding involving the construction, admission to probate, or validity of the will or involving any other matter affecting any part of the estate subject to this section.

(7) Property determined as exempt under this section shall be excluded from the value of the estate before residuary, intestate, or pretermitted or elective shares are determined.

(Laws 1974, ch. 74-106, §1; Laws 1975, ch. 75-220, § 19; Laws 1977, ch. 77-87, §10; Laws 1977, ch. 77-174, §1; Laws 1981, ch. 81-238, §1; Laws 1985, ch. 85- 79, §3; Laws 1987, ch. 87-226, §67. Amended by Laws 1998, ch. 98-421, §51, effective July 1, 1998; Laws 1999, ch. 99-220, §3, effective May 26, 1999; Laws 2001, ch. 2001-180, §3, effective June 7, 2001; Laws 2001, ch. 2001-226, § 39, effective January 1, 2002; Laws 2002, ch. 2002-387, § 1036, effective January 7, 2003; Laws 2006, ch. 2006-134, § 5, effective July 1, 2006; Laws 2006, ch. 2006-303, § 5, effective July 1, 2006.)

Rule 5.4061. Procedure to determine exempt property

(a) Petition. An interested person may file a petition to determine exempt property within the time allowed by law.

(b) Contents. The petition shall be verified by the petitioner and shall:

(1) describe the property and the basis on which it is claimed as exempt property; and

(2) state the name and address of the decedent's surviving spouse or, if none, the names and addresses of decedent's children entitled by law to the exempt property and the dates of birth of those who are minors.

(c) Order. The court shall determine each item of exempt property and its value and order the surrender of that property to the persons entitled to it.

(Added September 13, 1984, effective January 1, 1985 (458 So.2d 1079). Amended September 29, 1988, effective January 1, 1989 (537 So.2d 500); October 3, 1996, effective January 1, 1997 (683 So.2d 78).)

II. Minimum Rights of the Surviving Spouse

The law protects a surviving spouse from disinheritance by the decedent. Two justifications exist for limiting testamentary freedom in the context of spousal disinheritance: the support rationale and the marital contribution rationale. First, the decedent has a moral duty to support a surviving spouse even after the decedent's death. Second, it is considered unfair to allow a decedent to deprive the surviving spouse of the latter's contribution to the acquisition of the decedent's assets. Andra J. Hedrick, Note, Protection Against Spousal Disinheritance: A Critical Analysis of Tennessee's New Forced Share System, 28 U. Mem. L. Rev. 561, 562-563 (1998).

Surviving spouses enjoy different levels of protection against disinheritance depending on the law of the state with jurisdiction over the decedent's estate. *Id.* at 563. Such protections include dower, statutory forced share, and community property rights.

A. Dower

At common law, a surviving wife was protected from disinheritance by the concept of dower. The widow's dower interest consisted of a life estate in one-third of all real property of which her husband was seised (owned) at any time during the marriage (regardless of whether the husband actually owned the property at his death). Dower guaranteed the widow a share of the decedent's *real property* which could not be defeated by the husband's will or his inter vivos conveyances. That is, the grantee or devisee took the real property subject to the widow's dower right. Dower was an inchoate right, dependent on the wife's surviving her husband.

The husband's correlative right in his deceased wife's estate was termed curtesy. Curtesy consisted of a life estate in all (not simply one-third) of the lands of which his wife was seised at any time during the marriage. However, the husband only acquired his curtesy right if he fathered a child with his wife (regardless of whether that child survived).

The primary differences between dower and curtesy at common law may be summarized as follows: (1) curtesy entitled the husband to an estate in all the wife's inheritable freeholds, whereas dower entitled the widow to an interest in only one-third of the husband's; (2) curtesy attached to the wife's equitable as well as legal interests, whereas dower applied only to the husband's legal estates; (3) a requirement for curtesy was the birth of issue, whereas no such requirement pertained to the dower right; and (4) before the wife's death, curtesy was a present estate, whereas dower was only a protected expectancy before the husband's death. Hedrick, *supra*, at 570 n. 38 (citing George L. Haskins, Curtesy in the United States, 100 U. Pa. L. Rev. 196, 197 (1951)).

Gender-based distinctions regarding the rights of the surviving spouse have been found to violate equal protection. See, e.g., Stokes v. Stokes, 613 S.W.2d 372 (Ark. 1981) (finding dower statute violative of equal protection); Boan v. Watson, 316 S.E.2d 401 (S.C. 1984) (same). Today, a small number of states continue to protect the survivor's dower rights, but the rights are available to both men and women.

At one time, some states differentiated between the dower rights of state residents versus nonresidents. In Ferry v. Spokane, P. & S. Ry., 258 U.S. 314 (1922), the Supreme Court found that such a statute did not violate the privileges and immunities or equal protection clauses of the Constitution. The court upheld the constitutionality of an Oregon statute providing for dower, if the wife was an Oregon resident, in all of the lands of which the husband was seised at any time during the marriage, but restricting dower to the lands of which the husband died seised if the widow was a resident of another

state. The statute was repealed in 1969 (Laws 1969, ch. 591, §305).

As mentioned above, dower protected the surviving spouse from disinheritance and from creditors (i.e., beneficiaries and creditors took property subject to her dower right). However, dower has many disadvantages. It applies only to the decedent's real property and not to personal property. Dower provides only a life estate for the surviving spouse and not a fee interest. Finally, it is a clog on title. As a result, many states have abolished dower. See, e.g., Cal. Prob. Code §6412; UPC §2-113 (abolishing dower and curtesy). The abolition of dower and curtesy was attributable in large part to the transformation from an agrarian to an industrialized society. Hedrick, *supra*, at 571 n. 39.

In Florida, the law of dower was revised in 1968 so as to no longer require the husband's joinder in any conveyance by the wife (Fla. Stat. §708.08 cmt. explaining derivation of statute). In 1970, the legislature amended the state constitution to bring it into conformity with state law on dower (Laws 1970, ch. 70-4, §2). In 1973, widowers were given the same rights as widows. Trawick, *supra*, at 4-6 (This change operated from October 1, 1973, until July 1, 1975). Finally, in 1974, the legislature substituted the elective share for the common law doctrines of dower and curtesy (Fla. Stat. §732.2065). Trawick, *supra*, at §§4-4, 4-6. The elective share is discussed below.

The gradual abolition of dower raises interesting issues in the conflict of laws. See, e.g., In re Binkow's Estate, 120 So. 2d 15 (Fla. Dist. Ct. App. 1960 (determining that a widow, whose husband was domiciled in Florida, was entitled to dower, even though the law of Maryland and Michigan, where the property was situated, did not so hold).

§732.111. Abolition of dower

Dower and curtesy are abolished.

(Laws 1974, ch. 74-106, §1; Laws 1975, ch. 75-220, §12.)

§708.08. Married women's property rights

(1) Every married woman is empowered to take charge of and manage and control her separate property, to contract and to be contracted with, to sue and be sued, to sell, convey, transfer, mortgage, use, and pledge her real and personal property and to make, execute, and deliver instruments of every character without the joinder or consent of her husband in all respects as fully as if she were unmarried. Every married woman has and may exercise all rights and powers with respect to her separate property, income, and earnings and may enter into, obligate herself to perform, and enforce contracts or undertakings to the same extent and in like manner as if she were unmarried and without the joinder or consent of her husband. All conveyances, contracts, transfers, or mortgages of real property or any interest in it executed by a married woman without the joinder of her husband before or after the effective date of the 1968 Constitution of Florida are as valid and effective as though the husband had joined.

(2) Any married woman who conveyed or mortgaged her separate real property without the joinder of her husband before the effective date of the 1968 State Constitution, and any person claiming by, through, or under her, shall have 2 years after June 2, 1983, to file a notice of lis pendens and to bring an action based on the nonjoinder of the husband contesting the validity of any such conveyance or mortgage; and, if the action is not brought and a notice of lis pendens is not filed within the time allowed, she, and any person claiming by, through, or under her, shall be forever barred from bringing an action to contest the validity of the conveyance or mortgage. This subsection shall not be construed to revive any action that has been barred.

(Laws 1943, ch. 21932, §1; Laws 1970, ch. 70-4, §2; Laws 1983, ch. 83-67, §1.)

FLORIDA CONSTITUTION
Article 10, §5
Coverture and property: dower and curtesy

There shall be no distinction between married women and married men in the holding, control, disposition, or encumbering of their property, both real and personal; except that dower or curtesy may be established and regulated by law.

B. Forced Share and the Surviving Spouse's Election

Most jurisdictions today have replaced dower with the concept of a forced (or elective) share. A forced share enables the surviving spouse to take a certain portion of the decedent's estate if the decedent disinherits the spouse or fails to bequeath a minimum amount to the survivor. The surviving spouse has the

right to take a statutory share of the decedent's estate in lieu of the share that the survivor would have taken under the decedent's will. Thus, if a husband bequeaths his wife only a small portion of his estate, the wife has a choice: (1) to take the share given to her under the decedent's will or (2) refuse that testamentary gift and, instead, take her statutory share. Generally, the surviving spouse will choose whichever option yields a larger amount.

The amount of the forced share varies from jurisdiction to jurisdiction. Some jurisdictions simply specify that the surviving spouse's elective share is the "intestate share." Other jurisdictions provide:

- a fixed percentage of the net probate estate (ranging from one-third to one-half);
- a fixed percentage (e.g., ranging from one-third to one-half of the net probate estate depending on the number of children (the more children, the smaller the share));
- a minimum dollar amount plus a fixed percentage of any additional property in the net probate estate (e.g., the first $100,000 plus one-half the balance) (reflecting the influence of the pre-1990 UPC);
- a percentage of the estate varying with the length of the marriage (reflecting the influence of the current UPC).

The majority of forced-share jurisdictions provide for a statutory share that is equal to a fixed fraction of the decedent's estate. "The modern approach, however, is to determine the surviving spouse's statutory share according to the length of time in which the decedent and surviving spouse were married to each other, taking into account their individual and marital wealth." Hedrick, *supra*, at 565. These latter states are called "accrual-type elective share systems" and reflect the influence of the UPC, as revised in 1990, to include a redesigned forced-share system. By revising the forced-share provision, the drafters of the 1990 UPC attempted to take into account the partnership theory of marriage.

The forced share is distinguishable from dower in several ways. Unlike dower, the surviving spouse takes the elective share in fee. Also, the forced share applies to both real and personal property. However, in many states the elective share includes only assets that the decedent owned at death, i.e., the net probate estate. If the decedent made significant inter vivos gifts to third persons and thereby depleted the probate estate, the surviving spouse has no claim to those assets. Also, the elective share is subject to the claims of creditors. Dower protected the surviving spouse from the husband's inter vivos conveyances and creditors' claims.

Some states protect the surviving spouse from the decedent's inter vivos transfers by applying the elective share to certain asserts that pass outside probate. This approach (called the "augmented estate") is influenced by UPC §§ 2-201 et seq. The problem of the best manner of protecting the surviving spouse against the decedent's nonprobate transfers is discussed in Section IV of this chapter *infra*.

The surviving spouse generally must exercise the election within a fixed time period. For example, the UPC provides that the surviving spouse must make the election no later than either 9 months after the decedent's death or 6 months after the decedent's will was admitted to probate (whichever is later) (UPC §2-211).

Note that when the surviving spouse makes an election, that election may upset the decedent's estate plan. As a result, some of the legacies may have to be reduced (or abated) to provide for the surviving spouse's share. For a discussion of abatement, see Chapter XV, Section IIC *infra*.

In Florida, the surviving spouse has a right to an elective share that is equal to 30 percent of the "elective estate" (Fla. Stat. §732.2065).

The surviving spouse receives his or her elective share *in addition to* other statutory rights (homestead, exempt property and family allowance) (Fla. Stat. §732.2105(1)). After the surviving spouse files for an election, the surviving spouse is treated as if she or he predeceased the decedent for purposes of the administration of (the balance of) the decedent's estate (Fla. Stat. §732.2105(2)).

In 1999, the Florida legislature enacted the "augmented estate" to replace the surviving spouse's elective share. The doctrine is derived from the UPC's augmented estate concept (UPC §2-202 to §2-208). The statute applies to decedents who die after October 1, 2001.

The types of property that are included in the elective share are specified in Florida Statutes §732.2035. Subsections (2) to (8), include the decedent's interest in the following: multiple-party accounts, joint tenancy with right or survivorship or tenancy by the entirety, property transferred by the decedent to the extent that the transfer was revocable by the decedent alone or together with another, other transfers by the decedent if he or she had a right

to the enjoy the possession or use of the principal or income, cash surrender value of life insurance policies, pension benefits, some property transfers within a year of death, etc.

The statute also excludes some property from the augmented estate, particularly if the transfers were not intended as disinheritance devices, such as: transfers made by the decedent that are irrevocable, transfers made by the decedent with adequate consideration, and transfers made with the written consent of the decedent's spouse, etc. (Fla. Stat. §732.2045(1)).

Sometimes, decedents use inter vivos trusts as disinheritance devices. In Florida, property held in trust at the decedent's death may be excluded from the augmented estate if the following conditions exist: (1) the property was a trust asset continuously from October 1, 1999 and the decedent's death, (2) the decedent was not married to the surviving spouse when the property was transferred to the trust, and (3) the property was a nonmarital asset under Florida Statutes §61.075 [Florida's equitable distribution statute] immediately before the decedent's death (Fla. Stat. §732.2155(6)).

On attempts to defeat the surviving spouse's statutory rights, see Section IV *infra*.

§732.201. Surviving spouse's right to an elective share

The surviving spouse of a person who dies domiciled in Florida has the right to a share of the elective estate of the decedent as provided in this part, to be designated the elective share.

(Laws 1974, ch, 74-106, §1; Laws 1975, ch. 75-220, §13. Amended by Laws 1999, ch. 99-343, §1, effective October 1, 1999.)

§732.2035. Elective estate: defined

Except as provided in §732.2045, the elective estate consists of the sum of the values as determined under §732.2055 of the following property interests:

(1) The decedent's probate estate.

(2) The decedent's ownership interest in accounts or securities registered in "Pay On Death," "Transfer On Death," "In Trust For," or coownership with right of survivorship form. For this purpose, "decedent's ownership interest" means, in the case of accounts or securities held in tenancy by the entirety, one-half of the value of the account or security, and in all other cases, that portion of the accounts or securities which the decedent had, immediately before death, the right to withdraw or use without the duty to account to any person.

(3) The decedent's fractional interest in property, other than property described in subsection (2) or subsection (7), held by the decedent in joint tenancy with right of survivorship or in tenancy by the entirety. For this purpose, "decedent's fractional interest in property" means the value of the property divided by the number of tenants.

(4) That portion of property, other than property described in subsection (2), transferred by the decedent to the extent that at the time of the decedent's death the transfer was revocable by the decedent alone or in conjunction with any other person. This subsection does not apply to a transfer that is revocable by the decedent only with the consent of all persons having a beneficial interest in the property.

(5)(a) That portion of property, other than property described in subsection (3), subsection (4), or subsection (7), transferred by the decedent to the extent that at the time of the decedent's death:

1. The decedent possessed the right to, or in fact enjoyed the possession or use of, the income or principal of the property; or

2. The principal of the property could, in the discretion of any person other than the spouse of the decedent, be distributed or appointed to or for the benefit of the decedent.

In the application of this subsection, a right to payments under a commercial or private annuity, an annuity trust, a unitrust, or a similar arrangement shall be treated as a right to that portion of the income of the property necessary to equal the annuity, unitrust, or other payment.

(b) The amount included under this subsection is:

1. With respect to subparagraph (a)1., the value of the portion of the property to which the decedent's right or enjoyment related, to the extent the portion passed to or for the benefit of any person other than the decedent's probate estate; and

2. With respect to subparagraph (a)2., the value of the portion subject to the discretion, to the extent the portion passed to or for the benefit of any person other than the decedent's probate estate.

(c) This subsection does not apply to any property if the decedent's only interests in the property are that:

1. The property could be distributed to or for the benefit of the decedent only with the consent of all persons having a beneficial interest in the property; or

2. The income or principal of the property could be distributed to or for the benefit of the decedent only through the exercise or in default of an exercise of a general power of appointment held by any person other than the decedent; or

3. The income or principal of the property is or could be distributed in satisfaction of the decedent's obligation of support; or

4. The decedent had a contingent right to receive principal, other than at the discretion of any person, which contingency was beyond the control of the decedent and which had not in fact occurred at the decedent's death.

(6) The decedent's beneficial interest in the net cash surrender value immediately before death of any policy of insurance on the decedent's life.

(7) The value of amounts payable to or for the benefit of any person by reason of surviving the decedent under any public or private pension, retirement, or deferred compensation plan, or any similar arrangement, other than benefits payable under the federal Railroad Retirement Act [FN1] or the federal Social Security System. In the case of a defined contribution plan as defined in §414(i) of the Internal Revenue Code of 1986, [FN2] as amended, this subsection shall not apply to the excess of the proceeds of any insurance policy on the decedent's life over the net cash surrender value of the policy immediately before the decedent's death.

(8) Property that was transferred during the 1-year period preceding the decedent's death as a result of a transfer by the decedent if the transfer was either of the following types:

(a) Any property transferred as a result of the termination of a right or interest in, or power over, property that would have been included in the elective estate under subsection (4) or subsection (5) if the right, interest, or power had not terminated until the decedent's death.

(b) Any transfer of property to the extent not otherwise included in the elective estate, made to or for the benefit of any person, except:

1. Any transfer of property for medical or educational expenses to the extent it qualifies for exclusion from the United States gift tax under §2503(e) of the Internal Revenue Code, [FN3] as amended; and

2. After the application of subparagraph (b)1., the first $10,000 of property transferred to or for the benefit of each donee during the 1-year period, but only to the extent the transfer qualifies for exclusion from the United States gift tax under §2503(b) or (c) of the Internal Revenue Code, [FN4] as amended.

(c) Except as provided in paragraph (d), for purposes of this subsection:

1. A "termination" with respect to a right or interest in property occurs when the decedent transfers or relinquishes the right or interest, and, with respect to a power over property, a termination occurs when the power terminates by exercise, release, lapse, default, or otherwise.

2. A distribution from a trust the income or principal of which is subject to subsection (4), subsection (5), or subsection (9) shall be treated as a transfer of property by the decedent and not as a termination of a right or interest in, or a power over, property.

(d) Notwithstanding anything in paragraph (c) to the contrary:

1. A "termination" with respect to a right or interest in property does not occur when the right or interest terminates by the terms of the governing instrument unless the termination is determined by reference to the death of the decedent and the court finds that a principal purpose for the terms of the instrument relating to the termination was avoidance of the elective share.

2. A distribution from a trust is not subject to this subsection if the distribution is required by the terms of the governing instrument unless the event triggering the distribution is determined by reference to the death of the decedent and the court finds that a principal purpose of the terms of the governing instrument relating to the distribution is avoidance of the elective share.

(9) Property transferred in satisfaction of the elective share.

[FN1] 45 U.S.C.A. § 231 et seq.
[FN2] 26 U.S.C.A. § 414(i)
[FN3] 26 U.S.C.A. § 2503(e)
[FN4] 26 U.S.C.A. § 2503(b) or (c)

(Fla. St. 1997, §732.206; Laws 1975, ch. 75-220, §15. Renumbered as 732.2035 and amended by Laws 1999, ch. 99-343, §3, effective October 1, 1999. Amended by Laws 2001, ch. 2001-226, §20, effective October 1, 2001.)

§732.2045. Exclusions and overlapping application

(1) Exclusions.–Section 732.2035 does not apply to:

(a) Except as provided in §732.2155(4), any transfer of property by the decedent to the extent the transfer is irrevocable before the effective date of this subsection or after that date but before the date of the decedent's marriage to the surviving spouse.

(b) Any transfer of property by the decedent to the extent the decedent received adequate consideration in money or money's worth for the transfer.

(c) Any transfer of property by the decedent made with the written consent of the decedent's spouse. For this purpose, spousal consent to split-gift treatment under the United States gift tax laws does not constitute written consent to the transfer by the decedent.

(d) The proceeds of any policy of insurance on the decedent's life in excess of the net cash surrender value of the policy whether payable to the decedent's estate, a trust, or in any other manner.

(e) Any policy of insurance on the decedent's life maintained pursuant to a court order.

(f) The decedent's one-half of the property to which §§732.216-732.228 apply and real property that is community property under the laws of the jurisdiction where it is located.

(g) Property held in a qualifying special needs trust on the date of the decedent's death.

(h) Property included in the gross estate of the decedent for federal estate tax purposes solely because the decedent possessed a general power of appointment.

(i) Property which constitutes the protected homestead of the decedent whether held by the decedent or by a trust at the decedent's death.

(2) Overlapping application.–If §732.2035(1) and any other subsection of §732.2035 apply to the same property interest, the amount included in the elective estate under other subsections is reduced by the amount included under subsection (1). In all other cases, if more than one subsection of §732.2035 applies to a property interest, only the subsection resulting in the largest elective estate shall apply.

(Laws 1999, ch. 99-343, §4, effective October1, 1999. Amended by Laws 2001, ch. 2001-226, §21, effective October 1, 2001).

§732.2055. Manner of valuation of elective estate

For purposes of §732.2035, "value" means:

(1) In the case of any policy of insurance on the decedent's life includable under §732.2035(4), (5), or (6), the net cash surrender value of the policy immediately before the decedent's death.

(2) In the case of any policy of insurance on the decedent's life includable under §732.2035(8), the net cash surrender value of the policy on the date of the termination or transfer.

(3) In the case of amounts includable under §732.2035(7), the transfer tax value of the amounts on the date of the decedent's death.

(4) In the case of other property included under §732.2035(8), the fair market value of the property on the date of the termination or transfer, computed after deducting any mortgages, liens, or security interests on the property as of that date.

(5) In the case of all other property, the fair market value of the property on the date of the decedent's death, computed after deducting from the total value of the property:

(a) All claims paid or payable from the elective estate; and

(b) To the extent they are not deducted under paragraph (a), all mortgages, liens, or security interests on the property.

(Laws 1999, ch. 99-343, §5, effective October 1, 1999. Amended by Laws 2001, ch. 2001-226, § 22, effective October 1, 2001.)

§732.2065. Surviving spouse's elective share

The elective share is an amount equal to 30 percent of the elective estate.

(Laws 1975, ch. 75-220, §15; Laws 1981, ch. 81-27, §1. Renumbered from 732.207 and amended by Laws 1999, ch. 99-343, §6, effective October 1, 1999.)

§732.2075. Source from which elective share is payable

(1) Unless otherwise provided in the decedent's will or, in the absence of a provision in the decedent's will, in a trust referred to in the decedent's will, the following are applied first to satisfy the elective share:

(a) To the extent paid to or for the benefit of the surviving spouse, the proceeds of any term or other policy of insurance on the decedent's life if, at the time of decedent's death, the policy was owned by any person other than the surviving spouse.

(b) To the extent paid to or for the benefit of the surviving spouse, amounts payable under any plan or arrangement described in §732.2035(7).

(c) To the extent paid to or for the benefit of the surviving spouse, the decedent's one-half of any property described in §732.2045(1)(f).

(d) Property held for the benefit of the surviving spouse in a qualifying special needs trust.

(e) Property interests included in the elective estate that pass or have passed to or for the benefit of the surviving spouse, including interests that are contingent upon making the election, but only to the extent that such contingent interests do not diminish other property interests that would be applied to satisfy the elective share in the absence of the contingent interests.

(f) Property interests that would have satisfied the elective share under any preceding paragraph of this subsection but were disclaimed.

(2) If, after the application of subsection (1), the elective share is not fully satisfied, the unsatisfied balance shall be apportioned among the direct recipients of the remaining elective estate in the following order of priority:

(a) *Class 1*.--The decedent's probate estate and revocable trusts.

(b) *Class 2*.--Recipients of property interests, other than protected charitable interests, included in the elective estate under §732.2035(2), (3), or (6) and, to the extent the decedent had at the time of death the power to designate the recipient of the property, property interests, other than protected charitable interests, included under §732.2035(5) and (7).

(c) *Class 3*.--Recipients of all other property interests, other than protected charitable interests, included in the elective estate.

(d) *Class 4*.--Recipients of protected charitable lead interests, but only to the extent and at such times that contribution is permitted without disqualifying the charitable interest in that property for a deduction under the United States gift tax laws.

For purposes of this subsection, a protected charitable interest is any interest for which a charitable deduction with respect to the transfer of the property was allowed or allowable to the decedent or the decedent's spouse under the United States gift tax laws. A protected charitable lead interest is a protected charitable interest where one or more deductible interests in charity precede some other nondeductible interest or interests in the property.

(3) The contribution required of the decedent's probate estate and revocable trusts may be made in cash or in kind. In the application of this subsection, subsections (4) and (5) are to be applied to charge contribution for the elective share to the beneficiaries of the probate estate and revocable trusts as if all beneficiaries were taking under a common governing instrument.

(4) Unless otherwise provided in the decedent's will or, in the absence of a provision in the decedent's will, in a trust referred to in the decedent's will, any amount to be satisfied from the decedent's probate estate, other than from property passing to an inter vivos trust, shall be paid from the assets of the probate estate in the order prescribed in §733.805.

(5) Unless otherwise provided in the trust instrument or, in the decedent's will if there is no provision in the trust instrument, any amount to be satisfied from trust property shall be paid from the assets of the trust in the order provided for claims under §737.3054(2) and (3). A direction in the decedent's will is effective only for revocable trusts.

(Laws 1975, ch. 75-220, §15. Renumbered from 732.209 and amended by Laws 1999, ch. 99-343, §7, effective October 1, 1999. Amended by Laws 2001, ch. 2001-226, §23, effective October 1, 2001; Laws 2002, ch. 2002-82, §4, effective April 23, 2002.)

§732.2085. Liability of direct recipients and beneficiaries

(1) Only direct recipients of property included in the elective estate and the beneficiaries of the decedent's probate estate or of any trust that is a direct recipient, are liable to contribute toward satisfaction of the elective share.

(a) Within each of the classes described in §732.2075(2)(b), (c), and (d), each direct recipient is liable in an amount equal to the value, as determined under §732.2055, of the proportional part of the liability for all members of the class.

(b) Trust and probate estate beneficiaries who receive a distribution of principal after the decedent's death are liable in an amount equal to the value of the principal distributed to them multiplied by the contribution percentage of the distributing trust or estate. For this purpose, "contribution percentage" means the remaining unsatisfied balance of the trust or estate at the time of the distribution divided by the value of the trust or estate as determined under §732.2055. "Remaining unsatisfied balance" means the amount of liability initially apportioned to the trust or estate reduced by amounts or property previously contributed by any person in satisfaction of that liability.

(2) In lieu of paying the amount for which they are liable, beneficiaries who have received a distribution of property included in the elective estate and direct recipients other than the decedent's probate estate or revocable trusts, may:

(a) Contribute a proportional part of all property received; or

(b) With respect to any property interest received before the date of the court's order of contribution:

1. Contribute all of the property; or

2. If the property has been sold or exchanged prior to the date on which the spouse's election is filed, pay an amount equal to the value of the property, less reasonable costs of sale, on the date it was sold or exchanged.

In the application of paragraph (a), the "proportional part of all property received" is determined separately for each class of priority under §732.2075(2).

(3) If a person pays the value of the property on the date of a sale or exchange or contributes all of the property received, as provided in paragraph (2)(b):

(a) No further contribution toward satisfaction of the elective share shall be required with respect to that property.

(b) Any unsatisfied contribution is treated as additional unsatisfied balance and reapportioned to other recipients as provided in §732.2075 and this section.

(4) If any part of §732.2035 or §732.2075 is preempted by federal law with respect to a payment, an item of property, or any other benefit included in the elective estate, a person who, not for value, receives the payment, item of property, or any other benefit is obligated to return the payment, item of property, or benefit, or is personally liable for the amount of the payment or the value of that item of property or benefit, as provided in §§732.2035 and 732.2075, to the person who would have been entitled to it were that section or part of that section not preempted.

(Laws 1999, ch. 99-343, §8, effective October 1, 1999. Amended by Laws 2001, ch. 2001-226, §24, effective October 1, 2001.)

§732.2095. Valuation of property used to satisfy elective share

(1) Definitions.–As used in this section, the term:

(a) "Applicable valuation date" means:

1. In the case of transfers in satisfaction of the elective share, the date of the decedent's death.

2. In the case of property held in a qualifying special needs trust on the date of the decedent's death, the date of the decedent's death.

3. In the case of other property irrevocably transferred to or for the benefit of the surviving spouse during the decedent's life, the date of the transfer.

4. In the case of property distributed to the surviving spouse by the personal representative, the date of distribution.

5. Except as provided in subparagraphs 1, 2, and 3, in the case of property passing in trust for the surviving spouse, the date or dates the trust is funded in satisfaction of the elective share.

6. In the case of property described in §732.2035(2) or (3), the date of the decedent's death.

7. In the case of proceeds of any policy of insurance payable to the surviving spouse, the date of the decedent's death.

8. In the case of amounts payable to the surviving spouse under any plan or arrangement described in §732.2035(7), the date of the decedent's death.

9. In all other cases, the date of the decedent's death or the date the surviving spouse first comes into possession of the property, whichever occurs later.

(b) "Qualifying power of appointment" means a general power of appointment that is exercisable alone and in all events by the decedent's spouse in favor of the spouse or the spouse's estate. For this purpose, a general power to appoint by will is a qualifying power of appointment if the power may be exercised by the spouse in favor of the spouse's estate without the consent of any other person.

(c) "Qualifying invasion power" means a power held by the surviving spouse or the trustee of an elective share trust to invade trust principal for the health, support, and maintenance of the spouse. The power may, but need not, provide that the other resources of the spouse are to be taken into account in any exercise of the power.

(2) Except as provided in this subsection, the value of property for purposes of §732.2075 is the fair market value of the property on the applicable valuation date.

(a) If the surviving spouse has a life interest in property not in trust that entitles the spouse to the use of the property for life, the value of the spouse's interest is one-half of the value of the property on the applicable valuation date.

(b) If the surviving spouse has an interest in a trust, or portion of a trust, which meets the requirements of an elective share trust, the value of the spouse's interest is a percentage of the value of the principal of the trust, or trust portion, on the applicable valuation date as follows:

1. One hundred percent if the trust instrument includes both a qualifying invasion power and a qualifying power of appointment.

2. Eighty percent if the trust instrument includes a qualifying invasion power but no qualifying power of appointment.

3. Fifty percent in all other cases.

(c) If the surviving spouse is a beneficiary of a trust, or portion of a trust, which meets the requirements of a qualifying special needs trust, the value of the principal of the trust, or trust portion, on the applicable valuation date.

(d) If the surviving spouse has an interest in a trust that does not meet the requirements of either an elective share trust or a qualifying special needs trust, the value of the spouse's interest is the transfer tax value of the interest on the applicable valuation date; however, the aggregate value of all of the spouse's interests in the trust shall not exceed one-half of the value of the trust principal on the applicable valuation date.

(e) In the case of any policy of insurance on the decedent's life the proceeds of which are payable outright or to a trust described in paragraph (b), paragraph (c), or paragraph (d), the value of the policy for purposes of §732.2075 and paragraphs (b), (c), and (d) is the net proceeds.

(f) In the case of a right to one or more payments from an annuity or under a similar contractual arrangement or under any plan or arrangement described in §732.2035(7), the value of the right to payments for purposes of §732.2075 and paragraphs (b), (c), and (d) is the transfer tax value of the right on the applicable valuation date.

(Laws 1999, ch. 99-343, §9, effective October 1, 1999. Amended by Laws 2001, ch. 2001-226, §25, effective October 1, 2001.)

§732.2105. Effect of surviving spouse's election on other statutory entitlements

The elective share shall be in addition to homestead, exempt property, and allowances as provided in part IV.

(Laws 1975, ch. 75-220, §15. Renumbered from 732.208 and amended by Laws 1999, ch. 99-343, §10, effective October 1, 1999. Amended by Laws 2001, ch. 2001- 226, §26, effective October 1, 2001.)

§732.2125. Who has the right to elect

The right of election may be exercised:

(1) By the surviving spouse.

(2) With approval of the court having jurisdiction of the probate proceeding by an attorney in fact or a guardian of the property of the surviving spouse. The court shall determine the election as the best interests of the surviving spouse, during the spouse's probable lifetime, require.

(Laws 1975, ch. 75-220, §15. Renumbered from 732.210 and amended by Laws 1999, ch. 99-343, §12, effective October 1, 1999. Amended by Laws 2001, ch. 2001- 226, § 27, effective October 1, 2001.

§732.2135. Time of election; extensions; withdrawal

(1) Except as provided in subsection (2), the election must be filed on or before the earlier of the date that is 6 months after the date of service of a copy of the notice of administration on the surviving spouse, or an attorney in fact or guardian of the property of the surviving spouse, or the date that is 2 years after the date of the decedent's death.

(2) Within the period provided in subsection (1), the surviving spouse or an attorney in fact or guardian of the property of the surviving spouse may petition the court for an extension of time for making an election. For good cause shown, the court may extend the time for election. If the court grants the petition for an extension, the election must be filed within the time allowed by the extension.

(3) The surviving spouse or an attorney in fact, guardian of the property, or personal representative of the surviving spouse may withdraw an election on or before the earlier of the date that is 8 months after the date of the decedent's death or the date of a court order of contribution. If an election is withdrawn, the court may assess attorney's fees and costs against the surviving spouse or the surviving spouse's estate.

(4) A petition for an extension of the time for making the election or for approval to make the election shall toll the time for making the election.

(Laws 1975, ch. 75-220, §15. Renumbered from 732.212 and amended by Laws 1999, ch. 99-343, §13, effective October 1, 1999. Amended by Laws 2001, ch. 2001- 226, §28, effective October 1, 2001; Laws 2006, ch. 2006-134, §4, effective July 1, 2006.)

§732.2145. Court shall determine elective share and contribution

(1) The court shall determine the elective share and contribution. Contributions shall bear interest at the statutory rate beginning 90 days after the order of contribution. The order is prima facie correct in proceedings in any court or jurisdiction.

(2) Except as provided in subsection (3), the personal representative shall collect contribution from the recipients of the elective estate as provided in the court's order of contribution.

(a) If property within the possession or control of the personal representative is distributable to a beneficiary or trustee who is required to contribute in satisfaction of the elective share, the personal representative shall withhold from the distribution the contribution required of the beneficiary or trustee.

(b) If, after the order of contribution, the personal representative brings an action to collect contribution from property not within the personal representative's control, the judgment shall include the personal representative's costs and reasonable attorney's fees. The personal representative is not required to seek collection of any portion of the elective share from property not within the personal representative's control until after the entry of the order of contribution.

(3) A personal representative who has the duty under this section of enforcing contribution may be relieved of that duty by an order of the court finding that it is impracticable to enforce contribution in view of the improbability of obtaining a judgment or the improbability of collection under any judgment that might be obtained, or otherwise. The personal representative shall not be liable for failure to attempt collection if the attempt would have been economically impracticable.

(4) Nothing in this section limits the independent right of the surviving spouse to collect the elective share as provided in the order of contribution, and that right is hereby conferred. If the surviving spouse brings an action to enforce the order, the judgment shall include the surviving spouse's costs and reasonable attorney's fees.

(Laws 1999, ch. 99-343, §14, effective October 1, 1999. Amended by Laws 2001, ch. 2001-226, §29, effective October 1, 2001.)

§732.2155. Effective date and the effect of prior waivers

(1) Sections 732.201-732.2155 are effective on October 1, 1999, for all decedents dying on or after October 1, 2001. The law in effect prior to October 1, 1999, applies to decedents dying before October 1, 2001.

(2) Nothing in §§732.201-732.2155 modifies or applies to the rights of spouses under chapter 61.

(3) A waiver of elective share rights before the effective date of this section which is otherwise in compliance with the requirements of §732.702 is a waiver of all rights under §§ 732.201-732.2145.

(4) Notwithstanding anything in § 732.2045(1)(a) to the contrary, any trust created by the decedent before the effective date of §§732.201-732.2145 that meets the requirements of an elective share trust is treated as if the decedent created the trust after the effective date of these sections and in satisfaction of the elective share.

(5) Sections 732.201-732.2155 do not affect any interest in contracts entered into for adequate consideration in money or money's worth before October 1, 1999, to the extent that the contract was irrevocable at all times from October 1, 1999, until the date of the decedent's death.

(6) Sections 732.201--732.2155 do not affect any interest in property held, as of the decedent's death, in a trust, whether revocable or irrevocable, if:

(a) The property was an asset of the trust at all times between October 1, 1999, and the date of the decedent's death;

(b) The decedent was not married to the decedent's surviving spouse when the property was transferred to the trust; and

(c) The property was a nonmarital asset as defined in § 61.075 immediately prior to the decedent's death.

(Laws 1999, ch. 99-343, §15, effective October 1, 1999. Amended by Laws 2001, ch. 2001-226, §30, effective October 1, 2001.)

§732.223. Surviving spouse may seek to perfect title to property

If the title to any property to which §§732.216-732.228 apply was held by the decedent at the time of the decedent's death, title of the surviving spouse may be perfected by an order of the probate court or by execution of an instrument by the personal representative or the beneficiaries of the decedent with the approval of the probate court. The probate court in which the decedent's estate is being administered has no duty to discover whether property held by the decedent is property to which §§732.216-732.228 apply. The personal representative has no duty to discover whether property held by the decedent is property to which §§732.216-732.228 apply unless a written demand is made by the surviving spouse or the spouse's successor in interest within 3 months after service of a copy of the notice of administration on the surviving spouse or the spouse's successor in interest.

(Laws 1992, ch. 92-200, § 10. Amended by Laws 1997, ch. 97-102, § 957, effective July 1, 1997; Laws 2001, ch. 2001-226, § 35, effective Jan. 1, 2002.)

Rule 5.360. Procedure for filing petition for elective share

(a) Election. An election to take the elective share may be filed by the surviving spouse, or on behalf of the surviving spouse by an attorney-in-fact or guardian of the property of the surviving spouse.

(1) *Election by Surviving Spouse.* An electing surviving spouse shall file the election within the time required by law and promptly serve a copy of the election on the personal representative in the manner provided for service of formal notice.

(2) *Election by Attorney-in-Fact or Guardian of the Property of Surviving Spouse.*

(A) Petition for Approval. Before filing the election, the attorney-in-fact or guardian of the property of the surviving spouse shall petition the court having jurisdiction of the probate proceeding for approval to make the election. The petition for approval shall allege the authority to act on behalf of the surviving spouse and facts supporting the election.

(B) Notice of Petition. Upon receipt of the petition, the personal representative shall promptly serve a copy of the petition by formal notice on all interested persons.

(C) Filing the Election. Upon entry of an order authorizing the filing of an election, the attorney-in-fact or guardian of the property shall file the election within the later of the time provided by law or 30 days from service of the order and promptly serve a copy of the election on the personal representative in the manner provided for service of formal notice.

(b) Procedure for Election.

(1) *Extension.* Within the period provided by law to make the election, the surviving spouse or an attorney-in-fact or guardian of the property of the surviving spouse may petition the court for an extension of time for making an election or for approval to make the election. After notice and hearing the court for good cause shown may extend the time for election. If the court grants the petition for an extension, the election must be filed within the time allowed by the extension.

(2) *Withdrawal of Election.* The surviving spouse, an attorney-in-fact, a guardian of the property of the surviving spouse, or the personal representative of the surviving spouse's estate may withdraw the election within the time provided by law.

(3) *Service of Notice.* Upon receipt of an election the personal representative shall serve a notice of election within 20 days following service of the election, together with a copy of the election, on all interested persons in the manner provided for service of formal notice. The notice of election shall indicate the names and addresses of the attorneys for the surviving spouse and the personal representative and shall state that:

(A) persons receiving a notice of election may be required to contribute toward the satisfaction of the elective share;

(B) objections to the election must be served within 20 days after service of the copy of the notice of election; and

(C) if no objection to the election is timely served, an order determining the surviving spouse's entitlement to the elective share may be granted without further notice.

(4) *Objection to Election.* Within 20 days after service of the notice of election, an interested person may serve an objection to the election which shall state with particularity the grounds on which the objection is based. The objecting party shall serve copies of the objection on the surviving spouse and the personal representative. If an objection is served, the personal representative shall promptly serve a copy of the objection on all other interested persons who have not previously been served with a copy of the objection.

(c) Determination of Entitlement.

(1) *No Objection Served.* If no objection to the election is timely served, the court shall enter an order determining the spouse's entitlement to the elective share.

(2) *Objection Served.* If an objection to the election is timely served, the court shall determine the surviving spouse's entitlement to the elective share after notice and hearing.

(d) Procedure to Determine Amount of Elective Share and Contribution.

(1) *Petition by Personal Representative.* After entry of the order determining the surviving spouse's entitlement to the elective share, the personal representative shall file and serve a petition to determine the amount of the elective share. The petition shall

(A) give the name and address of each direct recipient known to the personal representative;

(B) describe the proposed distribution of assets to satisfy the elective share, and the time and manner of distribution; and

(C) identify those direct recipients, if any, from whom a specified contribution will be required and state the amount of contribution sought from each.

(2) *Service of Inventory.* The inventory of the elective estate required by rule 5.340, together with the petition, shall be served within 60 days after entry of the order determining entitlement to the elective share on all interested persons in the manner provided for service of formal notice.

(3) *Petition by Spouse.* If the personal representative does not file the petition to determine the amount of the elective share within 90 days from rendition of the order of entitlement, the electing spouse or the attorney-in-fact or the guardian of the property or personal representative of the electing spouse may file the petition specifying as particularly as is known the value of the elective share.

(4) *Objection to Amount of Elective Share.* Within 20 days after service of the petition to determine the amount of the elective share, an interested person may serve an objection to the amount of or distribution of assets to satisfy the elective share. The objection shall state with particularity the grounds on which the objection is based. The objecting party shall serve copies of the objection on the surviving spouse and the personal representative. If an objection is served, the personal representative shall promptly serve a copy of the objection on all interested persons who have not previously been served.

(5) *Determination of Amount of Elective Share and Contribution.*

(A) No Objection Served. If no objection is timely served to the petition to determine the amount of the elective share, the court shall enter an order on the petition.

(B) Objection Served. If an objection is timely served to the petition to determine the amount of the elective share, the court shall determine the amount of the elective share and contribution after notice and hearing.

(6) Order Determining Amount of Elective Share and Contribution. The order shall:

(A) set forth the amount of the elective share;

(B) identify the assets to be distributed to the surviving spouse in satisfaction of the elective share; and

(C) if contribution is necessary, specify the amount of contribution for which each direct recipient is liable.

(e) Relief from Duty to Enforce Contribution. A petition to relieve the personal representative from the duty to enforce contribution shall state the grounds on which it is based and notice shall be served on interested persons.

(Amended September 13, 1984, effective January 1, 1985 (458 So.2d 1079); September 29, 1988, effective January 1, 1989 (537 So.2d 500); September 24, 1992, effective January 1, 1993 (607 So.2d 1306); October 11, 2001 (807 So.2d 622); September 29, 2005, effective January 1, 2006 (912 So.2d 1178).)

C. Community Property Rights

Community property states offer the most protection to surviving spouses. There are nine community property states (Arizona, California, Idaho, Louisiana, Nevada, New Mexico, Texas, Washington, and Wisconsin).

Florida is not a community property jurisdiction. However, Florida law provides for the disposition of the property of persons who die domiciled in Florida and who have an interest in community property that they acquired while living in another jurisdiction (Fla. Stat. §§732.217-732.226). The statutory provisions are modeled after those of the Uniform Disposition of Community Property Rights at Death Act, adopted by the National Conference of Commissioners on Uniform State Laws in 1971. That Act has been adopted by 14 states (Alaska, Arkansas, Colorado, Connecticut, Florida, Hawaii, Kentucky, Michigan, Montana, New York, North Carolina, Oregon, Virginia, and Wyoming). NCCUSL, Disposition of Community Property Rights at Death, Legislative Fact Sheet, available at *www.nccusl.org* (last visited on February 11, 2007).

Based on the Florida statutory provisions, community property principles apply to the property owned by a decedent who owned community property at death in another jurisdiction. In community property states, each spouse has an undivided interest in any property acquired from spousal earnings during the marriage. During the marriage, the spouses' interests in the community property are present, existing, and equal. Upon the death of the decedent, the surviving spouse is considered to be the owner of half of the marital property dating from the beginning of the marriage. In Florida, the decedent only has the right to dispose of the decedent's half of the marital property either by "testamentary disposition or distribution under the laws of succession. . ." (Fla. Stat. §732.219). For that reason, the decedent's one-half of that property is not included in the elective estate. *Id.*

Note that a presumption operates in Florida regarding property acquired by the spouses during the marriage. Property that a Florida domiciliary acquires while domiciled in a community property state, "is presumed to have been acquired as, or to have become and remained, property to which these sections apply" (Fla. Stat. §732.218(1)).

The spouses can change the characterization of their property by agreement (Fla. Stat. §732.225).That is, property may be transmuted by a written agreement from

community property to separate property or vice versa.

§732.216. Title of Act

Sections 732.216-732.228 may be cited as the "Florida Uniform Disposition of Community Property Rights at Death Act."
(Laws 1992, ch. 92-200, §4.)

§732.217. Application

Sections 732.216-732.228 apply to the disposition at death of the following property acquired by a married person:

(1) Personal property, wherever located, which:

(a) Was acquired as, or became and remained, community property under the laws of another jurisdiction;

(b) Was acquired with the rents, issues, or income of, or the proceeds from, or in exchange for, community property; or

(c) Is traceable to that community property.

(2) Real property, except real property held as tenants by the entirety, which is located in this state, and which:

(a) Was acquired with the rents, issues, or income of, the proceeds from, or in exchange for, property acquired as, or which became and remained, community property under the laws of another jurisdiction; or

(b) Is traceable to that community property.

(Laws 1992, ch. 92-200, §5. Amended by Laws 2003, ch. 2003-154, §4, effective June 12, 2003.)

§732.218. Rebuttable presumptions

In determining whether §§732.216-732.228 apply to specific property, the following rebuttable presumptions apply:

(1) Property acquired during marriage by a spouse of that marriage while domiciled in a jurisdiction under whose laws property could then be acquired as community property is presumed to have been acquired as, or to have become and remained, property to which these sections apply.

(2) Real property located in this state, other than homestead and real property held as tenants by the entirety, and personal property wherever located acquired by a married person while domiciled in a jurisdiction under whose laws property could not then be acquired as community property and title to which was taken in a form which created rights of survivorship are presumed to be property to which these sections do not apply.

(Laws 1992, ch. 92-200, §6. Amended by Laws 2001, ch. 2001-226, §31, effective January 1, 2002.)

§732.219. Spousal rights in community property

Upon the death of a married person, one-half of the property to which §§732.216-732.228 apply is the property of the surviving spouse and is not subject to testamentary disposition by the decedent or distribution under the laws of succession of this state. One-half of that property is the property of the decedent and is subject to testamentary disposition or distribution under the laws of succession of this state. The decedent's one-half of that property is not in the elective estate.
(Laws 1992, ch. 92-200, §7. Amended by Laws 2001, ch. 2001-226, §32, effective January 1, 2002; Laws 2002, ch. 2002-1, §107, effective May 21, 2002.)

§732.221. Perfection of title of personal representative or beneficiary

If the title to any property to which §§732.216-732.228 apply is held by the surviving spouse at the time of the decedent's death, the personal representative or a beneficiary of the decedent may institute an action to perfect title to the property. The personal representative has no duty to discover whether any property held by the surviving spouse is property to which §§732.216-732.228 apply, unless a written demand is made by a beneficiary within 3 months after service of a copy of the notice of administration on the beneficiary or by a creditor within 3 months after the first publication of the notice to creditors.
(Laws 1992, ch. 92-200, §8. Amended by Laws 2001, ch. 2001-226, §33, effective January 1, 2002.)

§732.222. Purchaser for value or lender

(1) If a surviving spouse has apparent title to property to which §§732.216-732.228 apply, a purchaser for value or a lender taking a security interest in the property takes the interest in the property free of any rights of the personal representative or a beneficiary of the decedent.

(2) If a personal representative or a beneficiary of the decedent has apparent title to property to which §§732.216-732.228 apply, a purchaser for value or a lender taking a security interest in the property takes that interest in the property free of any rights of the surviving spouse.

(3) A purchaser for value or a lender need not inquire whether a vendor or borrower acted properly.

(4) The proceeds of a sale or creation of a security interest must be treated as the property transferred to the purchaser for value or a lender. *(Laws 1992, ch. 92-200, §9. Amended by Laws 1997,*

ch. 97-102, §956, effective July 1, 1997; Laws 2001, ch. 2001-226, §34, effective January 1, 2002.)

§732.223. Perfection of title of surviving spouse

If the title to any property to which §§732.216-732.228 apply was held by the decedent at the time of the decedent's death, title of the surviving spouse may be perfected by an order of the probate court or by execution of an instrument by the personal representative or the beneficiaries of the decedent with the approval of the probate court. The probate court in which the decedent's estate is being administered has no duty to discover whether property held by the decedent is property to which §§732.216-732.228 apply. The personal representative has no duty to discover whether property held by the decedent is property to which §§732.216-732.228 apply unless a written demand is made by the surviving spouse or the spouse's successor in interest within 3 months after service of a copy of the notice of administration on the surviving spouse or the spouse's successor in interest.

(Laws 1992, ch. 92-200, §10. Amended by Laws 1997, ch. 97-102, §957, effective July 1, 1997; Laws 2001, ch. 2001-226, §35, effective January 1, 2002.)

§732.224. Creditor's rights

Sections 732.216-732.228 do not affect rights of creditors with respect to property to which §§732.216-732.228 apply.

(Laws 1992, ch. 92-200, §11.)

§732.225. Acts of married persons

Sections 732.216-732.228 do not prevent married persons from severing or altering their interests in property to which these sections apply. The reinvestment of any property to which these sections apply in real property located in this state which is or becomes homestead property creates a conclusive presumption that the spouses have agreed to terminate the community property attribute of the property reinvested.

(Laws 1992, ch. 92-200, §12.)

§732.226. Limitations on testamentary disposition

Sections 732.216-732.228 do not authorize a person to dispose of property by will if it is held under limitations imposed by law preventing testamentary disposition by that person.

(Laws 1992, ch. 92-200, §13.)

III. Waiver by the Surviving Spouse

A spouse may renounce ("disclaim") any statutory rights in the other's estate. Spouses may do so either by a premarital agreement (sometimes called an "antenuptial agreement") or by an agreement executed during the marriage. Often, the marital parties agree to waive inheritance rights in order to protect the rights of the respective spouses' children from prior marriages.

Florida law specifies the rules by which the surviving spouse may waive rights in the decedent's estate. According to Florida law, a surviving spouse can waive rights to homestead, exempt property, and family allowance, whole or in part, before or after marriage) (Fla. Stat. §732.702 (1)). An effective waiver requires a written contract, signed by the waiving party in the presence of two subscribing witnesses. *Id.*

A surviving spouse may also waive his or her right to an elective share, a pretermitted share, preference in appointment as personal representative and must meet the above requirements to do so. *Id.*

The UPC, similarly, provides that spouses may waive property rights by premarital or marital agreements. Such agreements must be in writing, voluntary, and not unconscionable (UPC §2-213(a)). Spouses may also waive the family protection allowances and exemptions (UPC §2-213(a)). To contest such a waiver, the surviving spouse must show that the waiver was not executed voluntarily or that it was unconscionable at the time of execution and lacked fair disclosure (UPC §2-213(b)). See also Restatement (Third) of Property, *supra*, at §9.4.

§732.702. Waiver of rights by surviving spouse

(1) The rights of a surviving spouse to an elective share, intestate share, pretermitted share, homestead, exempt property, family allowance, and preference in appointment as personal representative of an intestate estate or any of those rights, may be waived, wholly or partly, before or after marriage, by a written contract, agreement, or waiver, signed by the waiving party in the presence of two subscribing witnesses. The requirement of witnesses shall be applicable only to contracts, agreements, or waivers signed by Florida residents after the effective date of this law. Any contract, agreement, or waiver executed by a nonresident of Florida, either before or after this law takes effect, is valid in this state if valid when executed under the laws of the state or country where it was executed, whether or not he or

she is a Florida resident at the time of death. Unless the waiver provides to the contrary, a waiver of "all rights," or equivalent language, in the property or estate of a present or prospective spouse, or a complete property settlement entered into after, or in anticipation of, separation, dissolution of marriage, or divorce, is a waiver of all rights to elective share, intestate share, pretermitted share, homestead, exempt property, family allowance, and preference in appointment as personal representative of an intestate estate, by the waiving party in the property of the other and a renunciation by the waiving party of all benefits that would otherwise pass to the waiving party from the other by intestate succession or by the provisions of any will executed before the written contract, agreement, or waiver.

(2) Each spouse shall make a fair disclosure to the other of that spouse's estate if the agreement, contract, or waiver is executed after marriage. No disclosure shall be required for an agreement, contract, or waiver executed before marriage.

(3) No consideration other than the execution of the agreement, contract, or waiver shall be necessary to its validity, whether executed before or after marriage.

(Laws 1974, ch. 74-106, §1; Laws 1975, ch. 75-220, §39; Laws 1977, ch. 77-87, §14. Amended by Laws 2001, ch. 2001-226, §56, effective January 1, 2002.)

IV. Attempts to Defeat the Spouse's Statutory Rights

A. Generally

A significant problem in forced-share jurisdictions is the protection of the surviving spouse's right to nonprobate assets (i.e., those assets that are not part of the probate estate). Such nonprobate assets often consist of joint tenancy property that passes by right of survivorship or life insurance proceeds. In some cases, testators use such assets as probate avoidance techniques—e.g., by holding joint property with someone other than the spouse or making life insurance proceeds payable to someone other than the spouse.

States approach this problem in different ways. Some states subject the decedent's inter vivos transfers to the "illusory transfer" test. These states subject property whose transfer is deemed illusory to the surviving spouse's elective share. McGovern & Kurtz, *supra*, §3.7 at 150. The Restatement (Second) of Property (Donative Transfers) §34.1(3)(1990), as well as the Restatement (Third) of Trusts §25, cmt. d (1996), both permit a surviving spouse to reach assets of a revocable trust created by the decedent (cited in McGovern & Kurtz, *supra*, at 150).

Other states invalidate those nonprobate transfers that are made fraudulently with an intent to deprive the surviving spouse of the elective share. *Id.* at 150-151. Other states simply include certain nonprobate assets when computing the elective share. *Id.* at 151. This last approach reflects the influence of the UPC (discussed *infra*).

726.105. Fraudulent transfers and creditors

(1) A transfer made or obligation incurred by a debtor is fraudulent as to a creditor, whether the creditor's claim arose before or after the transfer was made or the obligation was incurred, if the debtor made the transfer or incurred the obligation:

(a) With actual intent to hinder, delay, or defraud any creditor of the debtor; or

(b) Without receiving a reasonably equivalent value in exchange for the transfer or obligation, and the debtor:

1. Was engaged or was about to engage in a business or a transaction for which the remaining assets of the debtor were unreasonably small in relation to the business or transaction; or

2. Intended to incur, or believed or reasonably should have believed that he or she would incur, debts beyond his or her ability to pay as they became due.

(2) In determining actual intent under paragraph (1)(a), consideration may be given, among other factors, to whether:

(a) The transfer or obligation was to an insider.

(b) The debtor retained possession or control of the property transferred after the transfer.

(c) The transfer or obligation was disclosed or concealed.

(d) Before the transfer was made or obligation was incurred, the debtor had been sued or threatened with suit.

(e) The transfer was of substantially all the debtor's assets.

(f) The debtor absconded.

(g) The debtor removed or concealed assets.

(h) The value of the consideration received by the debtor was reasonably equivalent to the value of the asset transferred or the amount of the obligation incurred.

(i) The debtor was insolvent or became insolvent shortly after the transfer was made or the obligation was incurred.

(j) The transfer occurred shortly before or shortly after a substantial debt was incurred.

(k) The debtor transferred the essential assets of the business to a lienor who transferred the assets to an insider of the debtor.

(Laws 1987, ch. 87-79, §5. Amended by Laws 1997, ch. 97-102, §937, effective July 1, 1997.)

B. UPC Augmented Estate

The UPC also provides for an elective share for the surviving spouse. The elective share applies to protect surviving spouses of decedents who were domiciled at death in a state which adopted the UPC. A surviving spouse may elect to take a designated percentage of the "augmented estate" (UPC §2-202). The augmented estate is an estate that is conceptualized for the purpose of calculating the value of the surviving spouse's elective share. The concept signifies that the probate estate is "augmented" (increased) by certain inter vivos transfers of the decedent.

Specifically, the augmented estate takes into account:

- **the decedent's gross probate estate minus creditors' claims, funeral expenses and expenses of administration, and family protection allowances and exemptions (UPC §2-204);**
- **decedent's nonprobate transfers to others to the extent the decedent retained interests (such as a joint tenancy with right of survivorship, a revocable trust, life insurance owned by the decedent on the decedent's life, multiple-party accounts held in decedent's name with a right of survivorship in a third party, and powers of appointment) (UPC § 2-205(1)); or irrevocable transfers by the decedent to third persons within two years before death that would have been included in this category (UPC § 2-205(3));**
- **the surviving spouse's property which consisted of the decedent's nonprobate property that was derived from the decedent by reason of the latter's death (e.g., life insurance benefits, retirement plan benefits) (UPC § 2-206); and**
- **the surviving spouse's assets (i.e., assets earned during the marriage, acquired prior to marriage, and assets derived from the decedent and other persons) (UPC § 2-207(a)). The purpose of including the last two categories (assets derived from the decedent as a result of death and the surviving spouse's personal assets) in the augmented estate is to ensure that the augmented estate concept does not benefit surviving spouses with substantial personal assets.**

The original version of the UPC (promulgated in 1969) specified that the surviving spouse would take a fixed share (a one-third share) of the augmented estate. However, subsequent revisions in 1990 altered the percentage to take into consideration the length of the marriage. Spouses married at least 1 year may take 3 percent of the augmented estate; those married at least 5 years take 15 percent of the augmented estate; and those married 15 years or more are entitled to 50 percent of the augmented estate. Further, the Code suggests a minimum monetary amount of $50,000 regardless of the length of the marriage. The policy rationale for the 1990 UPC provisions is that marriage is a partnership in which each spouse earns an increasing interest in the estate of the other. The UPC expands the spouses' interest to all assets of both spouses and not merely marital property (unlike in community property states in which the spouse's one-half interest applies only to property acquired during the marriage).

As discussed above, Florida adopted a version of the UPC augmented estate in 1999.

C. Election Will

Sometimes, a testator attempts to bequeath or devise property that belongs to a beneficiary of the will (i.e., property that does not belong to the testator). Such situations commonly arise in wills of spouses who live in community property states (although the use of such election wills is not limited to marital partners).

For example, one spouse may attempt to effectuate a testamentary scheme that involves a testamentary gift of all of the community property (not merely the testator's half but the half that belongs to the other spouse). Because the decedent-spouse only has the right of testamentary disposition over the decedent's half of the community property (and

the decedent's separate property), the act of bequeathing all of the community property may serve to put the surviving spouse to an election.

The surviving spouse then has a choice: (1) to elect against the will (thereby retaining the survivor's property that was the subject of the testator's testamentary gift but renouncing any testamentary gift), or (2) to take under the will (thereby acquiescing in the testator's testamentary gift of the surviving spouse's property to another party). Clearly, the surviving spouse will choose the alternative that is financially most beneficial.

Most jurisdictions favor a construction that does not lead to an election by the surviving spouse. That is, if the testator's will bequeaths "all my property," courts are likely to interpret that bequest to encompass only the property over which the decedent has testamentary disposition (i.e., the testator's half of the community property and all of his or her separate property).

V. Protection from Disinheritance

A testator has the power to disinherit family members. This ability is inherent in the power of testamentary disposition. In order to disinherit an heir, the testator must execute a will that expressly disinherits the heir. The will must also dispose of all of the testator's property because any property that is not devised by the will may pass to the heir by the laws of intestate succession.

If the decedent attempts to disinherit a spouse, the surviving spouse may claim an elective share. The surviving spouse may claim that share regardless of whether the decedent's will disinherits the survivor entirely or bequeaths to the survivor part of the decedent's estate.

In some cases, a testator may unintentionally disinherit a family member. Given the jurisdiction, such family members may be protected from some types of unintentional disinheritance (discussed *infra*).

A. Spouses

Many jurisdictions protect certain family members (e.g., spouses, children) against unintentional disinheritance. These statutes are known as "pretermitted" (or omitted) heir statutes. American pretermission statutes date from the eighteenth century. McGovern & Kurtz, *supra*, §3.5 at 140. The English Wills Act of 1837 provided that marriage revoked the will of a spouse, and many jurisdictions follow this rule. Id., §3.6 at 145. Other jurisdictions revoke a will only if the testator both marries and has a child. *Id.*

The share given to an omitted spouse in many jurisdictions is the same as the intestate share. However, most omitted spouse statutes give a share of the net probate estate and do not include nonprobate property (such as trust property). *Id.*, §3.7 at 147.

The most common situation that results in unintentional omission of a spouse is the antenuptial will, i.e., a spouse who marries the testator after the testator executes a will. For example, Florida Statutes §732.301 provides that a surviving spouse who marries the decedent after the will was executed shall receive a share of the estate equal to the surviving spouse's intestate share (i.e., the share that the surviving spouse would have received if the testator had died intestate), unless certain conditions exist. That is, surviving spouses in Florida do *not* receive a share of the decedent's estate if the decedent provided for the spouse in the will (i.e. if the will makes *any* provision for the named person, whether identified as a "spouse" or in any other manner, such as a friend), if the decedent's failure to provide for the surviving spouse was intentional as evident from the will, or if the surviving spouse waived his or her rights (Fla. Stat. §732.301(1),(2),(3)).

To illustrate, in In re Dumas' Estate, 413 So. 2d 58 (Fla. Dist. Ct. App. 1982), James H. Dumas died, leaving his wife Daisy surviving. Before his marriage, he had executed a will leaving his estate to the daughter of his former spouse and to that stepdaughter's child. He did not make a new will after the marriage. The beneficiaries sought to probate the will. The court of appeals held that because the decedent was survived by his spouse and had no lineal descendants, the beneficiaries were not entitled to a share in his estate. Rather, Daisy, as a pretermitted spouse, should receive the entire estate.

Florida Statutes §733.805 governs the sources from which the pretermitted spouse's share is to be obtained.

Florida law applicable to pretermitted spouses is similar in many regards to the UPC. The UPC provides for an intestate share to a spouse in the antenuptial will situation (UPC §2-301), and does not permit the omitted spouse to take if evidence establishes that the omission was intentional (such as if the will shows an express intent to exclude the spouse from a subsequent marriage. However, the UPC has additional provisions precluding an omitted spouse that are not present in the Florida statute, e.g., if the surviving spouse received

transfers outside the will that were intended to be in lieu of a testamentary gift, or if the will was executed in "contemplation" of the marriage (UPC §2-301(a)(1)). Florida law fails to incorporate these provision because the Florida statute was based on an earlier version of the UPC.

Note that an expressly disinherited spouse can still take an elective share in many jurisdictions. However, that share may be smaller than the share specifically provided for an "omitted spouse." For example, under the UPC, the size of the elective share depends on the duration of the marriage.

A common scenario in antenuptial will situations occurs when a testator executes a will with a small provision for a "friend." Later, the testator marries the friend. "Most courts have held that such a devise does not bar an omitted spouse's claim unless the will was made in contemplation of the marriage, but there are also contrary decisions." McGovern & Kurtz, *supra*, §3.6, at 146. Cf. Estate of Moi, 2006 WL 3085601 (Wash. App. Ct. 2006) (holding that husband of two weeks was not an omitted spouse because the omitted spouse statute did not contain a contemplation-of-marriage test, and also because husband was named and provided for with $100,000 bequest in wife's will, even though as a friend).

§732.301. Share of omitted spouse

When a person marries after making a will and the spouse survives the testator, the surviving spouse shall receive a share in the estate of the testator equal in value to that which the surviving spouse would have received if the testator had died intestate, unless:

(1) Provision has been made for, or waived by, the spouse by prenuptial or postnuptial agreement;

(2) The spouse is provided for in the will; or

(3) The will discloses an intention not to make provision for the spouse.

The share of the estate that is assigned to the pretermitted spouse shall be obtained in accordance with s. 733.805.

(Laws 1974, ch. 74-106, §1; Laws 1975, ch. 75-220, §16; Laws 1977, ch. 77-87, §9.)

§733.805. Order of abatement

(1) Funds or property designated by the will shall be used to pay debts, family allowance, exempt property, elective share charges, expenses of administration, and devises, to the extent the funds or property is sufficient. If no provision is made or the designated fund or property is insufficient, the funds and property of the estate shall be used for these purposes, and to raise the shares of a pretermitted spouse and children, except as otherwise provided in subsections (3) and (4), in the following order:

(a) Property passing by intestacy.

(b) Property devised to the residuary devisee or devisees.

(c) Property not specifically or demonstratively devised.

(d) Property specifically or demonstratively devised.

(2) Demonstrative devises shall be classed as general devises upon the failure or insufficiency of funds or property out of which payment should be made, to the extent of the insufficiency. Devises to the decedent's surviving spouse, given in satisfaction of, or instead of, the surviving spouse's statutory rights in the estate, shall not abate until other devises of the same class are exhausted. Devises given for a valuable consideration shall abate with other devises of the same class only to the extent of the excess over the amount of value of the consideration until all others of the same class are exhausted. Except as herein provided, devises shall abate equally and ratably and without preference or priority as between real and personal property. When property that has been specifically devised or charged with a devise is sold or used by the personal representative, other devisees shall contribute according to their respective interests to the devisee whose devise has been sold or used. The amounts of the respective contributions shall be determined by the court and shall be paid or withheld before distribution is made.

(3) Section 733.817 shall be applied before this section is applied.

(4) In determining the contribution required under §733.607(2), subsections (1)-(3) of this section and §736.05053(2) shall be applied as if the beneficiaries of the estate and the beneficiaries of a trust described in §733.707(3), other than the estate or trust itself, were taking under a common instrument.

(Laws 1974, ch. 74-106, §1; Laws 1975, ch. 75-220, §88; Laws 1977, ch. 77-174, §1. Amended by Laws 1997, ch. 97-102, §1020, effective July 1, 1997; Laws 2001, ch. 2001-226, §156, effective January 1, 2002; Laws 2006, ch. 2006-217, §38, effective July 1, 2007.)

B. Children

Pretermitted heir statutes protect not only omitted spouses but also omitted children. However, children receive far less protection

than spouses. Pretermitted heir statutes generally provide a share for an omitted child born to the testator after the testator executed a will. The rationale for inclusion is based on presumed intent (i.e., the idea that a testator would have wanted to provide a share for such a child). Jurisdictions are more restrictive in their treatment of those omitted children who were alive at the time of the will execution.

Disinheritance of a child may stem from several reasons. The most common is inadvertence—either a child is unintentionally omitted from the will or no will is written after the child is born. Brian C. Brennan, Note, Disinheritance of Dependent Children: Why Isn't America Fulfilling Its Moral Obligation?, 14 Quinnipiac Prob. L.J. 125, 128-129 (1999). Intentional disinheritance on the other hand, may result from some parents' belief that disinheriting a child will force the child to work harder in life "to become a better person and a more contributing member of society," or the mistaken belief that existing legal provisions (family allowances, homestead exemptions, and personal property exemptions) will protect the child. *Id.* at 129-131. Finally, the increasing rate of divorce and remarriage leads to more frequent disinheritance of children from prior marriages as testators balance the needs of current families against those of previous ones. *Id.* at 131-132.

Only one state (Louisiana) guarantees children a forced share in their parents' estate. Policy reasons underlying this forced heirship include: furthering state interests in warding off intra-family litigation, promoting family solidarity, and preventing excessive concentrations of wealth. Brennan, *supra*, at 155. Louisiana adopted the French law of inheritance (the Napoleonic Code of 1803) in 1825, guanteeing children a forced share. The concept was enshrined in the state constitution. See La. Const. (art. XII, §5) (providing "no law shall abolish forced heirship"). In 1989-1990, the Louisiana state legislature placed restrictions on forced heirship in terms of age and competency. See La. Civ. Code art. 1493 (as amended in 1989 and 1990) (extinguishing forced heirship for persons who, upon the decedent's death, are competent and 23 years of age or older). The Louisiana Supreme Court subsequently declared these restrictions unconstitutional (Succession of Lauga, 624 So.2d 1156 (La. 1993); Succession of Terry, 624 So.2d 1201 (La. 1993)).

In 1995, however, by constitutional amendment, the Louisiana state legislature deleted the language "no law shall abolish forced heirship" and required the legislature to implement legislation restricting forced heirship to those children age 23 or younger but also permitting forced shares to issue (of any age) who were incompetent. See La. Constit. art. XII, §5 (amended by Acts 1995, No. 1321, Section 1, approved October 21, 1995, effective November 23, 1995) (cited in Brennan, *supra*, at 156 n. 228).

In other states, pretermitted heir statutes differ as to: (1) the existence of protection for living versus after-born children (i.e., some statutes only cover children born after the will was executed but not those omitted children who were alive at the time the will was executed); (2) protection for children versus other relatives of the testator (i.e., some statutes cover grandchildren as well, although UPC §2-302 protects children only and not other relatives); and (3) the type of evidence admissible to prove intention to disinherit (i.e., some statutes provide that only evidence on the face of the will is admissible whereas other states admit extrinsic evidence).

Some statutes provide that the will is revoked by the subsequent birth of children. The majority of states, however, permit the pretermitted heir to take an intestate share and give effect to the will insofar as possible.

Florida law protects only those children who were born to or adopted by the decedent after execution of the decedent's will (Fla. Stat. §732.302). Such children can receive an intestate share. An omitted child will not receive such a share of the estate if the child: (1) already received an equivalent share by way of an advancement, (2) if the will evidences an intent to exclude the child, or (3) if the testator had a different estate plan to bequeath substantially all of the estate to the other parent of the pretermitted child in a situation when the couple had one or more children.

Florida rules that govern the manner of satisfying the omitted child's share of the estate (Fla. Stat. §733.805) are analogous to those applying to satisfy the pretermitted spouse's share. On the rules of abatement, see Chapter XV, Section IIC, *infra*.

On disinheritance, see generally Susanna Blumenthal, The Deviance of the Will, Policing the Bounds of Testamentary Freedom in Nineteenth-Century America, 119 Harv. L. Rev. 959 (2006); Richard Lewis Brown, Undeserving Heirs? The Case of the "Terminated" Parent, 40 U. Rich. L. Rev. 547 (2006).

§732.302. Pretermitted child: eligibility and share

When a testator omits to provide by will for any of his or her children born or adopted after making the will and the child has not received a part of the testator's property equivalent to a child's part by way of advancement, the child shall receive a share of the estate equal in value to that which the child would have received if the testator had died intestate, unless:

(1) It appears from the will that the omission was intentional; or

(2) The testator had one or more children when the will was executed and devised substantially all the estate to the other parent of the pretermitted child and that other parent survived the testator and is entitled to take under the will.

The share of the estate that is assigned to the pretermitted child shall be obtained in accordance with §733.805.

(Laws 1974, ch. 74-106, §1; Laws 1975, ch. 75-220, §16. Amended by Laws 1997, ch. 97-102, §958, effective July 1, 1997; Laws 2001, ch. 2001-226, §36, effective January 1, 2002.)

§733.805. Order of abatement

(1) Funds or property designated by the will shall be used to pay debts, family allowance, exempt property, elective share charges, expenses of administration, and devises, to the extent the funds or property is sufficient. If no provision is made or the designated fund or property is insufficient, the funds and property of the estate shall be used for these purposes, and to raise the shares of a pretermitted spouse and children, except as otherwise provided in subsections (3) and (4), in the following order:

(a) Property passing by intestacy.

(b) Property devised to the residuary devisee or devisees.

(c) Property not specifically or demonstratively devised.

(d) Property specifically or demonstratively devised.

(2) Demonstrative devises shall be classed as general devises upon the failure or insufficiency of funds or property out of which payment should be made, to the extent of the insufficiency. Devises to the decedent's surviving spouse, given in satisfaction of, or instead of, the surviving spouse's statutory rights in the estate, shall not abate until other devises of the same class are exhausted. Devises given for a valuable consideration shall abate with other devises of the same class only to the extent of the excess over the amount of value of the consideration until all others of the same class are exhausted. Except as herein provided, devises shall abate equally and ratably and without preference or priority as between real and personal property. When property that has been specifically devised or charged with a devise is sold or used by the personal representative, other devisees shall contribute according to their respective interests to the devisee whose devise has been sold or used. The amounts of the respective contributions shall be determined by the court and shall be paid or withheld before distribution is made.

(3) Section 733.817 shall be applied before this section is applied.

(4) In determining the contribution required under §733.607(2), subsections (1)-(3) of this section and §736.05053(2) shall be applied as if the beneficiaries of the estate and the beneficiaries of a trust described in §733.707(3), other than the estate or trust itself, were taking under a common instrument.

(Laws 1974, ch. 74-106, §1; Laws 1975, ch. 75-220, §88; Laws 1977, ch. 77-174, §1. Amended by Laws 1997, ch. 97-102, §1020, effective July 1, 1997; Laws 2001, ch. 2001-226, §156, effective January 1, 2002; Laws 2006, ch. 2006-217, §38, effective July 1, 2007.)

C. Mortmain Statutes

Historically, some jurisdictions restricted the decedent's dispositions to charity. Such restrictions were called "mortmain" statutes. These statutes date to the thirteenth century in England. John R. Cunningham, Mortmain Statutes: The Dead Hand Still Survives, 27 Idaho L. Rev. 49 (1990/1991).

Mortmain (meaning "dead hand") statutes refers to the perpetual ownership of land by charitable organizations. "In thirteenth century England, the Crown was deeply concerned about the ownership of land by ecclesiastical and lay corporations." *Id.* Among the problems such ownership posed were: "(1) the loss of feudal incidents to the crown and lords because of the transfer of land from one generation to another, (2) the consequential restraint on the free alienability of land, and (3) the inability of religious organizations and persons to perform certain feudal burdens attaching to land ownership." *Id.* at 49-50.

In response, Parliament enacted forfeiture and mortmain statutes which provided that real property held by religious organizations had to be forfeited to the overlord and, if he refused, to the Crown. David Villar Patton, The

Queen, the Attorney General, and the Modern Charitable Fiduciary: A Historical Perspective on Charitable Enforcement Reform, 11 U. Fla. J.L. & Pub. Pol'y 131, 134 (2000).

The first comprehensive mortmain statute (the Statute of Mortmain) was enacted by Parliament in 1279. Shirley Norwood Jones, The Demise of Mortmain in the United States, 12 Miss. C. L. Rev. 407, 408 (1992). "Perhaps there was justification for the early English Mortmain statutes since at one time in England the church and other religious societies possessed nearly half of the real property in England." ***Id.***

Religious charities found a loophole by the conveyance of land to individuals for the use of a religious order. "By the 1390s, however, the mortmain statutes were expanded to include conveyances to individuals, and the loophole was closed." Patton, ***supra,*** **at 134. Parliament enacted subsequent legislation in the eighteenth century (9 Geo. 2, c. 36 (1736)), providing that all gifts of land to charity had to be made by a deed, sealed and delivered at least 12 months before the donor's death. McGovern & Kurtz,** ***supra,*** **§3.10 at 176.**

Although the English Mortmain Statute was not widely adopted in this country, many American jurisdictions enacted similar restrictions. Statutes were of two types. Some jurisdictions provided that charitable testamentary gifts were invalid unless the will was executed a specified ***time before death.*** **The policy underlying this type of statute was "to prevent the testator from being unduly influenced while under fear of impending death." Atkinson,** ***supra,*** **§35 at 136. Other jurisdictions enacted limitations on the** ***proportion of the estate*** **which might be devoted to charitable purposes.** ***Id.*** **at 135. Some state statutes incorporated both provisions. Statutes generally required that the testator had to be survived by certain close relatives who were the sole persons eligible to object.**

The Florida legislature enacted its mortmain statute (Fla. Stat. §731.19, now repealed) in 1933. Following enactment of the UPC, the Florida legislature enacted another version of the statute (Fla. Stat. §732.803, also repealed). The latter statute permitted the testator's spouse or lineal descendants to seek to invalidate a will that devised all or part of the testator's estate to charitable institutions unless the will was executed more than six months before the testator's death or the testator's prior will had the same charitable devise ("in substantially the same amount for the same purpose").

As of 1970, 11 states had a mortmain statute. Restatement (Third) of Property, v. 2, §9.6, Reporter's Note cmt. 3. By 1990, only Florida, Georgia, Idaho and Mississippi had mortmain-type statutes still in effect. Shriners Hospitals for Crippled Children v. Zrillic, 563 So.2d 64, 69 n. 5 (Fla. 1990).

Today, all mortmain statutes have been repealed by statute or declared unconstitutional (on equal protection and/or due process grounds). Restatement (Third) of Property, v. 2, §9.6 cmt. c. See, e.g., Estate of French v. Doyle, 365 A.2d 621 (D.C. App. 1976) (declaring statute unconstitutional on due process and equal protection grounds); Estate of Kinyon, 615 P.2d 174 (Mont. 1980); Shriner's Hosp. for Crippled Children v. Hester, 492 N.E.2d 153 (Ohio 1986) (declaring statute unconstitutional on equal protection grounds of the state and federal constitutions); Estate of Cavill, 329 A.2d 503 (Pa. 1974) (declaring statute unconstitutional on substantive due process grounds).

The Florida statute was declared unconstitutional in ***Shriner's Hospital, supra.*** **When a daughter (who had been disinherited) brought an action to set aside, under the Mortmain Statute, her mother's charitable bequest, the Florida supreme court held that the statute was unconstitutional based on equal protection grounds of the state and federal constitutions and an unconstitutional restraint on a testator's right to devise property under the state constitution (Art. 1, § 2). The Florida legislature repealed the statute in 1991. The Idaho statute, codified at Idaho Code §15-2-615(a), was finally repealed in 1994 (S.L. 1994, ch. 359, §1). See generally Elizabeth Barker Brandt, Estate of Kirk: Mortmain, Perpetuities, Extrinsic Evidence, Aaargh!, 39 Advocate (Idaho) 21 (July 1996).**

§732.803. Mortmain statute: restrictions on charitable devises (repealed)

(1) If a testator dies leaving lineal descendants or a spouse and his will devises part or all of the testator's estate:

(a) To a benevolent, charitable, educational, literary, scientific, religious, or missionary institution, corporation, association, or purpose,

(b) To this state, any other state or country, or a county, city, or town

in this or any other state or country, or

(c) To a person in trust for any such purpose or beneficiary, whether or not the trust appears on the face of the instrument making the devise, the devise shall be avoided in its entirety if one or more of the lineal descendants or a spouse who would receive any interest in the devise, if avoided, files written notice to this effect in the administration proceeding within 4 months after the date letters are issued, unless:

(d) The will was duly executed at least 6 months before the testator's death, or

(e) The testator made a valid charitable devise in substantially the same amount for the same purpose or to the same beneficiary, or to a person in trust for the same purpose or beneficiary, as was made in the last will or by a will or a series of wills duly executed immediately next to the last will, one of which was executed more than 6 months before the testator's death.

(2) The testator's making of a codicil that does not substantially change a charitable devise as herein defined within the 6-month period before the testator's death shall not render the charitable gift voidable under this section.

D. Negative Beneficiaries

A testator may desire to disinherit a particular person (so-called "negative beneficiary"). According to the common law rule, such a disinheritance provision is ineffective unless the testator makes an affirmative disposition of the entire estate. Thus, if a negative beneficiary becomes the testator's heir and some property passes intestate (because the testator has not named beneficiaries for all his or her property), the negative beneficiary will take an intestate share of that property. Frederic S. Schwartz, Models of the Will and Negative Disinheritance, 48 Mercer L. Rev. 1137, 1137-1138 (1997).

The Restatement (Third) of Property (§2.7) provides that a will may "expressly exclude or limit the right of an individual or class to succeed to property" passing by intestate succession. This provision thereby reverses the common law rule. The Restatement also addresses the effect of a negative will provision on the distribution of the intestate property. That is, if the testator expressly excludes or limits the right of an individual or class to take by intestate succession, any share of the decedent's intestate estate that would have passed to the disinherited person or class, passes as if the person or class made a disclaimer. Thus, for example, if the decedent provided that his only brother would take "$50 and no more," the brother is entitled to the $50. However, any share of the decedent's intestate share that would have passed to the brother instead passes to the brother's descendants by representation. *Id.* at §2.7, cmt. c. The revised UPC (§2-101) also authorizes negative wills.

Most American courts hold that the heir who is expressly disinherited may still be entitled to his intestate share if some or all of the testator's estate passes by intestacy. J. Andrew Heaton, Comment, The Intestate Claims of Heirs Excluded by Will: Should "Negative Wills" Be Enforced?, 52 U. Chi. L. Rev. 177, 177-178 (1985) (citing authorities including In re Estate of Levy, 196 So. 2d 255 (Fla. Dist. Ct. App. 1967) (holding that legacies passed to testator's son even though testator stated he was making no provision for his issue where will had no residuary clause and some property passed by way of intestacy). See also In re Estate of Scott, 659 So.2d 361 (Fla. Dist. Ct. App. 1995) (holding that statement in will that intentionally excluded her sister's children did not preclude them from taking under the antilapse statute when the sister predeceased the testator).

On negative wills, see also Paula A. Monopoli, 49 U. Miami L. Rev. 257 (1994) (advocating a behavior-based model to exclude inheritance by fathers who abandon or fail to support their children).

III
WILL EXECUTION

All states require that the testator comply with certain formalities in order for a will to be valid. This chapter explores these formal requirements. First, the chapter addresses the historical background and policies underlying the formalities. Second, it explores testamentary capacity and testamentary intent. Third, it examines requirements regarding a writing and the testator's signature. Fourth, it focuses on the rules regarding attestation by witnesses. Finally, it explores various types of wills (including holographic wills, oral wills, conditional wills, statutory wills, foreign and international wills, and the self-proved will).

I. INTRODUCTION

A. Terminology

A will disposes of property owned at death. A will may be one of the following types:

- **formally executed (also called "attested" or "witnessed");**
- **handwritten ("holographic"); or**
- **oral ("nuncupative").**

To be valid, a will must comply with certain statutory formalities (discussed *infra*). It is not essential that a document be called a "will" in order for it to serve as a will.

A *codicil* is a document that amends a will. In some cases, a codicil may do nothing more than revoke a prior will. A valid codicil must be executed with the requisite statutory formalities. If a codicil complies with the statutory requirements, it may be probated as a will (for example, if the will to which it is attached is not effective). It is not required that a codicil must call itself a "codicil" (or a "will") in order to serve as a testamentary instrument.

According to Florida law, the term "will" may include a codicil (Fla. Stat. §731.201 (37)). In addition, the term "will" may include a testamentary instrument which does no more than: (1) appoint an executor, (2) revoke a will, or (3) change another will. *Id.* That is, a will or codicil need not be dispositive.

The UPC recognizes several different wills: (1) the witnessed will (UPC §2-502(a)), (2) the holographic will (UPC §2-502(b)), (3) the foreign will (UPC §2-506), (4) the international will (UPC Art. II, Pt. 10, Uniform International Wills Act), and (5) the self-proved will (UPC §2-504).

Florida recognizes the following types of wills: (1) written *and* attested wills (Fla. Stat. §732.502), (2) military testamentary instruments (Fla. Stat. §732.502(3)) and (3) self-proved wills (Fla. Stat. §732.503) (discussed in Section II *infra*).

The term "personal representative" generally signifies an executor (the person who administers a testate estate) or an administrator (the person who administers an intestate estate). The term "fiduciary" includes both a personal representative and a trustee.

§731.201. Definitions: "beneficiary," "will," etc.

Subject to additional definitions in subsequent chapters that are applicable to specific chapters or parts, and unless the context otherwise requires, in this code, in §409.9101, and in chapters 736, 738, 739, and 744, the term:

. . .

(2) "Beneficiary" means heir at law in an intestate estate and devisee in a testate estate. The term "beneficiary" does not apply to an heir at law or a devisee after that person's interest in the estate has been satisfied. In the case of a devise to an existing trust or trustee, or to a trust or trustee described by will, the trustee is a beneficiary of the estate. Except as otherwise provided in this subsection, the beneficiary of the trust is not a beneficiary of the estate of which that trust or the trustee of that trust is a beneficiary. However, if each trustee is also a personal representative of the estate, each qualified beneficiary of the trust as defined in §736.0103(14) shall be regarded as a beneficiary of the estate.

(3) "Child" includes a person entitled to take as a child under this code by intestate succession from the parent whose relationship is involved, and excludes any person who is only a stepchild, a foster child, a grandchild, or a more remote descendant.

. . . .

(6) "Court" means the circuit court.

(7) "Curator" means a person appointed by the court to take charge of the estate of a decedent until letters are issued.

(8) "Devise," when used as a noun, means a testamentary disposition of real or personal property and, when used as a verb, means to dispose of real or personal property by will or trust. The term includes "gift," "give," "bequeath," "bequest," and "legacy." A devise is subject to charges for debts, expenses, and taxes as provided in this code, the will, or the trust.

(9) "Devisee" means a person designated in a will or trust to receive a devise. Except as otherwise provided in this subsection, in the case of a devise to

an existing trust or trustee, or to a trust or trustee of a trust described by will, the trust or trustee, rather than the beneficiaries of the trust, is the devisee. However, if each trustee is also a personal representative of the estate, each qualified beneficiary of the trust as defined in §736.0103(14) shall be regarded as a devisee.

(10) "Distributee" means a person who has received estate property from a personal representative or other fiduciary other than as a creditor or purchaser. A testamentary trustee is a distributee only to the extent of distributed assets or increments to them remaining in the trustee's hands. A beneficiary of a testamentary trust to whom the trustee has distributed property received from a personal representative is a distributee. For purposes of this provision, "testamentary trustee" includes a trustee to whom assets are transferred by will, to the extent of the devised assets.

....

(18) "Heirs" or "heirs at law" means those persons, including the surviving spouse, who are entitled under the statutes of intestate succession to the property of a decedent.

....

(21) "Interested person" means any person who may reasonably be expected to be affected by the outcome of the particular proceeding involved. In any proceeding affecting the estate or the rights of a beneficiary in the estate, the personal representative of the estate shall be deemed to be an interested person. In any proceeding affecting the expenses of the administration and obligations of a decedent's estate, or any claims described in § 733.702(1), the trustee of a trust described in § 733.707(3) is an interested person in the administration of the grantor's estate. The term does not include a beneficiary who has received complete distribution. The meaning, as it relates to particular persons, may vary from time to time and must be determined according to the particular purpose of, and matter involved in, any proceedings.

....

(24) "Parent" excludes any person who is only a stepparent, foster parent, or grandparent.

....

(28) "Probate of will" means all steps necessary to establish the validity of a will and to admit a will to probate.

....

(32) "Residuary devise" means a devise of the assets of the estate which remain after the provision for any devise which is to be satisfied by reference to a specific property or type of property, fund, sum, or statutory amount. If the will contains no devise which is to be satisfied by reference to a specific property or type of property, fund, sum, or statutory amount, "residuary devise" or "residue" means a devise of all assets remaining after satisfying the obligations of the estate.

....

(37) "Will" means an instrument, including a codicil, executed by a person in the manner prescribed by this code, which disposes of the person's property on or after his or her death and includes an instrument which merely appoints a personal representative or revokes or revises another will.

(Laws 1974, ch. 74-106, §1; Laws 1975, ch. 75-220, §4; Laws 1977, ch. 77-174, §1; Laws 1985, ch. 85-79, §2; Laws 1987, ch. 87-226, §66; Laws 1988, ch. 88-340, §1; Laws 1993, ch. 93-257, §7. Amended by Laws 1995, ch. 95- 401, §6, effective July 1, 1995; Laws 1997, ch. 97-102, §949, effective July 1, 1997; Laws 1998, ch. 98-421, § 52, effective July 1, 1998; Laws 2001, ch. 2001-226, §11, effective January 1, 2002; Laws 2002, ch. 2002-1, §106, effective May 21, 2002; Laws 2003, ch. 2003-154, §2, effective June 12, 2003; Laws 2005, ch. 2005-108, §2, effective July 1, 2005; Laws 2006, ch. 2006-217, §29, effective July 1, 2007.)

B. Historical Background

English common law reflected a different evolution for the distribution of personal property and the descent of real property. In the Middle Ages, ecclesiastical courts permitted distribution of personalty via oral wills called "testaments" (generally dictated to clerics) to a decedent's spouse, child, or another person of the decedent's choice. On the other hand, "primogeniture" governed inheritance of real property, i.e., land passed automatically to the eldest son. Individuals could not devise real property until the Statute of Wills of 1540. The Statute of Wills permitted wills of real property, provided that such instruments were in writing (although equity enforced oral devises of uses before that time). McGovern & Kurtz, *supra*, §4.1 at 182.

The subsequent Statute of Frauds of 1677 specified various formalities for the execution of wills (such as the requirement that devises of land be signed by the testator and subscribed by witnesses) and also limited the use of oral wills. The Statute of Wills ("Wills Act") of 1837 permitted persons to dispose of both real and personal property owned at death provided that certain formalities of execution were met. For the first time, the requirements for disposition of real and personal property were

the same. The Wills Act established a minimum age requirement for testamentary capacity, and also specified rules for amendments and revocation of wills.

Currently, all states have legislation on will execution that has been derived from the English Statute of Frauds of 1677 and the Wills Act of 1837. Christopher J. Caldwell, Comment, Should "E-Wills" Be Wills: Will Advances in Technology Be Recognized for Will Execution?, 63 U. Pitt. L. Rev. 467, 467 (2002).

II. Formalities of Will Execution

Every jurisdiction has a Wills Act that requires certain formalities for executing a valid will. All statutes mandate a writing, signature, and attestation by witnesses. Most jurisdictions require strict compliance with these statutory requirements. Such rigid adherence to formalism sometimes has led to harsh results and a defeat of testators' intent.

In an influential law review article in 1975, Professor John Langbein proposed liberalization of the formal requirements for will execution by means of a doctrine of "substantial compliance." John H. Langbein, Substantial Compliance with the Wills Act, 88 Harv. L. Rev. 489, 489 (1975). He advocated liberal judicial interpretation of jurisdictions' Wills Acts: fatally defective wills should still be admitted to probate if the will proponents could prove that the functions of the will formalities were satisfied.

Subsequently, Langbein modified his proposal, influenced by a statute enacted in South Australia. John H. Langbein, Excusing Harmless Errors in the Execution of Wills: A Report on Australia's Tranquil Revolution in Probate Law, 87 Colum. L. Rev. 1, 9 n. 31 (1987) (citing Wills Act Amendment Act (No. 2 of 1975), §9 amending Wills Act of 1936, §12(2), (8 S. Austral. Stat. 665)). That statute authorized probate courts to employ a "dispensing power" that excuses harmless errors. Probate courts could disregard the formal statutory requirements if the courts were satisfied beyond a reasonable doubt that "the document embodies the unequivocal intent of the testator." Langbein, *supra,* at 34.

Langbein termed the South Australian statute "a triumph of law reform." *Id.* at 1. He evaluated the operation of the Australian legislation by reviewing a decade of case law (41 cases) involving attestation problems (i.e., testators who had not signed in the presence of witnesses present at the same time), or signature problems (i.e., testators who either had not signed wills or not signed at the end of the will), or defective alteration cases. He concluded that courts were applying the doctrine effectively and that the new legislation had not undermined the Wills Act. He recommended that the United States enact similar legislation but with two improvements: (1) the reform should extend to revocation formalities, and (2) the standard of proof should be lowered to clear and convincing evidence. *Id.* at 53.

Langbein's influence was reflected in subsequent revisions to the Uniform Probate Code and also in the Restatement (Third) of Property (Wills and Other Donative Transfers). The 1990 revisions to Article II of the Uniform Probate Code (UPC §2-503) permitted courts to dispense with some statutory formalities (although which formalities are not specified) provided that the will proponents establish by clear and convincing evidence that the testator intended the instrument to constitute his or her will:

> Although a document or writing added upon a document was not executed in compliance with Section 2-502, the document or writing is treated as if it had been executed in compliance with that section if the proponent of the document or writing establishes by clear and convincing evidence that the decedent intended the document or writing to constitute (i) the decedent's will, (ii) a partial or complete revocation of the will, (iii) an addition to or an alteration of the will, or (iv) a partial or complete revival of his [or her] formerly revoked will or of a formerly revoked portion of the will.

UPC §2-503. The UPC thereby permitted liberal admission of extrinsic evidence to prove testamentary intent. Florida has no provision similar to UPC §2-503. For further discussion of the "harmless error rule," see Sean P. Milligan, Comment, The Effect of a Harmless Error in Executing a Will: Why Texas Should Adopt Section 2-503 of the Uniform Probate Code, 36 St. Mary's L.J. 787 (2005).

The Restatement (Third) of Property (Wills and Other Donative Transfers) §3.3 (1999), reflects a similar liberalizing trend by providing for a "harmless error" rule: "A harmless error in executing a will may be excused if the proponent establishes by clear and convincing evidence that the decedent adopted the document as his or her will."

Note that the 1990 revisions to the UPC reflected liberalization of other technical requirements for will execution. Specifically, the revisions included: codification of the conscious presence requirement, the change for holographs from "material provisions" to "material portions," and the allowance of a signature by the witnesses within a reasonable time after witnessing the testator's signing or acknowledgment. (These revisions are discussed *infra*.)

Florida law dates from the nineteenth century. Spain ceded Florida to the United States in 1821. Later that year, Andrew Jackson established a new territorial government. Florida became the 27th state in 1845. Beginning in 1823 until 1933, the Florida legislature adopted a number of statutes addressing wills and the administration of estates. The Probate Act of 1933 revised all former statutes pertaining to wills and the administration of estates. In the early 1970s, a probate reform movement followed promulgation of the Uniform Probate Code. The Florida legislature created the Florida Uniform Probate Code Study Commission to consider adoption of the Uniform Probate Code. However, rather than adopt the entire UPC, the Florida legislature decided to incorporate parts of the UPC into the Florida Probate Act of 1933. The current Florida Probate Code became effective in 1976. In 2001, the legislature undertook another revision of the Probate Code.

In addition to statutory and decisional law, Florida has rules that regulate probate practice. The Florida state constitution gives the state supreme court the right to adopt rules for practice and procedure in all courts. Probate rules became effective January 1, 1968 and have been amended several times since then. Trawick, *supra*, at §1-2.

The Florida Probate Code requires the following formalities for a valid will:

- the will must be in writing;
- the will must be signed at the end by the testator or by a proxy who signs the testator's name in the testator's presence and by the testator's direction;
- the testator must either sign or acknowledge his or her signature (or that a proxy has signed for him or her) in the presence of two witnesses; and
- the witnesses must sign the will in the presence of the testator and in the presence of each other.

Florida recognizes formally executed wills (i.e. written and attested documents) and also military testamentary instruments. The latter must comply with 10 U.S.C. §1044d. Federal legislation authorizes military testamentary instruments. Congress created a new will, the military testamentary instrument, by the enactment of the National Defense Authorization Act for 2001, Floyd D. Spence National Defense Authorization Act for Fiscal Year 2001, §551, Pub. L. No. 106-398, 114 Stat. 1654, 1654A-123 to -125 (2000) (codified as amended at 10 U.S.C. §1044d). The statute enables a military attorney to provide testamentary instruments that are valid in every U.S. jurisdiction.

To be valid in Florida, the military testamentary instrument must be executed: (1) by a person who is eligible for military legal assistance, (2) in the presence of military legal assistance counsel, and (3) in the presence of two disinterested witnesses (Fla. Stat. §732.502(3); 10 U.S.C. §1044d)).

A. Function of the Formalities

Several purposes explain the formalities for will execution. In a classic article, two commentators identified three functions of will formalities:

- a ritual or cautionary function (which reinforces the instrument as a will to the decedent as a deliberate and final decision);
- an evidentiary function (which provides the court with reliable evidence of testamentary intent); and
- a protective function (which safeguards the testator from improper acts of coercion, fraud, or undue influence).

Ashbel G. Gulliver & Catherine J. Tilson, Classification of Gratuitous Transfers, 51 Yale L.J. 1, 3-6 (1941). Subsequently, Professor John Langbein identified a fourth function:

- the channeling function (which identifies the instrument as a will in the larger community).

Langbein, Substantial Compliance, *supra*, at 491-498 (discussing the channeling function). The channeling function of law originated with Lon Fuller who suggested that the formalities of contract law provide "channels for the legally effective expression of intention." Lon L. Fuller, Consideration and Form, 41 Colum. L. Rev. 799, 801 (1941).

B. Testamentary Capacity

The Statute of Wills of 1540 permitted devises of real property by minors. However, Parliament soon amended the Statute to require that the testator of a devise of real property must be 21 years of age. Thomas Atkinson, Wills §50, at 230 (2d ed. 1953). Regarding testamentary capacity for the disposition of personal property, the civil law rule was that a boy had to be at least 14 years old and a girl at least 12 years old. *Id.* at 229. That rule was adopted by the ecclesiastical courts. *Id.* However, the Wills Act of 1837 established age 21 as the minimum age for both male and female testators and for dispositions of both real and personal property. *Id.* at 230.

Statutes in all jurisdictions now establish capacity to make a will. Most jurisdictions require that a testator be an adult and mentally competent. The majority of jurisdictions require that a testator be at least 18 years of age. Age 18 is also the minimum specified by UPC §2-501.

Some jurisdictions establish age 18 as the minimum, but permit exceptions. Thus, for example, in some states persons in military service or married persons may make wills, regardless of age. Florida law provides an exception for emancipated minors (Fla. Stat. §732.501). On emancipation, see Chapter IV *infra*.

American statutes include mental capacity by requiring that the testator be "of sound mind." That term is generally not defined. See, e.g., Fla. Stat. §732.501 (requiring that the testator be at least 18 years of age and "of sound mind"). The Florida requirements regarding age and "sound mind" are identical to those of UPC §2-501, except for a provision added by statutory amendment in Florida in 2001 (Laws 2001, ch. 2001-226, §41, effective January 1, 2002) permitting emancipated minors to execute a will.

Testamentary capacity (issues of mental capacity, undue influence, fraud, etc.) is explored further in Chapter IV *infra*.

§732.501. Who may make a will

Any person who is of sound mind and who is either 18 or more years of age or an emancipated minor may make a will.

(Laws 1974, ch. 74-106, §1; Laws 1975, ch. 75-220, §20. Amended by Laws 2001, ch. 2001-226, §41, effective January 1, 2002.)

C. Testamentary Intent

A testator must have the requisite intent to execute a valid will. Testamentary intent must be present at the time the testator signed the testamentary instrument. "Testamentary intent" refers to the testator's general intent that a *particular* document serve as a disposition of his or her property to be effective on death. See generally Emily Sherwin, Clear and Convincing Evidence of Testamentary Intent: The Search for a Compromise Between Formality and Adjudicative Justice, 34 Conn. L. Rev. 453 (2002).

D. Writing Requirement

All states require that a will be in writing. Florida law requires that a will must be in writing as well as signed and attested (Fla. Stat. §732.502). Florida does not recognize holographic wills or oral wills.

Currently, no state allows probate of a videotaped will. See Estate of Reed, 672 P.2d 829 (Wyo.1983) (holding that a tape-recorded will was not "in writing"). Some commentators, however, advocate videotaping the will execution ceremony to provide evidence of testamentary capacity and due execution for the probate process. Caldwell, *supra*, at 475. In 1985, Indiana became the first state to authorize by statute the admission of a videotaped will execution ceremony to show that the statutory requirements for execution were satisfied. John A. Warnick, The Ungrateful Living: An Estate Planner's Nightmare—The Trial Attorney's Dream, 24 Land & Water L. Rev. 401, 423 n. 114 (1989) (citing Ind. Code Ann. §29-1-5-3(d)). However, the section was repealed in 1989 by P.L. 262-1989, Sec. 1.

The issue of whether e-mail messages or a web site could qualify as a valid will has not yet arisen in case law. Warnick, *supra*, at 476. For further discussion, see "Electronic Signatures," Section E3 *infra*.

See generally Gerry W. Beyer, Video Requiem: Thy Will Be Done, Tr. & Est., July 1985, at 24; Gerry W. Beyer & William R. Buckley, Videotape and the Probate Process: The Nexus Grows, 42 Okla. L. Rev. 43 (1989); Lisa L. McGarry, Note, Videotaped Wills: An Evidentiary Tool or a Written Will Substitute?, 77 Iowa L. Rev. 1187, 1187 (1992); Terry Zickefoose, Videotaped Wills: Ready for Prime Time, 9 Prob. L.J. 139 (1989).

§732.502. Requirements for execution of wills

Every will must be in writing and executed as follows:

(1)(a) *Testator's signature.*--

1. The testator must sign the will at the end; or

2. The testator's name must be subscribed at the end of the will by some other person in the testator's presence and by the testator's direction.

(b) *Witnesses.*--The testator's:

1. Signing, or
2. Acknowledgment:
a. That he or she has previously signed the will, or
b. That another person has subscribed the testator's name to it,

must be in the presence of at least two attesting witnesses.
(c) *Witnesses' signatures.*--The attesting witnesses must sign the will in the presence of the testator and in the presence of each other.
(2) Any will, other than a holographic or nuncupative will, executed by a nonresident of Florida, either before or after this law takes effect, is valid as a will in this state if valid under the laws of the state or country where the will was executed. A will in the testator's handwriting that has been executed in accordance with subsection (1) shall not be considered a holographic will.
(3) Any will executed as a military testamentary instrument in accordance with 10 U.S.C. § 1044d, Chapter 53, by a person who is eligible for military legal assistance is valid as a will in this state.
(4) No particular form of words is necessary to the validity of a will if it is executed with the formalities required by law.
(5) A codicil shall be executed with the same formalities as a will.
(Laws 1974, ch. 74-106, §1; Laws 1975, ch. 75-220, §21; Laws 1977, ch. 77-87, §11. Amended by Laws 1997, ch. 97-102, §961, effective July 1, 1997; Laws 2001, ch. 2001-226, §42, effective January 1, 2002; Laws 2003, ch. 2003-154, §5, effective June 12, 2003.)

§733.204. Will in foreign language may be probated

(1) No will written in a foreign language shall be admitted to probate unless it is accompanied by a true and complete English translation.
(2) No personal representative who complies in good faith with the English translation of the will as established by the court shall be liable for doing so.
(Laws 1974, ch. 74-106, §1; Laws 1975, ch. 75-220, § 54; Laws 1977, ch. 77-174, §1. Amended by Laws 2001, ch. 2001-226, §88, effective January 1, 2002.)

Rule 5.216. Will in foreign language: procedure for admission to probate

A will written in a foreign language being offered for probate shall be accompanied by a true and complete English translation. In the order admitting the foreign language will to probate, the court shall establish the correct English translation. At any time during administration, any interested person may have the correctness of the translation redetermined after formal notice to all other interested persons.
(Added May 2, 2002 (824 So.2d 849).)

UNITED STATES CODE
§1044d. Military testamentary instruments: requirements for recognition

(a) Testamentary instruments to be given legal effect.--A military testamentary instrument--
(1) is exempt from any requirement of form, formality, or recording before probate that is provided for testamentary instruments under the laws of a State; and
(2) has the same legal effect as a testamentary instrument prepared and executed in accordance with the laws of the State in which it is presented for probate.
(b) Military testamentary instruments.--For purposes of this section, a military testamentary instrument is an instrument that is prepared with testamentary intent in accordance with regulations prescribed under this section and that--
(1) is executed in accordance with subsection (c) by (or on behalf of) a person, as a testator, who is eligible for military legal assistance;
(2) makes a disposition of property of the testator; and
(3) takes effect upon the death of the testator.
(c) Requirements for execution of military testamentary instruments.--An instrument is valid as a military testamentary instrument only if-
(1) the instrument is executed by the testator (or, if the testator is unable to execute the instrument personally, the instrument is executed in the presence of, by the direction of, and on behalf of the testator);
(2) the instrument is executed in the presence of a military legal assistance counsel acting as presiding attorney;
(3) the instrument is executed in the presence of at least two disinterested witnesses (in addition to the presiding attorney), each of whom attests to witnessing the testator's execution of the instrument by signing it; and
(4) the instrument is executed in accordance with such additional requirements as may be provided in regulations prescribed under this section.
(d) Self-proving military testamentary instruments.—

(1) If the document setting forth a military testamentary instrument meets the requirements of paragraph (2), then the signature of a person on the document as the testator, an attesting witness, a notary, or the presiding attorney, together with a written representation of the person's status as such and the person's military grade (if any) or other title, is prima facie evidence of the following:

(A) That the signature is genuine.

(B) That the signatory had the represented status and title at the time of the execution of the will.

(C) That the signature was executed in compliance with the procedures required under the regulations prescribed under subsection (f).

(2) A document setting forth a military testamentary instrument meets the requirements of this paragraph if it includes (or has attached to it), in a form and content required under the regulations prescribed under subsection (f), each of the following:

(A) A certificate, executed by the testator, that includes the testator's acknowledgment of the testamentary instrument.

(B) An affidavit, executed by each witness signing the testamentary instrument, that attests to the circumstances under which the testamentary instrument was executed.

(C) A notarization, including a certificate of any administration of an oath required under the regulations, that is signed by the notary or other official administering the oath.

(e) Statement to be included.—

(1) Under regulations prescribed under this section, each military testamentary instrument shall contain a statement that sets forth the provisions of subsection (a).

(2) Paragraph (1) shall not be construed to make inapplicable the provisions of subsection (a) to a testamentary instrument that does not include a statement described in that paragraph.

(f) Regulations.--Regulations for the purposes of this section shall be prescribed jointly by the Secretary of Defense and by the Secretary of Homeland Security with respect to the Coast Guard when it is not operating as a service in the Department of the Navy.

(g) Definitions.--In this section:

(1) The term "person eligible for military legal assistance" means a person who is eligible for legal assistance under section 1044 of this title.

(2) The term "military legal assistance counsel" means--

(A) a judge advocate (as defined in section 801(13) of this title); or

(B) a civilian attorney serving as a legal assistance officer under the provisions of section 1044 of this title.

(3) The term "State" includes the District of Columbia, the Commonwealth of Puerto Rico, the Commonwealth of the Northern Mariana Islands, and each possession of the United States.

(Pub.L. 106-398, §1 [Div. A, Title V, §551(a)], Oct. 30, 2000, 114 Stat. 1654, 1654A-123, and amended Pub.L. 107-296, Title XVII, §1704(b)(1), Nov. 25, 2002, 116 Stat. 2314.)

E. Testator's Signature

A valid will requires the signature of the testator. The Statute of Frauds of 1677 required that a will disposing of real property be signed by the testator but did not require a particular place for that signature. Atkinson, *supra*, §64 at 301. A few years later, the case of Lemayne v. Stanley, 3 Lev.1, 83 Eng. Rep. 545 (1681), held that the testator's name could appear at the top, bottom, or margin of the will and upheld the validity of a will that provided, "I, John Stanley, make this my last will."

All state wills legislation and the UPC (§2-502(a)(1)) include the requirement of a testator's signature. Most American jurisdictions follow the rule of Lemayne v. Stanley in failing to specify the place for that signature. Atkinson, *supra*, §64 at 301.

In contrast to the Statute of Frauds' requirement that a will could be signed anywhere, the English Wills Act of 1837 required that the will must be *subscribed*, i.e., signed at the "end." In 1982, England eliminated the subscription requirement. Nonetheless, a minority of jurisdictions (including Florida) still retain this requirement. McGovern & Kurtz, *supra*, §4.2 at 187-188; Fla. Stat.§732.502(1)(a)(1).

Although a will must be signed by the testator, the testator need not write a full or correct name. If a testator cannot write his signature (whether for reasons of illiteracy or illness), the testator's mark will suffice if intended by the testator as a "complete act" to authenticate the instrument. McGovern & Kurtz, *supra*, §64 at 297.

Some states require that the testator sign in the witnesses' presence. Many states, however, require that the testator sign *or* acknowledge the testator's signature or the will in the witnesses' presence. Thus, the testator could simply acknowledge the testator's signature to the witnesses or could simply acknowledge that the instrument before the witnesses is indeed the testator's will. This

situation commonly arises if the testator previously signed the will. See also Acknowledgment vs. Publication, Section F4 *infra.*

§732.502. Execution of wills: requirements

Every will must be in writing and executed as follows:

(1)(a) *Testator's signature.*—

1. The testator must sign the will at the end; or

2. The testator's name must be subscribed at the end of the will by some other person in the testator's presence and by the testator's direction. ....

[The remainder of the statute is reprinted *supra* in Section C.]

1. Subscription Requirement

In jurisdictions with a subscription requirement, troublesome cases sometimes arise regarding whether a will was subscribed if material appeared after the testator's signature. This problem necessitates judicial exploration of the "end" requirement. Case law has formulated two tests: the logical end and the physical end. McGovern & Kurtz, *supra*, §4.2 at 174. See also Bradley v. Bradley, 371 So. 2d 168, 170 (Fla. Dist. Ct. App. 1999) (discussing different tests).

Florida has adopted a liberal interpretation of the "logical end" requirement. Thus, Florida law permits the probate of a will in which the testator signed a printed will form not on the designated line, which appeared at the logical end of testamentary language, but rather after the printed words "Will of" in the identification section. In Bain v. Hill, 639 So. 2d 178 (Fla. Dist. Ct. App. 1994), the Florida District Court of Appeals admitted the will to probate, reasoning that the testator signed *temporally* at the "end" of her preparation of the will. Note that Florida law does not require the *witnesses* to sign at the end of the will.

The UPC requires that the will be signed but does not require that the signature appear in any particular place. See UPC §2-502 (specifying merely that the will must be signed by the testator or by a proxy).

2. Proxy Signature

Some states permit the will to be signed either by the testator or by another person (a proxy). See, e.g., Fla. Stat. §732.502(1)(a)(2) (permitting a proxy to subscribe the testator's name at the end of the will provided that the subscription is done in the testator's presence and at his or her direction).

The Uniform Probate Code (§2-502) also allows a will to be signed by the testator or by another on the testator's behalf. The 1990 revisions to the UPC adopted the rule that the proxy who signs the will at the testator's request must sign in the conscious presence of the testator (UPC §2502(a)(2)). On the presence requirement, see Section E5 *infra*.

3. Electronic Signatures

In an effort to make the law responsive to technological developments by protecting electronic transactions, Congress enacted the Electronic Signatures in Global and National Commerce Act (or "E-Sign Act"), Pub. L. No. 106-229, 114 Stat. 464 (2000). The Act does not require acceptance of electronic signatures but rather provides that such signatures may not be denied legal effect because they are in electronic form (i.e., not paper-based). However, the Act excludes electronic signatures that are used in testamentary instruments such as wills or testamentary trusts. Chandel Gauthreaux Hall, A Cursory Look at the E-Sign Act, 48 La. B.J. 452 (2001).

Similarly, the Uniform Electronic Transactions Act (UETA), 7A U.L.A. 20 (Supp. 2000), promulgated by NCCUSL, in 1999 also excludes wills and trusts. That Uniform Act provides:

UNIFORM ELECTRONIC TRANSACTIONS ACT

Section 3. Scope

(a) Except as otherwise provided in subsection (b), this [Act] applies to electronic records and electronic signatures relating to a transaction.

(b) This [Act] does not apply to a transaction to the extent it is governed by:

(1) a law governing the creation and execution of wills, codicils, or testamentary trusts;

. . .

F. Witnesses

1. Generally

The Wills Acts of the various jurisdictions require that a will must be attested (i.e., witnessed) by several persons. The Statute of Frauds required "three or four credible" witnesses. McGovern & Kurtz, *supra*, §4.3 at 189.

The Wills Act of 1837 required only two. *Id.* Today, almost all states (including Florida) as well as the Uniform Probate Code require that a will be signed by two witnesses (Fla. Stat. §732.502(1)(b); UPC §2-505(a)).

Most states require that the witnesses be "competent" or capable of giving testimony in court. In other words, the witness must understand the significance of taking an oath. See, e.g., Fla. Stat. §732.504. See also Competence vs. Interest, Section IIF3 *infra*.

Only a few states have minimum age requirements for *witnesses*. McGovern & Kurtz, *supra*, §4.3 at 189.

Often, witnesses' signatures appear in an "attestation clause." Such a clause declares that the instrument is a will, specifies the number of pages, recites the statutory requirements for execution, and includes the date of execution. Although no state requires such a clause, many states hold that the presence of such a clause raises a *rebuttable presumption* that the will was duly executed. Restatement (Third) of Property, *supra*, at §3.1, cmt. q.

Some statutes and case law address the order of the testator's signature and witnesses' attestation. That is, some jurisdictions require that the testator sign *prior to* attestation by witnesses.

Most states, however, follow the "continuous" (sometimes "contemporaneous") transaction approach and consider the attestation valid provided that the testator signs and the witnesses attest as part of a continuous transaction. Thus, it would not matter if the witnesses signed before the testator provided that everyone signed during the same transaction. Florida follows this view. See Bain v. Hill, 639 So. 2d 178 (Fla. Dist. Ct. App. 1994) (holding that so long as the witnesses saw the testator sign the will, and they signed it in his presence and in the presence of each other, the order in which the attestation occurred made no difference).

The UPC requires that the attestation occurs within a reasonable time after (1) the witness observes the testator sign, (2) the testator acknowledges his or her signature, or (3) the testator acknowledges the will (UPC §2-502(a)(3)).

The procedure for admitting a will to probate generally requires the admission of evidence by witnesses. Florida requires the admission of the evidence of only one witness (Fla. Stat. §733.201(2)). Although Florida law requires two witnesses for execution of a valid will (Fla. Stat. §732.502(1)(b)), that requirement does not extend to proving the will (i.e., admitting the will to probate). The two-witness requirement for due execution exists to protect the testator from fraud or undue influence.

To begin the probate process in Florida, a petitioner must offer proof of a will, unless the will is self-proved (discussed *infra* Section L). The petitioner must file a declaration under oath of one of the two witnesses to the will. That oath must be sworn before a circuit court judge, clerk, or a commissioner who has been appointed for that purpose (Fla. Stat. §733.201(2)). Sometimes, none of the witnesses can be located. In such a case, the personal representative (or a person without a pecuniary interest in the estate) may prove the will by a declaration under oath affirming his or her belief that the document is the decedent's will (Fla. Stat. §733.201(3)).

Three different issues arise regarding "presence" during an attestation by witnesses: (1) must the testator sign in the witnesses' presence? (2) must the witnesses sign in the testator's presence? and (3) must the witnesses sign in the presence of each other? These issues are discussed *infra*.

§732.502. Execution of wills: requirements

Every will must be in writing and executed as follows:

(1)(a) Testator's signature.--

1. The testator must sign the will at the end; or

2. The testator's name must be subscribed at the end of the will by some other person in the testator's presence and by the testator's direction.

(b) *Witnesses*.--The testator's:

1. Signing, or

2. Acknowledgment:

a. That he or she has previously signed the will, or

b. That another person has subscribed the testator's name to it, must be in the presence of at least two attesting witnesses.

(c) *Witnesses' signatures*.--The attesting witnesses must sign the will in the presence of the testator and in the presence of each other.

. . . .

(Laws 1974, ch. 74-106, §1; Laws 1975, ch. 75-220, §21; Laws 1977, ch. 77-87, §11. Amended by Laws 1997, ch. 97-102, §961, effective July 1, 1997; Laws 2001, ch. 2001-226, §42, effective January 1, 2002; Laws 2003, ch. 2003-154, §5, effective June 12, 2003.)

[The remainder of the statute is reprinted *supra* Section IID.]

§733.201. Proof of wills: testimony of witnesses

(1) Self-proved wills executed in accordance with this code may be admitted to probate without further proof.

(2) A will may be admitted to probate upon the oath of any attesting witness taken before any circuit judge, commissioner appointed by the court, or clerk.

(3) If it appears to the court that the attesting witnesses cannot be found or that they have become incompetent after the execution of the will or their testimony cannot be obtained within a reasonable time, a will may be admitted to probate upon the oath of the personal representative nominated by the will as provided in subsection (2), whether or not the nominated personal representative is interested in the estate, or upon the oath of any person having no interest in the estate under the will stating that the person believes the writing exhibited to be the true last will of the decedent.

(Laws 1974, ch. 74-106, §1; Laws 1975, ch. 75-220, §51. Amended by Laws 1997, ch. 97-102, §985, effective July 1, 1997; Laws 2001, ch. 2001-226, §85, effective January 1, 2002.)

2. Testator's Signature in the Witnesses' Presence

Most states do not require that the testator actually sign the will while in the witnesses' presence. That is, most states permit the testator to acknowledge his or her previously affixed signature to the witnesses. This situation is likely to arise when the testator first writes his or her signature on the will and then *subsequently* shows the instrument to the witnesses while asking them to serve as witnesses. The testator's acknowledgment can be by statements or gestures and can also be an acknowledgment of his or her signature by a proxy (third party).

The Florida Probate Code requires that the testator sign or acknowledge his or her signature in the presence of two witnesses who are present at the same time (Fla. Stat. §732.502(1)(b)).

3. Competence vs. Interest

a. Definition

Generally, statutes require that witnesses be "competent" or "credible" at the time of the execution of the will. This requirement refers to the witness's ability to give testimony in court to establish the validity of the will. The requirement was reflected in the Statute of Frauds and the UPC. The Statute of Frauds required that wills be attested by "credible" witnesses. McGovern & Kurtz, *supra*, §4.3 at 189. The UPC specifies that "any person generally competent to be a witness may act as a witness to a will" (UPC §2-505(a)). The UPC rule is the prevailing view. McGovern & Kurtz, *supra*. Florida law follows the UPC (Fla. Stat. §732.504(1)).

Competence is required at the time of execution. If a witness is competent at the time of the execution of the will but subsequently becomes incompetent, the will is nonetheless valid.

At common law, an interested witness was not considered competent to testify. An interested witness is someone who stands to take a pecuniary interest under the testator's will, such as a beneficiary. At common law (and in some states today), the spouse of a beneficiary was considered an interested witness (based on the doctrine of coverture in which the wife's legal identity merged with that of her husband's). An executor generally is not considered an interested witness, because the executor receives fees pursuant to statutory authority (i.e. the compensation is not prescribed by the will).

§732.504. Competent witness requirement

(1) Any person competent to be a witness may act as a witness to a will.

(2) A will or codicil, or any part of either, is not invalid because the will or codicil is signed by an interested witness.

(Laws 1974, ch. 74-106, §1; Laws 1975, ch. 75-220, §22; Laws 1977, ch. 77-174, §1; Laws 1979, ch. 79-400, §268.)

b. Effect on the Will

An important issue is the effect on the will of having an interested witness. At common law, attestation by an essential interested witness rendered the entire will void. However, the presence of an extra or "supernumerary" witness could validate the will.

The Model Probate Code (the predecessor to the Uniform Probate Code) provided for a purging statute. Under that approach, the essential interested witness forfeited any benefit under the will, but a witness

who was an heir of the testator's could take the lesser of: the beneficiary's share under the will or the beneficiary's intestate share in the decedent's estate.

> [A]n interested witness shall, unless the will is also attested by two disinterested witnesses, forfeit so much of the provisions therein made for him as in the aggregate exceeds in value, as of the date of the testator's death, what he would have received had the testator died intestate.

Model Probate Code §46(b). However, the will was not invalidated if attested by an interested witness. Many states still follow this approach.

The UPC adopted a *rule of nonforfeiture* in terms of the effect on the will of having an interested witness. An essential interested witness does not forfeit his or her share under the will (UPC §2-505(b)). Nor does having an interested witness invalidate the will. Rather, issues of undue influence are left to will contests. Florida adheres to the UPC rule (Fla. Stat. §732.504(2)).

4. Acknowledgment vs. Publication

As explained above, many states do not require that the testator sign in the witnesses' presence and instead permit the testator to "acknowledge" the testator's will or signature. Thus, the testator could simply confirm his or her signature to the witnesses or confirm that the instrument before the witnesses is indeed the testator's will. This situation might arise if the testator previously signed the will. Acknowledgment does not require any specific words; gestures may suffice.

Acknowledgment is different from publication. Some jurisdictions require that the testator "publish" his or her will. By publication, the testator declares to the witnesses that the instrument is his or her will and requests them to sign it. In jurisdictions with a publication requirement, there is no requirement that the witnesses have to know the contents of the will.

The UPC requires that the witnesses see either (1) the testator's signing or (2) the testator's acknowledgment of that signature or acknowledgment of the will (UPC §2-502(a)(3)). The UPC has no publication requirement. Florida law follows the UPC in both regards (Fla. Stat. §732.502(1) (b)). See, e.g., Estate of Beakes, 306 So. 2d 99 (Fla. 1974) (holding that Florida law does not require publication and that the attesting witnesses do not need to know, at the time they witness the will, that the instrument is in fact a will).

5. Witnesses' Signature in the Testator's Presence: Line of Sight vs. Conscious Presence Tests

Most statutes today require that witnesses sign the will "in the presence of the testator." The requirement derives from the Statute of Frauds's mandate that the witnesses sign a will devising real property in the testator's presence. McGovern & Kurtz, *supra*, §4.3 at 192.

Considerable controversy exists about the meaning of "presence." In the famous case of Cunningham v. Cunningham, 83 N.W. 58 (Minn. 1900), an ill testator signed his will while sitting on the edge of his bed. Two physicians, whom he requested to serve as witnesses, then witnessed the will at a table in an adjoining room (out of the testator's sight). When the contestants argued that the will was invalid because the attestation was outside the testator's "presence," as the statute required, the Minnesota Supreme Court disagreed. In upholding the will, the court explained the two tests for presence:

- the line-of-sight test (sometimes referred to as the "scope of vision" test), and
- the conscious presence test.

Under the former test, the testator either must see the attestation by witnesses or could have seen the attestation without a material change of his or her position. Under the latter test, the witnesses must sign within the testator's hearing, knowledge, and understanding. The *Cunningham* court adopted the more liberal conscious presence test. The court reasoned that, based on the circumstances (the testator knew what was being done, the attestation lasted only a few minutes, and he approved their signatures afterward), there was no possibility of fraud and the denial of probate would defeat the testator's intent. The majority view is the conscious presence test.

Must the witnesses sign at the same time? Most states do not require that the witnesses be together when they affix their signatures to the will. However, in Florida, the witnesses have to sign in the testator's presence *and* in the presence of each other (Fla. Stat. §732.502(1)(b)). For example, in Jordan v. Fehr, 902 So. 2d 198 (Fla. Dist. Ct. App. 2005), the appellate court held that the purported will was invalid because the evidence failed to establish that the decedent signed the document in the presence of the two attesting witnesses who were both present at the same time. That is, one attesting witness testified that he did not see the decedent sign the will, and the other attesting witness testified that he did not recall whether the first attesting witness was present when the decedent signed the will.

The UPC does not require the witnesses to sign in the testator's presence. Nor does the UPC require that the witnesses sign in each other's presence. Note that, unlike wills legislation in many states permitting a testator to acknowledge a previously affixed signature, statutes generally do not permit witnesses to acknowledge their previously affixed signatures.

Note also that attestations by witnesses after the death of the testator have been rejected by several jurisdictions. See In re Estate of Saueressig, 136 P.3d 201, 205 (Cal. 2006) (surveying jurisdictions and holding that the post-death subscription of a witness will not satisfy the statutory requirements because it would "erode the efficacy of the witnessing requirement as a safeguard against fraud or mistake"). However, the UPC would permit post-death attestation so long as the witnesses' affix their signatures "within a reasonable time" after the death of the testator (UPC §2-502(a)(3), Comment).

G. Holographic Wills

A holographic (sometimes called "olographic") will is a handwritten will. Holographic wills were permitted in English eccleasiastic courts beginning around 1600, but were abolished by the English Wills Act of 1837. R. H. Helmholz, The Origin of Holographic Wills in English Law, 15 J. Leg. Hist. 97 (1994). See also Gail B. Bird, Sleight of Handwriting: The Holographic Will in California, 21 Hast. L.J. 605 (1981).

Holographs are valid in over half the states. As of 1998, these included: Alaska, Arizona, Arkansas, California, Colorado, Hawaii, Idaho, Kentucky, Louisiana, Oklahoma, Maine, Maryland, Michigan, Mississippi, Montana, Nebraska, Nevada, New Jersey, New York, North Carolina, North Dakota, South Dakota, Tennessee, Texas, Utah, West Virginia, and Wyoming. Restatement (Third) of Property, *supra*, at §§3.1, 3.2. However, Maryland and New York limit holographic wills to persons in the armed services. *Id.* Holographic wills are also recognized by UPC §2-502(b).

Florida law does not recognize handwritten wills (or codicils) unless they are attested by two witnesses (Fla. Stat. §732.502(1)(b)). Holographs that are valid in other states are not recognized in Florida (Fla. Stat. §732.502(c)(2)).

The constitutionality of the Florida will execution statute was upheld in a case involving an unattested holographic will. In In re Olson's Estate, 181 So. 2d 642 (Fla. 1966), the Florida Supreme Court held that the statute governing execution of wills (the predecessor to Florida Statutes §732.502) requiring attestation by at least two witnesses was not an unwarranted restriction upon the disposition of property and was constitutional as applied to bar the probate of an unattested holographic will.

§732.502. Execution of wills: requirements

Every will must be in writing and executed as follows:

(1)(a) Testator's signature.--

1. The testator must sign the will at the end; or

2. The testator's name must be subscribed at the end of the will by some other person in the testator's presence and by the testator's direction.

(b) *Witnesses*.--The testator's:

1. Signing, or

2. Acknowledgment:

a. That he or she has previously signed the will, or

b. That another person has subscribed the testator's name to it,

must be in the presence of at least two attesting witnesses.

(c) *Witnesses' signatures*.--The attesting witnesses must sign the will in the presence of the testator and in the presence of each other.

(2) Any will, other than a holographic or nuncupative will, executed by a nonresident of Florida, either before or after this law takes effect, is valid as a will in this state if valid under the laws of the state or country where the will was executed. A will in the testator's handwriting that has been executed in accordance with subsection (1) shall not be considered a holographic will.

……

(Laws 1974, ch. 74-106, §1; Laws 1975, ch. 75-220, §21; Laws 1977, ch. 77-87, §11. Amended by Laws 1997, ch. 97-102, §961, effective July 1, 1997; Laws 2001, ch. 2001-226, §42, effective January 1, 2002; Laws 2003, ch. 2003-154, §5, effective June 12, 2003.)

[The remainder of the statute is reprinted in Section IID *supra*.]

H. Oral Wills

An oral or nuncupative will is a will that is spoken rather than written. Two general types of oral wills exist: the oral will that is uttered during the testator's last illness and the soldiers'/sailors' will. The former is an oral will that was spoken by the testator during his or her last illness before witnesses and soon afterward reduced to writing. A soldiers'/sailors' will is an oral will in which a soldier or sailor disposes of his personalty without the necessity for the usual formalities of will execution.

Oral wills date to Roman law when they were permitted for soldiers. McGovern & Kurtz, *supra*, §4.4 at 200. Historically, such wills were permitted for soldiers either as a reward for military service or because soldiers in active service could not comply easily with testamentary formalities. *Id.*

The Statute of Frauds of 1676 (which required wills of real property to be in writing) also regulated oral wills. By the Statute of Frauds, Parliament created a number of substantive requirements for the validity of oral wills of personal property valued in excess of £30. Lloyd Bonfield, Reforming the Requirements for Due Execution of Wills: Some Guidance from the Past, 70 Tul. L. Rev. 1893 (1996). The Statute of Frauds required that three persons (who acted at the testator's request) must "bear witness" that the testator's statements were his will. The testator must have spoken the statements during a last illness. And, the statements had to be spoken in the decedent's

> habitation or dwelling, or where he or she hath been resident for the space of ten days or more next before the making of such Will, except where such person was surprised or taken sick, being from his own home, and died before he returned to the place of his or her dwelling.

Cited in *id.* at 1911.

The Statute of Frauds also regulated the probate procedure for noncupative wills. Ecclesiastic courts had to receive testimony proving the validity of such wills within 6 months, unless the testimony or its substance was reduced to writing shortly after utterance (i.e., within 6 days). *Id.* at 1912. The Statute also limited the ability to revoke orally a clause, devise, or bequest in a written will. *Id.* The English Wills Act of 1837 abolished oral wills except for those of soldiers in active military service or sailors at sea (regarding disposition of personal property). McGovern & Kurtz, *supra*, §4.4 at 200.

The majority of states (including Florida) as well as the UPC (§2-506) refuse to recognize oral wills. McGovern & Kurtz, *supra*, §4.4 at 186. See also In re Estate of Corbin, 645 So. 2d 39 (Fla. Dist. Ct. App. 1994) (holding that a provision in a will was ineffective and resulted in intestacy, where the will devised property to the testator's daughter according to the testator's oral instructions).

The primary reasons for nonrecognition of oral wills is the fear of fraud. Those few jurisdictions that continue to recognize oral wills limit them to personal property and sometimes set a value on the property. Many of these states require that the oral will must be put into writing within a short period of time after the spoken will and, similarly, must be probated within a short period of time after the testator's death. Finally, many statutes have witnessing requirements.

I. Conditional Wills

A conditional will is a will whose validity is subject to a condition. That is, the effectiveness of the will is conditional upon an event, such as death from a particular cause. If the condition does not occur, then the will is not effective.

Traditionally, courts have been reluctant to find wills conditional, preferring to find that the condition merely expresses the testator's motivation for executing the will. The issue is whether the testator intended to make the occurrence of an event as a condition precedent to the operation of the will (in which case the instrument is denied probate if the condition is not fulfilled), or whether the testator stated the possibility of the event merely as the motive leading to execution of the will (in which case the will becomes effective on the testator's death even if the event never took place).

In a famous case, Estate of Taylor, 259 P.2d 1014 (Cal. 1953), the testator (Clark Taylor) was in the Navy when he wrote to a Mr. Lindsay, saying that in case "Davie Jones gets me out in the South Pacific," he wanted his "Bonds, and cash in the bank also the pay I will have coming" to go to an old friend Betty Black. *Id.* at 1015-1016. After Taylor left the Navy, he lived with the Black's family. He mentioned the letter repeatedly. At Taylor's death, Lindsay filed the letter for probate; an aunt of Taylor's contested it. The court admitted the will to probate, reasoning that the possibility of the testator's dying at sea was an inducement rather than a condition.

Florida case law occasionally addresses the validity of conditional (sometimes called "contingent") wills. In In re Nichols' Estate, 428 So. 2d 372 (Fla. Dist. Ct. App. 1983), the appellate court held that the will was not contingent and void because of a paragraph stating that it was made "in contemplation of marriage" for the reason that the word "contemplation" did not denote a contingency implying that the will would not be valid until the marriage occurred, but only referred to the fact that the will was intended to be valid even after the occurrence of an expected future event.

Also, in In re Estate of Dickerhoff, 267 So. 2d 388 (Fla. Dist. Ct. App. 1972), the testator's will (bequeathing her entire estate to her husband who subsequently predeceased her) provided that in the event of a common disaster, the estate would be divided between certain named individuals. The testator and her husband both died of natural causes (an eventuality that was not envisioned by the will). The court held that the common-disaster provision was conditional and therefore inoperative and that the estate should descend to the testator's heirs at law rather than the named individuals.

J. Statutory Will

A small number of states (California, Maine, Massachusetts, Michigan, New Mexico, and Wisconsin) have enacted a statutory will. Captain Theresa A. Bruno, The Deployment Will, 47 A.F. L. Rev. 211, 225 (1999). California was the first of these states to enact statutory will legislation in the 1980s. *Id.*

The statutory will (a type of "fill-in-the-blank" will) is a legislative effort to accommodate the large numbers of persons who would otherwise die intestate. Statutory wills permit testators to fill in blank spaces for beneficiaries, guardians for children, trustees, and executors of the estate. Florida does not recognize statutory wills.

K. Foreign and International Wills

Sometimes, a testator executes a will in a state or country that is different from that of the testator's domicile or place of death. Many states have statutes that recognize such wills. The Uniform Probate Code includes two statutory approaches to validate such wills. The first solution recognizes a foreign will that has been executed according to the requirements of other states or countries through a special choice of law rule (UPC §2-506). The second solution is the Uniform International Wills Act which authorizes a special procedure (UPC §§10-1001 to 10-1010) and specifies that wills executed pursuant to that procedure (in jurisdictions that have enacted the Act or that are signatories to an international convention) will be given effect in other jurisdictions.

UPC §2-506 recognizes the validity of any foreign instrument if executed in compliance with the law of any of the following jurisdictions:

- the place of execution,
- the testator's domicile at the time of execution,
- the testator's place of abode at the time of execution,
- the place of the testator's nationality at the time of execution,
- the testator's domicile at the time of death,
- the testator's place of abode at the time of death, or
- the testator's nationality at the time of death.

The Uniform International Wills Act, incorporated in the Uniform Probate Code, (Article II, Part 10), was promulgated by the National Conference of Commissioners on Uniform State Laws (NCCUSL) in 1977. Under the Act, a will is valid regardless of the place where it was executed, the location of the assets, or the nationality, domicile, or residence of the testator. The Act also implements an international convention calling for all countries and states to adopt a uniform formality for executing wills. The Act has been adopted by 13 states and the District of Columbia (but not Florida). See *www.nccusl.org/Update/uniformact_factsheets/uniformacts-fs-uiwa.asp* (last visited Feb. 28, 2007).

Florida law provides for recognition of wills executed by Florida *nonresidents*. According to Florida Statutes §732.502(2), a will executed by a nonresident of Florida may be admitted to probate in Florida provided that the will was validly executed under the laws of the state or country where the testator was located at the time of the execution of the will.

On the probate of wills in foreign languages, see Florida Statutes §733.204 and Rule 5.216 (reprinted in Section IID *supra*) requiring that English translations be attached.

§732.502. Execution of wills: recognition of wills of nonresidents

....

(2) Any will, other than a holographic or nuncupative will, executed by a nonresident of Florida, either before or after this law takes effect, is valid as a will in this state if valid under the laws of the state or country where the will was executed. A will in the testator's handwriting that has been executed in accordance with subsection (1) shall not be considered a holographic will.

....

(Laws 1974, ch. 74-106, §1; Laws 1975, ch. 75-220, § 21; Laws 1977, ch. 77-87, §11. Amended by Laws 1997, ch. 97-102, §961, effective July 1, 1997; Laws 2001, ch. 2001-226, §42, effective January 1, 2002; Laws 2003, ch. 2003-154, §5, effective June 12, 2003.)

L. Self-Proved Wills

Some states and the UPC (§2-504) provide for a "self-proved will" which consists of a witnessed will with a notarized affidavit in which the testator and witnesses affirm under oath that all the statutory requirements have been fulfilled. A self-proving affidavit resembles an attestation clause. However, because of the addition of the notarized statement under oath, a self-proved will facilitates probate by enabling the will to be admitted without the necessity of testimony by the subscribing witnesses.

Almost all states (including Florida) permit self-proving affidavits in connection with a will or codicil. Betsy Dupree-Kyle, Comment, Michigan Self-Proved Wills: What Are They and How Do They Work?, 2000 L. Rev. Mich. St. U. Det. C.L. 829, 830 (2000).

Sometimes, problems arise when a testator or witnesses sign only the self-proving affidavit and not the will. Jurisdictions differ as to whether the self-proving affidavit is incorporated into the will, serving as a substitute for the attestation clause (thereby requiring one set of signatures), or instead a two-step procedure requiring execution of a will and a separate affidavit (thereby requiring two sets of signatures). According to the majority approach, one set of signatures is sufficient to witness a will and to self-prove it. See, e.g., Estate of Dellinger, 793 N.E.2d 1041 (Ind. 2003).

The UPC includes alternative forms. One form permits the simultaneous execution of a will and affidavit, in which case the affidavit is part of the will itself. According to UPC §2-504(a). the testator and witnesses execute both the affidavit and will simultaneously. The second form pertains to the situation when an attested will is made self-proved after its execution (UPC §2-504(b)). In such a case, the will and affidavit have been executed separately. However, NCCUSL subsequently added subsection (c) to UPC §2-504 to clarify that a signature on the self-proving affidavit is considered a signature affixed to the will. See UPC §2-504(c) ("A signature affixed to a self-proving affidavit attached to a will is considered a signature affixed to the will, if necessary to prove the will's due execution").

UPC provisions for the self-proved will specify additional requirements (not required for the witnessed will generally): The testator must declare to witnesses that this will is the testator's last will, and the witnesses must sign in the testator's presence and hearing (UPC §504).

Florida case law establishes that signatures on the affidavit may serve as the necessary signatures on the will. See Estate of Charry, 359 So. 2d 544 (Fla. Dist. Ct. App. 1978) (rejecting the view that self-proved affidavit is not part of will and that signatures of testator and witnesses on affidavit are not on the will).

In Florida, self-proved wills are admitted to probate without additional proof (Fla. Stat. §733.201). Further, according to Florida Statutes §732.503, a will or codicil may be made self-proved (either at the time of execution orf subsequently by the testator's acknowledgment and affidavits by witnesses) provided that it is made before a notary and under oath. Eclavea & Lease, 17 Fla. Jur. 2d Decedents' Property §153.

On the history of self-proved wills, see Dupree-Kyle, *supra*, at 835-838. See also Bruce H. Mann, Self-Proving Affidavits and Formalism in Wills Adjudication, 63 Wash. U.L.Q. 39 (1985).

§732.503. Self-proof of will

(1) A will or codicil executed in conformity with § 732.502 may be made self-proved at the time of its execution or at any subsequent date by the acknowledgment of it by the testator and the affidavits of the witnesses, made before an officer authorized to administer oaths and evidenced by the officer's certificate attached to or following the will, in substantially the following form:

STATE OF FLORIDA COUNTY OF ________

I, ________, declare to the officer taking my acknowledgment of this instrument, and to the subscribing witnesses, that I signed this instrument as my will.

____

Testator

We, ________ and, ________ have been sworn by the officer signing below, and declare to that officer on our oaths that the testator declared the instrument to be the testator's will and signed it in our presence and that we each signed the instrument as a witness in the presence of the testator and of each other.

____

Witness

____

Witness

Acknowledged and subscribed before me by the testator, (type or print testator's name), who is personally known to me or who has produced (state type of identification--see § 117.05(5)(b)2.) as identification, and sworn to and subscribed before me by the witnesses, (type or print name of first witness) who is personally known to me or who has produced (state type of identification--see § 117.05(5)(b)2.) as identification and (type or print name of second witness) who is personally known to me or who has produced (state type of identification--see § 117.05(5)(b)2.) as identification, and subscribed by me in the presence of the testator and the subscribing witnesses, all on (date).

(Signature of Officer)

(Print, type, or stamp commissioned name and affix official seal)

(2) A will or codicil made self-proved under former law, or executed in another state and made self-proved under the laws of that state, shall be considered as self-proved under this section.

(Laws 1974, ch. 74-106, §1; Laws 1975, ch. 75-220, §21; Laws 1977, ch. 77-87, §12; Laws 1993, ch. 93-62, §8. Amended by Laws 1997, ch. 97-102, §962, effective July 1, 1997; Laws 1998, ch. 98-246, §18, effective January 1, 1999; Laws 2001, ch. 2001-226, §43, effective January 1, 2002.)

§733.201. Proof of will: self-proved wills

(1) Self-proved wills executed in accordance with this code may be admitted to probate without further proof.

(2) A will may be admitted to probate upon the oath of any attesting witness taken before any circuit judge, commissioner appointed by the court, or clerk.

(3) If it appears to the court that the attesting witnesses cannot be found or that they have become incompetent after the execution of the will or their testimony cannot be obtained within a reasonable time, a will may be admitted to probate upon the oath of the personal representative nominated by the will as provided in subsection (2), whether or not the nominated personal representative is interested in the estate, or upon the oath of any person having no interest in the estate under the will stating that the person believes the writing exhibited to be the true last will of the decedent.

(Laws 1974, ch. 74-106, §1; Laws 1975, ch. 75-220, §51. Amended by Laws 1997, ch. 97-102, §985, effective July 1, 1997; Laws 2001, ch. 2001-226, §85, effective January 1, 2002.)

M. Limitations on Transfers to Beneficiaries who Serve as Drafters

Some states invalidate donative transfers to certain classes of persons such as a drafter of the instrument as well as persons related by blood or marriage to the drafter. See, e.g., Cal. Probate Code §§21350 to 21356. The issue of donative transfers to beneficiaries who serve as drafters raises the specter of conflicts of interest and undue influence. On Undue Influence, see Chapter IV, Section IV.

Prior to the ABA's adoption of limitations on transfers to a beneficiary-draftsman, Florida had no special statutory provisions addressing such transfers. Rather, Florida law subsumed such transfers within the law of fiduciary duty and undue influence. See, e.g., Jacobs v. Vaillancourt, 634 So. 2d 667 (Fla. Dist. Ct. App. 1994) (holding that draftsman who was testatrix's son-in-law did not breach his fiduciary duty to testatrix's husband by drafting an estate plan created for the benefit of draftsman's wife and also that testatrix's husband was not under undue influence at the time he executed the instrument because son-in-law was not active in procurement of instrument).

The ABA promulgated limitations on transfers to beneficiaries who serve as drafters of testamentary instruments. The ABA Model Rules provide that a lawyer cannot prepare an instrument giving the lawyer (or a person "related" to the lawyer) a "substantial" gift unless the recipient (lawyer or third party) is related to the client. "Related" persons are defined, for purposes of the Rule, as a spouse,

child, grandchild, parent, grandparent or other relative or individual with whom the lawyer or the client maintains a close familial relationship. Florida has adopted this rule.

FLORIDA BAR RULE
Rule 4-1.8. Conflict of Interest; Prohibited and Other Transactions

. . .

(c) Gifts to Lawyer or Lawyer's Family. A lawyer shall not solicit any substantial gift from a client, including a testamentary gift, or prepare on behalf of a client an instrument giving the lawyer or a person related to the lawyer any substantial gift unless the lawyer or other recipient of the gift is related to the client. For purposes of this subdivision, related persons include a spouse, child, grandchild, parent, grandparent, or other relative with whom the lawyer or the client maintains a close, familial relationship.

. . . .

(Amended July 23, 1992, effective January 1, 1993 (605 So. 2d 252); April 25, 2002 (820 So. 2d 210); May 20, 2004 (875 So. 2d 448); March 23, 2006, effective May 22, 2006 (833 So. 2d 417).

IV
TESTAMENTARY CAPACITY

This chapter addresses issues of capacity to make a will. These issues include legal and mental capacity, fraud, duress, and undue influence. Such issues constitute grounds for contest of a will. For other requirements for will execution, see Chapter III, Section IIB. Will contests are also discussed in Chapter XIV, Section IIID.

I. Mental Capacity

A person must have legal capacity and mental capacity to execute a will. Most jurisdictions require that a testator be an adult and mentally competent. Statutes in all jurisdictions establish the minimum age to make a will. The majority of jurisdictions require that a testator be at least 18 years of age. Age 18 is also the minimum specified by the Uniform Probate Code (§2-501).

Some jurisdictions permit exceptions to the age requirement for persons in military service, married persons, or emancipated minors. See, e.g., Fla. Stat. §732.501 (permitting exception for emancipated minors).

Note: Emancipation enables a child to take on the legal status of an adult and also frees a parent from legal responsibility for the child. A minor in Florida becomes "emancipated" either based on the common law doctrine of emancipation (accomplished by marriage or military service) or, alternatively, by statute (Fla. Stat. §§743.01 et seq.). See also Ison v. Florida Sanitarium & Benevolent Assn., 302 So. 2d 200, 201 (Fla. Dist. Ct. App. 1974) (holding that father was not liable for daughter's medical expenses because daughter had voluntarily left the home).

In addition to legal capacity, a testator must have the mental capacity to execute a will. The first case to develop a doctrinal test for testamentary capacity was Pawlet, Marquess of Winchester's Case, 77 Eng. Rep. 287 (K.B. 1601), in which a testator's legitimate son challenged his father's bequest of the bulk of his estate to the father's nonmarital children. Eunice L. Ross & Thomas J. Reed, Will Contests §2:6 (2d ed. 2003 & Supp.).

The modern test for testamentary capacity, with its three-pronged requirement, derives from two subsequent English cases (sometimes referred to as the "*Greenwood-Baker* rule"). Greenwood v. Greenwood, 163 Eng. Rep. 930 (K.B. 1790), involved a challenge by the decedent's brother to the validity of title to real estate devised in the decedent's will. The brother argued that the will was the product of an unsound mind, claiming that the decedent was violent and insane at the time he executed it. Lord Kenyon charged the jury on the law of testamentary capacity, requiring that the testator understand: (1) what he possessed, and (2) who were the natural objects of his bounty. Later, Harwood v. Baker, 13 Eng. Rep. 117 (P.C. 1840), added the third requirement of the test for testamentary capacity—i.e., the testator must be able to form an intelligent distribution plan. *Harwood* involved a will contest by children of the decedent's first marriage who had been disinherited in favor of the decedent's second wife. Ross & Reed, *supra*, at §2:6. Florida adheres to this three-prong test for mental capacity. See, e.g., Raimi v. Furlong, 702 So.2d 1273, 1286 (Fla. Dist. Ct. App. 1997); In re Wilmott's Estate, 66 So.2d 465 (Fla. 1953).

American statutes include the requirement that the testator must be "of sound mind." That term is generally not defined. See, e.g., Fla. Stat. §732.501 (requiring that the testator be at least 18 years of age and "of sound mind").

The Florida requirements regarding age and "sound mind" are identical to those of UPC §2-501, except for a provision added by statutory amendment in Florida in 2001 (Laws 2001, ch. 2001-226, §41, effective January 1, 2002), permitting emancipated minors to execute a will.

By its inclusion of emancipated minors, the Florida statute is similar to that of the new Restatement (Third) of Property. The Restatement provides generally that "A person must have mental capacity in order to make or revoke a donative transfer." Restatement (Third) of Property (Wills & Don. Transfers) §8.1 (2003). In regard to the lack of capacity specifically due to minority, the Restatement specifies: "A minor does not have capacity to make a will. A purported will made by a minor is void." *Id.* at §8.2(a). The term "minor" is defined as a person who has not reached the age of majority (further defined as the age of 18 "unless an applicable statute provides otherwise") or one who lacks capacity "for the purpose in question" and one *"who is not emancipated."* *Id.* at §8.2(c) (emphasis added).

Testamentary capacity is determined at the *time of execution* of the will. Thomas E. Atkinson, Law of Wills §51 at p. 241 (2d ed. 1953); Trawick, *supra*, at §3-9. See also York v. Smith, 385 So. 2d 1110 (Fla. Dist. Ct. App. 1980) (testator's lack of capacity on date when he acknowledged his signature did not invalidate prior will because substantial evidence supported the finding that he possessed testamentary capacity when he executed the prior will); In re Blakey's Estate, App. 363 So. 2d 630 (Fla. Dist. Ct. App. 1978) (finding that testatrix possessed testamentary capacity during a lucid interval).

Evidence regarding the testator's mental condition before or after the execution of the will is important only insofar as it sheds light on his or her mental condition at the time of the will execution.

Courts admit a range of evidence on the subject of capacity, including evidence by subscribing witnesses, intimate acquaintances, and medical personnel (physicians, psychologists, psychiatrists).

Even a testator who is under an adjudication of mental incompetency may make a will. Chapman v. Campbell, 119 So. 2d 61 (Fla. Dist. Ct. App. 1960) (holding that the evidence amply supported the court order admitting a will to probate of a testator who had been previously declared incompetent). See also A.G. Barnett, Effect of Guardianship of Adult on Testamentary Capacity, 89 ALR 2d 1120 (1963 & Supp.); Trawick, *supra*, at §§3-9, 10-2.

Florida case law has held that the following, alone, do not establish mental incapacity: mental weakness, old age, physical weakness, alcohol or drug abuse, "eccentricity or peculiarity in appearance and behavior or penuriousness, passion or prejudice." Trawick, *supra*, at §10-2.

Mental derangement also is a ground for invalidating a will based on lack of capacity. The doctrinal rule for "insane delusion" derives from mid-nineteenth century case law. Ross & Reed, *supra*, at §2:9. In Dew v. Clark, 162 Eng. Rep. 410 (Prerog. 1826), a testator took a violent, unreasonable dislike to his daughter from his first marriage and disinherited her. His third wife subsequently committed him to an insane asylum. *Dew* announced the doctrine that invalidates a will because all or part of it is the product of the testator's insane delusion about a family member. Ross & Reed, *supra*, at §2:7.

The insane delusion doctrine was first adopted by Maryland in 1848 and shortly thereafter by New York and Pennsylvania. *Id.* However, the most frequently cited insane delusion case is American Seaman's Friends Society v. Hopper, 33 N.Y. 619, 1865 WL 4050 (1865), in which the decedent bequeathed his residuary estate to the American Seaman's Friends Society and disinherited his wife and blood relatives, including two nephews. A few years before his death, the decedent began to suspect his wife (then in her sixties) of carrying on an affair with several ministers (who were elderly and beyond reproach). He also believed that his nephews were involved with his wife in a conspiracy to murder him and that one nephew had caused him to fall against a hot stove (the nephew was not present in the house at the time). The appellate court denied probate of the decedent's will. *Hopper* set forth the requirement that the insane delusion must affect the dispositive provisions of the will in order to invalidate a will.

Florida courts have defined "insane delusion" as "a spontaneous conception and acceptance as a fact of that which has no real existence except in imagination. The conception must be persistently adhered to against all evidence and reason." Hooper v. Stokes, 145 So. 855, 856 (Fla. 1933). Furthermore, if the insane delusion pertains to a person who is the object of the testator's bounty and causes the testator to make a will he would not have made otherwise ("but for that delusion") (*id.*), then the will will be invalid.

In Miami Rescue Mission, Inc. v. Roberts, 943 So. 2d 274 (Fla. Dist. Ct. App. 2006), a testatrix, while hospitalized with severe pain and under the influence of pain medication, executed a will one day before she died. The will disinherited her longtime caregiver/friend (beneficiary of a prior will), and left her residuary estate instead to four charities. The appellate court affirmed the trial court's finding that the testatrix was suffering from an insane delusion because she had an unreasonable belief that her friend/caregiver was not visiting her and was not caring for her dog. The evidence established, however, that the caregiver visited the testatrix daily and each time reassured her that the dog was fine, but that on one visit the testatrix failed to recognize her. The trial court's conclusion was supported by the testimony of four doctors who explained how the medication affected the testatrix in the days before her death.

The Florida Probate Code also specifies the applicable burden of proof in will contests. Proponents of the will have the burden of proof of due execution. Contestants have the burden of proof of lack of capacity or revocation (Fla. Stat. §733.107; Fla. Prob. Rule §5.275 (implementing Fla. Stat. §733.107)). On will contests, see also Chapter IV, Section IIID.

For a recent proposal to improve assessments of testamentary capacity, see Pamela Champine, Expertise and Instinct in the Assessment of Testamentary Capacity, 51 Vill. L. Rev. 25(2006) (urging formulation of a new test on testamentary capacity to be administered by psychologists).

§732.501. Persons who may make a will

Any person who is of sound mind and who is either 18 or more years of age or an emancipated minor may make a will

(Laws 1974, ch. 74-106, §1; Laws 1975, ch. 75-220, §20. Amended by Laws 2001, ch. 2001-226, §41, effective January 1, 2002.)

II. Fraud

Fraud also is a ground for invalidating a will. "A will is invalid if the testator has been willfully deceived by the beneficiary as to the character or contents of the instrument, or as to extrinsic facts which are material to the disposition and in fact caused it." Atkinson, *supra*, §56 at 263.

In Florida, fraud constitutes a ground for invalidating a will or a portion thereof (Fla. Stat. §732.5165). Few Florida cases address fraud as a basis for invalidating a will. Trawick, *supra*, at §10-2.

Testamentary fraud takes many forms. Such fraud may consist of fraudulent concealment (by a statement or conduct) of relevant facts, knowingly with the intent to mislead, that prevents the decedent from acquiring knowledge of the truth. Or, the deceiver may fraudulently fail to reveal facts (fraudulent nondisclosure) to the testator, who (had he or she known the true facts) would have made a different disposition. Fraudulent concealment or fraudulent nondisclosure also operates when the wrongdoer has a fiduciary duty to disclose facts to the testator. Ross & Reed, *supra*, at §8:13.

"Scienter" is an essential element to prove fraud. Scienter requires that the deceiver made the misrepresentation either with knowledge of its falsity or with reckless disregard of the truth so as to induce the decedent to perform some testamentary act in reliance on the misrepresentation. *Id.*

Fraud may occur in the execution or inducement of a will. Either form of fraud can invalidate the entire will or only certain provisions. *Fraud in the execution* involves situations where the decedent is deceived into executing a particular document which he or she believes is another document. Or, pages of a document may be fraudulently substituted. *Id.*, at §8:10.

In contrast, *fraud in the inducement* refers to a misrepresentation or concealment of a material fact that induces the decedent to make a will other than that which he or she intended. See, e.g., In re Young, 738 N.Y.S.2d 100 (App. Div. 2001) (holding that there was no admissible evidence to support the claim of testatrix's son that his sister exerted fraud upon the testator to the effect that a disposition to the mentally disabled son would cause him to lose his Social Security benefits).

In the days before no-fault divorce, testamentary fraud cases frequently involved a spouse in a bigamous marriage with the testator. "The causation question then [arose] whether, had the testator not been deceived as to the bigamous marriage, a bequest would have been made to the deceitful spouse." Ross & Reed, *supra*, at §8:11. See, e.g., Estate of Carson, 194 P. 5 (Cal. 1920) (stating that if the bequest to the bigamous husband were the direct fruit of his fraud, such bequest is void, and concluding that it was not an unreasonable inference, from the fact that the wife had been so recently married when the will was made, that she left the bulk of her estate to her husband because she believed he was her lawful husband, and would not have done so if she had believed otherwise). Misrepresentations also may relate to the alleged death of a beneficiary or to facts about a beneficiary that would lead to an estrangement. If fraud is proven, the ensuing will may be invalidated.

Note that courts are more willing to admit extrinsic evidence to prove fraud than to prove mistake. Ross & Reed, *supra*, at §8:14.

Several remedies exist for fraudulently procured actions or inactions by testators (i.e., fraudulent procured revocation of a will, wrongful prevention of revocation, or fraudulent procurement of a new will). A tort remedy (termed "wrongful interference with the expectation of a bequest") may exist for fraudulent prevention of the execution of a will or codicil. The elements of the tort require plaintiff to prove: (1) the existence of the expectancy; (2) the defendants' intentional interference with that expectancy; (3) the existence of tortious conduct such as fraud, duress, or undue influence; and (4) a reasonable certainty that the devise to plaintiff would have been received but for defendant's interference. Ross & Reed, *supra,* at §8:8 (citing case law). Florida is among those jurisdictions that recognize a cause of action for wrongful interference with a testamentary expectancy. See, e.g., Davison v. Feuerherd, 391 So. 2d 799 (Fla. Dist. Ct. App. 1980) (holding that plaintiff was not precluded from maintaining an action for tortious interference with an expectancy because she had alleged testator's lack of testamentary capacity in a previous will contest).

An additional remedy in cases of fraudulent revocation of a will is to probate the will subsequently pursuant to a "lost or destroyed will" statute. Or, if execution or revocation of a will was prevented by fraud, the disappointed legatee may be the beneficiary of a constructive trust even if the will cannot be probated. If fraud induced a revocation *and* a new will, similarly, courts might probate the former will and impose a constructive trust or reform the substituted legacy. Ross & Reed, *supra*, at §8:8. See, e.g., Kramer v. Freedman, 272 So. 2d 195 (Fla. Dist. Ct. App. 1973), *reh'g denied*, 295 So. 2d 97 (1973)(holding that a constructive trust may be imposed where, through fraud or abuse of confidence, decedent's half-sisters made representations to share their estate with plaintiff and thereby induced decedent not to change his will).

III. Duress

Duress is also a ground to invalidate a will. Duress typically includes violence or threats of violence that induce the testator to make a will in favor of either the wrongdoer or a third party. Traditionally, duress signified threats involving life or limb, unjust civil imprisonment, criminal prosecution, imprisonment of decedent or a close relative, or wrongful seizure or damage to decedent's property. Subsequently, duress was broadened to include economic duress or business compulsion. Ross & Reed, *supra*, at §8:15.

Evidence establishing duress must be clear and convincing. In addition, causation must be proved—i.e., that the decedent's action or inaction would not have been undertaken but for the coercion. *Id.* at §8:17.

> The issue in duress is not whether a brave or firm decedent would have resisted the compulsion or been in fear from the threats, but whether the particular deceased undertook the testamentary action or inaction through compulsion or such fear as to preclude the exercise of free will and judgment.

Id. at §8:15.

Duress requires an "unlawful" threat. For example, in Rubenstein v. Sela, 672 P.2d 491 (Ariz. Ct. App. 1983), the court refused to permit a wife to invalidate a deed on the ground of duress because the husband's threat to leave her (if she did not) was not an unlawful act. Cited in McGovern & Kurtz, *supra*, §7.3 at 284.

Courts sometimes blur the lines between duress and undue influence. The former refers to a physical compulsion or threat-induced fear; the latter refers to unfair persuasion. Ross & Reed, *supra*, at §8:16.

Duress in the will context sometimes involves situations in which the decedent is prevented from executing a will, changing a will, or revoking a will. See, e.g., Blakeley v. Blakeley, 298 F.2d 635 (7th Cir. 1962); Pope v. Garrett, 211 S.W.2d 559 (Tex. 1948). Duress may also occur if the wrongdoer's actions are aimed at procuring the decedent's total or partial intestacy.

Restitutionary principles dictate the remedy for duress. The Restatement of Restitution specifies the remedy depending on the nature of the wrong. Ross & Reed, *supra*, at §8:14 (citing Restatement of Restitution §184, cmts. g, h). For example, if the wrongdoer's duress prevents execution of a will, the probate court cannot admit the will to probate. However, a court (probate court or equity court, depending on which court has jurisdiction) might impress a constructive trust against all the heirs in favor of the intended legatee(s). If the wrongdoer uses duress to induce a revocation of a will and substitution of a new will, the new will might be denied probate or a constructive trust imposed in favor of legatees under the prior will. If the wrongdoer uses duress to *prevent* the revocation of a will and execution of a new will, the will may be probated with the imposition of a construction trust in favor of the disappointed legatees.

Duress cases arise infrequently. In Wells v. Estate of Wells, 922 S.W.2d 715 (Ark. 1996), the state supreme court denied probate to a will that was offered for probate by decedent's stepson. Evidence revealed that the stepson isolated the decedent from her relatives when she was hospitalized for a heart attack (shortly before the will was executed), that the decedent telephoned her attorney claiming that her stepson had made her a prisoner, that he made her sign a pile of papers, and that she did not know what she had signed. A neighbor and niece testified that the stepson and his wife mistreated the decedent, and she feared him. The court found that the evidence supported a finding of duress and undue influence by the stepson. In Florida, the remedy of wrongful interference with a testamentary expectancy might provide a remedy to a disappointed legatee in analogous situations.

§732.5165. Will void for fraud, duress, mistake and undue influence

A will is void if the execution is procured by fraud, duress, mistake, or undue influence. Any part of the will is void if so procured, but the remainder of the will not so procured shall be valid if it is not invalid for other reasons.
(Laws 1975, ch. 75-220, §31.)

IV. Undue Influence

Undue influence, in conjunction with lack of mental capacity, is the most frequent ground for invalidating a will. Ray D. Madoff, Unmasking Undue Influence, 81 Minn. L. Rev. 571, 574 (1997). The wills of many famous people (e.g., Doris Duke, Georgia O'Keeffe, J. Seward Johnson, and Pearl S. Buck) have been challenged based on undue influence. *Id.* at 573.

Undue influence doctrine is similar to, and yet different from, the doctrines of fraud and duress. Like the doctrines of fraud and duress, the undue influence doctrine attempts to protect testators' rights to dispose freely of their property. *Id.* at 576. However, the doctrines reveal several inherent differences.

> The doctrine of fraud prevents a will from being given effect when the will is brought about through lies told to the testator. The doctrine of duress prevents a will from being given effect when the will is brought about through threats of harm to the testator. The undue influence doctrine is broader than each of these in that it invalidates a will when it is the result of any action that subverts the will of the testator and replaces the will of the testator with that of the one influencing.

Id. at 579-580.

Another difference between the doctrine of undue influence and mental capacity is that mental incapacity generally invalidates the entire will. However, a finding of undue influence may invalidate only that portion of the will that was unduly influenced.

The law of undue influence dates to an eighteenth-century English case. Ross & Reed, *supra*, at §2:8. In Mountain v. Bennet, 29 Eng. Rep. 1200 (Ex. 1787), the testator devised real property to his wife, whom he had secretly married shortly before executing his will. His heirs objected to the admission of the will to probate on the ground that the wife unduly influenced the decedent to make a will in her favor. Based in part on the widow's letter to her subsequent husband in which she gloated about the control she yielded over the decedent, the jury denied probate of the will.

The law of undue influence continued to develop in a subsequent will contest case, Kinleside v. Harrison, 161 Eng. Rep. 1196 (Prerog. 1818), which announced the doctrine that a confidential relationship between the testator and a person who benefits from the will raises a presumption of undue influence. Ross & Reed, *supra*, at §2:8. Finally, in 1828, the Prerogative Court decided Williams v. Goude, 162 Eng. Rep. 682 (Prerog. 1828), which announced the modern test for undue influence. In *Williams*, the testator's will preferred his wife's nephews over his only heirs, two nephews. Testator's nephews argued that the widow had urged him to favor her nephews. In upholding the testator's will, the court explained:

> The influence to vitiate an act must amount to force and coercion destroying free—it must not be the influence of affection and attachment—it must not be the mere desire of gratifying the wishes of another. . . . there must be proof that the act was obtained by this coercion—by importunity which could not be resisted. . . .

Id. at 684. These cases form the basis for American legal doctrine on undue influence. Ross & Reed, *supra*, at §2:8.

The first noteworthy American case on undue influence involved the will of a South Carolina planter who disinherited his relatives in favor of his mistress (a slave) and their nonmarital son. O'Neall ads. Farr, 30 S.C.L. 80, 1 Rich. 80 (S.C. 1844) (discussed in Ross & Reed, *supra*, at §2:10). The South Carolina Supreme Court reversed a jury verdict in favor of the relatives, and stated the law on undue influence which was similar to that of Williams v. Goude, *supra*.

By the 1860s, American law of undue influence required that any person who gained a benefit from a will by means of abuse of a confidential relationship could lose a testamentary gift, particularly if the beneficiary was not the natural object of the testator's bounty. Ross & Reed, *supra*, at §2:10. Early American cases attempted to determine the scope of influence that was "undue" and tended to define such influence by its absence (i.e., as requiring more than mere advice or persuasion). *Id.*

Undue influence currently may be proven by one of two methods:

- a showing of (1) susceptibility to undue influence, (2) opportunity to exert such influence, (3) a disposition to influence unduly to procure an improper favor, and (4) an unnatural result that is the effect of the supposed influence; or
- a showing of a confidential relationship and suspicious circumstances.

Courts frequently wrestle with what makes a disposition "unnatural." "[W]hat one frequently finds in the case law is a surprisingly straightforward and objective response to the question of what constitutes a 'natural' disposition: a 'natural' disposition is one which provides for a testator's heirs at law." Madoff, *supra*, at 590.

The presence of a confidential relationship plus "suspicious circumstances" gives rise to a *presumption* of undue influence. McGovern & Kurtz, *supra*, §7.3 at 306-308. The Restatement (Third) of Property (Wills and Other Donative Transfers) §8.3, cmt. g, also uses the term "suspicious circumstances" as an element raising the presumption. The Restatement mentions participation in procurement of a will as one of several examples of suspicious circumstances. See also Allen v. Gore, 387 So. 2d 535 (Fla. Dist. Ct. App. 1980) (holding that "the mere existence of a confidential relationship between decedent and beneficiary does not raise a presumption of undue influence unless accompanied by the element of active procurement").

The Florida Supreme Court has specified several factors for courts to consider in determinations of "active procurement," including:

> (a) the presence of the beneficiary at the execution of the will; (b) presence of the beneficiary on those occasions when the testator expressed a desire to make a will; (c) recommendation by the beneficiary of an attorney to draw the will; (d) knowledge of the contents of the will by the beneficiary prior to execution; (e) giving of instructions on preparation of the will by the beneficiary to the attorney drawing the will; (f) securing of witnesses to the will by the beneficiary; and (g) safekeeping of the will by the beneficiary subsequent to execution.

Newman v. Brecher, 887 So. 2d 384, 386 (Fla. Dist. Ct. App. 2004) (finding no undue influence because evidence of a niece transporting her aunt to the appointment with the attorney and remaining in the waiting room was not sufficient evidence of active procurement).
Classic confidential relationships are doctor-patient, pastor-parishioner, guardian-ward, priest-penitent, nurse-companion, and attorney-client. A relationship between family members is not necessarily a confidential relationship. "[T]he undue influence doctrine only categorizes family relationships as 'confidential' in very limited circumstances." Madoff, supra, at 584. Rather, a confidential relationship refers to a relationship in which one party dominates the other or in which one party depends on the other, such as for business decisionmaking. A confidential relationship "is generally defined as a relationship of trust and reliance whereby the testator reasonably believed that the confidant was acting in the testator's best interest." Id. at 583.

Florida is among the states that require that the undue influence involve coercion or destruction of the testator's free agency. Ross & Reed, *supra*, §7:3. See, e.g., Derovanesian v. Derovanesian, 857 So. 2d 240 (Fla. Dist. Ct. App. 2003), *review denied* (Fla. Jan. 26, 2004) (holding that testator's will and trust were not the products of undue influence, despite daughter's role in securing scrivener, her presence at will execution, and her knowledge of the contents, because testator was of an independent mind, had previously expressed the desire to leave her estate to her daughter, and the daughter was responding to the wishes of the testator, with whom she was living at time of testator's death).

According to Florida law, influence stemming from mere affection or acts of kindness does not rise to undue influence within the meaning of the rule. See, e.g., Carter v. Carter, 526 So. 2d 141 (Fla. Dist. Ct. App. 1988) (holding that sons' actions helping their mother change her will to restore one son's original share were "acts of dutiful sons" toward an aged mother rather than undue influence); Marston v. Churchill, 187 So. 762 (Fla. 1939) (affirming validity of will that left testatrix's property to young unmarried man who lived with her because of his kindness and consideration for her welfare).

Undue influence may also lead to invalidation of *inter vivos transfers*. For example, in In re Estate of Stetzko, 714 So. 2d 1087 (Fla. Dist. Ct. App. 1998), the decedent's siblings challenged certain inter vivos transfers by the testator to his longtime female caregiver, including a joint bank account, an annuity, transfer of his house, etc., all made within a few weeks of testator's death. The appellate court affirmed the trial court finding of a lack of undue influence, in light of evidence that the testator was healthy and handling his own affairs until just shortly before he died, that these transfers were motivated by his desire to repay the caregiver for her care of him and his wife while they were suffering from cancer, and that testator's siblings were not disinherited but rather received considerable assets from the probate estate and inter vivos transfers (totaling $110,316.).

See McGovern & Kurtz, *supra*, §7.3 at 302-303. See generally Madoff, *supra* (providing critique of traditional undue influence doctrine).

V. Right to Jury Trial

At common law, probate matters were decided by ecclesiastic courts and, hence, not subject to jury trials. In Florida, the right to a jury trial in will contest cases is not authorized either by statute or the state constitution. Eclavea & Lease, Probate and Contest of Testamentary Instruments, 18 Fla. Jur. 2d Decedents' Property §258. Therefore, such issues as undue influence and testamentary capacity that were traditionally decided by judges continue to be resolved by judges. See also Lavey v. Doig, 6 So. 259 (Fla. 1889) (affirming the denial of a right to jury trial in a will contest, explaining that the effect of the third section of the Bill of Rights of the 1868 Florida Constitution was not to extend the right to jury trial to any case not previously accorded that right).

However, a probate court may, in its discretion, submit an issue in a will contest to an advisory jury whose verdict the court may accept or reject. See, e.g., In re Fanelli's

Estate, 336 So. 2d 631 (Fla. Dist. Ct. App. 1976) (holding that any error in submitting the case to a jury was harmless where the verdict was not contrary to the manifest weight of the evidence and there was no showing that the conclusion would have been otherwise if cause had been tried by judge).

FLORIDA RULES OF CIVIL PROCEDURE

Rule 1.430. Right to jury trial

(a) *Right Preserved.* The right of trial by jury as declared by the Constitution or by statute shall be preserved to the parties inviolate.

(b) *Demand.* Any party may demand a trial by jury of any issue triable of right by a jury by serving upon the other party a demand therefor in writing at any time after commencement of the action and not later than 10 days after the service of the last pleading directed to such issue. The demand may be indorsed upon a pleading of the party.

(c) *Specification of Issues.* In the demand a party may specify the issues that the party wishes so tried; otherwise, the party is deemed to demand trial by jury for all issues so triable. If a party has demanded trial by jury for only some of the issues, any other party may serve a demand for trial by jury of any other or all of the issues triable by jury 10 days after service of the demand or such lesser time as the court may order.

(d) *Waiver.* A party who fails to serve a demand as required by this rule waives trial by jury. If waived, a jury trial may not be granted without the consent of the parties, but the court may allow an amendment in the proceedings to demand a trial by jury or order a trial by jury on its own motion. A demand for trial by jury may not be withdrawn without the consent of the parties.

(Amended July 26, 1972, effective January 1, 1973 (265 So.2d 21); July 16, 1992, effective January 1, 1993 (604 So.2d 1110).)

V
Will Doctrines, Extrinsic Evidence, and Mistake

I. Introduction

Will provisions must be interpreted and construed before the terms can be put into effect. The primary concern in interpreting a will is the determination of the testator's intent. Because of the difficulty of discovering the *unexpressed* intent of the testator, courts tend to emphasize reliance on the language used by the testator in the will.

If the language in the will is not conclusive, courts may resort to an examination of the surrounding circumstances and extrinsic evidence. However, if these efforts in turn are not successful, then courts conclude the process of interpretation of the instrument and employ instead various legal presumptions or rules of construction.

Interpretation is the process of determining the testator's intent, usually by reliance on the language of the will and/or extrinsic evidence.

When a court's attempt at interpretation fails (i.e., when the testator's intent cannot be determined), courts may resort to *construction*. *Construction* is the process of assigning a meaning to a testamentary provision when the testator's intent cannot be ascertained.

Some common rules of construction include: every expression in a will should be given effect if possible, preference should be given to an interpretation of a will that will avoid intestacy, all parts of an instrument should be construed as a whole, and words of a will are to be given their ordinary meaning unless a different intention can be ascertained.

In addition, a cardinal rule is that courts will not construe a will or admit extrinsic evidence if the terms of the will are clear and unambiguous. See In re Estate of Budny, 815 So. 2d 781, 782 (Fla. Dist. Ct. App. 2002) (refusing to admit evidence of the testator's intention to adeem a devise of real property, reasoning that extrinsic evidence may be admitted only when the testator's intent "is obscured by a discernible ambiguity or uncertainty arising from the language used").

II. Will Doctrines

A. Integration

Generally, when a testator executes a will, the document consists of several pages. The testamentary scheme might even include several different documents (e.g., wills, codicils, and other testamentary instruments such as trusts). Sometimes, it is difficult for courts to ascertain which instruments were intended to be part of the will. *Integration* involves the process of establishing which writings were intended by the testator to be part of his or her will.

Integration has two elements. First, the doctrine requires that the testator *intended* the separate writings to be part of the will. Second, the separate writings must have been *present at the time of execution* of the will.

Integration is facilitated by physical connection or internal coherence. Although the pages of a will are commonly fastened together at the time of the execution ceremony, this physical connection is not a requirement. According to the Restatement (Third) of Property (Wills & Don. Trans.) §3.5 (1999),

> [p]hysical connection does, however, support an inference that the physically-connected pages or other writings were present at the time of execution and that they were intended to be part of the will.

Alternatively, evidence of the will's internal coherence might support the integration doctrine. "Internal coherence is present if the pages or other writings appear to be part of a single document." *Id.* An inference might arise if the sentences spill over from one page to another (rather than each page having self-contained paragraphs), or the testator and witnesses initial each page, or each page is numbered in reference to the whole (i.e., "one of ten pages," "two of ten pages," etc.), or the will contains an attestation clause that refers to the number of pages in the entire document.

Occasional courts have suggested that physical connection or internal coherence is essential to the integration doctrine. However, the Restatement (Third) of Property disagrees and points out instead that "the actual decisions tend strongly to support the view that any evidence will suffice" provided that the two elements (above) are satisfied. *Id.*

Extrinsic evidence is admissible to prove the testator's intent to integrate two or more writings into a single will. *Id.*, at §3.5, cmt. d.

Integration problems frequently arise with holographic wills because such wills often are written informally. Cases are divided as to whether a signature on an envelope containing sheets of papers with will provisions can be integrated into a valid will. *Id.*, at §3.5. The Restatement adopts the "better view" that integration should be permitted in such cases. *Id.*

B. Incorporation by Reference

Incorporation by reference occurs when a testamentary instrument refers to a separate and distinct writing in an effort to give the latter testamentary significance. For example, by a will dated June 10, 2007, Testator (T) leaves $10,000 to "the person whose name I shall write in a letter dated this date and enclosed in an envelope with this will. I also leave the residue of my estate to my wife Wilma." T dies survived by Wilma but no issue or parents. A letter is found at T's death in his safe, physically attached to the will and dated June 10, 2007, with the name of T's niece Nancy. If T's will successfully incorporates the letter by reference, then Nancy will take the $10,000 and Wilma will take the residue. On the other hand, if T's attempted incorporation by reference fails, then the $10,000 gift to Nancy fails and Wilma takes the entire estate.

Language in the will must manifest the intent to incorporate the extrinsic document by reference. The will must be a valid testamentary instrument for the doctrine of incorporation by reference to apply.

Note that only writings may be incorporated, not physical objects. See Fla. Stat. §732.512(1) ("[a] *writing* in existence when a will is executed may be incorporated by reference") (emphasis added).

Pursuant to the incorporation by reference doctrine, the extrinsic writing generally has not been executed with the requisite testamentary formalities and need not be testamentary in character. Thus, the writing sought to be incorporated does not have to be signed or witnessed as required for a will.

Incorporation by reference has several requirements:

- the testator must have intended to incorporate the extrinsic writing into the will;
- the extrinsic writing must be in existence when the testator executed the will; and
- the will must sufficiently describe the extrinsic writing so that it is identified and conforms to the description in the will.

The second requirement above is sometimes referred to as "*the existing document rule.*" Thus, a testator generally cannot incorporate by reference a *future* document. Some courts require that the will refer to the extrinsic document as being an existing document when the will was executed, although UPC §2-510 does not hold to this strict requirement. McGovern & Kurtz, *supra*, §6.2 at 273. See also Restatement (Third) of Property, *supra*, at §3.6 (explaining that this additional requirement was imposed at common law but, because it is "intent-defeating," the Restatement does not adopt it as a requirement).

Incorporation by reference is distinguishable from integration. Integration occurs when the testator intends separate writings to be part of one testamentary instrument. However, under the integration doctrine, the will does not specifically refer to any extraneous documents or writings (as in incorporation by reference).

Florida Statutes §732.512 codifies the common law doctrine of incorporation by reference. Florida Statutes §732.512(1) is the same as UPC §2-510.

For applications of the Florida statute, see Lewis v. SunTrust Bank, 698 So.2d1276 (Fla. Dist. Ct. App. 1997) (holding that the terms of an inter vivos trust were not incorporated by reference into decedent's will because the will made no explicit reference to the trust, therefore a will provision appointing a trustee of the trust failed to supersede or revoke the terms of the trust); In re Estate of McGahee, 550 So. 2d 83 (Fla. Dist. Ct. App. 1989) (holding that the testator, by language used in his will, manifested an intent to incorporate by reference an attached holographic document disinheriting some of his children and that the will sufficiently described that attached holographic writing to permit its identification with the requisite certainty by virtue of his notation "attached [date of holograph]" and "reconfirmed"); Swan v. Florida Nat'l Bank of Miami, 445 So. 2d 622 (Fla. Dist. Ct. App. 1984) (holding that husband's will did not incorporate wife's inter vivos trust because the latter did not exist when he executed his will that provided that his estate should pass by her *testamentary* trust if she predeceased him).

Florida also adopted a related UPC provision (UPC §2-513) which was intended to relax execution formalities, especially for people who change their will frequently and informally by making lists of tangible personal property. See Fla. Stat. §732.515. Specifically, UPC §2-513 allows *a list* of tangible personal property to be incorporated by reference even if the list was prepared *after* the will was executed. That is, under limited circumstances, UPC §2-513 permits a separate writing to dispose of certain property even if the writing does not satisfy the traditional formulation of the incorporation by reference doctrine (because the writing came into existence after the execution of the will) or the doctrine of events of independent significance (because the extrinsic writing may not have independent significance). Lawrence H. Averill, Uniform Probate Code in a Nutshell 166 (3d ed. 1993). For the separate writing to be effective under the UPC, the writing must be signed by the testator, the items and devisees must be described sufficiently, the items must be personal property (and must not otherwise be disposed of by the testator's will), and there must be a reference to this writing in a valid will of the testator.

UPC Commentary bars use of the rule to transmit writings of indebtedness, documents of title, securities, and property used in trade or business. Unsigned holographic writings do not qualify under the provision. Averill, *supra*, at 167. The Florida statute incorporates some language from the UPC Commentary ("other than property used in trade or business") as an explicit exception to the Florida rule.

To illustrate the application of this provision, a testator executes a will on September 2, 2007, that leaves pieces of jewelry to "each of four friends whose name I will write on a piece of paper and enclose with this will. I leave the residue of my estate to my brother Bob." A piece of paper is found among the testator's papers at his death that is dated December 10, 2007. It is signed and lists the names of four of the testator's friends. How will the estate be distributed? Note that the list cannot be incorporated by reference into the will because the list was not in existence at the time that the will was executed. The list can be given effect to dispose of the jewelry, however, pursuant to Florida Statutes §732.515, because the will refers to the list, the list was signed by the testator, and the list described the items with reasonable certainty. Although the list has no significance apart from its effect on the will (because it exists only to dispose of property at the testator's death), the statute does not require independent significance.

The doctrine of incorporation by reference has sometimes been used to validate a "pour-over" to a previously established inter vivos trust. A "pour-over" provision is a will provision that specifies that part of the decedent's estate should go to an existing inter vivos trust. Some early courts invalidated a "pour-over" provision if the inter vivos trust agreement contained a reservation of the power to amend the trust – based on the reasoning that the will could not incorporate an amended trust by reference because the latter trust did not satisfy the existing document rule (i.e., it was not in existence when the will was executed). The Uniform Testamentary Addition to Trusts Act (UTATA), promulgated by NCCUSL in 1960 (and incorporated into the UPC of 1969 as UPC §2-511) clarified the law by permitting pour-over provisions in wills. Similar legislation has been enacted in nearly all of the states including Florida. See Fla. Stat. §732.513. On pour-over provisions, see Chapter IX, 3D *infra.*

§732.512. Incorporation by reference: requirements

(1) A writing in existence when a will is executed may be incorporated by reference if the language of the will manifests this intent and describes the writing sufficiently to permit its identification.

...

(Laws 1974, ch. 74-106, §1; Laws 1975, ch. 75-220, §27.)

§732. 515. Lists to dispose of property: requirements

A written statement or list referred to in the decedent's will shall dispose of items of tangible personal property, other than property used in trade or business, not otherwise specifically disposed of by the will. To be admissible under this section as evidence of the intended disposition, the writing must be signed by the testator and must describe the items and the devisees with reasonable certainty. The writing may be prepared before or after the execution of the will. It may be altered by the testator after its preparation. It may be a writing that has no significance apart from its effect upon the dispositions made by the will. If more than one otherwise effective writing exists, then, to the extent of any conflict among the writings, the provisions of the most recent writing revoke the inconsistent provisions of each prior writing.

(Laws 1974, ch. 74-106, §1; Laws 1975, ch. 75-220, §29. Amended by Laws 2001, ch. 2001-226, §48, effective January 1, 2002.)

§732.513. Pour-overs: validity

(1) A valid devise may be made to the trustee of a trust that is evidenced by a written instrument in existence at the time of making the will, or by a written instrument subscribed concurrently with making of the will, if the written instrument is identified in the will.

(2) The devise shall not be invalid for any or all of the following reasons:

(a) Because the trust is amendable or revocable, or both, by any person.

(b) Because the trust has been amended or revoked in part after execution of the will or a codicil to it.

(c) Because the trust instrument or any amendment to it was not executed in the manner required for wills.

(d) Because the only res of the trust is the possible expectancy of receiving, as a named beneficiary, a devise under a will or death benefits as described in §733.808, and even though the testator or other person has reserved any or all rights of ownership in the death benefit policy, contract, or plan, including the right to change the beneficiary.

(e) Because of any of the provisions of §689.075.

(3) The devise shall dispose of property under the terms of the instrument that created the trust as previously or subsequently amended.

(4) An entire revocation of the trust by an instrument in writing before the testator's death shall invalidate the devise or bequest.

(5) Unless the will provides otherwise, the property devised shall not be held under a testamentary trust of the testator but shall become a part of the principal of the trust to which it is devised.

(Laws 1974, ch. 74-106, §1; Laws 1975, ch. 75-74, §3; Laws 1975, ch. 75-220, §28; Laws 1988, ch. 88-340, §2. Amended by Laws 2001, ch. 2001-226, §46, effective January 1, 2002.

C. Republication by Codicil

A codicil is a document that amends or modifies a will. Sometimes, a codicil may do no more than appoint an executor or revoke an earlier will. That is, to be valid, a codicil does not have to make testamentary gifts. See, e.g., Fla. Stat. §731.201(36) (providing that a will or codicil is a valid testamentary instrument if it "merely appoints a personal representative or revokes or revises another will").

In order for a codicil to be valid, it must meet the same formal requirements as a will. See *id.* (will or codicil must be "executed by a person in the manner prescribed by this code").

When a testator executes a codicil to modify the provisions of will in whole or in part, a court will attempt to construe the will and codicil together. See, e.g., In re Campbell's Estate, 288 So. 2d 528, 530 (Fla. Dist. Ct. App. 1974) (finding that the provision in the codicil that conflicted with the will should prevail because the codicil provisions were "the last expression of the testator's intention").

The revocation of a will revokes all codicils (Fla. Stat. §732.509), although the revocation of a codicil does not necessarily revoke all prior wills.

A codicil that refers to an earlier will "republishes" it. McGovern & Kurtz, *supra*, §6.2 at 272. See also Restatement (Third) of Property, *supra*, at §3.6, cmt. d. That is, the will is considered to be executed at the later date of the codicil.

The origins of the doctrine of republication by codicil are traced to the common law rule that a will could not dispose of land acquired after the will was executed. At common law, a will could bequeath personal property—but not real property—that was acquired after the execution of the will. Only after the Wills Act of 1837 did English law permit a will to operate on real property that was acquired after the execution of the will. Restatement (Third) of Property, *supra*, at §3.4. The doctrine of republication by codicil developed to overcome this earlier rule.

Republication by codicil is a rule of construction designed to carry out the testator's probable intention. The doctrine will not be applied if its application would be contrary to that intent. See, e.g., In re Freedman's Estate 226 So.2d 423 (Fla. Dist. Ct. App. 1969) (holding that a codicil did not republish a will so as to enable a nonmarital child to qualify as a pretermitted heir because the original will specifically stated that the testator was not making any testamentary provision for that child). But cf. Azcunce v. Estate of Azcunce, 586 So. 2d 1216 (Fla. Dist. Ct. App. 1991) (holding that the second codicil republished the testator's original will so as to preclude a child (who was living at the time of the second codicil) as a pretermitted heir)).

The doctrine has been codified in Florida. See Fla. Stat. §§732.5105, 732.511. According to Florida Statutes §732.511, a revoked will or an

yes in Florida

invalid will can be republished (validated) by its reexecution or the execution of a codicil that republishes it (provided that the codicil is executed with the requisite statutory formalities).

§731.201. "Will" and "codicil": definitions

Subject to additional definitions in subsequent chapters that are applicable to specific chapters or parts, and unless the context otherwise requires, in this code, in §409.9101, and in chapters 737, 738, 739, and 744, the term:

...

(36) "Will" means an instrument, including a codicil, executed by a person in the manner prescribed by this code, which disposes of the person's property on or after his or her death and includes an instrument which merely appoints a personal representative or revokes or revises another will.

(Laws 1974, ch. 74-106, §1; Laws 1975, c. 75-220, §4; Laws 1977, ch. 77-174, §1; Laws 1985, c. 85-79, §2; Laws 1987, ch. 87-226, §66; Laws 1988, ch. 88-340, §1; Laws 1993, ch. 93-257, §7. Amended by Laws 1995, ch. 95- 401, §6, effective July 1, 1995; Laws 1997, ch. 97-102, §949, effective July 1, 1997; Laws 1998, ch. 98-421, §52, effective July 1, 1998; Laws 2001, ch. 2001-226, §11, effective January 1, 2002; Laws 2002, ch. 2002-1, §106, effective May 21, 2002; Laws 2003, ch. 2003-154, §2, effective June 12, 2003; Laws 2005, ch. 2005-108, §2, effective July 1, 2005.)

§732. 509. Revocation of a will revokes all codicils

Revocation of a will revokes all codicils to that will..

(Laws. 1974, ch. 74-106, §1; Laws. 1975, ch. 75-220, §26.)

§732. 5105. Republication by codicil doctrine: effect on will

The execution of a codicil referring to a previous will has the effect of republishing the will as modified by the codicil.

(Laws 1974, ch. 74-106, §1; Laws 1975, ch. 75-220, §26.)

§732. 511. Republication by a will by its re-execution

If a will has been revoked or if it is invalid for any other reason, it may be republished and made valid by its reexecution or the execution of a codicil republishing it with the formalities required by this law for the execution of wills.

(Laws 1974, ch. 74-106, §1; Laws 1975, ch. 75-220, §26.)

D. Acts of Independent Significance

Reference to events of independent significance allows the testator to make testamentary dispositions based on the occurrence or nonoccurrence of specified acts or facts. For example, Testator executes a will that contains a bequest of $10,000 "to the person who is my housekeeper at my death."

The doctrine permits a court to admit certain extrinsic evidence (evidence outside the will) in order to determine certain beneficiaries and certain property that pass under the testator's will. "A statement of its principle is that if a fact, be it an act or event, has significance other than to pass property at death, this significance entitles that fact to control and to determine the disposition of the property." Averill, *supra*, at 165.

Under the doctrine of incorporation by reference (discussed *supra*), a testator cannot affect his will by a *future* writing because only existing documents may be incorporated by reference into a will. However, by the doctrine of acts of independent significance, the testator may make a valid testamentary disposition based on future acts (e.g., future acts of a third person or the testator). For the doctrine to apply, these acts must have a significance distinct from their effect on the will (i.e., independent significance).

The doctrine of acts of independent significance is usually not codified. Averill, *supra*, at 165. However, following promulgation of the UPC, many jurisdictions enacted statutes addressing the doctrine. Florida Statutes §732.512 codifies the doctrine and is based on UPC §2-512. However, the Florida statute includes two different UPC statutes—one on incorporation by reference (UPC §2-510, codified as Fla. Stat. §732.512(a)) and one on events of independent significance (UPC §2-511, codified as Fla. Stat. §732.512(b)).

The UPC made a significant change in prior law by permitting the referenced act to occur *before or after the execution of the will* or *before or after the testator's death* (emphasis added) (UPC §2-512). See also Restatement (Third) of Property, *supra*, at §3.7.

§732.512. Acts of Independent Significance: requirements

...

(2) A will may dispose of property by reference to acts and events which have significance apart from their effect upon the dispositions made by the will,

whether they occur before or after the execution of the will or before or after the testator's death. The execution or revocation of a will or trust by another person is such an event.

(Laws 1974, ch. 74-106, §1; Laws 1975, ch. 75-220, §27.)

III. Extrinsic Evidence and Mistake

A central issue in the determination of the testator's intent is the admissibility of extrinsic evidence. Several bases exist for excluding evidence of the testator's intent that is not in writing, signed, and attested. McGovern & Kurtz, *supra*, §6.1 at 259. The Parol Evidence Rule provides that oral evidence shall not be admitted to vary the written terms of an agreement, such as a contract, a deed, or a will. Further, the Statute of Frauds requires transfers of real property to be in writing. And, wills legislation in all jurisdictions requires that testamentary instruments must comport with various statutory requirements. Unlike disputes involving contracts, when disputes arise regarding wills, one of the parties (i.e., the testator) is no longer alive to present evidence of intent. For this reason, as a general rule, courts are reluctant to admit extrinsic evidence, and specifically testimony regarding oral declarations of the testator. However, in limited circumstances, courts will admit extrinsic evidence of the testator's intent (discussed *infra*). See, e.g., In re Estate of Riggs, 643 So.2d 1132 (Fla. Dist. Ct. App. 1994) (holding that extrinsic, including parol, evidence should be considered *only* if the language used in the will is ambiguous and concluding that it was error to admit extrinsic evidence because the term "my entire estate" created no ambiguity).

Many states have "dead person's statutes" that bar testimony regarding oral communications between a witness and a person who is now deceased. The rationale of the bar is to protect decedents and their estates against false claims because the decedent is unavailable to testify. Florida law formerly had such a statute (Fla. Stat. §90.602) disqualifying a witness from testifying if (1) the witness was interested in the action; (2) the witness was being examined about an oral communication with a person now deceased or mentally incompetent; and (3) the testimony was offered against the estate of the decedent or the guardian of a mentally incompetent person.

The legislature repealed that statute effective June 30, 2005, and thereby adopted the majority view and the view of the federal courts (i.e., the Federal Rules of Evidence have no dead person's statute). Charles W. Ehrhardt, Hearsay: Statements of Personal or Family History, 1 Fla. Prac., Evidence §804.6 (2006). The primary motivation for the repeal was the concern that the statute often led to harsh results by making it impossible for persons to prove bona fide claims. "The statute's ultimate effect was to defeat legitimate claims against the decedent's estate instead of protecting it against false claims." Charles W. Ehrhardt, Witnesses: General Rule of Competency, 1 Fla. Prac., Evidence §602.2 (2006).

In place of the deadman's statute, the Florida legislature enacted a new hearsay exception (Fla. Stat. §90.804(2)). The exception was drafted as a method of protecting the estates of persons (particularly the elderly) against unscrupulous persons who would later claim that the decedent had made a binding oral contract with the witness prior to death "and that the estate would have no way to rebut the evidence if it was admitted." Ehrhardt, *supra*, at §602.2. The amendment provides:

> an exception for hearsay statements of a deceased or ill declarant regarding the same subject matter as a hearsay statements of the declarant which have been offered and admitted against her estate. The intent of the amendment was to provide the estate with a method of rebutting hearsay statements of a decedent when similar statements had been admitted against her estate.

Id., at §804.6. See also Fla. Stat. §90.804(2)(e). In weighing the testimony, the judge or jury can consider whether the witness has a pecuniary interest in the outcome.

Testators sometimes execute wills under a mistaken belief. Mistakes in wills take several forms: (1) mistake in omission, (2) mistake in execution, (3) mistake in misdescription, and (4) mistake in the inducement.

A *mistake in omission* results when the testator intends to make a particular gift or a gift to a particular beneficiary but fails to do so. According to the traditional rule, courts will not remedy a mistake in omission. In such situations, courts probate the will as written, refusing to correct the testator's mistake. Courts justify their reluctance to add omitted provisions either by reference to the Parol Evidence Rule (i.e., the addition of words would violate the Parol Evidence Rule) or the Statute of Wills (permitting an unnamed beneficiary to take, or unnamed property to pass, would permit a testamentary gift that violates the Statute of Wills). The primary concern here is with the possibility of fraud.

A *mistake in execution* occurs when the testator is mistaken about the particular instrument being executed. Mistakes in execution frequently arise when spouses execute mutual and reciprocal wills. Thus, a husband mistakenly executes a wife's will, and the wife mistakenly executes the husband's will. Traditionally, courts refuse to remedy a mistake in execution, finding that the requisite testamentary intent was lacking. (Recall that testamentary intent requires that the testator intend *this* instrument to operate as his or her will.) Courts explain that the husband did not intend for his wife's will to operate as his will; nor did the wife intend for her husband's will to operate as her will. See, e.g., In re Pavlinko's Estate, 148 A.2d 528 (Pa. 1959) (refusing to admit the will of the wife as the will of the husband).

However, courts have become more willing to correct such mistakes. For example, in In re Snide, 418 N.E.2d 656 (N.Y. 1981), a husband and wife mistakenly executed each other's will. The husband died first without realizing his mistake. The widow then introduced to probate the will that the husband had executed. The Surrogate's Court decreed that the husband's will could be reformed to substitute the husband's name wherever the wife's name appeared. The Appellate Division reversed, refusing to admit the document based on the traditional rule. The New York Court of Appeals reversed, granting relief through reformation, reasoning that the will was executed with the requisite formalities, the wills of husband and wife were identical, and the denial of relief would frustrate the testator's intent.

Mistakes in misdescription have several variations. Sometimes, the will reveals a mistake regarding a beneficiary's name. For example, a testatrix left property to "the French Orphans of France." No such society existed. Instead, the Fraternité Franco-Américaine, claiming the property as the successor to the "French War Orphans Relief," attempted to show that the decedent had dealt with its organization in the past. In response, the court corrected the provision to permit the charity to take. Estate of Regnier, 11 P.2d 639 (Cal. 1932). The traditional rule in such cases was termed "the plain meaning rule." That is, if the meaning was clearly expressed in the document, courts refused to admit extrinsic evidence to vary the description in the will (and permitted the property to pass intestate if the institution could not be identified).

In a famous case, an English court refused to remedy a mistake in misdescription in a bequest to a children's welfare organization. A Scottish testator mistakenly bequeathed a legacy to the "National Society for the Prevention of Cruelty to Children" (an organization headquartered in London with which he was unfamiliar) when he actually intended to bequeath the legacy to a different organization ("the Scottish National Society for the Prevention of Cruelty to Children") that was headquartered in Edinburgh where the testator lived. Scottish Nat'l Soc'y for the Prevention of Cruelty to Children, 111 L.T.R. 869 (1915).

The distinction between latent and patent ambiguity becomes especially relevant in misdescription cases. A *latent ambiguity* is an ambiguity that emerges in attempting to apply the will provision(s) to a particular person or property. At that point, it becomes apparent that no person or property conforms to the misdescription in the will. For example, a testatrix bequeathed her residuary estate to "my nephew Raymond and his wife Mabel." At the time the will was executed, the testator's nephew Raymond was married to Evelyn and divorced from his former wife Mabel. The latent ambiguity emerged when it became apparent that "Mabel" was not "Raymond's wife." Breckheimer v. Kraft, 273 N.E.2d 468 (Ill. App. Ct. 1971) (holding that parol evidence was admissible to explain the latent ambiguity).

A *patent ambiguity* is an ambiguity that is apparent on the face of the will. An example would be the same devise given to two different people. "I give Blackacre to A; I give Blackacre to B."

Under the traditional rule, courts admit extrinsic evidence to resolve a latent ambiguity but not a patent ambiguity. See, e.g., Perkins v. O'Donald, 82 So. 401 (Fla. 1919). For a recent case adhering to this doctrine, see Harbie v. Falk, 907 So. 2d 566 (Fla. Dist. Ct. App. 2005). In *Harbie*, a testator executed a will bequeathing one-half of his residuary estate to be distributed "among my children." The will also stated that "I have only one child at the time of this will, Rita Harbie." However, the will omitted to provide for an adult son from a previous marriage. When the son claimed a share of the estate, the court held that extrinsic evidence from the drafter of the will was admissible to resolve the "latent ambiguity" concerning whether the adult son was a beneficiary. The court reasoned that the existence of the second son, when the will claimed that there was only one child, created a latent ambiguity. But cf. Campbell v. Campbell, 489 So. 2d 774, 778 (Fla. Dist. Ct. App. 1986) (criticizing the "meaningless" distinction between latent and patent ambiguity).

Many misdescription cases reveal the traditional judicial reliance on the distinction between latent versus patent ambiguities. Thus, for example in Patch v. White, 117 U.S. 210 (1886), the testator devised to his brother real property that was described as: "Lot #6 in Square 403." In fact, the testator owned, and intended to devise, Lot #3 in Square 406. Extrinsic evidence revealed a latent ambiguity: a conflict between the description contained in the will and the subject matter of the gift. Adhering to the rule that if a latent ambiguity is only disclosed by extrinsic evidence, it may be removed by extrinsic evidence, the court held that extrinsic evidence was admissible to reveal the parcel that the testator actually owned. The court added that since the instrument revealed the testator's intention to dispose of all his property, the clause would be reformed.

As explained above, the traditional rule holds that only when the language of a will is ambiguous or uncertain can courts resort to extrinsic evidence in order to ascertain the intention of the testator. By the beginning of the 1980s, however, legal scholars announced that appellate courts in California, New Jersey, and New York had decided several cases that "may presage the abandonment of the ancient 'no-reformation' rule" (i.e., the rule that courts would not reform wills on the basis of mistake). John H. Langbein & Lawrence W. Waggoner, Reformation of Wills on the Ground of Mistake: Change of Direction in American Law?, 130 U. Pa. L. Rev. 521, 521 (1982).

A *mistake in the inducement* is a mistake which induces the testator to execute a will. Such a mistake can arise from the testator's incorrect belief about the conduct of, or assets owed to, a beneficiary. The testator makes a will based on that mistaken belief.

Traditionally, courts have been reluctant to remedy mistakes in the inducement of wills. According to the general rule, mistakes in the inducement, "relating as they do to facts outside the will itself, cannot be proved because such mistakes are wholly subjective in nature, and the question of what the testator would have done had he not been mistaken is too conjectural to be undertaken on the basis of extrinsic evidence." Max A. Yageman, Mistake in the Inducement in Wills, 1 Am. Jur. Proof of Facts 2d 323 (2002).

Early cases developed a common law exception to the general rule. According to this exception, some courts grant relief for mistakes in the inducement if: (1) the mistake is on the face of the will, and (2) the alternative disposition is also apparent on the face of the will. Thus, in Gifford v. Dyer, 2 R.I. 99 (R.I. 1852), the testatrix executed a will bequeathing her property to her brother-in-law and two nephews, stemming from her belief that her only son was dead. Her son had left home 10 years before and had not been heard from since. The court held that the appearance of the son did not revoke the will because the will contained no express mention of the testator's mistaken belief and any alternative disposition had she known the truth.

Courts are more willing to remedy fraud in the inducement than mistake in the inducement. In the former, a third party induces the testator to make a will or devise by fraudulently misrepresenting a material fact.

According to the modern trend, courts increasingly are more willing to admit extrinsic evidence, even in cases of patent ambiguity. See, e.g., Matter of Estate of Frietze, 966 P.2d 183 (N.M. Ct. App. 1998) (holding that extrinsic evidence was properly admitted to resolve an ambiguity posed by the testator's devising the same piece of real property, with two different legal descriptions, to two different beneficiaries, although declining to admit extrinsic evidence regarding another parcel where the will was not ambiguous).

On mistakes in the inducement of revocation of a will, see Chapter VI, Section III *infra*.

§90.804 Hearsay exceptions: oral communications with the decedent

(1) Definition of unavailability.– "Unavailability as a witness" means that the declarant:

(a) Is exempted by a ruling of a court on the ground of privilege from testifying concerning the subject matter of the declarant's statement;

(b) Persists in refusing to testify concerning the subject matter of the declarant's statement despite an order of the court to do so;

(c) Has suffered a lack of memory of the subject matter of his or her statement so as to destroy the declarant's effectiveness as a witness during the trial;

(d) Is unable to be present or to testify at the hearing because of death or because of then-existing physical or mental illness or infirmity; or

(e) Is absent from the hearing, and the proponent of a statement has been unable to procure the declarant's attendance or testimony by process or other reasonable means.

However, a declarant is not unavailable as a witness if such exemption, refusal, claim of lack of memory, inability to be present, or absence is due to the procurement or wrongdoing of the party who is the proponent of his or her statement in preventing the witness from attending or testifying.

(2) Hearsay exceptions.–The following are not excluded under s. 90.802, provided that the declarant is unavailable as a witness:

(a) *Former testimony*.--Testimony given as a witness at another hearing of the same or a different proceeding, or in a deposition taken in compliance with law in the course of the same or another proceeding, if the party against whom the testimony is now offered, or, in a civil action or proceeding, a predecessor in interest, had an opportunity and similar motive to develop the testimony by direct, cross, or redirect examination.

(b) *Statement under belief of impending death*.--In a civil or criminal trial, a statement made by a declarant while reasonably believing that his or her death was imminent, concerning the physical cause or instrumentalities of what the declarant believed to be impending death or the circumstances surrounding impending death.

(c) *Statement against interest*.--A statement which, at the time of its making, was so far contrary to the declarant's pecuniary or proprietary interest or tended to subject the declarant to liability or to render invalid a claim by the declarant against another, so that a person in the declarant's position would not have made the statement unless he or she believed it to be true. A statement tending to expose the declarant to criminal liability and offered to exculpate the accused is inadmissible, unless corroborating circumstances show the trustworthiness of the statement.

(d) *Statement of personal or family history*.--A statement concerning the declarant's own birth, adoption, marriage, divorce, parentage, ancestry, or other similar fact of personal or family history, including relationship by blood, adoption, or marriage, even though the declarant had no means of acquiring personal knowledge of the matter stated.

(e) *Statement by deceased or ill declarant similar to one previously admitted*.--In an action or proceeding brought against the personal representative, heir at law, assignee, legatee, devisee, or survivor of a deceased person, or against a trustee of a trust created by a deceased person, or against the assignee, committee, or guardian of a mentally incompetent person, when a declarant is unavailable as provided in paragraph (1)(d), a written or oral statement made regarding the same subject matter as another statement made by the declarant that has previously been offered by an adverse party and admitted in evidence.

(Laws 1976, ch. 76-237, §1. Amended by Laws 1990, ch. 90-139, §3, effective October 1, 1990; Laws 1990, ch. 90-174, §4, effective October 1, 1990; Laws 1995, ch. 95-147, §499, effective July 10, 1995; Laws 2005, ch. 2005-46, §2, effective July 1, 2005.)

VI
REVOCATION OF WILLS

This chapter addresses the revocation of wills. First, it explores the different methods of revocation. Then, it examines the common law doctrine of dependent relative revocation that permits a revocation to be disregarded. Next, it focuses on revival, i.e., the process of reinstating a revoked will. It then turns to the common law presumption regarding the revocation of a will. Finally, it examines limitations on the probate of a lost or destroyed will.

I. Introduction

A testator may revoke his or her will at any time after executing it. The methods of revocation are specified by state statute. The primary methods of revocation are: (1) revocation by operation of law, (2) revocation by physical act, and (3) revocation by subsequent written instrument.

To revoke a will, a testator (1) must have an intent to revoke (called *animus revocandi*), and (2) must comply with the statutory requirements regarding the methods of revocation. If a testator does not have the requisite intent and/or fails to comply with the statutory formalities, the revocation will be ineffective.

The intent to revoke and the actual revocation of the will must be concurrent. See, e.g., In re Estate of Dickson, 590 So. 2d 471, 473 (Fla. Dist. Ct. App. 1991) ("In order to revoke a valid will, there must be a joint operation of act and intention to revoke.") Note that if an attempted revocation is not effective, then the decedent's estate passes according to the will.

Florida Statutes §732.505 and §732.506 specify the requisite methods for revocation. First, a will may be revoked by a subsequent will or codicil that is inconsistent with the prior will or codicil even if the latter testamentary instrument does not *expressly* revoke the former (Fla. Stat. §732.505). Second, a testator may revoke a will by burning, tearing, canceling, obliterating, or otherwise destroying it, provided that the testator does so with the intent to revoke (Fla. Stat. §732.506).

Many jurisdictions recognize partial revocation of a will, following the Statute of Frauds provision that neither the will *nor any part thereof* may be revoked except in the prescribed manner (emphasis added). Atkinson, *supra*, §86 at 444. For example, Florida law (Fla. Stat. §6120) provides: "A will *or any part thereof* is revoked by any of the following [methods] (emphasis added)." See also UPC §2-507.

Many states do not permit partial revocation by physical act (i.e., they permit partial revocation only by subsequent instrument). Atkinson, *supra*, §86 at 444-445. For example, Florida law provides that a partial revocation of a will is not effective unless the statutory formalities required for execution of a will are complied with. Therefore, when a testator fails to observe the statutory formalities for the execution of a will, his or her attempt at partial revocation is invalid. Eclavea & Lease, Partial Revocation, 17 Fla. Jur. 2d Decedents' Property §189.

In Dahley v. Dahley, 866 So.2d 745 (Fla. Dist. Ct. App. 2004), the district court of appeal held that the testator's alterations to his will did not constitute a valid revocation or partial revocation. The decedent attempted to revoke portions of his will by lining through the name of the personal representative, placing the word "delete" over certain paragraphs, and placing his signature with the words, "Please draw up a new will making all changes noted here" on a note in the adjoining margin. The court held that these acts failed to meet the statutory requirements for revocation for the following reasons:

> [T]he father did not burn, tear, cancel, deface, obliterate, or destroy the will for the purpose of revocation. Rather, he apparently attempted to modify some but not all of the terms of his existing will. Additionally, and perhaps more importantly, the father did not sign the altered will at the end of the document, nor did he have any attesting witnesses to the altered document.

Id. at 748.

Similarly, in Taft v. Zack, 830 So. 2d 881 (Fla. Dist. Ct. App. 2002), the appellate court held that the testatrix's partial revocation was ineffective where the decedent had crossed out particular will provisions and had written "void" with her initials ("SZT") on the crossed-out portions. Because the testatrix did not sign the will at the end (or have a proxy do so) and there were no attesting witnesses (as required by (Fla. Stat. §732.502), the court determined that the partial revocation was ineffective and admitted the original will to probate.

When an attempted partial revocation of a will or codicil is found to be invalid, the will or codicil as originally written must be admitted to probate. Also, if a given jurisdiction does not recognize the doctrine of partial revocation, then any attempted partial revocation is ineffective and the will is admitted to probate unchanged.

The policy underlying such a prohibition is a concern with fraud (i.e., the fear that an interested beneficiary, rather than the testator, revoked the will in part).

Florida Statutes §733.109 sets out the procedure for revocation of the probate of a will. On will contests, see Chapter XIV *infra*.

§733.109. Proceeding to revoke probate of a will

(1) A proceeding to revoke the probate of a will shall be brought in the court having jurisdiction over the administration. Any interested person, including a beneficiary under a prior will, unless barred under §733.212 or §733.2123, may commence the proceeding before final discharge of the personal representative.

(2) Pending the determination of any petition for revocation of probate, the personal representative shall proceed with the administration of the estate as if no revocation proceeding had been commenced, except that no distribution may be made to beneficiaries in contravention of the rights of those who, but for the will, would be entitled to the property disposed of.

(3) Revocation of probate of a will shall not affect or impair the title to property purchased in good faith for value from the personal representative prior to an order of revocation.

(Laws 1974, ch. 74-106, §1; Laws 1975, ch. 75-220, §50; Laws 1977, ch. 77-87, §18; Laws 1977, ch. 77-104, §227. Amended by Laws 2001, ch. 2001-226, §84, effective January 1, 2002.)

§732.509. Effect of revocation of will

The revocation of a will revokes all codicils to that will.

(Laws 1974, ch. 74-106, §1; Laws 1975, ch. 75-220, §26.)

II. Methods of Revocation

A. Revocation by Operation of Law

Certain events may trigger a revocation of a will by operation of law. The purpose of statutes providing for revocation by operation of law is to effectuate the presumed intent of the testator. The most common triggering events are: marriage, the birth of issue, and divorce.

The English Wills Act of 1837 (7 Wm. IV & 1 Vict., c. 26, §§xviii, xix) provided that marriage revoked the will of either spouse. Atkinson, *supra*, §85 at 423. By this Wills Act, Parliament changed the former gender-based common law rule that a woman's will was revoked upon marriage (based on the fact that a married woman was under a common law disability preventing her from being able to make a will), but a man's will was not revoked unless he also had after-born children. *Id.* at 422, 424.

Many states today provide, similarly, that marriage has the effect of revoking a prior will. In some states, a marriage (after execution of a will) does not revoke the will if: (1) the will was "in contemplation of" the marriage or (2) the spouse was provided for (in some manner) in the will or (3) the spouse was provided for by nonprobate transfers with the intent that such transfers be in lieu of a testamentary share. Also, of course, a spouse may waive the right to inherit property from the decedent.

Most states revoke a *portion* of a testator's will if the will does not provide a minimal amount to the surviving spouse. In such cases, statutes provide that the surviving spouse receives a forced or elective share of the decedent's estate. For discussion of the forced share, see Chapter II, Section IIB *supra*.

Florida law provides some protection for a spouse and child(ren) who have been omitted from a will (Fla. Stat. §§732.301, 732.302) . See Chapter II, Section IVA and B *supra*. Omitted spouses may elect to take against a will. Although a spouse and/or children may receive an intestate share in some cases, this outcome does not have the effect of revoking the testator's will. The will is still probated and its provisions effectuated insofar as possible.

In some states, a divorce or annulment revokes a will or will provisions for the former spouse. Some states specify broadly the effect of the divorce or annulment (modeled after UPC §2-804). See, e.g., Cal. Prob. Code §6122) (providing that dissolution or annulment serves to revoke any testamentary dispositions to a former spouse, any will provisions conferring a general or special power of appointment on the former spouse, and any will provision nominating the former spouse as executor, trustee, conservator, or guardian).

Other states provide for a more limited effect of the divorce or annulment. See, e.g., Fla. Stat. §732.507(2) (providing that "Any provision of a will executed by a married person that affects the spouse of that person shall become void upon the divorce of that person or upon the dissolution or annulment of the marriage"). Note

that legal separations do not serve to exclude a former spouse from taking under the will because a legal separation does not terminate the marital status of the parties.

When a will provision is revoked by divorce, the property that would have passed to the former spouse passes instead as if the former spouse predeceased the testator. See, e.g., Fla. Stat. §732.507(2) (providing that the will is administered as if the former spouse had predeceased, absent an expression of contrary intent in the will, the dissolution, or divorce judgment).

Sometimes, spouses reconcile after having dissolved their relationship. In some states, remarriage revives those parts of the will formerly revoked by the divorce See, e.g., Cal. Prob. Code §§6122(b), 6122.1(b). According to the Restatement Third of Property (Wills & Other Donative Transfers) section 4.2(c), "A testamentary provision that was revoked by dissolution of the testator's marriage is revived if: (i) the testator remarried the former spouse, reexecuted the will, or executed a codicil indicating an intent to revive the previously revoked provision; or (ii) the dissolution of the marriage is nullified."

However, in Florida, according to case law, a will that is revoked by a divorce remains void despite the parties' subsequent remarriage to each other. Esclavea & Lease, Revocation by Operation of Law, 17 Fla. Jur. 2d Decedents' Property §201 (citing In re Guess' Estate, 213 So. 2d 638 (Fla. Dist. Ct. App. 1968); Bauer v. Reese, 161 So. 2d 678 (Fla. Dist. Ct. App. 1964)).

An interesting issue is whether the revocation-by-dissolution also applies to revoke testamentary bequests to third parties who are related to the former spouse. Note that UPC §2-804 revokes testamentary bequests to the former spouse as well as bequests to a "relative" of the former spouse (and revives testamentary bequests to these persons as well).

§732.507 Revocation by operation of law: marriage, birth, adoption, and divorce

(1) Neither subsequent marriage, birth, nor adoption of lineal descendants shall revoke the prior will of any person, but the pretermitted child or spouse shall inherit as set forth in §732.301and 732.302, regardless of the prior will.

(2) Any provision of a will executed by a married person that affects the spouse of that person shall become void upon the divorce of that person or upon the dissolution or annulment of the marriage. After the dissolution, divorce, or annulment, the will shall be administered and construed as if the former spouse had died at the time of the dissolution, divorce, or annulment of the marriage, unless the will or the dissolution or divorce judgment expressly provides otherwise.

(Laws 1974, ch. 74-106, §1; Laws 1975, ch. 75-220, §24; Laws 1990, ch. 90- 23, §3. Amended by Laws 2001, ch. 2001-226, §45, effective January 1, 2002.)

[Cross-referenced statutes are included below.]

§732.301. Pretermitted spouse: share, exceptions

When a person marries after making a will and the spouse survives the testator, the surviving spouse shall receive a share in the estate of the testator equal in value to that which the surviving spouse would have received if the testator had died intestate, unless:

(1) Provision has been made for, or waived by, the spouse by prenuptial or postnuptial agreement;

(2) The spouse is provided for in the will; or

(3) The will discloses an intention not to make provision for the spouse.

The share of the estate that is assigned to the pretermitted spouse shall be obtained in accordance with §733.805.

(Laws 1974, ch. 74-106, §1; Laws 1975, ch. 75-220, §16; Laws 1977, ch. 77-87, §9.)

§732.302. Pretermitted child: share, exceptions

When a testator omits to provide by will for any of his or her children born or adopted after making the will and the child has not received a part of the testator's property equivalent to a child's part by way of advancement, the child shall receive a share of the estate equal in value to that which the child would have received if the testator had died intestate, unless:

(1) It appears from the will that the omission was intentional; or

(2) The testator had one or more children when the will was executed and devised substantially all the estate to the other parent of the pretermitted child and that other parent survived the testator and is entitled to take under the will.

The share of the estate that is assigned to the pretermitted child shall be obtained in accordance with §733.805.

(Laws 1974, ch. 74-106, §1; Laws 1975, ch. 75-220, §16. Amended by Laws 1997, ch. 97-102, §958, eff.

July 1, 1997; Laws 2001, ch. 2001-226, §36, eff. Jan. 1, 2002.)

B. Revocation by Physical Act

State statutes generally require that the physical act of revocation must be performed with concurrent intent to revoke. Statutes specify the nature of the physical act that is legally sufficient to revoke a will. Many states reflect the influence of the Statute of Frauds that permitted "burning, canceling, tearing, or obliterating." The UPC and some states extend the necessary physical acts by the addition of language permitting "burning, tearing, canceling, obliterating, or *destroying the will*. . . ." (UPC §2-507) (emphasis added).

If the physical act is not legally sufficient, it will not constitute an effective revocation. In such cases, the will or will provision is still effective.

Note that "canceling" implies marking through the words but leaving them legible, such as by drawing lines through the words or writing "VOID" across the face of the will. However, "obliterating" the words renders them illegible.

At common law, any act of cancellation had to touch a *material* part of the will. Atkinson, *supra*, §86 at 439. The modern trend liberalizes this requirement so that any act of burning, tearing, or cancellation is sufficient. According to UPC §2-507(a)(2), "A burning, tearing, or canceling is a 'revocatory act on the will,' whether or not the burn, tear, or cancellation touched any of the words on the will."

Florida courts have wrestled with what legally sufficient acts are necessary for the revocation of a will. In re Estate of Dickson, 590 So.2d 471(Fla. Dist. Ct. App. 1991), the court of appeals determined that words of revocation written on a self-proved will (i.e., the affidavit accompanying the will), together with the obliteration of the notary's seal, were adequate to revoke a will. And, In re Wider's Estate, 62 So. 2d 422 (Fla. 1953), the Florida Supreme Court found that the testator's act of cutting out his signature and the signatures of witnesses was a sufficient act to revoke his will.

Many states (including Florida) permit *proxy revocations.* That is, the revocation does not have to be performed by the testator but rather may be accomplished by a third party, provided that the proxy does so "in the testator's presence and by the testator's direction" (Fla. Stat. §732.506). Proxies, thus, are permitted for revocation as well as for execution of a will (compare Fla. Stat. §732.501(1)(a)(2)).

Several Florida cases have addressed the validity of proxy revocations of wills. See, e.g., In re Bancker's Estate, 232 So. 2d 431 (Fla. Dist. Ct. App. 1970) (holding that destruction of will by flushing pieces of it down the toilet was ineffective act of revocation because testator was in another room and did not see the act); In re Estate of Gross, 144 So. 2d 861 (Fla. Dist. Ct. App. 1962) (holding that burning of will by proxy when testator was in a different city was ineffective act of revocation even though proxy was acting at testator's instructions). In Florida, the requirement that the proxy revocation be "in the presence" of the testator was added by statutory amendment in 1933. *Bancker's Estate*, 232 So. 2d at 432 (discussing history).

For a fascinating recent case involving an attempted will revocation by a proxy, see In re Estate of Boote, 198 S.W.3d 699 (Tenn. Ct. App. 2005) (holding that attorney's subsequent revocation of the testator's third codicil by shredding it outside the presence of the testator did not validly revoke it despite testator's explicit instruction to "Just tear the damn thing up" as he left the attorney's office weeks earlier).

§732.505. Revocation by subsequent instrument

A will or codicil, or any part of either, is revoked:

(1) By a subsequent inconsistent will or codicil, even though the subsequent inconsistent will or codicil does not expressly revoke all previous wills or codicils, but the revocation extends only so far as the inconsistency.

(2) By a subsequent will, codicil, or other writing executed with the same formalities required for the execution of wills declaring the revocation.

(Laws 1974, ch. 74-106, §1; Laws 1975, ch. 75-220, §23; Laws 1977, ch. 77-87, §13; Laws 1979, ch. 79-400, §269. Amended by Laws 2001, ch. 2001-226, §44, effective January 1, 2002.)

C. Revocation by Subsequent Written Instrument

A subsequent will may revoke a prior will in two ways: (1) expressly or (2) by implication. An express revocation by subsequent instrument may be entire or partial. UPC §2-507(a)(1). An example of an express revocation would be: "I, Jane Smith, do hereby revoke all prior wills and codicils."

A subsequent will also may revoke a prior will by implication, such as by inconsistency. For example, if Testator gave

Blackacre to A in his first will; but his second will gave Blackacre to B; then the devise of Blackacre to A has been revoked by inconsistency.

To constitute an effective revocation, the subsequent written instrument must comply with the statutory formalities for execution of a will. However, the subsequent instrument does not have to be a will or codicil or even be dispositive; it may do nothing more than revoke the prior will. See, e.g., Fla. Stat. §732.505(2) ("permitting revocation by other writing executed with the same formalities required for the executing of wills declaring the revocation").

According to the UPC, if a testator makes a complete disposition of his or her estate in a subsequent will, a presumption applies that the testator intended to revoke the prior will (rather than merely to supplement it) (UPC §2-507(c)) (cited in McGovern & Kurtz, *supra*, §5.1 at 236).

A holographic will may revoke a formally attested will, provided that the jurisdiction recognizes holographic instruments. McGovern & Kurtz, *supra*, §5.1 at 235-236. However, Florida does not recognize holographic wills. Eclavea & Lease, 18 Fla. Jur 2d Decedents' Property §214 (citing Fla. Stat. §732.502(1)(requiring wills to be executed with certain formalities); §732.502(2) (providing that wills of nonresidents that were validly executed elsewhere are valid in Florida—"except holographs")).

The Restatement (Third) of Property permits testators to make a handwritten alteration of a holographic will without re-signing the document. Restatement (Third) of Property, *supra*, at §3.2, cmt. f. The Restatement (Third) of Property also permits testators to make handwritten alterations of a previously executed attested will "if he or she signs the alteration and, if the statute so requires, dates it." *Id.*, cmt. g. The handwritten alteration of the formally attested will, then, is regarded as a holographic codicil.

§732.505. Revocation by subsequent instrument

A will or codicil, or any part of either, is revoked:

(1) By a subsequent inconsistent will or codicil, even though the subsequent inconsistent will or codicil does not expressly revoke all previous wills or codicils, but the revocation extends only so far as the inconsistency.

(2) By a subsequent will, codicil, or other writing executed with the same formalities required for the execution of wills declaring the revocation.

(Laws 1974, ch. 74-106, §1; Laws 1975, ch. 75-220, §23; Laws 1977, ch. 77-87, §13; Laws 1979, ch. 79-400, §269. Amended by Laws 2001, ch. 2001-226, §44, effective January 1, 2002.)

III. Dependent Relative Revocation

Dependent relative revocation is a common law doctrine that permits a court to disregard a valid revocation of a will in some cases. The situation generally arises when a testator makes a will but later revokes the will (or will provision) in order to effectuate a subsequent testamentary scheme. If the revocation of the will (or will provision) was dependent on, and relative to, a mistake, a court may disregard the revocation based on the testator's presumed intent.

A classic case of dependent relative revocation arises in the following situation involving revocation by physical act. The testator makes a bequest of $10,000 to each of the three children (A, B, and C) of his best friend. Later, he crosses out the $10,000 bequest to A and inserts instead $15,000. If the jurisdiction recognizes partial revocation by physical act, the testator's cancellation of the $10,000 to A could be an effective revocation. However, the $15,000 "codicil" fails because it does not comply with the statute of wills (either as a formally attested will or as a holographic instrument). A court might apply dependent relative revocation based on the testator's presumed intent. That is, the court might disregard the testator's revocation of the $10,000 gift to A in the belief that the revocation was dependent on and relative to a mistake (the effectiveness of the larger bequest). The presumed intent would be that the testator would clearly prefer for A to take $10,000 rather than zero.

Some jurisdictions impose a restriction on the doctrine and apply dependent relative revocation only where Will #1 was revoked by physical act, based on the theory that such revocations by physical act are inherently ambiguous.

Florida case law has long recognized the doctrine of dependent relative revocation. For example, in Stewart v. Johnson, 194 So. 869 (Fla. 1940), a decedent executed a will in 1937. In 1938, he executed another will. When the later will was held to be invalid because it lacked the requisite number of witnesses, the beneficiaries

under the first will claimed that the doctrine of dependent relative revocation should apply to re-establish the earlier will. Agreeing, the Florida Supreme Court concluded that the evidence that the testator referred to and incorporated part of the earlier will in the latter one, and that the testator did not intend to die intestate and believed that the new will effectively disposed of his estate, justified the probate of the earlier will on the basis of the dependent relative revocation doctrine.

A more recent case concerned the application of the doctrine to a will in which the decedent failed to exercise a power of appointment in accordance with its terms. In Rosoff v. Harding, 901 So.2d 1006 (Fla. Dist. Ct. App. 2005), appellant claimed that the court should apply the doctrine to revive the clause of a prior will in which the power was exercised. Refusing, the court concluded that the doctrine did not apply to re-establish the earlier will because the later will substantially changed the disposition of the testator's estate, and nothing in the later will demonstrated the testator's preference for the prior will's exercise of the power of appointment over the default disposition provided for in the power of appointment itself.

The doctrine of dependent relative revocation is premised on the testator's presumed intention. As the court stated in Wehrheim v. Golden Pond Assisted Living Facility, 905 So. 2d 1002 (Fla. Dist. Ct. App. 2005), the doctrine creates a rebuttable presumption that the testator would have preferred to revive his earlier bequests rather than let his property pass intestate. Sometimes, the similarities between the prior and subsequent wills support application of the doctrine (as in *Wehrheim, supra*).

IV. Revival of a Revoked Will

Revival is the process of reinstating a revoked will. The testator may *intentionally* revive a revoked will in two ways: (1) by re-executing the former will so that it complies with all the statutory formalities, or (2) by executing a new testamentary instrument (in accordance with statutory formalities) expressly providing that the former will is effective.

Revival becomes more problematic if the following sequence of events occurs:

- the testator executes a will (Will #1) and then revokes it by a subsequent written instrument (Will #2);
- the testator then revokes the subsequent revoking instrument (Will #2) by physical act (e.g., tearing up Will #2).

This sequence of events may lead to uncertainty regarding the testator's intent: Did the testator wish the first will to be revived, or did the testator wish to die intestate?

Courts have different responses to this situation. The common law followed a rule of *automatic revival*. That is, upon the revocation of a revoking instrument (Will #2), the former will (Will #1) was automatically revived. The theory for this approach was that a will was not effective until death. Therefore, Will #1 was never revoked by Will #2 because Will #2, having been revoked prior to death, was never effective. At the testator's death, Will #1 is given effect because it is the only will then in existence.

The majority of states now follow a *rebuttable presumption of anti-revival*. Under this approach, the former will (Will #1) is not revived unless evidence reveals that the testator intended this effect. If no evidence of intent to revive the former will is apparent, then the court determines that the testator died intestate. This approach is derived from the English Wills Act of 1837 limiting the circumstances in which a former will can be revived—only by re-execution or "by a duly executed codicil expressing an intention to revive it." Cited in McGovern & Kurtz, *supra*, §5.4 at 244. Some American jurisdictions adopted this rule but required that the testator's intent to revive had to be evidenced by the "terms" of the revoking instrument. That is, courts limited evidence of intent to the face of the will; therefore, statements by the testator regarding revival were inadmissible. This approach reflected an unwillingness to admit extrinsic evidence because of the possibility of fraud.

The UPC follows the anti-revival rule. However, the UPC liberalized the rule regarding the admission of extrinsic evidence that is sufficient to revive an earlier will. Under the UPC, revocation of a revoking instrument will revive the former will if the testator's intent to revive is evident "from the circumstances of the revocation of the subsequent will or from the testator's *contemporaneous or subsequent* declarations" (UPC §2-509(a) (emphasis added)). Thus, the UPC admits oral statements of the testator, including those that were made contemporaneously with the revocation as well as those that occurred after the revocation.

The UPC's dispensing power concept also might permit admission of extrinsic evidence. The dispensing power under UPC §2-503 applies to execution, revocation, alteration, and revival of wills. "A document, writing or even interlineation on a will might be treated as executed in compliance with the [UPC]'s will statute, if proponents of the document, writing or interlineation prove by clear and convincing evidence that the testator desired it to constitute a revival of a prior revoked clause or will." Averill, *supra*, at 156. The application of this provision has not yet been fully explored by the courts. *Id.* For discussion of the dispensing power generally, see Chapter IV, Section II *supra*.

The UPC has a provision somewhat analogous to the common law automatic revival doctrine in regard to remarriage of the decedent to a prior spouse. Upon the testator's remarriage to a previously divorced spouse (or in cases of remarriage following an annulment), the provisions for that former spouse are automatically revived by operation of law (UPC §2-804(d)). See also Cal. Prob. Code §§6122(b), 6122.1(b).

Like the UPC's dispensing power standard, the Restatement (Third) of Property requires "clear and convincing" evidence of the testator's intent to revive. Restatement (Third) of Property, *supra*, at §4.2, cmt. i.

The Restatement (Third) of Property §4.2 specifies different methods of revival based on the method of will revocation. A will revoked by physical act may be revived "if the testator: (i) reexecuted the will; (ii) executed a codicil indicating an intent to revive the previously revoked will; or (iii) performed an act on the will that clearly and convincingly demonstrates an intent to reverse the revocation." *Id.* at §4.2(b). However, a will revoked by a subsequent will may be revived "if the testator: (i) reexecuted the previously revoked will; (ii) executed a codicil indicating an intent to revive the previously revoked will; (iii) revoked the revoking will by act intending to revive the previously revoked will; or (iv) revoked the revoking will by another, later will whose terms indicate an intent to revive the previously revoked will." *Id.* at §4.2(a).

Some jurisdictions set forth special statutory provisions to revive a will (or will provision) that has been revoked by divorce if: "(i) the testator remarried the former spouse, reexecuted the will, or executed a codicil indicating an intent to revive the previously revoked provision; or (ii) the dissolution of the marriage is nullified." *Id.* at §4.2(c).

It is important, in applying the doctrine of revival, to determine whether the subsequent revoking instrument revoked the prior will entirely or partially. If the prior will is only revoked partially (i.e., the revoking instrument merely supersedes it), then the revocation of the revoking instrument automatically reinstates the superseded disposition. See also UPC §2-509(b).

In cases of revocation of a will, Florida follows the anti-revival rule. Thus, if a testator revokes a will that revokes a former will, such revocation will not revive the former will, even though the former will is in existence at the date of the revocation of the subsequent will (Fla. Stat. §732.508(1)).

Florida law treats the revocation of a will differently from revocation of a codicil. Revocation of a codicil to a will does not revoke the will. According to Florida Statutes §732.508(2), it is presumed that in revoking the codicil, a testator intended to reinstate the provisions of a will or codicil that were revoked by the revoked codicil, as if the revoked codicil had never been executed. In In re Estate of Griffis, 330 So. 2d 797 (Fla. Dist. Ct. App. 1976), a testator executed a will and three codicils (increasing and decreasing the share of his wife). He subsequently physically destroyed the second and later the third codicils. The executor argued that the codicils were not revoked, contending that a written instrument of revocation was required (and that even if they did revoke the codicils, the revocation did not revive language in the will and first codicil). However, the court of appeals disagreed and found that the revocation was effective and served to reestablish the first codicil and the pertinent language of the original will.

§732.508 Revival doctrine; effect of revocation of codicil

(1) The revocation by the testator of a will that revokes a former will shall not revive the former will, even though the former will is in existence at the date of the revocation of the subsequent will.

(2) The revocation of a codicil to a will does not revoke the will, and, in the absence of evidence to the contrary, it shall be presumed that in revoking the codicil the testator intended to reinstate the provisions of a will or codicil that were changed or revoked by the revoked codicil, as if the revoked codicil had never been executed.

(Laws 1974, ch. 74-106, §1; Laws 1975, ch. 75-220, §25.)

§732.511. Republication and reexecution of a revoked will

If a will has been revoked or if it is invalid for any other reason, it may be republished and made valid by its reexecution or the execution of a codicil republishing it with the formalities required by this law for the execution of wills.

(Laws 1974, ch. 74-106, §1; Laws 1975, ch. 75-220, § 26.)

V. Presumptions

A. Presumption of Revocation

At common law, if a will could not be found at the testator's death and was last traced to the testator's possession, the law presumed that the testator destroyed the will with the requisite intent. Many jurisdictions continue to apply this rebuttable presumption. Some jurisdictions also apply the presumption if the will is found in a mutilated condition in the testator's possession at death. Once the presumption applies, the proponent of the will must introduce evidence to overcome it.

Duplicate originals often present problems in terms of the application of this presumption. A duplicate will is one that meets all the statutory formalities (i.e., signed, attested, etc.). Some testators execute duplicate wills in the belief that such an act ensures against loss. Sometimes, only one of the duplicate originals is traced to the testator's possession. If the other duplicate cannot be found, a rebuttable presumption exists that the testator destroyed it with the intention of revoking both it and any other duplicates. 79 Am. Jur.2d Wills §575. However, if both duplicate original wills are found at the testator's death, but only one of them has been canceled, then courts apply a presumption that the will is not revoked. The rationale is that if testator intended revocation, he or she would have canceled both copies. *Id.*

In Daul v. Goff, 754 So. 2d 847 (Fla. Dist. Ct. App. 2000), the testatrix executed a will excluding her children and naming the Sheriffs' Youth Ranch as the beneficiary of her estate. The original will could not be found at her death. The personal representative petitioned to establish the will through admission of a photocopy. The court of appeal held that the personal representative had not overcome the presumption that the original will had been revoked. The court reasoned that when a testator has her will in her custody and it cannot be located after her death, a presumption arises that, in the absence of other evidence, she destroyed it with the intention of revoking it.

An earlier case, In re Estate of Washington, 56 So. 2d 545 (Fla. 1952) illustrates the type of evidence that is necessary to overcome the presumption of revocation. There, a witness testified that the decedent had confirmed her intention to leave her estate to the beneficiary named in her will several days before she died. Immediately after her death, two brothers (who were not beneficiaries) asked about the location of the decedent's deeds. A jar, which contained the decedent's important papers, was missing after the brothers' ransacked the home. Neither of the brothers explained their actions in court. The Florida Supreme Court held that the evidence was sufficient to sustain the finding that the presumption of revocation was rebutted.

B. Lost and Destroyed Will Statutes

A validly executed will that has been lost or destroyed may still be given effect in some circumstances. When a will cannot be found at death, several possibilities arise: (1) the will has been lost, (2) the will has been destroyed by the testator, or (3) the will has been destroyed by another person. At common law, ecclesiastical courts probated valid wills that were lost or destroyed when real property was involved and when proof of the contents could be established. Atkinson, *supra*, §97, at 506.

Today, in cases when a will cannot be found at death and it was last traced to the testator's possession, the presumption of revocation operates (see Section V, A *supra*). However, because of the concern that the loss of the will may be attributable to wrongdoing, jurisdictions permit probate of a lost or destroyed will under some circumstances.

Many jurisdictions have lost or destroyed will statutes that specify the requirements for probate of such wills. Generally, "a will lost, or mutilated without intent thereby to revoke, may be admitted to probate upon satisfactory proof of its contents and due execution." Atkinson, *supra*, §97, at 506. Many jurisdictions require proof of the contents and the facts of due execution by clear and convincing evidence.

Proof of the contents may consist of testimony by witnesses, or production of a copy, draft, or memorandum of the will made by the testator. *Id.*, §97 at 511. Proof of the facts of due execution may be by attesting witnesses or by proof of the witnesses' handwriting. *Id.*, §97 at 509. If the decedent's attorney had a copy of the will, that copy could be offered in evidence or the attorney could offer oral testimony to establish the terms of the will. Declarations of the testator, made before or after the execution, may serve as corroboration of the contents (although not proof of the provisions) or the facts of due execution. Atkinson, *supra*, §97 at 511.

New York's lost and destroyed will statute, enacted in 1827 (1 R.L. 364, Title I, Art. Third, sec. 89; New York Rev. Stats. 1846, Vol. 2, p. 133), was a model for that of other jurisdictions. The original New York statute read:

> No will . . . shall be allowed to be proved as a lost or destroyed will, unless the same shall be proved to have been in existence at the time of the death of the testator; or be shown to have been fraudulently destroyed, in the lifetime of the testator; nor unless its provisions shall be clearly and distinctly proved by at least two credible witnesses, a correct copy or draft being deemed equivalent to one witness.

Prior to 1850, New York courts maintained that the fraudulent destruction of a will did not amount to a revocation, and that if the contents of the will could be satisfactorily shown, the will would be admitted to probate. See In re Arbuckle's Estate, 220 P.2d 950, 956 (Cal. Ct. App. 1950) (explaining history of statute). New York courts interpreted the term "fraudulent" liberally. They required neither actual fraud, nor an intention to profit by the destruction of the will. They interpreted "fraudulent" to mean "constructive fraud." "The destruction of the will, without the knowledge or consent of the testatrix, in disregard of her intention and to the injury of the objects of her bounty, constitutes constructive fraud, and becomes a fraudulent destruction, within the meaning of section 143 of the Surrogate's Court Act." *Id.* at 957.

California adopted the New York statute. However, the San Francisco Earthquake and subsequent fire in 1906 highlighted the need for a statutory amendment to the lost and destroyed will statute because so many wills in attorneys' offices and financial institutions were destroyed. At that time, the California lost and destroyed will statute (Cal. Code Civ. Proc. §1339) provided:

> No will shall be proven as a lost or destroyed will, unless the same is proved to have been in existence at the time of the death of the testator, or is shown to have been fraudulently destroyed in the lifetime of the testator, nor unless its provisions are clearly and distinctly proved by at least two credible witnesses.

In 1907, the legislature amended the statute to enable probate of lost or destroyed wills that "have been fraudulently or *by public calamity* destroyed . . ." (Stats. 1907, ch. 100, p. 122) (emphasis added). Provisions of such wills still had to be proven by clear and convincing evidence and by at least two credible witnesses. See also In re Patterson's Estate, 102 P. 941 (Cal. 1909) (holding that the statutory amendment should be applied liberally to give effect to a will destroyed in the 1906 fire).

The California legislature in 1982 repealed this strict level of proof (i.e., the clear and convincing standard and two-credible-witnesses requirement) and replaced it with a preponderance standard and no minimum number of witnesses. Currently, California Probate Code §8223 requires merely that the petition for probate of a lost or destroyed will shall include a written statement of the testamentary words or their substance.

For many years, many state statutes, similar to those of California and New York, adhered to the requirement that the will must have been "fraudulently destroyed." Under such provisions, there was no need to prove actual fraud. Courts interpreted the language as requiring that the will must have been destroyed by a third party without the decedent's knowledge. See, e.g., In re Fox's Will, 174 N.E.2d 499 (N.Y. 1961) (holding that a will that had been destroyed in a Berlin bombing in 1944 could be admitted to probate, reasoning that the phrase "fraudulently destroyed" had nothing to do with the motive for destruction but solely with the agency of destruction, i.e., it was destroyed by someone other than the testator and without his authorization or direction).

The proponent of a will that has been lost or destroyed need not prove the exact words of the original will. Proof of the substance of the will is sufficient. See, e.g., In re Camp's Estate, 66 P.227 (Cal. 1901) (holding that where the testimony of two witnesses coincides as to the provisions in a lost portion of a will, the court is authorized to establish such provisions, although such witnesses may differ as to the exact language used by the testator). Also, if witnesses recall only a substantial portion of the will but not its entire contents, that portion could be admitted to probate. *Patterson's Estate*, *supra*.

To establish and probate a lost or destroyed will under the Florida statute, the specific contents of the lost will must be proved by the testimony of two disinterested witnesses or, if a correct copy is provided, it must be proved by one disinterested witness (Fla. Stat. §733.207).

In Walton v. Estate of Walton, 601 So. 2d 1266 (Fla. Dist. Ct. App. 1992), Mary Walton's original will could not be found after her death, giving rise to the presumption that she had

destroyed the will with the intention of revoking it. The intended beneficiaries (her nephew and his wife) petitioned to establish the will under the lost and destroyed will statute. The court of appeals found that the requirements for the establishment of a lost and destroyed will were met. The court determined that there was sufficient evidence to rebut the presumption of revocation because a copy of the will was presented to the court, testimony was offered by one disinterested witness (a minister who drafted the will and testified that it was a correct copy), and evidence was presented that the wife of an intestate heir had access to decedent's home and an opportunity to destroy the will herself, as well as a pecuniary interest in doing so.

A more recent case refused to probate a will pursuant to the lost and destroyed will statute because the witnesses attempting to prove the will were not disinterested. In In re Estate of Hatten, 880 So. 2d 1271 (Fla. Dist. Ct. App. 2004), the court of appeals held that the decedent's siblings (who were intended beneficiaries under a will that excluded other siblings) could not petition to establish the contents of a lost will allegedly destroyed by their brother because the siblings were not "disinterested" witnesses. Nonetheless, the court held that evidence of the contents of the will was admissible in the siblings' related action for interference with a testamentary expectancy under an exception to the hearsay rule for statements relating to execution, revocation, identification, or terms of declarant's will.

Note that in Florida, a cause of action is recognized for tortious interference with an expectancy. DeWitt v. Duce, 408 So. 2d 216 (Fla. 1981). The cause of action may be used where a wrongdoer has destroyed a will and the plaintiff is unable to reestablish the destroyed will in a probate proceeding under the applicable lost and destroyed will statute.

§732.207. Lost or destroyed wills: requirements to probate

Any interested person may establish the full and precise terms of a lost or destroyed will and offer the will for probate. The specific content of the will must be proved by the testimony of two disinterested witnesses, or, if a correct copy is provided, it shall be proved by one disinterested witness.

(Laws 1974, ch. 74-106, §1; Laws 1975, ch. 75-220, §57. Amended by Laws 2001, ch. 2001-226, §91, effective January 1, 2002.)

Rule 5.510. Establishment and probate of lost or destroyed will

(a) Proceeding. The establishment and probate of a lost or destroyed will shall be in one proceeding.

(b) Petition. The petition, in addition to reciting information required under these rules for petition for administration, shall include a statement of the facts constituting grounds on which relief is sought, and a statement of the contents of the will or, if available, a copy of the will.

(c) Testimony. The testimony of each witness in the proceeding shall be reduced to writing and filed and may be used as evidence in any contest of the will if the witness has died or moved from the state.

(d) Notice. No lost or destroyed will shall be admitted to probate unless formal notice has been given to those who, but for the will, would be entitled to the property thereby devised.

(e) Order. The order admitting the will to probate shall state in full its terms and provisions.

(Amended March 31, 1977, effective July 1, 1977 (344 So. 2d 828); September 13, 1984, effective January 1, 1985 (458 So. 2d 1079); September 29, 1988, effective January 1, 1989 (537 So. 2d 500); May 2, 2002 (824 So. 2d 849).)

VII
CONTRACTS TO MAKE WILLS

I. Introduction

A. Types of Contracts

A will contract is an agreement that requires a testator to make a particular testamentary disposition of property. It thereby restricts the testator's ability to make a different disposition.

Several types of will contracts exist:

- contracts to make a will;
- contracts to make a particular devise or bequest;
- contracts to die intestate;
- contracts to revoke a will;
- contracts not to revoke a will; and
- contracts not to contest a will.

Will contracts arise most frequently in two situations. First, a testator promises to make a bequest or devise in favor of a third person in consideration for the latter's services. Often such services involve caretaking for the testator for the remainder of his or her life. Such contracts are sometimes referred to as "life-care contracts." Second, two testators (generally spouses) make joint or mutual wills with reciprocal provisions that contain (or allegedly contain) a contract not to revoke their respective wills.

In the former case, the contract is breached when the testator fails to make the agreed-upon will (or the agreed-upon provision in a will). The party who has rendered services in reliance on the testator's promise discovers this fact after the testator's death. In the joint or mutual will situation, the surviving spouse breaches the agreement by disposing of his or her estate differently than previously promised.

Will contracts are governed by the law of contracts and not the law of succession. Thus, assume that a testator (T) makes a promise to leave his or her home to X. When T dies, X discovers that T left his home to Y, instead of to X, in breach of the contract. T's will will be probated (provided that it conforms to all the statutory requirements). X must pursue a remedy under the jurisdiction's applicable contract law. The contract must meet the given jurisdiction's requirements for a valid contract. If the court finds that the will contract is valid, the court may order specific performance, quantum meruit, damages for breach of contract, or a constructive trust. These remedies are discussed *infra*.

B. Historical Background

The law has long recognized the right of a person to enter into a contract to make a particular testamentary disposition. The only bar to such contracts is the Statute of Frauds' requirement that a contract regarding the transfer of real property must be in writing. However, even in cases in which the Statute of Frauds applies, courts commonly admitted extrinsic evidence and applied exceptions (e.g., part performance doctrine, etc., discussed *infra*) to permit proof of oral will contracts.

Before 1958, will contracts in Florida were subject to the same requirements as other oral or written contracts. Trawick, *supra,* at §3-3. However, in that year, the legislature codified the requirements for will contracts. Florida Statutes §731.051(1) (now repealed) required that all agreements to make a will be in writing and signed by the party whose personal representative was to be charged in the presence of two subscribing witnesses.

The effect of that codification was to tighten significantly the requirements for will contracts. In First Gulf Beach Bank and Trust Company v. Grubaugh, 330 So. 2d 205 (Fla. Dist. Ct. App. 1976), the court explained the legislative intent by saying that the statute

> Is not a typical statute of frauds. The statute of frauds already applied to contracts to make devises of realty. By the passage of a separate statute containing different wording, we believe the legislature had more in mind than simply extending the statute of frauds to contracts for bequests of personalty. Fla. Stat. §731.051 is specifically intended to require that one who contracts to make a will should do so with substantially the same formalities as when he executes his will.

Id. at 210.

Language in the 1958 statute (Fla. Stat. §731.051) stated explicitly that it would apply to agreements prior to the effective date of the legislation (January 1, 1958). However, in Keith v. Culp, 111 So. 2d 278 (Fla. Dist. Ct. App. 1959), a Florida court of appeals held that the provision of the statute conferring retroactive effect violated the Florida constitution (§17, Declaration of Rights) which prohibits the passage of any law impairing the obligation of contracts. *Keith* determined that the statute did not apply to an oral contract made before the effective date of the statute.

The 1958 Florida statute on will contracts was repealed in 1974 (Laws 1974, ch. 74-106, §1) with the enactment of the current statute (Fla. Stat. §732.701(1)). According to that statute, an agreement to make a will, to give a devise, not to revoke a will, not to revoke a devise, not to make a will, or not to make a devise is enforceable if the agreement is in writing and signed by the agreeing party in the presence of two attesting witnesses (Fla. Stat. §732.701(1)). A statutory amendment in 2001 (Laws 2001, ch. 2001-226, §55, effective January 1, 2002), inserted the current final sentence in subsection 1, providing for the validity of will contracts that are executed by nonresidents of Florida before or after the law took effect.

Some jurisdictions have stricter requirements for will contracts than Florida, stemming from a concern with the difficulty of proof of the contract. These states require that the will state the existence of the contract as well as its material terms. Many state statutes are modeled on the UPC (§2-514) providing that a will contract (defined as a contract to make a will or devise, not to revoke a will or devise or to die intestate) may be established by one of the following methods:

> (i) the provisions of a will stating the material provisions of the contract, (ii) an express reference in a will to a contract and extrinsic evidence proving the terms of the contract, or (iii) a writing signed by the decedent evidencing the contract.

See also Cal. Prob. Code §21700 (West Supp. 2004) (based on UPC§2-514).

On Florida will contracts generally, see Richard C. Milstein, Florida Wills (For Modest Estates), Powers of Attorney, and Health Care Advance Directives, Florida Bar CLE, § IVA3 (2002); Trawick, *supra*, at §3-3.

II. Proof of the Contract

The foremost problem in litigation involving will contracts is proof of the contract. This issue is especially important because one of the parties to the contract (the decedent) is no longer available to testify as to his or her understanding. Courts are worried that, after the death of the testator, self-interested parties will fabricate evidence of a contract by the testator to leave them his or her property.

In proving a will contract, a plaintiff may present testimony of various persons, such as the attorney who drafted the will, who can testify as to the parties' understanding that the wills were intended to be irrevocable. Or, the intended beneficiaries of the will contract might offer testimony of disinterested relatives. See, e.g., Somogyi's Estate v. Marosites, 389 So. 2d 244 (Fla. Dist. Ct. App. 1980) (holding that evidence of wife's sister, subscribing witness, divorced husband of testatrix's daughter, and minister, supported trial court finding that the spouses agreed to make a mutual will benefiting wife's daughters by a prior marriage).

Note that it is not necessary that a will contract contain an *explicit* provision against revocation. Laragione v. Hagan, 195 So. 2d 246 (Fla. Dist. Ct. App. 1967), *rev'd on other grounds*, 205 So. 2d 289 (Fla. 1967). Even without such a provision, courts can still find that the parties' understanding was to make their wills irrevocable. Further, will contracts need not be proved by disinterested witnesses. See *Laragione*, 195 So. 2d at 248 (finding that testimony of witness who was friend of deceased husband and plaintiffs should not have been disregarded in suit against wife's estate to enforce alleged oral contract between spouses to execute mutual wills in favor of plaintiffs).

A. Joint and Mutual Wills

Problems of proof arise most frequently in connection with joint and mutual wills. A joint will is a single document that is the will of two or more persons. In this situation, the same testamentary instrument is probated on the death of each of the testators. The joint will is frequently used by husbands and wives. Mutual wills are the separate testamentary documents of two persons that contain reciprocal provisions. For that reason, they are sometimes referred to as "reciprocal wills."

Joint wills and mutual wills are notorious litigation breeders because of the likelihood that such wills are contractual. For example, a husband's will may leave all his property to his wife if she survives him; but if she does not survive him (or after her death, if she does survive him), he provides that the property shall pass to the children of his prior marriage. The wife's will contains identical language: all the wife's property to the husband if he survives her; but if he does not survive her (or after his death, if he does survive her), then the property shall pass to the children of her prior marriage.

The fact that each will contains the same disposition indicates the possibility that the testators entered into an agreement as to the method of distribution of their respective estates and desired the survivor to be bound by that agreement. The problem arises after the death of the first spouse. At that time, the surviving spouse may change his or her will to provide only for his or her respective children. Then, the issue becomes whether the parties' mutual or reciprocal wills were based on a contract not to revoke their respective wills.

Will contracts between spouses may arise in conjunction with antenuptial agreements or marital settlement ("post-nuptial") agreements. See, e.g., Shuck v. Bank of America, 862 So. 2d 20 (Fla. Dist. Ct. App. 2003) (suit by widow to enforce antenuptial agreement that husband shall execute will or trust leaving her half of his assets); In re Rosenstein's Estate, 326 So. 2d 239 (Fla. Dist. Ct. App. 1976) (holding that the complaint set forth a valid cause of action against the executor on the basis of an antenuptial agreement to make a will naming plaintiff as beneficiary); Sharps v. Sharps, 219 So. 2d 735 (Fla. Dist. Ct. App. 1969) (holding that an antenuptial agreement was properly construed by the trial court to be a contract to make a will); Donner v. Donner, 302 So. 2d 452 (Fla. Dist. Ct. App. 1974) (addressing conflicts of law issues pertaining to marital separation agreement in which husband agreed to make will in favor of first wife).

Florida Statutes §732.702 governs the rights of a surviving spouse to an elective share, intestate share, pretermitted share, homestead, exempt property, family allowance, and preference in appointment as personal representative. A spouse may waive these rights either in an antenuptial or marital settlement agreement.

§732.701. Will contract: requirements and lack of presumption

No agreement to make a will, to give a devise, not to revoke a will, not to revoke a devise, not to make a will, or not to make a devise shall be binding or enforceable unless the agreement is in writing and signed by the agreeing party in the presence of two attesting witnesses. Such an agreement executed by a nonresident of Florida, either before or after this law takes effect, is valid in this state if valid when executed under the laws of the state or country where the agreement was executed, whether or not the agreeing party is a Florida resident at the time of death.

(2) The execution of a joint will or mutual wills neither creates a presumption of a contract to make a will nor creates a presumption of a contract not to revoke the will or wills.

(Laws 1974, ch. 74-106, §1; Laws 1975, ch. 75-220, §39. Amended by Laws 2001, ch. 2001-226, §55, effective January 1, 2002.)

§732.702. Spouse can waive rights

(1) The rights of a surviving spouse to an elective share, intestate share, pretermitted share, homestead, exempt property, family allowance, and preference in appointment as personal representative of an intestate estate or any of those rights, may be waived, wholly or partly, before or after marriage, by a written contract, agreement, or waiver, signed by the waiving party in the presence of two subscribing witnesses. The requirement of witnesses shall be applicable only to contracts, agreements, or waivers signed by Florida residents after the effective date of this law. Any contract, agreement, or waiver executed by a nonresident of Florida, either before or after this law takes effect, is valid in this state if valid when executed under the laws of the state or country where it was executed, whether or not he or she is a Florida resident at the time of death. Unless the waiver provides to the contrary, a waiver of "all rights," or equivalent language, in the property or estate of a present or prospective spouse, or a complete property settlement entered into after, or in anticipation of, separation, dissolution of marriage, or divorce, is a waiver of all rights to elective share, intestate share, pretermitted share, homestead, exempt property, family allowance, and preference in appointment as personal representative of an intestate estate, by the waiving party in the property of the other and a renunciation by the waiving party of all benefits that would otherwise pass to the waiving party from the other by intestate succession or by the provisions of any will executed before the written contract, agreement, or waiver.

(2) Each spouse shall make a fair disclosure to the other of that spouse's estate if the agreement, contract, or waiver is executed after marriage. No disclosure shall be required for an agreement, contract, or waiver executed before marriage.

(3) No consideration other than the execution of the agreement, contract, or waiver shall be necessary to its validity, whether executed before or after marriage.

(Laws 1974, ch. 74-106, §1; Laws 1975, ch. 75-220, §39; Laws 1977, ch. 77-87, §14. Amended by Laws 2001, ch. 2001-226, §56, effective January 1, 2002.)

§725.01. Statute of Frauds

No action shall be brought whereby to charge any executor or administrator upon any special promise to answer or pay any debt or damages out of her or his own estate, or whereby to charge the defendant upon any special promise to answer for the debt, default or miscarriage of another person or to charge any person upon any agreement made upon consideration of marriage, or upon any contract for the sale of lands, tenements or hereditaments, or of any uncertain interest in or concerning them, or for any lease thereof for a period longer than 1 year, or upon any agreement that is not to be performed within the space of 1 year from the making thereof, or whereby to charge any health care provider upon any guarantee, warranty, or assurance as to the results of any medical, surgical, or diagnostic procedure performed by any physician licensed under chapter 458, osteopathic physician licensed under chapter 459, chiropractic physician licensed under chapter 460, podiatric physician licensed under chapter 461, or dentist licensed under chapter 466, unless the agreement or promise upon which such action shall be brought, or some note or memorandum thereof shall be in writing and signed by the party to be charged therewith or by some other person by her or him thereunto lawfully authorized.

(Act Nov. 15, 1828, §10; Rev. St. 1892, §1995; Gen. St.1906, §2517; Rev. Gen. St. 1920, §3872; Comp. Gen. Laws 1927, §5779; Laws 1975, ch. 75-9, §10. Amended by Laws 1997, ch. 97-102, §933, effective July 1, 1997; Laws 1997, ch. 97-264, §60, effective July 1, 1997; Laws 1998, ch. 98-166, §§227, 294, effective July 1, 1998.)

[The statute of frauds provision applicable to the sale of goods is set forth in Florida Statutes §672.201 (omitted).]

B. Majority View: No Presumption of a Contract Not to Revoke

When two parties execute joint wills or mutual wills that contain identical provisions, some states presume that such wills are executed pursuant to a contract. However, under the majority view (followed by Florida), the execution of a joint will or mutual will does *not* create the presumption of a contract not to revoke the will or wills (Fla. Stat. §732.701(2)).

A significant contribution of the UPC (former §2-701, now §2-514) was to eliminate the presumption that the execution of a joint will or reciprocal wills constitutes a contract not to revoke. The Florida legislature adopted this provision in 1974 in Florida Statutes §732.701(2).

III. Breach

A. After Promisor's Death

Generally, claims on will contracts are brought after the promisor's death. Such claims may be brought either against the promisor's estate (in a suit against the personal representative) or against a third party (often a third party who has received benefits under the decedent's will).

As previously explained, the most common breaches of will contracts occur in two situations. First, a surviving spouse receives a disposition under the deceased spouse's will that was allegedly executed pursuant to a will contract. The surviving spouse subsequently revokes his or her will in breach of that contract and executes a new testamentary disposition. It is important to note that the surviving spouse has the *ability* to revoke his or her will even though doing so would constitute a breach of the will contract. Furthermore, the probate court will not deny admission to probate of a will merely because of the existence of a will contract calling for a different testamentary scheme. Rather, the plaintiff's remedy is under contract law not the law of succession.

In the second common breach of a will contract, a caregiver provides caretaking services for the decedent for many years in reliance on an alleged will contract that bequeaths or devises to the caregiver a significant portion of the decedent's estate. At the decedent's death, the caregiver discovers that the decedent's testamentary plan was not in conformity with the will contract.

Among the legal and equitable remedies which are available for a breach of a will contract are: damages for breach of contract, specific performance (sometimes called quasi-specific performance on the theory that specific performance is not possible after the death of one of the contracting parties); imposition of a

constructive trust on the assets of the testator's estate in favor of the intended beneficiaries of the will contract (to prevent unjust enrichment by someone who has received a benefit under the will which was allegedly in breach of the contract); and a claim for quantum meruit for the reasonable value of any services rendered to the decedent.

B. During Lifetimes of Contracting Parties

An issue which may arise is whether the contracting parties can revoke their will contract while both parties are alive. Most authorities allow either party to repudiate the will contract unilaterally at any time before performance. McGovern & Kurtz, *supra*, §4.9 at 212. Although the will contract is unilaterally revocable during the lifetimes of all the contracting parties, some states require that the breaching party give notice to the other so that the latter has the opportunity to change his or her will.

Note, however, that courts generally will not *enforce* contracts to make a will until the promisor's death. Thus, a promisee usually cannot bring an action (or the action does not accrue) before the promisor's death to compel compliance with the will contract. A Florida court of appeals joined the majority of jurisdictions in following this rule in In re Estate of Tensfeldt, 839 So. 2d 720 (Fla. Dist. Ct. App. 2003). In *Tensfeldt*, the testator's children brought an action against the estate of their father's second wife, seeking funds promised to them in their father's divorce decree from the father's first marriage to their mother. Their father had executed a new will after his second marriage that violated the provisions of the earlier marital settlement agreement. The court held that the cause of action to enforce the will contract accrued (and the five-year statute of limitations began to run) at the time of the testator's death (rather than when he breached the agreement by executing the new will).

In so ruling, the *Tensfeldt* court noted that some jurisdictions allow an action for breach of a will contract during the lifetime of the promisor or hold that the cause of action accrued during the promisor's lifetime. However, the court distinguished those cases by pointing out:

> those cases often involve a promise to devise a specific piece of property and a clear repudiation of that promise when the specific piece of property is conveyed to a third party, making performance by the promisor impossible [citations omitted]. That is not the case here....

Id. at 724 n.4 .

IV. Defenses

A. Statute of Frauds

A fundamental problem regarding enforcement of oral will contracts is that the Statute of Frauds requires contracts of real property to be in writing. Courts have interpreted contracts to devise land to fall under this provision. McGovern & Kurtz, *supra*, §4.9 at 227.

Many state courts traditionally hold that equitable doctrines bar defendants from relying on the Statute of Frauds as a defense in cases involving oral allegations of will contracts.

The part performance doctrine may be invoked in the life-care situation. The acts of a promisee generally consist of the performance of personal services for the promisor, such as providing a home, food and shelter, companionship, and nursing care. In some cases, the promisee may leave work, move, and make significant accommodations to provide care in return for the promised benefit. Such acts may satisfy the court as to the existence of a will contract and demonstrate hardship if the promisee does not obtain the promised benefit. That is, the performance of these acts by the promisee serve to corroborate the oral testimony as to the existence of the will contract. Given that such services are not normally rendered without expectation of reward, a court may reason that the promisee must have provided services based on the existence of a will contract. "This would be especially probable if no compensation was paid during the life of the alleged promisor." George Gleason Bogert et al., Trusts and Trustees: Constructive Trusts §480 (rev. 2d ed. 2002) [hereinafter Bogert].

Prior to the enactment of the 1958 Florida statute (codifying the requirements for will contracts), Florida courts permitted the part performance doctrine to remove an oral will contract from the Statute of Frauds. See First Gulf Beach Bank & Trust Co. v. Grubaugh, 330 So. 2d 205, 209-211 (Fla. Dist. Ct. App. 1976) (explaining history of statute). However, subsequent to the 1958 statute, Florida courts became more reluctant to recognize the part performance doctrine. See *id.* at 210 ("[t]o permit part performance or an unwitnessed writing to obviate the statute would be to thwart its obvious purpose" and holding that the aunt's

alleged contract to make a will leaving a nephew her estate if he cared for her until her death was not enforceable by virtue of his part performance for one year before she left his home voluntarily).

See also Renfro v. Dodge, 520 So. 2d 690 (Fla. Dist. Ct. App. 1988) (rejecting caregiver's defense of part performance and affirming trial court order limiting her recovery to quantum meruit); City of Hope v. Levin, 266 So. 2d 59 (Fla. Dist. Ct. App. 1972) (holding that alleged promise of corporation to name hospital in decedent's honor in exchange for her oral agreement to bequeath $250,000 did not constitute partial performance of the agreement and thus did not render Statute of Frauds inapplicable).

The defense of the Statute of Frauds must be affirmatively pleaded in Florida or its provisions are waived. See Staples v. Battisti, 191 So. 2d 583 (Fla. Dist. Ct. App. 1966); Cypen v. Frederick, 139 So. 2d 201 (Fla. Dist. Ct. App. 1962).

Another remedy in will contract cases is specific performance. The basis of an award of specific performance is to give the promisee the property for which he or she contracted. As a prerequisite to granting specific performance, courts require that the plaintiff's remedy at law be inadequate. Sometimes, courts prefer to use the remedy of constructive trust, rather than specific performance, because some courts reject the view that there can be a decree for specific performance of a contract to make a will that is in effect until death (i.e., courts are reluctant to issue decrees that require someone to do an act or to supervise personal matters). ***Id.***

B. Statute of Limitations

Another possible defense to a claim for breach of a will contract is the jurisdiction's applicable statute of limitations. Statutes of limitation encourage prompt resolution of controversies and reduce the risk of erroneous decisions stemming from the loss of evidence and witness testimony because of the passage of time. Philip J. Padovano, Civil Procedure, Actions, 5 Fla. Prac., Civil Practice §3.3 (2007).

Jurisdictions have different statutes of limitation that might apply to will contract claims. For example, Florida has a one-year statute of limitations for a claim for specific performance (Fla. Stat. §94.11 (5)(a), a four-year statute of limitations for actions on an oral contract (Fla. Stat. §95.11(3)(k), and a five-year statute of limitations for actions based on a written contract (Fla. Stat. §95.11(2)(b)). It is also possible that a disappointed legatee might sue under a creditors' claim statute. States have short statutes of limitations for the filing of "creditors' claims" against an estate. See, e.g., Fla. Stat. §733.702(1)) (creditor must file a claim within—the later of the following two periods—three months after the first publication of notice to creditors or within 30 days after personal service of notice on the creditor (if notice is required to be served on him or her)). The process of filing creditors' claims is discussed in Chapter XIV ***infra.***

§95.11. Statute of limitations

Actions other than for recovery of real property shall be commenced as follows:

(1) Within twenty years.--An action on a judgment or decree of a court of record in this state.

(2) Within five years.--

(a) An action on a judgment or decree of any court, not of record, of this state or any court of the United States, any other state or territory in the United States, or a foreign country.

(b) A legal or equitable action on a contract, obligation, or liability founded on a written instrument, except for an action to enforce a claim against a payment bond, which shall be governed by the applicable provisions of §§**255.05(10)** and **713.23(1)(e)**.

...

(3) Within four years....

(k) A legal or equitable action on a contract, obligation, or liability not founded on a written instrument, including an action for the sale and delivery of goods, wares, and merchandise, and on store accounts.

...

(5) Within one year.-

(a) An action for specific performance of a contract.

...

(6) Laches.--Laches shall bar any action unless it is commenced within the time provided for legal actions concerning the same subject matter regardless of lack of knowledge by the person sought to be held liable that the person alleging liability would assert his or her rights and whether the person sought to be held liable is injured or prejudiced by the delay. This subsection shall not affect application of laches at an earlier time in accordance with law.

...

(Laws 1872, ch. 1869, §10; Laws 1889, ch. 3900, §1; Rev. St. 1892, §1294; Gen. St. 1906, §1725; Laws 1919, ch. 7838, §10, subd. 19; Rev. Gen. St.1920, §2939; Comp. Gen. Laws 1927, §4663; Laws 1943, ch.

21892, §1; Laws 1947, ch. 24337, §7, subd. B; Laws 1957, ch. 57-1, §24; Laws 1959, ch. 59-188, §1; Laws 1967, ch. 67-284, §1; Laws 1971, ch. 71-254, §1; Laws 1973, ch. 73-333, §30; Laws 1974, ch. 74-382, §7; Laws 1975, ch. 75-9, §7; Laws 1977, ch. 77- 174, §1; Laws 1978, ch. 78-435, §11; Laws 1980, ch. 80-322, §1. Amended by Laws 1983, ch. 83-38, §34, effective May 16, 1983; Laws 1984, ch. 84-13, §1, effective May 3, 1984; Laws 1985, ch. 85-63, §1, effective July 30, 1985; Laws 1986, ch. 86-220, §139, effective Oct. 1, 1986; Laws 1986, ch. 86-231, §1, effective October 1, 1986; Laws 1986, ch. 86-272, §1, effective October 1, 1986; Laws 1988, ch. 88-397, §1, effective Oct. 1, 1988; Laws 1990, ch. 90-109, §20, effective January 1, 1991; Laws 1992, c. 92-102, § 1, effective April 8, 1992; Laws 1995, ch. 95-147, § 520, effective July 10, 1995; Laws 1995, ch. 95-283, § 2, effective June 15, 1995; Laws 1996, ch. 96-106, § 4, effective July 1, 1996; Laws 1996, ch. 96-167, § 1, effective July 1, 1996; Laws 1998, ch. 98-280, § 15, effective June 30, 1998; Laws 1999, ch. 99-5, § 2, effective July 29, 1999; Laws 1999, ch. 99-137, § 12, effective July 1, 1999; Laws 2001, ch. 2001-211, § 2, effective July 1, 2001; Laws 2005, ch. 2005-230, § 15, effective October 1, 2005; Laws 2005, ch. 2005-353, § 1, effective December 12, 2005; Laws 2006, ch. 2006-145, §1, effective July 1, 2006.)

V. Surviving Spouse's Statutory Rights

A question sometimes arises whether the rights of the third-party beneficiaries of the will contract should prevail over the forced heirship rights of the surviving spouse. This question involves a conflict of two policies: contractual rights versus family protection.

Case law divides on this question. Some jurisdictions subordinate the surviving spouse's forced share to the rights of the contract beneficiaries. See, e.g., Rubinstein v. Mueller, 225 N.E.2d 540 (N.Y. 1967); Estate of Beerenk, 241 A.2d 755 (Pa. 1968). On the other hand, other jurisdictions protect the forced heirship rights of the subsequent spouse. See Shimp v. Huff, 556 A.2d 252 (Md. 1989); Patecky v. Friend, 350 P.2d 170 (Or. 1960)

The majority view favors the rights of the third-party beneficiaries. Gregory v. Estate of Gregory, 866 S.W.2d 379, 382 (Ark. 1993) (citing authorities and adopting the majority view that subordinates the rights of the surviving spouse to the contract beneficiaries).

In contrast, Florida follows the minority view. Via v. Putnam, 656 So. 2d 460 (Fla. 1995), pitted a decedent's surviving spouse, who claimed a share of his estate under a pretermitted spouse statute, against the children of the decedent's first marriage, who claimed that the mutual wills executed by their parents (naming them residuary beneficiaries of their parents' estates) gave rise to a creditor's contract claim that had priority against the surviving spouse's claim against the estate. Although acknowledging that other jurisdictions' take a contrary view, the Florida Supreme Court held that the testator's surviving spouse prevailed as a pretermitted spouse over the rights of the testator's children as third-party beneficiaries. The court based its holding on the public policy of protecting the rights of a surviving spouse.

> The protection of the widow's interest in the estate of her husband has been in existence in Florida longer than we have been a state. We conclude that we have no authority to judicially modify the public policy protecting a surviving spouse's interest in the deceased spouse's estate by adopting this creditor-theory approach as an exception to the pretermitted spouse statute.

Id. at 466.

VIII
WILL SUBSTITUTES

This chapter addresses nontestamentary devices that enable property to be transferred at death without administration. States permit persons to dispose of their property at death through either testamentary dispositions or nontestamentary devices (called "will substitutes" or "nonprobate transfers"). Common will substitutes include: life insurance, multiple-party accounts, joint tenancy, deeds, gifts, and inter vivos trusts. (Inter vivos trusts are discussed in Chapter IX *infra*.)

I. Nonprobate Transfers Generally

A nonprobate transfer is a will substitute. A will substitute permits the property owner to enjoy certain rights of ownership during his or her lifetime while enabling the owner to transfer the property in a manner that avoids the subsequent costs and delay of the probate process.

II. Contracts

Some contracts contain provisions that direct the disposition of property at death. Property subject to such contracts passes directly to the designated recipient rather than through probate. Sometimes, family members of a decedent challenge the validity of contracts as "testamentary" documents which thereby fail to comply with a given jurisdiction's statute of wills. Such challenges arise because most state wills legislation fail to define the term "will." Today, contracts providing for at-death transfers (like many other will substitutes) have achieved considerable acceptance.

A. Life Insurance

1. General Characteristics

A life insurance policy is a contract. As such, its provisions are construed according to contract law. The insured (generally the owner of the policy) purchases life insurance from an insurance company (the insurer) by paying premiums. At the insured's death, the insurer pays the proceeds to the person(s) whom the insured has designated. The proceeds of the life insurance policy, similar to other nonprobate transfers, pass outside the estate.

The insured may make the proceeds of a life insurance policy payable either to a designated beneficiary or to the insured's estate. In the latter case, the proceeds will be subject to claims of the decedent's creditors. Insurance proceeds also may become part of the decedent's estate upon the failure of the primary and secondary beneficiaries to survive the decedent, or upon the disclaimer of a beneficiary.

An insured also may put the proceeds of life insurance in a trust (called a "life insurance trust"). This may be accomplished by several methods. The insured can have the proceeds paid directly to trustees who have been designated in the insured's will. Or, the insured could create an inter vivos trust and designate the trust as the beneficiary of the insurance policy. Life insurance trusts are especially useful if a beneficiary is a minor, thereby avoiding the cost and burden involved in property management by a guardian.

Life insurance has several advantages: (1) it is a valuable asset insofar as the proceeds are insulated from creditors' claims because they pass outside the probate estate; (2) it provides substitute income replacing the decedent's wages; (3) the beneficiary is not required to pay income tax on the proceeds; and (4) the proceeds provide a source of liquidity enabling heirs and beneficiaries to pay immediate expenses at the decedent's death (i.e., funeral, medical, taxes, etc.). Beyer, *supra*, §17.2 at 313.

The primary types of life insurance are term life and whole life. In a term life policy, the insurer pays proceeds to a beneficiary if the insured dies within a term specified by the policy. The policy is generally renewable but at an increased cost as the insured ages. In contrast, whole life insurance provides protection for a set amount of premiums or the insured's entire life and also builds up a cash reserve that may be used by the insured. Universal life insurance is a variation of whole life insurance that builds up a cash reserve but provides a better rate of return. *Id.* at 313-314.

An early concern reflected in case law was that life insurance was "testamentary" and therefore invalid for failure to comply with the Statute of Wills. Case law and statute now have eliminated this concern. See, e.g., Kansas City Life Ins. Co. v. Rainey, 182 S.W.2d 624 (Mo. 1944) (upholding the beneficiary designation under an annuity as a contract for the benefit of a third party and rejecting the claim that the policy was invalid as a testamentary disposition).

An annuity is a contract between an individual (the annuitant) and an insurance company or annuity provider for a guaranteed interest bearing policy with guaranteed income options. Generally, the beneficiary is the annuitant during his or her lifetime and (at the annuitant's death) the annuitant's surviving spouse and children.

Life insurance policies generally exempt the insurer from liability in case of death of the insured by suicide. The suicide exclusion is of longstanding origin and appears in all types of life insurance. The exclusion eliminates any recovery under the policy, aside from a refund of premiums paid, if the insured dies by suicide. Lee Hugh Goodman, Litigating the Suicide Exclusion in Life Insurance Policies, 20 Am. Jur. Proof of Facts 3d 227 (2002). The insurance company has the burden of establishing the affirmative defense of suicide.

The purchaser of life insurance on a person's life must have an "insurable interest" in the person's life. A person has an insurable interest in his or her own life, as well as that of a spouse, child, and parent.

In some states, life insurance is among the nonprobate assets that are included in the augmented estate. A few states have adopted the UPC's augmented estate concept. Laura A. Rosenbury, Two Ways to End a Marriage: Divorce or Death, 2005 Utah L. Rev. 1227, 1247 (2005). Florida adopted a version of the UPC's augmented estate in 1999. States have different approaches to the inclusion of life insurance as a nonprobate asset of the augmented estate.

In Florida, the elective share of the surviving spouse constitutes 30 percent of the augmented estate (Fla. Stat. §732.2065)). The Florida legislature chose to include life insurance in the elective estate to the extent that the decedent possessed a beneficial interest in the net cash surrender value of the policy immediately before death (Fla. Stat. §§732.2035(6), 732.2045(1)(d), 732. 2055(1)).

> **The Augmented Share Committee's justification for this choice [rather than including *all* the proceeds in the augmented estate] was that to subject all of the proceeds to the elective share would be a windfall to the spouse because the decedent's investment in the policy only depletes the decedent's estate to the extent of the policy premiums.**

Daniel A. Hanley & William T. Hennessey, Elective Share, Florida Bar CLE §§7-1, 7.69. For discussion of the elective share and the augmented estate, see Chapter III *supra*.

§624.02. "Insurance" defined

"Insurance" is a contract whereby one undertakes to indemnify another or pay or allow a specified amount or a determinable benefit upon determinable contingencies.

(Laws 1959, ch. 59-205, §2.)

§624.6011. "Kinds of Insurance" defined

Insurance shall be classified into the following "kinds of insurance":

(1) Life.
(2) Health.
(3) Property.
(4) Casualty.
(5) Surety.
(6) Marine.
(7) Title.

(Laws 1989, ch. 89-360, §38.)

§624.602. "Life insurance," defined

(1) "Life insurance" is insurance of human lives. The transaction of life insurance includes also the granting of annuity contracts, including, but not limited to, fixed or variable annuity contracts; the granting of endowment benefits, additional benefits in event of death or dismemberment by accident or accidental means, additional benefits in event of the insured's disability; and optional modes of settlement of proceeds of life insurance. Life insurance does not include workers' compensation coverages.

(2) A "life insurer" or "life insurance company" is an insurer engaged in the business of issuing life insurance contracts, including contracts of combined life and health and accident insurance.

(Laws 1959, ch. 59-205, §100; *Fla. St. 1969, §624.0401*; Laws 1977, ch. 77- 295, §1; Laws 1979, ch. 79-40, §82; Laws 1982, ch. 82-243, §79 (1st).)

§222.13. Life insurance policies: disposition of proceeds

(1) Whenever any person residing in the state shall die leaving insurance on his or her life, the said insurance shall inure exclusively to the benefit of the person for whose use and benefit such insurance is designated in the policy, and the proceeds thereof shall be exempt from the claims of creditors of the insured unless the insurance policy or a valid assignment thereof provides otherwise. Notwithstanding the foregoing, whenever the insurance, by designation or otherwise, is payable to the insured or to the insured's estate or to his or her executors, administrators, or assigns, the insurance proceeds shall become a part of the insured's estate for all purposes and shall be administered by the

personal representative of the estate of the insured in accordance with the probate laws of the state in like manner as other assets of the insured's estate.

(2) Payments as herein directed shall, in every such case, discharge the insurer from any further liability under the policy, and the insurer shall in no event be responsible for, or be required to see to, the application of such payments.

(Laws 1872, ch. 1864, §1; Rev. St. 1892, § 2347; Laws 1897, ch. 4555, §1; Laws 1903, ch. 5165, §1; Gen. St. 1906, §3154; Rev. Gen. St. 1920, §4977; Comp. Gen. Laws 1927, §7065; Laws 1955, ch. 29861, §1; Laws 1959, ch. 59-333, §1; Laws 1963, ch. 63-230, §1; Laws 1970, ch. 70-376, §1; Laws 1971, ch. 71- 355, §51. Amended by Laws 1995, ch. 95-147, § 202, effective July 10, 1995.)

§222.14. Cash surrender value: exemption from creditors

The cash surrender values of life insurance policies issued upon the lives of citizens or residents of the state and the proceeds of annuity contracts issued to citizens or residents of the state, upon whatever form, shall not in any case be liable to attachment, garnishment or legal process in favor of any creditor of the person whose life is so insured or of any creditor of the person who is the beneficiary of such annuity contract, unless the insurance policy or annuity contract was effected for the benefit of such creditor.

(Laws 1925, ch. 10154, §1; Comp. Gen. Laws 1927, §7066; Laws 1978, ch. 78-76, §1.)

2. Change of Beneficiary

Occasionally, an insured may wish to revoke a prior designation of a beneficiary. To effect any such change of beneficiary, the insured must comply with the policy requirements. For example, in Stringfellow v. Alexander, 117 So. 899 (Fla. 1928), the Florida Supreme Court held that when one takes out life insurance upon his own life and designates a person who has an insurable interest in the former's life as the beneficiary, the insured may not change the beneficiary without his or her consent, unless there exists a clause in the policy of insurance permitting it.

The life insurance company normally specifies the method of changing beneficiaries, such as by requiring a request from the insured that is filed with the insurer and indorsement of the change on the policy by the insurer.

The insured generally cannot alter the designation of beneficiary by means of a will. An exception to this rule is the "superwill" (or "blockbuster will") that enables a person to change the conditions and provisions of will substitutes through the use of testamentary instruments. The American Bar Association briefly considered (but rejected) model uniform superwill legislation in 1987. However, the state of Washington has enacted such a reform.

Washington's superwill statute (Wash. Rev. Code ch. 11.11) permits a testator to alter in a will the beneficiary designation of revocable living trusts and joint tenancy bank accounts with right of survivorship (but not life insurance). See generally Cynthia J. Artura, Comment, Superwill to the Rescue? How Washington's Statute Falls Short of Being a Hero in the Field of Trust and Probate Law, 74 Wash. L. Rev. 799 (1999) (criticizing the statute because its definition of nonprobate asset excludes life insurance policies and retirement plans, and recommending that the state legislature broaden the definition of nonprobate assets to include all nontestamentary revocable devices). UPC §6-101 provides that if the contract permits the owner to change the beneficiary by will, then the owner may do so.

At common law, and in absence of statute today, divorce does not revoke the designation of the former spouse as a life insurance beneficiary. Thus, where the insured dies without changing the designation of the former spouse as beneficiary, the rights of the former spouse-beneficiary cannot be abrogated by the insured's will.

Florida law (Fla. Stat. §732.507(2)) provides that divorce or annulment revokes any provision of a will that affects a former spouse. However, the statute does not apply to the beneficiary designation in a life insurance policy. Thus, in Cooper v. Muccitelli, 682 So. 2d 77 (Fla. 1996), the Florida Supreme Court held that the ex-spouse, as beneficiary of the decedent's life insurance policy, was entitled to the proceeds of the policy, even though the parties had divorced and executed a separation agreement containing a general release of claims that did not specifically mention the insurance policy.

State statutes with automatic revocation provisions may be preempted by federal laws governing employer-provided benefits. The United States Supreme Court has explored whether federal law preempted the Washington state operation-of-law-revocation statute providing that the designation of a spouse as the beneficiary of a nonprobate asset was revoked

automatically upon divorce (Wash. Rev. Code §11.07.010).

In Egelhoff v. Egelhoff, 532 U.S. 141 (2001), the Supreme Court determined whether the Employee Retirement Income Security Act of 1974 (ERISA), 88 Stat. 832, 29 U.S.C. §§1001 et seq., preempts the Washington State statute. In *Egelhoff*, the children from an intestate's first marriage sued the intestate's second wife, whose marriage to intestate had been dissolved shortly before his death, claiming entitlement to life insurance proceeds and pension plan benefits. The decedent was employed by the Boeing Company, which provided him with a life insurance policy and a pension plan—both governed by ERISA. The decedent had designated his second wife as the beneficiary under both and had failed to change that designation before his death. The United States Supreme Court held that federal law preempted the state statute providing for automatic revocation, upon divorce, of any designation of s spouse as beneficiary of a nonprobate asset. The Court ruled, therefore, that the benefits should be paid in accordance with federal law, i.e., the benefits should be paid in accordance with the plan documents that designated the wife as beneficiary.

§627.422. Policy may be assigned

A policy may be assignable, or not assignable, as provided by its terms. Subject to its terms relating to assignability, any life or health insurance policy under the terms of which the beneficiary may be changed upon the sole request of the policyowner may be assigned either by pledge or transfer of title, by an assignment executed by the policyowner alone and delivered to the insurer, whether or not the pledgee or assignee is the insurer. Any such assignment shall entitle the insurer to deal with the assignee as the owner or pledgee of the policy in accordance with the terms of the assignment, until the insurer has received at its home office written notice of termination of the assignment or pledge or written notice by or on behalf of some other person claiming some interest in the policy in conflict with the assignment.

(Laws 1959, ch. 59-205, §471; Fla. St. 1969, §627.0121; Laws 1982, ch. 82- 243, §372. Laws 1959, ch. 59-205, §471; Fla. St. 1969, §627.0121; Laws 1982, ch. 82- 243, §372.)

3. Effect of Simultaneous Death and Homicide on Life Insurance Benefits

Florida law (Fla. Stat. §732.601) provides for the distribution of life insurance benefits in the simultaneous death situation. When the insured and the beneficiary in a policy of life or accident insurance have both died and there is insufficient evidence that they died otherwise than simultaneously, the proceeds of the policy shall be distributed as if the insured had survived the beneficiary.

In addition, Florida law specifies the effect of a homicide on the distribution of life insurance benefits. The Florida slayer statute precludes a beneficiary of a life insurance policy from taking any benefit by virtue of slaying the insured. Specifically, Florida Statutes §732.802(3) provides that the beneficiary of a life insurance policy who "unlawfully and intentionally" kills the insurer is not entitled to any benefit under the policy. The policy becomes payable as if the slayer predeceased the insured. *Id.*

For further discussion of the slayer disqualification, see Chapter I, Section IIIE1 *supra*.

§732.601. Simultaneous Death Law: treatment of life insurance

Unless a contrary intention appears in the governing instrument:

(1) When title to property or its devolution depends on priority of death and there is insufficient evidence that the persons have died otherwise than simultaneously, the property of each person shall be disposed of as if that person survived.

(2) When two or more beneficiaries are designated to take successively by reason of survivorship under another person's disposition of property and there is insufficient evidence that the beneficiaries died otherwise than simultaneously, the property thus disposed of shall be divided into as many equal parts as there are successive beneficiaries and the parts shall be distributed to those who would have taken if each designated beneficiary had survived.

(3) When there is insufficient evidence that two joint tenants or tenants by the entirety died otherwise than simultaneously, the property so held shall be distributed one-half as if one had survived and one-half as if the other had survived. If there are more than two joint tenants and all of them so died, the property thus distributed shall be in the proportion that one bears to the number of joint tenants.

(4) When the insured and the beneficiary in a policy of life or accident insurance have died and there is insufficient evidence that they died otherwise than simultaneously, the proceeds of the policy shall be distributed as if the insured had survived the beneficiary.

(Laws 1974, ch. 74-106, §1; Laws 1975, ch. 75-220, §34. Amended by Laws 1997, ch. 97-102, §966, effective July 1, 1997; Laws 2001, ch. 2001-226, §50, effective January 1, 2002.)

§732.802. Killer not entitled to receive property or other benefits by reason of victim's death

(1) A surviving person who unlawfully and intentionally kills or participates in procuring the death of the decedent is not entitled to any benefits under the will or under the Florida Probate Code, and the estate of the decedent passes as if the killer had predeceased the decedent. Property appointed by the will of the decedent to or for the benefit of the killer passes as if the killer had predeceased the decedent.

(2) Any joint tenant who unlawfully and intentionally kills another joint tenant thereby effects a severance of the interest of the decedent so that the share of the decedent passes as the decedent's property and the killer has no rights by survivorship. This provision applies to joint tenancies with right of survivorship and tenancies by the entirety in real and personal property; joint and multiple-party accounts in banks, savings and loan associations, credit unions, and other institutions; and any other form of coownership with survivorship incidents.

(3) A named beneficiary of a bond, life insurance policy, or other contractual arrangement who unlawfully and intentionally kills the principal obligee or the person upon whose life the policy is issued is not entitled to any benefit under the bond, policy, or other contractual arrangement; and it becomes payable as though the killer had predeceased the decedent.

(4) Any other acquisition of property or interest by the killer, including a life estate in homestead property, shall be treated in accordance with the principles of this section.

(5) A final judgment of conviction of murder in any degree is conclusive for purposes of this section. In the absence of a conviction of murder in any degree, the court may determine by the greater weight of the evidence whether the killing was unlawful and intentional for purposes of this section.

(6) This section does not affect the rights of any person who, before rights under this section have been adjudicated, purchases from the killer for value and without notice property which the killer would have acquired except for this section, but the killer is liable for the amount of the proceeds or the value of the property. Any insurance company, bank, or other obligor making payment according to the terms of its policy or obligation is not liable by reason of this section unless prior to payment it has received at its home office or principal address written notice of a claim under this section.

(Laws 1974, ch. 74-106, §1; Laws 1975, ch. 75-220, §41; Laws 1982, ch. 82-71, §1.)

B. Multiple-Party Accounts

1. Generally

People often hold accounts in financial institutions in two or more names. These accounts are called "multiple-party" accounts. Such accounts provide a simple and inexpensive method for a depositor to specify the disposition of the funds upon death.

These accounts generally take the following forms:

- **joint account (e.g., an account payable to "X or Y");**
- **trust account (e.g., an account held as "X, in trust for Y"); or**
- **POD account (e.g., an account held as "X, payable on death to Y").**

Such accounts have caused litigation concerning such issues as: validity, ownership as between the parties of the multiple-party accounts and others, alteration of rights, rights at death (of the donee and surviving spouse), rights of creditors, and the protection of financial institutions.

To respond to these concerns, the National Conference of Commissioners on Uniform State Laws promulgated the Uniform Multiple-Person Accounts Act in 1969. The Act was incorporated subsequently as Article VI, Part I, of the Uniform Probate Code. The Uniform Multiple-Person Accounts Act was promulgated to encourage banks and credit unions to offer payable-on-death and "convenience" account forms for people who desire some of the incidents of joint accounts. See NCCUSL, Legislative Fact Sheet (explaining the history of the Act), http://www.nccusl.org (last visited March 13, 2007). The Act addresses (1) ownership of the

accounts during the owners' lifetimes; (2) the existence, validity, and revocability of survivors' benefits; and (3) the protection of financial institutions offering multiple-party accounts.

The Uniform Multiple-Person Accounts Act was revised in 1989. The revisions include:

> provision for an agency designation, optional statutory account forms, treatment of community property and other types of marital property, payments to minors under the Uniform Transfers to Minors Act , and extensive terminological and drafting simplifications and standardizations.

Prefatory Note, Uniform Multiple-Person Account Act (1989).

In 1994, Florida adopted legislation on multiple-party accounts to supplement existing law. Specifically, the state legislature enacted Florida Statutes §655.82 that authorizes pay-on-death accounts, provides applicable definitions, specifies rights with respect to such accounts, provides for payments from such accounts and specifies a form that may be used to select such an account. At the same time, the legislature enacted Florida Statutes §§711.50 to 711.512 adopting the Uniform Transfers on Death Security Registration Act to establish a procedure to allow the owner of securities to register the title of the securities in transfer-on-death form and also to enable an issuer, transfer agent, broker, or other intermediary to transfer the securities directly to the designated transferee on the owner's death. See 1994 Fla. Sess. Law Serv. Ch. 9C.S.S.B. 1228 and 1910) 94-216

According to Florida Statutes §655.82(e)), "[a] multiple-party account" is defined as "an account payable on request to one or more of two or more parties, whether or not a right of survivorship is mentioned." The statute specifies that a designated beneficiary of an account with a payable-on-death designation has *no right to ownership* of the proceeds of the account during the lifetime of any party (Fla. Stat. §655.82(2)).

However, on the death of one of the multiple parties in an account with a payable-on-death designation, the funds in the account belong to the surviving party (or parties). When a sole party dies (or the last surviving of two or more parties die), the remaining funds belong to the surviving beneficiary or beneficiaries (Fla. Stat. §655.82(3)). In the event that the account names two or more beneficiaries and if two or more of these persons survive, then the remaining funds belong to these persons in equal shares (without any right of survivorship between or among them). If no beneficiary survives (i.e. the beneficiary or beneficiaries predecease the owner(s) of the account), then the remaining funds belong to the estate of the last surviving party. *Id.*

The Code authorizes the creation of accounts in "convenience" form. Such accounts in the name of one person, designate another person (or persons) as agents with the right to make deposits to and to withdraw funds from such an account (Fla. Stat. §655.80(1)). On the death of the depositor, any balance is not payable to the agent but rather to other designated persons (Fla. Stat. §655.80(3)).

Finally, Florida law provides protection for financial institutions that offer multiple-party accounts. For example, in Sander v. Jaffe, 913 So. 2d 1205 (Fla. Dist. Ct. App. 2005), an appellate court held that a decedent's estate was entitled to reimbursement of funds that the decedent's daughter withdrew (and spent for her own use) from a joint account held in the names of the decedent and her children with right of survivorship. The daughter had argued that she was entitled to withdraw funds for her own benefit from the joint account because she was a title holder based on the right-of-survivorship provision. The appellate court rejected that argument, pointing out that the intent of Florida Statutes §655.78 (authorizing a financial institution to pay the account proceeds to either of two named account holders) is to protect the financial institution from liability for distributing funds from a multiple-party account to any of the individual account holders. According to the court, the statute was not intended to shape the relationship between the account holders themselves. *Id.* at 1207.

For further discussion of joint tenancy and tenancy by the entirety, see Section III *infra*.

§655.78. Deposit accounts in two or more names: payable to either

(1) Unless otherwise expressly provided in a contract, agreement, or signature card executed in connection with the opening or maintenance of an account, including a certificate of deposit, a deposit account in the names of two or more persons may be paid to, or on the order of, either or any of such persons or to, or on the order of, the guardian of the property of any such person who is incompetent, whether the other or others are competent. The check or other order for payment to any such person or guardian is a valid and sufficient release and

discharge of the obligation of the institution for funds transferred thereby.

(2) In the case of a credit union, a member may designate any person or persons to hold deposits with the member in joint tenancy with the right of survivorship; but a joint tenant, unless he or she is a member in his or her own right, may not be permitted to vote, obtain a loan, or hold office or be required to pay an entrance or membership fee.

(Laws 1992, ch. 92-303, §47, effective July 3, 1992. Amended by Laws 1997, ch. 97-102, §527, effective July 1, 1997.)

§655.79. Deposit accounts in two or more names: presumption as to vesting on death

(1) Unless otherwise expressly provided in a contract, agreement, or signature card executed in connection with the opening or maintenance of an account, including a certificate of deposit, a deposit account in the names of two or more persons shall be presumed to have been intended by such persons to provide that, upon the death of any one of them, all rights, title, interest, and claim in, to, and in respect of such deposit account, less all proper setoffs and charges in favor of the institution, vest in the surviving person or persons.

(2) The presumption created in this section may be overcome only by proof of fraud or undue influence or clear and convincing proof of a contrary intent. In the absence of such proof, all rights, title, interest, and claims in, to, and in respect of such deposits and account and the additions thereto, and the obligation of the institution created thereby, less all proper setoffs and charges in favor of the institution against any one or more of such persons, upon the death of any such person, vest in the surviving person or persons, notwithstanding the absence of proof of any donative intent or delivery, possession, dominion, control, or acceptance on the part of any person and notwithstanding that the provisions hereof may constitute or cause a vesting or disposition of property or rights or interests therein, testamentary in nature, which, except for the provisions of this section, would or might otherwise be void or voidable.

(3) This section does not abridge, impair, or affect the validity, effectiveness, or operation of any of the provisions of s§ 655.78 and 674.405 or the rights of institutions to make payments as therein provided.

(Laws 1992, ch. 92-303, §48, effective July 3, 1992.)

§655.80. Convenience accounts

(1) A convenience account is a deposit account, other than a certificate of deposit, in the name of one individual (principal), in which one or more other individuals have been designated as agents with the right to make deposits to and to withdraw funds from or draw checks on such account. The designation of agents, the substitution or removal of agents, or any other change in the contractual terms or provisions governing a convenience account may be made only by the principal. Except as otherwise provided in this section, the agency relationship created under this account is not affected by the subsequent death or incompetence of the principal.

(2) All rights, interests, and claims in, to, and in respect of, such deposits and convenience account and the additions thereto shall be those of the principal only.

(3) Any balance standing to the credit of a convenience account shall be paid to the guardian of the property of the principal, to any person designated in a court order entered pursuant to §735.206, to any person designated by letter or other writing as authorized by §735.301, or to the personal representative of the deceased principal's estate, upon presentation of effective written notice and, if applicable, proof of judicial appointment of such guardian or personal representative by a court of competent jurisdiction. No such court order or letter, written notice, or proof of judicial appointment is effective until it is served upon and received by an officer of the institution during regular banking hours and in such time and in such manner as to afford the institution a reasonable opportunity to act on it prior to the happening of any of the events described in §674.303. No other notice, knowledge, or other information shown to have been available to an institution affects its right to the protection provided by this section.

(4) Payment by an institution pursuant to this section is a valid and sufficient release and discharge to the institution from all claims for payments so paid.

(5) Without qualifying any other right to setoff or lien, and subject to any contractual provision, if the principal is indebted to the institution, the institution has a right to setoff against the account.

(Laws 1992, ch. 92-303, §49, effective July 3, 1992.).

§655.82. Payable-on-death accounts

(1) As used in this section:

(a) "Account" means a contract of deposit between a depositor and an institution, including, but not limited to, a checking account, savings account, certificate of deposit, and share account.

(b) "Beneficiary" means a person named as one to whom sums on deposit in an account are payable on request after death of all parties or for whom a party is named as trustee.

(c) "Devisee" means any person designated in a will to receive a testamentary disposition of real or personal property.

(d) "Heirs" means those persons, including a surviving spouse, who are entitled, under the laws of this state regarding intestate succession, to the property of a decedent.

(e) "Multiple-party account" means an account payable on request to one or more of two or more parties, whether or not a right of survivorship is mentioned.

(f) "Party" means a person who, by the terms of an account, has a present right, subject to request, to payment from the account other than as a beneficiary.

(g) "Payment" means disbursement of sums on deposit, and includes withdrawal, payment to a party or third person pursuant to check or other request, and a pledge of sums on deposit by a party, or a setoff, reduction, or other disposition of all or part of an account pursuant to a pledge.

(h) "Pay-on-death designation" means the designation of:

1. A beneficiary in an account payable on request to one party during the party's lifetime and on the party's death to one or more beneficiaries, or to one or more parties during their lifetimes and on death of all of them to one or more beneficiaries; or

2. A beneficiary in an account in the name of one or more parties as trustee for one or more beneficiaries if the relationship is established by the terms of the account and there is no subject of the trust other than the sums on deposit in the account, whether or not payment to the beneficiary is mentioned.

(i) "Personal representative" means an executor, administrator, curator, successor personal representative, special administrator, or any other person who performs substantially the same function under the law governing their status.

(j) "Receive," as it relates to notice to an institution, means receipt in the office or branch office of the institution in which the account is established, but if the terms of the account require notice at a particular place, in the place required.

(k) "Request" means a request for payment complying with all terms of the account, including special requirements concerning necessary signatures and regulations of the institution; but, for purposes of this section, if terms of the account condition payment on advance notice, a request for payment is treated as immediately effective and a notice of intent to withdraw is treated as a request for payment.

(l) "Successor" means any person, other than a creditor, who is entitled to property of a decedent under the decedent's will or otherwise.

(m) "Sums on deposit" means the balance payable on an account, including interest and dividends earned, whether or not included in the current balance, and any deposit of life insurance proceeds added to the account by reason of death of a party.

(n) "Terms of the account" means the deposit agreement and other terms and conditions, including the form, of the contract of deposit.

(2) A beneficiary in an account having a pay-on-death designation has no right to sums on deposit during the lifetime of any party.

(3) In an account with a pay-on-death designation:

(a) On the death of one of two or more parties, sums on deposit in the account belong to the surviving party or parties.

(b) On the death of the sole party or the last survivor of two or more parties, sums on deposit belong to the surviving beneficiary or beneficiaries. If two or more beneficiaries survive, sums on deposit belong to them in equal and undivided shares, and, unless otherwise provided in a depository agreement written between December 31, 1994, and July 1, 2001, there is no right of survivorship in the event of death of a beneficiary thereafter. If no beneficiary survives, sums on deposit belong to the estate of the last surviving party.

(4) A pay-on-death designation in a multiple-party account without right of survivorship is ineffective. For purposes of this section, designation of an account as a tenancy in common establishes that the account is without right of survivorship.

(5) The ownership right of a surviving party or beneficiary, or of the decedent's estate, in sums on deposit is subject to requests for payment made by a party before the party's death, whether paid by the institution before or after death, or unpaid. The surviving party or beneficiary, or the decedent's estate, is liable to the payee of an unpaid request for payment. The liability is limited to a proportionate share of the amount transferred under this section, to the extent necessary to discharge the request for payment.

(6) An institution, on request, may pay sums on deposit in an account with a pay-on-death designation to:

(a) One or more of the parties, whether or not another party is disabled, incapacitated, or deceased when the payment is requested and whether or not a party survives another party;

(b) The beneficiary or beneficiaries, if proof of death is presented to the institution showing that the beneficiary or beneficiaries survived all persons named as parties; or

(c) The personal representative, if any, or, if there is none, the heirs or devisees of a deceased party, if proof of death is presented to the institution showing that the deceased party was the survivor of all other persons named on the account either as a party or beneficiary.

(7) Payment made pursuant to this section discharges the institution from all claims for amounts so paid, whether or not the payment is consistent with the beneficial ownership of the account as between parties, beneficiaries, or their successors. Payment may be made whether or not a party or beneficiary is disabled, incapacitated, or deceased when payment is requested, received, or made.

(8) A beneficiary in an account at a credit union having a pay-on-death designation, unless the beneficiary is a member in her or his own right, may not be permitted to vote, obtain an extension of credit, or hold office or be required to pay an entrance or membership fee.

(9) The following is an example of the form of a contract of deposit that may be used to select a pay-on-death account for use by one or more parties:

SINGLE-PARTY ACCOUNT OR MULTIPLE-PARTY

ACCOUNT WITH PAY-ON-DEATH DESIGNATION

PARTIES (Name each party): ____________ ____________

OWNERSHIP (Select one and initial):

_______ SINGLE-PARTY ACCOUNT

_______ MULTIPLE-PARTY ACCOUNT

RIGHTS AT DEATH (Select one and initial):

_______ SINGLE-PARTY ACCOUNT

At death of the party, ownership passes as part of the party's estate.

_______ SINGLE-PARTY ACCOUNT WITH A PAY-ON-DEATH DESIGNATION

(Name one or more beneficiaries):

____________ ____________

At death of the party, ownership passes to the designated pay-on-death beneficiaries and is not part of the party's estate.

_______ MULTIPLE-PARTY ACCOUNT WITH RIGHT OF SURVIVORSHIP

At death of a party, ownership passes to the surviving party or parties.

_______ MULTIPLE-PARTY ACCOUNT WITH RIGHT OF SURVIVORSHIP AND A PAY-ON-DEATH DESIGNATION

(Name one or more beneficiaries):

____________ ____________

At death of the last surviving party, ownership passes to the designated pay-on-death beneficiaries and is not part of the last surviving party's estate.

(Laws 1994, ch. 94-216, §1, effective January 1, 1995. Amended by Laws 1997, ch. 97-102, §529, effective July 1, 1997; Laws 2001, ch. 2001-243, §21, effective June 15, 2001.)

§655.825. Deposits in trust

(1) Because deposits in trust are also accounts with a pay-on-death designation as described in §655.82, it is the intent of the Legislature that the provisions of §655.82 shall apply to and govern deposits in trust. References to §655.81 in any depository agreement shall be interpreted after the effective date of this act as references to § 655.82.

(2) This section shall take effect July 1, 2001, and shall apply to deposits made to a depository account created after December 31, 1994.

(Laws 2001, ch. 2001-243, §3, effective July 1, 2001.)

2. Florida Uniform Transfer-on-Death Registration Act

In 1994, the Florida legislature enacted the Florida Uniform Transfer-on-Death Security Registration Act (Fla. Stat. §§711.50-512). This legislation provides that ownership of any *security* that is registered in a "beneficiary form" by an owner dying on or after January 1, 1995, automatically passes to the designated beneficiary (or beneficiaries) upon the death of the sole owner (or the last surviving among multiple owners) (Fla. Stat. §711.507). The term "security" is broadly defined (Fla. Stat. §711.501(9)). See generally W. Fletcher Belcher, Jointly Held Assets, Litigation Under the Florida Probate Code, Florida Bar, LPC FL-CLE §5-42 (2003).

§711.50. Title

Sections 711.50-711.512 may be cited as the "Florida Uniform Transfer-on-Death Security Registration Act."

(Laws 1994, ch. 94-216, §3, effective January 1, 1995.)

§711.501. Applicable definitions

In §§711.50-711.512, unless the context otherwise requires, the term:

(1) "Beneficiary form" means a registration of a security which indicates the present owner of the security and the intention of the owner regarding the person who will become the owner of the security upon the death of the owner.

(2) "Devisee" means any person designated in a will to receive a disposition of real or personal property.

(3) "Heirs" means those persons, including the surviving spouse, who are entitled under the statutes of intestate succession to the property of a decedent.

(4) "Person" means an individual, a corporation, an organization, or other legal entity.

(5) "Personal representative" includes an executor, administrator, successor personal representative, special administrator, and persons who perform substantially the same function under the law governing their status.

(6) "Property" includes both real and personal property or any interest therein and means anything that may be the subject of ownership.

(7) "Register," including its derivatives, means to issue a certificate showing the ownership of a certificated security or, in the case of an uncertificated security, to initiate or transfer an account showing ownership of securities.

(8) "Registering entity" means a person who originates or transfers a security title by registration, and includes a broker maintaining security accounts for customers and a transfer agent or other person acting for or as an issuer of securities.

(9) "Security" means a share, participation, or other interest in property, in a business, or in an obligation of an enterprise or other issuer, and includes a certificated security, an uncertificated security, and a security account.

(10) "Security account" means:

(a) A reinvestment account associated with a security, a securities account with a broker, a cash balance in a brokerage account, cash, interest, earnings, or dividends earned or declared on a security in an account, a reinvestment account, or a brokerage account, whether or not credited to the account before the owner's death;

(b) An investment management account, investment advisory account, investment agency account, custody account, or any other type of account with a bank or trust company, including the securities in the account, the cash balance in the account, and cash equivalents, and any interest, earnings, or dividends earned or declared on a security in the account, whether or not credited to the account before the owner's death; or

(c) A cash balance or other property held for or due to the owner of a security as a replacement for or product of an account security, whether or not credited to the account before the owner's death.

(11) "State" includes any state of the United States, the District of Columbia, the Commonwealth of Puerto Rico, and any territory or possession subject to the legislative authority of the United States.

(Laws 1994, ch. 94-216, §3, effective January 1, 1995. Amended by Laws 2005, ch. 2005-85, §1, effective July 1, 2005.)

§711.502. Sole or multiple ownership: registration requirements

Only individuals whose registration of a security shows sole ownership by one individual or multiple ownership by two or more with right of survivorship, rather than as tenants in common, may obtain registration in beneficiary form. Multiple owners of a security registered in beneficiary form hold as joint tenants with right of survivorship, as tenants by the entireties, or as owners of community property held in survivorship form, and not as tenants in common.

(Laws 1994, ch. 94-216, §3, effective January 1, 1995.)

§711.503. Registration in beneficiary form; applicable law

A security may be registered in beneficiary form if the form is authorized by this or a similar statute of the state of organization of the issuer or registering entity, the location of the registering entity's principal office, the office of its transfer agent or its office making the registration, or by this or a similar statute of the law of the state listed as the owner's address at the time of registration. A registration governed by the law of a jurisdiction in which this or similar legislation is not in force or was not in force when a registration in beneficiary form was made is nevertheless presumed to be valid and authorized as a matter of contract law.

(Laws 1994, ch. 94-216, §3, effective January 1, 1995.)

§711.504. Registration must include designation of ownership at death

A security, whether evidenced by certificate or account, is registered in beneficiary form when the registration includes a designation of a beneficiary

to take the ownership at the death of the owner or the deaths of all multiple owners.
(Laws 1994, ch. 94-216, §3, effective January 1, 1995.)

§711.505. Various forms of registration in beneficiary form

Registration in beneficiary form may be shown by the words "transfer on death" or the abbreviation "TOD," or by the words "pay on death" or the abbreviation "POD," after the name of the registered owner and before the name of a beneficiary.
(Laws 1994, ch. 94-216, §3, effective January 1, 1995.)

§711.506. No effect on ownership during life of owner

The designation of a transfer-on-death beneficiary on a registration in beneficiary form has no effect on ownership until the owner's death. A registration of a security in beneficiary form may be canceled or changed at any time by the sole owner or all then-surviving owners without the consent of the beneficiary.
(Laws 1994, ch. 94-216, §3, effective January 1, 1995.)

§711.507. Ownership passes to surviving beneficiary at death of owner

On death of a sole owner or the last to die of all multiple owners, ownership of securities registered in beneficiary form passes to the beneficiary or beneficiaries who survive all owners. On proof of death of all owners and compliance with any applicable requirements of the registering entity, a security registered in beneficiary form may be reregistered in the name of the beneficiary or beneficiaries who survived the death of all owners. Until division of the security after the death of all owners, multiple beneficiaries surviving the death of all owners hold their interests as tenants in common. If no beneficiary survives the death of all owners, the security belongs to the estate of the deceased sole owner or the estate of the last to die of all multiple owners.
(Laws 1994, ch. 94-216, §3, effective January 1, 1995.)

§711.508. Registering entity may refuse request

(1) A registering entity is not required to offer or to accept a request for security registration in beneficiary form. If a registration in beneficiary form is offered by a registering entity, the owner requesting registration in beneficiary form assents to the protections given to the registering entity by §§711.50-711.512.

(2) By accepting a request for registration of a security in beneficiary form, the registering entity agrees that the registration will be implemented on death of the deceased owner as provided in §§711.50-711.512.

(3) A registering entity is discharged from all claims to a security by the estate, creditors, heirs, or devisees of a deceased owner if it registers a transfer of the security in accordance with §711.507 and does so in good faith reliance on the registration, on §§711.50-711.512, and on information provided to it by affidavit of the personal representative of the deceased owner, or by the surviving beneficiary or by the surviving beneficiary's representatives, or other information available to the registering entity. The protections of §§711.50-711.512 do not extend to a reregistration or payment made after a registering entity has received written notice from any claimant to any interest in the security objecting to implementation of a registration in beneficiary form. No other notice or other information available to the registering entity affects its right to protection under §§ 711.50-711.512.

(4) The protection provided by §§711.50-711.512 to the registering entity of a security does not affect the rights of beneficiaries in disputes between themselves and other claimants to ownership of the security transferred or its value or proceeds.
(Laws 1994, ch. 94-216, §3, effective January 1, 1995.)

§711.509. Nontestamentary transfer on death: effectiveness

(1) A transfer on death resulting from a registration in beneficiary form is effective by reason of the contract regarding the registration between the owner and the registering entity and §§711.50-711.512 and is not testamentary.

(2) Sections 711.50-711.512 do not limit the rights of creditors of security owners against beneficiaries and other transferees under other laws of this state.
(Laws 1994, ch. 94-216, §3, effectiev January 1, 1995.)

§711.51. Terms and conditions for registration

(1) A registering entity offering to accept registrations in beneficiary form may establish the terms and conditions under which it will receive

requests for registrations in beneficiary form, and requests for implementation of registrations in beneficiary form, including requests for cancellation of previously registered transfer-on-death beneficiary designations and requests for reregistration to effect a change of beneficiary. The terms and conditions so established may provide for proving death, avoiding or resolving any problems concerning fractional shares, designating primary and contingent beneficiaries, and substituting a named beneficiary's descendants to take in the place of the named beneficiary in the event of the beneficiary's death. Substitution may be indicated by appending to the name of the primary beneficiary the letters "LDPS," standing for "lineal descendants per stirpes." This designation substitutes a deceased beneficiary's descendants who survive the owner for a beneficiary who fails to so survive, the descendants to be identified and to share in accordance with the law of the beneficiary's domicile at the owner's death governing inheritance by descendants of an intestate. Other forms of identifying beneficiaries who are to take on one or more contingencies, and rules for providing proofs and assurances needed to satisfy reasonable concerns by registering entities regarding conditions and identities relevant to accurate implementation of registrations in beneficiary form, may be contained in a registering entity's terms and conditions.

(2) The following are illustrations of registrations in beneficiary form which a registering entity may authorize:

(a) Sole owner-sole beneficiary:
John S Brown TOD (or POD) John S Brown Jr.

(b) Multiple owners-sole beneficiary:
John S Brown Mary B Brown JT TEN TOD John S Brown Jr.

(c) Multiple owners-primary and secondary (substituted) beneficiaries:

1. John S Brown Mary B Brown JT TEN TOD John S Brown Jr SUB BENE Peter Q Brown; or

2. John S Brown Mary B Brown JT TEN TOD John S Brown Jr LDPS.

(Laws 1994, ch. 94-216, §3, effective January 1, 1995.)

§711.511. Rules of construction

(1) Sections 711.50-711.512 shall be liberally construed and applied to promote their underlying purposes and policy and to make uniform the laws with respect to the subject of these sections among states enacting them.

(2) Unless displaced by the particular provisions of §§711.50-711.512, the principles of law and equity supplement the provisions of these sections.

(Laws 1994, ch. 94-216, §3, effective January 1, 1995.)

§711.512. Applicable date

Sections 711.50-711.512 apply to registrations of securities in beneficiary form made before, on, or after January 1, 1995, by decedents dying on or after January 1, 1995.

(Laws 1994, ch. 94-216, §3, effective January 1, 1995.)

3. Totten Trusts (Savings Account Trusts)

A savings account trust (also called a "tentative trust" or "Totten Trust") (named after the case of In re Totten, 71 N.E. 748 (N.Y. 1904)), is a form of multiple-party bank account in which a person (a "depositor") deposits funds in the depositor's name as trustee for another person or persons. Totten Trusts are valid, by case law or statute, in the majority of jurisdictions.

Savings bank trusts have been in existence since the late nineteenth century. Historically, courts had difficulty determining the validity of such accounts at the death of the depositor. Compare Martin v. Funk, 75 N.Y. 134 (N.Y. 1878) (holding that a savings bank trust was sufficient to pass title to named beneficiary) *with* Brabrook v. Boston Five Cents Savings Bank, 104 Mass. 228 (Mass. 1870) (denying recovery because the passbooks were never in the beneficiary's possession). Early courts questioned whether these arrangements were invalid for failure to comply with a given jurisdiction's wills legislation. Even if courts determined that these arrangements were valid, other concerns emerged regarding the depositor's intent. That is, did the depositor intend to create a revocable or irrevocable trust? If the latter, did the depositor intend to create an irrevocable trust immediately or, rather, an irrevocable trust as to the balance, subject to the depositor's power to revoke any funds during his or her lifetime?

The landmark case of *In re Totten, supra*, established the validity of savings account trusts and also their revocable nature. *Totten* involved

a controversy between the administrator of the decedent's estate and the beneficiary of a savings account trust created by the decedent. The decedent had opened approximately 16 trust accounts (totalling approximately $40,000) and designated various beneficiaries. During her lifetime, she retained the passbooks and control of the deposits. She never stated her intention in opening these accounts. After her death, one of the beneficiaries (a nephew who had no knowledge of the accounts during decedent's lifetime) presented a claim against the estate. After surveying the law, the court concluded that the depositor of such an account establishes a trust that is revocable until the depositor dies or makes the gift irrevocable. If the depositor predeceases the beneficiary without revoking the gift, a presumption arises that an irrevocable trust was created as to the balance. *Totten*, 71 N.E. at 752.

Courts have specified that Totten Trusts, unlike other trusts with no implied power of revocation, are revocable based on judicial beliefs about the expectations of the depositor. Bogert et al., *supra*, at §47.

Generally, a depositor can revoke the savings account trust by: manifestation of such intent, withdrawal of any part of the whole of the funds on deposit (the withdrawal operating as a revocation to the extent of such withdrawal), or a disposition in the depositor's will of the deposit in favor of another beneficiary. The depositor can make the savings account trust *irrevocable* by: manifestation of such intent, delivery of the passbook to the beneficiary, or notice to the beneficiary. The trust becomes irrevocable also if the depositor predeceases the beneficiary without the depositor revoking the account, thereby entitling the beneficiary to the balance remaining in the account.

Totten Trusts have been recognized in Florida since 1956. In Seymour v. Seymour, 85 So. 2d 726 (Fla. 1956), a mother opened a savings account by means of a signature card that proclaimed that she held the account "in trust for [her son]." When she died, the administrator of her estate claimed the funds as part of her estate. The Florida Supreme Court held that, because the decedent took no steps during her lifetime to rebut the presumption of her initial act, her son was entitled to the proceeds in the account on her death. The court thereby adopted the common-law Totten Trust doctrine, saying "[w]e accept it without hesitation." *Id.* at 727.

In 1969, the Florida legislature enacted a statutory amendment (Fla. Stat. §689.075(2)) that recognized Totten Trusts despite the fact that the settlor of such trusts was also the trustee and the life beneficiary.

> The statutory amendment . . . was felt necessary to free Totten Trusts from the statutory requirements that trusts in some cases must be executed with the formalities of a will.

John G. Grimsley, Totten Trusts, Fla. Law of Trusts §15-6 (4th ed. 2006).

The Totten Trust doctrine was challenged subsequently in Litsey v. First Federal Savings & Loan Association of Tampa, 243 So. 2d 239 (Fla. Dist. Ct. App. 1972). The executor of a decedent's estate challenged the validity of 13 savings bank trusts naming the decedent's son and other relatives as beneficiaries, arguing "that the Totten Trust doctrine should be overruled or at least receded from in Florida because it is contrary to the Statute of Wills, the Florida policy against using joint accounts for testamentary purpose, and the policy against illusory and naked trusts." *Id.* at 241. Rejecting these arguments, the appellate court upheld the trusts and noted that the Totten Trust doctrine was a "firmly established rule of law in Florida." *Id.*

The Totten Trust doctrine finally was codified in 1992 (Fla. Stat. §655.81). However in 2001, pursuant to Florida Statutes §655.825, the legislature replaced Florida Statutes §655.81 with §655.82 (Laws 2001, ch. 2001-243, §20). The 2001 statutory amendment provided that the Florida statute on multiple-party accounts (i.e., legislation adopting the Uniform Multiple-Person Accounts Act, Fla. Stat. §655.82) should henceforth apply to Totten Trusts. (The Uniform Act, as promulgated by NCCUSL, treats accounts in the form of Totten Trusts as payable-on-death accounts.)

§655.825. Deposits in trust accounts; replacement of former §655.81 with §655.82

(1) Because deposits in trust are also accounts with a pay-on-death designation as described in §655.82, it is the intent of the Legislature that the provisions of §655.82 shall apply to and govern deposits in trust. References to §655.81 in any depository agreement shall be interpreted after the effective date of this act as references to § 655.82.

(2) This section shall take effect July 1, 2001, and shall apply to deposits made to a depository account created after December 31, 1994.

(Laws 2001, ch 2001-243, §3, effective July 1, 2001.)

§655.82. Payable-on-death accounts generally

(1) As used in this section:

(a) "Account" means a contract of deposit between a depositor and an institution, including, but not limited to, a checking account, savings account, certificate of deposit, and share account.

(b) "Beneficiary" means a person named as one to whom sums on deposit in an account are payable on request after death of all parties or for whom a party is named as trustee.

(c) "Devisee" means any person designated in a will to receive a testamentary disposition of real or personal property.

(d) "Heirs" means those persons, including a surviving spouse, who are entitled, under the laws of this state regarding intestate succession, to the property of a decedent.

(e) "Multiple-party account" means an account payable on request to one or more of two or more parties, whether or not a right of survivorship is mentioned.

(f) "Party" means a person who, by the terms of an account, has a present right, subject to request, to payment from the account other than as a beneficiary.

(g) "Payment" means disbursement of sums on deposit, and includes withdrawal, payment to a party or third person pursuant to check or other request, and a pledge of sums on deposit by a party, or a setoff, reduction, or other disposition of all or part of an account pursuant to a pledge.

(h) "Pay-on-death designation" means the designation of:

1. A beneficiary in an account payable on request to one party during the party's lifetime and on the party's death to one or more beneficiaries, or to one or more parties during their lifetimes and on death of all of them to one or more beneficiaries; or

2. A beneficiary in an account in the name of one or more parties as trustee for one or more beneficiaries if the relationship is established by the terms of the account and there is no subject of the trust other than the sums on deposit in the account, whether or not payment to the beneficiary is mentioned.

(i) "Personal representative" means an executor, administrator, curator, successor personal representative, special administrator, or any other person who performs substantially the same function under the law governing their status.

(j) "Receive," as it relates to notice to an institution, means receipt in the office or branch office of the institution in which the account is established, but if the terms of the account require notice at a particular place, in the place required.

(k) "Request" means a request for payment complying with all terms of the account, including special requirements concerning necessary signatures and regulations of the institution; but, for purposes of this section, if terms of the account condition payment on advance notice, a request for payment is treated as immediately effective and a notice of intent to withdraw is treated as a request for payment.

(l) "Successor" means any person, other than a creditor, who is entitled to property of a decedent under the decedent's will or otherwise.

(m) "Sums on deposit" means the balance payable on an account, including interest and dividends earned, whether or not included in the current balance, and any deposit of life insurance proceeds added to the account by reason of death of a party.

(n) "Terms of the account" means the deposit agreement and other terms and conditions, including the form, of the contract of deposit.

(2) A beneficiary in an account having a pay-on-death designation has no right to sums on deposit during the lifetime of any party.

(3) In an account with a pay-on-death designation:

(a) On the death of one of two or more parties, sums on deposit in the account belong to the surviving party or parties.

(b) On the death of the sole party or the last survivor of two or more parties, sums on deposit belong to the surviving beneficiary or beneficiaries. If two or more beneficiaries survive, sums on deposit belong to them in equal and undivided shares, and, unless otherwise provided in a depository agreement written between December 31, 1994, and July 1, 2001, there is no right of survivorship in the event of death of a beneficiary thereafter. If no beneficiary survives, sums on deposit belong to the estate of the last surviving party.

(4) A pay-on-death designation in a multiple-party account without right of survivorship is ineffective. For purposes of this section, designation of an account as a tenancy in common establishes that the account is without right of survivorship.

(5) The ownership right of a surviving party or beneficiary, or of the decedent's estate, in sums on deposit is subject to requests for payment made by a party before the party's death, whether paid by the institution before or after death, or unpaid. The

surviving party or beneficiary, or the decedent's estate, is liable to the payee of an unpaid request for payment. The liability is limited to a proportionate share of the amount transferred under this section, to the extent necessary to discharge the request for payment.

(6) An institution, on request, may pay sums on deposit in an account with a pay-on-death designation to:

(a) One or more of the parties, whether or not another party is disabled, incapacitated, or deceased when the payment is requested and whether or not a party survives another party;

(b) The beneficiary or beneficiaries, if proof of death is presented to the institution showing that the beneficiary or beneficiaries survived all persons named as parties; or

(c) The personal representative, if any, or, if there is none, the heirs or devisees of a deceased party, if proof of death is presented to the institution showing that the deceased party was the survivor of all other persons named on the account either as a party or beneficiary.

(7) Payment made pursuant to this section discharges the institution from all claims for amounts so paid, whether or not the payment is consistent with the beneficial ownership of the account as between parties, beneficiaries, or their successors. Payment may be made whether or not a party or beneficiary is disabled, incapacitated, or deceased when payment is requested, received, or made.

(8) A beneficiary in an account at a credit union having a pay-on-death designation, unless the beneficiary is a member in her or his own right, may not be permitted to vote, obtain an extension of credit, or hold office or be required to pay an entrance or membership fee.

(9) The following is an example of the form of a contract of deposit that may be used to select a pay-on-death account for use by one or more parties:

PARTIES (Name each party): ___________ ___________
OWNERSHIP (Select one and initial):
_______ SINGLE-PARTY ACCOUNT
_______ MULTIPLE-PARTY ACCOUNT
RIGHTS AT DEATH (Select one and initial):
_______ SINGLE-PARTY ACCOUNT
At death of the party, ownership passes as part of the party's estate.
_______ SINGLE-PARTY ACCOUNT WITH A PAY-ON-DEATH DESIGNATION
(Name one or more beneficiaries):

_______________ _______________
At death of the party, ownership passes to the designated pay-on-death beneficiaries and is not part of the party's estate.
_______ MULTIPLE-PARTY ACCOUNT WITH RIGHT OF SURVIVORSHIP
At death of a party, ownership passes to the surviving party or parties.
_______ MULTIPLE-PARTY ACCOUNT WITH RIGHT OF SURVIVORSHIP AND A PAY-ON-DEATH DESIGNATION
(Name one or more beneficiaries):

_______________ _______________

At death of the last surviving party, ownership passes to the designated pay-on-death beneficiaries and is not part of the last surviving party's estate.

(Laws 1994, ch. 94-216, §1, effective January 1, 1995. Amended by Laws 1997, ch. 97-102, §529, effective July 1, 1997; Laws 2001, ch. 2001-243, §21, effective June 15, 2001.)

§689.075. Validity of inter vivos trusts when settlor retains significant powers

(1) A trust which is otherwise valid and which complies with §737.111, including, but not limited to, a trust the principal of which is composed of real property, intangible personal property, tangible personal property, the possible expectancy of receiving as a named beneficiary death benefits as described in § 733.808, or any combination thereof, and which has been created by a written instrument shall not be held invalid or an attempted testamentary disposition for any one or more of the following reasons:

(a) Because the settlor or another person or both possess the power to revoke, amend, alter, or modify the trust in whole or in part;

(b) Because the settlor or another person or both possess the power to appoint by deed or will the persons and organizations to whom the income shall be paid or the principal distributed;

(c) Because the settlor or another person or both possess the power to add to, or withdraw from, the trust all or any part of the principal or income at one time or at different times;

(d) Because the settlor or another person or both possess the power to remove the trustee or trustees and appoint a successor trustee or trustees;

(e) Because the settlor or another person or both possess the power to control the trustee or trustees in the administration of the trust;

(f) Because the settlor has retained the right to receive all or part of the income of the trust during her or his life or for any part thereof;

(g) Because the settlor is, at the time of the execution of the instrument, or thereafter becomes, sole trustee.

(2) Nothing contained herein shall affect the validity of those accounts, including but not limited to bank accounts, share accounts, deposits, certificates of deposit, savings certificates, and other similar arrangements, heretofore or hereafter established at any bank, savings and loan association, or credit union by one or more persons, in trust for one or more other persons, which arrangements are, by their terms, revocable by the person making the same until her or his death or incompetency.

(3) The fact that any one or more of the powers specified in subsection (1) are in fact exercised once, or more than once, shall not affect the validity of the trust or its nontestamentary character.

(4) This section shall be applicable to trusts executed before or after July 1, 1969, by persons who are living on or after said date. However, the requirement of conformity with the formalities for the execution of wills as found in paragraph (1)(g) [FN1] shall not be imposed upon any trust executed prior to July 1, 1969.

(5) The amendment of this section, by chapter 75-74, Laws of Florida, is intended to clarify the legislative intent of this section at the time of its original enactment that it apply to all otherwise valid trusts which are created by written instrument and which are not expressly excluded by the terms of this section and that no such trust shall be declared invalid for any of the reasons stated in subsections (1) and (3) regardless of whether the trust involves or relates to an interest in real property.

[FN1] Laws 1995, ch. 95-401, §5, removed reference to the formalities for the execution of wills from paragraph (1)(g).

(Laws 1969, ch. 69-192, §§1, 2; Laws 1969, Ex. Sess., ch. 69-1747, §1; Laws 1971, ch. 71-126, §§1, 2; Laws 1973, ch. 73-333, §169; Laws 1974, ch. 74-78, §1; Laws 1975, ch. 75-74, §§1, 2. Amended by Laws 1995, ch. 95-401, §5, effective July 1, 1995; Laws 1997, ch. 97-102, § 756, effective July 1, 1997.)

III. Other Joint Forms of Ownership

Several forms of joint ownership exist. These include: joint tenancy, tenancy in common, and tenancy by the entirety. These forms of ownership are explained below.

A. Joint Tenancy

1. Characteristics

The most common form of joint ownership is joint tenancy. Joint tenancies may be created in both real and personal property. Atkinson, *supra*, §40 at 164. Upon the death of a joint tenant, the remaining joint tenant (or joint tenants) take the property by operation of law without the need for judicial proceedings. *Id.*, §28 at 103.

The common law presumed that a grant to two or more persons created a joint estate with the right of survivorship. However, today joint estates are disfavored. Atkinson, *supra*, §40 at 164.

At common law, a joint tenancy required four unities of interest, title, time, and possession. That is, the joint tenants must have:

- **the same and equal interests;**
- **rights that were created under the same instrument;**
- **interests that commenced at the same time; and**
- **the right to undivided possession.**

A joint tenant cannot devise his or her interest by will. If a joint tenant wants to devise his interest to someone other than the co-tenant(s), the former must *sever the tenancy* during his or her lifetime. That severance converts the joint tenancy into a tenancy in common as to the share conveyed, thereby enabling the original joint tenant to devise his or her interest. Note that if one of three or more joint tenants conveys his or her interest to one of the others, the grantee becomes a tenant in common as to the interest conveyed, but remains a joint tenant as to his or her original interest. Annot., Estates by Entirety in Personal Property, 64 ALR2d §10 (1959 & Supp. 2006).

Creation of a joint tenancy requires compliance with the relevant state statute. In Florida, creation of a joint tenancy requires that the instrument creating the interest contain an *express* provision regarding the right of survivorship. According to Florida Statutes §689.15, a devise, transfer or conveyance to two or more persons creates a tenancy in common, unless the instrument creating the estate "shall expressly provide for the right of survivorship."

Although early Florida case law required unequivocal language of survivorship, more recent cases hold that, for purposes of satisfying the requirement of Florida Statutes §689.15,

> language indicating that the account is payable to the survivor is sufficient, and that the court will look at all of the instruments that were a part of the transaction (e.g., depository agreement, signature card, savings passbook, ledger sheets, rules and regulations of the financial institution) to find the required language, and that its omission from certain of the documents is not fatal to the creation of a joint tenancy account with right of survivorship.

Belcher, Jointly Held Assets, *supra*, at §5.5 (citing case law). An exception to the rule requiring an express statement of the right of survivorship arises in case of estates by the entirety (discussed *infra*).

§689.15. Creation of estates requires express statement of the right to survivorship

The doctrine of the right of survivorship in cases of real estate and personal property held by joint tenants shall not prevail in this state; that is to say, except in cases of estates by entirety, a devise, transfer or conveyance heretofore or hereafter made to two or more shall create a tenancy in common, unless the instrument creating the estate shall expressly provide for the right of survivorship; and in cases of estates by entirety, the tenants, upon dissolution of marriage, shall become tenants in common.

(Act Nov. 17, 1829, §20; Rev. St. 1892, §1819; Gen. St. 1906, §2294; Rev. Gen. St. 1920, §3617; Comp. Gen. Laws 1927, §5482; Laws 1941, ch. 20954, §3; Laws 1973, ch. 73-300, §1.)

2. Distinguished from Tenancy in Common and Tenancy by the Entirety

Another form of co-ownership is a tenancy in common. The primary difference between a joint tenancy and a tenancy in common is that in the latter case, the co-tenant's interest passes into the co-tenant's probate estate. The interest then is distributed either according to the co-tenant's will or by intestate succession.

Still another form of joint ownership—similar to a joint tenancy but applicable only to spouses—is a tenancy by the entirety. That form of co-ownership has been recognized by case law in Florida since 1913 (English v. English, 63 So. 822 (Fla. 1913), and currently by statute (Fla. Stat. §689.11).

A tenancy by the entirety can exist in personal property as well as real property. Case law has recognized the following property in this form: shares of stock; bank accounts; certificates of deposit; promissory notes, mortgages, assignments of mortgage, and agreements for deed; checks payable to husband and wife; bearer bonds; objects of art and household furnishings. Belcher, *supra*, at §5.10.

A tenancy by the entirety depends on the existence of the marital relationship. Therefore, upon dissolution of the marriage, the parties become tenants in common by operation of law. Further, if the parties are not legally married, they cannot hold property in a tenancy by the entirety. See, e.g., Reinhardt v. Diedricks, 439 So. 2d 936 (Fla. Dist. Ct. App. 1983) (holding that, because a transfer of property to a man and a woman who were not married did not expressly provide for a right of survivorship, a tenancy in common was created and therefore upon his death, his heirs succeeded to his share of estate). See generally Stephen Lease, Survivorship Deeds, 19 Fla. Jur. 2d §11 (2007).

For a time, Florida treated tenancies by the entirety in real property differently from that in personal property. Prior to 2001, Florida law held that a presumption operated that a transfer of real property—but not personal property—to a husband and wife created a tenancy by the entirety. For personal property, the marital parties had to prove intention to create a tenancy by the entirety.

Beal Bank, SSB v. Almand & Assocs., 780 So. 2d 45 (Fla. 2001), changed that rule by treating personal property like real property in terms of applying the presumption of intent favoring tenancies by the entirety. In *Beal Bank*, a creditor of one of the spouses sought to garnish various joint accounts held by both spouses for a debt owed by one spouse individually. The title to some of the accounts was silent with respect to the type of ownership intended and another account listed the owners as joint tenants with right of survivorship. The Florida Supreme Court held that a presumption arose in each case favoring a tenancy by the entirety when personal property is owned by husband and wife. The court then concluded that

> when property is held as a tenancy by the entireties, only the creditors of both the husband and wife, jointly, may attach the tenancy by the entireties property; the property is not divisible on behalf of one spouse alone, and therefore it cannot be reached to satisfy the obligation of only one spouse.

***Id.* at 53. See also Buckeye Retirement Co., LLC, Ltd. V. Nassau Land & Trading Co., Inc., 943 So. 2d 223 (Fla. Dist. Ct. App. 2006) (holding that the debtor and his wife were entitled to dissolution of a writ of garnishment on an account they held as tenancy by the entirety where garnishment was for debt owed by debtor individually).**

It is not necessary, therefore, that the instrument expressly specify that a tenancy by the entirety has been created, provided that the property is owned by husband and wife. This rule is an exception to the requirement stated in Florida Statutes §689.15 that an instrument creating co-ownership in property must expressly state the right of survivorship.

A different statute provides for yet another method of creation of a tenancy by the entirety. Florida Statutes §689.11 provides that when one spouse owns real property and conveys it to the other spouse, a tenancy by the entirety may be created. This effect results from use of a deed that states the *purpose* to create such an estate or a deed that conveys the property to *both* spouses as grantees.

The Florida simultaneous death statute also applies to property held in tenancy by the entirety. According to Florida Statutes §732.601(3), when there is insufficient evidence that spouses who hold property in the form of tenancy by the entirety have died otherwise than simultaneously, the property shall be distributed one-half as if one had survived and one-half as if the other had survived. Application of the Florida slayer disqualification to property held as tenancy by the entirety is discussed in Section III, A, 3, *infra*.

See generally Carolyn J. Frantz & Hanoch Dagan, Properties of Marriage, 104 Colum. L. Rev. 75 (2004) (discussing forms of ownership of marital property).

§689.11. Conveyances between husband and wife create a tenancy by entireties

(1) A conveyance of real estate, including homestead, made by one spouse to the other shall convey the legal title to the grantee spouse in all cases in which it would be effectual if the parties were not married, and the grantee need not execute the conveyance. An estate by the entirety may be created by the action of the spouse holding title:

(a) Conveying to the other by a deed in which the purpose to create the estate is stated; or

(b) Conveying to both spouses.

(2) All deeds heretofore made by a husband direct to his wife or by a wife direct to her husband are hereby validated and made as effectual to convey the title as they would have been were the parties not married;

(3) Provided, that nothing herein shall be construed as validating any deed made for the purpose, or that operates to defraud any creditor or to avoid payment of any legal debt or claim; and

(4) Provided further that this section shall not apply to any conveyance heretofore made, the validity of which shall be contested by suit commenced within 1 year of the effective date of this law.

(Laws 1903, ch. 5147, §1; Gen. St. 1906, §2457; Rev. Gen. St. 1920, §3797; Comp. Gen. Laws 1927, §5670; Laws 1941, ch. 20954, §6; Laws 1947, ch. 23964, §1; Laws 1971, ch. 71-54, §1.)

§689.15. Creation of joint tenancy requires express statement of the right to survivorship

The doctrine of the right of survivorship in cases of real estate and personal property held by joint tenants shall not prevail in this state; that is to say, except in cases of estates by entirety, a devise, transfer or conveyance heretofore or hereafter made to two or more shall create a tenancy in common, unless the instrument creating the estate shall expressly provide for the right of survivorship; and in cases of estates by entirety, the tenants, upon dissolution of marriage, shall become tenants in common.

(Act Nov. 17, 1829, §20; Rev. St. 1892, §1819; Gen. St. 1906, §2294; Rev. Gen. St. 1920, §3617; Comp. Gen. Laws 1927, §5482; Laws 1941, ch. 20954, §3; Laws 1973, ch. 73-300, §1.)

§689.115. Tenancy by entireties created by mortgage made to husband and wife

Any mortgage encumbering real property, or any assignment of a mortgage encumbering real property, made to two persons who are husband and wife, heretofore or hereafter made, creates an estate by the entirety in such mortgage and the obligation secured thereby unless a contrary intention appears in such mortgage or assignment.

(Laws 1986, ch. 86-29, §1; Laws 1991, ch. 91-110, §21.)

§708.09. Married women's rights

Every married woman may enter into agreements and contracts with her husband, may become the partner of her husband or others, may give a power of attorney to her husband, and may execute powers conferred upon her by her husband, including the power to execute and acknowledge all instruments, including relinquishments of dower, conveying, transferring, or encumbering property, or any interest in it, owned by her, or by herself and her husband as tenants by the entirety, or by her husband. All powers of attorney heretofore executed by a wife to her husband and vice versa, and the execution of all documents executed thereunder, are hereby validated and confirmed.

(Laws 1943, ch. 21696, §1; Laws 1943, ch. 21932, §2; Laws 1970, ch. 70-4, §3.)

§708.10. Married women's rights: construction of law not to abolish tenancy by entireties

This law shall not be construed as:

(1) Relieving a husband from any duty of supporting and maintaining his wife and children;

(2) Abolishing estates by the entireties or any of the incidents thereof;

(3) Abolishing dower or any of the incidents thereof;

(4) Changing the rights of either husband or wife to participate in the distribution of the estate of the other upon his death, as may now or hereafter be provided by law;

(5) Dispensing with the joinder of husband and wife in conveying or mortgaging homestead property.

(Laws 1943, ch. 21932, §3.)

§732.601. Simultaneous Death Law

Unless a contrary intention appears in the governing instrument:

(1) When title to property or its devolution depends on priority of death and there is insufficient evidence that the persons have died otherwise than simultaneously, the property of each person shall be disposed of as if that person survived.

(2) When two or more beneficiaries are designated to take successively by reason of survivorship under another person's disposition of property and there is insufficient evidence that the beneficiaries died otherwise than simultaneously, the property thus disposed of shall be divided into as many equal parts as there are successive beneficiaries and the parts shall be distributed to those who would have taken if each designated beneficiary had survived.

(3) When there is insufficient evidence that two joint tenants or tenants by the entirety died otherwise than simultaneously, the property so held shall be distributed one-half as if one had survived and one-half as if the other had survived. If there are more than two joint tenants and all of them so died, the property thus distributed shall be in the proportion that one bears to the number of joint tenants.

(4) When the insured and the beneficiary in a policy of life or accident insurance have died and there is insufficient evidence that they died otherwise than simultaneously, the proceeds of the policy shall be distributed as if the insured had survived the beneficiary.

(Laws 1974, ch. 74-106, §1; Laws 1975, ch. 75-220, §34. Amended by Laws 1997, ch. 97-102, §966, effective July 1, 1997; Laws 2001, ch. 2001-226, §50, effective January 1, 2002.)

FLORIDA CONSTITUTION, Art. 10, §5

There shall be no distinction between married women and married men in the holding, control, disposition, or encumbering of their property, both real and personal; except that dower or curtesy may be established and regulated by law.

3. Severance of the Joint Tenancy

Severance of the joint tenancy extinguishes the right of survivorship. Severance must be accomplished during the lifetimes of the joint tenants. A will is ineffective to change the survivorship feature of a joint tenancy. (A frequent reason to sever the joint tenancy is to ensure that the co-tenant does not take the former's share at death.)

A severance of the joint tenancy may occur by mutual agreement of the parties or by any conduct that is inconsistent with one or more of the unities (i.e., possession, interest, title, or time) required to create a joint tenancy with right of survivorship. Belcher, *supra*, at §5.7.

Severance of the joint tenancy (or tenancy by the entirety) converts it into a tenancy in common. A joint tenant who kills another joint tenant (or a tenant by the entirety) effects a severance of the tenancy (Fla. Stat. §732.802(2). The killing results in disqualification of the slayer: that is, the decedent's share of the property passes as the decedent's property rather than passing automatically to the slayer by operation of law.

According to Florida law, a fraudulent transfer by one joint tenant of his interest does not cause a severance of the tenancy. See Perrott v. Frankie, 605 So. 2d 118 (Fla. Dist. Ct.

App. 1992) (holding that a father's transfer of an apartment building to his daughter as joint tenants with right of survivorship during pending litigation in order to protect the asset from the creditor was fraudulent and, therefore, that the property reverted to its prior status).

§732.802. Slayer disqualification: severance of joint tenancies and tenancies by the entireties

(1) A surviving person who unlawfully and intentionally kills or participates in procuring the death of the decedent is not entitled to any benefits under the will or under the Florida Probate Code, and the estate of the decedent passes as if the killer had predeceased the decedent. Property appointed by the will of the decedent to or for the benefit of the killer passes as if the killer had predeceased the decedent.

(2) Any joint tenant who unlawfully and intentionally kills another joint tenant thereby effects a severance of the interest of the decedent so that the share of the decedent passes as the decedent's property and the killer has no rights by survivorship. This provision applies to joint tenancies with right of survivorship and tenancies by the entirety in real and personal property; joint and multiple-party accounts in banks, savings and loan associations, credit unions, and other institutions; and any other form of coownership with survivorship incidents.

....

(Laws 1974, ch. 74-106, §1; Laws 1975, ch. 75-220, §41; Laws 1982, ch. 82-71, §1.)

B. Joint Ownership of Safe Deposit Boxes

Often, persons lease a safe deposit box jointly. The financial institution specifies the terms of the lease of the box. Those terms generally give the parties joint access to the box but do not change title to the contents.

> [T]he rental agreement is usually prepared by the safe-deposit box company on its printed form and is designed for its protection; often it does not represent the true understanding of the lessees. For these reasons, it is reasonable to deny that a joint tenancy can be created by this method.

Atkinson, *supra*, §40, at 167.

Florida law has regulations applicable to the lease of safe-deposit boxes. The regulations govern the right of access to a safe-deposit box, the liability of the financial institution in various situations, and remedies for nonpayment of box rental fees.

A Florida financial institution may make available safe-deposit boxes for the safekeeping of property and/or documents, provided that it issues a receipt for any such property or documents (Fla. Stat. §655.931).

The right of access to a safe-deposit box is regulated by (1) the agreement between the lessee and the financial institution, (2) the rules of the financial institution, and (3) state law. Florida law provides the following persons with access: lessees of the box, as well as fiduciaries and their agents (Fla. Stat. §655.93).

If the rental agreement for the safe-deposit box provides that access will be granted to either of two (or more) lessees, the financial institution must grant access to any of these lessees. William H. Danne, Safe-deposit Boxes and Safekeeping Facilities, 5 Fla. Jur. 2d §75 (2007). The lessee's signature on the access record (or the lessee's receipt for property) is a sufficient release of the lessor for purposes of liability (Fla. Stat. §655.937(2)).

If the financial institution receives satisfactory proof of the death of a lessee of the box, the institution must permit statutorily designated persons to open the safe-deposit box and examine the contents in the presence of an official of the institution (Fla. Stat. §655.935). Further, the financial institution must permit the aforementioned persons to conduct a search of the safe-deposit box for a will or burial instructions (Fla. Stat. §655.935(1), (2)). The financial institution may deny access to any person who refuses to comply with any of the institution's requirements or procedures (Fla. Stat. §655.939). The Code also regulates the delivery of the contents of the box to the personal representative (Fla. Stat. §955.936(1)).

A statutory amendment in 2006 clarified that the right of access of a co-lessee differs from that of a personal representative (Fla. Stat. §655.937(4)), and also specified procedures for opening a safety deposit box that is co-leased by a decedent in cases in which a lessee wants to examine the contents after the death of another lessee. Specifically, the statute provides that the surviving co-lessee(s) may make a written inventory of the box in the presence of another person (Fla. Stat. §655.937(5)). Those present at that time must verify the contents of the box by signing a copy of the inventory under penalty of perjury (*id.*). A different statute provides additional rules regarding the initial opening of a

safe-deposit box for purposes of conducting the inventory of the estate (Fla. Stat. §733.6065).

Occasionally, a lessee of a safe-deposit box fails to pay rent on the box. Florida law provides that the financial institution may enforce rental fee liability by opening the safe deposit box; disposing of the contents; and using the proceeds of the sale to satisfy the outstanding rental fees, cost of opening the box, and sale of the contents. However, the bank first must provide notice to the lessee(s). According to Florida law, if the rental fee has not been paid for a three-month period, the financial institution may send a notice to the last known address of the lessee informing him or her of the appropriate procedures for nonpayment (Fla. Stat. §655.94(1)). If the rental fee and accumulated charges remain unpaid for one year, the financial institution may send a subsequent notice informing the lessee that the contents will be sold at public auction and the proceeds deposited in an account to the credit of the lessee (Fla. Stat. §655.94(3)). After three years, however, if the property is still unclaimed, it is subject to the escheat provisions of the Florida Disposition of Unclaimed Property Act (Fla. Stat. §717.116). On escheat, see Chapter I *supra*.

Note that the issue of access to the box is different from the issue of title to the contents. See, e.g., Bechtel v. Bechtel's Estate, 330 So. 2d 217 (Fla. Dist. Ct. App. 1976), *appeal after remand*, 348 So. 2d 927 (Fla. Dist. Ct. App. 1977) (holding that that, despite wife's co-signing lease for safe deposit box, bearer bonds found in box were not held by husband and wife as tenants by the entirety so as to vest possession in widow after decedent's death).

§655.93. Applicable definitions regarding safe-deposit box legislation

As used in §§655.93-655.94, the term:

(1) "Lessee" means a person who contracts with a lessor for the use of a safe-deposit box.

(2) "Lessor" means a financial institution that rents safe-deposit facilities.

(3) "Safe-deposit box" means a safe-deposit box, vault, or other safe-deposit receptacle maintained by a lessor, and the rules relating thereto apply to property or documents kept in safekeeping in the financial institution's vault.

(Laws 1992, ch. 92-303, §60, effective July 3, 1992.)

§655.931. Authority to lease safe-deposit boxes

A financial institution may maintain and lease safe-deposit boxes and may accept property or documents for safekeeping if, except in the case of property or documents accepted through night depositories, it issues a receipt therefor.

(Laws 1992, ch. 92-303, §61, effective July 3, 1992.)

§655.932. Bank can lease box to minor

A lessor may lease a safe-deposit box to, and in connection therewith deal with, a minor with the same effect as if leasing to and dealing with a person of full legal capacity.

(Laws 1992, ch. 92-303, §62, effective July 3, 1992.)

§655.933. Bank may lease to fiduciary

If a safe-deposit box is made available by a lessor to one or more persons acting as fiduciaries, the lessor may, except as otherwise expressly provided in the lease or the writings pursuant to which such fiduciaries are acting, allow access thereto as follows:

(1) By any one or more of the persons acting as personal representatives.

(2) By any one or more of the persons otherwise acting as fiduciaries if authorized in writing, which writing is signed by all other persons so acting.

(3) By any agent authorized in writing, which writing is signed by all persons acting as fiduciaries.

(Laws 1992, ch. 92-303, §63, effective July 3, 1992.)

§655.934. Lessee's death: binding effect of transactions

If a lessor without knowledge of the death or of an order determining incapacity of the lessee deals with the lessee's agent in accordance with a written power of attorney or a durable family power of attorney signed by such lessee, the transaction binds the lessee's estate and the lessee.

(Laws 1992, ch. 92-303, § 64, effective July 3, 1992.)

§655.935. Bank shall permit search of safety-deposit box for will or burial instructions

If satisfactory proof of the death of the lessee is presented, a lessor shall permit the person named in a court order for the purpose, or if no order has been served upon the lessor, the spouse, a parent, an adult descendant, or a person named as a personal representative in a copy of a purported will produced by such person, to open and examine the contents of a safe-deposit box leased or coleased by a decedent, or any documents delivered by a decedent for safekeeping, in the presence of an officer of the lessor; and the lessor, if so requested by such person, shall deliver:

(1) Any writing purporting to be a will of the decedent, to the court having probate jurisdiction in the county in which the financial institution is located.

(2) Any writing purporting to be a deed to a burial plot or to give burial instructions, to the person making the request for a search.

(3) Any document purporting to be an insurance policy on the life of the decedent, to the beneficiary named therein.

No other contents may be removed pursuant to this section. Access granted pursuant to this section shall not be considered the initial opening of the safe-deposit box pursuant to § 733.6065 by a personal representative appointed by a court in this state.

(Laws 1992, ch. 92-303, §65, effective July 3, 1992. Amended by Laws 2006, ch. 2006-134, §1, effective July 1, 2006; Laws 2006, ch. 2006-213, § 67, effective October 1, 2006.)

§655.936. Bank shall deliver contents of box to personal representative

(1) Subject to the provisions of subsection (3), the lessor shall immediately deliver to a personal representative appointed by a court in this state, upon presentation of a certified copy of his or her letters of authority, all property deposited with it by the decedent for safekeeping, and shall grant the personal representative access to any safe-deposit box in the decedent's name and permit him or her to remove from such box any part or all of the contents thereof.

(2) If a personal representative of a deceased lessee has been appointed by a court of any other state, a lessor may, at its discretion, after 3 months from the issuance to such personal representative of his or her letters of authority, deliver to such personal representative all properties deposited with it for safekeeping and the contents of any safe-deposit box in the name of the decedent if at such time the lessor has not received written notice of the appointment of a personal representative in this state, and such delivery is a valid discharge of the lessor for all property or contents so delivered. A personal representative appointed by a court of any other state shall furnish the lessor with an affidavit setting forth facts showing the domicile of the deceased lessee to be other than this state and stating that there are no unpaid creditors of the deceased lessee in this state, together with a certified copy of his or her letters of authority. A lessor making delivery pursuant to this subsection shall maintain in its files a receipt executed by such personal representative which itemizes in detail all property so delivered.

(3) Notwithstanding the provisions of subsection (1), after the death of a lessee of a safe-deposit box, the lessor shall permit the initial opening of the safe-deposit box and the removal of the contents of the safe-deposit box in accordance with §733.6065.

(4) A lessor is not liable for damages or penalty by reason of any delivery made pursuant to this section.

(Laws 1992, ch. 92-303, §66, effective July 3, 1992. Amended by Laws 1997, ch. 97-102, §531, effective July 1, 1997; Laws 1997, ch. 97-240, §12, effective May 30, 1997; Laws 2001, ch. 2001-226, §3, effective January 1, 2002; Laws 2006, ch. 2006-134, §2, effective July 1, 2006; Laws 2006, ch. 2006-213, §68, effective October 1, 2006.)

§655.937. Access granted to either of two lessees

(1) Unless specifically provided in the lease or rental agreement to the contrary, if a safe-deposit box is rented or leased in the names of two or more lessees, access to the safe-deposit box will be granted to:

(a) Either or any of such lessees, regardless of whether or not the other lessee or lessees or any of them are living or competent.

(b) Subject to §655.933, those persons named in §655.933.

(c) Subject to §655.935, those persons named in §655.935.

(d) Subject to §733.6065, the personal representative of the estate of either or any of such lessees who is deceased, or the guardian of the property of either or any of such lessees who is incapacitated.

(2) In all cases described in subsection (1), the signature on the safe-deposit entry or access record, or the receipt or acquittance, in the case of property or documents otherwise held for safekeeping, is a valid and sufficient release and discharge to the lessor for granting access to such safe-deposit box or for the delivery of such property or documents otherwise held for safekeeping.

(3) A lessor may not be held liable for damages or penalty by reason of any access granted or delivery made pursuant to this section.

(4) The right of access by a colessee is separate from the rights and responsibilities of other persons who may be granted access to a safe-deposit box after

the death or incapacity of another colessee, and such right of access is not subject to the provisions of §655.935, §733.6065, or other requirements imposed upon personal representatives, guardians, or other fiduciaries.

(5) After the death of a colessee, the surviving colessee or any other person who is granted access to the safe-deposit box pursuant to this section may make a written inventory of the box, which must be conducted by the person making the request in the presence of one other person as specified in this subsection. Each person present shall verify the contents of the box by signing a copy of the inventory under penalty of perjury.

(a) If the person making the written inventory is a surviving colessee, the other person may be any other person granted access pursuant to this section, an employee of the institution where the box is located, or an attorney licensed in this state.

(b) If the person making the written inventory is not a surviving colessee, the other person may be a surviving colessee, an employee of the institution where the box is located, or an attorney licensed in this state.

(Laws 1992, ch. 92-303, §67, effective July 3, 1992. Amended by Laws 2006, ch. 2006-134, §3, effective July 1, 2006; Laws 2006, ch. 2006-213, §69, effective October 1, 2006.)

§655.938. Bank's responsibility if there are adverse claims to contents

(1) An adverse claim to the contents of a safe-deposit box, or to property held in safekeeping, is not sufficient to require the lessor to deny access to its lessee unless:

(a) The lessor is directed to do so by a court order issued in an action in which the lessee is served with process and named as a party by a name which identifies the lessee with the name in which the safe-deposit box is leased or the property held; or

(b) The safe-deposit box is leased or the property is held in the name of a lessee with the addition of words indicating that the contents or property are held in a fiduciary capacity, and the adverse claim is supported by a written statement of facts disclosing that it is made by, or on behalf of, a beneficiary and that there is reason to know that the fiduciary will misappropriate the trust property.

(2) A claim is also an adverse claim if one of several lessees claims, contrary to the terms of the lease, an exclusive right of access, or if one or more persons claim a right of access as agents or officers of a lessee to the exclusion of others as agents or officers, or if it is claimed that a lessee is the same person as one using another name.

(Laws 1992, ch. 92-303, §68, effective July 3, 1992.)

§655.939. Bank can deny access to a person for failure to comply with bank's rules

If any individual who has a right of access to a safe-deposit box is unwilling or unable for any reason or cause to comply with any of the lessor's normal requirements or procedures in connection with such access relating to security, safety, or protection, the lessor has the right to limit or deny access to the safe-deposit box by such individual unless all lessees of such safe-deposit box take such action as is necessary to ensure reasonable compliance with such security, safety, or protection requirements or procedures.

(Laws 1992, ch. 92-303, §69, effective July 3, 1992.)

§655.94. Remedies for nonpayment of rental fees

(1) If the rental due on a safe-deposit box has not been paid for 3 months, the lessor may send a notice by certified mail to the last known address of the lessee stating that the safe-deposit box will be opened and its contents stored at the expense of the lessee unless payment of the rental is made within 30 days. If the rental is not paid within 30 days from the mailing of the notice, the box may be opened in the presence of an officer of the lessor and of a notary public. The contents shall be sealed in a package by a notary public who shall write on the outside the name of the lessee and the date of the opening. The notary public shall execute a certificate reciting the name of the lessee, the date of the opening of the box, and a list of its contents. The certificate shall be included in the package, and a copy of the certificate shall be sent by certified mail to the last known address of the lessee. The package shall then be placed in the general vaults of the lessor at a rental not exceeding the rental previously charged for the box. The lessor has a lien on the package and its contents to the extent of any rental due and owing plus the actual, reasonable costs of removing the contents from the safe-deposit box.

(2) If the contents of the safe-deposit box have not been claimed within 1 year after the mailing of the certificate, the lessor may send a further notice to the last known address of the lessee stating that, unless the accumulated charges are paid within 30 days, the contents of the box will be sold at public auction at a specified time and place or, in the case of securities

listed on a stock exchange, will be sold upon the exchange on or after a specified date and unsalable items will be destroyed. The time, place, and manner of sale shall also be posted conspicuously on the premises of the lessor and advertised once in a newspaper of general circulation in the community. If the articles are not claimed, they may then be sold in accordance with the notice. The balance of the proceeds, after deducting accumulated charges, including the expenses of advertising and conducting the sale, shall be deposited to the credit of the lessee in any account maintained by the lessee, or, if none, shall be deemed a deposit account with the financial institution operating the safe-deposit facility, and shall be identified on the books of the financial institution as arising from the sale of contents of a safe-deposit box.

(3) Any documents or writings of a private nature, and having little or no apparent value, need not be offered for sale, but shall be retained, unless claimed by the owner, for the period specified for unclaimed contents, after which they may be destroyed.

(Laws 1992, ch. 92-303, §70, effective July 3, 1992. Amended by Laws 2004, ch. 2004-340, §12, effective July 1, 2004; Laws 2004, ch. 2004-390, §95, effective July 1, 2004.)

§733.6065. Opening safe-deposit box for purposes of inventory of estate

(1) Subject to the provisions of §655.936(2), the initial opening of a safe-deposit box that is leased or coleased by the decedent shall be conducted in the presence of any two of the following persons: an employee of the institution where the box is located, the personal representative, or the personal representative's attorney of record. Each person who is present must verify the contents of the box by signing a copy of the inventory under penalties of perjury. The personal representative shall file the safe-deposit box inventory, together with a copy of the box entry record from a date which is 6 months prior to the date of death to the date of inventory, with the court within 10 days after the box is opened. Unless otherwise ordered by the court, this inventory and the attached box entry record is subject to inspection only by persons entitled to inspect an inventory under §733.604(1). The personal representative may remove the contents of the box.

(2) The right to open and examine the contents of a safe-deposit box leased by a decedent, or any documents delivered by a decedent for safekeeping, and to receive items as provided for in §655.935 is separate from the rights provided for in subsection (1).

(Laws 2001, ch. 2001-226, §129, effective January 1, 2002. Amended by Laws 2006, ch. 2006-134, §7, effective July 1, 2006; Laws 2006, ch. 2006-213, §71, effective October 1, 2006.)

IV. Gifts

A. Inter Vivos Gifts

A gift is a gratuitous transfer of property to a donee by a donor with donative intent. Two types of gifts exist:

- **inter vivos gifts, and**
- **conditional gifts (such as gifts in contemplation of marriage and gifts in contemplation of impending death).**

A gift requires donative intent and delivery. However, courts sometimes find donative intent even without delivery. Other times, courts find that delivery is not sufficient to show donative intent. McGovern & Kurtz, *supra*, §4.5 at 204-205.

An inter vivos gift is a completed transfer. With limited exceptions (see Section B *infra*), it cannot be made revocable or conditional. Atkinson, *supra*, §45 at 200. See also Restatement (Third) Property, *supra*, at §6.1.

A valid inter vivos gift requires:

- **donative intent by a donor having capacity;**
- **delivery, so as to relinquish dominion and control by the donor; and**
- **acceptance by the donee (although acceptance may be presumed).**

To make a valid inter vivos gift, the property owner must presently divest himself or herself of ownership and control. If the donor intends for a gift to take effect in the future, it is merely a promise to make a gift.

Gifts of intangibles can be made by several methods. The first method is manual or actual delivery. However, some intangibles (i.e., certificates of deposit, bonds) may be subject to the additional rule of financial institutions that require notice of the transfer. McGovern & Kurtz, *supra*, §4.5 at 204. *Id.* Sometimes, a gift will be effective without actual delivery if the donor merely re-registers the intangibles in the donee's name even if the donee is unaware of the gift. *Id.*

The second method is delivery by a signed writing. *Id.* at 191. The writing indicates the donor's intent to give the item. In some cases, the gift will be effective if the donor gives the

signed writing without delivering the item itself. *Id.*

Traditionally, signing and delivering a check to a donee is not effective as an assignment of the donor's funds if the donor dies before the check is paid. That is, the order on the bank is considered revoked by the donor's death; the check is not enforceable against the estate. Atkinson, *supra*, §45 at 199; McGovern & Kurtz, *supra*, at 205.

The third method of delivery is symbolic (sometimes called "constructive"), such as by transferring a savings account book. Atkinson, *supra*, §45 at 202-203; McGovern & Kurtz, *supra*, §4.5 at 206. The bank book serves as a symbol or evidence of the item itself.

Delivery may be made to a third person acting on behalf of a donee, provided that the donor parts with dominion and control over the gift. If the donee already has possession of the item, delivery is unnecessary.

The Statute of Frauds requires that gifts of real property be in writing. However, courts sometimes give effect to oral gifts of land if the donee has taken possession and made valuable improvements. McGovern & Kurtz, *supra*, §4.5 at 203.

Spouses may make gifts to each other. The same elements of gift apply: donative intent, delivery, and acceptance by the donee. Case law addresses these elements. For example, in In re Kellman, 248 B.R. 430 (Bankr. M.D. Fla. 1999), the bankruptcy court held that a husband did not have the requisite donative intent when he added his wife's name to his credit union account in order to give her joint access merely in the event that he became disabled.

A gift that one spouse gives to the other spouse may become a marital asset subject to distribution in the event of a divorce. In Florida, the equitable distribution statute (Fla. Stat. §61.075(5)(b) provides authority for a divorce court to divide interspousal gifts in a dissolution proceeding.

If one spouse commingles funds (mixes separate property and marital property), a presumption may be created that that spouse made a gift to the other of an undivided half interest in the funds. For example, in Lakin v. Lakin, 901 So. 2d 186 (Fla. Dist. Ct. App. 2005), the appellate court held that funds that the husband inherited from his mother's estate lost their status as non-divisible non-marital assets when he deposited them in a joint account and therefore the funds were subject to equitable distribution in the divorce proceeding. See also Link v. Link, 897 So. 2d 533 (Fla. Dist. Ct. App. 2005) (holding that wife commingled non-marital life insurance proceeds with marital funds and thereby created a presumption of a gift to husband and that property was subject to equitable distribution in divorce proceeding). See generally Joseph J. Bassano et al., Transactions Between Spouses, Gifts, 25 Fla. Jur. 2d Family Law §407 (2007).

B. Conditional Gifts

Inter vivos gifts generally are a completed gratuitous transfer. Thus, they are neither revocable nor conditional. However, two types of gifts are exceptions to the rule:

- gifts in contemplation of marriage, and
- gifts in contemplation of death (called "gifts causa mortis").

1. Gifts in Contemplation of Marriage

During an engagement, the parties may give gifts to each other (such as an engagement ring). Many courts hold that an engagement ring is a conditional gift. Under this theory, A's gift to B of an engagement ring is conditioned on B's performance of an act (getting married). If the condition is not fulfilled (i.e., the marriage does not take place), then A may recover the gift.

At common law, fault barred recovery or retention of the engagement ring. Thus, the man could recover the ring if the woman unjustifiably ended the engagement or if the couple mutually dissolved it, but not if he unjustifiably terminated the engagement. In most states today, whether a party must return such a gift still depends on who was responsible (at fault) for terminating the engagement.

The fault-based rule is the majority rule. See, e.g., Clippard v. Pfefferkorn, 168 S.W.3d 616 (Mo. Ct. App. 2005). See also Brian L. Kruckenberg, Comment, "I Don't": Determining Ownership of the Engagement Ring When the Engagement Terminates (Herman v. Parrish, 942 P.2d 631 (Kan. 1997), 37 Washburn L.J. 425, 434 (1998)).

Florida follows the majority fault-based rule. In Gill v. Shively, 320 So. 2d 415 (Fla. Dist. Ct. App. 1975), the appellate court held that the donor stated a valid cause of action for return of an engagement ring after his fiancée broke off the engagement, reasoning that the ring was a conditional gift. Further, the court added that the statute that abolished causes of action for amatory torts (Fla. Stat. §771.01) did not abolish the cause of action for return of engagement rings.

However, according to the modern trend, fault is irrelevant. See, e.g., Fowler v. Perry, 830 N.E.2d 97, 105 (Ind. Ct. App. 2005)); Meyer v. Mitnick, 625 N.W.2d 136 (Mich. Ct. App. 2001); Benassi v. Back and Neck Pain Clinic, 629 N.W.2d 475 (Minn. Ct. App. 2001). See generally Rebecca Tushnet, Rules of Engagement, 107 Yale L.J. 2583 (1998).

§771.01. Abolition of amatory torts

The rights of action heretofore existing to recover sums of money as damage for the alienation of affections, criminal conversation, seduction or breach of contract to marry are hereby abolished. *(Laws 1945, ch. 23138, §1.)*

2. Gifts in Contemplation of Death (Gifts Causa Mortis)

A gift causa mortis is a gift of personal property by a person in apprehension of immediate death. Gifts causa mortis were influenced by Roman law. Atkinson, *supra*, §45 at 200 n.7. Gifts causa mortis are a hybrid type of transfer, enabling the property owner to secure most of the advantages of both a will and an inter vivos gift. *Id.* at 205.

Gifts causa mortis, like gifts generally, require donative intent and delivery. "[A]ny set of facts which would constitute good delivery for a gift inter vivos will satisfy this requirement of a gift causa mortis." *Id.* at 202. Delivery also is effective to a third person who is requested to give the property to the donee at the donor's death. *Id.*

The primary difference between gifts causa mortis and inter vivos gifts is the revocability of the former. Gifts causa mortis may be revoked by: (1) the donor's express act; (2) the donor's recovery from illness; or (3) the donor's survival of the donee. *Id.* at 204. Also, gifts causa mortis, unlike inter vivos gifts, may be subject to creditors' claims. "In case of insolvency of the donor's estate his personal representative is entitled to recover gifts causa mortis to the extent necessary to satisfy creditors." *Id.* Gifts causa mortis differ from wills in several ways. Wills must be in writing. Delivery is required for gifts causa mortis but not for legacies. Gifts causa mortis require immediate apprehension of death. And, wills can dispose of land but gifts causa mortis cannot. *Id.* at 205.

Several Florida cases address the validity of alleged gifts causa mortis. For example, in Josephson v. Kuhner, 139 So. 2d 440 (Fla. Dist. Ct. App. 1962), the appellate court held that three transfers of funds to joint bank accounts with right of survivorship that were made ten days before death to a landlord by a miserly, hospitalized, 81-year-old man were not valid gifts causa mortis. The court pointed out that such gifts are disfavored and must be established by stricter proof than that necessary for inter vivos gifts. Similarly, in Canova v. Florida Nat.'l Bank of Jacksonville, 60 So. 2d 627 (Fla. 1952), the Florida Supreme Court held that the plaintiff (caregiver of her elderly ill neighbor) failed to establish clear and convincing evidence of the requisite delivery to her of his savings account and the contents of his safety deposit box.

C. Gifts to Minors

Because minors lack legal capacity to manage property, property ownership for children requires special provisions. Common forms of management of property for minors are guardianships and trusts. However, each type involves shortcomings. Guardianships are cumbersome. Guardians must file a bond, submit accounts to a court, and obtain judicial approval for sales, investments, and distributions. Guardianships also terminate at age 18. McGovern & Kurtz, *supra*, §9.2 at 347. Inter vivos trusts are an alternative. However, trusts are a more expensive option, involving costs for creation and administration.

A preferable system, for modest gifts to minors, is the Uniform Gifts to Minors Act (UGMA) or its successor Uniform Transfers to Minors Act (UTMA). Every state has enacted a version of UGMA or UTMA, which enables an adult to give substantial gifts of property to a child, without the child having to assume control of the property. The National Conference of Commissioners on Uniform State Laws (NCCUSL) promulgated UGMA in 1956. UGMA stemmed from model legislation sponsored by the New York Stock Exchange to create a simple and inexpensive method to make inter vivos gifts of securities to minors. Security dealers were concerned that minors' right of disaffirmance of contracts posed hazards for brokers, and therefore made it difficult to sell securities and reinvest on minors' behalf.

Initially, UGMA applied only to inter vivos gifts of money, as well as securities, to minors. When UGMA was revised in 1965 and 1966, NCCUSL expanded the definition of custodial property (to include life insurance policies and annuity contracts) and the types of financial institutions that could serve as depositories, and also facilitated the designation of successor custodians. Prefatory Note, Uniform Transfers to

Minors Act, 8C U.L.A. 3-4 (2001). In addition, NCCUSL changed the title of the Act to replace the narrow term "gifts" with the broader term "transfers" to expand the types of possible transfers. Not all states enacted the 1966 revisions. Moreover, many states have revised their versions of UGMA since 1966 to include different kinds of property that are the subject of a gift and permitting transfers to custodians from other sources. As a result, considerable lack of uniformity exists. *Id.*

1. Transfer of Property into Custodianship

UTMA allows any kind of property (real or personal, tangible or intangible, and without limit), to be the subject of a transfer to a custodian for the benefit of a minor. It permits such transfers not only by inter vivos gifts, but also from such other sources as: trusts, estates, guardianships, and third-party debtors of a minor who does not have a conservator (e.g., parties against whom a minor has a tort claim or judgment, and depository institutions holding deposits or insurance companies issuing policies payable on death to a minor). *Id.*

A donor may make a transfer pursuant to UTMA by an express declaration (i.e., mentioning the Act) that the gift is made to a custodian in the name of the minor. For property that is in registered form, the transfer generally is completed by registering ownership in the name of the minor under the given jurisdiction's Uniform Transfers to Minors Act. Delivery to the minor is not required. A custodianship may be established only for the benefit of one minor. A "transfer" is irrevocable and indefeasibly vests ownership of the property interest in the minor.

2. Custodians: Eligibility, Duties

A person is eligible to serve as custodian if he or she has reached age 21. A trust company may also act as custodian. Only one custodian may serve. Death or incapacity of, or renunciation by, a custodian does not invalidate the transfer of property into the custodianship. In such cases, UTMA provides for the appointment of successor custodians.

A custodian first must take control of custodial property, including facilitating any necessary registration or recordation of custodial property. The custodian may act, without judicial involvement, to manage and invest custodial property.

3. Custodianships: Costs, Compensation, Investments, Expenditures

The custodian must exercise authority according to a high standard of care—i.e., the standard observed by a prudent person dealing with the property of another. The custodian may choose a broad range of allowable investments. However, custodial property should not be commingled with the custodian's personal property. Also, custodial property may not be placed in joint tenancy with a right of survivorship.

Custodians have broad discretion to use the custodial property for the minor's benefit. Under UTMA §14(a), the custodian may spend amounts according to what he or she considers "advisable" for the minor's "use and benefit." The UTMA "use and benefit" standard is broader than that of UGMA. (See UTMA §14 cmt.) Under UGMA (§4), the custodian is limited to use custodial property for the "support, maintenance, education, and benefit of the minor."

UTMA provides for reimbursement from custodial property by "reasonable compensation" for "reasonable expenses incurred in the performance of the custodian's duties." However, the custodian who is also a transferor may not receive compensation.

4. Distribution of Custodial Property

The age of distribution of custodial property depends on the manner in which the property is transferred. If property is transferred by means of an inter vivos gift, the exercise of a power of appointment, by will, or by the terms of a trust, then the property may be distributed to a minor at age 21. The age of distribution for other transfers (e.g., testamentary transfers through life insurance designation, an employee benefit plan, or a payable on death account) is tied to the age of majority in the enacting state. Paul M. Peterson, The Uniform Transfers to Minors Act: A Practitioner's Guide, 1995 Army Lawyer 3, 10 (1995). Some states allow the transferor to vary the age of distribution within a fixed range of ages (from 18 to 25). *Id.*

At the age designated for distribution, the custodianship terminates and the custodian may distribute the property. During the course of the custodianship, custodial property is indefeasibly vested in the minor. Any income received is attributed to the minor for tax purposes (whether or not actually distributed to the minor). Uniform Transfers to Minors Act, Prefatory Note.

5. Custodian's Liability

The expansion of the type of property interests that may be held in a custodial account increases the potential personal liability for both the minor and the custodian. As a result, UTMA limits the claims of third parties against the custodial property, and insulates the minor against personal liability unless he or she is personally at fault, and also insulates the custodian unless he or she is personally at fault or fails to disclose his custodial capacity in entering into a contract. *Id.* One possible remedy against a custodian is removal and appointment of a successor custodian. Courts may require custodians to pay damages for a breach of fiduciary duty that causes a loss of custodial property as well as the minor's attorneys fees. Peterson, *supra,* at 10.

UTMA also specifies the choice of law. A transferor designates the state law of choice by referring to a given jurisdiction in creating the custodianship. Courts of that state will follow the designation provided that the state has some minimum connections with the UTMA transaction. *Id.*

If property is transferred initially by a state that has adopted UGMA, but later enacts UTMA, UTMA provides that UTMA provisions will apply. This rule operates unless the application of UTMA would deprive the minor of rights in the property or would extend the age of distribution. *Id.*

On the Florida Uniform Transfers to Minors Act, see Jani Mauer, Uniform Transfers to Minors Act Accounts—Progress, Potential, and Pitfalls, 28 Nova L. Rev. 745 (2004); Steven Douglas Najarian, Uniform Transfers to Minors Act, 28 Fla. Jur. 2d Gifts 24 (2007).

§710.101. Title

This act may be cited as the "Florida Uniform Transfers to Minors Act."

(Laws 1985, ch. 85-95, §1.)

§710.102. Definitions

As used in this act, the term:

(1) "Adult" means an individual who has attained the age of 21 years.

(2) "Benefit plan" means a retirement plan and may include, but is not limited to, any pension, profit-sharing, stock-bonus, or stock-ownership plan or individual retirement account.

(3) "Broker" means a person lawfully engaged in the business of effecting transactions in securities or commodities for the person's own account or for the account of others.

(4) "Conservator" means a person appointed or qualified by a court to act as general, limited, or temporary guardian of a minor's property or a person legally authorized to perform substantially the same functions.

(5) "Court" means the circuit court.

(6) "Custodial property" means any interest in property transferred to a custodian under this act and the income from and proceeds of that interest in property.

(7) "Custodian" means a person so designated under §710.111 or a successor or substitute custodian designated under §710.121.

(8) "Financial institution" means a bank, trust company, savings institution, or credit union, chartered and supervised under state or federal law.

(9) "Legal representative" means an individual's personal representative or conservator.

(10) "Member of the minor's family" means the minor's parent, stepparent, spouse, grandparent, brother, sister, uncle, or aunt, whether of the whole or half blood or by adoption.

(11) "Minor" means an individual who has not attained the age of 21 years.

(12) "Person" means an individual, corporation, organization, or other legal entity.

(13) "Personal representative" means an executor, administrator, successor personal representative, or special administrator of a decedent's estate or a person legally authorized to perform substantially the same functions.

(14) "Qualified minor's trust" means a trust that meets the requirements of §2503(c) of the Internal Revenue Code of 1986, [FN1] as amended.

(15) "State" includes any state of the United States, the District of Columbia, the Commonwealth of Puerto Rico, and any territory or possession subject to the legislative authority of the United States.

(16) "Transfer" means a transaction that creates custodial property under §710.111.

(17) "Transferor" means a person who makes a transfer under this act.

(18) "Trust company" means a financial institution, corporation, or other legal entity, authorized to exercise general trust powers.

[FN1] 26 U.S.C.A. §2503(c).

(Laws 1985, ch. 85-95, §1. Amended by Laws 2005, ch. 2005-101, §3, effective June 1, 2005.)

§710.103. Scope and jurisdiction

(1) This act applies to a transfer that refers to this act in the designation under §710.111(1) by which the transfer is made if at the time of the transfer, the transferor, the minor, or the custodian is a resident of this state or the custodial property is located in this state. The custodianship so created remains subject to this act despite a subsequent change in residence of a transferor, the minor, or the custodian, or the removal of custodial property from this state.

(2) A person designated as custodian under this act is subject to personal jurisdiction in this state with respect to any matter relating to the custodianship.

(3) A transfer that purports to be made and which is valid under the Uniform Transfers to Minors Act, the Uniform Gifts to Minors Act, or a substantially similar act, of another state is governed by the law of the designated state and may be executed and is enforceable in this state if, at the time of the transfer, the transferor, the minor, or the custodian is a resident of the designated state or the custodial property is located in the designated state.

(Laws 1985, ch. 85-95, §1.)

§710.104. Nomination of custodian

(1) A person having the right to designate the recipient of property transferable upon the occurrence of a future event may revocably nominate a custodian to receive the property for a minor beneficiary upon the occurrence of the event by naming the custodian followed in substance by the words: "as custodian for (name of minor) under the Florida Uniform Transfers to Minors Act." The nomination may name one or more persons as substitute custodians to whom the property must be transferred, in the order named, if the first nominated custodian dies before the transfer or is unable, declines, or is ineligible to serve. The nomination may be made in a will, a trust, a deed, an instrument exercising a power of appointment, or in a writing designating a beneficiary of contractual rights, including, but not limited to, the right to a benefit plan, which is registered with or delivered to the payor, issuer, or other obligor of the contractual rights.

(2) A custodian nominated under this section must be a person to whom a transfer of property of that kind may be made under §710.111(1).

(3) The nomination of a custodian under this section does not create custodial property until the nominating instrument becomes irrevocable or a transfer to the nominated custodian is completed under §710.111. Unless the nomination of a custodian has been revoked, upon the occurrence of the future event the custodianship becomes effective and the custodian shall enforce a transfer of the custodial property pursuant to §710.111.

(Laws 1985, ch. 85-95, §1. Amended by Laws 2005, ch. 2005-101, §4, effective June 1, 2005.)

§710.105. Transfer by gift or exercise of power of appointment

A person may make a transfer by irrevocable gift to, or the irrevocable exercise of a power of appointment in favor of, a custodian for the benefit of a minor pursuant to §710.111.

(Laws 1985, ch. 85-95, §1.)

§710.106. Transfer by will or trust

(1) A personal representative or trustee may make an irrevocable transfer pursuant to §710.111 to a custodian for the benefit of a minor as authorized in the governing will or trust.

(2) If the testator or settlor has nominated a custodian under §710.104 to receive the custodial property, the transfer must be made to that person.

(3) If the testator or settlor has not nominated a custodian under §710.104, or all persons so nominated as custodian die before the transfer or are unable, decline, or are ineligible to serve, the personal representative or the trustee, as the case may be, shall designate the custodian from among those eligible to serve as custodian for property of that kind under §710.111(1).

(Laws 1985, ch. 85-95, §1.)

§710.107. Other transfer by fiduciary

(1) Subject to subsection (3), a personal representative or trustee may make an irrevocable transfer to another adult or trust company as custodian for the benefit of a minor pursuant to §710.111, in the absence of a will or under a will or trust that does not contain an authorization to do so.

(2) Subject to subsection (3), a conservator may make an irrevocable transfer to another adult or trust company as custodian for the benefit of the minor pursuant to §710.111.

(3) A transfer under subsection (1) or subsection (2) may be made only if:

(a) The personal representative, trustee, or conservator considers the transfer to be in the best interest of the minor;

(b) The transfer is not prohibited by or inconsistent with provisions of the applicable will, trust agreement, or other governing instrument; and

(c) The transfer is authorized by the court if it exceeds $10,000 in value.

(Laws 1985, ch. 85-95, §1.)

§710.108. Transfer by obligor

(1) Subject to subsections (2) and (3), a person not subject to §710.106 or §710.107 who holds property, including, but not limited to, a benefit plan, of a minor not having a conservator, or who owes a liquidated debt to a minor not having a conservator, may make an irrevocable transfer to a custodian for the benefit of the minor pursuant to §710.111.

(2) If a person having the right to do so under §710.104 has nominated a custodian under that section to receive the custodial property, the transfer must be made to that person.

(3) If no custodian has been nominated under §710.104, or all persons so nominated as custodian die before the transfer or are unable, decline, or are ineligible to serve, a transfer under this section may be made to an adult member of the minor's family or to a trust company unless the property exceeds $15,000 in value.

(Laws 1985, ch. 85-95, §1; Laws 1987, ch. 87-226, §61. Amended by Laws 2005, ch. 2005-101, §5, effective June 1, 2005.)

§710.109. Receipt for custodial property

A written acknowledgment of delivery by a custodian constitutes a sufficient receipt and discharge for custodial property transferred to the custodian pursuant to this act.

(Laws 1985, ch. 85-95, §1.)

§710.111. Manner of creating custodial property

(1) Custodial property is created and a transfer is made whenever:

(a) An uncertificated security or a certificated security in registered form is either:

1. Registered in the name of the transferor, an adult other than the transferor, or a trust company, followed in substance by the words: "as custodian for (name of minor) under the Florida Uniform Transfers to Minors Act"; or

2. Delivered if in certificated form, or any document necessary for the transfer of an uncertificated security is delivered, together with any necessary endorsement to an adult other than the transferor or to a trust company as custodian, accompanied by an instrument in substantially the form set forth in subsection (2);

(b) Money is paid or delivered to a broker or financial institution for credit to an account in the name of the transferor, an adult other than the transferor, or a trust company, followed in substance by the words: "as custodian for (name of minor) under the Florida Uniform Transfers to Minors Act";

(c) The ownership of a life or endowment insurance policy or annuity contract is either:

1. Registered with the issuer in the name of the transferor, an adult other than the transferor, or a trust company, followed in substance by the words: "as custodian for (name of minor) under the Florida Uniform Transfers to Minors Act"; or

2. Assigned in a writing delivered to an adult other than the transferor or to a trust company whose name in the assignment is followed in substance by the words: "as custodian for (name of minor) under the Florida Uniform Transfers to Minors Act";

(d) An irrevocable exercise of a power of appointment or an irrevocable present right to future payment under a contract is the subject of a written notification delivered to the payor, issuer, or other obligor that the right is transferred to the transferor, an adult other than the transferor, or a trust company, whose name in the notification is followed in substance by the words: "as custodian for (name of minor) under the Florida Uniform Transfers to Minors Act";

(e) An interest in real property is recorded in the name of the transferor, an adult other than the transferor, or a trust company, followed in substance by the words: "as custodian for (name of minor) under the Florida Uniform Transfers to Minors Act";

(f) A certificate of title issued by a department or agency of a state or of the United States which evidences title to tangible personal property is either:

1. Issued in the name of the transferor, an adult other than the transferor, or a trust company, followed in substance by the words: "as custodian for (name of minor) under the Florida Uniform Transfers to Minors Act"; or

2. Delivered to an adult other than the transferor or to a trust company, endorsed to that person followed in substance by the words: "as custodian for (name of minor) under the Florida Uniform Transfers to Minors Act"; or

(g) An interest in any property not described in paragraphs (a)-(f) is transferred to an adult other than the transferor or to a trust company by a written instrument in substantially the form set forth in subsection (2).

(2) An instrument in the following form satisfies the requirements of subparagraph (1)(a)2. and paragraph (1)(g):

"TRANSFER UNDER THE
FLORIDA UNIFORM TRANSFERS TO MINORS ACT

I, (name of transferor or name and representative capacity if a fiduciary) hereby transfer to (name of custodian) , as custodian for (name of minor) under the Florida Uniform Transfers to Minors Act, the following: (insert a description of the custodial property sufficient to identify it)

Dated: _____

(signature)

(name of custodian) acknowledges receipt of the property described above as custodian for the minor named above under the Florida Uniform Transfers to Minors Act.

Dated: _____

(signature of custodian) ."

(3) A transferor shall place the custodian in control of the custodial property as soon as practicable.
(Laws 1985, ch. 85-95, §1.)

§710.112. Only one minor and only one custodian

A transfer may be made only for one minor, and only one person may be the custodian. All custodial property held under this act by the same custodian for the benefit of the same minor constitutes a single custodianship.
(Laws 1985, ch. 85-95, §1.)

§710.113. Validity and effect of transfer

(1) The validity of a transfer made in a manner prescribed in this act is not affected by:

(a) Failure of the transferor to comply with §710.111(3) concerning possession and control;

(b) Designation of an ineligible custodian, except designation of the transferor in the case of property for which the transferor is ineligible to serve as custodian under §710.111(1); or

(c) Death or incapacity of a person nominated under §710.104 or designated under §710.111 as custodian or the disclaimer of the office by that person.

(2) A transfer made pursuant to §710.111 is irrevocable, and the custodial property is indefeasibly vested in the minor, but the custodian has all the rights, powers, duties, and authority provided in this act, and neither the minor nor the minor's legal representative has any right, power, duty, or authority with respect to the custodial property except as provided in this act.

(3) By making a transfer, the transferor incorporates in the disposition all the provisions of this act and grants to the custodian, and to any third person dealing with a person designated as custodian, the respective powers, rights, and immunities provided in this act.
(Laws 1985, ch. 85-95, §1.)

§710.114. Care of custodial property

(1) A custodian shall:

(a) Take control of custodial property;

(b) Register or record title to custodial property if appropriate; and

(c) Collect, hold, manage, invest, and reinvest custodial property.

(2) In dealing with custodial property, a custodian shall observe the standard of care that would be observed by a prudent person dealing with property of another and is not limited by any other statute restricting investments by fiduciaries. If a custodian has a special skill or expertise or is named custodian on the basis of representations of a special skill or expertise, the custodian shall use that skill or expertise. However, a custodian, in the custodian's discretion and without liability to the minor or the minor's estate, may retain any custodial property received from a transferor.

(3) A custodian may invest in or pay premiums on life insurance or endowment policies on the life of the minor only if the minor or the minor's estate is the sole beneficiary, or on the life of another person in whom the minor has an insurable interest only to the extent that the minor, the minor's estate, or the custodian in the capacity of custodian is the irrevocable beneficiary.

(4) A custodian at all times shall keep custodial property separate and distinct from all other property in a manner sufficient to identify it clearly as custodial property of the minor. Custodial property consisting of an undivided interest is so identified if the minor's interest is held as a tenant in common and is fixed. Custodial property subject to recordation is so identified if it is recorded, and custodial property subject to registration is so identified if it is either registered, or held in an

account designated, in the name of the custodian, followed in substance by the words: "as a custodian for (name of minor) under the Florida Uniform Transfers to Minors Act."

(5) A custodian shall keep records of all transactions with respect to custodial property, including information necessary for the preparation of the minor's tax returns, and shall make them available for inspection at reasonable intervals by a parent or legal representative of the minor or by the minor if the minor has attained the age of 14 years.
(Laws 1985, ch. 85-95, §1.)

§710.115. Powers of custodian

(1) A custodian, acting in a custodial capacity, has all the rights, powers, and authority over custodial property that unmarried adult owners have over their own property, but a custodian may exercise those rights, powers, and authority in that capacity only.

(2) This section does not relieve a custodian from liability for breach of §710.114.
(Laws 1985, ch. 85-95, §1.)

§710.116. Use of custodial property

(1) A custodian may deliver or pay to the minor or expend for the minor's benefit so much of the custodial property as the custodian considers advisable for the use and benefit of the minor, without court order and without regard to the duty or ability of the custodian personally or of any other person to support the minor, or to any other income or property of the minor which may be applicable or available for that purpose.

(2) A custodian may, without court order, transfer all or part of the custodial property to a qualified minor's trust. A transfer of property pursuant to this subsection terminates the custodianship to the extent of the property transferred.

(3) On petition of an interested person or the minor if the minor has attained the age of 14 years, the court may order the custodian to deliver or pay to the minor or expend for the minor's benefit so much of the custodial property as the court considers advisable for the use and benefit of the minor.

(4) A delivery, payment, or expenditure under this section is in addition to, not in substitution for, and does not affect any obligation of a person to support the minor.
(Laws 1985, ch. 85-95, §1. Amended by Laws 2005, ch. 2005-101, §6, effective June 1, 2005.)

§710.117. Custodian's expenses and compensation

(1) A custodian is entitled to reimbursement from custodial property for reasonable expenses incurred in the performance of the custodian's duties.

(2) Except for one who is a transferor under §710.105, a custodian has a noncumulative election during each calendar year to charge reasonable compensation for services performed during that year.

(3) Except as provided in §710.121(6), a custodian need not give a bond.
(Laws 1985, ch. 85-95, §1.)

§710.118. Exemption of third party from liability

A third person in good faith and without court order may act on the instructions of or otherwise deal with any person purporting to make a transfer or purporting to act in the capacity of a custodian and, in the absence of knowledge, is not responsible for determining:

(1) The validity of the purported custodian's designation;

(2) The propriety of, or the authority under this act for, any act of the purported custodian;

(3) The validity or propriety under this act of any instrument or instructions executed or given either by the person purporting to make a transfer or by the purported custodian; or

(4) The propriety of the application of any property of the minor delivered to the purported custodian.
(Laws 1985, ch. 85-95, §1.)

§710.119. Liability to third parties

(1) A claim based on:

(a) A contract entered into by a custodian acting in a custodial capacity;

(b) An obligation arising from the ownership or control of custodial property; or

(c) A tort committed during the custodianship,

may be asserted against the custodial property by proceeding against the custodian in the custodial capacity, whether or not the custodian or the minor is personally liable therefor.

(2) A custodian is not personally liable:

(a) On a contract properly entered into in the custodial capacity unless the custodian fails to reveal that capacity and to identify the custodianship in the contract; or

(b) For an obligation arising from control of custodial property or for a tort committed during the custodianship unless the custodian is personally at fault.

(3) A minor is not personally liable for an obligation arising from ownership of custodial property or for a tort committed during the custodianship unless the minor is personally at fault.
(Laws 1985, ch. 85-95, §1.)

§710.121. Removal and replacement of custodian

(1) A person nominated under §710.104 or designated under §710.111 as custodian may decline to serve by delivering a valid disclaimer under chapter 739 to the person who made the nomination or to the transferor or the transferor's legal representative. If the event giving rise to a transfer has not occurred and no substitute custodian able, willing, and eligible to serve was nominated under §710.104, the person who made the nomination may nominate a substitute custodian under §710.104; otherwise, the transferor or the transferor's legal representative shall designate a substitute custodian at the time of the transfer, in either case from among the persons eligible to serve as custodian for that kind of property under§710.111(1). The custodian so designated has the rights of a successor custodian.

(2) A custodian at any time may designate a trust company or an adult other than a transferor under §710.105 as successor custodian by executing and dating an instrument of designation before a subscribing witness other than the successor. If the instrument of designation does not contain or is not accompanied by the resignation of the custodian, the designation of the successor does not take effect until the custodian resigns, dies, becomes incapacitated, or is removed.

(3) A custodian may resign at any time by delivering written notice to the minor if the minor has attained the age of 14 years and to the successor custodian and by delivering the custodial property to the successor custodian.

(4) If a custodian is ineligible, dies, or becomes incapacitated without having effectively designated a successor and the minor has attained the age of 14 years, the minor may designate as successor custodian, in the manner prescribed in subsection (2), an adult member of the minor's family, a conservator of the minor, or a trust company. If the minor has not attained the age of 14 years or fails to act within 60 days after the ineligibility, death, or incapacity, the conservator of the minor becomes successor custodian. If the minor has no conservator or the conservator declines to act, the transferor, the legal representative of the transferor or of the custodian, an adult member of the minor's family, or any other interested person may petition the court to designate a successor custodian.

(5) A custodian who declines to serve under subsection (1) or resigns under subsection (3), or the legal representative of a deceased or incapacitated custodian, as soon as practicable, shall put the custodial property and records in the possession and control of the successor custodian. The successor custodian by action may enforce the obligation to deliver custodial property and records and becomes responsible for each item as received.

(6) A transferor, the legal representative of a transferor, an adult member of the minor's family, a guardian of the person of the minor, the conservator of the minor, or the minor if the minor has attained the age of 14 years may petition the court to remove the custodian for cause and designate a successor custodian other than a transferor under §710.105 or to require the custodian to give appropriate bond.
(Laws 1985, ch. 85-95, § 1. Amended by Laws 2005, ch. 2005-108, §4, effective July 1, 2005.)

§710.122. Minor may petition for an accounting

(1) A minor who has attained the age of 14 years, the minor's guardian of the person or legal representative, an adult member of the minor's family, a transferor, or a transferor's legal representative may petition the court for an accounting by the custodian or the custodian's legal representative or for a determination of responsibility, as between the custodial property and the custodian personally, for claims against the custodial property unless the responsibility has been adjudicated in an action under §710.119 to which the minor or the minor's legal representative was a party.

(2) A successor custodian may petition the court for an accounting by the predecessor custodian.

(3) The court, in a proceeding under this act or in any other proceeding, may require or permit the custodian or the custodian's legal representative to account.

(4) If a custodian is removed under §710.121(6), the court shall require an accounting and order delivery of the custodial property and records to the successor custodian and the execution of all instruments required for transfer of the custodial property.
(Laws 1985, ch. 85-95, §1.)

§710.123. Termination of custodianship

The custodian shall transfer in an appropriate manner the custodial property to the minor or to the minor's estate upon the earlier of:

(1) The minor's attainment of 21 years of age with respect to custodial property transferred under §710.105 or §710.106;

(2) The minor's attainment of age 18 with respect to custodial property transferred under §710.107 or §710.108; or

(3) The minor's death.

(Laws 1985, ch. 85-95, §1.)

§710.124. Applicability

This act applies to a transfer within the scope of §710.103 made after October 1, 1985, if:

(1) The transfer purports to have been made under the Florida Gifts to Minors Act (former §§710.01-710.10); or

(2) The instrument by which the transfer purports to have been made uses in substance the designation "as custodian under the Uniform Gifts to Minors Act" or "as custodian under the Uniform Transfers to Minors Act" of any other state, and the application of this act is necessary to validate the transfer.

(Laws 1985, ch. 85-95, §1; Laws 1987, ch. 87-226, §62.)

§710.125. Effect on existing custodianships

(1) Any transfer of custodial property as now defined in this act made before October 1, 1985, is validated notwithstanding that there was no specific authority in the Florida Gifts to Minors Act for the coverage of custodial property of that kind or for a transfer from that source at the time the transfer was made.

(2) This act applies to all transfers made before October 1, 1985, in a manner and form prescribed in the Florida Gifts to Minors Act, except insofar as the application impairs constitutionally vested rights or extends the duration of custodianships in existence on October 1, 1985.

(3) Sections 710.102-710.123 with respect to the age of a minor for whom custodial property is held under this act do not apply to custodial property held in a custodianship that terminated because of the minor's attainment of the age of 18 after January 1, 1975, and before October 1, 1985.

(Laws 1985, ch. 85-95, §1.)

§710.126. Policy of uniformity

This act shall be applied and construed to effectuate its general purpose to make uniform the law with respect to the subject of this act among states enacting it.

(Laws 1985, ch. 85-95, §1.)

IX
TRUST CREATION AND VALIDITY

This chapter focuses on the requirements for the creation of a valid trust. Trusts may be created expressly by an owner of property who intends to create a trust, or may be created by operation of law. The former trusts consist of private express trusts and charitable trusts (discussed in Chapter XIII *infra*). Trusts created by operation of law consist of constructive trusts and resulting trusts.

I. Introduction

A. Definitions

A trust is an arrangement in which the legal title to property is held by a trustee, but the equitable interest in the property belongs to a beneficiary or beneficiaries. According to the Restatement (Third) of Trusts §2 (2001), a trust is:

> **a fiduciary relationship with respect to property, arising from a manifestation of intention to create that relationship and subjecting the person who holds title to the property to duties to deal with it for the benefit of charity or for one or more persons, at least one of whom is not the sole trustee.**

The cardinal features of the trust are (1) the separation of legal and equitable interests, and (2) the fiduciary duty imposed on the trustee (the holder of legal title) to deal with the property for the benefit of the beneficiary (the holder of the equitable title).

The owner of the property is called the "trustor," "settlor," "grantor," or "donor." (The Restatement (Third) of Trusts §3 uses the term "settlor.") The person or corporation holding legal title is the "trustee." The third party who owns the equitable interest in the property is the "beneficiary" or "cestui que trust." The trust property is called the "corpus" or "res."

In Florida, a valid private express trust must meet the following requirements:

- **the settlor must have capacity to create a trust (Fla. Stat. §736.0402(1)(a));**
- **the settlor must indicate an intent to create the trust (Fla, Stat. §736.0402(1)(b));**
- **the trust must have property (Fla. Stat. §736.0401(1), (2));**
- **the trust must have a definite beneficiary (Fla. Stat. §736.0402(1)(c));**
- **the trust must have a purpose that is not illegal or against public policy (Fla. Stat. §736.0404)**

In 2006 the Florida legislature substantially revised Florida law relating to trusts. The legislature adopted a significant portion of the Uniform Trust Code (UTC), thereby creating the Florida Trust Code. The new Code adopts the following UTC definitions:

§736.0103. Definition

....

(3) "Ascertainable standard" means a standard relating to an individual's health, education, support, or maintenance within the meaning of §2041(b)(1)(A) or §2514(c)(1) of the Internal Revenue Code of 1986, as amended. [FN1]

(4) "Beneficiary" means a person who:

(a) Has a present of future beneficial interest in a trust, vested or contingent; or

(b) Holds a power of appointment over trust property in a capacity other than that of a trustee.

...

(10) "Interests of the beneficiaries" means the beneficial interests provided in the terms of the trust.

...

(13) "Property" means anything that may be the subject of ownership, real or personal, legal or equitable, or any interest therein.

(14) "Qualified beneficiary" means a living beneficiary who, on the date the beneficiary's qualification is determined:

(a) Is a distributee or permissible distributee of trust income or principal;

(b) Would be a distributee or permissible distributee of trust income or principal if the interests of the distributees described in paragraph (a) terminated on that date without causing the trust to terminate; or

(c) Would be a distributee or permissible distributee of trust income or principal if the trust terminated in accordance with its terms on that date.

(15) "Revocable," as applied to a trust, means revocable by the settlor without the consent of the trustee or a person holding an adverse interest.

(16) "Settlor" means a person, including a testator, who creates or contributes property to a trust. If more than one person contributes property to a trust, each person is a settlor of the portion of the trust property attributable to that person's contribution

except to the extent another person has the power to revoke or withdraw that portion.

(17) "Spendthrift provision" means a term of a trust that restrains both voluntary and involuntary transfer of a beneficiary's interest.

...

(19) "Terms of a trust" means the manifestation of the settlor's intent regarding a trust's provisions as expressed in the trust instrument or as may be established by other evidence that would be admissible in a judicial proceeding.

(20) "Trust instrument" means an instrument executed by a settlor that contains terms of the trust, including any amendment to the trust.

(21) "Trustee" means the original trustee and includes any additional trustee, any successor trustee, and any cotrustee.

[FN1] 26 U.S.C.A. § 2041(b)(1)(A) or § 2514(c)(1).

(Laws 2006, ch. 2006-217, §1, effective July 1, 2007.)

§736.0108. Place of administration of a trust

(1) Terms of a trust designating the principal place of administration of the trust are valid only if there is a sufficient connection with the designated jurisdiction. Without precluding other means for establishing a sufficient connection, terms of a trust designating the principal place of administration are valid and controlling if:

(a) A trustee's principal place of business is located in or a trustee is a resident of the designated jurisdiction; or

(b) All or part of the administration occurs in the designated jurisdiction. (2) Unless otherwise validly designated in the trust instrument, the principal place of administration of a trust is the trustee's usual place of business where the records pertaining to the trust are kept or, if the trustee has no place of business, the trustee's residence. In the case of cotrustees, the principal place of administration is: (a) The usual place of business of the corporate trustee, if there is only one corporate cotrustee; (b) The usual place of business or residence of the individual trustee who is a professional fiduciary, if there is only one such person and no corporate cotrustee; or otherwise

(c) The usual place of business or residence of any of the cotrustees as agreed on by the cotrustees.

(3) Notwithstanding any other provision of this section, the principal place of administration of a trust, for which a bank, association, or trust company organized under the laws of this state or bank or savings association organized under the laws of the United States with its main office in this state has been appointed trustee, shall not be moved or otherwise affected solely because the trustee engaged in an interstate merger transaction with an out-of-state bank pursuant to §658.2953 in which the out-of-state bank is the resulting bank.

(4) A trustee is under a continuing duty to administer the trust at a place appropriate to its purposes and its administration.

(5) Without precluding the right of the court to order, approve, or disapprove a transfer, the trustee, in furtherance of the duty prescribed by subsection (4), may transfer the trust's principal place of administration to another state or to a jurisdiction outside of the United States.

(6) The trustee shall notify the qualified beneficiaries of a proposed transfer of a trust's principal place of administration not less than 60 days before initiating the transfer. The notice of proposed transfer must include:

(a) The name of the jurisdiction to which the principal place of administration is to be transferred.

(b) The address and telephone number at the new location at which the trustee can be contacted.

(c) An explanation of the reasons for the proposed transfer

(d) The date on which the proposed transfer is anticipated to occur. (e) The date, not less than 60 days after the notice is provided, by which the qualified beneficiary must notify the trustee of an objection to the proposed transfer. (7) The authority of a trustee to act under this section without court approval to transfer a trust's principal place of administration is suspended if a qualified beneficiary files a lawsuit objecting to the proposed transfer on or before the date specified in the notice. The suspension is effective until the lawsuit is dismissed or withdrawn. (8) In connection with a transfer of the trust's principal place of administration, the trustee may transfer any of the trust property to a successor trustee designated in the terms of the trust or appointed pursuant to §736.0704.

(Laws 2006, ch. 2006-217, §1, effective July 1, 2007.)

B. Reasons for Establishing Trusts

Several reasons exist for establishing a trust. These include:

- **avoidance of probate with its delays and costs;**
- **providing property management for persons who are incompetent to do so or who prefer not to manage the property themselves;**
- **providing for successive enjoyment of property over several generations;**
- **securing tax benefits (by the use of irrevocable, but not revocable, trusts); and**
- **insulating trust property from the beneficiary's creditors.**

Restatement (Third) of Trusts §27, cmt. b. See generally McGovern & Kurtz, *supra*, §§9.1, 9.2 & 9.3 at 341-352.

C. Judicial Proceedings Regarding Trusts: Jurisdiction and Venue

The Florida Trust Code sets forth the legal rules applicable to judicial proceedings regarding trusts, such as those pertaining to jurisdiction and venue.

§736.0105. Code governs rules for judicial proceedings

...

(2) The terms of a trust prevail over any provision of this code except:

...

(d) The periods of limitation for commencing a judicial proceeding.

(e) The power of the court to take such action and exercise such jurisdiction as may be necessary in the interests of justice.

(f) The requirements under §736.0108(1) for the designation of a principal place of administration of the trust.

(g) The jurisdiction and venue provisions in §§736.0202, 736.0203, and 736.0204.

...

(Laws 2006, ch. 2006-217, §1, effective July 1, 2007.)

§736.0111. Parties may enter into binding nonjudicial settlement agreements

(1) For purposes of this section, the term "interested persons" means persons whose interest would be affected by a settlement agreement.

(2) Except as otherwise provided in subsection (3), interested persons may enter into a binding nonjudicial settlement agreement with respect to any matter involving a trust.

(3) A nonjudicial settlement agreement among the trustee and trust beneficiaries is valid only to the extent the terms and conditions could be properly approved by the court. A nonjudicial settlement may not be used to produce a result not authorized by other provisions of this code, including, but not limited to, terminating or modifying a trust in an impermissible manner.

(4) Matters that may be resolved by a nonjudicial settlement agreement include:

(a) The interpretation or construction of the terms of the trust.

(b) The approval of a trustee's report or accounting.

(c) The direction to a trustee to refrain from performing a particular act or the grant to a trustee of any necessary or desirable power.

(d) The resignation or appointment of a trustee and the determination of a trustee's compensation.

(e) The transfer of a trust's principal place of administration.

(f) The liability of a trustee for an action relating to the trust.

(5) Any interested person may request the court to approve or disapprove a nonjudicial settlement agreement.

(Laws 2006, ch. 2006-217, §1, effective July 1, 2007.)

§736.0201. Trust proceedings: role of court

(1) Except as provided in subsection (5) and §736.0206, proceedings concerning trusts shall be commenced by filing a complaint and shall be governed by the Florida Rules of Civil Procedure.

(2) The court may intervene in the administration of a trust to the extent the court's jurisdiction is invoked by an interested person or as provided by law.

(3) A trust is not subject to continuing judicial supervision unless ordered by the court.

(4) A judicial proceeding involving a trust may relate to the validity, administration, or distribution of a trust, including proceedings to:

(a) Determine the validity of all or part of a trust;

(b) Appoint or remove a trustee;

(c) Review trustees' fees;

(d) Review and settle interim or final accounts;

(e) Ascertain beneficiaries; determine any question arising in the administration or distribution of any trust, including questions of construction of trust instruments; instruct trustees; and determine the existence or nonexistence of any immunity, power, privilege, duty, or right;

(f) Obtain a declaration of rights; or

(g) Determine any other matters involving trustees and beneficiaries.

(5) A proceeding for the construction of a testamentary trust may be filed in the probate proceeding for the testator's estate. The proceeding shall be governed by the Florida Probate Rules.

(Laws 2006, ch. 2006-217, §2, effective July 1, 2007.)

§736.0202. Jurisdiction over trustee and beneficiary

(1) By accepting the trusteeship of a trust having its principal place of administration in this state or by moving the principal place of administration to this state, the trustee submits personally to the jurisdiction of the courts of this state regarding any matter involving the trust.

(2) With respect to their interests in the trust, the beneficiaries of a trust having its principal place of administration in this state are subject to the jurisdiction of the courts of this state regarding any matter involving the trust. By accepting a distribution from such a trust, the recipient submits personally to the jurisdiction of the courts of this state regarding any matter involving the distribution.

(3) This section does not preclude other methods of obtaining jurisdiction over a trustee, beneficiary, or other person receiving property from the trust.

(Laws 2006, ch. 2006-217, §2, effective July 1, 2007.)

§736.0203. Subject matter jurisdiction

The circuit court has original jurisdiction in this state of all proceedings arising under this code.

(Laws 2006, ch. 2006-217, §2, effective July 1, 2007.)

§736.0204. Venue

Venue for actions and proceedings concerning trusts, including those under §736.0201, may be laid in:

(1) Any county where the venue is proper under chapter 47;

(2) Any county where the beneficiary suing or being sued resides or has its principal place of business; or

(3) The county where the trust has its principal place of administration.

(Laws 2006, ch. 2006-217, §1, effective July 1, 2007.)

§736.0205. Trust proceedings relating to foreign trusts

Over the objection of a party, the court shall not entertain proceedings under §736.0201 for a trust registered, or having its principal place of administration, in another state unless all interested parties could not be bound by litigation in the courts of the state where the trust is registered or has its principal place of administration. The court may condition a stay or dismissal of a proceeding under this section on the consent of any party to jurisdiction of the state where the trust is registered or has its principal place of business, or the court may grant a continuance or enter any other appropriate order.

(Laws. 2006, ch. 2006-217, §1, effective July 1, 2007.)

§736.0206. Court may review employment of agents and compensation by trustees

(1) After notice to all interested persons, the court may review the propriety of the employment by a trustee of any person, including any attorney, auditor, investment adviser, or other specialized agent or assistant, and the reasonableness of any compensation paid to that person or to the trustee.

(2) If the settlor's estate is being probated, and the settlor's trust or the trustee of the settlor's trust is a beneficiary under the settlor's will, the trustee, any person employed by the trustee, or any interested person may have the propriety of employment and the reasonableness of the compensation of the trustee or any person employed by the trustee determined in the probate proceeding.

(3) The burden of proof of the propriety of the employment and the reasonableness of the compensation shall be on the trustee and the person employed by the trustee. Any person who is determined to have received excessive compensation from a trust for services rendered may be ordered to make appropriate refunds.

(4) Court proceedings to determine reasonable compensation of a trustee or any person employed by a trustee, if required, are a part of the trust administration process. The costs, including attorney's fees, of the person assuming the burden of

proof of propriety of the employment and reasonableness of the compensation shall be determined by the court and paid from the assets of the trust unless the court finds the compensation paid or requested to be substantially unreasonable. The court shall direct from which part of the trust assets the compensation shall be paid.

(5) The court may determine reasonable compensation for a trustee or any person employed by a trustee without receiving expert testimony. Any party may offer expert testimony after notice to interested persons. If expert testimony is offered, a reasonable expert witness fee shall be awarded by the court and paid from the assets of the trust. The court shall direct from which part of the trust assets the fee shall be paid.

(6) Persons given notice as provided in this section shall be bound by all orders entered on the complaint.

(7) In a proceeding pursuant to subsection (2), the petitioner may serve formal notice as provided in the Florida Probate Rules, and such notice shall be sufficient for the court to acquire jurisdiction over the person receiving the notice to the extent of the person's interest in the trust.

(Laws 2006, ch. 2006-217, §1, effective July 1, 2007.)

§736.0207. Contests of validity of trusts

An action to contest the validity of all or part of a trust may not be commenced until the trust becomes irrevocable, except this section does not prohibit such action by the guardian of the property of an incapacitated settlor.

(Laws 2006, ch. 2006-217, §1, effective July 1, 2007.)

II. Creation of a Trust

A. Common Methods

The most common methods of trust creation are: (1) a transfer or (2) a declaration of trust. The transfer of property from the owner to the trustee may be accomplished during the owner's life time (called an inter vivos or living trust) or may be accomplished at the owner's death (called a testamentary trust). To establish a trust by declaration, the owner declares that he or she holds property in trust for another. A declaration obviates the need for a transfer from the owner to the trustee because, in a trust created by declaration, the owner becomes the trustee.

Other methods of trust creation also exist. According to Florida law, a trust may be created not only by a declaration or transfer (either inter vivos or by will), but also by the exercise of a power of appointment in favor of a trustee (Fla. Stat. §736.0401). Trusts may also be created by will. However, such testamentary trusts must comply with the Statute of Wills (Fla. Stat. §737.111).

A valid trust does not require consideration. However, if the trust is created by means of a promise, then consideration is required according to contract law. Kimberly C. Simmons, Express Trusts, Consideration, 55A Fla. Jur.2d Trusts §20.

Statutes on the creation, validity, modification, and termination of trusts are set forth in Chapter 736, Part IV of Title 42, Estates and Trusts, of the Florida Statutes. The Florida Trust Code was enacted in 2006 (effective July 1, 2007), as Chapter 736 of the Florida Statutes (§§736.0101-736.1303). That Chapter also covers the law regarding trustees and beneficiaries; judicial proceedings concerning trusts; rights of third persons; investment of trust property; and payments of claims, debts, and expenses from a revocable trust of a deceased settlor. Other relevant provisions (e.g., those relating to trust property investment and portions of the Uniform Prudent Investor Act) are set forth in Chapter 518 of the Florida Statutes.

Modification and termination of trusts are discussed in Chapter X *infra*; the law regarding trustees is explored in Chapter XI *infra* and the law regarding beneficiaries in Chapter XII *infra*.

§736.0101. Title: Florida Trust Code

This chapter may be cited as the "Florida Trust Code" and for purposes of this chapter is referred to as the "code."

(Laws 2006 , ch. 217, §1, effective January 1, 2007.)

§736.0102. Scope: Code applies to various types of trusts

This code applies to express trusts, charitable or noncharitable, and trusts created pursuant to a law, judgment, or decrees that requires the trust to be administered in the manner of an express trust. This code does not apply to constructive or resulting trusts; conservatorships; custodial arrangements pursuant to the Florida Uniform Transfers to Minors Act; business trusts providing for certificates to be issued to beneficiaries, common trust funds; land trusts under §689.05; trusts created by the form of the account or by the deposit agreement at a financial institution; voting trusts; security arrangements; liquidation trusts; trusts for the primary purpose of paying debts, dividends, interest, salaries, wages, profits, pensions, or employee benefits of any kind; and any

arrangement under which a person nominee or escrowee for another.
(Laws 2006, ch. 217, §1, effective July 1, 2007.)

§736.0105. Scope: Code governs requirements for trust creation, duties and powers of trustee, rights of beneficiaries, etc.

(1) Except as otherwise provided in the terms of the trust, this code governs the duties and powers of a trustee, relations among trustees, and the rights and interests of a beneficiary.

(2) The terms of a trust prevail over any provision of this code except:

(a) The requirements for creating a trust.

(b) The duty of the trustee to act in good faith and in accordance with the terms and purposes of the trust and the interests of the beneficiaries.

(c) The requirement that a trust and its terms be for the benefit of the trust's beneficiaries, and that the trust have a purpose that is lawful, not contrary to public policy, and possible to achieve.

(d) The periods of limitation for commencing a judicial proceeding.

(e) The power of the court to take such action and exercise such jurisdiction as may be necessary in the interests of justice.

(f) The requirements under §736.0108(1) for the designation of a principal place of administration of the trust.

(g) The jurisdiction and venue provisions in §§736.0202, 736.0203, and 736.0204.

(h) The restrictions on the designation of representative under §736.0306.

(i) The formalities required under §736.0403(2) for the execution of a trust.

(j) The power of the court to modify or terminate a trust under §§736.0410-736.04115, except as provided in s. 736.04115(3)(b), and under §§736.0413, 736.0415, and 736.0416.

(k) The ability to modify a trust under §736.0412, except as provided in §736.0412(4)(b).

(l) The effect of a spendthrift provision and the rights of certain creditors and assignees to reach a trust as provided in part V.

(m) The trustee's duty under §736.05053 to pay expenses and obligations of the settlor's estate.

(n) The trustee's duty under s. 736.05055 to file a notice of trust at the settlor's death.

(o) The right of a trustee under §736.0701 to decline a trusteeship and the right of a trustee under §736.0705 to resign a trusteeship.

(p) The power of the court under §736.0702 to require, dispense with, modify, or terminate a bond.

(q) The power of the court under §736.0708(2) to adjust a trustee's compensation specified in the terms of the trust that is unreasonably low or high.

(r) The duty under §736.0813(1)(a) and (b) to notify qualified beneficiaries of an irrevocable trust of the existence of the trust, of the identity of the trustee, and of their rights to trust accountings.

(s) The duty under §736.0813(1)(c) and (d) to provide a complete copy of the trust instrument and to account to qualified beneficiaries.

(t) The duty under §736.0813(1)(e) to respond to the request of a qualified beneficiary of an irrevocable trust for relevant information about the assets and liabilities of the trust and the particulars relating to trust administration.

(u) The effect of an exculpatory term under §736.1011.

(v) The rights under §§736.1013-736.1017 of a person other than a trustee or beneficiary.

(w) The effect of a penalty clause for contesting a trust under §736.1108.

(Laws 2006 , ch. 217, §1, effective July 1, 2007.)

§736.0106. Common law and equitable principles

The common law of trusts and principles of equity supplement this code, except to the extend modified by this code or another law of this state.
(Laws 2006 , ch. 217, §1, effective July 1, 2007.)

§736.0401. Methods of trust creation

A trust may be created by:

(1) Transfer of property to another person as trustee during the settlor's lifetime or by will or other disposition taking effect on the settlor's death;

(2) Declaration by the owner of property that the owner holds identifiable property as trustee; or

(3) Exercise a power of appointment in favor of a trustee.

(Laws 2006, ch. 217, §4, effective July 1, 2007.)

§736.0402. Requirements for trust creation

(1) A trust is created only if:

(a) The settlor has capacity to create a trust.

(b) The settlor indicates an intent to create the trust.

(c) The trust has a definite beneficiary or is:

1. A charitable trust;

2. A trust for the care of an animal, as provided in §736.0408; or

3. A trust for a noncharitable purpose, as provided in §736.0409.

(d) The trustee has duties to perform.

(e) The same person is not the sole trustee and sole beneficiary.

(2) A beneficiary is definite if the beneficiary can be ascertained now or in the future, subject to any applicable rule against perpetuities.

(3) A power of a trustee to select a beneficiary from an indefinite class is valid. If the power is not exercised within a reasonable time, the power fails and the property subject to the power passes to the persons who would have taken the property had the power not been conferred.

(Laws 2006, ch. 217, §4, effective July 1, 2007.)

§737.111. Requirements for testamentary trusts

(1) The testamentary aspects of a trust defined in §731.201(34), are invalid unless the trust instrument is executed by the grantor with the formalities required for the execution of a will.

(2) The testamentary aspects of a trust created by a nonresident of Florida, either before or after this law takes effect, are not invalid because the trust does not meet the requirements of this section, if the trust is valid under the laws of the state or country where the settlor was at the time of execution.

(3) The testamentary aspects of an amendment to a trust are invalid unless the amendment is executed by the settlor with the same formalities as a will.

(4) For the purposes of this section, the term "testamentary aspects" means those provisions of the trust that dispose of the trust property on or after the death of the settlor other than to the settlor's estate.

(5) This section shall not apply to trusts established as part of an employee annuity described in §403 of the Internal Revenue Code of 1986, [FN1] as amended, an Individual Retirement Account as described in §408 of the Internal Revenue Code of 1986, [FN2] as amended, a Keogh (HR-10) Plan, or a retirement or other plan that is qualified under §401 of the Internal Revenue Code of 1986, [FN3] as amended.

(6) This section shall not apply to trust instruments executed prior to October 1, 1995.

[FN1] 26 U.S.C.A. §403.
[FN2] 26 U.S.C.A. §408.
[FN3] 26 U.S.C.A. §401.

(Laws 1995, ch. 95-401, §11, effective October 1, 1995. Amended by Laws 1997, ch. 97-240, §4, effective May 30, 1997; Laws 2001, ch. 2001-226, §193, effective January 1, 2002.)

B. Intent

A trust is created only if "the settlor properly manifests an intention to create a trust relationship." Restatement (Third) of Trusts §13. The settlor's intention to create a trust must be express, clear, and unequivocal. Judicial determination of the settlor's intent is not limited to the writing but includes an examination of the parties' acts and declarations. Intention also may be inferred from the surrounding circumstances.

"Particular words or a form of words is not required in creating a trust." Simmons, Express Trusts, Determination of Intent, 55A Fla. Jur.2d, Trusts, §22. According to the Restatement (Third) of Trusts §13 cmt. b, "[A] trust may be created without the settlor's use of words such as 'trust' or 'trustee.'" Also, the fact that the transferor uses the words "trust" or "trustee" is not dispositive on whether the owner had the requisite intention to create a trust. *Id.* The settlor does not have know that the relationship is called a trust or understand that characteristics of the trust relationship. *Id.* at cmt. a.

Sometimes, a particular problem arises in interpreting intent when a settlor uses precatory language to create a trust. Precatory language includes expressions of desire, wish, request, etc. Precatory language is regarded as creating a trust only if it appears that the settlor intended to impose an imperative obligation on the trustee and to exclude the exercise of discretion.

For example, in Lines v. Darden, 5 Fla. 51 (Fla. 1853), the testator in one clause bequeathed his entire estate to his daughter for life, to be divided equally among her children upon her death. The next clause expressed his "will and desire" that should either grandson reach the age of 21 or any granddaughter marry before the property was transferred to them, that grandchild shall receive a portion of the estate as a loan to manage and receive the benefits therefrom until the final distribution, when such property would be divided equally among the grandchildren. The Court held that this will did not create a trust for the benefit of the grandchildren, but merely conferred a discretionary power upon the testator's daughter.

If a testator expresses words of desire to an executor, courts traditionally construed such

language as a command, following the English rule. Restatement (Third) of Trusts §13 cmt. d. The inference that the testator's wish is a command is no longer followed.

The Restatement (Third) of Trusts lists several circumstances that may facilitate a determination of the testator's intent in the face of precatory language:

- specific terms and tenor of the words use;
- definiteness (of lack thereof) of the property involved;
- ease (or lack thereof) of ascertaining possible trust purposes and terms;
- specificity (or lack thereof) of the possible beneficiaries and their interests;
- interests, motives, and concerns that might have influenced the transferor;
- transferor's prior conduct, statements, and relationships regarding the beneficiaries;
- personal and fiduciary relationship between the transferor and the transferee;
- testator's other present or past dispositions; and
- the likelihood that a finding of trust would be desired by the transferor.

Id. at §13, cmt. d.

§736.0402. Requirements for creation

(1) A trust is created only if:

....

(b) The settlor indicates an intent to create the trust.

(Laws 2006, ch. 217, §4, effective July 1, 2007.)

C. Trust Property

A valid trust requires trust property. Trust property may consist of anything that may be the subject of ownership, and includes real and personal property. The trust property must be in existence when the trust is created. That is, the trust res cannot be an expectancy. Simmons, Express Trusts, Trust Res, 55A Fla. Jur.2d, Trusts, §16.

A settlor must have transferable title or an interest in property to create a valid trust. In addition, the owner of property must divest himself or herself of a property interest in that property by the creation of the trust. It is not necessary to trust creation that a *present* interest be transferred or that the beneficiary have a *present* right of enjoyment. That is, the beneficiary may receive a future interest because such a property interest is presently vested.

According to the aforementioned general rule, a trust res cannot be an expectancy interest. (Recall that a future interest is *not* an expectancy because the former is vested.) However, Florida law does permit as trust property an expectancy interest in certain designated death benefits: life insurance policies, designated benefit plans described in Florida Statutes §733.808, annuities or endowment contracts, and health or accident policies (Fla. Stat. §689.075).

A settlor may not retain the full equitable and legal ownership in property or else the doctrine of merger applies. See, e.g., Restatement (Third) of Trusts §69 (trust terminates if the legal and equitable title "become united in one person"); Unif. Trust Code §402(a)(5) (requiring division of title).

The retention of a power of revocation or the reservation of a life estate by the settlor of an inter vivos trust does not render a trust testamentary and invalid (Fla. Stat. §689.075 (1)(a) , (f)).

Florida Statutes §736.0401(1), (2) refer to the creation of a trust by the transfer of a property interest or the declaration of such an interest. Moreover, Florida Statutes §736.0106 provides that the common law of trusts will supplement the Code. The common law of trusts, as well as case law in Florida, has long held that the possession of existing, identifiable property is a requirement of a valid trust. See, e.g., In re Estate of Craft, 320 So. 2d 874 (Fla. Dist. Ct. App. 1975) (holding that the subject matter of the trust, i.e., eight shares of corporate stock from a block of 78 shares previously held by the trustee bank in the decedent's prior trust, was in existence at the time of the execution of the new will and creation of the new trust and was ascertainable with reasonable certainty through the testimony of the trust officer of the trustee bank and the writings of the decedent).

§689.075. Inter vivos trusts; powers retained by settlor

(1) A trust which is otherwise valid and which complies with §737.111, including, but not limited to, a trust the principal of which is composed of real property, intangible personal property, tangible personal property, the possible expectancy of receiving as a named beneficiary death benefits as described in §733.808, or any combination thereof, and which has been created by a written instrument shall not be held invalid or an attempted

testamentary disposition for any one or more of the following reasons:

(a) Because the settlor or another person or both possess the power to revoke, amend, alter, or modify the trust in whole or in part;

(b) Because the settlor or another person or both possess the power to appoint by deed or will the persons and organizations to whom the income shall be paid or the principal distributed;

(c) Because the settlor or another person or both possess the power to add to, or withdraw from, the trust all or any part of the principal or income at one time or at different times;

(d) Because the settlor or another person or both possess the power to remove the trustee or trustees and appoint a successor trustee or trustees;

(e) Because the settlor or another person or both possess the power to control the trustee or trustees in the administration of the trust;

(f) Because the settlor has retained the right to receive all or part of the income of the trust during her or his life or for any part thereof;

(g) Because the settlor is, at the time of the execution of the instrument, or thereafter becomes, sole trustee.

(2) Nothing contained herein shall affect the validity of those accounts, including but not limited to bank accounts, share accounts, deposits, certificates of deposit, savings certificates, and other similar arrangements, heretofore or hereafter established at any bank, savings and loan association, or credit union by one or more persons, in trust for one or more other persons, which arrangements are, by their terms, revocable by the person making the same until her or his death or incompetency.

(3) The fact that any one or more of the powers specified in subsection (1) are in fact exercised once, or more than once, shall not affect the validity of the trust or its nontestamentary character.

(4) This section shall be applicable to trusts executed before or after July 1, 1969, by persons who are living on or after said date. However, the requirement of conformity with the formalities for the execution of wills as found in paragraph (1)(g) shall not be imposed upon any trust executed prior to July 1, 1969.

(5) The amendment of this section, by chapter 75-74, Laws of Florida, is intended to clarify the legislative intent of this section at the time of its original enactment that it apply to all otherwise valid trusts which are created by written instrument and which are not expressly excluded by the terms of this section and that no such trust shall be declared invalid for any of the reasons stated in subsections (1) and (3) regardless of whether the trust involves or relates to an interest in real property.

(Laws 1969, ch. 69-192, §§1, 2; Laws 1969, Ex. Sess., ch. 69-1747, §1; Laws 1971, ch. 71-126, §§1, 2; Laws 1973, ch. 73-333, §169; Laws 1974, ch. 74-78, §1; Laws 1975, ch. 75-74, §§1, 2. Amended by Laws 1995, ch. 95-401, §5, effective July 1, 1995; Laws 1997, ch. 97-102, §756, effective July 1, 1997.)

§733.808. Designated death benefits may be corpus of trust

(1) Death benefits of any kind, including, but not limited to, proceeds of:

(a) An individual life insurance policy;

(b) A group life insurance policy;

(c) A benefit plan as defined by §710.102;

(d) An annuity or endowment contract; and

(e) A health or accident policy,

may be made payable to the trustee under a trust agreement or declaration of trust in existence at the time of the death of the insured, employee, or annuitant or the owner of or participant in the benefit plan. The death benefits shall be held and disposed of by the trustee in accordance with the terms of the trust as they appear in writing on the date of the death of the insured, employee, annuitant, owner, or participant. It shall not be necessary to the validity of the trust agreement or declaration of trust, whether revocable or irrevocable, that it have a trust corpus other than the right of the trustee to receive death benefits.

(2) Death benefits of any kind, including, but not limited to, proceeds of:

(a) An individual life insurance policy;

(b) A group life insurance policy;

(c) A benefit plan as defined in §710.102;

(d) An annuity or endowment contract; and

(e) A health or accident policy,

may be made payable to the trustee named, or to be named, in a written instrument that is admitted to probate as the last will of the insured, the owner of the policy, the employee, owner, or participant covered by the plan or contract, or any other person, whether or not the will is in existence at the time of designation. Upon the admission of the will to probate, the death benefits shall be paid to the trustee, to be held, administered, and disposed of in accordance with the terms of the trust or trusts created by the will.

(3) In the event no trustee makes proper claim to the proceeds from the insurance company or other obligor within a period of 6 months after the date of

the death of the insured, employee, annuitant, owner, or participant, or if satisfactory evidence is furnished to the insurance company or obligor within that period that there is, or will be, no trustee to receive the proceeds, payment shall be made by the insurance company or obligor to the personal representative of the person making the designation, unless otherwise provided by agreement with the insurer or obligor during the lifetime of the insured, employee, annuitant, owner, or participant.

(4) Death benefits payable as provided in subsection (1), subsection (2), or subsection (3), unless paid to a personal representative under the provisions of subsection (3), shall not be deemed to be part of the decedent's estate, and shall not be subject to any obligation to pay the expenses of the administration and obligations of the decedent's estate or for contribution required from a trust under §733.607(2) to any greater extent than if the proceeds were payable directly to the beneficiaries named in the trust.

(5) The death benefits held in trust may be commingled with any other assets that may properly come into the trust.

(6) This section does not affect the validity of any designation of a beneficiary of proceeds previously made that designates as beneficiary the trustee of any trust established under a trust agreement or declaration of trust or by will.

(Laws 1974, ch. 74-106, §1; Laws 1975, ch. 75-220, §91; Laws 1977, ch. 77-87, §38. Amended by Laws 2001, ch. 2001-226, §158, effective January 1, 2002; Laws 2005, ch. 2005-101, §7, effective June 1, 2005.)

D. Valid Trust Purpose

A trust requires a valid trust purpose. According to the Restatement (Third) of Trusts §29, a trust is illegal if it involves the commission of a crime or tort, or violates rules relating to perpetuities or public policy. The Uniform Trust Code §404 specifies, similarly, that the trust terms may not require the trustee to commit an act that is criminal, tortious, or contrary to public policy. In the same vein, Florida law (Fla. Stat. §736.0404) provides that the purposes of the trust must be lawful and not contrary to public policy. However, Florida law also specifies that the trust purposes must be possible to achieve. *Id.*

Sometimes, a settlor attempts to control the conduct of a beneficiary by means of a condition in a trust. If the condition is a *total* restraint on marriage, the condition is void and the beneficiary takes the property free of trust. However, *reasonable* restraints regarding marriage (e.g., pertaining to the religion of a prospective spouse) will be upheld. Also, a settlor may not insert a trust condition that encourages divorce (e.g., "I leave my property in trust for my daughter Rosa for life, but the trust will terminate and the proceeds be distributed to her if she divorces that no-good-bum Herbert"). However, a trust that provides for *support* of a beneficiary in the event of divorce or widowhood will be upheld ("I leave my property in trust to my daughter Rosa for life, but in the event that she becomes widowed or divorced, the trust will terminate to provide for her support"). Also, a trust created for the purpose of *defrauding creditors* or other persons is void.

A trust may be void *for lack of certainty* in its purpose or material terms. For example, the Restatement (Third) of Trusts §30 specifies that a private trust (or trust provision) may be unenforceable because of impossibility or indefiniteness.

Florida law also provides that a valid trust purpose is the care of an animal (Fla. Stat. §736.0402) (discussed in Section E *infra*). Florida law also specifies that a trustee may combine two or more trusts into a single trust or divide a trust into separate trusts, if the result would not "adversely affect achievement of the purposes of the trusts" (Fla. Stat. §736.0417).

§736.0404. Trust purposes

A trust may be created only to the extent the purposes of the trust are lawful, not contrary to public policy, and possible to achieve. A trust and its terms must be for the benefit of its beneficiaries.

(Laws 200 , ch. 217, §4, effective July 1, 2007.)

§736.0417. Combination and division of trusts absent impairment of trust purposes

(1) After notice to the qualified beneficiaries, a trustee may combine two or more trusts into a single trust or divide a trust into two or more separate trusts, if the result does not impair rights of any beneficiary or adversely affect achievement of the purposes of the trusts or trust, respectively.

(2) Subject to the terms of the trust, the trustee may take into consideration differences in federal tax attributes and other pertinent factors in administering the trust property of any separate account or trust, in making applicable tax elections, and in making distributions. A separate trust created by severance must be treated as a separate trust for all purposes from the date on which the severance is effective. The effective date of the severance may be

retroactive to a date before the date on which the trustee exercises such power.
(Laws 2006, ch. 2006-217, §4, effective July 1, 2007.)

E. Parties

A trust is generally created by the owner of property who is called the "trustor," "settlor," "grantor," or "donor." The person (or corporation) who holds legal title is the "trustee." The third party who owns the equitable interest in the property is the "beneficiary" or "cestui que trust." The trustee occupies a fiduciary relationship (i.e., requiring a high standard of conduct in handling the trust property) with the beneficiary.

A trust requires a trustee to hold legal title and to deal with the property for the benefit of the beneficiaries. However, according to the basic rule, a trust will not fail, at its inception or thereafter, for want of a trustee, i.e., because of the trustee's death, incapacity, resignation, or removal. That is, a court will appoint a successor unless the terms of the trust clearly specify that the trust may only continue as long as the designated trustee continues to act. For additional discussion of trustees, see Chapter XI *infra*.

A valid trust also requires a beneficiary (or beneficiaries) who holds equitable title and who has (or have) the right to enforce the trust. According to the general rule, a private express trust must have definite beneficiaries, or at least beneficiaries who will be definitely ascertainable within the period during which all interests must vest under the applicable state law pertaining to perpetuities. For additional discussion of beneficiaries, see Chapter XII *infra*. For discussion of trust duration, see *infra* this chapter, Section F.

Generally, a trust has at least three parties: a settlor, a trustee (or co-trustees), and one or more beneficiaries. However, the settlor and the trustee may be the same person such as when the settlor declares himself the trustee. Note that the same person may not be the sole trustee and the sole beneficiary or else the merger doctrine applies (i.e., merger of the legal and equitable interests). See, e.g., Restatement (Third) of Trusts §69 (trust terminates if the legal and equitable title "become united in one person"). In case of merger, the beneficiary takes free of the trust. However, a sole trustee may be one of several beneficiaries. Similarly, one of several co-trustees may be the sole beneficiary.

In Florida, a beneficiary of a trust may be a particular animal or animals, provided that that animal or animals was/were alive during the settlor's lifetime (Fla. Stat. §736.0408(1)). Such a trust terminates on the death of the animal or (if several) the death of the last surviving animal. *Id.* See also the discussion of "honorary trusts" in Section IIIE *infra*.

Florida law also dispenses with the definite beneficiaries requirement in some cases by permitting a trustee to make the selection of beneficiary (Fla. Stat. §736.0409). Such a trust may not be enforced for more than 21 years. *Id.*

§736.0402. Requirements for creation

(1) A trust is created only if:

...

(c) The trust has a definite beneficiary or is:

1. A charitable trust;

2. A trust for the care of an animal, as provided in §736.0408; or

3. A trust for a noncharitable purpose, as provided in §736.0409.

(d) The trustee has duties to perform.

(e) The same person is not the sole trustee and sole beneficiary.

(2) A beneficiary is definite if the beneficiary can be ascertained now or in the future,
subject to any applicable rule against perpetuities.

(3) A power of a trustee to select a beneficiary from an indefinite class is valid. If the power is not exercised within a reasonable time, the power fails and the property subject to the power passes to the persons who would have taken the property had the power not been conferred.
(Laws 2006, ch. 217, §4, effective July 1, 2007.)

§736.0408. Trust for care of animal

(1) A trust may be created to provide for the care of an animal alive during the settlor's lifetime. The trust terminates on the death of the animal or, if the trust was created to provide for the care of more than one animal alive during the settlor's lifetime, on the death of the last surviving animal.

(2) A trust authorized by this section may be enforced by a person appointed in the terms of the trust or, if no person is appointed, by a person appointed by the court. A person having an interest in the welfare of the animal may request the court to appoint a person to enforce the trust or to remove a person appointed.

(3) Property of a trust authorized by this section may be applied only to the intended use of the property, except to the extent the court determines that the value of the trust property exceeds the

amount required for the intended use. Except as otherwise provided in the terms of the trust, property not required for the intended use must be distributed to the settlor, if then living, otherwise as part of the settlor's estate.

(Laws 2006, ch. 2006-217, §4, effective July 1, 2007.)

§736.0409. Noncharitable trust without ascertainable beneficiary

(1) A trust may be created for a noncharitable purpose without a definite or definitely ascertainable beneficiary or for a noncharitable but otherwise valid purpose to be selected by the trustee. The trust may not be enforced for more than 21 years.

(2) A trust authorized by this section may be enforced by a person appointed in the terms of the trust or, if no person is appointed, by a person appointed by the court.

(3) Property of a trust is authorized by this section may be applied only to the intended use of the property, except to the extent the court determines that the value of the trust property exceeds the amount required for the intended use. Except as otherwise provided in the terms of the trust, property not required for the intended use must be distributed to the settlor, if then living, otherwise as part of the settlor's estate.

(Laws 2006, ch. 217, §4, effective July 1, 2007.)

F. Duration

In most jurisdictions, private express trusts are subject to the Rule Against Perpetuities. The purposes of the Rule are: (1) to promote alienability (to keep property productive), and (2) to limit dead hand control over property to enable trusts to respond to changing conditions (so that present property owners can use the property most productively).

According to the Rule Against Perpetuities, the duration of the trust cannot exceed a permissible period. That is, the Rule Against Perpetuities prohibits trusts in which the designation of beneficiaries will be delayed beyond a certain period of time ("the perpetuities period"). The Rule prohibits those interests that may remain contingent beyond the perpetuities period. All contingent future interests, both legal and equitable, are subject to the Rule. Future interests created in transferees (but not those retained by the transferor) are subject to the Rule.

Many states today follow the common law approach that specified the period of time as 21 years after the death of some life in being at the time of the creation of the interest, plus a period of gestation. The period begins to run, for irrevocable inter vivos trusts, from the time the settlor creates the trust (at declaration, execution of the instrument, or delivery if required). The period begins to run, for revocable inter vivos trusts, from the time when the trust is no longer revocable (usually at the settlor's death). For testamentary trusts (similar to wills), the period begins to run from the time the settlor (or testator) dies.

Many jurisdictions have enacted reforms to the Rule Against Perpetuities. Some jurisdictions adopt a "wait-and-see" approach that looks to actual, rather than possible, events in terms of whether the contingency happens within the period of the Rule. Other jurisdictions lengthen the common law period. Some jurisdictions permit judicial reformation of existing instruments to avoid a Rule violation (via a doctrine analogous to the cy pres doctrine, discussed in Chapter XIII *infra*) to make the trust conform to the settlor's intent as closely as possible. A few jurisdictions have abolished the Rule.

A significant number of states have enacted the Uniform Statutory Rules Against Perpetuities Act (USRAP) (UPC §§2-901 to 2-905). The Act was promulgated by NCCUSL in 1986, and amended in 1990 by adding Section 1(e). As of 2007, 26 states (including Florida) and the District of Columbia have adopted USRAP. Legislative Fact Sheet, http://nccusl.org/nccusl/uniformact_factsheets/uniformacts-fs-usrap.asp (last visited March 3, 2007). USRAP is set forth in Florida Statutes §689.225.

USRAP combines several of the aforementioned approaches, including adoption of a 90-year period within which to determine whether an interest either vests or terminates after its creation. "Ninety years represents an estimate of the actual time most extended future interests will take, at the outside, to vest. If they do not vest, 90 years is sufficient time to justify invalidating such interest." Legislative Fact Sheet, Summary, http://nccusl.org/nccusl/uniformact_factsheets/uniformacts-fs-usrap.asp (last visited March 3, 2007).

Florida amended its version of the USRAP in 2000 by changing the 90-year time limit to "360 years" for unvested property interests or powers of appointment contained in a trust (applicable to trusts created after December 31, 2000). According to the current version of the Florida Rule (Fla. Stat. §689.225(2)), a nonvested property interest in real or personal property is invalid unless: (1) when the interest was created, it was certain to vest or terminate within 21 years after the death of an individual then alive, or (2)

the interest either vests or terminates within 90 years (now 360 years for trusts created after December 31, 2000 "unless the terms of the trust require that all beneficial interests in the trust vest or terminate within a lesser period") (Fla. Stat. §689.225(2)(f)).

On these reforms, see generally McGovern & Kurtz, *supra*, §11.4 at 431-436; Stewart E. Sterk, Jurisdictional Competition to Abolish the Rule Against Perpetuities: R.I.P. for the R.A.P., 24 Cardozo L. Rev. 2097 (2003) (criticizing abolition of the Rule); Note, Dynasty Trusts and the Rule Against Perpetuities, 116 Harv. L. Rev. 2588 (2003) (examining state trends and the academic debate about the Rule's repeal).

§689.13. Rule against perpetuities inapplicable to dispositions of property for cemeteries

No disposition of property, or the income thereof, hereafter made for the maintenance or care of any public or private burying ground, churchyard, or other place for the burial of the dead, or any portion thereof, or grave made in perpetuity; but such disposition shall be held to be made for a charitable purpose or purposes.

(Laws 1931, ch. 14655, §1; Comp. Gen. Laws Supp. 1936, §5671(1).)

§689.225. Rule against perpetuities

(1) SHORT TITLE. --This section may be cited as the "Florida Uniform Statutory Rule Against Perpetuities."

(2) STATEMENT OF THE RULE.

(a) A nonvested property interest in real or personal property is invalid unless:

1. When the interest is created, it is certain to vest or terminate no later than 21 years after the death of an individual then alive; or

2. The interest either vests or terminates within 90 years after its creation.

(b) A general power of appointment not presently exercisable because of a condition precedent is invalid unless:

1. When the power is created, the condition precedent is certain to be satisfied or become impossible to satisfy no later than 21 years after the death of an individual then alive; or

2. The condition precedent either is satisfied or becomes impossible to satisfy within 90 years after its creation.

(c) A nongeneral power of appointment or a general testamentary power of appointment is invalid unless:

1. When the power is created, it is certain to be irrevocably exercised or otherwise to terminate no later than 21 years after the death of an individual then alive; or

2. The power is irrevocably exercised or otherwise terminates within 90 years after its creation.

(d) In determining whether a nonvested property interest or a power of appointment is valid under subparagraph (a)1., subparagraph (b)1., or subparagraph (c)1., the possibility that a child will be born to an individual after the individual's death is disregarded.

(e) If, in measuring a period from the creation of a trust or other property arrangement, language in a governing instrument (i) seeks to disallow the vesting or termination of any interest or trust beyond, (ii) seeks to postpone the vesting or termination of any interest or trust until, or (iii) seeks to operate in effect in any similar fashion upon, the later of:

1. The expiration of a period of time not exceeding 21 years after the death of a specified life or the survivor of specified lives, or upon the death of a specified life or the death of the survivor of specified lives in being at the creation of the trust or other property arrangement, or

2. The expiration of a period of time that exceeds or might exceed 21 years after the death of the survivor of lives in being at the creation of the trust or other property arrangement, that language is inoperative to the extent it produces a period of time that exceeds 21 years after the death of the survivor of the specified lives.

(f) As to any trust created after December 31, 2000, this section shall apply to a nonvested property interest or power of appointment contained in a trust by substituting 360 years in place of "90 years" in each place such term appears in this section unless the terms of the trust require that all beneficial interests in the trust vest or terminate within a lesser period.

(3) WHEN NONVESTED PROPERTY INTEREST OR POWER OF APPOINTMENT CREATED.

(a) Except as provided in paragraphs (b), (d), and (e) of this subsection and in paragraph (a) of subsection (6), the time of creation of a nonvested property interest or a power of appointment is determined under general principles of property law.

(b) For purposes of this section, if there is a person who alone can exercise a power created by a governing instrument to become the unqualified beneficial owner of a nonvested property interest or a property interest subject to a power of appointment described in paragraph (b) or paragraph (c) of subsection (2), the nonvested property interest or power of appointment is created when the power to become the unqualified beneficial owner terminates.

(c) For purposes of this section, a joint power with respect to community property or to marital property under the Uniform Marital Property Act held by individuals married to each other is a power exercisable by one person alone.

(d) For purposes of this section, a nonvested property interest or a power of appointment arising from a transfer of property to a previously funded trust or other existing property arrangement is created when the nonvested property interest or power of appointment in the original contribution was created.

(e) For purposes of this section, if a nongeneral or testamentary power of appointment is exercised to create another nongeneral or testamentary power of appointment, every nonvested property interest or power of appointment created through the exercise of such other nongeneral or testamentary power is considered to have been created at the time of the creation of the first nongeneral or testamentary power of appointment.

(4) REFORMATION. --Upon the petition of an interested person, a court shall reform a disposition in the manner that most closely approximates the transferor's manifested plan of distribution and is within the 90 years allowed by subparagraph (2)(a)2, subparagraph (2)(b)2, or subparagraph (2)(c)2. if:

(a) A nonvested property interest or a power of appointment becomes invalid under subsection (2);

(b) A class gift is not but might become invalid under subsection (2) and the time has arrived when the share of any class member is to take effect in possession or enjoyment; or

(c) A nonvested property interest that is not validated by subparagraph (2)(a)1. can vest but not within 90 years after its creation.

(5) EXCLUSIONS FROM STATUTORY RULE AGAINST PERPETUITIES. --Subsection (2) does not apply to:

(a) A nonvested property interest or a power of appointment arising out of a nondonative transfer, except a nonvested property interest or a power of appointment arising out of:

1. A premarital or postmarital agreement;
2. A separation or divorce settlement;
3. A spouse's election;
4. A similar arrangement arising out of a prospective, existing, or previous marital relationship between the parties;
5. A contract to make or not to revoke a will or trust;
6. A contract to exercise or not to exercise a power of appointment;
7. A transfer in satisfaction of a duty of support; or
8. A reciprocal transfer;

(b) A fiduciary's power relating to the administration or management of assets, including the power of a fiduciary to sell, lease, or mortgage property, and the power of a fiduciary to determine principal and income;

(c) A power to appoint a fiduciary;

(d) A discretionary power of a trustee to distribute principal before termination of a trust to a beneficiary having an indefeasibly vested interest in the income and principal;

(e) A nonvested property interest held by a charity, government, or governmental agency or subdivision, if the nonvested property interest is preceded by an interest held by another charity, government, or governmental agency or subdivision;

(f) A nonvested property interest in, or a power of appointment with respect to, a trust or other property arrangement forming part of a pension, profit-sharing, stock bonus, health, disability, death benefit, income deferral, or other current or deferred benefit plan for one or more employees, independent contractors, or their beneficiaries or spouses, to which contributions are made for the purpose of distributing to or for the benefit of the participants, or their beneficiaries or spouses, the property, income, or principal in the trust or other property arrangement, except a nonvested property interest or a power of appointment that is created by an election of a participant or a beneficiary or spouse; or

(g) A property interest, power of appointment, or arrangement that was not subject to the common-law rule against perpetuities or is excluded by another statute of this state.

(6) APPLICATION.

(a) Except as extended by paragraph (c), this section applies to a nonvested property interest or a power of appointment that is created on or after October 1, 1988. For purposes of this subsection, a nonvested property interest or a power of appointment created by the exercise of a power of appointment is created when the power is irrevocably exercised or when a revocable exercise becomes irrevocable.

(b) This section also applies to a power of appointment that was created before October 1, 1988, but only to the extent that it remains unexercised on October 1, 1988.

(c) If a nonvested property interest or a power of appointment was created before October 1, 1988, and is determined in a judicial proceeding commenced on or after October 1, 1988, to violate this state's rule against perpetuities as that rule existed before October 1, 1988, a court, upon the petition of an interested person, may reform the disposition in the manner that most closely approximates the transferor's manifested plan of distribution and is within the limits of the rule against perpetuities applicable when the nonvested property interest or power of appointment was created.

(7) RULE OF CONSTRUCTION. --With respect to any matter relating to the validity of an interest within the rule against perpetuities, unless a contrary intent appears, it shall be presumed that the transferor of the interest intended that the interest be valid. This section is the sole expression of any rule against perpetuities or remoteness in vesting in this state. No common-law rule against perpetuities or remoteness in vesting shall exist with respect to any interest or power regardless of whether such interest or power is governed by this section.

(8) UNIFORMITY OF APPLICATION AND CONSTRUCTION. --This section shall be applied and construed to effectuate its general purpose to make uniform the law with respect to the subject of this act among states enacting it.

(Stats. 2000,, ch. 245, §1, effective January 1, 2001.)

III. Types of Trusts

A. Introduction

Trusts may be classified in different ways. For example, trusts can be either inter vivos or testamentary in nature. Inter vivos trusts come into effect during the settlor's lifetime. Testamentary trusts are created by will and come into effect after the settlor's death. See, e.g., Uniform Trust Code § 401(1). See generally Simmons, Classification of Trusts, 55A Fla. Jur.2d Trusts §2.

A private trust is created for noncharitable beneficiaries, whereas a charitable trust is one created for charitable purposes. For discussion of charitable trusts, see Chapter XIII *infra*.

In addition, a trust may be revocable or irrevocable. A revocable trust can be terminated by the settlor, whereas an irrevocable trust cannot. For a discussion of trust modification and termination, see Chapter X *infra*.

Trusts also can be express or created by operation of law. An express trust is one arising from the settlor's expressed intent to create the trust. The settlor's intent may be evidenced by written or spoken words. Trusts created by operation of law (by judicial intervention) include constructive and resulting trusts (discussed *infra* this chapter).

Trusts also may be active or passive. According to the Restatement (Third) of Trusts §6(1), in an active trust, the trustee has affirmative duties to perform. In contrast, the trustee's sole duty in a passive trust "is not to interfere with the enjoyment of the trust property by the beneficiaries." *Id.* A passive trust is not a valid trust. Therefore the beneficiary is entitled to the property. *Id.* at §6(2). See also Fla. Stat. §736.0402(1)(d) requiring that the trustee have duties to perform in order to create a valid trust.

§736.0402. Requirements for creation

(1) A trust is created only if:

...

(d) The trustee has duties to perform.

(e) The same person is not the sole trustee and sole beneficiary.

(2) A beneficiary is definite if the beneficiary can be ascertained now or in the future,

subject to any applicable rule against perpetuities.

(3) A power of a trustee to select a beneficiary from an indefinite class is valid. If the power is not exercised within a reasonable time, the power fails and the property subject to the power passes to the persons who would have taken the property had the power not been conferred.

(Laws 2006 , ch. 217, §4, effective July 1, 2007.)

B. Oral vs. Written

Pursuant to the Statute of Frauds of 1677, the conveyance of all legal interest in land (including trusts of real property) had to be manifested by a writing. Today, most American jurisdictions (including Florida) have adopted the Statute of Fraud's requirement that trusts of real property have to be in writing. McGovern & Kurtz, *supra*, §4.6 at 201-202.

Such a writing may be signed by the settlor or trustee, depending on the circumstances. It need not constitute the specific writing that created the trust; rather, a subsequent written acknowledgment also suffices. *Id.* at 202.

Oral trusts of *personal property* are valid in most jurisdictions. Because of the possibility of fraud, some jurisdictions and the Uniform Trust Code (§406) require that such trusts be established by clear and convincing evidence.

Florida law requires that trusts consisting of real property must be in writing (Fla. Stat. §689.05). Additional requirements exist as to the methods of conveying any interest in real property: (1) a deed that is signed by the grantor in the presence of two subscribing witnesses and delivered, or (2) a will that is duly executed (i.e., complies with the Statute of Wills). Although Florida does not recognize oral trusts of real property (Fla. Stat. §736.0403), oral trusts for personal property are valid if proven by clear and convincing evidence (Fla. Stat. §736.0407).

§736.0403. Trusts created in other jurisdictions; formalities required for revocable trusts

(1) A trust not created by will is validly created if the creation of the trust complies with the law of the jurisdiction in which the trust instrument was executed or the law of the jurisdiction in which, at the time of creation, the settlor was domiciled.

(2) Notwithstanding subsection (1):

(a) No trust or confidence of or in any messuages, lands, tenements, or hereditaments shall arise or result unless the trust complies with the provisions of §689.05.

(b) The testamentary aspects of a revocable trust, executed by a settlor who is a domiciliary of this state at the time of execution, are invalid unless the trust instrument is executed by the settlor with the formalities required for the execution of a will in this state. For purposes of this subsection, the term "testamentary aspects" means those provisions of the trust instrument that dispose of the trust property on or after the death of the settlor other than to the settlor's estate.

(3) Paragraph (2)(b) does not apply to trusts established as part of an employee annuity described in §403 of the Internal Revenue Code of 1986, as amended, an individual retirement account as described in §408 of the Internal Revenue Code of 1986, as amended, a Keogh (HR-10) Plan, or a retirement or other plan that is qualified under §401 of the Internal Revenue Code of 1986, as amended.

(4) Paragraph (2)(b) applies to trusts created on or after the effective date of this code. Section 737.111, as in effect prior to the effective date of this code, continues to apply to trusts created before the effective date of this code.

(Laws 2006, ch. 217, §4, effective July 1, 2007.)

§736.0407. Clear and convincing evidence of oral trust required

Except as required by §736.0403 or a law other than this code, a trust need not be evidenced by a trust instrument but the creation of an oral trust and its terms may be established only by clear and convincing evidence.

(Laws 2006, ch. 217, §4, effective July 1, 2007.)

§689.05. Statutes of Frauds: creation of trusts in land must be in writing

All declarations and creations of trust and confidence of or in any messuages, lands, tenements or hereditaments shall be manifested and proved by some writing, signed by the party authorized by law to declare or create such trust or confidence, or by the party's last will and testament, or else they shall be utterly void and of none effect; provided, always, that where any conveyance shall be made of any lands, messuages or tenements by which a trust or confidence shall or may arise or result by the implication or construction of law, or be transferred or extinguished by the act and operation of law, then, and in every such case, such trust or confidence shall be of the like force and effect as the same would have been if this section had not been made, anything herein contained to the contrary in anywise notwithstanding.

(Laws 1997, ch. 102, §754.)

§689.06. Methods of conveyance of trusts in land

All grants, conveyances, or assignments of trust or confidence of or in any lands, tenements, or hereditaments, or of any estate or interest therein, shall be by deed signed and delivered, in the presence of two subscribing witnesses, by the party granting, conveying, or assigning, or by the party's attorney or agent thereunto lawfully authorized, or by last will and testament duly made and executed, or else the same shall be void and of no effect.

(Act Nov. 15, 1828, §3; Rev. St. 1892, §1952; Gen. St. 1906, §2453; Rev. Gen. St. 1920, §3792; Comp. Gen. Laws 1927, §5665; Laws 1980, ch. 80-219, §1. Amended by Laws 1997, ch. 97-102, §755, effective July 1, 1997.)

C. Trusts Created by Operation of Law

1. Resulting Trust

Some trusts arise by operation of law. Two types of trusts created by operation of law are: (1) resulting trusts and (2) constructive trusts.

A resulting trust is implied from the facts and circumstances of the case and is used to accomplish the presumed intent of the parties. Simmons, Resulting Trusts, 55A Fla. Jur.2d, Trusts, §85. In such a trust, the transferee has an obligation to convey title to the beneficiary. However, the transferee has no other obligations. The beneficiary may be the settlor or, if the settlor has died, the settlor's successor in interest. A resulting trust may be established in personal or real property. According to the Restatement (Third) of Trusts §7, a resulting trust is a "reversionary, equitable interest implied by law in property that is held by a transferee, in whole or in part, as trustee for the transferor or the transferor's successor in interest."

A resulting trust arises in three primary situations:

- an express trust fails,
- an express trust makes an incomplete disposition of property, or
- a purchase money resulting trust.

According to the Restatement (Third) of Trusts §8, a resulting trust arises when an express trust fails in whole or in part. The Restatement specifies two exceptions to this rule: the transferor manifested an intention that a resulting trust should not arise, or the trust fails for illegality, in which case public policy would dictate that unjust enrichment of a transferee is preferable to giving relief to the wrongdoer. *Id.* at §8(a), (b).

The purchase money resulting trust arises when one person pays the purchase price for certain property but title to that property is taken in the name of a different person. In such a case, a rebuttable presumption operates that the title holder holds the property on resulting trust for the person who paid the consideration. In some jurisdictions, if the title holder is a close relative (i.e., parent, child, spouse) of the property owner, then a rebuttable presumption arises that a gift took place.

According to the Restatement (Third) of Trusts §9, two exceptions exist to the purchase money resulting trust: if the transferor manifests an intention that no resulting trust should arise, or the transfer is made to accomplish an unlawful purpose, in which case a resulting trust does not arise based on public policy concerns. *Id.* at §9(1)(a), (b).

According to the Florida Statutes §736.0102, the Code (§§736.0101-736.1303) does not apply to resulting or constructive trusts. Also, Florida case law provides that the Statute of Frauds does not apply to resulting or constructive trusts. See, e.g., Stonely v. Moore, 851 So. 2d 905, 906 (Fla. Dist. Ct. App. 2003) (holding that trial court erred in granting summary judgment on the basis of the statute of frauds because "constructive or resulting trusts involving real estate can be based on parol evidence").

See generally McGovern & Kurtz, *supra*, §6.1 at 269-270.

§736.0102. Code not applicable to resulting or constructive trusts

This code applies to express trusts, charitable or noncharitable, and trusts created pursuant to a law, judgment, or decrees that requires the trust to be administered in the manner of an express trust. This code does not apply to constructive or resulting trusts; conservatorships; custodial arrangements pursuant to the Florida Uniform Transfers to Minors Act; business trusts providing for certificates to be issued to beneficiaries, common trust funds; land trusts under §689.05; trusts created by the form of the account or by the deposit agreement at a financial institution; voting trusts; security arrangements; liquidation trusts; trusts for the primary purpose of paying debts, dividends, interest, salaries, wages, profits, pensions, or employee benefits of any kind; and any arrangement under which a person nominee or escrowee for another.

(Laws 2006, ch. 217, §1, effective July 1, 2007.)

2. Constructive Trust

The second type of trust created by operation of law is a constructive trust. Such trusts arise entirely by operation of law, without regard to the intention of the parties to create a trust. Simmons, Classification as, and Distinction Between, Resulting and Constructive Trusts, 55A Fla. Jur.2d, Trusts, §82.

A constructive trust is an equitable remedy imposed by a court to prevent unjust enrichment. It is a restitutionary device to prevent a wrongdoer from enjoying a beneficial interest in property that was obtained by his or her wrongful act (e.g., fraud, breach of fiduciary duty, etc.). The court impresses a constructive trust on wrongfully acquired property in order to convey that property to the person (i.e., the beneficiary) who would have owned it but for the defendant's wrongful conduct. The wrongdoer then becomes a constructive trustee with the duty to transfer the property to the plaintiff. In an action to recover the trust property, the beneficiary has the right of "tracing." That is, he or she can follow the original trust property into its product and impress a constructive trust on that product.

A constructive trust also may arise by breach of a confidential relationship by which the trustee acquires property by fraud, misrepresentation, duress, abuse of confidence or other form of "unconscionable conduct," "which one in equity and good conscience" should not retain. Simmons, Definitions and Elements of Constructive Trust, 55A Fla. Jur.2d, Trusts, §98. A confidential relationship may exist in the case of a fiduciary relationship, or in the case of a moral, social, domestic, or merely personal relationship. Simmons, General Types of Relationships Considered Confidential, 55A Fla. Jur.2d, Trusts, §103.

Florida case law supports the imposition of a constructive trust in situations of mistake or fraud. For example, in In re Estate of Tolin, 622 So. 2d 988 (Fla. 1993), the Florida Supreme Court held that a constructive trust should be imposed on property conveyed by a codicil where the testator's intent to revoke the codicil was frustrated by his mistake in destroying a copy of the codicil rather than the original, and where the residual beneficiary of the codicil benefited at the expense of the testator's intended beneficiary. Further, a constructive trust may be imposed against the wrongdoer or a third party who was not engaged in the wrongful conduct but who was enriched thereby. Joseph v. Chanin, 940 So. 2d 483 (Fla. Dist. Ct. App. 2006) (granting relief to surviving joint tenant against beneficiary of other joint tenant's separate account, based on theory of conversion, but stating that constructive trust might also be a possible theory of recovery) .

On constructive trusts, see generally McGovern & Kurtz, *supra*, §6, at 249-250.

D. Pour-Over Trusts

A pour-over is a provision in a will that makes a gift of probate assets to an existing inter vivos trust. Use of such an estate planning measure enables a testator to devise property into a trust even though the trust has been altered subsequent to the execution of the will. McGovern & Kurtz, *supra*, §6.2 at 274. Such a provision is commonly called a "pour-over" provision, and such a trust is commonly called a "pour-over" trust.

Pour-over provisions are especially common as an estate planning devices because: (1) an inter vivos trust is easier to amend than a will (because an amendment to a will must conform with the jurisdiction's Statute of Wills); (2) an inter vivos trust can incorporate many types of assets (e.g., life insurance proceeds) to provide a unified dispositive scheme, and (3) the testator may pour over property into a trust that was created by a third party, such as a spouse. Beyer, *supra*, §9.6, at 193.

At common law, courts did not give effect to pour-over provisions because such provisions were thought to violate the Statute of Wills (by permitting disposition of property without compliance with the relevant wills legislation). Gradually, courts upheld pour-over dispositions based on the theories of either: (1) incorporation by reference (i.e., the will incorporates the terms of the trust by reference) or (2) facts of independent significance (i.e., the trust is a fact of independent significance). The former doctrine (incorporation) sufficed if the trust existed when the will was executed and remained unamended at the testator's death. However, if the trust had been amended since the execution of the will, then courts resorted to the doctrine of independent significance to validate the devise (because the trust, as amended, did not satisfy the preexisting document requirement of the incorporation by reference doctrine).

Subsequent legislation obviated the need for states to validate pour-over provisions by reliance on either the doctrine of incorporation by reference or facts of independent significance. Virtually all states now have adopted one of two versions of the Uniform Testamentary Additions to Trust Act (UTATA). In 1960, the National Conference of Commissioners on Uniform State Laws promulgated the original UTATA. The original Act was adopted in 44 states (including Florida). The purpose of the 1960 version was to address difficulties that arose from application of either the doctrine of incorporation by reference or the doctrine of independent significance. Under the early Act, property was governed by the trust terms in effect at the testator's death.

NCCUSL revised the Act in 1991. That version is incorporated into the Uniform Probate Code Article II as §2-511. The 1991 Act has been adopted by 15 states (but not Florida). The 1991 version no longer requires the trust to be in existence at the time the will was executed. The

trust can be created even from property that is poured over. Moreover, the property is governed by the current terms of the trust (i.e., not the trust terms in effect at the testator's death).

For additional background on the two versions of the UTATA and the state adoptions, see http://ncculs.org/nccusl/uniformact_factsheets/uniformacts-fs-tata.asp (last visited March 3, 2007).

The Florida version of the original UTATA is found at Florida Statutes §732.513. The Florida statute requires the trust *either* to be in existence at the time the will is made, *or* created concurrently with the will, provided that the trust is identified in the will. The trust can be amendable or revocable, can be amended or revoked in part any time after the execution of the will, and, as in the 1991 UTATA revision, the trust property can be entirely comprised of property to be poured over from the will.

The Restatement (Third) of Trusts §19 recognizes pour-over dispositions by will that add property to an irrevocable or revocable inter vivos trust, or that fund a trust unfunded during the testator's lifetime. According to the Restatement, such dispositions are effective if authorized by statute; validated by either the doctrine of incorporation by reference or facts of independent significance; or if the trust instrument, together with the will, either (1) "satisfies an applicable rule of substantial compliance, harmless error, or judicial dispensation," or (2) "otherwise satisfies the policies underlying the formal safeguards of the applicable Wills Act." *Id.*

For discussion of the application of will doctrines (incorporation by reference, facts of independent significance) to pour-over trusts, see Chapter V *supra*.

§732.513. Will may pour over assets to previously existing trust

(1) A valid devise may be made to the trustee of a trust that is evidenced by a written instrument in existence at the time of making the will, or by a written instrument subscribed concurrently with making of the will, if the written instrument is identified in the will.

(2) The devise shall not be invalid for any or all of the following reasons:

(a) Because the trust is amendable or revocable, or both, by any person.

(b) Because the trust has been amended or revoked in part after execution of the will or a codicil to it.

(c) Because the only res of the trust is the possible expectancy of receiving, as a named beneficiary, a devise under a will or death benefits as described in § 733.808, and even though the testator or other person has reserved any or all rights of ownership in the death benefit policy, contract, or plan, including the right to change the beneficiary.

(d) Because of any of the provisions of §689.075 [requirement of writing for trusts of real property].

(3) The devise shall dispose of property under the terms of the instrument that created the trust as previously or subsequently amended.

(4) An entire revocation of the trust by an instrument in writing before the testator's death shall invalidate the devise or bequest.

(5) Unless the will provides otherwise, the property devised shall not be held under a testamentary trust of the testator but shall become a part of the principal of the trust to which it is devised.

(Laws 2006 , ch. 217, §32, effective July 1, 2007.)

E. Honorary Trusts

An honorary trust may be defined as "a noncharitable trust which has no ascertained or ascertainable beneficiaries and so is not enforceable, but one in which the court permits the trustee, if willing, to carry out the purposes of the trust." Bogert, *supra*, at §166. That is, the trustee has only a moral, and not legal, obligation to carry out an hononary trust because there is no beneficiary capable of enforcing the trust.

Although courts uphold trusts benefiting the welfare of animals, in general, trusts naming particular animals as beneficiaries cannot be upheld either as charitable trusts or as private express trusts because animals are not legal persons. *Id.* at §35. However, English courts, historically, have used the "honorary trust" theory to validate trusts for specific animals (i.e. dogs and horses). *Id.* In an honorary trust, the settlor vests in the trustee the power to care for particular animals should the trustee choose to do so.

Honorary trusts have been upheld in this country for the following purposes: (1) manumission of slaves; (2) erection of sepulchral monuments; (3) care of graves; (4) care of definite groups of animals; and (5) saying of masses. William Fratcher, Bequests for Purposes, 56 Iowa L. Rev. 773, 801-802 (1971).

An honorary trust is void generally if it can last beyond the period of the Rule Against

Perpetuities. In Florida, trusts for the care of animals alive during the settlor's lifetime are authorized by statute (Fla. Stat. §736.0408). The statute circumvents the problem of not having a beneficiary capable of enforcing the trust by providing that a person appointed in the trust may seek enforcement of the trust, or the court may appoint a person to seek enforcement. *Id.* Additionally, a person "having an interest in the welfare of the animal may request the court to appoint a person to enforce the trust or to remove a person appointed." *Id.*

Bogert explains the arguments in favor of, and opposed to, upholding honorary trusts:

> **In support of the honorary trust theory it can be urged that their recognition will carry out the intent of the donor; that such trusts are not illegal or contrary to the public interest; that the settlor clearly intended to exclude his heirs, next of kin, and residuary legatees from any interest in the trust property and so invalidity and a consequent resulting trust for them should not be decreed; that the power of the successors of the settlor to intervene if the honorary trustee fails to carry out the provisions of the gift insures performance; and that there is some case authority for giving effect to such trusts as honorary.**
>
> **In opposition to honorary trusts it can be argued that a definite beneficiary and enforceability are inherent characteristics of a private trust which should not be discarded for a relatively unimportant reason; that the next of kin or heirs of a property owner are entitled to his property at his death, unless he gives his estate to others by will, and that in the situation under discussion there is no transfer by will of the equitable interest to any person; that a purpose or cause should not be permitted by the courts to take the place of a beneficiary in a noncharitable trust; that the carrying out of the terms of the gift is not apt to be insured by intervention by the successors of the testator, since it is unlikely that they will have the inclination or ability to watch the trustee over a period of years and go to the trouble and expense of seeking to secure the property; and that the small amount of case law approving the honorary trust is "anomalous and exceptional" and a "concession to human weakness or sentiment."**

Bogert, *supra*, at §166.

§736.0408. Trust for care of an animal

(1) A trust may be created to provide for the care of an animal alive during the settlor's lifetime. The trust terminates on the death of the animal or, if the trust was created to provide for the care of more than one animal alive during the settlor's lifetime, on the death of the last surviving animal.

(2) A trust authorized by this section may be enforced by a person appointed in the terms of the trust or, if no person is appointed, by a person appointed by the court. A person having an interest in the welfare of the animal may request the court to appoint a person to enforce the trust or to remove a person appointed.

(3) Property of a trust authorized by this section may be applied only to the intended use of the property, except to the extent the court determines that the value of the trust property exceeds the amount required for the intended use. Except as otherwise provided in the terms of the trust, property not required for the intended use must be distributed to the settlor, if then living, otherwise as part of the settlor's estate.

(Laws 2006, ch. 217, §4, effective July 1, 2007.)

F. Secret vs. Semi-Secret Trusts

Some trusts are secret or semi-secret. In a secret trust situation, a will makes an absolute gift and is silent on whether the testator intended a trust. However, subsequent evidence reveals an agreement between the donee and the testator that the donee would hold the property in trust for a beneficiary designated by the testator. In the semi-secret trust situation, the will reveals that the testator intended a trust; however, the beneficiary is not identified in the will.

A secret trust may be enforced without a writing if proven by clear and convincing evidence. The secret trust is enforced through a constructive trust. In contrast, in the semi-secret trust situation, courts traditionally hold that the trust fails and return the purported trust property to the settlor based on a resulting trust theory.

The Restatement (Third) of Trusts §18 recognizes secret trusts, and provides for their enforcement by constructive trust, in two situations: (1) if a testator bequeaths property in reliance on the beneficiary's agreement (express or implied) to hold the property in trust for a particular purpose and person(s), and (2) if a person dies intestate and relies on an heir's agreement (express or implied) to hold the property in trust for a particular purpose or person(s).

The different enforcement remedies have been criticized by commentators on various grounds. For example, one commentator notes

the "pretext" of imposing equitable relief in the form of a constructive trust in the secret trust situation.

> Courts have imposed an equitable constructive trust upon the named beneficiary to enforce the transfer over to the intended one. Courts thereby effectuate the testator's intent, despite her failure to comply fully with the statute of wills. The pretext for imposing a constructive trustee in this case is prevention of "wrong-doing" by the beneficiary, who might otherwise break his (implicit) promise to the testator to hand over the bequest. But, as usual, this contraption comprises an imperfect antidote to the statute [of wills]: For equity can only be summoned in the event of a wrong.

Adam J. Hirsch, Inheritance Law, Legal Contraptions, and the Problem of Doctrinal Change, 79 Or. L. Rev. 527, 558 n. 113 (2000).

McGovern argues out that the semi-secret trust constitutes a stronger case for relief because "the extrinsic evidence showing the intended beneficiaries is not inconsistent with the will but rather supplements it. . . ." McGovern & Kurtz, *supra*, §6.2 at 251. He points out that the Restatement of Trust makes semi-secret trusts enforceable, and dispenses with the higher burden of proof required for constructive trusts. Id. (citing Restatement (Third) of Trusts §18, cmts. c, h). Florida case law does not address secret or semi-secret trusts in testamentary instruments.

X
MODIFICATION AND TERMINATION OF TRUSTS

Once a trust is created, the provisions of the trust sometimes may be modified and even terminated. In some cases, a particular party, such as the settlor, trustee, or beneficiary, has the ability to modify the provisions of the trust. Such parties also may have the ability to terminate the trust, thereby causing distribution of the trust principal. In other cases, the court may modify the provisions of a trust or even terminate the trust if the circumstances warrant. This chapter focuses on the circumstances under which the parties and the court may alter and/or terminate a trust.

I. Settlor's Power to Modify or Revoke

A. Settlor's Power Limited by the Trust Terms

As a general rule, the settlor's power to modify or revoke is limited by the terms of the trust. After the trust is created, a settlor might want to modify it by changing the beneficiaries or by altering particular interests of the beneficiaries. Perhaps, the settlor might want to terminate the trust in order to recover the trust property for the settlor's needs or to subject the property to a different estate plan. Whether the settlor is able to do so in such cases depends on the terms of the instrument. That is, if the trust instrument expressly reserves the power to modify or revoke a trust, then the settlor may do so. See also Restatement (Third) of Trusts §63(1) ("The settlor of an inter vivos trust has power to revoke or modify the trust to the extent the terms of the trust so provide").

Sometimes, a settlor may provide for delegation of the power to modify or revoke to another person (i.e., a party or nonparty to the trust). The settlor may specify that that person may exercise the power only under certain conditions, such as the occurrence of a particular event. Bogert, *supra*, at §1000.

In addition, revocation of a trust instrument may occur due to fraud, duress, undue influence, or mistake. For example, if the instrument does not contain certain terms as intended, the settlor or other interested party may seek to have the trust reformed. Also, courts have reformed trust instruments to make them irrevocable where the parties so intended such as for tax purposes.

The Restatement (Third) of Trusts §61 provides that a trust terminates in whole or in part upon the expiration of a period or the happening of an event as provided by the trust terms; absent such terms, the trust terminates in whole or in part when the purpose of the trust is accomplished.

Section §62 of the Restatement (Third) of Trusts provides that a trust may be rescinded or reformed based on the same grounds as those upon which other transfers of property may be rescinded or reformed generally. The Restatement (Third) of Property §12.2 provides for modification of donative documents to achieve the settlor's tax objectives. The rationale for this last provision is probable intention, i.e., the donor would have desired the modification if the donor had realized that the desired tax objectives would not be achieved.

Courts may require a high standard of proof (i.e., clear and convincing evidence) to reform a trust because of mistake or fraud. See, e.g, Restatement (Third) of Property §12.1 cmt. e (specifying that the standard of proof for reformation of donative documents to correct mistakes is clear and convincing evidence). But cf. *id.* at §12.2 cmt. c (providing that, for purposes of modifying donative documents to achieve a donor's tax objectives, proof of these objectives may be established by a preponderance of the evidence). On reformation of trusts, see generally Bogert, *supra*, at §§991-1000.

In Florida, revocable trusts may be terminated by the settlor at any time (Fla. Stat. §736.0602). See also Fla. Stat. §736.0410 ("trust terminates to the extent the trust expires or is revoked or is properly distributed pursuant to the terms of the trust"). Revocable trusts that are created or funded by more than one settlor and that consist of community property may be revoked by either spouse alone; however, action by both spouses is required for purposes of amending such trusts (Fla. Stat. §736.0602(2)(a).

Florida law provides that a trust is void if procured by fraud, duress, mistake, or undue influence (Fla. Stat. §736.0405). And, Florida law adheres to the Restatement (Third) of Property in permitting the court to modify a trust to achieve a settlor's tax objectives (Fla. Stats. §736.0416).

A trust may also terminate if the trust becomes a passive trust, its purpose has been accomplished, or the performance of the trust has become impossible. Simmons, Express Trusts, Termination, In General, 55A Fla. Jur.2d 47. The death of the sole trustee (or the last surviving trustee of several trustees) does not terminate the trust because the legal title to the trust property passes to the trustee's personal representative. *Id.*

§736.0405. Trust is void if procured by fraud, duress, mistake, or undue influence

A trust is void if the creation of the trust is procured by fraud, duress, mistake, or undue influence. Any part of the trust is void if procured by such means, but the remainder of the trust not procured by such means is valid if the remainder is not invalid for other reasons.
(Laws 2006, ch. 217, §4, effective July 1, 2007.)

§736.0410. Methods of, and proceedings to disapprove, modification or termination

(1) In addition to the methods of termination prescribed by §§736.04113-736.0414 [judicial modification and modification by trustees], a trust terminates to the extent the trust expires or is revoked or is properly distributed pursuant to the terms of the trust.

(2) A proceeding to disapprove a proposed modification or termination under §736.0412 or a trust combination or division under §736.0417 may be commenced by any beneficiary.

(3) A proceeding to disapprove a proposed termination under §736.0414(1) may be commenced by any qualified beneficiary.
(Laws 2006, ch. 217, §4, effective July 1, 2007.)

§736.0415. Court may reform trust to correct mistakes

Upon application of a settlor or any interested person, the court may reform the terms of a trust, even if unambiguous, to conform the terms to the settlor's intent if it is proved by clear and convincing evidence that both the accomplishment of the settlor's intent and the terms of the trust were affected by a mistake of fact or law, whether in expression or inducement. In determining the settlor's original intent, the court may consider evidence relevant to the settlor's intent even though the evidence contradicts an apparent plain meaning of the trust instrument.
(Laws 2006, ch. 217, §4, effective July 1, 2007.)

§736.0416. Court may modify the trust to achieve a settlor's tax objectives

Upon application of any interested person, to achieve the settlor's tax objectives the court may modify the terms of a trust in a manner that is not contrary to the settlor's probable intent. The court may provide that the modification has a retroactive effect.
(Laws 2006, ch. 217, §4, effective July 1, 2007.)

§736.0601. Capacity of settlor to amend or terminate revocable trust

The capacity required to create, amend, revoke, or add property to a revocable trust, or to direct the actions of the trustee of a revocable trust, is the same as that required to make a will.
(Laws 2006, ch. 217, §6, effective July 1, 2007.)

§736.0602. Trust is presumed to be revocable; methods of revocation; joint action by spouses; notification; substantial compliance

(1) Unless the terms of a trust expressly provide that the trust is irrevocable, the settlor may revoke or amend the trust. This subsection does not apply to a trust created under an instrument executed before the effective date of this code.

(2) If a revocable trust is created or funded by more than one settlor:

(a) To the extent the trust consists of community property, the trust may be revoked by either spouse acting alone but may be amended only by joint action of both spouses;

(b) To the extent the trust consists of property other than community property, each settlor may revoke or amend the trust with regard to the portion of the trust property attributable to that settlor's contribution;

(c) Upon the revocation or amendment of the trust by fewer than all of the settlors, the trustee shall promptly notify the other settlors of the revocation or amendment.

(3) Subject to §736.0403(a), the settlor may revoke or amend a revocable trust:

(a) By substantial compliance with a method provided in the terms of the trust; or

(b) If the terms of the trust do not provide a method, by:

1. A later will or codicil that expressly refers to the trust or specifically devises property that

would otherwise have passed according to the terms of the trust; or

2. Any other method manifesting clear and convincing evidence of the settlor's intent.

(4) Upon revocation of a revocable trust, the trustee shall deliver the trust property as the settlor directs.

(5) A settlor's powers with respect to revocation, amendment, or distribution of trust property may be exercised by an agent under a power of attorney only as authorized by §709.08.

(6) A guardian of the property of the settlor may exercise a settlor's powers with respect to revocation, amendment or distribution of trust property only as provided in §744.441.

(7) A trustee who does not know that a trust has been revoked or amended is not liable for distributions made and other actions taken on the assumption that the trust had not been amended or revoked.

(Laws 2006, ch. 217, §6, effective July 1, 2007.)

§736.0603. Trustee's duties for revocable trust are owed to settlor; powers of withdrawal

(1) While a trust is revocable, the duties of the trustee are owed exclusively to the settlor.

(2) During the period the power may be exercised, the holder of a power of withdrawal has the right of a settlor of a revocable trust under this section to the extent of the property subject to the power.

(Laws 2006, ch. 217, §6, effective July 1, 2007.)

§736.0604. Limitation on action to contest validity of revocable trust

An action to contest the validity of a trust that was revocable at the settlor's death is barred, if not commenced within the earliest of:

(1) The time as provided in chapter 95; or

(2) Six months after the trustee sent the person a copy of the trust instrument and a notice informing the person of the trust's existence, of the trustee's name and address, and of the time allowed for commencing a proceeding.

(Laws 2006, ch. 217, §6, effective July 1, 2007.)

B. Presumptions of Revocability

Some trust instruments are silent regarding reservation of a power of modification or termination. Other trust instruments simply are unclear regarding reservation of these powers. Traditionally, in cases of ambiguity, the law often resorts to presumptions. According to the majority rule, a trust is presumed to be irrevocable unless a power of revocation is expressly reserved or may be implied from language in the instrument. Restatement (Second) of Trusts §330. On the other hand, a few states and the Uniform Trust Code §602 reverse the general rule: They presume that trusts are revocable unless expressly made irrevocable.

Florida law, prior to the adoption of the Uniform Trust Code (effective July 1, 2007), followed the majority rule that a trust is presumed irrevocable unless the instrument expressly reserves a power of revocation. However, Florida recently adopted §602 of the Uniform Trust Code, reversing this presumption. This section applies, however, only to trust instruments executed after this section becomes effective (July 1, 2007). All instruments executed prior to that date are governed by the former presumption.

As explained above, UTC §602(a) rejects the common law presumption that a trust is irrevocable. The commentary to the Restatement (Third) of Trusts points out that this UTC change is of little practical importance for professionally drafted trust instruments because such instruments specify the revocability or irrevocability of a trust. However, the change is important for instruments drafted by nonlawyers for which there is an inference that the trust was meant to be revocable. Cited in Restatement (Third) of Trusts §63, cmts. b, c, d.

The Restatement (Third) of Trusts §63 applies different presumptions of revocability based on *whether or not the settlor retained an interest in the trust.* These presumptions apply to reflect the settlor's unstated intentions. Thus, when the settlor fails expressly to provide whether a trust may be modified or revoked, in cases in which the settlor retains no interest in the trust, it is rebuttably presumed that the settlor has no power to modify or revoke the trust. In such a case, the trust may be compared to an outright gift in which the settlor reserves no beneficial interests. The presumption of irrevocability in this case mirrors general principles regarding inter vivos gifts. Restatement (Third) of Trusts §63 at cmt. c.

However, if the settlor fails expressly to provide whether a trust may be modified or revoked but has retained interests in the trust, the presumption is that "the trust is revocable or amendable by the settlor." The Restatement considers the settlor's retention of a power of appointment to be a "retained interest." In these cases of retained interests, "a presumption of revocability is justified by the risk of confusion

and doubts about a settlor's understanding." ***Id.*** **at c(1). Doubts regarding the settlor's intention are resolved in favor of the settlor. A presumption of revocability also serves to protect the settlor from unanticipated, adverse tax consequences.** ***Id.***

§736.0602. Presumption of revocability

(1) Unless the terms of a trust expressly provide that the trust is irrevocable, the settlor may revoke or amend the trust. This subsection does not apply to a trust created under an instrument executed before the effective date of this code.

....

(Laws 2006, ch. 217, §6, effective July 1, 2007.)

C. Methods of Revocation

Settlors who desire to revoke a trust must comply with the method(s) specified in the trust instrument or specified by law. If a method is specified by the instrument, that provision controls. If no method is specified, then any reasonable method may be used. Bogert, ***supra,*** **at §1001. If the settlor vests the power of revocation in two persons, then both persons must join in the act.** ***Id.***

The Florida Trust Code provides that the settlor may revoke a trust by any method that substantially complies with the terms of the trust (Fla. Stat. §736.0602(3)(a)). If the trust does not provide a method of revocation, the settlor may revoke the trust by a later will or codicil that disposes of property that would have been trust property, (Fla. Stat. §736.0602(3)(b)(1)), or alternatively by "any other method manifesting clear and convincing evidence of the settlor's intent" (Fla. Stat. §736.0602(3)(b)(2)).

The Uniform Trust Code §602(c)(1) liberalizes prior law by permitting merely "substantial compliance" with the prescribed method of revocation. Florida law also adopts a standard of proof that is followed by the Restatement (Third) of Trusts §63—the power to revoke "can be exercised in any way that provides clear and convincing evidence of the settlor's intention to do so." Cf. Fla. Stat. §736.0602(3)(b)(2)) (adopting standard of "clear and convincing evidence").

§736.0602. Presumption of revocability and methods of revocation

(1) Unless the terms of a trust expressly provide that the trust is irrevocable, the settlor may revoke or amend the trust. This subsection does not apply to a trust created under an instrument executed before the effective date of this code.

(2) If a revocable trust is created or funded by more than one settlor:

(a) To the extent the trust consists of community property, the trust may be revoked by either spouse acting alone but may be amended only by joint action of both spouses;

(b) To the extent the trust consists of property other than community property, each settlor may revoke or amend the trust with regard to the portion of the trust property attributable to that settlor's contribution;

(c) Upon the revocation or amendment of the trust by fewer than all of the settlors, the trustee shall promptly notify the other settlors of the revocation or amendment.

(3) Subject to §736.0403(a), the settlor may revoke or amend a revocable trust:

(a) By substantial compliance with a method provided in the terms of the trust; or

(b) If the terms of the trust do not provide a method, by:

1. A later will or codicil that expressly refers to the trust or specifically devises property that would otherwise have passed according to the terms of the trust; or

2. Any other method manifesting clear and convincing evidence of the settlor's intent.

(4) Upon revocation of a revocable trust, the trustee shall deliver the trust property as the settlor directs.

(5) A settlor's powers with respect to revocation, amendment, or distribution of trust property may be exercised by an agent under a power of attorney only as authorized by §709.08.

(6) A guardian of the property of the settlor may exercise a settlor's powers with respect to revocation, amendment or distribution of trust property only as provided in §744.441.

(7) A trustee who does not know that a trust has been revoked or amended is not liable for distributions made and other actions taken on the assumption that the trust had not been amended or revoked.

(Laws 2006, ch. 217, §6, effective July 1, 2007.)

D. Settlor as Sole Beneficiary

If a court determines that the settlor is the sole beneficiary of a trust, the settlor may terminate the trust. A sole beneficiary-settlor may terminate a trust even if: (1) the settlor has reserved no power of modification or revocation, (2) the trust is irrevocable, (3) the trust purposes

have not been fully accomplished, or (4) the trust has a spendthrift provision. The rationale for trust termination in such cases is that there is no problem concerning defeating the trust purpose against the settlor's wishes. See Genova v. Florida Nat. Bank of Palm Beach County, 433 So. 2d 1211 (Fla. Dist. Ct. App. 1983); Bogert, *supra*, at §1004.

A sole beneficiary-settlor has *no right* to terminate the trust during his lifetime if the trust property was supposed to pass by exercise of a power of appointment as specified by the settlor's *will*, and otherwise to his or her heirs. This result occurs because the settlor's heirs can be divested of their interests only by the exercise of the settlor's reserved power of testamentary appointment. Bogert, *supra*, at §1004.

E. Rights of Creditors in Face of Settlor's Power of Revocation

In some states, including Florida, creditors of the settlor may reach the trust property during the settlor's lifetime if the settlor retains the power to revoke the trust. See, e.g., Fla. Stat. §736.0505 (1)(a). Compare Restatement (Second) of Trusts §330 cmt. o ("Unless it is otherwise provided by statute a power of revocation reserved by the settlor cannot be reached by his creditors [who] can compel him to revoke the trust for their benefit").

Florida law also specifies the circumstances in which the assets of an *irrevocable* trust may be subject to the claims of the settlor's creditors. That is, a creditor (or assignee) of the settlor may reach the maximum amount that can be distributed to or for the settlor's benefit in an irrevocable trust (Fla. Stat. §736.0505 (1)(b)). These rules apply regardless of whether the terms of the trust contain a spendthrift provision (Fla. Stat. §736.0505 (1)).

§736.0505. Creditors claims against settlor

(1) Whether or not the terms of a trust contain a spendthrift provision, the following rules apply:

(a) The property of a revocable trust is subject to the claims of the settlor's creditors during the settlor's lifetime to the extent the property would not otherwise be exempt by law if owned directly by the settlor.

(b) With respect to an irrevocable trust, a creditor or assignee of the settlor may reach the maximum amount that can be distributed to or for the settlor's benefit. If a trust has more than one settlor, the amount the creditor or assignee of a particular settlor may reach may not exceed the settlor's interest in the portion of the trust attributable to that settlor's contribution.

(c) Notwithstanding the provisions of paragraph (b), the assets of an irrevocable trust may not be subject to the claims of an existing or subsequent creditor or assignee of the settlor, in whole or in part, solely because of the existence of a discretionary power granted to the trustee by the terms of the trust, or any other provision of law, to pay directly to the taxing authorities or to reimburse the settlor for any tax on trust income or principal which is payable by the settlor under the law imposing such tax.

(2) For purposes of this section:

(a) During the period the power may be exercised, the holder of a power of withdrawal is treated in the same manner as the settlor of a revocable trust to the extent of the property subject to the power.

(b) Upon the lapse, release, or waiver of the power, the holder is treated as the settlor of the trust only to the extent the value of the property affected by the lapse, release, or waiver exceeds the greater of the amount specified in:

1. Section 2041(b)(2) or §2514(e); or
2. Section 2503(b),

of the Internal Revenue Code of 1986, as amended.

(Laws 2006, ch. 217, §5, effective July 1, 2007.)

F. Other

The power to revoke generally includes the power to amend. The reservation of a power to revoke does not affect the validity of a trust.

Some jurisdictions, either by case law or statute, permit one of several settlors to revoke, See, e.g., Fla. Stat. §736.0602(2)(b) ("To the extent the trust consists of property other than community property, each settlor may revoke or amend the trust with regard to the portion of the trust property attributable to that settlor's contribution").

If the trust property consists of "community property," the Florida Trust Code provides that "the trust may be revoked by either spouse acting alone but may be amended only by joint action of both spouse." Fla. Stat. §736.0602.

Florida has adopted the Uniform Disposition of Community Property Rights at Death Act, Fla. Stat. §§732.216 to 732.228. The Act governs the disposition at death of property acquired by a married resident of Florida that would have been community property under the

laws of a community property state. It applies to personal property, wherever located, and real property that is located in Florida and was acquired with community property funds.

On trust termination, see generally Gail B. Bird, Trust Termination: Unborn, Living, and Dead Hands-Too Many Fingers in the Trust Pie, 36 Hast. L.J. 563 (1985); Ronald Chester, Modification and Termination of Trusts in the 21st Century: The Uniform Trust Code Leads a Quiet Revolution, 35 Real Property, Probate & Trust Journal 697 (2001); Edward C. Halbach, Jr., Uniform Acts, Restatements, & Trends in American Trust Law at Century's End, 88 Cal. L. Rev. 1877 (2000); Julia C. Walker, Get Your Dead Hands Off Me: Beneficiaries' Right to Terminate or Modify a Trust Under the Uniform Trust Code, 67 Mo. L. Rev. 443 (2002).

II. Power of the Trustee to Modify or Revoke

The trustee has the power to modify or terminate the trust only if expressly or impliedly authorized to do so by the terms of the instrument. Moreover, the trustee's power to modify or terminate must be exercised in accordance with fiduciary standards and the intent of the settlor (as expressed in the terms of the trust instrument).

Most instruments do not confer upon a trustee an express power to modify or revoke a trust. Even if the settlor agrees, the trustee has no power to terminate a trust unless the trust instrument expressly grants the trustee such a power. If the trustee declares the trust terminated or agrees with the settlor to do so, without authorization, the transaction is void. Bogert, *supra*, at §998.

However, in some circumstances, the trust instrument may indirectly give the trustee the authority to act in such a way that results in modification or termination of the trust. For example, the settlor might give the trustee discretion to invade principal. In that event, the exercise of the trustee's discretion to distribute all of the principal might lead to termination.

Alternatively, the settlor or state law might provide that if the value of the trust property falls below a certain amount, the trustee has discretion to terminate the trust and distribute the principal. For example, the Florida Trust Code (Fla. Stat. §736.0414) provides that the trustee may, after notice to qualified beneficiaries, terminate a trust with a total value of less than $50,000. Alternatively, the court may, upon application of a trustee or qualified beneficiary, modify or terminate the trust or change trustees if the court determines the value of the trust property is insufficient to justify the cost of administration.

In addition, many statutes authorize a trustee to combine similar trusts in order to take advantage of tax benefits (if the trusts are substantially similar), such as by permitting the trustees to make different decisions regarding taxes for each trust. See, e.g., Fla. Stat. §736.0417(1) ("After notice to the qualified beneficiaries, a trustee may combine two or more trusts into a single trust or divide a trust into two or more separate trusts, if the result does not impair rights of any beneficiary or adversely affect achievement of the purposes of the trusts or trust, respectively").

Note that whenever a trust is terminated, the trustee has a duty to act for a reasonable period in order to perform administrative tasks necessary for winding up the trust and distributing the trust property. During that period, the trustee must continue to exercise the powers granted or implied in the trust instrument that are appropriate to protect and preserve the trust property for distribution to the beneficiaries. See generally Bogert, *supra*, at §§992, 1010.

§736.0414. Trustee or court may terminate uneconomic trust

(1) After notice to the qualified beneficiaries, the trustee of a trust consisting of trust property having a total value less than $ 50,000 may terminate the trust if the trustee concludes that the value of the trust property is insufficient to justify the cost of administration.

(2) Upon application of a trustee or any qualified beneficiary, the court may modify or terminate a trust or remove the trustee and appoint a different trustee if the court determines that the value of the trust property is insufficient to justify the cost of administration.

(3) Upon termination of a trust under this section, the trustee shall distribute the trust property in a manner consistent with the purposes of the trust. The trustee may enter into agreements or make such other provisions that the trustee deems necessary or appropriate to protect the interests of the beneficiaries and the trustee and to carry out the intent and purposes of the trust.

(4) The existence of a spendthrift provision in the trust does not make this section inapplicable unless the trust instrument expressly provides that the trustee may not terminate the trust pursuant to this section.

(5) This section does not apply to an easement for conservation or preservation.
(Laws 2006, ch. 217, §4, effective July 1, 2007.)

§736.0417. Trustee may combine trusts

(1) After notice to the qualified beneficiaries, a trustee may combine two or more trusts into a single trust or divide a trust into two or more separate trusts, if the result does not impair rights of any beneficiary or adversely affect achievement of the purposes of the trusts or trust, respectively.

(2) Subject to the terms of the trust, the trustee may take into consideration differences in federal tax attributes and other pertinent factors in administering the trust property of any separate account or trust, in making applicable tax elections, and in making distributions. A separate trust created by severance must be treated as a separate trust for all purposes from the date on which the severance is effective. The effective date of the severance may be retroactive to a date before the date on which the trustee exercises such power.
(Laws 2006, ch. 217, §4, effective July 1, 2007.)

III. Beneficiaries' Power to Modify or Revoke

In most American jurisdictions, a trust can be modified or terminated at the beneficiaries' request, provided that (1) all the beneficiaries consent, (2) all are competent, and (3) if modification or termination will not interfere with a "material purpose" of the settlor. Under the traditional doctrine, the fact of some beneficiaries' being unborn, incompetent, or unascertainable prevents modification or termination. The material purpose requirement also has presented difficulties for beneficiaries who desire modification or termination. "Under the conventional American rule, courts defer to the settlor's intent and preserve the integrity of the trust regardless of the beneficiaries' desires." Walker, *supra*, at 447.

The traditional rule on trust modification and termination is termed the "Claflin doctrine," after the famous case of Claflin v. Claflin, 20 N.E. 545 (Mass. 1889). In *Claflin*, a testator established a trust for a son. Payments were to be made at defined intervals ($10,000 at age 21, $10,000 at age 25), with the remainder to be paid when the son reached the age of 30. At age 21, the son sought termination of the trust. The court refused, reasoning the premature termination would violate the intent of the testator.

Note that an exception to the *Claflin* doctrine is if the settlor is alive and joins the beneficiaries in giving consent (even if the modification or termination is inconsistent with a material purpose of the trust). In such cases, courts are not concerned with the material purpose because the settlor has acquiesced. See also Unif. Trust Code §411(a) (permitting modification or termination of a noncharitable irrevocable trust upon consent of the settlor and all beneficiaries even if such act would be inconsistent with a material purpose of the trust).

Under the traditional doctrine, courts were troubled by the best manner of protecting the interest of those trust beneficiaries who are unborn or unascertained. Then, in 1966, the United States District Court for the District of Columbia reached a creative solution to the problem. In Hatch v. Riggs National Bank, 361 F.2d 559 (D.C.C. 1966), a settlor wanted to modify a trust to provide her with needed income. She had created the trust 40 years earlier. The terms of the trust directed the trustees to pay the settlor the income for her life, and upon her death, to pay the corpus according to her testamentary power of appointment and, in default of the exercise of this power of appointment, to her next of kin. The problem was whether the settlor could modify the trust in the face of a spendthrift restriction and in the face of the interests of unborn contingent beneficiaries.

The district court decided to appoint a guardian ad litem to represent the interests of the unborn or unascertained beneficiaries. The court reasoned that the appointment was in accordance with "basic principles of trust law," also the use of a guardian ad litem was recognized in other jurisdictions (although in other contexts), and, in addition, statutes providing for the appointment of guardians ad litem (in other contexts) were "consistent with the Anglo-American system of law and adopted to promote the objectives of justice." *Id.* at 565.

In American trust law, the *Claflin* doctrine has been liberalized by two developments: (1) some states allow vicarious consent, for example by a guardian ad litem or virtual representation, on behalf of unborn or unascertainable beneficiaries; (2) some states attempt to expand the material purposes qualification in the doctrine. Halbach, Uniform Acts, *supra*, at 1900-1901. Virtual representation is the process by which an unrepresented person (such as an unborn child) may be represented by another beneficiary with a similar beneficial interest.

American law on trust modification and termination by the beneficiaries differs from that of England. In England, a trust may be modified or terminated if all the beneficiaries are adult, legally competent, and consent. It is only necessary to show that the modification or termination is beneficial to the beneficiaries. This rule is consistent with the English view that abhors restraints on alienation.

The English rule is derived from Saunders v. Vautier, Cr. & Ph. 240 (1841), in which the court terminated a trust and awarded the balance to the beneficiary earlier than authorized by the trust instrument. Finding that the settlor had no express motivation to withhold funds until the beneficiary reached majority, the court determined that the restriction on premature termination was arbitrary. "*Saunders* epitomized the notion of freely alienable property interests and represented the majority rule in the United States [prior to adoption of the *Claflin* doctrine]." Walker, *supra*, at 448.

In the 1950's, Parliament codified the English rule on trust modification and termination. Responding to the plea of trust beneficiaries seeking to modify trusts in order to avoid tax burdens caused by the reform of tax laws, Parliament enacted the Variation of Trusts Act of 1958 (6 & 7 Eliz. 2, ch. 53, § 1).

The Act provides that a court may consent to modification or termination of a trust on behalf of incompetent, minor, or unborn beneficiaries whenever the court finds it to the beneficiaries' advantage. The function of the court is to protect those who cannot protect themselves, considering educational and social benefits, and family dissension, as well as financial benefits. The settlor's intent is a relevant but not controlling consideration. Jesse Dukeminier & James E. Krier, The Rise of the Perpetual Trust, 50 UCLA L. Rev. 1303, 1329 (2003).

The American Law Institute in the Restatement (Third) of Trusts and NCCUSL in the Uniform Trust Code recently liberalized the *Claflin* doctrine. In cases in which all the beneficiaries desire modification or termination, both the Restatement (Third) of Trusts and the Uniform Trust Code §411(b) still require that modification or termination must not be inconsistent with a material purpose of the trust. However, under the Restatement (Third) of Trusts §65, if the modification or termination would be inconsistent with a material purpose of the trust, the beneficiaries need either the settlor's consent or judicial authorization (after the settlor's death). The test for judicial authorization or modification or termination in cases of unanimous consent by the beneficiaries is if "the reason for termination or modification outweighs the material purpose." Restatement (Third) of Trusts §65(2).

The Uniform Trust Code §411(b) also permits modification or termination if all the beneficiaries consent "if the court concludes that continuance of the trust is not necessary to achieve any material purpose of the trust." However, if not all beneficiaries consent to a proposed modification or termination, then a court may still approve modification or termination if both the following conditions are met: (1) if all the beneficiaries had consented, the trust could have been modified or terminated under this section; and (2) the interests of a beneficiary who does not consent will be adequately protected. Uniform Trust Code §411(b). Neither the Uniform Trust Code nor the Restatement (Third) of Trust presumes that the insertion of a spendthrift clause constitutes a material purpose barring modification or termination.

Like the UTC, Florida law (Fla. Stat. §736.0412(1)) provides for modification upon the unanimous agreement of all beneficiaries, but only after the death of the settlor. Unlike the UTC, the Florida statute does not require that the modification or termination must not impair the trust purposes.

The Florida Trust Code also provides for representation of beneficiaries who lack capacity or are unascertained. For example, Florida law allows representation by fiduciaries or parents (Fla. Stat. §736.0303), representation by a person with a "substantially identical interest" (Fla. Stat. §736.0304), and, finally, representation by a court-appointed representative if the other sections on representation do not apply (Fla. Stat. §736.0305). A trustee may not serve as a representative for a beneficiary, but the trust instrument may designate a representative who is not a trustee (Fla. Stat. §736.0306).

On judicial termination at the request of the beneficiaries when the trust purposes have been accomplished, see Bogert, *supra*, at §1007; on judicial termination at the request of the beneficiaries when the trust purposes have not been accomplished, see *id.* at §1008.

§736.0412. Beneficiaries may modify trust irrevocable trust

(1) After the settlor's death, a trust may be modified at any time as provided in §736.04113(2) upon the unanimous agreement of the trustee and all qualified beneficiaries.

(2) Modification of a trust as authorized in this section is not prohibited by a spendthrift clause or by a provision in the trust instrument that prohibits amendment or revocation of the trust.

(3) An agreement to modify a trust under this section is binding on a beneficiary whose interest is represented by another person under part III of this code.

(4) This section shall not apply to:

(a) Any trust created prior to January 1, 2001.

(b) Any trust created after December 31, 2000, if, under the terms of the trust, all beneficial interests in the trust must vest or terminate within the period prescribed by the rule against perpetuities in §689.225(2), notwithstanding §689.225(2)(f), unless the terms of the trust expressly authorize nonjudicial modification.

(c) Any trust for which a charitable deduction is allowed or allowable under the Internal Revenue Code until the termination of all charitable interests in the trust.

(5) For purposes of subsection (4), a revocable trust shall be treated as created when the right of revocation terminates.

(6) The provisions of this section are in addition to, and not in derogation of, rights under the common law to modify, amend, terminate, or revoke trusts.

(Laws 2006, ch. 217, §4, effective July 1, 2007.)

§736.0301. Binding effect of representation

(1) Notice, information, accountings, or reports given to a person who may represent and bind another person under this part may serve as a substitute for and have the same effect as notice, information, accountings, or reports given directly to the other person.

(2) Actions taken by a person who represents the interests of another person under this part are binding on the person whose interests are represented to the same extent as if the actions had been taken by the person whose interests are represented.

(3) Except as otherwise provided in §736.0602, a person under this part who represents a settlor lacking capacity may receive notice and give a binding consent on the settlor's behalf.

(4) A trustee is not liable for giving notice, information, accountings, or reports to a beneficiary who is represented by another person under this part, and nothing in this part prohibits the trustee from giving notice, information, accountings, or reports to the person represented.

Laws 2006 (S.B. 1170), ch. 217, §3, effective July 1, 2007.)

§736.0302. Holder of power of appointment may bind persons whose interests are subject to the power

(1) The holder of a power of appointment may represent and bind persons whose interests, as permissible appointees, takers in default, or otherwise, are subject to the power.

(2) Subsection (1) does not apply to:

(a) Any matter determined by the court to involve fraud or bad faith by the trustee;

(b) A power of a trustee to distribute trust property; or

(c) A power of appointment held by a person while the person is the sole trustee.

Laws 2006, ch. 217, §3, effective July 1, 2007.)

§736.0303.Representation by guardians, parents and fiduciaries

To the extent there is no conflict of interest between the representative and the person represented or among those being represented with respect to a particular question or dispute:

(1) A guardian of the property may represent and bind the estate that the guardian of the property controls.

(2) An agent having authority to act with respect to the particular question or dispute may represent and bind the principal.

(3) A trustee may represent and bind the beneficiaries of the trust.

(4) A personal representative of a decedent's estate may represent and bind persons interested in the estate.

(5) A parent may represent and bind the parent's unborn child, or the parent's minor child if a guardian of the property for the minor child has not been appointed.

Laws 2006, ch. 217, §3, effective July 1, 2007.)

§736.0304. Virtual representation: substantially similar interests

Unless otherwise represented, a minor, incapacitated, or unborn individual, or a person whose identity or location is unknown and not reasonably ascertainable, may be represented by and bound by another person having a substantially identical interest with respect to the particular question or dispute, but only to the extent there is no conflict of interest between the representative and the person represented.

Laws 2006, ch. 217, §3, effective July 1, 2007.)

§736.0305. Court may appoint representative for unrepresented interests

(1) If the court determines that an interest is not represented under this part, or that the otherwise available representation might be inadequate, the court may appoint a representative to receive notice, give consent, and otherwise represent, bind, and act on behalf of a minor, incapacitated, or unborn individual, or a person whose identity or location is unknown. If not precluded by a conflict of interest, a representative may be appointed to represent several persons or interests.

(2) A representative may act on behalf of the individual represented with respect to any matter arising under this code, whether or not a judicial proceeding concerning the trust is pending.

(3) In making decisions, a representative may consider general benefits accruing to the living members of the represented individual's family.

Laws 2006,, ch. 217, §3, effective July 1, 2007.)

§736.0306. Trust instrument may designate representatives of beneficiaries

(1) If authorized in the trust instrument, one or more persons may be designated to represent and bind a beneficiary and receive any notice, information, accounting, or report.

(2) Except as otherwise provided in this code, a person designated, as provided in subsection (1) may not represent and bind a beneficiary while that person is serving as trustee.

(3) Except as otherwise provided in this code, a person designated, as provided in subsection (1) may not represent and bind another beneficiary if the person designated also is a beneficiary, unless:

(a) That person was named by the settlor; or

(b) That person is the beneficiary's spouse or a grandparent or descendant of a grandparent of the beneficiary or the beneficiary's spouse.

(4) No person designated, as provided in subsection (1), is liable to the beneficiary whose interests are represented, or to anyone claiming through that beneficiary, for any actions or omissions to act made in good faith.

Laws 2006, ch. 217, §3, effective July 1, 2007.)

IV. Judicial Power to Modify

A court may modify the terms of the trust upon the application of the settlor or one or more beneficiaries. Judicial modification of a trust is the doctrine of "equitable deviation." Courts generally have the power to alter *administrative* provisions of a trust where a circumstance arises that is unknown or unanticipated by the settlor, of where a change is necessary to assure that the trust accomplished its purpose. Bogert, *supra*, at §§146, 994.

According to the general rule, although the court may modify administrative provisions of the trust, it may *not* modify *distributive* provisions. That is, a court may not introduce new beneficiaries, remove beneficiaries, or change the interests of the beneficiaries. *Id.* at §994.

The Restatement (Second) of Trusts §167 incorporated the traditional rule by providing for equitable deviation based on changed circumstances that were unknown or unanticipated by the settlor if "compliance would defeat or substantially impair the accomplished purpose of the trust." Commentary explained that a court should not "permit or direct the trustee to deviate from the terms of the trust merely because such deviation would be more advantageous to the beneficiaries than a compliance with such direction." *Id.*, cmt. b. Commentators have criticized the harshness of the rule precluding judicial modification of distributive provisions:

> The Restatement (Second) reflects an outmoded view of the world, based on a sentiment that Adam Smith called "piety to the dead." The Restatement provision assumes that a settlor would not want a deviation if its only purpose were to make trust beneficiaries better off, notwithstanding that most trusts are set up for just that reason—to provide advantages for beneficiaries by way of tax savings, competent management, protection from creditors, and so forth. The trust provisions, created at a given time, presumably aim to advantage the beneficiaries under the circumstances as they existed at that time. No one can see how circumstances will change, but we can reasonably suppose that, whatever happens, settlors would rather hold to the beneficial purposes of their trust than to precise terms that have come to be inconsistent with those purposes, given subsequent events. Trust law needs modernizing in this respect. . . .

Dukeminier & Krier, *supra*, at 1327.

In response to such criticisms, the Restatement (Third) of Trusts §66 liberalizes the traditional rule to permit a court to modify an administrative or distributive provision in cases of unanticipated circumstances where modification or deviation would further the trust purposes. The commentary suggests that the court may modify or permit deviation by the trustee of provisions governing management and administration of the trust property (e.g., prohibitions on sale of properties or acquisition of certain investments), or defining the beneficial interests of the beneficiaries (e.g., prohibitions on invasion of principal or accumulation of income). *Id.* at §66, cmt. b.

Under Restatement (Third) of Trusts §66, it is not required that the situation constitutes an emergency or jeopardizes the trust purposes. *Id.* at §66, cmt. a. For the classic case permitting judicial modification in case of emergencies, see Matter of Pulitzer, 249 N.Y.S. 975 (N.Y. 1932).

The Uniform Trust Code §412(a), similarly, has liberalized the equitable deviation doctrine to permit modification of administrative *or* distributive provisions. Some states statutes also permit modification of distributive provisions.

The Florida Code does not currently distinguish between administrative and distributive provisions. The Code allows a court to modify the terms of a trust if the purposes have been "fulfilled or have become illegal, impossible, wasteful, or impracticable" or because of circumstances unanticipated by the settlor (Fla. Stat. §736.04113(1)(a)).

In addition, under Florida Statutes §736.04115, the court has the discretion to modify the trust when "compliance with the terms of a trust is not in the best interests of the beneficiaries." Subsection (2) of that section sets forth various factors for the court to take into consideration in exercising its discretion, including: the settlor's intent, the current circumstances and best interests of the beneficiaries; the terms and purposes of the trust; the facts and circumstances surrounding the creation of the trust; and extrinsic evidence relevant to the proposed modification. The court is not precluded from modifying the trust because of the presence of a spendthrift provision.

Further, Florida Statutes §736.0414 provides that the court may modify or terminate an uneconomic trust. The court may terminate the trust or appoint a different trustee "if the court determines that the value of the trust property is insufficient to justify the cost of administration (Fla. Stat. §736.0414 (2)).

§736.04113. Court may modify irrevocable trust if modification would not defeat settlor's material purpose

(1) Upon the application of a trustee of the trust or any qualified beneficiary, a court at any time may modify the terms of a trust that is not then revocable in the manner provided in subsection (2), if:

(a) The purposes of the trust have been fulfilled or have become illegal, impossible, wasteful, or impracticable to fulfill;

(b) Because of circumstances not anticipated by the settlor, compliance with the terms of the trust would defeat or substantially impair the accomplishment of a material purpose of the trust; or

(c) A material purpose of the trust no longer exists.

(2) In modifying a trust under this section, a court may:

(a) Amend or change the terms of the trust, including terms governing distribution of the trust income or principal or terms governing administration of the trust;

(b) Terminate the trust in whole or in part;

(c) Direct or permit the trustee to do acts that are not authorized or that are prohibited by the terms of the trust; or

(d) Prohibit the trustee from performing acts that are permitted or required by the terms of the trust.

(3) In exercising discretion to modify a trust under this section:

(a) The court shall consider the terms and purposes of the trust, the facts and circumstances surrounding the creation of the trust, and extrinsic evidence relevant to the proposed modification.

(b) The court shall consider spendthrift provisions as a factor in making a decision, but the court is not precluded from modifying a trust because the trust contains spendthrift provisions.

(4) The provisions of this section are in addition to, and not in derogation of, rights under the common law to modify, amend, terminate, or revoke trusts.

Laws 2006, ch. 217, §4, effective July 1, 2007.)

§736.0414. Trustee and court may modify or terminate uneconomic trust

(1) After notice to the qualified beneficiaries, the trustee of a trust consisting of trust property having a total value less than $ 50,000 may terminate the trust if the trustee concludes that the value of the trust property is insufficient to justify the cost of administration.

(2) Upon application of a trustee or any qualified beneficiary, the court may modify or terminate a trust or remove the trustee and appoint a different trustee if the court determines that the value of the trust property is insufficient to justify the cost of administration.

(3) Upon termination of a trust under this section, the trustee shall distribute the trust property in a manner consistent with the purposes of the trust. The trustee may enter into agreements or make such other provisions that the trustee deems necessary or appropriate to protect the interests of the beneficiaries and the trustee and to carry out the intent and purposes of the trust.

(4) The existence of a spendthrift provision in the trust does not make this section inapplicable unless the trust instrument expressly provides that the trustee may not terminate the trust pursuant to this section.

(5) This section does not apply to an easement for conservation or preservation.

(Laws 2006, ch. 217, §4, effective July 1, 2007.)

§736.04115. Court may modify irrevocable trust if modification is in the best interests of the beneficiaries

(1) Without regard to the reasons for modification provided in §736.04113, if compliance with the terms of a trust is not in the best interests of the beneficiaries, upon the application of a trustee or any qualified beneficiary, a court may at any time modify a trust that is not then revocable as provided in §736.04113(2).

(2) In exercising discretion to modify a trust under this section:

(a) The court shall exercise discretion in a manner that conforms to the extent possible with the intent of the settlor, taking into account the current circumstances and best interests of the beneficiaries.

(b) The court shall consider the terms and purposes of the trust, the facts and circumstances surrounding the creation of the trust, and extrinsic evidence relevant to the proposed modification.

(c) The court shall consider spendthrift provisions as a factor in making a decision, but the court is not precluded from modifying a trust because the trust contains spendthrift provisions.

(3) This section shall not apply to:

(a) Any trust created prior to January 1, 2001.

(b) Any trust created after December 31, 2000, if:

1. Under the terms of the trust, all beneficial interests in the trust must vest or terminate within the period prescribed by the rule against perpetuities in §689.225(2), notwithstanding §689.225(2)(f).

2. The terms of the trust expressly prohibit judicial modification.

(4) For purposes of subsection (3), a revocable trust shall be treated as created when the right of revocation terminates.

(5) The provisions of this section are in addition to, and not in derogation of, rights under the common law to modify, amend, terminate, or revoke trusts.

(Laws 2006, ch. 217, §4, effective July 1, 2007.)

XI
TRUSTEES

This chapter explores aspects of the fiduciary office, including the selection, appointment, and qualification of trustees; compensation and indemnification of trustees; and resignation and removal of trustees. The chapter then turns to the general standard of conduct imposed by the law on trustees as well as the trustees' duties, powers, and liabilities. Note that the term "fiduciary" refers to both trustees and personal representatives. This chapter addresses only trustees' responsibilities. For a discussion of the responsibilities of personal representatives, see Chapter XIV *infra*.

I. Generally

The settlor may name one trustee or several co-trustees. A trustee's acceptance generally is not essential to the validity of the trust or to the effectiveness of a conveyance in trust. That is, it is possible to create a trust without notice to, or the consent of, a trustee. Although a trustee is an essential element of a valid trust, a familiar maxim is that equity will not permit a trust to fail for want of a trustee. Therefore, if the trust instrument does not name a trustee, or the designated trustee cannot or will not act, the court will appoint a trustee. A trust might fail only if the testator has manifested an intention that the existence of the trust depended on administration by a *particular* trustee. Austin Wakeman Scott, Abridgement of the Law of Trusts §35, at 88 (1960) [hereinafter Scott]. See also Restatement (Third) of Trusts §31.

Courts have held that if the settlor has delivered the subject matter of the trust or a deed of transfer, a trust is validly created at the time of the conveyance, regardless of whether the named trustee has notice or disclaims (refuses to serve). Scott, *supra*, §35 at 89.

Capacity of a trustee refers to the designated person's capacity (1) to take title to the property, (2) to hold title to the property, and (3) to administer the trust property to the same capacity as the beneficial owner. See Restatement (Third) of Trusts §32. Any person who can take title to property may take title to property as a trustee. However, some persons cannot administer the trust. For example, minors cannot administer a trust because their contracts are subject to disaffirmance (i.e., are voidable). Also, special requirements may be applicable to nonresident trustees. Some state statutes forbid the appointment of nonresident trustees (or the appointment of nonresidents as executors or administrators). Other state statutes provide that a nonresident can act only with a resident trustee. Bogert, *supra*, at §132.

A trustee may be either an individual or a corporation. Frequently, banks and trust companies are corporations that are chartered to conduct business as trustees, subject to state requirements. In Florida, trust companies incorporated under Florida law, and state and national banking and savings institutions authorized to act as trustee may all act as trustees (Fla. Stat. §660.41).

Some settlors establish a trust in a different state and designate a foreign corporation as trustee. In such cases, state statutes frequently authorize foreign corporations to transact limited types of business in the state without qualifying to do business within the state. Bogert, *supra*, at §132. See also Restatement (Third) of Trusts §33 ("A corporation has capacity to take and hold property in trust except as limited by law, and to administer trust property and act as trustee to the extent of the powers conferred upon it by law").

Most states that authorize a foreign corporation to administer testamentary trusts subject that foreign corporation to certain requirements. For example, some statutes require the foreign corporation to designate a state officer or other state resident as its agent for purposes of service of process within the state. Some statutes require the foreign corporation to file a bond or deposit cash or securities prior to administering the trust. Some states prohibit a foreign corporation from maintaining a branch in the state or from soliciting trust business within the state. The foreign corporation may have to obtain local letters of trusteeship. Bogert, *supra*, at §132. Florida law does not require local qualification by a foreign trustee under the newly adopted Florida Trust Code (Fla. Stat. §736.0112).

Today, an unincorporated association may serve as trustee if a given jurisdiction recognizes it as a legal entity for such purposes. See Restatement (Third) of Trusts §33(2) ("If a partnership, unincorporated association, or other entity has capacity to take and hold property for its own purposes, it has capacity to take, hold, and administer property in trust"). In contrast, at common law, an unincorporated association could not take or hold legal title to property for its own benefit or in trust for others. Scott, *supra*, §97 at 209. However, a trust would not fail in such cases because the court would appoint a new trustee. See, e.g., Wittmeier v. Heiligenstein, 139 N.E. 871 (Ill. 1923) (holding

that a wife's trust to a church, to pay her divorced husband $50 a month for his life plus his medical and funeral expenses, was invalid because an unincorporated association could not take as grantee; however, the inability of the trustee to take does not invalidate a deed where the settlor and beneficiary are both competent, and the property is of such a nature that it can be legally placed in trust).

A settlor may serve as trustee of an inter vivos trust that he or she created (as in the case of a trust created by a declaration). (For obvious reasons, a settlor cannot be a trustee of a testamentary trust that the settlor has created!) For a trust created by a declaration, delivery of the property is not required. The settlor merely must manifest an intention to hold the property in trust.

Also, a trust beneficiary can serve as trustee. However, the sole beneficiary may not be the sole trustee because of the merger doctrine. Note that merger does not result if one of several beneficiaries is one of the several trustees, if one of several beneficiaries is the sole trustee, if the sole beneficiary is one of several trustees, or if the group of beneficiaries is identical with the group of trustees. Scott, *supra*, §§99-99.5, at 210-212.

Florida statute specifies the methods by which a trustee may accept or decline trusteeship. Florida Statutes §736.0701(1) provides that a trustee may accept by "substantially complying" with a method of acceptance set forth in the trust, or if the trust does not indicate a method, accept by indication, i.e., accepting delivery of trust property or exercising powers of the trustee. However, certain actions do not indicate an acceptance of the trusteeship, such as acting to preserve the trust property, sending a written statement declining to a beneficiary, or inspection or investigation of trust property. *Id.* at §736.0701(3). Section 736.0701(2) states that a trustee may decline, and a trustee will be deemed to decline if he/she does not accept within a "reasonable time after knowing of the designation" as trustee.

Florida law also provides for methods of filling vacancies in the office of trustee. Florida Statutes §736.0704 defines the circumstances that constitute a vacancy. If a vacancy occurs in the office of a co-trustee, the court need not appoint a new trustee (Fla. Stat. §736.0704(2)).

In Florida, as in the Uniform Trust Code, co-trustees are not required to act by unanimous decision, but may act instead by majority vote (Fla. Stat. §736.0703(1)).

If the office of trustee becomes vacant, and the trust instrument fails to provide for a successor trustee or a method for appointing one, a court may appoint a new trustee. Bogert, *supra,* at §32. Florida law (Fla. Stat. §736.0704(3)) provides the following hierarchy to fill a vacant trustee office of a noncharitable trust: a person named in the trust instrument, a person appointed by unanimous agreement of the beneficiaries, then a person named by the court.

§736.0103. Definitions

...

(21) "Trustee" means the original trustee and includes any additional trustee, any successor trustee, and any cotrustee.

(Laws 2006, ch. 217, §7, effective July 1, 2007.)

§736.0108. Principal place of administration

(1) Terms of a trust designating the principal place of administration of the trust are valid only if there is a sufficient connection with the designated jurisdiction. Without precluding other means for establishing a sufficient connection, terms of a trust designating the principal place of administration are valid and controlling if:

(a) A trustee's principal place of business is located in or a trustee is a resident of the designated jurisdiction; or

(b) All or part of the administration occurs in the designated jurisdiction.

(2) Unless otherwise validly designated in the trust instrument, the principal place of administration of a trust is the trustee's usual place of business where the records pertaining to the trust are kept or, if the trustee has no place of business, the trustee's residence. In the case of cotrustees, the principal place of administration is:

(a) The usual place of business of the corporate trustee, if there is only one corporate cotrustee;

(b) The usual place of business or residence of the individual trustee who is a professional fiduciary, if there is only one such person and no corporate cotrustee; or otherwise

(c) The usual place of business or residence of any of the cotrustees as agreed on by the cotrustees.

(3) Notwithstanding any other provision of this section, the principal place of administration of a trust, for which a bank, association, or trust company organized under the laws of this state or bank or savings association organized under the laws of the United States with its main office in this state has been appointed trustee, shall not be moved or otherwise affected solely because the trustee engaged in an interstate merger transaction with an out-of-

state bank pursuant to §658.2953 in which the out-of-state bank is the resulting bank.

(4) A trustee is under a continuing duty to administer the trust at a place appropriate to its purposes and its administration.

(5) Without precluding the right of the court to order, approve, or disapprove a transfer, the trustee, in furtherance of the duty prescribed by subsection (4), may transfer the trust's principal place of administration to another state or to a jurisdiction outside of the United States.

(6) The trustee shall notify the qualified beneficiaries of a proposed transfer of a trust's principal place of administration not less than 60 days before initiating the transfer. The notice of proposed transfer must include:

(a) The name of the jurisdiction to which the principal place of administration is to be transferred.

(b) The address and telephone number at the new location at which the trustee can be contacted.

(c) An explanation of the reasons for the proposed transfer.

(d) The date on which the proposed transfer is anticipated to occur.

(e) The date, not less than 60 days after the notice is provided, by which the qualified beneficiary must notify the trustee of an objection to the proposed transfer.

(7) The authority of a trustee to act under this section without court approval to transfer a trust's principal place of administration is suspended if a qualified beneficiary files a lawsuit objecting to the proposed transfer on or before the date specified in the notice. The suspension is effective until the lawsuit is dismissed or withdrawn.

(8) In connection with a transfer of the trust's principal place of administration, the trustee may transfer any of the trust property to a successor trustee designated in the terms of the trust or appointed pursuant to §736.0704.

(Laws 2006, ch. 2006-217, §1, effective July 1, 2007.)

§736.0112. Qualification of foreign trustee

Unless otherwise doing business in this state, local qualification by a foreign trustee is not required for the trustee to receive distribution from a local estate. Nothing in this chapter shall affect the provisions of §660.41.

Laws 2006, ch. 217, §1, effective July 1, 2007.)

§660.41. Corporations; certain fiduciary functions prohibited

All corporations are prohibited from exercising any of the powers or duties and from acting in any of the capacities, within this state, as follows:

(1) As personal representative of the estate of any decedent, whether such decedent was a resident of this state or not, and whether the administration of the estate of such decedent is original or ancillary; however, if the personal representative of the estate of a nonresident decedent is a corporation duly authorized, qualified, and acting as such personal representative in the jurisdiction of the domicile of the decedent, it may as a foreign personal representative perform such duties and exercise such powers and privileges as are required, authorized, or permitted by §734.101.

(2) As receiver or trustee under appointment of any court in this state.

(3) As assignee, receiver, or trustee of any insolvent person or corporation or under any assignment for the benefit of creditors.

(4) As fiscal agent, transfer agent, or registrar of any municipal or private corporation, except that this prohibition shall not be so construed as to prevent banks, associations, and trust companies not located in this state from acting within the state where located as fiscal agent, transfer agent, or registrar of municipal or private corporations of this state. Nothing herein shall prevent any Florida corporation that is not a bank, association, or trust company and that does not have trust powers from being its own fiscal agent, transfer agent, or registrar concerning its own affairs, stock, or securities. Nothing herein shall prevent any Florida corporation or corporation having its principal place of business in Florida registered as a transfer agent with the Federal Deposit Insurance Corporation, the Comptroller of the Currency, the Board of Governors of the Federal Reserve System, or the Securities and Exchange Commission from acting as a transfer agent for any other private corporation. Nothing in this section or in any other law of this state shall be construed to prohibit a foreign bank, foreign association, or foreign trust company as trustee of any charitable foundation or endowment, employees' pension, retirement or profit-sharing trust, alone or together with a cotrustee, from: making loans or committing to make loans to any other person; contracting, in this state or elsewhere, with any person to acquire from such person a part or the entire interest in a loan which such person proposes to make, has heretofore made, or hereafter makes, together with a

like interest in any security instrument covering real or personal property in the state proposed to be given or hereafter or heretofore given to such person to secure or evidence such loan; servicing directly or entering into servicing contracts with persons, and enforcing in this state the loans made by it or obligations heretofore or hereafter acquired by it in the transaction of business outside this state or in the transaction of any business authorized or permitted hereby; or acquiring, holding, leasing, mortgaging, contracting with respect to, or otherwise protecting, managing, or conveying property in this state which has heretofore or may hereafter be assigned, transferred, mortgaged, or conveyed to it as security for, or in whole or in part in satisfaction of, a loan or loans made by it or obligations acquired by it in the transaction of any business authorized or permitted hereby. However, no such foreign bank, foreign association, or foreign trust company shall be deemed to be transacting business in this state, shall be required to qualify so to do, or shall be deemed to be unlawfully exercising powers or duties, acting in an unlawful or prohibited capacity, or violating any of the provisions of this section or of any other law of this state solely by reason of the performance of any of the acts or business hereinbefore permitted or authorized hereby; further, nothing herein shall be construed as authorizing or permitting any foreign bank, association, or trust company to maintain an office within this state.

This section does not apply to banks or associations and trust companies incorporated under the laws of this state and having trust powers, banks or associations and trust companies resulting from an interstate merger transaction with a Florida bank pursuant to §658.2953 and having trust powers, or national banking associations or federal associations authorized and qualified to exercise trust powers in Florida.

(Laws 1988 (H.B. 288), ch. 33, §4, (H.B. 654), ch. 111, §2. Amended by Laws 1991 (H.B. 2363), ch.110, §15, (S.B. 2280) ch. 307, §1; Laws 1992 (S.B. 210H) ch. 303, §§1, 214; Laws 1999 (S.B. 990), ch. 145, §1.)

§736.0701. Accepting or declining trusteeship

(1) Except as otherwise provided in subsection (3), a person designated as trustee accepts the trusteeship:

(a) By substantially complying with a method of acceptance provided in the terms of the trust; or

(b) If the terms of the trust do not provide a method or the method provided in the terms is not expressly made exclusive, by accepting delivery of the trust property, exercising powers or performing duties as trustee, or otherwise indicating acceptance of the trusteeship.

(2) A person designated as trustee who has not accepted the trusteeship may decline the trusteeship. A designated trustee who does not accept the trusteeship within a reasonable time after knowing of the designation is deemed to have declined the trusteeship.

(3) A person designated as trustee may, without accepting the trusteeship:

(a) Act to preserve the trust property if, within a reasonable time after acting, the person sends to a qualified beneficiary a written statement declining the trusteeship.

(b) Inspect or investigate trust property to determine potential liability under environmental or other law or for any other purpose.

(Laws 2006, ch. 217, §7, effective July 1, 2007.)

§736.0703. Cotrustees

(1) Cotrustees who are unable to reach a unanimous decision may act by majority decision.

(2) If a vacancy occurs in a cotrusteeship, the remaining cotrustees or a majority of the remaining cotrustees may act for the trust.

(3) A cotrustee must participate in the performance of a trustee's function unless the cotrustee is unavailable to perform the function because of absence, illness, disqualification under other provision of law, or other temporary incapacity or the cotrustee has properly delegated the performance of the function to another cotrustee.

(4) If a cotrustee is unavailable to perform duties because of absence, illness, disqualification under other law, or other temporary incapacity, and prompt action is necessary to achieve the purposes of the trust or to avoid injury to the trust property, the remaining cotrustee or a majority of the remaining cotrustees may act for the trust.

(5) A cotrustee may not delegate to another cotrustee the performance of a function the settlor reasonably expected the cotrustees to perform jointly. A cotrustee may revoke a delegation previously made.

(6) Except as otherwise provided in subsection (7), a cotrustee who does not join in an action of another cotrustee is not liable for the action.

(7) Each cotrustee shall exercise reasonable care to:

(a) Prevent a cotrustee from committing a breach of trust.

(b) Compel a cotrustee to redress a breach of trust.

(8) A dissenting cotrustee who joins in an action at the direction of the majority of the cotrustees and

who notifies any cotrustee of the dissent at or before the time of the action is not liable for the action.
(Laws 2006, ch. 217, §7, effective July 1, 2007.)

§736.0704. Vacancy in trusteeship; appointment of successor

(1) A vacancy in a trusteeship occurs if:

(a) A person designated as trustee declines the trusteeship;

(b) A person designated as trustee cannot be identified or does not exist;

(c) A trustee resigns;

(d) A trustee is disqualified or removed;

(e) A trustee dies; or

(f) A trustee is adjudicated to be incapacitated.

(2) If one or more cotrustees remain in office, a vacancy in a trusteeship need not be filled. A vacancy in a trusteeship must be filled if the trust has no remaining trustee.

(3) A vacancy in a trusteeship of a noncharitable trust that is required to be filled must be filled in the following order of priority:

(a) By a person named or designated pursuant to the terms of the trust to act as successor trustee.

(b) By a person appointed by unanimous agreement of the qualified beneficiaries.

(c) By a person appointed by the court.

(4) A vacancy in a trusteeship of a charitable trust that is required to be filled must be filled in the following order of priority:

(a) By a person named or designated pursuant to the terms of the trust to act as successor trustee.

(b) By a person selected by unanimous agreement of the charitable organizations expressly designated to receive distributions under the terms of the trust.

(c) By a person appointed by the court.

(5) The court may appoint an additional trustee or special fiduciary whenever the court considers the appointment necessary for the administration of the trust, whether or not a vacancy in a trusteeship exists or is required to be filled.
(Laws 2006, ch. 217, §7, effective July 1, 2007.)

A. Selection, Appointment, and Qualification

The settlor generally names a trustee. Sometimes, a settlor designates more than one trustee to act. By the terms of the trust, the settlor also can empower a third party to appoint a trustee.

Most trustees take office without the need to be appointed by a court. See Restatement (Third) of Trusts §34(1) ("Except as required by statute, a trustee designated by or selected in accordance with the terms of a trust may act without being appointed by the court"). For trustees who are appointed by a court (as in situations of vacancy in the office), the court clerk must issue a "certificate" of trustee upon application by the trustee. This certification is similar to letters issued to a personal representative that provide proof that the individual is qualified to act.

In Florida, the trustee is required to file notice of the trust with the court upon the death of the settlor (Fla. Stat. §736.05055).

"Qualification" generally refers to the need for the trustee to take an oath and/or post a performance bond. By taking an oath, the trust swears that he or she will faithfully carry out his or her duties. A bond affirms that the trustee will faithfully carry out his or her duties. The court generally sets the amount of the bond, payable by the trustee, based on the value of the trust corpus.

The Restatement (Third) of Trusts §34(3) specifies that "A trustee need not provide a performance bond except as required by statute, trust provision, or court order."

Florida law provides that a bond is only required if the court finds that one is needed to protect the interest of the beneficiaries or is required by the trust instrument (Fla. Stat. §736.0702(1)).

§736.0702. Trustee's bond

(1) A trustee shall give bond to secure performance of the trustee's duties only if the court finds that a bond is needed to protect the interests of the beneficiaries or is required by the terms of the trust and the court has not dispensed with the requirement

(2) The court may specify the amount of a bond, the trustee's liabilities under the bond, and whether sureties are necessary. The court may modify or terminate a bond at any time.
(Laws 2006, ch. 217, §7, effective July 1, 2007.)

§ 736.05055. Notice of trust

(1) Upon the death of a settlor of a trust described in §733.707(3) [a trust in which the grantor retains a power of revocation], the trustee must file a notice of trust with the court of the county of the settlor's domicile and the court having jurisdiction of the settlor's estate.

(2) The notice of trust must contain the name of the settlor, the settlor's date of death, the title of the trust, if any, the date of the trust, and the name and address of the trustee.

(3) If the settlor's probate proceeding has been commenced, the clerk shall notify the trustee in writing of the date of the commencement of the probate proceeding and the file number.

(4) The clerk shall file and index the notice of trust in the same manner as a caveat unless there exists a probate proceeding for the settlor's estate, in which case the notice of trust must be filed in the probate proceeding and the clerk shall send a copy to the personal representative.

(5) The clerk shall send a copy of any caveat filed regarding the settlor to the trustee, and the notice of trust to any caveator, unless there is a probate proceeding pending and the personal representative and the trustee are the same.

(6) Any proceeding affecting the expenses of the administration or obligations of the settlor's estate prior to the trustee filing a notice of trust are binding on the trustee.

(7) The trustee's failure to file the notice of trust does not affect the trustee's obligation to pay expenses of administration and obligations of the settlor's estate as provided in §733.607(2).

(Laws 2006, ch. 2006-217, §5, effective July 1, 2007.)

B. Compensation and Indemnification of Trustees

Trustees are entitled to compensation for their services. In early English law (followed by some American jurisdictions), trustees were expected to serve without compensation unless the terms of the trust provided otherwise. That rule has been changed in all states either by statute or case law. Scott, *supra*, §242 at 513. The amount of the trustee's compensation is fixed either by the terms of the trust instrument, by contract between settlor and trustee, by statute, or by judicial action. Bogert, *supra*, at §975. Trustees may agree to waive compensation.

Most states have statutes that govern the trustee's compensation in cases in which the settlor has not provided for compensation. There are three types of trustee compensation statutes. *Id.* The most common authorizes judicial discretion in providing "reasonable compensation." (The trustee requests a specific amount and the court determines if the amount is reasonable.) The second type of statute provides an entitlement to compensation, authorizing compensation from the trust estate without prior court authorization but subject to judicial review upon petition of an interested person. The third basic type of statute sets a fee schedule. *Id.*

The trend is to provide trustees with "reasonable compensation." See Uniform Probate Code §3-719 (personal representative is entitled to "reasonable compensation for his services"); Restatement (Third) of Trusts §38(1) ("A trustee is entitled to reasonable compensation out of the trust estate for services as trustee, unless the terms of the trust provide otherwise or the trustee agrees to forgo compensation"); Uniform Trust Code §708 (trustee is entitled to "compensation that is reasonable under the circumstances" if the terms of the trust do not specify the amount of compensation). Florida law follows this trend and has adopted the Uniform Trust Code provision (Fla. Stat. §736.0708).

According to Florida law, if the trust instrument provides for compensation, the court has discretion to deviate from the stated amount if the duties of the trustee are "substantially different from those contemplated when the trust was created" or if the amount stated in the trust instrument would be "unreasonably low or high" (Fla. Stat. §736.0708(2)). Florida law (Fla. Stat. §736.0708(3)) also allows a trustee to receive additional reasonable compensation if he or she "rendered other services in connection with the administration of the trust."

At common law, although trustees were not allowed compensation for their services (unless the trust instrument so provided), they were allowed indemnity (i.e., reimbursement) for expenses they properly incurred. Scott, *supra*, §244 at 522. Today, a trustee can be reimbursed from the trust property for expenses that are necessary for carrying out the purposes of the trust. See Restatement (Third) of Trusts §38(2) ("A trustee is entitled to indemnity out of the trust estate for expenses properly incurred in the administration of the trust"). Similarly, in Florida, a trustee is entitled to reimbursement for "reasonable expenses that were properly incurred in the administration of the trust" (Fla. Stat. §736.0709).

§736.0708. Compensation of trustee

(1) If the terms of a trust do not specify the trustee's compensation, a trustee is entitled to compensation that is reasonable under the circumstances.

(2) If the terms of a trust specify the trustee's compensation, the trustee is entitled to be compensated as specified, but the court may allow more or less compensation if:

(a) The duties of the trustee are substantially different from those contemplated when the trust was created; or

(b) The compensation specified by the terms of the trust would be unreasonably low or high.

(3) If the trustee has rendered other services in connection with the administration of the trust, the trustee shall also be allowed reasonable compensation for the other services rendered in addition to reasonable compensation as trustee.

(Laws 2006, ch. 217, §7, effective July 1, 2007.)

§736.0709. Reimbursement of expenses

(1) A trustee is entitled to be reimbursed out of the trust property, with interest as appropriate, for reasonable expenses that were properly incurred in the administration of the trust.

(2) An advance by the trustee of money for the protection of the trust gives rise to a lien against trust property to secure reimbursement with reasonable interest.

(Laws 2006, ch. 217, §7, effective July 1, 2007.)

C. Resignation and Removal

After a person agrees to serve as trustee, sometimes that trustee may wish to resign. "[I]f the trustee has once accepted the trust, he cannot relieve himself of his duties under the trust, unless he is permitted to resign." Scott, *supra*, §106 at 219. However, the trustee can only resign in accordance with the terms of the trust instrument, or by permission of court or consent of the beneficiaries. Restatement (Third) of Trusts §36. The trust instrument may permit the trustee to resign without the need for judicial proceedings (such as by notice to, or with consent of, the beneficiaries).

Note that resignation does not relieve the trustee from liability for breaches of trust that were committed before the resignation became effective. *Id.*, §36 cmt. d.

Under Florida law, a trustee may resign by giving 30 days notice to the beneficiaries, settlor (if living) and any co-trustees, or by approval of the court (Fla. Stat. §736.0705).

A trustee may also be removed from office. Absent statutorily enumerated grounds, the issue of removal is in the discretion of the court. The standard is whether the trustee's continuance in office would be detrimental to the trust. Florida law specifies the following grounds for judicial removal of trustees: a serious breach of trust; a lack of cooperation among co-trustees that substantially impairs the administration of the trust; unfitness, unwillingness or failure to administer the trust effectively; a substantial change in circumstances; or, all beneficiaries request removal and the court finds such removal serves the best interests of the beneficiaries (Fla. Stat. §736.0706).

The settlor, a co-trustee, or a beneficiary may request that the court remove a trustee, or the court may remove the trustee on its own initiative. *Id.* Courts are reluctant to remove trustees on grounds that were known to the settlor and existed at the time of trust creation.

Friction between the trustees or between the trustee and beneficiary generally is insufficient to justify removal of the trustee. Simmons, Grounds for Removal of Trustee, 55A Fla. Jur.2d §126. However, removal may be justified if the trustee's continuance would be detrimental to the interests of the trust.

A trustee who has resigned or has been removed still has the duties of a trustee and the powers to protect trust property until the trust property is delivered to the successor trustee (Fla. Stat. §736.0707(1)). This trustee must deliver the trust property to the successor trustee in a "reasonable time." *Id.* at §736.0707(2).

§736.0705. Resignation of trustee

(1) A trustee may resign:

(a) Upon at least 30 days' notice to the qualified beneficiaries, the settlor, if living, and all cotrustees; or

(b) With the approval of the court.

(2) In approving a resignation, the court may issue orders and impose conditions reasonably necessary for the protection of the trust property.

(3) Any liability of a resigning trustee or of any sureties on the trustee's bond for acts or omissions of the trustee is not discharged or affected by the trustee's resignation.

(Laws 2006, ch. 217, §7, effective July 1, 2007.)

§736.0706. Removal of trustee

(1) The settlor, a cotrustee, or a beneficiary may request the court to remove a trustee, or a trustee may be removed by the court on the court's own initiative.

(2) The court may remove a trustee if:

(a) The trustee has committed a serious breach of trust;

(b) The lack of cooperation among cotrustees substantially impairs the administration of the trust;

(c) Due to the unfitness, unwillingness, or persistent failure of the trustee to administer the trust effectively, the court determines that removal of the trustee best serves the interests of the beneficiaries; or

(d) There has been a substantial change of circumstances or removal is requested by all of the qualified beneficiaries, the court finds that removal of the trustee best serves the interests of all of the beneficiaries and is not inconsistent with a material purpose of the trust, and a suitable cotrustee or successor trustee is available.

(3) Pending a final decision on a request to remove a trustee, or in lieu of or in addition to removing a trustee, the court may order such appropriate relief under §736.1001(2) as may be necessary to protect the trust property or the interests of the beneficiaries.

(Laws 2006, ch. 217, §7, effective July 1, 2007.)

§736.0707. Delivery of property by former trustee

(1) Unless a cotrustee remains in office or the court otherwise orders and until the trust property is delivered to a successor trustee or other person entitled to the property, a trustee who has resigned or been removed has the duties of a trustee and the powers necessary to protect the trust property.

(2) A trustee who has resigned or been removed shall within a reasonable time deliver the trust property within the trustee's possession to the cotrustee, successor trustee, or other person entitled to the property, subject to the right of the trustee to retain a reasonable reserve for the payment of debts, expenses, and taxes. The provisions of this subsection are in addition to and are not in derogation of the rights of a removed or resigning trustee under the common law.

(Laws 2006, ch. 217, §7, effective July 1, 2007.)

II. Trustee's Standard of Care and Fiduciary Duties

A. Standard of Care

The trustee is required to conform to standards of conduct imposed by law. The standard of care and skill originally was developed by case law. Now, however, these standards of conduct have been codified by statute in most jurisdictions.

The trustee has a duty to manifest the care, skill, prudence, and diligence in the management of the trust as that of an ordinarily prudent person engaged in similar business affairs and with objectives similar to those of the trust in question. Bogert, *supra*, at §541. This is sometimes referred to as the *prudent person standard*. See Fla. Stat. §736.0804. Note that many states have enacted new prudent investor legislation (discussed *infra*).

Many jurisdictions, influenced by the Uniform Probate Code, have imposed a heightened standard of care on trustees. UPC §7-302 requires that the trustee must observe "the standards in dealing with the trust assets that would be observed by a prudent man dealing with the property of *another*" (emphasis added). This rule changes the former standard of care that required a trustee to observe the standards in dealing with trust assets that would be observed by a prudent man dealing with his or her *own* property.

Professional trustees (i.e., banks, trust companies) are held to a higher standard of care. If a trustee represents that he or she has a higher degree of skill than that possessed by the average individual, the trustee is held to a higher standard of care (UPC §7-302; Fla. Stat. §736.0806). Also, because the prudent person standard is an objective standard, a trustee will not be relieved from liability by arguing that he or she exercised lower-than-normal skill in managing the trust.

§736.0804. Prudent person standard

A trustee shall administer the trust as a prudent person would, by considering the purposes, terms, distribution requirements, and other circumstances of the trust. In satisfying this standard, the trustee shall exercise reasonable care, skill, and caution.

(Laws 2006, ch. 217, §8, effective July 1, 2007.)

§736.0806. Higher standard: trustee with special skills

A trustee who has special skills or expertise, or is named trustee in reliance on the trustee's representation that the trustee has special skills or expertise, shall use those special skills or expertise.

(Laws 2006, ch. 217, §8, effective July 1, 2007.)

B. Duties Generally

A trustee is subject to various fiduciary duties. If a trustee fails to comply with these duties, he or she can be held personally liable and even may be subject to criminal and/or civil penalties.

According to Florida law, a trustee has a duty to administer the trust in good faith, in accordance with its terms and purposes and in accordance with the Florida Trust Code (Fla. Stat. §736.0801).

A trustee has duties to both the trust and the beneficiaries. For example, the trustee may only

incur "reasonable" expenses in administering the trust (Fla. Stat. §736.0805) and must enforce and defend claims against the trust (Fla. Stat. §736.0811). The trustee must also pay the expenses of the settlor's estate (Fla. Stat. §736.5053). The trustee also has a duty to make distributions to those entitled to them under the trust (Fla. Stat. §§ 736.08147, 736.0817).

Additional duties regarding the investment of trust property are covered by the prudent investor rule (included in Section H *infra*) such as the duty to diversify the trust portfolio and review it to ensure that the trust property is productive (Fla. Stat. §518.11). Further, the trustee has a duty to keep the beneficiaries informed and to render accountings to them (Fla. Stat. §736.0813) (set forth in Section G, *infra*).

For a discussion of the trustee's duties with regard to discretionary powers, see also Chapter XII, Section B2b *infra*.).

§736.0801. Duty to administer trust

Upon acceptance of a trusteeship, the trustee shall administer the trust in good faith, in accordance with its terms and purposes and the interests of the beneficiaries, and in accordance with this code.

(Laws 2006, ch. 217, §8, effective July 1, 2007.)

§736.0805. Duty to incur only reasonable expenses of administration

In administering a trust, the trustee shall only incur expenses that are reasonable in relation to the trust property, the purposes of the trust, and the skills of the trustee.

(Laws 2006, ch. 217, §8, effective July 1, 2007.)

§736.0811. Duty to enforce and defend claims

A trustee shall take reasonable steps to enforce claims of the trust and to defend claims against the trust.

(Laws 2006, ch. 217, §8, effective July 1, 2007.)

§736.08147. Duty to distribute trust income

If a will or trust instrument granting income to the settlor's or testator's spouse for life is silent as to the time of distribution of income and the frequency of distributions, the trustee shall distribute all net income, as defined in chapter 738, to the spouse no less frequently than annually. This provision shall apply to any trust established before, on, or after July 1, 2007, unless the trust instrument expressly directs or permits net income to be distributed less frequently than annually.

(Laws 2006, ch. 217, §8, effective July 1, 2007.)

§736.05053. Duty to pay expenses and obligations of settlor's estate

(1) A trustee of a trust described in §733.707(3) shall pay to the personal representative of a settlor's estate any amounts that the personal representative certifies in writing to the trustee are required to pay the expenses of the administration and obligations of the settlor's estate. Payments made by a trustee, unless otherwise provided in the trust instrument, must be charged as expenses of the trust without a contribution from anyone. The interests of all beneficiaries of such a trust are subject to the provisions of this subsection; however, the payments must be made from assets, property, or the proceeds of the assets or property, other than assets proscribed in §733.707(3), that are included in the settlor's gross estate for federal estate tax purposes

(2) Unless a settlor provides by will, or designates in a trust described in §733.707(3) funds or property passing under the trust to be used as designated, the expenses of the administration and obligations of the settlor's estate must be paid from the trust in the following order

(a) Property of the residue of the trust remaining after all distributions that are to be satisfied by reference to a specific property or type of property, fund, or sum

(b) Property that is not to be distributed from specified or identified property or a specified or identified item of property

(c) Property that is to be distributed from specified or identified property or a specified or identified item of property.

(3) Trust distributions that are to be satisfied from specified or identified property must be classed as distributions to be satisfied from the general assets of the trust and not otherwise disposed of in the trust instrument on the failure or insufficiency of funds or property from which payment should be made, to the extent of the insufficiency. Trust distributions given for valuable consideration abate with other distributions of the same class only to the extent of the excess over the value of the consideration until all others of the same class are exhausted. Except as provided in this section, trust distributions abate equally and ratably and without preference or priority between real and personal property. When a specified or identified item of property that has been designated for distribution in the trust instrument or that is charged with a distribution is sold or taken by the trustee, other beneficiaries shall contribute according to their respective interests to the

beneficiary whose property has been sold or taken. Before distribution, the trustee shall determine the amounts of the respective contributions and such amounts must be paid or withheld before distribution is made.

(4) The trustee shall pay the expenses of trust administration, including compensation of trustees and attorneys of the trustees, before and in preference to the expenses of the administration and obligations of the settlor's estate.

(Laws 2006, ch. 217, §5, effective July 1, 2007.)

§736.08165. Duty to administer trust pending outcome of contest or other proceeding

(1) Pending the outcome of a proceeding filed to determine the validity of all or part of a trust or the beneficiaries of all or part of a trust, the trustee shall proceed with the administration of the trust as if no proceeding had been commenced, except no action may be taken and no distribution may be made to a beneficiary in contravention of the rights of those persons who may be affected by the outcome of the proceeding.

(2) Upon motion of a party and after notice to interested persons, a court, on good cause shown, may make an exception to the prohibition under subsection (1) and authorize the trustee to act or to distribute trust assets to a beneficiary subject to any conditions the court, in the court's discretion, may impose, including the posting of bond by the beneficiary.

(Laws 2006, ch. 2006-217, §8, effective July 1, 2007.)

§736.0817. Duty to distribute trust property at termination

Upon the occurrence of an event terminating or partially terminating a trust, the trustee shall proceed expeditiously to distribute the trust property to the persons entitled to the property, subject to the right of the trustee to retain a reasonable reserve for the payment of debts, expenses, and taxes. The provisions of this section are in addition to and are not in derogation of the rights of a trustee under the common law with respect to final distribution of a trust.

(Laws 2006, ch. 2006-217, §8, effective July 1, 2007.)

C. Duty to Take Control of and Preserve Trust Property

After a trustee accepts the office, he or she has a duty to take control of the assets of the trust. The trustee must locate the property and then ensure that the property becomes a trust asset (by registering corporate securities or recording real property in the name of the trust, for example). The trustee also has a duty to preserve the trust property. This duty requires that the trustee safeguards the assets by acquiring appropriate insurance (e.g., fire, theft) and placing valuable property in a secure location (e.g., a safe deposit box or safe).

After taking control of the trust property, the trustee has a duty to review the trust assets to make sure that they are appropriate for the trust. This duty is now incorporated in Florida's version of the prudent investor rule in Florida Statutes §518.11 (this section is included in Section H *infra*). The task must be accomplished within a reasonable time after accepting the trusteeship or receiving the trust property. This review entails: (1) disposing of bad investments or investments that the trustee is not permitted to make, according to the terms of the trust or state law; and (2) disposing of unproductive property. In addition, the trustee should review the trust property periodically thereafter to determine if the assets continue to be appropriate for the trust, and, if not, the trustee should dispose of these assets as well.

§736.0809. Duty to take control and protect trust property

A trustee shall take reasonable steps to take control of and protect the trust property.

(Laws 2006, ch. 217, §8, effective July 1, 2007.)

§736.0812. Duty to collect trust property from former trustee

A trustee shall take reasonable steps to compel a former trustee or other person to deliver trust property to the trustee and, except as provided in §736.08125, to redress a breach of trust known to the trustee to have been committed by a former trustee.

(Laws 2006, ch. 217, §8, effective July 1, 2007.)

D. Duty of Loyalty

The trustee has a duty of undivided loyalty in the administration of the trust. That is, the trustee must administer the trust solely in the interests of the beneficiaries. The duty of loyalty calls for the trustee to exclude consideration of his or her own interests, as well as the interests of third parties.

The trustee must not place himself or herself in a conflict of interest position in which personal interest or that of a third party is adverse to that of the beneficiary or beneficiaries. One type of conflict of interest that a trustee must avoid is "self-dealing." In cases of self-dealing, the trustee acts in such a way as to

benefit himself or herself. Examples of prohibited self-dealing include:

- to sell or lease of trust property to oneself as an individual;
- to sell or lease of individual property to the trust;
- (for a corporate trustee) to retain or acquire the corporation's own stock as a trust asset;
- to lend trust assets to oneself as an individual; or
- to acquire an interest in trust property for oneself as an individual.

Bogert, *supra*, at §543.

Most courts adopt a "*no-further-inquiry rule*" and do not consider good faith or fairness as defenses. The strict rule serves as a deterrence against acts of self-dealing. Some defenses have developed: (1) if the act is approved by a court, (2) if the act is authorized by the trust instrument, and (3) if the beneficiaries consent after full disclosure. In some situations, statutes authorize some forms of self-dealing.

If a trustee engages in self-dealing, for example by selling property owned as an individual to the trust, the beneficiary has the choice: to affirm the sale or set it aside (Fla. Stat. §§736.0802, 736.1002). The beneficiary may also require the trustee to account for any personal profit or loss to the trust (Fla. Stat. §736.1001-1002).

The Florida prohibition against self-dealing contains no defense for good faith. However, the transaction will not be voidable if: (1) the trust authorized the transaction, (2) the court approved the transaction, (3) the beneficiary did not commence judicial proceedings within the allotted time, (4) the beneficiary consented to or ratified the transaction or released the trustee, (5) the transaction involves a contract entered into by the trustee when he or she was not yet a trustee or nominated to be trustee, or (6) the settlor consented to the transaction while the trust was revocable (Fla. Stat. §736.0802).

In addition, a trustee of a trust that has multiple beneficiaries has a duty to administer the trust in an impartial manner so as to take into account the interest of all beneficiaries (Fla. Stat. §736.0803).

The Uniform Trust Code (and Florida law) prohibits certain acts of self dealing involving not only the trustee but also the trustee's relatives, such as: "[a] sale, encumbrance or other transaction involving the investment or management of the trust property" if it is entered into by the trustee with his or her spouse, descendants, siblings, parents, or their spouses (Unif. Trust Code §802(c); Fla. Stat. §736.0802(3)). See generally Karen E. Boxx, Of Punctilios and Paybacks: The Duty of Loyalty Under the Uniform Trust Code, 67 Mo. L. Rev. 279 (2002).

For discussion of an interesting case involving a breach of the duty of loyalty, see Jason L. Smith, Stegemeier v. Magness: An Analysis of a Trustee's Fiduciary Duty in Self-Interested Transactions, 14 Quinnipiac Prob. L.J. 605 (2000).

§736.0802. Trustee's duty of loyalty: scope

(1) As between a trustee and the beneficiaries, a trustee shall administer the trust solely in the interests of the beneficiaries.

(2) Subject to the rights of persons dealing with or assisting the trustee as provided in §736.1016, a sale, encumbrance, or other transaction involving the investment or management of trust property entered into by the trustee for the trustee's own personal account or which is otherwise affected by a conflict between the trustee's fiduciary and personal interests is voidable by a beneficiary affected by the transaction unless:

(a) The transaction was authorized by the terms of the trust;

(b) The transaction was approved by the court;

(c) The beneficiary did not commence a judicial proceeding within the time allowed by §736.1008;

(d) The beneficiary consented to the trustee's conduct, ratified the transaction, or released the trustee in compliance with §736.1012;

(e) The transaction involves a contract entered into or claim acquired by the trustee when that person had not become or contemplated becoming trustee; or

(f) The transaction was consented to in writing by a settlor of the trust while the trust was revocable.

(3) A sale, encumbrance, or other transaction involving the investment or management of trust property is presumed to be affected by a conflict between personal and fiduciary interests if the sale, encumbrance, or other transaction is entered into by the trustee with:

(a) The trustee's spouse;

(b) The trustee's descendants, siblings, parents, or their spouses;

(c) An officer, director, employee, agent, or attorney of the trustee; or

(d) A corporation or other person or enterprise in which the trustee, or a person that owns a significant interest in the trustee, has an interest that might affect the trustee's best judgment.

(4) A transaction not concerning trust property in which the trustee engages in the trustee's individual capacity involves a conflict between personal and fiduciary interests if the transaction concerns an opportunity properly belonging to the trust.

(5)

(a) An investment by a trustee authorized by lawful authority to engage in trust business, as defined in §658.12(20), in investment instruments, as defined in §660.25(6), that are owned or controlled by the trustee or its affiliate, or from which the trustee or its affiliate receives compensation for providing services in a capacity other than as trustee, is not presumed to be affected by a conflict between personal and fiduciary interests provided the investment otherwise complies with chapters 518 and 660 and the trustee complies with the disclosure requirements of this subsection.

(b) A trustee who invests trust funds in investment instruments that are owned or controlled by the trustee or its affiliate shall disclose the following to all qualified beneficiaries:

1. Notice that the trustee has invested trust funds in investment instruments owned or controlled by the trustee or its affiliate.

2. The identity of the investment instruments.

3. The identity and relationship to the trustee of any affiliate that owns or controls the investment instruments.

(c) A trustee who invests trust funds in investment instruments with respect to which the trustee or its affiliate receives compensation for providing services in a capacity other than as trustee shall disclose to all qualified beneficiaries, the nature of the services provided by the trustee or its affiliate, and all compensation, including, but not limited to, fees or commissions paid or to be paid by the account and received or to be received by an affiliate arising from such affiliated investment.

(d) Disclosure required by this subsection shall be made at least annually unless there has been no change in the method or increase in the rate at which such compensation is calculated since the most recent disclosure. The disclosure may be given in a trust disclosure document as defined in §736.1008, in a copy of the prospectus for the investment instrument, in any other written disclosure prepared for the investment instrument under applicable federal or state law, or in a written summary that includes all compensation received or to be received by the trustee and any affiliate of the trustee and an explanation of the manner in which such compensation is calculated, either as a percentage of the assets invested or by some other method.

(e) This subsection shall apply as follows:

1. This subsection does not apply to qualified investment instruments or to a trust for which a right of revocation exists.

2. For investment instruments other than qualified investment instruments, paragraphs (a), (b), (c), and (d) shall apply to irrevocable trusts created on or after July 1, 2007, which expressly authorize the trustee, by specific reference to this subsection, to invest in investment instruments owned or controlled by the trustee or its affiliate.

3. For investment instruments other than qualified investment instruments, paragraphs (a), (b), (c), and (d) shall apply to irrevocable trusts not described in subparagraph 2. only as follows:

a. Such paragraphs shall not apply until 60 days after the statement required in paragraph (f) is provided and no objection is made or any objection which is made has been terminated.

(I) An objection is made if, within 60 days after the date of the statement required in paragraph (f), a super majority of the eligible beneficiaries deliver to the trustee written objections to the application of this subsection to such trust. An objection shall be deemed to be delivered to the trustee on the date the objection is mailed to the mailing address listed in the notice provided in paragraph (f).

(II) An objection is terminated upon the earlier of the receipt of consent from a super majority of eligible beneficiaries of the class that made the objection or the resolution of the objection pursuant to this subparagraph.

(III) If an objection is delivered to the trustee, the trustee may petition the court for an order overruling the objection and authorizing the trustee to make investments under this subsection. The burden shall be on the trustee to show good cause for the relief sought.

(IV) Any qualified beneficiary may petition the court for an order to prohibit, limit, or restrict a trustee's authority to make investments under this subsection. The burden shall be upon the petitioning beneficiary to show good cause for the relief sought.

(V) The court may award costs and attorney's fees relating to any petition under this subparagraph in the same manner as in chancery actions. When costs and attorney's fees are to be paid out of the trust, the court, in its discretion, may direct from which part of the trust such costs and fees shall be paid.

b. The objection of a super majority of eligible beneficiaries under this subparagraph may thereafter be removed by the written consent of a super majority of the class or classes of those eligible beneficiaries that made the objection.

(f)

1. Any time prior to initially investing in any investment instrument described in this subsection other than a qualified investment instrument, the trustee of a trust described in subparagraph (e)3. shall provide to all qualified beneficiaries a statement containing the following:

a. The name, telephone number, street address, and mailing address of the trustee and of any individuals who may be contacted for further information.

b. A statement that, unless a super majority of the eligible beneficiaries objects to the application of this subsection to the trust within 60 days after the date the statement pursuant to this subsection was delivered, this subsection shall apply to the trust.

c. A statement that, if this subsection applies to the trust, the trustee will have the right to make investments in investment instruments, as defined in §660.25(6), which are owned or controlled by the trustee or its affiliate, or from which the trustee or its affiliate receives compensation for providing services in a capacity other than as trustee, and that the trustee or its affiliate may receive fees in addition to the trustee's compensation for administering the trust.

d. A statement by the trustee is not delivered if the statement is accompanied by another written communication other than a written communication by the trustee that refers only to the statement.

2. For purposes of paragraph (e) and this paragraph:

a. "Eligible beneficiaries" means:

(I) If at the time the determination is made there are one or more beneficiaries as described in §736.0103(14)(c), the beneficiaries described in §736.0103(14)(a) and (c); or

(II) If there is no beneficiary described in §736.0103(14)(c), the beneficiaries described in §736.0103(14)(a) and (b).

b. "Super majority of the eligible beneficiaries" means:

(I) If at the time the determination is made there are one or more beneficiaries as described in §736.0103(14)(c), at least two-thirds in interest of the beneficiaries described in §736.0103(14)(a) or two-thirds in interest of the beneficiaries described in §736.0103(14)(c), if the interests of the beneficiaries are reasonably ascertainable; otherwise, two-thirds in number of either such class; or

(II) If there is no beneficiary as described in §736.0103(14)(c), at least two-thirds in interest of the beneficiaries described in §736.0103(14)(a) or two-thirds in interest of the beneficiaries described in §736.0103(14)(b), if the interests of the beneficiaries are reasonably ascertainable; otherwise, two-thirds in number of either such class.

c. "Qualified investment instrument" means a mutual fund, common trust fund, or money market fund described in and governed by §736.0816(3).

d. An irrevocable trust is created upon execution of the trust instrument. If a trust that was revocable when created thereafter becomes irrevocable, the irrevocable trust is created when the right of revocation terminates.

(g) Nothing in this chapter is intended to create or imply a duty for the trustee to seek the application of this subsection to invest in investment instruments described in paragraph (a), and no inference of impropriety may be made as a result of a trustee electing not to invest trust assets in investment instruments described in paragraph (a).

(6) In voting shares of stock or in exercising powers of control over similar interests in other forms of enterprise, the trustee shall act in the best interests of the beneficiaries. If the trust is the sole owner of a corporation or other form of enterprise, the trustee shall elect or appoint directors or other managers who will manage the corporation or enterprise in the best interests of the beneficiaries

(7) This section does not preclude the following transactions, if fair to the beneficiaries:

(a) An agreement between a trustee and a beneficiary relating to the appointment or compensation of the trustee;

(b) A payment of reasonable compensation to the trustee;

(c) A transaction between a trust and another trust, the decedent's estate, or a guardian of the property of which the trustee is a fiduciary or in which a beneficiary has an interest;

(d) A deposit of trust money in a regulated financial service institution operated by the trustee; or

(e) An advance by the trustee of money for the protection of the trust

(8) This section does not preclude the employment of persons, including, but not limited to, attorneys, accountants, investment advisers, or agents, even if they are the trustee, an affiliate of the trustee, or otherwise associated with the trustee, to advise or assist the trustee in the exercise of any of the trustee's powers and to pay reasonable compensation and costs incurred in connection with such employment from the assets of the trust; to act without independent investigation on their recommendations; and, instead of acting personally, to employ one or more agents to perform any act of administration, whether or not discretionary.

(9) The court may appoint a special fiduciary to act with respect to any proposed transaction that might violate this section if entered into by the trustee.

(10) Payment of costs or attorney's fees incurred in any trust proceeding from the assets of the trust may be made by the trustee without the approval of any person and without court authorization, except that court authorization shall be required if an action has been filed or defense asserted against the trustee based upon a breach of trust. Court authorization is not required if the action or defense is later withdrawn or dismissed by the party that is alleging a breach of trust or resolved without a determination by the court that the trustee has committed a breach of trust.

(Laws 2006, ch. 217, §8, effective July 1, 2007.)

§736.0803. Impartiality

If a trust has two or more beneficiaries, the trustee shall act impartially in administering the trust property, giving due regard to the beneficiaries' respective interests.

(Laws 2006, ch. 217, §8, effective July 1, 2007.)

E. Duty to Identify and to Segregate Trust Property

A trustee has a duty to earmark the trust property, i.e., to identify and label the trust assets as properly belonging to the trust (Fla. Stat. §736.0810(3)). The trustee also has a duty to segregate the trust property and not to commingle it with his or her own assets (Fla. Stat. §736.0810(2)) or the assets of other trusts. Earmarking is important because failure to earmark may result in the trustee's personal creditors seizing trust property in the belief that the trustee owns it in his or her individual capacity.

At common law, a trustee was liable for all losses that resulted from failure to earmark. This strict rule has been liberalized, however, to make trustees liable only if the loss resulted from the failure to earmark. Thus, suppose a trustee fails to register corporate securities in the name of the trust (registering them in his or her own name instead) and the stock subsequently decreases in value. The trustee will not be liable if the loss was due to economic conditions. However, suppose the trustee fails to register corporate securities in the name of the trust and the trustee's creditor seizes the stock for payment of the trustee's individual debt. Then, the trustee will be liable for the loss.

Some state statutes permit trustees to commingle property from several trusts in a "common trust fund" for ease of management. Such funds permit a trustee to obtain lower costs, for example, on the sale of corporate stock. See Fla. Stat. §736.0810(4) (permitting a trustee to invest the property of two or more separate trusts if the trustee maintains adequate records).

§736.0810. Duty to identify and segregate trust property

(1) A trustee shall keep clear, distinct, and accurate records of the administration of the trust.

(2) A trustee shall keep trust property separate from the trustee's own property.

(3) Except as otherwise provided in subsection (4), a trustee shall cause the trust property to be designated so that the interest of the trust, to the extent feasible, appears in records maintained by a party other than a trustee or beneficiary.

(4) If the trustee maintains records clearly indicating the respective interests, a trustee may invest as a whole the property of two or more separate trusts.

(Laws 2006, ch. 217, §8, effective July 1, 2007.)

§736.08105. Duty to obtain marketable title of trust real property

A trustee holding title to real property received from a settlor or estate shall not be required to obtain title insurance or proof of marketable title until a marketable title is required for a sale or conveyance of the real property.

(Laws 2006, ch. 217, §8, effective July 1, 2007.)

F. Duty with Respect to Delegation

A trustee is not required to perform all acts involved in the administration of a trust. According to the traditional rule, a trustee may delegate *ministerial* duties but may not delegate *discretionary* duties.

Although the Restatement (Second) of Trusts §171 cmt. h prohibited delegation of the power to select investments, the Restatement (Third) of Trusts permits a trustee "in appropriate circumstances," to delegate discretionary acts involving "the selection of trust investments or the management of specialized investment programs, and to other activities of administration involving significant judgment." Restatement (Third) of Trusts §171 cmt. f.

A trend to permit trustees to delegate more of their discretionary duties began in 1964, with the promulgation of the Uniform Trustees' Powers Act. That Act permitted a trustee to employ agents to assist in the performance of the trustee's administrative duties. Such agents could help the trustee by performing any act of administration, whether discretionary or not. The Uniform Trustees' Powers Act was followed by the Uniform Prudent Investor Act (UPIA) in 1994. Taking into consideration modern portfolio theory, the UPIA adopts a "prudent investor standard" to replace the former "prudent person standard" regarding investment decisions—"recognizing that for many individual trustees, delegating some investment authority is actually the prudent approach." Susan N. Gary, Regulating the Management of Charities: Trust Law, Corporate Law and Tax Law, 21 U. Haw. L. Rev. 601-602 (1999).

The Uniform Trust Code and the Restatement (Third) of Trusts adopted the approach of the Uniform Prudent Investor Act in terms of delegation. Both permit trustees to delegate duties and powers to agents to the extent that a prudent trustee would delegate duties and powers that a prudent trustee would delegate and also require care in the selection and supervision of agents. "A trustee may delegate duties and powers that a prudent trustee of comparable skills could properly delegate under the circumstances." Unif. Trust Code §807(a) (derived from Uniform Prudent Investor Act §9). Florida has adopted this rule (Fla. Stat. §736.0807).

The Uniform Trust Codes makes the decision to delegate dependent on the particular facts and circumstances. "For example, delegating some administrative and reporting duties might be prudent for a family trustee but unnecessary for a corporate trustee." Unif. Trust Code §807(a) cmt. Note that the Uniform Trust Code provision applies only to delegation to agents, not to co-trustees (rules governing delegation to a co-trustee are set forth in Uniform Trust Code §703(e)).

§736.0807. Delegation by trustee

(1) A trustee may delegate duties and powers that a prudent trustee of comparable skills could properly delegate under the circumstances. The trustee shall exercise reasonable care, skill, and caution in

(a) Selecting an agent

(b) Establishing the scope and terms of the delegation, consistent with the purposes and terms of the trust

(c) Reviewing the agent's actions periodically, in order to monitor the agent's performance and compliance with the terms of the delegation

(2) In performing a delegated function, an agent owes a duty to the trust to exercise reasonable care to comply with the terms of the delegation

(3) A trustee who complies with subsection (1) is not liable to the beneficiaries or to the trust for an action of the agent to whom the function was delegated

(4) By accepting a delegation of powers or duties from the trustee of a trust that is subject to the law of this state, an agent submits to the jurisdiction of the courts of this state.

(Laws 2006, ch. 217, §8, effective July 1, 2007.)

§736.0808. Trustee may follow settlor's directions even if contrary to terms of trust

(1) Subject to §§736.0403(2) and 736.0602(3)(a), the trustee may follow a direction of the settlor that is contrary to the terms of the trust while a trust is revocable

(2) If the terms of a trust confer on a person other than the settlor of a revocable trust the power to direct certain actions of the trustee, the trustee shall act in accordance with an exercise of the power unless the attempted exercise is manifestly contrary to the terms of the trust or the trustee knows the attempted exercise would constitute a serious breach of a fiduciary duty that the person holding the power owes to the beneficiaries of the trust

(3) The terms of a trust may confer on a trustee or other person a power to direct the modification or termination of the trust

(4) A person, other than a beneficiary, who holds a power to direct is presumptively a fiduciary who, as such, is required to act in good faith with regard to

the purposes of the trust and the interests of the beneficiaries. The holder of a power to direct is liable for any loss that results from breach of a fiduciary duty.
(Laws 2006, ch. 217, §8, effective July 1, 2007.)

§736.1007. Trustee's attorney's fees

(1) If the trustee of a revocable trust retains an attorney to render legal services in connection with the initial administration of the trust, the attorney is entitled to reasonable compensation for those legal services, payable from the assets of the trust without court order. The trustee and the attorney may agree to compensation that is determined in a manner or amount other than the manner or amount provided in this section. The agreement is not binding on a person who bears the impact of the compensation unless that person is a party to or otherwise consents to be bound by the agreement. The agreement may provide that the trustee is not individually liable for the attorney's fees and costs.

(2) Unless otherwise agreed, compensation based on the value of the trust assets immediately following the settlor's death and the income earned by the trust during initial administration at the rate of 75 percent of the schedule provided in §733.6171(3)(a)-(h) is presumed to be reasonable total compensation for ordinary services of all attorneys employed generally to advise a trustee concerning the trustee's duties in initial trust administration.

(3) An attorney who is retained to render only limited and specifically defined legal services shall be compensated as provided in the retaining agreement. If the amount or method of determining compensation is not provided in the agreement, the attorney is entitled to a reasonable fee, taking into account the factors set forth in subsection (6).

(4) Ordinary services of the attorney in an initial trust administration include legal advice and representation concerning the trustee's duties relating to:

(a) Review of the trust instrument and each amendment for legal sufficiency and interpretation.

(b) Implementation of substitution of the successor trustee.

(c) Persons who must or should be served with required notices and the method and timing of such service.

(d) The obligation of a successor to require a former trustee to provide an accounting.

(e) The trustee's duty to protect, insure, and manage trust assets and the trustee's liability relating to these duties.

(f) The trustee's duty regarding investments imposed by the prudent investor rule.

(g) The trustee's obligation to inform and account to beneficiaries and the method of satisfaction of such obligations, the liability of the trust and trustee to the settlor's creditors, and the advisability or necessity for probate proceedings to bar creditors.

(h) Contributions due to the personal representative of the settlor's estate for payment of expenses of administration and obligations of the settlor's estate.

(i) Identifying tax returns required to be filed by the trustee, the trustee's liability for payment of taxes, and the due date of returns.

(j) Filing a nontaxable affidavit, if not filed by a personal representative.

(k) Order of payment of expenses of administration of the trust and order and priority of abatement of trust distributions.

(*l*) Distribution of income or principal to beneficiaries or funding of further trusts provided in the governing instrument.

(m) Preparation of any legal documents required to effect distribution.

(n) Fiduciary duties, avoidance of self-dealing, conflicts of interest, duty of impartiality, and obligations to beneficiaries.

(o) If there is a conflict of interest between a trustee who is a beneficiary and other beneficiaries of the trust, advice to the trustee on limitations of certain authority of the trustee regarding discretionary distributions or exercise of certain powers and alternatives for appointment of an independent trustee and appropriate procedures.

(p) Procedures for the trustee's discharge from liability for administration of the trust on termination or resignation.

(5) In addition to the attorney's fees for ordinary services, the attorney for the trustee shall be allowed further reasonable compensation for any extraordinary service. What constitutes an extraordinary service may vary depending on many factors, including the size of the trust. Extraordinary services may include, but are not limited to:

(a) Involvement in a trust contest, trust construction, a proceeding for determination of beneficiaries, a contested claim, elective share proceedings, apportionment of estate taxes, or other adversary proceedings or litigation by or against the trust.

(b) Representation of the trustee in an audit or any proceeding for adjustment, determination, or collection of any taxes.

(c) Tax advice on postmortem tax planning, including, but not limited to, disclaimer, renunciation of fiduciary commission, alternate valuation date, allocation of administrative expenses between tax returns, the QTIP or reverse QTIP election, allocation of GST exemption, qualification for Internal Revenue Code §§303 and 6166 privileges, deduction of last illness expenses, distribution planning, asset basis considerations, throwback rules, handling income or deductions in respect of a decedent, valuation discounts, special use and other valuation, handling employee benefit or retirement proceeds, prompt assessment request, or request for release from personal liability for payment of tax.

(d) Review of an estate tax return and preparation or review of other tax returns required to be filed by the trustee.

(e) Preparation of decedent's federal estate tax return. If this return is prepared by the attorney, a fee of one-half of 1 percent up to a value of $10 million and one-fourth of 1 percent on the value in excess of $10 million, of the gross estate as finally determined for federal estate tax purposes, is presumed to be reasonable compensation for the attorney for this service. These fees shall include services for routine audit of the return, not beyond the examining agent level, if required.

(f) Purchase, sale, lease, or encumbrance of real property by the trustee or involvement in zoning, land use, environmental, or other similar matters.

(g) Legal advice regarding carrying on of decedent's business or conducting other commercial activity by the trustee.

(h) Legal advice regarding claims for damage to the environment or related procedures.

(i) Legal advice regarding homestead status of trust real property or proceedings involving the status.

(j) Involvement in fiduciary, employee, or attorney compensation disputes.

(k) Considerations of special valuation of trust assets, including discounts for blockage, minority interests, lack of marketability, and environmental liability.

(6) Upon petition of any interested person in a proceeding to review the compensation paid or to be paid to the attorney for the trustee, the court may increase or decrease the compensation for ordinary services of the attorney for the trustee or award compensation for extraordinary services if the facts and circumstances of the particular administration warrant. In determining reasonable compensation, the court shall consider all of the following factors giving such weight to each as the court may determine to be appropriate:

(a) The promptness, efficiency, and skill with which the initial administration was handled by the attorney.

(b) The responsibilities assumed by, and potential liabilities of, the attorney.

(c) The nature and value of the assets that are affected by the decedent's death.

(d) The benefits or detriments resulting to the trust or the trust's beneficiaries from the attorney's services.

(e) The complexity or simplicity of the administration and the novelty of issues presented.

(f) The attorney's participation in tax planning for the estate, the trust, and the trust's beneficiaries and tax return preparation or review and approval.

(g) The nature of the trust assets, the expenses of administration, and the claims payable by the trust and the compensation paid to other professionals and fiduciaries.

(h) Any delay in payment of the compensation after the services were furnished.

(i) Any other relevant factors.

(7) The court may determine reasonable attorney's compensation without receiving expert testimony. Any party may offer expert testimony after notice to interested persons. If expert testimony is offered, an expert witness fee may be awarded by the court and paid from the assets of the trust. The court shall direct from what part of the trust the fee is to be paid.

(8) If a separate written agreement regarding compensation exists between the attorney and the settlor, the attorney shall furnish a copy to the trustee prior to commencement of employment and, if employed, shall promptly file and serve a copy on all interested persons. A separate agreement or a provision in the trust suggesting or directing the trustee to retain a specific attorney does not obligate the trustee to employ the attorney or obligate the attorney to accept the representation but, if the attorney who is a party to the agreement or who drafted the trust is employed, the compensation paid shall not exceed the compensation provided in the agreement.

(9) Court proceedings to determine compensation, if required, are a part of the trust administration process, and the costs, including fees for the trustee's attorney, shall be determined by the court and paid from the assets of the trust unless the court finds the attorney's fees request to be substantially unreasonable. The court shall direct from what part of the trust the fees are to be paid.

(10) As used in this section, the term "initial trust administration" means administration of a revocable trust during the period that begins with the death of the settlor and ends on the final distribution of trust assets outright or to continuing trusts created under the trust agreement but, if an estate tax return is required, not until after issuance of an estate tax closing letter or other evidence of termination of the estate tax proceeding. This initial period is not intended to include continued regular administration of the trust.

(Laws 2006, ch. 2006-217, §10, effective July 1, 2007.)

G. Duty to Report Information to the Beneficiaries and to Render Accounts

A trustee has a duty to keep the beneficiaries informed and to render accountings to them (Fla. Stat. §§736.0813-08135). Upon the request at the beneficiaries and at reasonable times, the trustee has a duty to give the beneficiary or beneficiaries complete and accurate information relative to the administration of the trust. The purpose of the requirement is to enable a beneficiary to enforce his or her rights. The duty to inform is derived from UPC §7-303 (1987).

§736.0813. Trustee's duty to inform and account to beneficiaries

The trustee shall keep the qualified beneficiaries of the trust reasonably informed of the trust and its administration.

(1) The trustee's duty to inform and account includes, but is not limited to, the following:

(a) Within 60 days after acceptance of the trust, the trustee shall give notice to the qualified beneficiaries of the acceptance of the trust and the full name and address of the trustee.

(b) Within 60 days after the date the trustee acquires knowledge of the creation of an irrevocable trust, or the date the trustee acquires knowledge that a formerly revocable trust has become irrevocable, whether by the death of the settlor or otherwise, the trustee shall give notice to the qualified beneficiaries of the trust's existence, the identity of the settlor or settlors, the right to request a copy of the trust instrument, and the right to accountings under this section.

(c) Upon reasonable request, the trustee shall provide a qualified beneficiary with a complete copy of the trust instrument.

(d) A trustee of an irrevocable trust shall provide a trust accounting, as set forth in §736.08135, to each qualified beneficiary annually and on termination of the trust or on change of the trustee.

(e) Upon reasonable request, the trustee shall provide a qualified beneficiary with relevant information about the assets and liabilities of the trust and the particulars relating to administration.

Paragraphs (a) and (b) do not apply to an irrevocable trust created before the effective date of this code, or to a revocable trust that becomes irrevocable before the effective date of this code. Paragraph (a) does not apply to a trustee who accepts a trusteeship before the effective date of this code.

(2) A qualified beneficiary may waive the trustee's duty to account under paragraph (1)(d). A qualified beneficiary may withdraw a waiver previously given. Waivers and withdrawals of prior waivers under this subsection must be in writing. Withdrawals of prior waivers are effective only with respect to accountings for future periods.

(3) The representation provisions of part III apply with respect to all rights of a qualified beneficiary under this section.

(4) As provided in §736.0603(1), the trustee's duties under this section extend only to the settlor while a trust is revocable.

(5) This section applies to trust accountings rendered for accounting periods beginning on or after January 1, 2008.

(Laws 2006, ch. 217, §8, effective July 1, 2007.)

§736.08135. Trust accounting: requirements

(1) A trust accounting must be a reasonably understandable report from the date of the last accounting or, if none, from the date on which the trustee became accountable, that adequately discloses the information required in subsection (2).

(2)

(a) The accounting must begin with a statement identifying the trust, the trustee furnishing the accounting, and the time period covered by the accounting.

(b) The accounting must show all cash and property transactions and all significant transactions affecting administration during the accounting period, including compensation paid to the trustee and the trustee's agents. Gains and losses realized during the accounting period and all receipts and disbursements must be shown.

(c) To the extent feasible, the accounting must identify and value trust assets on hand at the close of the accounting period. For each asset or class of assets reasonably capable of valuation, the accounting shall contain two values, the asset acquisition value or carrying value and the estimated current value. The accounting must identify each known noncontingent liability with an estimated current amount of the liability if known.

(d) To the extent feasible, the accounting must show significant transactions that do not affect the amount for which the trustee is accountable, including name changes in investment holdings, adjustments to carrying value, a change of custodial institutions, and stock splits.

(e) The accounting must reflect the allocation of receipts, disbursements, accruals, or allowances between income and principal when the allocation affects the interest of any beneficiary of the trust.

(f) The trustee shall include in the final accounting a plan of distribution for any undistributed assets shown on the final accounting.

(3) This section applies to all trust accountings rendered for any accounting periods beginning on or after January 1, 2003.

(Laws 2006, ch. 217, §8, effective July 1, 2007.)

H. Uniform Prudent Investor Act

The Uniform Prudent Investor Act (UPIA) was promulgated by the National Conference of Commissioners on Uniform State Laws (NCCUSL) in 1994. UPIA is modeled on the Restatement (Third) of Trusts: Prudent Investor Rule (1992).

NCCUSL promulgated UPIA to address shortcomings of the common law rules. For example, common law rules placed severe restrictions on the types of investments in which trustees could invest trust assets. Trustees were precluded from obtaining professional investment help. And, a trustee's performance was rated by the performance of each investment individually rather than on the performance of the whole portfolio.

Today, under UPIA, trusts are able to achieve a better rate of return for beneficiaries than at common law. Trustees can better protect the trust corpus by diversification. Trustees can invest to counter the effects of inflation. Trustees can obtain professional investment services. Trustees can take into account the changing character and kinds of assets that are available for investment. Trustees can utilize modern portfolio theory to guide their investment decisions. Trustees are judged on the overall performance of all the trust assets in a trust rather than specific assets. Trustees have a list of factors to consider in making investment decisions, such as "general economic conditions," "possible effect of inflation or deflation," "the expected total return from income and the appreciation of capital," and "other resources of the beneficiaries."

Approximately 44 states (and the District of Columbia) have enacted UPIA or substantially similar provisions (http://nccusl.org/nccusl/uniformact_factsheets/uniformacts-fs-upria.asp (last visited Mar. 5, 2007)). Florida has codified the prudent investor rule in Florida Statutes §518.11.

§518.11. Prudent Investor Rule

(1) A fiduciary has a duty to invest and manage investment assets as follows:

(a) The fiduciary has a duty to invest and manage investment assets as a prudent investor would considering the purposes, terms, distribution requirements, and other circumstances of the trust. This standard requires the exercise of reasonable care and caution and is to be applied to investments not in isolation, but in the context of the investment portfolio as a whole and as a part of an overall investment strategy that should incorporate risk and return objectives reasonably suitable to the trust, guardianship, or probate estate. If the fiduciary has special skills, or is named fiduciary on the basis of representations of special skills or expertise, the fiduciary is under a duty to use those skills.

(b) No specific investment or course of action is, taken alone, prudent or imprudent. The fiduciary may invest in every kind of property and type of investment, subject to this section. The fiduciary's investment decisions and actions are to be judged in terms of the fiduciary's reasonable business judgment regarding the anticipated effect on the investment portfolio as a whole under the facts and circumstances prevailing at the time of the decision or action. The prudent investor rule is a test of conduct and not of resulting performance.

(c) The fiduciary has a duty to diversify the investments unless, under the circumstances, the fiduciary believes reasonably it is in the interests of the beneficiaries and furthers the purposes of the trust, guardianship, or estate not to diversify.

(d) The fiduciary has a duty, within a reasonable time after acceptance of the trust, estate, or guardianship, to review the investment portfolio and to make and implement decisions concerning the retention and disposition of original preexisting investments in order to conform to the provisions of this section. The fiduciary's decision to retain or dispose of an asset may be influenced properly by the asset's special relationship or value to the purposes of the trust, estate, or guardianship, or to some or all of the beneficiaries, consistent with the trustee's duty of impartiality, or to the ward.

(e) The fiduciary has a duty to pursue an investment strategy that considers both the reasonable production of income and safety of capital, consistent with the fiduciary's duty of impartiality and the purposes of the trust, estate, or guardianship. Whether investments are underproductive or overproductive of income shall be judged by the portfolio as a whole and not as to any particular asset.

(f) The circumstances that the fiduciary may consider in making investment decisions include, without limitation, the general economic conditions, the possible effect of inflation, the expected tax consequences of investment decisions or strategies, the role each investment or course of action plays within the overall portfolio, the expected total return, including both income yield and appreciation of capital, and the duty to incur only reasonable and appropriate costs. The fiduciary may, but need not, consider related trusts, estates, and guardianships, and the income available from other sources to, and the assets of, beneficiaries when making investment decisions.

(2) The provisions of this section may be expanded, restricted, eliminated, or otherwise altered by express provisions of the governing instrument, whether the instrument was executed before or after the effective date of this section. An express provision need not refer specifically to this statute. The fiduciary is not liable to any person for the fiduciary's reasonable reliance on those express provisions.

(3) Nothing in this section abrogates or restricts the power of an appropriate court in proper cases:

(a) To direct or permit the trustee to deviate from the terms of the governing instrument; or

(b) To direct or permit the fiduciary to take, or to restrain the fiduciary from taking, any action regarding the making or retention of investments.

(4) The following terms or comparable language in the investment powers and related provisions of a governing instrument shall be construed as authorizing any investment or strategy permitted under this section: "investments permissible by law for investment of trust funds," "legal investments," "authorized investments," "using the judgment and care under the circumstances then prevailing that persons of prudence, discretion, and intelligence exercise in the management of their own affairs, not in regard to speculation but in regard to the permanent disposition of their funds, considering the probable income as well as the probable safety of their capital," "prudent trustee rule," "prudent person rule," and "prudent investor rule."

(5) This section applies to all existing and future fiduciary relationships subject to this section, but only as to acts or omissions occurring after October 1, 1993.

(Laws 1953, ch. 28154, §6; Laws 1993, ch. 93-257, §2. Amended by Laws 1997, ch. 97-98, §26, effective July 1, 1997; Laws 1997, ch. 97-103, §686, effective July 1, 1997.)

I. Uniform Principal and Income Allocation

A trustee has a fiduciary obligation to be fair both to the income beneficiaries during the management of the trust and also to the remainder beneficiaries. As part of their duties, trustees may be required to allocate income to certain beneficiaries and to pay expenses from particular assets before distribution of the trust property. Trustees must make the proper allocation of assets and charge the property disbursements to either income or principal.

Model legislation facilitates the difficult tasks of indemnification of principal versus income, its allocation, and apportionment. The original Uniform Principal and Income Act (UPAIA) was promulgated in 1931 and revised in 1962. The Act was widely adopted by 1997, when a new revision was promulgated.

The purpose of the new UPAIA (similar to that of the preceding Acts), is to provide procedures for trustees administering an estate in identifying principal versus income, and to ensure that the settlor's intention is the guiding principal. Importantly, the 1997 revision was necessary in order to enable principal and income allocation rules to accommodate prudent investor rules (the Uniform Prudent Investor Act was promulgated in 1994).

UPAIA is a default statute that operates when the trust instrument is silent. The Act establishes whether specific kinds of assets qualify as principal versus income. Next, the Act simplifies the allocation process by providing that any money received by a fiduciary is income, unless it fits within certain defined categories. The new Act provides for assets that were not within the scope of earlier versions of the Act, such as: derivatives, options, deferred payment obligations, and synthetic financial assets. The new legislation also provides better guidelines for apportionment than did earlier versions of the Act. For example, the new Act provides than an income receipt is principal if it is due before a decedent dies (for an estate) or

before an income interest begins (for a trust). However, after death or after an income interest begins, the interest is classified as income.

Also, the 1997 Act establishes rules that assure orderly distribution of income when a decedent dies or an income interest ends. Earlier versions of the Act did not address this distribution problem.

Significantly, the 1997 Act also accommodates the notions of prudent investment, modern portfolio theory, and total return that were not in existence at the time of the earlier Acts. The Act provides that a trustee must use prudent investment rules. For example, investment policy should be dependent upon the trustee's making the appropriate risk/return analysis and reaching investment decisions in light of that analysis. Also, one of the primary contributions of the 1997 Act (UPAIA §104) is to permit a trustee to adjust principal and income as dictated by the prudent investor standard when a trust provides for a fixed income for the income beneficiary. That is, the Act authorizes a trustee to make adjustments between principal and income that may be necessary if the income of a portfolio's total return is too small or too large because of investment decisions made pursuant to the prudent investor rule. The Act provides a list of factors that the trustee shall consider in making decisions and specifies the circumstances in which such adjustments are prohibited. Section 104 adds an important element of flexibility to the trustee's powers by authorizing adjustment between principal and income instead of merely applying traditional rules.

Finally, the 1997 Act has been modernized by the inclusion of a provision that deals with the problem of disbursements made because of environmental laws and by provisions that address imbalances posed by tax laws (i.e., the trustee is given the power to make adjustments between principal and income to correct inequities caused by tax laws).

To date, 41 states (including Florida) and the District of Columbia have enacted the Uniform Principal and Income Act (http://nccusl.org/nccusl/uniformact_factsheets/uniformacts-fs-upia.asp (last visited March 5, 2007)). The Florida version is set forth below.

§738.101. Florida Uniform Principal and Income Act

This chapter may be cited as the "Florida Uniform Principal and Income Act."

(Laws 2002, ch. 2002-42, §1, effective January 1, 2003.)

§738.102. Applicable definitions

As used in this chapter, the term:

(1) "Accounting period" means a calendar year unless another 12-month period is selected by a fiduciary. The term includes a portion of a calendar year or other 12-month period that begins when an income interest begins or ends when an income interest ends.

(2) "Beneficiary" means, in the case of a decedent's estate, an heir or devisee and, in the case of a trust, an income beneficiary or a remainder beneficiary.

(3) "Fiduciary" means a personal representative or a trustee. The term includes an executor, administrator, successor personal representative, special administrator, or a person performing substantially the same function.

(4) "Income" means money or property that a fiduciary receives as current return from a principal asset. The term includes a portion of receipts from a sale, exchange, or liquidation of a principal asset, to the extent provided in §§738.401-738.403 and §738.503.

(5) "Income beneficiary" means a person to whom net income of a trust is or may be payable.

(6) "Income interest" means the right of an income beneficiary to receive all or part of net income, whether the terms of the trust require the net income to be distributed or authorize the net income to be distributed in the trustee's discretion.

(7) "Mandatory income interest" means the right of an income beneficiary to receive net income that the terms of the trust require the fiduciary to distribute.

(8) "Net income" means the total receipts allocated to income during an accounting period minus the disbursements made from income during the period, plus or minus transfers under this chapter to or from income during the period.

(9) "Person" means an individual, corporation, business trust, estate, trust, partnership, limited liability company, association, joint venture, public corporation, or any other legal or commercial entity or a government or governmental subdivision, agency, or instrumentality.

(10) "Principal" means property held in trust for distribution to a remainder beneficiary when the trust terminates.

(11) "Remainder beneficiary" means a person entitled to receive principal when an income interest ends.

(12) "Terms of a trust" means the manifestation of the intent of a grantor or decedent with respect to the trust, expressed in a manner that admits of its proof

in a judicial proceeding, whether by written or spoken words or by conduct.

(13) "Trustee" includes an original, additional, or successor trustee, whether or not appointed or confirmed by a court.

(Laws 2002, ch. 2002-42. §1. effective January 1, 2003.)

§738.103. Fiduciary duties

(1) In allocating receipts and disbursements to or between principal and income, and with respect to any matter within the scope of §§738.201 and 738.202 and §§738.301-738.303, a fiduciary:

(a) Shall administer a trust or estate in accordance with the terms of the trust or the will, even if there is a different provision in this chapter.

(b) May administer a trust or estate by the exercise of a discretionary power of administration given to the fiduciary by the terms of the trust or the will, even if the exercise of the power produces a result different from a result required or permitted by this chapter.

(c) Shall administer a trust or estate in accordance with this chapter if the terms of the trust or the will do not contain a different provision or do not give the fiduciary a discretionary power of administration.

(d) Shall add a receipt or charge a disbursement to principal to the extent the terms of the trust and this chapter do not provide a rule for allocating the receipt or disbursement to or between principal and income.

(2) In exercising the power to adjust under §738.104(1) or a discretionary power of administration regarding a matter within the scope of this chapter, whether granted by the terms of a trust, a will, or this chapter, a fiduciary shall administer a trust or estate impartially, based on what is fair and reasonable to all of the beneficiaries, except to the extent the terms of the trust or the will clearly manifest an intention that the fiduciary shall or may favor one or more of the beneficiaries. A determination in accordance with this chapter is presumed to be fair and reasonable to all of the beneficiaries.

(Laws 2002, ch. 2002-42, §1, effective January 1, 2003.)

§738.104. Trustee's power to adjust between principal and income

(1) A trustee may adjust between principal and income to the extent the trustee considers necessary if the trustee invests and manages trust assets as a prudent investor, the terms of the trust describe the amount that may or shall be distributed to a beneficiary by referring to the trust's income, and the trustee determines, after applying the rules in §738.103(1), that the trustee is unable to comply with §738.103(2).

(2) In deciding whether and to what extent to exercise the power conferred by subsection (1), a trustee shall consider all factors relevant to the trust and its beneficiaries, including the following factors to the extent they are relevant:

(a) The nature, purpose, and expected duration of the trust.

(b) The intent of the grantor.

(c) The identity and circumstances of the beneficiaries.

(d) The needs for liquidity, regularity of income, and preservation and appreciation of capital.

(e) The assets held in the trust; the extent to which the assets consist of financial assets, interests in closely held enterprises, tangible and intangible personal property, or real property; the extent to which an asset is used by a beneficiary; and whether an asset was purchased by the trustee or received from the grantor.

(f) The net amount allocated to income under the other sections of this chapter and the increases or decreases in the value of the principal assets, which the trustee may estimate as to assets for which market values are not readily available

(g) Whether and to what extent the terms of the trust give the trustee the power to invade principal or accumulate income or prohibit the trustee from invading principal or accumulating income and the extent to which the trustee has exercised a power from time to time to invade principal or accumulate income.

(h) The actual and anticipated effect of economic conditions on principal and income and effects of inflation and deflation.

(i) The anticipated tax consequences of an adjustment.

(3) A trustee may not make an adjustment:

(a) That reduces the actuarial value of the income interest in a trust to which a person transfers property with the intent to qualify for a gift tax exclusion;

(b) That changes the amount payable to a beneficiary as a fixed annuity or a fixed fraction of the value of the trust assets;

(c) From any amount that is permanently set aside for charitable purposes under a will or the terms of a trust unless both income and principal are so set aside;

(d) If possessing or exercising the power to adjust causes an individual to be treated as the owner of all or part of the trust for income tax purposes and the individual would not be treated as the owner if the trustee did not possess the power to adjust;

(e) If possessing or exercising the power to adjust causes all or part of the trust assets to be included for estate tax purposes in the estate of an individual who has the power to remove a trustee or appoint a trustee, or both, and the assets would not be included in the estate of the individual if the trustee did not possess the power to adjust;

(f) If the trustee is a beneficiary of the trust; or

(g) If the trustee is not a beneficiary of the trust but the adjustment would benefit the trustee directly or indirectly, except that in the case of a trustee whose compensation for acting as trustee is based upon the value of trust assets, an adjustment that affects the value of trust assets shall not be deemed to benefit the trustee.

(4) If paragraph (3)(d), paragraph (3)(e), paragraph (3)(f), or paragraph (3)(g) applies to a trustee and there is more than one trustee, a cotrustee to whom the provision does not apply may make the adjustment unless the exercise of the power by the remaining trustee is not permitted by the terms of the trust.

(5)

(a) A trustee may release the entire power to adjust conferred by subsection (1) if the trustee desires to convert an income trust to a total return unitrust pursuant to §738.1041.

(b) A trustee may release the entire power to adjust conferred by subsection (1) or may release only the power to adjust from income to principal or the power to adjust from principal to income if the trustee is uncertain about whether possessing or exercising the power will cause a result described in paragraphs (3)(a)-(e) or paragraph (3)(g) or if the trustee determines that possessing or exercising the power will or may deprive the trust of a tax benefit or impose a tax burden not described in subsection (3).

(c) A release under this subsection may be permanent or for a specified period, including a period measured by the life of an individual. Notwithstanding anything contrary to this subsection, a release of the power to adjust pursuant to paragraph (a) shall remain effective only for as long as the trust is administered as a unitrust pursuant to §738.1041.

(6) Terms of a trust that limit a trustee's power to adjust between principal and income do not affect the application of this section unless it is clear from the terms of the trust that the terms are intended to deny the trustee the power to adjust conferred by subsection (1).

(7) Nothing in this chapter is intended to create or imply a duty to make an adjustment and no inference of impropriety shall be made as a result of a trustee not exercising the power to adjust conferred by subsection (1).

(8) With respect to a trust in existence on January 1, 2003:

(a) A trustee shall not have the power to adjust under this section until the statement required in subsection (9) is provided and either no objection is made or any objection which is made has been terminated.

1. An objection is made if, within 60 days after the date of the statement required in subsection (9), a super majority of the eligible beneficiaries deliver to the trustee a written objection to the application of this section to such trust. An objection shall be deemed to be delivered to the trustee on the date the objection is mailed to the mailing address listed in the notice provided in subsection (9).

2. An objection is terminated upon the earlier of the receipt of consent from a super majority of eligible beneficiaries of the class that made the objection, or the resolution of the objection pursuant to paragraph (c).

(b) An objection or consent under this section may be executed by a legal representative or natural guardian of a beneficiary without the filing of any proceeding or approval of any court.

(c) If an objection is delivered to the trustee, then the trustee may petition the circuit court for an order quashing the objection and vesting in such trustee the power to adjust under this section. The burden will be on the objecting beneficiaries to prove that the power to adjust would be inequitable, illegal, or otherwise in contravention of the grantor's intent. The court may award costs and attorney's fees relating to the trustee's petition in the same manner as in chancery actions. When costs and attorney's fees are to be paid out of the trust, the court may, in its discretion, direct from which part of the trust they shall be paid.

(d) If no timely objection is made or if the trustee is vested with the power to adjust by court order, the trustee may thereafter exercise the power to adjust without providing notice of its intent to do so unless, in vesting the trustee with the power to adjust, the court determines that unusual circumstances require otherwise.

(e)

1. If a trustee makes a good faith effort to comply with the notice provisions of subsection (9), but fails to deliver notice to one or more

beneficiaries entitled to such notice, neither the validity of the notice required under this subsection nor the trustee's power to adjust under this section shall be affected until the trustee has actual notice that one or more beneficiaries entitled to notice were not notified. Until the trustee has actual notice of the notice deficiency, the trustee shall have all of the powers and protections granted a trustee with the power to adjust under this chapter.

2. When the trustee has actual notice that one or more beneficiaries entitled to notice under subsection (9) were not notified, the trustee's power to adjust under this section shall cease until all beneficiaries who are entitled to such notice, including those who were previously provided with such notice, are notified and given the opportunity to object as provided for under this subsection.

(f) The objection of a super majority of eligible beneficiaries under this subsection shall be valid for a period of 1 year after the date of the notice set forth in subsection (9). Upon expiration of the objection, the trustee may thereafter give a new notice under subsection (9).

(g) Nothing in this section is intended to create or imply a duty of the trustee of a trust existing on January 1, 2003, to seek a power to adjust pursuant to this subsection or to give the notice described in subsection (9) if the trustee does not desire to have a power to adjust under this section, and no inference of impropriety shall be made as the result of a trustee not seeking a power to adjust pursuant to this subsection.

(9)

(a) A trustee of a trust in existence on January 1, 2003, that is not prohibited under subsection (3) from exercising the power to adjust shall, any time prior to initially exercising the power, provide to all eligible beneficiaries a statement containing the following:

1. The name, telephone number, street address, and mailing address of the trustee and of any individuals who may be contacted for further information;

2. A statement that unless a super majority of the eligible beneficiaries objects to the application of this section to the trust within 60 days after the date the statement pursuant to this subsection was served, §738.104 shall apply to the trust; and

3. A statement that, if §738.104 applies to the trust, the trustee will have the power to adjust between income and principal and that such a power may have an effect on the distributions to such beneficiary from the trust.

(b) The statement may contain information regarding a trustee's fiduciary obligations with respect to the power to adjust between income and principal under this section.

(c) The statement referred to in this subsection shall be served informally, in the manner provided in the Florida Rules of Civil Procedure relating to service of pleadings subsequent to the initial pleading. The statement may be served on a legal representative or natural guardian of a beneficiary without the filing of any proceeding or approval of any court.

(d) For purposes of subsection (8) and this subsection, the term:

1. "Eligible beneficiaries" means:

a. If at the time the determination is made there is one or more beneficiaries described in §736.0103(14)(c), the beneficiaries described in §736.0103(14)(a) and (c); or

b. If there is no beneficiary described in §736.0103(14)(c), the beneficiaries described in §736.0103(14)(a) and (b).

2. "Super majority of the eligible beneficiaries" means:

a. If at the time the determination is made there is one or more beneficiaries described in §736.0103(14)(c), at least two-thirds in interest of the beneficiaries described in §736.0103(14)(a) or two-thirds in interest of the beneficiaries described in §736.0103(14)(c), if the interests of the beneficiaries are reasonably ascertainable; otherwise, it means two-thirds in number of either such class; or

b. If there is no beneficiary described in §736.0103(14)(c), at least two-thirds in interest of the beneficiaries described in §736.0103(14)(a) or two-thirds in interest of the beneficiaries described in §736.0103(14)(b), if the interests of the beneficiaries are reasonably ascertainable, otherwise, two-thirds in number of either such class.

(10) A trust exists on January 1, 2003, if it is not revocable on January 1, 2003. A trust is revocable if revocable by the grantor alone or in conjunction with any other person. A trust is not revocable for purposes of this section if revocable by the grantor only with the consent of all persons having a beneficial interest in the property.

(11) This section shall be construed as pertaining to the administration of a trust and is applicable to any trust that is administered either in this state or under Florida law.

(Laws 2002, ch. 2002-42, §1. Amended by Laws 2003, ch. 2003-43, §1, effective May 23, 2003; Laws 2005, ch. 2005-85, §5, effective July 1, 2005; Laws 2006, ch. 2006-217, §40, effective July 1, 2007.

§738.1041. Total return unitrust

(1) For purposes of this section, the term:

(a) "Disinterested person" means a person who is not a "related or subordinate party" as defined in §672(c) of the United States Internal Revenue Code, 26 U.S.C. § 1 et seq., or any successor provision thereof, with respect to the person then acting as trustee of the trust and excludes the grantor and any interested trustee.

(b) "Fair market value" means the fair market value of assets held by the trust as otherwise determined under this chapter, reduced by all known noncontingent liabilities.

(c) "Income trust" means a trust, created by either an inter vivos or a testamentary instrument, which directs or permits the trustee to distribute the net income of the trust to one or more persons, either in fixed proportions or in amounts or proportions determined by the trustee and regardless of whether the trust directs or permits the trustee to distribute the principal of the trust to one or more such persons.

(d) "Interested distributee" means a person to whom distributions of income or principal can currently be made who has the power to remove the existing trustee and designate as successor a person who may be a "related or subordinate party," as defined in the Internal Revenue Code, 26 U.S.C. §672(c), with respect to such distributee.

(e) "Interested trustee" means an individual trustee to whom the net income or principal of the trust can currently be distributed or would be distributed if the trust were then to terminate and be distributed, any trustee whom an interested distributee has the power to remove and replace with a related or subordinate party as defined in paragraph (d), or an individual trustee whose legal obligation to support a beneficiary may be satisfied by distributions of income and principal of the trust.

(f) "Unitrust amount" means the amount determined by multiplying the fair market value of the assets as defined in paragraph (b) by the percentage calculated under paragraph (2)(b).

(2) A trustee may, without court approval, convert an income trust to a total return unitrust, reconvert a total return unitrust to an income trust, or change the percentage used to calculate the unitrust amount or the method used to determine the fair market value of the trust if:

(a) The trustee adopts a written statement regarding trust distributions that provides:

1. In the case of a trust being administered as an income trust, that future distributions from the trust will be unitrust amounts rather than net income, and indicates the manner in which the unitrust amount will be calculated and the method in which the fair market value of the trust will be determined.

2. In the case of a trust being administered as a total return unitrust, that:

a. Future distributions from the trust will be net income rather than unitrust amounts; or

b. The percentage used to calculate the unitrust amount or the method used to determine the fair market value of the trust will be changed, and indicates the manner in which the new unitrust amount will be calculated and the method in which the new fair market value of the trust will be determined;

(b) The trustee determines the terms of the unitrust under one of the following methods:

1. A disinterested trustee determines, or if there is no trustee other than an interested trustee, the interested trustee appoints a disinterested person who, in its sole discretion but acting in a fiduciary capacity, determines for the interested trustee:

a. The percentage to be used to calculate the unitrust amount, provided the percentage used is not greater than 5 percent nor less than 3 percent;

b. The method to be used in determining the fair market value of the trust; and

c. Which assets, if any, are to be excluded in determining the unitrust amount; or

2. The interested trustee or disinterested trustee administers the trust such that:

a. The percentage used to calculate the unitrust amount is 50 percent of the applicable federal rate as defined in the Internal Revenue Code, 26 U.S.C. §7520, in effect for the month the conversion under this section becomes effective and for each January thereafter; however, if the percentage calculated exceeds 5 percent, the unitrust percentage shall be 5 percent and if the percentage calculated is less than 3 percent, the unitrust percentage shall be 3 percent; and

b. The fair market value of the trust shall be determined at least annually on an asset-by-asset basis, reasonably and in good faith, in accordance with the provisions of §738.202(5), except the following property shall not be included in determining the value of the trust:

(I) Any residential property or any tangible personal property that, as of the first business day of the current valuation year, one or more current beneficiaries of the trust have or have had the right to occupy, or have or have had the right to possess or control (other than in his or her capacity as trustee of the trust), and instead the right of occupancy or the right to possession and control shall be deemed to be the unitrust amount with respect to such property; however, the unitrust amount shall be adjusted to take into account partial distributions from or receipt into the trust of such property during the valuation year.

(II) Any asset specifically given to a beneficiary and the return on investment on such property, which return on investment shall be distributable to such beneficiary.

(III) Any asset while held in a testator's estate;

(c) The trustee sends written notice of its intention to take such action, along with copies of such written statement and this section, and, if applicable, the determinations of either the trustee or the disinterested person to:

1. The grantor of the trust, if living.

2. All living persons who are currently receiving or eligible to receive distributions of income of the trust.

3. All living persons who would receive distributions of principal of the trust if the trust were to terminate at the time of the giving of such notice (without regard to the exercise of any power of appointment) or, if the trust does not provide for its termination, all living persons who would receive or be eligible to receive distributions of income or principal of the trust if the persons identified in subparagraph 2. were deceased.

4. All persons acting as advisers or protectors of the trust.

5. Notice under this paragraph shall be served informally, in the manner provided in the Florida Rules of Civil Procedure relating to service of pleadings subsequent to the initial pleading. Notice may be served on a legal representative or natural guardian of a person without the filing of any proceeding or approval of any court;

(d) At least one person receiving notice under each of subparagraphs (c)2. and 3. is legally competent; and

(e) No person receiving such notice objects, by written instrument delivered to the trustee, to the proposed action of the trustee or the determinations of the disinterested person within 60 days after service of such notice. An objection under this section may be executed by a legal representative or natural guardian of a person without the filing of any proceeding or approval of any court.

(3) If a trustee desires to convert an income trust to a total return unitrust, reconvert a total return unitrust to an income trust, or change the percentage used to calculate the unitrust amount or the method used to determine a fair market value of the trust but does not have the ability to or elects not to do it under subsection (2), the trustee may petition the circuit court for such order as the trustee deems appropriate. In that event, the court, in its own discretion or on the petition of such trustee or any person having an income or remainder interest in the trust, may appoint a disinterested person who, acting in a fiduciary capacity, shall present such information to the court as shall be necessary for the court to make a determination hereunder.

(4) All determinations made pursuant to sub-subparagraph (2)(b)2.b shall be conclusive if reasonable and made in good faith. Such determination shall be conclusively presumed to have been made reasonably and in good faith unless proven otherwise in a proceeding commenced by or on behalf of a person interested in the trust within the time provided in §736.1008. The burden will be on the objecting interested party to prove that the determinations were not made reasonably and in good faith.

(5) Following the conversion of an income trust to a total return unitrust, the trustee:

(a) Shall treat the unitrust amount as if it were net income of the trust for purposes of determining the amount available, from time to time, for distribution from the trust.

(b) May allocate to trust income for each taxable year of the trust, or portion thereof:

1. Net short-term capital gain described in the Internal Revenue Code, 26 U.S.C. §1222(5), for such year, or portion thereof, but only to the extent that the amount so allocated together with all other amounts allocated to trust income, as determined under the provisions of this chapter without regard to this section and §738.104, for such year, or portion thereof, does not exceed the unitrust amount for such year, or portion thereof.

2. Net long-term capital gain described in the Internal Revenue Code, 26 U.S.C. §1222(7), for such year, or portion thereof, but only to the extent that the amount so allocated together with all other amounts, including amounts described in subparagraph 1., allocated to trust income for such year, or portion thereof, does not exceed the unitrust amount for such year, or portion thereof.

(6) In administering a total return unitrust, the trustee may, in its sole discretion but subject to the provisions of the governing instrument, determine:

(a) The effective date of the conversion.

(b) The timing of distributions, including provisions for prorating a distribution for a short year in which a beneficiary's right to payments commences or ceases.

(c) Whether distributions are to be made in cash or in kind or partly in cash and partly in kind.

(d) If the trust is reconverted to an income trust, the effective date of such reconversion.

(e) Such other administrative issues as may be necessary or appropriate to carry out the purposes of this section.

(7) Conversion to a total return unitrust under the provisions of this section shall not affect any other provision of the governing instrument, if any, regarding distributions of principal.

(8) Any trustee or disinterested person who in good faith takes or fails to take any action under this section shall not be liable to any person affected by such action or inaction, regardless of whether such person received written notice as provided in this section and regardless of whether such person was under a legal disability at the time of the delivery of such notice. Such person's exclusive remedy shall be to obtain, under subsection (9), an order of the court directing the trustee to convert an income trust to a total return unitrust, to reconvert from a total return unitrust to an income trust, or to change the percentage used to calculate the unitrust amount. If a court determines that the trustee or disinterested person has not acted in good faith in taking or failing to take any action under this section, the provisions of §738.105(3) apply.

(9) If a majority in interest of either the income or remainder beneficiaries of an income trust has delivered to the trustee a written objection to the amount of the income distributions of the trust, and, if the trustee has failed to resolve the objection to the satisfaction of the objecting beneficiaries within 6 months from the receipt of such written objection, then the objecting beneficiaries may petition the court in accordance with subsection (3).

(10) This section shall be construed as pertaining to the administration of a trust and is applicable to any trust that is administered either in this state or under Florida law unless:

(a) The governing instrument reflects an intention that the current beneficiary or beneficiaries are to receive an amount other than a reasonable current return from the trust;

(b) The trust is a trust described in the Internal Revenue Code, 26 U.S.C. §170(f)(2)(B), §642(c)(5), §664(d), §2702(a)(3), or §2702(b);

(c) One or more persons to whom the trustee could distribute income have a power of withdrawal over the trust:

1. That is not subject to an ascertainable standard under the Internal Revenue Code, 26 U.S.C. §2041 or §2514, and exceeds in any calendar year the amount set forth in the Internal Revenue Code, 26 U.S.C. §2041(b)(2) or §2514(e); or

2. A power of withdrawal over the trust that can be exercised to discharge a duty of support he or she possesses;

(d) The governing instrument expressly prohibits use of this section by specific reference to the section. A provision in the governing instrument that, "The provisions of section 738.1041, Florida Statutes, as amended, or any corresponding provision of future law, shall not be used in the administration of this trust," or similar words reflecting such intent shall be sufficient to preclude the use of this section; or

(e) The trust is a trust with respect to which a trustee currently possesses the power to adjust under §738.104.

(11) The grantor of a trust may create an express total return unitrust which will become effective as provided in the trust document without requiring a conversion under this section. An express total return unitrust created by the grantor of the trust shall be treated as a unitrust under this section only if the terms of the trust document contain all of the following provisions:

(a) That distributions from the trust will be unitrust amounts and the manner in which the unitrust amount will be calculated and the method in which the fair market value of the trust will be determined.

(b) The percentage to be used to calculate the unitrust amount, provided the percentage used is not greater than 5 percent nor less than 3 percent.

(c) The method to be used in determining the fair market value of the trust.

(d) Which assets, if any, are to be excluded in determining the unitrust amount.

(Laws 2002, ch. 2002-42, §1, effective January 1, 2003. Amended by Laws 2003, ch. 2003-43, §2, effective May 23, 2003; Laws 2005, ch. 2005-85, §6, effective July 1, 2005.)

§738.105. Judicial control of fiduciary's discretionary powers

(1) A court shall not change a fiduciary's decision to exercise or not to exercise a discretionary power conferred by this chapter unless the court determines that the decision was an abuse of the fiduciary's discretion. A court shall not determine that a fiduciary abused its discretion merely because the court would have exercised the discretion in a different manner or would not have exercised the discretion.

(2) The decisions to which subsection (1) applies include:

(a) A determination under §738.104(1) of whether and to what extent an amount should be transferred from principal to income or from income to principal.

(b) A determination of the factors that are relevant to the trust and trust beneficiaries, the extent to which such factors are relevant, and the weight, if any, to be given to the relevant factors, in deciding whether and to what extent to exercise the power conferred by §738.104(1).

(3) If a court determines that a fiduciary has abused its discretion, the remedy shall be to restore the income and remainder beneficiaries to the positions they would have occupied if the fiduciary had not abused its discretion, according to the following rules:

(a) To the extent the abuse of discretion has resulted in no distribution to a beneficiary or a distribution that is too small, the court shall require the fiduciary to distribute from the trust to the beneficiary an amount the court determines will restore the beneficiary, in whole or in part, to his or her appropriate position.

(b) To the extent the abuse of discretion has resulted in a distribution to a beneficiary that is too large, the court shall restore the beneficiaries, the trust, or both, in whole or in part, to their appropriate positions by requiring the fiduciary to withhold an amount from one or more future distributions to the beneficiary who received the distribution that was too large or requiring that beneficiary to return some or all of the distribution to the trust.

(c) To the extent the court is unable, after applying paragraphs (a) and (b), to restore the beneficiaries, the trust, or both, to the positions they would have occupied if the fiduciary had not abused its discretion, the court may require the fiduciary to pay an appropriate amount from its own funds to one or more of the beneficiaries or the trust or both.

(4) Upon the filing of a petition by the fiduciary, the court having jurisdiction over the trust or estate shall determine whether a proposed exercise or nonexercise by the fiduciary of a discretionary power conferred by this chapter will result in an abuse of the fiduciary's discretion. If the petition describes the proposed exercise or nonexercise of the power and contains sufficient information to inform the beneficiaries of the reasons for the proposal, the facts upon which the fiduciary relies, and an explanation of how the income and remainder beneficiaries will be affected by the proposed exercise or nonexercise of the power, a beneficiary who challenges the proposed exercise or nonexercise has the burden of establishing that such exercise or nonexercise will result in an abuse of discretion.

(5) If an action is instituted alleging an abuse of discretion in the exercise or nonexercise of the power of adjustment conferred by §738.104(1) and the court determines that no abuse of discretion has occurred, the trustee's costs and attorney's fees incurred in defending the action shall be paid from the trust assets.

(Laws 2002, ch. 2002-42, §1, effective January 1, 2003.)

§738.201. Fiduciary shall determine and distribute net income

After a decedent dies, in the case of an estate, or after an income interest in a trust ends, the following rules apply:

(1) A fiduciary of an estate or of a terminating income interest shall determine the amount of net income and net principal receipts received from property specifically given to a beneficiary under the rules in §§738.301-738.706 which apply to trustees and the rules in subsection (5). The fiduciary shall distribute the net income and net principal receipts to the beneficiary who is to receive the specific property.

(2) A fiduciary shall determine the remaining net income of a decedent's estate or a terminating income interest under the rules in §§738.301-738.706 which apply to trustees and by:

(a) Including in net income all income from property used to discharge liabilities.

(b) Paying from income or principal, in the fiduciary's discretion, fees of attorneys, accountants, and fiduciaries; court costs and other expenses of administration; and interest on death taxes, but the fiduciary may pay those expenses from income of property passing to a trust for which the fiduciary claims an estate tax marital or charitable deduction only to the extent the payment of those expenses from income will not cause the reduction or loss of the deduction.

(c) Paying from principal all other disbursements made or incurred in connection with the settlement of a decedent's estate or the winding up of a terminating income interest, including debts, funeral expenses, disposition of remains, family allowances, and death taxes and related penalties that are apportioned to the estate or terminating income interest by the will, the terms of the trust, or applicable law.

(3) A fiduciary shall distribute to a beneficiary who receives a pecuniary amount outright the interest or any other amount provided by the will, the terms of the trust, or applicable law from net income determined under subsection (2) or from principal to the extent net income is insufficient. If a beneficiary is to receive a pecuniary amount outright from a trust after an income interest ends and no interest or other amount is provided for by the terms of the trust or applicable law, the fiduciary shall distribute the interest or other amount to which the beneficiary would be entitled under applicable law if the pecuniary amount were required to be paid under a will.

(4) A fiduciary shall distribute the net income remaining after distributions required by subsection (3) in the manner described in §738.202 to all other beneficiaries, including a beneficiary who receives a pecuniary amount in trust, even if the beneficiary holds an unqualified power to withdraw assets from the trust or other presently exercisable general power of appointment over the trust.

(5) A fiduciary may not reduce principal or income receipts from property described in subsection (1) because of a payment described in §738.701 or §738.702 to the extent the will, the terms of the trust, or applicable law requires the fiduciary to make the payment from assets other than the property or to the extent the fiduciary recovers or expects to recover the payment from a third party. The net income and principal receipts from the property are determined by including all of the amounts the fiduciary receives or pays with respect to the property, whether those amounts accrued or became due before, on, or after the date of a decedent's death or an income interest's terminating event, and by making a reasonable provision for amounts the fiduciary believes the estate or terminating income interest may become obligated to pay after the property is distributed.

(Laws 2002, ch. 2002-42, §1, effective January 1, 2003.)

§738.202 Beneficiary's right to receive assets

(1) Each beneficiary described in §738.201(4) is entitled to receive a portion of the net income equal to the beneficiary's fractional interest in undistributed principal assets, using values as of the distribution date. If a fiduciary makes more than one distribution of assets to beneficiaries to whom this section applies, each beneficiary, including one who does not receive part of the distribution, is entitled, as of each distribution date, to the net income the fiduciary has received after the date of death or terminating event or earlier distribution date but has not distributed as of the current distribution date.

(2) In determining a beneficiary's share of net income, the following rules apply:

(a) The beneficiary is entitled to receive a portion of the net income equal to the beneficiary's fractional interest in the undistributed principal assets immediately before the distribution date, including assets that later may be sold to meet principal obligations.

(b) The beneficiary's fractional interest in the undistributed principal assets shall be calculated without regard to property specifically given to a beneficiary and property required to pay pecuniary amounts not in trust.

(c) The beneficiary's fractional interest in the undistributed principal assets shall be calculated on the basis of the aggregate value of those assets as of the distribution date without reducing the value by any unpaid principal obligation.

(d) The distribution date for purposes of this section may be the date as of which the fiduciary calculates the value of the assets if that date is reasonably near the date on which assets are actually distributed.

(3) If a fiduciary does not distribute all of the collected but undistributed net income to each person as of a distribution date, the fiduciary shall maintain appropriate records showing the interest of each beneficiary in that net income.

(4) A fiduciary may apply the rules in this section, to the extent the fiduciary considers appropriate, to net gain or loss realized after the date of death or terminating event or earlier distribution date from the disposition of a principal asset if this section applies to the income from the asset.

(5) The value of trust assets shall be determined on an asset-by-asset basis and shall be conclusive if reasonable and determined in good faith. Determinations based on appraisals performed within 2 years before or after the valuation date shall be presumed reasonable. The value of trust assets

shall be conclusively presumed to be reasonable and determined in good faith unless proven otherwise in a proceeding commenced by or on behalf of a person interested in the trust within the time provided in §737.307.

(Laws 2002, ch. 2002-42, §1, effective January 1, 2003.)

§738.301 Determination of date when income beneficiary becomes entitled to net income

An income beneficiary is entitled to net income from the date on which the income interest begins.

(1) An income interest begins on the date specified in the terms of the trust or, if no date is specified, on the date an asset becomes subject to a trust or successive income interest.

(2) An asset becomes subject to a trust:

(a) On the date the asset is transferred to the trust in the case of an asset that is transferred to a trust during the transferor's life;

(b) On the date of a testator's death in the case of an asset that becomes subject to a trust by reason of a will, even if there is an intervening period of administration of the testator's estate; or

(c) On the date of an individual's death in the case of an asset that is transferred to a fiduciary by a third party because of the individual's death.

(3) An asset becomes subject to a successive income interest on the day after the preceding income interest ends, as determined under subsection (4), even if there is an intervening period of administration to wind up the preceding income interest.

(4) An income interest ends on the day before an income beneficiary dies or another terminating event occurs, or on the last day of a period during which there is no beneficiary to whom a trustee may distribute income.

(Laws 2002, ch. 2002-42, §1, effective January 1, 2003.)

§738.302 Trustee's apportionment of receipts and disbursements when decedent dies or income interest begins

(1) A trustee shall allocate an income receipt or disbursement other than one to which §738.201(1) applies to principal if the due date of the receipt or disbursement occurs before a decedent dies in the case of an estate or before an income interest begins in the case of a trust or successive income interest.

(2) A trustee shall allocate an income receipt or disbursement to income if the due date of the receipt or disbursement occurs on or after the date on which a decedent dies or an income interest begins and the due date is a periodic due date. An income receipt or disbursement shall be treated as accruing from day to day if the due date of the receipt or disbursement is not periodic or the receipt or disbursement has no due date. The portion of the receipt or disbursement accruing before the date on which a decedent dies or an income interest begins shall be allocated to principal and the balance shall be allocated to income.

(3) An item of income or an obligation is due on the date the payor is required to make a payment. If a payment date is not stated, there is no due date for the purposes of this chapter. Distributions to shareholders or other owners from an entity to which §738.401 applies are deemed to be due on the date fixed by the entity for determining who is entitled to receive the distribution or, if no date is fixed, on the declaration date for the distribution. A due date is periodic for receipts or disbursements that shall be paid at regular intervals under a lease or an obligation to pay interest or if an entity customarily makes distributions at regular intervals.

(4) Nothing in this section shall prevent the application of §733.817 to apportion tax to the income recipient under this section.

(Laws 2002, ch. 2002-42, §1, effective January 1, 2003.)

§738.303 Trustee's obligation to apportion when income interest ends

(1) For purposes of this section, "undistributed income" means net income received on or before the date on which an income interest ends. The term does not include an item of income or expense that is due or accrued or net income that has been added or is required to be added to principal under the terms of the trust. In the case of a trust being administered as a unitrust under §738.1041, the term "undistributed income" means the prorated unitrust amount computed on a daily basis through the date on which the income interest ends.

(2) When a mandatory income interest ends, the trustee shall pay to a mandatory income beneficiary who survives that date, or the estate of a deceased mandatory income beneficiary whose death causes the interest to end, the beneficiary's share of the undistributed income that is not disposed of under the terms of the trust unless the beneficiary has an unqualified power to revoke more than 5 percent of the trust immediately before the income interest ends. In the latter case, the undistributed income from the portion of the trust that may be revoked shall be added to principal.

(3) When a trustee's obligation to pay a fixed annuity or a fixed fraction of the value of the trust's assets ends, the trustee shall prorate the final

payment if and to the extent required by applicable law to accomplish a purpose of the trust or its grantor relating to income, gift, estate, or other tax requirements.

(Laws 2002, ch. 2002-42, §1, effective January 1, 2003.)

§738.401 Character of receipts that trustee shall allocate

(1) For purposes of this section, "entity" means a corporation, partnership, limited liability company, regulated investment company, real estate investment trust, common trust fund, or any other organization in which a trustee has an interest other than a trust or estate to which §738.402 applies, a business or activity to which §738.403 applies, or an asset-backed security to which §738.608 applies.

(2) Except as otherwise provided in this section, a trustee shall allocate to income money received from an entity.

(3) Except as otherwise provided in this section, a trustee shall allocate the following receipts from an entity to principal:

(a) Property other than money.

(b) Money received in one distribution or a series of related distributions in exchange for part or all of a trust's interest in the entity.

(c) Money received in total or partial liquidation of the entity.

(d) Money received from an entity that is a regulated investment company or a real estate investment trust if the money distributed represents short-term or long-term capital gain realized within the entity.

(4) If a trustee elects, or continues an election made by its predecessor, to reinvest dividends in shares of stock of a distributing corporation or fund, whether evidenced by new certificates or entries on the books of the distributing entity, the new shares shall retain their character as income.

(5) Money is received in partial liquidation:

(a) To the extent the entity, at or near the time of a distribution, indicates that such money is a distribution in partial liquidation; or

(b) If the total amount of money and property received in a distribution or series of related distributions is greater than 20 percent of the entity's gross assets, as shown by the entity's year-end financial statements immediately preceding the initial receipt.

(6) Money is not received in partial liquidation, nor may money be taken into account under paragraph (5)(b), to the extent such money does not exceed the amount of income tax a trustee or beneficiary must pay on taxable income of the entity that distributes the money.

(7) The following special rules shall apply to moneys or property received by a private trustee from entities described in this subsection:

(a) Moneys or property received from a targeted entity that is not an investment entity which do not exceed the trust's pro rata share of the undistributed cumulative net income of the targeted entity during the time an ownership interest in the targeted entity was held by the trust shall be allocated to income. The balance of moneys or property received from a targeted entity shall be allocated to principal.

(b) If trust assets include any interest in an investment entity, the designated amount of moneys or property received from the investment entity shall be treated by the trustee in the same manner as if the trustee had directly held the trust's pro rata share of the assets of the investment entity attributable to the distribution of such designated amount. Thereafter, distributions shall be treated as principal.

(c) For purposes of this subsection, the following definitions shall apply:

1. "Cumulative net income" means the targeted entity's net income as determined using the method of accounting regularly used by the targeted entity in preparing its financial statements, or if no financial statements are prepared, the net book income computed for federal income tax purposes, for every year an ownership interest in the entity is held by the trust. The trust's pro rata share shall be the cumulative net income multiplied by the percentage ownership of the trust.

2. "Designated amount" means moneys or property received from an investment entity during any year that is equal to the amount of the distribution that does not exceed the greater of:

a. The amount of income of the investment entity for the current year, as reported to the trustee by the investment entity for federal income tax purposes; or

b. The amount of income of the investment entity for the current year and the prior 2 years, as reported to the trustee by the investment entity for federal income tax purposes, less any distributions of moneys or property made by the investment entity to the trustee during the prior 2 years.

3. "Investment entity" means a targeted entity that normally derives 50 percent or more of its annual cumulative net income from

interest, dividends, annuities, royalties, rental activity, or other passive investments, including income from the sale or exchange of such passive investments.

4. "Private trustee" means a trustee who is an individual, but only if the trustee is unable to utilize the power to adjust between income and principal with respect to receipts from entities described in this subsection pursuant to §738.104. A bank, trust company, or other commercial trustee shall not be considered to be a private trustee.

5. "Targeted entity" means any entity that is treated as a partnership, subchapter S corporation, or disregarded entity pursuant to the Internal Revenue Code of 1986, as amended, other than an entity described in §738.403.

6. "Undistributed cumulative net income" means the trust's pro rata share of cumulative net income, less all prior distributions from the targeted entity to the trust that have been allocated to income.

(d) This subsection shall not be construed to modify or change any of the provisions of §§738.705 and 738.706 relating to income taxes.

(8) A trustee may rely upon a statement made by an entity about the source or character of a distribution, about the amount of profits of a targeted entity, or about the nature and value of assets of an investment entity if the statement is made at or near the time of distribution by the entity's board of directors or other person or group of persons authorized to exercise powers to pay money or transfer property comparable to those of a corporation's board of directors.

(Laws 2002, ch. 2002-42, §1, effective January 1, 2003. Amended by Laws 2003, ch. 2003-43, §4, effective May 23, 2003; Laws 2005, ch. 2005-85, §8, effective July1, 2005.)

§738.402 Distribution of income and principal from trust or estate

A trustee shall allocate to income an amount received as a distribution of income from a trust or an estate in which the trust has an interest other than a purchased interest and shall allocate to principal an amount received as a distribution of principal from such a trust or estate. If a trustee purchases an interest in a trust that is an investment entity, or a decedent or donor transfers an interest in such a trust to a trustee, §738.401 or §738.608 applies to a receipt from the trust.

(Laws 2002, ch. 2002-42, §1, effective January 1, 2003.)

§738.403. Allocation by trustee who conducts a business

(1) If a trustee who conducts a business or other activity determines that it is in the best interest of all the beneficiaries to account separately for the business or activity instead of accounting for the business or activity as part of the trust's general accounting records, the trustee may maintain separate accounting records for the transactions of such business or other activity, whether or not the assets of such business or activity are segregated from other trust assets.

(2) A trustee who accounts separately for a business or other activity may determine the extent to which the net cash receipts of such business or activity must be retained for working capital, the acquisition or replacement of fixed assets, and other reasonably foreseeable needs of the business or activity, and the extent to which the remaining net cash receipts are accounted for as principal or income in the trust's general accounting records. If a trustee sells assets of the business or other activity, other than in the ordinary course of the business or activity, the trustee shall account for the net amount received as principal in the trust's general accounting records to the extent the trustee determines that the amount received is no longer required in the conduct of the business.

(3) Activities for which a trustee may maintain separate accounting records include:

(a) Retail, manufacturing, service, and other traditional business activities.

(b) Farming.

(c) Raising and selling livestock and other animals.

(d) Management of rental properties.

(e) Extraction of minerals and other natural resources.

(f) Timber operations.

(g) Activities to which §738.608 applies.

(Laws 2002, ch. 2002-42, §1, effective January 1, 2003.)

§738.501 Trustee shall allocate certain assets to principal

A trustee shall allocate to principal:

(1) To the extent not allocated to income under this chapter, assets received from a transferor during the transferor's lifetime, a decedent's estate, a trust with a terminating income interest, or a payor under a contract naming the trust or its trustee as beneficiary.

(2) Money or other property received from the sale, exchange, liquidation, or change in form of a principal asset, including realized profit, subject to this section.

(3) Amounts recovered from third parties to reimburse the trust because of disbursements described in §738.702(1)(g) or for other reasons to the extent not based on the loss of income.

(4) Proceeds of property taken by eminent domain but a separate award made for the loss of income with respect to an accounting period during which a current income beneficiary had a mandatory income interest is income.

(5) Net income received in an accounting period during which there is no beneficiary to whom a trustee may or shall distribute income.

(6) Other receipts as provided in §§738.601-738.608.

(Laws 2002, ch. 2002-42, §1, effective January 1, 2003.)

§738.502 Allocation of receipts from rental property

To the extent a trustee accounts for receipts from rental property pursuant to this section, the trustee shall allocate to income an amount received as rent of real or personal property, including an amount received for cancellation or renewal of a lease. An amount received as a refundable deposit, including a security deposit or a deposit that is to be applied as rent for future periods, shall be added to principal and held subject to the terms of the lease and is not available for distribution to a beneficiary until the trustee's contractual obligations have been satisfied with respect to that amount.

(Laws 2002, ch. 2002-42, §1, effective January 1, 2003.)

§738.503 Allocation of interest or obligation to pay money

(1) An amount received as interest, whether determined at a fixed, variable, or floating rate, on an obligation to pay money to the trustee, including an amount received as consideration for prepaying principal, shall be allocated to income without any provision for amortization of premium.

(2) Except as otherwise provided herein, a trustee shall allocate to principal an amount received from the sale, redemption, or other disposition of an obligation to pay money to the trustee.

(3) The increment in value of a bond or other obligation for the payment of money bearing no stated interest but payable at a future time in excess of the price at which it was issued or purchased, if purchased after issuance, is distributable as income. If the increment in value accrues and becomes payable pursuant to a fixed schedule of appreciation, it may be distributed to the beneficiary who was the income beneficiary at this time of increment from the first principal cash available or, if none is available, when the increment is realized by sale, redemption, or other disposition. When unrealized increment is distributed as income but out of principal, the principal shall be reimbursed for the increment when realized. If, in the reasonable judgment of the trustee, exercised in good faith, the ultimate payment of the bond principal is in doubt, the trustee may withhold the payment of incremental interest to the income beneficiary.

(4) This section does not apply to an obligation to which §738.602, §738.603, §738.604, §738.605, §738.607, or §738.608 applies.

(Laws 2002, ch. 2002-42, §1, effective January 1, 2003.)

§738.504 Allocation of proceeds of insurance policies and similar contracts

(1) Except as otherwise provided in subsection (2), a trustee shall allocate to principal the proceeds of a life insurance policy or other contract in which the trust or its trustee is named as beneficiary, including a contract that insures the trust or its trustee against loss for damage to, destruction of, or loss of title to a trust asset. The trustee shall allocate dividends on an insurance policy to income if the premiums on the policy are paid from income and to principal if the premiums are paid from principal.

(2) A trustee shall allocate to income proceeds of a contract that insures the trustee against loss of occupancy or other use by an income beneficiary, loss of income, or, subject to §738.403, loss of profits from a business.

(3) This section does not apply to a contract to which §738.602 applies.

(Laws 2002, ch. 2002-42, §1, effective January 1, 2003.)

§738.601 Allocation if amount is insubstantial

If a trustee determines that an allocation between principal and income required by §738.602, §738.603, §738.604, §738.605, or §738.608 is insubstantial, the trustee may allocate the entire amount to principal unless one of the circumstances described in §738.104(3) applies to the allocation. This power may be exercised by a cotrustee in the circumstances described in §738.104(4) and may be released for the reasons and in the manner described in §738.104(5). An allocation is presumed to be insubstantial if:

(1) The amount of the allocation would increase or decrease net income in an accounting period, as

determined before the allocation, by less than 10 percent; or

(2) The value of the asset producing the receipt for which the allocation would be made is less than 10 percent of the total value of the trust's assets at the beginning of the accounting period.

(Laws 2002, ch. 2002-42, §1, effective January 1, 2003.)

§738.602 Allocation of deferred compensation, annuities, and similar payments

(1) For purposes of this section, "payment" means a payment that a trustee may receive over a fixed number of years or during the life of one or more individuals because of services rendered or property transferred to the payor in exchange for future payments. The term includes a payment made in money or property from the payor's general assets or from a separate fund created by the payor, including a private or commercial annuity, an individual retirement account, and a pension, profit-sharing, stock-bonus, or stock-ownership plan.

(2) With respect to payments that may be characterized as interest, dividends, or their equivalent:

(a) A trustee shall allocate to income in the following order:

1. First, payments characterized by the payor as interest or dividends or as a payment made in lieu of interest or dividends.

2. Second, all other payments to the extent that the trustee, reasonably and in good faith, determines that such payments represent interest, dividends, or their equivalent.

(b) A trustee shall allocate to principal the balance of any payment not characterized as, or otherwise determined to be, interest, dividends, or their equivalent.

(3) If no part of a payment is characterized as, or otherwise determined to be, interest, a dividend, or an equivalent payment and all or part of the payment is required to be made, a trustee shall allocate to income 10 percent of the part that is required to be made during the accounting period and the balance to principal. If no part of a payment is required to be made or the payment received is the entire amount to which the trustee is entitled, the trustee shall allocate the entire payment to principal. For purposes of this subsection, a payment is not "required to be made" to the extent the payment is made because the trustee exercises a right of withdrawal.

(4) If, to obtain an estate tax marital deduction for a trust, a trustee must allocate more of a payment to income than provided for by this section, the trustee shall allocate to income the additional amount necessary to obtain the marital deduction.

(5) This section does not apply to payments to which §738.603 applies.

(Laws 2002, ch. 2002-42, §1, effective January 1, 2003.)

§738.603 Allocation of receipts from liquidating asset

(1) For purposes of this section, "liquidating asset" means an asset the value of which will diminish or terminate because the asset is expected to produce receipts for a period of limited duration. The term includes a leasehold, patent, copyright, royalty right, and right to receive payments during a period of more than 1 year under an arrangement that does not provide for the payment of interest on the unpaid balance. The term does not include a payment subject to §738.602, resources subject to §738.604, timber subject to §738.605, an activity subject to §738.607, an asset subject to §738.608, or any asset for which the trustee establishes a reserve for depreciation under §738.703.

(2) A trustee shall allocate to income 10 percent of the receipts from a liquidating asset and the balance to principal.

(Laws 2002, ch. 2002-42, §1, effective January 1, 2003.)

§738.604. Allocation of receipts from interest in minerals, water, and other natural resources

(1) To the extent a trustee accounts for receipts from an interest in minerals or other natural resources pursuant to this section, the trustee shall allocate such receipts as follows:

(a) If received as nominal delay rental or nominal annual rent on a lease, a receipt shall be allocated to income.

(b) If received from a production payment, a receipt shall be allocated to income if and to the extent the agreement creating the production payment provides a factor for interest or its equivalent. The balance shall be allocated to principal.

(c) If an amount received as a royalty, shut-in-well payment, take-or-pay payment, bonus, or delay rental is more than nominal, 90 percent shall be allocated to principal and the balance to income.

(d) If an amount is received from a working interest or any other interest not provided for in paragraph (a), paragraph (b), or paragraph (c), 90 percent of the net amount received shall be allocated to principal and the balance to income.

(2) An amount received on account of an interest in water that is renewable shall be allocated to income. If the water is not renewable, 90 percent of the amount shall be allocated to principal and the balance to income.

(3) This chapter applies whether or not a decedent or donor was extracting minerals, water, or other natural resources before the interest became subject to the trust.

(4) If a trust owns an interest in minerals, water, or other natural resources on January 1, 2003, the trustee may allocate receipts from the interest as provided in this chapter or in the manner used by the trustee before January 1, 2003. If the trust acquires an interest in minerals, water, or other natural resources after January 1, 2003, the trustee shall allocate receipts from the interest as provided in this chapter.

(Laws 2002, ch. 2002-42, §1, effective January 1, 2003.)

§738.605. Allocation of receipts from sale of timber

(1) To the extent a trustee accounts for receipts from the sale of timber and related products pursuant to this section, the trustee shall allocate the net receipts:

(a) To income to the extent the amount of timber removed from the land does not exceed the rate of growth of the timber during the accounting periods in which a beneficiary has a mandatory income interest;

(b) To principal to the extent the amount of timber removed from the land exceeds the rate of growth of the timber or the net receipts are from the sale of standing timber;

(c) To or between income and principal if the net receipts are from the lease of timberland or from a contract to cut timber from land owned by a trust by determining the amount of timber removed from the land under the lease or contract and applying the rules in paragraphs (a) and (b); or

(d) To principal to the extent advance payments, bonuses, and other payments are not allocated pursuant to paragraph (a), paragraph (b), or paragraph (c).

(2) In determining net receipts to be allocated pursuant to subsection (1), a trustee shall deduct and transfer to principal a reasonable amount for depletion.

(3) This chapter applies whether or not a decedent or transferor was harvesting timber from the property before the property became subject to the trust.

(4) If a trust owns an interest in timberland on January 1, 2003, the trustee may allocate net receipts from the sale of timber and related products as provided in this chapter or in the manner used by the trustee before January 1, 2003. If the trust acquires an interest in timberland after January 1, 2003, the trustee shall allocate net receipts from the sale of timber and related products as provided in this chapter.

(Laws 2002, ch. 2002-42, §1, effective January 1, 2003.)

§738.606 Trustee's obligation regarding property not productive of income

(1) If a marital deduction is allowed for all or part of a trust the income of which is required to be distributed to the grantor's spouse and the assets of which consist substantially of property that does not provide the spouse with sufficient income from or use of the trust assets, and if the amounts the trustee transfers from principal to income under §738.104 and distributes to the spouse from principal pursuant to the terms of the trust are insufficient to provide the spouse with the beneficial enjoyment required to obtain the marital deduction, the spouse may require the trustee to make property productive of income, convert property within a reasonable time, or exercise the power conferred by §§738.104 and 738.1041. The trustee may decide which action or combination of actions to take.

(2) In cases not governed by subsection (1), proceeds from the sale or other disposition of an asset are principal without regard to the amount of income the asset produces during any accounting period.

(Laws 2002, ch. 2002-42, §1, effective January 1, 2003.)

§738.607. Trustee's obligation to account for derivatives and options

(1) For purposes of this section, "derivative" means a contract or financial instrument or a combination of contracts and financial instruments which gives a trust the right or obligation to participate in some or all changes in the price of a tangible or intangible asset or group of assets, or changes in a rate, an index of prices or rates, or other market indicator for an asset or a group of assets.

(2) To the extent a trustee does not account under §738.403 for transactions in derivatives, the trustee shall allocate to principal receipts from and disbursements made in connection with those transactions.

(3) If a trustee grants an option to buy property from the trust whether or not the trust owns the property when the option is granted, grants an option that permits another person to sell property to the trust, or acquires an option to buy property for the trust or an option to sell an asset owned by the trust, and the trustee or other owner of the asset is required to deliver the asset if the option is exercised, an amount received for granting the option shall be allocated to principal. An amount paid to acquire the option shall be paid from principal. A gain or loss realized upon the exercise of an option, including an option granted to a grantor of the trust for services rendered, shall be allocated to principal.
(Laws 2002, ch. 2002-42, §1, effective January 1, 2003.)

§738.608. Asset-backed securities

(1) For purposes of this section, "asset-backed security" means an asset the value of which is based upon the right given the owner to receive distributions from the proceeds of financial assets that provide collateral for the security. The term includes an asset that gives the owner the right to receive from the collateral financial assets only the interest or other current return or only the proceeds other than interest or current return. The term does not include an asset to which §738.401 or §738.602 applies.

(2) If a trust receives a payment from interest or other current return and from other proceeds of the collateral financial assets, the trustee shall allocate to income the portion of the payment which the payor identifies as being from interest or other current return and shall allocate the balance of the payment to principal.

(3) If a trust receives one or more payments in exchange for the trust's entire interest in an asset-backed security during a single accounting period, the trustee shall allocate the payments to principal. If a payment is one of a series of payments that will result in the liquidation of the trust's interest in the security over more than a single accounting period, the trustee shall allocate 10 percent of the payment to income and the balance to principal.
(Laws 2002, ch. 2002-42, §1, effective January 1, 2003.)

§738.701. Special disbursements from income

A trustee shall make the following disbursements from income to the extent they are not disbursements to which §738.201(2)(a) or (c) applies:

(1) One-half of the regular compensation of the trustee and of any person providing investment advisory or custodial services to the trustee.

(2) One-half of all expenses for accountings, judicial proceedings, or other matters that involve both the income and remainder interests.

(3) All of the other ordinary expenses incurred in connection with the administration, management, or preservation of trust property and the distribution of income, including interest, ordinary repairs, regularly recurring taxes assessed against principal, and expenses of a proceeding or other matter that concerns primarily the income interest.

(4) Recurring premiums on insurance covering the loss of a principal asset or the loss of income from or use of the asset.
(Laws 2002, ch. 2002-42, §1, effective January 1, 2003.)

§738.702. Special disbursements from principal

(1) A trustee shall make the following disbursements from principal:

(a) The remaining one-half of the disbursements described in §738.701(1) and (2).

(b) All of the trustee's compensation calculated on principal as a fee for acceptance, distribution, or termination and disbursements made to prepare property for sale.

(c) Payments on the principal of a trust debt.

(d) Expenses of a proceeding that concerns primarily principal, including a proceeding to construe the trust or to protect the trust or its property.

(e) Premiums paid on a policy of insurance not described in §738.701(4) of which the trust is the owner and beneficiary.

(f) Estate, inheritance, and other transfer taxes, including penalties, apportioned to the trust.

(g) Disbursements related to environmental matters, including reclamation, assessing environmental conditions, remedying and removing environmental contamination, monitoring remedial activities and the release of substances, preventing future releases of substances, collecting amounts from persons liable or potentially liable for the costs of such activities, penalties imposed under environmental laws or regulations and other payments made to comply with those laws or regulations, statutory or common law claims by third parties, and defending claims based on environmental matters.

(h) Payments representing extraordinary repairs or expenses incurred in making a capital improvement to principal, including special assessments; however, a trustee may establish an allowance for depreciation out of income to the extent permitted by §738.703.

(2) If a principal asset is encumbered with an obligation that requires income from that asset to be paid directly to the creditor, the trustee shall transfer from principal to income an amount equal to the income paid to the creditor in reduction of the principal balance of the obligation.

(Laws 2002, ch. 2002-42, §1, effective January 1, 2003.)

§738.703. Transfers from income to principal for depreciation

(1) For purposes of this section, "depreciation" means a reduction in value due to wear, tear, decay, corrosion, or gradual obsolescence of a fixed asset having a useful life of more than 1 year.

(2) A trustee may transfer to principal a reasonable amount of the net cash receipts from a principal asset that is subject to depreciation but may not transfer any amount for depreciation:

(a) Of that portion of real property used or available for use by a beneficiary as a residence or of tangible personal property held or made available for the personal use or enjoyment of a beneficiary;

(b) During the administration of a decedent's estate; or

(c) Under this section if the trustee is accounting under §738.403 for the business or activity in which the asset is used.

(3) The amount of depreciation taken for tax purposes with respect to an asset shall be presumed to be a reasonable amount of depreciation. An amount taken for depreciation shall not be considered unreasonable solely because it is greater or less than the amount taken for tax purposes.

(4) An amount transferred to principal need not be held as a separate fund.

(Laws 2002, ch. 2002-42, §1, effective January 1, 2003.)

§738.101. Florida Uniform Principal and Income Act

738.704 Transfers from income to reimburse principal.

(1) If a trustee makes or expects to make a principal disbursement described in this section, the trustee may transfer an appropriate amount from income to principal in one or more accounting periods to reimburse principal or to provide a reserve for future principal disbursements.

(2) Principal disbursements to which subsection (1) applies include the following, but only to the extent the trustee has not been and does not expect to be reimbursed by a third party:

(a) An amount chargeable to income but paid from principal because the amount is unusually large.

(b) Disbursements made to prepare property for rental, including tenant allowances, leasehold improvements, and broker's commissions.

(c) Disbursements described in §738.702(1)(g).

(3) If the asset the ownership of which gives rise to the disbursements becomes subject to a successive income interest after an income interest ends, a trustee may continue to transfer amounts from income to principal as provided in subsection (1).

(4) To the extent principal cash is not sufficient to pay the principal balance of payments due on mortgaged property, income may be applied to such payment in order to avoid a default on any mortgage or security interest securing the property. Income shall be reimbursed for such payments out of the first available principal cash. If the asset the ownership of which gives rise to the disbursements described in this subsection becomes subject to a successive income interest after an income interest ends, all rights of the initial income interest shall lapse, and amounts remaining due from principal shall not be a lien on the assets of the trust.

(Laws 2002, ch. 2002-42, §1, effective January 1, 2003.)

§738.705. Trustee's allocation of income taxes

(1) A tax required to be paid by a trustee based on receipts allocated to income shall be paid from income.

(2) A tax required to be paid by a trustee based on receipts allocated to principal shall be paid from principal, even if the tax is called an income tax by the taxing authority.

(3) A tax required to be paid by a trustee on the trust's share of an entity's taxable income shall be paid proportionately:

(a) From income to the extent receipts from the entity are allocated to income; and

(b) From principal to the extent:

1. Receipts from the entity are allocated to principal; and

2. The trust's share of the entity's taxable income exceeds the total receipts described in paragraph (a) and subparagraph 1.

(4) For purposes of this section, receipts allocated to principal or income shall be reduced by the

amount distributed to a beneficiary from principal or income for which the trust receives a deduction in calculating the tax.
(Laws 2002, ch. 2002-42, §1, effective January 1, 2003.)

§738.706. Adjustments between principal and income due to taxes

(1) A fiduciary may make adjustments between principal and income to offset the shifting of economic interests or tax benefits between income beneficiaries and remainder beneficiaries which arise from:

(a) Elections and decisions, other than those described in paragraph (b), that the fiduciary makes from time to time regarding tax matters;

(b) An income tax or any other tax that is imposed upon the fiduciary or a beneficiary as a result of a transaction involving or a distribution from the estate or trust; or

(c) The ownership by an estate or trust of an interest in an entity whose taxable income, whether or not distributed, is includable in the taxable income of the estate, trust, or a beneficiary.

(2) If the amount of an estate tax marital deduction or charitable contribution deduction is reduced because a fiduciary deducts an amount paid from principal for income tax purposes instead of deducting such amount for estate tax purposes, and as a result estate taxes paid from principal are increased and income taxes paid by an estate, trust, or beneficiary are decreased, each estate, trust, or beneficiary that benefits from the decrease in income tax shall reimburse the principal from which the increase in estate tax is paid. The total reimbursement shall equal the increase in the estate tax to the extent the principal used to pay the increase would have qualified for a marital deduction or charitable contribution deduction but for the payment. The proportionate share of the reimbursement for each estate, trust, or beneficiary whose income taxes are reduced shall be the same as such estate's, trust's, or beneficiary's proportionate share of the total decrease in income tax. An estate or trust shall reimburse principal from income.
(Laws 2002, ch. 2002-42, §1, effective January 1, 2003.)

§738.801. Allocations regarding expenses and improvements

(1) The provisions of §§738.701-738.705, so far as applicable and excepting those dealing with costs of, or assessments for, improvements to property, shall govern the apportionment of expenses between tenants and remaindermen when no trust has been created, subject to any agreement of the parties or specific direction of the taxing or other statutes, but when either tenant or remainderman has incurred an expense for the benefit of his or her own estate without consent or agreement of the other, he or she shall pay such expense in full.

(2) Subject to the exceptions stated in subsection (1), the cost of, or special taxes or assessments for, an improvement representing an addition of value to property forming part of the principal shall be paid by the tenant when the improvement is not reasonably expected to outlast the estate of the tenant. In all other cases a part only shall be paid by the tenant, while the remainder shall be paid by the remainderman. The part payable by the tenant shall be ascertainable by taking that percentage of the total that is found by dividing the present value of the tenant's estate by the present value of an estate of the same form as that of the tenant except that it is limited for a period corresponding to the reasonably expected duration of the improvement. The computation of present values of the estates shall be made on the expectancy basis set forth in the official mortality tables, and no other evidence of duration or expectancy shall be considered.
(Laws 2002, ch. 2002-42, §1, effective January 1, 2003.)

§738.802 Uniformity of application and construction

In applying and construing this act, consideration shall be given to the need to promote uniformity of the law with respect to the act's subject matter among states that enact such act.
(Laws 2002, ch. 2002-42, §1, effective January 1, 2003.)

§738.803 Severability

If any provision of this chapter or its application to any person or circumstance is held invalid, the invalidity shall not affect other provisions or applications of this chapter which can be given effect without the invalid provision or application, and to this end the provisions of this chapter are severable.
(Laws 2002, ch. 2002-42, §1, effective January 1, 2003.)

§738.804 Application to transactions; date

Except as provided in the trust instrument, the will, or this chapter, this chapter shall apply to any receipt or expense received or incurred and any disbursement made after January 1, 2003, by any trust or decedent's estate, whether established before or after January 1, 2003, and whether the asset involved was acquired by the trustee or personal representative before or after January 1, 2003. Receipts or expenses received or incurred and disbursements made before January 1, 2003, shall be governed by the law of this state in effect at the time of the event, except as otherwise expressly provided in the will or terms of the trust or in this chapter.

(Laws 2002, ch. 2002-42, §1, effective January 1, 2003.)

III. Trustees' Powers

A trustee must have a broad range of powers to carry out the acts that are necessary in the management of trust property. Such powers include, among others, the power to buy, sell, lease, borrow and lend money; encumber trust property; develop land; make repairs or improvements; continue a business that is part of the trust property; and insure trust property.

Traditionally, the settlor enumerated in the trust instrument the list of powers granted to a trustee. Sometimes, statutes set forth a list of such powers. Some trust powers also may be implied by the circumstances. Further, a court may grant additional powers beyond those authorized by the trust instrument or by statute, and also restrict those same powers.

A trust instrument may provide for *mandatory* powers for a trustee (i.e., requiring the trustee to take a certain action). Or, the trustee may have *discretionary* powers (permitting the trustee to use judgment in the use of a power).

In Florida, a trustee may exercise powers that are conferred by the terms of the trust without the need to obtain court authorization (Fla. Stat. §736.0815). The Florida standard for the exercise of a discretionary power by a trustee is: good faith, in accordance with the terms and purposes of the trust, and in the interests of the beneficiaries (Fla. Stat. §736.0814). Specific powers of the trustee are set forth in Florida Statutes §§736.0816-736.08163.

A. Generally

§736.0815. General powers of trustees

(1) A trustee, without authorization by the court, may, except as limited or restricted by this code, exercise:

(a) Powers conferred by the terms of the trust.

(b) Except as limited by the terms of the trust:

1. All powers over the trust property that an unmarried competent owner has over individually owned property.

2. Any other powers appropriate to achieve the proper investment, management, and distribution of the trust property.

3. Any other powers conferred by this code.

(2) The exercise of a power is subject to the fiduciary duties prescribed by this code.

(Laws 2006, ch. 217, §8, effective July 1, 2007.)

B. Specific Powers of Trustees

§736.0814. Standard for exercise of discretionary powers

(1) Notwithstanding the breadth of discretion granted to a trustee in the terms of the trust, including the use of such terms as "absolute," "sole," or "uncontrolled," the trustee shall exercise a discretionary power in good faith and in accordance with the terms and purposes of the trust and the interests of the beneficiaries. A court shall not determine that a trustee abused its discretion merely because the court would have exercised the discretion in a different manner or would not have exercised the discretion.

(2) Subject to subsection (3) and unless the terms of the trust expressly indicate that a rule in this subsection does not apply, a person who is a beneficiary and a trustee may not:

(a) Make discretionary distributions of either principal or income to or for the benefit of that trustee, except to provide for that trustee's health, education, maintenance, or support as described under §§2041 and 2514 of the Internal Revenue Code;

(b) Make discretionary allocations of receipts or expenses as between principal and income, unless the trustee acts in a fiduciary capacity whereby the trustee has no power to enlarge or shift any beneficial interest except as an incidental consequence of the discharge of the trustee's fiduciary duties;

(c) Make discretionary distributions of either principal or income to satisfy any of the trustee's legal support obligations; or

(d) Exercise any other power, including, but not limited to, the right to remove or to replace any trustee, so as to cause the powers enumerated in paragraph (a), paragraph (b), or paragraph (c) to be exercised on behalf of, or for the benefit of, a beneficiary who is also a trustee.

(3) Subsection (2) does not apply to:

(a) A power held by the settlor of the trust;

(b) A power held by the settlor's spouse who is the trustee of a trust for which a marital deduction, as defined in §2056(a) or §2523(a) of the Internal Revenue Code of 1986, as amended, was previously allowed;

(c) Any trust during any period that the trust may be revoked or amended by its settlor; or

(d) A trust if contributions to the trust qualify for the annual exclusion under §2503(c) of the Internal Revenue Code of 1986, as amended.

(4) A power whose exercise is limited or prohibited by subsection (2) may be exercised by the remaining trustees whose exercise of the power is not so limited or prohibited. If there is no trustee qualified to exercise the power, on petition by any qualified beneficiary, the court may appoint an independent trustee with authority to exercise the power.

(5) A person who has the right to remove or to replace a trustee does not possess nor may that person be deemed to possess, by virtue of having that right, the powers of the trustee that is subject to removal or to replacement.

(Laws 2006, ch. 217, §8, effective July 1, 2007.)

§736.0816. Scope of powers of a trustee

Except as limited or restricted by this code, a trustee may:

(1) Collect trust property and accept or reject additions to the trust property from a settlor, including an asset in which the trustee is personally interested, and hold property in the name of a nominee or in other form without disclosure of the trust so that title to the property may pass by delivery but the trustee is liable for any act of the nominee in connection with the property so held.

(2) Acquire or sell property, for cash or on credit, at public or private sale.

(3) Acquire an undivided interest in a trust asset, including, but not limited to, a money market mutual fund, mutual fund, or common trust fund, in which asset the trustee holds an undivided interest in any trust capacity, including any money market or other mutual fund from which the trustee or any affiliate or associate of the trustee is entitled to receive reasonable compensation for providing necessary services as an investment adviser, portfolio manager, or servicing agent. A trustee or affiliate or associate of the trustee may receive compensation for such services in addition to fees received for administering the trust provided such compensation is fully disclosed in writing to all qualified beneficiaries.

(4) Exchange, partition, or otherwise change the character of trust property.

(5) Deposit trust money in an account in a regulated financial service institution.

(6) Borrow money, with or without security, and mortgage or pledge trust property for a period within or extending beyond the duration of the trust and advance money for the protection of the trust.

(7) With respect to an interest in a proprietorship, partnership, limited liability company, business trust, corporation, or other form of business or enterprise, continue the business or other enterprise and take any action that may be taken by shareholders, members, or property owners, including, but not limited to, merging, dissolving, or otherwise changing the form of business organization or contributing additional capital.

(8) With respect to stocks or other securities, exercise the rights of an absolute owner, including, but not limited to, the right to:

(a) Vote, or give proxies to vote, with or without power of substitution, or enter into or continue a voting trust agreement.

(b) Hold a security in the name of a nominee or in other form without disclosure of the trust so that title may pass by delivery.

(c) Pay calls, assessments, and other sums chargeable or accruing against the securities, and sell or exercise stock subscription or conversion rights.

(d) Deposit the securities with a depositary or other regulated financial service institution.

(9) With respect to an interest in real property, construct, or make ordinary or extraordinary repairs to, alterations to, or improvements in, buildings or other structures, demolish improvements, raze existing or erect new party walls or buildings, subdivide or develop land, dedicate land to public use or grant public or private easements, and make or vacate plats and adjust boundaries.

(10) Enter into a lease for any purpose as lessor or lessee, including a lease or other arrangement for exploration and removal of natural resources, with or without the option to purchase or renew, for a period within or extending beyond the duration of the trust.

(11) Grant an option involving a sale, lease, or other disposition of trust property or acquire an option for the acquisition of property, including an option exercisable beyond the duration of the trust, and exercise an option so acquired.

(12) Insure the property of the trust against damage or loss and insure the trustee, trustee's agents, and beneficiaries against liability arising from the administration of the trust.

(13) Abandon or decline to administer property of no value or of insufficient value to justify the collection or continued administration of such property.

(14) Pay or contest any claim, settle a claim by or against the trust, and release, in whole or in part, a claim belonging to the trust.

(15) Pay taxes, assessments, compensation of the trustee and of employees and agents of the trust, and other expenses incurred in the administration of the trust.

(16) Allocate items of income or expense to trust income or principal, as provided by law.

(17) Exercise elections with respect to federal, state, and local taxes.

(18) Select a mode of payment under any employee benefit or retirement plan, annuity, or life insurance payable to the trustee, exercise rights under such plan, annuity, or insurance, including exercise of the right to indemnification for expenses and against liabilities, and take appropriate action to collect the proceeds.

(19) Make loans out of trust property, including, but not limited to, loans to a beneficiary on terms and conditions that are fair and reasonable under the circumstances, and the trustee has a lien on future distributions for repayment of those loans.

(20) Employ persons, including, but not limited to, attorneys, accountants, investment advisers, or agents, even if they are the trustee, an affiliate of the trustee, or otherwise associated with the trustee, to advise or assist the trustee in the exercise of any of the trustee's powers and pay reasonable compensation and costs incurred in connection with such employment from the assets of the trust and act without independent investigation on the recommendations of such persons.

(21) Pay an amount distributable to a beneficiary who is under a legal disability or who the trustee reasonably believes is incapacitated, by paying the amount directly to the beneficiary or applying the amount for the beneficiary's benefit, or by:

(a) Paying the amount to the beneficiary's guardian of the property or, if the beneficiary does not have a guardian of the property, the beneficiary's guardian of the person;

(b) Paying the amount to the beneficiary's custodian under a Uniform Transfers to Minors Act or custodial trustee under a Uniform Custodial Trust Act, and, for that purpose, creating a custodianship or custodial trust;

(c) Paying the amount to an adult relative or other person having legal or physical care or custody of the beneficiary, to be expended on the beneficiary's behalf, if the trustee does not know of a guardian of the property, guardian of the person, custodian, or custodial trustee; or

(d) Managing the amount as a separate fund on the beneficiary's behalf, subject to the beneficiary's continuing right to withdraw the distribution.

(22) On distribution of trust property or the division or termination of a trust, make distributions in divided or undivided interests, allocate particular assets in proportionate or disproportionate shares, value the trust property for those purposes, and adjust for resulting differences in valuation.

(23) Prosecute or defend, including appeals, an action, claim, or judicial proceeding in any jurisdiction to protect trust property or the trustee in the performance of the trustee's duties.

(24) Sign and deliver contracts and other instruments that are useful to achieve or facilitate the exercise of the trustee's powers.

(25) On termination of the trust, exercise the powers appropriate to wind up the administration of the trust and distribute the trust property to the persons entitled to the property, subject to the right of the trustee to retain a reasonable reserve for the payment of debts, expenses, and taxes.

(Laws 2006, ch. 217, §8, effective July 1, 2007.)

§ 736.08163. Specific powers regarding environmental laws

(1) From the creation of a trust until final distribution of the assets from the trust, the trustee has, without court authorization, the powers specified in subsection (2).

(2) Unless otherwise provided in the trust instrument, a trustee has the power, acting reasonably, to:

(a) Inspect or investigate, or cause to be inspected or investigated, property held by the trustee, including interests in sole proprietorships, partnerships, or corporations and any assets owned by any such business entity for the purpose of determining compliance with an environmental law affecting that property or to respond to an actual or threatened violation of an environmental law affecting that property;

(b) Take, on behalf of the trust, any action necessary to prevent, abate, or otherwise remedy an actual or potential violation of an environmental law affecting property held by the trustee, before or after initiation of an enforcement action by a governmental body;

(c) Refuse to accept property in trust if the trustee determines that any property to be donated or conveyed to the trustee is contaminated with a hazardous substance or is being used or has been used for an activity directly or indirectly involving a hazardous substance,

Facility payment power
facility of payment provision

which circumstance could result in liability to the trust or trustee or otherwise impair the value of the assets to be held;

(d) Settle or compromise at any time any claim against the trust or trustee that may be asserted by a governmental body or private party that involves the alleged violation of an environmental law affecting property of any trust over which the trustee has responsibility;

(e) Disclaim any power granted by any document, law, or rule of law that, in the sole judgment of the trustee, may cause the trustee to incur personal liability, or the trust to incur liability, under any environmental law;

(f) Decline to serve as a trustee, or having undertaken to serve as a trustee, resign at any time, if the trustee believes there is or may be a conflict of interest in its fiduciary capacity and in its individual capacity because of potential claims or liabilities that may be asserted against the trustee on behalf of the trust by reason of the type or condition of the assets held; or

(g) Charge against the income and principal of the trust the cost of any inspection, investigation, review, abatement, response, cleanup, or remedial action that this section authorizes the trustee to take and, if the trust terminates or closes or the trust property is transferred to another trustee, hold assets sufficient to cover the cost of cleaning up any known environmental problem.

(3) A trustee is not personally liable to any beneficiary or any other person for a decrease in value of assets in a trust by reason of the trustee's compliance or efforts to comply with an environmental law, specifically including any reporting requirement under that law.

(4) A trustee that acquires ownership or control of a vessel or other property, without having owned, operated, or materially participated in the management of that vessel or property before assuming ownership or control as trustee, is not considered an owner or operator for purposes of liability under chapter 376, chapter 403, or any other environmental law. A trustee that willfully, knowingly, or recklessly causes or exacerbates a release or threatened release of a hazardous substance is personally liable for the cost of the response, to the extent that the release or threatened release is attributable to the trustee's activities. This subsection does not preclude the filing of claims against the assets that constitute the trust held by the trustee or the filing of actions against the trustee in its representative capacity and in any such action, an award or judgment against the trustee must be satisfied only from the assets of the trust.

(5) The acceptance by the trustee of the property or a failure by the trustee to inspect or investigate the property does not create any inference as to whether there is liability under an environmental law with respect to that property.

(6) For the purposes of this section, the term "hazardous substance" means a substance defined as hazardous or toxic, or any contaminant, pollutant, or constituent thereof, or otherwise regulated, by an environmental law.

(7) This section does not apply to any trust created under a document executed before July 1, 1995, unless the trust is amendable and the settlor amends the trust at any time to incorporate the provisions of this section.

(Laws 2006, ch. 217, §8, effective July 1, 2007.)

IV. Liability of Trustees to Beneficiaries

A. Liability for Breach of Trust

A trustee's violation of any duty that the trustee owes the beneficiary is a breach trust (Fla. Stat. §736.1001(1)). A range of remedies are available for a breach of trust, including: compelling the trustee to perform duties, enjoining the trustee from committing the breach of trust, compelling the trustee to redress the breach, appointing a receiver to take possession of the trust property, reducing or denying the trustee's compensation, and removing the trustee (Fla. Stat. §736.1001(2)).

Most Florida statutory provisions on the trustee's liabilities for breach are derived from the Uniform Trust Code.

§736.1003. Trustee's liability for breach of trust

Absent a breach of trust, a trustee is not liable to a beneficiary for a loss or depreciation in the value of trust property or for not having made a profit.

(Laws 2006, ch. 217, §10, effective July 1, 2007.)

§736.1012. Trustee's liability if beneficiary consents, releases, or ratifies breach

A trustee is not liable to a beneficiary for breach of trust if the beneficiary consented to the conduct constituting the breach, released the trustee from liability for the breach, or ratified the transaction constituting the breach, unless:

(1) The consent, release, or ratification of the beneficiary was induced by improper conduct of the trustee; or

(2) At the time of the consent, release, or ratification, the beneficiary did not know of the

beneficiary's rights or of the material facts relating to the breach.
(Laws 2006, ch. 2006-217, §10, effective July 1, 2007.)

§736.08125. Liability of successor trustee

(1) A successor trustee is not personally liable for actions taken by any prior trustee, nor does any successor trustee have a duty to institute any proceeding against any prior trustee, or file any claim against any prior trustee's estate, for any of the prior trustee's actions as trustee under any of the following circumstances:

(a) As to a successor trustee who succeeds a trustee who was also the settlor of a trust that was revocable during the time that the settlor served as trustee;

(b) As to any beneficiary who has waived any accounting required by §736.0813, but only as to the periods included in the waiver;

(c) As to any beneficiary who has released the successor trustee from the duty to institute any proceeding or file any claim;

(d) As to any person who is not an eligible beneficiary; or

(e) As to any eligible beneficiary:

1. If a super majority of the eligible beneficiaries have released the successor trustee;

2. If the eligible beneficiary has not delivered a written request to the successor trustee to institute an action or file a claim against the prior trustee within 6 months after the date of the successor trustee's acceptance of the trust, if the successor trustee has notified the eligible beneficiary in writing of acceptance by the successor trustee in accordance with §736.0813(1)(a) and that writing advises the beneficiary that, unless the beneficiary delivers the written request within 6 months after the date of acceptance, the right to proceed against the successor trustee will be barred pursuant to this section; or

3. For any action or claim that the eligible beneficiary is barred from bringing against the prior trustee.

(2) For the purposes of this section, the term:

(a) "Eligible beneficiaries" means:

1. At the time the determination is made, if there are one or more beneficiaries as described in §736.0103(14)(c), the beneficiaries described in §736.0103(14)(a) and (c); or

2. If there is no beneficiary as described in §736.0103(14)(c), the beneficiaries described in §736.0103(14)(a) and (b).

(b) "Super majority of eligible beneficiaries" means at least two-thirds in interest of the eligible beneficiaries if the interests of the eligible beneficiaries are reasonably ascertainable, otherwise, at least two-thirds in number of the eligible beneficiaries.

(3) Nothing in this section affects any liability of the prior trustee or the right of the successor trustee or any beneficiary to pursue an action or claim against the prior trustee.
(Laws 2006, ch. 217, §8, effective July 1, 2007.)

§ 736.0507. Personal liability of trustee

Except to the extent of the trustee's interest in the trust other than as a trustee, trust property is not subject to personal obligations of the trustee, even if the trustee becomes insolvent or bankrupt.
(Laws 2006, ch. 2006-217, §5, effective July 1, 2007.)

B. Remedies for Breach of Trust

§736.1001. Remedies for trustee's breach of trust

(1) A violation by a trustee of a duty the trustee owes to a beneficiary is a breach of trust.

(2) To remedy a breach of trust that has occurred or may occur, the court may:

(a) Compel the trustee to perform the trustee's duties;

(b) Enjoin the trustee from committing a breach of trust;

(c) Compel the trustee to redress a breach of trust by paying money or restoring property or by other means;

(d) Order a trustee to account;

(e) Appoint a special fiduciary to take possession of the trust property and administer the trust;

(f) Suspend the trustee;

(g) Remove the trustee as provided in §736.706;

(h) Reduce or deny compensation to the trustee;

(i) Subject to §736.1016, void an act of the trustee, impose a lien or a constructive trust on trust property, or trace trust property wrongfully disposed of and recover the property or its proceeds; or

(j) Order any other appropriate relief.

(3) As an illustration of the remedies available to the court and without limiting the court's discretion as provided in subsection (2), if a breach of trust

results in the favoring of any beneficiary to the detriment of any other beneficiary or consists of an abuse of the trustee's discretion:

(a) To the extent the breach of trust has resulted in no distribution to a beneficiary or a distribution that is too small, the court may require the trustee to pay from the trust to the beneficiary an amount the court determines will restore the beneficiary, in whole or in part, to his or her appropriate position.

(b) To the extent the breach of trust has resulted in a distribution to a beneficiary that is too large, the court may restore the beneficiaries, the trust, or both, in whole or in part, to their appropriate positions by requiring the trustee to withhold an amount from one or more future distributions to the beneficiary who received the distribution that was too large or by requiring that beneficiary to return some or all of the distribution to the trust.

(Laws 2006, ch. 217, §10, effective July 1, 2007.)

C. Measure of Liability for Breach of Trust

§736.1002. Damages for trustee's breach of trust

(1) A trustee who commits a breach of trust is liable for the greater of:

(a) The amount required to restore the value of the trust property and trust distributions to what they would have been if the breach had not occurred, including lost income, capital gain, or appreciation that would have resulted from proper administration; or

(b) The profit the trustee made by reason of the breach.

(2) Except as otherwise provided in this subsection, if more than one person, including a trustee or trustees, is liable to the beneficiaries for a breach of trust, each liable person is entitled to pro rata contribution from the other person or persons. A person is not entitled to contribution if the person committed the breach of trust in bad faith. A person who received a benefit from the breach of trust is not entitled to contribution from another person to the extent of the benefit received.

(3) In determining the pro rata shares of liable persons in the entire liability for a breach of trust:

(a) Their relative degrees of fault shall be the basis for allocation of liability.

(b) If equity requires, the collective liability of some as a group shall constitute a single share.

(c) Principles of equity applicable to contribution generally shall apply.

(4) The right of contribution shall be enforced as follows:

(a) Contribution may be enforced by separate action, whether or not judgment has been entered in an action against two or more liable persons for the same breach of trust.

(b) When a judgment has been entered in an action against two or more liable persons for the same breach of trust, contribution may be enforced in that action by judgment in favor of one judgment defendant against any other judgment defendants by motion upon notice to all parties to the action.

(c) If there is a judgment for breach of trust against the liable person seeking contribution, any separate action by that person to enforce contribution must be commenced within 1 year after the judgment has become final by lapse of time for appeal or after appellate review.

(d) If there is no judgment for the breach of trust against the liable person seeking contribution, the person's right of contribution is barred unless the person has:

1. Discharged by payment the common liability within the period of the statute of limitations applicable to the beneficiary's right of action against the liable person and the person has commenced an action for contribution within 1 year after payment, or

2. Agreed, while action is pending against the liable person, to discharge the common liability and has within 1 year after the agreement paid the liability and commenced the person's action for contribution.

(5) The beneficiary's recovery of a judgment for breach of trust against one liable person does not of itself discharge other liable persons from liability for the breach of trust unless the judgment is satisfied. The satisfaction of the judgment does not impair any right of contribution.

(6) The judgment of the court in determining the liability of several defendants to the beneficiary for breach of trust is binding upon such defendants in determining the right of such defendants to contribution.

(7) Subsection (2) applies to all causes of action for breach of trust pending on July 1, 2007, under which causes of action the right of contribution among persons jointly and severally liable is involved and to all causes of action filed after July 1, 2007.

(Laws 2006, ch. 217, §10, effective July 1, 2007.)

D. Limitations and Exculpation

§736.1008. Limitations on claims against trustees for breach of trust

(1) Except as provided in subsection (2), all claims by a beneficiary against a trustee for breach of trust are barred as provided in chapter 95 as to:

(a) All matters adequately disclosed in a trust disclosure document issued by the trustee, with the limitations period beginning on the date of receipt of adequate disclosure.

(b) All matters not adequately disclosed in a trust disclosure document if the trustee has issued a final trust accounting and has given written notice to the beneficiary of the availability of the trust records for examination and that any claims with respect to matters not adequately disclosed may be barred unless an action is commenced within the applicable limitations period provided in chapter 95. The limitations period begins on the date of receipt of the final trust accounting and notice.

(2) Unless sooner barred by adjudication, consent, or limitations, a beneficiary is barred from bringing an action against a trustee for breach of trust with respect to a matter that was adequately disclosed in a trust disclosure document unless a proceeding to assert the claim is commenced within 6 months after receipt from the trustee of the trust disclosure document or a limitation notice that applies to that disclosure document, whichever is received later.

(3) When a trustee has not issued a final trust accounting or has not given written notice to the beneficiary of the availability of the trust records for examination and that claims with respect to matters not adequately disclosed may be barred, a claim against the trustee for breach of trust based on a matter not adequately disclosed in a trust disclosure document accrues when the beneficiary has actual knowledge of the trustee's repudiation of the trust or adverse possession of trust assets, and is barred as provided in chapter 95.

(4) As used in this section, the term:

(a) "Trust disclosure document" means a trust accounting or any other written report of the trustee. A trust disclosure document adequately discloses a matter if the document provides sufficient information so that a beneficiary knows of a claim or reasonably should have inquired into the existence of a claim with respect to that matter.

(b) "Trust accounting" means an accounting that adequately discloses the information required by and that substantially complies with the standards set forth in §736.08135.

(c) "Limitation notice" means a written statement of the trustee that an action by a beneficiary against the trustee for breach of trust based on any matter adequately disclosed in a trust disclosure document may be barred unless the action is commenced within 6 months after receipt of the trust disclosure document or receipt of a limitation notice that applies to that trust disclosure document, whichever is later. A limitation notice may but is not required to be in the following form: "An action for breach of trust based on matters disclosed in a trust accounting or other written report of the trustee may be subject to a 6-month statute of limitations from the receipt of the trust accounting or other written report. If you have questions, please consult your attorney."

(5) For purposes of this section, a limitation notice applies to a trust disclosure document when the limitation notice is:

(a) Contained as a part of the trust disclosure document or as a part of another trust disclosure document received within 1 year prior to the receipt of the latter trust disclosure document;

(b) Accompanied concurrently by the trust disclosure document or by another trust disclosure document that was received within 1 year prior to the receipt of the latter trust disclosure document;

(c) Delivered separately within 10 days after the delivery of the trust disclosure document or of another trust disclosure document that was received within 1 year prior to the receipt of the latter trust disclosure document. For purposes of this paragraph, a limitation notice is not delivered separately if the notice is accompanied by another written communication, other than a written communication that refers only to the limitation notice; or

(d) Received more than 10 days after the delivery of the trust disclosure document, but only if the limitation notice references that trust disclosure document and:

1. Offers to provide to the beneficiary on request another copy of that trust disclosure document if the document was received by the beneficiary within 1 year prior to receipt of the limitation notice; or

2. Is accompanied by another copy of that trust disclosure document if the trust disclosure document was received by the beneficiary 1 year or more prior to the receipt of the limitation notice.

(6) This section applies to trust accountings for accounting periods beginning on or after January 1, 2008, and to written reports, other than trust

accountings, received by a beneficiary on or after January 1, 2008.
(Laws 2006, ch. 2006-217, §10, effective July 1, 2007.)

§736.1009. Trustee is not liable for reasonable reliance on trust instrument

A trustee who acts in reasonable reliance on the terms of the trust as expressed in the trust instrument is not liable to a beneficiary for a breach of trust to the extent the breach resulted from the reliance.
(Laws 2006, ch. 2006-217, §10, effective July 1, 2007.)

§736.1010. Limitation on liability for ignorance of event affecting administration or distribution

If the happening of an event, including marriage, divorce, performance of educational requirements, or death, affects the administration or distribution of a trust, a trustee who has exercised reasonable care to ascertain the happening of the event is not liable for a loss resulting from the trustee's lack of knowledge.
(Laws 2006, ch. 2006-217, §10, effective July 1, 2007.)

§736.1011. Exculpation of trustee by terms of the trust

(1) A term of a trust relieving a trustee of liability for breach of trust is unenforceable to the extent that the term:

(a) Relieves the trustee of liability for breach of trust committed in bad faith or with reckless indifference to the purposes of the trust or the interests of the beneficiaries; or

(b) Was inserted into the trust instrument as the result of an abuse by the trustee of a fiduciary or confidential relationship with the settlor.

(2) An exculpatory term drafted or caused to be drafted by the trustee is invalid as an abuse of a fiduciary or confidential relationship unless the trustee proves that the exculpatory term is fair under the circumstances and that the term's existence and contents were adequately communicated directly to the settlor.
(Laws 2006, ch. 2006-217, §10, effective July 1, 2007.).

V. Liability of Trustees to Third Persons

Often, a trustee often must deal with third parties during the administration of the trust. Such transactions may result in claims asserted by third parties against the trustee in the trustee's representative or individual capacity. Statutes regulate the nature and extent of the trustee's liability to third parties.

According to Florida law, a trustee may be liable for claims based on contract, tort, or those involving the ownership and control of the trust property (Fla. Stat. §736.1013). In some cases, the trustee may be personally liable (i.e., liable in his or her individual capacity). For example, a trustee may be personally liable on a contract entered into during the administration of the trust if the trustee entered into the agreement in the trustee's fiduciary capacity without disclosing the trustee's fiduciary capacity (Fla. Stat. §736.1013(3)). On the other hand, a trustee is personally liable for obligations regarding torts committed in the course of administering the trust or regarding ownership or control of trust property only if the trustee is personally at fault (Fla. Stat. §736.1013(2)). Judicial proceedings may determine whether the trust is liable or the trustee is personally liable (Fla. Stat. §736.1013(4)).

§736.1013. Limitations on personal liability of trustee: disclosure, etc.

(1) Except as otherwise provided in the contract, a trustee is not personally liable on a contract properly entered into in the trustee's fiduciary capacity in the course of administering the trust if the trustee in the contract disclosed the fiduciary capacity.

(2) A trustee is personally liable for torts committed in the course of administering a trust or for obligations arising from ownership or control of trust property only if the trustee is personally at fault.

(3) A claim based on a contract entered into by a trustee in the trustee's fiduciary capacity, on an obligation arising from ownership or control of trust property, or on a tort committed in the course of administering a trust may be asserted in a judicial proceeding against the trustee in the trustee's fiduciary capacity, whether or not the trustee is personally liable for the claim.

(4) Issues of liability between the trust estate and the trustee individually may be determined in a proceeding for accounting, surcharge, or indemnification or in any other appropriate proceeding.
(Laws 2006, ch. 2006-217, §10, effective July 1, 2007.)

§736.1016. Protection of person who assists or deals with trustee in good faith

(1) A person other than a beneficiary who in good faith assists a trustee or who in good faith and for value deals with a trustee, without knowledge that the trustee is exceeding or improperly exercising the trustee's powers, is protected from liability as if the trustee properly exercised the power.

(2) A person other than a beneficiary who in good faith deals with a trustee is not required to inquire into the extent of the trustee's powers or the propriety of their exercise.

(3) A person who in good faith delivers assets to a trustee need not ensure their proper application.

(4) A person other than a beneficiary who in good faith assists a former trustee or who in good faith and for value deals with a former trustee, without knowledge that the trusteeship has terminated, is protected from liability as if the former trustee were still a trustee.

(5) Comparable protective provisions of other laws relating to commercial transactions or transfer of securities by fiduciaries prevail over the protection provided by this section.

(Laws 2006, ch. 2006-217, §10, effective. July 1, 2007.)

XII
BENEFICIARIES

This chapter explores the nature and extent of the beneficiary's interest. It addresses the rights of a beneficiary to enforce a beneficial interest. Then the chapter turns to the transferability of the beneficial interests and the susceptibility of these interests to the claims of creditors.

I. Nature of the Beneficiary's Interest

A. Generally

A private express trust requires a definite beneficiary or beneficiaries. The reason for this requirement is that a trust must have ascertainable beneficiaries in order to enforce it. (Note that charitable trusts are not subject to the rule requiring definite beneficiaries because charitable trusts are enforced by the state Attorney General.)

A trust may be created for a single beneficiary or several beneficiaries. In the case of several beneficiaries, it is common to have successive beneficiaries, i.e., one or more beneficiaries who are entitled to the enjoyment of the trust property in succession.

A trust may be created for an unborn beneficiary. "[A] trust can be created in favor of a person who has not yet come into existence as long as there is a possibility that he may come into existence." Austin Wakeman Scott & William Franklin Fratcher, The Law of Trusts §112.3 at 166 (4th ed., 1987) [hereinafter Scott & Fratcher]. Also, a trust can be created for a minor. A minor has capacity to take and hold title to property even though the minor cannot manage the property. Legal entities such as corporations or partnerships may be beneficiaries of trusts provided they are empowered by state law to take and hold title to property. Further, the settlor can designate as trust beneficiaries the members of a class ("my children," "my nephews and nieces") provided that the class members are ascertainable. On class gifts, see Chapter XV *infra*.

If the settlor fails to name a beneficiary, the trust fails and a resulting trust arises. In some cases, a beneficiary who is not specifically named in the instrument may be identified by resort to extrinsic facts, such as by use of the doctrine of facts or acts of independent significance. (For discussion of this doctrine, see Chapter V *supra*.)

The settlor also may be the beneficiary of the trust—either the sole beneficiary or one of several beneficiaries. (For example, it is common for a settlor to transfer property in trust to pay the income to the settlor for life and then, on the settlor's death, to convey the property to other beneficiaries.) The fact that the settlor is the sole beneficiary does not render the trust invalid. However, a settlor cannot create a trust to insulate himself or herself from creditors' claims. (For discussion of the ability of a settlor to terminate a trust when he or she is the sole beneficiary, see Chapter X *supra*.) Although the settlor can be the sole beneficiary of a trust, a sole trustee cannot be the sole beneficiary. Bogert, *supra*, at §129. In the latter case, the doctrine of merger applies (i.e., the legal and beneficial interests would merge) and the trust fails. Note that the merger doctrine does not apply when that when there are multiple settlors, at least one of which is a trustee, and one or more of those settlors are also beneficiaries during the lifetime of the settlors.

§736.0103. "Beneficiary" defined, generally

...

(4) "Beneficiary" means a person who:

(a) Has a present or future beneficial interest in a trust, vested or contingent; or

(b) Holds a power of appointment over trust property in a capacity other than that of a trustee.

....

(Laws 2006, ch. 2006-217, §1, effective July 1, 2007.)

B. Disclaimer by a Beneficiary

A beneficiary does not have to accept the property interest given by the settlor. Refusal of an inheritance is termed "disclaimer" or "renunciation." Beneficiaries of wills or trusts, as well as heirs, may disclaim a property interest. One of the primary motivations for a disclaimer is to reduce tax liabilities.

State law generally specifies the requirements for disclaimer, such as the interests that may be disclaimed and the procedure for doing so. In the event of a disclaimer, the disclaimed property passes as if the beneficiary predeceased the settlor. A disclaimer is irrevocable.

Florida has enacted the Uniform Disclaimer of Property Interests Act (1999), 8A U.L.A. 166-75 (2003). UDPIA, promulgated by NCCUSL in 1999 (and incorporated into section 2-801 of the Uniform Probate Code in 2002), has been adopted by 12 states and the District of Columbia. The current Florida version of the Act is reprinted below.

UDPIA revises an earlier uniform act that was promulgated in 1978. NCCUSL promulgated

three different acts in 1978 to address disclaimers of various property interests: (1) the Uniform Disclaimer of Property Interests Act (for states without prior law on disclaimers), (2) Uniform Disclaimer of Transfers by Will, Intestacy or Appointment Act (for disclaimers of interests in estates), and (3) Uniform Disclaimer of Transfers under Nontestamentary Instruments Act (for disclaimers of nonprobate transfers). In 1999, NCCUSL replaced these three acts with the revised UDPIA.

UDPIA permits disclaimers by the following: an heir in an intestate estate, a devisee of a will, a beneficiary of a trust or other nontestamentary transfer, a joint tenant in a joint tenancy with right of survivorship, a trustee of a trust, any other fiduciary acting in a fiduciary capacity, and a donee of a power of appointment.

For historical background on the law of disclaimers, see Jon Finelli, *In re Costas*: The Misapplication of Section 548(A) to Disclaimer Law, 14 Am. Bankr. Inst. L. Rev. 567 (2006).

According to Florida law, a disclaimer must (1) be made in a writing that is identified as such, (2) describe the interest that is being renounced, (3) be signed, witnessed, and acknowledged, and (4) be delivered (Fla. Stat. §739.104(3)).

The right to disclaim is not precluded by the insertion by the testator or trustor of a spendthrift restriction prohibiting voluntary or involuntary assignments)(Fla. Stat. §739.104(1)). On spendthrift restrictions in trusts, see Chapter XII *infra*.

§739.102. UDPIA definitions

As used in this chapter, the term:

(1) "Benefactor" means the creator of the interest that is subject to a disclaimer.

(2) "Beneficiary designation" means an instrument, other than an instrument creating or amending a trust, naming the beneficiary of:

(a) An annuity or insurance policy;

(b) An account with a designation for payment on death;

(c) A security registered in beneficiary form;

(d) A pension, profit-sharing, retirement, or other employment-related benefit plan; or

(e) Any other nonprobate transfer at death.

(3) "Disclaimant" means the person to whom a disclaimed interest or power would have passed had the disclaimer not been made.

(4) "Disclaimed interest" means the interest that would have passed to the disclaimant had the disclaimer not been made.

(5) "Disclaimer" means the refusal to accept an interest in or power over property. The term includes a renunciation.

(6) "Fiduciary" means a personal representative, trustee, agent acting under a power of attorney, guardian, or other person authorized to act as a fiduciary with respect to the property of another person.

(7) "Future interest" means an interest that takes effect in possession or enjoyment, if at all, later than the time of its creation.

(8) "Insolvent" means that the sum of a person's debts is greater than all of the person's assets at fair valuation. A person is presumed to be "insolvent" if the person is generally not paying his or her debts as they become due.

(9) "Jointly held property" means property held in the names of two or more persons under an arrangement in which all holders have concurrent interests and under which the last surviving holder is entitled to the whole of the property. Jointly held property does not include property held as tenants by the entirety.

(10) "Person" includes individuals, ascertained and unascertained, living or not living, whether entitled to an interest by right of intestacy or otherwise; a government, governmental subdivision, agency, or instrumentality; and a public corporation.

(11) "Time of distribution" means the time when a disclaimed interest would have taken effect in possession or enjoyment.

(12) "Trust" means:

(a) An express trust (including an honorary trust or a trust under §736.0408), charitable or noncharitable, with additions thereto, whenever and however created; and

(b) A trust created pursuant to a statute, judgment, or decree which requires the trust be administered in the manner of an express trust.

As used in this chapter, the term "trust" does not include a constructive trust or a resulting trust.

(Laws 2005, ch. 2005-108, §1, effective July 1, 2005. Amended by Laws 2006, ch. 2006-217, §43, effective July 1, 2007.)

§739.103. Scope

This chapter applies to disclaimers of any interest in or power over property, whenever created. Except as provided in §739.701, this chapter is the exclusive means by which a disclaimer may be made under Florida law.

(Laws 2005, ch. 2005-108, §1, effective July 1, 2005.)

§739.104. Power to disclaim: requirements

(1) A person may disclaim, in whole or in part, conditionally or unconditionally, any interest in or power over property, including a power of appointment. A person may disclaim the interest or power even if its creator imposed a spendthrift provision or similar restriction on transfer or a restriction or limitation on the right to disclaim. A disclaimer shall be unconditional unless the disclaimant explicitly provides otherwise in the disclaimer.

(2) With court approval, a fiduciary may disclaim, in whole or part, any interest in or power over property, including a power of appointment. Without court approval, a fiduciary may disclaim, in whole or in part, any interest in or power over property, including a power of appointment, if and to the extent that the instrument creating the fiduciary relationship explicitly grants the fiduciary the right to disclaim. In the absence of a court-appointed guardian, notwithstanding anything in chapter 744 to the contrary, without court approval, a natural guardian under §744.301 may disclaim on behalf of a minor child of the natural guardian, in whole or in part, any interest in or power over property, including a power of appointment, which the minor child is to receive solely as a result of another disclaimer, but only if the disclaimed interest or power does not pass to or for the benefit of the natural guardian as a result of the disclaimer.

(3) To be effective, a disclaimer must be in writing, declare the writing as a disclaimer, describe the interest or power disclaimed, and be signed by the person making the disclaimer and witnessed and acknowledged in the manner provided for deeds of real estate to be recorded in this state. In addition, for a disclaimer to be effective, an original of the disclaimer must be delivered or filed in the manner provided in §739.301.

(4) A partial disclaimer may be expressed as a fraction, percentage, monetary amount, term of years, limitation of a power, or any other interest or estate in the property.

(5) A disclaimer becomes irrevocable when any conditions to which the disclaimant has made the disclaimer subject are satisfied and when the disclaimer is delivered or filed pursuant to §739.301 or it becomes effective as provided in §§739.201-739.207, whichever occurs later.

(6) A disclaimer made under this chapter is not a transfer, assignment, or release.

(*Laws 2005, ch. 2005-108, §1, effective July 1, 2005.* Amended by Laws 2006, ch. 2006-1, §103, effective July 4, 2006.)

§739.202. Disclaimer of rights of survivorship in jointly held property

(1) Upon the death of a holder of jointly held property:

(a) If, during the deceased holder's lifetime, the deceased holder could have unilaterally regained a portion of the property attributable to the deceased holder's contributions without the consent of any other holder, another holder may disclaim, in whole or in part, a fractional share of that portion of the property attributable to the deceased holder's contributions determined by dividing the number one by the number of joint holders alive immediately after the death of the holder to whose death the disclaimer relates.

(b) For all other jointly held property, another holder may disclaim, in whole or in part, a fraction of the whole of the property the numerator of which is one and the denominator of which is the product of the number of joint holders alive immediately before the death of the holder to whose death the disclaimer relates multiplied by the number of joint holders alive immediately after the death of the holder to whose death the disclaimer relates.

(2) A disclaimer under subsection (1) takes effect as of the death of the holder of jointly held property to whose death the disclaimer relates.

(3) An interest in jointly held property disclaimed by a surviving holder of the property passes as if the disclaimant predeceased the holder to whose death the disclaimer relates.

(Laws 2005, ch. 2005-108, §1, effective July 1, 2005.)

§739.201. Disclaimer of interest in property

Except for a disclaimer governed by §739.202, §739.203, or §739.204, the following rules apply to a disclaimer of an interest in property:

(1) The disclaimer takes effect as of the time the instrument creating the interest becomes irrevocable or, if the interest arose under the law of intestate succession, as of the time of the intestate's death.

(2) The disclaimed interest passes according to any provision in the instrument creating the interest providing explicitly for the disposition of the interest, should it be disclaimed, or of disclaimed interests in general.

(3) If the instrument does not contain a provision described in subsection (2), the following rules apply:

(a) If the disclaimant is an individual, the disclaimed interest passes as if the disclaimant had died immediately before the interest was created, unless under the governing instrument or other applicable law the disclaimed interest is contingent on surviving to the time of distribution, in which case the disclaimed interest passes as if the disclaimant had died immediately before the time for distribution. However, if, by law or under the governing instrument, the descendants of the disclaimant would share in the disclaimed interest by any method of representation had the disclaimant died before the time of distribution, the disclaimed interest passes only to the descendants of the disclaimant who survive the time of distribution. For purposes of this subsection, a disclaimed interest is created at the death of the benefactor or such earlier time, if any, that the benefactor's transfer of the interest is a completed gift for federal gift tax purposes. Also for purposes of this subsection, a disclaimed interest in a trust described in §733.707(3) shall pass as if the interest had been created under a will.

(b) If the disclaimant is not an individual, the disclaimed interest passes as if the disclaimant did not exist.

(c) Upon the disclaimer of a preceding interest, a future interest held by a person other than the disclaimant takes effect as if the disclaimant had died or ceased to exist immediately before the time of distribution, but a future interest held by the disclaimant is not accelerated in possession or enjoyment as a result of the disclaimer.

(Laws 2005, ch. 2005-108, §1, effective July 1, 2005.)

§739.203. Disclaimer of property held as tenancy by the entirety

(1) The survivorship interest in property held as a tenancy by the entirety to which the survivor succeeds by operation of law upon the death of the cotenant may be disclaimed as provided in this chapter. For purposes of this chapter only, the deceased tenant's interest in property held as a tenancy by the entirety shall be deemed to be an undivided one-half interest.

(2) A disclaimer under subsection (1) takes effect as of the death of the deceased tenant to whose death he disclaimer relates.

(3) The survivorship interest in property held as a tenancy by the entirety disclaimed by the surviving tenant passes as if the disclaimant had predeceased the tenant to whose death the disclaimer relates.

(4) A disclaimer of an interest in real property held as tenants by the entirety does not cause the disclaimed interest to be homestead property for purposes of descent and distribution under §§732.401 and 732.4015.

(Laws 2005, ch. 2005-108, §1, effective. July 1, 2005.)

§739.301. Delivery of disclaimer

(1) Subject to subsections (2) through (12), delivery of a disclaimer may be effected by personal delivery, first-class mail, or any other method that results in its receipt. A disclaimer sent by first-class mail shall be deemed to have been delivered on the date it is postmarked. Delivery by any other method shall be effective upon receipt by the person to whom the disclaimer is to be delivered under this section.

(2) In the case of a disclaimer of an interest created under the law of intestate succession or an interest created by will, other than an interest in a testamentary trust:

(a) The disclaimer must be delivered to the personal representative of the decedent's estate; or

(b) If no personal representative is serving when the disclaimer is sought to be delivered, the disclaimer must be filed with the clerk of the court in any county where venue of administration would be proper.

(3) In the case of a disclaimer of an interest in a testamentary trust:

(a) The disclaimer must be delivered to the trustee serving when the disclaimer is delivered or, if no trustee is then serving, to the personal representative of the decedent's estate; or

(b) If no personal representative is serving when the disclaimer is sought to be delivered, the disclaimer must be filed with the clerk of the court in any county where venue of administration of the decedent's estate would be proper.

(4) In the case of a disclaimer of an interest in an inter vivos trust:

(a) The disclaimer must be delivered to the trustee serving when the disclaimer is delivered;

(b) If no trustee is then serving, it must be filed with the clerk of the court in any county where the filing of a notice of trust would be proper; or

(c) If the disclaimer is made before the time the instrument creating the trust becomes irrevocable, the disclaimer must be delivered to the grantor of the revocable trust or the transferor of the interest or to such person's legal representative.

(5) In the case of a disclaimer of an interest created by a beneficiary designation made before the time the designation becomes irrevocable, the disclaimer must be delivered to the person making

the beneficiary designation or to such person's legal representative.

(6) In the case of a disclaimer of an interest created by a beneficiary designation made after the time the designation becomes irrevocable, the disclaimer must be delivered to the person obligated to distribute the interest.

(7) In the case of a disclaimer by a surviving holder of jointly held property, or by the surviving tenant in property held as a tenancy by the entirety, the disclaimer must be delivered to the person to whom the disclaimed interest passes or, if such person cannot reasonably be located by the disclaimant, the disclaimer must be delivered as provided in subsection (2).

(8) In the case of a disclaimer by an object, or taker in default of exercise, of a power of appointment at any time after the power was created:

(a) The disclaimer must be delivered to the holder of the power or to the fiduciary acting under the instrument that created the power; or

(b) If no fiduciary is serving when the disclaimer is sought to be delivered, the disclaimer must be filed with a court having authority to appoint the fiduciary.

(9) In the case of a disclaimer by an appointee of a nonfiduciary power of appointment:

(a) The disclaimer must be delivered to the holder, the personal representative of the holder's estate, or the fiduciary under the instrument that created the power; or

(b) If no fiduciary is serving when the disclaimer is sought to be delivered, the disclaimer must be filed with a court having authority to appoint the fiduciary.

(10) In the case of a disclaimer by a fiduciary of a power over a trust or estate, the disclaimer must be delivered as provided in subsection (2), subsection (3), or subsection (4) as if the power disclaimed were an interest in property.

(11) In the case of a disclaimer of a power exercisable by an agent, other than a power exercisable by a fiduciary over a trust or estate, the disclaimer must be delivered to the principal or the principal's representative.

(12) Notwithstanding subsection (1), delivery of a disclaimer of an interest in or relating to real estate shall be presumed upon the recording of the disclaimer in the office of the clerk of the court of the county or counties where the real estate is located.

(13) A fiduciary or other person having custody of the disclaimed interest is not liable for any otherwise proper distribution or other disposition made without actual notice of the disclaimer or, if the disclaimer is barred under §739.402, for any otherwise proper distribution or other disposition made in reliance on the disclaimer, if the distribution or disposition is made without actual knowledge of the facts constituting the bar of the right to disclaim.

(Laws 2005, ch. 2005-108, §1, effective July 1, 2005.)

§739.401. Disclaimer permitted at any time

A disclaimer may be made at any time unless barred under §739.402.

(Laws 2005, ch. 2005-108, §1, effective July 1, 2005.)

§739.402. Disclaimer may be barred or limited

(1) A disclaimer is barred by a written waiver of the right to disclaim.

(2) A disclaimer of an interest in property is barred if any of the following events occur before the disclaimer becomes effective:

(a) The disclaimer accepts the interest sought to be disclaimed;

(b) The disclaimant voluntarily assigns, conveys, encumbers, pledges, or transfers the interest sought to be disclaimed or contracts to do so;

(c) The interest sought to be disclaimed is sold pursuant to a judicial sale; or

(d) The disclaimant is insolvent when the disclaimer becomes irrevocable.

(3) A disclaimer, in whole or in part, of the future exercise of a power held in a fiduciary capacity is not barred by its previous exercise.

(4) A disclaimer, in whole or in part, of the future exercise of a power not held in a fiduciary capacity is not barred by its previous exercise unless the power is exercisable in favor of the disclaimant.

(5) A disclaimer of an interest in, or a power over, property which is barred by this section is ineffective.

(Laws 2005, ch. 2005-108, §1, effective July 1, 2005.)

§739.501. Effectiveness of disclaimer for tax purposes

Notwithstanding any other provision of this chapter, if, as a result of a disclaimer or transfer, the disclaimed or transferred interest is treated pursuant to the provisions of §2518 of the Internal Revenue Code of 1986 [FN1] as never having been transferred to the disclaimant, the disclaimer or transfer is effective as a disclaimer under this chapter.

[FN1] 26 U.S.C.A. § 2518.

(Laws 2005, ch. 2005-108, §1, effective July 1, 2005.)

§739.601. Need to record disclaimer of interest in real property

(1) A disclaimer of an interest in or relating to real estate does not provide constructive notice to all persons unless the disclaimer contains a legal description of the real estate to which the disclaimer relates and unless the disclaimer is filed for recording in the office of the clerk of the court in the county or counties where the real estate is located.

(2) An effective disclaimer meeting the requirements of subsection (1) constitutes constructive notice to all persons from the time of filing. Failure to record the disclaimer does not affect its validity as between the disclaimant and persons to whom the property interest or power passes by reason of the disclaimer.

(Laws 2005, ch. 2005-108, §1, effective July 1, 2005.)

C. Beneficiaries' Rights

1. General Limitations

The rights and interests of the beneficiaries in a trust are limited by the settlor (based on the terms of the trust) and state law. For example, the settlor may insert a spendthrift limitation on the rights of the beneficiary (discussed *infra* Section C2). And, state law may specify the beneficiary's ability to modify or terminate the trust, and the trustee's duties vis a vis the beneficiaries (such as the trustee's duty to inform and render accounts to the beneficiaries).

§739.0105. Code governs rights and interests of beneficiaries

(1) Except as otherwise provided in the terms of the trust, this code governs the duties and powers of a trustee, relations among trustees, and the rights and interests of a beneficiary.

(2) The terms of a trust prevail over any provision of this code except:

(a) The requirements for creating a trust.

(b) The duty of the trustee to act in good faith and in accordance with the terms and purposes of the trust and the interests of the beneficiaries.

(c) The requirement that a trust and its terms be for the benefit of the trust's beneficiaries, and that the trust have a purpose that is lawful, not contrary to public policy, and possible to achieve.

(d) The periods of limitation for commencing a judicial proceeding.

(e) The power of the court to take such action and exercise such jurisdiction as may be necessary in the interests of justice.

(f) The requirements under §736.0108(1) for the designation of a principal place of administration of the trust.

(g) The jurisdiction and venue provisions in §§736.0202, 736.0203, and 736.0204.

(h) The restrictions on the designation of representative under §736.0306.

(i) The formalities required under §736.0403(2) for the execution of a trust.

(j) The power of the court to modify or terminate a trust under §§736.0410-736.04115, except as provided in §736.04115(3)(b), and under §§736.0413, 736.0415, and 736.0416.

(k) The ability to modify a trust under §736.0412, except as provided in §736.0412(4)(b).

(l) The effect of a spendthrift provision and the rights of certain creditors and assignees to reach a trust as provided in part V.

(m) The trustee's duty under §736.05053 to pay expenses and obligations of the settlor's estate.

(n) The trustee's duty under §736.05055 to file a notice of trust at the settlor's death.

(o) The right of a trustee under §736.0701 to decline a trusteeship and the right of a trustee under §736.0705 to resign a trusteeship.

(p) The power of the court under §736.0702 to require, dispense with, modify, or terminate a bond.

(q) The power of the court under §736.0708(2) to adjust a trustee's compensation specified in the terms of the trust that is unreasonably low or high.

(r) The duty under §736.0813(1)(a) and (b) to notify qualified beneficiaries of an irrevocable trust of the existence of the trust, of the identity of the trustee, and of their rights to trust accountings.

(s) The duty under §736.0813(1)(c) and (d) to provide a complete copy of the trust instrument and to account to qualified beneficiaries.

(t) The duty under §736.0813(1)(e) to respond to the request of a qualified beneficiary of an irrevocable trust for relevant information about the assets and liabilities of the trust and the particulars relating to trust administration.

(u) The effect of an exculpatory term under §736.1011.

(v) The rights under §736.1013-736.1017 of a person other than a trustee or beneficiary.

(w) The effect of a penalty clause for contesting a trust under §736.1108.

(Laws 2006, ch. 2006-217, §1, effective July 1, 2007.)

2. Restrictions on Voluntary and Involuntary Transfers

a. Voluntary Transfer

The beneficiary of a trust generally can transfer his or her equitable interest in the trust. However, if the beneficiary is an income beneficiary, the beneficiary may transfer only his or her interest in the trust income because the transferee cannot acquire a greater estate than that possessed by the beneficiary.

A beneficiary can transfer an equitable interest either inter vivos or by will, in whole or in part, either absolutely or in trust. Thus, the beneficiary's interest is freely alienable unless the interest is made inalienable either by the terms of the trust or by statute. Scott & Fratcher, *supra*, §132, at 4-5. It is now held that the beneficiary has an interest in property and not merely a right of action against the trustee. *Id.*, §132 at 3.

To transfer an interest in a trust, the beneficiary must manifest an intention to transfer the interest either by express words or otherwise. The beneficiary can transfer his or her interest without the consent of, or notice to, the trustee unless the terms of the trust provide otherwise. *Id.*, §136 at 19. However, if the trustee does not have notice of the transfer, the trustee is under no liability for continuing to make payments to the original beneficiary.

b. Involuntary Transfer

The beneficiary's interest also may be subject to involuntary transfer. According to the modern trend, trust assets increasingly are available to creditors. Creditors can enforce their claims by several means, including attachment, garnishment, or execution. However, the creditor acquires only the same rights as the beneficiary.

Certain types of trusts contain restrictions on the beneficiary's interest. The most common type of protective trust is the *spendthrift trust*. In a spendthrift trust (more accurately, a spendthrift provision in a trust), the beneficiary's interest is not subject to either voluntary alienation by the beneficiary or involuntary alienation in the form of attachment by creditors. Such a provision also prevents a beneficiary from requesting that the trust be terminated prematurely. Other types of trusts with spendthrift-like restrictions are discussed *infra*.

Spendthrift trusts have been recognized by Florida case law since 1850. See Strong v. Willis, 3 Fla. 124 (Fla. 1850) (upholding validity of decedent's trust for his wife and children, to be held by them free of his debts, against a claim by a contractor who built the family home). Spendthrift trusts are authorized in many states by statute. See, e.g., Fla. Stat. §§736.0502 et seq.

In Florida, spendthrift trusts are subject to certain qualifications. For example, such trusts may not be created by the settlor to insulate himself or herself from creditors. See, e.g., In re Williams, 118 B.R. 812 (Bankr. N.D. Fla. 1990) (holding that, where a beneficiary exercises control over a retirement plan—as in having the right to direct the investment of the funds or the ability to withdraw his contributions in hardship circumstances—the plan no longer qualifies as a spendthrift trust under state law, and any interest held by the debtor will become part of the bankruptcy estate).

The significance of the spendthrift restriction, from the perspective of a creditor, is that the beneficiary's interest is not subject to enforcement of a money judgment until the beneficiary receives that interest (Fla. Stat. §736.0502(3)) ("a creditor or assignee of the beneficiary may not reach the interest or a distribution by the trustee *before receipt of the interest or distribution by the beneficiary*") (emphasis added).

Spendthrift trusts are subject to certain statutory exceptions. According to the Restatement (Second) of Trusts §157, particular classes of claimants may reach the interest of a beneficiary despite a spendthrift limitation. These claimants include: a spouse or child of the beneficiary for support, creditors who furnish necessary services or supplies to a beneficiary, creditors who furnish services or materials that benefit a beneficiary, or the state or federal government to satisfy a claim against the beneficiary. Many states have codified some or all of these exceptions. See, e.g., Fla. Stat. §736.0503.

As aforementioned, a beneficiary has the right to disclaim an interest in a spendthrift trust. That is, the right to disclaim is not precluded by the insertion by the testator or trustor of a spendthrift restriction prohibiting voluntary or involuntary assignments)(Fla. Stat. §739.104(1)).

Some trusts are similar to spendthrift trusts in terms of the imposition of restrictions on the ability of creditors to attach a beneficial interest. Several types of protective trusts exist, such as those for support and maintenance, or discretionary trusts. Whereas a spendthrift trust is a direct restraint on voluntary or involuntary alienation of a beneficial interest in a trust, these other protective trusts *indirectly* protect against alienation, for example, by providing for

forfeiture of the beneficiary's interest in case of a certain event or for the exercise of a trustee's discretion as to payment. Simmons, Spendthrift and Similar Protective Trusts, 55A Fla. Jur.2d Trusts §76. (In discretionary trusts, a trustee has discretion regarding how much, if any, income to give a beneficiary from the trust.)

§736.0501. Court may authorize creditor to reach beneficiary's interest

To the extent a beneficiary's interest is not subject to a spendthrift provision, the court may authorize a creditor or assignee of the beneficiary to reach the beneficiary's interest by attachment of present or future distributions to or for the benefit of the beneficiary or by other means. The court may limit the award to such relief as is appropriate under the circumstances.

(Laws. 2006, ch. 2006-217, §1, effective July 1, 2007.)

§736.0502. Spendthrift provisions: validity

(1) A spendthrift provision is valid only if the provision restrains both voluntary and involuntary transfer of a beneficiary's interest. This subsection does not apply to any trust in existence on the effective date of this code.

(2) A term of a trust providing that the interest of a beneficiary is held subject to a spendthrift trust, or words of similar import, is sufficient to restrain both voluntary and involuntary transfer of the beneficiary's interest.

(3) A beneficiary may not transfer an interest in a trust in violation of a valid spendthrift provision and, except as otherwise provided in this part, a creditor or assignee of the beneficiary may not reach the interest or a distribution by the trustee before receipt of the interest or distribution by the beneficiary.

(4) A valid spendthrift provision does not prevent the appointment of interests through the exercise of a power of appointment.

(Laws 2006, ch. 2006-217, §1, effective July 1, 2007.)

§736.0503. Special exceptions to spendthrift provisions: support, services to protect beneficiary's interest, state/federal claims

(1) As used in this section, the term "child" includes any person for whom an order or judgment for child support has been entered in this or any other state.

(2) To the extent provided in subsection (3), a spendthrift provision is unenforceable against:

(a) A beneficiary's child, spouse, or former spouse who has a judgment or court order against the beneficiary for support or maintenance.

(b) A judgment creditor who has provided services for the protection of a beneficiary's interest in the trust.

(c) A claim of this state or the United States to the extent a law of this state or a federal law so provides.

(3) Except as otherwise provided in this subsection, a claimant against which a spendthrift provision may not be enforced may obtain from a court, or pursuant to the Uniform Interstate Family Support Act, an order attaching present or future distributions to or for the benefit of the beneficiary. The court may limit the award to such relief as is appropriate under the circumstances. Notwithstanding this subsection, the remedies provided in this subsection apply to a claim by a beneficiary's child, spouse, former spouse, or a judgment creditor described in paragraph (2)(a) or paragraph (2)(b) only as a last resort upon an initial showing that traditional methods of enforcing the claim are insufficient.

(Laws 2006, ch. 2006-217, §1, effective July 1, 2007.)

§736.0504. Discretionary trusts; effect of spendthrift provision

(1) Whether or not a trust contains a spendthrift provision, a creditor of a beneficiary may not compel a distribution that is subject to the trustee's discretion, even if:

(a) The discretion is expressed in the form of a standard of distribution; or

(b) The trustee has abused the discretion.

(2) If the trustee's discretion to make distributions for the trustee's own benefit is limited by an ascertainable standard, a creditor may not reach or compel distribution of the beneficial interest except to the extent the interest would be subject to the creditor's claim were the beneficiary not acting as trustee.

(3) This section does not limit the right of a beneficiary to maintain a judicial proceeding against a trustee for an abuse of discretion or failure to comply with a standard for distribution.

(Laws 2006, ch. 2006-217, §1, effective July 1, 2007.)

§736.0506. Overdue distribution

(1) As used in this section, the term "mandatory distribution" means a distribution of income or principal the trustee is required to make to a

beneficiary under the terms of the trust, including a distribution on termination of the trust. The term does not include a distribution subject to the exercise of the trustee's discretion, even if:

(a) The discretion is expressed in the form of a standard of distribution; or

(b) The terms of the trust authorizing a distribution couple language of discretion with language of direction.

(2) A creditor or assignee of a beneficiary may reach a mandatory distribution of income or principal, including a distribution upon termination of the trust, if the trustee has not made the distribution to the beneficiary within a reasonable time after the designated distribution date, whether or not a trust contains a spendthrift provision.

(Laws 2006, ch. 2006-217, §5, effective July 1, 2007.)

II. Remedies of the Beneficiary

Statutes often specify the remedies available to beneficiaries for a trustee's breach of trust. For a discussion of the beneficiaries' remedies under Florida law, see Chapter XI, Section IV *supra*.

XIII
CHARITABLE TRUSTS

This chapter explores the general nature of charitable trusts, the definition of charitable purposes, the rules applicable to charitable trustees and beneficiaries, the special rules regarding modification of charitable trusts (the "cy pres" doctrine), the constitutional limits (race- and gender-based) on testamentary gifts for charitable purposes, and the enforcement of charitable trusts.

I. Introduction

A. Definition of Charity

Courts frequently have to determine whether a particular gift is "charitable" based on a theoretical definition or purpose. Often, construction of the terms "charity" and "charitable purposes" arises in cases involving exemption from state taxes. Bogert, *supra*, at §361.

The meaning of "charitable" under both federal and state tax law is distinct from the definition of "charitable" in trust law. In reality, however, the American law of charitable trusts is intimately connected with the statutory requirements for charitable tax exemption. Ilana H. Eisenstein, Comment, Keeping Charity in Charitable Trust Law: The Barnes Foundation and the Case for Consideration of Public Interest in Administration of Charitable Trusts, 151 U. Pa. L. Rev. 1747, 1760-1761 (2003).

Frequently, state law defines "charitable trust" by reference to the definition in the Internal Revenue Code of those organizations that are exempt from taxation (IRC §4947(a)). See, e.g., Fla. Stat. §736.1201 (referring to the IRC). Definitions of the term "charitable" in tax law are extremely influential (although not necessarily dispositive) in judicial determinations of the validity of charitable trusts and charitable purposes. The definition of "charity" for purposes of charitable trusts generally is broader than the definition used by the Internal Revenue Service. McGovern & Kurtz, *supra*, §9.7 at 390. In order for a charitable trust to acquire tax-exempt status under federal income tax law, the trust must comply with requirements specified by the Internal Revenue Code. Various sections of the Internal Revenue Code and Treasury regulations issued thereunder specify the types of organizations and charitable purposes that qualify for tax-exempt status.

Note that courts have validated charitable trusts by determining that various synonyms used by settlors (e.g., "benevolent," "beneficent," "eleemosynary") have the same meaning as the term "charitable." See, e.g., People v. Cogswell, 45 P. 270, 271 (Cal. 1896) ("'Eleemosynary' has come in the law to be interchangeable with the word 'charitable'").

B. Origins of Charitable Trusts

Charitable trusts have been traced as far back as the fourteenth century. In 1601, Parliament codified the law of charitable trusts with the enactment of the Statute of Charitable Uses, 43 Eliz., c. 4 (Eng.). The Statute had two objectives: to enumerate those trust purposes that could qualify as charitable, and to provide for a method of investigation and enforcement of charitable trusts.

The public attitude toward charitable trusts has changed throughout American history, as explained below:

- The American law of trusts was inherited from British common law, and with it came the taint of British aristocracy. In the early republic, many states adopted highly restrictive laws regulating charitable trusts because they saw them as remnants of colonial law. Until the late nineteenth century, "charity was associated with privilege, with the dead hand, with established churches, with massive wealth in perpetuity"—with distinctly un-American ideals. Only the wealthy could afford to create enduring foundations; thus, such entities were considered part and parcel of the problems of inherited privilege.
- In the latter part of the nineteenth century, however, American attitudes toward charity began to change. Philanthropy came to be seen as a substitute for government action and socialist values. Greater reverence for private property and individualism led to increased respect for donors and their wishes. The rise of the great philanthropists, particularly Andrew Carnegie and John D. Rockefeller, created a new public perception that private wealth could be a "public trust" benefiting all society, rather than simply a marker of elite privilege. These

> changes led to more favorable treatment of charitable trusts and greater respect for philanthropists and their charitable designs.

Eisenstein, *supra*, at 1756.

In the nineteenth century, the United States Supreme Court examined the validity of charitable trusts in two cases. In Trustees of Philadelphia Baptist Ass'n v. Hart's Executors, 17 U.S. (4 Wheat.) 1 (1819), the Court determined whether a private trust established for charitable purposes was invalid for lack of a definite beneficiary when the jurisdiction had repealed the Statute of Charitable Uses. In 1790, a Virginia citizen, Silas Hart, executed a will bequeathing property to "the Baptist Association [as] a perpetual fund for the education of youths of the Baptist denomination, who shall appear promising for the ministry. . . ." In 1792, Virginia, like many American states in post-Revolutionary America, had repealed all statutes derived from English laws, including the Statute of Charitable Uses. Thus, in 1795, when the testator died, the jurisdiction had no legislation recognizing charitable trusts. The Supreme Court held that Virginia's repeal of the Statute of Charitable Uses deprived the Chancery Court of power to enforce the trust, and that there was no known common law validating such private trusts established for charitable purposes and having no definite beneficiaries.

The Court revisited the issue of the validity of charitable trusts in Vidal v. Girard's Executors, 43 U.S. (2 How.) 127 (1844). Banker Stephen Girard bequeathed his $7 million estate to the City of Philadelphia to establish a school for poor, white male orphans. His heirs challenged the will. The Statute of Charitable Uses, although not repealed (as in Virginia), was not in force in Pennsylvania. Justice Story, the noted scholar of equity jurisprudence, held that recognition of charitable trusts did not depend on enactment by the jurisdiction of the English Statute of Charitable Uses. Based on historical analysis, Story explained that charitable trusts had been enforced in Chancery long before Parliament's enactment of the Statute of Charitable Uses. That decision effectively overruled *Trustees of Philadelphia Baptist Association* and validated charitable trusts.

C. Private Express Trusts Distinguished

Charitable trusts manifest some similarities to, as well as differences from, private express trusts. Like private express trusts, charitable trusts arise from the intention of a settlor to create a trust. A charitable trust may be created by use of the same methods as those to create private express trusts, and may be inter vivos or testamentary.

However, charitable trusts benefit the community rather than individuals. They are not subject to the rule requiring definite beneficiaries. In fact, they must have *indefinite beneficiaries*. They are enforced by the state Attorney General (rather than the beneficiaries). Also, they constitute an exception to the Rule Against Perpetuities, which limits the duration of private express trusts, and therefore may continue indefinitely.

Finally, charitable trusts receive tax advantages.

> A charitable trust benefits from tax-exempt status in two ways. First, the organization itself does not incur tax liabilities on any income earned or on property or assets held. Second, income tax deductibility and estate tax benefits encourage donors to give money to an established charitable organization or to found a new charitable trust.

Eisenstein, *supra*, at 1760.

FLORIDA STATUTES
§736.1201. Definitions

As used in this part:

(1) "Charitable organization" means an organization described in §501(c)(3) of the Internal Revenue Code [FN1] and exempt from tax under §501(a) of the Internal Revenue Code. [FN2]

(2) "Internal Revenue Code" means the Internal Revenue Code of 1986, as amended. [FN3]

(3) "Private foundation trust" means a trust, including a trust described in §4947(a)(1) of the Internal Revenue Code, [FN4] as defined in §509(a) of the Internal Revenue Code. [FN5]

(4) "Split interest trust" means a trust for individual and charitable beneficiaries that is subject to the provisions of §4947(a)(2) of the Internal Revenue Code.

(5) "State attorney" means the state attorney for the judicial circuit of the principal place of administration of the trust pursuant to §736.0108.

[FN1] 26 U.S.C.A. §501(c)(3).
[FN2] 26 U.S.C.A. §501(a).
[FN3] 26 U.S.C.A. §1 et seq.
[FN4] 26 U.S.C.A. §4947(a)(1).
[FN5] 26 U.S.C.A. §509(a).

(Laws 2006, ch. 2006-217, §12, effective July 1, 2007.)

INTERNAL REVENUE CODE

§501. Organizations exempt from taxation

(a) Exemption from taxation.—An organization described in subsection (c) or (d) or section 401(a) shall be exempt from taxation under this subtitle unless such exemption is denied under section 502 or 503.

(b) Tax on unrelated business income and certain other activities.—An organization exempt from taxation under subsection (a) shall be subject to tax to the extent provided in parts II, III, and VI of this subchapter, but (notwithstanding parts II, III, and VI of this subchapter) shall be considered an organization exempt from income taxes for the purpose of any law which refers to organizations exempt from income taxes.

(c) List of exempt organizations.—The following organizations are referred to in subsection (a):

(1) Any corporation organized under Act of Congress which is an instrumentality of the United States but only if such corporation—

(A) is exempt from Federal income taxes—

(i) under such Act as amended and supplemented before July 18, 1984, or

(ii) under this title without regard to any provision of law which is not contained in this title and which is not contained in a revenue Act, or

(B) is described in subsection (l).

(2) Corporations organized for the exclusive purpose of holding title to property, collecting income therefrom, and turning over the entire amount thereof, less expenses, to an organization which itself is exempt under this section. Rules similar to the rules of subparagraph (G) of paragraph (25) shall apply for purposes of this paragraph.

(3) Corporations, and any community chest, fund, or foundation, organized and operated exclusively for religious, charitable, scientific, testing for public safety, literary, or educational purposes, or to foster national or international amateur sports competition (but only if no part of its activities involve the provision of athletic facilities or equipment), or for the prevention of cruelty to children or animals, no part of the net earnings of which inures to the benefit of any private shareholder or individual, no substantial part of the activities of which is carrying on propaganda, or otherwise attempting, to influence legislation (except as otherwise provided in subsection (h)), and which does not participate in, or intervene in (including the publishing or distributing of statements), any political campaign on behalf of (or in opposition to) any candidate for public office.

. . . .

(August 16, 1954, ch. 736, 68A Stat. 163; March 13, 1956, ch. 83, §5(2), 70 Stat. 49; April 22, 1960, Pub. L. 86-428, §1, 74 Stat. 54; July 14, 1960, Pub. L. 86-667, §1, 74 Stat. 534; Oct. 16, 1962, Pub. L. 87-834, §8(d), 76 Stat. 997; Feb. 2, 1966, Pub. L. 89-352, §1, 80 Stat. 4; Nov. 8, 1966, Pub. L. 89-800, §6(a), 80 Stat. 1515; June 28, 1968, Pub. L. 90-364, Title I, §109(a), 82 Stat. 269; December 30, 1969, Pub. L. 91-172, Title I, §§101(j)(3) to (6), 121(b)(5)(A), (6)(A), 83 Stat. 526, 527, 541; December 31, 1970, Pub. L. 91-618, §1, 84 Stat. 1855; August 29, 1972, Pub. L. 92-418, §1(a), 86 Stat. 656; June 8, 1974, Pub. L. 93-310, §3(a), 88 Stat. 235; January 3, 1975, Pub. L. 93-625, §10(c), 88 Stat. 2119; Oct. 4, 1976, Pub. L. 94-455, Title XIII, §§1307(a)(1), (d)(1)(A), 1312(a), 1313(a), Title XIX, §1906(b)(13)(A), Title XXI, §§2113(a), 2134(b), 90 Stat. 1720, 1727, 1730, 1834, 1907, 1927; Oct. 20, 1976, Pub. L. 94-568, §§1(a), 2(a), 90 Stat. 2697; Feb. 10, 1978, Pub. L. 95-227, §4(a), 92 Stat. 15; August 15, 1978, Pub. L. 95-345, §1(a), 92 Stat. 481; Nov. 6, 1978, Pub. L. 95-600, Title VII, §703(b)(2), (g)(2)(B), 92 Stat. 2939, 2940; April 1, 1980, Pub. L. 96-222, Title I, §108(b)(2)(B), 94 Stat. 226; September 26, 1980, Pub. L. 96-364, Title II, §209(a), 94 Stat. 1290; December 24, 1980, Pub. L. 96-601, §3(a), 94 Stat. 3496; December 28, 1980, Pub. L. 96-605, Title I, §106(a), 94 Stat. 3523; December 29, 1981, Pub. L. 97-119, Title I, §103(c)(1), 95 Stat. 1638; September 3, 1982, Pub. L. 97-248, Title II, §286(a), Title III, §354(a), (b), 96 Stat. 569, 640, 641; January 12, 1983, Pub. L. 97-448, Title III, §306(b)(5), 96 Stat. 2406; July 18, 1984, Pub. L. 98-369, Div. A, Title X, §§1032(a), 1079, Div. B, Title VIII, §2813(b), 98 Stat. 1033, 1056, 1206; April 7, 1986, Pub. L. 99-272, Title XI, §11012(b), 100 Stat. 260; Oct. 22, 1986, Pub. L. 99-514, Title X, §§1012(a), 1024(b), Title XI, §§1109(a), 1114(b)(14), Title XVI, §1603(a), Title XVIII, §§1879(k)(1), 1899A(15), 100 Stat. 2390, 2406, 2435, 2451, 2768, 2909, 2959; December 22, 1987, Pub. L. 100-203, Title X, §10711(a)(2), 101 Stat. 1330-464; Nov. 10, 1988, Pub. L. 100-647, Title I, §§1010(b)(4), 1011(c)(7)(D), 1016(a)(1)(A), (2) to (4), 1018(u)(14), (15), (34), Title II, §2003(a)(1), (2), Title VI, §6202(a), 102 Stat. 3451, 3458, 3573, 3574, 3590, 3592, 3597 to 3598, 3730; August 9, 1989, Pub. L. 101-73, Title XIV, §1402(a), 103 Stat. 550; Oct. 24, 1992, Pub. L. 102-486, Title XIX, §1940(a), 106 Stat.

3034; August 10, 1993, Pub. L. 103-66, Title XIII, §13146(a), (b), 107 Stat. 443; July 30, 1996, Pub. L. 104-168, Title XIII, §1311(b)(1), 110 Stat. 1478; August 20, 1996, Pub. L. 104-188, Title I, §§1114(a), 1704(j)(5), 110 Stat. 1759, 1882; August 21, 1996, Pub. L. 104-191, Title III, §§341(a), 342(a), 110 Stat. 2070; August 5, 1997, Pub. L. 105-33, Title IV, §4041(a), 111 Stat. 360; August 5, 1997, Pub. L. 105-34, Title I, §101(c), Title IX, §§963(a), (b), 974(a), 111 Stat. 799, 892, 898; July 22, 1998, Pub. L. 105-206, Title VI, §6023(6), (7), 112 Stat. 825; June 7, 2001, Pub. L. 107-16, Title VI, §611(d)(3)(C), 115 Stat. 98; December 21, 2001, Pub. L. 107-90, Title II, §202, 115 Stat. 890; November 11, 2003, Pub. L. 108-121, Title 1 §§105(a), 108(a), 117 Stat. 1338, 1339; April 10, 2004, Pub. L. 108-218, Title II, 206(a), (b), 118 Stat. 610; October 22, 2004, Pub. L. 108-357, Title III, Subititle B, §319(a), (b), 118 Stat. 1470; August 8, 2004, P.L. 109-58, Title XIII, Subtitle A, §1304(a), (b) 110 Stat. 997. Amended by December 21, 2005, Pub. L. 109-135, Title IV, Subititle A, §412(bb), (cc), 110 Stat. 2639.)

§4947. Charitable trust defined; certain nonexempt trusts

(a) Application of tax.—

(1) Charitable trusts.—For purposes of part II of subchapter F of chapter 1 (other than section 508(a), (b), and (c)) and for purposes of this chapter, a trust which is not exempt from taxation under section 501(a), all of the unexpired interests in which are devoted to one or more of the purposes described in section 170(c)(2)(B), and for which a deduction was allowed under section 170, 545(b)(2), 556(b)(2), 642(c), 2055, 2106(a)(2), or 2522 (or the corresponding provisions of prior law), shall be treated as an organization described in section 501(c)(3). For purposes of section 509(a)(3)(A), such a trust shall be treated as if organized on the day on which it first becomes subject to this paragraph.

(2) Split-interest trusts.—In the case of a trust which is not exempt from tax under section 501(a), not all of the unexpired interests in which are devoted to one or more of the purposes described in section 170(c)(2)(B), and which has amounts in trust for which a deduction was allowed under section 170, 545(b)(2), 556(b)(2), 642(c), 2055, 2106(a)(2), or 2522, section 507 (relating to termination of private foundation status), section 508(e) (relating to governing instruments) to the extent applicable to a trust described in this paragraph, section 4941 (relating to taxes on self-dealing), section 4943 (relating to taxes on excess business holdings) except as provided in subsection (b)(3), section 4944 (relating to investments which jeopardize charitable purpose) except as provided in subsection (b)(3), and section 4945 (relating to taxes on taxable expenditures) shall apply as if such trust were a private foundation. This paragraph shall not apply with respect to—

(A) any amounts payable under the terms of such trust to income beneficiaries, unless a deduction was allowed under section 170(f)(2)(B), 2055(e)(2)(B), or 2522(c)(2)(B),

(B) any amounts in trust other than amounts for which a deduction was allowed under section 170, 545(b)(2), 556(b)(2), 642(c), 2055, 2106(a)(2), or 2522, if such other amounts are segregated from amounts for which no deduction was allowable, or

(C) any amounts transferred in trust before May 27, 1969.

(3) Segregated amounts.—For purposes of paragraph (2)(B), a trust with respect to which amounts are segregated shall separately account for the various income, deduction, and other items properly attributable to each of such segregated amounts.

(b) Special rules.—

(1) Regulations.—The Secretary shall prescribe such regulations as may be necessary to carry out the purposes of this section.

(2) Limit to segregated amounts.—If any amounts in the trust are segregated within the meaning of subsection (a)(2)(B) of this section, the value of the net assets for purposes of subsections (c)(2) and (g) of section 507 shall be limited to such segregated amounts.

(3) Sections 4943 and 4944.—Sections 4943 and 4944 shall not apply to a trust which is described in subsection (a)(2) if—

(A) all the income interest (and none of the remainder interest) of such trust is devoted solely to one or more of the purposes described in section 170(c)(2)(B), and all amounts in such trust for which a deduction was allowed under section 170, 545(b)(2), 556(b)(2), 642(c), 2055, 2106(a)(2), or 2522 have an aggregate value not more than 60 percent of the aggregate fair market value of all amounts in such trusts, or

(B) a deduction was allowed under section 170, 545(b)(2), 556(b)(2), 642(c), 2055, 2106(a)(2), or 2522 for amounts payable under the terms of such trust to every remainder beneficiary but not to any income beneficiary.

(4) Section 507.—The provisions of section 507(a) shall not apply to a trust which is described

in subsection (a)(2) by reason of a distribution of qualified employer securities (as defined in section 664(g)(4)) to an employee stock ownership plan (as defined in section 4975(e)(7)) in a qualified gratuitous transfer (as defined by section 664(g)).
(December 30, 1969, Pub. L. 91-172, Title I, §101(b), 83 Stat. 517. Amended by October 4, 1976, Pub. L. 94-455, Title XIX, §1906(b) (13) (A), 90 Stat. 1834; August 5, 1997, Pub. L. 105-34, Title XV, §1530(c)(9), , 111 Stat. 1079; June 7, 2001, Pub. L. 107-16, Title V, §542(e)(4), , 115 Stat. 85; October 22, 2004, Pub. L. 109-357, Title IV, §413(c)(30), 118 Stat. 1509.)

TREASURY REGULATION §1.501(c)(3)-1(d)(2)

. . .

(2) **Charitable defined**. The term 'charitable' is used in section 501(c)(3) in its generally accepted legal sense and is therefore, not to be construed as limited by the separate enumeration in section 501(c)(3) of other tax-exempt purposes which may fall within the broad outlines of 'charity' as developed by judicial decisions. Such terms include: Relief of the poor and distressed or of the underprivileged; advancement of religion; advancement of education or science; erection or maintenance of public buildings, monuments, or works, lessening of the burdens of Government; and promotion of social welfare by organizations designed to accomplish any of the above purposes, or (i) to lessen neighborhood tensions; (ii) to eliminate prejudice and discrimination; (iii) to defend human and civil rights secured by law; or (iv) to combat community deterioration and juvenile delinquency. The fact that an organization which is organized and operated for the relief of indigent persons may receive voluntary contributions from the persons intended to be relieved will not necessarily prevent such organizations from being exempt as an organization organized and operated exclusively for charitable purposes. The fact that an organization, in carrying out its primary purpose, advocates social or civic changes or presents opinion on controversial issues with the intention of molding public opinion or creating public sentiment to an acceptance of its views does not preclude such organization from qualifying under section 501(c)(3) so long as it is not an 'action' organization of any one of the types described in paragraph (c)(3) of this section.
(November 26, 1960, T.D. 6500, 25 FR 11737. Amended by January 11, 1961, T.D. 6525, 26 R 189; December 12, 1967, T.D. 6939, 32 FR 17661; August 16, 1967, T.D. 7428, 41 FR 34620; August 31, 1990, T.D. 8308, 55 FR 35587.)

D. Application of Florida Law to Charitable Trusts

The Florida legislature enacted the Uniform Trust Code in 2006 (effective July 1, 2007). The new Code applies to express trusts that are both charitable and noncharitable (Fla. Stat. §736.0102; Unif. Trust Code §102). Except as otherwise provided, the provisions of the Code apply retroactively. For matters that are not addressed in the new Trust Code, the new Code provides for resort to the common law and "principles of equity" (Fla. Stat. §736.0106; Unif. Trust Code §106). See generally David J. Powell, The New Florida Trust Code, Part I, 80 Fla. B.J. 24 (July/Aug. 2006) (explaining key provisions of the new Code).

The distinction between "beneficiary" and "qualified beneficiary" (as those terms are used in Florida Statutes §§736.0103, 736.0110) is explained in the Commentary to the Uniform Trust Code definitional section:

> The definition of "beneficiary" includes only those who hold beneficial interests of the trust. Because a charitable trust is not created to benefit ascertainable beneficiaries but to benefit the community [as stated in Section 405a of the Uniform Trust Code] persons receiving distributions from a charitable trust are not beneficiaries as that term is defined in this Code. However, pursuant to Section 110(b) [of the Uniform Trust Code, codified at Fla. Stat. §736.0110], also granted rights of a qualified beneficiary under the Code are charitable organizations expressly designated to receive distributions under the terms of a charitable trust [in enumerated circumstances].

Unif. Trust Code §103, cmt.

The Florida Trust Code also incorporates Uniform Trust Code provisions regulating the requirements for trust creation (Unif. Trust Code §402, codified as Fla. Stat. §736.0402), charitable purposes and enforcement (Unif. Trust Code §405, codified as Fla. Stat. §736.0405), modification of charitable trusts (Unif. Trust Code §413, codified as Fla. Stat. §736.0413), and vacancies in trustees (Unif. Trust Code §704, codified as Fla. Stat. §736.0704).

Commentary to the Uniform Trust Code (Article 4) explains that the particular provisions for creation, charitable purposes, and

enforcement merely codify traditional doctrine. The provision on trust purposes specifies the same charitable purposes listed in the Restatement (Third) of Trusts §28, and Restatement (Second) of Trusts §368. (See Unif. Trust Code, §405 cmt.) If a trust that states a general charitable intent is silent as to a particular charitable trust purpose or the beneficiary of a charitable trust, the trust does not fail. Rather, the Code permits a court to make the selection consistent with the settlor's intention (to the extent it can be ascertained) (Unif. Trust Code §405(b), codified as Fla. Stat. §736.0405(2)).

§736.0102. Scope

This code applies to express trusts, charitable or noncharitable, and trusts created pursuant to a law, judgment, or decree that requires the trust to be administered in the manner of an express trust. This code does not apply to constructive or resulting trusts; conservatorships; custodial arrangements pursuant to the Florida Uniform Transfers to Minors Act; [FN1] business trusts providing for certificates to be issued to beneficiaries; common trust funds; land trusts under §689.05; trusts created by the form of the account or by the deposit agreement at a financial institution; voting trusts; security arrangements; liquidation trusts; trusts for the primary purpose of paying debts, dividends, interest, salaries, wages, profits, pensions, or employee benefits of any kind; and any arrangement under which a person is nominee or escrowee for another.

[FN1] F.S.A. §710.101 et seq.

(Laws 2006, ch. 2006-217, §1, effective July 1, 2007.)

§736.0103. Definitions

Unless the context otherwise requires, in this code:

. . .

(4) "Beneficiary" means a person who:

(a) Has a present or future beneficial interest in a trust, vested or contingent; or

(b) Holds a power of appointment over trust property in a capacity other than that of trustee.

. . .

(5) "Charitable trust" means a trust, or portion of a trust, created for a charitable purpose as described in §736.0405(1).

. . . .

(14) "Qualified beneficiary" means a living beneficiary who, on the date the beneficiary's qualification is determined:

(a) Is a distributee or permissible distributee of trust income or principal;

(b) Would be a distributee or permissible distributee of trust income or principal if the interests of the distributees described in paragraph (a) terminated on that date without causing the trust to terminate; or

(c) Would be a distributee or permissible distributee of trust income or principal if the trust terminated in accordance with its terms on that date.

(Laws 2006, ch. 2006-217, §1, effective July 1, 2007.)

§736.0106. Common law and equitable principles

The common law of trusts and principles of equity supplement this code, except to the extent modified by this code or another law of this state.

(Laws 2006, ch. 2006-217, §1, effective July 1, 2007.)

§736.0110. Qualified beneficiaries

(1) A charitable organization expressly designated to receive distributions under the terms of a charitable trust has the rights of a qualified beneficiary under this code if the charitable organization, on the date the charitable organization's qualification is being determined:

(a) Is a distributee or permissible distributee of trust income or principal;

(b) Would be a distributee or permissible distributee of trust income or principal on termination of the interests of other distributees or permissible distributees then receiving or eligible to receive distributions; or

(c) Would be a distributee or permissible distributee of trust income or principal if the trust terminated on that date.

(2) A person appointed to enforce a trust created for the care of an animal or another noncharitable purpose as provided in §736.0408 or §736.0409 has the rights of a qualified beneficiary under this code.

(3) The Attorney General may assert the rights of a qualified beneficiary with respect to a charitable trust having its principal place of administration in this state.

(Laws 2006, ch 2006-217, §1, effective July 1, 2007.)

§736.0402. Trust creation

(1) A trust is created only if:

(a) The settlor has capacity to create a trust.

(b) The settlor indicates an intent to create the trust.

(c) The trust has a definite beneficiary or is:

1. A charitable trust;

2. A trust for the care of an animal, as provided in §736.0408; or

3. A trust for a noncharitable purpose, as provided in §736.0409.

(d) The trustee has duties to perform.

(e) The same person is not the sole trustee and sole beneficiary.

(2) A beneficiary is definite if the beneficiary can be ascertained now or in the future, subject to any applicable rule against perpetuities.

(3) A power of a trustee to select a beneficiary from an indefinite class is valid. If the power is not exercised within a reasonable time, the power fails and the property subject to the power passes to the persons who would have taken the property had the power not been conferred.

(Laws 2006, ch. 2006-217, §4, effective July 1, 2007.)

II. Charitable Purposes

The Preamble to the English Statute of Charitable Uses enumerated several purposes that were recognized as charitable. Courts frequently refer to that list to identify those purposes that are charitable. Courts generally hold that any purpose is charitable that falls within a type designated in the Preamble, or that is analogous thereto (although the original list was not intended to be complete). As recognized by the Statute of Charitable Uses, charitable purposes include the following:

> The relief of aged, impotent and poor people; the maintenance of maimed and sick soldiers and mariners; the support of schools of learning, free schools, and scholars of universities; repairs of bridges, ports, havens, causeways, churches, seabanks, and highways; education and preferment of orphans; the relief, stock, and maintenance of houses of correction; marriage of poor maids; aid and help of young tradesmen, handicraftsmen, and persons decayed; relief or redemption of prisoners and captives; aid of poor inhabitants concerning payments of fifteenths, setting out of soldiers, and other taxes.

43 Eliz. c. 4 (1601). Gradually, courts have enlarged the scope of charitable purposes.

Definitions of charitable purposes in both the Restatements and the Uniform Trust Code are derived from the Statute of Charitable Uses. According to Uniform Trust Code §405(a), a charitable trust may be created for the following charitable purposes: the relief of poverty; the advancement of education or religion; the promotion of health, governmental, or municipal purposes; or other purposes the accomplishment of which is beneficial to the community. The above rule restates the charitable purposes listed in the Restatement (Third) of Trusts §28 and the Restatement (Second) of Trusts §368.

The determination of whether the settlor's purpose is charitable is made by a court. That is, the settlor's opinion of whether a purpose is charitable is irrelevant. See, e.g., Shenandoah Valley Nat'l Bank v. Taylor, 63 S.E.2d 786 (Va. 1951) (holding that a charitable trust was invalid as an educational trust, despite the fact that the testator had directed that payments be made to school children at Easter and Christmas to be used in furtherance of their education).

Charitable trusts are subject to the restriction that the trust purpose must not be illegal or contrary to public policy. Unif. Trust Code §404 ("A trust may be created only to the extent its purposes are lawful, not contrary to public policy, and possible to achieve. A trust and its terms must be for the benefit of its beneficiaries."). See also Restatement (Third) of Trusts §29 ("An intended trust or trust provision is invalid if: (a) its purpose is unlawful or its performance calls for the commission of a criminal or tortious act; (b) it violates rules relating to perpetuities; or (c) it is contrary to public policy").

If the settlor states a general charitable purpose, and neglects to set forth either a specific purpose or beneficiary (ies), the court may select the particular purpose or beneficiary (ies) or delegate the task to a trustee. Unif. Trust Code §405(b).

Charitable trusts must be dedicated exclusively to charitable objectives, even if only for a period of time (e.g., charitable remainder trusts). As explained above, a charitable trust has to be for a charitable purpose. However, a trust can be both charitable and noncharitable simultaneously. Such trusts are termed *split-interest trusts*. A common type of such trusts is a private express trust for the settlor's surviving spouse for life, followed by a charitable remainder trust devoting the remainder to a charitable organization.

Trusts to satisfy a personal whim of the donor do not have sufficient community benefit. For the same reason, trusts that are established to disseminate beliefs that are either irrational or inconsequential are not valid.

III. Beneficiaries

Charitable trusts are exempt from the rule applicable to private express trusts requiring definite beneficiaries. Whereas definite beneficiaries are necessary to enforce a private express trust, the state Attorney General is the public representative charged with the enforcement of charitable trusts.

Actually, the more narrow the class of beneficiaries, the more likely a charitable trust runs the danger of being invalid.

> **If the trust provides for the distribution of charitable benefits to a single individual, or a very small group of definite persons, it can be said that the public or community benefit is nonexistent or so small as to be negligible. Here the type of benefit to be given by the trust is appropriate for a charitable trust, but the benefit is not to be so widely distributed as to make the trust one of general interest. Illustrations of this type of case are to be found in trusts to educate a particular named person, or to prepare a designated relative of the settlor for the ministry. These trusts provide some educational or religious benefits, but not to such an extent as to give the state any interest in the enforcement of the trust.**

Bogert, *supra*, at §363.

§736.0405. Charitable purposes

(1) A trust may be created for charitable purposes. Charitable purposes include, but are not limited to, the relief of poverty; the advancement of arts, sciences, education, or religion; and the promotion of health, governmental, or municipal purposes.

(2) If the terms of a charitable trust do not indicate a particular charitable purpose or beneficiary, the court may select one or more charitable purposes or beneficiaries. The selection must be consistent with the settlor's intent to the extent such intent can be ascertained.

(3) The settlor of a charitable trust, among others, has standing to enforce the trust.

(Laws 2006, ch. 2006-217, §4, effective July 1, 2007.)

IV. Trustees

Trustees of charitable trusts are charged with fulfilling the trust purposes for the designated class of beneficiaries and in accordance with the settlor's intent. The duties of trustees of charitable trusts are similar to those of private express trusts. However, the trustees of charitable trusts may be subject to additional statutory duties.

Misconduct by a trustee of a charitable trust, similar to misconduct by a trustee of a private express trust, may result in the trustee's removal from the administration of the trust. In a famous case of trustee misconduct, a Hawaii probate court reorganized one of the nation's richest charitable trusts by removal of four of the five trustees of the Kamehameha Schools Bishop Estate (and acceptance of the resignation of the fifth). The charitable trust was established over a century ago by the will of Princess Bernice Pauahi Bishop, the last descendant of Hawaiian King Kamehameha. The princess devised 400,000 acres of land in a charitable trust for the education of Hawaiian children. In re Estate of Bishop, 499 P.2d 670, 673 (Haw. 1972).

On the *Bishop* case, see Robert Mahealani M. Seto & Lynne Marie Kohm, Of Princesses, Charities, Trustees, and Fairytales: A Lesson of the Simple Wishes of Princess Bernice Pauahi Bishop, 21 Haw. L. Rev. 393 (1999); Robert Whitman & Kumar Paturi, Improving Mechanisms for Resolving Complaints of Powerless Trust Beneficiaries, 16 Quinnipiac Prob. L.J. 64, 81-84 (2002) (discussing *Bishop* litigation).

The Uniform Trust Code addresses vacancies in the trusteeship of charitable trusts (i.e., those vacancies that are required to be filled). Such vacancies must be filled in a particular order of priority: by persons designated in the trust instrument, by persons selected by a charitable organization that is expressly designated to receive distributions under the terms of the trust, and finally by persons who are appointed by the court (Unif. Trust Code §704, codified as Fla. Stat. §736.0704). The Florida Code does not include suggested UTC language that would require approval of persons as trustees and selected by a charitable organization (the second order of priority above) to be subject to the concurrence of the state attorney general. Compare Unif. Trust Code §704 (d)(2), with Fla. Stat. §736.0704 (4)(b).

For an interesting case on the eligibility to serve as a charitable trustee, see In re Estate of Coleman, 317 A.2d 631 (Pa. 1974) (holding that the settlor's requirement that spouses of charitable trustees must be Protestant was an unreasonable condition, unrelated to the settlor's charitable intentions, and not appropriate for judicial enforcement).

§736.0704. Vacancy in trusteeship

(1) A vacancy in a trusteeship occurs if:

(a) A person designated as trustee declines the trusteeship;

(b) A person designated as trustee cannot be identified or does not exist;

(c) A trustee resigns;

(d) A trustee is disqualified or removed;

(e) A trustee dies; or

(f) A trustee is adjudicated to be incapacitated.

(2) If one or more cotrustees remain in office, a vacancy in a trusteeship need not be filled. A vacancy in a trusteeship must be filled if the trust has no remaining trustee.

(3) A vacancy in a trusteeship of a noncharitable trust that is required to be filled must be filled in the following order of priority:

(a) By a person named or designated pursuant to the terms of the trust to act as successor trustee.

(b) By a person appointed by unanimous agreement of the qualified beneficiaries.

(c) By a person appointed by the court.

(4) A vacancy in a trusteeship of a charitable trust that is required to be filled must be filled in the following order of priority:

(a) By a person named or designated pursuant to the terms of the trust to act as successor trustee.

(b) By a person selected by unanimous agreement of the charitable organizations expressly designated to receive distributions under the terms of the trust.

(c) By a person appointed by the court.

(5) The court may appoint an additional trustee or special fiduciary whenever the court considers the appointment necessary for the administration of the trust, whether or not a vacancy in a trusteeship exists or is required to be filled.

(Laws 2006, ch. 2006-217, §7, effective July 1, 2007.)

§736.1202. Application of Part

Except as otherwise provided in the trust, the provisions of this part apply to all private foundation trusts and split interest trusts, whether created or established before or after November 1, 1971, and to all trust assets acquired by the trustee before or after November 1, 1971.

(Laws 2006, ch. 2006-217, §12, effective July 1, 2007.)

§736.1203. Trustees of private foundations

Except as provided in §736.1205, the trustee of a private foundation trust or a split interest trust has the duties and powers conferred on the trustee by this part.

(Laws 2006, ch. 2006-217, §12, effective July 1, 2007.)

§736.1204. Limitations on powers and duties of trustees of a private foundation trust or a split interest trust

(1) In the exercise of a trustee's powers, including the powers granted by this part, a trustee has a duty to act with due regard to the trustee's obligation as a fiduciary, including a duty not to exercise any power in such a way as to:

(a) Deprive the trust of an otherwise available tax exemption, deduction, or credit for tax purposes;

(b) Deprive a donor of a trust asset or tax deduction or credit; or

(c) Operate to impose a tax on a donor, trust, or other person.

For purposes of this subsection, the term "tax" includes, but is not limited to, any federal, state, or local excise, income, gift, estate, or inheritance tax.

(2) Except as provided in §736.1205, a trustee of a private foundation trust shall make distributions at such time and in such manner as not to subject the trust to tax under §4942 of the Internal Revenue Code. [FN1]

(3) Except as provided in subsection (4) and in §736.1205, a trustee of a private foundation trust, or a split interest trust to the extent that the split interest trust is subject to the provisions of §4947(a)(2) of the Internal Revenue Code, [FN2] in the exercise of the trustee's powers shall not:

(a) Engage in any act of self-dealing as defined in §4941(d) of the Internal Revenue Code; [FN3]

(b) Retain any excess business holdings as defined in §4943(c) of the Internal Revenue Code; [FN4]

(c) Make any investments in a manner that subjects the foundation to tax under §4944 of the Internal Revenue Code; [FN5] or

(d) Make any taxable expenditures as defined in §4945(d) of the Internal Revenue Code. [FN6]

(4) Paragraphs (3)(b) and (c) shall not apply to a split interest trust if:

(a) All the interest from income, and none of the remainder interest, of the trust is devoted solely to one or more of the purposes described in

§170(c)(2)(B) of the Internal Revenue Code, [FN7] and all amounts in the trust for which a deduction was allowed under §170, §545(b)(2), §556(b)(2), §642(c), §2055, §2106(a)(2), or §2522 of the Internal Revenue Code [FN8] have an aggregate fair market value of not more than 60 percent of the aggregate fair market value of all amounts in the trust; or

(b) A deduction was allowed under §170, §545(b)(2), §556(b)(2), §642(c), §2055, §2106(a)(2), or §2522 of the Internal Revenue Code for amounts payable under the terms of the trust to every remainder beneficiary but not to any income beneficiary.

[FN1] 26 U.S.C.A. § 4942.
[FN2] 26 U.S.C.A. § 4947(a)(2).
[FN3] 26 U.S.C.A. § 4941(d).
[FN4] 26 U.S.C.A. § 4943(c).
[FN5] 26 U.S.C.A. § 4944.
[FN6] 26 U.S.C.A. § 4945(d).
[FN7] U.S.C.A. § 170(c)(2)(B).
[FN8] 26 U.S.C.A. § 170, § 545(b)(2), § 556(b)(2), § 642(c), § 2055, § 2106, or § 2522.

(Laws 2006, ch. 2006-217, §12, effective July 1, 2007.)

§736.1205. Notice that this Part is inapplicable

In the case of a power to make distributions, if the trustee determines that the governing instrument contains provisions that are more restrictive than §736.1204(2), or if the trust contains other powers, inconsistent with the provisions of §736.1204(3) that specifically direct acts by the trustee, the trustee shall notify the state attorney when the trust becomes subject to this part. Section 736.1204 does not apply to any trust for which notice has been given pursuant to this section unless the trust is amended to comply with the terms of this part.
(Laws 2006, ch. 2006-217, §12, effective July 1, 2007.)

§736.1206. Trustee may amend trust instrument for tax purposes

(1) In the case of a trust that is solely for a named charitable organization or organizations and for which the trustee does not possess any discretion concerning the distribution of income or principal among two or more such organizations, the trustee may amend the governing instrument to comply with the provisions of §736.1204(2) with the consent of the named charitable organization or organizations.

(2) In the case of a charitable trust that is not subject to the provisions of subsection (1), the trustee may amend the governing instrument to comply with the provisions of §736.1204(2) with the consent of the state attorney.
(Laws 2006, ch. 2006-217, §12, effective July 1, 2007.)

§736.1207. Court has power to permit deviation from restrictions on trustees' powers and duties

This part does not affect the power of a court to relieve a trustee from any restrictions on the powers and duties that are placed on the trustee by the governing instrument or applicable law for cause shown and on complaint of the trustee, state attorney, or an affected beneficiary and notice to the affected parties.
(Laws 2006, ch. 2006-217, §12, effective July 1, 2007.)

§736.1208. Trustee may release power to select charitable donees

(1) The trustee of a trust, all of the unexpired interests in which are devoted to one or more charitable purposes, may release a power to select charitable donees unless the creating instrument provides otherwise.

(2) The release of a power to select charitable donees may apply to all or any part of the property subject to the power and may reduce or limit the charitable organizations, or classes of charitable organizations, in whose favor the power is exercisable.

(3) A release shall be effected by a duly acknowledged written instrument signed by the trustee and delivered as provided in subsection (4).

(4) Delivery of a release shall be accomplished as follows:

(a) If the release is accomplished by specifying a charitable organization or organizations as beneficiary or beneficiaries of the trust, by delivery of a copy of the release to each designated charitable organization.

(b) If the release is accomplished by reducing the class of permissible charitable organizations, by delivery of a copy of the release to the state attorney.

(5) If a release is accomplished by specifying a public charitable organization or organizations as beneficiary or beneficiaries of the trust, the trust at all times thereafter shall be operated exclusively for the benefit of, and be supervised by, the specified public charitable organization or organizations.

(Laws 2006, ch. 2006-217, §12, effective July 1, 2007.)

§736.1209. Election to come under this Part

With the consent of that organization or organizations, a trustee of a trust for the benefit of a public charitable organization or organizations may come under §736.0838(5) by filing with the state attorney an election, accompanied by the proof of required consent. Thereafter the trust shall be subject to §736.1208(5).

(Laws 2006, ch. 2006-217, §12, effective July 1, 2007.)

§736.1210. Interpretation to effect state's intent

This part shall be interpreted to effectuate the intent of the state to preserve, foster, and encourage gifts to, or for the benefit of, charitable organizations.

(Laws 2006, ch. 2006-217, §12, effective July 1, 2007.)

V. Modification

Under the *cy pres doctrine* [pronounced "see prey" and rhymes with "replay"], when a charitable trust becomes impossible or impracticable, a court will substitute another beneficiary in a manner that approaches the original purpose as closely as possible. The cy pres rule allows the court to direct the disposition of the trust property for a related charitable purpose, keeping as closely as possible to the settlor's intent. The doctrine confers flexibility on charitable trusts to meet changing social conditions. The name "cy pres" is derived from the Norman French expression meaning "so near" (*si pres*).

Application of the doctrine depends on two requirements: (1) the original purpose has become impossible or impracticable, or unforeseen changed circumstances would defeat or substantially impair the accomplishment of the trust purposes, and (2) the settlor had a general charitable intent. Most courts interpret narrowly the requirement that the original purpose has become impossible or impracticable. According to the second requirement, courts will not apply the cy pres doctrine if the testator would have preferred that the gift fail if the original purpose could not be accomplished. However, "courts almost never find that a donor did not exhibit general charitable intent." Bernstein, *supra*, at 1771.

The cy pres doctrine differs from the power of equitable deviation applicable to private express trusts. The cy pres doctrine is unique to charitable trusts. Courts have the power to change the administration of both charitable and private trusts as to time and methods of payments and other features of trust administration, and thus to sanction a deviation from the terms in many ways. However, the power to permit deviation does not extend (as does the cy pres doctrine) to altering the trust beneficiaries and the size of their interests and thus to revise the gifts which the settlor intended. Bogert, *supra*, at §431.

Although the origins of the cy pres doctrine are unclear, it has been suggested that ecclesiastic judges struggled to save gifts for the benefit of the Church or other religious institutions. *Id.* Because donors often made death-bed charitable gifts to ensure their salvation, "it was natural that chancery, with its ecclesiastical bias, should think that the testator would have desired the substitution of any other similar plan which would bring about a result similar to the original gift." *Id.*

In England, two forms of the cy pres doctrine existed: judicial and prerogative. The latter power, exercisable by the Crown, has never been recognized in this country. Aversion to the prerogative power stemmed from "association of the doctrine with royal abuses." Bernstein, *supra*, at 1771. See, e.g., DaCosta v. De Pas, Amb. 228 (1754) (applying the prerogative power to direct that a gift to educate Jews in their religion should be applied to instruct children in a foundling hospital in the Christian religion).

Most states recognize the cy pres doctrine by case law. A few jurisdictions recognize the doctrine by statute. See, e.g., Fla. Stat. §736.0413.

Certain limitations on the cy pres doctrine exist. Courts will not apply the doctrine if the settlor has provided in the trust instrument that, should the charitable gift fail, the trust shall terminate and cy pres should not be applied. In this case, the trust res passes to the settlor or the settlor's successors via a resulting trust. Nor will a court apply the cy pres doctrine if the settlor provided for an alternative charitable disposition should the original charitable gift prove impossible or impracticable. Burr v. Brooks, 393 N.E.2d 1091 (Ill. Ct. App. 1979).

The doctrine may apply when the charitable trust is frustrated either at the beginning of the

trust or else subsequently during the administration of the trust.

A famous case, Estate of Buck, 35 Cal. Rptr.2d 442 (Ct. App. 1994), involved a charitable trust established by Beryl Buck and her husband to benefit the needy residents of a particular California county, Marin County. The trustees unsuccessfully attempted to use the cy pres doctrine to broaden the terms to include a 5-county area. In response to this (and other cases), one scholar has issued a "call for a departure from the 'pure' model of cy pres, which adheres as rigidly as possible to the donor's original intent, and for adoption of one of several modified versions, each of which would allow some consideration of public interest or charitable efficiency." Bernstein, *supra*, at 1771.

In a more recent case, a St. Louis dentist created a trust with a remainder interest (after the death of his nieces and nephews) to the Washington University Dental School. However, upon the death of the last designated niece and nephew, the university had closed the Dental School. In an action for declaratory relief by the settlor's heirs, the trial court determined that the settler had manifested a general charitable intent and applied the cy pres doctrine in favor of Washington University to establish two dental-related professorships in the dentist's name. Obermeyer v. Bank of America, 140 S.W.3d 18, 23 (Mo. 2004).

The provision on modification of charitable trusts of the Uniform Trust Code codifies and modifies traditional doctrine. According to the commentary in the Uniform Trust Code, the Code

> **authorizes the court to apply cy pres not only if the original means becomes impossible or unlawful but also if the means become impracticable or wasteful. Section 413 also creates a presumption of general charitable intent. Upon failure of the settlor's original plan, the court cannot divert the trust property to a noncharity unless the terms of the trust expressly so provide. Furthermore, absent a contrary provision in the terms of the trust, limits are placed on when a gift over to a noncharity can take effect upon failure or impracticality of the original charitable purpose. The gift over is effective only if, when the provision takes effect, the trust property is to revert to the settlor and the settlor is still living, or fewer than 21 years have elapsed since the date of the trust's creation.**

Unif. Trust Code, Article 4, cmt.

Note that the Uniform Trust Code modifies the traditional cy pres doctrine by *presuming* that a settler has a general charitable intent in cases when the settlor's particular charitable purpose becomes impossible or impracticable (rather than leaving the matter entirely to judicial determination) Unif. Trust Code §413 cmt. "Under subsection (a), if the particular purpose for which the trust was created becomes impracticable, unlawful, impossible to achieve, or wasteful, the trust does not fail." *Id.* Rather the court will modify the terms or distribute the property in a manner consistent with the settlor's charitable purposes. *Id.*

The Florida Code does not contain the UTC provision on charitable trust modification (Unif. Trust Code §413 (b)) concerning the manner in which trust property passes to a noncharitable beneficiary upon failure of a particular charitable purpose. That provision invalidates a gift over to a noncharitable beneficiary when a particular charitable purpose fails unless the property reverts to a living settlor or fewer than 21 years have lapsed since the trust's creation. (See Unif. Trust Code §413 cmt.). Conversely, the Florida Code includes a provision on charitable trust modification that is not specified in the UTC. The Florida Code provides: "A proceeding to modify or terminate a trust under this section may be commenced by a settlor, a trustee, or any qualified beneficiary" (Fla. Stat. §736.0413(2)).

See generally Rob Atkinson, Reforming Cy Pres Reform, 44 Hastings L. J. 1111 (1993); Evelyn Brody, The Limits of Charity Fiduciary Law, 57 Md. L. Rev. 1400 (1998); W. Dudley McCarter, Charitable Trusts Are Favorites of Equity, 60 J. Mo. Bar 213 (2004); Note, Phantom Selves: The Search for a General Charitable Intent in the Application of the Cy Pres Doctrine, 40 Stan. L. Rev. 973 (1988).

§736.0413. Cy pres doctrine

(1) If a particular charitable purpose becomes unlawful, impracticable, impossible to achieve, or wasteful, the court may apply the doctrine of cy pres to modify or terminate the trust by directing that the trust property be applied or distributed, in whole or in part, in a manner consistent with the settlor's charitable purposes.

(2) A proceeding to modify or terminate a trust under this section may be commenced by a settlor, a trustee, or any qualified beneficiary.

(Laws 2006, ch. 2006-217, §4, effective July 1, 2007.)

VI. Enforcement

A. Judicial

Charitable trusts may be subject to constitutional limitations. Courts may refuse to enforce charitable trusts that discriminate on the basis of race or gender, reasoning that such trusts violate the Equal Protection Clause. Traditionally, courts viewed charitable trusts that discriminated on the basis of race or gender as private arrangements. They held that "private discrimination" was permissible provided it did not implicate the Constitution. Specifically, such trusts were considered private arrangements if they did not involve state action (such as public officials who served as their trustees).

Increasingly, however, courts have been prone to invalidate some types of discriminatory charitable trusts, especially those that discriminate on the basis of race. The last case to uphold a racially discriminatory charitable trust was First National Bank v. Danforth, 523 S.W.2d 808 (Mo. 1975), *cert. denied sub nom.* Sutt v. First Nat'l Bank, 421 U.S. 992 (1975).

The law concerning racially discriminatory charitable trusts was influenced by two cases: In re Girard Coll. Trusteeship, 138 A.2d 844 (Pa. 1958), and Evans v. Newton, 382 U.S. 296 (1966). James W. Colliton, Race and Sex Discrimination in Charitable Trusts, 12 Cornell J.L. & Pub. Pol'y 274, 278 (2003). In the *Girard College* case, a settlor established an institution, with the city of Philadelphia as trustee, to provide for the training of "poor male white orphan children." In the latter case, a settlor gave property, naming the city of Macon, Georgia as trustee, to be used as a park for white people only.

In the *Girard College* case, the United States Supreme Court held that the trust violated the Fourteenth Amendment. Pennsylvania v. Bd. of Dirs. of City Trusts, 353 U.S. 230 (1957). The Pennsylvania Supreme Court affirmed the Orphan's Court decision that substituted private trustees in an effort to remedy the constitutional shortcoming. Despite this effort, the Third Circuit Court of Appeals found impermissible state involvement. Pennsylvania v. Brown, 392 F.2d 120 (3d. Cir. 1968).

In *Newton*, the Georgia court tried a similar strategy to remedy the constitutional problem by appointing private individuals to replace the public trustees. The United States Supreme Court rejected this ploy, finding that the trust still violated the Constitution because the park benefited by municipal services (police protection, garbage collection, etc.). In Evans v. Abney, 396 U.S. 435 (1970), the Supreme Court affirmed the state court decision that the trust failed and the property reverted to the settlor's heirs.

Since these cases, courts have refused to uphold racially discriminatory trusts. See, e.g., Connecticut Bank & Trust Co. v. Johnson Memorial Hospital, 294 A.2d 586 (Conn. 1972) (invalidating a trust to provide Medicare for whites only); Coffee v. Rice University, 408 S.W.2d 269 (Tex. Civ. App. 1966) (upholding a jury verdict allowing the university trustees to admit nonwhite students); Grant v. Medlock, 349 S.E.2d 655 (S.C. Ct. App. 1986) (eliminating a racial restriction in a trust establishing a home for the aged for only white persons); Home for Incurables of Baltimore City v. University of Maryland Medical System Corp., 797 A.2d 746 (Md. 2002) (invalidating a restriction in a trust created for the benefit of Keswick Home to provide accommodations for only white patients) (all cited and discussed in Colliton, *supra*, at 282-286).

However, the judicial response to gender-based charitable trusts has not been as uniform. With rare exception, courts have upheld such trusts. For example, cases in the late 1970s and early 1980s "demonstrate the willingness of courts . . . to permit sex discrimination in charitable trusts" (Colliton, *supra*, at 289). For example, in Shapiro v. Columbia Union National Bank, 576 S.W.2d 310 (Mo. 1978), the court upheld a trust providing scholarships for boys, reasoning that there was no state action despite the fact that state university officials processed scholarship applications and made tentative awards subject to the private trustee's approval. And, in In re Estate of Wilson, 452 N.E.2d 1228 (N.Y. 1983), the court upheld trusts establishing a scholarship fund for "young men," permitted them to continue without the involvement of public officials, despite state action consisting of significant involvement on the part of public officials in certifying and selecting the beneficiaries.

In contrast, the Supreme Court of New Hampshire subsequently eliminated trust provisions that limited scholarships to male public high school students. In In re Certain Scholarship Funds, 575 A.2d 1325 (N.H. 1990), the court based its decision on the Equal Protection Clause of the state constitution and the state cy pres statute. See also Ebitz v. Pioneer National Bank, 361 N.E.2d 225 (Mass. 1977) (affirming a decision interpreting a charitable trust for "worthy and ambitious young men" to include women).

One commentator argues that both gender-based and racially discriminatory trusts violate public policy and should not be enforced under traditional trust law. Colliton, *supra*. He bases his argument on the fact that charitable trusts are "essentially public entities that serve public purposes" (*id.* at 292), and benefit from generous treatment by the law (in the form of exemptions from federal income taxation, application of the cy pres doctrine, and freedom from limitations of the Rule Against Perpetuities) (*id.* at 293).

Note that the Uniform Trust Code deviates from the Restatement (Second) of Trusts (§391) regarding enforcement of charitable trusts. That is, the UTC confers standing on a *settlor* to enforce a charitable trust (§405(c), codified as Fla. Stat. §736.0405(3)). This recognition does not exclude enforcement by either the state attorney general or persons with special interests (Unif. Trust Code §405 cmt.)

Florida law follows the UTC in allowing proceedings to modify or terminate charitable trusts by settlors, trustees, or any qualified beneficiary (Fla. Stat. §736.0413(2)).

B. Governmental

In most jurisdictions, the state Attorney General is authorized to investigate charitable trusts to ensure that their charitable purposes are being effectuated. Some states authorize enforcement by a similar public official or administrative agency.

> The history and purposes of this standing doctrine make clear that public enforcement is predicated on the paramount importance of the public interest in the administration of charitable trusts. The attorney general acts under the parens *patriae* power, which has its roots in the "ancient powers of guardianship over persons under disability and of protectorship of the public interest." This power, historically held by the English king, has been adopted in the United States by state and federal governments through common law and state statutes.

Bernstein, *supra*, at 1766.

State law often specifies the duties and responsibilities of the Attorney General vis à vis charitable trusts. Some states have adopted the Uniform Supervision of Trustees for Charitable Purposes Act (7C U.L.A. 372 (2000)), promulgated by the National Conference on Uniform State Laws in 1954. Pursuant to this statute, the trustees of charitable trusts and charitable corporations must report the existence of the trust to the state attorney general's office and must submit periodic reports to that office. The Act also authorizes the state attorney general to institute proceedings to investigate and supervise the charitable entities.

For an interesting case involving the attorney general's role in the supervision of a charitable trust, see In re Milton Hershey School Trust, 807 A.2d 324 (Pa. Commw. Ct. 2002) (granting the state attorney general's request for an injunction to the sale of the trust's controlling interest in Hershey Foods Corp.).

In addition to the Attorney General, most states permit parties with a "special interest" to sue to enforce the fiduciary duty of charitable trustees. To qualify, a party must prove that he or she is entitled to benefit from the trust and that such entitlement is different from that of the public. Jurisdictions vary in the persons they recognize as parties with "special interests." However, absent statutory authorization, standing generally does not extend to the next of kin, taxpayers, or the settlor. Bernstein, *supra*, at 1766. See also Restatement (Second) of Trusts §391 ("A suit can be maintained for the enforcement of a charitable trust by the Attorney General or other public officer, or by a co-trustee, or by a person who has a special interest in the enforcement of the charitable trust, but not by persons who have no special interest or by the settlors or his heirs, personal representatives or next-of-kin."); Restatement (Third) of Trusts §405(c) ("The settlor of a charitable trust, among others, may maintain a proceeding to enforce the trust").

For discussion of charitable trusts, see generally Alison Manolovici Cody, Success in New Jersey: Using the Charitable Trust Doctrine to Preserve Women's Reproductive Services When Hospitals Become Catholic, 57 N.Y.U. Ann. Surv. Am. L. 323 (2000); James J. Fishman, Improving Charitable Accountability, 62 Md. L. Rev. 218 (2003); Robert Mahealani M. Seto & Lynne Marie Kohm, Of Princesses, Charities, Trustees, and Fairytales: A Lesson of the Simple Wishes of Princess Bernice Pauahi Bishop, 21 Haw. L. Rev. 393 (1999); Jennifer L. Komoroski, Note, The Hershey Trust's Quest to Diversify: Redefining the State Attorney General's Role When Charitable Trusts Wish to Diversify, 45 Wm. & Mary L. Rev. 1769 (2004).

XIV
Fiduciary Administration

This chapter explores the fundamentals of fiduciary administration. It explores issues of jurisdiction, probate of an estate, appointment and tasks of the personal representative, and the disposition of estates without administration (or with simplified administration).

I. Generally

A court must have jurisdiction to assert authority over a decedent's estate. Subject matter jurisdiction in Florida for the administration of estates is vested in the circuit court (Fla. Stat. §26.012).

A petitioner must establish the requisite jurisdictional facts by a verified petition (including date and place of death, domicile of the decedent in the state at the time of death, and a statement of the approximate value and nature of the assets, etc.) (Rule 5.200).

Venue for the probate of wills and the granting of letters (i.e., the authority to administer an estate) is in the county of the decedent's domicile (Fla. Stat. §733.101). Any person wishing to make an objection to jurisdiction or venue must do so within a limited period of time (Fla. Stat. §733.212(3)).

For a recent challenge to venue in a Florida probate proceeding, see Parker v. Estate of Bealer, 890 So. 2d 508 (Fla. Dist. Ct. App. 2005) (affirming order confirming venue, and reasoning that the beneficiary had been properly served with notice in the state where the testator died, given that notice was served on the beneficiary's attorney in another state who was handling matters on behalf of the beneficiary on issues related to the testator's business).

§26.012. Jurisdiction of circuit court

(1) Circuit courts shall have jurisdiction of appeals from county courts. . . .

(2) They shall have exclusive original jurisdiction:

(a) In all actions at law not cognizable by the county courts;

(b) Of proceedings relating to the settlement of the estates of decedents and minors, the granting of letters testamentary, guardianship, involuntary hospitalization, the determination of incompetency, and other jurisdiction usually pertaining to courts of probate;

. . . .

(5) A circuit court is a trial court.

(Laws 1972, ch. 72-404, §3; Laws 1974, ch. 74-209, §1; Laws 1977, ch. 77-119, §1; Laws 1980, ch. 80-399, §1; Laws 1981, ch. 81-178, §1; Laws 1981, ch. 81- 259, §22; Laws 1982, ch. 82-37, §12; Laws 1984, ch. 84-303, § 2; Laws 1991, ch. 91-112, §5; Laws 1994, ch. 94-353, §27; Laws 1995, ch. 95-280, §52. Amended by Laws 1998, ch. 98-280, §3, effective June 30, 1998; Laws 2004, ch. 2004-11, §1, effective October 1, 2004.)

§733.101. Venue of probate proceedings

(1) The venue for probate of wills and granting letters shall be:

(a) In the county in this state where the decedent was domiciled.

(b) If the decedent had no domicile in this state, then in any county where the decedent's property is located.

(c) If the decedent had no domicile in this state and possessed no property in this state, then in the county where any debtor of the decedent resides.

(2) For the purpose of this section, a married woman whose husband is an alien or a nonresident of Florida may establish or designate a separate domicile in this state.

(3) Whenever a proceeding is filed laying venue in an improper county, the court may transfer the action in the same manner as provided in the Florida Rules of Civil Procedure. Any action taken by the court or the parties before the transfer is not affected by the improper venue.

(Laws 1974, ch. 74-106, §1; Laws 1975, ch. 75-220, §46. Amended by Laws 1997, ch. 97-102, §981, effective July 1, 1997; Laws 2001, ch. 2001-226, §78, effective January 1, 2002.)

§733.212. Notice of administration; filing of objections

. . .

(3) Any interested person on whom a copy of the notice of administration is served must object to the validity of the will, the qualifications of the personal representative, the venue, or the jurisdiction of the court by filing a petition or other pleading requesting relief in accordance with the Florida Probate Rules on or before the date that is 3 months after the date of service of a copy of the notice of administration on the objecting person, or those objections are forever barred. . . .

(Laws 1974, ch. 74-106, §1; Laws 1975, ch. 75-220, §60; Laws 1977, ch. 77-104, §227; Laws 1988, ch. 88-340, §3; Laws 1989, ch. 89-340, §2; Laws 1990, ch. 90-23, §2; Laws 1993, ch. 93-257, §8. Amended by Laws 1995, ch. 95-401, §7, effective October 1, 1995; Laws 1999, ch. 99-397, §191, effective July 1, 1999; Laws 2001, ch. 2001-226, §94, effective January 1, 2002; Laws 2003, ch. 2003-154, §8, effective June 12, 2003; Laws 2006, ch. 2006-134, §6, effective July 1, 2006.)

[For the rest of this statute, see Section II, B, 2.]

Rule 5.200. Petition for Administration

The petition for administration shall be verified by the petitioner and shall contain:

(a) a statement of the interest of the petitioner, the petitioner's name and address, and the name and office address of the petitioner's attorney;

(b) the name, last known address, social security number, date and place of death of the decedent, and state and county of the decedent's domicile;

(c) so far as is known, the names and addresses of the surviving spouse, if any, and the beneficiaries and their relationship to the decedent and the date of birth of any who are minors;

(d) a statement showing venue;

(e) the priority, under the code, of the person whose appointment as the personal representative is sought and a statement that the person is qualified to serve under the laws of Florida;

(f) a statement whether domiciliary or principal proceedings are pending in another state or country, if known, and the name and address of the foreign personal representative and the court issuing letters;

(g) a statement of the approximate value and nature of the assets;

(h) in an intestate estate, a statement that after the exercise of reasonable diligence the petitioner is unaware of any unrevoked wills or codicils, or if the petitioner is aware of any unrevoked wills or codicils, a statement why the wills or codicils are not being probated, or otherwise a statement of the facts concerning any such will or codicil;

(i) in a testate estate, a statement identifying all unrevoked wills and codicils being presented for probate, and a statement that the petitioner is unaware of any other unrevoked will or codicil or, if the petitioner is aware of any other unrevoked wills or codicils, a statement why the other wills or codicils are not being probated; and

(j) in a testate estate, a statement that the original of the decedent's last will is in the possession of the court or accompanies the petition, or that an authenticated copy of a will deposited with or probated in another jurisdiction or that an authenticated copy of a notarial will, the original of which is in the possession of a foreign notary, accompanies the petition.

(Amended March 31, 1977, effective July 1, 1977 (344 So.2d 828); September 29, 1988, effective January 1, 1989 (537 So.2d 500); September 24, 1992, effective January 1, 1993 (607 So.2d 1306); May 2, 2002 (824 So.2d 849).

II. Opening Estate Administration

"Probate" refers to the court-supervised administration of a decedent's estate for a decedent who died testate (with a valid will) or intestate (without a valid will). For a decedent who died testate, probate proceedings are initiated by the filing of a petition for probate of the decedent's will and for letters testamentary. For a decedent who died intestate, probate proceedings are initiated by a petition for letters of administration.

The stages of estate administration include: probating the will (for testate decedents), appointing a personal representative (for testate or intestate estates), marshalling the assets, conducting an inventory, determining and paying the decedent's debts, paying administration expenses and taxes, and transferring title to the estate property to the beneficiaries or heirs.

Not all of a decedent's property is subject to probate. For example, inter vivos trusts, joint tenancy property, and life insurance proceeds pass outside the estate. Probate also may be avoided regarding a decedent's real and personal property that passes to a surviving spouse pursuant to a proceeding for a protected homestead or a family allowance (Fla. Stat. §§13650 et seq.). In addition, summary distribution proceedings may occur in cases involving small estates (see Section VI *infra*).

Sometimes, a will is proved before someone other than a Florida circuit court. In such cases, the probate court must issue a "commission," i.e., a document granting authority to an appointee (who is called a "commissioner") to enable the appointee to require witnesses to appear and testify. The commissioner then renders that testimony to the court that issued the commission. See Fla. Stat. §733.201(2).

A. Generally

§733.105. Determination of beneficiaries

(1) When property passes by intestate succession or the will is unclear and there is doubt about:

(a) Who is entitled to receive any part of the property, or

(b) The shares and amounts that any person is entitled to receive,

any interested person may petition the court to determine beneficiaries or their shares.

(2) Any personal representative who makes distribution or takes any other action pursuant to an order determining beneficiaries shall be fully protected.

(3) A separate civil action to determine beneficiaries may be brought when an estate has not been administered.
(Laws 1974, ch. 74-106, §1; Laws 1975, ch. 75-220, §48; Laws 1977, ch. 77-104, §226; Laws 1977, ch. 77-174, §1. Amended by Laws 1997, ch. 97-102, §983, effective July 1, 1997; Laws 2001, ch. 2001-226, §81, effectiive January 1, 2002.)

§733.201. Proof of wills

(1) Self-proved wills executed in accordance with this code may be admitted to probate without further proof.

(2) A will may be admitted to probate upon the oath of any attesting witness taken before any circuit judge, commissioner appointed by the court, or clerk.

(3) If it appears to the court that the attesting witnesses cannot be found or that they have become incompetent after the execution of the will or their testimony cannot be obtained within a reasonable time, a will may be admitted to probate upon the oath of the personal representative nominated by the will as provided in subsection (2), whether or not the nominated personal representative is interested in the estate, or upon the oath of any person having no interest in the estate under the will stating that the person believes the writing exhibited to be the true last will of the decedent.
(Laws 1974, ch. 74-106, §1; Laws 1975, ch. 75-220, §51. Amended by Laws 1997, ch. 97-102, §985, effective July 1, 1997; Laws 2001, ch. 2001-226, §85, effective January 1, 2002.)

§733.202. Petition

Any interested person may petition for administration.
(Laws 1974, ch. 74-106, §1; Laws 1975, ch. 75-220, §52; Laws 1977, ch. 77-87, §9; Laws 1992, ch. 92-200, §19. Amended by Laws 1997, ch. 97-102, §986, effective July 1, 1997; Laws 2001, ch. 2001-226, §86, effective January 1, 2002.)

B. Notice

Florida Statutes §§731.301 et seq. govern notice generally in probate proceedings. If a petitioner is entitled to preference in appointment, he or she is not required to give notice prior to the issuance of letters (i.e., the commencement of estate administration) (Rule 5.201). However, petitioners who are not entitled to preference in appointment must give formal notice to all persons who are entitled to priority of appointment as personal representation (and who have not waived notice). *Id.*

Florida Probate Rule 5.040 below specifies the requirements for formal as well as informal notice. According to the rule, unless the Probate Code or Probate Rules require formal notice, the term "notice" means informal notice. Informal notice shall be served as provided in Rule 5.041(b).

Following appointment to the office of personal representative, the representative must serve a copy of the notice of administration on the surviving spouse, beneficiaries, trustees of designated trusts, and persons who may be entitled to exempt property (Fla. Stat. §733.212).

If a caveat (an objection) is filed, then formal notice must be given to all interested persons. (A caveat is defined as a document that may be filed by any interested person, including a creditor, that requires notice (Rule 5.260).

Before 2002, the personal representative was required to publish a "notice of administration" in a newspaper that informed the decedent's creditors of the need to file their claims against the estate. However, in that year, the legislature enacted a statute (Fla. Stat. §733.2121) to provide for a different form of notice to creditors. The personal representative now is required to publish a notice specifically to creditors (informing them of the time limitations), and to make the requisite publication in a designated manner (i.e., once a week for two consecutive weeks in a newspaper published in the county, or if none, a newspaper of general circulation in that county) (Fla. Stat. §733.2121(2)). In addition, the personal representative must serve notice on particular persons who are known to him or her (certain designated persons) (Fla. Stat. §733.212(1)). For decedents who are 55 years or older, the personal representative must also serve a copy of the notice on the Agency for Health Care Administration (Fla. Stat. §733.2121(3)(d)).

The new statute was a response to constitutional concerns stemming from the United States Supreme Court decision in Tulsa v. Pope, 485 U.S. 478 (1988), requiring a personal representative to promptly make a diligent search to determine the creditors who are reasonably ascertainable and to serve a notice on them. Previously, the United States Supreme Court held, in Mullane v. Central Hanover Bank, 339 U.S. 306 (1950), that notice was required to trust beneficiaries that is "reasonably calculated under the circumstances" to inform interested parties of the pendency of any action and provide them with a reasonable opportunity to be heard. However, it was unclear subsequently whether *Mullane* notice was required to creditors. *Tulsa* answered that question in the affirmative.

1. Generally

§731.301. Notice

(1) When notice to an interested person of a petition or other proceeding is required, the notice shall be given to the interested person or that person's attorney as provided in the Florida Probate Rules.

(2) Formal notice shall be sufficient to acquire jurisdiction over the person receiving formal notice to the extent of the person's interest in the estate.

(3) Persons given notice of any proceeding shall be bound by all orders entered in that proceeding.

(Laws 1974, ch. 74-106, §1; Laws 1975, ch. 75-220, §5; Laws 1977, ch. 77-87, §3; Laws 1977, ch. 77-174, §1; Laws 1993, ch. 93-257, §1. Amended by Laws 1995, ch. 95-211, §64, effective July 10, 1995; Laws 1997, ch. 97-102, §950, effective July 1, 1997; Laws 2001, ch. 2001-226, § 12, effective January 1, 2002.)

Rule 5.040. Notice

(a) Formal Notice

(1) When formal notice is given, a copy of the pleading or motion shall be served on interested persons, together with a notice requiring the person served to serve written defenses on the person giving notice within 20 days after service of the notice, exclusive of the day of service, and to file the original of the written defenses with the clerk of the court either before service or immediately thereafter, and notifying the person served that failure to serve written defenses as required may result in a judgment or order for the relief demanded in the pleading or motion, without further notice.

(2) After service of formal notice, informal notice of any hearing on the pleading or motion shall be served on interested persons, provided that if no written defense is served within 20 days after service of formal notice on an interested person, the pleading or motion may be considered ex parte as to that person, unless the court orders otherwise.

(3) Formal notice shall be served:

(A) by sending a copy by any commercial delivery service requiring a signed receipt or by any form of mail requiring a signed receipt as follows:

(i) to the attorney representing an interested person; or

(ii) to an interested person who has filed a request for notice at the address given in the request for notice; or

(iii) to an incapacitated person to the person's usual place of abode and to the person's legal guardian, if any, at the guardian's usual place of abode or regular place of business; or, if there is no legal guardian, to the incapacitated person at the person's usual place of abode and on the person, if any, having care or custody of the incapacitated person at the usual place of abode or regular place of business of such custodian; or

(iv) on any other individual to the individual's usual place of abode or to the place where the individual regularly conducts business; or

(v) on a corporation or other business entity to its registered office in Florida or its principal business office in Florida or, if neither is known after reasonable inquiry, to its last known address; or

(B) as provided in the Florida Rules of Civil Procedure for service of process; or

(C) as otherwise provided by Florida law for service of process.

(4) Service of formal notice pursuant to subdivision (3)(A) shall be complete on receipt of the notice. Proof of service shall be by verified statement of the person giving the notice; and there shall be attached to the verified statement the signed receipt or other evidence satisfactory to the court that delivery was made to the addressee or the addressee's agent.

(5) If service of process is made pursuant to Florida law, proof of service shall be made as provided therein.

(b) Informal Notice. When informal notice of a petition or other proceeding is required or permitted, it shall be served as provided in rule 5.041(b).

(c) "Notice" Defined. In these rules, the Florida Probate Code, and the Florida Guardianship Law "notice" shall mean informal notice unless formal notice is specified.

(d) Formal Notice Optional. Formal notice may be given in lieu of informal notice at the option of the person giving notice unless the court orders otherwise. When formal notice is given in lieu of informal notice, formal notice shall be given to all interested persons entitled to notice.

(Amended March 31, 1977, effective July 1, 1977 (344 So.2d 828); September 4, 1980, effective January 1, 1981 (387 So.2d 949); September 13, 1984, effective January 1, 1985 (458 So.2d 1079); September 29, 1988, effective January 1, 1989 (537 So.2d 500); August 22, 1991, effective October 1, 1991 (584 So.2d 964); September 24, 1992, effective January 1, 1993 (607 So.2d 1306); October 3, 1996, effective January 1, 1997 (683 So.2d 78); September 28, 2000, effective January 1, 2001 (778 So.2d 272); September 29, 2005, effective January 1, 2006 (912 So.2d 1178).)

Rule 5.041. Service of Pleadings and Papers

(a) Service; When Required. Unless the court orders otherwise, every petition or motion for an order determining rights of an interested person, and every other pleading or paper filed in the particular proceeding which is the subject matter of such petition or motion, except applications for witness subpoenas, shall be served on interested persons unless these rules, the Florida Probate Code, or the Florida Guardianship Law provides otherwise. No service need be made on interested persons against whom a default has been entered, or against whom the matter may otherwise proceed ex parte, unless a new or additional right or demand is asserted.

(b) Service; How Made. When service is required or permitted to be made on an interested person represented by an attorney, service shall be made on the attorney unless service on the interested person is ordered by the court. Except when serving formal notice, or when serving a motion, pleading, or other paper in the manner provided for service of formal notice, service shall be made by delivering or mailing a copy of the motion, pleading, or other paper to the attorney or interested person at the last known address or, if no address is known, leaving it with the clerk of the court. Service by mail shall be complete upon mailing except when serving formal notice or when making service in the manner of formal notice. Delivery of a copy within this rule shall be complete upon

(1) handing it to the attorney or to the interested person; or

(2) leaving it at the attorney's or interested person's office with a clerk or other person in charge thereof; or

(3) if there is no one in charge, leaving it in a conspicuous place therein; or

(4) if the office is closed or the person to be served has no office, leaving it at the person's usual place of abode with some person of his or her family above 15 years of age and informing that person of the contents; or

(5) transmitting it by facsimile to the attorney's or interested person's office with a cover sheet containing the sender's name, firm, address, telephone number, facsimile number, and the number of pages transmitted. When delivery is made by facsimile, a copy shall also be served by any other method permitted by this rule. Facsimile delivery occurs when transmission is complete.

Service by delivery after 4:00 p.m. shall be deemed to have been made on the next day that is not a Saturday, Sunday, or legal holiday.

(c) Service; Numerous Interested Persons. In proceedings when the interested persons are unusually numerous, the court may regulate the service contemplated by these rules on motion or on its initiative in a manner as may be found to be just and reasonable.

(d) Filing. All original papers shall be filed either before service or immediately thereafter. If the original of any bond or other paper is not placed in the court file, a certified copy shall be so placed by the clerk.

(e) Filing With Court Defined. The filing of papers with the court as required by these rules shall be made by filing them with the clerk, except that the judge may permit the papers to be filed with the judge in which event the judge shall note the filing date and transmit the papers to the clerk. The date of filing is that shown on the face of each paper by the judge's notation or the clerk's time stamp, whichever is earlier.

(f) Certificate of Service. When any attorney shall certify in substance:

> "I certify that a copy hereof has been served on (here insert name or names) by (delivery) (mail) (fax) on (date).
>
> ______________________________
>
> ______________________
>
> Attorney"

the certificate shall be taken as prima facie proof of service in compliance with these rules except in case of formal notice or service in the manner of formal notice. A person not represented by an attorney shall certify in the same manner, but the certificate must be verified.

(g) Service of Orders.

(1) A copy of all orders or judgments determining rights of an interested person shall be transmitted by the court or under its direction at the time of entry of the order or judgment to all interested persons in the particular proceeding.

(2) This subdivision (g) is directory, and a failure to comply with it does not affect the order or judgment or its finality.

(Added September 13, 1984, effective January 1, 1985 (458 So.2d 1079). Amended September 24, 1992, effective January 1, 1993 (607 So.2d 1306); October 3, 1996, effective January 1, 1997 (683 So.2d 78); September 28, 2000, effective January 1, 2001 (778 So.2d 272); September 29, 2005, effective January 1, 2006 (912 So.2d 1178).)

2. Notice at Death

§731.303. Representation

In the administration of or in judicial proceedings involving estates of decedents or trusts, the following apply:

(1) Persons are bound by orders binding others in the following cases:

(a) Orders binding the sole holder or all coholders of a power of revocation or a general, special, or limited power of appointment, including one in the form of a power of amendment or revocation to the extent that the power has not become unexercisable in fact, bind all persons to the extent that their interests, as persons who may take by virtue of the exercise or nonexercise of the power, are subject to the power.

(b) To the extent there is no conflict of interest between them or among the persons represented:

1. Orders binding a guardian of the property bind the ward.
2. Orders binding a trustee bind beneficiaries of the trust in proceedings to probate a will, in establishing or adding to a trust, in reviewing the acts or accounts of a prior fiduciary, and in proceedings involving creditors or other third parties. However, for purposes of this section, a conflict of interest shall be deemed to exist when each trustee of a trust that is a beneficiary of the estate is also a personal representative of the estate.
3. Orders binding a personal representative bind persons interested in the undistributed assets of a decedent's estate, in actions or proceedings by or against the estate.

(c) An unborn or unascertained person, or a minor or any other person under a legal disability, who is not otherwise represented is bound by an order to the extent that person's interest is represented by another party having the same or greater quality of interest in the proceeding.

(2) Orders binding a guardian of the person shall not bind the ward.

(3) In proceedings involving the administration of estates or trusts, notice is required as follows:

(a) Notice as prescribed by law shall be given to every interested person, or to one who can bind the interested person as described in paragraph (1)(a) or paragraph (1)(b). Notice may be given both to the interested person and to another who can bind him or her.

(b) Notice is given to unborn or unascertained persons who are not represented pursuant to paragraph (1)(a) or paragraph (1)(b) by giving notice to all known persons whose interests in the proceedings are the same as, or of a greater quality than, those of the unborn or unascertained persons.

(4) If the court determines that representation of the interest would otherwise be inadequate, the court may, at any time, appoint a guardian ad litem to represent the interests of an incapacitated person, an unborn or unascertained person, a minor or any other person otherwise under a legal disability, or a person whose identity or address is unknown. If not precluded by conflict of interest, a guardian ad litem may be appointed to represent several persons or interests.

(5) When a sole holder or coholder of a general, special, or limited power of appointment, including an exercisable power of amendment or revocation over property in an estate or trust, is bound by:

(a) Agreements, waivers, consents, or approvals; or

(b) Accounts, trust accountings, or other written reports that adequately disclose matters set forth therein,

then all persons who may take by virtue of, and whose interests are subject to, the exercise or nonexercise of the power are also bound, but only to the extent of their interests which could otherwise be affected by the exercise or nonexercise of the power.

(Laws 1974, ch. 74-106, §1; Laws 1975, ch. 75-220, §7; Laws 1977, ch. 77-87, §5; Laws 1977, ch. 77-174, §1; Laws 1988, ch. 88-217, §1; Laws 1992, ch. 92-200, §3. Amended by Laws 1997, ch. 97-102, §951, effective July 1, 1997; Laws 2001, ch. 2001-226, §13, effective January 1, 2002; Laws 2002, ch. 2002-82, §3, effective April 23, 2002; Laws 2003, ch. 2003-154, §3, effective June 12, 2003.)

§733.2121. Notice to creditors; filing of claims

(1) Unless creditors' claims are otherwise barred by §733.710, the personal representative shall promptly publish a notice to creditors. The notice shall contain the name of the decedent, the file number of the estate, the designation and address of the court in which the proceedings are pending, the name and address of the personal representative, the name and address of the personal representative's attorney, and the date of first publication. The notice shall state that creditors must file claims against the estate with the court during the time periods set forth in §733.702, or be forever barred.

(2) Publication shall be once a week for 2 consecutive weeks, in a newspaper published in the county where the estate is administered or, if there is no newspaper published in the county, in a newspaper of general circulation in that county.

(3)

(a) The personal representative shall promptly make a diligent search to determine the names and addresses of creditors of the decedent who are reasonably ascertainable, even if the claims are unmatured, contingent, or unliquidated, and shall promptly serve a copy of the notice on those creditors. Impracticable and extended searches are not required. Service is not required on any creditor who has filed a claim as provided in this part, whose claim has been paid in full, or whose claim is listed in a personal representative's timely filed proof of claim.

(b) The personal representative is not individually liable to any person for giving notice under this section, even if it is later determined that notice was not required. The service of notice to creditors in accordance with this section shall not be construed as admitting the validity or enforceability of a claim.

(c) If the personal representative in good faith fails to give notice required by this section, the personal representative is not liable to any person for the failure. Liability, if any, for the failure is on the estate.

(d) If a decedent at the time of death was 55 years of age or older, the personal representative shall promptly serve a copy of the notice to creditors and provide a copy of the death certificate on the Agency for Health Care Administration within 3 months after the first publication of the notice to creditors, unless the agency has already filed a statement of claim in the estate proceedings.

(e) If the Department of Revenue has not previously been served with a copy of the notice to creditors, then service of the inventory on the Department of Revenue shall be the equivalent of service of a copy of the notice to creditors.

(4) Claims are barred as provided in §§733.702 and 733.710.

(Laws 2001, ch. 2001-226, §95, effective January 1, 2002. Amended by Laws 2003, ch. 2003-154, §9, effective June 12, 2003; Laws 2005, ch. 2005-140, §4, effective July 1, 2005.)

Rule 5.060. Request for notices and copies of pleadings

(a) Request. Any interested person who desires notice of proceedings in the estate of a decedent or ward may file a separate written request for notice of further proceedings, designating therein such person's residence and post office address. When such person's residence or post office address changes, a new designation of such change shall be filed in the proceedings. A person filing such request, or address change, shall also deliver a copy thereof to the clerk, who shall forthwith mail it to the attorney for the personal representative or guardian, noting on the original the fact of mailing.

(b) Notice and Copies. A party filing a request shall be served thereafter by the moving party with notice of further proceedings and with copies of subsequent pleadings and papers as long as the party is an interested person.

(Amended September 4, 1980, effective January 1, 1981 (387 So.2d 949); September 29, 1988, effective January 1, 1989 (537 So.2d 500); September 24, 1992, effective January 1, 1993 (607 So.2d 1306).)

Rule 5.201. Notice of petition for administration

Except as may otherwise be required by these rules or the Florida Probate Code, no notice need be given of the petition for administration or the issuance of letters when it appears that the petitioner is entitled to preference of appointment. Before letters shall be issued to any person who is not entitled to preference, formal notice shall be served on all known persons qualified to act as personal representative and entitled to preference equal to or greater than the applicant, unless those entitled to preference waive it in writing.

(Added September 29, 1988, effective January 1, 1989 (537 So.2d 500).)

Rule 5.240. Notice of administration

(a) Service. The personal representative shall promptly serve a copy of the notice of administration on the following persons who are known to the personal representative and who were not previously served under section 733.2123, Florida Statutes:

(1) the decedent's surviving spouse;

(2) all beneficiaries;

(3) a trustee of any trust described in section 733.707(3), Florida Statutes and each beneficiary of the trust as defined in section 737.303(4)(b), if each trustee is also a personal representative of the estate; and

(4) persons who may be entitled to exempt property

in the manner provided for service of formal notice. The personal representative may similarly serve a copy of the notice on any devisee under another will or heirs or others who claim or may claim an interest in the estate.

(b) Contents. The notice shall state:

(1) the name of the decedent, the file number of the estate, the designation and address of the court in which the proceedings are pending, whether the estate is testate or intestate, and, if testate, the date of the will and any codicils;

(2) the name and address of the personal representative and of the personal representative's attorney;

(3) that any interested person on whom the notice is served who challenges the validity of the will, the qualifications of the personal representative, venue, or jurisdiction of the court is required to file any objections with the court in the manner provided in the Florida Probate Rules within the time required by law or those objections are forever barred;

(4) that any person entitled to exempt property is required to file a petition for determination of exempt property within the time provided by law or the right to exempt property is deemed waived; and

(5) that a surviving spouse seeking an elective share must file an election to take elective share within the time provided by law.

(c) Copy of Will. Unless the court directs otherwise, the personal representative of a testate estate shall, upon written request, furnish a copy of the will and all codicils admitted to probate to any person on whom the notice of administration was served.

(d) Objections. Objections to the validity of the will shall follow the form and procedure set forth in these rules pertaining to revocation of probate. Objections to the qualifications of the personal representative shall follow the form and procedure set forth in these rules pertaining to removal of a personal representative. Objections to the venue or jurisdiction of the court shall follow the form and procedure set forth in the Florida Rules of Civil Procedure.

(Amended March 31, 1977, effective July 1, 1977 (344 So.2d 828); September 13, 1984, effective January 1, 1985 (458 So.2d 1079); September 29, 1988, effective January 1, 1989 (537 So.2d 500); August 22, 1991, effective October 1, 1991 (584 So.2d 964); September 24, 1992, effective January 1, 1993 (607 So.2d 1306); October 3, 1996, effective January 1, 1997 (683 So.2d 78); May 2, 2002 (824 So.2d 849); June 19, 2003, (848 So.2d 1069); September 29, 2005, effective January1, 2006 (912 So.2d 1178).)

Rule 5.241. Notice to creditors

(a) Publication and Service. Unless creditors' claims are otherwise barred by law, the personal representative shall promptly publish a notice to creditors and serve a copy of the notice on all creditors of the decedent who are reasonably ascertainable and, if required by law, on the Agency for Health Care Administration. Service of the notice shall be either in the manner provided for informal notice, or in the manner provided for service of formal notice at the option of the personal representative. Service on one creditor by a chosen method shall not preclude service on another creditor by another method.

(b) Contents. The notice to creditors shall contain the name of the decedent, the file number of the estate, the designation and address of the court, the name and address of the personal representative and of the personal representative's attorney, and the date of first publication of the notice to creditors. The notice shall require all creditors to file all claims against the estate with the court, within the time provided by law.

(c) Method of Publication and Proof. Publication shall be made as required by law. The personal representative shall file proof of publication with the court within 45 days after the date of first publication of the notice to creditors.

(d) Statement Regarding Creditors. Within 4 months after the date of the first publication of notice to creditors, the personal representative shall file a verified statement that diligent search has been made to ascertain the name and address of each person having a claim against the estate. The statement shall indicate the name and address of each person at that time known to the personal representative who has or may have a claim against the estate and whether such person was served with the notice to creditors or otherwise received actual notice of the information contained in the notice to creditors; provided that the statement need not include persons who have filed a timely claim or who were included in the personal representative's proof of claim.

(Added May 2, 2002 (824 So.2d 849). Amended September 29, 2005, effective January 1, 2006 (912 So.2d 1178).)

[Note: Caveat proceedings permit a decedent's creditor or other interested person to be notified when letters of administration are issued. Thereafter, the caveator must take appropriate action to protect the caveator's interests. Rule 5.260 treats the creditor caveator differently from other caveators.]

Rule 5.260. Caveat; Proceedings

(a) Filing. Any creditor or interested person other than a creditor may file a caveat with the court.

(b) Contents. The caveat shall contain the decedent's name, the decedent's social security number or date of birth, if known, a statement of the interest of the caveator in the estate, and the name, specific mailing address, and residence address of the caveator.

(c) Resident Agent of Caveator; Service. If the caveator is not a resident of Florida, the caveator shall file a designation of the name and specific mailing address and residence address of a resident in the county where the caveat is filed as the caveator's agent for service of notice. The written acceptance by the person appointed as resident agent shall be filed with the designation or included in the caveat. The designation and acceptance shall constitute the consent of the caveator that service of notice upon the designated resident agent shall bind the caveator. If the caveator is represented by an attorney admitted to practice in Florida who signs the caveat, it shall not be necessary to designate a resident agent under this rule.

(d) Filing After Commencement. If at the time of the filing of any caveat the decedent's will has been admitted to probate or letters of administration have been issued, the clerk shall forthwith notify the caveator in writing of the date of issuance of letters and the names and addresses of the personal representative and the personal representative's attorney.

(e) Creditor. When letters of administration issue after the filing of a caveat by a creditor, the clerk shall forthwith notify the caveator, in writing, advising the caveator of the date of issuance of letters and the names and addresses of the personal representative and the personal representative's attorney, unless notice has previously been served on the caveator. A copy of any notice given by the clerk, together with a certificate of the mailing of the original notice, shall be filed in the estate proceedings.

(f) Other Interested Persons; Before Commencement. After the filing of a caveat by an interested person other than a creditor, the court shall not admit a will of the decedent to probate or appoint a personal representative without service of formal notice on the caveator or the caveator's designated agent.

(Amended March 31, 1977, effective July 1, 1977 (344 So.2d 828); September 13, 1984, effective January 1, 1985 (458 So.2d 1079); September 24, 1992, effective January 1, 1993 (607 So.2d 1306).)

§733.212. Notice of administration; filing of objections

(1) The personal representative shall promptly serve a copy of the notice of administration on the following persons who are known to the personal representative:

(a) The decedent's surviving spouse;

(b) Beneficiaries;

(c) The trustee of any trust described in §733.707(3) and each beneficiary of the trust as defined in §737.303(4)(b), if each trustee is also a personal representative of the estate; and

(d) Persons who may be entitled to exempt property in the manner provided for service of formal notice, unless served under §733.2123. The personal representative may similarly serve a copy of the notice on any devisees under a known prior will or heirs or others who claim or may claim an interest in the estate.

(2) The notice shall state:

(a) The name of the decedent, the file number of the estate, the designation and address of the court in which the proceedings are pending, whether the estate is testate or intestate, and, if testate, the date of the will and any codicils.

(b) The name and address of the personal representative and the name and address of the personal representative's attorney.

(c) That any interested person on whom a copy of the notice of administration is served must file on or before the date that is 3 months after the date of service of a copy of the notice of administration on that person any objection that challenges the validity of the will, the qualifications of the personal representative, the venue, or the jurisdiction of the court.

(d) That persons who may be entitled to exempt property under §732.402 will be deemed to have waived their rights to claim that property as exempt property unless a petition for determination of exempt property is filed by such persons or on their behalf on or before the later of the date that is 4 months after the date of service of a copy of the notice of administration on such persons or the date that is 40 days after the date of termination of any proceeding involving the construction, admission to probate, or validity of the will or involving any other matter affecting any part of the exempt property.

(e) That an election to take an elective share must be filed on or before the earlier of the date that is 6 months after the date of service of a copy of the notice of administration on the surviving spouse, or an attorney in fact or a guardian of the property of the surviving spouse, or the date that is 2 years after the date of the decedent's death.

(3) Any interested person on whom a copy of the notice of administration is served must object to the validity of the will, the qualifications of the personal representative, the venue, or the jurisdiction of the court by filing a petition or other pleading requesting relief in accordance with the Florida Probate Rules on or before the date that is 3 months after the date of service of a copy of the notice of administration on the objecting person, or those objections are forever barred.

(4) The appointment of a personal representative or a successor personal representative shall not extend or renew the period for filing objections under this section, unless a new will or codicil is admitted.

(5) The personal representative is not individually liable to any person for giving notice under this section, regardless of whether it is later determined that notice was not required by this section. The service of notice in accordance with this section shall not be construed as conferring any right.

(6) If the personal representative in good faith fails to give notice required by this section, the personal representative is not liable to any person for the failure. Liability, if any, for the failure is on the estate.

(7) If a will or codicil is subsequently admitted to probate, the personal representative shall promptly serve a copy of a new notice of administration as required for an initial will admission.

(8) For the purpose of determining deadlines established by reference to the date of service of a copy of the notice of administration in cases in which such service has been waived, service shall be deemed to occur on the date the waiver is filed.

(Laws 1974, ch. 74-106, §1; Laws 1975, ch. 75-220, §60; Laws 1977, ch. 77-104, §227; Laws 1988, ch. 88-340, §3; Laws 1989, ch. 89-340, §2; Laws 1990, ch. 90-23, §2; Laws 1993, ch. 93-257, §8. Amended by Laws 1995, ch. 95-401, §7, effective October 1, 1995; Laws 1999, ch. 99-397, §191, effective July 1, 1999; Laws 2001, ch. 2001-226, §94, effective January 1, 2002; Laws 2003, ch. 2003-154, §8, effective June 12, 2003; Laws 2006, ch. 2006-134, §6, effective July 1, 2006.)

§733.2123. Adjudication before issuance of letters

A petitioner may serve formal notice of the petition for administration on interested persons. A copy of the will offered for probate shall be attached to the notice. No person who is served with formal notice of the petition for administration prior to the issuance of letters or who has waived notice may challenge the validity of the will, testacy of the decedent, qualifications of the personal representative, venue, or jurisdiction of the court, except in the proceedings before issuance of letters.

(Laws 1975, ch. 75-220, §60; Laws 1981, ch. 81-27, §2. Amended by Laws 1997, ch. 97-102, §987, effective July 1, 1997; Laws 2001, ch. 2001-226, §96, effective January 1, 2002.)

§733.701. Notifying creditors

Unless creditors' claims are otherwise barred by §733.710, every personal representative shall cause notice to creditors to be published and served under §733.2121.

(Laws 1974, ch. 74-106, §1; Laws 1975, ch. 75-220, §83; Laws 1977, ch. 77-87, §33; Laws 1989, ch. 89-340, §4. Amended by Laws 2001, ch. 2001-226, §145, effective January 1, 2002; Laws 2003, ch. 2003-154, §31, effective June 12, 2003.)

[Note: Creditors' claims are discussed *infra* in Section IVC.]

3. Waiver of Notice

§731.302. Waiver and consent by interested person

Subsequent to the filing of a petition for administration, an interested person, including a guardian ad litem, administrator ad litem, guardian of the property, personal representative, trustee, or other fiduciary, or a sole holder or all coholders of a power of revocation or a power of appointment, may waive, to the extent of that person's interest or the interest which that person represents, subject to the provisions of §§731.303 and 733.604, any right or notice or the filing of any document, exhibit, or schedule required to be filed and may consent to any action or proceeding which may be required or permitted by this code.

(Laws 1974, ch. 74-106, §1; Laws 1975, ch. 75-220, §6; Laws 1977, ch. 77-87, §4; Laws 1979, ch. 79-400, §267; Laws 1984, ch. 84-106, §3. Amended by Laws 2003, ch. 2003-154, §25, effective June 12, 2003.)

Rule 5.180. Waiver and consent

(a) Waiver. An interested person, including a guardian ad litem, administrator ad litem, guardian of the property, or, if none, the natural guardian, personal representative, trustee, or other fiduciary, or a sole holder or all co-holders of a power of revocation or a power of appointment, may in writing

(1) *waive*:

(A) formal notice;

(B) informal notice;

(C) service including service of notice of administration;

(D) disclosure of the amount of compensation either paid to or to be paid to the personal representatives, attorneys, accountants, appraisers, or other agents employed by the personal representative;

(E) disclosure of prior or proposed distribution of assets;

(F) any right or notice or the filing of any document, exhibit, or schedule required to be filed;

(G) any other proceedings or matters permitted to be waived by law or by these rules; and

(2) waive or consent on the person's own behalf and on behalf of those the person represents to the extent there is no conflict of interest.

(b) Contents of Waiver. A waiver of disclosure of the amount of, or manner of determining, compensation shall be signed by each party bearing the impact of the compensation and shall be filed with the court. The waiver shall contain language declaring that the waiving party has actual knowledge of the amount and manner of determining the compensation and, in addition, either:

(1) that the party has agreed to the amount and manner of determining that compensation and waives any objection to payment; or

(2) that the party has the right to petition the court to decrease the compensation and waives that right.

(Amended March 31, 1977, effective July 1, 1977 (344 So.2d 828); September 13, 1984, effective January 1, 1985 (458 So.2d 1079); September 29, 1988, effective January 1, 1989 (537 So.2d 500); September 24, 1992, effective January 1, 1993 (607 So.2d 1306); October 3, 1996, effective January 1, 1997 (683 So.2d 78).)

III. Probate of Estate

A. Proof of Will

The estate administration process begins with the filing of a petition for administration. If the decedent died testate (with a will), the will generally accompanies the petition (Rule 5.200j).

If the will was written in a foreign language, a copy of an English translation must accompany the will (Fla. Stat. §733.204).

If a will has been lost or destroyed, the terms of the will may be offered for probate. In order to prove the terms of the will, the testimony of two disinterested witnesses is necessary (Fla. Stat. §733.207). However, if a copy of the will exists, then the testimony of only one disinterested witness is required. *Id.*

Proof of a will is not necessary if the will is "self-proved." A "self-proved will" is a will that includes an affidavit signed by the testator and witnesses before a notary (Fla. Stat. §732.503). A self-proved will establishes a prima facie case of due execution. Blits v. Blits, 468 So. 2d 320 (Fla. Dist. Ct. App. 1985) (holding that an affidavit by the attorney who drew up testator's will that was present at the time of execution and stated that the will was executed in compliance with Florida law was sufficient to establish a prima facie case of formal execution).

Sometimes, it may be difficult to locate the decedent's will. Florida legislation provides that a custodian of a will must deposit the will with the clerk of the court having venue of the estate within 10 days after receiving information of the testator's death (Fla. Stat. §732.901). In some cases, a search for the will must be made of the testator's safe deposit box. The safe-deposit-box search procedure (both the initial search for the will as well as the initial inventory by the personal representative) is regulated by Florida Statutes §§655.935, 655.936, 733.6065, and Probate Rule 5.342.

Another prerequisite to commencing estate administration is the establishment of death. Evidence of death must be filed by the personal representative or any petitioner interested in the estate. Establishment of death must be filed not only to open estate administration but also for the determination of beneficiaries, determination of homestead rights, probate of a will without administration, and disposition without administration (summary disposition) (Rule 5.205(a)). The court may waive this requirement (Rule 5.205(b).

In cases of missing persons (or those with unexplained absences), a common law presumption of death operated. Any unexplained absence for more than seven years raised a presumption that the individual was dead. Florida Statute §731.103(3) codified the presumption and reduces the time period to five years. Legislation in 2003 added subsection 3, which permits the establishment of death for a person missing less than 5 years upon proof that the absent person was exposed to a specific peril of death (for example, a natural disaster).

1. Generally

Rule 5.200. Petition for administration

The petition for administration shall be verified by the petitioner and shall contain:

(a) a statement of the interest of the petitioner, the petitioner's name and address, and the name and office address of the petitioner's attorney;

(b) the name, last known address, social security number, date and place of death of the decedent, and state and county of the decedent's domicile;

(c) so far as is known, the names and addresses of the surviving spouse, if any, and the beneficiaries and their relationship to the decedent and the date of birth of any who are minors;

(d) a statement showing venue;

(e) the priority, under the code, of the person whose appointment as the personal representative is sought and a statement that the person is qualified to serve under the laws of Florida;

(f) a statement whether domiciliary or principal proceedings are pending in another state or country, if known, and the name and address of the foreign personal representative and the court issuing letters;

(g) a statement of the approximate value and nature of the assets;

(h) in an intestate estate, a statement that after the exercise of reasonable diligence the petitioner is unaware of any unrevoked wills or codicils, or if the petitioner is aware of any unrevoked wills or codicils, a statement why the wills or codicils are not being probated, or otherwise a statement of the facts concerning any such will or codicil;

(i) in a testate estate, a statement identifying all unrevoked wills and codicils being presented for probate, and a statement that the petitioner is unaware of any other unrevoked will or codicil or, if the petitioner is aware of any other unrevoked wills or codicils, a statement why the other wills or codicils are not being probated; and

(j) in a testate estate, a statement that the original of the decedent's last will is in the possession of the court or accompanies the petition, or that an authenticated copy of a will deposited with or probated in another jurisdiction or that an authenticated copy of a notarial will, the original of which is in the possession of a foreign notary, accompanies the petition.

(Amended March 31, 1977, effective July 1, 1977 (344 So.2d 828); September 29, 1988, effective January 1, 1989 (537 So.2d 500); September 24,

1992, effective January 1, 1993 (607 So.2d 1306); May 2, 2002 (824 So.2d 849).)

§732.901. Production of wills

(1) The custodian of a will must deposit the will with the clerk of the court having venue of the estate of the decedent within 10 days after receiving information that the testator is dead. The custodian must supply the testator's date of death or social security number to the clerk upon deposit.

(2) Upon petition and notice, the custodian of any will may be compelled to produce and deposit the will as provided in subsection (1). All costs, damages, and a reasonable attorney's fee shall be adjudged to petitioner against the delinquent custodian if the court finds that the custodian had no just or reasonable cause for failing to deposit the will.

(Laws 1974, ch. 74-106, §1; Laws 1975, ch. 75-220, §44; Laws 1992, ch. 92- 200, §18. Amended by Laws 1997, ch. 97-102, §972, effective July 1, 1997; Laws 2001, ch. 2001-226, §59, effectiev January 1, 2002.)

§733.103. Effect of probate

(1) Until admitted to probate in this state or in the state where the decedent was domiciled, the will shall be ineffective to prove title to, or the right to possession of, property of the testator.

(2) In any collateral action or proceeding relating to devised property, the probate of a will in Florida shall be conclusive of its due execution; that it was executed by a competent testator, free of fraud, duress, mistake, and undue influence; and that the will was unrevoked on the testator's death.

(Laws 1974, ch. 74-106, §1; Laws 1975, ch. 75-220, §48; Laws 1977, ch. 77-87, §17; Laws 1977, ch. 77-174, §1. Amended by Laws 2001, ch. 2001-226, §79, effective January 1, 2002.)

§733.201. Proof of wills

(1) Self-proved wills executed in accordance with this code may be admitted to probate without further proof.

(2) A will may be admitted to probate upon the oath of any attesting witness taken before any circuit judge, commissioner appointed by the court, or clerk.

(3) If it appears to the court that the attesting witnesses cannot be found or that they have become incompetent after the execution of the will or their testimony cannot be obtained within a reasonable time, a will may be admitted to probate upon the oath of the personal representative nominated by the will as provided in subsection (2), whether or not the nominated personal representative is interested in the estate, or upon the oath of any person having no interest in the estate under the will stating that the person believes the writing exhibited to be the true last will of the decedent.

(Laws 1974, ch. 74-106, §1; Laws 1975, ch. 75-220, §51. Amended by Laws 1997, ch. 97-102, §985, effective July 1, 1997; Laws 2001, ch. 2001-226, §85, effective January 1, 2002.)

§733.213. Probate as prerequisite to judicial construction of will

A will may not be construed until it has been admitted to probate.

(Laws 1974, ch. 74-106, §1; Laws 1975, ch. 75-220, §61. Amended by Laws 2001, ch. 2001-226, §97, effective January 1, 2002.)

2. Establishment of Death

§731.103. Evidence as to death or status

In proceedings under this code and under chapter 736, the following additional rules relating to determination of death and status are applicable:

(1) An authenticated copy of a death certificate issued by an official or agency of the place where the death purportedly occurred is prima facie proof of the fact, place, date, and time of death and the identity of the decedent.

(2) A copy of any record or report of a governmental agency, domestic or foreign, that a person is alive, missing, detained, or, from the facts related, presumed dead is prima facie evidence of the status and of the dates, circumstances, and places disclosed by the record or report.

(3) A person who is absent from the place of his or her last known domicile for a continuous period of 5 years and whose absence is not satisfactorily explained after diligent search and inquiry is presumed to be dead. The person's death is presumed to have occurred at the end of the period unless there is evidence establishing that death occurred earlier. Evidence showing that the absent person was exposed to a specific peril of death may be a sufficient basis for the court determining at any time after such exposure that he or she died less than 5 years after the date on which his or her absence commenced. A petition for this determination shall be filed in the county in Florida where the decedent maintained his or her domicile or in any county of this state if the decedent was not a resident of Florida at the time his or her absence commenced.

(4) This section does not preclude the establishment of death by direct or circumstantial evidence prior to expiration of the 5-year time period set forth in subsection (3).

(Laws 1974, ch. 74-106, §1; Laws 1975, ch. 75-220, §2. Amended by Laws 1997, ch. 97-102, §946, effective July 1, 1997; Laws 2003, ch. 2003-154,

§1, effective June 12, 2003; Laws 2006, ch. 2006-217, §27, effective July 1, 2007.)

§733.209. Estates of missing persons

Any interested person may petition to administer the estate of a missing person; however, no personal representative shall be appointed until the court determines the missing person is dead.

(Laws 1974, ch. 74-106, §1; Laws 1975, ch. 75-220, §59. Amended by Laws 2001, ch. 2001-226, §93, effective January 1, 2002.)

Rule 5.205. Filing Evidence of Death

(a) Requirements for Filing. A copy of an official record of the death of a decedent shall be filed by the personal representative, if any, or the petitioner in each of the following proceedings and at the times specified:

(1) *Administration of decedent's estate*: not later than 3 months following the date of the first publication of the notice to creditors.

(2) *Ancillary proceedings*: not later than 3 months following the date of first publication of notice to creditors.

(3) *Summary administration*: at any time prior to entry of the order of summary administration.

(4) *Disposition without administration*: at the time of filing the application for disposition without administration.

(5) *Determination of beneficiaries*: at any time prior to entry of the final judgment determining beneficiaries.

(6) Determination of protected homestead: at any time prior to entry of the final judgment determining protected homestead status of real property.

(7) Probate of will without administration: at any time prior to entry of the order admitting will to probate.

(b) Waiver. On verified petition by the personal representative, if any, or the petitioner the court may enter an order dispensing with this rule, without notice or hearing.

(c) Authority to Require Filing. The court may, without notice or hearing, enter an order requiring the personal representative, if any, or the petitioner to file a copy of an official record of death at any time during the proceedings.

(Added September 4, 1980, effective January 1, 1981 (387 So.2d 949). Amended September 13, 1984, effective January 1, 1985 (458 So.2d 1079); September 29, 1988, effective January 1, 1989 (537 So.2d 500); September 24, 1992, effective January 1, 1993 (607 So.2d 1306); May 2, 2002 (824 So.2d 849); June 19, 2003 (848 So.2d 1069).)

3. Special Types of Wills

§732.503. Self-proof of will

(1) A will or codicil executed in conformity with §732.502 may be made self-proved at the time of its execution or at any subsequent date by the acknowledgment of it by the testator and the affidavits of the witnesses, made before an officer authorized to administer oaths and evidenced by the officer's certificate attached to or following the will, in substantially the following form:

STATE OF FLORIDA COUNTY OF ________

I, ________, declare to the officer taking my acknowledgment of this instrument, and to the subscribing witnesses, that I signed this instrument as my will.

____

Testator

We, ________ and, ________ have been sworn by the officer signing below, and declare to that officer on our oaths that the testator declared the instrument to be the testator's will and signed it in our presence and that we each signed the instrument as a witness in the presence of the testator and of each other.

____

Witness

____

Witness

Acknowledged and subscribed before me by the testator, (type or print testator's name), who is personally known to me or who has produced (state type of identification--see §117.05(5)(b)2.) as identification, and sworn to and subscribed before me by the witnesses, (type or print name of first witness) who is personally known to me or who has produced (state type of identification--see §117.05(5)(b)2.) as identification and (type or print name of second witness) who is personally known to me or who has produced (state type of identification--see §117.05(5)(b)2.) as identification, and subscribed by me in the presence of the testator and the subscribing witnesses, all on (date).

(Signature of Officer)

(Print, type, or stamp commissioned name and affix official seal)

(2) A will or codicil made self-proved under former law, or executed in another state and made self-proved under the laws of that state, shall be considered as self-proved under this section.

(Laws 1974, ch. 74-106, §1; Laws 1975, ch. 75-220, §21; Laws 1977, ch. 77-87, §12; Laws 1993, ch. 93-62, §8. Amended by Laws 1997, ch. 97-102, §962, effective July 1, 1997; Laws 1998, ch. 98-

246, §18, effective January 1, 1999; Laws 2001, ch. 2001-226, §43, effective January 1, 2002.)

§733.201. Proof of self-proved wills

(1) Self-proved wills executed in accordance with this code may be admitted to probate without further proof....

(Laws 1974, ch. 74-106, §1; Laws 1975, ch. 75-220, §51. Amended by Laws 1997, ch. 97-102, §985, effective July 1, 1997; Laws 2001, ch. 2001-226, §85, effective January 1, 2002.)

§733.204. Probate of a will written in a foreign language

(1) No will written in a foreign language shall be admitted to probate unless it is accompanied by a true and complete English translation.

(2) No personal representative who complies in good faith with the English translation of the will as established by the court shall be liable for doing so.

(Laws 1974, ch. 74-106, §1; Laws 1975, ch. 75-220, §54; Laws 1977, ch. 77-174, §1. Amended by Laws 2001, ch. 2001-226, §88, effective January 1, 2002.)

Rule 5.216. Will Written in Foreign Language

A will written in a foreign language being offered for probate shall be accompanied by a true and complete English translation. In the order admitting the foreign language will to probate, the court shall establish the correct English translation. At any time during administration, any interested person may have the correctness of the translation redetermined after formal notice to all other interested persons.

(Added May 2, 2002 (824 So.2d 849).)

§733.205. Probate of notarial will

(1) When a copy of a notarial will in the possession of a notary entitled to its custody in a foreign state or country, the laws of which state or country require that the will remain in the custody of the notary, duly authenticated by the notary, whose official position, signature, and seal of office are further authenticated by an American consul, vice consul, or other American consular officer within whose jurisdiction the notary is a resident, or whose official position, signature, and seal of office have been authenticated according to the requirements of the Hague Convention of 1961, is presented to the court, it may be admitted to probate if the original could have been admitted to probate in this state.

(2) The duly authenticated copy shall be prima facie evidence of its purported execution and of the facts stated in the certificate in compliance with subsection (1).

(3) Any interested person may oppose the probate of such a notarial will or may petition for revocation of probate of such a notarial will, as in the original probate of a will in this state.

(Laws 1974, ch. 74-106, §1; Laws 1975, ch. 75-220, §55. Amended by Laws 2001, ch. 2001-226, §89, effective January 1, 2002; Laws 2003, ch. 2003-154, §7, effective June 12, 2003.)

§733.206. Probate of will of resident after foreign probate

(1) If a will of any person who dies a resident of this state is admitted to probate in any other state or country through inadvertence, error, or omission before probate in this state, the will may be admitted to probate in this state if the original could have been admitted to probate in this state.

(2) An authenticated copy of the will, foreign proof of the will, the foreign order of probate, and any letters issued shall be filed instead of the original will and shall be prima facie evidence of its execution and admission to foreign probate.

(3) Any interested person may oppose the probate of the will or may petition for revocation of the probate of the will, as in the original probate of a will in this state.

(Laws 1974, ch. 74-106, §1; Laws 1975, ch. 75-220, §56. Amended by Laws 2001, ch. 2001-226, §90, effective January 1, 2002.)

§733.207. Establishment and probate of lost or destroyed will

Any interested person may establish the full and precise terms of a lost or destroyed will and offer the will for probate. The specific content of the will must be proved by the testimony of two disinterested witnesses, or, if a correct copy is provided, it shall be proved by one disinterested witness.

(Laws 1974, ch. 74-106, §1; Laws 1975, ch. 75-220, §57. Amended by Laws 2001, ch. 2001-226, §91, effective January 1, 2002.)

§733.208. Discovery of later will

On the discovery of a later will or codicil, any interested person may petition to revoke the probate of the earlier will or to probate the later will or codicil. No will or codicil may be offered after the testate or intestate estate has been completely administered and the personal representative discharged.

(Laws 1974, ch. 74-106, §1; Laws 1975, ch. 75-220, §58. Amended by Laws 2001, ch. 2001-226, §92, effective January 1, 2002.)

Rule 5.215. Authenticated Copy of Will

An authenticated copy of a will may be admitted to probate if the original could be admitted to probate in Florida.
(Added May 2, 2002 (824 So.2d 849).)

Rule 5.230. Commission to Prove Will

(a) Petition. On petition the court may appoint a commissioner to take the oath of any person qualified to prove the will under Florida law. The petition shall set forth the date of the will and the place where it was executed, if known; the names of the witnesses and address of the witness whose oath is to be taken; and the name, title, and address of the proposed commissioner.

(b) Commission. The commission shall be directed to any person who is authorized to administer an oath by the laws of Florida, the United States of America, or the state or country where the witness may be found, and it shall empower the commissioner to take the oath of the witness to prove the will and shall direct the commissioner to certify the oath and file the executed commission, copy of the will, oath of the witness, and certificate of commissioner. An oath of the commissioner is not required.

(c) Mailing or Delivery. The petitioner or the petitioner's attorney shall cause the commission, together with a copy of the will, the oath, and the certificate of commissioner, to be mailed or delivered to the commissioner.

(d) Filing. The executed commission, copy of the will, oath of the witness, and certificate of commissioner shall be filed.

(e) Objections. Objections to the validity of the will shall follow the form and procedure set forth in these rules pertaining to revocation of probate. Objections to the qualifications of the personal representative shall follow the form and procedure set forth in these rules pertaining to removal of personal representatives. Objections to the venue or jurisdiction of the court shall follow the form and procedure set forth in the Florida Rules of Civil Procedure.
(Amended September 13, 1984, effective January 1, 1985 (458 So.2d 1079); September 29, 1988, effective January 1, 1989 (537 So.2d 500); September 24, 1992, effective January 1, 1993 (607 So.2d 1306).)

4. Search of Safety-Deposit Boxes

§655.935 Search procedure on death of lessee

If satisfactory proof of the death of the lessee is presented, a lessor shall permit the person named in a court order for the purpose, or if no order has been served upon the lessor, the spouse, a parent, an adult descendant, or a person named as a personal representative in a copy of a purported will produced by such person, to open and examine the contents of a safe-deposit box leased or coleased by a decedent, or any documents delivered by a decedent for safekeeping, in the presence of an officer of the lessor; and the lessor, if so requested by such person, shall deliver:

(1) Any writing purporting to be a will of the decedent, to the court having probate jurisdiction in the county in which the financial institution is located.

(2) Any writing purporting to be a deed to a burial plot or to give burial instructions, to the person making the request for a search.

(3) Any document purporting to be an insurance policy on the life of the decedent, to the beneficiary named therein.

No other contents may be removed pursuant to this section. Access granted pursuant to this section shall not be considered the initial opening of the safe-deposit box pursuant to §733.6065 by a personal representative appointed by a court in this state.
(Added by Laws 1992, ch. 92-303, §65, effective July 3, 1992. Amended by Laws 2006, ch. 2006-134, §1, effective July 1, 2006; Laws 2006, ch. 2006-213, §67, effective October 1, 2006.)

§655.936. Delivery of safe-deposit box contents or property held in safekeeping to personal representative

(1) Subject to the provisions of subsection (3), the lessor shall immediately deliver to a personal representative appointed by a court in this state, upon presentation of a certified copy of his or her letters of authority, all property deposited with it by the decedent for safekeeping, and shall grant the personal representative access to any safe-deposit box in the decedent's name and permit him or her to remove from such box any part or all of the contents thereof.

(2) If a personal representative of a deceased lessee has been appointed by a court of any other state, a lessor may, at its discretion, after 3 months from the issuance to such personal representative of his or her letters of authority, deliver to such personal representative all properties deposited with it for safekeeping and the contents of any safe-deposit box in the name of the decedent if at such time the lessor has not received written notice of the appointment of a personal representative in this state, and such delivery is a valid discharge of the lessor for all property or contents so delivered. A personal representative appointed by a court of any other state shall furnish the lessor with an affidavit setting forth facts showing the domicile of the deceased lessee to be other than this state and stating that there are no unpaid creditors of the deceased lessee in this state, together with a certified copy of his or her letters of authority. A

lessor making delivery pursuant to this subsection shall maintain in its files a receipt executed by such personal representative which itemizes in detail all property so delivered.

(3) Notwithstanding the provisions of subsection (1), after the death of a lessee of a safe-deposit box, the lessor shall permit the initial opening of the safe-deposit box and the removal of the contents of the safe-deposit box in accordance with §733.6065..

(4) A lessor is not liable for damages or penalty by reason of any delivery made pursuant to this section.

(Added by Laws 1992, ch. 92-303, §66, effective July 3, 1992. Amended by Laws 1997, ch. 97-102, §531, effective July 1, 1997; Laws 1997, ch. 97-240, §12, effective May 30, 1997; Laws 2001, ch. 2001-226, §3, effective January 1, 2002; Laws 2006, ch. 2006-134, §2, effective July 1, 2006; Laws 2006, ch. 2006-213, §68, effective October 1, 2006.)

§733.6065. Opening safe-deposit box

(1) Subject to the provisions of §655.936(2), the initial opening of a safe-deposit box that is leased or coleased by the decedent shall be conducted in the presence of any two of the following persons: an employee of the institution where the box is located, the personal representative, or the personal representative's attorney of record. Each person who is present must verify the contents of the box by signing a copy of the inventory under penalties of perjury. The personal representative shall file the safe-deposit box inventory, together with a copy of the box entry record from a date which is 6 months prior to the date of death to the date of inventory, with the court within 10 days after the box is opened. Unless otherwise ordered by the court, this inventory and the attached box entry record is subject to inspection only by persons entitled to inspect an inventory under §733.604(1). The personal representative may remove the contents of the box.

(2) The right to open and examine the contents of a safe-deposit box leased by a decedent, or any documents delivered by a decedent for safekeeping, and to receive items as provided for in §655.935 is separate from the rights provided for in subsection (1).

(Laws 2001, ch. 2001-226, §129, effective January 1, 2002. Amended by Laws 2006, ch. 2006-134, §7, effective July 1, 2006; Laws 2006, ch. 2006-213, §71, effective October 1, 2006.)

Rule 5.342. Inventory of safe-deposit box

(a) Filing. The personal representative shall file an inventory of the contents of the decedent's safe-deposit box within 10 days of the initial opening of the box by the personal representative or the personal representative's attorney of record. The inventory shall include a copy of the financial institution's entry record for the box from a date that is six months prior to the decedent's date of death to the date of the initial opening by the personal representative or the personal representative's attorney of record.

(b) Verification. Each person who was present at the initial opening must verify the contents of the box by signing a copy of the inventory under penalties of perjury.

(c) Service. The personal representative shall serve a copy of the inventory on the surviving spouse, each heir at law in an intestate estate, each residuary beneficiary in a testate estate, and any other interested person who may request it in writing. The personal representative shall file proof of such service.

(Added June 19, 2003 (848 So.2d 1069).)

5. Revocation of Probate

§733.109. Proceeding to revoke

(1) A proceeding to revoke the probate of a will shall be brought in the court having jurisdiction over the administration. Any interested person, including a beneficiary under a prior will, unless barred under §733.212 or §733.2123, may commence the proceeding before final discharge of the personal representative.

(2) Pending the determination of any petition for revocation of probate, the personal representative shall proceed with the administration of the estate as if no revocation proceeding had been commenced, except that no distribution may be made to beneficiaries in contravention of the rights of those who, but for the will, would be entitled to the property disposed of.

(3) Revocation of probate of a will shall not affect or impair the title to property purchased in good faith for value from the personal representative prior to an order of revocation.

(Laws 1974, ch. 74-106, §1; Laws 1975, ch. 75-220, §50; Laws 1977, ch. 77-87, §18; Laws 1977, ch. 77-104, §227. Amended by Laws 2001, ch. 2001-226, §84, effective January 1, 2002.)

[Note: On the filing of notice of administration to beneficiaries and creditors, see Section II, B2 ("Notice for Purposes of Commencing Administration").]

B. Contest of Will

A will contest is a challenge to the validity of a decedent's will. Florida legislation specifies the procedure for filing an objection to probate of a will (Fla. Stat. §733.212). Statutory restrictions regulate the persons who may bring such contests (*id.*) and the grounds for a contest (Fla. Stat. §732.5165).

Will contests generally begin by a petition to revoke probate of a will. Florida law sets forth the rules for such proceedings. A challenge by any "interested person on whom notice is served" must occur within the later of (1) three months after the date of first publication of notice of administration, or (2) 30 days after the date of service of the notice. Objections may pertain to the validity of the will, the qualifications of the personal representative, venue, or jurisdiction (Fla. Stat. §733.212(3)).

Will contests consist of claims that the will was not executed with the requisite formalities (Fla. Stat. §732.502); or a testator was not mentally competent (Fla. Stat. §732.501); or the presence of undue influence, fraud, duress or mistake (Fla. Stat. §732.5165); or the will has been previously revoked (Fla. Stat. §732.505). Trawick, *supra*, at §10-2. See Fla. Stat. §§732.501 et seq.

The Florida Code also specifies the applicable burden of proof in will contests. Proponents of the will have the burden of proof of due execution. Contestants have the burden of proof of lack of capacity or revocation (Fla. Stat. §733.107). See also Fla. Prob. Rule §5.275 (implementing Fla. Stat. §733.107).

A will that is procured by fraud, duress, undue influence, or mistake shall be void. If only a provision of a will is procured by fraud, duress, undue influence or mistake, only that provision will be void (Fla. Stat. §732.5165).

The Code governs the law applicable to "no-contest clauses" (i.e., will provisions that penalize an heir or beneficiary who brings an unsuccessful challenge to a will). In a majority of jurisdictions, no-contest clauses are not enforceable against a beneficiary who brings a contest provided that the beneficiary has probable cause. According to Florida Statutes §732.517, a no-contest clause in a will (defined as a provision that purports either to penalize a person for bringing a contest or for "instituting other proceedings relating to the estate") is unenforceable.

An amendment in 2002 to Florida Statutes §733.107 provides that the presumption of undue influence is a "presumption shifting the burden of proof under §§90.301-90.304 [defining presumptions affecting the burden of proof]." According to this statutory amendment, when the presumption of undue influence arises, the burden shifts to the alleged wrongdoer to prove that there was no undue influence. Before the amendment, the presumption of undue influence merely shifted to the contestant the burden of going forward with the evidence. See generally Steven G. Nilsson, Florida's New Statutory Presumption of Undue Influence: Does it Change the Law or Merely Clarify?, 77 Fla. B.J. 20 (2003).

On the grounds for will contests, see also Chapter IV *supra* on testamentary capacity.

§732.517. Penalty clause for contest

A provision in a will purporting to penalize any interested person for contesting the will or instituting other proceedings relating to the estate is unenforceable.

(Laws 1974, ch. 74-106, §1; Laws 1975, ch. 75-220, 32.)

§733.2123. Adjudication before issuance of letters

A petitioner may serve formal notice of the petition for administration on interested persons. A copy of the will offered for probate shall be attached to the notice. No person who is served with formal notice of the petition for administration prior to the issuance of letters or who has waived notice may challenge the validity of the will, testacy of the decedent, qualifications of the personal representative, venue, or jurisdiction of the court, except in the proceedings before issuance of letters.

(Laws 1975, ch. 75-220, §60; Laws 1981, ch. 81-27, §2. Amended by Laws 1997, ch. 97-102, §987, effective July 1, 1997; Laws 2001, ch. 2001-226, §96, effective January 1, 2002.)

§733.107. Burden of proof in contests; presumption of undue influence

(1) In all proceedings contesting the validity of a will, the burden shall be upon the proponent of the will to establish prima facie its formal execution and attestation. Thereafter, the contestant shall have the burden of establishing the grounds on which the probate of the will is opposed or revocation is sought.

(2) The presumption of undue influence implements public policy against abuse of fiduciary or confidential relationships and is therefore a presumption shifting the burden of proof under §§90.301-90.304.

(Laws 1974, ch. 74-106, § 1; Laws 1975, ch. 75-220, § 50. Amended by Laws 2001, ch. 2001-226, § 83, effective January 1, 2002; Laws 2002, ch. 2002-82, § 5, effective April 23, 2002.)

Rule 5.240. Notice of Administration

. . **(d) Objections.** Objections to the validity of the will shall follow the form and procedure set forth in these rules pertaining to revocation of probate. Objections to the qualifications of the personal representative shall follow the form and procedure set forth in these rules pertaining to removal of a personal representative. Objections to the venue or jurisdiction of the court shall follow the form and procedure set forth in the Florida Rules of Civil Procedure.

(Amended March 31, 1977, effective July 1, 1977 (344 So.2d 828); September 13, 1984, effective January 1, 1985 (458 So.2d 1079); September 29, 1988, effective January 1, 1989 (537 So.2d 500); August 22, 1991, effective October 1, 1991 (584 So.2d 964); September 24, 1992, effective January 1, 1993 (607 So.2d 1306); October 3, 1996, effective January 1, 1997 (683 So.2d 78); May 2, 2002 (824 So.2d 849); June 19, 2003, (848 So.2d 1069); September 29, 2005, effective January1, 2006 (912 So.2d 1178).)

Rule 5.275. Burden of Proof in Will Contests

In all proceedings contesting the validity of a will, the burden shall be upon the proponent of the will to establish prima facie its formal execution and attestation. Thereafter, the contestant shall have the burden of establishing the grounds on which the probate of the will is opposed or revocation sought.

(Added September 29, 1988, effective January 1, 1989 (537 So.2d 500).)

733.212. Notice of administration; filing of objections

....

(3) Any interested person on whom a copy of the notice of administration is served must object to the validity of the will, the qualifications of the personal representative, the venue, or the jurisdiction of the court by filing a petition or other pleading requesting relief in accordance with the Florida Probate Rules on or before the date that is 3 months after the date of service of a copy of the notice of administration on the objecting person, or those objections are forever barred.

(4) The appointment of a personal representative or a successor personal representative shall not extend or renew the period for filing objections under this section, unless a new will or codicil is admitted.

....

(Amended September 13, 1984, effective January 1, 1985 (458 So.2d 1079); September 29, 1988, effective January 1, 1989 (537 So.2d 500); September 29, 2005, effective January 1, 2006 (912 So.2d 1178).)

Rule 5.025. Adversary Proceedings

(a) Specific Adversary Proceedings. The following shall be adversary proceedings unless otherwise ordered by the court: proceedings to remove a personal representative, surcharge a personal representative, remove a guardian, surcharge a guardian, probate a lost or destroyed will or later-discovered will, determine beneficiaries, construe a will, cancel a devise, partition property for the purposes of distribution, determine pretermitted share, determine amount of elective share and contribution, and for revocation of probate of a will.

(b) Declared Adversary Proceedings. Other proceedings may be declared adversary by service on interested persons of a separate declaration that the proceeding is adversary.

(1) If served by the petitioner, the declaration shall be served with the petition to which it relates.

(2) If served by the respondent, the declaration and a written response to the petition shall be served at the earlier of:

(A) within 20 days after service of the petition, or

(B) prior to the hearing date on the petition.

(3) When the declaration is served by a respondent, the petitioner shall promptly serve formal notice on all other interested persons.

(c) Adversary Status by Order. The court may determine any proceeding to be an adversary proceeding at any time.

(d) Notice and Procedure in Adversary Proceedings.

(1) Petitioner shall serve formal notice.

(2) After service of formal notice, the proceedings, as nearly as practicable, shall be conducted similar to suits of a civil nature and the Florida Rules of Civil Procedure shall govern, including entry of defaults.

(3) The court on its motion or on motion of any interested person may enter orders to avoid undue delay in the main administration.

(4) If a proceeding is already commenced when an order is entered determining the proceeding to be adversary, it shall thereafter be conducted as an adversary proceeding. The order shall require interested persons to serve written defenses, if any, within 20 days from the date of the order. It shall not be necessary to re-serve the petition except as ordered by the court.

(5) When the proceedings are adversary, the caption of subsequent pleadings, as an extension of the probate caption, shall include the name of the first petitioner and the name of the first respondent.

(Amended March 31, 1977, effective July 1, 1977 (344 So.2d 828); September 13, 1984, effective January 1, 1985 (458 So.2d 1079); September 29, 1988, effective January 1, 1989 (537 So.2d 500); September 24, 1992, effective January 1, 1993 (607 So.2d 1306); October 11, 2001 (807 So.2d 622); January 10, 2002 (816 So.2d 1095).)

§732.5165. Effect of fraud, duress, mistake, and undue influence

A will is void if the execution is procured by fraud, duress, mistake, or undue influence. Any part of the will is void if so procured, but the

remainder of the will not so procured shall be valid if it is not invalid for other reasons.
(Laws 1975, ch. 75-220, §31.)

IV. Appointment of Personal Representative

A personal representative is an officer of the court and acts in a fiduciary capacity. A personal representative who administers the estate of a decedent generally is either: (1) an "executor" who is named by a decedent in his or her will, or (2) an "administrator" if the decedent dies without a valid will.

Florida law also authorizes other representatives. A "curator" is a person appointed to take charge of an estate until the appointment of a personal representative (Fla. Stat. §731.201(7)). An "administrator ad litem" administers an estate when there is no personal representative (Fla. Stat. §733.308) or the personal representative has a conflict of interest (Rule 5.120). See generally Trawick, *supra*, §5-5 n.23 (suggesting that the statute and Probate Rule conflict because they provide for different reasons for appointment of administrators ad litem). Finally, an "executor de son tort" is a person who performs acts of estate administration without the authority to do so.

Occasionally, *joint* personal representatives may be appointed. In such cases, a *majority* of the personal representatives is required for acts involving the administration of the estate (for wills executed after October 1, 1987). This restriction does not apply if the will provides otherwise, any joint personal representative receives property due the estate, an emergency exists and the concurrence of the other personal representatives cannot be easily obtained, or one personal representative has been delegated by the others to act on behalf of the estate (Fla. Stat. §733.615(1)).

On the advantages and disadvantages of choosing a personal representative who is a beneficiary versus an independent fiduciary, see Dan P. Heller et al., Fiduciaries, Basic Estate Planning in Florida §§12.3, 12.4 (2006).

A. Generally

§731.201. General definitions

Subject to additional definitions in subsequent chapters that are applicable to specific chapters or parts, and unless the context otherwise requires, in this code, in §409.9101, and in chapters 736, 738, 739, and 744, the term:...

(7) "Curator" means a person appointed by the court to take charge of the estate of a decedent until letters are issued.

...

(15) "Foreign personal representative" means a personal representative of another state or a foreign country.

. . .

(22) "Letters" means authority granted by the court to the personal representative to act on behalf of the estate of the decedent and refers to what has been known as letters testamentary and letters of administration. All letters shall be designated "letters of administration."

. . .

(25) "Personal representative" means the fiduciary appointed by the court to administer the estate and refers to what has been known as an administrator, administrator cum testamento annexo, administrator de bonis non, ancillary administrator, ancillary executor, or executor.

(26) "Petition" means a written request to the court for an order.

...

(28) "Probate of will" means all steps necessary to establish the validity of a will and to admit a will to probate.

. . .

(Laws 1974, ch. 74-106, § 1; Laws 1975, ch. 75-220, § 4; Laws 1977, ch. 77-174, § 1; Laws 1985, ch. 85-79, § 2; Laws 1987, ch. 87-226, § 66; Laws 1988, ch. 88-340, § 1; Laws 1993, ch. 93-257, § 7. Amended by Laws 1995, ch. 95- 401, § 6, effective July 1, 1995; Laws 1997, ch. 97-102, § 949, effective July 1, 1997; Laws 1998, ch. 98-421, § 52, effective July 1, 1998; Laws 2001, ch. 2001-226, § 11, effective January 1, 2002; Laws 2002, ch. 2002-1, § 106, effective May 21, 2002; Laws 2003, ch. 2003-154, § 2, effective June 12, 2003; Laws 2005, ch. 2005-108, § 2, effective July 1, 2005; Laws 2006, ch. 2006-217, § 29, effective July 1, 2007.)

§733.308. Administrator ad litem

When an estate must be represented and the personal representative is unable to do so, the court shall appoint an administrator ad litem without bond to represent the estate in that proceeding. The fact that the personal representative is seeking reimbursement for claims against the decedent does not require appointment of an administrator ad litem.
(Laws 1974, ch. 74-106, §1; Laws 1975, ch. 75-220, §65. Amended by Laws 2001, ch. 2001-226, §103, effective January 1, 2002.)

733.309. Executor de son tort

No person shall be liable to a creditor of a decedent as executor de son tort, but any person taking, converting, or intermeddling with the property of a decedent shall be liable to the personal representative or curator, when appointed, for the value of all the property so taken or converted and for all damages to the

estate caused by the wrongful action. This section shall not be construed to prevent a creditor of a decedent from suing anyone in possession of property fraudulently conveyed by the decedent to set aside the fraudulent conveyance.
(Laws 1974, ch. 74-106, §1; Laws 1975, ch. 75-220, §65. Amended by Laws 1997, ch. 97-102, §991, effective July 1, 1997; Laws 2001, ch. 2001-226, §104, effective January 1, 2002.)

Rule 5.120. Administrator Ad Litem and Guardian Ad Litem

(a) Appointment. When it is necessary that the estate of a decedent or a ward be represented in any probate or guardianship proceeding and there is no personal representative of the estate or guardian of the ward, or the personal representative or guardian is or may be interested adversely to the estate or ward, or is enforcing the personal representative's or guardian's own debt or claim against the estate or ward, or the necessity arises otherwise, the court may appoint an administrator ad litem or a guardian ad litem, as the case may be, without bond or notice for that particular proceeding. At any point in a proceeding, a court may appoint a guardian ad litem to represent the interests of an incapacitated person, an unborn or unascertained person, a minor or any other person otherwise under a legal disability, or a person whose identity or address is unknown, if the court determines that representation of the interest otherwise would be inadequate. If not precluded by conflict of interest, a guardian ad litem may be appointed to represent several persons or interests. The administrator ad litem or guardian ad litem shall file an oath to discharge all duties faithfully and upon the filing shall be qualified to act. No process need be served upon the administrator ad litem or guardian ad litem, but such person shall appear and defend as directed by the court.

(b) Petition. The petition for appointment of a guardian ad litem shall state to the best of petitioner's information and belief:

(1) the name and residence address of each minor or incapacitated person and birth date of each minor who has an interest in the proceedings;

(2) the name and address of any guardian appointed for each minor or incapacitated person;

(3) the name and residence address of any living natural guardians or living natural guardian having legal custody of each minor or incapacitated person;

(4) a description of the interest in the proceedings of each minor or incapacitated person; and

(5) the facts showing the necessity for the appointment of a guardian ad litem.

(c) Notice. Within 10 days after appointment, the petitioner shall deliver or mail conformed copies of the petition for appointment of a guardian ad litem and order to any guardian, or if there is no guardian, to the living natural guardians or the living natural guardian having legal custody of the minor or incapacitated person.

(d) Report. The guardian ad litem shall deliver or mail conformed copies of any written report or finding of the guardian ad litem's investigation and answer filed in the proceedings, petition for compensation and discharge, and the notice of hearing on the petition to any guardian, or in the event that there is no guardian, to the living natural guardians or the living natural guardian having legal custody of the minor or incapacitated person.

(e) Service of Petition and Order. Within 10 days after appointment, the petitioner for an administrator ad litem shall deliver or mail conformed copies of the petition for appointment and order to the attorney of record of each beneficiary and to each known beneficiary not represented by an attorney of record.

(f) Enforcement of Judgments. When an administrator ad litem or guardian ad litem recovers any judgment or other relief, it shall be enforced as other judgments. Execution shall issue in favor of the administrator ad litem or guardian ad litem for the use of the estate or ward and the money collected shall be paid to the personal representative or guardian, or as otherwise ordered by the court.

(g) Claim of Personal Representative. The fact that the personal representative is seeking reimbursement for claims against the decedent paid by the personal representative does not require appointment of an administrator ad litem.
(Amended March 31, 1977, effective July 1, 1977 (344 So.2d 828); September 29, 1988, effective January 1, 1989 (537 So.2d 500); September 24, 1992, effective January 1, 1993 (607 So.2d 1306).)

§733.501. Curators

(1) When it is necessary, the court may appoint a curator after formal notice to the person apparently entitled to letters of administration. The curator may be authorized to perform any duty or function of a personal representative. If there is great danger that any of the decedent's property is likely to be wasted, destroyed, or removed beyond the jurisdiction of the court and if the appointment of a curator would be delayed by giving notice, the court may appoint a curator without giving notice.

(2) Bond shall be required of the curator as the court deems necessary. No bond shall be required of banks and trust companies as curators.

(3) Curators shall be allowed reasonable compensation for their services, and the court may consider the provisions of §733.617.

(4) Curators shall be subject to removal and surcharge.
(Laws 1974, ch. 74-106, §1; Laws 1975, ch. 75-220, §69; Laws 1977, ch. 77-174, §1. Amended by Laws 1997, ch. 97-102, §995, effective July 1, 1997; Laws 2001, ch. 2001-226, §112, effective January 1, 2002; Laws 2002, ch. 2002-1, §108, effective May 21, 2002.)

§733.615. Joint personal representatives; when joint action required

(1) If two or more persons are appointed joint personal representatives, and unless the will provides otherwise, the concurrence of all joint personal representatives appointed pursuant to a will or codicil executed prior to October 1, 1987, or appointed to administer an intestate estate of a decedent who died prior to October 1, 1987, or of a majority of joint personal representatives appointed pursuant to a will or codicil executed on or after October 1, 1987, or appointed to administer an intestate estate of a decedent dying on or after October 1, 1987, is required on all acts connected with the administration and distribution of the estate. This restriction does not apply when any joint personal representative receives and receipts for property due the estate, when the concurrence required under this subsection cannot readily be obtained in the time reasonably available for emergency action necessary to preserve the estate, or when a joint personal representative has been delegated to act for the others.

(2) Where action by a majority of the joint personal representatives appointed is authorized, a joint personal representative who has not joined in exercising a power is not liable to the beneficiaries or to others for the consequences of the exercise, and a dissenting joint personal representative is not liable for the consequences of an action in which the dissenting personal representative joins at the direction of the majority of the joint personal representatives, if the dissent is expressed in writing to the other joint personal representatives at or before the time of the action.

(3) A person dealing with a joint personal representative without actual knowledge that joint personal representatives have been appointed, or if advised by a joint personal representative that the joint personal representative has authority to act alone for any of the reasons mentioned in subsection (1), is as fully protected in dealing with that joint personal representative as if that joint personal representative possessed and properly exercised the power.
(Laws 1974, ch. 74-106, §1; Laws 1975, ch. 75-220, §79; Laws 1987, ch. 87- 317, §1; Laws 1988, ch. 88-340, §4. Amended by Laws 1997, ch. 97-102, §1013, effective July 1, 1997; Laws 2001, ch. 2001-226, §139, effective January 1, 2002.)

B. Qualification, Appointment, and Removal

All states specify the persons who are entitled to appointment as personal representatives and who have the power to administer an estate. The appointment of the personal representative becomes effective following issuance of "letters testamentary" (for the estate of a decedent who died testate) or "letters of administration" (for the estate of a decedent who died intestate).

An executor who is named in the decedent's will has the right to be appointed personal representative unless he or she declines to act or is statutorily disqualified.

Florida Statutes §§733.302-733.305 specify the qualifications of the personal representative. To be appointed, a person must have capacity and be a resident of Florida at the time of the decedent's death (Fla. Stat. §§733.302). Persons who are prohibited from serving include: felons, persons who are unable for physical or mental reasons to perform the requisite duties, and minors (Fla. Stat. §§733.303(1)).

Nonresidents of the state may serve as personal representatives only in limited situations, if the person is (1) an adopted child or adoptive parent of the decedent; (2) related to the decedent ("by lineal consanguinity"); (3) a spouse, brother, sister, uncle, aunt, nephew, or niece of the decedent (or "someone related by lineal consanguinity to any such person"); or (4) the spouse of any person otherwise qualified (Fla. Stat. §733.304).

For a trenchant criticism of the Florida rule restricting nonresidents' serving as personal representations, see David T. Smith, The Potential Personal Representative: Ready, Willing, But Perhaps Unable to Act in Florida, 48 Fla. L. Rev. 675, 691 (1996) ("the only pragmatic justification for the existence of section 733.304 [is] protectionism [to] 'keep the personal representative business at home'").

Statutes typically specify an order of appointment for granting letters of administration. In a testate estate, preference is given to: (1) the person nominated in the will, (2) the person selected by a majority of those "persons entitled to the estate," and (3) a devisee (Fla. Stat. §733.301(1)(a)). In contrast, in intestate estates, the order of priority is: (1) the surviving spouse, (2) the person selected by a "majority in interest of the heirs," and (3) the heir "nearest in degree." In the last case, if more than one heir shares the same degree of proximity, then the court may select the "best qualified" (Fla. Stat. §733.301(1)(b)).

1. Generally

§733.301. Preference in appointment of personal representative

(1) In granting letters of administration, the following order of preference shall be observed:

(a) In testate estates:

1. The personal representative, or his or her successor, nominated by the will or pursuant to a power conferred in the will.

2. The person selected by a majority in interest of the persons entitled to the estate.

3. A devisee under the will. If more than one devisee applies, the court may select the one best qualified.

(b) In intestate estates:

1. The surviving spouse.

2. The person selected by a majority in interest of the heirs.

3. The heir nearest in degree. If more than one applies, the court may select the one best qualified.

(2) A guardian of the property of a ward who if competent would be entitled to appointment as, or to select, the personal representative may exercise the right to select the personal representative.

(3) In either a testate or an intestate estate, if no application is made by any of the persons described in subsection (1), the court shall appoint a capable person; but no person may be appointed under this subsection:

(a) Who works for, or holds public office under, the court.

(b) Who is employed by, or holds office under, any judge exercising probate jurisdiction.

(4) After letters have been granted in either a testate or an intestate estate, if a person who was entitled to, and has not waived, preference over the person appointed at the time of the appointment and on whom formal notice was not served seeks the appointment, the letters granted may be revoked and the person entitled to preference may have letters granted after formal notice and hearing.

(5) After letters have been granted in either a testate or an intestate estate, if any will is subsequently admitted to probate, the letters shall be revoked and new letters granted.

(Laws 1974, ch. 74-106, §1; Laws 1975, ch. 75-220, §62; Laws 1977, ch. 77-87, §21; Laws 1977, ch. 77-174, §1. Amended by Laws 1997, ch. 97-102, §988, effective July 1, 1997; Laws 2001, ch. 2001-226, §98, effective January 1, 2002.)

§733.302. Who may be appointed personal representative

Subject to the limitations in this part, any person who is sui juris and is a resident of Florida at the time of the death of the person whose estate is to be administered is qualified to act as personal representative in Florida.

(Laws 1974, ch. 74-106, §1; Laws 1975, ch. 75-220, §63; Laws 1979, ch. 79-343, §5. Amended by Laws 1997, ch. 97-102, §989, effective July 1, 1997; Laws 2001, ch. 2001-226, §99, effective January 1, 2002.)

§733.303. Persons not qualified

(1) A person is not qualified to act as a personal representative if the person:

(a) Has been convicted of a felony.

(b) Is mentally or physically unable to perform the duties.

(c) Is under the age of 18 years.

(2) If the person named as personal representative in the will is not qualified, letters shall be granted as provided in §733.301.

(Laws 1974, ch. 74-106, §1; Laws 1975, ch. 75-220, §63; Laws 1977, ch. 77-87, §22. Amended by Laws 1997, ch. 97-102, §990, effective July 1, 1997.)

§733.304. Nonresidents

A person who is not domiciled in the state cannot qualify as personal representative unless the person is:

(1) A legally adopted child or adoptive parent of the decedent;

(2) Related by lineal consanguinity to the decedent;

(3) A spouse or a brother, sister, uncle, aunt, nephew, or niece of the decedent, or someone related by lineal consanguinity to any such person; or

(4) The spouse of a person otherwise qualified under this section.

(Laws 1974, ch. 74-106, §1; Laws 1975, ch. 75-220, §63; Laws 1979, ch. 79-343, §6.)

§733.305. Trust companies and other corporations and associations

(1) All trust companies incorporated under the laws of Florida, all state banking corporations and state savings associations authorized and qualified to exercise fiduciary powers in Florida, and all national banking associations and federal savings and loan associations authorized and qualified to exercise fiduciary powers in Florida shall be entitled to act as personal representatives and curators of estates.

(2) When a qualified corporation has been named as a personal representative in a will and subsequently transfers its business and assets to, consolidates or merges with, or is in any manner provided by law succeeded by, another qualified corporation, on the death of the testator, the successor corporation may qualify as personal representative unless the will provides otherwise.

(3) A corporation authorized and qualified to act as a personal representative as a result of merger or consolidation shall succeed to the rights and duties of all predecessor corporations as the

personal representative of estates upon filing proof in the court, and without a new appointment. A purchase of substantially all the assets and the assumption of substantially all the liabilities shall be deemed a merger for the purpose of this section.
(Laws 1974, ch. 74-106, §1; Laws 1975, ch. 75-220, §63; Laws 1977, ch. 77-174, §1; Laws 1981, ch. 81-27, §3. Amended by Laws 2001, ch. 2001-226, §100, effective January 1, 2002.)

§733.306. Effect of appointment of debtor

The appointment of a debtor as personal representative shall not extinguish the debt due the decedent.
(Laws 1974, ch. 74-106, §1; Laws 1975, ch. 75-220, §63. Amended by Laws 2001, ch. 2001-226, §101, effective January 1, 2002.)

§733.307. Succession of administration

The personal representative of the estate of a deceased personal representative is not authorized to administer the estate of the first decedent. On the death of a sole or surviving personal representative, the court shall appoint a successor personal representative to complete the administration of the estate.
(Laws 1974, ch. 74-106, §1; Laws 1975, ch. 75-220, § 64. Amended by Laws 2001, ch. 2001-226, §102, effective January 1, 2002.)

§733.3101. Personal representative not qualified

Any time a personal representative knows or should have known that he or she would not be qualified for appointment if application for appointment were then made, the personal representative shall promptly file and serve a notice setting forth the reasons. A personal representative who fails to comply with this section shall be personally liable for costs, including attorney's fees, incurred in any removal proceeding, if the personal representative is removed. This liability shall be cumulative to any other provided by law.
(Laws 2001, ch. 2001-226, §105, effective January 1, 2002.)

Rule 5.110. Address designation for personal representative or guardian; designation of resident agent and acceptance

(a) Address Designation of Personal Representative or Guardian. Before letters are issued, the personal representative or guardian shall file a designation of its residence street address and mailing address.

(b) Designation of Resident Agent. Before letters are issued, a personal representative or guardian shall file a designation of resident agent for service of process or notice, and the acceptance by the resident agent. A designation of resident agent is not required if a personal representative or guardian is (1) a corporate fiduciary having an office in Florida, or (2) a Florida Bar member who is a resident of and has an office in Florida. The designation shall contain the name, residence street address, and mailing address of the resident agent. A Florida office street address and mailing address for the attorney as resident agent may be designated in lieu of a residence address.

(c) Residency Requirement. A resident agent, other than a member of The Florida Bar who is a resident of Florida, must be a resident of the county where the proceedings are pending.

(d) Acceptance by Resident Agent. The resident agent shall sign a written acceptance of its designation.

(e) Incorporation in Other Pleadings. The designation of the address of the personal representative or guardian, the designation of resident agent, or acceptance may be incorporated in the petition for administration, the petition for appointment of guardian, or the personal representative's or guardian's oath.

(f) Effect of Designation and Acceptance. The designation of and acceptance by the resident agent shall constitute consent to service of process or notice on the agent and shall be sufficient to bind the personal representative or guardian:

(1) in its representative capacity in any action; and

(2) in its personal capacity only in those actions in which the personal representative or guardian is sued personally for claims arising from the administration of the estate or guardianship.

(g) Successor Agent. If the resident agent dies, resigns, or is unable to act for any other reason, the personal representative or guardian shall appoint a successor agent within 10 days after receiving notice that such event has occurred.
(Amended September 13, 1984, effective January 1, 1985 (458 So.2d 1079); September 29, 1988, effective January 1, 1989 (537 So.2d 500); September 24, 1992, effective January 1, 1993 (607 So.2d 1306); September 28, 2000, effective January 1, 2001 (778 So.2d 272).)

Rule 5.235. Issuance of letters, bond

(a) Appointment of Personal Representative. After the petition for administration is filed and the will, if any, is admitted to probate:

(1) the court shall appoint the person entitled and qualified to be personal representative;

(2) the court shall determine the amount of any bond required. The clerk may approve the bond in the amount determined by the court; and

(3) any required oath or designation of, and acceptance by, a resident agent shall be filed.

(b) Issuance of Letters. Upon compliance with all of the foregoing, letters shall be issued to the personal representative.

(c) Bond. On petition by any interested person or on the court's own motion, the court may waive the requirement of filing a bond, require a personal representative or curator to give bond, increase or decrease the bond, or require additional surety.

(Added September 29, 1988, effective January 1, 1989 (537 So.2d 500). Amended September 24, 1992, effective January 1, 1993 (607 So.2d 1306); October 3, 1996, effective January 1, 1997 (683 So.2d 78).)

§733.302. Who may be appointed personal representative

Subject to the limitations in this part, any person who is sui juris and is a resident of Florida at the time of the death of the person whose estate is to be administered is qualified to act as personal representative in Florida.

(Laws 1974, ch. 74-106, §1; Laws 1975, ch. 75-220, §63; Laws 1979, ch. 79-343, §5. Amended by Laws 1997, ch. 97-102, §989, effective July 1, 1997; Laws 2001, ch. 2001-226, §99, effective January 1, 2002.)

2. Oath and Bond

As a general rule, a personal representative is required to take an oath before issuance of letters of administration (Rule 5.320). In taking the oath, the personal representative faithfully promises to administer the estate of the decedent.

The personal representative also must give bond. However, the decedent's will or the court may waive the requirement of a bond (Fla. Stat. §733.402). The bond requirement is not applicable to corporate fiduciaries (Fla. Stat. §733.402(3)).

Rule 5.320. Oath of Personal Representative

Before the granting of letters of administration, the personal representative shall file an oath to faithfully administer the estate of the decedent. If the petition is verified by the prospective personal representative individually, the oath may be incorporated in the petition or in the designation of resident agent.

(Amended September 24, 1992, effective January 1, 1993 (607 So.2d 1306).)

§733.402. Bond of fiduciary; when required; form

(1) Unless the bond requirement has been waived by the will or by the court, every fiduciary to whom letters are granted shall execute and file a bond with surety, as defined in §45.011, to be approved by the clerk without a service fee. The bond shall be payable to the Governor and the Governor's successors in office, conditioned on the performance of all duties as personal representative according to law. The bond must be joint and several.

(2) No bond shall be void or invalid because of an informality in it or an informality or illegality in the appointment of the fiduciary. The bond shall have the same force as if the appointment had been legally made and the bond executed in proper form.

(3) The requirements of this section shall not apply to banks and trust companies authorized by law to act as personal representative.

(4) On petition by any interested person or on the court's own motion, the court may waive the requirement of filing a bond, require a bond, increase or decrease the bond, or require additional surety.

(Laws 1974, ch. 74-106, §1; Laws 1975, ch. 75-220, §67; Laws 1977, ch. 77-87, §24; Laws 1977, ch. 77-174, §1. Amended by Laws 1997, ch. 97-102, §992, effective July 1, 1997; Laws 2001, ch. 2001-226, §107, effective January 1, 2002.)

§733.403. Amount of bond

All bonds required by this part shall be in the penal sum that the court deems sufficient after consideration of the gross value of the estate, the relationship of the personal representative to the beneficiaries, exempt property and any family allowance, the type and nature of assets, known creditors, and liens and encumbrances on the assets.

(Laws 1974, ch. 74-106, §1; Laws 1975, ch. 75-220, §67. Amended by Laws 2001, ch. 2001-226, §108, effective January 1, 2002.)

§733.404. Liability of surety

No surety for any personal representative or curator shall be charged beyond the value of the assets of an estate because of any omission or mistake in pleading or of false pleading of the personal representative or curator.

(Laws 1974, ch. 74-106, §1; Laws 1975, ch. 75-220, §68. Amended by Laws 2001, ch. 2001-226, §109, effective January 1, 2002.)

§733.405. Release of surety

(1) Subject to the limitations of this section, on the petition of any interested person, the surety is entitled to be released from liability for the future acts and omissions of the fiduciary.

(2) Pending the hearing of the petition, the court may restrain the fiduciary from acting, except to preserve the estate.

(3) On hearing, the court shall enter an order prescribing the amount of the new bond for the

fiduciary and the date when the bond shall be filed. If the fiduciary fails to give the new bond, the fiduciary shall be removed at once, and further proceedings shall be had as in cases of removal.

(4) The original surety shall remain liable in accordance with the terms of its original bond for all acts and omissions of the fiduciary that occur prior to the approval of the new surety and filing and approval of the bond. The new surety shall be liable on its bond only after the filing and approval of the new bond.

(Laws 1974, ch. 74-106, §1; Laws 1975, ch. 75-220, §68. Amended by Laws 1997, ch. 97-102, §993, effective July 1, 1997; Laws 2001, ch. 2001-226, §110, effective January 1, 2002.)

§733.406. Bond premium allowable as expense of administration

A personal representative or other fiduciary required to give bond shall pay the reasonable premium as an expense of administration.

(Laws 1899, ch. 4716, §1; Gen. St. 1906, §2789; Rev. Gen. St. 1920, §4336; Comp. Gen. Laws 1927, §6299; Laws 1945, ch. 22858, §7; Fla. St. 1957, §648.05; Laws 1959, ch. 59-205, §613; Fla. St. 1969, §627.0902; Fla. St. 1981, §627.753; Laws 1982, ch. 82-243, §566. Amended by Laws 1997, ch. 97-102, §994, effective July 1, 1997; Laws 2001, ch. 2001-226, §111, effective January 1, 2002.)

Rule 5.235. Issuance of Letters, Bond

(a) Appointment of Personal Representative. After the petition for administration is filed and the will, if any, is admitted to probate:

(1) the court shall appoint the person entitled and qualified to be personal representative;

(2) the court shall determine the amount of any bond required. The clerk may approve the bond in the amount determined by the court; and

(3) any required oath or designation of, and acceptance by, a resident agent shall be filed.

(b) Issuance of Letters. Upon compliance with all of the foregoing, letters shall be issued to the personal representative.

(c) Bond. On petition by any interested person or on the court's own motion, the court may waive the requirement of filing a bond, require a personal representative or curator to give bond, increase or decrease the bond, or require additional surety.

(Added September 29, 1988, effective January 1, 1989 (537 So.2d 500). Amended September 24, 1992, effective January 1, 1993 (607 So.2d 1306); October 3, 1996, effective January 1, 1997 (683 So.2d 78).)

3. Removal of Personal Representative

Persons may sometimes desire the *removal* of a personal representative. Removal can be accomplished by means of a petition to the court. Alternatively, the court on its own motion may seek removal of a personal representative to protect the estate or interested persons. Florida Statutes §733.504 governs the grounds for removal.

The Code specifies several grounds for removal, including: misuse of funds, lack of capacity to execute the duties of office, failure to give bond or comply with a court order, conviction of a felony, revocation of the will that appointed the personal representative, or a conflict of interest that may interfere with the administration of the estate.

A petition for removal must be filed in the same court that issued the letters of administration (Fla. Stat. §733.505).

On the grounds and procedures for removal, see James G. Pressly, Jr., Removal of Personal Representative and Surcharge (Chapter 9), Litigation Under Florida Probate Code, Florida Bar CLE 9-1 (2003).

§733.504. Removal of personal representative; causes for removal

A personal representative may be removed and the letters revoked for any of the following causes, and the removal shall be in addition to any penalties prescribed by law:

(1) Adjudication of incompetency.

(2) Physical or mental incapacity rendering the personal representative incapable of the discharge of his or her duties.

(3) Failure to comply with any order of the court, unless the order has been superseded on appeal.

(4) Failure to account for the sale of property or to produce and exhibit the assets of the estate when so required.

(5) Wasting or maladministration of the estate.

(6) Failure to give bond or security for any purpose.

(7) Conviction of a felony.

(8) Insolvency of, or the appointment of a receiver or liquidator for, any corporate personal representative.

(9) Holding or acquiring conflicting or adverse interests against the estate that will or may interfere with the administration of the estate as a whole. This cause of removal shall not apply to the surviving spouse because of the exercise of the right to the elective share, family allowance, or exemptions, as provided elsewhere in this code.

(10) Revocation of the probate of the decedent's will that authorized or designated the appointment of the personal representative.

(11) Removal of domicile from Florida, if domicile was a requirement of initial appointment.

(12) The personal representative would not now be entitled to appointment.

(Laws 1974, ch. 74-106, §1; Laws 1975, ch. 75-220, §69; Laws 1977, ch. 77-174, §1. Amended by Laws 1997, ch. 97-102, §998, effective July 1, 1997; Laws 2001, ch. 2001-226, §117, effective January 1, 2002.)

§733.505. Jurisdiction in removal proceedings

A petition for removal shall be filed in the court having jurisdiction of the administration.

(Laws 1974, ch. 74-106, §1; Laws 1975, ch. 75-220, § 70. Amended by Laws 2001, ch. 2001-226, §118, effective January 1, 2002.)

§733.506. Proceedings for removal

Proceedings for removal of a personal representative may be commenced by the court or upon the petition of an interested person. The court shall revoke the letters of a removed personal representative. The removal of a personal representative shall not exonerate the removed personal representative or the removed personal representative's surety from any liability.

(Laws 1974, ch. 74-106, §1; Laws 1975, ch. 75-220, §71. Amended by Laws 2001, ch. 2001-226, §119, effective January 1, 2002.)

§733.508. Accounting and discharge of removed personal representatives

(1) A removed personal representative shall file and serve a final accounting of that personal representative's administration.

(2) After determination and satisfaction of the liability, if any, of the removed personal representative, after compensation of that personal representative and the attorney and other persons employed by that personal representative, and upon receipt of evidence that the estate assets have been delivered to the successor fiduciary, the removed personal representative shall be discharged, the bond released, and the surety discharged.

(Laws 1974, ch. 74-106, §1; Laws 1975, ch. 75-220, §72. Amended by Laws 1997, ch. 97-102, §999, effective July 1, 1997; Laws 2001, ch. 2001-226, §122, effective January 1, 2002.)

§733.509. Surrender of assets upon removal

Upon entry of an order removing a personal representative, the removed personal representative shall immediately deliver all estate assets, records, documents, papers, and other property of or concerning the estate in the removed personal representative's possession or control to the remaining personal representative or successor fiduciary.

(Laws 1974, ch. 74-106, §1; Laws 1975, ch. 75-220, §73. Amended by Laws 2001, ch. 2001-226, §123, effective January 1, 2002.)

Rule 5.025. Adversary proceedings

(a) Specific Adversary Proceedings. The following shall be adversary proceedings unless otherwise ordered by the court: proceedings to remove a personal representative, surcharge a personal representative, remove a guardian, surcharge a guardian, probate a lost or destroyed will or later-discovered will, determine beneficiaries, construe a will, cancel a devise, partition property for the purposes of distribution, determine pretermitted share, determine amount of elective share and contribution, and for revocation of probate of a will.

(b) Declared Adversary Proceedings. Other proceedings may be declared adversary by service on interested persons of a separate declaration that the proceeding is adversary.

(1) If served by the petitioner, the declaration shall be served with the petition to which it relates.

(2) If served by the respondent, the declaration and a written response to the petition shall be served at the earlier of:

(A) within 20 days after service of the petition, or

(B) prior to the hearing date on the petition.

(3) When the declaration is served by a respondent, the petitioner shall promptly serve formal notice on all other interested persons.

(c) Adversary Status by Order. The court may determine any proceeding to be an adversary proceeding at any time.

(d) Notice and Procedure in Adversary Proceedings

(1) Petitioner shall serve formal notice.

(2) After service of formal notice, the proceedings, as nearly as practicable, shall be conducted similar to suits of a civil nature and the Florida Rules of Civil Procedure shall govern, including entry of defaults.

(3) The court on its motion or on motion of any interested person may enter orders to avoid undue delay in the main administration.

(4) If a proceeding is already commenced when an order is entered determining the proceeding to be adversary, it shall thereafter be conducted as an adversary proceeding. The order shall require interested persons to serve written defenses, if any, within 20 days from the date of the order. It shall not be necessary to re-serve the petition except as ordered by the court.

(5) When the proceedings are adversary, the caption of subsequent pleadings, as an

extension of the probate caption, shall include the name of the first petitioner and the name of the first respondent.

(Amended March 31, 1977, effective July 1, 1977 (344 So.2d 828); September 13, 1984, effective January 1, 1985 (458 So.2d 1079); September 29, 1988, effective January 1, 1989 (537 So.2d 500); September 24, 1992, effective January 1, 1993 (607 So.2d 1306); October 11, 2001 (807 So.2d 622); January 10, 2002 (816 So.2d 1095).)

Rule 5.310. Disqualification of personal representative; notification

Any personal representative who was not qualified to act at the time of appointment or who would not be qualified for appointment if application for appointment were then made shall immediately file and serve on all interested persons a notice describing:

(a) the reason the personal representative was not qualified at the time of appointment; or

(b) the reason the personal representative would not be qualified for appointment if application for appointment were then made and the date on which the disqualifying event occurred.

The personal representative's notice shall state that any interested person may petition to remove the personal representative.

(Amended September 24, 1992, effective January 1, 1993 (607 So.2d 1306); May 2, 2002 (824 So.2d 849).)

Rule 5.440. Proceedings for removal

(a) Commencement of Proceeding. The court on its own motion may remove, or any interested person by petition may commence a proceeding to remove, a personal representative. A petition for removal shall state the facts constituting the grounds upon which removal is sought, and shall be filed in the court having jurisdiction over the administration of the estate.

(b) Accounting. A removed personal representative shall file an accounting within 30 days after removal.

(c) Delivery of Records and Property. A removed personal representative shall, immediately after removal or within such time prescribed by court order, deliver to the remaining personal representative or to the successor fiduciary all of the records of the estate and all of the property of the estate.

(d) Failure to File Accounting or Deliver Records and Property. If a removed personal representative fails to file an accounting or fails to deliver all property of the estate and all estate records under the control of the removed personal representative to the remaining personal representative or to the successor fiduciary within the time prescribed by this rule or by court order, the removed personal representative shall be subject to contempt proceedings.

(Amended September 4, 1980, effective January 1, 1981 (387 So.2d 949); September 13, 1984, effective January 1, 1985 (458 So.2d 1079); September 29, 1988, effective January 1, 1989 (537 So.2d 500); September 24, 1992, effective January 1, 1993 (607 So.2d 1306); May 2, 2002 (824 So.2d 849).)

4. Resignation of Personal Representative

The personal representative may resign after taking office. However, the resignation is subject to notice to all interested persons and the court's approval—provided that "the interests of the estate are not jeopardized by the resignation" (Fla. Stat. §733.502).

Note, however, that resignation of a personal representative will not exonerate the fiduciary (or his or her surety) from liability. *Id.*

§733.502. Resignation of personal representative

A personal representative may resign. After notice to all interested persons, the court may accept the resignation and then revoke the letters of the resigning personal representative if the interests of the estate are not jeopardized by the resignation. The acceptance of the resignation shall not exonerate the personal representative or the surety from liability.

(Laws 1974, ch. 74-106, §1; Laws 1975, ch. 75-220, §69; Laws 1977, ch. 77-87, §25. Amended by Laws 1997, ch. 97-102, §996, effective July 1, 1997; Laws 2001, ch. 2001-226, §113, effective January 1, 2002.)

§733.503. Appointment of successor upon resignation

When the personal representative's resignation is accepted, the court shall appoint a personal representative or shall appoint a curator to serve until a successor personal representative is appointed.

(Laws 1974, ch. 74-106, §1; Laws 1975, ch. 75-220, §69. Amended by Laws 1997, ch. 97-102, §997, effective July 1, 1997; Laws 2001, ch. 2001-226, §114, effective January 1, 2002.)

§733.5035. Surrender of assets after resignation

When the resignation has been accepted by the court, all estate assets, records, documents, papers, and other property of or concerning the estate in the resigning personal representative's possession or control shall immediately be surrendered to the successor fiduciary. The court may establish the conditions and specify the assets and records, if any, that the resigning personal representative may retain until the final accounting of the resigning personal representative has been approved.

(Laws 2001, ch. 2001-226, §115, effective January 1, 2002.)

§733.5036. Accounting and discharge following resignation

(1) A resigning personal representative shall file and serve a final accounting of the personal representative's administration.

(2) After determination and satisfaction of the liability, if any, of the resigning personal representative, after compensation of the personal representative and the attorney and other persons employed by the personal representative, and upon receipt of evidence that undistributed estate assets have been delivered to the successor fiduciary, the personal representative shall be discharged, the bond released, and the surety discharged.

(Laws 2001, ch. 2001-226, §116, effective January 1, 2002.)

Rule 5.430. Resignation of personal Representative

(a) Resignation. A personal representative may resign with court approval.

(b) Petition for Resignation. The personal representative seeking to resign shall file a petition for resignation. The petition shall be verified and shall state:

(1) the personal representative desires to resign and be relieved of all powers, duties, and obligations as personal representative;

(2) the status of the estate administration and that the interests of the estate will not be jeopardized if the resignation is accepted;

(3) whether a proceeding for accounting, surcharge, or indemnification or other proceeding against the resigning personal representative is pending; and

(4) whether the appointment of a successor fiduciary is necessary. If the petition nominates a successor fiduciary, it shall state the nominee's priority under the Florida Probate Code, if any, and that the nominee is qualified to serve under the laws of Florida.

(c) Service. The petition shall be served by formal notice on all interested persons and the personal representative's surety, if any.

(d) Appointment of Successor. Before accepting the resignation, the court shall determine the necessity for appointment of a successor fiduciary. If there is no joint personal representative serving, the court shall appoint a successor fiduciary.

(e) Acceptance of Resignation. The court may accept the resignation and revoke the letters of the resigning personal representative if the interests of the estate are not jeopardized. Acceptance of the resignation shall not exonerate the resigning personal representative or the resigning personal representative's surety from liability.

(f) Delivery of Records and Property. The resigning personal representative shall immediately upon acceptance of the resignation by the court deliver to the remaining personal representative or the successor fiduciary all of the records of the estate and all property of the estate, unless otherwise directed by the court.

(g) Petition for Discharge; Accounting. The resigning personal representative shall file an accounting and a petition for discharge within 30 days after the date that the letters of the resigning personal representative are revoked by the court. The petition for discharge shall be verified and shall state:

(1) that the letters of the resigning personal representative have been revoked;

(2) that the resigning personal representative has surrendered all undistributed estate assets, records, documents, papers, and other property of or concerning the estate to the remaining personal representative or the successor fiduciary; and

(3) the amount of compensation paid or to be paid the resigning personal representative and the attorney and other persons employed by the resigning personal representative.

(h) Notice, Filing, and Objections to Accounting. Notice of, filing of, and objections to the accounting of the resigning personal representative shall be as provided in rule 5.345.

(i) Notice of Filing and Objections to Petition for Discharge.

(1) Notice of filing and a copy of the petition for discharge shall be served on all interested persons. The notice shall state that objections to the petition for discharge must be filed within 30 days after the later of service of the petition or service of the accounting on that interested person.

(2) Any interested person may file an objection to the petition for discharge within 30 days after the later of service of the petition or service of the accounting on that interested person. Any objection not filed within such time shall be deemed abandoned. An objection shall be in writing and shall state with particularity the item or items to which the objection is directed and the grounds on which the objection is based.

(3) The objecting party shall serve a copy of the objection on the resigning personal representative and other interested persons.

(4) Any interested person may set a hearing on the objections. Notice of the hearing shall be given to the resigning personal representative and other interested persons.

(j) Failure to File Accounting or Deliver Records or Property. The resigning personal representative shall be subject to contempt proceedings if the resigning personal representative fails to file an accounting or fails to deliver all property of the estate and all estate records under the control of the resigning personal representative to the remaining personal representative or the successor fiduciary within the time prescribed by this rule or by court order.

(k) Discharge. The court shall enter an order discharging the resigning personal representative and releasing the surety on any bond after the court is satisfied that the resigning personal representative has delivered all records and property of the estate to the remaining personal representative or the successor fiduciary; that all objections, if any, to the accounting of the resigning personal representative have been withdrawn, abandoned, or judicially resolved; and that the liability of the resigning personal representative has been determined and satisfied.

(Amended September 29, 1988, effective January 1, 1989 (537 So.2d 500); September 24, 1992, effective January 1, 1993 (607 So.2d 1306); June 19, 2003 (848 So.2d 1069).)

5. Filling Vacancies in Office of Personal Representative

The Florida Code provides for the filling of vacancies in the office of personal representative. Vacancies may occur if the personal representative resigns, is removed, becomes disabled or disqualified, or dies. In testate situations, a decedent's will often provides for such eventualities.

Generally when a vacancy occurs in the office of personal representative, the court will appoint a successor. However, if multiple personal representatives are administering an estate, the surviving personal representative(s) may continue unless the will provides otherwise. Trawick, *supra*, at §5-11. The court may also appoint a curator if no personal representative has been appointed.

Specific statutory provisions apply to the filling of vacancies after the *resignation* or *death* of a personal representation. Following a personal representative's resignation (which is subject to court approval), the court must appoint either a successor personal representative or a curator to serve until a successor personal representative is appointed (Fla. Stat. §733.503).

Upon the death of a personal representative, Florida Statutes §733.307 similarly provides that the court shall appoint a successor to complete the estate administration.

§733.307. Succession of administration

The personal representative of the estate of a deceased personal representative is not authorized to administer the estate of the first decedent. On the death of a sole or surviving personal representative, the court shall appoint a successor personal representative to complete the administration of the estate.

(Laws 1974, ch. 74-106, §1; Laws 1975, ch. 75-220, § 64. Amended by Laws 2001, ch. 2001-226, §102, effective January 1, 2002.)

§733.308. Administrator ad litem

When an estate must be represented and the personal representative is unable to do so, the court shall appoint an administrator ad litem without bond to represent the estate in that proceeding. The fact that the personal representative is seeking reimbursement for claims against the decedent does not require appointment of an administrator ad litem.

(Laws 1974, ch. 74-106, §1; Laws 1975, ch. 75-220, §65. Amended by Laws 2001, ch. 2001-226, §103, effective January 1, 2002.)

733.503. Appointment of successor upon resignation

When the personal representative's resignation is accepted, the court shall appoint a personal representative or shall appoint a curator to serve until a successor personal representative is appointed.

(Laws 1974, ch. 74-106, §1; Laws 1975, ch. 75-220, §69. Amended by Laws 1997, ch. 97-102, §997, effective July 1, 1997; Laws 2001, ch. 2001-226, §114, effective January 1, 2002.)

§733.5061. Appointment of successor upon removal

When a personal representative is removed, the court shall appoint a personal representative or shall appoint a curator to serve until a successor personal representative is appointed.

(Laws 2001, ch. 2001-226, §120, effective January 1, 2002.)

§733.614. Powers and duties of successor personal representative

A successor personal representative has the same power and duty as the original personal representative to complete the administration and distribution of the estate as expeditiously as possible, but shall not exercise any power made personal to the personal representative named in the will without court approval.

(Laws 1974, ch. 74-106, §1; Laws 1975, ch. 75-220, §78. Amended by Laws 1997, ch. 97-102, §1012, effective July 1, 1997; Laws 2001, ch. 2001-226, §138, effective January 1, 2002.)

§733.616. Powers of surviving personal representatives

Unless otherwise provided by the terms of the will or a court order, every power exercisable by joint personal representatives may be exercised by the one or more remaining after the appointment of one or more is terminated. If one or more, but not all, nominated as joint personal representatives are not appointed, those appointed may exercise all powers granted to those nominated.

(Laws 1974, ch. 74-106, §1; Laws 1975, ch. 75-220, §79. Amended by Laws 2001, ch. 2001-226, §140, effective January 1, 2002.)

C. Compensation

The personal representative receives compensation for fulfilling his or her responsibilities. If the personal representative has rendered "ordinary services," the compensation is based on the value of the estate (Fla. Stat. §733.617(1), (2)). On the other hand, if the personal representative has rendered "extraordinary services," the court may authorize additional compensation (Fla. Stat. §733.617(3)). Compensation for extraordinary services requires court approval (Fla. Stat. §733.617(7). A personal representative may renounce all or part of the compensation (Fla. Stat. §733.617(4).

A personal representative who is also an attorney is entitled to fees for legal services rendered to the estate as well as compensation for serving as personal representative (Fla. Stat. §733.617(6).

The statutory fee schedule for the personal representative's compensation is not applicable if the testator provides in the will for a different compensation scheme based on specific criteria (Fla. Stat. §733.617(4)).

If an estate is administered by two personal representatives and the value of the estate is $100,000 or more, then each personal representative is entitled to the full commission allowed to a sole personal representative (Fla. Stat. §733.617(5)). A different result ensues if there are more than two personal representatives. See *id*.

§733.106 Costs and attorney's fees

(1) In all probate proceedings costs may be awarded as in chancery actions.

(2) A person nominated as personal representative, or any proponent of a will if the person so nominated does not act within a reasonable time, if in good faith justified in offering the will in due form for probate, shall receive costs and attorney's fees from the estate even though probate is denied or revoked.

(3) Any attorney who has rendered services to an estate may be awarded reasonable compensation from the estate.

(4) When costs and attorney's fees are to be paid from the estate, the court may direct from what part of the estate they shall be paid.

(Laws 1974, ch. 74-106, §1; Laws 1975, ch. 75-220, §49. Amended by Laws 1997, ch. 97-102, §984, effective July 1, 1997; Laws 2001, ch. 2001-226, §82, effective January 1, 2002.)

§733.617. Compensation of personal representative

(1) A personal representative shall be entitled to a commission payable from the estate assets without court order as compensation for ordinary services. The commission shall be based on the compensable value of the estate, which is the inventory value of the probate estate assets and the income earned by the estate during administration.

(2) A commission computed on the compensable value of the estate is presumed to be reasonable compensation for a personal representative in formal administration as follows:

(a) At the rate of 3 percent for the first $1 million.

(b) At the rate of 2.5 percent for all above $1 million and not exceeding $5 million.

(c) At the rate of 2 percent for all above $5 million and not exceeding $10 million.

(d) At the rate of 1.5 percent for all above $10 million.

(3) In addition to the previously described commission, a personal representative shall be allowed further compensation as is reasonable for any extraordinary services including, but not limited to:

(a) The sale of real or personal property.

(b) The conduct of litigation on behalf of or against the estate.

(c) Involvement in proceedings for the adjustment or payment of any taxes.

(d) The carrying on of the decedent's business.

(e) Dealing with protected homestead.

(f) Any other special services which may be necessary for the personal representative to perform.

(4) If the will provides that a personal representative's compensation shall be based upon specific criteria, other than a general reference to commissions allowed by law or words of similar import, including, but not limited to, rates, amounts, commissions, or reference to the personal representative's regularly published schedule of fees in effect at the decedent's date of death, or words of similar import, then a personal representative shall be entitled to compensation in accordance with that provision. However, except for references in the will to the personal

representative's regularly published schedule of fees in effect at the decedent's date of death, or words of similar import, if there is no written contract with the decedent regarding compensation, a personal representative may renounce the provisions contained in the will and be entitled to compensation under this section. A personal representative may also renounce the right to all or any part of the compensation.

(5) If the probate estate's compensable value is $100,000 or more, and there are two representatives, each personal representative is entitled to the full commission allowed to a sole personal representative. If there are more than two personal representatives and the probate estate's compensable value is $100,000 or more, the compensation to which two would be entitled must be apportioned among the personal representatives. The basis for apportionment shall be one full commission allowed to the personal representative who has possession of and primary responsibility for administration of the assets and one full commission among the remaining personal representatives according to the services rendered by each of them respectively. If the probate estate's compensable value is less than $100,000 and there is more than one personal representative, then one full commission must be apportioned among the personal representatives according to the services rendered by each of them respectively.

(6) If the personal representative is a member of The Florida Bar and has rendered legal services in connection with the administration of the estate, then in addition to a fee as personal representative, there also shall be allowed a fee for the legal services rendered.

(7) Upon petition of any interested person, the court may increase or decrease the compensation for ordinary services of the personal representative or award compensation for extraordinary services if the facts and circumstances of the particular administration warrant. In determining reasonable compensation, the court shall consider all of the following factors, giving weight to each as it determines to be appropriate:

(a) The promptness, efficiency, and skill with which the administration was handled by the personal representative;

(b) The responsibilities assumed by and the potential liabilities of the personal representative;

(c) The nature and value of the assets that are affected by the decedent's death;

(d) The benefits or detriments resulting to the estate or interested persons from the personal representative's services;

(e) The complexity or simplicity of the administration and the novelty of the issues presented;

(f) The personal representative's participation in tax planning for the estate and the estate's beneficiaries and in tax return preparation, review, or approval;

(g) The nature of the probate, nonprobate, and exempt assets, the expenses of administration, the liabilities of the decedent, and the compensation paid to other professionals and fiduciaries;

(h) Any delay in payment of the compensation after the services were furnished; and

(i) Any other relevant factors.

(Laws 1974, ch. 74-106, §1; Laws 1975, ch. 75-220, §80; Laws 1976, ch. 76-172, §1; Laws 1988, ch. 88-340, §5; Laws 1990, ch. 90-129, §1; Laws 1993, ch. 93-257, §10. Amended by Laws 1995, ch. 95-401, §1, effective January 1, 1996; Laws 2001, ch. 2001-226, §141, effective January 1, 2002; Laws 2002, ch. 2002-1, §109, effective May 21, 2002.)

§733.6171. Compensation of attorney for the personal representative

(1) Attorneys for personal representatives shall be entitled to reasonable compensation payable from the estate assets without court order.

(2) The attorney, the personal representative, and persons bearing the impact of the compensation may agree to compensation determined in a different manner than provided in this section. Compensation may also be determined in a different manner than provided in this section if the manner is disclosed to the parties bearing the impact of the compensation and if no objection is made as provided for in the Florida Probate Rules.

(3) Compensation for ordinary services of attorneys in formal estate administration is presumed to be reasonable if based on the compensable value of the estate, which is the inventory value of the probate estate assets and the income earned by the estate during the administration as provided in the following schedule:

(a) One thousand five hundred dollars for estates having a value of $40,000 or less.

(b) An additional $750 for estates having a value of more than $40,000 and not exceeding $70,000.

(c) An additional $750 for estates having a value of more than $70,000 and not exceeding $100,000.

(d) For estates having a value in excess of $100,000, at the rate of 3 percent on the next $900,000.

(e) At the rate of 2.5 percent for all above $1 million and not exceeding $3 million.

(f) At the rate of 2 percent for all above $3 million and not exceeding $5 million.

(g) At the rate of 1.5 percent for all above $5 million and not exceeding $10 million.

(h) At the rate of 1 percent for all above $10 million.

(4) In addition to fees for ordinary services, the attorney for the personal representative shall be allowed further reasonable compensation for any extraordinary service. What is an extraordinary service may vary depending on many factors, including the size of the estate. Extraordinary services may include, but are not limited to:

(a) Involvement in a will contest, will construction, a proceeding for determination of beneficiaries, a contested claim, elective share proceeding, apportionment of estate taxes, or any adversarial proceeding or litigation by or against the estate.

(b) Representation of the personal representative in audit or any proceeding for adjustment, determination, or collection of any taxes.

(c) Tax advice on postmortem tax planning, including, but not limited to, disclaimer, renunciation of fiduciary commission, alternate valuation date, allocation of administrative expenses between tax returns, the QTIP or reverse QTIP election, allocation of GST exemption, qualification for Internal Revenue Code §§6166 and 303 privileges, deduction of last illness expenses, fiscal year planning, distribution planning, asset basis considerations, handling income or deductions in respect of a decedent, valuation discounts, special use and other valuation, handling employee benefit or retirement proceeds, prompt assessment request, or request for release of personal liability for payment of tax.

(d) Review of estate tax return and preparation or review of other tax returns required to be filed by the personal representative.

(e) Preparation of the estate's federal estate tax return. If this return is prepared by the attorney, a fee of one-half of 1 percent up to a value of $10 million and one-fourth of 1 percent on the value in excess of $10 million of the gross estate as finally determined for federal estate tax purposes, is presumed to be reasonable compensation for the attorney for this service. These fees shall include services for routine audit of the return, not beyond the examining agent level, if required.

(f) Purchase, sale, lease, or encumbrance of real property by the personal representative or involvement in zoning, land use, environmental, or other similar matters.

(g) Legal advice regarding carrying on of the decedent's business or conducting other commercial activity by the personal representative.

(h) Legal advice regarding claims for damage to the environment or related procedures.

(i) Legal advice regarding homestead status of real property or proceedings involving that status and services related to protected homestead.

(j) Involvement in fiduciary, employee, or attorney compensation disputes.

(k) Proceedings involving ancillary administration of assets not subject to administration in this state.

(5) Upon petition of any interested person, the court may increase or decrease the compensation for ordinary services of the attorney or award compensation for extraordinary services if the facts and circumstances of the particular administration warrant. In determining reasonable compensation, the court shall consider all of the following factors, giving weight to each as it determines to be appropriate:

(a) The promptness, efficiency, and skill with which the administration was handled by the attorney.

(b) The responsibilities assumed by and the potential liabilities of the attorney.

(c) The nature and value of the assets that are affected by the decedent's death.

(d) The benefits or detriments resulting to the estate or interested persons from the attorney's services.

(e) The complexity or simplicity of the administration and the novelty of issues presented.

(f) The attorney's participation in tax planning for the estate and the estate's beneficiaries and tax return preparation, review, or approval.

(g) The nature of the probate, nonprobate, and exempt assets, the expenses of administration, the liabilities of the decedent, and the compensation paid to other professionals and fiduciaries.

(h) Any delay in payment of the compensation after the services were furnished.

(i) Any other relevant factors.

(6) If a separate written agreement regarding compensation exists between the attorney and the decedent, the attorney shall furnish a copy to the personal representative prior to commencement of employment, and, if employed, shall promptly file and serve a copy on all interested persons. Neither a separate agreement nor a provision in the will suggesting or directing that the personal representative retain a specific attorney will obligate the personal representative to employ the attorney or obligate the attorney to accept the representation, but if the attorney who is a party to the agreement or who drafted the will is employed, the compensation paid shall not exceed the compensation provided in the agreement or in the will.

(Laws 1993, ch. 93-257, §4. Amended by Laws 1995, ch. 95-401, §2, effective July 1, 1995; Laws

2001, ch. 2001-226, §142, effective January 1, 2002.)

§733.6175. Judicial review of the employment of agents and of compensation

(1) The court may review the propriety of the employment of any person employed by the personal representative and the reasonableness of any compensation paid to that person or to the personal representative.

(2) Court proceedings to determine reasonable compensation of the personal representative or any person employed by the personal representative, if required, are a part of the estate administration process, and the costs, including attorneys' fees, of the person assuming the burden of proof of propriety of the employment and reasonableness of the compensation shall be determined by the court and paid from the assets of the estate unless the court finds the requested compensation to be substantially unreasonable. The court shall direct from which part of the estate the compensation shall be paid.

(3) The burden of proof of propriety of the employment and the reasonableness of the compensation shall be upon the personal representative and the person employed. Any person who is determined to have received excessive compensation from an estate for services rendered may be ordered to make appropriate refunds.

(4) The court may determine reasonable compensation for the personal representative or any person employed by the personal representative without receiving expert testimony. Any party may offer expert testimony after notice to interested persons. If expert testimony is offered, a reasonable expert witness fee shall be awarded by the court and paid from the assets of the estate. The court shall direct from what part of the estate the fee shall be paid.

(Laws 1976, ch. 76-172, §2. Amended by Laws 1997, ch. 97-102, §1014, effective July 1, 1997; Laws 2001, ch. 2001-226, §143, effective January 1, 2002.)

Rule 5.355. Proceedings for review of employment of agents and compensation

After notice to all interested persons and upon petition of an interested person bearing all or a part of the impact of the payment of compensation to the personal representative or any person employed by the personal representative, the propriety of the employment and the reasonableness of the compensation or payment may be reviewed by the court. The petition shall state the grounds on which it is based. The burden of proving the propriety of the employment and the reasonableness of the compensation shall be upon the personal representative and the person employed by the personal representative. Any person who is determined to have received excessive compensation from an estate may be ordered to make appropriate refunds.

(Added September 29, 1988, effective January 1, 1989 (537 So.2d 500). Amended September 24, 1992, effective January 1, 1993 (607 So.2d 1306); October 3, 1996, effective January 1, 1997 (683 So.2d 78).)

V. Duties and Powers of Personal Representatives

A. Standard of Care

In Florida, a personal representative is charged with the same fiduciary duty of care as a trustee (Fla. Stat. §§733.602, 733.603). If the fiduciary has special skills, however, he or she has a duty to exercise those skills (Fla. Stat. §737.302).

The personal representative has a duty to settle and distribute the estate of the decedent in accordance with the decedent's will and the dictates of the law "as expeditiously and efficiently as is consistent with the best interests of the estate" (Fla. Stat. §733.602(1). In addition, the personal representation must act "for the best interests of interested persons, including creditors." ***Id.***

§733.602. General duties

(1) A personal representative is a fiduciary who shall observe the standards of care applicable to trustees as described by §737.302. A personal representative is under a duty to settle and distribute the estate of the decedent in accordance with the terms of the decedent's will and this code as expeditiously and efficiently as is consistent with the best interests of the estate. A personal representative shall use the authority conferred by this code, the authority in the will, if any, and the authority of any order of the court, for the best interests of interested persons, including creditors.

....

(Laws 1974, ch. 74-106, §1; Laws 1975, ch. 75-220, §74; Laws 1977, ch. 77-87, §27; Laws 1977, ch. 77-174, §1; Laws 1979, ch. 79-400, §270; Laws 1989, ch. 89-340, §3. Amended by Laws 1997, ch. 97-102, §1001, effective July 1, 1997; Laws 2001, ch. 2001-226, §125, effective January 1, 2002.)

§733.609. Improper exercise of power; breach of fiduciary duty

(1) A personal representative's fiduciary duty is the same as the fiduciary duty of a trustee of an express trust, and a personal representative is liable to interested persons for damage or loss

resulting from the breach of this duty. In all actions for breach of fiduciary duty or challenging the exercise of or failure to exercise a personal representative's powers, the court shall award taxable costs as in chancery actions, including attorney's fees.

(2) When awarding taxable costs, including attorney's fees, under this section, the court in its discretion may direct payment from a party's interest, if any, in the estate or enter a judgment which may be satisfied from other property of the party, or both.

(3) This section shall apply to all proceedings commenced hereunder after the effective date, without regard to the date of the decedent's death.

(Laws 1974, ch. 74-106, §1; Laws 1975, ch. 75-220, §78. Amended by Laws 1997, ch. 97-102, §1006, effective July 1, 1997; Laws 2001, ch. 2001-226, §132, effective January 1, 2002; Laws 2003, ch. 2003-154, §11, effective June 12, 2003.)

§737.302. Trustee's standard of care and performance

Except as otherwise provided by the trust instrument, the trustee shall observe the standards in §518.11 regarding investments by fiduciaries when dealing with the trust assets. If the trustee has special skills, or is named trustee on the basis of representations of special skills or expertise, the trustee is under a duty to use those skills.

(Laws 1974, ch. 74-106, §1; Laws 1975, ch. 75-221, §6; Laws 1993, ch. 93- 257, §13.)

§518.11. Investments by fiduciaries; prudent investor rule

(1) A fiduciary has a duty to invest and manage investment assets as follows:

(a) The fiduciary has a duty to invest and manage investment assets as a prudent investor would considering the purposes, terms, distribution requirements, and other circumstances of the trust. This standard requires the exercise of reasonable care and caution and is to be applied to investments not in isolation, but in the context of the investment portfolio as a whole and as a part of an overall investment strategy that should incorporate risk and return objectives reasonably suitable to the trust, guardianship, or probate estate. If the fiduciary has special skills, or is named fiduciary on the basis of representations of special skills or expertise, the fiduciary is under a duty to use those skills.

(b) No specific investment or course of action is, taken alone, prudent or imprudent. The fiduciary may invest in every kind of property and type of investment, subject to this section. The fiduciary's investment decisions and actions are to be judged in terms of the fiduciary's reasonable business judgment regarding the anticipated effect on the investment portfolio as a whole under the facts and circumstances prevailing at the time of the decision or action. The prudent investor rule is a test of conduct and not of resulting performance.

(c) The fiduciary has a duty to diversify the investments unless, under the circumstances, the fiduciary believes reasonably it is in the interests of the beneficiaries and furthers the purposes of the trust, guardianship, or estate not to diversify.

(d) The fiduciary has a duty, within a reasonable time after acceptance of the trust, estate, or guardianship, to review the investment portfolio and to make and implement decisions concerning the retention and disposition of original preexisting investments in order to conform to the provisions of this section. The fiduciary's decision to retain or dispose of an asset may be influenced properly by the asset's special relationship or value to the purposes of the trust, estate, or guardianship, or to some or all of the beneficiaries, consistent with the trustee's duty of impartiality, or to the ward.

(e) The fiduciary has a duty to pursue an investment strategy that considers both the reasonable production of income and safety of capital, consistent with the fiduciary's duty of impartiality and the purposes of the trust, estate, or guardianship. Whether investments are underproductive or overproductive of income shall be judged by the portfolio as a whole and not as to any particular asset.

(f) The circumstances that the fiduciary may consider in making investment decisions include, without limitation, the general economic conditions, the possible effect of inflation, the expected tax consequences of investment decisions or strategies, the role each investment or course of action plays within the overall portfolio, the expected total return, including both income yield and appreciation of capital, and the duty to incur only reasonable and appropriate costs. The fiduciary may, but need not, consider related trusts, estates, and guardianships, and the income available from other sources to, and the assets of, beneficiaries when making investment decisions.

(2) The provisions of this section may be expanded, restricted, eliminated, or otherwise altered by express provisions of the governing instrument, whether the instrument was executed before or after the effective date of this section. An express provision need not refer specifically to this statute. The fiduciary is not liable to any person for the fiduciary's reasonable reliance on those express provisions.

(3) Nothing in this section abrogates or restricts the power of an appropriate court in proper cases:

(a) To direct or permit the trustee to deviate from the terms of the governing instrument; or

(b) To direct or permit the fiduciary to take, or to restrain the fiduciary from taking, any action regarding the making or retention of investments.

(4) The following terms or comparable language in the investment powers and related provisions of a governing instrument shall be construed as authorizing any investment or strategy permitted under this section: "investments permissible by law for investment of trust funds," "legal investments," "authorized investments," "using the judgment and care under the circumstances then prevailing that persons of prudence, discretion, and intelligence exercise in the management of their own affairs, not in regard to speculation but in regard to the permanent disposition of their funds, considering the probable income as well as the probable safety of their capital," "prudent trustee rule," "prudent person rule," and "prudent investor rule."

(5) This section applies to all existing and future fiduciary relationships subject to this section, but only as to acts or omissions occurring after October 1, 1993.

(Laws 1953, ch. 28154, §6; Laws 1993, ch. 93-257, §2. Amended by Laws 1997, ch. 97-98, §26, effective July 1, 1997; Laws 1997, ch. 97-103, §686, effective July 1, 1997.)

B. Estate Management

The personal representative is charged with preserving and managing estate assets for the benefit of beneficiaries, heirs, and creditors. To accomplish this task, the personal representative has many tasks to perform during the administration of the estate, such as marshalling the assets, conducting an inventory, paying creditors' claims, and making preliminary and final distributions of the assets.

1. General Provisions

The Florida Code confers broad powers on the personal representative to perform many tasks during the administration of the estate without the necessity of securing a court order. These powers are designated in Florida Statutes §733.612.

Certain exceptions apply, however, that mandate court approval. For example, court approval is required to continue a decedent's unincorporated business after a four-month period (Fla. Stat. §733.612(22)(b)). Court approval also is required to sell real property if the will does not grant a power of sale (Fla. Stat. §733.613). [These statutes are included *infra* in Section V, B4 and B5.]

§733.601. Time of accrual of duties and powers

The duties and powers of a personal representative commence upon appointment. The powers of a personal representative relate back in time to give acts by the person appointed, occurring before appointment and beneficial to the estate, the same effect as those occurring after appointment. A personal representative may ratify and accept acts on behalf of the estate done by others when the acts would have been proper for a personal representative.

(Laws 1974, ch. 74-106, §1; Laws 1975, ch. 75-220, §74. Amended by Laws 1997, ch. 97-102, §1000, effective July 1, 1997; Laws 2001, ch. 2001-226, §124, effective January 1, 2002.)

§733.602. General duties

(1) A personal representative is a fiduciary who shall observe the standards of care applicable to trustees as described by §737.302. A personal representative is under a duty to settle and distribute the estate of the decedent in accordance with the terms of the decedent's will and this code as expeditiously and efficiently as is consistent with the best interests of the estate. A personal representative shall use the authority conferred by this code, the authority in the will, if any, and the authority of any order of the court, for the best interests of interested persons, including creditors.

(2) A personal representative shall not be liable for any act of administration or distribution if the act was authorized at the time. Subject to other obligations of administration, a probated will is authority to administer and distribute the estate according to its terms. An order of appointment of a personal representative is authority to distribute apparently intestate assets to the heirs of the decedent if, at the time of distribution, the personal representative is not aware of a proceeding challenging intestacy or a proceeding questioning the appointment or fitness to continue. Nothing in this section affects the duty of the personal representative to administer and distribute the estate in accordance with the rights of interested persons.

(Laws 1974, ch. 74-106, §1; Laws 1975, ch. 75-220, §74; Laws 1977, ch. 77-87, §27; Laws 1977, ch. 77-174, §1; Laws 1979, ch. 79-400, §270; Laws 1989, ch. 89-340, §3. Amended by Laws 1997, ch. 97-102, §1001, effective July 1, 1997; Laws 2001, ch. 2001-226, §125, effective January 1, 2002.)

§733.603. Personal representative to proceed without court order

A personal representative shall proceed expeditiously with the settlement and distribution of a decedent's estate and, except as otherwise specified by this code or ordered by the court, shall do so without adjudication, order, or direction of the court. A personal representative

may invoke the jurisdiction of the court to resolve questions concerning the estate or its administration.
(Laws 1974, ch. 74-106, §1; Laws 1975, ch. 75-220, §75. Amended by Laws 1997, ch. 97-102, §1002, effective July 1, 1997; Laws 2001, ch. 2001-226, §126, effective January 1, 2002.)

§733.612. Transactions authorized for the personal representative; exceptions

Except as otherwise provided by the will or court order, and subject to the priorities stated in §733.805, without court order, a personal representative, acting reasonably for the benefit of the interested persons, may properly:

(1) Retain assets owned by the decedent, pending distribution or liquidation, including those in which the personal representative is personally interested or that are otherwise improper for fiduciary investments.

(2) Perform or compromise, or, when proper, refuse to perform, the decedent's contracts. In performing the decedent's enforceable contracts to convey or lease real property, among other possible courses of action, the personal representative may:

(a) Convey the real property for cash payment of all sums remaining due or for the purchaser's note for the sum remaining due, secured by a mortgage on the property.

(b) Deliver a deed in escrow, with directions that the proceeds, when paid in accordance with the escrow agreement, be paid as provided in the escrow agreement.

(3) Receive assets from fiduciaries or other sources.

(4) Invest funds as provided in §§518.10-518.14, considering the amount to be invested, liquidity needs of the estate, and the time until distribution will be made.

(5) Acquire or dispose of an asset, excluding real property in this or another state, for cash or on credit and at public or private sale, and manage, develop, improve, exchange, partition, or change the character of an estate asset.

(6) Make ordinary or extraordinary repairs or alterations in buildings or other structures; demolish improvements; or erect new party walls or buildings.

(7) Enter into a lease, as lessor or lessee, for a term within, or extending beyond, the period of administration, with or without an option to renew.

(8) Enter into a lease or arrangement for exploration and removal of minerals or other natural resources or enter into a pooling or unitization agreement.

(9) Abandon property when it is valueless or so encumbered, or in a condition, that it is of no benefit to the estate.

(10) Vote, or refrain from voting, stocks or other securities in person or by general or limited proxy.

(11) Pay calls, assessments, and other sums chargeable or accruing against, or on account of, securities, unless barred by the provisions relating to claims.

(12) Hold property in the name of a nominee or in other form without disclosure of the interest of the estate, but the personal representative is liable for any act of the nominee in connection with the property so held.

(13) Insure the assets of the estate against damage or loss and insure against personal and fiduciary liability to third persons.

(14) Borrow money, with or without security, to be repaid from the estate assets or otherwise, other than real property, and advance money for the protection of the estate.

(15) Extend, renew, or in any manner modify any obligation owing to the estate. If the personal representative holds a mortgage, security interest, or other lien upon property of another person, he or she may accept a conveyance or transfer of encumbered assets from the owner in satisfaction of the indebtedness secured by its lien instead of foreclosure.

(16) Pay taxes, assessments, and other expenses incident to the administration of the estate.

(17) Sell or exercise stock subscription or conversion rights or consent, directly or through a committee or other agent, to the reorganization, consolidation, merger, dissolution, or liquidation of a corporation or other business enterprise.

(18) Allocate items of income or expense to either estate income or principal, as permitted or provided by law.

(19) Employ persons, including, but not limited to, attorneys, accountants, auditors, appraisers, investment advisers, and others, even if they are one and the same as the personal representative or are associated with the personal representative, to advise or assist the personal representative in the performance of administrative duties; act upon the recommendations of those employed persons without independent investigation; and, instead of acting personally, employ one or more agents to perform any act of administration, whether or not discretionary. Any fees and compensation paid to a person who is the same as, associated with, or employed by, the personal representative shall be taken into consideration in determining the personal representative's compensation.

(20) Prosecute or defend claims or proceedings in any jurisdiction for the protection of the estate and of the personal representative.

(21) Sell, mortgage, or lease any personal property of the estate or any interest in it for cash, credit, or for part cash or part credit, and with or without security for the unpaid balance.

(22) Continue any unincorporated business or venture in which the decedent was engaged at the time of death:

(a) In the same business form for a period of not more than 4 months from the date of appointment, if continuation is a reasonable means of preserving the value of the business, including good will.

(b) In the same business form for any additional period of time that may be approved by court order.

(23) Provide for exoneration of the personal representative from personal liability in any contract entered into on behalf of the estate.

(24) Satisfy and settle claims and distribute the estate as provided in this code.

(25) Enter into agreements with the proper officer or department head, commissioner, or agent of any department of the government of the United States, waiving the statute of limitations concerning the assessment and collection of any federal tax or any deficiency in a federal tax.

(26) Make partial distribution to the beneficiaries of any part of the estate not necessary to satisfy claims, expenses of administration, taxes, family allowance, exempt property, and an elective share, in accordance with the decedent's will or as authorized by operation of law.

(27) Execute any instruments necessary in the exercise of the personal representative's powers.

(Laws 1974, ch. 74-106, § 1; Laws 1975, ch. 75-220, § 78; Laws 1976, ch. 76-172, § 3; Laws 1977, ch. 77-87, § 31; Laws 1977, ch. 77-174, §1; Laws 1979, ch. 79- 400, §271. Amended by Laws 1997, ch. 97-102, §1009, effective July 1, 1997; Laws 2001, ch. 2001-226, §135, effective January 1, 2002.)

2. Taking Control of Decedent's Property

The personal representative has a duty to take control of the decedent's property, and preserve and protect it for the heirs or beneficiaries. When performing these tasks, however, the personal representative may leave any real or tangible personal property with "the person presumptively entitled to it unless possession of the property by the personal representative will be necessary for purposes of administration"—unless the will provides otherwise (Fla. Stat. §733.607(1)). Not only does the personal representative have a duty to manage, protect, and preserve the estate until distribution but also he or she "shall take all steps reasonably necessary to do so." ***Id.***

The personal representative may (but is not required to) take possession of protected homestead property in order to protect it for the heir or devisee who has an interest in the property in cases in which the heir or devisee is not residing there (Fla. Stat. §733.608(2)).

§733.607. Possession of estate

(1) Except as otherwise provided by a decedent's will, every personal representative has a right to, and shall take possession or control of, the decedent's property, except the protected homestead, but any real property or tangible personal property may be left with, or surrendered to, the person presumptively entitled to it unless possession of the property by the personal representative will be necessary for purposes of administration. The request by a personal representative for delivery of any property possessed by a beneficiary is conclusive evidence that the possession of the property by the personal representative is necessary for the purposes of administration, in any action against the beneficiary for possession of it. The personal representative shall take all steps reasonably necessary for the management, protection, and preservation of the estate until distribution and may maintain an action to recover possession of property or to determine the title to it.

(2) If, after providing for statutory entitlements and all devises other than residuary devises, the assets of the decedent's estate are insufficient to pay the expenses of the administration and obligations of the decedent's estate, the personal representative is entitled to payment from the trustee of a trust described in §733.707(3), in the amount the personal representative certifies in writing to be required to satisfy the insufficiency.

(Laws 1974, ch. 74-106, §1; Laws 1975, ch. 75-220, §77; Laws 1977, ch. 77-87, §28; Laws 1993, ch. 93-257, §9. Amended by Laws 1995, ch. 95-401, §9, effective October 1, 1995; Laws 1997, ch. 97-102, §1005, effective July 1, 1997; Laws 2001, ch. 2001-226, §130, effective January 1, 2002.)

§733.608. General power of the personal representative

(1) All real and personal property of the decedent, except the protected homestead, within this state and the rents, income, issues, and profits from it shall be assets in the hands of the personal representative:

(a) For the payment of devises, family allowance, elective share, estate and inheritance taxes, claims, charges, and expenses of the administration and obligations of the decedent's estate.

(b) To enforce contribution and equalize advancement.

(c) For distribution.

(2) If property that reasonably appears to the personal representative to be protected homestead is not occupied by a person who appears to have an interest in the property, the personal representative is authorized, but not required, to

take possession of that property for the limited purpose of preserving, insuring, and protecting it for the person having an interest in the property, pending a determination of its homestead status. If the personal representative takes possession of that property, any rents and revenues may be collected by the personal representative for the account of the heir or devisee, but the personal representative shall have no duty to rent or otherwise make the property productive.

(3) If the personal representative expends funds or incurs obligations to preserve, maintain, insure, or protect the property referenced in subsection (2), the personal representative shall be entitled to a lien on that property and its revenues to secure repayment of those expenditures and obligations incurred. These expenditures and obligations incurred, including, but not limited to, fees and costs, shall constitute a debt owed to the personal representative that is charged against and which may be secured by a lien on the protected homestead, as provided in this section. The debt shall include any amounts paid for these purposes after the decedent's death and prior to the personal representative's appointment to the extent later ratified by the personal representative in the court proceeding provided for in this section.

(a) On the petition of the personal representative or any interested person, the court having jurisdiction of the administration of the decedent's estate shall adjudicate the amount of the debt after formal notice to the persons appearing to have an interest in the property.

(b) The persons having an interest in the protected homestead shall have no personal liability for the repayment of the above noted debt. The personal representative may enforce payment of the debt through any of the following methods:

1. By foreclosure of the lien as provided in this section;

2. By offset of the debt against any other property in the personal representative's possession that otherwise would be distributable to any person having an interest in the protected homestead, but only to the extent of the fraction of the total debt owed to the personal representative the numerator of which is the value of that person's interest in the protected homestead and the denominator of which is the total value of the protected homestead; or

3. By offset of the debt against the revenues from the protected homestead received by the personal representative.

(4) The personal representative's lien shall attach to the property and take priority as of the date and time a notice of that lien is recorded in the official records of the county where that property is located, and the lien may secure expenditures and obligations incurred, including, but not limited to, fees and costs made before or after recording the notice. The notice of lien may be recorded prior to the adjudication of the amount of the debt. The notice of lien also shall be filed in the probate proceeding, but failure to do so shall not affect the validity of the lien. A copy of the notice of lien shall be served by formal notice upon each person appearing to have an interest in the property. The notice of lien shall state:

(a) The name and address of the personal representative and the personal representative's attorney;

(b) The legal description of the property;

(c) The name of the decedent and also, to the extent known to the personal representative, the name and address of each person appearing to have an interest in the property; and

(d) That the personal representative has expended or is obligated to expend funds to preserve, maintain, insure, and protect the property and that the lien stands as security for recovery of those expenditures and obligations incurred, including, but not limited to, fees and costs.

Substantial compliance with the foregoing provisions shall render the notice in comportment with this section.

(5) The lien shall terminate upon the earliest of:

(a) Recording a satisfaction or release signed by the personal representative in the official records of the county where the property is located;

(b) The discharge of the personal representative when the estate administration is complete;

(c) One year from the recording of the lien in the official records unless a proceeding to determine the debt or enforce the lien has been filed; or

(d) The entry of an order releasing the lien.

(6) Within 14 days after receipt of the written request of any interested person, the personal representative shall deliver to the requesting person at a place designated in the written request an estoppel letter setting forth the unpaid balance of the debt secured by the lien referred to in this section. After complete satisfaction of the debt secured by the lien, the personal representative shall record within 30 days after complete payment, a satisfaction of the lien in the official records of the county where the property is located. If a judicial proceeding is necessary to compel compliance with the provisions of this subsection, the prevailing party shall be entitled to an award of attorney's fees and costs.

(7) The lien created by this section may be foreclosed in the manner of foreclosing a mortgage under the provisions of chapter 702.

(8) In any action for enforcement of the debt described in this section, the court shall award

taxable costs as in chancery actions, including reasonable attorney's fees.

(9) A personal representative entitled to recover a debt for expenditures and obligations incurred, including, but not limited to, fees and costs, under this section may be relieved of the duty to enforce collection by an order of the court finding:

(a) That the estimated court costs and attorney's fees in collecting the debt will approximate or exceed the amount of the recovery; or

(b) That it is impracticable to enforce collection in view of the improbability of collection.

(10) A personal representative shall not be liable for failure to attempt to enforce collection of the debt if the personal representative reasonably believes it would have been economically impracticable.

(11) The personal representative shall not be liable for failure to take possession of the protected homestead or to expend funds on its behalf. In the event that the property is determined by the court not to be protected homestead, subsections (2)-(10) shall not apply and any liens previously filed shall be deemed released upon recording of the order in the official records of the county where the property is located.

(12) Upon the petition of an interested party to accommodate a sale or the encumbrance of the protected homestead, the court may transfer the lien provided for in this section from the property to the proceeds of the sale or encumbrance by requiring the deposit of the proceeds into a restricted account subject to the lien. The court shall have continuing jurisdiction over the funds deposited. The transferred lien shall attach only to the amount asserted by the personal representative, and any proceeds in excess of that amount shall not be subject to the lien or otherwise restricted under this section. Alternatively, the personal representative and the apparent owners of the protected homestead may agree to retain in escrow the amount demanded as reimbursement by the personal representative, to be held there under the continuing jurisdiction of the court pending a final determination of the amount properly reimbursable to the personal representative under this section.

(13) This act shall apply to estates of decedents dying after the date on which this act becomes a law.

(Laws 1974, ch. 74-106, §1; Laws 1975, ch. 75-220, §77; Laws 1977, ch. 77-87, §29. Amended by Laws 2001, ch. 2001-226, §131, effective January 1, 2002; Laws 2003, ch. 2003-154, §10, effective June 12, 2003.)

§733.609. Improper exercise of power; breach of fiduciary duty

(1) A personal representative's fiduciary duty is the same as the fiduciary duty of a trustee of an express trust, and a personal representative is liable to interested persons for damage or loss resulting from the breach of this duty. In all actions for breach of fiduciary duty or challenging the exercise of or failure to exercise a personal representative's powers, the court shall award taxable costs as in chancery actions, including attorney's fees.

(2) When awarding taxable costs, including attorney's fees, under this section, the court in its discretion may direct payment from a party's interest, if any, in the estate or enter a judgment which may be satisfied from other property of the party, or both.

(3) This section shall apply to all proceedings commenced hereunder after the effective date, without regard to the date of the decedent's death.

(Laws 1974, ch. 74-106, §1; Laws 1975, ch. 75-220, §78. Amended by Laws 1997, ch. 97-102, §1006, effective July 1, 1997; Laws 2001, ch. 2001-226, §132, effective January 1, 2002; Laws 2003, ch. 2003-154, §11, effective June 12, 2003.)

§733.614. Powers and duties of successor personal representative

A successor personal representative has the same power and duty as the original personal representative to complete the administration and distribution of the estate as expeditiously as possible, but shall not exercise any power made personal to the personal representative named in the will without court approval.

(Laws 1974, ch. 74-106, §1; Laws 1975, ch. 75-220, §78. Amended by Laws 1997, ch. 97-102, §1012, effective July 1, 1997; Laws 2001, ch. 2001-226, §138, effective January 1, 2002.)

Rule 5.330. Execution by Personal Representative

Notwithstanding any other provisions of these rules, the personal representative shall sign the:

(a) inventory;

(b) accountings;

(c) petition for sale or confirmation of sale or encumbrance of real or personal property;

(d) petition to continue business of decedent;

(e) petition to compromise or settle claim;

(f) petition to purchase on credit;

(g) petition for distribution and discharge; and

(h) resignation of personal representative.

(Amended September 29, 1988, effective January 1, 1989 (537 So.2d 500); September 24, 1992, effective January 1, 1993 (607 So.2d 1306).)

Rule 5.341. Estate information

On reasonable request in writing, the personal representative shall provide an interested person with information about the estate and its administration.

(Added May 2, 2002 (824 So.2d 849).)

Rule 5.402. Notice of lien on protected homestead

(a) Filing. If the personal representative has recorded a notice of lien on protected homestead, the personal representative shall file a copy of the recorded notice in the probate proceeding.

(b) Contents. The notice of lien shall contain:

(1) the name and address of the personal representative and the personal representative's attorney;

(2) the legal description of the real property;

(3) to the extent known, the name and address of each person appearing to have an interest in the property; and

(4) a statement that the personal representative has expended or is obligated to expend funds to preserve, maintain, insure, or protect the property and that the lien stands as security for recovery of those expenditures and obligations incurred, including fees and costs.

(c) Service. A copy of the recorded notice of lien shall be served on interested persons in the manner provided for service of formal notice.

(Added September 29, 2005, effective January 1, 2006 (912 So.2d 1178).)

Rule 5.403. Proceedings to determine amount of lien on protected homestead

(a) Petition. A personal representative or interested person may file a petition to determine the amount of any lien on protected homestead.

(b) Contents. The petition shall be verified by the petitioner and shall state:

(1) the name and address of the personal representative and the personal representative's attorney;

(2) the interest of the petitioner;

(3) the legal description of the real property;

(4) to the extent known, the name and address of each person appearing to have an interest in the property; and

(5) to the extent known, the amounts paid or obligated to be paid by the personal representative to preserve, maintain, insure, or protect the protected homestead, including fees and costs.

(c) Service. The petition shall be served on interested persons by formal notice.

(Added September 29, 2005, effective January 1, 2006 (912 So.2d 1178).)

Rule 5.404. Notice of taking possession of protected homestead

(a) Filing of Notice. If a personal representative takes possession of what appears reasonably to be protected homestead pending a determination of its homestead status, the personal representative shall file a notice of that act.

(b) Contents of Notice. The notice shall contain:

(1) a legal description of the property;

(2) a statement of the limited purpose for preserving, insuring, and protecting it for the heirs or devisees pending a determination of the homestead status;

(3) the name and address of the personal representative and the personal representative's attorney;

(4) if known, the location, date, and time the petition to determine homestead status will be heard, and

(5) if the personal representative is in possession when the notice is filed, the date the personal representative took possession.

(c) Service of Notice. The notice shall be served in the manner provided for service of formal notice on interested persons and on any person in actual possession of the property.

(Added May 2, 2002 (824 So.2d 849). Amended September 29, 2005, effective January 1, 2006 (912 So.2d 1178).)

Rule 5.405. Proceedings to determine protected homestead real property

(a) Petition. An interested person may file a petition to determine protected homestead real property owned by the decedent.

(b) Contents. The petition shall be verified by the petitioner and shall state:

(1) the date of the decedent's death;

(2) the county of the decedent's domicile at the time of death;

(3) the name of the decedent's surviving spouse and the names and dates of birth of the decedent's surviving lineal descendants;

(4) a legal description of the property owned by the decedent on which the decedent resided; and

(5) any other facts in support of the petition.

(c) Order. The court's order on the petition shall describe the real property and determine whether any of the real property constituted the protected homestead of the decedent. If the court determines that any of the real property was the protected homestead of the decedent, the order shall identify the person or persons entitled to the protected homestead real property and define the interest of each.

(Added September 13, 1984, effective January 1, 1985 (458 So.2d 1079). Amended September 29, 1988, effective January 1, 1989 (537 So.2d 500);

September 24, 1992, effective January 1, 1993 (607 So.2d 1306); October 3, 1996, effective January 1, 1997 (683 So.2d 78); May 2, 2002 (824 So.2d 849).)

3. Investments and Purchase of Property

The personal representative may make investments without court order according to the prudent investor rule (see Fla. Stat. §§518.10-518.14).

§733.612. Transactions authorized for the personal representative; exceptions

Except as otherwise provided by the will or court order, and subject to the priorities stated in §733.805, without court order, a personal representative, acting reasonably for the benefit of the interested persons, may properly: . . .

(3) Receive assets from fiduciaries or other sources.

(4) Invest funds as provided in §§518.10-518.14, considering the amount to be invested, liquidity needs of the estate, and the time until distribution will be made.

(5) Acquire or dispose of an asset, excluding real property in this or another state, for cash or on credit and at public or private sale, and manage, develop, improve, exchange, partition, or change the character of an estate asset.

. . . .

[For the rest of this section, see Section V, A,1 *supra*]

§518.11. Investments by fiduciaries; prudent investor rule

(1) A fiduciary has a duty to invest and manage investment assets as follows:

(a) The fiduciary has a duty to invest and manage investment assets as a prudent investor would considering the purposes, terms, distribution requirements, and other circumstances of the trust. This standard requires the exercise of reasonable care and caution and is to be applied to investments not in isolation, but in the context of the investment portfolio as a whole and as a part of an overall investment strategy that should incorporate risk and return objectives reasonably suitable to the trust, guardianship, or probate estate. If the fiduciary has special skills, or is named fiduciary on the basis of representations of special skills or expertise, the fiduciary is under a duty to use those skills.

(b) No specific investment or course of action is, taken alone, prudent or imprudent. The fiduciary may invest in every kind of property and type of investment, subject to this section. The fiduciary's investment decisions and actions are to be judged in terms of the fiduciary's reasonable business judgment regarding the anticipated effect on the investment portfolio as a whole under the facts and circumstances prevailing at the time of the decision or action. The prudent investor rule is a test of conduct and not of resulting performance.

(c) The fiduciary has a duty to diversify the investments unless, under the circumstances, the fiduciary believes reasonably it is in the interests of the beneficiaries and furthers the purposes of the trust, guardianship, or estate not to diversify.

(d) The fiduciary has a duty, within a reasonable time after acceptance of the trust, estate, or guardianship, to review the investment portfolio and to make and implement decisions concerning the retention and disposition of original preexisting investments in order to conform to the provisions of this section. The fiduciary's decision to retain or dispose of an asset may be influenced properly by the asset's special relationship or value to the purposes of the trust, estate, or guardianship, or to some or all of the beneficiaries, consistent with the trustee's duty of impartiality, or to the ward.

(e) The fiduciary has a duty to pursue an investment strategy that considers both the reasonable production of income and safety of capital, consistent with the fiduciary's duty of impartiality and the purposes of the trust, estate, or guardianship. Whether investments are underproductive or overproductive of income shall be judged by the portfolio as a whole and not as to any particular asset.

(f) The circumstances that the fiduciary may consider in making investment decisions include, without limitation, the general economic conditions, the possible effect of inflation, the expected tax consequences of investment decisions or strategies, the role each investment or course of action plays within the overall portfolio, the expected total return, including both income yield and appreciation of capital, and the duty to incur only reasonable and appropriate costs. The fiduciary may, but need not, consider related trusts, estates, and guardianships, and the income available from other sources to, and the assets of, beneficiaries when making investment decisions.

(2) The provisions of this section may be expanded, restricted, eliminated, or otherwise altered by express provisions of the governing instrument, whether the instrument was executed before or after the effective date of this section. An express provision need not refer specifically to this statute. The fiduciary is not liable to any person for the fiduciary's reasonable reliance on those express provisions.

(3) Nothing in this section abrogates or restricts the power of an appropriate court in proper cases:

(a) To direct or permit the trustee to deviate from the terms of the governing instrument; or

(b) To direct or permit the fiduciary to take, or to restrain the fiduciary from taking, any action regarding the making or retention of investments.

(4) The following terms or comparable language in the investment powers and related provisions of a governing instrument shall be construed as authorizing any investment or strategy permitted under this section: "investments permissible by law for investment of trust funds," "legal investments," "authorized investments," "using the judgment and care under the circumstances then prevailing that persons of prudence, discretion, and intelligence exercise in the management of their own affairs, not in regard to speculation but in regard to the permanent disposition of their funds, considering the probable income as well as the probable safety of their capital," "prudent trustee rule," "prudent person rule," and "prudent investor rule."

(5) This section applies to all existing and future fiduciary relationships subject to this section, but only as to acts or omissions occurring after October 1, 1993.

(Laws 1953, ch. 28154, §6; Laws 1993, ch. 93-257, §2. Amended by Laws 1997, ch. 97-98, §26, effective July 1, 1997; Laws 1997, ch. 97-103, §686, effective July 1, 1997.)

§518.112. Delegation of investment functions

(1) A fiduciary may delegate any part or all of the investment functions, with regard to acts constituting investment functions that a prudent investor of comparable skills might delegate under the circumstances, to an investment agent as provided in subsection (3), if the fiduciary exercises reasonable care, judgment, and caution in selecting the investment agent, in establishing the scope and specific terms of any delegation, and in reviewing periodically the agent's actions in order to monitor overall performance and compliance with the scope and specific terms of the delegation.

(2)

(a) The requirements of subsection (1) notwithstanding, a fiduciary that administers an insurance contract on the life or lives of one or more persons may delegate without any continuing obligation to review the agent's actions, certain investment functions with respect to any such contract as provided in subsection (3), to any one or more of the following persons as investment agents:

1. The trust's settlor if the trust is one described in §733.707(3);

2. Beneficiaries of the trust or estate, regardless of the beneficiary's interest therein, whether vested or contingent;

3. The spouse, ancestor, or descendant of any person described in subparagraph 1 or subparagraph 2;

4. Any person or entity nominated by a majority of the beneficiaries entitled to receive notice under paragraph (3)(b); or

5. An investment agent if the fiduciary exercises reasonable care, judgment, and caution in selecting the investment agent and in establishing the scope and specific terms of any delegation.

(b) The delegable investment functions under this subsection include:

1. A determination of whether any insurance contract is or remains a proper investment;

2. A determination of whether or not to exercise any policy option available under such contracts;

3. A determination of whether or not to diversify such contracts relative to one another or to other assets, if any, administered by the fiduciary; or

4. An inquiry about changes in the health or financial condition of the insured or insureds relative to any such contract.

(c) Until the contract matures and the policy proceeds are received, a fiduciary that administers insurance contracts under this subsection is not obligated to diversify nor allocate other assets, if any, relative to such insurance contracts.

(3) A fiduciary may delegate investment functions to an investment agent under subsection (1) or subsection (2), if:

(a) In the case of a guardianship, the fiduciary has obtained court approval.

(b) In the case of a trust or estate, the fiduciary has given written notice, of its intention to begin delegating investment functions under this section, to all beneficiaries, or their legal representative, eligible to receive distributions from the trust or estate within 30 days of the delegation unless such notice is waived by the eligible beneficiaries entitled to receive such notice. This notice shall thereafter, until or unless the beneficiaries eligible to receive income from the trust or distributions from the estate at the time are notified to the contrary, authorize the trustee or legal representative to delegate investment functions pursuant to this subsection. This discretion to revoke the delegation does not imply under subsection (2) any continuing obligation to review the agent's actions.

1. Notice to beneficiaries eligible to receive distributions from the trust from the estate, or their legal representatives shall be

sufficient notice to all persons who may join the eligible class of beneficiaries in the future.

2. Additionally, as used herein, legal representative includes one described in §731.303, without any requirement of a court order, an attorney-in-fact under a durable power of attorney sufficient to grant such authority, a legally appointed guardian, or equivalent under applicable law, any living, natural guardian of a minor child, or a guardian ad litem.

3. Written notice shall be:

a. By any form of mail or by any commercial delivery service, approved for service of process by the chief judge of the judicial circuit in which the trust has its principal place of business at the date of notice, requiring a signed receipt;

b. As provided by law for service of process; or

c. By an elisor as may be provided in the Florida Rules of Civil Procedure.

Notice by mail or by approved commercial delivery service is complete on receipt of notice. Proof of notice must be by verified statement of the person mailing or sending notice, and there must be attached thereto the signed receipt or other satisfactory evidence that delivery was effected on the addressee or on the addressee's agent. Proof of notice must be maintained among the trustee's permanent records.

(4) If all requirements of subsection (3) are satisfied, the fiduciary shall not be responsible otherwise for the investment decisions nor actions or omissions of the investment agent to which the investment functions are delegated.

(5) The investment agent shall, by virtue of acceptance of its appointment, be subject to the jurisdiction of the courts of this state.

(6) In performing a delegated function, the investment agent shall be subject to the same standards as the fiduciary.

(Laws 1993, ch. 93-257, §3. Amended by Laws 1997, ch. 97-240, §8, effective May 30, 1997.)

4. Power of Sale: Real Property

The personal representative has the power to sell, mortgage or lease real property without court approval and without a showing of necessity if the decedent's will confers a power of sale (Fla. Stat. §733.613(2).

On the other hand, if the will does not confer a power of sale (or the testator has limited the power of sale so that it cannot be exercised), then the personal representative must secure court approval for a sale of real property (Fla. Stat. §733.613(1)).

§733.612. Transactions authorized for the personal representative; exceptions

Except as otherwise provided by the will or court order, and subject to the priorities stated in §733.805, without court order, a personal representative, acting reasonably for the benefit of the interested persons, may properly:

. . .

(2) Perform or compromise, or, when proper, refuse to perform, the decedent's contracts. In performing the decedent's enforceable contracts to convey or lease real property, among other possible courses of action, the personal representative may:

(a) Convey the real property for cash payment of all sums remaining due or for the purchaser's note for the sum remaining due, secured by a mortgage on the property.

(b) Deliver a deed in escrow, with directions that the proceeds, when paid in accordance with the escrow agreement, be paid as provided in the escrow agreement.

. . .

[For the rest of this statute, see Section V, A, 1 *supra*.]

§733.613. Personal representative's right to sell real property

(1) When a personal representative of an intestate estate, or whose testator has not conferred a power of sale or whose testator has granted a power of sale but the power is so limited by the will or by operation of law that it cannot be conveniently exercised, shall consider that it is for the best interest of the estate and of those interested in it that real property be sold, the personal representative may sell it at public or private sale. No title shall pass until the court authorizes or confirms the sale. No bona fide purchaser shall be required to examine any proceedings before the order of sale.

(2) When a decedent's will confers specific power to sell or mortgage real property or a general power to sell any asset of the estate, the personal representative may sell, mortgage, or lease, without authorization or confirmation of court, any real property of the estate or any interest therein for cash or credit, or for part cash and part credit, and with or without security for unpaid balances. The sale, mortgage, or lease need not be justified by a showing of necessity, and the sale pursuant to power of sale shall be valid.

(3) In a sale or mortgage which occurs under a specific power to sell or mortgage real property, or under a court order authorizing or confirming that act, the purchaser or lender takes title free of claims of creditors of the estate and entitlements of estate beneficiaries, except existing mortgages or other liens against real property are not affected.

(Laws 1974, ch. 74-106, §1; Laws 1975, ch. 75-220, §78. Amended by Laws 1997, ch. 97-102,

§1011, effective July 1, 1997; Laws 2001, ch. 2001-226, §137, effective January 1, 2002.)

Rule 5.370. Sales of real property where no power conferred

(a) Petition. When authorization or confirmation of the sale of real property is required, the personal representative shall file a verified petition setting forth the reasons for the sale, a description of the real property sold or proposed to be sold, and the price and terms of the sale.

(b) Order. If the sale is authorized or confirmed, the order shall describe the real property. An order authorizing a sale may provide for the public or private sale of the real property described therein, in parcels or as a whole. An order authorizing a private sale shall specify the price and terms of the sale. An order authorizing a public sale shall specify the type of notice of sale to be given by the personal representative.

(Amended September 13, 1984, effective January 1, 1985 (458 So.2d 1079); October 3, 1996, effective January 1, 1997 (683 So.2d 78).)

Rule 5.370. Sales of real property where no power conferred

(a) Petition. When authorization or confirmation of the sale of real property is required, the personal representative shall file a verified petition setting forth the reasons for the sale, a description of the real property sold or proposed to be sold, and the price and terms of the sale.

(b) Order. If the sale is authorized or confirmed, the order shall describe the real property. An order authorizing a sale may provide for the public or private sale of the real property described therein, in parcels or as a whole. An order authorizing a private sale shall specify the price and terms of the sale. An order authorizing a public sale shall specify the type of notice of sale to be given by the personal representative.

(Amended September 13, 1984, effective January 1, 1985 (458 So.2d 1079); October 3, 1996, effective January 1, 1997 (683 So.2d 78).)

§518.10. Fiduciary defined as used in §§518.11-518.14

For the purpose of §§518.11-518.14, a "fiduciary" is defined as an executor, administrator, trustee, guardian (except any guardian holding funds received from or currently in receipt of funds from the United States Department of Veterans Affairs, to the extent of those funds alone), or other person, whether individual or corporate, who by reason of a written agreement, will, court order, or other instrument has the responsibility for the acquisition, investment, reinvestment, exchange, retention, sale, or management of money or property of another.

(Laws 1953, ch. 28154, §5; Laws 1993, ch. 93-268, §28.)

5. Operation of Decedent's Business

The Florida Probate Code permits a personal representative to continue the decedent's unincorporated business for up to four months if "continuation is a reasonable means of preserving the value of the business, including good will" (Fla. Stat. §733.612(22)). After that period, however, the personal representative must secure court approval. Florida Probate Rule 5.350 specifies the procedure for obtaining court approval in the latter case.

One commentator notes that: "Probably the most commonly litigated subject of claimed mismanagement is in connection with continuation of the decedent's business." Pressley, *supra*, at §9.19.

§733.612. Transactions authorized for the personal representative; exceptions

Except as otherwise provided by the will or court order, and subject to the priorities stated in §733.805, without court order, a personal representative, acting reasonably for the benefit of the interested persons, may properly:

...

(22) Continue any unincorporated business or venture in which the decedent was engaged at the time of death:

(a) In the same business form for a period of not more than 4 months from the date of appointment, if continuation is a reasonable means of preserving the value of the business, including good will.

(b) In the same business form for any additional period of time that may be approved by court order.

[For the rest of this statute, see Section V, A, 1 *supra*.]

Rule 5.330. Execution by personal representative

Notwithstanding any other provisions of these rules, the personal representative shall sign the:

(a) inventory;

(b) accountings;

(c) petition for sale or confirmation of sale or encumbrance of real or personal property;

(d) petition to continue business of decedent;

(e) petition to compromise or settle claim;

(f) petition to purchase on credit;

(g) petition for distribution and discharge; and

(h) resignation of personal representative.
(Amended September 29, 1988, effective January 1, 1989 (537 So.2d 500); September 24, 1992, effective January 1, 1993 (607 So.2d 1306).)

Rule 5.350. Continuance of unincorporated business or venture

(a) Separate Accounts and Reports. In the conduct of an unincorporated business or venture, the personal representative shall keep separate, full, and accurate accounts of all receipts and expenditures and make reports as the court may require.

(b) Petition. If the personal representative determines it to be in the best interest of the estate to continue an unincorporated business or venture beyond the time authorized by statute or will, the personal representative shall file a verified petition which shall include:

(1) a statement of the nature of that business or venture;

(2) a schedule of specific assets and liabilities;

(3) the reasons for continuation;

(4) the proposed form and times of accounting for that business or venture;

(5) the period for which the continuation is requested; and

(6) any other information pertinent to the petition.

(c) Order. If the continuation is authorized, the order shall state:

(1) the period for which that business or venture is to continue;

(2) the particular powers of the personal representative in the continuation of that business or venture; and

(3) the form and frequency of accounting by that business or venture.

(d) Petition by Interested Person. Any interested person, at any time, may petition the court for an order regarding the operation of, accounting for, or termination of an unincorporated business or venture, and the court shall enter an order thereon.
(Amended September 13, 1984, effective January 1, 1985 (458 So.2d 1079); September 29, 1988, effective January 1, 1989 (537 So.2d 500).)

6. Personal Representative's Purchase of Estate Property

A purchase or sale of estate property by the personal representative in his or her official capacity to himself or herself individually is generally considered a conflict of interest and a breach of the duty of loyalty. Such a transaction is voidable by any interested party absent consent and full and fair disclosure or unless the will authorized the transaction or the transaction was subject to court approval after notice to interested parties (Fla. Stat. §733.610).

§733.610. Sale, encumbrance, or transaction involving conflict of interest

Any sale or encumbrance to the personal representative or the personal representative's spouse, agent, or attorney, or any corporation or trust in which the personal representative has a substantial beneficial interest, or any transaction that is affected by a conflict of interest on the part of the personal representative, is voidable by any interested person except one who has consented after fair disclosure, unless:

(1) The will or a contract entered into by the decedent expressly authorized the transaction; or

(2) The transaction is approved by the court after notice to interested persons.
(Laws 1974, ch. 74-106, §1; Laws 1975, ch. 75-220, §78. Amended by Laws 1997, ch. 97-102, §1007, effective July 1, 1997; Laws 2001, ch. 2001-226, §133, effective January 1, 2002.)

§733.6121. Personal representative: powers as to environmental issues relating to administration

(1) Except as otherwise provided by the will or by court order, and subject to §733.805, the personal representative has, without court authorization, the powers specified in subsection (2).

(2) A personal representative has the power, acting reasonably and for the benefit of the interested persons:

(a) To inspect or investigate, or cause to be inspected or investigated, property subject to administration, including interests in sole proprietorships, partnerships, or corporations and any assets owned by such a business entity for the purpose of determining compliance with an environmental law affecting that property or to respond to an actual or threatened violation of an environmental law affecting that property;

(b) To take, on behalf of the estate, any action necessary to prevent, abate, or otherwise remedy an actual or potential violation of an environmental law affecting property subject to administration, either before or after initiation of an enforcement action by a governmental body;

(c) To settle or compromise at any time any claim against the estate or the personal representative that may be asserted by a governmental body or private party which involves the alleged violation of an environmental law affecting property subject to administration over which the personal representative has responsibility;

(d) To disclaim any power granted by any document, statute, or rule of law which, in the sole judgment of the personal representative, could cause the personal representative to incur personal liability, or the estate to incur liability, under any environmental law;

(e) To decline to serve as a personal representative, or having undertaken to serve, to resign at any time, if the personal representative believes that there is or could be a conflict of interest because of potential claims or liabilities that could be asserted on behalf of the estate by reason of the type or condition of the assets held; or

(f) To charge against the assets of the estate the cost of any inspection, investigation, review, abatement, response, cleanup, or remedial action considered reasonable by the personal representative; and, in the event of the closing or termination of the estate or the transfer of the estate property to another personal representative, to hold moneys sufficient to cover the cost of cleaning up any known environmental problem.

(3) A personal representative is not personally liable to any beneficiary or any other party for a decrease in value of assets in an estate by reason of the personal representative's compliance or efforts to comply with an environmental law, specifically including any reporting requirement under that law.

(4) A personal representative who acquires ownership or control of a vessel or other property without having owned, operated, or materially participated in the management of that vessel or property before assuming ownership or control as personal representative is not considered an owner or operator for purposes of liability under chapter 376, chapter 403, or any other environmental law. A personal representative who willfully, knowingly, or recklessly causes or exacerbates a release or threatened release of a hazardous substance is personally liable for the cost of the response, to the extent that the release or threatened release is attributable to the personal representative's activities. This subsection does not preclude the filing of claims against the assets that constitute the estate held by the personal representative or the filing of actions against the personal representative as representative of the estate. In such an action, an award or judgment against the personal representative must be satisfied only from the assets of the estate.

(5) Neither the acceptance by the personal representative of the property or a failure by the personal representative to inspect or investigate the property creates any inference of liability under an environmental law with respect to that property.

(6) For the purposes of this section, the term "environmental law" means a federal, state, or local law, rule, regulation, or ordinance that relates to protection of the environment or human health, and the term "hazardous substance" means a substance, material, or waste defined as hazardous or toxic, or any contaminant, pollutant, or constituent thereof, or otherwise regulated by an environmental law.

(7) This section applies to any estate admitted to probate on or after July 1, 1995.

(Laws 1995, ch. 95-401, §18, effective July 1, 1995. Amended by Laws 1997, ch. 97-102, §1010, effective July 1, 1997; Laws 2001, ch. 2001-226, §136, effective January 1, 2002.)

7. Actions and Proceedings By or Against the Personal Representative

§733.612. Transactions authorized for the personal representative; exceptions

Except as otherwise provided by the will or court order, and subject to the priorities stated in §733.805, without court order, a personal representative, acting reasonably for the benefit of the interested persons, may properly:

...

(20) Prosecute or defend claims or proceedings in any jurisdiction for the protection of the estate and of the personal representative.....

[For the rest of this statute, see Section V, A, 1 *supra.*]

§733.104. Suspension of statutes of limitation in favor of the personal representative

(1) If a person entitled to bring an action dies before the expiration of the time limited for the commencement of the action and the cause of action survives, the action may be commenced by that person's personal representative before the later of the expiration of the time limited for the commencement of the action or 12 months after the decedent's death.

(2) If a person against whom a cause of action exists dies before the expiration of the time limited for commencement of the action and the cause of action survives, if a claim is timely filed, the expiration of the time limited for commencement of the action shall not apply.

(Laws 1974, ch. 74-106, §1; Laws 1975, ch. 75-220, §48; Laws 1977, ch. 77-174, §1. Amended by Laws 1997, ch. 97-102, §982, effective July 1, 1997; Laws 2001, ch. 2001-226, §80, effective January 1, 2002.)

B. Inventory

The personal representative must file a document called an "inventory" with the court during estate administration. This document constitutes a public record of all assets that are owned by the decedent as of the date of death that are subject to probate administration. (Note, however, that the homestead must be included even though it is not subject to probate administration (Rule 5.340(a)). The primary purposes of the inventory are to advise the beneficiaries and heirs of the assets and their value, and also to enable the court to determine such matters as bond, family allowance, etc.

Florida law governs the procedures for preparation and filing of the inventory. The personal representative must file the inventory within 60 days after issuance of letters. An amended or supplemental inventory must be filed if the personal representative subsequently discovers additional property (Fla. Stat. §733.604(2)), or to correct the value of assets (*id.*).

Personal service of the inventory is required on designated individuals, including the surviving spouse, heirs (in an intestate estate), residuary beneficiaries ((in a testate estate), any interested person who requests a copy, and also the Florida Department of Revenue (Rule 5.340(d)).

§733.604. Inventory

(1) Unless an inventory has been previously filed, a personal representative shall file a verified inventory of property of the estate, listing it with reasonable detail and including for each listed item its estimated fair market value at the date of the decedent's death. Unless otherwise ordered by the court for good cause shown, the inventory or amended or supplementary inventory is subject to inspection only by the clerk of the court, the clerk's representative, the personal representative, the personal representative's attorney, and other interested persons.

(2) If the personal representative learns of any property not included in the original inventory, or learns that the estimated value or description indicated in the original inventory for any item is erroneous or misleading, the personal representative shall file a verified amended or supplementary inventory showing any new items and their estimated value at the date of the decedent's death, or the revised estimated value or description.

(3) Upon written request to the personal representative, a beneficiary shall be furnished a written explanation of how the inventory value for an asset was determined, or, if an appraisal was obtained, a copy of the appraisal, as follows:

(a) To a residuary beneficiary or heir in an intestate estate, regarding all inventoried assets.

(b) To any other beneficiary, regarding all assets distributed or proposed to be distributed to that beneficiary. The personal representative must notify each beneficiary of that beneficiary's rights under this subsection. Neither a request nor the failure to request information under this subsection affects any rights of a beneficiary in subsequent proceedings concerning any accounting of the personal representative or the propriety of any action of the personal representative.

(Laws 1974, ch. 74-106, §1; Laws 1975, ch. 75-220, §76; Laws 1980, ch. 80-127, §1; Laws 1984, ch. 84-106, §4; Laws 1985, ch. 85-72, §1; Laws 1985, ch. 85- 342, §29; Laws 1987, ch. 87-266, §68. Amended by Laws 1995, ch. 95-401, §28, effective July 1, 1995; Laws 1997, ch. 97-102, §1003, effective July 1, 1997; Laws 1997, ch. 97-240, §13, effective May 30, 1997; Laws 2001, ch. 2001-226, §127, effective January 1, 2002.)

Rule 5.330. Execution by personal representative

Notwithstanding any other provisions of these rules, the personal representative shall sign the:

(a) inventory;

(b) accountings;

(c) petition for sale or confirmation of sale or encumbrance of real or personal property;

(d) petition to continue business of decedent;

(e) petition to compromise or settle claim;

(f) petition to purchase on credit;

(g) petition for distribution and discharge; and

(h) resignation of personal representative.

(Amended September 29, 1988, effective January 1, 1989 (537 So.2d 500); September 24, 1992, effective January 1, 1993 (607 So.2d 1306).)

Rule 5.340. Inventory

(a) Contents and Filing. Unless an inventory has been previously filed, the personal representative shall file an inventory of the estate within 60 days after issuance of letters. The inventory shall contain notice of the beneficiaries' rights under subdivision (e), list the estate with reasonable detail and include for each listed item (excluding real property appearing to be protected homestead property) its estimated fair market value at the date of the decedent's death. Real property appearing to be protected homestead property shall be listed and so designated.

(b) Extension. On petition the time for filing the inventory may be extended by the court for cause shown without notice, except that the personal representative shall serve copies of the petition and order on the persons described in subdivision (d).

(c) Amendments. A supplementary or amended inventory containing the information required by subdivision (a) as to each affected item shall be filed and served by the personal representative if:

(1) the personal representative learns of property not included in the original inventory; or

(2) the personal representative learns that the estimated value or description indicated in the original inventory for any item is erroneous or misleading; or

(3) the personal representative determines the estimated fair market value of an item whose value was described as unknown in the original inventory.

(d) Service. The personal representative shall serve a copy of the inventory and all supplemental and amended inventories on the Department of Revenue, the surviving spouse, each heir at law in an intestate estate, each residuary beneficiary in a testate estate, and any other interested person who may request it in writing. The personal representative shall file proof of such service.

(e) Information. On reasonable request in writing the personal representative shall provide a beneficiary with information to which the beneficiary is entitled by law.

(f) Elective Share Proceedings. Upon entry of an order determining the surviving spouse's entitlement to the elective share, the personal representative shall file an inventory of the property entering into the elective estate which shall identify the direct recipient, if any, of that property. The personal representative shall serve the inventory of the elective estate as provided in rule 5.360. Service of an inventory of the elective estate on the Department of Revenue is not required. On reasonable request in writing the personal representative shall provide an interested person with a written explanation of how the inventory value for an asset was determined and shall permit an interested person to examine appraisals on which the inventory values are based.

(g) Verification. All inventories shall be verified by the personal representative.

(Amended September 4, 1980, effective January 1, 1981 (387 So.2d 949); September 13, 1984, effective January 1, 1985 (458 So.2d 1079); November 30, 1984, effective January 1, 1985 (460 So.2d 906); September 29, 1988, effective January 1, 1989 (537 So.2d 500); September 24, 1992, effective January 1, 1993 (607 So.2d 1306); October 11, 2001 (807 So.2d 622); January 10, 2002 (816 So.2d 1095); May 2, 2002 (824 So.2d 849).)

Rule 5.342. Inventory of safe-deposit box

(a) Filing. The personal representative shall file an inventory of the contents of the decedent's safe-deposit box within 10 days of the initial opening of the box by the personal representative or the personal representative's attorney of record. The inventory shall include a copy of the financial institution's entry record for the box from a date that is six months prior to the decedent's date of death to the date of the initial opening by the personal representative or the personal representative's attorney of record.

(b) Verification. Each person who was present at the initial opening must verify the contents of the box by signing a copy of the inventory under penalties of perjury.

(c) Service. The personal representative shall serve a copy of the inventory on the surviving spouse, each heir at law in an intestate estate, each residuary beneficiary in a testate estate, and any other interested person who may request it in writing. The personal representative shall file proof of such service.

(Added June 19, 2003 (848 So.2d 1069).)

§733.6065. Opening safe-deposit box

(1) Subject to the provisions of §655.936(2), the initial opening of a safe-deposit box that is leased or coleased by the decedent shall be conducted in the presence of any two of the following persons: an employee of the institution where the box is located, the personal representative, or the personal representative's attorney of record. Each person who is present must verify the contents of the box by signing a copy of the inventory under penalties of perjury. The personal representative shall file the safe-deposit box inventory, together with a copy of the box entry record from a date which is 6 months prior to the date of death to the date of inventory, with the court within 10 days after the box is opened. Unless otherwise ordered by the court, this inventory and the attached box entry record is subject to inspection only by persons entitled to inspect an inventory under §733.604(1). The personal representative may remove the contents of the box.

(2) The right to open and examine the contents of a safe-deposit box leased by a decedent, or any documents delivered by a decedent for safekeeping, and to receive items as provided for in §655.935 is separate from the rights provided for in subsection (1).

(Laws 2001, ch. 2001-226, §129, effective January 1, 2002. Amended by Laws 2006, ch. 2006-134, §7, effective July 1, 2006; Laws 2006, ch. 2006-213, §71, effective October 1, 2006.)

C. Payment of Creditors' Claims

Certain statutory provisions regulate the procedure for payment of creditors' claims. Creditors must file their claims in the manner specified. Compliance with these statutory regulations is a prerequisite to the creditor's ability to maintain a subsequent action on the claim. If the creditor does not file a claim in a timely manner, the claim will be barred (Fla. Stat. §703.703(3)). Short claim periods facilitate the expeditious settlement of estates.

The personal representative has the responsibility to give proper notice to creditors. Whereas notice by publication formerly was sufficient, personal service is now required for those creditors who are known and reasonably ascertainable. Tulsa Professional Collection Servs., Inc. v. Pope, 485 U.S. 478 (1988). In Florida, a personal representative must file a verified statement within four months after the date of first publication affirming that a diligent search for creditors has been conducted and that creditors have received proper notice (Rule 5.241(e)).

A creditor must file a statement of claim within three months after the first publication of notice to creditors or within 30 days after personal service of notice on the creditor (if notice is required to be served on him or her – whichever is later (Fla. Stat. §733.702(1)). The creditor must file the claim even if the personal representative has recognized the claim by partial payment or otherwise (Fla. Stat. §733.702(1)).

The claim must be in writing (Fla. Stat. §733.703(1). Pursuant to Florida law, some creditors are exempt from the requirement of filing a claim in the probate proceeding. See Fla. Stat. §733.702(4).

§733.701. Notifying creditors

Unless creditors' claims are otherwise barred by §733.710, every personal representative shall cause notice to creditors to be published and served under §733.2121.

(Laws 1974, ch. 74-106, §1; Laws 1975, ch. 75-220, §83; Laws 1977, ch. 77-87, §33; Laws 1989, ch. 89-340, §4. Amended by Laws 2001, ch. 2001-226, §145, effective January 1, 2002; Laws 2003, ch. 2003-154, §31, effective June 12, 2003.)

§733.702. Limitations on presentation of claims

(1) If not barred by §733.710, no claim or demand against the decedent's estate that arose before the death of the decedent, including claims of the state and any of its political subdivisions, even if the claims are unmatured, contingent, or unliquidated; no claim for funeral or burial expenses; no claim for personal property in the possession of the personal representative; and no claim for damages, including, but not limited to, an action founded on fraud or another wrongful act or omission of the decedent, is binding on the estate, on the personal representative, or on any beneficiary unless filed in the probate proceeding on or before the later of the date that is 3 months after the time of the first publication of the notice to creditors or, as to any creditor required to be served with a copy of the notice to creditors, 30 days after the date of service on the creditor, even though the personal representative has recognized the claim or demand by paying a part of it or interest on it or otherwise. The personal representative may settle in full any claim without the necessity of the claim being filed when the settlement has been approved by the interested persons.

(2) No cause of action, including, but not limited to, an action founded upon fraud or other wrongful act or omission, shall survive the death of the person against whom the claim may be made, whether or not an action is pending at the death of the person, unless a claim is filed within the time periods set forth in this part.

(3) Any claim not timely filed as provided in this section is barred even though no objection to the claim is filed unless the court extends the time in which the claim may be filed. An extension may be granted only upon grounds of fraud, estoppel, or insufficient notice of the claims period. No independent action or declaratory action may be brought upon a claim which was not timely filed unless an extension has been granted by the court. If the personal representative or any other interested person serves on the creditor a notice to file a petition for an extension, the creditor shall be limited to a period of 30 days from the date of service of the notice in which to file a petition for extension.

(4) Nothing in this section affects or prevents:

(a) A proceeding to enforce any mortgage, security interest, or other lien on property of the decedent.

(b) To the limits of casualty insurance protection only, any proceeding to establish liability that is protected by the casualty insurance.

(c) The filing of a cross-claim or counterclaim against the estate in an action instituted by the estate; however, no recovery on a cross-claim or counterclaim shall exceed the estate's recovery in that action.

(5) The Department of Revenue may file a claim against the estate of a decedent for taxes due under chapter 199 after the expiration of the time for filing claims provided in subsection (1), if the department files its claim within 30 days after the service of the inventory. Upon filing of the estate tax return with the department as provided in §198.13, or to the extent the inventory or estate tax

return is amended or supplemented, the department has the right to file a claim or to amend its previously filed claim within 30 days after service of the estate tax return, or an amended or supplemented inventory or filing of an amended or supplemental estate tax return, as to the additional information disclosed.

(6) Nothing in this section shall extend the limitations period set forth in §733.710.

(Laws 1974, ch. 74-106, §1; Laws 1975, ch. 75-220, §84; Laws 1980, ch. 80-127, §2; Laws 1981, ch. 81-27, §4; Laws 1983, ch. 83-216, §160; Laws 1984, ch. 84-106, §5; Laws 1985, ch. 85-79, §4; Laws 1988, ch. 88-340, §6; Laws 1989, ch. 89-340, §5; Laws 1990, ch. 90-23, §4. Amended by Laws 1997, ch. 97-102, §1016, effective July 1, 1997; Laws 2001, ch. 2001-226, §146, effective January 1, 2002; Laws 2002, ch. 2002-82, §6, effective April 23, 2002.)

§733.703. Form and manner of presenting claim

(1) A creditor shall file a written statement of the claim. No additional charge may be imposed by a claimant who files a claim against the estate.

(2) Within the time allowed by §733.702, the personal representative may file a proof of claim of all claims he or she has paid or intends to pay. A claimant whose claim is listed in a personal representative's proof of claim shall be deemed to have filed a statement of the claim listed. Except as provided otherwise in this part, the claim shall be treated as if the claimant had filed it.

(Laws 1974, ch. 74-106, §1; Laws 1975, ch. 75-220, §84; Laws 1981, ch. 81-27, §5; Laws 1985, ch. 85-79, §5; Laws 1989, ch. 89-340, §6. Amended by Laws 2001, ch. 2001-226, §147, effective January 1, 2002.)

§733.704. Amendment of claims

If a bona fide attempt to file a claim is made but the claim is defective as to form, the court may permit the amendment of the claim at any time.

(Laws 1974, ch. 74-106, §1; Laws 1975, ch. 75-220, § 85; Laws 1977, ch. 77-174, §1. Amended by Laws 2001, ch. 2001-226, §148, effective January 1, 2002.)

§733.705. Payment of and objection to claims

(1) The personal representative shall pay all claims within 1 year from the date of first publication of notice to creditors, provided that the time shall be extended with respect to claims in litigation, unmatured claims, and contingent claims for the period necessary to dispose of those claims pursuant to subsections (5), (6), (7), and (8). The court may extend the time for payment of any claim upon a showing of good cause. No personal representative shall be compelled to pay the debts of the decedent until after the expiration of 5 months from the first publication of notice to creditors. If any person brings an action against a personal representative within the 5 months on any claim to which the personal representative has not filed an objection, the plaintiff shall not receive any costs or attorneys' fees, nor shall the judgment change the class of the claim for payment under this code.

(2) On or before the expiration of 4 months from the first publication of notice to creditors or within 30 days from the timely filing or amendment of a claim, whichever occurs later, a personal representative or other interested person may file a written objection to a claim. If an objection is filed, the person filing it shall serve a copy of the objection as provided by the Florida Probate Rules. The failure to serve a copy of the objection constitutes an abandonment of the objection. For good cause, the court may extend the time for filing or serving an objection to any claim. Objection to a claim constitutes an objection to an amendment of that claim unless the objection is withdrawn.

(3) If the objection is filed by a person other than the personal representative, the personal representative may apply to the court for an order relieving him or her from the obligation to defend the estate in an independent action or for the appointment of the objector as administrator ad litem to defend the action. Fees for the attorney for the administrator ad litem may be awarded as provided in §733.106(3). If costs or attorney's fees are awarded from or against the estate, the probate court may charge or apportion that award as provided in §733.106(4).

(4) An objection by an interested person to a personal representative's proof of claim shall state the particular item or items to which the interested person objects and shall be filed and served as provided in subsection (2). Issues of liability as between the estate and the personal representative individually for items listed in a personal representative's proof of claim shall be determined in the estate administration, in a proceeding for accounting or surcharge, or in another appropriate proceeding, whether or not an objection has been filed. If an objection to an item listed as to be paid in a personal representative's proof of claim is filed and served, and the personal representative has not paid the item, the other subsections of this section shall apply as if a claim for the item had been filed by the claimant; but if the personal representative has paid the claim after listing it as to be paid, issues of liability as between the estate and the personal representative individually shall be determined in the manner provided for an item listed as paid.

(5) The claimant is limited to a period of 30 days from the date of service of an objection within which to bring an independent action upon the claim, or a declaratory action to establish the

validity and amount of an unmatured claim which is not yet due but which is certain to become due in the future, or a declaratory action to establish the validity of a contingent claim upon which no cause of action has accrued on the date of service of an objection and that may or may not become due in the future, unless an extension of this time is agreed to by the personal representative in writing before it expires. For good cause, the court may extend the time for filing an action or proceeding after objection is filed. No action or proceeding on the claim may be brought against the personal representative after the time limited above, and the claim is barred without court order. If an objection is filed to the claim of any creditor and the creditor brings an action to establish the claim, a judgment establishing the claim shall give it no priority over claims of the same class to which it belongs.

(6) A claimant may bring an independent action or declaratory action upon a claim which was not timely filed pursuant to §733.702(1) only if the claimant has been granted an extension of time to file the claim pursuant to §733.702(3).

(7) If an unmatured claim has not become due before the time for distribution of an estate, the personal representative may prepay the full amount of principal plus accrued interest due on the claim, without discount and without penalty, regardless of any prohibition against prepayment or provision for penalty in any instrument on which the claim is founded. If the claim is not prepaid, no order of discharge may be entered until the creditor and personal representative have filed an agreement disposing of the claim, or in the absence of an agreement until the court provides for payment by one of the following methods:

(a) Requiring the personal representative to reserve such assets as the court determines to be adequate to pay the claim when it becomes due; in fixing the amount to be reserved, the court may determine the value of any security or collateral to which the creditor may resort for payment of the claim and may direct the reservation, if necessary, of sufficient assets to pay the claim or to pay the difference between the value of any security or collateral and the amount necessary to pay the claim. If the estate is insolvent, the court may direct a proportionate amount to be reserved. The court shall direct that the amount reserved be retained by the personal representative until the time that the claim becomes due, and that so much of the reserved amount as is not used for payment be distributed according to law;

(b) Requiring that the claim be adequately secured by a mortgage, pledge, bond, trust, guaranty, or other security, as may be determined by the court, the security to remain in effect until the time the claim becomes due, and so much of the security or collateral as is not needed for payment be distributed according to law; or

(c) Making provisions for the disposition or satisfaction of the claim as are equitable, and in a manner so as not to delay unreasonably the closing of the estate.

(8) If no cause of action has accrued on a contingent claim before the time for distribution of an estate, no order of discharge may be entered until the creditor and the personal representative have filed an agreement disposing of the claim or, in the absence of an agreement, until:

(a) The court determines that the claim is adequately secured or that it has no value,

(b) Three months from the date on which a cause of action accrues upon the claim, provided that no action on the claim is then pending,

(c) Five years from the date of first publication of notice to creditors, or

(d) The court provides for payment of the claim upon the happening of the contingency by one of the methods described in paragraph (a), paragraph (b), or paragraph (c) of subsection (7),

whichever occurs first. No action or proceeding on the claim may be brought against the personal representative after the time limited above, and the claim is barred without court order. If an objection is filed to the claim of any creditor and the creditor brings an action to establish the claim, a judgment establishing the claim shall give it no priority over claims of the same class to which it belongs.

(9) Interest shall be paid by the personal representative on written obligations of the decedent providing for the payment of interest. On all other claims, interest shall be allowed and paid beginning 5 months from the first publication of the notice to creditors.

(10) The court may determine all issues concerning claims or matters not requiring trial by jury.

(11) An order for extension of time authorized under this section may be entered only in the estate administration proceeding.

(Laws 1974, ch. 74-106, §1; Laws 1975, ch. 75-220, §86; Laws 1977, ch. 77-87, §34; Laws 1977, ch. 77-174, §1; Laws 1984, ch. 84-25, §1; Laws 1986, ch. 86- 249, §1; Laws 1988, ch. 88-340, §7; Laws 1989, ch. 89-340, §7; Laws 1991, ch. 91-61, §2. Amended by Laws 1997, ch. 97-102, §1017, effective July 1, 1997; Laws 2001, ch. 2001-226, §149, effective January 1, 2002.)

§733.706. Executions and levies

Except upon approval by the court, no execution or other process shall issue on or be levied against property of the estate. An order approving execution or other process to be levied against property of the estate may be entered only in the estate administration proceeding. Claims on all judgments against a decedent shall be filed in the same manner as other claims against estates of decedents. This section shall not be construed to prevent the enforcement of mortgages, security interests, or liens encumbering specific property. *(Laws 1974, ch. 74-106, §1; Laws 1975, ch. 75-220, §86; Laws 1989, ch. 89-340, §8.)*

§733.707. Order of payment of expenses and obligations

(1) The personal representative shall pay the expenses of the administration and obligations of the decedent's estate in the following order:

(a) Class 1.--Costs, expenses of administration, and compensation of personal representatives and their attorneys fees and attorneys fees awarded under §733.106(3).

(b) Class 2.--Reasonable funeral, interment, and grave marker expenses, whether paid by a guardian, the personal representative, or any other person, not to exceed the aggregate of $6,000.

(c) Class 3.--Debts and taxes with preference under federal law, and claims pursuant to §§409.9101 and 414.28.

(d) Class 4.--Reasonable and necessary medical and hospital expenses of the last 60 days of the last illness of the decedent, including compensation of persons attending the decedent.

(e) Class 5.--Family allowance.

(f) Class 6.--Arrearage from court-ordered child support.

(g) Class 7.--Debts acquired after death by the continuation of the decedent's business, in accordance with §733.612(22), but only to the extent of the assets of that business.

(h) Class 8.--All other claims, including those founded on judgments or decrees rendered against the decedent during the decedent's lifetime, and any excess over the sums allowed in paragraphs (b) and (d).

(2) After paying any preceding class, if the estate is insufficient to pay all of the next succeeding class, the creditors of the latter class shall be paid ratably in proportion to their respective claims.

(3) Any portion of a trust with respect to which a decedent who is the grantor has at the decedent's death a right of revocation, as defined in paragraph (e), either alone or in conjunction with any other person, is liable for the expenses of the administration and obligations of the decedent's estate to the extent the decedent's estate is insufficient to pay them as provided in §733.607(2).

(a) For purposes of this subsection, any trusts established as part of, and all payments from, either an employee annuity described in §403 of the Internal Revenue Code of 1986, [FN1] as amended, an Individual Retirement Account, as described in §408 of the Internal Revenue Code of 1986, [FN2] as amended, a Keogh (HR-10) Plan, or a retirement or other plan established by a corporation which is qualified under s. 401 of the Internal Revenue Code of 1986, [FN3] as amended, shall not be considered a trust over which the decedent has a right of revocation.

(b) For purposes of this subsection, any trust described in §664 of the Internal Revenue Code of 1986, [FN4] as amended, shall not be considered a trust over which the decedent has a right of revocation.

(c) This subsection shall not impair any rights an individual has under a qualified domestic relations order as that term is defined in §414(p) of the Internal Revenue Code of 1986, [FN5] as amended.

(d) For purposes of this subsection, property held or received by a trust to the extent that the property would not have been subject to claims against the decedent's estate if it had been paid directly to a trust created under the decedent's will or other than to the decedent's estate, or assets received from any trust other than a trust described in this subsection, shall not be deemed assets of the trust available to the decedent's estate.

(e) For purposes of this subsection, a "right of revocation" is a power retained by the decedent, held in any capacity, to:

1. Amend or revoke the trust and revest the principal of the trust in the decedent; or

2. Withdraw or appoint the principal of the trust to or for the decedent's benefit.

[FN1] 26 U.S.C.A. §403.
[FN2] 26 U.S.C.A. §408.
[FN3] 26 U.S.C.A. §401.
[FN4] 26 U.S.C.A. §664.
[FN5] 26 U.S.C.A. §414(p).

(Laws 1974, ch. 74-106, §1; Laws 1975, ch. 75-220, §86; Laws 1977, ch. 77-87, §35; Laws 1985, ch. 85-79, §7; Laws 1987, ch. 87-226, §69; Laws 1993, ch. 93-208, §20; Laws 1993, ch. 93-257, §11. Amended by Laws 1995, ch. 95-401, §10, effective July 1, 1995; Laws 1997, ch. 97-102, §1018, effective July 1, 1997; Laws 1997, ch. 97-240, §3, effective May 30, 1997; Laws 2001, ch. 2001-226, §150, effective January 1, 2002.)

§733.708. Compromise

When a proposal is made to compromise any claim, whether in suit or not, by or against the estate of a decedent or to compromise any question concerning the distribution of a decedent's estate, the court may enter an order authorizing the compromise if satisfied that the compromise will be for the best interest of the interested persons. The order shall relieve the personal representative of liability or responsibility for the compromise. Claims against

the estate may not be compromised until after the time for filing objections to claims has expired.
(Laws 1974, ch. 74-106, § 1; Laws 1975, ch. 75-220, § 86. Amended by Laws 2001, ch. 2001-226, § 151, effective January 1, 2002.)

§733.710. Limitations on claims against estates

(1) Notwithstanding any other provision of the code, 2 years after the death of a person, neither the decedent's estate, the personal representative, if any, nor the beneficiaries shall be liable for any claim or cause of action against the decedent, whether or not letters of administration have been issued, except as provided in this section.

(2) This section shall not apply to a creditor who has filed a claim pursuant to §733.702 within 2 years after the person's death, and whose claim has not been paid or otherwise disposed of pursuant to §733.705.

(3) This section shall not affect the lien of any duly recorded mortgage or security interest or the lien of any person in possession of personal property or the right to foreclose and enforce the mortgage or lien.
(Laws 1974, ch. 74-106, § 1; Fla.St.1974, Supp. § 733.108; Laws 1975, ch. 75- 220, § 50; Laws 1977, ch. 77-87, §36; Laws 1989, ch. 89-340, §9. Amended by Laws 2001, ch. 2001-226, §152, effective January 1, 2002.)

§735.2063. Notice to creditors

(1) Any person who has obtained an order of summary administration may publish a notice to creditors according to the relevant requirements of §733.2121, notifying all persons having claims or demands against the estate of the decedent that an order of summary administration has been entered by the court. The notice shall specify the total value of the estate and the names and addresses of those to whom it has been assigned by the order.

(2) If proof of publication of the notice is filed with the court, all claims and demands of creditors against the estate of the decedent who are not known or are not reasonably ascertainable shall be forever barred unless the claims and demands are filed with the court within 3 months after the first publication of the notice.
(Laws 1980, ch. 80-203, §3. Amended by Laws 2001, ch. 2001-226, §182, effective January 1, 2002; Laws 2003, ch. 2003-154, §13, effective June 12, 2003.)

Rule 5.241. Notice to creditors

(a) Publication and Service. Unless creditors' claims are otherwise barred by law, the personal representative shall promptly publish a notice to creditors and serve a copy of the notice on all creditors of the decedent who are reasonably ascertainable and, if required by law, on the Agency for Health Care Administration. Service of the notice shall be either in the manner provided for informal notice, or in the manner provided for service of formal notice at the option of the personal representative. Service on one creditor by a chosen method shall not preclude service on another creditor by another method.

(b) Contents. The notice to creditors shall contain the name of the decedent, the file number of the estate, the designation and address of the court, the name and address of the personal representative and of the personal representative's attorney, and the date of first publication of the notice to creditors. The notice shall require all creditors to file all claims against the estate with the court, within the time provided by law.

(c) Method of Publication and Proof. Publication shall be made as required by law. The personal representative shall file proof of publication with the court within 45 days after the date of first publication of the notice to creditors.

(d) Statement Regarding Creditors. Within 4 months after the date of the first publication of notice to creditors, the personal representative shall file a verified statement that diligent search has been made to ascertain the name and address of each person having a claim against the estate. The statement shall indicate the name and address of each person at that time known to the personal representative who has or may have a claim against the estate and whether such person was served with the notice to creditors or otherwise received actual notice of the information contained in the notice to creditors; provided that the statement need not include persons who have filed a timely claim or who were included in the personal representative's proof of claim.
(Added May 2, 2002 (824 So.2d 849). Amended September 29, 2005, effective January 1, 2006 (912 So.2d 1178).)

Rule 5.490. Form and Manner of Presenting Claim

(a) Form. A creditor's statement of claim shall be verified and filed with the clerk and shall state:

(1) the basis for the claim;

(2) the amount claimed;

(3) the name and address of the creditor;

(4) the security for the claim, if any; and

(5) whether the claim is due or involves an uncertainty and, if not due, then the due date and, if contingent or unliquidated, the nature of the uncertainty.

(b) Copy. At the time of filing the claim, the creditor shall also furnish the clerk with a copy thereof.

(c) Mailing. The clerk shall mail a copy of claims, noting the fact and date of mailing on the original, to the attorney for the personal representative unless all personal representatives file a notice directing that copies of claims be mailed to a designated personal representative or attorney of record. Absent designation, a copy of claims shall be mailed to the attorney for the personal representative named first in the letters of administration.

(d) Validity of Claim. Failure to deliver or receive a copy of the claim shall not affect the validity of the claim.

(e) Amending Claims. If a claim as filed is sufficient to notify interested persons of its substance but is otherwise defective as to form, the court may permit the claim to be amended at any time.

(Amended September 13, 1984, effective January 1, 1985 (458 So.2d 1079); September 29, 1988, effective January 1, 1989 (537 So.2d 500).)

Rule 5.496. Form and manner of objecting to claim

(a) Filing. An objection to a claim, other than a personal representative's proof of claim, shall be in writing and shall be filed on or before the expiration of 4 months from the first publication of notice to creditors or within 30 days from the timely filing or amendment of the claim, whichever occurs later.

(b) Service. A personal representative or other interested person who files an objection to the claim shall serve a copy of the objection on the claimant within 10 days after the filing of the objection. If the objection is filed by an interested person other than the personal representative, a copy of the objection shall also be served on the personal representative within 10 days after the filing of the objection.

(c) Notice to Claimant. An objection shall contain a statement that the claimant is limited to a period of 30 days from the date of service of an objection within which to bring an action as provided by law.

(Added September 24, 1992, effective January 1, 1993 (607 So.2d 1306). Amended June 19, 2003 (848 So.2d 1069); September 29, 2005, effective January 1, 2006 (912 So.2d 1178).)

Rule 5.498. Personal representative's proof of claim

(a) Contents. A personal representative's proof of claim shall state:

(1) the basis for each claim;

(2) the amount claimed;

(3) the name and address of the claimant;

(4) the security for the claim, if any;

(5) whether the claim is matured, unmatured, contingent, or unliquidated;

(6) whether the claim has been paid or is to be paid; and

(7) that any objection to a claim listed as to be paid shall be filed no later than 4 months from first publication of the notice to creditors or 30 days from the date of the filing of the proof of claim, whichever occurs later.

(b) Service. The proof of claim shall be served on all interested persons and all claimants listed in the proof of claim at the time of filing, or immediately thereafter.

(Added September 29, 2005, effective January 1, 2006 (912 So.2d 1178).)

Rule 5.499. Form and manner of objecting to personal representative's proof of claim

(a) Filing. An objection to a personal representative's proof of claim shall be in writing and shall be filed on or before the expiration of 4 months from the first publication of notice to creditors or within 30 days from the timely filing of the proof of claim, whichever occurs later.

(b) Contents. The objection shall identify the particular claim or claims listed as to be paid to which objection is made.

(c) Service. The objector shall serve a copy of the objection on the personal representative and on each claimant to which the objection relates within 10 days after the filing of the objection.

(d) Notice to Claimant. An objection shall contain a statement that the claimant is limited to a period of 30 days from the date of service of an objection within which to bring an action as provided by law. If the claim objected to is paid prior to the objection being filed, the claim shall be treated as if it were listed on the proof of claim as paid.

(Added September 29, 2005, effective January 1, 2006 (912 So.2d 1178).)

D. Accounting

The personal representative must file periodic accounts with the court. Accountings permit an opportunity for a court to review the propriety of the representative's management of the estate. Several types of accountings exist, including interim accounts and final accountings.

A personal representative *may* choose to file an interim accounting, or the court may require such an accounting (Rule 5.345(a)). The personal representative *must* file an interim accounting in cases of resignation or removal or when a curator is succeeded by a successor (Rule 5.345(a)). For a criticism of the rule, see Trawick, *supra*, at §6-19 (pointing out that these required accountings are really "final accountings" rather than interim accountings).

Rule 5.400 specifies the procedure for the final accounting prior to the personal representative's discharge from office. (See *infra* Section G "Closing the Estate.").

A personal representative must give interested persons information about the

estate when requested to do so in writing (Rule 5.341).

Rule 5.330. Execution by personal representative

Notwithstanding any other provisions of these rules, the personal representative shall sign the:

(a) inventory;

(b) accountings;

(c) petition for sale or confirmation of sale or encumbrance of real or personal property;

(d) petition to continue business of decedent;

(e) petition to compromise or settle claim;

(f) petition to purchase on credit;

(g) petition for distribution and discharge; and

(h) resignation of personal representative.

(Amended September 29, 1988, effective January 1, 1989 (537 So.2d 500); September 24, 1992, effective January 1, 1993 (607 So.2d 1306).)

Rule 5.341. Estate information

On reasonable request in writing, the personal representative shall provide an interested person with information about the estate and its administration.

(Added May 2, 2002 (824 So.2d 849).)

Rule 5.345. Accountings other than personal representatives' final accountings

(a) Applicability and Accounting Periods. This rule applies to the interim accounting of any fiduciary of a probate estate, the accounting of a personal representative who has resigned or been removed, and the accounting of a curator upon the appointment of a successor fiduciary. The fiduciary may elect to file an interim accounting at any time, or the court may require an interim or supplemental accounting. The ending date of the accounting period for any accounting to which this rule applies shall be as follows:

(1) For an interim accounting, any date selected by the fiduciary, including a fiscal or calendar year, or as may be determined by the court.

(2) For the accounting of a personal representative who has resigned or has been removed, the date the personal representative's letters are revoked.

(3) For a curator who has been replaced by a successor fiduciary, the date of appointment of the successor fiduciary.

(b) Notice of Filing. Notice of filing and a copy of any accounting to which this rule applies shall be served on all interested persons. The notice shall state that objections to the accounting must be filed within 30 days from the date of service of notice.

(c) Objection. Any interested person may file an objection to any accounting to which this rule applies within 30 days from the date of service of notice on that person. Any objection not filed within 30 days from the date of service shall be deemed abandoned. An objection shall be in writing and shall state with particularity the item or items to which the objection is directed and the grounds upon which the objection is based.

(d) Service of Objections. The objecting party shall serve a copy of the objection on the fiduciary filing the accounting and other interested persons.

(e) Disposition of Objections and Approval of Accountings. The court shall sustain or overrule any objection filed as provided in this rule. If no objection is filed, any accounting to which this rule applies shall be deemed approved 30 days from the date of service of the accounting on interested persons.

(f) Substantiating Papers. On reasonable written request, the fiduciary shall permit an interested person to examine papers substantiating items in any accounting to which this rule applies.

(g) Supplemental Accountings. The court, on its own motion or on that of any interested person, may require a fiduciary who has been replaced by a successor fiduciary to file a supplemental accounting, the beginning date of which shall be the ending date of the accounting as specified in subdivision (a) of this rule and the ending date of which is the date of delivery of all of the estate's property to the successor fiduciary, or such other date as the court may order.

(h) Verification. All accountings shall be verified by the fiduciary filing the accounting.

(Amended March 31, 1977, effective July 1, 1977 (344 So.2d 828); September 4, 1980, effective January 1, 1981 (387 So.2d 949); September 13, 1984, effective January 1, 1985 (458 So.2d 1079); September 24, 1992, effective January 1, 1993 (607 So.2d 1306); May 2, 2002 (824 So.2d 849); September 29, 2005, effective January 1, 2006 (912 So.2d 1178).)

Rule 5.346. Fiduciary accounting

(a) Contents. A fiduciary accounting shall include:

(1) all cash and property transactions since the date of the last accounting or, if none, from the commencement of administration, and

(2) a schedule of assets at the end of the accounting period.

(b) Accounting Standards. The following standards are required for the accounting of all transactions occurring on or after January 1, 1994:

(1) Accountings shall be stated in a manner that is understandable to persons who are not familiar with practices and terminology peculiar to the administration of estates and trusts.

(2) The accounting shall begin with a concise summary of its purpose and content.

(3) The accounting shall contain sufficient information to put interested persons on notice as to all significant transactions affecting administration during the accounting period.

(4) The accounting shall contain 2 values in the schedule of assets at the end of the accounting period, the asset acquisition value or carrying value, and estimated current value.

(5) Gains and losses incurred during the accounting period shall be shown separately in the same schedule.

(6) The accounting shall show significant transactions that do not affect the amount for which the fiduciary is accountable.

(c) Accounting Format. A model format for an accounting is attached to this rule as Appendix A.

(d) Verification. All accountings shall be verified by the fiduciary filing the accounting.

(Added September 29, 1988, effective January 1, 1989 (537 So.2d 500). Amended September 24, 1992, effective January 1, 1993 (607 So.2d 1306); October 3, 1996, effective January 1, 1997 (683 So.2d 78); May 2, 2002 (824 So.2d 849); September 29, 2005, effective January 1, 2006 (912 So.2d 1178).)

Rule 5.350. Continuance of unincorporated business or venture

(a) Separate Accounts and Reports. In the conduct of an unincorporated business or venture, the personal representative shall keep separate, full, and accurate accounts of all receipts and expenditures and make reports as the court may require.

(b) Petition. If the personal representative determines it to be in the best interest of the estate to continue an unincorporated business or venture beyond the time authorized by statute or will, the personal representative shall file a verified petition which shall include:

(1) a statement of the nature of that business or venture;

(2) a schedule of specific assets and liabilities;

(3) the reasons for continuation;

(4) the proposed form and times of accounting for that business or venture;

(5) the period for which the continuation is requested; and

(6) any other information pertinent to the petition.

(c) Order. If the continuation is authorized, the order shall state:

(1) the period for which that business or venture is to continue;

(2) the particular powers of the personal representative in the continuation of that business or venture; and

(3) the form and frequency of accounting by that business or venture.

(d) Petition by Interested Person. Any interested person, at any time, may petition the court for an order regarding the operation of, accounting for, or termination of an unincorporated business or venture, and the court shall enter an order thereon.

(Amended September 13, 1984, effective January 1, 1985 (458 So.2d 1079); September 29, 1988, effective January 1, 1989 (537 So.2d 500).)

§733.5036. Accounting and discharge following resignation

(1) A resigning personal representative shall file and serve a final accounting of the personal representative's administration.

(2) After determination and satisfaction of the liability, if any, of the resigning personal representative, after compensation of the personal representative and the attorney and other persons employed by the personal representative, and upon receipt of evidence that undistributed estate assets have been delivered to the successor fiduciary, the personal representative shall be discharged, the bond released, and the surety discharged.

(Laws 2001, ch. 2001-226, §116, effective January 1, 2002.)

Rule 5.400. Distribution and discharge

(a) Petition for Discharge; Final Accounting. A personal representative who has completed administration except for distribution shall file a final accounting and a petition for discharge including a plan of distribution.

(b) Contents.

The petition for discharge shall contain a statement:

(1) that the personal representative has fully administered the estate;

(2) that all claims which were presented have been paid, settled, or otherwise disposed of;

(3) that the personal representative has paid or made provision for taxes and expenses of administration;

(4) showing the amount of compensation paid or to be paid to the personal representative, attorneys, accountants, appraisers, or other agents employed by the personal representative and the manner of determining that compensation;

(5) showing a plan of distribution which shall include:

(A) a schedule of all prior distributions;

(B) the property remaining in the hands of the personal representative for distribution;

(C) a schedule describing the proposed distribution of the remaining assets; and

(D) the amount of funds retained by the personal representative to pay expenses that are incurred in the distribution of the remaining assets and termination of the estate administration;

(6) that any objections to the accounting, the compensation paid or proposed to be paid, or the proposed distribution of assets must be filed within 30 days from the date of service of the last of the petition for discharge or final accounting; and also that within 90 days after filing of the objection, a notice of hearing thereon must be served or the objection is abandoned; and

(7) that objections, if any, shall be in writing and shall state with particularity the item or items to which the objection is directed and the grounds on which the objection is based.

(c) Closing Estate; Extension. The final accounting and petition for discharge shall be filed and served on interested persons within 12 months after issuance of letters for estates not required to file a federal estate tax return, otherwise within 12 months from the date the return is due, unless the time is extended by the court for cause shown after notice to interested persons. The petition to extend time shall state the status of the estate and the reason for the extension.

(d) Distribution. The personal representative shall promptly distribute the estate property in accordance with the plan of distribution, unless objections are filed as provided in these rules.

(e) Discharge. On receipt of evidence that the estate has been fully administered and properly distributed, the court shall enter an order discharging the personal representative and releasing the surety on any bond.

(Amended March 31, 1977, effective July 1, 1977 (344 So.2d 828); September 4, 1980, effective January 1, 1981 (387 So.2d 949); September 13, 984, effective January 1, 1985 (458 So.2d 1079); September 29, 1988, effective January 1, 1989 (537 So.2d 500); September 24, 1992, effective January 1, 1993 (607 So.2d 1306); October 3, 1996, effective January 1, 1997 (683 So.2d 78); September 29, 2005, effective January 1, 2006 (912 So.2d 1178).)

§733.508. Accounting and discharge of removed personal representatives upon removal

(1) A removed personal representative shall file and serve a final accounting of that personal representative's administration.

(2) After determination and satisfaction of the liability, if any, of the removed personal representative, after compensation of that personal representative and the attorney and other persons employed by that personal representative, and upon receipt of evidence that the estate assets have been delivered to the successor fiduciary, the removed personal representative shall be discharged, the bond released, and the surety discharged.

(Laws 1974, ch. 74-106, §1; Laws 1975, ch 75-220, §72. Amended by Laws 1997, ch 97-102, §999, effective July 1, 1997; Laws 2001, ch. 2001-226, §122, effective January 1, 2002.)

E. Distribution

A personal representative is permitted to make a preliminary distribution of an estate before the time for closing and distributing the estate (Fla. Stat. §733.801). According to the statute, a beneficiary may not compel the personal representative to distribute any assets until five months after the personal representative's appointment.

Florida Statutes §733.612 constitutes a general grant of authority to the personal representative to perform certain types of transactions. Subsection 26 permits the personal representative to make partial distributions to beneficiaries of any part of the estate "not necessary to satisfy claims, expenses of administration, taxes, family allowance, exempt property, and an elective share, in accordance with the decedent's will or as authorized by operation of law."

Florida Statutes §733.812 provides that any improper distribution must be returned (or its value must be repaid with interest if the claimant no longer has the property). Further, a court may require a distributee to give bond to refund any amounts needed for payment of devises, family allowance, taxes, creditors' claims, a surviving spouse's elective share, expenses of administration, and equalization for advancements (Fla. Stat. §733.802(3)).

A personal representative makes preliminary distributions typically when the distributees' entitlement to estate property is not in dispute and the value of the estate is deemed sufficient. Several primary reasons exist for preliminary distributions of estates. They facilitate earlier enjoyment of the property by beneficiaries or heirs, favor public policy for speedy distribution of estates, and may avoid the need for payment of a family allowance (for example, if assets would have to be sold to fund the allowance).

On final distributions, see Section F *infra*. On closing the estate, see Section G *infra*.

Rule 5.400. Distribution and discharge

(a) Petition for Discharge; Final Accounting. A personal representative who has completed administration except for distribution shall file a final accounting and a petition for discharge including a plan of distribution.

(b) Contents. The petition for discharge shall contain a statement:

(1) that the personal representative has fully administered the estate;

(2) that all claims which were presented have been paid, settled, or otherwise disposed of;

(3) that the personal representative has paid or made provision for taxes and expenses of administration;

(4) showing the amount of compensation paid or to be paid to the personal representative, attorneys, accountants, appraisers, or other agents employed by the personal representative and the manner of determining that compensation;

(5) showing a plan of distribution which shall include:

(A) a schedule of all prior distributions;

(B) the property remaining in the hands of the personal representative for distribution;

(C) a schedule describing the proposed distribution of the remaining assets; and

(D) the amount of funds retained by the personal representative to pay expenses that are incurred in the distribution of the remaining assets and termination of the estate administration;

(6) that any objections to the accounting, the compensation paid or proposed to be paid, or the proposed distribution of assets must be filed within 30 days from the date of service of the last of the petition for discharge or final accounting; and also that within 90 days after filing of the objection, a notice of hearing thereon must be served or the objection is abandoned; and

(7) that objections, if any, shall be in writing and shall state with particularity the item or items to which the objection is directed and the grounds on which the objection is based.

(c) Closing Estate; Extension. The final accounting and petition for discharge shall be filed and served on interested persons within 12 months after issuance of letters for estates not required to file a federal estate tax return, otherwise within 12 months from the date the return is due, unless the time is extended by the court for cause shown after notice to interested persons. The petition to extend time shall state the status of the estate and the reason for the extension.

(d) Distribution. The personal representative shall promptly distribute the estate property in accordance with the plan of distribution, unless objections are filed as provided in these rules.

(e) Discharge. On receipt of evidence that the estate has been fully administered and properly distributed, the court shall enter an order discharging the personal representative and releasing the surety on any bond.

(Amended March 31, 1977, effective July 1, 1977 (344 So.2d 828); September 4, 1980, effective January 1, 1981 (387 So.2d 949); September 13, 1984, effective January 1, 1985 (458 So.2d 1079); September 29, 1988, effective January 1, 1989 (537 So.2d 500); September 24, 1992, effective January 1, 1993 (607 So.2d 1306); October 3, 1996, effective January 1, 1997 (683 So.2d 78); September 29, 2005, effective January 1, 2006 (912 So.2d 1178).)

Rule 5.401. Objections to petition for discharge or final accounting

(a) Objections. An interested person may object to the petition for discharge or final accounting within 30 days after the service of the later of the petition or final accounting on that interested person.

(b) Contents. Written objections to the petition for discharge or final accounting must state with particularity the items to which the objections are directed and must state the grounds on which the objections are based.

(c) Service. Copies of the objections shall be served by the objector on the personal representative and interested persons not later than 30 days after the last date on which the petition for discharge or final accounting was served on the objector.

(d) Hearing on Objections. Any interested person may set a hearing on the objections. Notice of the hearing shall be given to all interested persons. If a notice of hearing on the objections is not served within 90 days of filing of the objections, the objections shall be deemed abandoned and the personal representative may make distribution as set forth in the plan of distribution.

(e) Order on Objections. The court shall sustain or overrule any objections to the petition for discharge and final accounting and shall determine a plan of distribution.

(f) Discharge. On receipt of evidence that the estate has been distributed according to the plan determined by the court and the claims of creditors have been paid or otherwise disposed of, the court shall enter an order discharging the personal representative and releasing the surety on any bond.

(Added September 13, 1984, effective January 1, 1985 (458 So.2d 1079). Amended September 29, 1988, effective January 1, 1989 (537 So.2d 500); October 3, 1996, effective January 1, 1997 (683 So.2d 78).)

§733.612. Transactions authorized for the personal representative; exceptions

Except as otherwise provided by the will or court order, and subject to the priorities stated in §733.805, without court order, a personal representative, acting reasonably for the benefit of the interested persons, may properly:

(1) Retain assets owned by the decedent, pending distribution or liquidation, including those in which the personal representative is personally interested or that are otherwise improper for fiduciary investments.

...

(26) Make partial distribution to the beneficiaries of any part of the estate not necessary to satisfy claims, expenses of administration, taxes, family allowance, exempt property, and an elective share, in accordance with the decedent's will or as authorized by operation of law.

....

(Laws 1974, ch. 74-106, §1; Laws 1975, ch. 75-220, §78; Laws 1976, ch. 76-172, §3; Laws 1977, ch. 77-87, §31; Laws 1977, ch. 77-174, §1; Laws 1979, ch. 79- 400, §271. Amended by Laws 1997, ch. 97-102, § 1009, effective July 1, 1997; Laws 2001, ch. 2001-226, §135, effective January 1, 2002.)

§733.801. Delivery of devises and distributive shares

(1) No personal representative shall be required to pay or deliver any devise or distributive share or to surrender possession of any land to any beneficiary until the expiration of 5 months from the granting of letters.

(2) Except as otherwise provided in the will, the personal representative shall pay as an expense of administration the reasonable expenses of storage, insurance, packing, and delivery of tangible personal property to a beneficiary.

(Laws 1974, ch. 74-106, §1; Laws 1975, ch. 75-220, §86. Amended by Laws 2001, ch. 2001-226, §153, effective January 1, 2002.)

§733.802. Proceedings for compulsory payment of devises or distributive interest

(1) Before final distribution, no personal representative shall be compelled:

(a) To pay a devise in money before the final settlement of the personal representative's accounts,

(b) To deliver specific personal property devised, unless the personal property is exempt personal property,

(c) To pay all or any part of a distributive share in the personal estate of a decedent, or

(d) To surrender land to any beneficiary,

unless the beneficiary establishes that the property will not be required for the payment of debts, family allowance, estate and inheritance taxes, claims, elective share of the surviving spouse, charges, or expenses of administration or to provide funds for contribution or to enforce equalization in case of advancements.

(2) An order directing the surrender of real property or the delivery of personal property by the personal representative to the beneficiary shall be conclusive in favor of bona fide purchasers for value from the beneficiary or distributee as against the personal representative and all other persons claiming by, through, under, or against the decedent or the decedent's estate.

(3) If the administration of the estate has not been completed before the entry of an order of partial distribution, the court may require the person entitled to distribution to give a bond with sureties as prescribed in §45.011, conditioned on the making of due contribution for the payment of devises, family allowance, estate and inheritance taxes, claims, elective share of the spouse, charges, expenses of administration, and equalization in case of advancements, plus any interest on them.

(Laws 1974, ch. 74-106, § 1; Laws 1975, ch. 75-220, § 86; Laws 1977, ch. 77-87, § 37; Laws 1977, ch. 77-174, § 1; Laws 1979, ch. 79-400, § 272. Amended by Laws 1997, ch. 97-102, § 1019, effective July 1, 1997; Laws 2001, ch. 2001-226, §54, effective January 1, 2002.)

§733.803. Exoneration

The specific devisee of any encumbered property shall be entitled to have the encumbrance on devised property paid at the expense of the residue of the estate only when the will shows that intent. A general direction in the will to pay debts does not show that intent.

(Laws 1974, ch. 74-106, § 1; Laws 1975, ch. 75-220, § 86. Amended by Laws 2001, ch. 2001-226, § 155, effective January 1, 2002.)

§733.809. Right of retainer

The amount of a noncontingent indebtedness due from a beneficiary to the estate or its present value, if not due, may be offset against that beneficiary's interest. However, that beneficiary shall have the benefit of any defense that would be available in a direct proceeding for recovery of the debt.

(Laws 1974, ch. 74-106, §1; Laws 1975, ch. 75-220, §91; Laws 1977, ch. 77-87, §39. Amended by Laws 1997, ch. 97-102, § 1022, effective July 1, 1997; Laws 2001, ch. 2001-226, §159, effective January 1, 2002.)

§733.810. Distribution in kind; valuation

(1) Assets shall be distributed in kind unless:

(a) A general power of sale is conferred;

(b) A contrary intention is indicated by the will or trust; or

(c) Disposition is made otherwise under the provisions of this code.

(2) Any pecuniary devise, family allowance, or other pecuniary share of the estate or trust may be satisfied in kind if:

(a) The person entitled to payment has not demanded cash;

(b) The property is distributed at fair market value as of its distribution date; and

(c) No residuary devisee has requested that the asset remain a part of the residuary estate.

(3) When not practicable to distribute undivided interests in a residuary asset, the asset may be sold.

(4) When the fiduciary under a will or trust is required, or has an option, to satisfy a pecuniary devise or transfer in trust, to or for the benefit of the surviving spouse, with an in-kind distribution, at values as finally determined for federal estate tax purposes, the fiduciary shall, unless the governing instrument otherwise provides, satisfy the devise or transfer in trust by distribution of assets, including cash, fairly representative of the appreciated or depreciated value of all property available for that distribution, taking into consideration any gains and losses realized from a prior sale of any property not devised specifically, generally, or demonstratively.

(5) A personal representative or a trustee is authorized to distribute any distributable assets, non-pro rata among the beneficiaries subject to the fiduciary's duty of impartiality.

(Laws 1974, ch. 74-106, §1; Laws 1975, ch. 75-220, §92; Laws 1977, ch. 77-87, §40. Amended by Laws 2001, ch. 2001-226, §160, effective January 1, 2002.)

§733.811. Distribution; right or title of distributee

If a distributee receives from a fiduciary an instrument transferring assets in kind, payment in distribution, or possession of specific property, the distributee has succeeded to the estate's interest in the assets as against all persons interested in the estate. However, the fiduciary may recover the assets or their value if the distribution was improper.

(Laws 1974, ch. 74-106, § 1; Laws 1975, ch. 75-220, § 93. Amended by Laws 2001, ch. 2001-226, § 161, effective January 1, 2002.)

§733.812. Improper distribution or payment; liability of distributee or payee

A distributee or a claimant who was paid improperly must return the assets or funds received, and the income from those assets or interest on the funds since distribution or payment, unless the distribution or payment cannot be questioned because of adjudication, estoppel, or limitations. If the distributee or claimant does not have the property, its value at the date of disposition, income thereon, and gain received by the distributee or claimant must be returned.

(Laws 1974, ch. 74-106, §1; Laws 1975, ch. 75-220, §92. Amended by Laws 1997, ch. 97-102, §1023, effective July 1, 1997; Laws 2001, ch. 2001-226, §162, effective January 1, 2002.)

§733.813. Purchasers from distributees protected

If property distributed in kind, or a security interest in that property, is acquired by a purchaser or lender for value from a distributee, the purchaser or lender takes title free of any claims of the estate and incurs no personal liability to the estate, whether or not the distribution was proper. The purchaser or lender need not inquire whether a personal representative acted properly in making the distribution in kind.

(Laws 1974, ch. 74-106, §1; Laws 1975, ch. 75-220, §93. Amended by Laws 2001, ch. 2001-226, §163, effective January 1, 2002.)

§733.814. Partition for purpose of distribution

When two or more beneficiaries are entitled to distribution of undivided interests in any property, the personal representative or any beneficiary may petition the court before the estate is closed to partition the property in the same manner as provided by law for civil actions of partition. The court may direct the personal representative to sell any property that cannot be partitioned without prejudice to the owners and that cannot be allotted equitably and conveniently.

(Laws 1974, ch. 74-106, §1; Laws 1975, ch. 75-220, §93. Amended by Laws 2001, ch. 2001-226, §164, effective January 1, 2002.)

§733.815. Private contracts among interested persons

Subject to the rights of creditors and taxing authorities, interested persons may agree among themselves to alter the interests, shares, or amounts to which they are entitled in a written contract executed by them. The personal representative shall abide by the terms of the contract, subject to the personal representative's obligation to administer the estate for the benefit of interested persons who are not parties to the contract, and to pay costs of administration. Trustees of a testamentary trust are interested persons for the purposes of this section. Nothing in this section relieves trustees of any duties owed to beneficiaries of trusts.

(Laws 1974, ch. 74-106, §1; Laws 1975, ch. 75-220, §94. Amended by Laws 1997, ch. 97-102, §1024, effective July 1, 1997; Laws 2001, ch. 2001-226, §165, effective January 1, 2002.)

§733.816. Disposition of unclaimed property held by personal representatives

(1) In all cases in which there is unclaimed property in the hands of a personal representative that cannot be distributed or paid because of the

inability to find the lawful owner or because no lawful owner is known or because the lawful owner refuses to accept the property after a reasonable attempt to distribute it and after notice to that lawful owner, the court shall order the personal representative to sell the property and deposit the proceeds and cash already in hand, after retaining those amounts provided for in subsection (4), with the clerk and receive a receipt, and the clerk shall deposit the funds in the registry of the court to be disposed of as follows:

(a) If the value of the funds is $500 or less, the clerk shall post a notice for 30 days at the courthouse door giving the amount involved, the name of the personal representative, and the other pertinent information that will put interested persons on notice.

(b) If the value of the funds is over $500, the clerk shall publish the notice once a month for 2 consecutive months in a newspaper of general circulation in the county.

After the expiration of 6 months from the posting or first publication, the clerk shall deposit the funds with the Chief Financial Officer after deducting the clerk's fees and the costs of publication.

(2) Upon receipt of the funds, the Chief Financial Officer shall deposit them to the credit of the State School Fund, to become a part of the school fund. All interest and all income that may accrue from the money while so deposited shall belong to the fund. The funds so deposited shall constitute and be a permanent appropriation for payments by the Chief Financial Officer in obedience to court orders entered as provided by subsection (3).

(3) Within 10 years from the date of deposit with the Chief Financial Officer, on written petition to the court that directed the deposit of the funds and informal notice to the Department of Legal Affairs, and after proof of entitlement, any person entitled to the funds before or after payment to the Chief Financial Officer and deposit as provided by subsection (1) may obtain a court order directing the payment of the funds to that person. All funds deposited with the Chief Financial Officer and not claimed within 10 years from the date of deposit shall escheat to the state for the benefit of the State School Fund.

(4) The personal representative depositing assets with the clerk is permitted to retain from the funds a sufficient amount to pay final costs of administration chargeable to the assets accruing between the deposit of the funds with the clerk of the court and the order of discharge. Any funds so retained which are surplus shall be deposited with the clerk prior to discharge of the personal representative.

(5)

(a) If a person entitled to the funds assigns the right to receive payment or part payment to an attorney or private investigative agency which is duly licensed to do business in this state pursuant to a written agreement with that person, the Department of Financial Services is authorized to make distribution in accordance with the assignment.

(b) Payments made to an attorney or private investigative agency shall be promptly deposited into a trust or escrow account which is regularly maintained by the attorney or private investigative agency in a financial institution located in this state and authorized to accept these deposits.

(c) Distribution by the attorney or private investigative agency to the person entitled to the funds shall be made within 10 days following final credit of the deposit into the trust or escrow account at the financial institution, unless a party to the agreement protests the distribution in writing before it is made.

(d) The department shall not be civilly or criminally liable for any funds distributed pursuant to this subsection, provided the distribution is made in good faith.

(Laws 1974, ch. 74-106, §1; Laws 1975, ch. 75-220, §95; Laws 1985, ch. 85-79, §6; Laws 1989, ch. 89-291, § 5; Laws 1989, ch. 89-299, §10. Amended by Laws 1995, ch. 95-401, §21, effective July 1, 1995; Laws 1997, ch. 97-102, §1025, effective July 1, 1997; Laws 2001, ch. 2001-226, §166, effective January 1, 2002; Laws 2003, ch. 2003-261, §1897, effective June 26, 2003.)

§733.817. Apportionment of estate taxes

(1) For purposes of this section:

(a) "Fiduciary" means a person other than the personal representative in possession of property included in the measure of the tax who is liable to the applicable taxing authority for payment of the entire tax to the extent of the value of the property in possession.

(b) "Governing instrument" means a will, trust agreement, or any other document that controls the transfer of an asset on the occurrence of the event with respect to which the tax is being levied.

(c) "Gross estate" means the gross estate, as determined by the Internal Revenue Code [FN1] with respect to the federal estate tax and the Florida estate tax, and as that concept is otherwise determined by the estate, inheritance, or death tax laws of the particular state, country, or political subdivision whose tax is being apportioned.

(d) "Included in the measure of the tax" means that for each separate tax that an interest may incur, only interests included in the measure of that particular tax are considered. The term "included in the measure of the tax" does not include any interest, whether passing under the will or not, to the extent the interest is initially deductible from the gross estate, without regard to any subsequent reduction of the deduction by reason of the charge of any part of the applicable tax to the interest. The term "included in the measure of the tax" does not include interests or amounts that are not included in the gross estate but are included in the amount upon which the applicable tax is computed, such as adjusted taxable gifts with respect to the federal estate tax. If an election is required for deductibility, an interest is not "initially deductible" unless the election for deductibility is allowed.

(e) "Internal Revenue Code" means the Internal Revenue Code of 1986, as amended from time to time.

(f) "Net tax" means the net tax payable to the particular state, country, or political subdivision whose tax is being apportioned, after taking into account all credits against the applicable tax except as provided in this section. With respect to the federal estate tax, "net tax" is determined after taking into account all credits against the tax except for the credit for foreign death taxes.

(g) "Nonresiduary devise" means any devise that is not a residuary devise.

(h) "Nonresiduary interest" in connection with a trust means any interest in a trust which is not a residuary interest.

(i) "Recipient" means, with respect to property or an interest in property included in the gross estate, an heir at law in an intestate estate, devisee in a testate estate, beneficiary of a trust, beneficiary of an insurance policy, annuity, or other contractual right, surviving tenant, taker as a result of the exercise or in default of the exercise of a general power of appointment, person who receives or is to receive the property or an interest in the property, or person in possession of the property, other than a creditor.

(j) "Residuary devise" has the meaning set forth in §731.201(31).

(k) "Residuary interest," in connection with a trust, means an interest in the assets of a trust which remain after provision for any distribution that is to be satisfied by reference to a specific property or type of property, fund, sum, or statutory amount.

(l) "Revocable trust" means a trust as described in §733.707(3).

(m) "State" means any state, territory, or possession of the United States, the District of Columbia, and the Commonwealth of Puerto Rico.

(n) "Tax" means any estate tax, inheritance tax, generation skipping transfer tax, or other tax levied or assessed under the laws of this or any other state, the United States, any other country, or any political subdivision of the foregoing, as finally determined, which is imposed as a result of the death of the decedent, including, without limitation, the tax assessed pursuant to §4980A of the Internal Revenue Code. The term also includes any interest and penalties imposed in addition to the tax. Unless the context indicates otherwise, the term "tax" means each separate tax.

(o) "Temporary interest" means an interest in income or an estate for a specific period of time or for life or for some other period controlled by reference to extrinsic events, whether or not in trust.

(p) "Tentative Florida tax" with respect to any property means the net Florida estate tax that would have been attributable to that property if no tax were payable to any other state in respect of that property.

(q) "Value" means the pecuniary worth of the interest involved as finally determined for purposes of the applicable tax after deducting any debt, expense, or other deduction chargeable to it for which a deduction was allowed in determining the amount of the applicable tax. A lien or other encumbrance is not regarded as chargeable to a particular interest to the extent that it will be paid from other interests. The value of an interest shall not be reduced by reason of the charge against it of any part of the tax.

(2) An interest in protected homestead shall be exempt from the apportionment of taxes.

(3) The net tax attributable to the interests included in the measure of each tax shall be determined by the proportion that the value of each interest included in the measure of the tax bears to the total value of all interests included in the measure of the tax. Notwithstanding the foregoing:

(a) The net tax attributable to interests included in the measure of the tax by reason of §2044 of the Internal Revenue Code [FN2] shall be determined in the manner provided for the federal estate tax in §2207A of the Internal Revenue Code, [FN3] and the amount so determined shall be deducted from the tax to determine the net tax attributable to all remaining interests included in the measure of the tax.

(b) The foreign tax credit allowed with respect to the federal estate tax shall be allocated among the recipients of interests finally charged with the payment of the foreign tax in reduction of any federal estate tax chargeable to the recipients of the foreign interests, whether or not any federal estate tax is attributable to the foreign interests. Any excess of the foreign tax credit shall be applied to reduce proportionately the net amount of federal estate tax chargeable to the remaining recipients of the interests included in the measure of the federal estate tax.

(c) The reduction in the Florida tax on the estate of a Florida resident for tax paid to other states shall be allocated as follows:

1. If the net tax paid to another state is greater than or equal to the tentative Florida tax attributable to the property subject to tax in the other state, none of the Florida tax shall be attributable to that property.

2. If the net tax paid to another state is less than the tentative Florida tax attributable to the property subject to tax in the other state, the net Florida tax attributable to the property subject to tax in the other state shall be the excess of the amount of the tentative Florida tax attributable to the property over the net tax payable to the other state with respect to the property.

3. Any remaining net Florida tax shall be attributable to property included in the measure of the Florida tax exclusive of property subject to tax in other states.

4. The net federal tax attributable to the property subject to tax in the other state shall be determined as if it were located in the state.

(d) The net tax attributable to a temporary interest, if any, shall be regarded as attributable to the principal that supports the temporary interest.

(4)

(a) Except as otherwise effectively directed by the governing instrument, if the Internal Revenue Code, including, but not limited to, §§2032A(c)(5), 2206, 2207, 2207A, 2207B, and 2603, [FN4] applies to apportion federal tax against recipients of certain interests, all net taxes, including taxes levied by the state attributable to each type of interest, shall be apportioned against the recipients of all interests of that type in the proportion that the value of each interest of that type included in the measure of the tax bears to the total of all interests of that type included in the measure of the tax.

(b) The provisions of this subsection do not affect allocation of the reduction in the Florida tax as provided in this section with respect to estates of Florida residents which are also subject to tax in other states.

(5) Except as provided above or as otherwise directed by the governing instrument, the net tax attributable to each interest shall be apportioned as follows:

(a) For property passing under the decedent's will:

1. The net tax attributable to nonresiduary devises shall be charged to and paid from the residuary estate whether or not all interests in the residuary estate are included in the measure of the tax. If the residuary estate is insufficient to pay the net tax attributable to all nonresiduary devises, the balance of the net tax attributable to nonresiduary devises shall be apportioned among the recipients of the nonresiduary devises in the proportion that the value of each nonresiduary devise included in the measure of the tax bears to the total of all nonresiduary devises included in the measure of the tax.

2. The net tax attributable to residuary devises shall be apportioned among the recipients of the residuary devises included in the measure of tax in the proportion that the value of each residuary devise included in the measure of the tax bears to the total of all residuary devises included in the measure of the tax.

(b) For property passing under the terms of any trust other than a trust created in the decedent's will:

1. The net tax attributable to nonresiduary interests shall be charged to and paid from the residuary portion of the trust, whether or not all interests in the residuary portion are included in the measure of the tax. If the residuary portion of the trust is insufficient to pay the net tax attributable to all nonresiduary interests, the balance of the net tax attributable to nonresiduary interests shall be apportioned among the recipients of the nonresiduary interests in the proportion that the value of each nonresiduary interest included in the measure of the tax bears to the total of all nonresiduary interests included in the measure of the tax.

2. The net tax attributable to residuary interests shall be apportioned among the recipients of the residuary interests included in the measure of the tax in the proportion that the value of each residuary interest included in the measure of the tax bears to the total of all residuary interests included in the measure of the tax.

(c) The net tax attributable to an interest in protected homestead shall be apportioned against the recipients of other interests in the estate or passing under any revocable trust in the following order:

1. Class I: Recipients of interests not disposed of by the decedent's will or revocable trust that are included in the measure of the federal estate tax.

2. Class II: Recipients of residuary devises and residuary interests that are included in the measure of the federal estate tax.

3. Class III: Recipients of nonresiduary devises and nonresiduary interests that are

included in the measure of the federal estate tax. The net tax apportioned to a class, if any, pursuant to this paragraph shall be apportioned among the recipients in the class in the proportion that the value of the interest of each bears to the total value of all interests included in that class.

(d) In the application of this subsection, paragraphs (a), (b), and (c) shall be applied to apportion the net tax to the recipients of the estate and the recipients of the decedent's revocable trust as if all recipients, other than the estate or trusts themselves, were taking under a common instrument.

(e) The net tax imposed under §4980A of the Internal Revenue Code [FN5] shall be apportioned among the recipients of the interests included in the measure of that tax in the proportion that the value of the interest of each bears to the total value of all interests included in the measure of that tax.

(f) The net tax that is not apportioned under paragraphs (a), (b), and (c), including, but not limited to, the net tax attributable to interests passing by intestacy, jointly held interests passing by survivorship, insurance, properties in which the decedent held a reversionary or revocable interest, and annuities, shall be apportioned among the recipients of the remaining interests that are included in the measure of the tax in the proportion that the value of each such interest bears to the total value of all the remaining interests included in the measure of the tax.

(g) If the court finds that it is inequitable to apportion interest, penalties, or both, in the manner provided in paragraphs (a)-(f), the court may assess liability for the payment thereof in the manner it finds equitable.

(h)

1. To be effective as a direction for payment of tax in a manner different from that provided in this section, the governing instrument must direct that the tax be paid from assets that pass pursuant to that governing instrument, except as provided in this section.

2. If the decedent's will provides that the tax shall be apportioned as provided in the decedent's revocable trust by specific reference to the trust, the direction in the revocable trust shall be deemed to be a direction contained in the will and shall control with respect to payment of taxes from assets passing under both the will and the revocable trust.

3. A direction in the decedent's will to pay tax from the decedent's revocable trust is effective if a contrary direction is not contained in the trust agreement.

4. For a direction in a governing instrument to be effective to direct payment of taxes attributable to property not passing under the governing instrument from property passing under the governing instrument, the governing instrument must expressly refer to this section, or expressly indicate that the property passing under the governing instrument is to bear the burden of taxation for property not passing under the governing instrument. A direction in the governing instrument to the effect that all taxes are to be paid from property passing under the governing instrument whether attributable to property passing under the governing instrument or otherwise shall be effective to direct the payment from property passing under the governing instrument of taxes attributable to property not passing under the governing instrument.

5. If there is a conflict as to payment of taxes between the decedent's will and the governing instrument, the decedent's will controls, except as follows:

a. The governing instrument shall be given effect with respect to any tax remaining unpaid after the application of the decedent's will.

b. A direction in a governing instrument to pay the tax attributable to assets that pass pursuant to the governing instrument from assets that pass pursuant to that governing instrument shall be effective notwithstanding any conflict with the decedent's will, unless the tax provision in the decedent's will expressly overrides the conflicting provision in the governing instrument.

(6) The personal representative or fiduciary shall not be required to transfer to a recipient any property reasonably anticipated to be necessary for the payment of taxes. Further, the personal representative or fiduciary shall not be required to transfer any property to the recipient until the amount of the tax due from the recipient is paid by the recipient. If property is transferred before final apportionment of the tax, the recipient shall provide a bond or other security for his or her apportioned liability in the amount and form prescribed by the personal representative or fiduciary.

(7)

(a) The personal representative may petition at any time for an order of apportionment. If no administration has been commenced at any time after 90 days from the decedent's death, any fiduciary may petition for an order of apportionment in the court in which venue would be proper for administration of the decedent's estate. Formal notice of the petition for order of apportionment shall be given to all interested persons. At any time after 6 months from the decedent's death, any recipient may petition the court for an order of apportionment.

(b) The court shall determine all issues concerning apportionment. If the tax to be apportioned has not been finally determined, the court shall determine the probable tax due or to become due from all interested persons, apportion the probable tax, and retain jurisdiction over the parties and issues to modify the order of apportionment as appropriate until after the tax is finally determined.

(8)

(a) If the personal representative or fiduciary does not have possession of sufficient property otherwise distributable to the recipient to pay the tax apportioned to the recipient, whether under this section, the Internal Revenue Code, or the governing instrument, if applicable, the personal representative or fiduciary shall recover the deficiency in tax so apportioned to the recipient:

1. From the fiduciary in possession of the property to which the tax is apportioned, if any; and

2. To the extent of any deficiency in collection from the fiduciary, or to the extent collection from the fiduciary is excused pursuant to subsection (9) and in all other cases, from the recipient of the property to which the tax is apportioned, unless relieved of this duty as provided in subsection (9).

(b) In any action to recover the tax apportioned, the order of apportionment shall be prima facie correct.

(c) In any action for the enforcement of an order of apportionment, the court shall award taxable costs as in chancery actions, including reasonable attorney's fees, and may award penalties and interest on the unpaid tax in accordance with equitable principles.

(d) This subsection shall not authorize the recovery of any tax from any company issuing insurance included in the gross estate, or from any bank, trust company, savings and loan association, or similar institution with respect to any account in the name of the decedent and any other person which passed by operation of law on the decedent's death.

(9)

(a) A personal representative or fiduciary who has the duty under this section of collecting the apportioned tax from recipients may be relieved of the duty to collect the tax by an order of the court finding:

1. That the estimated court costs and attorney's fees in collecting the apportioned tax from a person against whom the tax has been apportioned will approximate or exceed the amount of the recovery;

2. That the person against whom the tax has been apportioned is a resident of a foreign country other than Canada and refuses to pay the apportioned tax on demand; or

3. That it is impracticable to enforce contribution of the apportioned tax against a person against whom the tax has been apportioned in view of the improbability of obtaining a judgment or the improbability of collection under any judgment that might be obtained, or otherwise.

(b) A personal representative or fiduciary shall not be liable for failure to attempt to enforce collection if the personal representative or fiduciary reasonably believes it would have been economically impracticable.

(10) Any apportioned tax that is not collected shall be reapportioned in accordance with this section as if the portion of the property to which the uncollected tax had been apportioned had been exempt.

(11) Nothing in this section shall limit the right of any person who has paid more than the amount of the tax apportionable to that person, calculated as if all apportioned amounts would be collected, to obtain contribution from those who have not paid the full amount of the tax apportionable to them, calculated as if all apportioned amounts would be collected, and that right is hereby conferred. In any action to enforce contribution, the court shall award taxable costs as in chancery actions, including reasonable attorney's fees.

(12) Nothing herein contained shall be construed to require the personal representative or fiduciary to pay any tax levied or assessed by any foreign country, unless specific directions to that effect are contained in the will or other instrument under which the personal representative or fiduciary is acting.

[FN1] 26 U.S.C.A. § 1 et seq.
[FN2] 26 U.S.C.A. § 4980A.
[FN3] 26 U.S.C.A. § 2044.
[FN4] 26 U.S.C.A. § 2207A.
[FN5] 26 U.S.C.A. §§ 2032A(c)(5), 2206, 2207, 2207A, 2207B, 2603.

(Laws 1974, ch. 74-106, § 1; Laws 1975, ch. 75-220, § 95; Laws 1977, ch. 77-87, § 41; Laws 1979, ch. 79-400, § 273; Laws 1992, ch. 92-200, § 20. Amended by Laws 1997, ch. 97-102, § 1026, effective July 1, 1997. Laws 1997, ch. 97-240, § 9, effective October 1, 1998; Laws 2000, ch. 2000-159, § 13, effective July 4, 2000; Laws 2001, ch. 2001-226, § 167, effective January 1, 2002.)

F. Closing the Estate

Upon completion of administration, the personal representative must file a petition for final distribution and provide an accounting to the court and interested parties. Final distribution takes place only after the personal representative files such an accounting (although an accounting sometimes may be waived).

Rule 5.330 authorizes a personal representative to prepare the petition for distribution and discharge. The personal representative should obtain a receipt from a distributee any time that estate property is distributed. Trawick, supra, at §11-4 n.14.

After a personal representative has complied with the terms of the order for final distribution, the personal representative is entitled to be discharged from liability. Occasionally, however, estate property may be discovered after an estate has been closed. If such a discovery necessitates subsequent administration of the estate, the court will again appoint a personal representative.

§733.802. Proceedings for compulsory payment of devises or distributive interest

(1) Before final distribution, no personal representative shall be compelled:

(a) To pay a devise in money before the final settlement of the personal representative's accounts,

(b) To deliver specific personal property devised, unless the personal property is exempt personal property,

(c) To pay all or any part of a distributive share in the personal estate of a decedent, or

(d) To surrender land to any beneficiary,

unless the beneficiary establishes that the property will not be required for the payment of debts, family allowance, estate and inheritance taxes, claims, elective share of the surviving spouse, charges, or expenses of administration or to provide funds for contribution or to enforce equalization in case of advancements.

(2) An order directing the surrender of real property or the delivery of personal property by the personal representative to the beneficiary shall be conclusive in favor of bona fide purchasers for value from the beneficiary or distributee as against the personal representative and all other persons claiming by, through, under, or against the decedent or the decedent's estate.

(3) If the administration of the estate has not been completed before the entry of an order of partial distribution, the court may require the person entitled to distribution to give a bond with sureties as prescribed in §45.011, conditioned on the making of due contribution for the payment of devises, family allowance, estate and inheritance taxes, claims, elective share of the spouse, charges, expenses of administration, and equalization in case of advancements, plus any interest on them.

(Laws 1974, ch. 74-106, §1; Laws 1975, ch. 75-220, §86; Laws 1977, ch. 77-87, §37; Laws 1977, ch. 77-174, §1; Laws 1979, ch. 79-400, §272. Amended by Laws 1997, ch. 97-102, §1019, effective July 1, 1997; Laws 2001, ch. 2001-226, §154, effective January 1, 2002.

§733.901. Final discharge

(1) After administration has been completed, the personal representative shall be discharged.

(2) The discharge of the personal representative shall release the personal representative and shall bar any action against the personal representative, as such or individually, and the surety.

(Laws 1974, ch. 74-106, §1; Laws 1975, ch. 75-220, §96; Laws 1977, ch. 77-87, §42; Laws 1977, ch. 77-174, §1; Laws 1981, ch. 81-27, §6. Amended by Laws 1995, ch. 95-401, §29, effective July 1, 1995; Laws 1997, ch. 97-102, §1027, effective July 1, 1997; Laws 2001, ch. 2001-226, §168, effective January 1, 2002.)

§733.903. Subsequent administration

The final settlement of an estate and the discharge of the personal representative shall not prevent further administration. The order of discharge may not be revoked based upon the discovery of a will or later will.

(Laws 1974, ch. 74-106, §1; Laws 1975, ch. 75-220, §96; Laws 1988, ch. 88-110, §1. Amended by Laws 2001, ch. 2001-226, §169, effective January 1, 2002.)

Rule 5.400. Distribution and discharge

(a) Petition for Discharge; Final Accounting. A personal representative who has completed administration except for distribution shall file a final accounting and a petition for discharge including a plan of distribution.

(b) Contents.

The petition for discharge shall contain a statement:

(1) that the personal representative has fully administered the estate;

(2) that all claims which were presented have been paid, settled, or otherwise disposed of;

(3) that the personal representative has paid or made provision for taxes and expenses of administration;

(4) showing the amount of compensation paid or to be paid to the personal representative, attorneys, accountants, appraisers, or other agents employed by the personal representative and the manner of determining that compensation;

(5) showing a plan of distribution which shall include:

(A) a schedule of all prior distributions;

(B) the property remaining in the hands of the personal representative for distribution;

(C) a schedule describing the proposed distribution of the remaining assets; and

(D) the amount of funds retained by the personal representative to pay expenses that are incurred in the distribution of the remaining assets and termination of the estate administration;

(6) that any objections to the accounting, the compensation paid or proposed to be paid, or the proposed distribution of assets must be filed within 30 days from the date of service of the last of the petition for discharge or final accounting; and also that within 90 days after filing of the objection, a notice of hearing thereon must be served or the objection is abandoned; and

(7) that objections, if any, shall be in writing and shall state with particularity the item or items to which the objection is directed and the grounds on which the objection is based.

(c) Closing Estate; Extension. The final accounting and petition for discharge shall be filed and served on interested persons within 12 months after issuance of letters for estates not required to file a federal estate tax return, otherwise within 12 months from the date the return is due, unless the time is extended by the court for cause shown after notice to interested persons. The petition to extend time shall state the status of the estate and the reason for the extension.

(d) Distribution. The personal representative shall promptly distribute the estate property in accordance with the plan of distribution, unless objections are filed as provided in these rules.

(e) Discharge. On receipt of evidence that the estate has been fully administered and properly distributed, the court shall enter an order discharging the personal representative and releasing the surety on any bond.

(Amended March 31, 1977, effective July 1, 1977 (344 So.2d 828); September 4, 1980, effective January 1, 1981 (387 So.2d 949); September 13, 1984, effective January 1, 1985 (458 So.2d 1079); September 29, 1988, effective January 1, 1989 (537 So.2d 500); September 24, 1992, effective January 1, 1993 (607 So.2d 1306); October 3, 1996, effective January 1, 1997 (683 So.2d 78); September 29, 2005, effective January 1, 2006 (912 So.2d 1178).)

Rule 5.460. Subsequent administration

(a) Petition. If, after an estate is closed, additional property of the decedent is discovered or if further administration of the estate is required for any other reason, any interested person may file a petition for further administration of the estate. The petition shall be filed in the same probate file as the original administration.

(b) Contents. The petition shall state:

(1) the name, address, and interest of the petitioner in the estate;

(2) the reason for further administration of the estate;

(3) the description, approximate value, and location of any asset not included among the assets of the prior administration; and

(4) a statement of the relief sought.

(c) Order. The court shall enter such orders as appropriate. Unless required, the court need not revoke the order of discharge, reissue letters, or require bond.

(Amended September 13, 1984, effective January 1, 1985 (458 So.2d 1079).)

G. Liability of Personal Representative

Florida legislation sets forth the situations in which the personal representative is personally liable. Generally, the personal representative is not personally for acts of estate management except for designated contracts and torts committed during estate management.

A personal representative may be personally liable (1) on a contract for attorney's fees, (2) if he or she executes a contract that fails to reveal his or her representative capacity and identify the estate in the contract, or (3) if the contract provides for personal liability (Fla. Stat. §733.619(1)). In addition, the personal representative may be personally liable for "obligations arising from ownership or control of the estate or for torts committed in the course of administration of the estate only if personally at fault." Id.

Issues of a personal representative's liability are determined in a proceeding for "accounting, surcharge, or indemnification, or other appropriate proceeding" (Fla. Stat. §733.619(4)).

§733.105. Determination of beneficiaries

(1) When property passes by intestate succession or the will is unclear and there is doubt about:

(a) Who is entitled to receive any part of the property, or

(b) The shares and amounts that any person is entitled to receive,

any interested person may petition the court to determine beneficiaries or their shares.

(2) Any personal representative who makes distribution or takes any other action pursuant to an order determining beneficiaries shall be fully protected.

(3) A separate civil action to determine beneficiaries may be brought when an estate has not been administered.

(Laws 1974, ch. 74-106, §1; Laws 1975, ch. 75-220, §48; Laws 1977, ch. 77-104, §226; Laws 1977, ch. 77-174, §1. Amended by Laws 1997, ch. 97-102, §983, effective July 1, 1997; Laws 2001, ch. 2001-226, §81, effective January 1, 2002.)

§733.609. Improper exercise of power; breach of fiduciary duty

(1) A personal representative's fiduciary duty is the same as the fiduciary duty of a trustee of an express trust, and a personal representative is liable to interested persons for damage or loss resulting from the breach of this duty. In all actions for breach of fiduciary duty or challenging the exercise of or failure to exercise a personal representative's powers, the court shall award taxable costs as in chancery actions, including attorney's fees.

(2) When awarding taxable costs, including attorney's fees, under this section, the court in its discretion may direct payment from a party's interest, if any, in the estate or enter a judgment which may be satisfied from other property of the party, or both.

(3) This section shall apply to all proceedings commenced hereunder after the effective date, without regard to the date of the decedent's death.

(Laws 1974, ch. 74-106, §1; Laws 1975, ch. 75-220, §78. Amended by Laws 1997, ch. 97-102, §1006, effective July 1, 1997; Laws 2001, ch. 2001-226, §132, effective January 1, 2002; Laws 2003, ch. 2003-154, §11, effective June 12, 2003.)

§733.611. Persons dealing with the personal representative

Except as provided in §733.613(1), a person who in good faith either assists or deals for value with a personal representative is protected as if the personal representative acted properly. The fact that a person knowingly deals with the personal representative does not require the person to inquire into the authority of the personal representative. A person is not bound to see to the proper application of estate assets paid or delivered to the personal representative. This protection extends to instances in which a procedural irregularity or jurisdictional defect occurred in proceedings leading to the issuance of letters, including a case in which the alleged decedent is alive. This protection is in addition to any protection afforded by comparable provisions of the laws relating to commercial transactions and laws simplifying transfers of securities by fiduciaries.

(Laws 1974, ch. 74-106, §1; Laws 1975, ch. 75-220, §78; Laws 1977, ch. 77-87, §30; Laws 1977, ch. 77-174, §1. Amended by Laws 1997, ch. 97-102, §1008, effective July 1, 1997; Laws 2001, ch. 2001-226, §134, effective January 1, 2002.)

§733.6121. Personal representative; powers as to environmental issues relating to administration

(1) Except as otherwise provided by the will or by court order, and subject to §733.805, the personal representative has, without court authorization, the powers specified in subsection (2).

(2) A personal representative has the power, acting reasonably and for the benefit of the interested persons:

(a) To inspect or investigate, or cause to be inspected or investigated, property subject to administration, including interests in sole proprietorships, partnerships, or corporations and any assets owned by such a business entity for the purpose of determining compliance with an environmental law affecting that property or to respond to an actual or threatened violation of an environmental law affecting that property;

(b) To take, on behalf of the estate, any action necessary to prevent, abate, or otherwise remedy an actual or potential violation of an environmental law affecting property subject to administration, either before or after initiation of an enforcement action by a governmental body;

(c) To settle or compromise at any time any claim against the estate or the personal representative that may be asserted by a governmental body or private party which involves the alleged violation of an environmental law affecting property subject to administration over which the personal representative has responsibility;

(d) To disclaim any power granted by any document, statute, or rule of law which, in the sole judgment of the personal representative, could cause the personal representative to incur personal liability, or the estate to incur liability, under any environmental law;

(e) To decline to serve as a personal representative, or having undertaken to serve, to resign at any time, if the personal representative believes that there is or could be a conflict of interest because of potential claims or liabilities that could be asserted on behalf of the estate by reason of the type or condition of the assets held; or

(f) To charge against the assets of the estate the cost of any inspection, investigation, review, abatement, response, cleanup, or remedial action considered reasonable by the personal representative; and, in the event of the closing or termination of the estate or the transfer of the estate property to another personal representative, to hold moneys sufficient to cover the cost of cleaning up any known environmental problem.

(3) A personal representative is not personally liable to any beneficiary or any other party for a

decrease in value of assets in an estate by reason of the personal representative's compliance or efforts to comply with an environmental law, specifically including any reporting requirement under that law.

(4) A personal representative who acquires ownership or control of a vessel or other property without having owned, operated, or materially participated in the management of that vessel or property before assuming ownership or control as personal representative is not considered an owner or operator for purposes of liability under chapter 376, chapter 403, or any other environmental law. A personal representative who willfully, knowingly, or recklessly causes or exacerbates a release or threatened release of a hazardous substance is personally liable for the cost of the response, to the extent that the release or threatened release is attributable to the personal representative's activities. This subsection does not preclude the filing of claims against the assets that constitute the estate held by the personal representative or the filing of actions against the personal representative as representative of the estate. In such an action, an award or judgment against the personal representative must be satisfied only from the assets of the estate.

(5) Neither the acceptance by the personal representative of the property or a failure by the personal representative to inspect or investigate the property creates any inference of liability under an environmental law with respect to that property.

(6) For the purposes of this section, the term "environmental law" means a federal, state, or local law, rule, regulation, or ordinance that relates to protection of the environment or human health, and the term "hazardous substance" means a substance, material, or waste defined as hazardous or toxic, or any contaminant, pollutant, or constituent thereof, or otherwise regulated by an environmental law.

(7) This section applies to any estate admitted to probate on or after July 1, 1995.

(Laws 1995, ch. 95-401, §18, effective July 1, 1995. Amended by Laws 1997, ch. 97-102, §1010, effective July 1, 1997; Laws 2001, ch. 2001-226, §136, effective January 1, 2002.)

§733.619. Individual liability of personal representative

(1) Unless otherwise provided in the contract, a personal representative is not individually liable on a contract, except a contract for attorney's fee, properly entered into as fiduciary unless the personal representative fails to reveal that representative capacity and identify the estate in the contract.

(2) A personal representative is individually liable for obligations arising from ownership or control of the estate or for torts committed in the course of administration of the estate only if personally at fault.

(3) Claims based on contracts, except a contract for attorney's fee, entered into by a personal representative as a fiduciary, on obligations arising from ownership or control of the estate, or on torts committed in the course of estate administration, may be asserted against the estate by proceeding against the personal representative in that capacity, whether or not the personal representative is individually liable.

(4) Issues of liability as between the estate and the personal representative individually may be determined in a proceeding for accounting, surcharge, or indemnification, or other appropriate proceeding.

(Laws 1975, ch. 75-220, §82; Laws 1977, ch. 77-87, §32; Laws 1977, ch. 77-104, §228. Amended by Laws 1997, ch. 97-102, §1015, effective July 1, 1997; Laws 2001, ch. 2001-226, §144, effective January 1, 2002.)

§733.708. Compromise

When a proposal is made to compromise any claim, whether in suit or not, by or against the estate of a decedent or to compromise any question concerning the distribution of a decedent's estate, the court may enter an order authorizing the compromise if satisfied that the compromise will be for the best interest of the interested persons. The order shall relieve the personal representative of liability or responsibility for the compromise. Claims against the estate may not be compromised until after the time for filing objections to claims has expired.

(Laws 1974, ch. 74-106, §1; Laws 1975, ch. 75-220, §86. Amended by Laws 2001, ch. 2001-226, §151, effective January 1, 2002.)

H. Nondomiciliary Decedents

Estates are administered at the place of the decedent's domicile (termed "principal" or "domiciliary" administration). However, in order to satisfy the policy of protection of creditors' rights, assets must be administered in each state in which property is found at the decedent's death. As a result, administration sometimes occurs in locations other than that of the decedent's domicile. Nondomiciliary administration (i.e., administration in Florida of a nonresident's estate) is termed "ancillary administration."

Florida Statutes §§733.101, 734.102 govern proceedings that involve the administration of an estate of a nondomiciliary decedent. Florida Statutes §733.101(1)(b) specifies the venue for probate proceedings involving the property of a nonresident decedent – in any county where the decedent owned property.

See, e.g., In re Estate of Barteau,736 So.2d 57 (Fla. Dist. Ct. App. 1999) (holding that a will executed in another state by a domiciliary of that state, and probated in the other state, is subject to the jurisdiction of Florida courts for the determination of the validity of that will when it is presented in Florida for the purpose of devising real property in Florida, and thereby holding that a Mexican will was subject to the jurisdiction of a Florida court in the county where the real property was located for a determination of the validity of the will).

If a decedent dies leaving no property in the state of Florida, probate proceedings may be held in any county where any debtor of the decedent resides (Fla. Stat. §733.101(1)(c)).

The Code sets forth a preference for the appointment of an ancillary personal representative in a testate as well as intestate estate (Fla. Stat. §734.102). If the decedent left a will, priority is given to the person designated in the decedent's will (if qualified in Florida) (Fla. Stat. §734.102(1)). In an intestate estate, the domiciliary personal representative has priority (if qualified in Florida). Id.

According to Florida Statutes §734.102(4)), the procedure for appointment of an ancillary personal representative is the same as that of any other personal representative. An ancillary personal representative has the same authority as other personal representatives in Florida to manage an estate (§734.102(77)). Further, an ancillary personal representative must comply with the same statutory requirements as other personal representatives regarding creditors' claims (Fla. Stat. §734.102(5)).

§733.101. Venue of probate proceedings

(1) The venue for probate of wills and granting letters shall be:

(a) In the county in this state where the decedent was domiciled.

(b) If the decedent had no domicile in this state, then in any county where the decedent's property is located.

(c) If the decedent had no domicile in this state and possessed no property in this state, then in the county where any debtor of the decedent resides.

(2) For the purpose of this section, a married woman whose husband is an alien or a nonresident of Florida may establish or designate a separate domicile in this state.

(3) Whenever a proceeding is filed laying venue in an improper county, the court may transfer the action in the same manner as provided in the Florida Rules of Civil Procedure. Any action taken by the court or the parties before the transfer is not affected by the improper venue.

(Laws 1974, ch. 74-106, §1; Laws 1975, ch. 75-220, §46. Amended by Laws 1997, ch. 97-102, §981, effective July 1, 1997; Laws 2001, ch. 2001-226, §78, effective January 1, 2002.)

§734.102. Ancillary administration

(1) If a nonresident of this state dies leaving assets in this state, credits due from residents in this state, or liens on property in this state, a personal representative specifically designated in the decedent's will to administer the Florida property shall be entitled to have ancillary letters issued, if qualified to act in Florida. Otherwise, the foreign personal representative of the decedent's estate shall be entitled to have letters issued, if qualified to act in Florida. If the foreign personal representative is not qualified to act in Florida and the will names an alternate or successor who is qualified to act in Florida, the alternate or successor shall be entitled to have letters issued. Otherwise, those entitled to a majority interest of the Florida property may have letters issued to a personal representative selected by them who is qualified to act in Florida. If the decedent dies intestate and the foreign personal representative is not qualified to act in Florida, the order of preference for appointment of a personal representative as prescribed in this code shall apply. If ancillary letters are applied for by other than the domiciliary personal representative, prior notice shall be given to any domiciliary personal representative.

(2) Ancillary administration shall be commenced as provided by the Florida Probate Rules.

(3) If the will and any codicils are executed as required by the code, they shall be admitted to probate.

(4) The ancillary personal representative shall give bond as do personal representatives generally. All proceedings for appointment and administration of the estate shall be as similar to those in original administrations as possible.

(5) Unless creditors' claims are otherwise barred by s733.710, the ancillary personal representative shall cause a notice to creditors to be served and published according to the requirements of chapter 733. Claims not filed in accordance with chapter 733 shall be barred as provided in §733.702.

(6) After the payment of all expenses of administration and claims against the estate, the court may order the remaining property held by the ancillary personal representative transferred to the foreign personal representative or distributed to the beneficiaries.

(7) Ancillary personal representatives shall have the same rights, powers, and authority as other personal representatives in Florida to manage and settle estates; to sell, lease, or mortgage local property; and to raise funds for the payment of debts, claims, and devises in the domiciliary jurisdiction. No property shall be sold, leased, or mortgaged to pay a debt or claim that is

barred by any statute of limitation or of nonclaim of this state.

(Laws 1974, ch. 74-106, §1; Laws 1975, ch. 75-220, §98; Laws 1977, ch. 77-87, §43; Laws 1977, ch. 77-174, §1. Amended by Laws 1997, ch. 97-102, §1029, effective July 1, 1997; Laws 2001, ch. 2001-226, §171, effective January 1, 2002.)

Rule 5.470. Ancillary administration

(a) Petition. The petition for ancillary letters shall include an authenticated copy of so much of the domiciliary proceedings as will show:

(1) for a testate estate the will, petition for probate, order admitting the will to probate, and authority of the personal representative; or

(2) for an intestate estate the petition for administration and authority of the personal representative to act.

(b) Notice. Before ancillary letters shall be issued to any person, formal notice shall be given to:

(1) all known persons qualified to act as ancillary personal representative and whose entitlement to preference of appointment is equal to or greater than petitioner's and who have not waived notice or joined in the petition; and

(2) all domiciliary personal representatives who have not waived notice or joined in the petition.

(c) Probate of Will. On filing the authenticated copy of a will, the court shall determine whether the will complies with Florida law to entitle it to probate. If it does comply, the court shall admit the will to probate.

(Amended September 13, 1984, effective January 1, 1985 (458 So.2d 1079); September 24, 1992, effective January 1, 1993 (607 So.2d 1306); October 3, 1996, effective January 1, 1997 (683 So.2d 78); September 29, 2005, effective January 1, 2006 (912 So.2d 1178).)

Rule 5.475. Ancillary administration, short form

(a) Filing Requirements. The foreign personal representative of a testate estate that meets the requirements of section 734.1025, Florida Statutes, may file with the clerk in the county where any property is located an authenticated copy of so much of the transcript of the foreign proceedings as will show:

(1) the probated will and all probated codicils of the decedent;

(2) the order admitting them to probate;

(3) the letters or their equivalent; and

(4) the part of the record showing the names of the beneficiaries of the estate or an affidavit of the foreign personal representative reciting that the names are not shown or not fully disclosed by the foreign record and specifying the names.

On presentation of the foregoing, the court shall admit the will and any codicils to probate if they comply with section 732.502(1) or section 732.502(2), Florida Statutes

(b) Notice to Creditors. After complying with the foregoing requirements, the foreign personal representative may cause a notice to creditors to be published as required by these rules.

(c) Claims Procedure. The procedure for filing or barring claims and objecting to them and for suing on them shall be the same as for other estates, except as provided in this rule.

(d) Order. If no claims are filed against the estate within the time allowed, the court shall enter an order adjudging that notice to creditors has been duly published and proof thereof filed and that no claims have been filed against the estate or that all claims have been satisfied.

(e) Notification of Claims Filed. If any claim is filed against the estate within the time allowed, the clerk shall send to the foreign personal representative a copy of the claim and a notice setting a date for a hearing to appoint an ancillary personal representative. At the hearing, the court shall appoint an ancillary personal representative according to the preferences as provided by law.

(f) Objections to Claims. If an ancillary personal representative is appointed pursuant to this rule, the procedure for filing, objecting to, and suing on claims shall be the same as for other estates, except that the ancillary personal representative appointed shall have not less than 30 days from the date of appointment within which to object to any claim filed.

(Added September 29, 1988, effective January 1, 1989 (537 So.2d 500). Amended September 24, 1992, effective January 1, 1993 (607 So.2d 1306); September 29, 2005, effective January 1, 2006 (912 So.2d 1178).)

VI. Disposition of Estates Without (or with Simplified) Administration

A decedent's estate may qualify for summary probate proceedings. Summary probate results in the disposition of the decedent's assets without the necessity for lengthy, costly probate proceedings. These proceedings generally permit the collection and transfer of certain property without administration or with simplified administration.

The primary situations in Florida law that give rise to summary probate proceedings are: (1) small estates, or (2) estates that consist of limited personal property.

The rationale for summary administration in cases of small estates is to facilitate settlement of such estates to insure support

for dependents of a deceased breadwinner who possessed few assets.

Summary administration may be requested either by a beneficiary or a person named in the will as personal representative (Fla. Stat. §735.202). In addition, the petition may be filed at any time during estate administration (Fla. Stat. §735.2055).

In seeking summary administration, the petitioner must make provision for creditors. Specifically, before the entry of the order for summary administration, the petitioner must (1) make a "diligent search and reasonable inquiry" for known or reasonably ascertainable creditors, (2) serve a copy of the petition on such creditors, and (3) make provision for payment for these creditors (Fla. Stat. §735.206(2)).

In 2002, Rule 5.210 was revised to permit a new proceeding of "probate without administration" for situations in which the decedent died testate but left no assets subject to administration in Florida.

A. Small Estates

Summary administration is available in Florida if the estate is less than $75,000 or if the decedent has been dead for more than two years (Fla. Stat. §735.201(2)). In the determination of the value of the estate that would make the estate eligible for this form of administration, property that is exempt from creditors' claims is not included. *Id.*

An additional requirement applies if the decedent left a will. Then summary administration is available only if the will does not specifically require administration of the estate. *Id.* at §735.201(1)).

§735.201. Summary administration; nature of proceedings

Summary administration may be had in the administration of either a resident or nonresident decedent's estate, when it appears:

(1) In a testate estate, that the decedent's will does not direct administration as required by chapter 733.

(2) That the value of the entire estate subject to administration in this state, less the value of property exempt from the claims of creditors, does not exceed $75,000 or that the decedent has been dead for more than 2 years.

(Laws 1974, ch. 74-106, § 1; Laws 1975, ch. 75-220, § 105; Laws 1980, ch. 80-203, § 2; Laws 1989, ch. 89-340, § 13. Amended by Laws 2001, ch. 2001-226, § 179, effective January 1, 2002.)

§735.202. May be administered in the same manner as other estates

The estate may be administered in the same manner as the administration of any other estate, or it may be administered as provided in this part.

(Laws 1974, ch. 74-106, § 1; Laws 1975, ch. 75-220, § 106.)

§735.203. Petition for summary administration

(1) A petition for summary administration may be filed by any beneficiary or person nominated as personal representative in the decedent's will offered for probate. The petition must be signed and verified by the surviving spouse, if any, and any beneficiaries.

(2) If a person named in subsection (1) has died, is incapacitated, or is a minor, or has conveyed or transferred all interest in the property of the estate, then, as to that person, the petition must be signed and certified by:

(a) The personal representative, if any, of a deceased person or, if none, the surviving spouse, if any, and the beneficiaries;

(b) The guardian of an incapacitated person or a minor; or

(c) The grantee or transferee of any of them shall be authorized to sign and verify the petition instead of the beneficiary or surviving spouse.

(3) The joinder in, or consent to, a petition for summary administration is not required of a beneficiary who will receive full distributive share under the proposed distribution. Any beneficiary not joining or consenting shall receive formal notice of the petition.

(Laws 1974, ch. 74-106, § 1; Laws 1975, ch. 75-220, § 107; Laws 1977, ch. 77-174, § 1. Amended by Laws 2001, ch. 2001-226, § 180, effective January 1, 2002.)

§735.2055. Filing of petition

The petition for summary administration may be filed at any stage of the administration of an estate if it appears that at the time of filing the estate would qualify.

(Laws 1977, ch. 77-87, § 47.)

§735.206. Summary administration distribution

(1) Upon the filing of the petition for summary administration, the will, if any, shall be proved in accordance with chapter 733 and be admitted to probate.

(2) Prior to entry of the order of summary administration, the petitioner shall make a diligent search and reasonable inquiry for any known or reasonably ascertainable creditors, serve a copy of the petition on those creditors, and make

provision for payment for those creditors to the extent that assets are available.

(3) The court may enter an order of summary administration allowing immediate distribution of the assets to the persons entitled to them.

(4) The order of summary administration and distribution so entered shall have the following effect:

(a) Those to whom specified parts of the decedent's estate, including exempt property, are assigned by the order shall be entitled to receive and collect the parts and to have the parts transferred to them. They may maintain actions to enforce the right.

(b) Debtors of the decedent, those holding property of the decedent, and those with whom securities or other property of the decedent are registered are authorized and empowered to comply with the order by paying, delivering, or transferring to those specified in the order the parts of the decedent's estate assigned to them by the order, and the persons so paying, delivering, or transferring shall not be accountable to anyone else for the property.

(c) After the entry of the order, bona fide purchasers for value from those to whom property of the decedent may be assigned by the order shall take the property free of all claims of creditors of the decedent and all rights of the surviving spouse and all other beneficiaries.

(d) Property of the decedent that is not exempt from claims of creditors and that remains in the hands of those to whom it may be assigned by the order shall continue to be liable for claims against the decedent until barred as provided in the code. Any known or reasonably ascertainable creditor who did not receive notice and for whom provision for payment was not made may enforce the claim and, if the creditor prevails, shall be awarded reasonable attorney's fees as an element of costs against those who joined in the petition.

(e) The recipients of the decedent's property under the order of summary administration shall be personally liable for a pro rata share of all lawful claims against the estate of the decedent, but only to the extent of the value of the estate of the decedent actually received by each recipient, exclusive of the property exempt from claims of creditors under the constitution and statutes of Florida.

(f) After 2 years from the death of the decedent, neither the decedent's estate nor those to whom it may be assigned shall be liable for any claim against the decedent, unless proceedings have been taken for the enforcement of the claim.

(g) Any heir or devisee of the decedent who was lawfully entitled to share in the estate but who was not included in the order of summary administration and distribution may enforce all rights in appropriate proceedings against those who procured the order and, if successful, shall be awarded reasonable attorney's fees as an element of costs.

(Laws 1974, ch. 74-106, § 1; Laws 1975, ch. 75-220, § 108; Laws 1977, ch. 77-87, § 48; Laws 1977, ch. 77-174, § 1; Laws 1989, ch. 89-340, § 14. Amended by Laws 1997, ch. 97-102, § 1035, effective July 1, 1997; Laws 2001, ch. 2001-226, § 181, effective January 1, 2002.)

§735.2063. Notice to creditors

(1) Any person who has obtained an order of summary administration may publish a notice to creditors according to the relevant requirements of §733.2121, notifying all persons having claims or demands against the estate of the decedent that an order of summary administration has been entered by the court. The notice shall specify the total value of the estate and the names and addresses of those to whom it has been assigned by the order.

(2) If proof of publication of the notice is filed with the court, all claims and demands of creditors against the estate of the decedent who are not known or are not reasonably ascertainable shall be forever barred unless the claims and demands are filed with the court within 3 months after the first publication of the notice.

(Laws 1980, ch. 80-203, § 3. Amended by Laws 2001, ch. 2001-226, § 182, effective January 1, 2002; Laws 2003, ch. 2003-154, § 13, effective June 12, 2003.)

Rule 5.210. Probate of Wills Without Administration

A petition to admit a decedent's will to probate without administration shall be verified by the petitioner and shall contain:

(a) a statement of the interest of the petitioner, the petitioner's name and address, and the name and office address of the petitioner's attorney;

(b) the name, last known address, social security number, date and place of death of the decedent, and state and county of the decedent's domicile;

(c) so far as is known, the names and addresses of the surviving spouse, if any, and the beneficiaries and their relationships to the decedent, and the date of birth of any who are minors;

(d) a statement showing venue;

(e) a statement whether domiciliary or principal proceedings are pending in another state or country, if known, and the name and address of the foreign personal representative and the court issuing letters;

(f) a statement that there are no assets subject to administration in Florida;

(g) a statement identifying all unrevoked wills and codicils being presented for probate and a statement that the petitioner is unaware of any other unrevoked will or codicil or, if the petitioner is aware of any other unrevoked wills or codicils, a statement why the other wills or codicils are not being probated; and

(h) a statement that the original of the decedent's last will is in the possession of the court or accompanies the petition, or that an authenticated copy of a will deposited with or probated in another jurisdiction or that an authenticated copy of a notarial will, the original of which is in the possession of a foreign notary, accompanies the petition.

(Amended September 13, 1984, effective January 1, 1985 (458 So.2d 1079); September 29, 1988, effective January 1, 1989 (537 So.2d 500); September 24, 1992, effective January 1, 1993 (607 So.2d 1306); October 3, 1996, effective January 1, 1997 (683 So.2d 78); May 2, 2002 (824 So.2d 849).)

Rule 5.530. Summary Administration

(a) Petition. The petition shall be verified and shall contain the statements required by law and the following:

(1) Facts showing that the petitioners are entitled to summary administration.

(2) A schedule of all assets required by law to be listed and the estimated value of each, separately designating protected homestead and exempt property.

(3) One of the following shall be included:

(A) A statement that the estate is not indebted.

(B) A statement that all creditors' claims are barred.

(C) A statement that the petitioners have made diligent search and reasonable inquiry for any known or reasonably ascertainable creditors, the name of each creditor, the nature of the debt, the amount of the debt and whether the amount is estimated or exact, and when the debt is due. If provision for payment of the debt has been made other than in the proposed order of distribution, the following information shall be shown:

(i) The name of the person who will pay the debt.

(ii) The creditor's written consent for substitution or assumption of the debt by another person.

(iii) The amount to be paid if the debt has been compromised.

(iv) If the debt is to be paid in other than 1 lump sum or as directed by court order, the time and method of payment.

(4) A schedule of proposed distribution of all probate assets and the person to whom each asset is to be distributed.

(b) Testate Estate. In a testate estate, on the filing of the petition for summary administration, the decedent's will shall be proved and admitted to probate.

(c) Order. If the court determines that the decedent's estate qualifies for summary administration, it shall enter an order distributing the probate assets and specifically designating the person to whom each asset is to be distributed.

(Amended March 31, 1977, effective July 1, 1977 (344 So.2d 828); September 13, 1984, effective January 1, 1985 (458 So.2d 1079); September 29, 1988, effective January 1, 1989 (537 So.2d 500); September 24, 1992, effective January 1, 1993 (607 So.2d 1306); May 2, 2002 (824 So.2d 849); September 29, 2005, effective January 1, 2006 (912 So.2d 1178).)

B. Disposition of Personal Property Without Administration

No administration is required in Florida if a decedent left limited personal property. The Code defines the type of property: property that is exempt from creditors' claims (such as household furnishings and automobiles, etc.), and also "nonexempt personal property" (i.e., personal property that is not exempt from creditors' claims), provided that the value of the latter does not exceed "the sum of the amount of preferred funeral expenses and reasonable and necessary medical and hospital expenses of the last 60 days of the last illness" (Fla. Stat. §733.301(1)). Florida law permits the use of an informal procedure for the disposition of such property. (Fla. Stat. §733.301(2)).

§735.301. Disposition without administration

(1) No administration shall be required or formal proceedings instituted upon the estate of a decedent leaving only personal property exempt under the provisions of §732.402, personal property exempt from the claims of creditors under the Constitution of Florida, and nonexempt personal property the value of which does not exceed the sum of the amount of preferred funeral expenses and reasonable and necessary medical and hospital expenses of the last 60 days of the last illness.

(2) Upon informal application by affidavit, letter, or otherwise by any interested party, and if the court is satisfied that subsection (1) is applicable, the court, by letter or other writing under the seal of the court, may authorize the payment, transfer, or disposition of the personal property, tangible or intangible, belonging to the decedent to those persons entitled.

(3) Any person, firm, or corporation paying, delivering, or transferring property under the authorization shall be forever discharged from liability thereon.
(Laws 1974, ch. 74-106, § 1; Laws 1975, ch. 75-220, § 111; Laws 1977, ch. 77-87, § 50; Laws 1977, ch. 77-174, § 1; Laws 1979, ch. 79-400, § 275. Amended by Laws 1998, ch. 98-421, § 52, effective July 1, 1998; Laws 2001, ch. 2001-226, § 184, effective January 1, 2002.)

§732.402. Exempt property

(1) If a decedent was domiciled in this state at the time of death, the surviving spouse, or, if there is no surviving spouse, the children of the decedent shall have the right to a share of the estate of the decedent as provided in this section, to be designated "exempt property."

(2) Exempt property shall consist of:

(a) Household furniture, furnishings, and appliances in the decedent's usual place of abode up to a net value of $10,000 as of the date of death.

(b) All automobiles held in the decedent's name and regularly used by the decedent or members of the decedent's immediate family as their personal automobiles.

(c) Stanley G. Tate Florida Prepaid College Program contracts purchased and Florida College Savings agreements established under part IV of chapter 1009.

(d) All benefits paid pursuant to §112.1915.

(3) Exempt property shall be exempt from all claims against the estate except perfected security interests thereon.

(4) Exempt property shall be in addition to protected homestead, statutory entitlements, and property passing under the decedent's will or by intestate succession.

(5) Property specifically or demonstratively devised by the decedent's will to any devisee shall not be included in exempt property. However, persons to whom property has been specifically or demonstratively devised and who would otherwise be entitled to it as exempt property under this section may have the court determine the property to be exempt from claims, except for perfected security interests thereon, after complying with the provisions of subsection (6).

(6) Persons entitled to exempt property shall be deemed to have waived their rights under this section unless a petition for determination of exempt property is filed by or on behalf of the persons entitled to the exempt property on or before the later of the date that is 4 months after the date of service of the notice of administration or the date that is 40 days after the date of termination of any proceeding involving the construction, admission to probate, or validity of the will or involving any other matter affecting any part of the estate subject to this section.

(7) Property determined as exempt under this section shall be excluded from the value of the estate before residuary, intestate, or pretermitted or elective shares are determined.
(Laws 1974, ch. 74-106, §1; Laws 1975, ch. 75-220, §19; Laws 1977, ch. 77-87, §10; Laws 1977, ch. 77-174, §1; Laws 1981, ch. 81-238, §1; Laws 1985, ch. 85- 79, §3; Laws 1987, ch. 87-226, §67. Amended by Laws 1998, ch. 98-421, §51, effective July 1, 1998; Laws 1999, ch. 99-220, §3, effective May 26, 1999; Laws 2001, ch. 2001-180, §3, effective June 7, 2001; Laws 2001, ch. 2001-226, §39, effective January 1, 2002; Laws 2002, ch. 2002-387, §1036, effective January 7, 2003; Laws 2006, ch. 2006-134, §5, effective July 1, 2006; Laws 2006, ch. 2006-303, §5, effective July 1, 2006.)

XV
Special Constructional Problems of Wills, Trusts, and Other Instruments

This chapter explores constructional problems involving dispositive provisions that arise because of changes either in estate assets after the will is executed (i.e., loss or destruction of an asset), or life changes that affect the beneficiaries (i.e., births and deaths). The chapter examines such distributive problems as ademption, satisfaction, abatement, and exoneration. It also addresses constructional problems in the determination of beneficiaries, such as lapse and class gifts.

I. Introduction: Classification of Testamentary Gifts

It is helpful to understand the classification of testamentary gifts for purposes of resolving some constructional problems, in particular problems involving the doctrines of abatement, ademption, and satisfaction.

A testamentary gift may be classified as follows:

- specific gift, i.e., a transfer of specifically identifiable property ("I leave my pearl necklace to my niece Alice");
- general gift, i.e., a transfer from the general assets of the estate ("I leave $5000 to my nephew Bob");
- demonstrative gift, i.e., a general gift, payable from a specific source ("I leave $10,000 to my daughter-in-law Carole, payable out of my brokerage account at Charles Schwab, and if this is insufficient then out of my other property");
- residuary gift, i.e., the property that remains after all specific and general gifts have been made ("I give the residue of my estate to my husband Daniel").

In Florida, the definition of the various testamentary gifts is provided by case law rather than statute. See cases cited in Esclavea & Lease, Legacies and Devises: Definitions, 18 Fla. Jur. 2d Decedents' Property §402.

II. Constructional Problems in the Disposition of Property

A. Ademption Doctrine

Ademption occurs when a specific gift that was the subject of a testamentary instrument is not in the transferor's estate at death. Several events may lead to ademption, such as:

- the decedent disposes of the property to the intended beneficiary of the will or to a third person, perhaps by means of gift or sale (sometimes referred to as "ademption by satisfaction"),
- the gift was destroyed during the decedent's lifetime (sometimes referred to as "ademption by extinction"), or
- the property underwent a "change in form" (explained *infra*).

See generally Trawick, *supra*, at §8-5.

If a specific gift of real or personal property is not in the decedent's estate at death, the property is considered "adeemed." The effect of ademption is to extinguish the intended beneficiary's rights. The intended beneficiary then has no right to other estate assets (or money). Only specific gifts can be adeemed.

Because of the harshness of the ademption doctrine (resulting in extinguishing the testamentary gift), the UPC sets forth statutory exceptions that avoid ademption in certain situations (UPC §2-608). Florida has enacted two nonademption provisions similar to those of UPC. Pursuant to Florida Statutes §732.606(1), if the decedent was placed under a guardianship after executing the will and the specifically devised property was sold by the guardian, then the intended beneficiary has the right to a cash award equal to the net sale price of the property. Similarly, if a condemnation award or insurance proceeds are paid to the guardian to compensate for the loss of property that was the subject of a specific devise, then the specific devisee has the right to a general pecuniary devise equal to the condemnation award or the insurance proceeds (Fla. Stat. §732.606(1)).

The rationale for the above rule is presumed intent. That is, the adjudication of guardianship prevented the transferor from being able to execute a new instrument to account for the change in form. An exception applies if (1) the guardianship terminates for the reason that the testator has regained competence and (2) the testator survives for at least a year. The exception may be explained because the testator, having regained competence, has the opportunity to execute a new will to account for the change in form of the property.

Florida law also governs the role of ademption when specifically devised securities (such as corporate stock) *increase or decrease* after the execution of the will due to stock splits, dividends, or other distributions or in cases in which the specifically devised securities *change in form.* The problem arises because the number of shares in the estate may differ from the amount designated in the testator's will. The difference in shares might result from either the decedent's actions or the corporation's acts. For example, the decedent may have sold some of the shares of the stock before death or the corporation may have issued a stock dividend or stock split.

Pursuant to Florida Statutes §732.605(1), in cases of increase or decrease of specifically devised securities, if the testator devised a particular security ("100 shares of IBM stock"), then the devisee is entitled to: (a) the amount of those securities that remain in the estate; (b) "any additional or other securities of the same entity" provided that the action resulting in the increase or decrease was initiated by the entity ("excluding any acquired by exercise of purchase options"); (c) securities that derive from the specifically devised securities as a result of merger, consolidation, reorganization, or other "similar action initiated by the entity"; or (d) any securities of the specifically devised security that result from any reinvestment plan.

Note that the statute does not apply if the testator made a gift of a *cash equivalent* ("$10,000 of IBM stock"). Michael D. Simon & William T. Hennessey, Will Construction, Litigation Under Florida Probate Code, Florida Bar CLE §7.20 (2003). Note also that if the statutory exemptions apply, then the intent of the testator is irrelevant. *Id.* (citing Owen v. Wilson, 399 So. 2d 498 (Fla. Dist. Ct. App. 1981)).

§732.605. Ademption: changes in securities

(1) If the testator intended a specific devise of certain securities rather than their equivalent value, the specific devisee is entitled only to:

(a) As much of the devised securities as is a part of the estate at the time of the testator's death.

(b) Any additional or other securities of the same entity owned by the testator because of action initiated by the entity, excluding any acquired by exercise of purchase options.

(c) Securities of another entity owned by the testator as a result of a merger, consolidation, reorganization, or other similar action initiated by the entity.

(d) Securities of the same entity acquired as a result of a plan of reinvestment.

(2) Distributions before death with respect to a specifically devised security, whether in cash or otherwise, which are not provided for in subsection (1) are not part of the specific devise.

(Laws 1974, ch. 74-106, §1; Laws 1975, ch. 75-220, §37. Amended by Laws 2001, ch. 2001-226, §53, effective January 1, 2002.)

§732.606. Ademption exceptions: guardianship, condemnation, insurance

(1) If specifically devised property is sold by a guardian of the property or if a condemnation award or insurance proceeds are paid to a guardian of the property, the specific devisee has the right to a general pecuniary devise equal to the net sale price, the condemnation award, or the insurance proceeds. This subsection does not apply if, subsequent to the sale, condemnation, or casualty, it is adjudicated that the disability of the testator has ceased and the testator survives the adjudication by 1 year. The right of the specific devisee under this subsection is reduced by any right described in subsection (2).

(2) A specific devisee has the right to the remaining specifically devised property and:

(a) Any balance of the purchase price owing from a purchaser to the testator at death because of sale of the property plus any security interest.

(b) Any amount of a condemnation award for the taking of the property unpaid at death.

(c) Any proceeds unpaid at death on fire or casualty insurance on the property.

(d) Property owned by the testator at death as a result of foreclosure, or obtained instead of foreclosure, of the security for the specifically devised obligation.

(Laws 1974, ch. 74-106, §1; Laws 1975, ch. 75-220, §38. Amended by Laws 1997, ch. 97-102, §969, effective July 1, 1997; Laws 2001, ch. 2001-226, §54, effective January 1, 2002.)

strict identity rule of florida

B. Satisfaction Doctrine

Inter vivos gifts from the decedent to heirs or beneficiaries sometimes may be deemed in "satisfaction" (in part or in whole) of the at-death transfer. The applicable intestate doctrine is termed "advancement," and requires either the decedent's written contemporaneous declaration of an intent to deduct the gift from the heir's share of the estate or the heir's written acknowledgment that the gift is to be deducted (discussed in Chapter I, Section V *supra*). The effect of the satisfaction doctrine is the reduction of the testamentary gift by the amount of the inter vivos gift (or sometimes extinction of the gift).

The testate doctrine is termed "satisfaction" (sometimes "ademption by satisfaction"). For the doctrine of satisfaction to apply, Florida Statutes §732.609 requires:

- a testamentary declaration of intent that the inter vivos gift will be deducted from the testamentary gift, *or*
- the transferor's contemporaneous written statement of intent that the gift is to be deducted from the testamentary gift (or is in satisfaction of the devise), *or*
- the transferee's written acknowledgement that the gift is in satisfaction of the testamentary gift.

The gift is valued as of the time the heir or transferee came into possession or enjoyment of the gift or as of the time of decedent's death, whichever occurs first (Fla. Stat. §732.609).

§732.609. Satisfaction rule: requirements

Property that a testator gave to a person in the testator's lifetime is treated as a satisfaction of a devise to that person, in whole or in part, only if the will provides for deduction of the lifetime gift, the testator declares in a contemporaneous writing that the gift is to be deducted from the devise or is in satisfaction of the devise, or the devisee acknowledges in writing that the gift is in satisfaction. For purposes of part satisfaction, property given during the testator's lifetime is valued at the time the devisee came into possession or enjoyment of the property or at the time of the death of the testator, whichever occurs first.

(Laws 1974, ch. 74-106, §1; Laws 1975, ch. 75-220, §38.)

C. Abatement

The abatement doctrine is triggered when the assets in the testator's estate are insufficient to satisfy all of the testamentary gifts. Abatement provides a method by which the shares of some or all beneficiaries are reduced. Abatement problems most frequently occur because the value of the estate has been depleted by payments of debts, expenses of estate administration, taxes, expenses of last illness, funeral and/or burial costs, or the assertion of statutory rights by a spouse or pretermitted heir.

Most states specify, by case law or statute, an order of abatement that applies in the absence of any contrary indication in the will as to how devises shall be reduced. The usual order of abatement is: (1) intestate property is reduced first; then (2) residuary gifts; (3) general gifts; and (4) specific gifts and demonstrative gifts are reduced last. Within each category, gifts also abate ratably, e.g., each general gift would be reduced proportionately.

The common law distinguished between real and personal property for abatement purposes. That is, at common law, personal property in a given category was exhausted before reduction of real property from that category. Modern statutes generally reject this distinction. See, e.g., Fla. Stat. §733.805 (providing no priority for abatement purposes between real and personal property). Some states (like Florida) provide preferential treatment for spouses, i.e., gifts to the testator's spouse abate last. See, e.g., Fla. Stat. §733.805(2).

The UPC also follows the normal order of abatement when a pretermitted child claims a share. However, the UPC departs from the general rule if a spouse claims an elective share and authorizes pro rata abatement (UPC §§2-210, 3-902(a)).

Florida law follows the general order of abatement for both pretermitted spouses and pretermitted children. See Fla. Stat. §732.301 (pretermitted spouse), §732.302 (pretermitted child), §733.805(1) (order of abatement). For Florida law regulating the sources from which the spouse's elective share is payable, see Florida Statutes §732.2075.

A recent Florida case questioned whether the rules governing homestead rights should prevail over abatement rules. In In re Estate of Mahaney, 903 So. 2d 234 (Fla. Dist. Ct. App. 2005), the appellate court held that the general rules governing abatement do not take precedence over the protection afforded to homestead property by the state constitution.

§732.301. Pretermitted spouse: share, waiver, and abatement

When a person marries after making a will and the spouse survives the testator, the surviving spouse shall receive a share in the estate of the testator equal in value to that which the surviving spouse would have received if the testator had died intestate, unless:

(1) Provision has been made for, or waived by, the spouse by prenuptial or postnuptial agreement;

(2) The spouse is provided for in the will; or

(3) The will discloses an intention not to make provision for the spouse.

The share of the estate that is assigned to the pretermitted spouse shall be obtained in accordance with §733.805.

(Laws 1974, ch. 74-106, §1; Laws 1975, ch. 75-220, §16; Laws 1977, ch. 77-87, §9.)

§732.302. Pretermitted child: share, exceptions, and abatement

When a testator omits to provide by will for any of his or her children born or adopted after making the will and the child has not received a part of the testator's property equivalent to a child's part by way of advancement, the child shall receive a share of the estate equal in value to that which the child would have received if the testator had died intestate, unless:

(1) It appears from the will that the omission was intentional; or

(2) The testator had one or more children when the will was executed and devised substantially all the estate to the other parent of the pretermitted child and that other parent survived the testator and is entitled to take under the will.

The share of the estate that is assigned to the pretermitted child shall be obtained in accordance with §733.805.

(Laws 1974, ch. 74-106, §1; Laws 1975, ch. 75-220, §16. Amended by Laws 1997, ch. 97-102, §958, effective July 1, 1997; Laws 2001, ch. 2001-226, §36, effective January 1, 2002.)

§732.2075. Sources from which to satisfy spouse's elective share

(1) Unless otherwise provided in the decedent's will or, in the absence of a provision in the decedent's will, in a trust referred to in the decedent's will, the following are applied first to satisfy the elective share:

(a) To the extent paid to or for the benefit of the surviving spouse, the proceeds of any term or other policy of insurance on the decedent's life if, at the time of decedent's death, the policy was owned by any person other than the surviving spouse.

(b) To the extent paid to or for the benefit of the surviving spouse, amounts payable under any plan or arrangement described in §732.2035(7).

(c) To the extent paid to or for the benefit of the surviving spouse, the decedent's one-half of any property described in §732.2045(1)(f).

(d) Property held for the benefit of the surviving spouse in a qualifying special needs trust.

(e) Property interests included in the elective estate that pass or have passed to or for the benefit of the surviving spouse, including interests that are contingent upon making the election, but only to the extent that such contingent interests do not diminish other property interests that would be applied to satisfy the elective share in the absence of the contingent interests.

(f) Property interests that would have satisfied the elective share under any preceding paragraph of this subsection but were disclaimed.

(2) If, after the application of subsection (1), the elective share is not fully satisfied, the unsatisfied balance shall be apportioned among the direct recipients of the remaining elective estate in the following order of priority:

(a) *Class 1.*--The decedent's probate estate and revocable trusts.

(b) *Class 2.*--Recipients of property interests, other than protected charitable interests, included in the elective estate under §732.2035(2), (3), or (6) and, to the extent the decedent had at the time of death the power to designate the recipient of the property, property interests, other than protected charitable interests, included under §732.2035(5) and (7).

(c) *Class 3.*--Recipients of all other property interests, other than protected charitable interests, included in the elective estate.

(d) *Class 4.*--Recipients of protected charitable lead interests, but only to the extent and at such times that contribution is permitted without disqualifying the charitable interest in that property for a deduction under the United States gift tax laws.

For purposes of this subsection, a protected charitable interest is any interest for which a charitable deduction with respect to the transfer of the property was allowed or allowable to the decedent or the decedent's spouse under the United States gift tax laws. A protected charitable lead interest is a protected charitable interest where one or more deductible interests in charity precede some other nondeductible interest or interests in the property.

(3) The contribution required of the decedent's probate estate and revocable trusts may be made in cash or in kind. In the application of this subsection, subsections (4) and (5) are to be applied to charge contribution for the elective share to the beneficiaries of the probate estate and revocable trusts as if all beneficiaries were taking under a common governing instrument.

(4) Unless otherwise provided in the decedent's will or, in the absence of a provision in the decedent's will, in a trust referred to in the decedent's will, any amount to be satisfied from the decedent's probate estate, other than from property passing to an inter vivos trust, shall be paid from the assets of the probate estate in the order prescribed in §733.805.

(5) Unless otherwise provided in the trust instrument or, in the decedent's will if there is no provision in the trust instrument, any amount to be satisfied from trust property shall be paid from the assets of the trust in the order provided for claims under §737.3054(2) and (3). A direction in the decedent's will is effective only for revocable trusts.

(Laws 1975, ch. 75-220, §15. Renumbered from 732.209 and amended by Laws 1999, ch. 99-343, §7, effective October 1, 1999. Amended by Laws 2001, ch. 2001-226, §23, effective October 1, 2001; Laws 2002, ch. 2002-82, §4, effective April 23, 2002.)

§733.805. Order of abatement

(1) Funds or property designated by the will shall be used to pay debts, family allowance, exempt property, elective share charges, expenses of administration, and devises, to the extent the funds or property is sufficient. If no provision is made or the designated fund or property is insufficient, the funds and property of the estate shall be used for these purposes, and to raise the shares of a pretermitted spouse and children, except as otherwise provided in subsections (3) and (4), in the following order:

(a) Property passing by intestacy.

(b) Property devised to the residuary devisee or devisees.

(c) Property not specifically or demonstratively devised.

(d) Property specifically or demonstratively devised.

(2) Demonstrative devises shall be classed as general devises upon the failure or insufficiency of funds or property out of which payment should be made, to the extent of the insufficiency. Devises to the decedent's surviving spouse, given in satisfaction of, or instead of, the surviving spouse's statutory rights in the estate, shall not abate until other devises of the same class are exhausted. Devises given for a valuable consideration shall abate with other devises of the same class only to the extent of the excess over the amount of value of the consideration until all others of the same class are exhausted. Except as herein provided, devises shall abate equally and ratably and without preference or priority as between real and personal property. When property that has been specifically devised or charged with a devise is sold or used by the personal representative, other devisees shall contribute according to their respective interests to the devisee whose devise has been sold or used. The amounts of the respective contributions shall be determined by the court and shall be paid or withheld before distribution is made.

(3) Section 733.817 shall be applied before this section is applied.

(4) In determining the contribution required under §733.607(2), subsections (1)-(3) of this section and §736.05053(2) shall be applied as if the beneficiaries of the estate and the beneficiaries of a trust described in § 733.707(3), other than the estate or trust itself, were taking under a common instrument.

(Laws 1974, ch. 74-106, §1; Laws 1975, ch. 75-220, §88; Laws 1977, ch. 77-174, §1. Amended by Laws 1997, ch. 97-102, §1020, effective July 1, 1997; Laws 2001, ch. 2001-226, §156, effective January 1, 2002; Laws 2006, ch. 2006-217, §38, effective July 1, 2007.)

[Cross-referenced statutes are below.]

§733.607. Personal representative's right to possession of estate and payment from trust for insufficiency

(1) Except as otherwise provided by a decedent's will, every personal representative has a right to, and shall take possession or control of, the decedent's property, except the protected homestead, but any real property or tangible personal property may be left with, or surrendered to, the person presumptively entitled to it unless possession of the property by the personal representative will be necessary for purposes of administration. The request by a personal representative for delivery of any property possessed by a beneficiary is conclusive evidence that the possession of the property by the personal representative is necessary for the purposes of administration, in any action against the beneficiary for possession of it. The personal representative shall take all steps reasonably

necessary for the management, protection, and preservation of the estate until distribution and may maintain an action to recover possession of property or to determine the title to it.

(2) If, after providing for statutory entitlements and all devises other than residuary devises, the assets of the decedent's estate are insufficient to pay the expenses of the administration and obligations of the decedent's estate, the personal representative is entitled to payment from the trustee of a trust described in §733.707(3), in the amount the personal representative certifies in writing to be required to satisfy the insufficiency.

(Laws 1974, ch. 74-106, §1; Laws 1975, ch. 75-220, §77; Laws 1977, ch. 77-87, §28; Laws 1993, ch. 93-257, §9. Amended by Laws 1995, ch. 95-401, §9, effective October 1, 1995; Laws 1997, ch. 97-102, §1005, effective July 1, 1997; Laws 2001, ch. 2001-226, §130, effective January 1, 2002.)

§733.707. Priority of expenses of administration

(1) The personal representative shall pay the expenses of the administration and obligations of the decedent's estate in the following order:

(a) *Class 1.*--Costs, expenses of administration, and compensation of personal representatives and their attorneys fees and attorneys fees awarded under §733.106(3).

(b) *Class 2.*--Reasonable funeral, interment, and grave marker expenses, whether paid by a guardian, the personal representative, or any other person, not to exceed the aggregate of $6,000.

(c) *Class 3.*--Debts and taxes with preference under federal law, and claims pursuant to §§409.9101 and 414.28.

(d) *Class 4.*--Reasonable and necessary medical and hospital expenses of the last 60 days of the last illness of the decedent, including compensation of persons attending the decedent.

(e) *Class 5.*--Family allowance.

(f) *Class 6.*--Arrearage from court-ordered child support.

(g) *Class 7.*--Debts acquired after death by the continuation of the decedent's business, in accordance with §733.612(22), but only to the extent of the assets of that business.

(h) *Class 8.*--All other claims, including those founded on judgments or decrees rendered against the decedent during the decedent's lifetime, and any excess over the sums allowed in paragraphs (b) and (d).

(2) After paying any preceding class, if the estate is insufficient to pay all of the next succeeding class, the creditors of the latter class shall be paid ratably in proportion to their respective claims.

(3) Any portion of a trust with respect to which a decedent who is the grantor has at the decedent's death a right of revocation, as defined in paragraph (e), either alone or in conjunction with any other person, is liable for the expenses of the administration and obligations of the decedent's estate to the extent the decedent's estate is insufficient to pay them as provided in §733.607(2).

(a) For purposes of this subsection, any trusts established as part of, and all payments from, either an employee annuity described in §403 of the Internal Revenue Code of 1986, [FN1] as amended, an Individual Retirement Account, as described in §408 of the Internal Revenue Code of 1986, [FN2] as amended, a Keogh (HR-10) Plan, or a retirement or other plan established by a corporation which is qualified under §401 of the Internal Revenue Code of 1986, [FN3] as amended, shall not be considered a trust over which the decedent has a right of revocation.

(b) For purposes of this subsection, any trust described in §664 of the Internal Revenue Code of 1986, [FN4] as amended, shall not be considered a trust over which the decedent has a right of revocation.

(c) This subsection shall not impair any rights an individual has under a qualified domestic relations order as that term is defined in §414(p) of the Internal Revenue Code of 1986, [FN5] as amended.

(d) For purposes of this subsection, property held or received by a trust to the extent that the property would not have been subject to claims against the decedent's estate if it had been paid directly to a trust created under the decedent's will or other than to the decedent's estate, or assets received from any trust other than a trust described in this subsection, shall not be deemed assets of the trust available to the decedent's estate.

(e) For purposes of this subsection, a "right of revocation" is a power retained by the decedent, held in any capacity, to:

1. Amend or revoke the trust and revest the principal of the trust in the decedent; or

2. Withdraw or appoint the principal of the trust to or for the decedent's benefit.

[FN1] 26 U.S.C.A. § 403.
[FN2] 26 U.S.C.A. § 408.
[FN3] 26 U.S.C.A. § 401.

[FN4] 26 U.S.C.A. § 664.
[FN5] 26 U.S.C.A. § 414(p).

(Laws 1974, ch. 74-106, §1; Laws 1975, ch. 75-220, §86; Laws 1977, ch. 77-87, §35; Laws 1985, ch. 85-79, §7; Laws 1987, ch. 87-226, §69; Laws 1993, ch. 93-208, §20; Laws 1993, ch. 93-257, §11. Amended by Laws 1995, ch. 95-401, §10, effective July 1, 1995; Laws 1997, ch. 97-102, §1018, effective July 1, 1997; Laws 1997, ch. 97-240, §3, effective May 30, 1997; Laws 2001, ch. 2001- 226, §150, effective January 1, 2002.)

§733.817. Apportionment of estate taxes

(1) For purposes of this section:

(a) "Fiduciary" means a person other than the personal representative in possession of property included in the measure of the tax who is liable to the applicable taxing authority for payment of the entire tax to the extent of the value of the property in possession.

(b) "Governing instrument" means a will, trust agreement, or any other document that controls the transfer of an asset on the occurrence of the event with respect to which the tax is being levied.

(c) "Gross estate" means the gross estate, as determined by the Internal Revenue Code [FN1] with respect to the federal estate tax and the Florida estate tax, and as that concept is otherwise determined by the estate, inheritance, or death tax laws of the particular state, country, or political subdivision whose tax is being apportioned.

(d) "Included in the measure of the tax" means that for each separate tax that an interest may incur, only interests included in the measure of that particular tax are considered. The term "included in the measure of the tax" does not include any interest, whether passing under the will or not, to the extent the interest is initially deductible from the gross estate, without regard to any subsequent reduction of the deduction by reason of the charge of any part of the applicable tax to the interest. The term "included in the measure of the tax" does not include interests or amounts that are not included in the gross estate but are included in the amount upon which the applicable tax is computed, such as adjusted taxable gifts with respect to the federal estate tax. If an election is required for deductibility, an interest is not "initially deductible" unless the election for deductibility is allowed.

(e) "Internal Revenue Code" means the Internal Revenue Code of 1986, as amended from time to time.

(f) "Net tax" means the net tax payable to the particular state, country, or political subdivision whose tax is being apportioned, after taking into account all credits against the applicable tax except as provided in this section. With respect to the federal estate tax, "net tax" is determined after taking into account all credits against the tax except for the credit for foreign death taxes.

(g) "Nonresiduary devise" means any devise that is not a residuary devise.

(h) "Nonresiduary interest" in connection with a trust means any interest in a trust which is not a residuary interest.

(i) "Recipient" means, with respect to property or an interest in property included in the gross estate, an heir at law in an intestate estate, devisee in a testate estate, beneficiary of a trust, beneficiary of an insurance policy, annuity, or other contractual right, surviving tenant, taker as a result of the exercise or in default of the exercise of a general power of appointment, person who receives or is to receive the property or an interest in the property, or person in possession of the property, other than a creditor.

(j) "Residuary devise" has the meaning set forth in §731.201(31).

(k) "Residuary interest," in connection with a trust, means an interest in the assets of a trust which remain after provision for any distribution that is to be satisfied by reference to a specific property or type of property, fund, sum, or statutory amount.

(l) "Revocable trust" means a trust as described in §733.707(3).

(m) "State" means any state, territory, or possession of the United States, the District of Columbia, and the Commonwealth of Puerto Rico.

(n) "Tax" means any estate tax, inheritance tax, generation skipping transfer tax, or other tax levied or assessed under the laws of this or any other state, the United States, any other country, or any political subdivision of the foregoing, as finally determined, which is imposed as a result of the death of the decedent, including, without limitation, the tax assessed pursuant to §4980A of the Internal Revenue Code. The term also includes any interest and penalties imposed in addition to the tax. Unless the context indicates otherwise, the term "tax" means each separate tax.

(o) "Temporary interest" means an interest in income or an estate for a specific period of time or for life or for some other period controlled by reference to extrinsic events, whether or not in trust.

(p) "Tentative Florida tax" with respect to any property means the net Florida estate tax that would have been attributable to that property if no tax were payable to any other state in respect of that property.

(q) "Value" means the pecuniary worth of the interest involved as finally determined for purposes of the applicable tax after deducting any debt, expense, or other deduction chargeable to it for which a deduction was allowed in determining the amount of the applicable tax. A lien or other encumbrance is not regarded as chargeable to a particular interest to the extent that it will be paid from other interests. The value of an interest shall not be reduced by reason of the charge against it of any part of the tax.

(2) An interest in protected homestead shall be exempt from the apportionment of taxes.

(3) The net tax attributable to the interests included in the measure of each tax shall be determined by the proportion that the value of each interest included in the measure of the tax bears to the total value of all interests included in the measure of the tax. Notwithstanding the foregoing:

(a) The net tax attributable to interests included in the measure of the tax by reason of §2044 of the Internal Revenue Code [FN2] shall be determined in the manner provided for the federal estate tax in §2207A of the Internal Revenue Code, [FN3] and the amount so determined shall be deducted from the tax to determine the net tax attributable to all remaining interests included in the measure of the tax.

(b) The foreign tax credit allowed with respect to the federal estate tax shall be allocated among the recipients of interests finally charged with the payment of the foreign tax in reduction of any federal estate tax chargeable to the recipients of the foreign interests, whether or not any federal estate tax is attributable to the foreign interests. Any excess of the foreign tax credit shall be applied to reduce proportionately the net amount of federal estate tax chargeable to the remaining recipients of the interests included in the measure of the federal estate tax.

(c) The reduction in the Florida tax on the estate of a Florida resident for tax paid to other states shall be allocated as follows:

1. If the net tax paid to another state is greater than or equal to the tentative Florida tax attributable to the property subject to tax in the other state, none of the Florida tax shall be attributable to that property.

2. If the net tax paid to another state is less than the tentative Florida tax attributable to the property subject to tax in the other state, the net Florida tax attributable to the property subject to tax in the other state shall be the excess of the amount of the tentative Florida tax attributable to the property over the net tax payable to the other state with respect to the property.

3. Any remaining net Florida tax shall be attributable to property included in the measure of the Florida tax exclusive of property subject to tax in other states.

4. The net federal tax attributable to the property subject to tax in the other state shall be determined as if it were located in the state.

(d) The net tax attributable to a temporary interest, if any, shall be regarded as attributable to the principal that supports the temporary interest.

(4)

(a) Except as otherwise effectively directed by the governing instrument, if the Internal Revenue Code, including, but not limited to, §§2032A(c)(5), 2206, 2207, 2207A, 2207B, and 2603, [FN4] applies to apportion federal tax against recipients of certain interests, all net taxes, including taxes levied by the state attributable to each type of interest, shall be apportioned against the recipients of all interests of that type in the proportion that the value of each interest of that type included in the measure of the tax bears to the total of all interests of that type included in the measure of the tax.

(b) The provisions of this subsection do not affect allocation of the reduction in the Florida tax as provided in this section with respect to estates of Florida residents which are also subject to tax in other states.

(5) Except as provided above or as otherwise directed by the governing instrument, the net tax attributable to each interest shall be apportioned as follows:

(a) For property passing under the decedent's will:

1. The net tax attributable to nonresiduary devises shall be charged to and paid from the residuary estate whether or not all interests in the residuary estate are included in the measure of the tax. If the residuary estate is insufficient to pay the net tax attributable to all nonresiduary devises, the balance of the net tax attributable to nonresiduary devises shall be apportioned among the recipients of the nonresiduary devises in the proportion that the value of each nonresiduary devise included in the measure of the tax bears to the total of all

nonresiduary devises included in the measure of the tax.

2. The net tax attributable to residuary devises shall be apportioned among the recipients of the residuary devises included in the measure of tax in the proportion that the value of each residuary devise included in the measure of the tax bears to the total of all residuary devises included in the measure of the tax.

(b) For property passing under the terms of any trust other than a trust created in the decedent's will:

1. The net tax attributable to nonresiduary interests shall be charged to and paid from the residuary portion of the trust, whether or not all interests in the residuary portion are included in the measure of the tax. If the residuary portion of the trust is insufficient to pay the net tax attributable to all nonresiduary interests, the balance of the net tax attributable to nonresiduary interests shall be apportioned among the recipients of the nonresiduary interests in the proportion that the value of each nonresiduary interest included in the measure of the tax bears to the total of all nonresiduary interests included in the measure of the tax.

2. The net tax attributable to residuary interests shall be apportioned among the recipients of the residuary interests included in the measure of the tax in the proportion that the value of each residuary interest included in the measure of the tax bears to the total of all residuary interests included in the measure of the tax.

(c) The net tax attributable to an interest in protected homestead shall be apportioned against the recipients of other interests in the estate or passing under any revocable trust in the following order:

1. Class I: Recipients of interests not disposed of by the decedent's will or revocable trust that are included in the measure of the federal estate tax.

2. Class II: Recipients of residuary devises and residuary interests that are included in the measure of the federal estate tax.

3. Class III: Recipients of nonresiduary devises and nonresiduary interests that are included in the measure of the federal estate tax. The net tax apportioned to a class, if any, pursuant to this paragraph shall be apportioned among the recipients in the class in the proportion that the value of the interest of each bears to the total value of all interests included in that class.

(d) In the application of this subsection, paragraphs (a), (b), and (c) shall be applied to apportion the net tax to the recipients of the estate and the recipients of the decedent's revocable trust as if all recipients, other than the estate or trusts themselves, were taking under a common instrument.

(e) The net tax imposed under §4980A of the Internal Revenue Code [FN5] shall be apportioned among the recipients of the interests included in the measure of that tax in the proportion that the value of the interest of each bears to the total value of all interests included in the measure of that tax.

(f) The net tax that is not apportioned under paragraphs (a), (b), and (c), including, but not limited to, the net tax attributable to interests passing by intestacy, jointly held interests passing by survivorship, insurance, properties in which the decedent held a reversionary or revocable interest, and annuities, shall be apportioned among the recipients of the remaining interests that are included in the measure of the tax in the proportion that the value of each such interest bears to the total value of all the remaining interests included in the measure of the tax.

(g) If the court finds that it is inequitable to apportion interest, penalties, or both, in the manner provided in paragraphs (a)-(f), the court may assess liability for the payment thereof in the manner it finds equitable.

(h)

1. To be effective as a direction for payment of tax in a manner different from that provided in this section, the governing instrument must direct that the tax be paid from assets that pass pursuant to that governing instrument, except as provided in this section.

2. If the decedent's will provides that the tax shall be apportioned as provided in the decedent's revocable trust by specific reference to the trust, the direction in the revocable trust shall be deemed to be a direction contained in the will and shall control with respect to payment of taxes from assets passing under both the will and the revocable trust.

3. A direction in the decedent's will to pay tax from the decedent's revocable trust is effective if a contrary direction is not contained in the trust agreement.

4. For a direction in a governing instrument to be effective to direct payment of taxes attributable to property not passing under the

governing instrument from property passing under the governing instrument, the governing instrument must expressly refer to this section, or expressly indicate that the property passing under the governing instrument is to bear the burden of taxation for property not passing under the governing instrument. A direction in the governing instrument to the effect that all taxes are to be paid from property passing under the governing instrument whether attributable to property passing under the governing instrument or otherwise shall be effective to direct the payment from property passing under the governing instrument of taxes attributable to property not passing under the governing instrument.

5. If there is a conflict as to payment of taxes between the decedent's will and the governing instrument, the decedent's will controls, except as follows:

a. The governing instrument shall be given effect with respect to any tax remaining unpaid after the application of the decedent's will.

b. A direction in a governing instrument to pay the tax attributable to assets that pass pursuant to the governing instrument from assets that pass pursuant to that governing instrument shall be effective notwithstanding any conflict with the decedent's will, unless the tax provision in the decedent's will expressly overrides the conflicting provision in the governing instrument.

(6) The personal representative or fiduciary shall not be required to transfer to a recipient any property reasonably anticipated to be necessary for the payment of taxes. Further, the personal representative or fiduciary shall not be required to transfer any property to the recipient until the amount of the tax due from the recipient is paid by the recipient. If property is transferred before final apportionment of the tax, the recipient shall provide a bond or other security for his or her apportioned liability in the amount and form prescribed by the personal representative or fiduciary.

(7)

(a) The personal representative may petition at any time for an order of apportionment. If no administration has been commenced at any time after 90 days from the decedent's death, any fiduciary may petition for an order of apportionment in the court in which venue would be proper for administration of the decedent's estate. Formal notice of the petition for order of apportionment shall be given to all interested persons. At any time after 6 months from the decedent's death, any recipient may petition the court for an order of apportionment.

(b) The court shall determine all issues concerning apportionment. If the tax to be apportioned has not been finally determined, the court shall determine the probable tax due or to become due from all interested persons, apportion the probable tax, and retain jurisdiction over the parties and issues to modify the order of apportionment as appropriate until after the tax is finally determined.

(8)

(a) If the personal representative or fiduciary does not have possession of sufficient property otherwise distributable to the recipient to pay the tax apportioned to the recipient, whether under this section, the Internal Revenue Code, or the governing instrument, if applicable, the personal representative or fiduciary shall recover the deficiency in tax so apportioned to the recipient:

1. From the fiduciary in possession of the property to which the tax is apportioned, if any; and

2. To the extent of any deficiency in collection from the fiduciary, or to the extent collection from the fiduciary is excused pursuant to subsection (9) and in all other cases, from the recipient of the property to which the tax is apportioned, unless relieved of this duty as provided in subsection (9).

(b) In any action to recover the tax apportioned, the order of apportionment shall be prima facie correct.

(c) In any action for the enforcement of an order of apportionment, the court shall award taxable costs as in chancery actions, including reasonable attorney's fees, and may award penalties and interest on the unpaid tax in accordance with equitable principles.

(d) This subsection shall not authorize the recovery of any tax from any company issuing insurance included in the gross estate, or from any bank, trust company, savings and loan association, or similar institution with respect to any account in the name of the decedent and any other person which passed by operation of law on the decedent's death.

(9)

(a) A personal representative or fiduciary who has the duty under this section of collecting the apportioned tax from recipients may be relieved of the duty to collect the tax by an order of the court finding:

1. That the estimated court costs and attorney's fees in collecting the apportioned tax from a person against whom the tax has been apportioned will approximate or exceed the amount of the recovery;

2. That the person against whom the tax has been apportioned is a resident of a foreign country other than Canada and refuses to pay the apportioned tax on demand; or

3. That it is impracticable to enforce contribution of the apportioned tax against a person against whom the tax has been apportioned in view of the improbability of obtaining a judgment or the improbability of collection under any judgment that might be obtained, or otherwise.

(b) A personal representative or fiduciary shall not be liable for failure to attempt to enforce collection if the personal representative or fiduciary reasonably believes it would have been economically impracticable.

(10) Any apportioned tax that is not collected shall be reapportioned in accordance with this section as if the portion of the property to which the uncollected tax had been apportioned had been exempt.

(11) Nothing in this section shall limit the right of any person who has paid more than the amount of the tax apportionable to that person, calculated as if all apportioned amounts would be collected, to obtain contribution from those who have not paid the full amount of the tax apportionable to them, calculated as if all apportioned amounts would be collected, and that right is hereby conferred. In any action to enforce contribution, the court shall award taxable costs as in chancery actions, including reasonable attorney's fees.

(12) Nothing herein contained shall be construed to require the personal representative or fiduciary to pay any tax levied or assessed by any foreign country, unless specific directions to that effect are contained in the will or other instrument under which the personal representative or fiduciary is acting.

[FN1] 26 U.S.C.A. §1 et seq.
[FN2] 26 U.S.C.A. §4980A.
[FN3] 26 U.S.C.A. §2044.
[FN4] 26 U.S.C.A. §2207A.
[FN5] 26 U.S.C.A. §§2032A(c)(5), 2206, 2207, 2207A, 2207B, 2603.

(Laws 1974, ch. 74-106, §1; Laws 1975, ch. 75-220, §95; Laws 1977, ch. 77-87, §41; Laws 1979, ch. 79-400, §273; Laws 1992, ch. 92-200, §20. Amended by Laws 1997, ch. 97-102, §1026, effective July 1, 1997. Laws 1997, ch. 97-240, §9, effective October 1, 1998; Laws 2000, ch. 2000-159, §13, effective July 4, 2000; Laws 2001, ch. 2001-226, §167, effective January 1, 2002.)

[Florida Statutes §737.3054 was repealed, effective July 1, 2007.]

D. Exoneration

At common law, a presumption of exoneration applied when a will contained a specific devise of property that was subject to a loan (e.g., a mortgage). That is, a rebuttable presumption applied that such obligations should be discharged by the personal representative from the assets of the estate before distribution of the estate to the devisee. The devisee of encumbered property would take the property free of the encumbrance.

The modern trend reverses the common law presumption, and adopts a nonexoneration rule. For example, the UPC provides that a devise passes *subject to* any mortgage interest (i.e., without the right of exoneration), and that any general testamentary directive to pay debts is not applicable (UPC §2-607). Florida Statutes §733.803 is similar. See also In re Estate of Sterner, 450 So. 2d 1256 (Fla. Dist. Ct. App. 1984) (holding that the codicil demonstrated the testator's intent to devise the property free of encumbrances).

§733.803. Nonexoneration rule

The specific devisee of any encumbered property shall be entitled to have the encumbrance on devised property paid at the expense of the residue of the estate only when the will shows that intent. A general direction in the will to pay debts does not show that intent.

(Laws 1974, ch. 74-106, §1; Laws 1975, ch. 75-220, §86. Amended by Laws 2001, ch. 2001-226, §155, effective January 1, 2002.)

II. Constructional Problems in the Determination of Beneficiaries

A. Lapse

Testamentary gifts to a beneficiary who predeceases the testator lapse, i.e., fail. The common law made a distinction between *void* gifts and *lapsed* gifts. A testamentary gift was *void* if the devisee predeceased the testator by

dying *before* execution of the will. However, if the devisee predeceased the testator by dying *after* execution of the will but before the death of the testator, the gift *lapsed*. In modern usage, both situations generally qualify as lapse. "The distinction [between void and lapsed gifts] is of no consequence in modern law, and is not perpetuated in [the Restatement (Third) of Property]. Both types are subsumed herein under the term 'lapsed devises.'" Restatement (Third) Property: Wills, *supra*, at §5.5 cmt. a. A lapsed gift passes to (1) a designated alternative beneficiary, *or* (2) if no alternative beneficiary has been named, to a residuary beneficiary, *or* (3) if neither of the above, then by intestacy.

All states today have "anti-lapse" statutes which abrogate lapse in cases when the recipient of the testamentary gift is a close relative. Anti-lapse statutes specify substitute takers for lapsed gifts. Such statutes typically provide that the devised property passes to the *issue* of the deceased devisee provided that the issue survive the testator. The statutes are based on presumed intent. Statutes do not apply if the predeceased devisee died without descendants. Restatement (Third) Property: Wills, *supra*, at §5.5 cmt. e. Generally, issue of the predeceased devisee who are more remote than children take by representation. McGovern & Kurtz, *supra*, §8.3 at 329. See also Restatement (Third) Property: Wills, *supra*, at §5.5 cmt. d.

Statutes vary in terms of the requisite familial relationship *between the testator and the predeceased beneficiary* that evoke application of the anti-lapse doctrine. That is, the "protected devisees" vary. Some anti-lapse statutes are narrow and avoid lapse only if the predeceased devisee was a descendant of the testator (i.e., child or grandchild). However, most anti-lapse statutes define the requisite familial relationship more broadly. These statutes avoid lapse if the predeceased devisee was a grandparent of the testator or a descendant of grandparents. Restatement (Third) of Property: Wills, *supra*, at §5.5 cmt. c. See, e.g., UPC §2-603(b) (applying to devises to the testator's grandparent or a descendant of the testator's grandparent). Some statutes are so broad that they avoid lapse if the predeceased beneficiary is kin of the testator's *spouse*. See, e.g., UPC §2-603(b) (applying to devises to a predeceased stepchild of the testator).

Note that anti-lapse statutes do not apply if the testator has expressed a contrary intent. According to the Restatement (Third) of Property: Wills, *supra*, at §5.5 cmt. f., many anti-lapse statutes recognize a contrary intent only if expressed in the will. The revised Uniform Probate Code §2-601, however, allows the admission of extrinsic evidence on the question of contrary intent.

Testamentary gifts may fail for other reasons than because the beneficiary predeceases the testator. For example, lapse also may arise if a beneficiary is disqualified (i.e., due to disclaimer, divorce, or homicide), or if the beneficiary is an interested witness. In such cases, even though the beneficiary survives the testator, statutes may provide for substitute takers. McGovern & Kurtz, *supra*, §8.3 at 333.

Florida law addresses lapse in Florida Statutes §732.603. If the predeceased devisee is either a grandparent or a lineal descendant of a grandparent of the testator, then the statute permits the descendants of the predeceased devisee to take the gift per stirpes (Fla. Stat. §732.603(1)). The rule applies if the devisee is dead at the time of execution of the will or dies after execution of the will (but before the testator). The rule is applicable unless the testator has expressed a contrary intent in the will. Note that a predeceased devisee's spouse would not be a substitute taker under the statute because he or she is not a "surviving descendant" of the devisee.

What happens if the anti-lapse statute is not applicable? Pursuant to Florida Statutes §732.604(1), a nonresiduary devise that fails becomes part of the residue. The Florida Probate Code also addresses the lapse of a residuary gift. A residuary devise that fails passes to the other residuary devisees (Fla. Stat. 732.604(2)). If the entire residue fails (or if the will has no residuary clause), then the residue of the estate passes by intestate succession. Michael D. Simon & William T. Hennessey, Will Construction, Litigation Under Florida Probate Code, Florida Bar CLE §7.20 (2003).

732.603. Antilapse provisions for predeceased devisees; class gifts

[Text of section effective July 1, 2007]

(1) Unless a contrary intent appears in the will, if a devisee who is a grandparent, or a descendant of a grandparent, of the testator:

(a) Is dead at the time of the execution of the will;

(b) Fails to survive the testator; or

(c) Is required by the will or by operation of law to be treated as having predeceased the testator,

a substitute gift is created in the devisee's surviving descendants who take per stirpes the property to which the devisee would have been entitled had the devisee survived the testator.

(2) When a power of appointment is exercised by will, unless a contrary intent appears in the document creating the power of appointment or in the testator's will, if an appointee who is a grandparent, or a descendant of a grandparent, of the donor of the power:

(a) Is dead at the time of the execution of the will or the creation of the power;

(b) Fails to survive the testator; or

(c) Is required by the will, the document creating the power, or by operation of law to be treated as having predeceased the testator,

a substitute gift is created in the appointee's surviving descendants who take per stirpes the property to which the appointee would have been entitled had the appointee survived the testator. Unless the language creating a power of appointment expressly excludes the substitution of the descendants of an object of a power for the object, a surviving descendant of a deceased object of a power of appointment may be substituted for the object whether or not the descendant is an object of the power.

(3) In the application of this section:

(a) Words of survivorship in a devise or appointment to an individual, such as "if he survives me," or to "my surviving children," are a sufficient indication of an intent contrary to the application of subsections (1) and (2). Words of survivorship used by the donor of the power in a power to appoint to an individual, such as the term "if he survives the donee," or in a power to appoint to the donee's "then surviving children," are a sufficient indication of an intent contrary to the application of subsection (2).

(b) The term:

1. "Appointment" includes an alternative appointment and an appointment in the form of a class gift.

2. "Appointee" includes:

a. A class member if the appointment is in the form of a class gift.

b. An individual or class member who was deceased at the time the testator executed his or her will as well as an individual or class member who was then living but who failed to survive the testator.

3. "Devise" also includes an alternative devise and a devise in the form of a class gift.

4. "Devisee" also includes:

a. A class member if the devise is in the form of a class gift.

b. An individual or class member who was deceased at the time the testator executed his or her will as well as an individual or class member who was then living but who failed to survive the testator.

(4) This section applies only to outright devises and appointments. Devises and appointments in trust, including to a testamentary trust, are subject to §736.1106.

(Laws 1974, ch. 74-106, §1; Laws 1975, ch. 75-220, §36. Amended by Laws 1997, ch. 97-102, §967, effective July 1, 1997; Laws 2001, ch. 2001-226, § 51, effective January 1, 2002; Laws 2003, ch. 2003-154, §6, effective June 12, 2003; Laws 2006, ch. 2006-217, §33, effective July 1, 2007.)

§732.604. Failure of residuary devise: treated like class gifts

(1) Except as provided in §732.603, if a devise other than a residuary devise fails for any reason, it becomes a part of the residue.

(2) Except as provided in §732.603, if the residue is devised to two or more persons and the devise to one of the residuary devisees fails for any reason, that devise passes to the other residuary devisee, or to the other residuary devisees in proportion to their interests in the residue.

(Laws 1974, ch. 74-106, §1; Laws 1975, ch. 75-220, §37. Amended by Laws 1997, ch. 97-102, §968, effective July 1, 1997; Laws 2001, ch. 2001-226, § 52, effective January 1, 2002; Laws 2003, ch. 2003-154, §29, effective June 12, 2003.)

B. Class Gifts

Sometimes, a testator devises a gift to a designated *class* of beneficiaries. For example, class gift language applies to bequests to such aggregate groups as "children," or "nephews and nieces." A class gift is a gift to a group, without naming the takers individually.

Occasionally, a testator may devise property to *both* a group and individuals, e.g., "to my nephews and nieces, John, Thomas, and Barbara." The aggregate designation suggests a class gift, but the testator's naming of the individual relatives contradicts the former designation. Some cases hold that such a gift is treated as one to named individuals (i.e., not a class gift). However, courts are divided on the issue. McGovern & Kurtz, *supra*, §8.3 at 332.

Florida courts have held that such a bequest to a named beneficiary raises a presumption that the gift is *not* a class gift. In In re Eltzeroth's Estate, 83 So. 2d 772 (Fla. 1955), the Florida

Supreme Court held that a testamentary gift to two named persons was not a class gift. The named persons were designated as "the children" of the testatrix and stepchildren of the testator, and "who share equally." But, in the event that either of the two named children was not living at the death of testator and testatrix, then the testatrix provided that the portion bequeathed to him was bequeathed to his children. The court determined that the bequest was a gift to individuals, and therefore that where one child died simultaneously with his children before the death of testator, the gift to such child's children lapsed and passed intestate. The court reasoned that testamentary language that the beneficiaries shall take "share and share" alike has been held to show that the gift is not one to a class.

Courts often must make difficult determinations whether a particular bequest is a class gift. For example, in In re McCune's Estate, 214 So. 2d 56 (Fla. Dist. Ct. App. 1968), the trial court invalidated a testamentary bequest to the widows of named male beneficiaries of a trust because it was too indefinite a class gift and violated the Rule Against Perpetuities. The court of appeals reversed, holding that no class gift was intended because no "aggregate sum" was to be divided among the widows. Rather, each widow was to take individually the interest that had been her husband's, and each interest was independent of that of the widows of the other male beneficiaries. As such, the bequest was valid even though the identity of the remaindermen could not yet be determined.

According to the traditional rule, the determination of whether a particular devise is a class gift depends on the testator's intent. However, a testator's intent is often difficult to determine. Courts may look to whether the testator was "aggregate"-minded, as in *McCune's Estate, supra*.

Once the determination is made that the testator intended a class gift, special rules are applicable. For example, if any "class member" predeceases the decedent without issue, the share of that predeceased devisee passes to the other members of the class (absent a contrary provision in the will).

Suppose a devisee of a class gift predeceases the testator but dies leaving issue surviving. Then, his or her issue take the share of the predeceased devisee, based on the application of most anti-lapse statutes to class gifts (e.g., UPC §2-603(a)(4)). See also McGovern & Kurtz, *supra*, §8.3, at 332.

Further, the UPC would save the gift for the issue of the predeceased "class member" in cases where the class member died *before* or after the execution of the instrument (UPC §2-603(a)(4)). (Recall that a gift was void at common law if the class member was already dead.). Florida law also follows this rule (Fla. Stat. §732.603(4) (b)(definition of "devisee")).

In Florida, membership in the class generally is determined at the time of the testator's death. This is called the "class closing doctrine." Estate Planning, Wills, Classes of Persons, 10 Florida Jur. Forms Legal & Bus. §35:300 (2006). However, sometimes the determination of class membership must take into account a contingency that has to occur before a gift vests. For example, in In re Estate of Winters, 162 So. 2d 282 (Fla. Dist. Ct. App. 1964), the court of appeals held that class membership is determined as of the time the first member of a class becomes entitled to possession. The testator's will gave the residue in equal shares to the children of the testatrix's son provided they were over 18, but placed the balance in trust for the use of the minor children until they reached 18. The court held that that provision did not indicate an intention that the determination of shares be made at the time of testatrix' death. Rather, the court reasoned that the class of beneficiaries was subject to closure only when at least one member of the class attained the age of 18 years.

According to Florida law, the inclusion of adoptees and nonmarital children in class gift language depends on whether such persons are entitled to inherit under state laws of intestate succession (Fla. Stat. §732.608).

§732.603. Antilapse provisions for predeceased devisees; class gifts

(1) Unless a contrary intent appears in the will, if a devisee who is a grandparent, or a descendant of a grandparent, of the testator:

(a) Is dead at the time of the execution of the will;

(b) Fails to survive the testator; or

(c) Is required by the will or by operation of law to be treated as having predeceased the testator,

a substitute gift is created in the devisee's surviving descendants who take per stirpes the property to which the devisee would have been entitled had the devisee survived the testator.

(2) When a power of appointment is exercised by will, unless a contrary intent appears in the document creating the power of appointment or in the testator's will, if an appointee who is a

grandparent, or a descendant of a grandparent, of the donor of the power:

(a) Is dead at the time of the execution of the will or the creation of the power;

(b) Fails to survive the testator; or

(c) Is required by the will, the document creating the power, or by operation of law to be treated as having predeceased the testator,

a substitute gift is created in the appointee's surviving descendants who take per stirpes the property to which the appointee would have been entitled had the appointee survived the testator. Unless the language creating a power of appointment expressly excludes the substitution of the descendants of an object of a power for the object, a surviving descendant of a deceased object of a power of appointment may be substituted for the object whether or not the descendant is an object of the power.

(3) In the application of this section:

(a) Words of survivorship in a devise or appointment to an individual, such as "if he survives me," or to "my surviving children," are a sufficient indication of an intent contrary to the application of subsections (1) and (2). Words of survivorship used by the donor of the power in a power to appoint to an individual, such as the term "if he survives the donee," or in a power to appoint to the donee's "then surviving children," are a sufficient indication of an intent contrary to the application of subsection (2).

(b) The term:

1. "Appointment" includes an alternative appointment and an appointment in the form of a class gift.

2. "Appointee" includes:

a. A class member if the appointment is in the form of a class gift.

b. An individual or class member who was deceased at the time the testator executed his or her will as well as an individual or class member who was then living but who failed to survive the testator.

3. "Devise" also includes an alternative devise and a devise in the form of a class gift.

4. "Devisee" also includes:

a. A class member if the devise is in the form of a class gift.

b. An individual or class member who was deceased at the time the testator executed his or her will as well as an individual or class member who was then living but who failed to survive the testator.

(4) This section applies only to outright devises and appointments. Devises and appointments in trust, including to a testamentary trust, are subject to s736.1106.

(Laws 1974, ch. 74-106, §1; Laws 1975, ch. 75-220, §36. Amended by Laws 1997, ch. 97-102, §967, effective July 1, 1997; Laws 2001, ch. 2001-226, § 51, effective January 1, 2002; Laws 2003, ch. 2003-154, §6, effective June 12, 2003; Laws 2006, ch. 2006-217, §33, effective July 1, 2007.)

§732.608. Class gifts: adoptees and nonmarital children

Adopted persons and persons born out of wedlock are included in class gift terminology and terms of relationship, in accordance with rules for determining relationships for purposes of intestate succession.

(Laws 1974, ch. 74-106, §1; Laws 1975, ch. 75-220, §38.)

§736.1106. Antilapse doctrine applied to beneficiaries of future interests under trusts

(1) As used in this section, the term:

(a) "Beneficiary" means the beneficiary of a future interest and includes a class member if the future interest is in the form of a class gift.

(b) "Distribution date," with respect to a future interest, means the time when the future interest is to take effect in possession or enjoyment. The distribution date need not occur at the beginning or end of a calendar day, but can occur at a time during the course of a day.

(c) "Future interest" includes an alternative future interest and a future interest in the form of a class gift.

(d) "Future interest under the terms of a trust" means a future interest created by an inter vivos or testamentary transfer to an existing trust or creating a trust or by an exercise of a power of appointment to an existing trust directing the continuance of an existing trust, designating a beneficiary of an existing trust, or creating a trust.

(e) "Surviving beneficiary" or "surviving descendant" means a beneficiary or a descendant who did not predecease the distribution date or is not deemed to have predeceased the distribution date by operation of law.

(2) A future interest under the terms of a trust is contingent upon the beneficiary surviving the distribution date. Unless a contrary intent appears in the trust instrument, if a beneficiary of a future interest under the terms of a trust fails to survive the distribution date, and the deceased beneficiary leaves surviving descendants, a substitute gift is created in

the beneficiary's surviving descendants. They take per stirpes the property to which the beneficiary would have been entitled if the beneficiary had survived the distribution date.

(3) In the application of this section:

(a) Words of survivorship attached to a future interest are a sufficient indication of an intent contrary to the application of this section.

(b) A residuary clause in a will is not a sufficient indication of an intent contrary to the application of this section, whether or not the will specifically provides that lapsed or failed devises are to pass under the residuary clause.

(4) If, after the application of subsections (2) and (3), there is no surviving taker, the property passes in the following order:

(a) If the future interest was created by the exercise of a power of appointment, the property passes under the donor's gift-in-default clause, if any, which clause is treated as creating a future interest under the terms of a trust.

(b) If no taker is produced by the application of paragraph (a) and the trust was created in a nonresiduary devise or appointment in the transferor's will, the property passes under the residuary clause in the transferor's will. For purposes of this section, the residuary clause is treated as creating a future interest under the terms of a trust.

(c) If no taker is produced by the application of paragraph (a) or paragraph (b), the property passes to those persons, including the state, and in such shares as would succeed to the transferor's intestate estate under the intestate succession law of the transferor's domicile if the transferor died when the disposition is to take effect in possession or enjoyment.

For purposes of paragraphs (b) and (c), the term "transferor" with respect to a future interest created by the exercise of a power of appointment, means the donor if the power was a nongeneral power and the donee if the power was a general power.

(5) This section applies to all trusts other than trusts that were irrevocable before the effective date of this code.

(Laws 2006, ch. 2006-217, §11, effective July 1, 2007.)

XVI
Health Care Decisionmaking: Planning for Disability and Death

Considerable public attention has focused in recent years on the issue of health care decisionmaking, including the withdrawal of treatment for terminally ill individuals or for other persons who lose the capacity to control their own treatment. This chapter explores the statutory provisions that are applicable to persons who are elderly or disabled as well as those persons who wish to plan for disability.

I. Protective Services Generally for Disabled Adults and the Elderly

The growing elderly population has prompted legislation offering various protective services for the aged and disabled. Currently, more than half of the states have such statutes. Many of these statutes prohibit physical abuse or neglect of an elder, "dependent," or "vulnerable" adult. A few states also prohibit "emotional abuse" of such persons. Some states include penalties for failure to report elder abuse. Geralyn M. Passaro, Claims of Exploitation of the Elderly in the Sale of Financial Products, 80 Fla. B.J. 81 (Oct. 2006).

The Florida legislature enacted the Adult Protective Services Act (Fla. Stat. §§415.101-415.113) in 1973. The intent of the legislation was "to provide for the detection and correction of abuse, neglect, and exploitation through social services and criminal investigations and to establish a program of protective services [for the elderly and disabled]" (Fla. Stat. §415.101).

Hayes v. Guardianship of Thompson, 2006 WL 3228916 (Fla. 2006). illustrates the application of the Act. The Department of Children and Families (DCF) filed a petition under the Adult Protective Services Act to remove an 81-year-old woman from her nephew's home because of poor living conditions. The circuit court granted the petition and ordered that DCF place her in an appropriate facility, apply for eligible financial benefits on her behalf, secure available medical and legal services, provide casework for the purpose of planning and providing needed services, provide for medical and psychiatric examinations if needed, and file a petition to determine capacity and to appoint a guardian. See also S.S. v. Department of Children & Family Servs., 805 So. 2d 879 (Fla. Ct. App. 2001) (holding that daughter who failed to call for help after mother fell, based on mother's request, was not mother's "caregiver," and thus could not be found to have abused, neglected, or exploited mother).

The Florida legislation defines abuse as: a willful or threatened act "which causes or is likely to cause significant impairment to a vulnerable adult's physical, mental, or emotional health" (Fla. Stat. §415.102(1)). Abuse includes both acts and omissions (*id.*). A victim is a "vulnerable adult," defined as "a person 18 years of age or older whose ability to perform the normal activities of daily living or to provide for his or her own care or protection is impaired due to a mental, emotional, long-term physical, or developmental disability or dysfunctioning, or brain damage, or the infirmities of aging" (Fla. Stat. §415.102(26)). The statutory scheme requires mandatory reporting of abuse (Fla. Stat. §415.1034).

Unlike legislation in many states, the Florida Act creates a private cause of action that enables the abused adult to recover actual and punitive damages from the perpetrator (Fla. Stat. §415.1111.) Such an action may be brought by the victim, the victim's guardian, a person or organization acting on behalf of the victim (with the consent of the victim or guardian), or the personal representative of the estate of a deceased victim (without regard to whether the cause of death resulted from the abuse, neglect, or exploitation). *Id.* The statute permits recovery of attorneys' fees and costs as well as damages. *Id.*

§415.101. Adult Protective Services Act; legislative findings and intent to provide services

(1) Sections 415.101-415.113 may be cited as the "Adult Protective Services Act."

(2) The Legislature recognizes that there are many persons in this state who, because of age or disability, are in need of protective services. Such services should allow such an individual the same rights as other citizens and, at the same time, protect the individual from abuse, neglect, and exploitation. It is the intent of the Legislature to provide for the detection and correction of abuse, neglect, and exploitation through social services and criminal investigations and to establish a program of protective services for all disabled adults or elderly persons in need of them. It is intended that the mandatory reporting of such cases will cause the

protective services of the state to be brought to bear in an effort to prevent further abuse, neglect, and exploitation of disabled adults or elderly persons. In taking this action, the Legislature intends to place the fewest possible restrictions on personal liberty and the exercise of constitutional rights, consistent with due process and protection from abuse, neglect, and exploitation. Further, the Legislature intends to encourage the constructive involvement of families in the care and protection of disabled adults or elderly persons.

(Laws 1973, ch. 73-176, §§1 to 11; Fla. St. 1973, §828.043; Laws 1977, ch. 77-174, §1; Laws 1979, ch. 79-287, §§3, 5; Laws 1979, ch. 79-298, §15; Laws 1980, ch. 80-293, §1; Fla. St. 1981, §827.09(1); Laws 1983, ch. 83-82, §1; Laws 1985, ch. 85-81, §61; Laws 1986, ch. 86-220, §27; Laws 1995, ch. 95- 418, §93.)

§415.1034. Mandatory reporting of abuse

(1) Mandatory reporting.--

(a) Any person, including, but not limited to, any:

1. Physician, osteopathic physician, medical examiner, chiropractic physician, nurse, paramedic, emergency medical technician, or hospital personnel engaged in the admission, examination, care, or treatment of vulnerable adults;

2. Health professional or mental health professional other than one listed in subparagraph 1.;

3. Practitioner who relies solely on spiritual means for healing;

4. Nursing home staff; assisted living facility staff; adult day care center staff; adult family-care home staff; social worker; or other professional adult care, residential, or institutional staff;

5. State, county, or municipal criminal justice employee or law enforcement officer;

6. An employee of the Department of Business and Professional Regulation conducting inspections of public lodging establishments under §509.032;

7. Florida advocacy council member or long-term care ombudsman council member; or

8. Bank, savings and loan, or credit union officer, trustee, or employee, who knows, or has reasonable cause to suspect, that a vulnerable adult has been or is being abused, neglected, or exploited shall immediately report such knowledge or suspicion to the central abuse hotline.

(b) To the extent possible, a report made pursuant to paragraph (a) must contain, but need not be limited to, the following information:

1. Name, age, race, sex, physical description, and location of each victim alleged to have been abused, neglected, or exploited.

2. Names, addresses, and telephone numbers of the victim's family members.

3. Name, address, and telephone number of each alleged perpetrator.

4. Name, address, and telephone number of the caregiver of the victim, if different from the alleged perpetrator.

5. Name, address, and telephone number of the person reporting the alleged abuse, neglect, or exploitation.

6. Description of the physical or psychological injuries sustained.

7. Actions taken by the reporter, if any, such as notification of the criminal justice agency.

8. Any other information available to the reporting person which may establish the cause of abuse, neglect, or exploitation that occurred or is occurring.

(2) Mandatory reports of death.--Any person who is required to investigate reports of abuse, neglect, or exploitation and who has reasonable cause to suspect that a vulnerable adult died as a result of abuse, neglect, or exploitation shall immediately report the suspicion to the appropriate medical examiner, to the appropriate criminal justice agency, and to the department, notwithstanding the existence of a death certificate signed by a practicing physician. The medical examiner shall accept the report for investigation pursuant to §406.11 and shall report the findings of the investigation, in writing, to the appropriate local criminal justice agency, the appropriate state attorney, and the department. Autopsy reports maintained by the medical examiner are not subject to the confidentiality requirements provided for in §415.107.

(Laws 1995, ch. 95-418, § 96; Laws 1997, ch. 97-98, § 10; Laws 1997, ch. 97-264, § 42. Amended by Laws 1998, ch. 98-166, § 256, effective July 1, 1998; Laws 2000, ch. 2000-263, § 21, effective July 1, 2000; Laws 2000, ch. 2000-318, § 2, effective July 1, 2000; Laws 2000, ch. 2000-349, § 28, effective September 1, 2000.)

§415.102. Applicable definitions of terms

As used in §§415.101-415.113, the term:

(1) "Abuse" means any willful act or threatened act by a relative, caregiver, or household member which causes or is likely to cause significant impairment to a vulnerable adult's physical, mental,

or emotional health. Abuse includes acts and omissions.

(2) "Alleged perpetrator" means a person who has been named by a reporter as the person responsible for abusing, neglecting, or exploiting a vulnerable adult.

(3) "Capacity to consent" means that a vulnerable adult has sufficient understanding to make and communicate responsible decisions regarding the vulnerable adult's person or property, including whether or not to accept protective services offered by the department.

(4) "Caregiver" means a person who has been entrusted with or has assumed the responsibility for frequent and regular care of or services to a vulnerable adult on a temporary or permanent basis and who has a commitment, agreement, or understanding with that person or that person's guardian that a caregiver role exists. "Caregiver" includes, but is not limited to, relatives, household members, guardians, neighbors, and employees and volunteers of facilities as defined in subsection (8). For the purpose of departmental investigative jurisdiction, the term "caregiver" does not include law enforcement officers or employees of municipal or county detention facilities or the Department of Corrections while acting in an official capacity.

(5) "Deception" means a misrepresentation or concealment of a material fact relating to services rendered, disposition of property, or the use of property intended to benefit a vulnerable adult.

(6) "Department" means the Department of Children and Family Services.

(7)

(a) "Exploitation" means a person who:

1. Stands in a position of trust and confidence with a vulnerable adult and knowingly, by deception or intimidation, obtains or uses, or endeavors to obtain or use, a vulnerable adult's funds, assets, or property with the intent to temporarily or permanently deprive a vulnerable adult of the use, benefit, or possession of the funds, assets, or property for the benefit of someone other than the vulnerable adult; or

2. Knows or should know that the vulnerable adult lacks the capacity to consent, and obtains or uses, or endeavors to obtain or use, the vulnerable adult's funds, assets, or property with the intent to temporarily or permanently deprive the vulnerable adult of the use, benefit, or possession of the funds, assets, or property for the benefit of someone other than the vulnerable adult.

(b) "Exploitation" may include, but is not limited to:

1. Breaches of fiduciary relationships, such as the misuse of a power of attorney or the abuse of guardianship duties, resulting in the unauthorized appropriation, sale, or transfer of property;

2. Unauthorized taking of personal assets;

3. Misappropriation, misuse, or transfer of moneys belonging to a vulnerable adult from a personal or joint account; or

4. Intentional or negligent failure to effectively use a vulnerable adult's income and assets for the necessities required for that person's support and maintenance.

(8) "Facility" means any location providing day or residential care or treatment for vulnerable adults. The term "facility" may include, but is not limited to, any hospital, state institution, nursing home, assisted living facility, adult family-care home, adult day care center, residential facility licensed under chapter 393, adult day training center, or mental health treatment center.

(9) "False report" means a report of abuse, neglect, or exploitation of a vulnerable adult to the central abuse hotline which is not true and is maliciously made for the purpose of:

(a) Harassing, embarrassing, or harming another person;

(b) Personal financial gain for the reporting person;

(c) Acquiring custody of a vulnerable adult; or

(d) Personal benefit for the reporting person in any other private dispute involving a vulnerable adult.

The term "false report" does not include a report of abuse, neglect, or exploitation of a vulnerable adult which is made in good faith to the central abuse hotline.

(10) "Fiduciary relationship" means a relationship based upon the trust and confidence of the vulnerable adult in the caregiver, relative, household member, or other person entrusted with the use or management of the property or assets of the vulnerable adult. The relationship exists where there is a special confidence reposed in one who in equity and good conscience is bound to act in good faith and with due regard to the interests of the vulnerable adult. For the purposes of this part, a fiduciary relationship may be formed by an informal agreement between the vulnerable adult and the other person and does not require a formal declaration or court order for its existence. A fiduciary relationship includes, but is not limited to, court-appointed or voluntary guardians, trustees,

attorneys, or conservators of a vulnerable adult's assets or property.

(11) "Guardian" means a person who has been appointed by a court to act on behalf of a person; a preneed guardian, as provided in chapter 744; or a health care surrogate expressly designated as provided in chapter 765.

(12) "In-home services" means the provision of nursing, personal care, supervision, or other services to vulnerable adults in their own homes.

(13) "Intimidation" means the communication by word or act to a vulnerable adult that that person will be deprived of food, nutrition, clothing, shelter, supervision, medicine, medical services, money, or financial support or will suffer physical violence.

(14) "Lacks capacity to consent" means a mental impairment that causes a vulnerable adult to lack sufficient understanding or capacity to make or communicate responsible decisions concerning person or property, including whether or not to accept protective services.

(15) "Neglect" means the failure or omission on the part of the caregiver or vulnerable adult to provide the care, supervision, and services necessary to maintain the physical and mental health of the vulnerable adult, including, but not limited to, food, clothing, medicine, shelter, supervision, and medical services, which a prudent person would consider essential for the well-being of a vulnerable adult. The term "neglect" also means the failure of a caregiver or vulnerable adult to make a reasonable effort to protect a vulnerable adult from abuse, neglect, or exploitation by others. "Neglect" is repeated conduct or a single incident of carelessness which produces or could reasonably be expected to result in serious physical or psychological injury or a substantial risk of death.

(16) "Obtains or uses" means any manner of:

(a) Taking or exercising control over property;

(b) Making any use, disposition, or transfer of property;

(c) Obtaining property by fraud, willful misrepresentation of a future act, or false promise; or

(d)

1. Conduct otherwise known as stealing; larceny; purloining; abstracting; embezzlement; misapplication; misappropriation; conversion; or obtaining money or property by false pretenses, fraud, or deception; or

2. Other conduct similar in nature.

(17) "Position of trust and confidence" with respect to a vulnerable adult means the position of a person who:

(a) Is a parent, spouse, adult child, or other relative by blood or marriage;

(b) Is a joint tenant or tenant in common;

(c) Has a legal or fiduciary relationship, including, but not limited to, a court-appointed or voluntary guardian, trustee, attorney, or conservator; or

(d) Is a caregiver or any other person who has been entrusted with or has assumed responsibility for the use or management of the vulnerable adult's funds, assets, or property.

(18) "Protective investigation" means acceptance of a report from the central abuse hotline alleging abuse, neglect, or exploitation as defined in this section; investigation of the report; determination as to whether action by the court is warranted; and referral of the vulnerable adult to another public or private agency when appropriate .

(19) "Protective investigator" means an authorized agent of the department who receives and investigates reports of abuse, neglect, or exploitation of vulnerable adults.

(20) "Protective services" means services to protect a vulnerable adult from further occurrences of abuse, neglect, or exploitation. Such services may include, but are not limited to, protective supervision, placement, and in-home and community-based services.

(21) "Protective supervision" means those services arranged for or implemented by the department to protect vulnerable adults from further occurrences of abuse, neglect, or exploitation.

(22) "Psychological injury" means an injury to the intellectual functioning or emotional state of a vulnerable adult as evidenced by an observable or measurable reduction in the vulnerable adult's ability to function within that person's customary range of performance and that person's behavior.

(23) "Records" means all documents, papers, letters, maps, books, tapes, photographs, films, sound recordings, videotapes, or other material, regardless of physical form or characteristics, made or received pursuant to a protective investigation.

(24) "Sexual abuse" means acts of a sexual nature committed in the presence of a vulnerable adult without that person's informed consent. "Sexual abuse" includes, but is not limited to, the acts defined in §794.011(1)(h), fondling, exposure of a vulnerable adult's sexual organs, or the use of a vulnerable adult to solicit for or engage in prostitution or sexual performance. "Sexual abuse" does not include any act intended for a valid medical purpose or any act that may reasonably be construed to be normal caregiving action or appropriate display of affection.

(25) "Victim" means any vulnerable adult named in a report of abuse, neglect, or exploitation.

(26) "Vulnerable adult" means a person 18 years of age or older whose ability to perform the normal activities of daily living or to provide for his or her own care or protection is impaired due to a mental, emotional, long-term physical, or developmental disability or dysfunctioning, or brain damage, or the infirmities of aging.

(27) "Vulnerable adult in need of services" means a vulnerable adult who has been determined by a protective investigator to be suffering from the ill effects of neglect not caused by a second party perpetrator and is in need of protective services or other services to prevent further harm.

(Laws 1973, ch. 73-176, §§1 to 11; Fla. St. 1973, §828.043; Laws 1977, ch. 77-174, §1; Laws 1979, ch. 79-287, §§3, 5; Laws 1979, ch. 79-298, §15; Laws 1980, ch. 80-293, §1; Fla. St. 1981, §827.09(2); Laws 1983, ch. 83-82, §1; Laws 1986, ch. 86-220, §28; Laws 1987, ch. 87-238, §29; Laws 1989, ch. 89-294, §26; Laws 1990, ch. 90-50, §1; Laws 1990, ch. 90-306, §44; Laws 1991, ch. 91-57, §1; Laws 1995, ch. 95-210, §35; Laws 1995, ch. 95-418, §94; Laws 1997, ch. 97-98, §9; Laws 1997, ch. 97-101, §127; Laws 1997, ch. 97-264, §41. Amended by Laws 1998, ch. 98-182, §1, effective July 1, 1998; Laws 2000, ch. 2000-153, §68, effective July 4, 2000; Laws 2000, ch. 2000-349, §26, effective September 1, 2000; Laws 2003, ch. 2003-57, §4, effective May 30, 2003; Laws 2006, ch. 2006-131, §1, effective June 9, 2006; Laws 2006, ch. 2006-227, §57, effective July 1, 2006.)

§415.103. Central abuse hotline to receive reports of abuse

(1) The department shall establish and maintain a central abuse hotline that receives all reports made pursuant to §415.1034 in writing or through a single statewide toll-free telephone number. Any person may use the statewide toll-free telephone number to report known or suspected abuse, neglect, or exploitation of a vulnerable adult at any hour of the day or night, any day of the week. The central abuse hotline must be operated in such a manner as to enable the department to:

(a) Accept reports for investigation when there is a reasonable cause to suspect that a vulnerable adult has been or is being abused, neglected, or exploited.

(b) Determine whether the allegations made by the reporter require an immediate, 24-hour, or next-working-day response priority.

(c) When appropriate, refer calls that do not allege the abuse, neglect, or exploitation of a vulnerable adult to other organizations that might better resolve the reporter's concerns.

(d) Immediately identify and locate prior reports of abuse, neglect, or exploitation through the central abuse hotline.

(e) Track critical steps in the investigative process to ensure compliance with all requirements for all reports.

(f) Maintain data to facilitate the production of aggregate statistical reports for monitoring patterns of abuse, neglect, or exploitation.

(g) Serve as a resource for the evaluation, management, and planning of preventive and remedial services for vulnerable adults who have been subject to abuse, neglect, or exploitation.

(2) Upon receiving an oral or written report of known or suspected abuse, neglect, or exploitation of a vulnerable adult, the central abuse hotline must determine if the report requires an immediate onsite protective investigation. For reports requiring an immediate onsite protective investigation, the central abuse hotline must immediately notify the department's designated protective investigative district staff responsible for protective investigations to ensure prompt initiation of an onsite investigation. For reports not requiring an immediate onsite protective investigation, the central abuse hotline must notify the department's designated protective investigative district staff responsible for protective investigations in sufficient time to allow for an investigation to be commenced within 24 hours. At the time of notification of district staff with respect to the report, the central abuse hotline must also provide any known information on any previous report concerning a subject of the present report or any pertinent information relative to the present report or any noted earlier reports.

(3) The department shall set standards, priorities, and policies to maximize the efficiency and effectiveness of the central abuse hotline.

(Laws 1973, ch. 73-176, §§1 to 11; Fla. St. 1973, §828.043; Laws 1977, ch. 77-174, §1; Laws 1979, ch. 79-287, §§3, 5; Laws 1979, ch. 79-298, §15; Laws 1980, ch. 80-293, §1; Fla. St. 1981, §827.09(4), (6); Laws 1983, ch. 83-82, §1; Laws 1986, ch. 86-163, §67; Laws 1986, ch. 86-220, §29; Laws 1987, ch. 87-238, §30; Laws 1988, ch. 88-337, §16; Laws 1989, ch. 89-294, §27; Laws 1990, ch. 90-50, §2; Laws 1990, ch. 90-306, §45; Laws 1991, ch. 91-57, §2; Laws 1991, ch. 91-71, §14; Laws 1995, ch. 95-210, §36; Laws 1995, ch. 95-418, §95. Amended by Laws 2000, ch. 2000-349, §27, effective September 1, 2000.)

§415.1035. Facility's duty to inform residents of the right to report abuse and duty to facilitate reporting

The department shall work cooperatively with the Agency for Health Care Administration, the Agency for Persons with Disabilities, and the Department of Elderly Affairs to ensure that every facility that serves vulnerable adults informs residents of their right to report abusive, neglectful, or exploitive practices. Each facility must establish appropriate policies and procedures to facilitate such reporting.

(Laws 1995, ch. 95-418, §97. Amended by Laws 2000, ch. 2000-349, §29, effective September 1, 2000; Laws 2006, ch. 2006-227, §58, effective July 1, 2006.)

§415.1036. Immunity for good faith reports of abuse

(1) Any person who participates in making a report under §415.1034 or participates in a judicial proceeding resulting therefrom is presumed to be acting in good faith and, unless lack of good faith is shown by clear and convincing evidence, is immune from any liability, civil or criminal, that otherwise might be incurred or imposed. This section does not grant immunity, civil or criminal, to any person who is suspected of having abused, neglected, or exploited, or committed any illegal act upon or against, a vulnerable adult. Further, a resident or employee of a facility that serves vulnerable adults may not be subjected to reprisal or discharge because of the resident's or employee's actions in reporting abuse, neglect, or exploitation pursuant to § 415.1034.

(2) Any person who makes a report under §415.1034 has a civil cause of action for appropriate compensatory and punitive damages against any person who causes detrimental changes in the employment status of the reporting party by reason of the reporting party's making the report. Any detrimental change made in the residency or employment status of such a person, such as, but not limited to, discharge, termination, demotion, transfer, or reduction in pay or benefits or work privileges, or negative evaluations, within 120 days after the report is made establishes a rebuttable presumption that the detrimental action was retaliatory.

(Laws 1995, ch. 95-418, §98. Amended by Laws 2000, ch. 2000-349, §30, effective September 1, 2000.)

§415.104. Investigations procedures and law enforcement involvement in cases of abuse

(1) The department shall, upon receipt of a report alleging abuse, neglect, or exploitation of a vulnerable adult, begin within 24 hours a protective investigation of the facts alleged therein. If a caregiver refuses to allow the department to begin a protective investigation or interferes with the conduct of such an investigation, the appropriate law enforcement agency shall be contacted for assistance. If, during the course of the investigation, the department has reason to believe that the abuse, neglect, or exploitation is perpetrated by a second party, the appropriate law enforcement agency and state attorney shall be orally notified. The department and the law enforcement agency shall cooperate to allow the criminal investigation to proceed concurrently with, and not be hindered by, the protective investigation. The department shall make a preliminary written report to the law enforcement agencies within 5 working days after the oral report. The department shall, within 24 hours after receipt of the report, notify the appropriate Florida local advocacy council, or long-term care ombudsman council, when appropriate, that an alleged abuse, neglect, or exploitation perpetrated by a second party has occurred. Notice to the Florida local advocacy council or long-term care ombudsman council may be accomplished orally or in writing and shall include the name and location of the vulnerable adult alleged to have been abused, neglected, or exploited and the nature of the report.

(2) Upon commencing an investigation, the protective investigator shall inform all of the vulnerable adults and alleged perpetrators named in the report of the following:

(a) The names of the investigators and identifying credentials from the department.

(b) The purpose of the investigation.

(c) That the victim, the victim's guardian, the victim's caregiver, and the alleged perpetrator, and legal counsel for any of those persons, have a right to a copy of the report at the conclusion of the investigation.

(d) The name and telephone number of the protective investigator's supervisor available to answer questions.

(e) That each person has the right to obtain his or her own attorney.

Any person being interviewed by a protective investigator may be represented by an attorney, at the person's own expense, or may choose to have another person present. The other person present may not be an alleged perpetrator in any report currently under investigation. Before participating in such interview, the other person present shall execute an agreement to comply with the confidentiality requirements of §§415.101-415.113. The absence of an attorney or other person does not prevent the department from proceeding with other aspects of the investigation, including interviews with other persons. In an investigative interview with a vulnerable adult, the protective investigator may conduct the interview with no other person present.

(3) For each report it receives, the department shall perform an onsite investigation to:

(a) Determine that the person is a vulnerable adult as defined in §415.102.

(b) Determine whether the person is a vulnerable adult in need of services, as defined in §415.102.

(c) Determine the composition of the family or household, including the name, address, date of birth, social security number, sex, and race of each person in the household.

(d) Determine whether there is an indication that a vulnerable adult is abused, neglected, or exploited.

(e) Determine the nature and extent of present or prior injuries, abuse, or neglect, and any evidence thereof.

(f) Determine, if possible, the person or persons apparently responsible for the abuse, neglect, or exploitation, including name, address, date of birth, social security number, sex, and race.

(g) Determine the immediate and long-term risk to each vulnerable adult through utilization of standardized risk assessment instruments.

(h) Determine the protective, treatment, and ameliorative services necessary to safeguard and ensure the vulnerable adult's well-being and cause the delivery of those services.

(4) No later than 60 days after receiving the initial report, the designated protective investigative staff of the department shall complete the investigation and notify the guardian of the vulnerable adult, the vulnerable adult, and the caregiver of any recommendations of services to be provided to ameliorate the causes or effects of abuse, neglect, or exploitation.

(5) Whenever the law enforcement agency and the department have conducted independent investigations, the law enforcement agency shall, within 5 working days after concluding its investigation, report its findings to the state attorney and to the department.

(6) Upon receipt of a report which alleges that an employee or agent of the department acting in an official capacity has committed an act of abuse, neglect, or exploitation, the department shall commence, or cause to be commenced, a protective investigation and shall notify the state attorney in whose circuit the alleged abuse, neglect, or exploitation occurred.

(7) With respect to any case of reported abuse, neglect, or exploitation of a vulnerable adult, the department, when appropriate, shall transmit all relevant reports to the state attorney of the circuit where the incident occurred.

(8) Within 15 days after completion of the state attorney's investigation of a case reported to him or her pursuant to this section, the state attorney shall report his or her findings to the department and shall include a determination of whether or not prosecution is justified and appropriate in view of the circumstances of the specific case.

(9) The department shall not use a warning, reprimand, or disciplinary action against an employee, found in that employee's personnel records, as the sole basis for a finding of abuse, neglect, or exploitation.

(Laws 1973, ch. 73-176, §§1 to 11; Fla. St. 1973, §828.043; Laws 1977, ch. 77-174, §1; Laws 1979, ch. 79-287, §§3, 5; Laws 1979, ch. 79-298, §15; Laws 1980, ch. 80-293, §1; Fla. St. 1981, §827.09(5), (7), (11); Laws 1983, ch. 83-82, §1; Laws 1984, ch. 84-226, §5; Laws 1985, ch. 85-143, §2; Laws 1986, ch. 86-220, §30; Laws 1987, ch. 87-238, §31; Laws 1988, ch. 88-337, §17; Laws 1989, ch. 89-294, §28; Laws 1990, ch. 90-50, §3; Laws 1990, ch. 90-306, §46; Laws 1991, ch. 91-57, §3; Laws 1997, ch. 97-103, §64. Amended by Laws 1999, ch. 99-8, §200, effective June 29, 1999; Laws 2000, ch. 2000-263, §22, effective July 1, 2000; Laws 2000, ch. 2000-349, §31, effective September 1, 2000.)

§415.1045. Evidence of abuse: photographs, videotapes, medical exam, privileged communications, confidentiality

(1) Photographs and videotapes.--

(a) The protective investigator, while investigating a report of abuse, neglect, or exploitation, may take or cause to be taken photographs and videotapes of the vulnerable adult, and of his or her environment, which are relevant to the investigation. All photographs and videotapes taken during the course of the protective investigation are confidential and exempt from public disclosure as provided in §415.107.

(b) Any photographs or videotapes made pursuant to this subsection, or copies thereof, must be sent to the department as soon as possible.

(2) Medical examinations.--

(a) With the consent of the vulnerable adult who has the capacity to consent or the vulnerable adult's guardian, or pursuant to §415.1051, the department may cause the vulnerable adult to be referred to a licensed physician or any emergency department in a hospital or health care facility for medical examination, diagnosis, or treatment if any of the following circumstances exist:

1. The areas of trauma visible on the vulnerable adult indicate a need for medical examination;

2. The vulnerable adult verbally complains or otherwise exhibits signs or symptoms indicating a need for medical attention as a consequence of suspected abuse, neglect, or exploitation; or

3. The vulnerable adult is alleged to have been sexually abused.

(b) Upon admission to a hospital or health care facility, with the consent of the vulnerable adult who has capacity to consent or that person's guardian, or pursuant to §415.1051, the medical staff of the facility may examine, diagnose, or treat the vulnerable adult. If a person who has legal authority to give consent for the provision of medical treatment to a vulnerable adult has not given or has refused to give such consent, examination and treatment must be limited to reasonable examination of the patient to determine the medical condition of the patient and treatment reasonably necessary to alleviate the medical condition or to stabilize the patient pending a determination by the court of the department's petition authorizing protective services. Any person may seek an expedited judicial intervention under rule 5.900 of the Florida Probate Rules concerning medical treatment procedures.

(c) Medical examination, diagnosis, and treatment provided under this subsection must be paid for by third-party reimbursement, if available, or by the vulnerable adult, if he or she is able to pay; or, if he or she is unable to pay, the department shall pay the costs within available emergency services funds.

(d) Reports of examination, diagnosis, and treatment made under this subsection, or copies thereof, must be sent to the department as soon as possible.

(e) This subsection does not obligate the department to pay for any treatment other than that necessary to alleviate the immediate presenting problems.

(3) Abrogation of privileged communications.--The privileged quality of communication between husband and wife and between any professional and the professional's patient or client, and any other privileged communication except that between attorney and client or clergy and person, as such communication relates to both the competency of the witness and to the exclusion of confidential communications, does not apply to any situation involving known or suspected abuse, neglect, or exploitation of a vulnerable adult and does not constitute grounds for failure to report as required by §415.1034, for failure to cooperate with law enforcement or the department in its activities under §§415.101-415.113, or for failure to give evidence in any judicial or administrative proceeding relating to abuse, neglect, or exploitation of a vulnerable adult.

(4) Medical, social, or financial records or documents.--

(a) The protective investigator, while investigating a report of abuse, neglect, or exploitation, must have access to, inspect, and copy all medical, social, or financial records or documents in the possession of any person, caregiver, guardian, or facility which are relevant to the allegations under investigation, unless specifically prohibited by the vulnerable adult who has capacity to consent.

(b) The confidentiality of any medical, social, or financial record or document that is confidential under state law does not constitute grounds for failure to:

1. Report as required by §415.1034;

2. Cooperate with the department in its activities under §§415.101-415.113;

3. Give access to such records or documents; or

4. Give evidence in any judicial or administrative proceeding relating to abuse, neglect, or exploitation of a vulnerable adult.

(5) Access to records and documents.--If any person refuses to allow a law enforcement officer or the protective investigator to have access to, inspect, or copy any medical, social, or financial record or document in the possession of any person, caregiver, guardian, or facility which is relevant to the allegations under investigation, the department may petition the court for an order requiring the person to allow access to the record or document. The petition

must allege specific facts sufficient to show that the record or document is relevant to the allegations under investigation and that the person refuses to allow access to such record or document. If the court finds by a preponderance of the evidence that the record or document is relevant to the allegations under investigation, the court may order the person to allow access to and permit the inspection or copying of the medical, social, or financial record or document.

(6) Working agreements.--By March 1, 2004, the department shall enter into working agreements with the jurisdictionally responsible county sheriffs' office or local police department that will be the lead agency when conducting any criminal investigation arising from an allegation of abuse, neglect, or exploitation of a vulnerable adult. The working agreement must specify how the requirements of this chapter will be met. The Office of Program Policy Analysis and Government Accountability shall conduct a review of the efficacy of the agreements and report its findings to the Legislature by March 1, 2005. For the purposes of such agreement, the jurisdictionally responsible law enforcement entity is authorized to share Florida criminal history and local criminal history information that is not otherwise exempt from §119.07(1) with the district personnel. A law enforcement entity entering into such agreement must comply with §943.0525. Criminal justice information provided by such law enforcement entity shall be used only for the purposes specified in the agreement and shall be provided at no charge. Notwithstanding any other provision of law, the Department of Law Enforcement shall provide to the department electronic access to Florida criminal justice information which is lawfully available and not exempt from §119.07(1), only for the purpose of protective investigations and emergency placement. As a condition of access to such information, the department shall be required to execute an appropriate user agreement addressing the access, use, dissemination, and destruction of such information and to comply with all applicable laws and rules of the Department of Law Enforcement.

(Laws 1995, ch. 95-418, §99. Amended by Laws 1998, ch. 98-182, §2, effective July 1, 1998; Laws 2000, ch. 2000-349, §32, effective September 1, 2000; Laws 2002, ch. 2002-174, §4, effective April 24, 2002; Laws 2003, ch. 2003-262, §1, effective July 1, 2003.)

§415.105. Consent of victim, withdrawal of victim's consent and interference with victim's consent

(1) Protective services with consent.--If the department determines through its investigation that a vulnerable adult demonstrates a need for protective services or protective supervision, the department shall immediately provide, or arrange for the provision of, protective services or protective supervision, including in-home services, provided that the vulnerable adult consents. A vulnerable adult in need of services as defined in §415.102 shall be referred to the community care for disabled adults program, or to the community care for the elderly program administered by the Department of Elderly Affairs.

(2) Withdrawal of consent.--If the vulnerable adult withdraws consent to the receipt of protective services or protective supervision, the services may not be provided, except pursuant to §415.1051.

(3) Interference with the provision of protective services.--When any person refuses to allow the provision of protective services to a vulnerable adult who has the capacity to consent to services, the department shall petition the court for an order enjoining the person from interfering with the provision of protective services. The petition must allege specific facts sufficient to show that the vulnerable adult is in need of protective services and that the person refuses to allow the provision of such services . If the court finds by clear and convincing evidence that the vulnerable adult is in need of protective services and that the person refuses to allow the provision of such services, the court may issue an order enjoining the person from interfering with the provision of protective services to the vulnerable adult.

(Laws 1973, ch. 73-176, §§1 to 11; Fla. St. 1973, §828.043; Laws 1977, ch. 77-174, §1; Laws 1979, ch. 79-287, §§3, 5; Laws 1979, ch. 79-298, §15; Laws 1980, ch. 80-293, §1; Fla. St. 1981, §827.09(7), (8); Laws 1983, ch. 83-82, §1; Laws 1986, ch. 86-220, §31; Laws 1989, ch. 89-294, §29; Laws 1995, ch. 95-144, §21; Laws 1995, ch. 95-210, §37; Laws 1995, ch. 95- 418, §100. Amended by Laws 1998, ch. 98-182, §3, effective July 1, 1998; Laws 2000, ch. 2000-349, §33, effective September 1, 2000.)

§415.1051. Protective services interventions: lack of consent, notice, hearing, costs

(1) Nonemergency protective services interventions.--If the department has reasonable cause to believe that a vulnerable adult or a

vulnerable adult in need of services is being abused, neglected, or exploited and is in need of protective services but lacks the capacity to consent to protective services, the department shall petition the court for an order authorizing the provision of protective services.

(a) Nonemergency protective services petition.--The petition must state the name, age, and address of the vulnerable adult, allege specific facts sufficient to show that the vulnerable adult is in need of protective services and lacks the capacity to consent to them, and indicate the services needed.

(b) Notice.--Notice of the filing of the petition and a copy of the petition must be given to the vulnerable adult, to that person's spouse, guardian, and legal counsel, and, when known, to the adult children or next of kin of the vulnerable adult. Such notice must be given at least 5 days before the hearing.

(c) Hearing.--

1. The court shall set the case for hearing within 14 days after the filing of the petition. The vulnerable adult and any person given notice of the filing of the petition have the right to be present at the hearing. The department must make reasonable efforts to ensure the presence of the vulnerable adult at the hearing.

2. The vulnerable adult has the right to be represented by legal counsel at the hearing. The court shall appoint legal counsel to represent a vulnerable adult who is without legal representation.

3. The court shall determine whether:

a. Protective services, including in-home services, are necessary.

b. The vulnerable adult lacks the capacity to consent to the provision of such services.

(d) Hearing findings.--If at the hearing the court finds by clear and convincing evidence that the vulnerable adult is in need of protective services and lacks the capacity to consent, the court may issue an order authorizing the provision of protective services. If an order for protective services is issued, it must include a statement of the services to be provided and designate an individual or agency to be responsible for performing or obtaining the essential services on behalf of the vulnerable adult or otherwise consenting to protective services on behalf of the vulnerable adult.

(e) Continued protective services.--

1. No more than 60 days after the date of the order authorizing the provision of protective services, the department shall petition the court to determine whether:

a. Protective services will be continued with the consent of the vulnerable adult pursuant to this subsection;

b. Protective services will be continued for the vulnerable adult who lacks capacity;

c. Protective services will be discontinued; or

d. A petition for guardianship should be filed pursuant to chapter 744.

2. If the court determines that a petition for guardianship should be filed pursuant to chapter 744, the court, for good cause shown, may order continued protective services until it makes a determination regarding capacity.

(f) Costs.--The costs of services ordered under this section must be paid by the perpetrator if the perpetrator is financially able to do so; or by third-party reimbursement, if available. If the vulnerable adult is unable to pay for guardianship, application may be made to the public guardian for public guardianship services, if available.

(2) Emergency protective services intervention.--If the department has reasonable cause to believe that a vulnerable adult is suffering from abuse or neglect that presents a risk of death or serious physical injury to the vulnerable adult and that the vulnerable adult lacks the capacity to consent to emergency protective services, the department may take action under this subsection. If the vulnerable adult has the capacity to consent and refuses consent to emergency protective services, emergency protective services may not be provided.

(a) Emergency entry of premises.--If, upon arrival at the scene of the incident, consent is not obtained for access to the alleged victim for purposes of conducting a protective investigation under this subsection and the department has reason to believe that the situation presents a risk of death or serious physical injury, a representative of the department and a law enforcement officer may forcibly enter the premises. If, after obtaining access to the alleged victim, it is determined through a personal assessment of the situation that no emergency exists and there is no basis for emergency protective services intervention under this subsection, the department shall terminate the emergency entry.

(b) Emergency removal from premises.--If it appears that the vulnerable adult lacks the capacity to consent to emergency protective services and that the vulnerable adult, from the personal observations of the representative of the department and specified medical personnel or law enforcement officers, is likely to incur a risk of death or serious physical injury if such person is not immediately removed from the premises, then the representative of the department shall transport or arrange for the transportation of the vulnerable adult to an appropriate medical or protective services facility in order to provide emergency protective services. Law enforcement personnel have a duty to transport when medical transportation is not available or needed and the vulnerable adult presents a threat of injury to self or others. If the vulnerable adult's caregiver or guardian is present, the protective investigator must seek the caregiver's or guardian's consent pursuant to subsection (4) before the vulnerable adult may be removed from the premises, unless the protective investigator suspects that the vulnerable adult's caregiver or guardian has caused the abuse, neglect, or exploitation. The department shall, within 24 hours after providing or arranging for emergency removal of the vulnerable adult, excluding Saturdays, Sundays, and legal holidays, petition the court for an order authorizing emergency protective services.

(c) Emergency medical treatment.--If, upon admission to a medical facility, it is the opinion of the medical staff that immediate medical treatment is necessary to prevent serious physical injury or death, and that such treatment does not violate a known health care advance directive prepared by the vulnerable adult, the medical facility may proceed with treatment to the vulnerable adult. If a person with legal authority to give consent for the provision of medical treatment to a vulnerable adult has not given or has refused to give such consent, examination and treatment must be limited to reasonable examination of the patient to determine the medical condition of the patient and treatment reasonably necessary to alleviate the emergency medical condition or to stabilize the patient pending court determination of the department's petition authorizing emergency protective services. Any person may seek an expedited judicial intervention under rule 5.900 of the Florida Probate Rules concerning medical treatment procedures.

(d) Emergency protective services petition.--A petition filed under this subsection must state the name, age, and address of the vulnerable adult and allege the facts constituting the emergency protective services intervention and subsequent removal of the vulnerable adult or provision of in-home services, the facts relating to the capacity of the vulnerable adult to consent to services, the efforts of the department to obtain consent, and the services needed or delivered.

(e) Notice.--Notice of the filing of the emergency protective services petition and a copy of the petition must be given to the vulnerable adult, to that person's spouse, to that person's guardian, if any, to legal counsel representing the vulnerable adult, and, when known, to adult children or next of kin of the vulnerable adult. Such notice must be given at least 24 hours before any hearing on the petition for emergency protective services.

(f) Hearing.--When emergency removal has occurred under this subsection, a hearing must be held within 4 days after the filing of the emergency protective services petition, excluding Saturday, Sunday, and legal holidays, to establish reasonable cause for grounds to continue emergency protective services.

1. The court shall determine, by clear and convincing evidence, whether an emergency existed which justified the emergency protective services intervention, whether the vulnerable adult is in need of emergency protective services, whether the vulnerable adult lacks the capacity to consent to emergency protective services, and whether:

a. Emergency protective services will continue with the consent of the vulnerable adult;

b. Emergency protective services will continue without the consent of the vulnerable adult; or

c. Emergency protective services will be discontinued.

2. The vulnerable adult has the right to be represented by legal counsel at the hearing. The court shall appoint legal counsel to represent a vulnerable adult who is without legal representation.

3. The department must make reasonable efforts to ensure the presence of the vulnerable adult at the hearing.

4. If an order to continue emergency protective services is issued, it must state the services to be provided and designate an individual or agency to be responsible for performing or obtaining the essential services, or otherwise consenting to protective services on behalf of the vulnerable adult.

(g) Continued emergency protective services.--

1. Not more than 60 days after the date of the order authorizing the provision of emergency protective services, the department shall petition the court to determine whether:

a. Emergency protective services will be continued with the consent of the vulnerable adult;

b. Emergency protective services will be continued for the vulnerable adult who lacks capacity;

c. Emergency protective services will be discontinued; or

d. A petition should be filed under chapter 744.

2. If it is decided to file a petition under chapter 744, for good cause shown, the court may order continued emergency protective services until a determination is made by the court.

(h) Costs.--The costs of services ordered under this section must be paid by the perpetrator if the perpetrator is financially able to do so, or by third-party reimbursement, if available.

(3) Protective services order.--In ordering any protective services under this section, the court shall adhere to the following limitations:

(a) Only such protective services as are necessary to ameliorate the conditions creating the abuse, neglect, or exploitation may be ordered, and the court shall specifically designate the approved services in the order of the court.

(b) Protective services ordered may not include a change of residence, unless the court specifically finds such action is necessary to ameliorate the conditions creating the abuse, neglect, or exploitation and the court gives specific approval for such action in the order. Placement may be made to such facilities as adult family-care homes, assisted living facilities, or nursing homes, or to other appropriate facilities. Placement may not be made to facilities for the acutely mentally ill, except as provided in chapter 394.

(c) If an order to continue emergency protective services is issued, it must include the designation of an individual or agency to be responsible for performing or obtaining the essential services on behalf of the vulnerable adult or otherwise consenting to protective services on behalf of the vulnerable adult.

(4) Protective services interventions with caregiver or guardian present.--

(a) When a vulnerable adult who lacks the capacity to consent has been identified as the victim, the protective investigator must first request consent from the caregiver or guardian, if present, before providing protective services or protective supervision, unless the protective investigator suspects that the caregiver or guardian has caused the abuse, neglect, or exploitation.

(b) If the caregiver or guardian agrees to engage or provide services designed to prevent further abuse, neglect, or exploitation, the department may provide protective supervision.

(c) If the caregiver or guardian refuses to give consent or later withdraws consent to agreed-upon services, or otherwise fails to provide needed care and supervision, the department may provide emergency protective services as provided in subsection (2). If emergency protective services are so provided, the department must then petition the court for an order to provide emergency protective services under subsection (3).

(5) Interference with court-ordered protective services.--When a court order exists authorizing protective services for a vulnerable adult who lacks capacity to consent and any person interferes with the provision of such court-ordered protective services, the appropriate law enforcement agency shall enforce the order of the court.

(6) Limitations.--This section does not limit in any way the authority of the court or a criminal justice officer, or any other duly appointed official, to intervene in emergency circumstances under existing statutes. This section does not limit the authority of any person to file a petition for guardianship under chapter 744.

(Laws 1995, ch. 95-418, §101; Laws 1997, ch. 97-98, §11. Amended by Laws 2000, ch. 2000-349, §34, effective September 1, 2000; Laws 2006, ch. 2006-131, §2, effective June 9, 2006.)

§415.1052. Interference with investigation or services

(1) If, upon arrival of the protective investigator, any person refuses to allow the department to begin a protective investigation, interferes with the department's ability to conduct such an investigation, or refuses to give access to the vulnerable adult, the appropriate law enforcement agency must be contacted to assist the department in commencing the protective investigation.

(2) When any person refuses to allow the provision of protective services to the vulnerable adult who has the capacity to consent to services, the department shall petition the court for an order enjoining the person from interfering with the provision of protective services. The petition must allege specific facts sufficient to show that the vulnerable adult is in need of protective services and that the person refuses to allow the provision of such services. If the court finds by clear and convincing evidence that the

vulnerable adult is in need of protective services and that the person refuses to allow the provision of such services, the court may issue an order enjoining the person from interfering with the provision of protective services to the vulnerable adult.

(Laws 1995, ch. 95-418, §102. Amended by Laws 2000, ch. 2000-349, §35, effective September 1, 2000.)

§415.1055. Notification to proper administrative authorities

(1) Upon receipt of a report that alleges that an employee or agent of the department, the Agency for Persons with Disabilities, or the Department of Elderly Affairs, acting in an official capacity, has committed an act of abuse, neglect, or exploitation, the department shall notify the state attorney in whose circuit the abuse, neglect, or exploitation occurred. This notification may be oral or written.

(2) If at any time during a protective investigation the department has reasonable cause to believe that a vulnerable adult has been abused, neglected, or exploited by another person, the state attorney having jurisdiction in the county in which the abuse, neglect, or exploitation occurred shall be notified immediately, either orally or in writing.

(3) If at any time during a protective investigation the department has reasonable cause to believe that a vulnerable adult has been abused, neglected, or exploited by another person, the appropriate law enforcement agency shall be immediately notified. Such agency may begin a criminal investigation concurrent with or independent of the protective investigation of the department. This notification may be oral or written.

(4) If at any time during a protective investigation the department has reasonable cause to believe that abuse, neglect, or exploitation of a vulnerable adult has occurred within a facility that receives Medicaid funds, the department shall notify the Medicaid Fraud Control Unit within the Department of Legal Affairs, Office of the Attorney General, in order that it may begin an investigation concurrent with the protective investigation of the department. This notification may be oral or written.

(5) If at any time during a protective investigation the department has reasonable cause to believe that an employee of a facility, as defined in §415.102, is the alleged perpetrator of abuse, neglect, or exploitation of a vulnerable adult, the department shall notify the Agency for Health Care Administration, Division of Health Quality Assurance, in writing.

(6) If at any time during a protective investigation the department has reasonable cause to believe that professional licensure violations have occurred, the department shall notify the Division of Medical Quality Assurance within the Department of Health. This notification must be in writing.

(7) The department shall notify the state attorney having jurisdiction in the county in which the abuse, neglect, or exploitation occurred if evidence indicates that further criminal investigation is warranted. This notification must be in writing.

(8) At the conclusion of a protective investigation at a facility, the department shall notify either the Florida local advocacy council or long-term care ombudsman council of the results of the investigation. This notification must be in writing.

(9) When a report involving a guardian of the person or property, or both, is received, the department shall notify the probate court having jurisdiction over the guardianship, in writing.

(10) When a report has been received and the department has reason to believe that a vulnerable adult resident of a facility licensed by the Agency for Health Care Administration or the Agency for Persons with Disabilities has been the victim of abuse, neglect, or exploitation, the department shall provide a copy of its investigation to the appropriate agency. If the investigation determines that a health professional licensed or certified under the Department of Health may have abused, neglected, or exploited a vulnerable adult, the department shall also provide a copy to the Department of Health.

(Laws 1995, ch. 95-418, §103; Laws 1997, ch. 97-98, §12. Amended by Laws 1998, ch. 98-166, §30, effective July 1, 1998; Laws 1998, ch. 98-182, §4, effective July 1, 1998; Laws 2000, ch. 2000-153, §69, effective July 4, 2000; Laws 2000, ch. 2000-263, §23, effective July 1, 2000; Laws 2000, ch. 2000-349, §36, effective September 1, 2000; Laws 2006, ch. 2006-227, §59, effective July 1, 2006.)

§415.106. Duty of various stage agencies to cooperate with the investigation of abuse

(1) All criminal justice agencies have a duty and responsibility to cooperate fully with the department so as to enable the department to fulfill its responsibilities under §§415.101-415.113. Such duties include, but are not limited to, forced entry, emergency removal, emergency transportation, and the enforcement of court orders obtained under§§415.101-415.113.

(2) To ensure coordination, communication, and cooperation with the investigation of abuse, neglect,

or exploitation of vulnerable adults, the department shall develop and maintain interprogram agreements or operational procedures among appropriate departmental programs and the State Long-Term Care Ombudsman Council, the Florida Statewide Advocacy Council, and other agencies that provide services to vulnerable adults. These agreements or procedures must cover such subjects as the appropriate roles and responsibilities of the department in identifying and responding to reports of abuse, neglect, or exploitation of vulnerable adults; the provision of services; and related coordinated activities.

(3) To the fullest extent possible, the department shall cooperate with and seek cooperation from all appropriate public and private agencies, including health agencies, educational agencies, social service agencies, courts, organizations, or programs providing or concerned with human services related to the prevention, identification, or treatment of abuse, neglect, or exploitation of vulnerable adults.

(Laws 1973, ch. 73-176, §§1 to 11; Fla. St. 1973, §828.043; Laws 1977, ch. 77-174, §1; Laws 1979, ch. 79-287, §§3, 5; Laws 1979, ch. 79-298, §15; Laws 1980, ch. 80-293, §1; Fla. St. 1981, §827.09(9); Laws 1983, ch. 83-82, §1; Laws 1986, ch. 86-220, §32; Laws 1993, ch. 93-177, §27; Laws 1995, ch. 95-418, §104. Amended by Laws 2000, ch. 2000-263, §24, effective July 1, 2000; Laws 2000, ch. 2000-349, §37, effective September 1, 2000.)

§415.107. All reports and records must be confidential

(1) In order to protect the rights of the individual or other persons responsible for the welfare of a vulnerable adult, all records concerning reports of abuse, neglect, or exploitation of the vulnerable adult, including reports made to the central abuse hotline, and all records generated as a result of such reports shall be confidential and exempt from §§119.07(1) and may not be disclosed except as specifically authorized by §§415.101-415.113.

(2) Upon the request of the committee chairperson, access to all records shall be granted to staff of the legislative committees with jurisdiction over issues and services related to vulnerable adults, or over the department. All confidentiality provisions that apply to the Department of Children and Family Services continue to apply to the records made available to legislative staff under this subsection.

(3) Access to all records, excluding the name of the reporter which shall be released only as provided in subsection (6), shall be granted only to the following persons, officials, and agencies:

(a) Employees or agents of the department, the Agency for Persons with Disabilities, the Agency for Health Care Administration, or the Department of Elderly Affairs who are responsible for carrying out protective investigations, ongoing protective services, or licensure or approval of nursing homes, assisted living facilities, adult day care centers, adult family-care homes, home care for the elderly, hospices, residential facilities licensed under chapter 393, or other facilities used for the placement of vulnerable adults.

(b) A criminal justice agency investigating a report of known or suspected abuse, neglect, or exploitation of a vulnerable adult.

(c) The state attorney of the judicial circuit in which the vulnerable adult resides or in which the alleged abuse, neglect, or exploitation occurred.

(d) Any victim, the victim's guardian, caregiver, or legal counsel, and any person who the department has determined might be abusing, neglecting, or exploiting the victim.

(e) A court, by subpoena, upon its finding that access to such records may be necessary for the determination of an issue before the court; however, such access must be limited to inspection in camera, unless the court determines that public disclosure of the information contained in such records is necessary for the resolution of an issue then pending before it.

(f) A grand jury, by subpoena, upon its determination that access to such records is necessary in the conduct of its official business.

(g) Any appropriate official of the Florida advocacy council or long-term care ombudsman council investigating a report of known or suspected abuse, neglect, or exploitation of a vulnerable adult.

(h) Any appropriate official of the department, the Agency for Persons with Disabilities, the Agency for Health Care Administration, or the Department of Elderly Affairs who is responsible for:

1. Administration or supervision of the programs for the prevention, investigation, or treatment of abuse, neglect, or exploitation of vulnerable adults when carrying out an official function; or

2. Taking appropriate administrative action concerning an employee alleged to have perpetrated abuse, neglect, or exploitation of a vulnerable adult in an institution.

(i) Any person engaged in bona fide research or auditing. However, information identifying the subjects of the report must not be made available to the researcher.

(j) Employees or agents of an agency of another state that has jurisdiction comparable to the jurisdiction described in paragraph (a).

(k) The Public Employees Relations Commission for the sole purpose of obtaining evidence for appeals filed pursuant to §447.207. Records may be released only after deletion of all information that specifically identifies persons other than the employee.

(l) Any person in the event of the death of a vulnerable adult determined to be a result of abuse, neglect, or exploitation. Information identifying the person reporting abuse, neglect, or exploitation shall not be released. Any information otherwise made confidential or exempt by law shall not be released pursuant to this paragraph.

(4) The Department of Health, the Department of Business and Professional Regulation, and the Agency for Health Care Administration may have access to a report, excluding the name of the reporter, when considering disciplinary action against a licensee or certified nursing assistant pursuant to allegations of abuse, neglect, or exploitation.

(5) The department may release to any professional person such information as is necessary for the diagnosis and treatment of, and service delivery to, a vulnerable adult or the person perpetrating the abuse, neglect, or exploitation.

(6) The identity of any person reporting abuse, neglect, or exploitation of a vulnerable adult may not be released, without that person's written consent, to any person other than employees of the department responsible for protective services, the central abuse hotline, or the appropriate state attorney or law enforcement agency. This subsection grants protection only for the person who reported the abuse, neglect, or exploitation and protects only the fact that the person is the reporter. This subsection does not prohibit the subpoena of a person reporting the abuse, neglect, or exploitation when deemed necessary by the state attorney or the department to protect a vulnerable adult who is the subject of a report, if the fact that the person made the report is not disclosed.

(7) For the purposes of this section, the term "access" means a visual inspection or copy of the hard-copy record maintained in the district.

(8) Information in the central abuse hotline may not be used for employment screening.

(Laws 1973, ch. 73-176, §§1 to 11; Fla. St. 1973, §828.043; Laws 1977, ch. 77-174, §1; Laws 1979, ch. 79-287, §§3, 5; Laws 1979, ch. 79-298, §15; Laws 1980, ch. 80-293, §1; Fla. St. 1981, §827.09(10); Laws 1983, ch. 83-82, §1; Laws 1986, ch. 86-220, §33; Laws 1987, ch. 87-238, §32; Laws 1988, ch. 88-219, §7; Laws 1988, ch. 88-337, §18; Laws 1989, ch. 89-170, §4; Laws 1989, ch. 89-294, §30; Laws 1990, ch. 90-50, §4; Laws 1990, ch. 90-208, §7; Laws 1990, ch. 90-306, §47; Laws 1991, ch. 91-57, §4; Laws 1991, ch. 91-71, §15; Laws 1992, ch. 92-58, §§43, 47; Laws 1993, ch. 93-39, §31; Laws 1993, ch. 93-214, §15; Laws 1994, ch. 94-218, §57; Laws 1995, ch. 95-210, §38; Laws 1995, ch. 95-418, §106; Laws 1996, ch. 96-406, §267. Amended by Laws 1998, ch. 98-111, §1, effective July 1, 1998; Laws 1998, ch. 98-182, §9, effective July 1, 1998; Laws 1998, ch. 98-255, §2, effective May 28, 1998; Laws 1998, ch. 98-280, §41, effective June 30, 1998; Laws 2000, ch. 2000-153, §70, effective July 4, 2000; Laws 2000, ch. 2000-263, §25, effective July 1, 2000; Laws 2000, ch. 2000-349, §38, effective September 1, 2000; Laws 2006, ch. 2006-131, §3, effective June 9, 2006; Laws 2006, ch. 2006-227, §60, effective July 1, 2006.)

§415.1071. Release of confidential information upon good cause

(1) Any person or organization, including the Department of Children and Family Services, may petition the court for an order making public the records of the Department of Children and Family Services which pertain to investigations of alleged abuse, neglect, or exploitation of a vulnerable adult. The court shall determine whether good cause exists for public access to the records sought or a portion thereof. In making this determination, the court shall balance the best interests of the vulnerable adult who is the focus of the investigation together with the privacy right of other persons identified in the reports against the public interest. The public interest in access to such records is reflected in §119.01(1), and includes the need for citizens to know of and adequately evaluate the actions of the Department of Children and Family Services and the court system in providing vulnerable adults of this state with the protections enumerated in §415.101. However, this subsection does not contravene §415.107, which protects the name of any person reporting the abuse, neglect, or exploitation of a vulnerable adult.

(2) In cases involving serious bodily injury to a vulnerable adult, the Department of Children and Family Services may petition the court for an order for the immediate public release of records of the department which pertain to the protective investigation. The petition must be personally served upon the vulnerable adult, the vulnerable adult's legal guardian, if any, and any person named as an alleged perpetrator in the report of abuse, neglect, or exploitation. The court must determine whether good

cause exists for the public release of the records sought no later than 24 hours, excluding Saturdays, Sundays, and legal holidays, after the date the department filed the petition with the court. If the court does not grant or deny the petition within the 24-hour time period, the department may release to the public summary information including:

(a) A confirmation that an investigation has been conducted concerning the alleged victim.

(b) The dates and brief description of procedural activities undertaken during the department's investigation.

(c) The date of each judicial proceeding, a summary of each participant's recommendations made at the judicial proceeding, and the ruling of the court.

The summary information shall not include the name of, or other identifying information with respect to, any person identified in any investigation. In making a determination to release confidential information, the court shall balance the best interests of the vulnerable adult who is the focus of the investigation together with the privacy rights of other persons identified in the reports against the public interest for access to public records. However, this subsection does not contravene §415.107, which protects the name of any person reporting abuse, neglect, or exploitation of a vulnerable adult.

(3) When the court determines that good cause for public access exists, the court shall direct that the department redact the name of and other identifying information with respect to any person identified in any protective investigation report until such time as the court finds that there is probable cause to believe that the person identified committed an act of alleged abuse, neglect, or exploitation.

(Laws 2004, ch. 2004-335, §18, effective October 1, 2004.)

§415.1099. Certain fees must not be charged

In all proceedings under §§415.101-415.113, court fees must not be charged to the department; to any party to a petition; to any legal custodian of records, documents, or persons; or to any adult named in a summons. In a proceeding under §§415.101-415.113, witness fees are not allowed to the department; to any party to a petition; to any legal custodian of records, documents, or persons; or to any adult named in a summons.

(Laws 1995, ch. 95-418, §108.)

§415.1102. Multidisciplinary adult protection teams

(1) Subject to an appropriation, the department may develop, maintain, and coordinate the services of one or more multidisciplinary adult protection teams in each of the districts of the department. As used in this section, the term "multidisciplinary adult protection team" means a team of two or more persons who are trained in the prevention, identification, and treatment of abuse of elderly persons, as defined in §430.602, or of dependent persons and who are qualified to provide a broad range of services related to abuse of elderly or dependent persons.

(2) Such teams may be composed of, but need not be limited to:

(a) Psychiatrists, psychologists, or other trained counseling personnel;

(b) Police officers or other law enforcement officers;

(c) Medical personnel who have sufficient training to provide health services;

(d) Social workers who have experience or training in preventing the abuse of elderly or dependent persons; and

(e) Public guardians as described in part IX of chapter 744.

(3) The department shall utilize and convene the teams to supplement the protective services activities of the protective services program of the department.

(4) This section does not prevent a person from reporting under §415.1034 all suspected or known cases of abuse, neglect, or exploitation of a vulnerable adult. The role of the teams is to support activities of the protective services program and to provide services deemed by the teams to be necessary and appropriate to abused, neglected, and exploited vulnerable adults upon referral. Services must be provided with the consent of the vulnerable adult or that person's guardian, or through court order.

(5) If an adult protection team is providing certain services to abused, neglected, or exploited vulnerable adults, other offices and units of the department shall avoid duplicating those services.

(Laws 1989, ch. 89-294, §32; Laws 1990, ch. 90-306, §48; Laws 1995, ch. 95-418, §109. Amended by Laws 1998, ch. 98-182, §6, effective July 1, 1998; Laws 2000, ch. 2000-153, §71, effective July 4, 2000; Laws 2000, ch. 2000-349, §39, effective September 1, 2000; Laws 2003, ch. 2003-262, §2, effective July 1, 2003.)

§415.1105. Department shall develop training programs

(1) The department shall develop rules governing preservice and inservice training for adult protective investigation staff and, within available resources, shall provide appropriate preservice and inservice training to such staff.

(2) Within available resources, the department shall cooperate with other appropriate agencies in developing and providing preservice and inservice training programs for those persons specified in §415.1034(1)(a).

(Laws 1995, ch. 95-418, §110.)

§415.111. Criminal penalties for failure to report abuse

(1) A person who knowingly and willfully fails to report a case of known or suspected abuse, neglect, or exploitation of a vulnerable adult, or who knowingly and willfully prevents another person from doing so, commits a misdemeanor of the second degree, punishable as provided in §775.082 or §775.083.

(2) A person who knowingly and willfully makes public or discloses any confidential information contained in the central abuse hotline, or in other computer systems, or in the records of any case of abuse, neglect, or exploitation of a vulnerable adult, except as provided in §§415.101-415.113, commits a misdemeanor of the second degree, punishable as provided in §775.082 or § 775.083.

(3) A person who has custody of records and documents the confidentiality of which is abrogated under §415.1045(3) and who refuses to grant access to such records commits a misdemeanor of the second degree, punishable as provided in §775.082 or § 775.083.

(4) If the department or its authorized agent has determined after its investigation that a report is false, the department shall, with the consent of the alleged perpetrator, refer the reports to the local law enforcement agency having jurisdiction for an investigation to determine whether sufficient evidence exists to refer the case for prosecution for filing a false report as defined in §415.102. During the pendency of the investigation by the local law enforcement agency, the department must notify the local law enforcement agency of, and the local law enforcement agency must respond to, all subsequent reports concerning the same vulnerable adult in accordance with §415.104 or §415.1045. If the law enforcement agency believes that there are indicators of abuse, neglect, or exploitation, it must immediately notify the department, which must assure the safety of the vulnerable adult. If the law enforcement agency finds sufficient evidence for prosecution for filing a false report, it must refer the case to the appropriate state attorney for prosecution.

(5) A person who knowingly and willfully makes a false report of abuse, neglect, or exploitation of a vulnerable adult, or a person who advises another to make a false report, commits a felony of the third degree, punishable as provided in §775.082 or §775.083.

(a) The department shall establish procedures for determining whether a false report of abuse, neglect, or exploitation of a vulnerable adult has been made and for submitting all identifying information relating to such a false report to the local law enforcement agency as provided in this subsection and shall report annually to the Legislature the number of reports referred.

(b) Anyone making a report who is acting in good faith is immune from any liability under this subsection.

(Laws 1973, ch. 73-176, §§1 to 11; Fla. St. 1973, §828.043; Laws 1977, ch. 77-174, §1; Laws 1979, ch. 79-287, §§3, 5; Laws 1979, ch. 79-298, §15; Laws 1980, ch. 80-293, §1; Fla. St. 1981, §827.09(15)(a), (b); Laws 1983, ch. 83- 82, §1; Laws 1986, ch. 86-220, §36; Laws 1988, ch. 88-337, §19; Laws 1989, ch. 89-322, §1; Laws 1990, ch. 90-306, §49; Laws 1991, ch. 91-57, §5; Laws 1991, ch. 91-71, §16; Laws 1991, ch. 91-224, §250; Laws 1991, ch. 91-258, §1; Laws 1995, ch. 95-140, §4; Laws 1995, ch. 95-158, §20; Laws 1995, ch. 95-418, §111; Laws 1996, ch. 96-293, §7. Amended by Laws 1998, ch. 98-111, §2, effective July 1, 1998; Laws 1998, ch. 98-182, §10, effective July 1, 1998; Laws 2000, ch. 2000-349, §40, effective September 1, 2000; Laws 2002, ch. 2002-70, §4, effective July 1, 2002.)

§415.1111. Private causes of action against perpetrators

A vulnerable adult who has been abused, neglected, or exploited as specified in this chapter has a cause of action against any perpetrator and may recover actual and punitive damages for such abuse, neglect, or exploitation. The action may be brought by the vulnerable adult, or that person's guardian, by a person or organization acting on behalf of the vulnerable adult with the consent of that person or that person's guardian, or by the personal representative of the estate of a deceased victim without regard to whether the cause of death resulted from the abuse, neglect, or exploitation. The action may be brought in any court of competent jurisdiction to enforce such action and to recover actual and punitive damages for any deprivation of or infringement on the rights of a vulnerable adult. A party who prevails in any such action may be entitled to recover reasonable attorney's fees, costs of the action, and damages. The remedies provided in this section are in addition to and cumulative with other legal and administrative remedies available to a vulnerable adult. Notwithstanding the foregoing, any civil action for damages against any licensee or entity who establishes, controls, conducts, manages, or operates a facility licensed under part II of chapter 400 relating to its operation of the licensed facility shall be brought pursuant to §400.023, or against any licensee or entity who establishes, controls, conducts, manages, or operates a facility licensed under part I of chapter 429 relating to its operation of the licensed facility shall be brought pursuant to §429.29. Such licensee or entity shall not be vicariously liable for the acts or omissions of its employees or agents or any other third party in an action brought under this section.

(Laws 1995, ch. 95-418, §112; Laws 1996, ch. 96-418, §23. Amended by Laws 2000, ch. 2000-349, §41, effective September 1, 2000; Laws 2001, ch. 2001-45, §12, effective May 15, 2001; Laws 2006, ch. 2006-197, §86, effective July 1, 2006.)

§415.1113. Administrative fines for false reports

(1) In addition to any other penalty authorized by this section, chapter 120, or other law, the department may impose a fine, not to exceed $10,000 for each violation, upon a person who knowingly and willfully makes a false report of abuse, neglect, or exploitation of a vulnerable adult, or a person who counsels another to make a false report.

(2) If the department alleges that a person has knowingly and willfully filed a false report with the central abuse hotline, the department must file a notice of intent that alleges the name, age, and address of the individual; the facts constituting the allegation that the individual made a false report; and the administrative fine that the department proposes to impose on the person. Each time that a false report is made constitutes a separate violation.

(3) The notice of intent to impose the administrative fine must be served by certified mail, return receipt requested, upon the person alleged to have filed the false report and upon the person's legal counsel, if any.

(4) Any person alleged to have filed the false report is entitled to an administrative hearing under chapter 120 before the imposition of the fine becomes final. The person must request an administrative hearing within 60 days after receipt of the notice of intent by filing a request with the department. Failure to request an administrative hearing within 60 days after receipt of the notice of intent constitutes a waiver of the right to a hearing, making the administrative fine final.

(5) At the hearing, the department must prove by clear and convincing evidence that the person knowingly and willfully filed a false report with the central abuse hotline. The person has the right to be represented by legal counsel at the hearing.

(6) In determining the amount of fine to be imposed, if any, the following factors must be considered:

(a) The gravity of the violation, including the probability that serious physical or emotional harm to any person will result or has resulted, the severity of the actual or potential harm, and the nature of the false allegation.

(b) Actions taken by the false reporter to retract the false report as an element of mitigation, or, in contrast, to encourage an investigation on the basis of false information.

(c) Any previous false reports filed by the same individual.

(7) A decision by the department, following the administrative hearing, to impose an administrative fine for filing a false report constitutes final agency action within the meaning of chapter 120. Notice of the imposition of the administrative fine must be served upon the person and upon the person's legal counsel, by certified mail, return receipt requested, and must state that the person may seek judicial review of the administrative fine under §120.68.

(8) All amounts collected under this section must be deposited into the Operations and Maintenance Trust Fund within the Adult Services Program of the department.

(9) A person who is determined to have filed a false report of abuse or neglect is not entitled to confidentiality. Subsequent to the conclusion of all administrative or other judicial proceedings concerning the filing of a false report, the name of the false reporter and the nature of the false report must be made public, pursuant to §119.01(1). Such information is admissible in any civil or criminal proceeding.

(10) Any person who makes a report and acts in good faith is immune from any liability under this section and continues to be entitled to have the confidentiality of his or her identity maintained.

(Laws 1995, ch. 95-418, §113; Laws 1997, ch. 97-103, §68. Amended by Laws 1998, ch. 98-111, §3, effective July 1, 1998; Laws 1998, ch. 98-182, §11, effective July 1, 1998; Laws 1999, ch. 99-8, §201,

effective June 29, 1999; Laws 2000, ch. 2000-349, §42, effective September 1, 2000.)

§415.1115. Speedy trial provisions

In a civil action in which a person over the age of 65 is a party, such party may move the court to advance the trial on the docket. The presiding judge, after consideration of the age and health of the party, may advance the trial on the docket. The motion may be filed and served with the initial complaint or at any time thereafter.

(Laws 1991, ch. 91-251, §1; Fla. St. 1993, §415.114; Laws 1995, ch. 95- 418, §115.)

§415.112. Promulgation of rules for implementation of Act

The department shall promulgate rules for the implementation of §§415.101-415.113.

(Laws 1973, ch. 73-176, §§1 to 11; Fla. St. 1973, §828.043; Laws 1977, ch. 77-174, §1; Laws 1979, ch. 79-287, §§3, 5; Laws 1979, ch. 79-298, §15; Laws 1980, ch. 80-293, §1; Fla. St. 1981, §827.09(14); Laws 1983, ch. 83-82, §1; Laws 1986, ch. 86-220, §37.)

§415.113. Exclusion for treatment by spiritual means

Nothing in §§415.101-415.112 shall be construed to mean a person is abused, neglected, or in need of emergency or protective services for the sole reason that the person relies upon and is, therefore, being furnished treatment by spiritual means through prayer alone in accordance with the tenets and practices of a well-recognized church or religious denomination or organization; nor shall anything in such sections be construed to authorize, permit, or require any medical care or treatment in contravention of the stated or implied objection of such person. Such construction does not:

(1) Eliminate the requirement that such a case be reported to the department;

(2) Prevent the department from investigating such a case; or

(3) Preclude a court from ordering, when the health of the individual requires it, the provision of medical services by a licensed physician or treatment by a duly accredited practitioner who relies solely on spiritual means for healing in accordance with the tenets and practices of a well-recognized church or religious denomination or organization.

(Laws 1985, ch. 85-143, §1; Laws 1995, ch. 95-418, §114. Amended by Laws 2000, ch. 2000-349, §43, effective September 1, 2000.)

II. Powers of Attorney

Estate planning traditionally focused on the disposition of wealth *after death*. However, the increase in life expectancy and the growing population of elderly persons prompted a need for legislatures to address planning for mental and/or physical disability. Several estate planning tools (such as durable powers of attorney, designations of health care agents, and health care advance directives) exist for such purposes.

A power of attorney is an agency relationship that enables one person to act in the place of another. The person who grants authority is termed the "principal," whereas the person who is given the authority to act is termed the "agent" or "attorney-in-fact." (The term "attorney-in-fact" merely signifies an agent, not a lawyer.)

An agency relationship, in some ways, is similar to a trust. For example, an agent is a fiduciary, like a trustee. However, whereas a trustee has powers that are implied by common law or statute, agency law "only sparingly implies powers and strictly construes express powers." William M. McGovern, Jr., Trusts, Custodianships, and Durable Powers of Attorney, 27 Real Prop., Prob. & Trust J. 33 (1992) (cited in McGovern & Kurtz, *supra*, §9.2 at 351).

According to the traditional rule, an agent's powers terminate at the death or incapacity of the principal. Therefore, an agency relationship cannot be used for health care planning when the principal became incapacitated. A "durable" power of attorney is required that will not be affected by the disability of the principal. The principal must execute the durable power while he or she is legally competent. Note that a durable power survives disability but not death; it terminates at the death of the principal (although acts of an agent who does not have knowledge of the principal's death may be binding). McGovern, *supra* (citing UPC §5-504).

To address the need for planning for health care, disability, and death, the National Conference of Commissioners on Uniform State Laws (NCCUSL) promulgated a series of uniform acts. NCCUSL approved the Uniform Durable Power of Attorney Act in 1979 and revised it in 1987. That Act subsequently was included in revisions of the Uniform Probate Code (Article V, Part V). Most states (but not Florida) have adopted this legislation although with some variations. See Durable Power of Attorney, Legislative Factsheet (listing 43 states and the District of Columbia and Virgin Islands),

available at www.nccusl.org/Update/uniformacts_factsheets/uniformacts-fs-udpaa.asp (last visited April 26, 2007).

In 1982, NCCUSL promulgated the Model Health-Care Consent Act, which addressed broad issues of consent to treatment but not issues involving the dying patient. That legislation enables a person to transfer health care decisionmaking to a health care representative. To address the specific issues facing dying patients, the Uniform Law Commissioners approved the Uniform Rights of the Terminally Ill Act in 1985 (amended in 1989).

In 1988, NCCUSL adopted the Uniform Statutory Power of Attorney Act (USPAA) to provide a standardized form to facilitate the creation of a power of attorney. The Uniform Law Commissioners approved USPAA in recognition of the problem that agents bearing power-of-attorney documents often have their powers refused or disregarded in transactions on a principal's behalf. This difficulty frequently necessitates the need for an agent to seek judicial enforcement of his or her legitimately exercised powers. USPAA includes a comprehensive list of powers for an agent, enabling a principal to choose (by a check-off list) the desired specific or general powers. Fewer than a dozen states adopted this legislation. Although health care decisionmaking issues are not expressly included among USPAA powers, Section 2 of the Act and the form itself permit the power of attorney to remain in effect after the disability of the principal if that is permitted by other laws of the state.

In 1993, NCCUSL approved the Uniform Health-Care Decisions Act (UHCDA) which assists persons and the medical profession to designate a health care agent to choose a particular course of medical treatment. It addresses the general problem of health care decisionmaking and the specific issue of the withdrawal of life support. The legislation was designed to promote uniformity among the various state statutes by replacing existing living will, power of attorney for health care, and family health care consent statutes (Florida has not adopted this Act).

In July 2006, NCCUSL approved a new Uniform Power of Attorney Act that supersedes the Uniform Statutory Form Power of Attorney Act of 1988. The new Act stemmed from a recognition of the need for legislation prompted by NCCUSL's review of different states' power of attorney legislation. That survey found that, despite the earlier Uniform Durable Power of Attorney Act, most states had enacted a variety of provisions on the following topics: 1) the authority of multiple agents; 2) the authority of a later-appointed fiduciary or guardian; 3) the impact of dissolution or annulment of the principal's marriage to the agent; 4) activation of contingent powers; 5) the authority to make gifts; and 6) standards for agent conduct and liability. In a renewed effort to achieve uniformity,

> [t]he Act codifies both state legislative trends and collective best practices, and strikes a balance between the need for flexibility and acceptance of an agent's authority and the need to prevent and redress financial abuse."

Unif. Power of Attorney Act, Prefatory Note., available at www.law.upenn.edu/bll/ulc/dpoaa/2006final.htm (last visited April 26, 2007).

The federal government also has enacted legislation addressing patients' health care decisionmaking. In 1990, Congress enacted the Patient Self-Determination Act (PSDA), 42 U.S.C. §1395cc (f)(2000). The PSDA makes the provision of information about advance directives to patients in health care facilities a condition for the receipt of federal Medicare funds to health care facilities. That is, all health care providers who contract with Medicare or Medicaid must inform patients of their rights, under state law, regarding health care decisionmaking, such as the right to accept or reject medical treatment as well as the right to execute advance health care directives.

Florida law permits durable powers of attorney (Fla. Stat. §§709.01 et seq), designations of health care surrogates (Fla. Stat. §§765.201 et seq) and health care advance directives (such as living wills) (Fla. Stat. §§765.301 et seq).

According to Florida law, the durable power of attorney survives the subsequent incapacity of the principal except as otherwise provided in the Act. Florida Statutes §709.08 explains methods of creation and revocation of a durable power of attorney; eligibility to serve as attorney-in-fact; the effect of a delegation, revocation or filing of a petition to determine incapacity; the property subject to a durable power of attorney; powers of the attorney-in-fact and limitations thereon; reliance by third parties; liability of physicians who make determinations of incapacity; and the authority of the nominee when the principal is dead.

Note that an attorney in fact can "make all health care decisions on behalf of the principal, including, but not limited to, those set forth in chapter 765." (Fla. Stat. §709.08 (7), 6(c)). Note also that an attorney-in-fact cannot execute or

revoke any will or codicil on behalf of the principal; cannot create, amend, or revoke any disposition effective at the principal's death; and cannot transfer assets to an existing trust created by the principal—unless the power of attorney document expressly confers that authority (Fla. Stat. §709.08 (7), 4, 5).

A primary advantage of a durable power of attorney is to permit an individual to designate someone to help manage his or her affairs in the event of incapacity, rather than to have a court do so via adversarial guardianship proceedings. See, e.g., Smith v. Lynch, 821 So. 2d 1197 (Fla. Dist. Ct. App. 2002) (holding that appointment of guardian was not warranted because ward, now found to be incompetent, had previously executed a durable power of attorney).

Formerly, only a family member could be designated in a durable power of attorney as an attorney-in-fact. However, in 1990, the Florida legislature revised Florida Statutes §709.08(2) to permit any adult as an attorney-in-fact or even a financial institution with trust powers or a non-profit corporation (as defined).

Although the durable power of attorney may be used for some medical decisions (following the Florida legislature's expansion in 1990 of the powers exercisable by an attorney-in-fact), the use of a health care advance directive may be preferable.

> **First, [the latter] is a more specific document. Second, clients may wish to avoid mingling the separate areas of property management and health care, or have different individuals perform different tasks.**

Ryland F. Mahathey, Basic Estate Planning in Florida, Planning for Disability (chapter 3) §3.23 (2006). Health Care Advance Directives are set forth in Section III *infra*.

§709.01. Power of attorney; nominee's authority following death of principal

If any agent, constituted by power of attorney or other authority, shall do any act for his or her principal which would be lawful if such principal were living, the same shall be valid and binding on the estate of said principal, although he or she may have died before such act was done; provided, the party treating with such agent dealt bona fide, not knowing at the time of the doing of such act that such principal was dead. An affidavit, executed by the attorney in fact or agent setting forth that he or she has not or had not, at the time of doing any act pursuant to the power of attorney, received actual knowledge or actual notice of the death of the principal, or notice of any facts indicating his or her death, shall in the absence of fraud be conclusive proof of the absence of knowledge or notice by the agent of the death of the principal at such time. If the exercise of the power requires the execution and delivery of any instrument which is recordable under the laws of this state, such affidavit shall likewise be recordable. No report or listing, either official or otherwise, of "missing" or "missing in action" regarding any person in connection with any activity pertaining to or connected with the prosecution of any hostilities in which the United States is then engaged, as such words "missing" or "missing in action" are used in military parlance, shall constitute or be interpreted as constituting actual knowledge or actual notice of the death of such principal, or notice of any facts indicating the death of such person, or shall operate to revoke the agency.

(Laws 1945, ch. 23011, §1; Laws 1967, ch. 67-453, §1. Amended by Laws 1997, ch. 97-102, §793, effective July 1, 1997.)

§709.08. Durable power of attorney: methods of creation, eligibility of persons to serve as attorney in fact, powers of attorney in fact, reliance, notice, liability

(1) Creation of durable power of attorney.--A durable power of attorney is a written power of attorney by which a principal designates another as the principal's attorney in fact. The durable power of attorney must be in writing, must be executed with the same formalities required for the conveyance of real property by Florida law, and must contain the words: "This durable power of attorney is not affected by subsequent incapacity of the principal except as provided in §709.08, Florida Statutes"; or similar words that show the principal's intent that the authority conferred is exercisable notwithstanding the principal's subsequent incapacity, except as otherwise provided by this section. The durable power of attorney is exercisable as of the date of execution; however, if the durable power of attorney is conditioned upon the principal's lack of capacity to manage property as defined in §744.102(12)(a), the durable power of attorney is exercisable upon the delivery of affidavits in paragraphs (4)(c) and (d) to the third party.

(2) Who may serve as attorney in fact.--The attorney in fact must be a natural person who is 18 years of age or older and is of sound mind, or a financial institution, as defined in chapter 655, with

trust powers, having a place of business in this state and authorized to conduct trust business in this state. A not-for-profit corporation, organized for charitable or religious purposes in this state, which has qualified as a court-appointed guardian prior to January 1, 1996, and which is a tax-exempt organization under 26 U.S.C. §501(c)(3), may also act as an attorney in fact. Notwithstanding any contrary clause in the written power of attorney, no assets of the principal may be used for the benefit of the corporate attorney in fact, or its officers or directors.

(3) Notwithstanding the provisions of this section, a proceeding to determine incapacity must not affect any authority of the attorney in fact to make health care decisions for the principal, including, but not limited to, those defined in chapter 765, unless otherwise ordered by the court. If the principal has executed a health care advance directive designating a health care surrogate pursuant to chapter 765, the terms of the directive will control if the two documents are in conflict unless the durable power of attorney is later executed and expressly states otherwise.

(4) Protection without notice; good faith acts; affidavits.--

(a) Any third party may rely upon the authority granted in a durable power of attorney that is not conditioned on the principal's lack of capacity to manage property until the third party has received notice as provided in subsection (5). A third party may, but need not, require the attorney in fact to execute an affidavit pursuant to paragraph (c).

(b) Any third party may rely upon the authority granted in a durable power of attorney that is conditioned on the principal's lack of capacity to manage property as defined in §744.102(12)(a) only after receiving the affidavits provided in paragraphs (c) and (d), and such reliance shall end when the third party has received notice as provided in subsection (5).

(c) An affidavit executed by the attorney in fact must state where the principal is domiciled, that the principal is not deceased, and that there has been no revocation, partial or complete termination by adjudication of incapacity or by the occurrence of an event referenced in the durable power of attorney, or suspension by initiation of proceedings to determine incapacity or to appoint a guardian of the durable power of attorney at the time the power of attorney is exercised. A written affidavit executed by the attorney in fact under this paragraph may, but need not, be in the following form:

STATE OF __________

COUNTY OF __________

Before me, the undersigned authority, personally appeared (attorney in fact) ("Affiant"), who swore or affirmed that:

1. Affiant is the attorney in fact named in the Durable Power of Attorney executed by (principal) ("Principal") on (date) .

2. This Durable Power of Attorney is currently exercisable by Affiant. The principal is domiciled in (insert name of state, territory, or foreign country) .

3. To the best of the Affiant's knowledge after diligent search and inquiry:

a. The Principal is not deceased; and

b. There has been no revocation, partial or complete termination by adjudication of incapacity or by the occurrence of an event referenced in the durable power of attorney, or suspension by initiation of proceedings to determine incapacity or to appoint a guardian.

4. Affiant agrees not to exercise any powers granted by the Durable Power of Attorney if Affiant attains knowledge that it has been revoked, partially or completely terminated, suspended, or is no longer valid because of the death or adjudication of incapacity of the Principal.

____

(Affiant)

Sworn to (or affirmed) and subscribed before me this ____ day of (month), (year) , by (name of person making statement)

(Signature of Notary Public-State of Florida)

(Print, Type, or Stamp Commissioned Name of Notary Public)

Personally Known OR Produced Identification (Type of Identification Produced)

(d) A determination that a principal lacks the capacity to manage property as defined in §744.102(12)(a) must be made and evidenced by the affidavit of a physician licensed to practice medicine pursuant to chapters 458 and 459 as of the date of the affidavit. A judicial determination that the principal lacks the capacity to manage property pursuant to chapter 744 is not required prior to the determination by the physician and the execution of the affidavit. For purposes of this section, the physician executing the affidavit must be the primary physician who has responsibility for the treatment and care of the principal. The affidavit executed by a physician must state where the physician is licensed to practice medicine, that the physician is the primary physician who has responsibility for the treatment and care of the principal, and that the physician believes that the principal lacks the capacity to manage property as defined in §744.102(12)(a). The affidavit may, but need not, be in the following form:

STATE OF__________

COUNTY OF__________

Before me, the undersigned authority, personally appeared (name of physician) , Affiant, who swore or affirmed that:

1. Affiant is a physician licensed to practice medicine in (name of state, territory, or foreign country) .

2. Affiant is the primary physician who has responsibility for the treatment and care of (principal's name) .

3. To the best of Affiant's knowledge after reasonable inquiry, Affiant believes that the principal lacks the capacity to manage property, including taking those actions necessary to obtain, administer, and dispose of real and personal property, intangible property, business property, benefits, and income.

____

(Affiant)

Sworn to (or affirmed) and subscribed before me this ___ day of (month), (year), by (name of person making statement)

(Signature of Notary Public-State of Florida)

(Print, Type, or Stamp Commissioned Name of Notary Public)

Personally Known OR Produced Identification

(Type of Identification Produced)

(e) A physician who makes a determination of incapacity to manage property under paragraph (d) is not subject to criminal prosecution or civil liability and is not considered to have engaged in unprofessional conduct as a result of making such determination, unless it is shown by a preponderance of the evidence that the physician making the determination did not comply in good faith with the provisions of this section.

(f) A third party may not rely on the authority granted in a durable power of attorney conditioned on the principal's lack of capacity to manage property as defined in §744.102(12)(a) when any affidavit presented has been executed more than 6 months prior to the first presentation of the durable power of attorney to the third party.

(g) Third parties who act in reliance upon the authority granted to the attorney in fact under the durable power of attorney and in accordance with the instructions of the attorney in fact must be held harmless by the principal from any loss suffered or liability incurred as a result of actions taken prior to receipt of written notice pursuant to subsection (5). A person who acts in good faith upon any representation, direction, decision, or act of the attorney in fact is not liable to the principal or the principal's estate, beneficiaries, or joint owners for those acts.

(h) A durable power of attorney may provide that the attorney in fact is not liable for any acts or decisions made by the attorney in fact in good faith and under the terms of the durable power of attorney.

(5) Notice.--

(a) A notice, including, but not limited to, a notice of revocation, notice of partial or complete termination by adjudication of incapacity or by the occurrence of an event referenced in the durable power of attorney, notice of death of the principal, notice of suspension by initiation of proceedings to determine incapacity or to appoint a guardian, or other notice, is not effective until written notice is served upon the attorney in fact or any third persons relying upon a durable power of attorney.

(b) Notice must be in writing and served on the person or entity to be bound by the notice. Service may be by any form of mail that requires a signed receipt or by personal delivery as provided for service of process. Service is complete when received by interested persons or entities specified in this section and in chapter 48, where applicable. In the case of a financial institution as defined in chapter 655, notice, when not mailed, must be served during regular business hours upon an officer or manager of the financial institution at the financial institution's principal place of business in Florida and its office where the power of attorney or account was presented, handled, or administered. Notice by mail to a financial institution must be mailed to the financial institution's principal place of business in this state and its office where the power of attorney or account was presented, handled, or administered. Except for service of court orders, a third party served with notice must be given 14 calendar days after service to act upon that notice. In the case of a financial institution, notice must be served before the occurrence of any of the events described in §674.303.

(6) Property subject to durable power of attorney.--Unless otherwise stated in the durable power of attorney, the durable power of attorney applies to any interest in property owned by the principal, including, without limitation, the principal's interest in all real property, including homestead real property; all personal property, tangible or intangible; all property held in any type of joint tenancy, including a tenancy in common, joint tenancy with right of survivorship, or a tenancy by the entirety; all property over which the principal holds a general, limited, or special power of appointment; choses in action; and all other contractual or statutory rights or elections, including, but not limited to, any rights or elections in any probate or similar proceeding to which the principal is or may become entitled.

(7) Powers of the attorney in fact and limitations.--

(a) Except as otherwise limited by this section, by other applicable law, or by the durable power of attorney, the attorney in fact has full authority to perform, without prior court approval, every act authorized and specifically enumerated in the durable power of attorney. Such authorization may include, except as otherwise limited in this section:

1. The authority to execute stock powers or similar documents on behalf of the principal and delegate to a transfer agent or similar person the authority to register any stocks, bonds, or other securities either into or out of the principal's or nominee's name.

2. The authority to convey or mortgage homestead property. If the principal is married, the attorney in fact may not mortgage or convey homestead property without joinder of the spouse of the principal or the spouse's legal guardian. Joinder by a spouse may be accomplished by the exercise of authority in a durable power of attorney executed by the joining spouse, and either spouse may appoint the other as his or her attorney in fact.

(b) Notwithstanding the provisions of this section, an attorney in fact may not:

1. Perform duties under a contract that requires the exercise of personal services of the principal;

2. Make any affidavit as to the personal knowledge of the principal;

3. Vote in any public election on behalf of the principal;

4. Execute or revoke any will or codicil for the principal;

5. Create, amend, modify, or revoke any document or other disposition effective at the principal's death or transfer assets to an existing trust created by the principal unless expressly authorized by the power of attorney; or

6. Exercise powers and authority granted to the principal as trustee or as court-appointed fiduciary.

(c) If such authority is specifically granted in the durable power of attorney, the attorney in fact may make all health care decisions on behalf of the principal, including, but not limited to, those set forth in chapter 765.

(8) Standard of care.--Except as otherwise provided in paragraph (4)(e), an attorney in fact is a fiduciary who must observe the standards of care applicable to trustees as described in §736.0901. The attorney in fact is not liable to third parties for any act pursuant to the durable power of attorney if the act was authorized at the time. If the exercise of the power is improper, the attorney in fact is liable to interested persons as described in §731.201 for damage or loss resulting from a breach of fiduciary duty by the attorney in fact to the same extent as the trustee of an express trust.

(9) Multiple attorneys in fact; when joint action required.--Unless the durable power of attorney provides otherwise:

(a) If a durable power of attorney is vested jointly in two attorneys in fact by the same instrument, concurrence of both is required on all acts in the exercise of the power.

(b) If a durable power of attorney is vested jointly in three or more attorneys in fact by the same instrument, concurrence of a majority is required in all acts in the exercise of the power.

(c) An attorney in fact who has not concurred in the exercise of authority is not liable to the principal or any other person for the consequences of the exercise. A dissenting attorney in fact is not liable for the consequences of an act in which the attorney in fact joins at the direction of the majority of the joint attorneys in fact if the attorney in fact expresses such dissent in writing to any of the other joint attorneys in fact at or before the time of the joinder.

(d) If the attorney in fact has accepted appointment either expressly in writing or by acting under the power, this section does not excuse the attorney in fact from liability for failure either to participate in the administration of assets subject to the power or for failure to attempt to prevent a breach of fiduciary obligations thereunder.

(10) Powers of remaining attorney in fact.--Unless the durable power of attorney provides otherwise, all authority vested in multiple attorneys in fact may be exercised by the one or more that remain after the death, resignation, or incapacity of one or more of the multiple attorneys in fact.

(11) Damages and costs.--In any judicial action under this section, including, but not limited to, the unreasonable refusal of a third party to allow an attorney in fact to act pursuant to the power, and challenges to the proper exercise of authority by the attorney in fact, the prevailing party is entitled to damages and costs, including reasonable attorney's fees.

(12) Application.--This section applies to only those durable powers of attorney executed on or after October 1, 1995.

(13) Partial invalidity.--If any provision of this section or its application to any person or circumstance is held invalid, the invalidity does not affect other provisions or applications of this section which can be given effect without the invalid provision or application and to this end the provisions of this section are severable.

(Laws 1974, ch. 74-245, §1; Laws 1977, ch. 77-272, §1; Laws 1983, ch. 83-139, §1. Amended by Laws 1988, ch. 88-36, §1, effective May 12, 1988; Laws 1990, ch. 90-232, §24, effective October 1, 1990; Laws 1992, ch. 92-71, §1, effective October 1, 1992; Laws 1992, ch. 92-199, §8, effective April 10, 1992; Laws 1995, ch. 95- 401, §17, effective October 1, 1995; Laws 1997, ch. 97-102, §796, effective July 1, 1997; Laws 1997, ch. 97-240, §2, effective May 30, 1997; Laws 1999, ch. 99-6, §29, effective June 29, 1999; Laws 2001, ch. 2001-241, §1, effective January 1, 2002; Laws 2002, ch. 2002-1, §104, effective May 21, 2002; Laws 2003, ch. 2003-154, §22, effective June 12, 2003; Laws 2004, ch. 2004-260, §16, effective July 1, 2004; Laws 2006, ch. 2006-178, §31, effective July 1, 2006; Laws 2006, ch. 2006-217, §24, effective July 1, 2007.)

III. Health Care Surrogate Act

A type of a power of attorney that specifically applies to health care decisionmaking is the "power of attorney for health care." That document designates an agent to make health care decisions for the principal. Florida Statutes §§765.201 et seq. (termed the "Health Care Surrogate Act") govern powers of attorney for health care.

The Florida legislature first permitted individuals to designate agents for health care decisions in 1990. Specifically, the legislature extended the durable power of attorney to some medical decisions and simultaneously authorized the "health care surrogate" (under repealed Florida Statutes Chapter 745). In 1992, the legislature enacted a newly revised Chapter 765 to expand the options available to health care decisionmaking. The new Chapter (now retitled "Health Care Advance Directives") includes some former statutory provisions on health care surrogates and living wills.

A health care surrogate has powers that are specified in Florida Statutes §765.205. The surrogate has general authority to make health care decisions for the principal as well as the authority to: provide informed consent; have access to medical records; apply for benefits for the principal; and to authorize the admission, discharge, or transfer of the principal to or from a health care facility. See generally Ryland F. Mahathey, Planning for Disability, Basic Estate Planning in Florida, Florida Bar CLE §3.33 (2006).

Chapter 765. Health Care Advance Directives

Part II. Health Care Surrogate

§765.201. Title

Sections 765.202-765.205 may be cited as the "Florida Health Care Surrogate Act."

(Laws 1992, ch. 92-199, §3.)

§765.202. Requirements for designation of a health care surrogate

(1) A written document designating a surrogate to make health care decisions for a principal shall be signed by the principal in the presence of two subscribing adult witnesses. A principal unable to sign the instrument may, in the presence of witnesses, direct that another person sign the principal's name as required herein. An exact copy of the instrument shall be provided to the surrogate.

(2) The person designated as surrogate shall not act as witness to the execution of the document designating the health care surrogate. At least one person who acts as a witness shall be neither the principal's spouse nor blood relative.

(3) A document designating a health care surrogate may also designate an alternate surrogate provided the designation is explicit. The alternate surrogate may assume his or her duties as surrogate for the principal if the original surrogate is unwilling or unable to perform his or her duties. The principal's failure to designate an alternate surrogate shall not invalidate the designation.

(4) If neither the designated surrogate nor the designated alternate surrogate is able or willing to make health care decisions on behalf of the principal and in accordance with the principal's instructions, the health care facility may seek the appointment of a proxy pursuant to part IV.

(5) A principal may designate a separate surrogate to consent to mental health treatment in the event that the principal is determined by a court to be incompetent to consent to mental health treatment and a guardian advocate is appointed as provided under §394.4598. However, unless the document designating the health care surrogate expressly states otherwise, the court shall assume that the health care surrogate authorized to make health care decisions under this chapter is also the principal's choice to make decisions regarding mental health treatment.

(6) Unless the document states a time of termination, the designation shall remain in effect until revoked by the principal.

(7) A written designation of a health care surrogate executed pursuant to this section establishes a rebuttable presumption of clear and convincing evidence of the principal's designation of the surrogate.

(Laws 1992, ch. 92-199, §3; Laws 1994, ch. 94-183, §8; Laws 1996, ch. 96-169, §49. Amended by Laws 1997, ch. 97-102, §1797, effective July 1, 1997.)

765.203. Suggested form

A written designation of a health care surrogate executed pursuant to this chapter may, but need not be, in the following form:

DESIGNATION OF HEALTH CARE SURROGATE

Name:
_________(Last)_________(First)_________(Middle Initial)_________

In the event that I have been determined to be incapacitated to provide informed consent for medical treatment and surgical and diagnostic procedures, I wish to designate as my surrogate for health care decisions:

Name:
____
____

Address:
____
____

Phone: ________________________________

If my surrogate is unwilling or unable to perform his or her duties, I wish to designate as my alternate surrogate:

Name:
____
____

Address:
____
____

Phone: ________________

I fully understand that this designation will permit my designee to make health care decisions, except for anatomical gifts, unless I have executed an anatomical gift declaration pursuant to law, and to provide, withhold, or withdraw consent on my behalf; to apply for public benefits to defray the cost of health care; and to authorize my admission to or transfer from a health care facility.

Additional instructions (optional):

____
____
____
____
____
____
____

I further affirm that this designation is not being made as a condition of treatment or admission to a health care facility. I will notify and send a copy of this document to the following persons other than my surrogate, so they may know who my surrogate is.

Name:

____
____

Name:

____
____
____
____
____
____

Signed:

____
____

Date:

____
____

(Laws 1992, ch. 92-199, §3. Amended by Laws 1997, ch. 97-102, §1145, effective July 1, 1997; Laws 2000, ch. 2000-295, §9, effective June 15, 2000.)

§765.204. Capacity of principal, presumption, procedure

(1) A principal is presumed to be capable of making health care decisions for herself or himself unless she or he is determined to be incapacitated. Incapacity may not be inferred from the person's voluntary or involuntary hospitalization for mental illness or from her or his mental retardation.

(2) If a principal's capacity to make health care decisions for herself or himself or provide informed consent is in question, the attending physician shall evaluate the principal's capacity and, if the physician concludes that the principal lacks capacity, enter that evaluation in the principal's medical record. If the attending physician has a question as to whether the principal lacks capacity, another physician shall also evaluate the principal's capacity, and if the second physician agrees that the principal lacks the capacity to make health care decisions or provide informed consent, the health care facility shall enter both physician's evaluations in the principal's medical record. If the principal has designated a health care surrogate or has delegated authority to make health care decisions to an attorney in fact under a durable power of attorney, the facility shall notify such surrogate or attorney in fact in writing that her or his authority under the instrument has commenced, as provided in chapter 709 or §765.203.

(3) The surrogate's authority shall commence upon a determination under subsection (2) that the principal lacks capacity, and such authority shall remain in effect until a determination that the principal has regained such capacity. Upon commencement of the surrogate's authority, a surrogate who is not the principal's spouse shall notify the principal's spouse or adult children of the principal's designation of the surrogate. In the event the attending physician determines that the principal has regained capacity, the authority of the surrogate shall cease, but shall recommence if the principal subsequently loses capacity as determined pursuant to this section.

(4) A determination made pursuant to this section that a principal lacks capacity to make health care decisions shall not be construed as a finding that a principal lacks capacity for any other purpose.

(5) In the event the surrogate is required to consent to withholding or withdrawing life-prolonging procedures, the provisions of part III shall apply.

(Laws 1992, ch. 92-199, §3. Amended by Laws 1997, ch. 97-102, §1146, effective July 1, 1997; Laws 1999, ch. 99-331, §22, effective October 1, 1999; Laws 2000, ch. 2000-295, §10, effective June 15, 2000.)

§765.205. Powers and duties of the surrogate, effect of guardianship

(1) The surrogate, in accordance with the principal's instructions, unless such authority has been expressly limited by the principal, shall:

(a) Have authority to act for the principal and to make all health care decisions for the principal during the principal's incapacity.

(b) Consult expeditiously with appropriate health care providers to provide informed consent, and make only health care decisions for the principal which he or she believes the principal would have made under the circumstances if the principal were capable of making such decisions. If there is no indication of what the principal would have chosen, the surrogate may consider the patient's best interest in deciding that proposed treatments are to be withheld or that treatments currently in effect are to be withdrawn.

(c) Provide written consent using an appropriate form whenever consent is required, including a physician's order not to resuscitate.

(d) Be provided access to the appropriate medical records of the principal.

(e) Apply for public benefits, such as Medicare and Medicaid, for the principal and have access to information regarding the principal's income and assets and banking and financial records to the extent required to make application. A health care provider or facility may not, however, make such application a condition of continued care if the principal, if capable, would have refused to apply.

(2) The surrogate may authorize the release of information and medical records to appropriate persons to ensure the continuity of the principal's health care and may authorize the admission, discharge, or transfer of the principal to or from a health care facility or other facility or program licensed under chapter 400 or chapter 429.

(3) If, after the appointment of a surrogate, a court appoints a guardian, the surrogate shall continue to make health care decisions for the principal, unless the court has modified or revoked the authority of the surrogate pursuant to §744.3115. The surrogate may be directed by the court to report the principal's health care status to the guardian.

(Laws 1992, ch. 92-199, §3; Laws 1994, ch. 94-183, §9; Laws 1996, ch. 96-169, §50. Amended by Laws 1999, ch. 99-331, §23, effective Oct. 1, 1999; Laws 2000, ch. 2000-295, §11, effective June 15, 2000; Laws 2001, ch. 2001- 250, §6, effective July 15, 2001; Laws 2001, ch. 2001-277, §135, effective July 1, 2001; Laws 2006, ch. 2006-197, § 106, effective July 1, 2006.)

IV. Health Care Advance Directives

Health care advance directives exist to enable an individual to plan, in advance, for medical needs that may arise upon incapacity. Such directives are authorized by Florida Statutes §§765.101 et seq.

In 1992 the Florida legislature enacted newly revised Chapter 765 to expand the options available for health care planning. The new Chapter 765 (now retitled "Health Care Advance Directives") included some previous statutory provisions on living wills and health care surrogates.

Currently, Chapter 765 includes five parts: (1) general provisions (including definitions) (Fla. Stat. §§765.101-765.113); (2) health care surrogates (Fla. Stat. §§765.201-205); (3) "life-prolonging procedures" (including living wills) (Fla. Stat. §§765.301-310), (4) procedures to follow in the absence of the use of advance directives (Fla. Stat. §§765.401 and 765.404); and (5) anatomical gifts (this last section was added subsequently in 2001) (Fla. Stat. §§765.510-546).

Florida provisions on health care surrogates are set form in Part III infra. Living wills are discussed in Part V infra.

Chapter 765. Health Care Advance Directives

Part I. General Provisions

§765.101. Applicable definitions

As used in this chapter:

(1) "Advance directive" means a witnessed written document or oral statement in which instructions are given by a principal or in which the principal's desires are expressed concerning any aspect of the principal's health care, and includes, but is not limited to, the designation of a health care surrogate, a living will, or an anatomical gift made pursuant to part V of this chapter.

(2) "Attending physician" means the primary physician who has responsibility for the treatment and care of the patient.

(3) "Close personal friend" means any person 18 years of age or older who has exhibited special care and concern for the patient, and who presents an affidavit to the health care facility or to the attending or treating physician stating that he or she is a friend of the patient; is willing and able to become involved in the patient's health care; and has maintained such regular contact with the patient so as to be familiar with the patient's activities, health, and religious or moral beliefs.

(4) "End-stage condition" means an irreversible condition that is caused by injury, disease, or illness which has resulted in progressively severe and permanent deterioration, and which, to a reasonable degree of medical probability, treatment of the condition would be ineffective.

(5) "Health care decision" means:

(a) Informed consent, refusal of consent, or withdrawal of consent to any and all health care, including life-prolonging procedures and mental health treatment, unless otherwise stated in the advance directives.

(b) The decision to apply for private, public, government, or veterans' benefits to defray the cost of health care.

(c) The right of access to all records of the principal reasonably necessary for a health care surrogate to make decisions involving health care and to apply for benefits.

(d) The decision to make an anatomical gift pursuant to part V of this chapter.

(6) "Health care facility" means a hospital, nursing home, hospice, home health agency, or health maintenance organization licensed in this state, or any facility subject to part I of chapter 394.

(7) "Health care provider" or "provider" means any person licensed, certified, or otherwise authorized by law to administer health care in the ordinary course of business or practice of a profession.

(8) "Incapacity" or "incompetent" means the patient is physically or mentally unable to communicate a willful and knowing health care decision. For the purposes of making an anatomical gift, the term also includes a patient who is deceased.

(9) "Informed consent" means consent voluntarily given by a person after a sufficient explanation and disclosure of the subject matter involved to enable that person to have a general understanding of the treatment or procedure and the medically acceptable alternatives, including the substantial risks and hazards inherent in the proposed treatment or procedures, and to make a knowing health care decision without coercion or undue influence.

(10) "Life-prolonging procedure" means any medical procedure, treatment, or intervention, including artificially provided sustenance and hydration, which sustains, restores, or supplants a spontaneous vital function. The term does not include the administration of medication or performance of medical procedure, when such medication or procedure is deemed necessary to provide comfort care or to alleviate pain.

(11) "Living will" or "declaration" means:

(a) A witnessed document in writing, voluntarily executed by the principal in accordance with §765.302; or

(b) A witnessed oral statement made by the principal expressing the principal's instructions concerning life-prolonging procedures.

(12) "Persistent vegetative state" means a permanent and irreversible condition of unconsciousness in which there is:

(a) The absence of voluntary action or cognitive behavior of any kind.

(b) An inability to communicate or interact purposefully with the environment.

(13) "Physician" means a person licensed pursuant to chapter 458 or chapter 459.

(14) "Principal" means a competent adult executing an advance directive and on whose behalf health care decisions are to be made.

(15) "Proxy" means a competent adult who has not been expressly designated to make health care decisions for a particular incapacitated individual, but who, nevertheless, is authorized pursuant to §765.401 to make health care decisions for such individual.

(16) "Surrogate" means any competent adult expressly designated by a principal to make health care decisions on behalf of the principal upon the principal's incapacity.

(17) "Terminal condition" means

a condition caused by injury, disease, or illness from which there is no reasonable medical probability of recovery and which, without treatment, can be expected to cause death.

(Laws 1992, ch. 92-199, §2; Laws 1994, ch. 94-183, §3; Laws 1996, ch. 96-169, §46. Amended by Laws 1999, ch. 99-331, §16, effective October 1, 1999; Laws 2001, ch. 2001-250, §3, effective July 15, 2001; Laws 2001, ch. 2001-277, §131, effective July 1, 2001; Laws 2006, ch. 2006-1, §104, effective July 4, 2006; Laws 2006, ch. 2006-178, §28, effective July 1, 2006.)

§765.102. Legislative findings and intent; additional definitions

(1) The Legislature finds that every competent adult has the fundamental right of self-determination regarding decisions pertaining to his or her own health, including the right to choose or refuse medical treatment. This right is subject to certain interests of society, such as the protection of human life and the preservation of ethical standards in the medical profession.

(2) To ensure that such right is not lost or diminished by virtue of later physical or mental incapacity, the Legislature intends that a procedure be established to allow a person to plan for incapacity by executing a document or orally designating another person to direct the course of his or her medical treatment upon his or her incapacity. Such procedure should be less expensive and less

restrictive than guardianship and permit a previously incapacitated person to exercise his or her full right to make health care decisions as soon as the capacity to make such decisions has been regained.

(3) The Legislature recognizes that for some the administration of life-prolonging medical procedures may result in only a precarious and burdensome existence. In order to ensure that the rights and intentions of a person may be respected even after he or she is no longer able to participate actively in decisions concerning himself or herself, and to encourage communication among such patient, his or her family, and his or her physician, the Legislature declares that the laws of this state recognize the right of a competent adult to make an advance directive instructing his or her physician to provide, withhold, or withdraw life-prolonging procedures, or to designate another to make the treatment decision for him or her in the event that such person should become incapacitated and unable to personally direct his or her medical care.

(4) The Legislature recognizes the need for all health care professionals to rapidly increase their understanding of end-of-life and palliative care. Therefore, the Legislature encourages the professional regulatory boards to adopt appropriate standards and guidelines regarding end-of-life care and pain management and encourages educational institutions established to train health care professionals and allied health professionals to implement curricula to train such professionals to provide end-of-life care, including pain management and palliative care.

(5) For purposes of this chapter:

(a) Palliative care is the comprehensive management of the physical, psychological, social, spiritual, and existential needs of patients. Palliative care is especially suited to the care of persons who have incurable, progressive illnesses.

(b) Palliative care must include:

1. An opportunity to discuss and plan for end-of-life care.

2. Assurance that physical and mental suffering will be carefully attended to.

3. Assurance that preferences for withholding and withdrawing life-sustaining interventions will be honored.

4. Assurance that the personal goals of the dying person will be addressed.

5. Assurance that the dignity of the dying person will be a priority.

6. Assurance that health care providers will not abandon the dying person.

7. Assurance that the burden to family and others will be addressed.

8. Assurance that advance directives for care will be respected regardless of the location of care.

9. Assurance that organizational mechanisms are in place to evaluate the availability and quality of end-of-life, palliative, and hospice care services, including the evaluation of administrative and regulatory barriers.

10. Assurance that necessary health care services will be provided and that relevant reimbursement policies are available.

11. Assurance that the goals expressed in subparagraphs 1.-10. will be accomplished in a culturally appropriate manner.

(6) The Department of Elderly Affairs, the Agency for Health Care Administration, and the Department of Health shall jointly create a campaign on end-of-life care for purposes of educating the public. This campaign should include culturally sensitive programs to improve understanding of end-of-life care issues in minority communities.

(Laws 1992, ch. 92-199, §2. Amended by Laws 1997, ch. 97-102, §1144, effective July 1, 1997; Laws 1999, ch. 99-331, §17, effective October 1, 1999; Laws 2000, ch. 2000-295, §7, effective June 15, 2000; Laws 2001, ch. 2001-250, §4, effective July 15, 2001; Laws 2001, ch. 2001-277, §§132, 133, effective July 1, 2001.)

§765.103. Effect of an existing advance directive

Any advance directive made prior to October 1, 1999, shall be given effect as executed, provided such directive was legally effective when written.

(Laws 1992, ch. 92-199, §2. Amended by Laws 1999, ch. 99-331, §18, effective October 1, 1999.)

§765.104. Right of principal to amend or revoke at any time

(1) An advance directive or designation of a surrogate may be amended or revoked at any time by a competent principal:

(a) By means of a signed, dated writing;

(b) By means of the physical cancellation or destruction of the advance directive by the principal or by another in the principal's presence and at the principal's direction;

(c) By means of an oral expression of intent to amend or revoke; or

(d) By means of a subsequently executed advance directive that is materially different from a previously executed advance directive.

(2) Unless otherwise provided in the advance directive or in an order of dissolution or annulment of marriage, the dissolution or annulment of marriage of the principal revokes the designation of the principal's former spouse as a surrogate.

(3) Any such amendment or revocation will be effective when it is communicated to the surrogate, health care provider, or health care facility. No civil or criminal liability shall be imposed upon any person for a failure to act upon an amendment or revocation unless that person has actual knowledge of such amendment or revocation.

(4) Any patient for whom a medical proxy has been recognized under §765.401 and for whom any previous legal disability that precluded the patient's ability to consent is removed may amend or revoke the recognition of the medical proxy and any uncompleted decision made by that proxy. The amendment or revocation takes effect when it is communicated to the proxy, the health care provider, or the health care facility in writing or, if communicated orally, in the presence of a third person.

(Laws 1992, ch. 92-199, §2; Laws 1996, ch. 96-169, §47. Amended by Laws 1999, ch. 99-331, §19, effective October 1, 1999; Laws 2002, ch. 2002-195, §12, effective April 29, 2002.)

§765.105. Persons who may review surrogate's or proxy's decision

The patient's family, the health care facility, or the attending physician, or any other interested person who may reasonably be expected to be directly affected by the surrogate or proxy's decision concerning any health care decision may seek expedited judicial intervention pursuant to rule 5.900 of the Florida Probate Rules, if that person believes:

(1) The surrogate or proxy's decision is not in accord with the patient's known desires or the provisions of this chapter;

(2) The advance directive is ambiguous, or the patient has changed his or her mind after execution of the advance directive;

(3) The surrogate or proxy was improperly designated or appointed, or the designation of the surrogate is no longer effective or has been revoked;

(4) The surrogate or proxy has failed to discharge duties, or incapacity or illness renders the surrogate or proxy incapable of discharging duties;

(5) The surrogate or proxy has abused powers; or

(6) The patient has sufficient capacity to make his or her own health care decisions.

(Laws 1992, ch. 92-199, §2; Laws 1994, ch. 94-183, §4.)

§765.106. Rights herein do not impair existing rights

The provisions of this chapter are cumulative to the existing law regarding an individual's right to consent, or refuse to consent, to medical treatment and do not impair any existing rights or responsibilities which a health care provider, a patient, including a minor, competent or incompetent person, or a patient's family may have under the common law, Federal Constitution, State Constitution, or statutes of this state.

(Laws 1992, ch. 92-199, §2; Laws 1994, ch. 94-183, §5.)

§765.107. Construction relative to judicial consent law

(1) This chapter shall not be construed to repeal by implication any provision of §766.103, the Florida Medical Consent Law. For all purposes, the Florida Medical Consent Law shall be considered an alternative to provisions of this section.

(2) Procedures provided in this chapter permitting the withholding or withdrawal of life-prolonging procedures do not apply to a person who never had capacity to designate a health care surrogate or execute a living will.

(Laws 1992, ch. 92-199, §2. Amended by Laws 1999, ch. 99-331, § 20, effective October 1, 1999.)

§765.108. Advance directive shall not affect life insurance

The making of an advance directive pursuant to the provisions of this chapter shall not affect the sale, procurement, or issuance of any policy of life insurance, nor shall such making of an advance directive be deemed to modify the terms of an existing policy of life insurance. No policy of life insurance will be legally impaired or invalidated by the withholding or withdrawal of life-prolonging procedures from an insured patient in accordance with the provisions of this chapter, nor by any other treatment decision made according to this chapter, notwithstanding any term of the policy to the contrary. A person shall not be required to make an advance directive as a condition for being insured for, or receiving, health care services.

(Laws 1992, ch. 92-199, §2.)

§765.109. Health care providers: immunity for compliance with advance directive

(1) A health care facility, provider, or other person who acts under the direction of a health care facility or provider is not subject to criminal prosecution or civil liability, and will not be deemed to have engaged in unprofessional conduct, as a result of carrying out a health care decision made in accordance with the provisions of this chapter. The surrogate or proxy who makes a health care decision on a patient's behalf, pursuant to this chapter, is not subject to criminal prosecution or civil liability for such action.

(2) The provisions of this section shall apply unless it is shown by a preponderance of the evidence that the person authorizing or effectuating a health care decision did not, in good faith, comply with the provisions of this chapter.

(Laws 1992, ch. 92-199, §2.)

§765.110. Discipline of health care personnel for lack of compliance: notice of rights, forms, and forced execution or waiver of directive

(1) A health care facility, pursuant to Pub. L. No. 101-508, §§4206 and 4751, [FN1] shall provide to each patient written information concerning the individual's rights concerning advance directives and the health care facility's policies respecting the implementation of such rights, and shall document in the patient's medical records whether or not the individual has executed an advance directive.

(2) A health care provider or health care facility may not require a patient to execute an advance directive or to execute a new advance directive using the facility's or provider's forms. The patient's advance directives shall travel with the patient as part of the patient's medical record.

(3) A health care provider or health care facility shall be subject to professional discipline and revocation of license or certification, and a fine of not more than $1,000 per incident, or both, if the health care provider or health care facility, as a condition of treatment or admission, requires an individual to execute or waive an advance directive.

(4) The Department of Elderly Affairs for hospices and, in consultation with the Department of Elderly Affairs, the Department of Health for health care providers; the Agency for Health Care Administration for hospitals, nursing homes, home health agencies, and health maintenance organizations; and the Department of Children and Family Services for facilities subject to part I of chapter 394 shall adopt rules to implement the provisions of the section.

[FN1] See 42 U.S.C.A. §§ 1395i-3, 1395cc, 1395bbb, 1396a and 1396r.

(Laws 1992, ch. 92-199, §2; Laws 1994, ch. 94-183, §6; Laws 1994, ch. 94-218, §243; Laws 1996, ch. 96-169, §48. Amended by Laws 1999, ch. 99- 8, §284, effective June 29, 1999; Laws 1999, ch. 99-331, §21, effective October 1, 1999.)

§765.1103. Provider's duty to provide information regarding pain management

(1) A patient shall be given information concerning pain management and palliative care when he or she discusses with the attending or treating physician, or such physician's designee, the diagnosis, planned course of treatment, alternatives, risks, or prognosis for his or her illness. If the patient is incapacitated, the information shall be given to the patient's health care surrogate or proxy, court-appointed guardian as provided in chapter 744, or attorney in fact under a durable power of attorney as provided in chapter 709. The court-appointed guardian or attorney in fact must have been delegated authority to make health care decisions on behalf of the patient.

(2) Health care providers and practitioners regulated under chapter 458, chapter 459, or chapter 464 must, as appropriate, comply with a request for pain management or palliative care from a patient under their care or, for an incapacitated patient under their care, from a surrogate, proxy, guardian, or other representative permitted to make health care decisions for the incapacitated patient. Facilities regulated under chapter 395, chapter 400, or chapter 429 must comply with the pain management or palliative care measures ordered by the patient's physician.

(Laws 2000, ch. 2000-295, §8, effective June 15, 2000. Amended by Laws 2001, ch. 2001-250, §5, effective July 15, 2001; Laws 2001, ch. 2001-277, §134, effective July 1, 2001; Laws 2006, ch. 2006-197, §105, effective July 1, 2006.)

§765.1105. Transfer of a patient required following provider's refusal to comply with directive

(1) A health care provider or facility that refuses to comply with a patient's advance directive, or the treatment decision of his or her surrogate, shall make reasonable efforts to transfer the patient to another health care provider or facility that will comply with

the directive or treatment decision. This chapter does not require a health care provider or facility to commit any act which is contrary to the provider's or facility's moral or ethical beliefs, if the patient:

(a) Is not in an emergency condition; and

(b) Has received written information upon admission informing the patient of the policies of the health care provider or facility regarding such moral or ethical beliefs.

(2) A health care provider or facility that is unwilling to carry out the wishes of the patient or the treatment decision of his or her surrogate because of moral or ethical beliefs must within 7 days either:

(a) Transfer the patient to another health care provider or facility. The health care provider or facility shall pay the costs for transporting the patient to another health care provider or facility; or

(b) If the patient has not been transferred, carry out the wishes of the patient or the patient's surrogate, unless the provisions of § 765.105 apply.

(Laws 1992, ch. 92-199, §4; Laws 1994, ch. 94-183, §11. Amended by Laws 1997, ch. 97-102, §1148, effective July 1, 1997. Renumbered as §765.1105 and amended by Laws 1999, ch. 99-331, §30, effective Oct. 1, 1999.)

§765.1115. Liability for falsification, concealment, destruction, amendment or revocation of advance directive

(1) Any person who willfully conceals, cancels, defaces, obliterates, or damages an advance directive without the principal's consent or who falsifies or forges the revocation or amendment of an advance directive of another, and who thereby causes life-prolonging procedures to be utilized in contravention of the previously expressed intent of the principal, commits a felony of the third degree, punishable as provided in §§775.082, 775.083, or 775.084.

(2) Any person who falsifies or forges the advance directive of another or who willfully conceals or withholds personal knowledge of the revocation of an advance directive, with the intent to cause a withholding or withdrawal of life-prolonging procedures contrary to the wishes of the principal, and who thereby because of such act directly causes life-prolonging procedures to be withheld or withdrawn and death to be hastened, commits a felony of the second degree, punishable as provided in §§775.082, 775.083, or 775.084.

(Laws 1992, ch. 92-199, §4. Renumbered from 765.13 and amended by Laws 1999, ch. 99-331, §31, effective Oct. 1, 1999.)

§765.112. Recognition of out-of-state advance directives

An advance directive executed in another state in compliance with the law of that state or of this state is validly executed for the purposes of this chapter.

(Laws 1992, ch. 92-199, § 2.)

§765.113. Exclusions on consent: abortion, shock therapy, psychosurgery, experimental treatments

Unless the principal expressly delegates such authority to the surrogate in writing, or a surrogate or proxy has sought and received court approval pursuant to rule 5.900 of the Florida Probate Rules, a surrogate or proxy may not provide consent for:

(1) Abortion, sterilization, electroshock therapy, psychosurgery, experimental treatments that have not been approved by a federally approved institutional review board in accordance with 45 C.F.R. part 46 or 21 C.F.R. part 56, or voluntary admission to a mental health facility.

(2) Withholding or withdrawing life-prolonging procedures from a pregnant patient prior to viability as defined in § 390.0111(4).

(Laws 1992, ch. 92-199, §2; Laws 1994, ch. 94-183, §7. Amended by Laws 1999, ch. 99-3, §87, effective June 29, 1999.)

V. Living Wills

Beginning in the 1970s, many states enacted statutes authorizing *living wills*. A living will is a document that includes written instructions regarding health care (i.e., end-of-life decisions) in the event of an individual's becoming incapacitated. California was the first state to enact a living will statute in 1976. The statute was entitled "the Natural Death Act" and was a model for many states' Natural Death Acts legislation Jeanine Lewis, Chapter 658: California's Health Care Decisions Act, 31 McGeorge L. Rev. 501, 509 (2000).

State legislatures began enacting legislation authorizing living wills in response to In re Quinlan, 355 A.2d 647 (N.J. 1976). In *Quinlan*, the New Jersey Supreme Court held that the decision to remove a young woman in a persistent vegetative state from a respirator was protected by the constitutional right to privacy. From 1976 to 1980, ten states enacted living will statutes. In the next five years, another 29 states did so. See Martha S. Swartz, "Conscience Clauses" or "Unconscionable Clauses": Personal Beliefs versus Professional

Responsibilities, 6 Yale J. Health Pol'y, L. & Ethics 269, 283-84, n.61 (2006).

Early living will legislation was limited to individuals who faced a "terminal illness." The *Quinlan* case, *supra*, brought to light the possibility that people who were in persistent vegetative states might also benefit from advance directives. In recognition of this problem, many states broadened the scope of their Natural Death Acts by specifying additional conditions that set in motion advance directives, adding nutrition and hydration to the forms of life-sustaining treatment that could be withdrawn, prohibiting recognition of a living will for pregnant patients, and deleting time limitations on the validity of an advance directive. Lewis, *supra,* at 509.

Florida enacted its living will statute in 1984, codified as Chapter 765, "Right to Decline Life-Prolonging Procedure Act of Florida," Fla. Stat. §§765.01-15 (West 1984).

A similar period of law reform followed another "right to die" case. In Cruzan v. Mo. Dept. of Health, 497 U.S. 261 (1990), the United States Supreme Court upheld the state's right to require clear and convincing evidence of an incompetent's wishes prior to the withdrawal of life-sustaining treatment from a patient in a persistent vegetative state.

The Florida legislature also responded to this second wave of law reform. In 1992, the Florida legislature significantly revised the law regarding health care decisionmaking by repealing Chapter 765 (living wills) as well as Chapter 745 (health care surrogates), and incorporating provisions of those sections into a new Chapter 765, retitled "Health Care Advance Directives."

The provisions on living wills currently are set forth in Chapter 765, Florida Statutes §§765.301 et seq. (subtitled "Life-Prolonging Procedure Act of Florida"). The Florida provisions, similar to living will legislation in many jurisdictions, require execution of the document by a patient who is competent, concurring diagnoses by physicians, and attestation by unrelated persons who would not profit from the declarant's death. Specifically, statute provides that the procedure for making a living will requires execution by "any competent adult" (termed a "principal") who may make a living will "at any time" (Fla. Stat. §765.302(1). A person must have one of three conditions for the living will to be operative: (1) a "terminal condition," an (2) "end-stage condition" or (3) be in a persistent vegetative state. *Id.* For definitions of those terms, see Fla. Stat. §765.101 *supra.*

The living will must be signed by the patient in the presence of two witnesses, one of whom is not "a spouse or blood relative" (Fla. Stat. §765.302(1)). The patient has the responsibility to notify the attending or treating physician that he or she has executed a living will (Fla. Stat. §765.302(2)). For the living will to become operative, the patient's condition (one of the three above) must be confirmed by the patient's treating physician and another consulting physician—both of whom must also determine that the patient "does not have a reasonable medical probability of recovering capacity so that the right could be exercised directly by the principal" (Fla. Stat. §765.304). If the living will conforms to the statutory requirements, it evokes a rebuttable presumption of clear and convincing evidence of the patient's wishes (Fla. Stat. §765.302(3)).

The Act also distinguishes suicide ("withholding of life-sustaining treatment. . . does not, for any purpose, constitute a suicide") and specifies that the statute should not be construed to authorize mercy killing or euthanasia (Fla. Stat. §765.309). The statute provides a suggested form for the document that is optional (Fla. Stat. §765.303).

Florida courts have wrestled with several cases involving the right to withdraw life sustaining treatment from comatose patients. For example, in John F. Kennedy Mem'l Hosp., Inc. v. Bludworth, 452 So. 2d 921, 926 (Fla. 1984), the Florida Supreme Court relied on *Quinlan*, *supra*, to support the conclusion that the right of a comatose and terminally ill patient to refuse life-sustaining measures could be exercised by family members and that the patient (who had executed a living will) did not need a court-appointed guardian and court approval to terminate life-sustaining treatment.

Recently, the case of 26-year-old Terri Schiavo sparked considerable controversy. After physicians diagnosed Schiavo in a persistent vegetative state, her husband sought to withdraw her artificial life sustaining treatment. Her parents (the Schindlers) objected, disputing the husband's claims about her wishes and the diagnosis. Following several lawsuits brought by the parents and Florida Governor Jeb Bush, the husband prevailed. In re Guardianship of Schiavo, 780 So.2d 176 (Fla. Dist. Ct. App. 2001); In re Schiavo, 851 So. 2d 182 (Fla. Dist. Ct. App. 2003); Bush v. Shiavo, 866 So. 2d 136 (Fla. Dist. Ct. App. 2004). After Schiavo's feeding tube was removed in 2003, the Florida legislature required its reinsertion by adopting a law that was later ruled unconstitutional. Bush v. Schiavo, 885 So. 2d 321 (Fla. 2004), *cert. denied*,

543 U.S. 1121 (2005). Congress then enacted a special statute granting jurisdiction for de novo review of the case in federal court. P.L. 109-3, 119 Stats. 15 (Mar. 21, 2005). Subsequently, the Eleventh Circuit Court of Appeals also ruled against the parents' claims. Schiavo ex rel. Schindler v. Schiavo, 403 F.3d 1223 (11th Cir.), *stay denied*, 544 U.S. 945 (2005); 403 F.2d 1289 (11th Cir. 2005).

The family continued to battle over the manner of disposition of the young woman's remains and the inscription on her gravestone. See Mitch Stacy, Schiavo Kin: Marker Not Meant to Anger Her Parents, Intelligencer, June 22, 2005, at 7B. For accounts of the controversy, see Michael Schiavo, Terri: The Truth (2005); Mary & Robert Schindler, A Life That Matters: The Legacy of Terri Schiavo: A Lesson for Us All (2005).

Chapter 765. Health Care Advance Directives Part III. Life-Prolonging Procedures

§765.301. Title

Sections 765.302-765.309 may be cited as the "Life-Prolonging Procedure Act of Florida."

(Laws 1992, ch. 92-199, §4. Amended by Laws 1999, ch. 99-331, §24, effective October 1, 1999.)

§765.302. Requirements for execution of living will: competency, medical conditions, attestation, notice, presumption

(1) Any competent adult may, at any time, make a living will or written declaration and direct the providing, withholding, or withdrawal of life-prolonging procedures in the event that such person has a terminal condition, has an end-stage condition, or is in a persistent vegetative state. A living will must be signed by the principal in the presence of two subscribing witnesses, one of whom is neither a spouse nor a blood relative of the principal. If the principal is physically unable to sign the living will, one of the witnesses must subscribe the principal's signature in the principal's presence and at the principal's direction.

(2) It is the responsibility of the principal to provide for notification to her or his attending or treating physician that the living will has been made. In the event the principal is physically or mentally incapacitated at the time the principal is admitted to a health care facility, any other person may notify the physician or health care facility of the existence of the living will. An attending or treating physician or health care facility which is so notified shall promptly make the living will or a copy thereof a part of the principal's medical records.

(3) A living will, executed pursuant to this section, establishes a rebuttable presumption of clear and convincing evidence of the principal's wishes.

(Laws 1992, ch. 92-199, §4. Amended by Laws 1997, ch. 97-102, §1147, effective July 1, 1997; Laws 1999, ch. 99-331, §25, effective October 1, 1999.)

§765.303. Suggested form of a living will

(1) A living will may, BUT NEED NOT, be in the following form:

Living Will

Declaration made this ___ day of ___, (year), I, _________, willfully and voluntarily make known my desire that my dying not be artificially prolonged under the circumstances set forth below, and I do hereby declare that, if at any time I am incapacitated and

(initial) I have a terminal condition

or (initial) I have an end-stage condition

or (initial) I am in a persistent vegetative state

and if my attending or treating physician and another consulting physician have determined that there is no reasonable medical probability of my recovery from such condition, I direct that life-prolonging procedures be withheld or withdrawn when the application of such procedures would serve only to prolong artificially the process of dying, and that I be permitted to die naturally with only the administration of medication or the performance of any medical procedure deemed necessary to provide me with comfort care or to alleviate pain.

It is my intention that this declaration be honored by my family and physician as the final expression of my legal right to refuse medical or surgical treatment and to accept the consequences for such refusal.

In the event that I have been determined to be unable to provide express and informed consent regarding the withholding, withdrawal, or continuation of life-prolonging procedures, I wish to designate, as my surrogate to carry out the provisions of this declaration:

Name:
____
____

Address:

____

____

____

Zip Code: ________________________________

Phone: __________________________________

I understand the full import of this declaration, and I am emotionally and mentally competent to make this declaration.

Additional Instructions (optional):

____

____

____

(Signed)

Witness

Address

Phone

Witness

Address

Phone

(2) The principal's failure to designate a surrogate shall not invalidate the living will.

(Laws 1992, ch. 92-199, §4. Amended by Laws 1999, ch. 99-6, §35, effective June 29, 1999; Laws 1999, ch. 99-331, §26, effective October 1, 1999; Laws 2000, ch. 2000-295, §12, effective June 15, 2000.)

§765.304. Physician may proceed pursuant to living will absent patient's designation of surrogate

(1) If a person has made a living will expressing his or her desires concerning life-prolonging procedures, but has not designated a surrogate to execute his or her wishes concerning life-prolonging procedures or designated a surrogate under part II, the attending physician may proceed as directed by the principal in the living will. In the event of a dispute or disagreement concerning the attending physician's decision to withhold or withdraw life-prolonging procedures, the attending physician shall not withhold or withdraw life-prolonging procedures pending review under §765.105. If a review of a disputed decision is not sought within 7 days following the attending physician's decision to withhold or withdraw life-prolonging procedures, the attending physician may proceed in accordance with the principal's instructions.

(2) Before proceeding in accordance with the principal's living will, it must be determined that:

(a) The principal does not have a reasonable medical probability of recovering capacity so that the right could be exercised directly by the principal.

(b) The principal has a terminal condition, has an end-stage condition, or is in a persistent vegetative state.

(c) Any limitations or conditions expressed orally or in a written declaration have been carefully considered and satisfied.

(Laws 1992, ch. 92-199, §4; Laws 1994, ch. 94-183, §10. Amended by Laws 1999, ch. 99-331, §27, effective October 1, 1999.)

§765.305. Duties of health care surrogate absent living will

(1) In the absence of a living will, the decision to withhold or withdraw life-prolonging procedures from a patient may be made by a health care surrogate designated by the patient pursuant to part II unless the designation limits the surrogate's authority to consent to the withholding or withdrawal of life-prolonging procedures.

(2) Before exercising the incompetent patient's right to forego treatment, the surrogate must be satisfied that:

(a) The patient does not have a reasonable medical probability of recovering capacity so that the right could be exercised by the patient.

(b) The patient has an end-stage condition, the patient is in a persistent vegetative state, or the patient's physical condition is terminal.

(Laws 1992, ch. 92-199, §4. Amended by Laws 1999, ch. 99-331, §28, effective October 1, 1999; Laws 2000, ch. 2000-295, § 13, effective June 15, 2000.)

§765.306. Determination of patient's capacity and condition

In determining whether the patient has a terminal condition, has an end- stage condition, or is in a persistent vegetative state or may recover capacity, or whether a medical condition or limitation referred to in an advance directive exists, the patient's attending or treating physician and at least one other consulting physician must separately examine the patient. The findings of each such examination must be documented in the patient's medical record and signed by each examining physician before life-prolonging procedures may be withheld or withdrawn.

(Laws 1992, ch. 92-199, §4; Laws 1994, ch. 94-183, §13. Amended by Laws 1999, ch. 99-331, §29, effective October 1, 1999; Laws 2000, ch. 2000-295, §14, effective June 15, 2000.)

§765.309. Prohibition of mercy killing and euthanasia; suicide distinguished

(1) Nothing in this chapter shall be construed to condone, authorize, or approve mercy killing or euthanasia, or to permit any affirmative or deliberate act or omission to end life other than to permit the natural process of dying.

(2) The withholding or withdrawal of life-prolonging procedures from a patient in accordance with any provision of this chapter does not, for any purpose, constitute a suicide.

(Laws 1992, ch. 92-199, § 4.)

VI. Failure to Execute Advance Directive

Florida legislation provides for health care decisionmaking in case the patient fails to execute an advance directive. If the patient has not executed a living will or designated a heath care surrogate, health care decisions may be made for the patient by a "proxy." The proxy is appointed by the court from a list of persons in a designated order of priority: a judicially appointed guardian, spouse, adult child, (or if more than one child exists) a majority of the children, a parent of the patient, a sibling of the patient, a relative who has exhibited "special care and concern" for the patient, and finally, a licensed clinical social worker. (Fla. Stat. §764.401.)

§765.401. Court may appoint proxy in absence of advance directive or surrogate designation

(1) If an incapacitated or developmentally disabled patient has not executed an advance directive, or designated a surrogate to execute an advance directive, or the designated or alternate surrogate is no longer available to make health care decisions, health care decisions may be made for the patient by any of the following individuals, in the following order of priority, if no individual in a prior class is reasonably available, willing, or competent to act:

(a) The judicially appointed guardian of the patient or the guardian advocate of the person having a developmental disability as defined in §393.063, who has been authorized to consent to medical treatment, if such guardian has previously been appointed; however, this paragraph shall not be construed to require such appointment before a treatment decision can be made under this subsection;

(b) The patient's spouse;

(c) An adult child of the patient, or if the patient has more than one adult child, a majority of the adult children who are reasonably available for consultation;

(d) A parent of the patient;

(e) The adult sibling of the patient or, if the patient has more than one sibling, a majority of the adult siblings who are reasonably available for consultation;

(f) An adult relative of the patient who has exhibited special care and concern for the patient and who has maintained regular contact with the patient and who is familiar with the patient's activities, health, and religious or moral beliefs; or

(g) A close friend of the patient.

(h) A clinical social worker licensed pursuant to chapter 491, or who is a graduate of a court-approved guardianship program. Such a proxy must be selected by the provider's bioethics committee and must not be employed by the provider. If the provider does not have a bioethics committee, then such a proxy may be chosen through an arrangement with the bioethics committee of another provider. The proxy will be notified that, upon request, the provider shall make available a second physician, not involved in the patient's care to assist the proxy in evaluating treatment. Decisions to withhold or withdraw life-prolonging procedures will be reviewed by the facility's bioethics committee. Documentation of efforts to locate proxies from prior classes must be recorded in the patient record.

(2) Any health care decision made under this part must be based on the proxy's informed consent and on the decision the proxy reasonably believes the patient would have made under the circumstances. If there is no indication of what the patient would have chosen, the proxy may consider the patient's best interest in deciding that proposed treatments are to be withheld or that treatments currently in effect are to be withdrawn.

(3) Before exercising the incapacitated patient's rights to select or decline health care, the proxy must comply with the provisions of §§765.205 and 765.305, except that a proxy's decision to withhold or withdraw life-prolonging procedures must be supported by clear and convincing evidence that the decision would have been the one the patient would have chosen had the patient been competent or, if there is no indication of what the patient would have chosen, that the decision is in the patient's best interest.

(4) Nothing in this section shall be construed to preempt the designation of persons who may consent to the medical care or treatment of minors established pursuant to §743.0645.

(Laws 1992, ch. 92-199, §5; Laws 1994, ch. 94-183, §12. Amended by Laws 1999, ch. 99-331, §32, effective October 1, 1999; Laws 2000, ch. 2000-295, §15, effective June 15, 2000; Laws 2001, ch. 2001-250, §7, effective July 15, 2001; Laws 2001, ch. 2001-277, §136, effective July 1, 2001; Laws 2002, ch. 2002- 195, §13, effective April 29, 2002; Laws 2003, ch. 2003-57, §5, effective May 30, 2003.)

§765.404. Special procedures regarding persons in persistent vegetative state who lack advance directives

For persons in a persistent vegetative state, as determined by the attending physician in accordance with currently accepted medical standards, who have no advance directive and for whom there is no evidence indicating what the person would have wanted under such conditions, and for whom, after a reasonably diligent inquiry, no family or friends are available or willing to serve as a proxy to make health care decisions for them, life-prolonging procedures may be withheld or withdrawn under the following conditions:

(1) The person has a judicially appointed guardian representing his or her best interest with authority to consent to medical treatment; and

(2) The guardian and the person's attending physician, in consultation with the medical ethics committee of the facility where the patient is located, conclude that the condition is permanent and that there is no reasonable medical probability for recovery and that withholding or withdrawing life-prolonging procedures is in the best interest of the patient. If there is no medical ethics committee at the facility, the facility must have an arrangement with the medical ethics committee of another facility or with a community-based ethics committee approved by the Florida Bio-ethics Network. The ethics committee shall review the case with the guardian, in consultation with the person's attending physician, to determine whether the condition is permanent and there is no reasonable medical probability for recovery. The individual committee members and the facility associated with an ethics committee shall not be held liable in any civil action related to the performance of any duties required in this subsection.

(Laws 1999, ch. 99-331, §33, effective October 1, 1999.)

VII. Anatomical Gifts

An individual has the ability to donate his or her body or organs for research or transplantation (Fla. Stat. §§765.510-.522). The act may be accomplished by executing: (1) a Uniform Donor Card (see Fla. Stat. §765.514(2)(b), or (2) a signed, witnessed statement of intent (such as a living will), or (3) a valid will that so provides. However, testamentary anatomical gifts may not be effectuated if the will does not come to light at the appropriate time. An anatomical gift is considered irrevocable (Fla. Stat. §765.512(1)), unless the gift is subsequently revoked in the specified manner (Fla. Stat. §765.516).

If an individual has not made an effective anatomical gift, a relative may do so. "However, relatives are often too emotionally distraught to make these decisions. Further complications will arise if relatives disagree. " Richard C. Milstein, Florida Wills (for Modest Estates), Powers of Attorney, and Health Care Advance Directives, Health Issues and Organ Donations: Anatomical Gifts, Florida Bar CLE 1, Z(3) (2002).

Chapter 765. Health Care Advance Directives

Part V. Anatomical Gifts

§765.510. Legislative findings and intent

Because of the rapid medical progress in the fields of tissue and organ preservation, transplantation of tissue, and tissue culture, and because it is in the public interest to aid the medical developments in these fields, the Legislature in enacting this part intends to encourage and aid the development of reconstructive medicine and surgery and the development of medical research by facilitating premortem and postmortem authorizations for donations of tissue and organs. It is the purpose of this part to regulate the gift of a body or parts of a body, the gift to be made after the death of a donor. *(Laws 1974, ch. 74-106, §1; Laws 1975, ch. 75-220, §45; Laws 1984, ch. 84-264, §3. Renumbered from §732.910, by Laws 2001, ch. 2001-226, §60, effective January 1, 2002.)*

§765.511. Applicable definitions

As used in this part, the term:

(1) "Bank" or "storage facility" means a facility licensed, accredited, or approved under the laws of any state for storage of human bodies or parts thereof.

(2) "Death" means the absence of life as determined, in accordance with currently accepted medical standards, by the irreversible cessation of all respiration and circulatory function, or as determined, in accordance with §382.009, by the irreversible cessation of the functions of the entire brain, including the brain stem.

(3) "Donor" means an individual who makes a gift of all or part of his or her body.

(4) "Hospital" means a hospital licensed, accredited, or approved under the laws of any state and includes a hospital operated by the United States Government or a state, or a subdivision thereof, although not required to be licensed under state laws.

(5) "Physician" or "surgeon" means a physician or surgeon licensed to practice under chapter 458 or chapter 459 or similar laws of any state. "Surgeon" includes dental or oral surgeon.

(Laws 1974, ch. 74-106, §1; Laws 1975, ch. 75-220, §45; Laws 1997, ch. 97- 102, § 973; Laws 1998, ch. 98-68, §5. Renumbered from §732.911, by Laws 2001, ch. 2001-226, §61, effective January 1, 2002.)

§765.512. Requirements for donors of anatomical gifts

(1) Any person who may make a will may give all or part of his or her body for any purpose specified in §765.510, the gift to take effect upon death. An anatomical gift made by an adult donor and not revoked by the donor as provided in §765.516 is irrevocable after the donor's death. A family member, guardian, representative ad litem, or health care surrogate of an adult donor who has made an anatomical gift pursuant to subsection (2) may not modify, deny, or prevent a donor's wish or intent to make an anatomical gift from being made after the donor's death.

(2) If the decedent has executed an agreement concerning an anatomical gift, by signing an organ and tissue donor card, by expressing his or her wish to donate in a living will or advance directive, or by signifying his or her intent to donate on his or her driver's license or in some other written form has indicated his or her wish to make an anatomical gift, and in the absence of actual notice of contrary indications by the decedent, the document is evidence of legally sufficient informed consent to donate an anatomical gift and is legally binding. Any surrogate designated by the decedent pursuant to part II of this chapter may give all or any part of the decedent's body for any purpose specified in §765.510.

(3) If the decedent has not executed an agreement concerning an anatomical gift or designated a surrogate pursuant to part II of this chapter to make an anatomical gift pursuant to the conditions of subsection (2), a member of one of the classes of persons listed below, in the order of priority stated and in the absence of actual notice of contrary indications by the decedent or actual notice of opposition by a member of the same or a prior class, may give all or any part of the decedent's body for any purpose specified in §765.510:

(a) The spouse of the decedent;

(b) An adult son or daughter of the decedent;

(c) Either parent of the decedent;

(d) An adult brother or sister of the decedent;

(e) A grandparent of the decedent;

(f) A guardian of the person of the decedent at the time of his or her death; or

(g) A representative ad litem who shall be appointed by a court of competent jurisdiction forthwith upon a petition heard ex parte filed by any person, which representative ad litem shall ascertain that no person of higher priority exists who objects to the gift of all or any part of the decedent's body and that no evidence exists of the decedent's having made a communication expressing a desire that his or her body or body parts not be donated upon death;

but no gift shall be made by the spouse if any adult son or daughter objects, and provided that those of higher priority, if they are reasonably available, have been contacted and made aware of the proposed gift, and further provided that a reasonable search is made to show that there would have been no objection on religious grounds by the decedent.

(4) If the donee has actual notice of contrary indications by the decedent or, in the case of a spouse making the gift, an objection of an adult son or

daughter or actual notice that a gift by a member of a class is opposed by a member of the same or a prior class, the donee shall not accept the gift.

(5) The person authorized by subsection (3) may make the gift after the decedent's death or immediately before the decedent's death.

(6) A gift of all or part of a body authorizes:

(a) Any examination necessary to assure medical acceptability of the gift for the purposes intended.

(b) The decedent's medical provider, family, or a third party to furnish medical records requested concerning the decedent's medical and social history.

(7) Once the gift has been made, the rights of the donee are paramount to the rights of others, except as provided by §765.517.

(Laws 1974, ch. 74-106, §1; Laws 1975, ch. 75-220, §45; Laws 1984, ch. 84-264, §4; Laws 1985, ch. 85-62, §62; Laws 1995, ch. 95-423, §5; Laws 1997, ch. 97-102, §974; Laws 1998, ch. 98-68, §6; Laws 1999, ch. 99-331, §12. Renumbered from §732.912, and amended by Laws 2001, ch. 2001-226, §62, effective January 1, 2002. Amended by Laws 2003, ch. 2003-46, §2, effective July 1, 2003.)

§765.513. Recipients of anatomical gifts

The following persons or entities may become donees of gifts of bodies or parts of them for the purposes stated:

(1) Any hospital, surgeon, or physician for medical or dental education or research, advancement of medical or dental science, therapy, or transplantation.

(2) Any accredited medical or dental school, college, or university for education, research, advancement of medical or dental science, or therapy.

(3) Any bank or storage facility for medical or dental education, research, advancement of medical or dental science, therapy, or transplantation.

(4) Any individual specified by name for therapy or transplantation needed by him or her.

However, the Legislature declares that the public policy of this state prohibits restrictions on the possible recipients of an anatomical gift on the basis of race, color, religion, sex, national origin, age, physical handicap, health status, marital status, or economic status, and such restrictions are hereby declared void and unenforceable.

(Laws 1974, ch. 74-106, §1; Laws 1975, ch. 75-220, §45; Laws 1994, ch. 94- 305, §1; Laws 1997, ch. 97-102, §975; Laws 1998, ch. 98-68, §7. Renumbered from §732.913 by Laws 2001, ch. 2001-226, §63, effective January 1, 2002.)

§765.514. Procedures for making anatomical gifts

(1) A gift of all or part of the body under §765.512(1) may be made by will. The gift becomes effective upon the death of the testator without waiting for probate. If the will is not probated or if it is declared invalid for testamentary purposes, the gift is nevertheless valid to the extent that it has been acted upon in good faith.

(2)(a) A gift of all or part of the body under §765.512(1) may also be made by a document other than a will. The gift becomes effective upon the death of the donor. The document must be signed by the donor in the presence of two witnesses who shall sign the document in the donor's presence. If the donor cannot sign, the document may be signed for him or her at the donor's direction and in his or her presence and the presence of two witnesses who must sign the document in the donor's presence. Delivery of the document of gift during the donor's lifetime is not necessary to make the gift valid.

(b) The following form of written instrument shall be sufficient for any person to give all or part of his or her body for the purposes of this part:

UNIFORM DONOR CARD

The undersigned hereby makes this anatomical gift, if medically acceptable, to take effect on death. The words and marks below indicate my desires:

I give:

(a) ___ any needed organs or parts;

(b) ___ only the following organs or parts

[Specify the organ(s) or part(s)]

for the purpose of transplantation, therapy, medical research, or education;

(c) ___ my body for anatomical study if needed. Limitations or special wishes, if any:

(If applicable, list specific donee)

Signed by the donor and the following witnesses in the presence of each other:

(Signature of donor) (Date of birth of donor)

(Date signed) (City and State)

(Witness) (Witness)

(Address) (Address)

(3) The gift may be made to a donee specified by name. If the donee is not specified by name, the gift may be accepted by the attending physician as donee upon or following the donor's death. If the gift is made to a specified donee who is not available at the time and place of death, the attending physician may accept the gift as donee upon or following death in the absence of any expressed indication that the donor desired otherwise. However, the Legislature declares that the public policy of this state prohibits restrictions on the possible recipients of an anatomical gift on the basis of race, color, religion, sex, national origin, age, physical handicap, health status, marital status, or economic status, and such restrictions are hereby declared void and unenforceable. The physician who becomes a donee under this subsection shall not participate in the procedures for removing or transplanting a part.

(4) Notwithstanding §765.517(2), the donor may designate in his or her will or other document of gift the surgeon or physician to carry out the appropriate procedures. In the absence of a designation or if the designee is not available, the donee or other person authorized to accept the gift may employ or authorize any surgeon or physician for the purpose.

(5) Any gift by a member of a class designated in §765.512(3) must be made by a document signed by that person or made by that person's witnessed telephonic discussion, telegraphic message, or other recorded message.

(Laws 1974, ch. 74-106, §1; Laws 1975, ch. 75-220, §45; Laws 1983, ch. 83-171, §1; Laws 1994, ch. 94-305, §2; Laws 1995, ch. 95-423, §6; Laws 1997, ch. 97-102, §976; Laws 1998, ch. 98-68, §8; Laws 1999, ch. 99-331, §13. Renumbered from §732.914 and amended by Laws 2001, ch. 2001-226, §64, effective Jan. 1, 2002.)

§765.515. Delivery of document: delivery not essential to validity; various methods of delivery, donor registry

(1) If a gift is made through the program established by the Agency for Health Care Administration and the Department of Highway Safety and Motor Vehicles under the authority of §765.521, the completed donor registration card shall be delivered to the Department of Highway Safety and Motor Vehicles and processed in a manner specified in subsection (4), but delivery is not necessary to the validity of the gift. If the donor withdraws the gift, the records of the Department of Highway Safety and Motor Vehicles shall be updated to reflect such withdrawal.

(2) If a gift is not made through the program established by the Agency for Health Care Administration and the Department of Highway Safety and Motor Vehicles under the authority of §765.521 and is made by the donor to a specified donee, the document, other than a will, may be delivered to the donee to expedite the appropriate procedures immediately after death, but delivery is not necessary to the validity of the gift. Such document may be deposited in any hospital, bank, storage facility, or registry office that accepts such documents for safekeeping or for facilitation of procedures after death.

(3) On the request of any interested party upon or after the donor's death, the person in possession shall produce the document for examination.

(4) The Agency for Health Care Administration and the Department of Highway Safety and Motor Vehicles shall develop and implement an organ and tissue donor registry which shall record, through electronic means, organ and tissue donation documents submitted through the driver license identification program or by other sources. The registry shall be maintained in a manner which will allow, through electronic and telephonic methods, immediate access to organ and tissue donation documents 24 hours a day, 7 days a week. Hospitals, organ and tissue procurement agencies, and other parties identified by the agency by rule shall be allowed access through coded means to the information stored in the registry. Costs for the organ and tissue donor registry shall be paid from the Florida Organ and Tissue Donor Education and Procurement Trust Fund created by §765.52155. Funds deposited into the Florida Organ and Tissue Donor Education and Procurement Trust Fund shall be utilized by the Agency for Health Care Administration for maintaining the organ and tissue donor registry and for organ and tissue donor education.

(Laws 1974, ch. 74-106, §1; Laws 1975, ch. 75-220, §45; Laws 1983, ch. 83-171, §2; Laws 1987, ch. 87-372, §1; Laws 1995, ch. 95-423, §7; Laws 1996, ch. 96-418, §33; Laws 1998, ch. 98-68, §9; Fla. St. 2000, Renumbered from §732.915, and amended by Laws 2001, ch. 2001-226, §65, effective January 1, 2002.)

§765.516. Methods of amendment of anatomical gifts and revocation of the gift

(1) A donor may amend the terms of or revoke an anatomical gift by:

(a) The execution and delivery to the donee of a signed statement.

(b) An oral statement that is made in the presence of two persons, one of whom must not be a family member, and communicated to the donor's family or attorney or to the donee.

(c) A statement during a terminal illness or injury addressed to an attending physician, who must communicate the revocation of the gift to the procurement organization that is certified by the state.

(d) A signed document found on or about the donor's person.

(2) Any gift made by a will may also be amended or revoked in the manner provided for amendment or revocation of wills or as provided in subsection (1).

(Laws 1974, ch. 74-106, §1; Laws 1975, ch. 75-220, §45; Laws 1983, ch. 83-171, §3; Laws 1995, ch. 95-423, §8; Laws 1997, ch. 97-102, §977; Laws 1998, ch. 98-68, §10. Renumbered from §732.916, by Laws 2001, ch. 2001-226, §66, effective January 1, 2002. Amended by Laws 2003, ch. 2003-46, §3, effective July 1, 2003.)

§765.517. Duties of recipients of gifts, time of death, medical tests of donor, expenses

(1) The donee, as specified under the provisions of §765.515(2), may accept or reject the gift. If the donee accepts a gift of the entire body or a part of the body to be used for scientific purposes other than a transplant, the donee may authorize embalming and the use of the body in funeral services, subject to the terms of the gift. If the gift is of a part of the body, the donee shall cause the part to be removed without unnecessary mutilation upon the death of the donor and before or after embalming. After removal of the part, custody of the remainder of the body vests in the surviving spouse, next of kin, or other persons under obligation to dispose of the body.

(2) The time of death shall be determined by a physician who attends the donor at the donor's death or, if there is no such physician, the physician who certifies the death. After death and in the absence of other qualified personnel, this physician may participate in, but shall not obstruct, the procedures to preserve the donor's organs or tissues and shall not be paid or reimbursed by, nor be associated with or employed by, an organ procurement organization, tissue bank, or eye bank. This physician shall not participate in the procedures for removing or transplanting a part.

(3) The organ procurement organization, tissue bank, or eye bank, or hospital medical professionals under the direction thereof, may perform any and all tests to evaluate the deceased as a potential donor and any invasive procedures on the deceased body in order to preserve the potential donor's organs. These procedures do not include the surgical removal of an organ or penetrating any body cavity, specifically for the purpose of donation, until a properly executed donor card or document is located or, if a properly executed donor card or document cannot be located, a person specified in §765.512(3) has been located, has been notified of the death, and has granted legal permission for the donation.

(4) All reasonable additional expenses incurred in the procedures to preserve the donor's organs or tissues shall be reimbursed by the organ procurement organization, tissue bank, or eye bank.

(5) A person who acts in good faith and without negligence in accord with the terms of this part or under the anatomical gift laws of another state or a foreign country is not liable for damages in any civil action or subject to prosecution for his or her acts in any criminal proceeding.

(6) The provisions of this part are subject to the laws of this state prescribing powers and duties with respect to autopsies.

(Laws 1974, ch. 74-106, §1; Laws 1975, ch. 75-220, §45; Laws 1983, ch. 83-171, §4; Laws 1995, ch. 95-423, §9; Laws 1997, ch. 97-102, §978; Laws 1999, ch. 99-331, §14. Renumbered from §732.917 and amended by Laws 2001, ch. 2001-226, §67, effective January 1, 2002.)

§765.518. Gifts of eyes, eye banks, forms, names of donors

(1) Any state, county, district, or other public hospital may purchase and provide the necessary facilities and equipment to establish and maintain an eye bank for restoration of sight purposes.

(2) The Department of Education may have prepared, printed, and distributed:

(a) A form document of gift for a gift of the eyes.

(b) An eye bank register consisting of the names of persons who have executed documents for the gift of their eyes.

(c) Wallet cards reciting the document of gift.

(Laws 1974, ch. 74-106, §1; Laws 1975, ch. 75-220, §45; Laws 1977, ch. 77-147, §462. Renumbered from §732.918, by Laws 2001, ch. 2001-226, §68, effective January 1, 2002.)

§765.5185. Procedures for medical examiners to remove corneas

(1) In any case in which a patient is in need of corneal tissue for a transplant, a district medical examiner or an appropriately qualified designee with training in ophthalmologic techniques may, upon request of any eye bank authorized under §765.518, provide the cornea of a decedent whenever all of the following conditions are met:

(a) A decedent who may provide a suitable cornea for the transplant is under the jurisdiction of the medical examiner and an autopsy is required in accordance with §406.11.

(b) No objection by the next of kin of the decedent is known by the medical examiner.

(c) The removal of the cornea will not interfere with the subsequent course of an investigation or autopsy.

(2) Neither the district medical examiner nor the medical examiner's appropriately qualified designee nor any eye bank authorized under §765.518 may be held liable in any civil or criminal action for failure to obtain consent of the next of kin.

(Laws 1977, ch. 77-172, §1; Laws 1978, ch. 78-191, §1; Laws 1997, ch. 97- 102, §979; Fla. St. 2000, §732.9185. Renumbered from §732.9185 by Laws 2001, ch. 2001-226, §69, effective January 1, 2002. Amended by Laws 2002, ch. 2002- 1, §111, effective May 21, 2002.)

§765.519. Procedures for funeral directors to remove eyes

With respect to a gift of an eye as provided for in this part, a licensed funeral director as defined in chapter 497 who has completed a course in eye enucleation and has received a certificate of competence from the Department of Ophthalmology of the University of Florida School of Medicine, the University of South Florida School of Medicine, or the University of Miami School of Medicine may enucleate eyes for gift after proper certification of death by a physician and in compliance with the intent of the gift as defined in this chapter. No properly certified funeral director acting in accordance with the terms of this part shall have any civil or criminal liability for eye enucleation.

(Laws 1974, ch. 74-106, §1; Laws 1975, ch. 75-220, §45; Laws 1980, ch. 80-157, §1. Renumbered from §732.919, by Laws 2001, ch. 2001-226, §70, effective January 1, 2002. Amended by Laws 2004, ch. 2004-301, §148, effective October 1, 2005.)

§765.521. DMV policy of encouraging organ donations

(1) The Agency for Health Care Administration and the Department of Highway Safety and Motor Vehicles shall develop and implement a program encouraging and allowing persons to make anatomical gifts as a part of the process of issuing identification cards and issuing and renewing driver licenses. The donor registration card distributed by the Department of Highway Safety and Motor Vehicles shall include the material specified by §765.514(2)(b) and may require such additional information, and include such additional material, as may be deemed necessary by that department. The Department of Highway Safety and Motor Vehicles shall also develop and implement a program to identify donors, which program shall include notations on identification cards, driver licenses, and driver records or such other methods as the department may develop. This program shall include, after an individual has completed a donor registration card, making a notation on the front of the driver license or identification card that clearly indicates the individual's intent to donate the individual's organs or tissue. A notation on an individual's driver license or identification card that the individual intends to donate organs or tissues is deemed sufficient to satisfy all requirements for consent to organ or tissue donation. The Agency for Health Care Administration shall provide the necessary supplies and forms through funds appropriated from general revenue or contributions from interested voluntary, nonprofit organizations. The Department of Highway Safety and Motor Vehicles shall provide the necessary recordkeeping system through funds appropriated from general revenue. The Department of Highway Safety and Motor Vehicles and the Agency for Health Care Administration shall incur no liability in connection with the performance of any acts authorized herein.

(2) The Department of Highway Safety and Motor Vehicles, after consultation with and concurrence by the Agency for Health Care Administration, shall adopt rules to implement the provisions of this section according to the provisions of chapter 120.

(3) Funds expended by the Agency for Health Care Administration to carry out the intent of this section shall not be taken from any funds appropriated for patient care.

(Laws 1975, ch. 75-71, §1; Laws 1977, ch. 77-16, §1; Laws 1977, ch. 77-147, §463; Laws 1977, ch. 77-174, §1; Laws 1980, ch. 80-134, §1, 2; Laws 1983, ch. 83-171, §5; Laws 1995, ch. 95-423, §10. Renumbered

from §732.921 and amended by Laws 2001, ch. 2001-226, §71, effective January 1, 2002.)

§765.5215. Public education program encouraging anatomical gifts

The Agency for Health Care Administration, subject to the concurrence of the Department of Highway Safety and Motor Vehicles, shall develop a continuing program to educate and inform medical professionals, law enforcement agencies and officers, high school children, state and local government employees, and the public regarding the laws of this state relating to anatomical gifts and the need for anatomical gifts.

(1) The program is to be implemented with the assistance of the organ and tissue donor education panel as provided in §765.5216 and with the funds collected under §320.08047 and 322.08(6)(b). Existing community resources, when available, must be used to support the program, and volunteers may assist the program to the maximum extent possible. The Agency for Health Care Administration may contract for the provision of all or any portion of the program. When awarding such contract, the agency shall give priority to existing nonprofit groups that are located within the community, including within the minority communities specified in subsection (2). The program aimed at educating medical professionals may be implemented by contract with one or more medical schools located in the state.

(2) The Legislature finds that particular difficulties exist in making members of the various minority communities within the state aware of laws relating to anatomical gifts and the need for anatomical gifts. Therefore, the program shall include, as a demonstration project, activities especially targeted at providing such information to the nonwhite, Hispanic, and Caribbean populations of the state.

(3) The Agency for Health Care Administration shall, no later than March 1 of each year, submit a report to the Legislature containing statistical data on the effectiveness of the program in procuring donor organs and the effect of the program on state spending for health care.

(4) The Agency for Health Care Administration, in furtherance of its educational responsibilities regarding organ and tissue donation, shall have access to the buildings and workplace areas of all state agencies and political subdivisions of the state.

(Laws 1985, ch. 85-247, §1; Laws 1995, ch. 95-423, §11; Laws 1999, ch. 99-248, §65. Renumbered from §732.9215, by Laws 2001, ch. 2001-226, §72, effective January 1, 2002. Amended by Laws 2002, ch. 2002-1, §112, effective May 21, 2002.)

§765.52155. Creation of Florida Organ and Tissue Donor Education and Procurement Trust Fund

The Florida Organ and Tissue Donor Education and Procurement Trust Fund is hereby created, to be administered by the Agency for Health Care Administration. Funds shall be credited to the trust fund as provided for in general law.

(Laws 1995, ch. 95-316, §1; Laws 1996, ch. 96-418, §29. Renumbered from §732.92155, by Laws 2001, ch. 2001-226, §73, effective January 1, 2002.)

§765.5216. Creation of Organ and Tissue Donor Education Panel to encourage, educate, and represent public

(1) The Legislature recognizes that there exists in the state a shortage of organ and tissue donors to provide the organs and tissue that could save lives or enhance the quality of life for many Floridians. The Legislature further recognizes the need to encourage the various minority populations of Florida to donate organs and tissue. It is the intent of the Legislature that the funds collected pursuant to §§320.08047 and 322.08(6)(b) be used for educational purposes aimed at increasing the number of organ and tissue donors, thus affording more Floridians who are awaiting organ or tissue transplants the opportunity for a full and productive life.

(2) There is created within the Agency for Health Care Administration a statewide organ and tissue donor education panel, consisting of 12 members, to represent the interests of the public with regard to increasing the number of organ and tissue donors within the state. The panel and the Organ and Tissue Procurement and Transplantation Advisory Board established in §765.543 shall jointly develop, subject to the approval of the Agency for Health Care Administration, education initiatives pursuant to §765.5215, which the agency shall implement. The membership must be balanced with respect to gender, ethnicity, and other demographic characteristics so that the appointees reflect the diversity of the population of this state. The panel members must include:

(a) A representative from the Agency for Health Care Administration, who shall serve as chairperson of the panel.

(b) A representative from a Florida licensed organ procurement organization.

(c) A representative from a Florida licensed tissue bank.

(d) A representative from a Florida licensed eye bank.

(e) A representative from a Florida licensed hospital.

(f) A representative from the Division of Driver Licenses of the Department of Highway Safety and Motor Vehicles, who possesses experience and knowledge in dealing with the public.

(g) A representative from the family of an organ, tissue, or eye donor.

(h) A representative who has been the recipient of a transplanted organ, tissue, or eye, or is a family member of a recipient.

(i) A representative who is a minority person as defined in former § 381.81.

(j) A representative from a professional association or public relations or advertising organization.

(k) A representative from a community service club or organization.

(l) A representative from the Department of Education.

(3) All members of the panel shall be appointed by the Secretary of Health Care Administration to serve a term of 2 years, except that, initially, six members shall be appointed for 1-year terms and six members shall be appointed for 2- year terms.

(4) Members of the panel shall receive no compensation but shall be reimbursed for per diem and travel expenses by the agency in accordance with the provisions of §112.061, while engaged in the performance of their duties.

(5) The panel shall meet at least semiannually or upon the call of the chairperson or the Secretary of Health Care Administration.

(Laws 1995, ch. 95-423, §12; Laws 1998, ch. 98-68, §11; Laws 1999, ch. 99-248, §66; Laws 2000, ch. 2000-305, §25. Renumbered from §732.9216, by Laws 2001, ch. 2001-226, §74, effective January 1, 2002. Amended by Laws 2002, ch. 2002-1, §113, effective May 21, 2002; Laws 2003, ch. 2003-1, §103, effective July 1, 2003.)

§765.522. Duties of hospital personnel to ascertain existence of donor documents

(1) When used in this section, "hospital" means any establishment licensed under chapter 395 except psychiatric and rehabilitation hospitals.

(2) Where, based on accepted medical standards, a hospital patient is a suitable candidate for organ or tissue donation, the hospital administrator or the hospital administrator's designee shall, at or near the time of death, access the organ and tissue donor registry created by §765.515(4) to ascertain the existence of a donor card or document executed by the decedent. In the absence of a donor card, organ donation sticker or organ donation imprint on a driver's license, or other properly executed document, the hospital administrator or designee shall request:

(a) The patient's health care surrogate, as permitted in §765.512(2); or

(b) If the patient does not have a surrogate, or the surrogate is not reasonably available, any of the persons specified in §765.512(3), in the order and manner of priority stated in §765.512(3),

to consent to the gift of all or any part of the decedent's body for any purpose specified in this part. Except as provided in §765.512, in the absence of actual notice of opposition, consent need only be obtained from the person or persons in the highest priority class reasonably available.

(3) A gift made pursuant to a request required by this section shall be executed pursuant to § 765.514.

(4) The Agency for Health Care Administration shall establish rules and guidelines concerning the education of individuals who may be designated to perform the request and the procedures to be used in making the request. The agency is authorized to adopt rules concerning the documentation of the request, where such request is made.

(5) There shall be no civil or criminal liability against any organ procurement organization, eye bank, or tissue bank certified under §765.542, or against any hospital or hospital administrator or designee, when complying with the provisions of this part and the rules of the Agency for Health Care Administration or when, in the exercise of reasonable care, a request for organ donation is inappropriate and the gift is not made according to this part and the rules of the Agency for Health Care Administration.

(6) The hospital administrator or a designee shall, at or near the time of death of a potential organ donor, directly notify the affiliated Health Care Financing Administration designated organ procurement organization of the potential organ donor. This organ procurement organization must offer any organ from such a donor first to patients on a Florida-based local or state organ sharing transplant list. For the purpose of this subsection, the term "transplant list" includes certain categories of national or regional organ sharing for patients of exceptional need or exceptional match, as approved or mandated by the United Network for Organ Sharing. This notification must not be made to a tissue bank or eye bank in lieu of the organ procurement organization unless the tissue bank or

eye bank is also a Health Care Financing Administration designated organ procurement organization.
(Laws 1986, ch. 86-212, §1; Laws 1987, ch. 87-372, §2; Laws 1995, ch. 95- 423, §13; Laws 1997, ch. 97-102, §980; Laws 1998, ch. 98-68, §12; Laws 1999, ch. 99-331, §15. Renumbered from §732.922, and amended by Laws 2001, ch. 2001-226, §75, effective January 1, 2002. Amended by Laws 2003, ch. 2003-1, §104, effective July 1, 2003.)

§765.53. Creation of state advisory counsel of licensed physicians

(1) There is hereby created within the Agency for Health Care Administration a statewide technical Organ Transplant Advisory Council consisting of twelve members to represent the interests of the public and the clients of the Department of Health or the agency. The members shall be physicians licensed according to chapter 458 or chapter 459. A person employed by the agency may not be appointed as a member of the council.

(2) The Secretary of Health Care Administration shall appoint all members of the council to serve a term of 2 years.

(3) The Secretary of Health Care Administration shall fill each vacancy on the council for the balance of the unexpired term. Priority consideration must be given to the appointment of an individual whose primary interest, experience, or expertise lies with clients of the Department of Health and the agency. If an appointment is not made within 120 days after a vacancy occurs on the council, the vacancy must be filled by the majority vote of the council.

(4) The members of the council shall elect a chairperson. The term of the chairperson shall be for 2 years, and an individual may not serve as chairperson for more than two consecutive terms.

(5) Members of the council shall receive no compensation, but shall be reimbursed for per diem and travel expenses by the Agency for Health Care Administration in accordance with the provisions of §112.061 while engaged in the performance of their duties.

(6) The responsibilities of the council shall be to recommend to the Agency for Health Care Administration indications for adult and pediatric organ transplants. The council shall also formulate guidelines and standards for organ transplants and for the development of End Stage Organ Disease and Tissue/Organ Transplant programs. The recommendations, guidelines, and standards developed by the council are applicable only to those health programs funded through the Agency for Health Care Administration.

(7) The council shall meet at least annually or upon the call of the chairperson or the Secretary of Health Care Administration.
(Laws 1986, ch. 86-208, §1; Laws 1986, ch. 86-220, §88; Fla. St. 1989, §381.602; Laws 1991, ch. 91-49, §8; Laws 1991, ch. 91-297, §52; Laws 1994, ch. 94-305, §3; Laws 1997, ch. 97-101, §50. Amended by Laws 1999, ch. 99-299, §1, effective January 1, 2000; Laws 2000, ch. 2000-305, §6, effective October 1, 2000. Renumbered from §381.0602, by Laws 2003, ch. 2003-1, §33, effective July 1, 2003.)

§765.541. Establishment of program for certification of agencies that procure organ transplants

The Agency for Health Care Administration shall:

(1) Establish a program for the certification of organizations, agencies, or other entities engaged in the procurement of organs, tissues, and eyes for transplantation;

(2) Adopt rules that set forth appropriate standards and guidelines for the program. These standards and guidelines must be substantially based on the existing laws of the Federal Government and this state and the existing standards and guidelines of the United Network for Organ Sharing (UNOS), the American Association of Tissue Banks (AATB), the South-Eastern Organ Procurement Foundation (SEOPF), the North American Transplant Coordinators Organization (NATCO), and the Eye Bank Association of America (EBAA). In addition, the Agency for Health Care Administration shall, before adopting these standards and guidelines, seek input from all organ procurement organizations, tissue banks, and eye banks based in this state;

(3) Collect, keep, and make available to the Governor and the Legislature information regarding the numbers and disposition of organs and tissues procured by each certified entity;

(4) Monitor participating facilities and agencies for program compliance; and

(5) Provide for the administration of the Organ and Tissue Procurement and Transplantation Advisory Board.
(Laws 1991, ch. 91-271, §2; Laws 1994, ch. 94-305, §5. Renumbered from §381.6021 by Laws 2003, ch. 2003-1, §33, effective July 1, 2003.)

§765.542. Requirement of certification for procurement agencies

(1) An organization, agency, or other entity may not engage in the practice of organ procurement in this state without being designated as an organ procurement organization by the secretary of the United States Department of Health and Human Services and being appropriately certified by the Agency for Health Care Administration. As used in this subsection, the term "procurement" includes the retrieval, processing, or distribution of human organs. A physician or organ procurement organization based outside this state is exempt from these certification requirements if:

(a) The organs are procured for an out-of-state patient who is listed on, or referred through, the United Network for Organ Sharing System; and

(b) The organs are procured through an agreement of an organ procurement organization certified by the state.

(2) An organization, agency, or other entity may not engage in tissue procurement in this state unless it is appropriately certified by the Agency for Health Care Administration. As used in this subsection, the term "procurement" includes any retrieval, processing, storage, or distribution of human tissue for transplantation.

(3) An organization, agency, or other entity may not engage in the practice of eye procurement in this state without being appropriately certified by the Agency for Health Care Administration. As used in this subsection, the term "procurement" includes the retrieval, processing, or distribution of human eye tissue. Funeral directors or direct disposers that retrieve eye tissue for an eye bank certified under this subsection are exempt from the certification requirements under this subsection.

(4) A limited certificate may be issued to a tissue bank or eye bank, certifying only those components of procurement which the bank has chosen to perform. The Agency for Health Care Administration may issue a limited certificate if it determines that the tissue bank or eye bank is adequately staffed and equipped to operate in conformity with the rules adopted under this section.

(Laws 1991, ch. 91-271, §3; Laws 1994, ch. 94-305, §6. Renumbered from §381.6022 by Laws 2003, ch. 2003-1, §33, effective July 1, 2003.)

§765.543. Creation and duties of Organ and Tissue Procurement and Transplantation Advisory Board

(1) There is hereby created the Organ and Tissue Procurement and Transplantation Advisory Board, which shall consist of 14 members who are appointed by and report directly to the Secretary of Health Care Administration. The membership must be regionally distributed and must include:

(a) Two representatives who have expertise in vascular organ transplant surgery;

(b) Two representatives who have expertise in vascular organ procurement, preservation, and distribution;

(c) Two representatives who have expertise in musculoskeletal tissue transplant surgery;

(d) Two representatives who have expertise in musculoskeletal tissue procurement, processing, and distribution;

(e) A representative who has expertise in eye and cornea transplant surgery;

(f) A representative who has expertise in eye and cornea procurement, processing, and distribution;

(g) A representative who has expertise in bone marrow procurement, processing, and transplantation;

(h) A representative from the Florida Pediatric Society;

(i) A representative from the Florida Society of Pathologists; and

(j) A representative from the Florida Medical Examiners Commission.

(2) The advisory board members may not be compensated for their services except that they may be reimbursed for their travel expenses as provided by law. Members of the board shall be appointed for 3-year terms of office.

(3) The board shall:

(a) Assist the Agency for Health Care Administration in the development of necessary professional qualifications, including, but not limited to, the education, training, and performance of persons engaged in the various facets of organ and tissue procurement, processing, preservation, and distribution for transplantation;

(b) Assist the Agency for Health Care Administration in monitoring the appropriate and legitimate expenses associated with organ and tissue procurement, processing, and distribution for transplantation and developing methodologies to assure the uniform statewide reporting of data to facilitate the accurate and timely evaluation of the organ and tissue procurement and transplantation system;

(c) Provide assistance to the Florida Medical Examiners Commission in the development of appropriate procedures and protocols to assure continued improvement in the approval and release of potential organ and tissue donors by the district medical examiners and associate medical examiners;

(d) Develop with and recommend to the Agency for Health Care Administration the necessary procedures and protocols required to assure that all residents of this state have reasonable access to available organ and tissue transplantation therapy and that residents of this state can be reasonably assured that the statewide procurement transplantation system will be able to fulfill their organ and tissue requirements within the limits of the available supply and according to the severity of their medical condition and need; and

(e) Develop with and recommend to the Agency for Health Care Administration any changes to the laws of this state or administrative rules or procedures required to assure that the statewide organ and tissue procurement and transplantation system will be able to function smoothly, effectively, and efficiently, in accordance with the Federal Anatomical Gift Act and in a manner that assures the residents of this state that no person or entity profits from the altruistic voluntary donation of organs or tissues.

(Laws 1991, ch. 91-271, §4; Laws 1994, ch. 94-305, §7. Amended by Laws 2000, ch. 2000-305, §7, effective October 1, 2000. Renumbered from §381.6023 by Laws 2003, ch. 2003-1, §33, effective July 1, 2003.)

§765.544. Application fees for procurement agencies

(1) The Agency for Health Care Administration shall collect an initial application fee of $1,000 from organ procurement organizations and tissue banks and $500 from eye banks. The fee must be submitted with each application for initial certification and is nonrefundable.

(2) The Agency for Health Care Administration shall assess annual fees to be used, in the following order of priority, for the certification program, the advisory board, maintenance of the organ and tissue donor registry, and the organ and tissue donor education program in the following amounts, which may not exceed $35,000 per organization:

(a) Each general organ procurement organization shall pay the greater of $1,000 or 0.25 percent of its total revenues produced from procurement activity in this state by the certificateholder during its most recently completed fiscal year or operational year.

(b) Each bone and tissue procurement agency or bone and tissue bank shall pay the greater of $1,000 or 0.25 percent of its total revenues from procurement and processing activity in this state by the certificateholder during its most recently completed fiscal year or operational year.

(c) Each eye bank shall pay the greater of $500 or 0.25 percent of its total revenues produced from procurement activity in this state by the certificateholder during its most recently completed fiscal year or operational year.

(3) The Agency for Health Care Administration shall provide by rule for administrative penalties for the purpose of ensuring adherence to the standards of quality and practice required by this chapter and rules of the agency for continued certification.

(4)

(a) Proceeds from fees, administrative penalties, and surcharges collected pursuant to subsections (2) and (3) must be deposited into the Florida Organ and Tissue Donor Education and Procurement Trust Fund created by §765.52155.

(b) Moneys deposited in the trust fund pursuant to this section must be used exclusively for the implementation, administration, and operation of the certification program and the advisory board, for maintaining the organ and tissue donor registry, and for organ and tissue donor education.

(5) As used in this section, the term "procurement activity in this state" includes the bringing into this state for processing, storage, distribution, or transplantation of organs or tissues that are initially procured in another state or country.

(Laws 1991, ch. 91-271, §5; Laws 1994, ch. 94-305, §8; Laws 1996, ch. 96-418, §32. Amended by Laws 1998, ch. 98-68, §3, effective May 21, 1998; Laws 1998, ch. 98-68, §4, effective July 1, 1999; Laws 2002, ch. 2002-1, §54, effective May 21, 2002. Renumbered from §381.6024 by Laws 2003, ch. 2003-1, §33, effective July 1, 2003.)

§765.545. Requirements of medical training for certain agency staff

Organ procurement organizations, tissue banks, and eye banks may employ coordinators, who are registered nurses, physician's assistants, or other medically trained personnel who meet the relevant standards for organ procurement organizations, tissue banks, or eye banks as adopted by the Agency for Health Care Administration under §765.541, to assist in the medical management of organ donors or in the surgical procurement of cadaveric organs, tissues, or eyes for transplantation or research. A coordinator who assists in the medical management of organ donors or in the surgical procurement of cadaveric organs, tissues, or eyes for transplantation or research must do so under the direction and supervision of a licensed physician medical director pursuant to rules and guidelines to be adopted by the Agency for Health Care Administration. With the exception of organ procurement surgery, this supervision may be indirect supervision. For purposes of this section, the term "indirect supervision" means that the medical director is responsible for the medical actions of the coordinator, that the coordinator is operating under protocols expressly approved by the medical director, and that the medical director or his or her physician designee is always available, in person or by telephone, to provide medical direction, consultation, and advice in cases of organ, tissue, and eye donation and procurement. Although indirect supervision is authorized under this section, direct physician supervision is to be encouraged when appropriate.

(Laws 1991, ch. 91-271, §6; Laws 1994, ch. 94-305, §9; Laws 1995, ch. 95-148, §1035. Renumbered from §381.6025 and amended by Laws 2003, ch. 2003- 1, §34, effective July 1, 2003.)

§765.546. Procurement of cadaveric organs for transplant by out-of-state physicians

Any physician currently licensed to practice medicine and surgery in the United States may surgically procure in this state cadaveric organs for transplant if:

(1) The organs are being procured for an out-of-state patient who is listed on, or referred through, the United Network for Organ Sharing System; and

(2) The organs are being procured through the auspices of an organ procurement organization certified in this state.

(Laws 1991, ch. 91-271, §7. Renumbered from §381.6026 by Laws 2003, ch. 2003-1, §33, effective July 1, 2003.)

Part II

~

Restatement (Third) of Property: Wills and Other Donative Transfers, Vols. 1 & 2 (1999, 2003)

Restatement (Third) of Property: Wills and Other Donative Transfers, Vols. 1 & 2 (1999, 2003)

TABLE OF CONTENTS

RESTATEMENT (THIRD) OF PROPERTY: WILLS AND OTHER DONATIVE TRANSFERS, vol. 1 (1999)

RESTATEMENT (THIRD) OF PROPERTY: WILLS AND OTHER DONATIVE TRANSFERS, vol. 2 (2003)

RESTATEMENT (THIRD) OF PROPERTY: WILLS AND OTHER DONATIVE TRANSFERS, vol. 1 (1999)

Chapter 1: DEFINITIONS AND BASIC PRINCIPLES

§1.1 Probate Estate

(a) A decedent's "probate estate" is the estate subject to administration under applicable laws relating to decedents' estates. The probate estate consists of property owned by the decedent at death and property acquired by the decedent's estate at or after the decedent's death.

(b) The "net probate estate" is the probate estate after deduction for family, exempt property, and homestead allowances, claims against the estate (including funeral expenses and expenses of administration), and taxes for which the estate is liable. Subject to overriding claims and rights provided by applicable law, such as the right of the decedent's surviving spouse to take an elective share or to elect other marital rights, the decedent's net probate estate passes to the decedent's heirs or devisees by intestate or testate succession.

§1.2 Requirement of Surviving the Decedent

An individual who fails to survive the decedent cannot take as an heir or a devisee.

§1.3 Noncitizens

Except as otherwise provided by applicable statute, the fact that an individual, or an individual through whom he or she claims, is not or was not a citizen of the United States does not disqualify the individual from acquiring or transmitting property through testate or intestate succession

Chapter 2: INTESTACY

§2.1 General Principles and Definitions

(a) A decedent who dies without a valid will dies intestate. A decedent who dies with a valid will that does not dispose of all of the decedent's net probate estate dies partially intestate.

(b) The decedent's intestate estate, consisting of that part of the decedent's net probate estate that is not disposed of by a valid will, passes at the decedent's death to the decedent's heirs as provided by statute.

§2.2 Intestate Share of Surviving Spouse

An intestate decedent's surviving spouse takes a share of the intestate estate as provided by statute. The exact share differs among the states. Not infrequently, the spouse takes the entire intestate estate if the decedent leaves no surviving descendants or parents and, in some states, if the decedent also leaves no other specified relative such as a descendant of a parent. Older statutes tend to reduce the spouse's share to a fraction such as one-half or one-third when the decedent leaves a surviving descendant or another specified relative. Under the Revised Uniform Probate Code, the surviving spouse takes either the entire intestate estate or a specified lump sum plus a specified percentage of the excess, if any, depending on what other relatives survive the decedent.

§2.3 Intestate Share of Surviving Descendants

(a) An intestate decedent's surviving descendants take the entire intestate estate if the decedent leaves no surviving spouse, and they take any portion of the intestate estate not passing to the surviving spouse if the decedent leaves a surviving spouse.

(b) The decedent's surviving descendants take by representation. There are several systems of representation.

§2.4 Intestate Share of Surviving Ancestors and Collateral Relatives

(a) If an intestate decedent leaves no surviving spouse and no surviving descendants, nearly all intestacy statutes grant the intestate estate to the second parentela (the decedent's surviving parents or, if deceased, to the parent's surviving descendants) and if no member of the second parentela survives the decedent, to the third parentela (the decedent's grandparents or, if deceased, to the grantparent's surviving descendants).

(b) If no member of the second or third parentela survives the decedent, the intestacy statutes diverge, but most follow one of two patterns. Either the intestate estate escheats to the state, or the intestate estate passes per capita to the decedent's nearest kindred as determined by the civil-law method, with the relatives having the nearer common ancestor taking exclusively under some statutes. Under statutes of the latter sort, the estate escheats to the state only if the decedent leaves no surviving kindred.

§2.5 Parent and Child Relationship

For purposes of intestate succession by, from, or through an individual:

(1) An individual is the child of his or her genetic parents, whether or not they are married to each other, except as otherwise provided in paragraph (2) or (5) or as other facts and circumstances warrant a different result.

(2) An adopted individual is a child of his or her adoptive parent or parents.

> (A) If the adoption removes the child from the families of both of the genetic parents, the child is not a child of either genetic parent.
>
> (B) If the adoption is by a relative of either genetic parent, or by the spouse or surviving spouse of such a relative, the individual remains a child of both genetic parents.
>
> (C) If the adoption is by a stepparent, the adopted stepchild is not only a child of the adoptive stepparent but is also a child of the genetic parent who is married to the stepparent. Under several intestacy statutes, including the Uniform Probate Code, the adopted stepchild is also a child of the other genetic parent for purposes of inheritance from and through that parent, but not for purposes of inheritance from or through the child.

(3) A stepchild who is not adopted by his or her stepparent is not the stepparent's child.

(4) A foster child is not the child of his or her foster parent or parents.

(5) A parent who has refused to acknowledge or has abandoned his or her child, or a person whose parental rights have been terminated, is barred from inheriting from or through the child.

§2.6 Advancements

An inter vivos gift made by an intestate decedent to an individual who, at the decedent's death, is an heir is treated as an advancement against the heir's intestate share if the decedent indicated in a contemporaneous writing, or if the heir acknowledged in writing, that the gift was so to operate.

§2.7 Negative Wills

A decedent's will may expressly exclude or limit the right of an individual or class to succeed to property of the decedent passing by intestate succession.

Chapter 3: EXECUTION OF WILLS

A. Execution Formalities

§3.1 Attested Wills
§3.2 Holographic Wills
§3.3 Excusing Harmless Errors

B. Related Doctrines

§3.4 Republication by Codicil
§3.5 Integration of Multiple Pages or Writings Into a Single Will
§3.6 Incorporation by Reference
§3.7 Independent Significance
§3.8 Pour-Over Devises
§3.9 Testamentary Disposition by Unattested Writing

§3.1 Attested Wills

A will is validly executed if it is in writing and is signed by the testator and by a specified number of attesting witnesses under procedures provided by applicable law.

§3.2 Holographic Wills

Statutes in many states provide that a will, though unwitnessed, is validly executed if it is written in the testator's handwriting and signed by the testator, and, under some statutes, dated in the testator's handwriting.

§3.3 Excusing Harmless Errors

A harmless error in executing a will may be excused if the proponent establishes by clear and convincing evidence that the decedent adopted the document as his or her will.

Comment

. . . b. Excusing harmless errors. . . . The requirement of a writing is so fundamental to the purpose of the execution formalities that it cannot be excused as harmless under the principle of this Restatement. Only a harmless error in executing a document can be excused under this Restatement.

Among the defects in execution that can be excused, the lack of a signature is the hardest to excuse. An unsigned will raises a serious but not insuperable doubt about whether the testator adopted the document as his or her will. A particularly attractive case for excusing the lack of the testator's signature is a crossed will case, in which, by mistake, a wife signs her husband's will and the husband signs his wife's will. Because attestation makes a more modest contribution to the purpose of the formalities, defects in compliance with attestation procedures are more easily excused. . . .

c. Scope of harmless-error rule. The harmless-error rule established in this section applies not only to defective execution but also to the validity of attempts to revoke a will or to revive a revoked will, topics covered in Chapter 4. . . .

§3.4 Republication by Codicil

A will is treated as if it were executed when its most recent codicil was executed, whether or not the codicil expressly republishes the prior will, unless the effect of so treating it would be inconsistent with the testator's intent.

§3.5 Integration of Multiple Pages or Writings Into a Single Will

To be treated as part of a page or other writing must be present when the will is executed and must be intended to be part of the will.

§3.6 Incorporation by Reference

A writing that is not valid as a will but is in existence when a will is executed may be incorporated by reference into the will if the will manifests an intent to incorporate the writing and the writing to be incoporated is identified with reasonable certainty.

§3.7 Independent Significance

The meaning of a dispositive or other provision may be supplied or affected by an external circumstance referred to in the will, unless the external circumstance has no significance apart from its effect upon the will.

§3.8 Pour-Over Devises

(a) A "pour-over" devise is a provision in a will that (i) adds property to an inter vivos trust or (ii) funds a trust that was not funded during the testator's lifetime but whose terms are in a trust instrument that was executed during the testator's lifetime.

(b) A pour-over devise may be validated by statute, by incorporation by reference, or by independent significance.

§3.9 Testamentary Disposition by Unattested Writing

When permitted by statute, a will may devise property as provided in a separate unattested writing even though the writing has no independent significance and does not satisfy the requirements for incorporation by reference.

Chapter 4: REVOCATION OF WILLS

§4.1 Revocation of Wills
§4.2 Revival of Revoked Wills

§4.1 Revocation of Wills

(a) A testator may revoke his or her will in whole or in part by subsequent will or by revocatory act.

(b) The dissolution of the testator's marraige is a change in circumstance that presumptively revokes any provision in the testator's will in favor of his or her former spouse. Neither marriage nor marriage followed by birth of issue is a chance in circumstance that revokes a will or any part of a will.

Comment

. . . *j. Presumption if lost or mutilated will traced to testator's possession.* If a will is traced to the testator's possession and cannot be found after death, there are three plausible explanations for its absence: The testator destroyed it with the intent to revoke; the will was accidentally destroyed or lost; or the will was wrongfully destroyed or suppressed by someone dissatisfied with its terms. Of these plausible explanations, the law presumes that the testator destroyed the will with intent to revoke it.

If a will is traced to the testator's possession and it is found after death with a revocatory act performed on it, . . . the law presumes that the testator performed the act on the will with intent to revoke it.

The presumption that the testator destroyed the will or performed some other revocatory act on it with intent to revoke is rebuttable. . . .

l. Act performed by another. Even if the testator did not perform a revocatory act on the will with intent to revoke, the will is still revoked by act if the testator directed another to perform the act and if the other person performed the act in the testator's presence. . . .

m. Revocation of codicil by act—effect on will. The revocation by act of a codicil to a will does not revoke the will, but the revocation is presumed to revive portions of the will that the codicil revoked. See §4.2, Comment g.

n. Revocation of will by act—effect on codicil. The revocation of a will by act does not revoke a codicil to the will. If the codicil depends on the revoked will for its meaning, however, the codicil may have no effect as a matter of construction. . . .

§4.2 Revival of Revoked Wills

(a) A will that was revoked by a later will is revived if the testator: (i) reexecuted the previously revoked will; (ii) executed a codicil indicating an intent to revive the previously revoked will; (iii) revoked the revoking will by act intending to revive the previously revoked will; or (iv) revoked the revoking will by another, later will whose terms indicate an intent to revive the previously revoked will.

(b) A will that was revoked by act is revived if the testator: (i) reexecuted the will; (ii) executed a codicil indicating an intent to revive the previously revoked will; or (iii) performed an act on the will that clearly and convincingly demonstrates an intent to reverse the revocation.

(c) A testamentary provision that was revoked by dissolution of the testator's marriage is revived if: (i) the testator remarried thc former spouse, reexecuted the will, or executed a codicil indicating an intent to revive the previously revoked provision; or (ii) the dissolution of hte marriage is nullified.

§4.3 Ineffective Revocation (Dependent Relative Revocation)

(a) A partial or complete revocation of a will is presumptively ineffective if the testator made the revocation:

(1) in connection with an attempt to achieve a dispositive objective that fails under applicable law, or

(2) because of a false assumption of law, or because of a false belief about an objective fact, that is either recited in the revoking instrument or established by clear and convincing evidence.

(b) The presumption established in subsection (a) is rebutted if allowing the revocation to remain in effect would be more consistent with the testator's probable intention.

Chapter 5: POST-EXECUTION EVENTS AFFECTING WILLS

§5.1 Classification of Devises

Devises are classified as specific, general, demonstrative, or residuary:

(1) A specific devise is a testamentary disposition of a specifically identified asset.

(2) A general devise is a testamentary disposition, usually of a specified amount of money or quantity of property, that is payable from the general assets of the estate.

(3) A demonstrative devise is a testamentary disposition, usually of a specified amount of money or quantity of property, that is primarily payable from a designated source, but is secondarily payable from the general assets of the estate to the extent that the primary source is insufficient.

(4) A residuary devise is a testamentary disposition of property of the testator's net probate estate not disposed of by a specific, general, or demonstrative devise.

§5.2 Failure ("Ademption") of Specific Devises by Extinction

(a) If specifically devised property, in its original or in a changed form, is in the testator's estate at death, the devisee is entitled to the specifically devised property.

(b) If specifically devised property is not in the testator's estate at death, the devisee is entitled to any proceeds unpaid at death of (i) any sale, (ii) any condemnation award, or (iii) any insurance on or other recovery for damage to or loss of the property.

(c) Subject to subsection (b), if specifically devised property is not in the testator's estate at death, the specific devise fails unless failure of the devise would be inconsistent with the testator's intent.

§5.3 Effect of Stock Splits, Stock Dividends, and Other Distributions on Devises of a Specified Number of Securities

A devise of a specified number of securities carries with it any additional securities acquired by the testator after executing the will to the extent that the post-execution acquisitions resulted from the testator's ownership of the described securities.

§5.4 Ademption by Satisfaction

An inter vivos gift made by a testator to a devisee or to a member of the devisee's family adeems the devise by satisfaction, in whole or in part, if the testator indicated in a contemporaneous writing, or if the devisee acknowledged in writing, that the gift was so to operate.

§5.5 Antilapse Statutes

Antilapse statutes typically provide, as a rebuttable rule of construction, that devises to certain relatives who predecease the testator pass to specified substitute takers, usually the descendants of the predeceased devisee who survive the testator.

Comment

. . . Antilapse statutes establish a strong rule of construction, designed to carry out probable intent. They are based on the constructional preference against disinheriting a line of descent, which in turn implements the constructional preference for preserving equality among different lines of descent. . . .

h. Contrary intent; survival language. An often litigated question is whether language requiring the devisee to survive the testator, without more, constitutes a sufficient expression of a contrary intent to defeat the antilapse statute. The majority view is that such language signifies a contrary intent. Because such a survival provision is often boiler-plate form-book language, the testator may not understand that such language could disinherit the line of descent headed by the deceased devisee. When the testator is older than the devisee and hence does not expect the devisee to die first, or if the devisee was childless when the will was executed, it seems especially unlikely that a provision requiring the devisee to survive the testator was intended to disinherit the devisee's descendants. . . .

. . . As indicated [*supra*], antilapse statutes are based on the constructional preference against disinheriting a line of descent. As explained in §11.3, . . . that constructional preference

is strongest when applied to direct descendants of the donor (sometimes called *lineal* descendants). The preference . . . becomes somewhat weaker the farther removed the ancestor is to the donor. . . .

o. Lapse in the residue; rejection of the no-residue-of-a-residue rule. For the purpose of determining what happens to the share of a residuary devisee who fails to survive the testator, a residuary clause that devises the residue to two or more persons is treated as if it created a class gift, even if the devise is not in the form of a class gift. The contrary rule, sometimes called the *no-residue-of-a-residue rule*, is not followed in modern statutory law, including the Uniform Probate Code, nor in this Restatement. Thus, if an antilapse statute does not apply, the share of a residuary devisee that fails for any reason passes to the other residuary devisee, or if more than one, to the other residuary devisees in proportion to the interest of each in the remaining part of the residue. A residuary devise lapses and passes to intestacy only if an antilapse statute does not apply and no residuary devisee survives the testator. . . .

RESTATEMENT (THIRD) OF PROPERTY: WILLS AND OTHER DONATIVE TRANSFERS, vol. 2 (2003)

Chapter 6: GIFTS

§6.1 Requirements Applicable to All Gifts of Property

§6.2 Gifts of Personal Property

§6.3 Gifts of Land

§6.1 Requirements Applicable to All Gifts of Property

(a) To make a gift of property, the donor must transfer an ownership interest to the donee without consideration and with donative intent.

(b) Acceptance by the donee is required for a gift to become complete. Acceptance is presumed, subject to the donee's right to refuse or disclaim.

§6.2 Gifts of Personal Property

The transfer of personal property, necessary to perfect a gift, may be made

(1) by delivering the property to the donee or

(2) by inter vivos donative document.

§6.3 Gifts of Land

The transfer of land, necessary to perfect a gift, must be evidenced in a writing that is executed in compliance with the formalities required by the applicable statute of frauds.

Chapter 7: WILL SUBSTITUTES

§7.1 Will Substitute—Definition and Validity

(a) A will substitute is an arrangement respecting property or contract rights that is established during the donor's life, under which (1) the right to possession or enjoyment of the property or to a contractual payment shifts outside of probate to the donee at the donor's death; and (2) substantial lifetime rights of dominion, control, possession, or enjoyment are retained by the donor.

(b) To be valid, a will substitute need not be executed in compliance with the statutory formalities required for a will.

§7.2 Application of Will Doctrines to Will Substitutes

Although a will substitute need not be executed in compliance with the statutory formalities required for a will, such an arrangement is, to the extent appropriate, subject to substantive restrictions on testation and to rules of construction and other rules applicable to testamentary dispositions.

Comment

. . . A will substitute is subject to [wills'] rules of construction only to the extent appropriate. . . .

Historically, some of the rules of construction were formulated only for wills because wills then constituted the principal means of transmitting property at death. Some rules of construction were placed in the probate code, which led the legislature to draft them as rules applicable to wills. As will substitutes have proliferated and become alternative means of passing property at death, legislatures and courts have sometimes been slow to expand the scope of these rules to transactions to which they should be fully applicable in policy. This Restatement (along with Restatement Third, Trusts, the Revised Uniform Probate Code, and the Uniform Trust Code) moves toward the policy of unifying the law of wills and will substitutes. . . .

Chapter 8: INVALIDITY DUE TO THE DONOR'S INCAPACITY OR ANOTHER'S WRONGDOING

A. Donor's Capacity

B. Protection Against Wrongdoing

C. No Contest Clauses

§8.1 Requirement of Mental Capacity

(a) A person must have mental capacity in order to make or revoke a donative transfer.

(b) If the donative transfer is in the form of a will, a revocable will substitute, or a revocable gift, the testator or donor must be capable of knowing and understanding in a general way the nature and extent of his or her property, the natural objects of his or her bounty, and the disposition that he or she is making of that property, and must also be capable of relating these documents to one another and forming an orderly desire regarding the disposition of that property.

(c) If the donative transfer is in the form of an irrevocable gift, the donor must have the mental capacity necessary to make or revoke a will and must also be capable of understanding the effect that the gift may have on the future financial security of the donor and of anyone who may be dependent on the donor.

§8.2 Incapacity Due to Minority

(a) A minor does not have capacity to make a will. A purported will made by a minor is void.

(b) A minor does not have capacity to make a gift. A purported gift made by a minor is voidable, not void. Before reaching majority, the minor may disaffirm the gift. After reaching minority, the minor may either disaffirm or ratify the gift. The failure to disaffirm within a reasonable time after reaching majority constitutes a ratification of the gift.

(c) For purposes of this section, a "minor" is a person who has not reached the age of majority or the age of capacity for the purpose in question and who is not emancipated. The age of majority is 18, unless an applicable statute provides otherwise.

§8.3 Undue Influence, Duress, or Fraud

(a) A donative transfer is invalid to the extent that it was procured by undue influence, duress, or fraud.

(b) A donative transfer is procured by undue influence if the wrongdoer exerted such influence over the donor that it overcame the donor's free will and cuased the donor to make a donative transfer that the donor would not otherwise have made.

(c)A donative transfer is procured by duress if the wrongdoer threatened to perform or did perform a wrongful act that coerced the donor into making a donative transfer that the donor would not otherwise have made.

(d) A donative transfer is procured by fraud if the wrongdoer knowingly or recklessly made a false representation to the donor about a material fact that was intended to and did lead the donor to make a donative transfer that the donor would not otherwise have made.

§8.4 Homicide—The Slayer Rule

(a) A slayer is denied any right to benefit from the wrong. For purposes of this section, a slayer is a person who, without legal excuse or justification, is responsible for the felonious and intentional killing of another.

(b) Whether or not a person is a slayer is determined in a civil proceeding under the preponderance of the evidence standard rather than beyond a reasonable doubt. For purposes of the civil proceeding, however, a final judgment of conviction for the felonious and intentional killing of the decedent in a criminal proceeding conclusively establishes the convicted person as the decedent's slayer.

§8.5 No Contest Clauses

A provision in a donative document purporting to rescind a donative transfer to, or a fiduciary appointment of, any person who institutes a proceeding challenging the validity of all or part of the donative document is enforceable unless probable cause existed for instituting the proceeding.

Comment

a. Scope. . . This section only addresses the validity of a no contest clause that pertains to proceedings that challenge the validity of a donative document (or a portion of such a document). A clause that purports to prohibit beneficiaries from enforcing fiduciary duties owed to the beneficiaries by trustees or other fiduciaries does not fall within the scope of this section. Although sometimes couched as a no contest clause, such a measure functions as an exculpation clause and is governed by the standards applying to such clauses. . .
.

d. Construction of no contest clauses. No contest clauses are construed narrowly, consistent with their terms. The institution of a proceeding to contest a will or other donative transfer, or to challenge a particular provision, upon any of the grounds within the scope of the no contest clause, normally violates the clause. In the absence of specific language to the contrary, the clause should be construed to be violated regardless of whether the action is subsequently withdrawn immediately after its institution, prior to a hearing, at the trial, or at any time thereafter. The mere filing of a paper that is intended solely to procure time to ascertain the facts upon which the decision to institute a proceeding must rest should not be construed to constitute the institution of an action to contest or to challenge. . . .

A suit to construe, reform, or modify the language of a donative document is not a contest of the document and hence is not a violation of a no contest clause, unless the construction, reformation, or modification advocated by the person bringing the suit would invalidate the donative document or any of its provisions. . . . A proceeding brought by a beneficiary for the purpose of resolving an ambiguity, or for reforming or modifying the document, valid under all possible constructions or valid under the construction advocated by the beneficiary, is not a contest as that term is used in this section. In such a case, the beneficiary is seeking merely to determine and to protect the donor's intention and is not seeking to circumvent it. . . .

i. Donative transfers other than wills. This section applies to no contest clauses in all donative documents, not only in wills. No contest clauses have traditionally appeared more frequently in wills than in other donative documents. With the increase in the use of revocable inter vivos trusts as will substitutes, no contest clauses and clauses restraining challenges of particular provisions in those trusts serve the same purpose as do such clauses in wills, and the same test applies to determine the validity of those clauses in the two comparable situations. . . .

Chapter 9: PROTECTIONS AGAINST DISINHERITANCE

A. Protections Against Unintentional Disinheritance

§9.1 Surviving Spouse's Elective Share—Noncommunity Property States Other Than Those That Have Adopted a Revised Uniform Probate-Code Type Statute
§9.2 Surviving Spouse's Elective Share Under the Revised Uniform Probate Code
§9.3 Before-Tax Treatment of an Election
§9.4 Premarital or Marital Agreement

B. Protections Against Unintentional Disinheritance

§9.5 Protection of Surviving Spouse Against Unintentional Disinheritance by a Premarital Will
§9.6 Protection of Child or Descendant Against Unintentional Disinheritance
§9.7 Mortmain Abolished

§9.1 Surviving Spouse's Elective Share—Noncommunity Property States Other Than Those That Have Adopted a Revised Uniform Probate-Code Type Statute

(a) In nearly all of the non-community property states, the decedent's surviving spouse is entitled to elect a share of the decedent's property. The exact share differs among the states. The predominant share in the states that have not adopted a Revised Uniform Probate Code-type statute is one-third.

(b) In a state whose statute subjects the decedent's probate estate and specified nonprobate assets to the elective share, the elective-share fraction is applied to the sum of the value of the probate estate and the value of the specified nonprobate assets.

(c) In a state whose statute subjects the decedent's "estate" to the elective share, the elective share is applied to the value of the decedent's estate which, for purposes of calculating the elective share, includes (i) the value of the decedent's probate estate, (ii) the value of property owned or owned in substance by the decedent immediately before death that passed outside of probate at the decedent's death to donees other than the surviving spouse, and (iii) the value of irrevocable gifts to donees other than the surviving spouse made by the decedent in anticipation of imminent death.

§9.2 Surviving Spouse's Elective Share Under the Revised Uniform Probate Code

(a) Under the Revised Uniform Probate Code, the decedent's surviving spouse is entitled to an elective-share amount calculated by applying a specified percentage to the augmented estate. The percentage increases with the length of the marriage until it reaches a maximum of 50 percent, which is the percentage applicable to a marriage that has lasted 15 years or longer.

(b) The augmented estate consists of the sum of four components:

(1) the value of the decedent's net probate estate;

(2) the value of the decedent's nonprobate transfers to persons other than the surviving spouse;

(3) the value of the decedent's nonprobate transfers to the surviving spouse; and

(4) the value of the surviving spouse's net assets at the decedent's death, plus the surviving spouse's nonprobate transfers to others.

(c) In satisfying the elective-share amount, the decedent's probate and nonprobate transfers to the surviving spouse and the marital portion of the surviving spouse's assets are applied first. If these amounts equal or exceed the elective-share amount, the surviving spouse is not entitled to an additional amount. If the elective-share amount is not satisfied from these terms, the decedent's probate and nonprobate transfers to others are proportionately liable to satisfy the balance.

§9.3 Before-Tax Treatment of an Election

The amount of the elective share is calculated by applying the elective-share fraction or percentage to the estate or augmented estate without reduction by the amount of any tax liability imposed on (i) the decedent's estate by an applicable estate or similar transfer tax or (ii) the recipients of property from a decedent's estate by an applicable inheritance or similar tax.

§9.4 Premarital or Marital Agreement

(a) The elective share and other statutory rights accruing to a surviving spouse may be waived, wholly or partially, or otherwise altered, before or during marriage, by a written agreement that was signed by both parties. An agreement that was entered into before marriage is a premarital agreement. An agreement that was entered into during marriage is a marital agreement. Consideration is not necessary to the enforcement of a premarital or a marital agreement.

(b) For a premarital or marital agreement to be enforceable against the surviving spouse, the enforcing party must show that the surviving spouse's consent was informed and was not obtained by undue influence or duress.

(c) A rebuttable presumption arises that the requirements of subsection (b) are satisfied, shifting the burden of proof to the surviving spouse to show that his or her consent was not informed or was obtained under undue influence or duress, if the enforcing party shows that:

(1) before the agreement's execution, (i) the surviving spouse knew, at least approximately, the decedent's assets and asset values, income, and liabilities; or (ii) the decedent or his or her representative provided in timely fashion to the surviving spouse a written statement accurately disclosing the decedent's significant assets and asset values, income, and liabilities; and either

(2) the surviving spouse was represented by independent legal counsel; or

(3) if the surviving spouse was not represented by independent legal counsel, (i) the decedent or the decedent's representative advised the surviving spouse, in timely fashion, to obtain independent legal counsel, and if the surviving spouse was needy, offered to pay for the costs of the surviving spouse's representation; and (ii) the agreement stated, in language easily understandable by an adult of ordinary intelligence with no legal training, the nature of any rights or claims otherwise arising at death that were altered by the agreement, and the nature of that alteration.

§9.5 Protection of Surviving Spouse Against Unintentional Disinheritance by a Premarital Will

(a) Under the Original or Revised Uniform Probate Code, the testator's surviving spouse is entitled to a specified share of the testator's estate if the testator's will was executed before the marriage unless:

(1) the will or other evidence indicates that the will was made in contemplation of the marriage;

(2) the will expresses the intention that it be effective notwithstanding any subsequent marriage; or

(3) the testator provided for the spouse by transfer outside the will and the intent that the transfer be in lieu of a testamentary provision is shown by the testator's statements or is reasonably inferred from the amount of the transfer or other evidence.

(b) Under the Original Uniform Probate Code, the surviving spouse's share is the share that the spouse would have received if the testator had died intestate, but the spouse is only entitled to that share if the premarital will fails to provide for the surviving spouse. In satisfying the spouse's share, the devises made by the premarital will will abate according to the rules of abatement for the payment of claims.

(c) Under the Revised Uniform Probate Code, the surviving spouse's share is the share that the spouse would have received if the testator had died intestate as to that portion of the testator's estate, if any, that is not devised to the testator's children of a prior marriage or their descendants (or that does not pass to such descendants under an antilapse or other statute). Any devise in the premarital will to the surviving spouse counts toward satisfying the spouse's entitlement.

§9.6 Protection of Child or Descendant Against Unintentional Disinheritance

(a) A child of the testator, or under some statutes a descendant of the testator, who was not provided for in the testator's will may be entitled to a specified share of the testator's estate as provided by statute. Most of the statutes, including the Original and Revised Uniform Probate Code, only protect a child who was born or adopted after the will was executed.

(b) A child of the testator who was not provided for in the testator's will because the testator thought that the child was dead may be entitled to a specified share of the testator's estate as provided by statute.

(c) The omitted child or descendant is entitled to the specified share unless a contrary intent or other statutory exception is established.

§9.7 Mortmain Abolished

Any rule that a charitable devise is invalid if it exceeds a certain proportion of the testator's estate or if it is contained in a will that was executed within a certain time before the testator's death is abolished.

Chapter 10: GENERAL PRINCIPLES

§10.1 Donor's Intention Controls the Meaning of a Donative Document and Is Given Effect to the Maximum Extent Allowable by Law

The controlling consideration in determining the meaning of a donative document is the donor's intention. The donor's intention is given effect to the maximum extent allowable by law.

§10.2 Permissible Evidence for Determining Donor's Intention

In seeking to determine the donor's intention, all relevant evidence, whether direct or circumstantial, may be considered, including the text of the donative document and relevant extrinsic evidence.

Chapter 11: RESOLVING AMBIGUITIES

§11.1 Ambiguity Defined

An ambiguity in a donative document is an uncertainty in meaning that is revealed by the text or by extrinsic evidence other than direct evidence of intention contradicting the plain meaning of the text.

§11.2 Resolving Ambiguities in Accordance with the Donor's Intention

(a) An ambiguity to which no rule of construction or constructional preference applies is resolved by construing the text of the donative document in accordance with the donor's intention, to the extent that the donor's intention is established by a preponderance of the evidence.

(b) Ambiguities to which no rule of construction or constructional preference applies include those arising when:

(1) the text or extrinsic evidence (other than direct evidence contradicting the plain meaning of

the text) reveals a mistaken description of persons or property.

(2) the text reveals an apparent mistaken inclusion or omission.

(3) extrinsic evidence (other than direct evidence contradicting the plain meaning of the text) reveals that the donor's personal usage differs from the ordinary meaning of a term used in the text.

Comment on Subsection (a)

d. Extrinsic evidence. Once an ambiguity, patent, or latent is established, direct as well as circumstantial evidence of the donor's intention may be considered in resolving the ambiguity in accordance with the donor's intention. . . .

e. Construction by fiduciary or other payor. In resolving an ambiguity in a donative document, the construction placed on the document by the fiduciary (or other payor) is not entitled to a presumption of correctness in ligitation. The court resolves the matter de novo. The position is different, however, if the donative document grants the fiduciary (or other payor) authority to resolve questions of construction and provides that the fiduciary's decision shall be binding on all interested parties. In such cases, the clause does not make the fiduciary's decision controlling but does entitle it to a strong presumption of correctness that is to be set aside only if it is arbitrary or made in bad faith. On the analogous question of reviewing a fiduciary's decisions regarding the exercise of discretionary distributive powers, see Restatement Third, Trusts §50. . . .

§11.3 Rules of Construction and Constructional Preferences

(a) An ambiguity to which a rule of construction applies is resolved by the rule of construction, unless evidence establishes that the donor had a different intention.

(b) In the absence of an applicable rule of construction, an ambiguity to which a constructional preference applies is resolved by the constructional preference, unless evidence establishes that the donor had a different intention. If conflicting constructional preferences apply, the constructional preference that is most persuasive in the circumstances prevails unless evidence establishes that the donor had a different intention.

(c) The foundational constructional preference is for the construction that is more in accord with common intention than other plausible constructions. Constructional preferences derived from the preference for common intention include the constructional preferences for:

(1) the construction that is more in accord with the donor's general dispositive plan than other plausible constructions.

(2) the construction that renders the document more effective than other plausible constructions, including the construction that favors completeness of disposition and the construction that avoids illegality.

(3) the construction that favors family members over non-family members, the construction that favors close family members over more remote family members, and the construction that does not disinherit a line of descent.

(4) the construction that gives more favorable tax consequences than other plausible constructions.

(5) the construction that accords with the transferor's contractual obligations.

(6) the construction that is more in accord with public policy than other plausible constructions.

Comment on Subsections (a) and (b)

. . . *b. Constructional preferences distinguished from rules of construction.* Constructional preferences are general in nature. They provide general guidance for construing a wide variety of ambiguities in donative documents. Because of their generality, more than one constructional preference can apply to a particular ambiguity. Usually, the overlapping constructional preferences point to the same result, but not always; they sometimes conflict.

Rules of construction are specific in nature. They provide guidance for resolving specific situations or construing specific terms. Rules of construction are derived from one or more constructional preferences. For example, the rule of construction embodied in the antilapse statutes is derived from the constructional preference for avoiding disinheritance of a line of descent. The rule of construction that presumes an intent to include adopted children in class gifts is derived from the constructional preferences for the construction that carries out common intention and for the construction that accords with public policy. Because rules of construction, in contrast to constructional preferences, address relatively delimited problems, rules of construction ought not to overlap or conflict with one another within the law of a given jurisdiction.

Once a constructional preference or a set of overlapping constructional preferences have crystallized into a rule of construction, the rule of construction becomes the exclusive source of attributed intention for resolving ambiguities to which it applies, displacing the antecedent constructional preferences. To the extent that antecedent constructional preferences conflict with one another when applied to the type of ambiguity at issue, the conflict is resolved by adopting the rule of construction. The rule of construction is based upon the constructional preference or preferences deemed to carry the most weight for that situation. Thus, an ambiguity to which a rule of construction applies is resolved by considering only the rule of construction together with evidence of the donor's intention. Antecedent constructional preferences are no longer considered.

c. "Construction" versus "interpretation." As noted in §10.1, Comment b, this Restatement uses the word "construction" to designate the final product of the process of determining the meaning of a donative document (apart from exceptional cases in which reformation or modification is warranted (see Chapter 12)). Textwriters and courts sometimes state that there are two distinct processes involved in determining the meaning of a donative document. Under this conception, "interpretation" refers to the process of searching for the donor's actual intention by looking to the text of the document and extrinsic evidence. "Construction" refers to the process of attributing intention from constructional preferences and rules of construction. The process of interpretation is sometimes thought to occur first, followed by construction only when interpretation fails.

Interpretation and construction are not completely distinct processes, however, nor are they applied sequentially. Interpretation and construction are part of a single process. Distinguishing between actual and attributed intention is useful in determining which governs if the two conflict. Actual intention, when sufficiently established, always overcomes attributed intention. The key notion, however, is "when sufficiently established." Although constructional preferences and rules of construction are sometimes referred to as "default rules," this does not mean that they only govern in default of evidence of actual intention. The term, properly understood, means that they govern in default of sufficiently persuasive evidence of contrary actual intention.

In deciding whether actual intention is sufficiently established to overcome attributed intention, the process of construction requires all factors to be brought to bear simultaneously and conflicting factors to be considered against each other. This is a single process. Take, for example, a case in which there is an applicable constructional preference or rule of construction. It would misdescribe the process to say that the constructional preference or rule of construction ought to be consulted only if there is *no* evidence of actual intention. Rather, the constructional preference or rule of construction is considered together with any evidence of actual intention. Evidence of actual intention may itself consist of conflicting elements, some supporting the constructional preference or rule of construction and some contradicting it.

d. Considering a constructional preference or a rule of construction with evidence of actual intention. Because the primary objective of construction is to give effect to actual intention, to the extent that actual intention can be established, constructional preferences and rules of construction yield when a different intention is found. In determining whether the donor's actual intention overcomes a constructional preference or rule of construction, both the text of the document read as an entirety and extrinsic evidence of the donor's intention may be considered, as described in §10.2, unless consideration of extrinsic evidence is precluded by statute. . . . Extrinsic evidence and inferences derived from the text of the document tending to support as well as tending to overcome a constructional preference or a rule of construction must be considered as part of a single process. The single nature of this process is described in Comment c.

Sometimes a codified rule of construction provides that it prevails unless the donative document, another specified document, or one of a list of specified documents expressly provides otherwise. Since constructional preferences are seldom codified, it is uncommon to find a similar statutory provision regarding a constructional preference. Nevertheless, if a statute provides that a particular constructional preference or rule of construction can only be rebutted by an express statement in a document, extrinsic evidence may not be considered to support, rebut, or contradict the constructional preference or rule of construction. If, however, the elements prescribed in §12.1 are satisfied, the appropriate document can be reformed to insert language into its text expressly stating an intention contrary to the constructional preference or rule of construction. . . .

Some constructional preferences and rules of construction have more force and are therefore more difficult to rebut than others. Because constructional preferences are general in nature, two or more constructional preferences might apply in a given case and point to the same result or to differing results. If such overlapping constructional preferences lead to the same result, they reinforce each other and are more difficult to rebut. If they lead to differing results, they tend to neutralize each other unless the trier of fact determines that one is more weighty than the other in the particular case. The ambiguity in such a case is resolved by considering each of the constructional preferences together with evidence of the donor's intention to determine which resolution of the ambiguity is the most persuasive in the circumstances.

A rule of construction based on one or more strong constructional preferences is especially difficult to rebut. For example, because the rule of construction reflected in antilapse statutes derives from the strong constructional preference against disinheriting a line of descent, antilapse Statutes are especially difficult to rebut. . . .

Chapter 12: REFORMING AND MODIFYING DONATIVE DOCUMENTS

§12.1 Reforming Donative Documents to Correct Mistakes

A donative document, though unambiguous, may be reformed to conform the text to the donor's intention if it is established by clear and convincing evidence (1) that a mistake of fact or law, whether in expression or inducement, affected specific terms of the document; and (2) what the donor's intention was. In determining whether these elements have been established by clear and convincing evidence, direct evidence of intention contradicting the plain meaning of the text as well as other evidence of intention may be considered.

Comment

. . . *b. Rationale.* When a donative document is unambiguous, evidence suggesting that the terms of the document vary from intention is inherently suspect but possibly correct. The law deals with situations of inherently suspicious but possibly correct evidence in either of two ways. One is to exclude the evidence altogether, in effect denying a remedy in cases in which the evidence is genuine and persuasive. The other is to consider the evidence, but guard against giving effect to fraudulent or mistaken evidence by imposing an above-normal standard of proof. In choosing between exclusion and high-safeguard allowance of extrinsic evidence, this Restatement adopts the latter. Only high-safeguard allowance of extrinsic evidence achieves the primary objective of giving effect to the donor's intention. To this end, the full range of direct and circumstantial evidence relevant to the donor's intention described in §10.2 may be considered in a reformation action.

Equity rests the rationale for reformation on two related grounds: giving effect to the donor's intention and preventing unjust enrichment. . . .

c. Historical background. The reformation doctrine for donative documents other than wills is well established. Equity has long recognized that deeds of gifts, inter vivos trusts, life insurance contracts, and other donative documents can be reformed if it is established by clear and convincing evidence: (1) that a mistake of fact or law, whether in expression or inducement, affected specific terms of the document; and (2) what the donor's intention was. Reformation of these documents is granted, on an adequate showing of proof, even after the death of the donor.

This action unifies the law of wills and will substitutes by applying to wills the standards that govern other donative documents. Until recently, courts have not allowed reformation of wills. The denial of a reformation remedy for wills was predicated on observance of the Statute of Wills, which requires that wills be executed in accordance with certain formalities. See §3.1. Reforming a will, it was feared, would often require inserting language that was not executed in accordance with the statutory formalities. Section 11.2, however, authorizes inserting language to resolve *ambiguities* in accordance with the donor's intention. [M]odern authority is moving away from insistence on strict compliance with the statutory formalities on the question of initial execution of wills. Section 3.3 adopts the position that a harmless error in executing a will may be excused "if the proponent establishes by clear and convincing evidence that the decedent adopted the document as his or her will." See also Restatement Second, Property (Donative Transfers) §33.1, Comment g. The Revised Uniform Probate Code §2-503 also adopts a harmless-error rule. Under the Revised UPC, a document or writing on a document that was not executed in compliance with the statutory formalities is treated as if it had been properly executed "if the proponent of the document or writing establishes by clear and convincing evidence that the decedent intended the document or writing to constitute . . . the decedent's will. . . ."

The trend away from insisting on strict compliance with statutory formalities is based on a growing acceptance of the broader principle that mistake, whether in execution or in expression, should not be allowed to defeat intention. A common principle underlies the principle of this section, which authorizes reformation of unambiguous donative documents (including wills) to correct mistakes, and the movement (1) to excuse defective execution under §3.3 and (2) to authorize insertion of language to resolve ambiguities in donative documents under §11.2.

The important difference between §11.2 and this section is the burden of proof. Ambiguity shows that the donative document contains an inadequate expression of the donor's intention. Here, because there is no ambiguity, clear and convincing evidence is required to establish that the document does not adequately express intention. . . .

d. Plain-meaning rule disapproved. The so-called plain-meaning rule is disapproved to the extent that the rule purports to exclude extrinsic evidence of the donor's intention. . . .

§12.2 Modifying Donative Documents to Achieve Donor's Tax Objectives

A donative document may be modified, in a manner that does not violate the donor's probable intention, to achieve the donor's tax objectives.

Comment

a. Scope note. . . The term "modification" rather than "reformation" is used in this section to distinguish the situation covered here from the situation covered by §12.1, in which the donative document fails to express the donor's original, particularized intention. . . .

Part III

~

Restatement (Third) of Trusts, Vols. 1 & 2 (2003)

RESTATEMENT (THIRD) OF TRUSTS, VOLS. 1 & 2 (2003)

TABLE OF CONTENTS

Chapter 9. Beneficiaries

Part 4. Nature of Beneficiaries' Rights and Interests

CHAPTER 10. EXTENT AND ENFORCEABILITY OF BENEFICIAL INTERESTS

CHAPTER 11. VOLUNTARY AND INVOLUNTARY TRANFSERS OF BENEFICIAL INTERESTS; GENERAL PRINCIPLES

Part 5. Modification and Termination of Trusts

CHAPTER 13. MODIFICATION AND TERMINATION OF TRUSTS

Part 1. Nature, Characteristics, and Types of Trusts

Chapter 1: DEFINITIONS AND DISTINCTIONS

§1. Scope of this Restatement

Trusts dealt with in this Restatement include:

(a) trusts as defined in §2;
(b) charitable trusts (see §28); and
(c) resulting trusts (see §§7, 8, and 9).

§2. Definition of Trust

A trust, as the term is used in this Restatement when not qualified by the word "resulting" or "constructive," is a fiduciary relationship with respect to property, arising from a manifestation of intention to create that relationship and subjecting the person who holds title to the property to duties to deal with it for the benefit of charity or for one or more persons, at least one of whom is not the sole trustee.

Comment

b. Fiduciary relationship. . . . Despite the differences in the legal circumstances and responsibilities of various fiduciaries, one characteristic is common to all: A person in a fiduciary relationship to another is under a duty to act for the benefit of the other as to matters within the scope of the relationship. (Fiduciary duties may, in the circumstances of certain trust relationships, technically exist but not be effectively enforceable; the situation arises to the extent the trustee holds a power of revocation or a presently exercisable general power of appointment or withdrawal. . . .)

d. Title, ownership, and interests. . . . Although trust beneficiaries have equitable title, a trustee's title to trust property may be either legal or equitable. Although it is usually true (and is, unfortunately, often stated without qualification in cases and texts) that the trustee has legal title, in some instances the trustee will hold only an equitable title. . . .

f. The elements of a trust. In the strict, traditional sense, a trust involves three elements: (1) a trustee, who holds the trust property and is subject to duties to deal with it for the benefit of one or more others; (2) one or more beneficiaries, to whom and for whose benefit the trustee owes the duties with respect to the trust property; and (3) trust property, which is held by the trustee for the beneficiaries. In a more comprehensive sense, the trust purpose is often included in discussions of the elements of trusts, as in Part 3 (specifically Chapter 6) of this Restatement.

Although all of these elements are present in a complete trust, either or both of elements (1) and (2) above may be temporarily absent without destroying the trust or preventing its creation. . . .

§3. Settlor, Trust Property, Trustee, and Beneficiary

(1) The person who creates a trust is the settlor.

(2) The property held in trust is the trust property.

(3) The person who holds property in trust is the trustee.

(4) A person for whose benefit property is held in trust is a beneficiary.

§4. Terms of the Trust

The phrase "terms of the trust" means the manifestation of intention of the settlor with respect to the trust provisions expressed in a manner that admits of its proof in judicial proceedings.

Comment

d. Trusts created inter vivos by written instrument. If a trust is created by a transaction inter vivos and is evidenced by a written instrument, the terms of the trust are determined by the provisions of the governing instrument as interpreted in light of all the relevant circumstances and such direct evidence of the intention of the settlor with respect to the trust as is not denied consideration because of a statute of frauds, the parol-evidence rule, or some other rule of law. On the statutes of frauds, see §§22-24 (and cf. §20), and on the parol-evidence rule, see §21. See generally Restatement Third, Property (Wills and Other Donative Transfers) §10.2 and §§11.1-11.3.

The "provisions of the governing instrument" include the terms of any statute incorporated or made applicable by other provisions of that instrument. . . .

f. Trusts created by court order. If a trust is established by an order of court and is to be administered as an express trust, the terms of the trust are determined by the provisions of the court order as interpreted in accordance with general rules governing interpretation of judgments.

g. Trusts created by statute. Some forms of trusts that are created by statute, especially public retirement systems or pension funds, and sometimes public land trusts, school land trusts, or trusts for benefit of native populations, are administered as express trusts, the terms of which are either set forth in the statute or are supplied by the default rules of general trust law. . . .

§5. Trusts and Other Relationships

The following are not trusts:

(a) successive legal estates;

(b) decedents' estates;

(c) guardianships and conservatorships;

(d) receiverships and bankruptcy trusteeships;

(e) durable powers of attorney and other agencies;

(f) bailments and leases;

(g) corporations, partnerships, and other business associations;

(h) conditions and equitable charges;

(i) contracts to convey or certain contracts for the benefit of third parties;

(j) assignments or partial assignments of choses in action;

(k) relationships of debtors to creditors;

(l) mortgages, deeds of trust, pledges, liens, and other security arrangements.

§6. Active and Passive Trusts; The Statute of Uses

(1) A trust is active if, by the terms of the trust, the trustee has affirmative duties to perform; a trust is passive if the trustee's sole duty is not to interfere with the enjoyment of the trust property by the beneficiaries.

(2) A beneficiary of a passive trust is entitled to receive, upon demand, transfer of the property passively held for that beneficiary.

(3) If the Statute of Uses or similar statute applies to property of a trust, the trustee's title to that property is extinguished and the title is held by the beneficiary or beneficiaries in accordance with the equitable interests of each.

Chapter 2: RESULTING TRUSTS

§7. Nature and Definition of Resulting Trusts

A resulting trust is a reversionary, equitable interest implied by law in property that is held by a transferee, in whole or in part, as trustee for the transferor or the transferor's successors in interest.

§8. When Express Trust Fails in Whole or in Part

Where the owner of property makes a donative transfer and manifests an intention that the transferee is to hold the property in trust but the intended trust fails in whole or in part, or the trust is or will be fully performed without exhausting or fully utilizing the trust estate, the transferee holds the trust estate or the appropriate portion or interest therein on resulting trust for the transferor or the transferor's successors in interest, unless

(a) the transferor manifested an intention that a resulting trust should not arise, or

(b) the trust fails for illegality and the policy against permitting unjust enrichment of a transferee is outweighed by the policy against giving relief to one who has entered into an illegal transaction.

Comment

a. In general. . . . [If] a deed or will is ineffective to transfer title to the property to the intended trustee or a substitute trustee, no resulting trust arises by reason of the failure of the intended inter vivos or testamentary trust. The title to the property remains (with no need of the resulting-trust device) either in the would-be transferor or in the personal representative or beneficiaries of the testator's estate.

a(1). Successors in interest defined. If a testamentary disposition is not a residuary disposition, the decedent's successors in interest are normally determined by the residuary provisions of the will. Otherwise—that is, if the will contains no applicable residuary clause or if the trust disposition is itself residuary and there is no alternative disposition—the successors in interest are the testator's intestate successors, specifically the decedent's heirs at law.

If a testamentary trust comes into operation but thereafter is fully performed, or subsequently fails in whole or in part, the trustee then holds the appropriate property or interests on resulting trust for the testator's successors in interest. The initial step in determining these successors is as stated in the preceding paragraph. This is because the testator died leaving this reversionary interest to (that is, the possibility of a resulting trust later arising for) those original residuary or intestate successors from the very outset. Then, when the resulting trust eventually occurs, the interests of those various successors will have to be traced, if and as necessary, through possible subsequent assignments, insolvency proceedings, and decedents' estates, and ultimately then into the hands of the initial successors' respective successors in interest, who at the time of the resulting trust will also be successors in interest to the testator. In any of the foregoing situations, the successor in interest (or one of the successors) may be the State, for want of other successors.

Similarly, if an inter vivos express trust comes into existence but later is fully performed or wholly or partially fails, the reversionary interest based on this possibility remained in the settlor from the outset. If the settlor is dead when the resulting trust arises, and if the reversion has by then been voluntarily or involuntarily alienated, the successors in interest are determined by tracing the retained interest through the settlor's estate, or assignments or insolvency proceedings, and onward into the hands of the current interest holders, essentially as described in the preceding paragraph. The beneficiaries of the resulting trust are those so determined. . . .

§9. Purchase-Money Resulting Trusts

(1) Except as stated in Subsection (2), where a transfer of property is made to one person and the purchase price is paid by another, a resulting trust arises in favor of the person by whom the purchase price is paid unless

(a) the latter manifests an intention that no resulting trust should arise, or

(b) the transfer is made to accomplish an unlawful purpose, in which case a resulting trust does not arise if the policy against unjust enrichment of the transferee is outweighed by the policy against giving relief to a person who has entered into an illegal transaction.

(2) Where a transfer of property is made to one person and the purchase price is paid by another and the transferee is a spouse, descendant, or other natural object of the bounty of the person by whom the purchase price is paid, a resulting trust does not arise unless the latter manifests an intention that the transferee should not have the beneficial interest in the property.

Part 2. Creation of Trusts

Chapter 3: BASIC PRINCIPLES AND REQUIREMENTS

§10. Methods of Creating a Trust

Except as prevented by the doctrine of merger (§69), a trust may be created by:

(a) a transfer by the will of a property owner to another person as trustee for one or more persons; or

(b) a transfer inter vivos by a property owner to another person as trustee for one or more persons; or

(c) a declaration by an owner of property that he or she holds that property as trustee for one or more persons; or

(d) an exercise of a power of appointment by appointing property to a person as trustee for one or more persons who are objects of the power; or

(e) a promise or beneficiary designation that creates enforceable rights in a person who immediately or later holds those rights as trustee, or who pursuant to those rights later receives property as trustee, for one or more persons.

Comment

Comment on Clause (c)

e. Declaration of trust. If the owner of property declares himself or herself trustee of the property for the benefit of one or more others, or for the declarant and one or more others, a trust is created, even though there is no transfer of the title to the trust property to another and even though no consideration is received for the declaration. . . .

A statute of frauds may require a signed writing in order for a declaration of trust to be enforceable. See §22. . . .

[E]xcept as precluded by statute, a trust may be established by the settlor's signing of an instrument that begins, essentially, "I hereby declare myself trustee of the property listed in Schedule A attached hereto" or "O, as settlor, hereby transfers to O, as trustee, the property listed in the attached Schedule A," even though in either case the document is not supported at the time of execution, or by the time of the settlor's death or incompetency, by other acts or other documents of transfer or title. In short, the trust instrument may serve as an instrument of transfer (i.e., as a "deed" of gift or conveyance). . . .

Comment on Clause (e)

g. Trust created by enforceable promise or beneficiary designation. Where a property owner makes a nonbinding promise to create a trust in the future, no trust is thereby created. If the property owner later establishes the trust by inter vivos or testamentary transfer or by declaration, the trust is created by the transfer or declaration (see Comments d and e) and not by the promise.

Similarly, when a property owner makes a contractually binding promise to establish a trust by inter vivos or testamentary transfer or by declaration and later performs by making the promised transfer or declaration, ordinarily the trust is created at the time of performance, whether the transfer or declaration is made voluntarily or involuntarily. In this situation, the trust and the trustee's fiduciary duties ordinarily come into existence at the time of the settlor's performance and not at the time the binding promise is made. . . .

If, however, a person makes or causes to be made an enforceable promise to pay money or transfer property to another as trustee, and if the person (with the expressed or implied acceptance of the intended trustee) also manifests an intention immediately to create a trust of the promisee's rights, a trust is created at the time of the contract, with a chose in action (the rights under that contract) then being held for the beneficiaries by the trustee. . . .

§11. Capacity of a Settlor to Create a Trust

(1) A person has capacity to create a trust by will to the same extent that the person has capacity to devise or bequeath the property free of trust.

(2) A person has capacity to create a revocable inter vivos trust by transfer to another or by declaration to the same extent that the person has capacity to create a trust by will.

(3) A person has capacity to create an irrevocable inter vivos trust by transfer to another or by declaration to the same extent that the person has capacity to transfer the property inter vivos free of trust in similar circumstances.

(4) A person has capacity to create a trust by exercising a power of appointment to the same extent that the person has capacity to create a trust of his or her own property under Subsection (1), (2), or (3) above, as appropriate to the type of transfer and trust being created.

(5) Under some circumstances, an agent under a durable power of attorney or the legal representative of a property owner who is under disability may create a trust on behalf of the property owner.

Comment

Comment on Subsection (3)

c. Irrevocable inter vivos trusts. A property owner who has capacity to transfer property by outright gift inter vivos ordinarily has capacity to create an irrevocable trust during life. A property owner who does not have the capacity to make a gift lacks capacity to establish an irrevocable trust.

Rules concerning gift-making capacity are not peculiar to the law of trusts and are not within the scope of this Restatement. See generally Restatement Third, Property (Wills and Other Donative Transfers) §8.1, Comment d. In general, however, this is a standard slightly higher than that for a will because, in addition to factors that testators must be capable of understanding, irrevocable donative transfers during life require an ability to understand the effects the disposition may have on the future financial security of the settlor/donor and of those who may be dependent on him or her.

Some irrevocable inter vivos trusts, however, are not donative, or at least not entirely. Trusts are sometimes created as a result of negotiations, as in the case of a trust that is established as part of a commercial transaction or in settlement of an adversary legal proceeding, such as an action for divorce. For these situations, higher standards are normally appropriate. Again, however, these rules are not peculiar to the law of trusts and are not within the scope of this Restatement. See generally Restatement Second, Contracts §12, on capacity to contract. . . .

Comment on Subsection (5)

f. Acts on behalf of owner under disability. Transfers of property belonging to minors and legally incompetent adults may be made in the course of managing their financial affairs by their guardians, conservators, or other legal representatives, or by the agent (attorney in fact) of an incompetent adult appointed and acting under a durable power of attorney executed before the principal's incapacity. The legal representative or holder of a durable power of attorney may also make charitable and other inter vivos gifts of the property of a minor or incompetent person, including gift-transfers in trust, but only to the extent authorized by the appropriate court or, expressly or impliedly, by the terms of the durable power.

Ordinarily, under principles of "substituted judgment" . . ., a court may authorize a legal representative to make such transfers of the minor's or mentally incompetent person's property as would be reasonable as a matter of the property owner's personal, family, tax, and estate-planning objectives. Under many statutes, however, by express provision or judicial interpretation, courts do not have power to authorize legal representatives to make wills for minors or legally incompetent persons. Similarly, under many durable-power-of-attorney statutes, it is not legally permissible for the terms of a durable power to authorize an agent to make a will for an incapacitated principal.

Nevertheless, even under statutes that preclude the making of wills for persons under legal disability, a court or the terms of a durable power may for some purposes authorize a legal representative or agent to create, amend, or revoke, or to transfer additional property to, a revocable trust or other will-substitute arrangement. See Uniform Trust Code §602(e) and (f); and compare generally Restatement Third, Property (Wills and Other Donative Transfers) §8.1, Comments k and l, and Restatement Second, Property (Donative Transfers) §§34.4(2) and 34.5. For example, despite a restriction against making a will for an incompetent person, it is proper for a court or principal to authorize a legal representative or agent to establish, modify, or enlarge a revocable inter vivos trust to serve purposes that are financially advantageous to the estate, such as probate avoidance and managerial efficiency.

The trust's distributive provisions, however, present more sensitive issues, which turn on the policy underlying the typical statute's will-making prohibition. Distributions directed or authorized by the provisions of a revocable trust established by a legal representative or agent must be consistent either: (i) with inter vivos gifts the legal representative or agent could be empowered to make directly (supra); or (ii) with post-death dispositions that, under the statute, the court may, or the terms of the durable power may and do, authorize the legal representative or agent to make of the affected property of the incompetent person.

In the second situation (alternative (ii), above), the effect of a statutory prohibition against will making by legal representatives or agents depends on the reasons underlying that prohibition. The underlying policy may reflect a narrow purpose (based on efficiency and tradition) of precluding the use of a particular device (a will) that relies on the safeguards of probate and of specific, well-established statutory formalities; or the will-making prohibition may instead manifest a more general, substantive policy against post-death dispositions by these fiduciaries that would alter the plan of disposition established by intestate succession or by an existing will executed by a person who has subsequently become incompetent.

The breadth and generality of the latter policy would ordinarily apply by analogy (cf. §25(2) and Comments d and e thereto) to limit the post-death distributive provisions of a revocable inter vivos trust created by a legal representative or agent to dispositions that conform to the disposition of the affected property that would result, as the case may be, by operation of law or under the incompetent person's existing estate plan. Any departure from that pre-incompetency scheme of disposition would then be permissible only to the extent the adversely affected, expectant beneficiaries consent to relinquish some or all of their expected interests.

On the other hand, if the underlying policy is a narrow one that applies only to the making of wills by legal representatives or agents, and not to their use of will substitutes, the foregoing limitations on post-death distributive provisions (preceding paragraph) do not apply to the creation of revocable trusts by these fiduciaries.

Ultimately, the nature and breadth of the policy indicated by a will-making prohibition are matters of statutory interpretation. Durable-power-of-attorney legislation and principles of substituted judgment under conservatorship, guardianship, and other such statutes are designed to preserve for persons under disability much of the flexibility in financial management and planning that other property owners enjoy. Estate planning is fundamental to the objectives ordinarily implicit in such statutes; and sound, flexible planning requires actions that reflect not only the property owner's evolving circumstances and likely objectives but also changes in the law and in the personal and financial circumstances of potential beneficiaries. Furthermore, these statutes allow donative dispositions only with court authorization or as a result of authorization granted by a competent principal, with judicial scrutiny available for cases in which it is alleged that an agent's fiduciary authority has been exceeded or abused.

Accordingly, prohibitions against will making are generally to be strictly construed to prevent only the use of a particular device, the will, and not as reflecting a more general, substantive policy that extends to and prohibits the use of other methods of planning and accomplishing properly justified post-death disposition of estates of persons under disability.

In many states, the general preference for narrow construction is reinforced by statutes that, while prohibiting the making of wills, expressly enable a court or principal to authorize the use or amendment of certain other post-death dispositions or will substitutes. Some such statutes, for example, refer specifically to creating, amending, or enlarging revocable trusts, whereas other statutes or sections may authorize the closely related actions of selecting or changing post-death beneficial rights—such as beneficiary designations and payment options—under life insurance policies, retirement plans, and the like.

A conservator, guardian, or other legal representative or an agent under a durable power of attorney may be authorized by court or the terms of a durable power to exercise a settlor's expressed or implied rights to withdraw funds or amend terms of a revocable trust in accordance with the foregoing principles applicable to the creation of revocable trusts by these fiduciaries. That is, legal representatives and agents may be authorized to exercise the incompetent settlor's reserved powers not only in circumstances and ways that are appropriate to the current needs of the settlor and the settlor's family but also as appropriate to the settlor's estate-planning objectives, based on (i) the principles of substituted judgment or the terms of the durable power and on (ii) what is proper in light of the policies underlying any applicable statutory prohibition against the making of wills by such fiduciaries. . . .

§12. Trust Creation Induced by Undue Influence, Duress, Fraud, or Mistake

A transfer in trust or declaration of trust can be set aside, or the terms of a trust can be reformed, upon the same grounds as those upon which a transfer of property not in trust can be set aside or reformed.

§13. Intention to Create Trust

A trust is created only if the settlor properly manifests an intention to create a trust relationship.

§14. Notice and Acceptance Not Required to Create Trust

A trust can be created without notice to or acceptance by any beneficiary or trustee.

§15. Consideration Not Required to Create Trust

The owner of property can create a trust of the property by will or by declaration or transfer inter vivos, whether or not consideration is received for doing so.

§16. Ineffective Inter Vivos Transfers

(1) If a property owner undertakes to make a donative inter vivos disposition in trust by transferring property to another as trustee, an express trust is not created if the property owner fails during life to complete the contemplated transfer of the property. In some circumstances, however, the trust intention of such a property owner who dies or becomes incompetent may be given effect by constructive trust in order to prevent unjust enrichment of the property owner's successors in interest.

(2) If a property owner intends to make an outright gift inter vivos but fails to make the transfer that is required in order to do so, the gift intention will not be given effect by treating it as a declaration of trust.

Comment

b. Intended inter vivos transfer to another as trustee: Effective or ineffective? When an owner of property intends to create an inter vivos trust other than by declaration, the owner must transfer the property to the intended trustee. If the property owner attempts to make a transfer in trust but the intended transfer is not effective, no express trust is created.

An intended or contemplated transfer in trust may be ineffective for a number of reasons. The transfer may not be completed for want of delivery of the subject matter or instrument of transfer; or it may be ineffective because a would-be settlor does not own the intended trust property at the time of the purported transfer. In cases of these types, no trust is created. In the latter of these situations, however, actions of the would-be settlor after acquiring the intended trust property, considered together with the initial manifestation of trust intent, may serve to perfect the transfer and thereby create the trust at the later time. . . .

In the first of the above-mentioned situations, where there has been no delivery, the title to the property ordinarily (but see Comment c) remains in the owner free of trust. Even when an owner of property surrenders possession of it or of a document of transfer in a manner that otherwise would be sufficient to transfer the property to a trustee, if the property owner does not intend to make a presently effective transfer there is no transfer of the title. Accordingly, no trust is created and the owner retains title to the property, ordinarily free of trust. Again, however, subsequent actions of the property owner, considered together with the initial manifestation of trust intention, may constitute delivery, thereby completing the transfer and bringing the trust into being.

On the other hand, delivery sufficient to pass title to a trustee, like transfers to others as donees of outright gifts, may occur without handing over the property or an instrument of transfer to the intended trustee. Thus, a delivery may be made in escrow or may be accomplished by acts of constructive or symbolic delivery performed with the requisite intention to make a present transfer. . . .

Furthermore, if the owner of property transfers it to another with the intention that it be held immediately in trust, a trust may then arise even though by the terms of the trust the settlor reserves the power to revoke and modify the trust in whole or in part. . . . Similarly, a declaration of trust is not incomplete, nor is it a mere expression of an intention to create a trust in the future, simply because of the declarant's reservation of power to revoke and amend (§25(1)). In either of these situations the revocable inter vivos trust may be created even though the terms of the revocable trust also include the reservation to the settlor of a life interest in the property, and even though the transfer or declaration of trust thereby serves primarily as a substitute for a will (*id.*). . . .

Unless the contrary is expressly provided in an applicable statute, or is necessarily implied from its provisions, formalities prescribed for the creation of a recordable document, or otherwise for protection of or from third parties, need not be satisfied in order to make a valid donative transfer, that is, one that is effective as between the transferor and the transferee(s). See Restatement Second, Property (Donative Transfers) §32.3, Comment a.

Good practice certainly calls for the use of additional formalities and the taking of appropriate further steps, such as changes of registration, or the execution and recordation of deeds to land. Nevertheless, a writing signed by the settlor, or a trust agreement signed by the settlor and trustee, manifesting the settlor's present intention thereby to transfer specified property (such as all property listed on an attached schedule) is sufficient to create a trust. . . .

The rights and interests of transferees may be later perfected with respect to third parties, and for the protection of third parties, by steps taken by the settlor or, even following the settlor's death or incompetency, by court order or other procedures appropriate to the circumstances and applicable law or practice. Compare also the discussion of declarations of trust. . . . §10, Comment e.

c. Incomplete transfer sometimes given effect by constructive trust. Sometimes an attempted inter vivos transfer is ineffective to create an express trust even though the property owner has taken all the steps that would be required of the owner personally in order to implement the transfer in the intended manner. In such a case, the acts and circumstances may nevertheless satisfy the underlying legal policy of determining, by objective and reliable evidence, that the property owner had arrived at a definite, considered intention to create a trust. . . .

Cases of this type may arise because the title to intended trust property remains in a would-be settlor as a result of some technical defect or incompleteness in the intended transfer. For example, a person named as trustee may be dead or otherwise incapable of taking title to the intended trust property. . . . Similarly, an intended transfer may remain incomplete because an essentially ministerial act has not been performed. For example, a property owner may have placed property in the hands of his or her own agent with instruction to complete delivery promptly or as soon as conveniently possible (or at some time or upon the occurrence of some event that would have been expected to occur soon within the property owner's lifetime) but without need of further direction or action by the property owner.

In these various situations, if the property owner becomes legally incompetent or dies, it may be appropriate for a court of equity to compel the legal representative of the incompetent property owner or the deceased property owner's successors in interest to transfer property upon the intended trust. Provided the property owner had not expressly or impliedly by inaction manifested an intention to retain or reacquire the property free of trust, a constructive trust may be enforced to prevent the unjust enrichment that would occur if the property owner's successors in interest were allowed to retain or acquire property that is satisfactorily shown to have been intended to benefit others. This is so even though, at the time of death or incompetency, the property owner personally had the right to terminate or modify the agent's authority or to refuse to correct a defect in the intended transfer. [S]ee generally and compare Restatement of Restitution §164.

In some of these cases, of course, it may be difficult to determine whether the property owner had formed a sufficiently definite intention presently to proceed with the creation of the trust, or whether the owner had simply manifested an intention gratuitously to create a trust at some future time. Such questions are inevitably ones for interpretation. The critical issue in these cases is likely to be whether or not, under the chosen manner of making the transfer, it had been contemplated that the property owner personally would take some further action or make some further manifestation of intention before the transfer to the intended trustee was to be completed. Events and circumstances, however, may provide a negative answer to this question and satisfy the underlying policies by supplying both the evidentiary certainty and the likelihood of deliberation that support carrying out a trust intention. Thus, in a given situation the steps actually taken may supply the objective, reliable manifestations of intention needed to show that the now deceased or legally incompetent property owner had made a serious, definite decision to proceed with a transfer in trust (whether revocable or irrevocable), with no showing that this objective had been abandoned. . . .

Illustrations . . .

7. O, the owner of Blackacre, executes a deed by which she might convey Blackacre to T as trustee for B for life, remainder to B's issue. Because of her imminent departure on a business trip to Europe, O hands the deed to her financial adviser, A, asking him to act as her agent to make delivery to T as soon as A has an opportunity to do so. O dies in an automobile accident in Europe shortly after arriving there and before A has an opportunity to make delivery to T. Although O could have telephoned A immediately before her death to terminate his authority as her agent, and although title to Blackacre remained in A, O's personal representative or other successors in interest can be compelled to transfer Blackacre to T in trust for the intended purposes and beneficiaries.

The result in Illustration 7 is not based on dilatory conduct on the part of A or otherwise confined to cases that invite application of the maxim that equity treats as done what ought to have been done. . . .

Chapter 4: FORMALITIES: TRUSTS CREATED BY WILL

§17. Creation of Testamentary Trusts
§18. Secret Trusts
§19. "Pour-Over" Dispositions by Will

§17. Creation of Testamentary Trusts

(1) A testamentary trust is one created by a valid will.

(2) Except as provided in §19, a trust is created by a will if the intention to create the trust and other elements essential to the creation of a testamentary trust (ordinarily, identification of the trust property,

the beneficiaries, and the purposes of the trust) can be ascertained from

(a) the will itself; or

(b) an existing instrument properly incorporated by reference into the will; or

(c) facts referred to in the will that have significance apart from their effect upon the disposition of the property bequeathed or devised by the will.

§18. Secret Trusts

(1) Where a testator devises or bequeaths property to a person in reliance on the devisee's or legatee's expressed or implied agreement to hold the property upon a particular trust, no express trust is created, but the devisee or legatee holds the property upon a constructive trust for the agreed purposes and persons.

(2) Where a property owner dies intestate relying upon the expressed or implied agreement of an intestate successor to hold upon a particular trust the property acquired by intestate succession, no express trust is created, but the intestate successor holds the property upon a constructive trust for the agreed purposes and persons.

Comment

a. In general. Sometimes decedents by will or intestate succession leave property to a devisee or intestate successor who has agreed to hold the property upon a particular trust pursuant to an expressed or implied agreement with the decedent, but the terms of the trust (and often the intention to create a trust) do not appear in a will. (The term "devisee," here and generally today, includes "legatee.")

Where the person dies intestate, or the testator's will manifests no intention to create a trust, the expression "secret trust" is commonly used, as it is in this Restatement. Where the will reveals the intention to create the trust but not its terms, the expression "semi-secret trust" is used, generally and in this Restatement.

When a constructive trust is imposed under the rules stated in this Section in a situation of this type, it arises out of an intended express trust that is unenforceable because of the failure to satisfy the requirements of the Wills Act. In such a case, the testate or intestate successor would be unjustly enriched if permitted to retain the property, and is therefore chargeable as a constructive trustee.

It is arguable that, if a secret-trust agreement is shown, the testate or intestate successor should be chargeable as a constructive trustee (or, in the case of a semi-secret trust, as trustee of a resulting trust) for the estate of the decedent rather than for the intended beneficiaries. This would suffice to prevent the recipient from being unjustly enriched. The same evidence that shows the intended trust, however, also shows that the other (albeit innocent) beneficiaries of the decedent's estate would be unjustly enriched by such a result. In addition, the rule of this Section is supported by the great weight of authority in secret-trust cases . . . and by the lesser risk of unwarranted litigation in the semi-secret-trust cases. . . .

§19. "Pour-Over" Dispositions by Will

Where a will contains a testamentary disposition for the purpose of adding property to an irrevocable or revocable inter vivos trust, or for the purpose of funding a trust pursuant to the terms of an instrument of trust executed but not funded during the testator's lifetime, the intended disposition is effective if and as:

(a) provided by statute;

(b) validated by the doctrine of incorporation by reference or by the doctrine of facts of independent significance; or

(c) the trust instrument, together with the will, either

(i) satisfies an applicable rule of substantial compliance, harmless error, or judicial dispensation, or

(ii) otherwise satisfies the policies underlying the formal safeguards of the applicable Wills Act.

Chapter 5: FORMALITIES: CREATION OF INTER VIVOS TRUSTS

§20. Validity of Oral Inter Vivos Trusts

Except as required by a statute of frauds, a writing is not necessary to create an enforceable inter vivos trust, whether by declaration, by transfer to another as trustee, or by contract.

§21. The Parol-Evidence Rule

(1) In the absence of fraud, duress, undue influence, mistake, or other ground for reformation or rescission, if the owner of property:

(a) transfers it inter vivos to another person by a writing that states that the transferee is to take the property for the transferee's own benefit, extrinsic evidence may not be used to show that the transferee was intended to hold the property in trust; or

(b) transfers it inter vivos to another person by a writing that states that the transferee is to hold the property upon a particular trust, extrinsic evidence may not be used to show that the transferee was intended to hold the property upon a different trust or to take it beneficially; or

(c) by a writing declares that the property owner holds the property upon a particular trust, extrinsic evidence may not be used to show that the owner intended to hold the property upon a different trust or to hold it free of trust.

(2) If the owner of property transfers it inter vivos to another person by a writing that does not state either that the transferee is to take the property for the transferor's own benefit or that the transferee is to hold it upon a particular trust, except as excluded by a statute of frauds or other statute, extrinsic evidence may be used to show that the transferee was to hold the property in trust for either the transferor or one or more third parties, or for some combination of the transferor, the transferee, and one or more third parties.

§22. Writing Required by Statute of Frauds

(1) In order to create an enforceable express inter vivos trust of property for which a statute of frauds requires a writing, the writing must be signed as provided in §23 and must

(a) manifest the trust intention, and

(b) reasonably identify the trust property, the beneficiaries, and the purposes of the trust.

(2) The writing required by a statute of frauds

(a) may consist of several writings,

(b) need not be intended as the expression of a trust, and

(c) continues to satisfy the statute-of-frauds requirement even though later lost or destroyed.

§23 Signing Requirement: When and By Whom?

(1) Where the owner of property declares that he or she holds it upon a trust for which a statute of frauds requires a writing, a writing evidencing the trust as provided in §22 is sufficient to satisfy the statute if it is signed by the declarant

(a) before or at the time of the declaration, or

(b) after the time of the declaration but before the declarant has transferred the property.

(2) Where the owner of property transfers it inter vivos to another person upon an inter vivos trust for which a statute of frauds requires a writing, a writing evidencing the trust as provided in §22 is sufficient to satisfy the statute if it is signed:

(a) by the transferor before or at the time of the transfer; or

(b) by the transferee

(i) before or at the time of the transfer, or

(ii) after the transfer was made to the transferee but before the transferee has transferred the property to a third person.

§24. Result of Noncompliance with Statute of Frauds

(1) Where a property owner creates an oral inter vivos trust for which a statute of frauds requires a writing, the trustee

(a) can properly perform the intended express trust, or

(b) can be compelled to perform the intended express trust if it later becomes enforceable on the basis of part performance.

(2) Where an owner of property transfers it to another upon an inter vivos trust for which a statute of frauds requires a writing, but no writing is properly signed (§23) evidencing the intended trust (§22), and the transferee refuses and cannot be compelled to perform it as an express trust under Clause (b) of Subsection (1), the transferee holds upon a constructive trust for the intended beneficiaries and purposes if

(a) the transfer was procured by fraud, undue influence, or duress, or

(b) the transferee at the time of the transfer was in a confidential relation to the transferor.

(3) Where an owner of property transfers it to another upon an inter vivos trust for which a statute of frauds requires a writing, but no writing is properly signed (§23) evidencing the intended trust (§22) and the rule of Subsection (2) does not apply, and the transferee refuses and cannot be compelled under Clause (b) of Subsection (1) to perform the intended express trust, the transferee can be compelled to hold the property either upon resulting trust or upon constructive trust for the transferor, except when the transferor is incompetent or dead and a constructive trust for the intended beneficiaries and purposes is necessary as a means of preventing unjust enrichment of successors in interest of the transferor.

(4) Where an owner of property orally declares a trust that is unenforceable because of a statute of frauds and cannot be compelled to perform the trust under Clause (b) of Subsection (1), the declarant holds the property free of enforceable trust, except when the declarant is incompetent or dead and a constructive trust for the intended beneficiaries and purposes is necessary as a means of preventing unjust enrichment of successors in interest of the declarant.

§25. Validity and Effect of Revocable Inter Vivos Trust

(1) A trust that is created by the settlor's declaration of trust, or by inter vivos transfer to another, or by beneficiary designation or other payment under a life-insurance policy, employee-benefit or retirement arrangement, or other contract is not rendered testamentary merely because the settlor retains extensive rights such as a beneficial interest for life, powers to revoke and modify the trust, and the right to serve as or control the trustee,

or because the trust is funded in whole or in part or comes into existence at or after the death of the settlor, or because the trust is intended to serve as a substitute for a will.

(2) A trust that is not testamentary is not subject to the formal requirements of §17 or to procedures for the administration of a decedent's estate; nevertheless, a trust is ordinarily subject to substantive restrictions on testation and to rules of construction and other rules applicable to testamentary dispositions, and in other respects the property of such a trust is ordinarily treated as though it were owned by the settlor.

Comment

a. Scope, background, and rationale of this Section. Revocable inter vivos (or living) trusts are useful and widely used as a legitimate means of avoiding the costs and delays typically associated with the processes of administering decedents' estates in this country. This is because probate administration is not required for assets transferred to the trustee inter vivos, or for funds payable to the trustee by nonprobate arrangements, such as pension or life insurance beneficiary designations. Assets added to the trust by will, however, are subject to estate administration before they are distributed to the trustee. (On such "pour-over" arrangements, see §19.)

Living trusts also are used as means of providing property management for settlors late in life, often on a contingent or standby basis by settlors who initially at least serve as their own trustees but designate successors to assume responsibility in the event the settlor resigns or becomes incompetent. Thus, for management of the trust estate, the relatively developed principles and processes associated with trust administration (see §§74 and 97, as well as §§76-89) in general are substituted for the heavily court-dependent concepts and procedures of conservatorship.

Occasionally, settlors find additional motivation for the use of revocable trusts rather than wills—reasons such as privacy or, in some states, the avoidance of probate courts' retained jurisdiction over testamentary trusts, with what may be perceived as more intrusive supervision than the relationship of equity courts to inter vivos (or "non-court") trusts. Under some state inheritance-tax systems, tax considerations also may encourage the use of living trusts as receptacles for life insurance proceeds or death benefits under retirement plans.

In short, despite modern efforts to simplify the probate process and the modern and ongoing development of the durable powers of attorney for property management, revocable trusts created by declaration or by transfer to another are often preferred by property owners as means of holding and disposing of their property. Accordingly, the revocable trust is widely used as a legally accepted substitute for the will as the central document of an estate plan, usually in conjunction with pour-over wills (§19) and often with durable powers of attorney . . . , the latter more for trust funding than for asset management.

The law offers a variety of different means of transferring property to others or of creating property rights and interests in beneficiaries, each with its own set of procedures and formalities. These same means are available for creating trusts and conferring equitable property interests on trust beneficiaries, with the declaration of trust offering an additional means of trust creation. See generally §10. Thus, for example, just as it is not necessary to comply with the formalities of Statutes of Wills for a beneficiary to receive insurance proceeds or periodic payments after the death of an insured policy owner, or to receive death benefits under various settlement options under a decedent's pension plan, so, too, may insurance proceeds or plan benefits be paid to a trustee on the death of the insured or plan participant based on the usual policy or plan formalities and without need to comply with those of a Wills Act.

With widespread legislative and judicial endorsement over the years, supported by experience as well as popular interest, the revocable trust has become well established in American law as a socially useful and successful device for property management, especially late in life, and for the disposition of property (outright or in further trust) following the settlor's death. . . .

Issues of formality and procedure aside, however, the availability of nontestamentary methods of making disposition should not mean that substantive policies applicable to testamentary dispositions have no application. Thus, increasingly, statutes and case law in the various states are coming to recognize, as this Restatement provides, that the rights of the spouses and creditors of testators and of settlors of revocable trusts are fundamentally alike, because both the testator and the settlor have retained their complete control over the property that is subject to the will or trust instrument. Similarly, whatever the technicalities of concept and terminology, the interests the revocable-trust beneficiaries will receive on the death of the settlor should, generally at least, receive the same treatment and should be subject to the same rules of construction as the "expectancies" of devisees.

Thus, this Restatement recognizes and gives effect to a property owner's right to choose among different forms and procedures for disposition of property. Yet it seeks to treat functional equivalents similarly, and not to allow choice of form either to provide an escape from serious, substantive policies or to cause the loss of properly relevant aids in essentially constructional matters. Such a policy of treating revocable trusts and their settlors and beneficiaries in like manner to the treatment accorded testators and will beneficiaries, both during life and after the death of the settlor or testator, has long been explicit in the federal income and transfer tax systems. See, e.g., Internal Revenue Code §§671-677 (income tax), §§2036 and 3038 (estate tax), §2511 with Treasury Regulation §25.2511-2(c) (gift tax), and §2652(a) (generation-skipping transfer tax). Early, traditional, and still-developing doctrine in trust and probate law has been neither so clear nor so consistent.

In brief, the fundamental and pervasive policy underlying this Section and related rules of this Restatement is that diverse forms of revocable trusts (i) are valid without compliance with Wills Act formalities but (ii) absent persuasive reason for departure, are subject to the same restrictions (such as spousal rights) and other rules and constructional aids that are applicable to wills. In other substantive respects (such as creditors' rights), the property held in a revocable trust is ordinarily to be treated as if it were property of the settlor and not of the beneficiaries.

Unless a contrary intent is manifested or the rights of the spouses are significantly altered by the trust terms, community property transferred by husband and wife to a jointly created revocable inter vivos trust remains community property. . . .

e. Rights of creditors and other matters. Although a revocable trust is nontestamentary and is therefore not subject to the Wills Act or to the usual procedures of estate administration, property held in the trust is subject to the claims of creditors of the settlor or of the deceased settlor's estate if the same property belonging to the settlor or the estate would be subject to the claims of the creditors, taking account of homestead rights and other exemptions.

This result is not dependent on the trust being "illusory" or "testamentary," or on the transfer being a fraudulent conveyance, but is based on the sound public policy of basing the rights of creditors on the substance rather than the form of the debtor's property rights. Nor is the result affected by the presence of a spendthrift provision in the terms of the trust (see §58(2)) or by whether a creditor's claim arose before or after the transfer.

Whether other assets of the settlor must first be exhausted and other questions involving priority among creditors or among various categories of intended beneficiaries of a deceased debtor are not within the scope of this Restatement. . . .

e(1). Statutory protections against oversight and aids in construction. In addition to the limitations on testamentary disposition represented by statutes discussed in Comment d and less directly by claims of creditors (above), an array of statutes are found throughout the various American jurisdictions that are designed as protections or aids against oversight or inadequacies in the planning and drafting of wills. These statutes often fail specifically to address revocable inter vivos trusts or other will-substitute dispositions. (*Common law* rules or principles of construction normally apply to revocable and irrevocable inter vivos trusts as well as to testamentary trusts.) . . .

Illustrative are pretermitted-heir statutes that, despite differences in their breadth and other details, usually provide intestate shares of a decedent's estate at least for children born after the making of a will that does not by class gift or otherwise make provision, as defined by the statute, for them. Analogous statutes in some states, especially where intestate shares of surviving spouses are significantly greater than their elective shares, make provision in certain circumstances for survivors of marriages entered after the execution of wills.

Other examples include anti-lapse statutes, usually providing substitute gifts for the issue of certain legatees and devisees who predecease testators, and statutes primarily providing for revocation of will provisions for spouses in cases in which divorce occurs after the making of a will.

Statutes of these various types are generally based on legislative judgments concerning probabilities of intention and yield to contrary intent that is shown by types of evidence allowed by the legislation. Sound policy suggests that a property owner's choice of form in using a revocable trust rather than a will as the central instrument of an estate plan should not deprive that property owner and the objects of his or her bounty of appropriate aids and safeguards intended to achieve likely intentions. Thus, although a particular statute of this general type fails to address trusts that are revocable but nontestamentary, the legislation should ordinarily be applied as if trust dispositive provisions that are to be carried out after the settlor's death had been made by will.

e(2). Limits on public benefits and resources. Somewhat analogous problems may arise from quite different types of federal and state legislation or administrative regulations, involving such matters as public benefit programs and governmentally allocated opportunities. Examples range from matters of eligibility and reimbursement for welfare benefits and services to issues about the allocation of entitlements or licenses with respect to water resources, communications media, and the like. . . .

Illustrations

11. W transfers the bulk of her estate to T in trust for W for life, the trust to continue thereafter for the benefit of her husband H for life, with remainder thereafter to be distributed to W's issue. W reserves the power to revoke or amend the trust. A number of years later W and H are divorced; W dies shortly thereafter, and H is still alive. It is provided by statute that a divorce revokes provisions for the former spouse in a will executed before the divorce, with the provisions of the will to be carried out as if the former spouse had predeceased the testator. The provision for H in W's revocable living trust is revoked (see Comment e(1)); the issue are entitled to distribution of the trust property although H is still alive.

12. S owns two ranches, Blackacre and Whiteacre, and her brother B owns a ranch called Greenacre. The Scarce and Subsidized Water Act (SASWA) limits the water allocation each applicant may receive—"directly or indirectly," according to SASWA Regulations. S transfers all of her real and personal property, except for Whiteacre and some personal items, to T in trust for the benefit and use of S during her lifetime, and upon her death to distribute one-half of the trust property to B and the rest to certain nieces and nephews. S reserves the power to revoke or amend the trust. T applies for and obtains a SASWA water allocation for Blackacre. Soon thereafter, S and B also apply for water allocations, respectively, for Whiteacre and Greenacre. For purposes of their eligibility for water allocations, in the absence of an explicit SASWA provision to the contrary, the SASWA allocation to the trust for Blackacre is treated as an allocation to S and not to B (see Comment e(2)). . . .

§26. Tentative ("Totten" or Bank-Account) Trusts

Where a person makes a deposit in an account with a bank or similar financial institution in the depositor's own name "as trustee" or "in trust" for another, the presumption is that the depositor intends to establish a "tentative trust." The depositor may modify or revoke a tentative trust and may, from time to time, withdraw any or all of the funds on deposit. On the death of the depositor, the trust is enforceable by the beneficiary as to any funds then remaining on deposit, unless the depositor has revoked the trust.

. . . *c. Revocation and termination of tentative trust.* A tentative trust can properly be revoked by the depositor at any time during life by a manifestation of intention to do so. No particular formalities are necessary to manifest that intention.

Thus, the trust is terminated by withdrawal of all the funds or by transferring them to a different account. If any part of the deposit is withdrawn during the depositor's lifetime, this operates as a revocation of the trust to the extent of the withdrawal; and the beneficiary will be entitled only to the amount remaining on deposit at the death of the depositor. The nature or terms of the account may be changed by the depositor's direction to the savings institution. In addition, the right to funds remaining in the account at the depositor's death may be changed by agreement between the beneficiary and the depositor. . . .

Where there are multiple depositors, or if there are multiple persons designated as trustees, one of whom is the depositor, it is presumed that there is a right of survivorship between or among the "trustees" of the trust, which remains a tentative trust as long as a trustee and a beneficiary survive. The death of the beneficiary (or of the last survivor of multiple beneficiaries) of a tentative trust prior to the death of the depositor (or last trustee) terminates the trust, even though the depositor (or last trustee) later dies without having manifested an intention to revoke the trust and without having withdrawn the amount on deposit. In such a case, the personal representative of the depositor (or last trustee), not the personal representative of the beneficiary, will be entitled to the amount of deposit; and even an anti-lapse statute that ordinarily applies to other revocable trusts . . . does not apply to tentative trusts. . . .

In the absence of a statute to the contrary, a tentative trust may be revoked in whole or in part by the depositor's will, either by express provision or by necessary implication. The conservator of a depositor who becomes incompetent may, with such court permission as may be required by law, withdraw some or all of the tentative-trust funds as necessary for the welfare of the depositor and appropriate members of his or her family. . . .

d. Creditors' rights, family protection, and rules of will construction. The creditors of a person who establishes a tentative trust can reach the funds on deposit, as may the personal representative of a deceased depositor if assets otherwise available in the estate administration are insufficient to pay debts and funeral, last-illness, and administration expenses.

The tentative trust, like other revocable inter vivos trusts, is subject to restrictions on testamentary disposition and also to pretermitted-heir and omitted-spouse protections. . . .

Part 3. Elements of Trusts

Chapter 6: TRUST PURPOSES

§27. Purposes For Which a Trust Can Be Created

(1) Subject to the rules of §29, a trust may be created for charitable purposes (see §28) or for private purposes, or for a combination of charitable and private purposes.

(2) Subject to the special rules of §§46(2) and 47, a private trust, its terms, and its administration must be for the benefit of its beneficiaries, who must be identified or ascertainable as provided in §44. (On charitable trusts, see §28.)

Comment

Comment on Subsection (1)

a. Charitable and private purposes. Except as provided in §§46(2) and 47 (on certain trust provisions for "indefinite beneficiaries" and "noncharitable purposes," respectively), permissible purposes of trusts that are the subject of this Restatement are confined to those that are charitable ("charitable trusts") and those that are for the benefit of persons who are definite or will be ascertainable in compliance with rules regulating perpetuities ("private trusts"). Furthermore, trust purposes and provisions must not be unlawful or contrary to public policy (§29).

Trusts may have mixed charitable and private purposes. Thus, for example, a trust may be created to provide concurrent benefits for both charitable and private purposes, either by fixed portions or discretionary distributions. More frequently, so-called "split-interest" trusts are created to benefit the settlor or family members for term or life periods and thereafter to benefit charity, or vice versa. . . .

. . . Some purposes that a reasonable individual might believe worthwhile may fall short of the standard of charity for which a charitable trust may be established. On such cases, see §47.

Often the purposes of private trusts are not specified but must be inferred from the interests conferred on the various beneficiaries, whose identities and interests are subject to the requirements of definiteness discussed in Chapter 9 (especially §§44 through 47). . . .

Comment on Subsection (2)

b. Private trusts. The general purpose of a private trust is to benefit identified or identifiable beneficiaries (see §§44-46) in accordance with their respective interests in the trust. Within this general private purpose, a given trust may and most likely will serve multiple objectives or purposes (see *b(1)* below).

The settlor of a particular trust has considerable latitude in specifying the manner in which a trust purpose is to be pursued. In order to be valid, however, administrative and other provisions must reasonably relate to a trust purpose and must not have the effect of diverting the trust's funds or administration from that purpose in support of a purpose that does not meet the private- or charitable-purpose requirement of Subsection (1), as qualified by §47 (on general and specific noncharitable "purpose" trusts). . . .

§28. Charitable Purposes

Charitable trust purposes include:

(a) the relief of poverty;

(b) the advancement of knowledge or education;

(c) the advancement of religion;

(d) the promotion of health;

(e) governmental or municipal purposes; and

(f) other purposes that are beneficial to the community.

General Comment

a. The general nature of charitable trusts and purposes. . . .

The discussion in this Section of dispositions that are charitable does not necessarily provide a complete enumeration of charitable purposes. Other purposes of the same general character are likewise charitable. The common element of charitable purposes is that they are designed to accomplish objects that are beneficial to the community—i.e., to the public or indefinite members thereof—without also serving what amount to private trust purposes . . . . As long as the purposes to which the property of the trust is to be devoted are charitable, however, the motives of the settlor in creating the trust are immaterial.

A trust purpose is charitable if its accomplishment is of such social interest or benefit to the community as to justify permitting the property to be devoted to the purpose in perpetuity and to justify the various other special privileges that are typically allowed to charitable trusts.

There is no fixed standard to determine what purposes are of such interest to the community, for the interests of the community vary with time and place. Trust-law definitions of charity are not limited by those used in federal, state, and local tax law; nor are tax-law definitions necessarily limited to charitable purposes recognized by the trust law. Of the generally agreed purposes stated in this Section, it is Clause (f) (Comment *l*) that provides the greatest flexibility and also presents the most definitional issues at the margin. . . .

a(2). Controversial ideas and unpopular causes. If the general purposes for which a trust is created are such that they may be reasonably thought to promote the social interest of the community, the mere fact that a majority of the people or of the members of a court believe that the particular purpose of the settlor is unwise or not well adapted to its social objective does not prevent the trust from being charitable. Thus, a trust to promote a particular religious doctrine or a particular system of taxation is charitable even though the view to be promoted has but a modest number of adherents. The role of the court in deciding whether a purpose is charitable is not to attempt to decide which of conflicting views of the social or community interest is more beneficial or appropriate but to decide whether the trust purpose or the view to be promoted is sufficiently useful or reasonable to be of such benefit or interest to the community, including through a marketplace of ideas, as to justify the perpetual existence and other privileges of a charitable trust. Thus, a trust to establish a museum to exhibit what a testator regarded as objects of art but which testimony establishes to be of no artistic value, or a trust to publish and distribute a testator's views that are irrational or other writings that are of no literary or educational value, is not charitable. The line between what is charitable and what is not is sometimes a difficult one to draw, for the difference may be one of degree and the line may be drawn differently at different times and in different places. For trusts that do not qualify as either private or charitable trusts, see the limited duration and acceptance of "trusts for noncharitable purposes" in §47. . . .

d. Duration of charitable trusts. A charitable trust is not invalid although by its terms it is to continue for an indefinite or unlimited period of time. This is unlike the rules for private trusts, in which the interests of the beneficiaries must vest within the period of the applicable rule against perpetuities, and under which a provision that a private trust shall be indestructible (i. e., is not to be terminated even upon the consent of all beneficiaries) beyond the period of the rule is invalid. See §29(b) . . . .

Charitable trusts may be of unlimited duration, although dispositions over to charitable purposes following private trusts are subject to the rule against perpetuities, as are dispositions over to private purposes upon termination of charitable trusts. On the other hand, even after the perpetuities period would have expired, a shift over from one charitable purpose or trust to another is permissible because, it is often said, the property is "vested in charity." . . .

e. Trusts with mixed charitable and other purposes. A trust is not invalid, although it might not be a charitable trust, merely because it includes private trust interests (§27(2)) or a "noncharitable purpose" (§47) as well as the designated charitable purpose.

If the charitable and other purposes are distinctly divided either by time or into separate and independent shares, the period or share devoted to charity will be treated as a charitable trust just as if separate trusts had been created for the different purposes. Where there is no such separation by time or by independent shares, the trust is valid, but such a mixed charitable and private trust is subject to the rule against perpetuities as a private trust; and if the trust similarly combines charitable purposes with a noncharitable purpose, the trust is subject to the rules and limitations of noncharitable-purpose trusts under §47. . . .

f. Consistency with law and public policy. Like other trusts, charitable trusts are subject to the rule of §29 that trust purposes and provisions must not be unlawful or contrary to public policy.

It is particularly common, however, for provisions to be included in various types of charitable trusts, especially those created for educational or health purposes or for the relief of poverty, limiting the direct benefits or eligibility to persons of a particular national origin, religion, gender, sexual orientation, age group, political affiliation, or other characteristics or background. Of course, federal and state constitutions, legislation, and other binding expressions of applicable law and policy are to be respected in the administration of trusts and in determining the enforceability of the terms of trusts. These matters, and such implicit issues as what may constitute state action, are beyond the scope of this Restatement. The issue for present purposes, however, remains what provisions of this general type may, as a matter of trust law and policy, be inconsistent with the nature of charitable purposes.

Provisions of these types in charitable trusts are not valid if they involve invidious discrimination (see below). Where a restriction or preference is invalid, or the particular charitable disposition cannot be carried out because the intended recipient refuses to accept it due to a restrictive provision or preference the intended recipient deems objectionable, an issue arises concerning the application of the doctrine of cy pres. See §67. . . .

It is not always possible to state with certainty what constitutes an "invidious" form of discrimination for these purposes. What the law of charitable trusts does or does not allow inevitably varies from time to time and place to place, as well as from context to context. For example, trust-law policies regarding restrictions on gender, sexual orientation, or age are especially sensitive to context, as the scope of more general statutory and constitutional protections evolve in these matters. . . . Some generalizations are nevertheless possible.

When a scholarship or other form of assistance or opportunity is to be awarded on a basis that, for example, explicitly excludes potential beneficiaries on the basis of membership in a particular racial, ethnic, or religious group, the restriction is ordinarily invidious and therefore unenforceable. Thus, a trust to provide land and maintenance for a playground from which Black children are excluded, or a trust to support a scholarship program for which no Roman Catholic may apply, is not enforceable under those terms as a charitable trust. Similarly, although the exclusions are not explicit, a trust to provide research grants for which only "white, Anglo-Saxon Protestants" may apply is invidious and noncharitable.

This does not mean that a criterion such as gender, religion, or national origin may not be used in a charitable trust when it is a reasonable element of a settlor's charitable purpose and charitable motivation. Thus, the requirement that the purpose be of charitable character does not prevent alumnae or friends of a women's college from endowing a professorial chair or library fund for that college, or a Jewish man from leaving money to a university to establish a scholarship program, in the betterment of his religion as he sees it, to enable a rabbi or two each year to study in that university's philosophy department. Nor does it mean that a Norwegian immigrant who became wealthy in this country cannot establish a program of an otherwise charitable nature to aid, solely or by preference, other Norwegian immigrants or the children of Norwegian immigrants. Similarly, the law of charitable trusts as such does not object to what is sometimes called "affirmative action," attempting to respond to a social problem in its own terms, at least as reasonably perceived by a substantial (even if not majority) segment of society or of the affected community. . . .

Comment on Clause (f)

l. Promotion of other purposes beneficial to the community. A trust is charitable if it is established for the promotion of purposes that are of a character sufficiently of interest or beneficial to the community to justify permitting the property to be devoted forever to their accomplishment and to justify whatever other special privileges may be accorded to charitable trusts. . . .

The trusts encompassed by this Comment may involve any of a large, indefinite array of purposes in addition to (or overlapping) those that are dealt with in the preceding Comments but that are nevertheless held to promote the social interests of the community, and are therefore upheld as falling within the scope of charity. It is not possible adequately and accurately to enumerate all purposes of this type, for in deciding whether a particular purpose falls within the present clause, much depends on the time and the place at which the question arises. In each such case, as under some other clauses of this Section, particularly some cases involving purposes that are arguably educational, the question for potential judicial determination is whether at the time when the question arises and in the state in which it arises the purpose is one that might reasonably be held to be of community or social interest. The mere fact that a trust is created for the benefit of members of a community outside the state, however, does not prevent the trust from being charitable. Thus, a trust for the benefit of impoverished residents of another state, or to establish a school or hospital in a foreign country, is charitable.

A trust to prevent or alleviate the suffering of animals is charitable. . . . So also is a trust to establish or support a home or to provide care for stray animals, although a trust to provide for the settlor's own pets is not charitable (see, however, §47). . . .

A trust may be charitable although the accomplishment of the purpose for which the trust is created involves a change in the existing law. If the purpose of the trust is to bring about a change in the law by illegal means, however, such as by revolution, bribery, or illegal lobbying, or bringing improper pressure to bear upon members of the legislature, the purpose is not charitable. Cf. §29. Certainly a trust to promote general improvement in the law, whether by financial support of the work of a law-revision commission or through the support of research projects so directed, is charitable. The mere fact, however, that the purpose of a trust is to advocate and bring about a *particular* change of law does not prevent the purpose from being charitable. . . ..

Although a trust to promote the success of a particular political party is not charitable, the development and dissemination of information advocating or seeking to improve understanding of a particular set of social, economic, or political views is charitable, whether because it is educational (Comment h) or because it contributes to a marketplace of ideas that is beneficial to the community. Thus, on the one hand, a trust the income of which is to be used in the discretion of the chairperson of a political party to assist in the election of members of that party or otherwise to promote its interests is not charitable. On the other hand, if the promotion of a particular cause or socio-economic perspective is charitable, the mere fact that one or another of the political parties advocates that cause or viewpoint does not make the promotion of that cause or set of views noncharitable. Accordingly, a trust to promote a policy either of free trade or of protective tariffs is charitable although different political parties may take different stands on these policies or their current applications. . . .

§29. Purposes and Provisions That Are Unlawful or Against Public Policy

An intended trust or trust provision is invalid if:

(a) its purpose is unlawful or its performance calls for the commission of a criminal or tortious act;

(b) it violates rules relating to perpetuities; or

(c) it is contrary to public policy.

Comment on Clause (a)

b. Voidable transfers contrasted. The types of situations addressed in Clause (a) involve impermissible purposes or provisions of the trust itself. Analogous but different are trusts that may fail in whole or in part because a third party is entitled to set aside the settlor's transfer to the trustee or to reach the property in the trustee's hands. Illustrative are cases in which the settlor's property had been illegally acquired by the settlor and cases in which the settlor's transfer to the trust constitutes a fraudulent transfer under applicable creditors' rights law. . . .

Comment on Clause (c)

i. Nature and rationale of public-policy limits on trust provisions. The rules allowing and limiting the use of trusts, and the time-divided property ownership usually associated with deadhand control, reflect a compromise between free disposition of private property and other values (see §27 and Introductory Note to this Chapter). So also does the rule of Clause (c) of this Section, and ensuing Comments j-l involving trust benefits conditioned upon the beneficiary's future conduct.

The private trust is tolerated, even treasured, in the common-law world for the flexibility it offers to property owners in planning and designing diverse beneficial interests and financial protections over time, individually tailored as the particular property owner deems best to the varied needs, abilities, and circumstances of particular family members and others whom the owner chooses to benefit. Yet these societal and individual advantages are properly to be balanced against other social values and the effects of deadhand control on the subsequent conduct or personal freedoms of others, and also against the burdens a former owner's unrestrained dispositions might place on courts to interpret and enforce individualized interests and conditions.

The simplest examples of trusts or provisions that offend public policy are those that tend to encourage criminal or tortious conduct on the part of beneficiaries. . . .

Policies concerned with deadhand control limit the use of trusts in ways that do not apply to living individuals in the direct disposition of their property. Thus, a policy of fostering free family interaction or privacy between individuals, or simply society's tolerance of human frailty, traditionally exempts acts of property owners (and even their outright dispositions by will) from restrictions that would apply to personally intrusive or socially dubious conditions in the distributive provisions of irrevocable trusts. Furthermore, the "rigor mortis" of deadhand control is not present while a property owner is able to respond to persuasion and evolving circumstances.

Thus, although one is free to give property to another or to withhold it, it does not follow that one may give in trust with whatever terms or conditions one may wish to attach. This is particularly so of provisions that the law views as exerting a socially undesirable influence on the exercise or nonexercise of fundamental rights that significantly affect the personal lives of beneficiaries and often of others as well. See Scope note, Comment i(2), below. Also compare §28, Comment f, on "invidious" restrictions in charitable trusts.

In cases of the types considered in the Comments that follow, simple and precise rules of validity or invalidity frequently cannot be stated. This is particularly so because of the need to weigh the often worthy concerns and objectives of settlors against the objectionable effects or tendencies of conditions attached to beneficial interests, each of which involves specific terms and personal and overall estate-planning contexts that may vary subtly but significantly from situation to situation. Furthermore, in these various situations, remedial flexibility is required to reconcile (i) the policy objection to a provision with (ii) a motive or goal of the settlor that is legally acceptable in whole or in part as an effort to protect the beneficiary's interest or the trust property.

i(1). Consequences of invalidity; reformation. Ordinarily, if a beneficial interest in a trust is to be conferred or is to terminate upon an invalid condition (whether, in form, precedent or subsequent), the interest becomes effective or continues as if the condition had not been imposed, or as if the settlor's requirements or restrictions were satisfied. A different result may be reached, however, to avoid distorting the settlor's underlying general plan for allocating his or her estate among family members. Furthermore, if the settlor provides for a certain disposition in case of a condition's invalidity, that direction will be respected unless it would have the effect of deterring a beneficiary from asserting the rule of this Clause (c) of this Section.

In addition, a provision that is not to be upheld as written but is susceptible of adaptation to accommodate both public-policy concerns and legitimate settlor objectives may be so adapted by the court. The rule allowing reformation under the Comments that follow is rather like the use of equitable approximation (i.e., reformation) in cases of violations of the rule against perpetuities. . . .

i(2). Scope note. The policies restraining deadhand control in Clause (c) of this Section do not apply to outright dispositions conditioned on conduct prior to the death of the testator, or prior to the time a revocable trust becomes irrevocable. See Restatement Second, Property (Donative Transfers) §6.1, Comment c; although the Property Restatement's rules on behavior restraints apply to nontrust as well as trust dispositions in various forms, those rules (as here) only address restraints on "future conduct."

Some of the personal relationships or freedoms considered in Comments j through l may be protected in some fashion by federal or state statutes or constitutions (such as religious freedom). These Comments, however, involve rules and policies of the trust law and limit the purposes and terms of trusts in ways that are not based on statutory or constitutional safeguards, although trust law may be influenced by policies underlying such protections.

j. Family relationships. A trust or a condition or other provision in the terms of a trust is ordinarily (see below) invalid if it tends to encourage disruption of a family relationship or to discourage formation or resumption of such a relationship. See also Restatement Second, Contracts §§189-191.

Thus, a trust provision normally may not terminate a beneficial interest if a beneficiary and spouse who are living apart should resume living together, or confer a beneficial interest upon a beneficiary if he or she obtains a divorce or legal separation. Similarly, a trust provision is ordinarily invalid if it would tend to induce termination of a long-established relationship of cohabitation without marriage.

In addition, a trust provision is ordinarily invalid if it tends seriously to interfere with or inhibit the exercise of a beneficiary's freedom to obtain a divorce (creating a risk, e.g., of encouraging financial dependency upon an abusive relationship) or the exercise of freedom to marry, either by limiting the beneficiary's selection of a spouse or by unduly postponing the time of marriage. A fundamental exception, however, permits termination of a beneficial interest of the settlor's spouse in the event of the spouse's remarriage or, if the restraint is reasonable under all the circumstances . . . , termination of a beneficial interest of the surviving spouse of one who is or would have been a natural object of the settlor's bounty. . . .

The policy against undermining family relationships applies as well to trust provisions that discourage a person from living with or caring for a parent or child or from social interaction with siblings.

Clause (c) of this Section is generally concerned with the objective effects of a provision rather than with the settlor's underlying motive(s). Nevertheless, a subjective inquiry into the settlor's reasons for including a provision in a trust may be relevant. Thus, it may be shown that the settlor's motive was to provide for special needs that might arise in the event of the beneficiary's divorce, or to provide support for a beneficiary until marriage or for a child who feels unable to return to a parent's home. A provision of this type may be upheld despite the incidental influence it may have on the beneficiary's decision(s) affecting a marriage or family relationship. Such a condition may even relieve financial pressure on a beneficiary to remain in or enter a marriage. Similarly, in making or increasing provision for a beneficiary upon divorce from a particular spouse, a settlor may be motivated by reasonable concern over that spouse's financial irresponsibility or an apparent gambling or substance addiction.

The credibility of any such explanation is diminished, however, and its socially undesirable influence aggravated, when the provision does not take the form of discretionary distributions appropriately tailored to the alleged risk or to the beneficiary's needs and the availability of other means of meeting those needs. Moreover, a provision may reflect a mixture of motives or may provide some other basis for finding it invalid as written despite an acceptable purpose. In cases of these various types, a provision may fail in its original form but nevertheless be judicially reformed to accomplish the permissible objectives (possibly with fiduciary discretion over distributions) while removing or minimizing socially undesirable effects. Speculation about a settlor's motives and other difficulties inherent in these cases may be eased by this remedial flexibility under which an all-or-nothing decision is not required. . . .

k. Religious freedom. Individuals are normally free during life to promote their theological views among others, and to create charitable trusts during life or at death to support or advance a chosen religion (see §28, Clause (b)). But the use of private trusts that create financial pressure regarding the future religious choices of beneficiaries is a different matter. A trust provision is ordinarily invalid if its enforcement would tend to restrain the religious freedom of the beneficiary by offering a financial inducement to embrace or reject a particular faith or set of beliefs concerning religion. Illustrative is a provision granting or terminating a beneficial interest only if the beneficiary should adopt or abandon a particular religious faith. . . .

On the other hand, trust provisions would ordinarily be upheld if reasonably designed (or reformed) to protect beneficial interests or trust property from adverse financial implications associated with a beneficiary's present or future religious commitments. . . .

l. Careers and conduct. It is not contrary to public policy for a trust provision to encourage a beneficiary to be a productive member of society or to pursue a particular career or form of training, as long as the effect of the provision is not punitive or so rewarding as to be coercive. Thus, a settlor may validly create a trust or include a provision solely to finance a beneficiary's higher education, or a particular type of education, or to facilitate pursuit of a particular type of career (such as religious or social service) by compensating for the financial services that tend to be associated with the career choice.

Different policy considerations are presented, however, by a provision to distribute the corpus of a trust to its income beneficiary only if the beneficiary becomes a surgeon, or to terminate a beneficiary's interests for abandoning a particular career or for failing to take it up by a stated age. In cases of this type, society's interest in a property owner's freedom of disposition must be weighed against the risk of excessive influence on a personal decision significantly affecting the life of the beneficiary and perhaps others. The social concerns here involve not only the increased risk of an unsuitable decision being made or adhered to by the beneficiary but also the burdens and difficulties of judicial interpretation and enforcement of such interpretations.

Trust provisions intended or likely to induce a change or a continuation of a beneficiary's personal habits or conduct ordinarily are not against public policy. But Compare Comments *j* and *k* above, that where a provision is unnecessarily punitive or unreasonably intrusive into significant personal decisions or interests, or involves an unreasonable restraint on personal associations, the provision may be invalid. . . .

m. Capricious purposes; sound administration of trust. It is against public policy to enforce a trust provision that would divert distributions or administration from the interests of the beneficiaries to other purposes that are capricious or frivolous . . . , detrimental to the community, or otherwise (with limited exceptions . . .) neither private nor charitable in character. See §27.

Similarly, a trust provision may not be enforced if to do so would undermine proper administration of the trust. Thus, a provision that purports to prevent a court from removing a trustee will be disregarded if removal appears appropriate to proper administration of the trust; and an arbitrary restriction on the appointment of trustees or successor trustees may be invalid if not reasonably related to the trust purposes. A provision is also invalid to the extent it purports to relieve the trustee altogether from accountability and the duty to provide information to beneficiaries (see §§82, 83), or to relieve the trustee from liability even for dishonest or reckless acts (see §87, §96, and §§76-79). See generally Chapters 14 through 18, and cf. Restatement Second, Property (Donative Transfers) §9.2 and Restatement Third, Property (Wills and Other Donative Transfers) §8.5.

This principle does not, however, prevent a settlor from prescribing administrative provisions designed to serve a reasonable view of the beneficiaries' best interests or to express a widely even if not generally held view of business ethics or morality. . . .

§30. Impossibility and Indefiniteness

A private trust, or a provision in the terms of a trust, may be unenforceable because of impossibility or indefiniteness.

Chapter 7: THE TRUSTEE

§31. Trust Does Not Fail for Lack of Trustee

A trust does not fail because no trustee is designated or because the designated trustee declines, is unable, or ceases to act, unless the trust's creation or continuation depends on a specific person serving as trustee; a proper court will appoint a trustee as necessary and appropriate (see §34).

§32. Capacity of Individual to Be Trustee

A natural person, including a settlor or beneficiary, has capacity

(a) to take and hold property in trust to the extent the person has capacity to take and hold the property as beneficial owner; and

(b) to administer trust property and act as trustee to the same extent the person would have capacity to deal with the property as beneficial owner.

§33. Corporations and Other Entities as Trustees

(1) A corporation has capacity to take and hold property in trust except as limited by law, and to administer trust property and act as trustee to the extent of the powers conferred upon it by law.

(2) If a partnership, unincorporated association, or other entity has capacity to take and hold property for its own purposes, it has capacity to take, hold, and administer property in trust.

§34. Appointment of Trustees

(1) Except as required by statute, a trustee designated by or selected in accordance with the

terms of a trust may act without being appointed or confirmed by an order of court.

(2) If the appointment of a trustee is not provided for or made pursuant to the terms of the trust, the trustee will be appointed by a proper court.

(3) A trustee need not provide a performance bond except as required by statute, trust provision, or court order.

§35. Acceptance or Renunciation of Trusteeship

(1) A designated trustee may accept the trusteeship either by words or by conduct.

(2) A designated trustee who has not accepted the trusteeship may decline it.

§36. Resignation of Trustee

A trustee who has accepted the trust can properly resign:

(a) in accordance with the terms of the trust;

(b) with the consent of all beneficiaries; or

(c) upon terms approved by a proper court.

§37. Removal of Trustee

A trustee may be removed

(a) in accordance with the terms of the trust; or

(b) for cause by a proper court.

Comment

. . .*d. Removal by court; judicial discretion.* A court may remove a trustee whose continuation in that role would be detrimental to the interests of the beneficiaries. See Comment e. The matter is largely left to the discretion of the trial court, but is subject to review for abuse of discretion.

The court may act on the petition of any beneficiary, co-trustee, or other interested party, or on its own motion (see generally §94). The trustee is entitled to due process, with notice and an opportunity to be heard, although the court may suspend a trustee's powers (including, if necessary, by appointing a temporary trustee) pending a removal hearing.

e. Grounds for removal. The following are illustrative, but not exhaustive, of possible grounds for a court to remove a trustee: lack of capacity to administer the trust (see §32); unfitness, whether due to insolvency, diminution of physical vigor or mental acuity, substance abuse, want of skill, or the inability to understand fiduciary standards and duties; acquisition of a conflicting interest (cf. Comment f(1)); refusal or inability to give bond, if bond is required (see §34, Comment a); repeated or flagrant failure or delay in providing proper information or accountings to beneficiaries (see §§82 and 83); the commission of a crime, particularly one involving dishonesty; gross or continued inadequacies in matters of investment (see §§90-92); changes in the place of trust administration, location of beneficiaries, or other developments causing serious geographic inconvenience to the beneficiaries or to the administration of the trust; unwarranted preference to the interests of one or more beneficiaries; a pattern of indifference toward some or all of the beneficiaries; or unreasonable or corrupt failure to cooperate with a co-trustee.

Not every breach of trust warrants removal of the trustee (*cf.* Comment g), but serious or repeated misconduct, even unconnected with the trust itself, may justify removal. . . .

e(1). Friction between trustee and beneficiaries. Friction between the trustee and some of the beneficiaries is not a sufficient ground for removing the trustee unless it interferes with the proper administration of the trust. . . .

f. Trustee named by settlor. The court will less readily remove a trustee named by the settlor than one appointed by a court. . . .

Ordinarily, a court will not remove a trustee named by the settlor upon a ground that was known to the settlor at the time the trustee was designated, even though a court would not itself have appointed that person as trustee. In cases of unfitness to serve (*supra*), however, a court may remove a trustee even upon a ground known to the settlor at the time of designation.

f(1). Conflicting interests. Thus, the fact that the trustee named by the settlor is one of the beneficiaries of the trust, or would otherwise have conflicting interests, is not a sufficient ground for removing the trustee or refusing to confirm the appointment. This is so even though the trustee has broad discretion in matters of distribution and investment.

A trustee's removal may be warranted, however, by a conflict of interests that existed but was unknown to the settlor at the time of the designation, or that came into being at a later time.

Furthermore, when a beneficiary serves as trustee or when other conflict-of-interest situations exist, the conduct of the trustee in the administration of the trust will be subject to especially careful scrutiny. . . .

g. Alternatives to removal of trustee. Courts may grant more limited relief to deal with cases in which removal is not necessary or appropriate.

For example, conflict-of-interest problems might be ameliorated by the appointment of an additional trustee, or by the appointment of a trustee ad litem to handle a specific, conflict-sensitive transaction. . . .

§38. Trustee's Compensation and Indemnification

(1) A trustee is entitled to reasonable compensation out of the trust estate for services as trustee, unless the terms of the trust provide otherwise or the trustee agrees to forgo compensation.

(2) A trustee is entitled to indemnity out of the trust estate for expenses properly incurred in the administration of the trust.

Comment

Comment on Subsection (1)

c. Amount of compensation. . . . The reasonable compensation rule applies where there is no statute dealing with trustee compensation.

Trustees ordinarily receive some compensation periodically and, when the trust terminates, additional compensation for their special responsibilities at that time.

c(1). Determining reasonable compensation. Trial courts have discretion in determining reasonable compensation, but their determinations are subject to review for abuse of discretion.

Local custom is a factor to be considered in determining compensation. Other relevant factors are: the trustee's skill, experience and facilities, and the time devoted to trust duties; the amount and character of the trust property; the degree of difficulty, responsibility, and risk assumed in administering the trust, including in making discretionary distributions; the nature and costs of services rendered by others; and the quality of the trustee's performance.

The amount of compensation received by a trustee is relevant in determining whether certain costs of others' services are reimbursable under Subsection (2). This is particularly so of costs of hiring advisors, agents, and others to render services expected or normally to be performed by the trustee. Conversely, even proper expenses of this type may affect what is reasonable compensation for the trustee. . . . On the requirement that expenses be properly incurred, see generally §88.

Absent a statute so requiring, the trustee's compensation need not be approved by a court, but a trustee who has taken excessive compensation may be ordered to refund it. To make the possibility of judicial review meaningful, beneficiaries should be informed of compensation being taken by the trustee. On the extent to which a trustee is protected by a court decree, or by approval or acquiescence of beneficiaries, see §83 (on accounting) and §§97 (beneficiary consent) and 98 (laches). . . .

e. The terms of the trust. When the terms of a trust provide that the trustee is to receive a certain compensation or no compensation, the trustee's right to compensation is ordinarily governed by that provision. It is a question of interpretation whether such a provision applies also to successor trustees.

If the amount of compensation provided by the terms of the trust is or becomes unreasonably high or unreasonably low, the court may allow a smaller or larger compensation, or may allow the trustee to resign. See §36. . . .

l. Several trustees. When there are two or more co-trustees, compensation that is fixed by statute or trust provision ordinarily is to be divided among them in accordance with the relative value of their services. . . .

In the aggregate, the reasonable fees for multiple trustees may be higher than for a single trustee, because the normal duty of each trustee to participate in all aspects of administration (see §81, and cf. §80) can be expected not only to result in some duplication of effort but also to contribute to the quality of administration. . . .

§39. Exercise of Powers by Multiple Trustees

Unless otherwise provided by the terms of the trust, if there are two trustees their powers may be exercised only by concurrence of both of them, absent an emergency or a proper delegation; but if there are three or more trustees their powers may be exercised by a majority.

Comment

a. Basic rule and rationale. If a trust has two trustees, they must concur in order to exercise powers of the trusteeship. If there are three or more trustees and they disagree, the decision of the majority controls, although when feasible all trustees must be consulted before decisions are made. . . ..

For purposes of this rule, the number of trustees in office at the time of the action is controlling, rather than the original number of trustees. . . .

Traditionally, the majority-rule principle has applied only to charitable trusts; in private trusts all the trustees had to agree in order to take action. Considerations of sound and efficient administration, however, tend to be better served by the rule stated in this Section. This is evidenced not only by widespread drafting practice but also by the fact that most states today provide for majority rule by statute. . . . See also Uniform Trustees Powers Act §6; Uniform Trusts Act (1937) §11; and Uniform Trust Code §703(a).

These statutory provisions and the rule of this Section ordinarily protect a dissenting trustee from liability for an act authorized by the majority, while preserving the co-trustee's duty normally to participate in deliberations and decisionmaking and to act reasonably to prevent a breach of trust. . . .

Chapter 8: TRUST PROPERTY

§40. Any Property May Be Trust Property

Subject to the rule of §29, a trustee may hold in trust any interest in any type of property.

§41. Expectancies; Nonexistent Property Interests

An expectation or hope of receiving property in the future, or an interest that has not come into existence or has ceased to exist, cannot be held in trust.

§42. Extent and Nature of Trustee's Title

Unless a different intention is manifested, or the settlor owned only a lesser interest, the trustee takes a nonbeneficial interest of unlimited duration in the trust property and not an interest limited to the duration of the trust.

Chapter 9: BENEFICIARIES

§43. Persons Who May Be Beneficiaries

A person who would have capacity to take and hold legal title to the intended trust property has capacity to be a beneficiary of a trust of that property; ordinarily, a person who lacks capacity to hold legal title to property may not be a trust beneficiary.

§44. Definite-Beneficiary Requirement

A trust is not created, or if created will not continue, unless the terms of the trust provide a beneficiary who is ascertainable at the time or who may later become ascertainable within the period and terms of the rule against perpetuities.

§45. Members of a Definite Class as Beneficiaries

The members of a definite class of persons can be the beneficiaries of a trust.

§46. Members of an Indefinite Class as Beneficiaries

(1) Except as stated in Subsection (2), where the owner of property transfers it upon intended trust for the members of an indefinite class of persons, no trust is created.

(2) If the transferee is directed to distribute the property to such members of the indefinite class as the transferee shall select, the transferee holds the property in trust with power but no duty to distribute the property to such class members as the transferee may select; to whatever extent the power (presumptively personal) is not exercised, the transferee will then hold for reversionary beneficiaries implied by law.

Comment

Comment on Subsection (1)

b. *Where an equal division is directed among, or a specified amount is to be paid to, all members of the class.* If the only beneficial provision of an intended trust directs the trust property to be divided in equal shares among all of the members of an indefinite class, no member of the class can maintain a proceeding to enforce the intended trust, nor can anyone else. Because the intended trustee is under no enforceable duty to carry out the testator's direction, no trust is created. Moreover, since the total membership of the class cannot be ascertained, it is impossible to make an equal distribution among all of the members of the class, even if the intended trustee wishes to do so.

Similarly, where a testator directs the trustee to pay a specified sum to every member of an indefinite class, the intended trust provision for those class members fails. Accordingly, in these circumstances, the intended trustee holds the property upon resulting trust for the testator's estate.

Although a disposition is expressed simply as a trust for the members of an indefinite class, a literal interpretation would seem doubtful as a matter of transferor intention and (unless the transferor is alive to take by resulting trust) would wholly defeat whatever specific objective the transferor had in mind. An interpretation is therefore preferred that would give the disposition some effect reasonably consistent with the transferor's general objective. Thus, the disposition may be interpreted as intended to create a trust for members of the described class as determined or selected by the designated trustee, in which case the situation falls within Subsection (2). See Comment d. Or, if the disposition is interpreted as one intended to benefit those members of an otherwise indefinite class that are or may become identifiable in a manner described in §44 . . . , a valid trust is created. See §45. . . .

Comment on Subsection (2)

c. Background and comparison: powers of appointment. Subsection (2) addresses situations in which a property owner conveys or devises property to a person who is directed, not merely authorized, by the terms of the intended trust to distribute the property to persons to be selected by the trustee from an indefinite class of intended beneficiaries. This situation is discussed hereafter in Comment d.

Different from those situations and much more frequent are instances of valid transfers in trust for the benefit of definite beneficiaries under which one or more of the beneficiaries, or occasionally a trustee or other person, is granted a power of appointment by which the trust property or remainder may be (i.e., is authorized but not required to be) appointed to or for one or more "objects" (permissible appointees) of the power.

Under well-established doctrine, the objects of powers of appointment may properly consist of classes that are either definite or indefinite; powers of appointment may even be general, with no limit whatever with respect to permissible appointees. . . .

d. Beneficiaries to be selected by trustee. Occasionally, a testator leaves property to another upon an intended trust for members of an indefinite class to be selected by the devisee, intending thereby to impose upon the devisee, as trustee, a duty to make selections and to hold and administer the property in the meantime solely for the members of the class. This presents a problem that differs significantly from that in Comment b but that similarly arises from the requirement that a trust have definite beneficiaries.

d(1). Example. Instead of attempting to create a trust simply for all of the members of an indefinite class (as in Subsection (1) and Comment b), the testator leaves property to a person who, as trustee, is directed to liquidate the property and to distribute all of its proceeds in equal shares to those of the testator's "friends" whom the trustee shall select.

This trust, as written, fails for lack of definite beneficiaries capable of enforcing the intended fiduciary duty of selection. See Reporter's Notes. The settlor's intended trust purpose, however, need not fail altogether: That the trustee cannot be required to select the beneficiaries, and that a court will not direct a recalcitrant trustee to make equal distribution to class members too indefinite to be ascertained, nor even remove and replace the trustee, does not mean that the trustee cannot be allowed to make the selections if willing to do so.

The result of this example is that the devisee holds the property upon a trust, adapted by operation of law, for reversionary beneficiaries (the same persons who would take by resulting trust under §8 if the trust had immediately and completely failed), subject to the interests of potential beneficiaries later to be identified by the devisee's exercise of a nonmandatory power of selection. (On the validity of such a trust, cf. §44, Comments a and c; Comment c, above, on powers of appointment; and §45, Comment g.) Thus, the law simply treats the defective disposition as having a trust effect approximating that stated by the testator. Instead of complete failure, with an immediate resulting trust, there is a legally implied reversion to take effect only in default of selection.

d(2). Rationale. A testator can create a trust expressly for the people who would be his or her own heirs (or residuary beneficiaries), subject to an express power of appointment by which the trustee is allowed to appoint among an indefinite class of objects. (See Comment c.) Or the testator could have created a trust for beneficiaries authorized to be appointed later by the trustee, with either an express gift or one implied by law (a reversionary or "resulting trust" interest) in favor of the testator's estate . . . .

Therefore, if an intended trust that purports to require the trustee to select distributees from an indefinite class (such as "friends") fails as written, then, rather than to have the purpose fail altogether, the testator's purpose would be better served—and no policy of the law is violated (see Comment c)— by treating the will as having created an adapted version of the intended trust. This results in an enforceable trust for a definite though unexpressed (legally implied) class of reversionary beneficiaries, whose interests are subject, by legal adaptation, to a nonmandatory power in the trustee to select other distributees.

In brief, if a devisee can properly make distributions where merely authorized to do so, there is no reason why a devisee should be precluded from doing so where directed to do so. In neither case can the devisee be compelled to make the distributions, but in both cases a willing devisee should be permitted to carry out the testator's intention. This rule also serves to remove (or at least to reduce to technical questions) any issue of whether a particular power was or was not intended by the settlor to be mandatory.

Under the rule of Subsection (2), the primary purpose of the adapted trust will fail only to the extent the trustee (i) refuses to make selections, (ii) selects beneficiaries to receive some of the property but declines to make additional selections, (iii) fails to make selections within the specified time or the otherwise implied "reasonable period" for doing so, or (iv) dies without having exercised the power.

d(3). Selection power presumed personal. The preceding paragraph assumes, as is normally presumed, that the power of selection in any such case (like the typical power of appointment) was intended by the settlor to be personal to the designated trustee. . . .

On the other hand, if the testator in the Example above (Comment d(1)) had designated or provided a means for designating a substitute or successor trustee, the power of selection in the adapted trust would pass to the substitute or successor upon the initially designated trustee's disclaimer, resignation, incapacity, or death before the power is exercised or expires.

Similarly, if no substitute or successor was designated but the testator's intention is shown not to depend on the designated person serving as trustee . . . , then the selection power as well as the trusteeship in the adapted trust would pass to a court-appointed substitute or successor trustee. . . .

g. Enforcement of adapted trust. In no event is the devisee in the situation in Subsection (2) permitted to keep or misappropriate the property. Either the power of selection must be exercised or the trust property must be returned to the settlor's estate. See Comment d.

The heirs or other successors in interest of the settlor can maintain a proceeding to prevent or redress a breach of trust, or to compel the trustee to convey the trust property to them if the power is not exercised within the period specified in the will or, if none is specified, within a reasonable period fixed by the court. Thus, the devisee holds the property upon an enforceable trust for the legally implied reversionary beneficiaries, subject to a power in the devisee (trustee) voluntarily to select and make distribution among members of the class.

A situation may arise in which the named trustee disclaims the office or resigns, dies, or becomes incapacitated before the power in the adapted trust is exercised and, although the power is not personal to that trustee (see Comment d(3)), no substitute or successor is designated in the will. In such a case, either the testator's successors in interest or a person who fits within the class description may petition the court for appointment of another trustee. So may the testator's personal representative if the named trustee in such a case predeceases the testator, as may the personal representative, conservator, or guardian of a trustee who survives the testator but dies or becomes incapacitated before the exercise or expiration of a nonpersonal power. . . .

§47. Trusts for Noncharitable Purposes

(1) If the owner of property transfers it in trust for indefinite or general purposes, not limited to charitable purposes, the transferee holds the property as trustee with the power but not the duty to distribute or apply the property for such purposes; if and to whatever extent the power (presumptively personal) is not exercised, the trustee holds the property for distribution to reversionary beneficiaries implied by law.

(2) If the owner of property transfers it in trust for a specific noncharitable purpose and no definite or ascertainable beneficiary is designated, unless the purpose is capricious, the transferee holds the property as trustee with power, exercisable for a specified or reasonable period of time normally not to exceed 21 years, to apply the property to the designated purpose; to whatever extent the power is not exercised (although this power is *not* presumptively personal), or the property exceeds what reasonably may be needed for the purpose, the trustee holds the property, or the excess, for distribution to reversionary beneficiaries implied by law.

General Comment

a. Scope and basic principles. This Section is concerned with what are often called "purpose" or "honorary" trusts. These are a special form of noncharitable trust in which the purpose as expressed by the settlor is normally unenforceable. Thus, a testator may seek to establish a trust (1) for a noncharitable purpose that is general or indefinite (compare §46(2) dealing with indefinite beneficiaries) or (2) for a specific noncharitable purpose. In either case, for lack of a definite beneficiary, the trust is not enforceable in accordance with its intended terms.

Although reversionary interests arise in these cases by operation of law (compare §§7, 8 on "resulting trusts"), the primary question is whether the intended purpose should fail entirely or whether the devisee who wishes to do so may carry out the intended purpose. That is, does the devisee hold the property in trust for the testator's successors in interest, with a "power" (rather than a duty) to divest those successors in whole or in part by making distributions for the noncharitable purpose? Cf. §46(2) on "adapted trusts" in the private-trust context.

The rule of this Section also applies to trust provisions for either general or definite noncharitable purposes. In either case, there is no definite beneficiary to enforce the particular provision, even if the trust has identifiable express beneficiaries (§§44 and 45) to enforce it in other respects. The provision for the noncharitable purpose is unenforceable as written, leaving again the question of whether that purpose may be carried out through a power, even at the expense of express interests of ascertainable beneficiaries.

These questions are addressed, with affirmative answers, in Subsections (1) and (2) of this Section . . . . The underlying principles are similar to those applicable to the indefinite-beneficiaries situations in §46(2). . . .

The *adapted trust* rule of this Section does not apply to intended trusts for purposes that are capricious (see Comment e) or otherwise contrary to public policy. See generally §29(c).

d(2). Special duration rule: care of pets and graves. An adapted trust is allowed a period reasonably appropriate to accomplish the settlor's legally permissible purpose, although a period specified by the settlor is normally accepted if reasonably related to the purpose. Generally, however, regardless of how the reasonable period is determined, the period may not exceed 21 years, by analogy to the period of the rule against perpetuities. . . .

The 21-year period is neither sacred nor necessarily suitable to all cases of adapted trust powers. If an adapted trust for the care of a pet is worth allowing at all . . . , it makes sense to allow it to continue for the life of the pet, although not a human "life in being" for perpetuities purposes (but see below). Also, a trust power to maintain a grave should be allowed for the lifetime of the decedent's spouse and children or of other concerned individuals designated in the will . . . , all lives in being at the testator's death.

These exceptions to the 21-year limit are based on the special nature of the permissible noncharitable objective and the modest commitment of resources involved. . . .

f. Successor trustee enforcement. In the case of an adapted trust under either Subsection (1) or (2), the devisee may retain the power to direct the distribution or application of trust funds while declining or resigning from the trusteeship. A substitute or successor may be appointed by court, or by other means described in §34 Comments c and c(1).

A proceeding to prevent or redress a breach of trust, or to replace a trustee-power holder, may be brought (i) by the personal representative of the settlor or of a trustee who dies while in office, (ii) by any of the settlor's successors in interest, or (iii) by a person identifiably interested in the purpose of the power, such as the person caring for a pet or a member of the immediate family of a decedent for whom masses, grave care, or a monument is to be provided. . . .

§48. Beneficiaries Defined; Incidental Benefits

A person is a beneficiary of a trust if the settlor manifests an intention to give the person a beneficial interest; a person who merely benefits incidentally from the performance of the trust is not a beneficiary.

Part 4. Nature of Beneficiaries' Rights and Interests

Chapter 10: EXTENT AND ENFORCEABILITY OF BENEFICIAL INTERESTS

§49. Extent of Beneficiaries' Interests

Except as limited by law or public policy (see §29), the extent of the interest of a trust beneficiary depends upon the intention manifested by the settlor.

§50. Enforcement and Construction of Discretionary Interests

(1) A discretionary power conferred upon the trustee to determine the benefits of a trust beneficiary is subject to judicial control only to prevent misinterpretation or abuse of the discretion by the trustee.

(2) The benefits to which a beneficiary of a discretionary interest is entitled, and what may constitute an abuse of discretion by the trustee, depend on the terms of the discretion, including the proper construction of any accompanying standards, and on the settlor's purposes in granting the discretionary power and in creating the trust.

Comment

General Comment

a. Scope of Section. The powers of trustees and the discharge of trusteeship responsibilities regularly involve the exercise of discretion, or fiduciary judgment, with which courts do not interfere except to prevent abuse. . . .

This Section deals with situations in which trustees are granted discretion with respect to beneficiaries' rights to trust benefits. For these situations, the terminology "discretionary trust" or "discretionary interest" is used in this Restatement whether or not the terms of the trust provide standards (see Comments d, e, and f) to limit or guide the trustee's exercise of the discretionary power.

Situations of this type range from the typical power to invade principal for an income beneficiary to the discretionary trust that calls for distributions or applications of income, or of income and principal, for the support of a designated beneficiary (often a surviving spouse, elderly parent, or underage child) or for the benefit of "any one or more" of a group of beneficiaries, such as the settlor's spouse and issue. The trustee may have discretion whether or not to make payments to a particular beneficiary; or the trustee may have discretion only to determine the time, manner, and amount of distributions, pursuant to a particular standard or otherwise. A power's "discretionary" character may be implied from its being attached to a standard, such as a simple direction to pay "amounts appropriate to B's support."

The commentary that follows is concerned not only with the trustee's duties but also with the ability of beneficiaries of these discretionary interests to enforce their rights, and thus with the extent of the beneficiaries' interests. Comments b and c address the limited but important judicial authority to control a trustee's exercise of discretion, while Comments d, e, and f examine the meaning and effects of various standards and omissions frequently encountered in trust terms accompanying a grant of discretion.

A trustee's discretionary power with respect to trust benefits is to be distinguished from a power of appointment. The latter is not subject to fiduciary obligations and may be exercised arbitrarily within the scope of the power. That an appointment may not be made to persons who are not objects (i.e., not permissible appointees) of a power of appointment, see Restatement Second, Property (Donative Transfers) §20.1; "fraud on powers" is discussed in id. §§20.2-20.4; and cf. §§16.1, 16.2 (on contracts to appoint). (Tax law generally does not categorize powers in this manner, and even traditional property-law distinctions between fiduciary powers and powers of appointment may be difficult to draw; this is especially so because a true power of appointment can be conferred upon one who is also a trustee, although a power that runs with the office of trustee is strongly presumed to be a fiduciary power.). . .

Comment on Subsection (1)

b. Judicial review and control of trustee's discretion. A court will not interfere with a trustee's exercise of a discretionary power when that exercise is reasonable and not based on an improper interpretation of the terms of the trust. Thus, judicial intervention is not warranted merely because the court would have differently exercised the discretion. . . .

Furthermore, a court will intervene where the exercise of a power is left to the judgment of a trustee who improperly fails to exercise that judgment. Thus, even where a trustee has discretion whether or not to make any payments to a particular beneficiary, the court will interpose if the trustee, arbitrarily or without knowledge of or inquiry into relevant circumstances, fails to exercise the discretion. . . .

c. Effect of extended discretion. Although the discretionary character of a power of distribution does not ordinarily authorize the trustee to act beyond the bounds of reasonable judgment (Comment b), a settlor may manifest an intention to grant the trustee greater than ordinary latitude in exercising discretionary judgment. How does such an intention affect the duty of the trustee and the role of the court?

It is contrary to sound policy, and a contradiction in terms, to permit the settlor to relieve a "trustee" of all accountability. (Cf. §87, and also §76.) Once it is determined that the authority over trust distributions is held in the role of trustee (contrast nonfiduciary powers mentioned in Comment a), words such as "absolute" or "unlimited" or "sole and uncontrolled" are not interpreted literally. Even under the broadest grant of fiduciary discretion, a trustee must act honestly and in a state of mind contemplated by the settlor. Thus, the court will not permit the trustee to act in bad faith or for some purpose or motive other than to accomplish the purposes of the discretionary power. Except as the power is for the trustee's personal benefit, the court will also prevent the trustee from failing to act, either arbitrarily or from a misunderstanding of the trustee's duty or authority.

Within these limits, it is a matter of interpretation to ascertain the degree to which the settlor's use of language of extended (e.g., "absolute") discretion manifests an intention to relieve the trustee of normal judicial supervision and control in the exercise of a discretionary power over trust distributions. . . .

Comment on Subsection (2)

d. Meaning of frequently used standards. The terms of trusts usually provide some standards or guidelines concerning the purposes the settlor has in mind in creating a discretionary interest. Reasonably definite or objective standards serve to assure a beneficiary some minimum level of benefits, even when other standards are included to grant broad latitude with respect to additional benefits. On the trustee's duty to inform beneficiaries of the bases upon which discretionary distributions have been or will be made, see Comment b.

Sometimes trust terms express no standards or other clear guidance concerning the purposes of a discretionary power, or about the relative priority intended among the various beneficiaries. Even then a general standard of reasonableness, or at least of good-faith judgment, will apply to the trustee (Comment b), based on the extent of the trustee's discretion, the various beneficial interests created, the beneficiaries' circumstances and relationships to the settlor, and the general purposes of the trust.

d(1). General observations. This Comment is concerned with the construction of expressions frequently used in the terms of discretionary powers, and particularly with the types of benefits likely to be encompassed by typical standards. (The manner in which other resources available to a beneficiary relate to various standards is considered hereafter in Comment e; and Comment f discusses multiple beneficiaries or groups as concurrent discretionary distributees.) Presumed meanings yield to findings of actual contrary intention and also may be affected by context and the more general purpose(s) of the trust and the estate plan of which it is a part. See Comment g. Thus, distributions to which a discretionary beneficiary would ordinarily be entitled by a standard might properly be withheld if distribution would divert funds from other beneficiaries or purposes without achieving the purpose of the discretionary power.

d(2). Support or maintenance. The terms "support" and "maintenance" are normally construed as synonyms, even when this treats the terms as redundant. Probably the most common guides used in grants of discretion, these terms are sometimes accompanied by a reference to the beneficiary's accustomed standard of living or station in life. That level of intended support is normally implied from "support" or "maintenance" even without an express reference to the beneficiary's customary lifestyle. Whether this accustomed style is expressed or implied, a lower level of distributions may be justifiable if the trust estate is modest relative to the probable future needs of the beneficiary.

The accustomed manner of living for these purposes is ordinarily that enjoyed by the beneficiary at the time of the settlor's death or at the time an irrevocable trust is created. The distributions appropriate to that lifestyle not only increase to compensate for inflation but also may increase to meet subsequent increases in the beneficiary's needs resulting, for example, from deteriorating health or from added burdens appropriately assumed for the needs of another. See Illustration 5. Also, if a beneficiary becomes accustomed over time to a higher standard of living, that standard may become the appropriate standard of support if consistent with the trust's level of productivity and not inconsistent with an apparent priority among beneficiaries or other purpose of the settlor. Furthermore, distributions allowing the beneficiary an increased standard of living may be appropriate if, in light of the productivity of the trust estate, the eventual result would otherwise favor the remainder beneficiaries over the present beneficiary to a degree unlikely to have been intended by the settlor. "Productivity" for these purposes refers not only to trust income but also to a pattern of appreciation beyond maintenance of purchasing power, such as might result from a growth-oriented investment program. . . .

Under the usual construction of a support standard (supra) it would not be reasonable (Comment b), or even a result contemplated by the settlor (Comment c), for the trustee to provide only bare essentials for a beneficiary who had enjoyed a relatively comfortable lifestyle. (This is so even though the discretionary power is couched in terms of amounts the trustee considers "necessary" for the beneficiary's support.) The standard ordinarily entitles a beneficiary to distributions sufficient for accustomed living expenses, extending to such items as regular mortgage payments, property taxes, suitable health insurance or care, existing programs of life and property insurance, and continuation of accustomed patterns of vacation and of charitable and family giving. Reasonable additional comforts or "luxuries" that are within the means of many individuals of like station in life, such as a special vacation of a type the beneficiary had never before taken, may be borderline as entitlements but would normally be within the permissible range of the trustee's judgment, even without benefit of a grant of extended discretion (Comment c).

Without additional language suggesting a broader standard (infra), however, even with extended discretion, the terms "support" and "maintenance" do not normally encompass payments that are unrelated to support but merely contribute in other ways to a beneficiary's contentment or happiness. Thus, these terms do not authorize distributions to enlarge the beneficiary's personal estate or to enable the making of extraordinary gifts. See Illustration 3; but also compare Comment g.

A support standard normally covers not only the beneficiary's own support but also that of persons for whom provision is customarily made as a part of the beneficiary's accustomed manner of living. This generally includes the support of members of the beneficiary's household and the costs of suitable education (infra) for the beneficiary's children. The beneficiary is entitled also to receive reasonable amounts for the support of a current spouse, and of minor children who reside elsewhere but for whom the beneficiary either chooses or is required to provide support. Additional amounts to cover the beneficiary's support obligation to a former spouse would normally be within the trustee's reasonable discretion. (These matters of construction differ from but may be relevant to the question, discussed in §60, whether a beneficiary's discretionary interest may be reached in satisfaction of claims for spousal or child support.)

d(3). Other standards and supplementary language. Other terms or language may be used with or instead of a support standard to define or guide a trustee's discretionary authority with respect to trust distributions. These provisions may permit or even entitle beneficiaries to receive greater or lesser, or different, benefits than would have been authorized under a support provision standing alone. Sometimes, however, additional language adds little or nothing to what "support" might imply.

Supplementary terminology may affect the degree of generosity appropriate to a beneficiary's support, or it may suggest a special emphasis. For example, the term "education," without elaboration, is ordinarily construed as extending to payment of living expenses as well as fees and other costs of attending an institution of higher education, or the beneficiary's pursuit of a program of trade or technical training, and the like, as may be reasonably suitable to the individual and to the trust funds available for the purpose.

Similarly, without more, references to "health," "medical care," and the like in the terms of a discretionary power may be useful to inform beneficiary expectations or guide an inexperienced trustee, but presumptively they provide merely for health and medical benefits like those normally implied by a support standard. Thus, if the intention is to assure the beneficiary some special form of education, or expensive home care when not cost efficient, further elaboration would be helpful. Even a grant of extended discretion is likely to make it more difficult, if the trustee does not act generously, for a beneficiary to compel a trustee to follow a particular course of action (see Comment c).

Language of "comfort" often accompanies a support standard. Whether modifying support (e.g., "comfortable support" or "support in reasonable comfort") or as an additional standard ("support and comfort"), the normal construction is the same: the language adds nothing to the usual meaning of accustomed support (supra) for a beneficiary whose lifestyle is already at least reasonably comfortable. Such terms, however, would tend to elevate the appropriate standard for a beneficiary whose accustomed lifestyle has been more modest. "Comfort," in isolation, normally has like effect, impliedly referring to a comfortable level of support. On the other hand, stronger language, such as "generous" support, may permit and encourage the trustee to allow, and may even require, some reasonable enhancement of the beneficiary's lifestyle; but it falls short of a "happiness" standard (*infra*) in that the benefits still must normally be support-related. . . .

Although one effect of authorizing distributions for the "benefit," "best interests," or "welfare" of a beneficiary is to suggest a support standard, these terms tend also to authorize discretionary expenditures that fall beyond the usual scope of a purely support-related standard. For example, a "benefit" standard might make it reasonable for a trustee to make substantial distributions to provide a beneficiary with capital needed to start a business. (See also loans to beneficiaries, infra this Comment.) Terms of this type, however, lack the objective quality of a term such as "support." Thus, they may not facilitate a beneficiary's efforts to obtain judicial intervention to compel distributions by the trustee. On the other hand, the presence of less objective terminology in a discretionary standard may diminish the relevance of the beneficiary's other resources, except a parent's obligation to support a minor beneficiary. See Comment e.

The terms of a discretionary standard occasionally include stronger language, such as the word "happiness." Such language suggests an intention that the trustee's judgment be exercised generously and without relatively objective limitation. Although "happiness" alone expresses no objective minimum of entitlements (which to some extent may nevertheless be readily implied), the primary effect of such a term is to immunize from challenge by remainder beneficiaries almost any reasonably affordable distributions. This, however, does not mean that the trustee cannot properly resist any reasonable request by the beneficiary, because the decision remains one within the fiduciary discretion of the trustee. . . .

d(5). Post-death obligations. A question may arise, following the death of the beneficiary of a discretionary interest, whether a support or other standard authorizes or requires the trustee to pay the beneficiary's funeral and last-illness expenses and debts incurred by the beneficiary for support. Ultimately, the question is one of interpretation when the terms of the trust are unclear, with the presumption being that the trustee has discretion to pay these debts and expenses.

A duty to do so is presumed only to the extent that (i) probate estate, revocable trust, and other assets available for these purposes are insufficient or (ii) the trustee, during the beneficiary's lifetime, either agreed to make payment or unreasonably delayed in responding to a claim by the beneficiary for which the terms of the trust would have required payment while the beneficiary was alive. (A deceased beneficiary's estate may also recover distributions the trustee had a duty to make but did not make during the beneficiary's lifetime.)

d(6). Loans to beneficiaries. Sometimes a beneficiary requests funds for a purpose that falls within the reasonable discretion of the trustee but which the applicable standard would not require the trustee to furnish. If the trustee is reluctant for some reason to make the requested distribution, and particularly if the trustee's concern is one of impartiality, the trustee has discretion to make a loan or advance to the beneficiary. The loan need not qualify as a prudent investment under §90 [Restatement Third, Trusts (Prudent Investor Rule) §227]. It Is a form of discretionary benefit, and may be made at a market rate of interest or at low or no interest. . . .

e. Significance of beneficiary's other resources. It is important to ascertain whether a trustee, in determining the distributions to be made to a beneficiary under an objective standard (such as a support standard), (i) is *required* to take account of the beneficiary's other resources, (ii) is *prohibited* from doing so, or (iii) is to consider the other resources but has some discretion in the matter. If the trust provisions do not address the question, the general rule of construction presumes the last of these.

Specifically, with several qualifications (below), the presumption is that the trustee is to take the beneficiary's other resources into account in determining whether and in what amounts distributions are to be made, except insofar as, in the trustee's discretionary judgment, the settlor's intended treatment of the beneficiary or the purposes of the trust will in some respect be better accomplished by not doing so.

One qualification is that, if the discretionary power is one to invade principal for (or to distribute additional income to) a beneficiary who is entitled to all or a specific part of the trust income, or to an annuity or unitrust amount, the trustee must take the mandatory distributions into account before making additional payments under the discretionary power. . . .

Another qualification is that, to the extent and for as long as the discretionary interest is intended to provide for the support, education, or health care of a beneficiary (or group of beneficiaries, Comment f) for periods during which a beneficiary probably was not expected to be self-supporting, the usual inference is that the trustee is not to deny or reduce payments for these purposes because of a beneficiary's personal resources. (But contrast the effect of another's duty to support the beneficiary, Comment e(3)).

Furthermore, in cases of nonobjective standards (e.g., "benefit" or "happiness"), other resources have less direct relevance than with regard to additional amounts necessary to maintain an accustomed lifestyle, for example. Those resources, however, may have some bearing on the overall reasonableness of an exercise of the discretionary authority.

As a rule of construction, the above presumption, with its qualifications, does not apply when the settlor expresses a different intent or if the presumption is contrary to purposes or terms of the trust as interpreted in light of circumstances and other evidence of the settlor's intention (§4). Thus, the settlor may manifest an intention that other resources are not to be taken into account (as in an absolute gift of support) or that they must be (as in a provision for payments "only if and as needed" to maintain an accustomed standard of living), with the trustee to have no discretion in the matter. (Contrast, however, the common phrase "necessary for support," which without more normally does not limit the trustee's discretion in this way.) On factors relevant to this question of interpretation, see Comment g.

A grant of extended discretion (Comment c) does not relieve the trustee of a duty to take into account, or of a duty to disregard, a beneficiary's other resources, although the extended discretion is a factor to be considered in the process of interpretation. If, under the general rule of construction, the trustee has discretion in the matter the trustee has greater latitude in exercising that discretion when the settlor has used language of extended discretion in granting the power of distribution. . . .

e(2). What other resources are to be considered? Where a trustee is to take a beneficiary's other resources into account in deciding whether and in what amounts to make discretionary payments to satisfy a standard, those resources normally include the beneficiary's income and other periodic receipts, such as pension or other annuity payments and court-ordered support payments.

A trustee may have discretion, and perhaps a duty, to take account of the principal of the beneficiary's personal estate, depending on the terms and purposes of the discretionary power and other purposes of the trust. . . .

e(4). Public benefits. If a discretionary beneficiary is or may be eligible to receive public benefits, this factor, like the availability of other resources generally, is to be taken into account by the trustee under the usual rule of construction. Thus, to the extent consistent with the terms and purposes of the trust, and allowable by applicable benefits statutes (see Reporter's Notes), the presumption is that the trustee's discretion should be exercised in a manner that will avoid either disqualifying the beneficiary for other benefits or expending trust funds for purposes for which public funds would otherwise be available. . . .

Chapter 11: VOLUNTARY AND INVOLUNTARY TRANFSERS OF BENEFICIAL INTERESTS; GENERAL PRINCIPLES

§51. Voluntary Transfers Inter Vivos

Except as provided in Chapter 12, a beneficiary of a trust can transfer his or her beneficial interest during life to the same extent as a similar legal interest.

§52. Intention to Transfer

(1) To transfer a beneficial interest in a trust, the beneficiary must manifest an intention to make a present transfer; consideration is not essential to such a transfer.

(2) A promise to transfer an interest in the future is enforceable only if the requirements for an enforceable contract are satisfied.

(3) A transfer by a beneficiary can be rescinded upon the same grounds as the transfer of a legal interest.

§53. Need for a Writing

(1) A writing is not necessary to transfer a trust beneficiary's interest.

(2) If a statute requires the assignment of an interest in a trust to be in writing and signed by the assignor, the applicable principles are as stated in §§22-24.

§54. Effect of Success ive Transfers

Where the beneficiary of a trust makes successive transfers of an interest, the first transferee is entitled to the interest unless the subsequent transferee prevails under principles of estoppel.

§55. Transfers at Death

(1) If the interest of a deceased beneficiary of a trust does not terminate or fail by reason of the beneficiary's death, the interest devolves by will or intestate succession in the same manner as a corresponding legal interest.

(2) Where a statute gives a surviving spouse an elective share of the deceased beneficiary's estate, equitable interests of the deceased beneficiary's estate are included in determining that share.

§56. Rights of Beneficiary's Creditors

Except as stated in Chapter 12, creditors of a trust beneficiary, or of a deceased beneficiary's estate, can subject the interest of the beneficiary to the satisfaction of their claims, except insofar as a corresponding legal interest is exempt from creditors' claims.

Comment

a. Scope of Section. . . . The rule of this Section applies to all beneficial interests in a trust. Thus, subject to the rules of Chapter 12 and applicable exemptions (Comment d), creditors may reach a beneficiary's right to receive the trust income or an annuity or unitrust payments. They may also attach a beneficiary's right to discretionary distributions, subject to the practical limitations described in §60. The rule of this Section applies as well to all forms of future interests in trust, except to the extent that a policy of applicable law precludes or limits creditors' access to contingent or other uncertain legal interests. . . .

Creditors may also reach a beneficiary's right to withdraw trust property or to demand distribution of a stated or formula amount . . . , including a power periodically to compel payments of stated or percentage amounts. This power to require periodic distributions (although arguably a series of general powers) is treated for this purpose as an annuity or unitrust interest. . . .

e. Procedure for reaching beneficiary's interest. Except as modified by statute, a creditor can subject the beneficiary's interest to the satisfaction of a claim under the rule of this Section after having attempted to satisfy the claim out of legal interests of the beneficiary, or when it appears that an attempt to do so would be unsuccessful or insufficiently productive.

In the appropriate proceedings, the court will give creditors relief that is fair and reasonable under the circumstances. If the beneficiary has only a right to the trust income or a right periodically to receive ascertainable or discretionary (but see §60) payments, the court will normally direct the trustee to make the payments to the creditor until the claim, with interest, is satisfied. The court, however, may order less than all of the payments to be made to the creditor, leaving some distributions for the actual needs of the beneficiary and his or her family. ("Actual needs" are not based on a "station-in-life" standard of support and require that account also be taken of the beneficiary's other available resources.) . . .

In some circumstances, the court may order a sale of the beneficiary's interest and payment of the creditor's claim from the proceeds. Sale may be appropriate when it appears unlikely that the debt can be satisfied from distribution(s) within a reasonable time, particularly when the beneficiary's interest is a future interest. Even then the uncertainty or remoteness of the interest may be such that its forced sale would produce little relative to its value to the beneficiary, and perhaps also too little to satisfy the creditor's claim. In that case, unless a loan or other arrangement can be obtained, it would be appropriate for the court to grant the creditor a lien on the beneficiary's interest, to be realized if and when it falls into possession. . . .

§57. Forfeiture for Voluntary or Involuntary Alienation

Except with respect to an interest retained by the settlor, the terms of a trust may validly provide that an interest shall terminate or become discretionary upon an attempt by the beneficiary to transfer it or by the beneficiary's creditors to reach it, or upon the bankruptcy of the beneficiary.

§58. Spendthrift Trusts: Validity and General Effect

(1) Except as stated in Subsection (2), and subject to the rules in Comment *b* (ownership equivalence)

and §59, if the terms of a trust provide that a beneficial interest shall not be transferable by the beneficiary or subject to claims of the beneficiary's creditors, the restraint on voluntary and involuntary alienation of the interest is valid.

(2) A restraint on the voluntary and involuntary alienation of a beneficial interest retained by the settlor of a trust is invalid.

Comment

General Comment

a. Terminology, background, and scope of Section. The term "spendthrift trust" refers to a trust that restrains voluntary and involuntary alienation of all or any of the beneficiaries' interests. The extent of the protection such a trust offers is considered hereafter in Comment d. Spendthrift protection is not limited to beneficiaries who are legally incompetent or who, as a practical matter, lack the ability to manage their finances in a responsible manner.

A spendthrift trust is to be distinguished from a discretionary trust but may or may not also contain discretionary interests, which are considered in §60 (and §50). A spendthrift restraint may or may not also contain a forfeiture provision of the type discussed in §57. . . .

Spendthrift restraints are not permitted under English law and have been rejected by a few American cases. The vast majority of decisions in this country, however, have accepted the spendthrift trust doctrine essentially as stated above in Subsections (1) and (2) but differ in some matters discussed hereafter in this commentary, and also in matters discussed in §59.

A number of states have enacted legislation codifying the law of spendthrift trusts. A few statutes contain significant departures from the rules stated here, such as by allowing restraints on income but not principal interests or otherwise limiting the extent of the protection allowed (e.g., to the beneficiary's support). Some statutes make all trusts spendthrift trusts unless the settlor provides otherwise, or restrain involuntary but not voluntary alienation with respect to all trusts.

The rules of this Section have long been recognized under federal bankruptcy law. Current Bankruptcy Code §541(c)(2) states that a "restriction on the transfer of a beneficial interest of a debtor in a trust that is enforceable under applicable nonbankruptcy law" is to be honored in bankruptcy. . . .

Comment on Subsection (1)

b. Requirements for a valid spendthrift trust. Subsection (2) invalidates a spendthrift clause to the extent it is intended to apply to any interest of a beneficiary who is also the settlor of the trust. . . .

b(1). Absence of ownership equivalence. An intended spendthrift restraint is also invalid with respect to a nonsettlor's interests in trust property over which the beneficiary has the equivalent of ownership, entitling the beneficiary to demand immediate distribution of the property. . . .

b(2). Restraint on both voluntary and involuntary alienation. A spendthrift trust is one that restrains both voluntary and involuntary alienation.

b(3). Required manifestation of spendthrift intention. The settlor must manifest the intention to create a spendthrift trust. No particular form of wording is necessary for this purpose, as long as the requisite intention can be discerned from the terms of the trust (as defined in §4). It is sufficient if a settlor simply provides that the trust "is to be a spendthrift trust.". . .

d(1). Rights of beneficiary's purported transferees. Persons who have received a purported assignment of a beneficiary's interest in a spendthrift trust do not thereby acquire that beneficial interest. This does not mean, however, that the purported transfer has no effect. The beneficiary's act has the effect of an authorization to the trustee to distribute to the purported transferee whatever distributions the beneficiary is entitled to receive and has purported to assign, but the authorization is revocable at any time. Thus, a spendthrift restraint merely prevents the beneficiary from making an irrevocable transfer of his or her beneficial interest.

A trustee who pays funds to a purported assignee in accordance with a beneficiary's unrevoked assignment is protected, but must cease doing so upon instruction from the beneficiary. A trustee, however, is under no duty either to the beneficiary or to the purported assignee to accept this authorization to act on behalf of the beneficiary. . . .

If the beneficiary of a spendthrift interest purports to transfer it to another for value but later revokes the assignment and the trustee's authority pursuant to it, the beneficiary is liable to that other person. Although that person cannot reach the beneficiary's interest under the trust, satisfaction of the claim can be obtained from other property of the beneficiary or from trust funds after they have been distributed to the beneficiary.

d(2). Rights of beneficiary's creditors. A spendthrift trust protects the income and principal interests of its beneficiaries from the claims of their creditors as long as the income or principal in question is properly held in the trust. . . .

f. Circumstances in which beneficiary is settlor. The rule of Subsection (2) is not limited to cases in which the beneficiary actually conveyed the property to the trust or executed the trust instrument, or was designated as settlor. It is sufficient, for example, that the beneficiary pay the consideration in return for which another transferred the property to fund the trust.

If a beneficiary transfers part of the property or supplies part of the consideration to fund a trust, the beneficiary is ordinarily settlor to the extent of a fractional portion appropriate to reflect his or her proportionate share of the funding. . . .

Where a spendthrift trust is created by the will of one spouse in favor of the other, the surviving spouse does not become the settlor of the trust for purposes of the rule of this Section merely because she or he waives a right to insist on a statutory forced share of the deceased spouse's estate. (See Reporter's Notes on the different treatment of community-property spousal elections.)

f(1). Renunciations. Where the income beneficiary of a residuary trust under the will of another is also designated to receive a specific devise under that will but properly disclaims the devise, the disclaimer is not a transfer to the residuary trust even though it would normally have the effect of enlarging that trust (see §51, Comment f). Thus, the beneficiary is not the settlor of the enlarged portion of the trust, and a spendthrift provision in the trust terms is valid with respect to the beneficiary's life interest in all of the enlarged trust.

If, however, the beneficiary's renunciation is not a proper disclaimer, it would be treated as a transfer (id.); if the devised property then passes to the residuary trust the beneficiary would be treated as settlor to the extent of the property so added.

Similarly, if an income beneficiary of a trust properly disclaims a power of withdrawal or other presently exercisable general power of appointment over all or a portion of the trust estate, the beneficiary has not acquired an equivalent of ownership that invalidates a spendthrift restraint applicable to the income interest in the appointive property under the rule of Comment b; and the disclaimer is not treated as a transfer of the appointive property to the trust . . . to cause the beneficiary to be treated as settlor of the trust or portion thereof.

On the other hand, if the beneficiary had made a belated renunciation or other release (including a lapse, by allowing expiration) of the power, the beneficiary would have the equivalent of ownership until the time of the release, which—as a transfer (*id.*)—would have made the beneficiary settlor of the trust thereafter to the extent of the property previously subject to the power. Thus, any spendthrift restraint that would otherwise be applicable to the beneficiary's interest would be invalid, initially under Comment b and subsequently under this Subsection (2). . . .

§59. Spendthrift Trusts: Exceptions for Particular Types of Claims

The interest of a beneficiary in a valid spendthrift trust can be reached in satisfaction of an enforceable claim against the beneficiary for

(a) support of a child, spouse, or former spouse; or

(b) services or supplies provided for necessities or for the protection of the beneficiary's interest in the trust.

General Comment

a. Scope of the rule. The rule stated in this Section allows certain categories of creditors to reach beneficial interests in spendthrift trusts that are valid under the rule of §58, including discretionary interests in those trusts. The creditor's special advantage in being able to attach a discretionary interest is limited by the nature of the interest, as described in §60.

a(1). Governmental claims. It is implicit in the rule of this Section, as a statement of the common law, that governmental claimants, and other claimants as well, may reach the interest of a beneficiary of a spendthrift trust to the extent provided by federal law or an applicable state statute. Governmental claims and claims under governmentally assisted programs are often granted this special status. . . .

a(2). Other exceptions. The exceptions to spendthrift immunity stated in this Section are not exclusive. Special circumstances or evolving policy may justify recognition of other exceptions, allowing the beneficiary's interest to be reached by certain creditors in appropriate proceedings (on which see §56, Comment e).

In some circumstances, to permit attachment despite the spendthrift restraint may not undermine, and may even support, the protective purposes of the trust or some policy of the law. On the other hand, the advantage thus conferred on select creditors over others who cannot attach the interest but must pursue funds in the hands of the beneficiary, after distribution (see §58, Comment d), is not always appropriate as a matter of fairness and sound policy. Unlike the exceptions in Comments b through d, possible exceptions in situations of this type require case-by-case weighing of relevant considerations or evolving policies.

The nature or a pattern of tortious conduct by a beneficiary, for example, may on policy grounds justify a court's refusal to allow spendthrift immunity to protect the trust interest and the lifestyle of that beneficiary, especially one whose willful or fraudulent conduct or persistently reckless behavior causes serious harm to others. . . .

Comment on Clause (a)

b. Support claims. A beneficial interest in a spendthrift trust can be reached to satisfy an enforceable claim by the beneficiary's spouse or children for support. It can also be reached in satisfaction of a claim by a former spouse for support or alimony (on "compensatory spousal payments," see Reporter's Notes).

Although a spendthrift clause can often be construed as not intended to exclude the beneficiary's dependents, that is neither the rationale nor the limit of this exception to the general effect (§58, Comment d) of spendthrift protection. On public-policy grounds, the beneficiary should not be permitted to enjoy a beneficial interest in a trust while neglecting the support of dependents. The resulting advantage over other creditors (compare §58, Comment d) is also based on policy considerations. . . .

The right to benefits under the spendthrift interest, however, cannot be anticipated by execution sale, even in the case of a future interest. Nor can the support claimant assign to others the rights he or she acquires by attachment.

The beneficiary's interest may be attached through an appropriate proceeding in which the court has equitable discretion to determine whether all or only a portion of the trust distributions should be allocated to the support claimant, taking account of the beneficiary's actual need for some part of the distributions. Compare §56, Comment e. . . .

Comment on Clause (b)

c. Debts incurred for beneficiary's necessities. The interest of a beneficiary of a spendthrift trust can be reached to satisfy an enforceable claim by one, such as a physician or grocer, who renders necessary services or furnishes necessary supplies to the beneficiary. To the extent the person's claim is excessive in amount, however, or if the person has acted officiously, the claim cannot be enforced against the spendthrift interest.

Failure to give enforcement to appropriate claims of this type would tend to undermine the beneficiary's ability to obtain necessary goods and assistance; and a refusal to enforce such claims is not essential to a settlor's purpose of protecting the beneficiary.

d. Debts incurred to protect beneficiary's interest. The interest of a beneficiary in a spendthrift trust can be reached to satisfy an enforceable claim for services rendered or materials furnished to the beneficiary for the purpose of preserving his or her beneficial interest. . . .

§60. Transfer or Attachment of Discretionary Interests

Subject to the rules stated in §§58 and 59 (on spendthrift trusts), if the terms of a trust provide for a beneficiary to receive distributions in the trustee's discretion, a transferee or creditor of the beneficiary is entitled to receive or attach any distributions the trustee makes or is required to make in the exercise of that discretion after the trustee has knowledge of the transfer or attachment. The amounts a creditor can reach may be limited to provide for the beneficiary's needs (Comment *c*), or the amounts may be increased where the beneficiary either is the settlor (Comment *f*) or holds the discretionary power to determine his or her own distributions (Comment *g*).

Comment

a. Scope of the rule. The rule of this Section allows a beneficiary's assignee to receive discretionary distributions to which the beneficiary would otherwise be entitled, and allows creditors of the beneficiary to attach his or her discretionary interest. The rule does not apply if the beneficiary's interest is subject to a valid spendthrift restraint under the rules of §58 unless the situation falls within an exception under §59.

This Section recognizes special rules for discretionary interests retained by a settlor (compare §58(2)) and for trusts in which the beneficiary, as trustee or otherwise, holds the discretionary authority to determine his or her own distributions (compare §58, Comment c). These rules (in Comments f and g, respectively) expand the amount such a beneficiary's creditors may reach.

The rules stated in this Section and its commentary apply to whatever extent a beneficiary's interest is discretionary. Thus, if the beneficiary is entitled to all of the trust's net income but only to principal in the trustee's discretion, the Section applies to the provision for invasion of principal but not to the income interest. Also, the Section prevents the trustee not only from making payments to the beneficiary but also from making "distributions" by applying funds directly for the beneficiary's benefit contrary to the rights of the transferee or creditor. (On the latter, see especially Comment c.)

"Discretionary interests" for purposes of this Section include those encompassed by §50 (see especially §50, Comment a). Thus, this Section applies where trustees are granted discretionary authority over benefits, regardless of whether the trust terms provide simply for the beneficiary's support, provide other or additional standards, or express no standards to limit or guide the trustee's exercise of discretion. For purposes of this Section, however, unlike §50 (see §50, Comment a), discretionary interests also include powers by which beneficiaries who are not trustees may determine their own benefits pursuant to any form of standards, but which are not equivalent to ownership under §58, Comment c. . . .

b. Application to transferees. In the absence of a valid restraint on voluntary alienation, the beneficiary of a discretionary interest can properly assign that interest to another. The assignee, however, acquires only what the beneficiary had. Thus, if the interest is for the designated beneficiary's lifetime, the assignee takes a life interest pur autre vie—that is, for the life of the assigning beneficiary. (See Chapter 11, Introductory Note.) Standards governing the trustee's exercise of discretion still refer to the assigning beneficiary and his or her circumstances. Thus, to the extent the trustee may refuse or limit payments to or for the beneficiary, the trustee may refuse or limit payments to the assignee.

Whether or not the transferee could compel the trustee to make distributions (see Comments e-e(2)), if the trustee with knowledge of the assignment does make discretionary distributions they must be made to the transferee and not to the beneficiary-assignor. . . .

c. Rights of creditors. In the absence of a valid restraint on involuntary alienation (under §58 or a statute), the creditors of the beneficiary of a discretionary interest may attach that interest and may subject it to the satisfaction of enforceable claims by appropriate process as described in §56, Comment e. The interest, however, is not subject to execution sale. Furthermore, if an expressed or implied purpose of the discretionary interest is to provide for the beneficiary's support, health care, or education, in establishing the portion of each distribution allocated to the payment of claims the court is to take account of the beneficiary's actual needs in maintaining a reasonable level of support, care, and education. (Compare the court's equitable discretion in the spendthrift-trust exception in §59, Comment b, and more generally in §56, Comment e. Also contrast the generous station-in-life standard typical of discretionary "support" provisions, §50, Comment d, and the flexibility a trustee usually has in considering a beneficiary's other resources, §50, Comment e, neither of which is appropriate here.)

If the trustee has been served with process in a proceeding by a creditor to reach the beneficiary's interest, the trustee is personally liable to the creditor for any amount paid to or applied for the benefit of the beneficiary in disregard of the rights of the creditor, in the absence of a valid spendthrift provision (§58) applicable to the creditor (see §59). . . .

e. Can discretionary distributions be compelled by beneficiary's transferee or creditors? A transferee or creditor of a trust beneficiary cannot compel the trustee to make discretionary distributions if the beneficiary personally could not do so. It is rare, however, that the beneficiary's circumstances, the terms of the discretionary power, and the purposes of the trust leave the beneficiary so powerless. The exercise or non-exercise of fiduciary discretion is always subject to judicial review to prevent abuse. What might constitute an abuse, however, is not only affected by the extent of the trustee's discretion, standards applicable to its exercise, and purposes of the trust, but also by the beneficiary's circumstances and the effect discretionary decisions will have on the discretionary beneficiary and on others in relation to the fulfillment of trust purposes. See generally §50 and its commentary, especially Comment d(1). . . .

f. Where discretionary beneficiary is settlor. Where the trustee of an irrevocable trust has discretionary authority to pay to the settlor or apply for the settlor's benefit as much of the income or principal as the trustee may determine appropriate, creditors of the settlor can reach the maximum amount the trustee, in the proper exercise of fiduciary discretion, could pay to or apply for the benefit of the settlor. Where the beneficiary is the settlor of only a portion of the trust, the amount the creditor can reach under this rule is limited to that portion of the trust estate. . . .

g. Where beneficiary holds discretionary power. Sometimes a beneficiary is trustee of the discretionary trust, with authority to determine his or her own benefits. In such a case, a rule similar to that of Comment f applies, with creditors able to reach from time to time the maximum amount the trustee-beneficiary can properly take. As in other nonsettlor-beneficiary situations, the court may reserve a portion of that amount for the beneficiary's actual needs for reasonable support, health care, and education (Comment c). . . .

The rule does not apply, however, if the discretionary power is held jointly with another person who, in exercising the discretionary authority, has fiduciary duties to other beneficiaries of the trust. . . .

Part 5. Modification and Termination of Trusts

Chapter 13: MODIFICATION AND TERMINATION OF TRUSTS

Introductory Note [to Chapter 13] . . .

Liberalized rules and their rationale. At various points throughout this Chapter, traditional rules concerning revocation, termination, and modification are relaxed somewhat, or in some instances clarified, to facilitate the making of changes in the terms of trusts. This reflects both (i) modern trends in legislative policy and judicial decisions and (ii) practical considerations arising from other developments in or affecting estate planning. . . .

As life in the estate-planning world becomes increasingly complex, mainly with changing tax rules and concerns, which tend also to invite the use of longer-term trusts, the parties to trusts and the courts increasingly, and understandably, encounter instances of apparent oversight and human error. . . .

[P]roblems of error and oversight appear to have increased as broader segments of the population have come to recognize the utility of trusts for an expanding variety of purposes, with many settlors relying on advice and implementation not only by less expert or independent members of the legal profession but also by nonlawyers. . . .

Still another set of reasons underlying the selective liberalization of the rules considered in this Chapter is possibly more fundamental: the growing recognition that trusts should serve the beneficiaries' best interests (§27(2); and also the growing recognition that, realistically, this greater flexibility is more likely to aid than to undermine settlor objectives. . . .

§61. Completion of Period or Purpose for Which Trust Created

A trust will terminate in whole or in part upon the expiration of a period or the happening of an event as provided by the terms of the trust; in the absence of such a provision in the terms of the trust, termination will occur in whole or in part when the purpose(s) of the trust or severable portion thereof are accomplished.

§62. Rescission and Reformation

A trust may be rescinded or reformed upon the same grounds as those upon which a transfer of property not in trust may be rescinded or reformed.

Comment

. . . *b. Clarification and correction of terms of trust.* On resolving uncertainties of meaning where the terms of a donative document are ambiguous, see Restatement Third, Property (Wills and Other Donative Transfers) §§11.1-11.3.

Even if the will or other instrument creating a donative testamentary or inter vivos trust is unambiguous, the terms of the trust may be reformed by the court to conform the text to the intention of the settlor if the following are established by clear and convincing evidence: (1) that a mistake of fact or law, whether in expression or inducement, affected the specific terms of the document; and (2) what the settlor's intention was. Restatement Third, Property (Wills and Other Donative Transfers) §12.1 (noting that direct evidence of intention contradicting the plain meaning of the text, as well as other evidence of intention, may be considered).

§63. Power of Settlor to Revoke or Modify

(1) The settlor of an inter vivos trust has power to revoke or modify the trust to the extent the terms of the trust (§4) so provide.

(2) If the settlor has failed expressly to provide whether the trust is subject to a retained power of revocation or amendment, the question is one of interpretation. (See presumptions in Comment *c*.)

(3) Absent contrary provision in the terms of the trust, the settlor's power to revoke or modify the trust can be exercised in any way that provides clear and convincing evidence of the settlor's intention to do so.

Comment

Comment on Subsections (1) and (2)

b. The "terms of the trust." The phrase "terms of the trust" means the settlor's intention concerning the trust provisions, manifested in a manner that admits of its proof in judicial proceedings. See §4.

If the terms of the trust are otherwise expressed in writing but fail to provide whether or to what extent the settlor reserves the power to revoke or modify the trust, the writing is incomplete and its meaning uncertain. Accordingly, the writing does not prevent the admission of extrinsic evidence to prove the settlor's intention to either retain or relinquish power to revoke or amend the trust, or the admission of evidence to prove an intent to limit any such power. . . .

c. Presumptions regarding revocability. Where the settlor has failed expressly to provide whether a trust is subject to revocation or amendment, if the settlor has retained no interest in the trust (other than by resulting trust, §8), it is rebuttably presumed that the settlor has no power to revoke or amend the trust. If, however, the settlor has failed expressly to provide whether the trust is revocable or amendable but has retained an interest in the trust (other than by resulting trust), the presumption is that the trust is revocable and amendable by the settlor. . . .

Comment on Subsection (3)

. . .

i. Where method of revocation or amendment specified. If the terms of the trust reserve to the settlor a power to revoke or amend the trust exclusively by a particular procedure, the settlor can exercise the power only by substantial compliance with the method prescribed. . . .

k. Trust with multiple settlors. If a revocable trust has more than one settlor, unless the terms of the trust provide otherwise, each settlor ordinarily (but see exceptions below) may revoke or amend the trust with regard to that portion of the trust property attributable to the settlor's contribution. . . .

l. Settlor under legal incapacity. Where a settlor who has retained the power to revoke or amend a trust becomes legally incompetent, the power may be exercised by an agent under a durable power of attorney if and to the extent expressly authorized by the terms of the durable power or by the terms of the trust. The agent in such a case acts in a fiduciary capacity and, except as the settlor-principal specifies otherwise, for purposes similar to the substituted-judgment concept in conservatorship law.

Similarly, unless the trust terms provide otherwise, the settlor's power to revoke or amend a revocable trust may be exercised by a conservator, guardian, or other legal representative if and to the extent authorized by the appropriate court. . . .

§64. Termination or Modification by Trustee, Beneficiary, or Third Party

(1) Except as provided in §§65 and 68, the trustee or beneficiaries of a trust have only such power to terminate the trust or to change its terms as is granted by the terms of the trust.

(2) The terms of a trust may grant a third party a power with respect to termination or modification of the trust; such a third-party power is presumed to be held in a fiduciary capacity.

§65. Termination or Modification by Consent of Beneficiaries

(1) Except as stated in Subsection (2), if all of the beneficiaries of an irrevocable trust consent, they can compel the termination or modification of the trust.

(2) If termination or modification of the trust under Subsection (1) would be inconsistent with a material purpose of the trust, the beneficiaries cannot compel its termination or modification except with the consent of the settlor or, after the settlor's death, with authorization of the court if it determines that the reason(s) for termination or modification outweigh the material purpose.

Comment

a. Scope, background, and general principles. With the rule of this Section contrast the rule of §66, which depends upon a finding of unanticipated circumstances but does not require beneficiary consent.

. . .

Although Subsection (2) is not a part of the English law, that subsection recognizes the prevalent American view under the so-called Claflin doctrine (Claflin v. Claflin, 149 Mass. 19, 20 N.E. 454 (1889)).

While the rule against perpetuities requires only the timely vesting of interests and does not directly limit the duration of trusts, the rule of Subsection (2) ceases to apply after the perpetuities period has expired, and the Claflin doctrine no longer restricts the beneficiaries' power to terminate or modify the trust under Subsection (1). . . .

Comment on Subsection (1)

b. Requirement that all beneficiaries consent. The rule of Subsection (1) requires that consent be obtained from or on behalf of all potential beneficiaries, including those who lack capacity. This requirement of unanimous consent also includes, for example, beneficiaries who are relatively unlikely ever to receive distributions, those whose interests arise by operation of law (i.e., reversionary, or "resulting trust," interests), and persons who hold powers of appointment under the trust, as well as those who would take in default of the exercise of any but a presently exercisable general power (on which see §74). See generally §48, Comment a, defining trust beneficiary. Also included among those whose consent is required are successors in interest of prior beneficiaries, and the potential unborn (including after-adopted) or unascertainable beneficiaries so often provided for by class description, as in a seemingly simple trust designed to pay income to A for life and then to distribute the principal to A's descendants who are living at her death. . . .

[In some cases], the requirements of Subsection (1) are likely to be difficult to satisfy. The consent of potential beneficiaries who cannot consent for themselves, however, may be provided by guardians ad litem, by court appointed or other legally authorized representatives, or through representation by other beneficiaries under the doctrine of virtual representation. . . .

As a practical matter, however, the necessary consents may not be obtainable in many situations. This is not only because some beneficiaries may dissent from a termination or modification plan but also because of fiduciary inhibitions on the part of those called upon to represent the interests of others. The technical and practical problems of representing others are particularly challenging whenever more is involved than mutually beneficial modification of administrative provisions. . . .

Comment on Subsection (2)

d. The material-purpose restriction. Under the rule of Subsection (2), even all of the beneficiaries acting together ordinarily cannot compel termination of a trust if its continuance is necessary to carry out a material purpose of the trust. Similarly, the beneficiaries ordinarily cannot compel modification of the trust if the modification is inconsistent with a material purpose of the trust.

Because the rights of the beneficiaries are thus limited out of respect for serious objectives that appear to have motivated the settlor in creating the trust, however, the material-purpose restriction does not apply if the settlor is alive, legally competent, and content to waive it. Also, the restriction becomes unimportant and does not apply if the material purpose is no longer relevant or cannot be accomplished in any event. Furthermore, following the death or incapacity of the settlor, an appropriate court may authorize the termination of a trust under this Section if it determines that the reason(s) offered in support of the beneficiaries' petition for termination outweigh, at the time, the concerns or objectives reflected in the material purpose.

The line is not always easy to draw between a "material purpose" on the one hand and, on the other, specific intentions that are deemed less important so that the Claflin doctrine does not protect them. Occasionally, a settlor expressly states in the will, trust agreement, or declaration of trust that a specific purpose is the primary purpose or a material purpose of the trust. Otherwise, the identification and weighing of purposes under this Section frequently involve a relatively subjective process of interpretation and application of judgment to a particular situation, much as purposes or underlying objectives of settlors in other respects are often left to be inferred from specific terms of a trust, the nature of the various interests created, and the circumstances surrounding the creation of the trust. The question is narrower and more focused, although not necessarily easier, when applied to a specific modification rather than to the termination of the trust. . . .

Material purposes are not readily inferred. A finding of such a purpose generally requires some showing of a particular concern or objective on the part of the settlor, such as concern with regard to a beneficiary's management skills, judgment, or level of maturity. Thus, a court may look for some circumstantial or other evidence indicating that the trust arrangement represented to the settlor more than a method of allocating the benefits of property among multiple intended beneficiaries, or a means of offering to the beneficiaries (but not imposing on them) a particular advantage. Sometimes, of course, the very nature or design of a trust suggests its protective nature or some other material purpose. . . .

. . . A trust plan to provide successive enjoyment is not itself sufficient to indicate, for example, that the settlor had a material purpose of depriving the beneficiaries of the property management or otherwise of protecting them from the risks of their own judgment. In the absence of additional circumstances indicating a further purpose, the inference is that the trust was intended merely to allow one or more persons to enjoy the benefits of the property during the period of the trust and to allow the other beneficiary or beneficiaries to receive the property thereafter. . . .

e. Discretionary and spendthrift trusts. If the interests of one or more of the beneficiaries of a trust are subject to restraints on alienation (see §§58, 59), or if the terms of the trust provide support or other discretionary benefits for some or all of the beneficiaries (see §50), this may supply some indication that the settlor had a material purpose—a protective purpose—that would be inconsistent with allowing the beneficiaries to terminate the trust. Nevertheless, spendthrift restrictions are not sufficient in and of themselves to establish, or to create a presumption of, a material purpose that would prevent termination by consent of all of the beneficiaries. This is also true, in many contexts, of discretionary provisions. . . .

§66. Power of Court to Modify: Unanticipated Circumstances

(1) The court may modify an administrative or distributive provision of a trust, or direct or permit the trustee to deviate from an administrative or distributive provision, if because of circumstances not anticipated by the settlor the modification or deviation will further the purposes of the trust.

(2) If a trustee knows or should know of circumstances that justify judicial action under Subsection (1) with respect to an administrative provision, and of the potential of those circumstances to cause substantial harm to the trust or its beneficiaries, the trustee has a duty to petition the court for appropriate modification of or deviation from the terms of the trust.

Comment

Comment on Subsection (1)

a. Scope and purpose of Section. With the rule of this Section, contrast the rule of §65, which requires the consent of all beneficiaries but does not depend on a finding of unanticipated circumstances.

This Section — the so-called "equitable deviation" doctrine — applies to both charitable and private trusts. Although the unanticipated circumstances in cases falling under this Section are likely to be circumstances that have changed since the creation of the trust, the rule of the Section does not require changed circumstances. It is sufficient that the settlor was unaware of the circumstances in establishing the terms of the trust.

It is not necessary under this Section that the situation be so serious as to constitute an "emergency" or to jeopardize the accomplishment of the trust purposes.

The objective of the rule allowing judicial modification (or deviation) and the intended consequences of its application are not to disregard the intention of a settlor. The objective is to give effect to what the settlor's intent probably would have been had the circumstances in question been anticipated.

b. Operation of Section. The terms of the trust that the court may modify, or from which the court may authorize deviation by the trustee, may be provisions governing the management or administration of the trust estate or they may be provisions defining the beneficial interests or entitlements of the various trust beneficiaries. . . .

§67. Failure of Designated Charitable Purpose: The Doctrine of Cy Pres

Unless the terms of the trust provide otherwise, where property is placed in trust to be applied to a designated charitable purpose and it is or becomes unlawful, impossible, or impracticable to carry out that purpose, or to the extent it is or becomes wasteful to apply all of the property to the designated purpose, the charitable trust will not fail but the court will direct application of the property or appropriate portion thereof to a charitable purpose that reasonably approximates the designated purpose.

Comment

a. The cy pres doctrine: background and scope of the rule. The rule stated in this Section is called the doctrine of cy pres. The expression indicates the principle that, when the exact intention of the settlor is not to be carried out, the intention will be given effect "as nearly" as may be. . . .

The cy pres doctrine's modern rationale rests primarily in the perpetual duration allowed charitable trusts and in the resulting risk that designated charitable purposes may become obsolete as the needs and circumstances of society evolve over time, not to mention the sometimes unanticipated extent of decrease or increase in the funds available from a given trust. . . .

b. Contrary intention of settlor. Just as it is against the policy of the trust law to permit wasteful or seriously inefficient use of resources dedicated to charity, trust law also favors an interpretation that would sustain a charitable trust and avoid the return of the trust property to the settlor or successors in interest. . . . Accordingly, when the particular purpose of a charitable trust fails, in whole or in part, the rule of this Section makes the cy pres power applicable (thus presuming the existence of what is often called a general charitable purpose) unless the terms of the trust (defined in §4) express a contrary intention. . . .

A trust provision expressing the settlor's own choice of an alternative charitable purpose will be carried out, without need to apply the cy pres doctrine. . . .

The mere fact that the terms of the trust provide that property shall be devoted "forever" to a particular charitable purpose, or that it shall be devoted "only" to that purpose, or that the property is given "upon condition" that it be applied to that purpose, does not necessarily indicate the absence of a more general charitable commitment on the part of the settlor. Such language may merely emphasize the intention of the settlor that the property should not be applied to other charitable purposes as long as it is practicable to apply it to the specific purpose. Thus, such language alone does not sufficiently express an intention that cy pres should not apply and that the trust is to terminate if it should become illegal, impossible, or impracticable to carry out the particular purpose.

Even though the terms of a trust contain an express provision precluding the application of cy pres to alter the trust purpose, this does not prevent application of the so-called equitable-deviation doctrine of §66 to modify the means by which the purpose is to be accomplished.

c. Causes for failure of designated purpose. Under what circumstances will the particular purpose intended by the settlor not be carried out or continued, so that the court will either modify the trust cy pres or give effect to a trust provision calling for termination? It is not sufficient merely that it can be demonstrated that the trust funds could be better spent on some other purpose. Certainly, however, the particular purpose will fail if it is or becomes illegal or impossible to carry it out, or if the purpose is no longer charitable (as defined in §28, see especially Comment a). The doctrine of cy pres may also be applied, even though it is possible to carry out the particular purpose of the settlor, if to do so would not accomplish the settlor's charitable objective, or would not do so in a reasonable way. In such a case, it is "impracticable" to carry out the particular purpose in the sense in which that word is used in this Section. . . .

c(1). Surplus funds. Another type of case appropriate to the application of cy pres, when not precluded by the terms of the trust, is a situation in which the amount of property held in the trust exceeds what is needed for the particular charitable purpose to such an extent that the continued expenditure of all of the funds for that purpose, although possible to do, would be wasteful. . . .

d. New purpose; manner of cy pres application. In applying the cy pres doctrine, it is sometimes stated that the property must be applied to a purpose as near as possible to that designated by the terms of the intended trust. Increasingly, however, courts have recognized (as does the rule of this Section) that the substitute or supplementary purpose need not be the nearest possible but one reasonably similar or close to the settlor's designated purpose, or "falling within the general charitable purpose" of the settlor. This is especially so when the particular purpose becomes impossible or impracticable of accomplishment long after the creation of the trust or when, among purposes reasonably close to the original, one has a distinctly greater usefulness than the others that have been identified. This more liberal application of cy pres is appropriate both because settlors' probable preferences are almost inevitably a matter of speculation in any event and because it is reasonable to suppose that among relatively similar purposes charitably inclined settlors would tend to prefer those most beneficial to their communities.

In framing a scheme for the application of property cy pres, the court will consider evidence suggesting what the wishes of the settlor probably would have been if the circumstances had been anticipated. Such an assessment may look to whatever evidence is available concerning the attitudes and interests that appear to have motivated the settlor's selection of the particular purpose. Thus, it would be especially appropriate to consult the donor if available. In other situations, the circumstances of the trust's creation may be revealing, as may the settlor's relationships, social or religious affiliations, personal background, charitable-giving history, and the like. For example, a settlor's adviser may be able to reveal that a devise to a particular institution for a specific project or purpose began with a desire to benefit that institution and was then shaped to address some institutional interest, need, or opportunity; or the opposite might be revealed, with the settlor having a strong desire to encourage a particular field of study or research, or a particular charitable activity, and then settling upon an institution that appeared suitable. In the former case, if the precise plan does not work out or the funds prove to be excessive for the purpose, a court would probably decide to look for a different but related subject or activity at the chosen institution. In the latter case, the court would probably decide that the special interest of the settlor should be pursued at a nearby or comparable institution.

The cy pres power is vested in the court, not in the trustee or the Attorney General, who is, however, a necessary party entitled to notice of the proceeding. . . .

§68. Dividing and Combining Trusts

The trustee may divide a trust into two or more trusts or combine two or more trusts into a single trust, if doing so does not adversely affect the rights of any beneficiary or the accomplishment of the trust purposes.

§69. Merger

If the legal title to the trust property and the entire beneficial interest become united in one person, the trust terminates.

PART IV

~

UNIFORM ANATOMICAL GIFT ACT (REVISED, 2006)

UNIFORM ANATOMICAL GIFT ACT (REVISED, 2006)

TABLE OF CONTENTS

Prefatory Note

As of January, 2006 there were over 92,000 individuals on the waiting list for organ transplantation, and the list keeps growing. It is estimated that approximately 5,000 individuals join the waiting list each year. See "Organ Donation: Opportunities for Action," Institute of Medicine of the National Academies (2006) www.nap.edu. Every hour another person in the United States dies because of the lack of an organ to provide a life saving organ transplant.

The lack of organs results from the lack of organ donors. For example, according to the Scientific Registry of Transplant Recipients in 2005 when there were about 90,000 people on the organ transplant waiting list, there were 13,091 individuals who died under the age of 70 using cardiac and brain death criteria and who were eligible to be organ donors. Of these, only 58% or 7,593 were actual donors who provided just over 23,000 organs. Living donors, primarily of kidneys, contributed about 6,800 more organs. Between them about 28,000 organs were transplanted into patients on the waiting list in 2005. (See www.optn.org).

The 2005 data on cadaveric organ donors suggests there were 5,498 individuals who died that year that could have been donors who weren't and that had they been organ donors there would have been approximately 17,000 additional organs potentially available for transplantation. (See generally, www.unos.org and www.ustransplant.org). However, these numbers to some extent are only estimates. First, they exclude individuals dying over the age of 70. Second, the data are self reported for eligible donors. Indicative of the absence of precision in this area is the report from the Institute of Medicine. According to the IOM, it has been estimated that donor-eligible deaths range between 10,500 and 16,800 per year. See Organ Donation: Opportunities for Action," Institute of Medicine of the National Academies (2006) at page 27. www.nap.edu Using the 2005 figures for deceased organ donors, this would suggest that between approximately 3,000 and 9,000 decedents could have been donors but weren't. Further, if one assumes an average of three solid organs recovered from each of them, there could be between 9,000 and 27,000 more organs that might have been available to transplant into individuals on the waiting list.

The data for eye and tissue is, however, more encouraging. On an annual basis there are approximately 50,000 eye donors and tissue donors and over 1,000,000 ocular and tissue transplants.

This Revised Uniform Anatomical Gift Act ("UAGA") is promulgated by the National Conference of Commissioners on Uniform State Laws ("NCCUSL") to address in part the critical organ shortage by providing additional ways for making organ, eye, and tissue donations. The original UAGA was promulgated by NCCUSL in 1968 and promptly enacted by all states. In 1987, the UAGA was revised and updated, but only 26 states adopted that version. Since 1987, many states have adopted non-uniform amendments to their anatomical gift acts. The law among the various states is no longer uniform and harmonious, and the diversity of law is an impediment to transplantation. Furthermore the federal government has been increasingly active in the organ transplant process.

Since 1987, there also have been substantial improvements in the technology and practice of organ, eye, and tissue transplantation and therapy. And, the need for organs, eyes, and tissue for research and education has increased to assure more successful transplantations and therapies. The improvements in technology and the growing needs of the research community have correspondingly increased the need for more donors.

This 2006 Revised UAGA is promulgated with the substantial and active participation of the major stakeholders representing donors, recipients, doctors, procurement organizations, regulators, and others affected.... The following stakeholders were actively engaged in the dialogue working for a consensus that could and should be adopted on a uniform basis to facilitate the anatomical gifts of human bodies and parts: American Bar Association, American Medical Association, American Lung Association, Association of Organ Procurement Organizations, American Association of Tissue Banks, Eye Bank Association of America, Health Law Institute and Center for Race and Bioethics, Life Alaska Donor Services, Musculoskeletal Transplant Foundation, National Association of Medical Examiners, National Disease Research Interchange, National Kidney Foundation, North American Transplant Coordinators Organization, RTI Donor Services, United Network for Organ Sharing (UNOS) and United States Department of Health & Human Services. In addition, there were many who contributed their views and comments by correspondence, including the Funeral Consumers Alliance, Inc. and Funeral Ethics Organization.

This act adheres to the significant policy determinations reflected in existing anatomical gift acts. First, the act is designed to encourage the making of anatomical gifts. Second, the act is designed to honor and respect the autonomy interest of individuals to make or not to make an anatomical gift of their body or parts. Third, the act preserves the current anatomical gift system founded upon altruism by requiring a positive affirmation of an intent to make a gift and prohibiting the sale and purchase of organs. This act includes a number of provisions, discussed below, that enhance these policies.

History of 1968 and 1987 Acts

The first reported medical transplant occurred in the third century. However, medical miracles flowing from transplants are truly a modern story beginning in the first decade of the twentieth century with the first successful transplant of a cornea. But, not until three events occurred in the twentieth century, in addition to the development of surgical techniques to effectuate a transplant, could transplants become a viable option to save and meaningfully extend lives.

The first event was the development in the late 1960s of the first set of neurological criteria for determining death. These criteria allowed persons to be declared dead upon the cessation of all brain activity. Ultimately these criteria, together with the historic measure of determining death by cessation of circulation and respiration, were incorporated into Section 1 of the Uniform Determination of Death Act providing that: "An individual who has sustained either (1) irreversible cessation of circulatory and respiratory function, or (2) irreversible cessation of all functions of the entire brain, including the brain stem, is dead."

The second event, following shortly after Dr. Christian Barnard's successful transplant of a heart in November, 1967, was this Conference's adoption of the first Uniform Anatomical Gift Act. In short order, every jurisdiction uniformly adopted the 1968 Act. The most significant contribution of the 1968 Act was to create a right to donate organs, eyes, and tissue. This right was not clearly recognized at common law. By creating this right, individuals became empowered to donate their parts or their loved one's parts to save or improve the lives of others.

The last event was the development of immunosuppressive drugs that prevented organ recipients from rejecting transplanted organs. This permitted many more successful organ transplants, thus contributing to the rapid growth in the demand for organs and the need for changes in the law to facilitate the making of anatomical gifts.

In 1987, a revised Uniform Anatomical Gift Act was promulgated to address changes in circumstances and in practice. Only 26 jurisdictions enacted the 1987 revision. Consequently, there is significant non-uniformity between states with the 1968 Act and those with the 1987 revisions. Neither of those acts comports with changes in federal law adopted subsequent to the 1987 Act relating to the role of hospitals and procurement organization in securing organs, eyes, and tissues for transplantation. And, both of them have impediments that are inconsistent with a policy to encourage donation.

The two previous anatomical gift acts, as well as this act, adhere to an "opt in" principle as its default rule. Thus, an individual becomes a donor only if the donor or someone acting on the donor's behalf affirmatively makes an anatomical gift. The system universally adopted in this country is contrary to the system adopted in some countries, primarily in Europe, where an individual is deemed to be a donor unless the individual or another person acting on the individual's behalf "opts out." This other system is known as "presumed consent." While there are proponents of presumed consent who believe the concept of presumed consent could receive in the future a favorable reception in this country, the professional consensus appears to be not to replace the present opt-in principle at this time....

Scope of the 2006 Revised Act

This act is limited in scope to donations from deceased donors as a result of gifts made before or after their deaths. Although recently there has been a significant increase in so-called "living donations," where a living donor immediately donates an organ (typically a kidney or a section of a liver) to a recipient, donations by living donors are not covered in this act because they raise distinct and difficult legal issues that are more appropriate for a separate act.

A majority of donors or prospective donors are candidates for donation of eyes or tissue, but only a small percentage of individuals die under circumstances that permit an anatomical gift of an organ. To procure an anatomical gift for transplantation, therapy, research, or education, a donor or prospective donor must be declared dead (see Uniform Determination of Death Act). In cases of potential organ donation, measures necessary to ensure the medical suitability of an organ for transplantation or therapy are administered to a patient who is dead or near death to determine if the patient could be a prospective donor.

Pursuant to federal law, when a donor or a patient who could be a prospective donor is dead or near death, a procurement organization, or a designee, must be notified. The organization begins to develop a medical and social history to determine whether the dying or deceased individual's body might be medically suitable for donation. If the body of a dying or deceased person might be medically suitable for donation, the procurement organization checks for evidence of a donation, if not otherwise known, and seeks consent to donation from authorized persons, if necessary. In the case of an organ, the organ procurement organization obtains from the Organ Procurement and Transplantation Network ("OPTN") a prioritized list of potential recipients from the national organ waiting list and takes the necessary steps to see that the organ finds its way to the appropriate recipient. If eye or tissue is donated, the appropriate procurement organization procures the eye or tissue and takes the necessary steps to screen, test, process, store, or distribute them as required for transplantation, therapy, research, or education. All must be done expeditiously.

Recent technological innovations have increased the types of organs that can be transplanted, the demand for organs, and the range of individuals who can donate or receive an organ, thereby increasing the number of organs available each year and the number of transplantations that occur each year. Nonetheless, the number of deaths for lack of available organs also has increased. While the Commissioners are under no illusion that any anatomical gift act can fully satisfy the need for organs, any change that could increase the supply of organs and thus save lies is an improvement.

Transplantation occurs across state boundaries and requires speed and efficiency if the organ is to be successfully transplanted into a recipient. There simply is no time for researching and conforming to variations of the laws among the states. Thus, uniformity of state law is highly desirable. Furthermore, the decision to be a donor is a highly personal decision of great generosity and deserves the highest respect from the law. Because current state anatomical gift laws are out of harmony with both federal procurement and allocation policies and do not fully respect the autonomy interests of donors, there is a need to harmonize state law with federal policy as well as to improve the manner in which anatomical gifts can be made and respected.

Summary of the Changes in the Revised Act

This revision retains the basic policy of the 1968 and 1987 anatomical gift acts by retaining and strengthening the "opt-in" system that honors the free choice of an individual to donate the individual's organ (a process known in the organ transplant community as "first person consent" or "donor designation"). This revision also preserves the right of other persons to make an anatomical gift of a decedent's organs if the decedent had not made a gift during life. And, it strengthens the right of an individual not to donate the individual's organs by signing a refusal that also bars others from making a gift of the individual's organs after the individual's death. This revision:

1. Honors the choice of an individual to be or not to be a donor and strengthens the language barring others from overriding a donor's decision to make an anatomical gift (Section 8);
2. Facilitates donations by expanding the list of those who may make an anatomical gift for another individual during that individual's lifetime to include health-care agents and, under certain circumstances, parents or guardians (Section 4);
3. Empowers a minor eligible under other law to apply for a driver's license to be a donor (Section 4);
4. Facilitates donations from a deceased individual who made no lifetime choice by adding to the list of persons who can make a gift of the deceased individual's body or parts the following persons: the person who was acting as the decedent's agent under a power of attorney for health care at the time of the decedent's death, the decedent's adult grandchildren, and an adult who exhibited special care and concern for the decedent (Section 9) and defines the meaning of "reasonably available" which is relevant to who can make an anatomical gift of a decedent's body or parts (Section 2(23));
5. Permits an anatomical gift by any member of a class where there is more than one person in the class so long as no objections by other class members are known and, if an objection is known, permits a majority of the members of the class who are reasonably available to make the gift without having to take account of a known objection by any class member who is not reasonably available (Section 9);
6. Creates numerous default rules for the interpretation of a document of gift that lacks specificity regarding either the persons to receive the gift or the purposes of the gift or both (Section 11);
7. Encourages and establishes standards for donor registries (Section 20);
8. Enables procurement organizations to gain access to documents of gifts in donor registries, medical records, and the records of a state motor vehicle department (Sections 14 and 20);
9. Resolves the tension between a health-care directive requesting the withholding or withdrawal of life support systems and anatomical gifts by permitting measures necessary to ensure the medical suitability of organs for intended transplantation or therapy to be administered (Sections 14 and 21);
10. Clarifies and expands the rules relating to cooperation and coordination between procurement organizations and coroners or medical examiners (Sections 22 and 23);
11. Recognizes anatomical gifts made under the laws of other jurisdictions (Section 19); and
12. Updates the act to allow for electronic records and signatures (Section 25).

In addition, Section 2 provides a number of new definitions that are used in the substantive provisions of the act to clarify and expand the opportunities for anatomical gifts. These include: adult, agent, custodian, disinterested witness, donee, donor registry, driver's license, eye bank, guardian, know, license, minor, organ procurement organization, parent, prospective donor, reasonably available, recipient, record, sign, tissue, tissue bank, and transplant hospital.

Section 4 authorizes individuals to make anatomical gifts of their bodies or parts. It also permits certain persons, other than donors, to make an anatomical gift on behalf of a donor during the donor's lifetime. The expanded list includes agents acting under a health-care power of attorney or other record, parents of unemancipated minors, and guardians. The section also recognizes that it is appropriate that minors who can apply for a driver's license be empowered to make anatomical gifts, but, under Section 8(g), either parent can revoke the gift if the minor dies under the age of 18.

Section 5 recognizes that, since the adoption of the previous versions of this act, some states and many private organizations have created donor registries for the purpose of making anatomical gifts. Thus, in addition to evidencing a gift on a donor card or driver's license, this act allows for the making of anatomical gifts on donor registries. It also permits gifts to be made on state-issued identification cards and, under limited circumstances, to be made orally. Except for oral gifts, there is no witnessing requirement to make an anatomical gift.

Section 6 permits anatomical gifts to be amended or revoked by the execution of a later-executed record or by inconsistent documents of gifts. It also permits revocation by destruction of a document of gift and, under limited circumstances, permits oral revocations.

Section 7 permits an individual to sign a refusal that bars all other persons from making an anatomical gift of the individual's body or parts. A refusal generally can be made by a signed record, a will, or, under limited circumstances, orally. By permitting refusals, this act recognizes the autonomy interest of an individual either to be or not to be a donor. The section also recognizes that a refusal can be revoked.

Section 8 substantially strengthens the respect due a decision to make an anatomical gift. While the 1987 Act provided that a donor's anatomical gift was irrevocable (except by the donor), until quite recently it had been a common practice for procurement organizations to seek affirmation of the gift from the donor's family. This could result in unnecessary delays in the recovery of organs as well as a reversal of a donor's donation decision. Section 8 intentionally disempowers families from making or revoking anatomical gifts in contravention of a donor's wishes. Thus, under the strengthened language of this act, if a donor had made an anatomical gift, there is no reason to seek consent from the donor's family as they have no right to give it legally. See Section 8(a). Of course, that would not bar, nor should it bar, a procurement organization from advising the donor's family of the donor's express wishes, but that conversation should focus more on what procedures will be followed to carry out the donor's wishes and on answering a family's questions about the process rather than on seeking approval of the donation. A limited exception applies if the donor is a minor at the time of death. In this case, either parent may amend or revoke the donor's anatomical gift. See Section 8(g).

Section 8 also recognizes that some decisions of a donor are inherently ambiguous, making it appropriate to adopt rules that favor the making of anatomical gifts. For example, a donor's revocation of a gift of a part is not to be construed as a refusal for others to make gifts of other parts. Likewise, a donor's gift of one part is not to be construed as a refusal that would bar others from making gifts of other parts absent an express, contrary intent.

Section 9 sets forth a prioritized list of classes of persons who can make an anatomical gift of a decedent's body or part if the decedent was neither a donor nor had signed a refusal. The list is more expansive than under previous versions of this act. It includes persons acting as agents at the decedent's death, adult grandchildren, and close friends.

Section 10 deals with the manner of making, amending, or revoking an anatomical gift following the decedent's death.

Section 11 deals with the passing of parts to named persons and more generally to eye banks, tissue banks, and organ procurement organizations. In part, the section is designed to harmonize this act with federal law, particularly with respect to organs donated for transplantation or therapy. The National Organ Transplant Act created the Organ Procurement and Transplantation Network ("OPTN") to facilitate the nationwide, equitable distribution of organs. Currently, United Network Organ Sharing ("UNOS") operates the OPTN under contract with the U.S. Department of Health and Human Services. When an organ donor dies, the donor's organs, barring the rare instance of a donation to a named individual, are recovered by the organ procurement organization for the service area in which the donor dies, as custodian of the organs, to be allocated by it either locally, regionally, or nationally in accordance with allocation policies established by the OPTN.

Section 11 includes two important improvements to previous versions of this act. First, it creates a priority for transplantation or therapy over research or education when an anatomical gift is made for all four purposes in a document of gift that fails to establish a priority.

Second, it specifies the person to whom a part passes when the document of gift merely expresses a "general intent" to be an "organ donor." This type of general designation is common on a driver's license. Under Section 11(f) a general statement of intent to be a donor results only in an anatomical gift of the donor's eyes, tissues, and organs (not the whole body) for transplantation or therapy. Since a general statement of intent to be an organ donor does not result in the making of an anatomical gift of the whole body, or any part, for research or education, more specific language is required to make such a gift.

Section 11(b) provides that, if an anatomical gift of the decedent's body or parts does not pass to a named person designated in a document of gift, it passes to a procurement organization typically for transplantation or therapy and possibly for research or education. Custody of a body or part that is the subject of an anatomical gift that cannot be used for any intended purpose passes to the "person under obligation to dispose of the body or parts." See Section 11(i).

Section 11(j) prohibits a person from accepting an anatomical gift if the person knows that the gift was not validly made. For this purpose, if a person knows that an anatomical gift was made on a document of gift, the person is deemed to know of a refusal to make a gift if the refusal is on the same document of gift.

Lastly, Section 11(k) clarifies that nothing in this act affects the allocation of organs for transplantation or therapy except to the extent there has been a gift to a named recipient. See

Section 11(a)(2). The allocation of organs is administered exclusively under policies of the Organ Procurement and Transplantation Network.

In part, Section 14 has been redrafted to accord with controlling federal law when applicable. The federal rules require hospitals to notify an organ procurement organization or third party designated by the organ procurement organization of an individual whose death is imminent or who has died in the hospital to increase donation opportunity, and thus, transplantation. See 42 CFR §482.45 (Medicare and Medicaid Programs: Conditions of Participation: Identification of Potential Organ, Tissue, and Eye Donors and Transplant Hospitals' Provision of Transplant-Related Data). The right of the procurement organization to inspect a patient's medical records in Section 14(e) does not violate HIPAA. See 45 CFR §164.512(h) ("A covered entity may use or disclose protected health information to organ procurement organizations or other entities engaged in the procurement, banking, or transplantation of cadaveric organs, eyes, or tissue for the purpose of facilitating organ, eye, or tissue donation and transplantation"). Section 14(c) permits measures necessary to ensure the medical suitability of parts to be administered to a patient who is being evaluated to determine whether the patient has organs that are medically suitable for transplantation.

Section 17 and Section 18 deal with liability and immunity, respectively. (Section 16, dealing with the sale of parts, also provides for potential liabilities but is essentially the same as prior law). Section 17 includes a new provision establishing criminal sanctions for falsifying the making, amending, or revoking of an anatomical gift. Section 18, in substance, is the same as the 1987 Act providing immunity for "good faith" efforts to comply with this act. However, while the act contains no provisions relating to bad faith it is important to note that other laws of the state and federal governments may provide for further remedies and sanctions for bad faith, including those under regulatory rules, licensing requirements, Unfair and Deceptive Practices acts, and the common law.

Section 18(c) provides that in determining whether an individual has a right to make an anatomical gift under Section 9, a person, such as an organ procurement organization, may rely on the individual's representation regarding the individual's relationship to the donor or prospective donor.

Section 19 sets forth rules relating to the validity of documents of gift executed outside of the state while providing that any document of gift shall be interpreted in accordance with the laws of the state.

Section 20 authorizes an appropriate state agency to establish or contract for the establishment of a donor registry. It also provides that a registry can be established without a state contract. While this act does not specify in great detail what could or should be on a donor registry, it does mandate minimum requirements for all registries. First, the registry must provide a database that allows a donor or other person authorized to make an anatomical gift to include in the registry a statement or symbol that the donor has made a gift. Second, at or near the death of a donor or prospective donor, the registry must be accessible to all procurement organizations to obtain information relevant to determine whether the donor or prospective donor has made, amended, or revoked an anatomical gift. Lastly, the registry must be accessible on a twenty four hour, seven day a week basis.

Section 21 creates a default rule to adjust the tension that might exist between preserving organs to assure their medical suitability for transplantation or therapy and the expression of intent by a prospective donor in either a declaration or advance health-care directive not to have life prolonged by use of life support systems. The default rule under this act is that measures necessary to ensure the medical suitability of an organ for transplantation or therapy may not be withheld or withdrawn from the prospective donor. A prospective donor could expressly provide otherwise in the declaration or advance health-care directive.

Sections 22 and 23 represent a complete revision of the relationship of the [coroner] [medical examiner] to the anatomical gift process. Previous versions of this act permitted the [coroner] [medical examiner], under limited circumstances, to make anatomical gifts of the eyes of a decedent in the [coroner's] [medical examiner's] possession. In light of a series of Section 1983 lawsuits in which the [coroner's] [medical examiner's] actions were held to violate the property rights of surviving family members, see, e.g., Brotherton v. Cleveland, 923 F.2d 477 (6th Cir. 1991), the authority of the [coroner] [medical examiner] to make anatomical gifts was deleted from this act. Parts, with the rare exception discussed in the comments to Section 9, can be recovered for the purpose of transplantation, therapy, research, or education from a decedent whose body is under the jurisdiction of the [coroner] [medical examiner] only if there was an anatomical gift of those parts under Section 5 or Section 10 of this act.

This act includes a series of new provisions in Sections 22 and 23 relating to the relationship between the [coroner] [medical examiner] and procurement organizations. These provisions should encourage meaningful cooperation between these groups in hopes of increasing the number of anatomical gifts. Importantly, the section does not permit a [coroner] [medical examiner] to make an anatomical gift.

§1. Short title.

This [act] may be cited as the Revised Uniform Anatomical Gift Act.

§2. Definitions.

In this [act]:

(1) "Adult" means an individual who is at least [18] years of age.

(2) "Agent" means an individual:

(A) authorized to make health-care decisions on the principal's behalf by a power of attorney for health care; or

(B) expressly authorized to make an anatomical gift on the principal's behalf by any other record signed by the principal.

(3) "Anatomical gift" means a donation of all or part of a human body to take effect after the donor's death for the purpose of transplantation, therapy, research, or education.

(4) "Decedent" means a deceased individual whose body or part is or may be the source of an anatomical gift. The term includes a stillborn infant and, subject to restrictions imposed by law other than this [act], a fetus.

(5) "Disinterested witness" means a witness other than the spouse, child, parent, sibling, grandchild, grandparent, or guardian of the individual who makes, amends, revokes, or refuses to make an anatomical gift, or another adult who exhibited special care and concern for the individual. The term does not include a person to which an anatomical gift could pass under Section 11.

(6) "Document of gift" means a donor card or other record used to make an anatomical gift. The term includes a statement or symbol on a driver's license, identification card, or donor registry.

(7) "Donor" means an individual whose body or part is the subject of an anatomical gift.

(8) "Donor registry" means a database that contains records of anatomical gifts and amendments to or revocations of anatomical gifts.

(9) "Driver's license" means a license or permit issued by the [state department of motor vehicles] to operate a vehicle, whether or not conditions are attached to the license or permit.

(10) "Eye bank" means a person that is licensed, accredited, or regulated under federal or state law to engage in the recovery, screening, testing, processing, storage, or distribution of human eyes or portions of human eyes.

(11) "Guardian" means a person appointed by a court to make decisions regarding the support, care, education, health, or welfare of an individual. The term does not include a guardian ad litem.

(12) "Hospital" means a facility licensed as a hospital under the law of any state or a facility operated as a hospital by the United States, a state, or a subdivision of a state.

(13) "Identification card" means an identification card issued by the [state department of motor vehicles].

(14) "Know" means to have actual knowledge.

(15) "Minor" means an individual who is under [18] years of age.

(16) "Organ procurement organization" means a person designated by the Secretary of the United States Department of Health and Human Services as an organ procurement organization.

(17) "Parent" means a parent whose parental rights have not been terminated.

(18) "Part" means an organ, an eye, or tissue of a human being. The term does not include the whole body.

(19) "Person" means an individual, corporation, business trust, estate, trust, partnership, limited liability company, association, joint venture, public corporation, government or governmental subdivision, agency, or instrumentality, or any other legal or commercial entity.

(20) "Physician" means an individual authorized to practice medicine or osteopathy under the law of any state.

(21) "Procurement organization" means an eye bank, organ procurement organization, or tissue bank.

(22) "Prospective donor" means an individual who is dead or near death and has been determined by a procurement organization to have a part that could be medically suitable for transplantation, therapy, research, or education. The term does not include an individual who has made a refusal.

(23) "Reasonably available" means able to be contacted by a procurement organization without undue effort and willing and able to act in a timely manner consistent with existing medical criteria necessary for the making of an anatomical gift.

(24) "Recipient" means an individual into whose body a decedent's part has been or is intended to be transplanted.

(25) "Record" means information that is inscribed on a tangible medium or that is stored in an electronic or other medium and is retrievable in perceivable form.

(26) "Refusal" means a record created under Section 7 that expressly states an intent to bar other persons from making an anatomical gift of an individual's body or part.

(27) "Sign" means, with the present intent to authenticate or adopt a record:

(A) to execute or adopt a tangible symbol; or

(B) to attach to or logically associate with the record an electronic symbol, sound, or process.

(28) "State" means a state of the United States, the District of Columbia, Puerto Rico, the United States Virgin Islands, or any territory or insular possession subject to the jurisdiction of the United States.

(29) "Technician" means an individual determined to be qualified to remove or process parts by an appropriate organization that is licensed, accredited, or regulated under federal or state law. The term includes an enucleator.

(30) "Tissue" means a portion of the human body other than an organ or an eye. The term does not include blood unless the blood is donated for the purpose of research or education.

(31) "Tissue bank" means a person that is licensed, accredited, or regulated under federal or state law to engage in the recovery, screening, testing, processing, storage, or distribution of tissue.

(32) "Transplant hospital" means a hospital that furnishes organ transplants and other medical and surgical specialty services required for the care of transplant patients.

Legislative note: If this state does not license "hospitals", the definition of "hospital" should include a reference to the facility or facilities with equivalent functions by an additional sentence such as the following: "The term includes an acute care facility."

§3. Applicability.

This [act] applies to an anatomical gift or amendment to, revocation of, or refusal to make an anatomical gift, whenever made.

§4. Who may make anatomical gift before donor's death.

Subject to Section 8, an anatomical gift of a donor's body or part may be made during the life of the donor for the purpose of transplantation, therapy, research, or education in the manner provided in Section 5 by:

(1) the donor, if the donor is an adult or if the donor is a minor and is:

(A) emancipated; or

(B) authorized under state law to apply for a driver's license because the donor is at least [insert the youngest age at which an individual may apply for any type of driver's license] years of age;

(2) an agent of the donor, unless the power of attorney for health care or other record prohibits the agent from making an anatomical gift;

(3) a parent of the donor, if the donor is an unemancipated minor; or

(4) the donor's guardian.

§5. Manner of making anatomical gift before donor's death.

(a) A donor may make an anatomical gift:

(1) by authorizing a statement or symbol indicating that the donor has made an anatomical gift to be imprinted on the donor's driver's license or identification card;

(2) in a will;

(3) during a terminal illness or injury of the donor, by any form of communication addressed to at least two adults, at least one of whom is a disinterested witness; or

(4) as provided in subsection (b).

(b) A donor or other person authorized to make an anatomical gift under Section 4 may make a gift by a donor card or other record signed by the donor or other person making the gift or by authorizing that a statement or symbol indicating that the donor has made an anatomical gift be included on a donor registry. If the donor or other person is physically unable to sign a record, the record may be signed by another individual at the direction of the donor or other person and must:

(1) be witnessed by at least two adults, at least one of whom is a disinterested witness, who have signed at the request of the donor or the other person; and

(2) state that it has been signed and witnessed as provided in paragraph (1).

(c) Revocation, suspension, expiration, or cancellation of a driver's license or identification card upon which an anatomical gift is indicated does not invalidate the gift.

(d) An anatomical gift made by will takes effect upon the donor's death whether or not the will is probated. Invalidation of the will after the donor's death does not invalidate the gift.

§6. Amending or revoking anatomical gift before donor's death.

(a) Subject to Section 8, a donor or other person authorized to make an anatomical gift under Section 4 may amend or revoke an anatomical gift by:

(1) a record signed by:

(A) the donor;

(B) the other person; or

(C) subject to subsection (b), another individual acting at the direction of the donor or the other person if the donor or other person is physically unable to sign; or

(2) a later-executed document of gift that amends or revokes a previous anatomical gift or portion of an anatomical gift, either expressly or by inconsistency.

(b) A record signed pursuant to subsection (a)(1)(C) must:

(1) be witnessed by at least two adults, at least one of whom is a disinterested witness, who have signed at the request of the donor or the other person; and

(2) state that it has been signed and witnessed as provided in paragraph (1).

(c) Subject to Section 8, a donor or other person authorized to make an anatomical gift under Section 4 may revoke an anatomical gift by the destruction or cancellation of the document of gift, or the portion of the document of gift used to make the gift, with the intent to revoke the gift.

(d) A donor may amend or revoke an anatomical gift that was not made in a will by any form of communication during a terminal illness or injury addressed to at least two adults, at least one of whom is a disinterested witness.

(e) A donor who makes an anatomical gift in a will may amend or revoke the gift in the manner provided for amendment or revocation of wills or as provided in subsection (a).

§7. Refusal to make anatomical gift; effect of refusal.

(a) An individual may refuse to make an anatomical gift of the individual's body or part by:

(1) a record signed by:

(A) the individual; or

(B) subject to subsection (b), another individual acting at the direction of the individual if the individual is physically unable to sign;

(2) the individual's will, whether or not the will is admitted to probate or invalidated after the individual's death; or

(3) any form of communication made by the individual during the individual's terminal illness or injury addressed to at least two adults, at least one of whom is a disinterested witness.

(b) A record signed pursuant to subsection (a)(1)(B) must:

(1) be witnessed by at least two adults, at least one of whom is a disinterested witness, who have signed at the request of the individual; and

(2) state that it has been signed and witnessed as provided in paragraph (1).

(c) An individual who has made a refusal may amend or revoke the refusal:

(1) in the manner provided in subsection (a) for making a refusal;

(2) by subsequently making an anatomical gift pursuant to Section 5 that is inconsistent with the refusal; or

(3) by destroying or canceling the record evidencing the refusal, or the portion of the record used to make the refusal, with the intent to revoke the refusal.

(d) Except as otherwise provided in Section 8(h), in the absence of an express, contrary indication by the individual set forth in the refusal, an individual's unrevoked refusal to make an anatomical gift of the individual's body or part bars all other persons from making an anatomical gift of the individual's body or part.

§8. Preclusive effect of anatomical gift, amendment, or revocation.

(a) Except as otherwise provided in subsection (g) and subject to subsection (f), in the absence of an express, contrary indication by the donor, a person other than the donor is barred from making, amending, or revoking an anatomical gift of a donor's body or part if the donor made an anatomical gift of the donor's body or part under Section 5 or an amendment to an anatomical gift of the donor's body or part under Section 6.

(b) A donor's revocation of an anatomical gift of the donor's body or part under Section 6 is not a refusal and does not bar another person specified in Section 4 or 9 from making an anatomical gift of the donor's body or part under Section 5 or 10.

(c) If a person other than the donor makes an unrevoked anatomical gift of the donor's body or part under Section 5 or an amendment to an anatomical gift of the donor's body or part under Section 6, another person may not make, amend, or revoke the gift of the donor's body or part under Section 10.

(d) A revocation of an anatomical gift of a donor's body or part under Section 6 by a person other than the donor does not bar another person from making an anatomical gift of the body or part under Section 5 or 10.

(e) In the absence of an express, contrary indication by the donor or other person authorized to make an anatomical gift under Section 4, an anatomical gift of a part is neither a refusal to give another part nor a limitation on the making of an anatomical gift of another part at a later time by the donor or another person.

(f) In the absence of an express, contrary indication by the donor or other person authorized to make an anatomical gift under Section 4, an anatomical gift of a part for one or more of the purposes set forth in Section 4 is not a limitation on the making of an anatomical gift of the part for any of the other purposes by the donor or any other person under Section 5 or 10.

(g) If a donor who is an unemancipated minor dies, a parent of the donor who is reasonably available may revoke or amend an anatomical gift of the donor's body or part.

(h) If an unemancipated minor who signed a refusal dies, a parent of the minor who is reasonably available may revoke the minor's refusal.

§9. Who may make anatomical gift of decedent's body or part.

(a) Subject to subsections (b) and (c) and unless barred by Section 7 or 8, an anatomical gift of a decedent's body or part for purpose of transplantation, therapy, research, or education may be made by any member of the following classes of persons who is reasonably available, in the order of priority listed:

(1) an agent of the decedent at the time of death who could have made an anatomical gift under Section 4(2) immediately before the decedent's death;

(2) the spouse of the decedent;

(3) adult children of the decedent;

(4) parents of the decedent;

(5) adult siblings of the decedent;

(6) adult grandchildren of the decedent;

(7) grandparents of the decedent;

(8) an adult who exhibited special care and concern for the decedent;

(9) the persons who were acting as the [guardians] of the person of the decedent at the time of death; and

(10) any other person having the authority to dispose of the decedent's body.

(b) If there is more than one member of a class listed in subsection (a)(1), (3), (4), (5), (6), (7), or (9) entitled to make an anatomical gift, an anatomical gift may be made by a member of the class unless that member or a person to which the gift may pass under Section 11 knows of an objection by another member of the class. If an objection is known, the gift may be made only by a majority of the members of the class who are reasonably available.

(c) A person may not make an anatomical gift if, at the time of the decedent's death, a person in a prior class under subsection (a) is reasonably available to make or to object to the making of an anatomical gift.

§10. Manner of making, amending, or revoking anatomical gift of decedent's body or part.

(a) A person authorized to make an anatomical gift under Section 9 may make an anatomical gift by a document of gift signed by the person making the gift or by that person's oral communication that is electronically recorded or is contemporaneously reduced to a record and signed by the individual receiving the oral communication.

(b) Subject to subsection (c), an anatomical gift by a person authorized under Section 9 may be amended or revoked orally or in a record by any member of a prior class who is reasonably available. If more than one member of the prior class is reasonably available, the gift made by a person authorized under Section 9 may be:

(1) amended only if a majority of the reasonably available members agree to the amending of the gift; or

(2) revoked only if a majority of the reasonably available members agree to the revoking of the gift or if they are equally divided as to whether to revoke the gift.

(c) A revocation under subsection (b) is effective only if, before an incision has been made to remove a part from the donor's body or before invasive procedures have begun to prepare the recipient, the procurement organization, transplant hospital, or physician or technician knows of the revocation.

§11. Persons that may receive anatomical gift; purpose of anatomical gift.

(a) An anatomical gift may be made to the following persons named in the document of gift:

(1) a hospital; accredited medical school, dental school, college, or university; organ procurement organization; or other appropriate person, for research or education;

(2) subject to subsection (b), an individual designated by the person making the anatomical gift if the individual is the recipient of the part;

(3) an eye bank or tissue bank.

(b) If an anatomical gift to an individual under subsection (a)(2) cannot be transplanted into the individual, the part passes in accordance with subsection (g) in the absence of an express, contrary indication by the person making the anatomical gift.

(c) If an anatomical gift of one or more specific parts or of all parts is made in a document of gift that does not name a person described in subsection (a) but identifies the purpose for which an anatomical gift may be used, the following rules apply:

(1) If the part is an eye and the gift is for the purpose of transplantation or therapy, the gift passes to the appropriate eye bank.

(2) If the part is tissue and the gift is for the purpose of transplantation or therapy, the gift passes to the appropriate tissue bank.

(3) If the part is an organ and the gift is for the purpose of transplantation or therapy, the gift passes to the appropriate organ procurement organization as custodian of the organ.

(4) If the part is an organ, an eye, or tissue and the gift is for the purpose of research or education, the gift passes to the appropriate procurement organization.

(d) For the purpose of subsection (c), if there is more than one purpose of an anatomical gift set forth in the document of gift but the purposes are not set forth in any priority, the gift must be used for transplantation or therapy, if suitable. If the gift cannot be used for transplantation or therapy, the gift may be used for research or education.

(e) If an anatomical gift of one or more specific parts is made in a document of gift that does not name a person described in subsection (a) and does not identify the purpose of the gift, the gift may be used only for transplantation or therapy, and the gift passes in accordance with subsection (g).

(f) If a document of gift specifies only a general intent to make an anatomical gift by words such as "donor", "organ donor", or "body donor", or by a symbol or statement of similar import, the gift may be used only for transplantation or therapy, and the gift passes in accordance with subsection (g).

(g) For purposes of subsections (b), (e), and (f) the following rules apply:

(1) If the part is an eye, the gift passes to the appropriate eye bank.

(2) If the part is tissue, the gift passes to the appropriate tissue bank.

(3) If the part is an organ, the gift passes to the appropriate organ procurement organization as custodian of the organ.

(h) An anatomical gift of an organ for transplantation or therapy, other than an anatomical gift under subsection (a)(2), passes to the organ procurement organization as custodian of the organ.

(i) If an anatomical gift does not pass pursuant to subsections (a) through (h) or the decedent's body or part is not used for transplantation, therapy, research, or education, custody of the body or part passes to the person under obligation to dispose of the body or part.

(j) A person may not accept an anatomical gift if the person knows that the gift was not effectively made under Section 5 or 10 or if the person knows that the decedent made a refusal under Section 7 that was not revoked. For purposes of the subsection, if a person knows that an anatomical gift was made on a document of gift, the person is deemed to know of any amendment or revocation of the gift or any refusal to make an anatomical gift on the same document of gift.

(k) Except as otherwise provided in subsection (a)(2), nothing in this [act] affects the allocation of organs for transplantation or therapy.

§12. Search and notification.

(a) The following persons shall make a reasonable search of an individual who the person reasonably believes is dead or near death for a document of gift or other information identifying the individual as a donor or as an individual who made a refusal:

(1) a law enforcement officer, firefighter, paramedic, or other emergency rescuer finding the individual; and

(2) if no other source of the information is immediately available, a hospital, as soon as practical after the individual's arrival at the hospital.

(b) If a document of gift or a refusal to make an anatomical gift is located by the search required by subsection (a)(1) and the individual or deceased individual to whom it relates is taken to a hospital, the person responsible for conducting the search shall send the document of gift or refusal to the hospital.

(c) A person is not subject to criminal or civil liability for failing to discharge the duties imposed by this section but may be subject to administrative sanctions.

§13. Delivery of document of gift not required; right to examine.

(a) A document of gift need not be delivered during the donor's lifetime to be effective.

(b) Upon or after an individual's death, a person in possession of a document of gift or a refusal to make an anatomical gift with respect to the individual shall allow examination and copying of the document of gift or refusal by a person authorized to make or object to the making of an anatomical gift with respect to the individual or by a person to which the gift could pass under Section 11.

§14. Rights and duties of procurement organization and others.

(a) When a hospital refers an individual at or near death to a procurement organization, the organization shall make a reasonable search of the records of the [state department of motor vehicles] and any donor registry that it knows exists for the geographical area in which the individual resides to ascertain whether the individual has made an anatomical gift.

(b) A procurement organization must be allowed reasonable access to information in the records of the [state department of motor vehicles] to ascertain whether an individual at or near death is a donor.

(c) When a hospital refers an individual at or near death to a procurement organization, the organization may conduct any reasonable examination necessary to ensure the medical suitability of a part that is or could be the subject of an anatomical gift for transplantation, therapy, research, or education from a donor or a prospective donor. During the examination period, measures necessary to ensure the medical suitability of the part may not be withdrawn unless the hospital or procurement organization knows that the individual expressed a contrary intent.

(d) Unless prohibited by law other than this [act], at any time after a donor's death, the person to which a part passes under Section 11 may conduct any reasonable examination necessary to ensure the medical suitability of the body or part for its intended purpose.

(e) Unless prohibited by law other than this [act], an examination under subsection (c) or (d) may include an examination of all medical and dental records of the donor or prospective donor.

(f) Upon the death of a minor who was a donor or had signed a refusal, unless a procurement organization knows the minor is emancipated, the procurement organization shall conduct a reasonable search for the parents of the minor and provide the parents with an opportunity to revoke or amend the anatomical gift or revoke the refusal.

(g) Upon referral by a hospital under subsection (a), a procurement organization shall make a reasonable search for any person listed in Section 9 having priority to make an anatomical gift on behalf of a prospective donor. If a procurement organization receives information that an anatomical gift to any other person was made, amended, or revoked, it shall promptly advise the other person of all relevant information.

(h) Subject to Sections 11(i) and 23, the rights of the person to which a part passes under Section 11 are superior to the rights of all others with respect to the part. The person may accept or reject an anatomical gift in whole or in part. Subject to the terms of the document of gift and this [act], a person that accepts an anatomical gift of an entire body may allow embalming, burial or cremation, and use of remains in a funeral service. If the gift is of a part, the person to which the part passes under Section 11, upon the death of the donor and before embalming, burial, or cremation, shall cause the part to be removed without unnecessary mutilation.

(i) Neither the physician who attends the decedent at death nor the physician who determines the time of the decedent's death may participate in the procedures for removing or transplanting a part from the decedent.

(j) A physician or technician may remove a donated part from the body of a donor that the physician or technician is qualified to remove.

§15. Coordination of procurement and use.

Each hospital in this state shall enter into agreements or affiliations with procurement organizations for coordination of procurement and use of anatomical gifts.

§16. Sale or purchase of parts prohibited.

(a) Except as otherwise provided in subsection (b), a person that for valuable consideration, knowingly purchases or sells a part for transplantation or therapy if removal of a part from an individual is intended to occur after the individual's death commits a [[felony] and upon conviction is subject to a fine not exceeding [$50,000] or imprisonment not exceeding [five] years, or both][class[ ] felony].

(b) A person may charge a reasonable amount for the removal, processing, preservation, quality control, storage, transportation, implantation, or disposal of a part.

§17. Other prohibited acts.

A person that, in order to obtain a financial gain, intentionally falsifies, forges, conceals, defaces, or obliterates a document of gift, an amendment or revocation of a document of gift, or a refusal commits a [[felony] and upon conviction is subject to a fine not exceeding [$50,000] or imprisonment not exceeding [five] years, or both] [class] [felony].

§18. Immunity.

(a) A person that acts in accordance with this [act] or with the applicable anatomical gift law of another state, or attempts in good faith to do so, is not liable for the act in a civil action, criminal prosecution, or administrative proceeding.

(b) Neither the person making an anatomical gift nor the donor's estate is liable for any injury or damage that results from the making or use of the gift.

(c) In determining whether an anatomical gift has been made, amended, or revoked under this [act], a person may rely upon representations of an individual listed in Section 9(a)(2), (3), (4), (5), (6), (7), or (8) relating to the individual's relationship to the donor or prospective donor unless the person knows that the representation is untrue.

§19. Law governing validity; choice of law as to execution of document of gift; presumption of validity.

(a) A document of gift is valid if executed in accordance with:

(1) this [act];

(2) the laws of the state or country where it was executed; or

(3) the laws of the state or country where the person making the anatomical gift was domiciled, has a place of residence, or was a national at the time the document of gift was executed.

(b) If a document of gift is valid under this section, the law of this state governs the interpretation of the document of gift.

(c) A person may presume that a document of gift or amendment of an anatomical gift is valid unless that person knows that it was not validly executed or was revoked.

§20. Donor registry.

(a) The [insert name of appropriate state agency] may establish or contract for the establishment of a donor registry.

(b) The [state department of motor vehicles] shall cooperate with a person that administers any donor registry that this state establishes, contracts for, or recognizes for the purpose of transferring to the donor registry all relevant information regarding a donor's making, amendment to, or revocation of an anatomical gift.

(c) A donor registry must:

(1) allow a donor or other person authorized under Section 4 to include on the donor registry a statement or symbol that the donor has made, amended, or revoked an anatomical gift;

(2) be accessible to a procurement organization to allow it to obtain relevant information on the donor registry to determine, at or near death of the donor or a prospective donor, whether the donor or prospective donor has made, amended, or revoked an anatomical gift; and

(3) be accessible for purposes of paragraphs (1) and (2) seven days a week on a 24-hour basis.

(d) Personally identifiable information on a donor registry about a donor or prospective donor may not be used or disclosed without the express consent of the donor, prospective donor, or person that made the anatomical gift for any purpose other than to determine, at or near death of the donor or prospective donor, whether the donor or prospective donor has made, amended, or revoked an anatomical gift.

(e) This section does not prohibit any person from creating or maintaining a donor registry that is not established by or under contract with the state. Any such registry must comply with subsections (c) and (d).

Legislative Note: If the state has an existing donor registry statute, it should consider whether this section is necessary. It should also consider whether subsections (c) and (d), and Section 14(g)(last sentence), should be incorporated into its existing statute. Subsection (b) may be deleted if the state department of motor vehicles is the agency specified in subsection (a).

§21. Effect of anatomical gift on advance health-care directive.

(a) In this section:

(1) "Advance health-care directive" means a power of attorney for health care or a record signed by a prospective donor containing the prospective donor's direction concerning a health-care decision for the prospective donor.

(2) "Declaration" means a record signed by a prospective donor specifying the circumstances under which a life support system may be withheld or withdrawn from the prospective donor.

(3) "Health-care decision" means any decision made regarding the health care of the prospective donor.

(b) If a prospective donor has a declaration or advance health-care directive, measures necessary to ensure the medical suitability of an organ for transplantation or therapy may not be withheld or withdrawn from the prospective donor, unless the declaration expressly provides to the contrary.

§22. Cooperation between [coroner] [medical examiner] and procurement organization.

(a) A [coroner] [medical examiner] shall cooperate with procurement organizations to maximize the opportunity to recover anatomical gifts for the purpose of transplantation, therapy, research, or education.

(b) If a [coroner] [medical examiner] receives notice from a procurement organization that an anatomical gift might be available or was made with respect to a decedent whose body is under the jurisdiction of the [coroner] [medical examiner] and a post-mortem examination is going to be performed, unless the [coroner] [medical examiner] denies recovery in accordance with Section 23, the [coroner] [medical examiner] or designee shall conduct a post-mortem examination of the body or the part in a manner and within a period compatible with its preservation for the purposes of the gift.

(c) A part may not be removed from the body of a decedent under the jurisdiction of a [coroner] [medical examiner] for transplantation, therapy, research, or education unless the part is the subject of an anatomical gift. The body of a decedent under the jurisdiction of the [coroner] [medical examiner] may not be delivered to a person for research or education unless the body is the subject of an anatomical gift. This subsection does not preclude a [coroner] [medical examiner] from performing the medicolegal investigation upon the body or parts of a decedent under the jurisdiction of the [coroner] [medical examiner].

§23. Facilitation of anatomical gift from decedent whose body is under jurisdiction of [coroner] [medical examiner].

(a) Upon request of a procurement organization, a [coroner] [medical examiner] shall release to the procurement organization the name, contact information, and available medical and social history of a decedent whose body is under the jurisdiction of the [coroner] [medical examiner]. If the decedent's body or part is medically suitable for transplantation, therapy, research, or education, the [coroner] [medical examiner] shall release post-mortem examination results to the procurement organization. The procurement organization may make a subsequent disclosure of the post-mortem examination results or other information received from the [coroner] [medical examiner] only if relevant to transplantation or therapy.

(b) The [coroner] [medical examiner] may conduct a medicolegal examination by reviewing all medical records, laboratory test results, x-rays, other diagnostic results, and other information that any person possesses about a donor or prospective donor whose body is under the jurisdiction of the [coroner] [medical examiner] which the [coroner] [medical examiner] determines may be relevant to the investigation.

(c) A person that has any information requested by a [coroner] [medical examiner] pursuant to subsection (b) shall provide that information as expeditiously as possible to allow the [coroner] [medical examiner] to conduct the medicolegal investigation within a period compatible with the preservation of parts for the purpose of transplantation, therapy, research, or education.

(d) If an anatomical gift has been or might be made of a part of a decedent whose body is under the jurisdiction of the [coroner] [medical examiner] and a post-mortem examination is not required, or the [coroner] [medical examiner] determines that a post-mortem examination is required but that the recovery of the part that is the subject of an anatomical gift will not interfere with the examination, the [coroner] [medical examiner] and procurement organization shall cooperate in the timely removal of the part from the decedent for the purpose of transplantation, therapy, research, or education.

(e) If an anatomical gift of a part from the decedent under the jurisdiction of the [coroner] [medical examiner] has been or might be made, but the [coroner] [medical examiner] initially believes that the recovery of the part could interfere with the post-mortem investigation into the decedent's cause or manner of death, the [coroner] [medical examiner] shall consult with the procurement organization or physician or technician designated by the procurement organization about the proposed recovery. After consultation, the [coroner] [medical examiner] may allow the recovery.

(f) Following the consultation under subsection (e), in the absence of mutually agreed-upon protocols to resolve conflict between the [coroner] [medical examiner] and the procurement organization, if the [coroner] [medical examiner] intends to deny recovery, the [coroner] [medical examiner] or designee, at the request of the procurement organization, shall attend the removal procedure for the part before making a final determination not to allow the procurement organization to recover the part. During the removal procedure, the [coroner] [medical examiner] or designee may allow recovery by the procurement organization to proceed, or, if the [coroner] [medical examiner] or designee reasonably believes that the part may be involved in determining the decedent's cause or manner of death, deny recovery by the procurement organization.

(g) If the [coroner] [medical examiner] or designee denies recovery under subsection (f), the [coroner] [medical examiner] or designee shall:

(1) explain in a record the specific reasons for not allowing recovery of the part;

(2) include the specific reasons in the records of the [coroner] [medical examiner]; and

(3) provide a record with the specific reasons to the procurement organization.

(h) If the [coroner] [medical examiner] or designee allows recovery of a part under subsection (d), (e), or (f), the procurement organization, upon request, shall cause the physician or technician who removes the part to provide the [coroner] [medical examiner] with a record describing the condition of the part, a biopsy, a photograph, and any other information and observations that would assist in the post-mortem examination.

(i) If a [coroner] [medical examiner] or designee is required to be present at a removal procedure under subsection (f), upon request the procurement organization requesting the recovery of the part shall reimburse the [coroner] [medical examiner] or designee for the additional costs incurred in complying with subsection (f).

Legislative Note: Section 23 could be incorporated into the provisions of the state's code where the provisions relating to a coroner or medical examiner are codified rather than included in this act. If codified in that manner, the definitions in Section 2 of "anatomical gift", "donor", "eye bank", "organ procurement organization", "part", "procurement organization", "prospective donor" (first sentence only), "tissue", and "tissue bank" also should be included.

§24. Uniformity of application and construction.

In applying and construing this uniform act, consideration must be given to the need to promote uniformity of the law with respect to its subject matter among states that enact it.

§25. Relation to Electronic Signatures in Global and National Commerce Act.

This act modifies, limits, and supersedes the Electronic Signatures in Global and National Commerce Act, 15 U.S.C. Section 7001 et seq., but does not modify, limit or supersede Section 101(a) of that act, 15 U.S.C. Section 7001, or authorize electronic delivery of any of the notices described in Section 103(b) of that act, 15 U.S.C. Section 7003(b).

§26. Repeals.

The following acts and parts of acts are repealed:

(1) [Uniform Anatomical Gift Act];

(2)

(3)

§27. Effective Date.

This [act] takes effect __________________.

PART V

~

UNIFORM POWER OF ATTORNEY ACT (2006)

Uniform Power of Attorney Act (2006)

TABLE OF CONTENTS

Prefatory Note

The catalyst for the Uniform Power of Attorney Act (the "Act") was a national review of state power of attorney legislation. The review revealed growing divergence among states' statutory treatment of powers of attorney. The original Uniform Durable Power of Attorney Act ("Original Act"), last amended in 1987, was at one time followed by all but a few jurisdictions. Despite initial uniformity, the review found that a majority of states had enacted non-uniform provisions to deal with specific matters upon which the Original Act is silent. The topics about which there was increasing divergence included: 1) the authority of multiple agents; 2) the authority of a later-appointed fiduciary or guardian; 3) the impact of dissolution or annulment of the principal's marriage to the agent; 4) activation of contingent powers; 5) the authority to make gifts; and 6) standards for agent conduct and liability. Other topics about which states had legislated, although not necessarily in a divergent manner, included: successor agents, execution requirements, portability, sanctions for dishonor of a power of attorney, and restrictions on authority that has the potential to dissipate a principal's property or alter a principal's estate plan.

A national survey was then conducted by the Joint Editorial Board for Uniform Trust and Estate Acts (JEB) to ascertain whether there was actual divergence of opinion about default rules for powers of attorney or only the lack of a detailed uniform model. The survey was distributed to probate and elder law sections of all state bar associations, to the fellows of the American College of Trust and Estate Counsel, the leadership of the ABA Section of Real Property, Probate and Trust Law and the National Academy of Elder Law Attorneys, as well as to special interest list serves of the ABA Commission on Law and Aging. Forty-four jurisdictions were represented in the 371 surveys returned.

The survey responses demonstrated a consensus of opinion in excess of seventy percent that a power of attorney statute should:

1) provide for confirmation that contingent powers are activated;
2) revoke a spouse-agent's authority upon the dissolution or annulment of the marriage to the principal;
3) include a portability provision;
4) require gift making authority to be expressly stated in the grant of authority;
5) provide a default standard for fiduciary duties;
6) permit the principal to alter the default fiduciary standard;
7) require notice by an agent when the agent is no longer willing or able to act;
8) include safeguards against abuse by the agent;
9) include remedies and sanctions for abuse by the agent;
10) protect the reliance of other persons on a power of attorney; and
11) include remedies and sanctions for refusal of other persons to honor a power of attorney.

Informed by the review and the survey results, the Conference's drafting process also incorporated input from the American College of Trust and Estate Counsel, the ABA Section of Real Property, Probate and Trust Law, the ABA Commission on Law and Aging, the Joint Editorial Board for Uniform Trust and Estate Acts, the National Conference of Lawyers and Corporate Fiduciaries, the American Bankers Association, AARP, other professional groups, as well as numerous individual lawyers and corporate counsel. As a result of this process, the Act codifies both state legislative trends and collective best practices, and strikes a balance between the need for flexibility and acceptance of an agent's authority and the need to prevent and redress financial abuse.

While the Act contains safeguards for the protection of an incapacitated principal, the Act is primarily a set of default rules that preserve a principal's freedom to choose both the extent of an agent's authority and the principles to govern the agent's conduct. Among the Act's features that enhance drafting flexibility are the statutory definitions of powers in Article 2, which can be incorporated by reference in an individually drafted power of attorney or selected for inclusion on the optional statutory form provided in Article 3. The statutory definitions of enumerated powers are an updated version of those in the Uniform Statutory Form Power of Attorney Act (1988), which the Act supersedes. The national review found that eighteen jurisdictions had adopted some type of statutory form power of attorney. The decision to include a statutory form power of attorney in the Act was based on this trend and the proliferation of power of attorney forms currently available to the public.

Sections 119 and 120 of the Act address the problem of persons refusing to accept an agent's authority. Section 119 provides protection from liability for persons that in good faith accept an acknowledged power of attorney. Section 120 sanctions refusal to accept an acknowledged power of attorney unless the refusal meets limited statutory exceptions. An alternate Section 120 is provided for states that may wish to limit sanctions to refusal of an acknowledged statutory form power of attorney.

In exchange for mandated acceptance of an agent's authority, the Act does not require persons that deal with an agent to investigate the agent or the agent's actions. Instead, safeguards against abuse are provided through heightened requirements for granting authority that could dissipate the principal's property or alter the principal's estate plan (Section 201(a)), provisions that set out the agent's duties and liabilities (Sections 114 and 117) and by specification of the categories of persons that have standing to request judicial review of the agent's conduct (Section 116). The following provides a brief overview of the entire Act.

Overview of the Uniform Power of Attorney Act

The Act consists of 4 articles. The basic substance of the Act is located in Articles 1 and 2. Article 3 contains the optional statutory form and Article 4 consists of miscellaneous provisions dealing with general application of the Act and repeal of certain prior acts.

Article 1 – General Provisions and Definitions – Section 102 lists definitions which are useful in interpretation of the Act. Of particular note is the definition of "incapacity" which replaces the term "disability" used in the Original Act. The definition of "incapacity" is consistent with the standard for appointment of a conservator under Section 401 of the Uniform Guardianship and Protective Proceedings Act as amended in 1997. Another significant change in terminology from the Original Act is the use of "agent" in place of the term "attorney in fact." The term "agent" was also used in the Uniform Statutory Form Power of Attorney Act and is intended to clarify confusion in the lay public about the meaning of "attorney in fact." Section 103 provides that the Act is to apply broadly to all powers of attorney, but excepts from the Act powers of attorney for health care and certain specialized powers such as those coupled with an interest or dealing with proxy voting.

Another innovation is the default rule in Section 104 that a power of attorney is durable unless it contains express language indicating otherwise. This change from the Original Act reflects the view that most principals prefer their powers of attorney to be durable as a hedge against the need for guardianship. While the Original Act was silent on execution requirements for a power of attorney, Section 105 requires the principal's signature and provides that an acknowledged signature is presumed genuine. Section 106 recognizes military powers of attorney and powers of attorney properly executed in other states or countries, or which were properly executed in the state of enactment prior to the Act's effective date. Section 107 states a choice of law rule for determining the law that governs the meaning and effect of a power of attorney.

Section 108 addresses the relationship of the agent to a later court-appointed fiduciary. The Original Act conferred upon a conservator or other later-appointed fiduciary the same power to revoke or amend the power of attorney as the principal would have had prior to incapacity. In contrast, the Act reserves this power to the court and states that the agent's authority continues until limited, suspended, or terminated by the court. This approach reflects greater deference for the previously expressed preferences of the principal and is consistent with the state legislative trend that has departed from the Original Act.

The default rule for when a power of attorney becomes effective is stated in Section 109. Unless the principal specifies that it is to become effective upon a future date, event, or contingency, the authority of an agent under a power of attorney becomes effective when the power is executed. Section 109 permits the principal to designate who may determine when contingent powers are triggered. If the trigger for contingent powers is the principal's incapacity, Section 109 provides that the person designated to make that determination has the authority to act as the principal's personal representative under the Health Insurance Portability and Accountability Act (HIPAA) for purposes of accessing the principal's health-care information and communicating with the principal's health-care provider. This provision does not, however, confer on the designated person the authority to make health-care decisions for the principal. If the trigger for contingent powers is incapacity but the principal has not designated anyone to make the determination, or the person authorized is unable or unwilling to make the determination, the determination may be made by a physician or licensed psychologist, who must find that the principal's ability to manage property or business affairs is impaired, or by an attorney at law, judge, or appropriate governmental official, who must find that the principal is missing, detained, or unable to return to the United States.

The bases for termination of a power of attorney are covered in Section 110. In response to concerns expressed in the JEB survey, the Act provides as the default rule that authority granted to a principal's spouse is revoked upon the commencement of proceedings for legal separation, marital dissolution or annulment.

Sections 111 through 118 address matters related to the agent, including default rules for coagents and successor agents (Section 111), reimbursement and compensation (Section 112), an agent's acceptance of appointment (Section 113), and the agent's duties (Section 114). Section 115 provides that a principal may lower the standard of liability for agent conduct subject to a minimum level of accountability for actions taken dishonestly, with an improper motive, or with reckless indifference to the purposes of the power of attorney or the best interest of the principal. Section 116 sets out a comprehensive list of persons that may petition the court to review the agent's conduct and Section 117 addresses agent liability. An agent may resign by following the notice procedures described in Section 118.

Sections 119 and 120 are included in the Act to address the frequently reported problem of persons refusing to accept a power of attorney.

Section 119 protects persons that in good faith accept an acknowledged power of attorney without actual knowledge that the power of attorney is revoked, terminated, or invalid or that the agent is exceeding or improperly exercising the agent's powers. Subject to statutory exceptions, alternative Sections 120 impose liability for refusal to accept a power of attorney. Alternative A sanctions refusal of an acknowledged power of attorney and Alternative B sanctions only refusal of an acknowledged statutory form power of attorney.

Sections 121 through 123 address the relationship of the Act to other law. Section 121 clarifies that the Act is supplemented by the principles of common law and equity to the extent those principles are not displaced by a specific provision of the Act, and Section 122 further clarifies that the Act is not intended to supersede any law applicable to financial institutions or other entities. With respect to remedies, Section 123 provides that the remedies under the Act are not exclusive and do not abrogate any other cause of action or remedy that may be available under the law of the enacting jurisdiction.

Article 2 – Authority – The Act offers the drafting attorney enhanced flexibility whether drafting an individually tailored power of attorney or using the statutory form. Like the Uniform Statutory Form Power of Attorney Act, Sections 204 through 217 of the Act set forth detailed descriptions of authority relating to subjects such as "real property," "retirement plans," and "taxes," which a principal, pursuant to Section 202, may incorporate in full into the power of attorney either by a reference to the short descriptive term for the subject used in the Act or to the section number. Section 202 further states that a principal may modify in a power of attorney any authority incorporated by reference. The definitions in Article 2 also provide meaning for authority with respect to subjects enumerated on the optional statutory form in Article 3. Section 203 applies to all incorporated authority and grants of general authority, providing further detail on how the authority is to be construed.

Article 2 also addresses concerns about authority that might be used to dissipate the principal's property or alter the principal's estate plan. Section 201(a) lists specific categories of authority that cannot be implied from a grant of general authority, but which may be granted only through express language in the power of attorney. Section 201(b) contains a default rule prohibiting an agent that is not an ancestor, spouse, or descendant of the principal from creating in the agent or in a person to whom the agent owes a legal obligation of support an interest in the principal's property, whether by gift, right of survivorship, beneficiary designation, disclaimer, or otherwise.

Article 3 – Statutory Forms – The optional form in Article 3 is designed for use by lawyers as well as lay persons. It contains, in plain language, instructions to the principal and agent. Step-by-step prompts are given for designation of the agent and successor agents, and grant of general and specific authority. In the section of the form addressing general authority, the principal must initial the subjects over which the principal wishes to delegate general authority to the agent. In the section of the form addressing specific authority, the Section 201(a) categories of specific authority are listed, preceded by a warning to the principal about the potential consequences of granting such authority to an agent. The principal is instructed to initial only the specific categories of actions that the principal intends to authorize. Article 3 also contains a sample agent certification form.

Article 4 – Miscellaneous Provisions – The miscellaneous provisions in Article 4 clarify the relationship of the Act to other law and pre-existing powers of attorney. Enacting jurisdictions should repeal their existing power of attorney statutes, including, if applicable, the Uniform Durable Power of Attorney Act, The Uniform Statutory Form Power of Attorney Act, and Article 5, Part 5 of the Uniform Probate Code.

ARTICLE 1. GENERAL PROVISIONS

§101. Short title.

This [act] may be cited as the Uniform Power of Attorney Act.

§102. Definitions.

In this [act]:

(1) "Agent" means a person granted authority to act for a principal under a power of attorney, whether denominated an agent, attorney-in-fact, or otherwise. The term includes an original agent, coagent, successor agent, and a person to which an agent's authority is delegated.

(2) "Durable," with respect to a power of attorney, means not terminated by the principal's incapacity.

(3) "Electronic" means relating to technology having electrical, digital, magnetic, wireless, optical, electromagnetic, or similar capabilities.

(4) "Good faith" means honesty in fact.

(5) "Incapacity" means inability of an individual to manage property or business affairs because the individual:

(A) has an impairment in the ability to receive and evaluate information or make or communicate decisions even with the use of technological assistance; or

(B) is:

(i) missing;

(ii) detained, including incarcerated in a penal system; or

(iii) outside the United States and unable to return.

(6) "Person" means an individual, corporation, business trust, estate, trust, partnership, limited liability company, association, joint venture, public corporation, government or governmental subdivision, agency, or instrumentality, or any other legal or commercial entity.

(7) "Power of attorney" means a writing or other record that grants authority to an agent to act in the place of the principal, whether or not the term power of attorney is used.

(8) "Presently exercisable general power of appointment," with respect to property or a property interest subject to a power of appointment, means power exercisable at the time in question to vest absolute ownership in the principal individually, the principal's estate, the principal's creditors, or the creditors of the principal's estate. The term includes a power of appointment not exercisable until the occurrence of a specified event, the satisfaction of an ascertainable standard, or the passage of a specified period only after the occurrence of the specified event, the satisfaction of the ascertainable standard, or the passage of the specified period. The term does not include a power exercisable in a fiduciary capacity or only by will.

(9) "Principal" means an individual who grants authority to an agent in a power of attorney.

(10) "Property" means anything that may be the subject of ownership, whether real or personal, or legal or equitable, or any interest or right therein.

(11) "Record" means information that is inscribed on a tangible medium or that is stored in an electronic or other medium and is retrievable in perceivable form.

(12) "Sign" means, with present intent to authenticate or adopt a record:

(A) to execute or adopt a tangible symbol; or

(B) to attach to or logically associate with the record an electronic sound, symbol, or process.

(13) "State" means a state of the United States, the District of Columbia, Puerto Rico, the United States Virgin Islands, or any territory or insular possession subject to the jurisdiction of the United States.

(14) "Stocks and bonds" means stocks, bonds, mutual funds, and all other types of securities and financial instruments, whether held directly, indirectly, or in any other manner. The term does not include commodity futures contracts and call or put options on stocks or stock indexes.

Legislative Note: An enacting jurisdiction should review its respective guardianship, conservatorship, or other protective proceedings statutes and amend, if necessary for consistency, the definition of incapacity.

§103. Applicability.

This [act] applies to all powers of attorney except:

(1) a power to the extent it is coupled with an interest in the subject of the power, including a power given to or for the benefit of a creditor in connection with a credit transaction;

(2) a power to make health-care decisions;

(3) a proxy or other delegation to exercise voting rights or management rights with respect to an entity; and

(4) a power created on a form prescribed by a government or governmental subdivision, agency, or instrumentality for a governmental purpose.

§104. Power of attorney is durable.

A power of attorney created under this [act] is durable unless it expressly provides that it is terminated by the incapacity of the principal.

§105. Execution of power of attorney.

A power of attorney must be signed by the principal or in the principal's conscious presence by another individual directed by the principal to sign the principal's name on the power of attorney. A signature on a power of attorney is presumed to be genuine if the principal acknowledges the signature before a notary public or other individual authorized by law to take acknowledgments.

§106. Validity of power of attorney.

(a) A power of attorney executed in this state on or after [the effective date of this [act]] is valid if its execution complies with Section 105.

(b) A power of attorney executed in this state before [the effective date of this [act]] is valid if its execution complied with the law of this state as it existed at the time of execution.

(c) A power of attorney executed other than in this state is valid in this state if, when the power of attorney was executed, the execution complied with:

(1) the law of the jurisdiction that determines the meaning and effect of the power of attorney pursuant to Section 107; or

(2) the requirements for a military power of attorney pursuant to 10 U.S.C. Section 1044b [, as amended].

(d) Except as otherwise provided by statute other than this [act], a photocopy or electronically transmitted copy of an original power of attorney has the same effect as the original.

[Legislative Note: The brackets in subsections (a) and (b) of this section indicate where an enacting jurisdiction may elect to insert the actual effective date of the Act.]

§107. Meaning and effect of power of attorney.

The meaning and effect of a power of attorney is determined by the law of the jurisdiction indicated in the power of attorney and, in the absence of an indication of jurisdiction, by the law of the jurisdiction in which the power of attorney was executed.

§108. Nomination of [conservator or guardian]; relation of agent to court-appointed fiduciary.

(a) In a power of attorney, a principal may nominate a [conservator or guardian] of the principal's estate or [guardian] of the principal's person for consideration by the court if protective proceedings for the principal's estate or person are begun after the principal executes the power of attorney. [Except for good cause shown or disqualification, the court shall make its appointment in accordance with the principal's most recent nomination.]

(b) If, after a principal executes a power of attorney, a court appoints a [conservator or guardian] of the principal's estate or other fiduciary charged with the management of some or all of the principal's property, the agent is accountable to the fiduciary as well as to the principal. [The power of attorney is not terminated and the agent's authority continues unless limited, suspended, or terminated by the court.]

[Legislative Note: The brackets in this section indicate areas where an enacting jurisdiction should reference its respective guardianship, conservatorship, or other protective proceedings statutes and amend, if necessary for consistency, the terminology and substance of the bracketed language.]

§109. When power of attorney effective.

(a) A power of attorney is effective when executed unless the principal provides in the power of attorney that it becomes effective at a future date or upon the occurrence of a future event or contingency.

(b) If a power of attorney becomes effective upon the occurrence of a future event or contingency, the principal, in the power of attorney, may authorize one or more persons to determine in a writing or other record that the event or contingency has occurred.

(c) If a power of attorney becomes effective upon the principal's incapacity and the principal has not authorized a person to determine whether the principal is incapacitated, or the person authorized is unable or unwilling to make the determination, the power of attorney becomes effective upon a determination in a writing or other record by:

(1) a physician [or licensed psychologist] that the principal is incapacitated within the meaning of Section 102(5)(A); or

(2) an attorney at law, a judge, or an appropriate governmental official that the principal is incapacitated within the meaning of Section 102(5)(B).

(d) A person authorized by the principal in the power of attorney to determine that the principal is incapacitated may act as the principal's personal representative pursuant to the Health Insurance Portability and Accountability Act, Sections 1171 through 1179 of the Social Security Act, 42 U.S.C. Section 1320d, [as amended,] and applicable regulations, to obtain access to the principal's health-care information and communicate with the principal's health-care provider.

[Legislative Note: The phrase "or licensed psychologist" is bracketed in subsection (c)(1) to indicate where an enacting jurisdiction should insert the appropriate designation for the mental health professional or professionals in that jurisdiction who are qualified to make capacity determinations. An enacting jurisdiction should also review its respective guardianship, conservatorship, or other protective proceedings statutes and amend, if necessary for consistency, the definition of incapacity.]

§110. Termination of power of attorney or agent's authority.

(a) A power of attorney terminates when:

(1) the principal dies;

(2) the principal becomes incapacitated, if the power of attorney is not durable;

(3) the principal revokes the power of attorney;

(4) the power of attorney provides that it terminates;

(5) the purpose of the power of attorney is accomplished; or

(6) the principal revokes the agent's authority or the agent dies, becomes incapacitated, or resigns, and the power of attorney does not provide for another agent to act under the power of attorney.

(b) An agent's authority terminates when:

(1) the principal revokes the authority;

(2) the agent dies, becomes incapacitated, or resigns;

(3) an action is filed for the [dissolution] or annulment of the agent's marriage to the principal

or their legal separation, unless the power of attorney otherwise provides; or

(4) the power of attorney terminates.

(c) Unless the power of attorney otherwise provides, an agent's authority is exercisable until the authority terminates under subsection (b), notwithstanding a lapse of time since the execution of the power of attorney.

(d) Termination of an agent's authority or of a power of attorney is not effective as to the agent or another person that, without actual knowledge of the termination, acts in good faith under the power of attorney. An act so performed, unless otherwise invalid or unenforceable, binds the principal and the principal's successors in interest.

(e) Incapacity of the principal of a power of attorney that is not durable does not revoke or terminate the power of attorney as to an agent or other person that, without actual knowledge of the incapacity, acts in good faith under the power of attorney. An act so performed, unless otherwise invalid or unenforceable, binds the principal and the principal's successors in interest.

(f) The execution of a power of attorney does not revoke a power of attorney previously executed by the principal unless the subsequent power of attorney provides that the previous power of attorney is revoked or that all other powers of attorney are revoked.

[Legislative Note: The word "dissolution" is bracketed in subsection (b)(3) to indicate where an enacting jurisdiction should insert that jurisdiction's term for divorce or marital dissolution.]

§111. Coagents and successor agents.

(a) A principal may designate two or more persons to act as coagents. Unless the power of attorney otherwise provides, each coagent may exercise its authority independently.

(b) A principal may designate one or more successor agents to act if an agent resigns, dies, becomes incapacitated, is not qualified to serve, or declines to serve. A principal may grant authority to designate one or more successor agents to an agent or other person designated by name, office, or function. Unless the power of attorney otherwise provides, a successor agent:

(1) has the same authority as that granted to the original agent; and

(2) may not act until all predecessor agents have resigned, died, become incapacitated, are no longer qualified to serve, or have declined to serve.

(c) Except as otherwise provided in the power of attorney and subsection (d), an agent that does not participate in or conceal a breach of fiduciary duty committed by another agent, including a predecessor agent, is not liable for the actions of the other agent.

(d) An agent that has actual knowledge of a breach or imminent breach of fiduciary duty by another agent shall notify the principal and, if the principal is incapacitated, take any action reasonably appropriate in the circumstances to safeguard the principal's best interest. An agent that fails to notify the principal or take action as required by this subsection is liable for the reasonably foreseeable damages that could have been avoided if the agent had notified the principal or taken such action.

§112. Reimbursement and compensation of agent.

Unless the power of attorney otherwise provides, an agent is entitled to reimbursement of expenses reasonably incurred on behalf of the principal and to compensation that is reasonable under the circumstances.

§113. Agent's acceptance.

Except as otherwise provided in the power of attorney, a person accepts appointment as an agent under a power of attorney by exercising authority or performing duties as an agent or by any other assertion or conduct indicating acceptance.

§114. Agent's duties.

(a) Notwithstanding provisions in the power of attorney, an agent that has accepted appointment shall:

(1) act in accordance with the principal's reasonable expectations to the extent actually known by the agent and, otherwise, in the principal's best interest;

(2) act in good faith; and

(3) act only within the scope of authority granted in the power of attorney.

(b) Except as otherwise provided in the power of attorney, an agent that has accepted appointment shall:

(1) act loyally for the principal's benefit;

(2) act so as not to create a conflict of interest that impairs the agent's ability to act impartially in the principal's best interest;

(3) act with the care, competence, and diligence ordinarily exercised by agents in similar circumstances;

(4) keep a record of all receipts, disbursements, and transactions made on behalf of the principal;

(5) cooperate with a person that has authority to make health-care decisions for the principal to carry out the principal's reasonable expectations to the extent actually known by the agent and, otherwise, act in the principal's best interest; and

(6) attempt to preserve the principal's estate plan, to the extent actually known by the agent, if preserving the plan is consistent with the

principal's best interest based on all relevant factors, including:

(A) the value and nature of the principal's property;

(B) the principal's foreseeable obligations and need for maintenance;

(C) minimization of taxes, including income, estate, inheritance, generation-skipping transfer, and gift taxes; and

(D) eligibility for a benefit, a program, or assistance under a statute or regulation.

(c) An agent that acts in good faith is not liable to any beneficiary of the principal's estate plan for failure to preserve the plan.

(d) An agent that acts with care, competence, and diligence for the best interest of the principal is not liable solely because the agent also benefits from the act or has an individual or conflicting interest in relation to the property or affairs of the principal.

(e) If an agent is selected by the principal because of special skills or expertise possessed by the agent or in reliance on the agent's representation that the agent has special skills or expertise, the special skills or expertise must be considered in determining whether the agent has acted with care, competence, and diligence under the circumstances.

(f) Absent a breach of duty to the principal, an agent is not liable if the value of the principal's property declines.

(g) An agent that exercises authority to delegate to another person the authority granted by the principal or that engages another person on behalf of the principal is not liable for an act, error of judgment, or default of that person if the agent exercises care, competence, and diligence in selecting and monitoring the person.

(h) Except as otherwise provided in the power of attorney, an agent is not required to disclose receipts, disbursements, or transactions conducted on behalf of the principal unless ordered by a court or requested by the principal, a guardian, a conservator, another fiduciary acting for the principal, a governmental agency having authority to protect the welfare of the principal, or, upon the death of the principal, by the personal representative or successor in interest of the principal's estate. If so requested, within 30 days the agent shall comply with the request or provide a writing or other record substantiating why additional time is needed and shall comply with the request within an additional 30 days.

§115. Exoneration of agent.

A provision in a power of attorney relieving an agent of liability for breach of duty is binding on the principal and the principal's successors in interest except to the extent the provision:

(1) relieves the agent of liability for breach of duty committed dishonestly, with an improper motive, or with reckless indifference to the purposes of the power of attorney or the best interest of the principal; or

(2) was inserted as a result of an abuse of a confidential or fiduciary relationship with the principal.

§116. Judicial relief.

(a) The following persons may petition a court to construe a power of attorney or review the agent's conduct, and grant appropriate relief:

(1) the principal or the agent;

(2) a guardian, conservator, or other fiduciary acting for the principal;

(3) a person authorized to make health-care decisions for the principal;

(4) the principal's spouse, parent, or descendant;

(5) an individual who would qualify as a presumptive heir of the principal;

(6) a person named as a beneficiary to receive any property, benefit, or contractual right on the principal's death or as a beneficiary of a trust created by or for the principal that has a financial interest in the principal's estate;

(7) a governmental agency having regulatory authority to protect the welfare of the principal;

(8) the principal's caregiver or another person that demonstrates sufficient interest in the principal's welfare; and

(9) a person asked to accept the power of attorney.

(b) Upon motion by the principal, the court shall dismiss a petition filed under this section, unless the court finds that the principal lacks capacity to revoke the agent's authority or the power of attorney.

§117. Agent's liability.

An agent that violates this [act] is liable to the principal or the principal's successors in interest for the amount required to:

(1) restore the value of the principal's property to what it would have been had the violation not occurred; and

(2) reimburse the principal or the principal's successors in interest for the attorney's fees and costs paid on the agent's behalf.

§118. Agent's resignation; notice.

Unless the power of attorney provides a different method for an agent's resignation, an agent may resign by giving notice to the principal and, if the principal is incapacitated:

(1) to the [conservator or guardian], if one has been appointed for the principal, and a coagent or successor agent; or

(2) if there is no person described in paragraph (1), to:

(A) the principal's caregiver;

(B) another person reasonably believed by the agent to have sufficient interest in the principal's welfare; or

(C) a governmental agency having authority to protect the welfare of the principal.

[Legislative Note: The brackets in this section indicate where the enacting jurisdiction should review its respective guardianship, conservatorship, or other protective proceedings statutes and amend, if necessary for consistency, the bracketed language.]

§119. Acceptance of and reliance upon acknowledged power of attorney.

(a) For purposes of this section and Section 120, "acknowledged" means purportedly verified before a notary public or other individual authorized to take acknowledgements.

(b) A person that in good faith accepts an acknowledged power of attorney without actual knowledge that the signature is not genuine may rely upon the presumption under Section 105 that the signature is genuine.

(c) A person that in good faith accepts an acknowledged power of attorney without actual knowledge that the power of attorney is void, invalid, or terminated, that the purported agent's authority is void, invalid, or terminated, or that the agent is exceeding or improperly exercising the agent's authority may rely upon the power of attorney as if the power of attorney were genuine, valid and still in effect, the agent's authority were genuine, valid and still in effect, and the agent had not exceeded and had properly exercised the authority.

(d) A person that is asked to accept an acknowledged power of attorney may request, and rely upon, without further investigation:

(1) an agent's certification under penalty of perjury of any factual matter concerning the principal, agent, or power of attorney;

(2) an English translation of the power of attorney if the power of attorney contains, in whole or in part, language other than English; and

(3) an opinion of counsel as to any matter of law concerning the power of attorney if the person making the request provides in a writing or other record the reason for the request.

(e) An English translation or an opinion of counsel requested under this section must be provided at the principal's expense unless the request is made more than seven business days after the power of attorney is presented for acceptance.

(f) For purposes of this section and Section 120, a person that conducts activities through employees is without actual knowledge of a fact relating to a power of attorney, a principal, or an agent if the employee conducting the transaction involving the power of attorney is without actual knowledge of the fact.

Alternative A

§120. Liability for refusal to accept acknowledged power of attorney.

(a) Except as otherwise provided in subsection (b):

(1) a person shall either accept an acknowledged power of attorney or request a certification, a translation, or an opinion of counsel under Section 119(d) no later than seven business days after presentation of the power of attorney for acceptance;

(2) if a person requests a certification, a translation, or an opinion of counsel under Section 119(d), the person shall accept the power of attorney no later than five business days after receipt of the certification, translation, or opinion of counsel; and

(3) a person may not require an additional or different form of power of attorney for authority granted in the power of attorney presented.

(b) A person is not required to accept an acknowledged power of attorney if:

(1) the person is not otherwise required to engage in a transaction with the principal in the same circumstances;

(2) engaging in a transaction with the agent or the principal in the same circumstances would be inconsistent with federal law;

(3) the person has actual knowledge of the termination of the agent's authority or of the power of attorney before exercise of the power;

(4) a request for a certification, a translation, or an opinion of counsel under Section 119(d) is refused;

(5) the person in good faith believes that the power is not valid or that the agent does not have the authority to perform the act requested, whether or not a certification, a translation, or an opinion of counsel under Section 119(d) has been requested or provided; or

(6) the person makes, or has actual knowledge that another person has made, a report to the [local adult protective services office] stating a good faith belief that the principal may be subject to physical or financial abuse, neglect, exploitation, or abandonment by the agent or a person acting for or with the agent.

(c) A person that refuses in violation of this section to accept an acknowledged power of attorney is subject to:

(1) a court order mandating acceptance of the power of attorney; and

(2) liability for reasonable attorney's fees and costs incurred in any action or proceeding that

confirms the validity of the power of attorney or mandates acceptance of the power of attorney.

[Legislative Note: Section 120 enumerates the bases for legitimate refusals of a power of attorney as well as sanctions for refusals that violate the Act. Alternatives A and B are identical except that Alternative B applies only to acknowledged statutory form powers of attorney while Alternative A applies to all acknowledged powers of attorney.

Under both alternatives, the phrase "local adult protective services office" is bracketed to indicate where an enacting jurisdiction should insert the appropriate designation for the governmental agency with regulatory authority to protect the welfare of the principal]

Alternative B

§120. Liability for refusal to accept acknowledged statutory form power of attorney.

(a) In this section, "statutory form power of attorney" means a power of attorney substantially in the form provided in Section 301 or that meets the requirements for a military power of attorney pursuant to 10 U.S.C. Section 1044b [, as amended].

(b) Except as otherwise provided in subsection (c):

(1) a person shall either accept an acknowledged statutory form power of attorney or request a certification, a translation, or an opinion of counsel under Section 119(d) no later than seven business days after presentation of the power of attorney for acceptance;

(2) if a person requests a certification, a translation, or an opinion of counsel under Section 119(d), the person shall accept the statutory form power of attorney no later than five business days after receipt of the certification, translation, or opinion of counsel; and

(3) a person may not require an additional or different form of power of attorney for authority granted in the statutory form power of attorney presented.

(c) A person is not required to accept an acknowledged statutory form power of attorney if:

(1) the person is not otherwise required to engage in a transaction with the principal in the same circumstances;

(2) engaging in a transaction with the agent or the principal in the same circumstances would be inconsistent with federal law;

(3) the person has actual knowledge of the termination of the agent's authority or of the power of attorney before exercise of the power;

(4) a request for a certification, a translation, or an opinion of counsel under Section 119(d) is refused;

(5) the person in good faith believes that the power is not valid or that the agent does not have the authority to perform the act requested, whether or not a certification, a translation, or an opinion of counsel under Section 119(d) has been requested or provided; or

(6) the person makes, or has actual knowledge that another person has made, a report to the [local adult protective services office] stating a good faith belief that the principal may be subject to physical or financial abuse, neglect, exploitation, or abandonment by the agent or a person acting for or with the agent.

(d) A person that refuses in violation of this section to accept an acknowledged statutory form power of attorney is subject to:

(1) a court order mandating acceptance of the power of attorney; and

(2) liability for reasonable attorney's fees and costs incurred in any action or proceeding that confirms the validity of the power of attorney or mandates acceptance of the power of attorney.

[Legislative Note: Section 120 enumerates the bases for legitimate refusals of a power of attorney as well as sanctions for refusals that violate the Act. Alternatives A and B are identical except that Alternative B applies only to acknowledged statutory form powers of attorney while Alternative A applies to all acknowledged powers of attorney.

Under both alternatives, the phrase "local adult protective services office" is bracketed to indicate where an enacting jurisdiction should insert the appropriate designation for the governmental agency with regulatory authority to protect the welfare of the principal.]

§121. Principles of law and equity.

Unless displaced by a provision of this [act], the principles of law and equity supplement this [act].

§122. Laws applicable to financial institutions and entities.

This [act] does not supersede any other law applicable to financial institutions or other entities, and the other law controls if inconsistent with this [act].

§123. Remedies under other law.

The remedies under this [act] are not exclusive and do not abrogate any right or remedy under the law of this state other than this [act].

ARTICLE 2. AUTHORITY

§201. Authority that requires specific grant; grant of general authority.

(a) An agent under a power of attorney may do the following on behalf of the principal or with the principal's property only if the power of attorney expressly grants the agent the authority and exercise of the authority is not otherwise prohibited by another agreement or instrument to which the authority or property is subject:

(1) create, amend, revoke, or terminate an inter vivos trust;

(2) make a gift;

(3) create or change rights of survivorship;

(4) create or change a beneficiary designation;

(5) delegate authority granted under the power of attorney;

(6) waive the principal's right to be a beneficiary of a joint and survivor annuity, including a survivor benefit under a retirement plan; [or]

(7) exercise fiduciary powers that the principal has authority to delegate[; or

(8) disclaim property, including a power of appointment].

(b) Notwithstanding a grant of authority to do an act described in subsection (a), unless the power of attorney otherwise provides, an agent that is not an ancestor, spouse, or descendant of the principal, may not exercise authority under a power of attorney to create in the agent, or in an individual to whom the agent owes a legal obligation of support, an interest in the principal's property, whether by gift, right of survivorship, beneficiary designation, disclaimer, or otherwise.

(c) Subject to subsections (a), (b), (d), and (e), if a power of attorney grants to an agent authority to do all acts that a principal could do, the agent has the general authority described in Sections 204 through 216.

(d) Unless the power of attorney otherwise provides, a grant of authority to make a gift is subject to Section 217.

(e) Subject to subsections (a), (b), and (d), if the subjects over which authority is granted in a power of attorney are similar or overlap, the broadest authority controls.

(f) Authority granted in a power of attorney is exercisable with respect to property that the principal has when the power of attorney is executed or acquires later, whether or not the property is located in this state and whether or not the authority is exercised or the power of attorney is executed in this state.

(g) An act performed by an agent pursuant to a power of attorney has the same effect and inures to the benefit of and binds the principal and the principal's successors in interest as if the principal had performed the act.

[Legislative Note: The phrase "or disclaim property, including a power of appointment" is in brackets in subsection (a) and should be deleted if under the law of the enacting jurisdiction a fiduciary has authority to disclaim an interest in, or power over, property and the jurisdiction does not wish to restrict that authority by the Uniform Power of Attorney Act. See Unif. Disclaimer of Property Interests Acts § 5(b) (2006) (providing, "[e]xcept to the extent a fiduciary's right to disclaim is expressly restricted or limited by another statute of this State or by the instrument creating the fiduciary relationship, a fiduciary may disclaim, in whole or part, any interest in or power over property, including a power of appointment . . . ."). See also Section 301 Legislative Note.]

§202. Incorporation of authority.

(a) An agent has authority described in this [article] if the power of attorney refers to general authority with respect to the descriptive term for the subjects stated in Sections 204 through 217 or cites the section in which the authority is described.

(b) A reference in a power of attorney to general authority with respect to the descriptive term for a subject in Sections 204 through 217 or a citation to a section of Sections 204 through 217 incorporates the entire section as if it were set out in full in the power of attorney.

(c) A principal may modify authority incorporated by reference.

§203. Construction of authority generally.

Except as otherwise provided in the power of attorney, by executing a power of attorney that incorporates by reference a subject described in Sections 204 through 217 or that grants to an agent authority to do all acts that a principal could do pursuant to Section 201(c), a principal authorizes the agent, with respect to that subject, to:

(1) demand, receive, and obtain by litigation or otherwise, money or another thing of value to which the principal is, may become, or claims to be entitled, and conserve, invest, disburse, or use anything so received or obtained for the purposes intended;

(2) contract in any manner with any person, on terms agreeable to the agent, to accomplish a purpose of a transaction and perform, rescind, cancel, terminate, reform, restate, release, or modify the contract or another contract made by or on behalf of the principal;

(3) execute, acknowledge, seal, deliver, file, or record any instrument or communication the agent considers desirable to accomplish a purpose of a

transaction, including creating at any time a schedule listing some or all of the principal's property and attaching it to the power of attorney;

(4) initiate, participate in, submit to alternative dispute resolution, settle, oppose, or propose or accept a compromise with respect to a claim existing in favor of or against the principal or intervene in litigation relating to the claim;

(5) seek on the principal's behalf the assistance of a court or other governmental agency to carry out an act authorized in the power of attorney;

(6) engage, compensate, and discharge an attorney, accountant, discretionary investment manager, expert witness, or other advisor;

(7) prepare, execute, and file a record, report, or other document to safeguard or promote the principal's interest under a statute or regulation;

(8) communicate with any representative or employee of a government or governmental subdivision, agency, or instrumentality, on behalf of the principal;

(9) access communications intended for, and communicate on behalf of the principal, whether by mail, electronic transmission, telephone, or other means; and

(10) do any lawful act with respect to the subject and all property related to the subject.

§204. Real property.

Unless the power of attorney otherwise provides, language in a power of attorney granting general authority with respect to real property authorizes the agent to:

(1) demand, buy, lease, receive, accept as a gift or as security for an extension of credit, or otherwise acquire or reject an interest in real property or a right incident to real property;

(2) sell; exchange; convey with or without covenants, representations, or warranties; quitclaim; release; surrender; retain title for security; encumber; partition; consent to partitioning; subject to an easement or covenant; subdivide; apply for zoning or other governmental permits; plat or consent to platting; develop; grant an option concerning; lease; sublease; contribute to an entity in exchange for an interest in that entity; or otherwise grant or dispose of an interest in real property or a right incident to real property;

(3) pledge or mortgage an interest in real property or right incident to real property as security to borrow money or pay, renew, or extend the time of payment of a debt of the principal or a debt guaranteed by the principal;

(4) release, assign, satisfy, or enforce by litigation or otherwise a mortgage, deed of trust, conditional sale contract, encumbrance, lien, or other claim to real property which exists or is asserted;

(5) manage or conserve an interest in real property or a right incident to real property owned or claimed to be owned by the principal, including:

(A) insuring against liability or casualty or other loss;

(B) obtaining or regaining possession of or protecting the interest or right by litigation or otherwise;

(C) paying, assessing, compromising, or contesting taxes or assessments or applying for and receiving refunds in connection with them; and

(D) purchasing supplies, hiring assistance or labor, and making repairs or alterations to the real property;

(6) use, develop, alter, replace, remove, erect, or install structures or other improvements upon real property in or incident to which the principal has, or claims to have, an interest or right;

(7) participate in a reorganization with respect to real property or an entity that owns an interest in or right incident to real property and receive, and hold, and act with respect to stocks and bonds or other property received in a plan of reorganization, including:

(A) selling or otherwise disposing of them;

(B) exercising or selling an option, right of conversion, or similar right with respect to them; and

(C) exercising any voting rights in person or by proxy;

(8) change the form of title of an interest in or right incident to real property; and

(9) dedicate to public use, with or without consideration, easements or other real property in which the principal has, or claims to have, an interest.

§205. Tangible personal property.

Unless the power of attorney otherwise provides, language in a power of attorney granting general authority with respect to tangible personal property authorizes the agent to:

(1) demand, buy, receive, accept as a gift or as security for an extension of credit, or otherwise acquire or reject ownership or possession of tangible personal property or an interest in tangible personal property;

(2) sell; exchange; convey with or without covenants, representations, or warranties; quitclaim; release; surrender; create a security interest in; grant options concerning; lease; sublease; or, otherwise dispose of tangible personal property or an interest in tangible personal property;

(3) grant a security interest in tangible personal property or an interest in tangible personal property as security to borrow money or pay, renew, or extend the time of payment of a debt of the principal or a debt guaranteed by the principal;

(4) release, assign, satisfy, or enforce by litigation or otherwise, a security interest, lien, or other claim on behalf of the principal, with respect to tangible personal property or an interest in tangible personal property;

(5) manage or conserve tangible personal property or an interest in tangible personal property on behalf of the principal, including:

(A) insuring against liability or casualty or other loss;

(B) obtaining or regaining possession of or protecting the property or interest, by litigation or otherwise;

(C) paying, assessing, compromising, or contesting taxes or assessments or applying for and receiving refunds in connection with taxes or assessments;

(D) moving the property from place to place;

(E) storing the property for hire or on a gratuitous bailment; and

(F) using and making repairs, alterations, or improvements to the property; and

(6) change the form of title of an interest in tangible personal property.

§206. Stocks and bonds.

Unless the power of attorney otherwise provides, language in a power of attorney granting general authority with respect to stocks and bonds authorizes the agent to:

(1) buy, sell, and exchange stocks and bonds;

(2) establish, continue, modify, or terminate an account with respect to stocks and bonds;

(3) pledge stocks and bonds as security to borrow, pay, renew, or extend the time of payment of a debt of the principal;

(4) receive certificates and other evidences of ownership with respect to stocks and bonds; and

(5) exercise voting rights with respect to stocks and bonds in person or by proxy, enter into voting trusts, and consent to limitations on the right to vote.

§207. Commodities and options.

Unless the power of attorney otherwise provides, language in a power of attorney granting general authority with respect to commodities and options authorizes the agent to:

(1) buy, sell, exchange, assign, settle, and exercise commodity futures contracts and call or put options on stocks or stock indexes traded on a regulated option exchange; and

(2) establish, continue, modify, and terminate option accounts.

§208. Banks and other financial institutions.

Unless the power of attorney otherwise provides, language in a power of attorney granting general authority with respect to banks and other financial institutions authorizes the agent to:

(1) continue, modify, and terminate an account or other banking arrangement made by or on behalf of the principal;

(2) establish, modify, and terminate an account or other banking arrangement with a bank, trust company, savings and loan association, credit union, thrift company, brokerage firm, or other financial institution selected by the agent;

(3) contract for services available from a financial institution, including renting a safe deposit box or space in a vault;

(4) withdraw, by check, order, electronic funds transfer, or otherwise, money or property of the principal deposited with or left in the custody of a financial institution;

(5) receive statements of account, vouchers, notices, and similar documents from a financial institution and act with respect to them;

(6) enter a safe deposit box or vault and withdraw or add to the contents;

(7) borrow money and pledge as security personal property of the principal necessary to borrow money or pay, renew, or extend the time of payment of a debt of the principal or a debt guaranteed by the principal;

(8) make, assign, draw, endorse, discount, guarantee, and negotiate promissory notes, checks, drafts, and other negotiable or nonnegotiable paper of the principal or payable to the principal or the principal's order, transfer money, receive the cash or other proceeds of those transactions, and accept a draft drawn by a person upon the principal and pay it when due;

(9) receive for the principal and act upon a sight draft, warehouse receipt, or other document of title whether tangible or electronic, or other negotiable or nonnegotiable instrument;

(10) apply for, receive, and use letters of credit, credit and debit cards, electronic transaction authorizations, and traveler's checks from a financial institution and give an indemnity or other agreement in connection with letters of credit; and

(11) consent to an extension of the time of payment with respect to commercial paper or a financial transaction with a financial institution.

§209. Operation of entity or business.

Subject to the terms of a document or an agreement governing an entity or an entity ownership interest, and unless the power of attorney otherwise provides, language in a power of attorney granting general authority with respect to operation of an entity or business authorizes the agent to:

(1) operate, buy, sell, enlarge, reduce, or terminate an ownership interest;

(2) perform a duty or discharge a liability and exercise in person or by proxy a right, power,

privilege, or option that the principal has, may have, or claims to have;

(3) enforce the terms of an ownership agreement;

(4) initiate, participate in, submit to alternative dispute resolution, settle, oppose, or propose or accept a compromise with respect to litigation to which the principal is a party because of an ownership interest;

(5) exercise in person or by proxy, or enforce by litigation or otherwise, a right, power, privilege, or option the principal has or claims to have as the holder of stocks and bonds;

(6) initiate, participate in, submit to alternative dispute resolution, settle, oppose, or propose or accept a compromise with respect to litigation to which the principal is a party concerning stocks and bonds;

(7) with respect to an entity or business owned solely by the principal:

(A) continue, modify, renegotiate, extend, and terminate a contract made by or on behalf of the principal with respect to the entity or business before execution of the power of attorney;

(B) determine:

(i) the location of its operation;

(ii) the nature and extent of its business;

(iii) the methods of manufacturing, selling, merchandising, financing, accounting, and advertising employed in its operation;

(iv) the amount and types of insurance carried; and

(v) the mode of engaging, compensating, and dealing with its employees and accountants, attorneys, or other advisors;

(C) change the name or form of organization under which the entity or business is operated and enter into an ownership agreement with other persons to take over all or part of the operation of the entity or business; and

(D) demand and receive money due or claimed by the principal or on the principal's behalf in the operation of the entity or business and control and disburse the money in the operation of the entity or business;

(8) put additional capital into an entity or business in which the principal has an interest;

(9) join in a plan of reorganization, consolidation, conversion, domestication, or merger of the entity or business;

(10) sell or liquidate all or part of an entity or business;

(11) establish the value of an entity or business under a buy-out agreement to which the principal is a party;

(12) prepare, sign, file, and deliver reports, compilations of information, returns, or other papers with respect to an entity or business and make related payments; and

(13) pay, compromise, or contest taxes, assessments, fines, or penalties and perform any other act to protect the principal from illegal or unnecessary taxation, assessments, fines, or penalties, with respect to an entity or business, including attempts to recover, in any manner permitted by law, money paid before or after the execution of the power of attorney.

§210. Insurance and annuities.

Unless the power of attorney otherwise provides, language in a power of attorney granting general authority with respect to insurance and annuities authorizes the agent to:

(1) continue, pay the premium or make a contribution on, modify, exchange, rescind, release, or terminate a contract procured by or on behalf of the principal which insures or provides an annuity to either the principal or another person, whether or not the principal is a beneficiary under the contract;

(2) procure new, different, and additional contracts of insurance and annuities for the principal and the principal's spouse, children, and other dependents, and select the amount, type of insurance or annuity, and mode of payment;

(3) pay the premium or make a contribution on, modify, exchange, rescind, release, or terminate a contract of insurance or annuity procured by the agent;

(4) apply for and receive a loan secured by a contract of insurance or annuity;

(5) surrender and receive the cash surrender value on a contract of insurance or annuity;

(6) exercise an election;

(7) exercise investment powers available under a contract of insurance or annuity;

(8) change the manner of paying premiums on a contract of insurance or annuity;

(9) change or convert the type of insurance or annuity with respect to which the principal has or claims to have authority described in this section;

(10) apply for and procure a benefit or assistance under a statute or regulation to guarantee or pay premiums of a contract of insurance on the life of the principal;

(11) collect, sell, assign, hypothecate, borrow against, or pledge the interest of the principal in a contract of insurance or annuity;

(12) select the form and timing of the payment of proceeds from a contract of insurance or annuity; and

(13) pay, from proceeds or otherwise, compromise or contest, and apply for refunds in connection with, a tax or assessment levied by a taxing authority with respect to a contract of insurance or annuity or its proceeds or liability accruing by reason of the tax or assessment.

§211. Estates, trusts, and other beneficial interests.

(a) In this section, "estates, trusts, and other beneficial interests" means a trust, probate estate, guardianship, conservatorship, escrow, or custodianship or a fund from which the principal is, may become, or claims to be, entitled to a share or payment.

(b) Unless the power of attorney otherwise provides, language in a power of attorney granting general authority with respect to estates, trusts, and other beneficial interests authorizes the agent to:

(1) accept, receive, receipt for, sell, assign, pledge, or exchange a share in or payment from the fund;

(2) demand or obtain money or another thing of value to which the principal is, may become, or claims to be, entitled by reason of the fund, by litigation or otherwise;

(3) exercise for the benefit of the principal a presently exercisable general power of appointment held by the principal;

(4) initiate, participate in, submit to alternative dispute resolution, settle, oppose, or propose or accept a compromise with respect to litigation to ascertain the meaning, validity, or effect of a deed, will, declaration of trust, or other instrument or transaction affecting the interest of the principal;

(5) initiate, participate in, submit to alternative dispute resolution, settle, oppose, or propose or accept a compromise with respect to litigation to remove, substitute, or surcharge a fiduciary;

(6) conserve, invest, disburse, or use anything received for an authorized purpose; [and]

(7) transfer an interest of the principal in real property, stocks and bonds, accounts with financial institutions or securities intermediaries, insurance, annuities, and other property to the trustee of a revocable trust created by the principal as settlor [; and

(8) reject, renounce, disclaim, release, or consent to a reduction in or modification of a share in or payment from the fund].

§212. Claims and litigation.

Unless the power of attorney otherwise provides, language in a power of attorney granting general authority with respect to claims and litigation authorizes the agent to:

(1) assert and maintain before. a court or administrative agency a claim, claim for relief, cause of action, counterclaim, offset, recoupment, or defense, including an action to recover property or other thing of value, recover damages sustained by the principal, eliminate or modify tax liability, or seek an injunction, specific performance, or other relief;

(2) bring an action to determine adverse claims or intervene or otherwise participate in litigation;

(3) seek an attachment, garnishment, order of arrest, or other preliminary, provisional, or intermediate relief and use an available procedure to effect or satisfy a judgment, order, or decree;

(4) make or accept a tender, offer of judgment, or admission of facts, submit a controversy on an agreed statement of facts, consent to examination, and bind the principal in litigation;

(5) submit to alternative dispute resolution, settle, and propose or accept a compromise;

(6) waive the issuance and service of process upon the principal, accept service of process, appear for the principal, designate persons upon which process directed to the principal may be served, execute and file or deliver stipulations on the principal's behalf, verify pleadings, seek appellate review, procure and give surety and indemnity bonds, contract and pay for the preparation and printing of records and briefs, receive, execute, and file or deliver a consent, waiver, release, confession of judgment, satisfaction of judgment, notice, agreement, or other instrument in connection with the prosecution, settlement, or defense of a claim or litigation;

(7) act for the principal with respect to bankruptcy or insolvency, whether voluntary or involuntary, concerning the principal or some other person, or with respect to a reorganization, receivership, or application for the appointment of a receiver or trustee which affects an interest of the principal in property or other thing of value;

(8) pay a judgment, award, or order against the principal or a settlement made in connection with a claim or litigation; and

(9) receive money or other thing of value paid in settlement of or as proceeds of a claim or litigation.

§213. Personal and family maintenance.

(a) Unless the power of attorney otherwise provides, language in a power of attorney granting general authority with respect to personal and family maintenance authorizes the agent to:

(1) perform the acts necessary to maintain the customary standard of living of the principal, the principal's spouse, and the following individuals, whether living when the power of attorney is executed or later born:

(A) the principal's children;

(B) other individuals legally entitled to be supported by the principal; and

(C) the individuals whom the principal has customarily supported or indicated the intent to support;

(2) make periodic payments of child support and other family maintenance required by a court or governmental agency or an agreement to which the principal is a party;

(3) provide living quarters for the individuals described in paragraph (1) by:

(A) purchase, lease, or other contract; or

(B) paying the operating costs, including interest, amortization payments, repairs, improvements, and taxes, for premises owned by the principal or occupied by those individuals;

(4) provide normal domestic help, usual vacations and travel expenses, and funds for shelter, clothing, food, appropriate education, including postsecondary and vocational education, and other current living costs for the individuals described in paragraph (1);

(5) pay expenses for necessary health care and custodial care on behalf of the individuals described in paragraph (1);

(6) act as the principal's personal representative pursuant to the Health Insurance Portability and Accountability Act, Sections 1171 through 1179 of the Social Security Act, 42 U.S.C. Section 1320d, [as amended,] and applicable regulations, in making decisions related to the past, present, or future payment for the provision of health care consented to by the principal or anyone authorized under the law of this state to consent to health care on behalf of the principal;

(7) continue any provision made by the principal for automobiles or other means of transportation, including registering, licensing, insuring, and replacing them, for the individuals described in paragraph (1);

(8) maintain credit and debit accounts for the convenience of the individuals described in paragraph (1) and open new accounts; and

(9) continue payments incidental to the membership or affiliation of the principal in a religious institution, club, society, order, or other organization or to continue contributions to those organizations.

(b) Authority with respect to personal and family maintenance is neither dependent upon, nor limited by, authority that an agent may or may not have with respect to gifts under this [act].

§214. Benefits from governmental programs or civil or military service.

(a) In this section, "benefits from governmental programs or civil or military service" means any benefit, program or assistance provided under a statute or regulation including Social Security, Medicare, and Medicaid.

(b) Unless the power of attorney otherwise provides, language in a power of attorney granting general authority with respect to benefits from governmental programs or civil or military service authorizes the agent to:

(1) execute vouchers in the name of the principal for allowances and reimbursements payable by the United States or a foreign government or by a state or subdivision of a state to the principal, including allowances and reimbursements for transportation of the individuals described in Section 213(a)(1), and for shipment of their household effects;

(2) take possession and order the removal and shipment of property of the principal from a post, warehouse, depot, dock, or other place of storage or safekeeping, either governmental or private, and execute and deliver a release, voucher, receipt, bill of lading, shipping ticket, certificate, or other instrument for that purpose;

(3) enroll in, apply for, select, reject, change, amend, or discontinue, on the principal's behalf, a benefit or program;

(4) prepare, file, and maintain a claim of the principal for a benefit or assistance, financial or otherwise, to which the principal may be entitled under a statute or regulation;

(5) initiate, participate in, submit to alternative dispute resolution, settle, oppose, or propose or accept a compromise with respect to litigation concerning any benefit or assistance the principal may be entitled to receive under a statute or regulation; and

(6) receive the financial proceeds of a claim described in paragraph (4) and conserve, invest, disburse, or use for a lawful purpose anything so received.

§215. Retirement plans.

(a) In this section, "retirement plan" means a plan or account created by an employer, the principal, or another individual to provide retirement benefits or deferred compensation of which the principal is a participant, beneficiary, or owner, including a plan or account under the following sections of the Internal Revenue Code:

(1) an individual retirement account under Internal Revenue Code Section 408, 26 U.S.C. Section 408 [, as amended];

(2) a Roth individual retirement account under Internal Revenue Code Section 408A, 26 U.S.C. Section 408A [, as amended];

(3) a deemed individual retirement account under Internal Revenue Code Section 408(q), 26 U.S.C. Section 408(q) [, as amended];

(4) an annuity or mutual fund custodial account under Internal Revenue Code Section 403(b), 26 U.S.C. Section 403(b) [, as amended];

(5) a pension, profit-sharing, stock bonus, or other retirement plan qualified under Internal Revenue Code Section 401(a), 26 U.S.C. Section 401(a) [, as amended];

(6) a plan under Internal Revenue Code Section 457(b), 26 U.S.C. Section 457(b) [, as amended]; and

(7) a nonqualified deferred compensation plan under Internal Revenue Code Section 409A, 26 U.S.C. Section 409A [, as amended].

(b) Unless the power of attorney otherwise provides, language in a power of attorney granting general authority with respect to retirement plans authorizes the agent to:

(1) select the form and timing of payments under a retirement plan and withdraw benefits from a plan;

(2) make a rollover, including a direct trustee-to-trustee rollover, of benefits from one retirement plan to another;

(3) establish a retirement plan in the principal's name;

(4) make contributions to a retirement plan;

(5) exercise investment powers available under a retirement plan; and

(6) borrow from, sell assets to, or purchase assets from a retirement plan.

§216. Taxes.

Unless the power of attorney otherwise provides, language in a power of attorney granting general authority with respect to taxes authorizes the agent to:

(1) prepare, sign, and file federal, state, local, and foreign income, gift, payroll, property, Federal Insurance Contributions Act, and other tax returns, claims for refunds, requests for extension of time, petitions regarding tax matters, and any other tax-related documents, including receipts, offers, waivers, consents, including consents and agreements under Internal Revenue Code Section 2032A, 26 U.S.C. Section 2032A, [as amended,] closing agreements, and any power of attorney required by the Internal Revenue Service or other taxing authority with respect to a tax year upon which the statute of limitations has not run and the following 25 tax years;

(2) pay taxes due, collect refunds, post bonds, receive confidential information, and contest deficiencies determined by the Internal Revenue Service or other taxing authority;

(3) exercise any election available to the principal under federal, state, local, or foreign tax law; and

(4) act for the principal in all tax matters for all periods before the Internal Revenue Service, or other taxing authority.

§217. Gifts.

(a) In this section, a gift "for the benefit of" a person includes a gift to a trust, an account under the Uniform Transfers to Minors Act, and a tuition savings account or prepaid tuition plan as defined under Internal Revenue Code Section 529, 26 U.S.C. Section 529 [, as amended].

(b) Unless the power of attorney otherwise provides, language in a power of attorney granting general authority with respect to gifts authorizes the agent only to:

(1) make outright to, or for the benefit of, a person, a gift of any of the principal's property, including by the exercise of a presently exercisable general power of appointment held by the principal, in an amount per donee not to exceed the annual dollar limits of the federal gift tax exclusion under Internal Revenue Code Section 2503(b), 26 U.S.C. Section 2503(b), [as amended,] without regard to whether the federal gift tax exclusion applies to the gift, or if the principal's spouse agrees to consent to a split gift pursuant to Internal Revenue Code Section 2513, 26 U.S.C. 2513, [as amended,] in an amount per donee not to exceed twice the annual federal gift tax exclusion limit; and

(2) consent, pursuant to Internal Revenue Code Section 2513, 26 U.S.C. Section 2513, [as amended,] to the splitting of a gift made by the principal's spouse in an amount per donee not to exceed the aggregate annual gift tax exclusions for both spouses.

(c) An agent may make a gift of the principal's property only as the agent determines is consistent with the principal's objectives if actually known by the agent and, if unknown, as the agent determines is consistent with the principal's best interest based on all relevant factors, including:

(1) the value and nature of the principal's property;

(2) the principal's foreseeable obligations and need for maintenance;

(3) minimization of taxes, including income, estate, inheritance, generation-skipping transfer, and gift taxes;

(4) eligibility for a benefit, a program, or assistance under a statute or regulation; and

(5) the principal's personal history of making or joining in making gifts.

ARTICLE 3. STATUTORY FORMS

[Legislative Note: An enacting jurisdiction should review its respective statutory requirements for acknowledgments and for the recording of documents and amend, where necessary for conformity with those requirements, the statutory forms provided in Sections 301 and 302.]

§301. Statutory Form Power of Attorney.

A document substantially in the following form may be used to create a statutory form power of attorney that has the meaning and effect prescribed by this [act].

[INSERT NAME OF JURISDICTION]

STATUTORY FORM POWER OF ATTORNEY

IMPORTANT INFORMATION

This power of attorney authorizes another person (your agent) to make decisions concerning your property for you (the principal). Your agent will be able to make decisions and act with respect to your property (including your money) whether or not you are able to act for yourself. The meaning of authority over subjects listed on this form is explained in the Uniform Power of Attorney Act [insert citation].

This power of attorney does not authorize the agent to make health-care decisions for you.

You should select someone you trust to serve as your agent. Unless you specify otherwise, generally the agent's authority will continue until you die or revoke the power of attorney or the agent resigns or is unable to act for you.

Your agent is entitled to reasonable compensation unless you state otherwise in the Special Instructions.

This form provides for designation of one agent. If you wish to name more than one agent you may name a coagent in the Special Instructions. Coagents are not required to act together unless you include that requirement in the Special Instructions.

If your agent is unable or unwilling to act for you, your power of attorney will end unless you have named a successor agent. You may also name a second successor agent.

This power of attorney becomes effective immediately unless you state otherwise in the Special Instructions.

If you have questions about the power of attorney or the authority you are granting to your agent, you should seek legal advice before signing this form.

DESIGNATION OF AGENT

I ____

name the following

(Name of Principal)

person as my agent:

Name of Agent:

____

Agent's Address:

____

Agent's Telephone Number:

____

DESIGNATION OF SUCCESSOR AGENT(S)
(OPTIONAL)
If my agent is unable or unwilling to act for me, I name as my successor agent:

Name of Successor Agent:

____

Successor Agent's Address:

____

Successor Agent's Telephone Number:

____

If my successor agent is unable or unwilling to act for me, I name as my second successor agent:

Name of Second Successor Agent:

____

Second Successor Agent's Address:

____

Second Successor Agent's Telephone Number:

____

GRANT OF GENERAL AUTHORITY

I grant my agent and any successor agent general authority to act for me with respect to the following subjects as defined in the Uniform Power of Attorney Act [insert citation]:

(INITIAL each subject you want to include in the agent's general authority. If you wish to grant general authority over all of the subjects you may initial "All Preceding Subjects" instead of initialing each subject.)

(___) Real Property

(___) Tangible Personal Property

(___) Stocks and Bonds

(___) Commodities and Options

(___) Banks and Other Financial Institutions

(___) Operation of Entity or Business

(___) Insurance and Annuities

(___) Estates, Trusts, and Other Beneficial Interests

(___) Claims and Litigation

(___) Personal and Family Maintenance

(___) Benefits from Governmental Programs or Civil or Military Service

(___) Retirement Plans

(___) Taxes

(___) All Preceding Subjects

GRANT OF SPECIFIC AUTHORITY (OPTIONAL)

My agent MAY NOT do any of the following specific acts for me UNLESS I have INITIALED the specific authority listed below:

(CAUTION: Granting any of the following will give your agent the authority to take actions that could significantly reduce your property or change how your property is distributed at your death. INITIAL ONLY the specific authority you WANT to give your agent.)

(___) Create, amend, revoke, or terminate an inter vivos trust

(___) Make a gift, subject to the limitations of the Uniform Power of Attorney Act [insert citation to Section 217 of the act] and any special instructions in this power of attorney

(___) Create or change rights of survivorship

(___) Create or change a beneficiary designation

(___) Authorize another person to exercise the authority granted under this power of attorney

(___) Waive the principal's right to be a beneficiary of a joint and survivor annuity, including a survivor benefit under a retirement plan

(___) Exercise fiduciary powers that the principal has authority to delegate

[(___) Disclaim or refuse an interest in property, including a power of appointment]

LIMITATION ON AGENT'S AUTHORITY

An agent that is not my ancestor, spouse, or descendant MAY NOT use my property to benefit the agent or a person to whom the agent owes an obligation of support unless I have included that authority in the Special Instructions.

SPECIAL INSTRUCTIONS (OPTIONAL)

You may give special instructions on the following lines:

____
____
____
____
____
____
____
____
____
____

EFFECTIVE DATE

This power of attorney is effective immediately unless I have stated otherwise in the Special Instructions.

NOMINATION OF [CONSERVATOR OR GUARDIAN] (OPTIONAL)

If it becomes necessary for a court to appoint a [conservator or guardian] of my estate or [guardian] of my person, I nominate the following person(s) for appointment:

Name of Nominee for [conservator or guardian] of my estate:

____
____

Nominee's Address:
____
____

Nominee's Telephone Number:
____

Name of Nominee for [guardian] of my person:

____
____

Nominee's Address:
____
____

Nominee's Telephone Number:
____

RELIANCE ON THIS POWER OF ATTORNEY

Any person, including my agent, may rely upon the validity of this power of attorney or a copy of it unless that person knows it has terminated or is invalid.

SIGNATURE AND ACKNOWLEDGMENT

____
____

Your Signature

(Date)

____

Your Name Printed

____

____

Your Address

____

Your Telephone Number

State of ______________________

[County] of______________________

This document was acknowledged before me on ______________________,

(Date)

by_________________________________.

(Name of Principal)

____

(Seal, if any)

Signature of Notary

My commission expires: ____________________

[This document prepared by:

____

____

IMPORTANT INFORMATION FOR AGENT

Agent's Duties

When you accept the authority granted under this power of attorney, a special legal relationship is created between you and the principal. This relationship imposes upon you legal duties that continue until you resign or the power of attorney is terminated or revoked. You must:

(1) do what you know the principal reasonably expects you to do with the principal's property or, if you do not know the principal's expectations, act in the principal's best interest;

(2) act in good faith;

(3) do nothing beyond the authority granted in this power of attorney; and

(4) disclose your identity as an agent whenever you act for the principal by writing or printing the name of the principal and signing your own name as "agent" in the following manner:

(Principal's Name) by (Your Signature) as Agent

Unless the Special Instructions in this power of attorney state otherwise, you must also:

(1) act loyally for the principal's benefit;
(2) avoid conflicts that would impair your ability to act in the principal's best interest;
(3) act with care, competence, and diligence;
(4) keep a record of all receipts, disbursements, and transactions made on behalf of the principal;
(5) cooperate with any person that has authority to make health-care decisions for the principal to do what you know the principal reasonably expects or, if you do not know the principal's expectations, to act in the principal's best interest; and
(6) attempt to preserve the principal's estate plan if you know the plan and preserving the plan is consistent with the principal's best interest.

Termination of Agent's Authority

You must stop acting on behalf of the principal if you learn of any event that terminates this power of attorney or your authority under this power of attorney. Events that terminate a power of attorney or your authority to act under a power of attorney include:

(1) death of the principal;
(2) the principal's revocation of the power of attorney or your authority;
(3) the occurrence of a termination event stated in the power of attorney;
(4) the purpose of the power of attorney is fully accomplished; or
(5) if you are married to the principal, a legal action is filed with a court to end your marriage, or for your legal separation, unless the Special Instructions in this power of attorney state that such an action will not terminate your authority.

Liability of Agent

The meaning of the authority granted to you is defined in the Uniform Power of Attorney Act [insert citation]. If you violate the Uniform Power of Attorney Act [insert citation] or act outside the authority granted, you may be liable for any damages caused by your violation.

If there is anything about this document or your duties that you do not understand, you should seek legal advice.

[Legislative Note: The brackets which precede the words "Statutory Form Power of Attorney" indicate where the enacting jurisdiction should insert the name of the jurisdiction. An indication of the jurisdiction in a power of attorney is important to establish what law supplies the default rules and statutory definitions for interpretation of the power of attorney (see Section 107 and Comment). Likewise, the brackets in the first paragraph of the "Important Information" section of the form indicate where the enacting jurisdiction should insert the citation for its codification of the Uniform Power of Attorney Act.]

In the "Grant of Specific Authority" section of the form, the phrase "Disclaim or refuse an interest in property, including a power of appointment" is in brackets and should be deleted if under the law of the enacting jurisdiction a fiduciary has authority to disclaim an interest in, or power over, property and the jurisdiction does not wish to restrict that authority by the Uniform Power of Attorney Act. See Unif. Disclaimer of Property Interests Acts § 5(b) (2006) (providing, "[e]xcept to the extent a fiduciary's right to disclaim is expressly restricted or limited by another statute of this State or by the instrument creating the fiduciary relationship, a fiduciary may disclaim, in whole or part, any interest in or power over property, including a power of appointment . . . ."). See also Section 201 Legislative Note.

The brackets in the "Nomination of Conservator or Guardian" section of the form indicate areas where an enacting jurisdiction should review its respective guardianship, conservatorship, or other protective proceedings statutes and amend, if necessary for consistency, the terminology and substance of the bracketed language.

The bracketed language "This document prepared by:" at the conclusion of the "Signature and Acknowledgment" section of the form may be omitted or amended as necessary to conform to the jurisdiction's statutory requirements for acknowledgments or the recording of documents.

§302. Agent's Certification.

The following optional form may be used by an agent to certify facts concerning a power of attorney.

AGENT'S CERTIFICATION AS TO THE VALIDITY OF POWER OF ATTORNEY AND AGENT'S AUTHORITY

State of ______________________

[County] of______________________]

I, ______________________________ (Name of Agent), [certify] under penalty of perjury that ______________________________(Name of Principal) granted me authority as an agent or successor agent in a power of attorney dated ____________________.

I further [certify] that to my knowledge:

(1) the Principal is alive and has not revoked the Power of Attorney or my authority to act under the Power of Attorney and the Power of Attorney and my authority to act under the Power of Attorney have not terminated;

(2) if the Power of Attorney was drafted to become effective upon the happening of an event or contingency, the event or contingency has occurred;

(3) if I was named as a successor agent, the prior agent is no longer able or willing to serve; and

(4)

____
____
____
____
____
____

(Insert other relevant statements)

SIGNATURE AND ACKNOWLEDGMENT

____
____

Agent's Signature (Date)

____

Agent's Name Printed

____

____

Agent's Address

____

Agent's Telephone Number

____

This document was acknowledged before me on

____________________,
(Date)

by______________________________.
(Name of Agent)

____

(Seal, if any)

Signature of Notary

My commission expires: ____________________

[This document prepared by:

____

[Legislative Note: The phrase "certify" is bracketed in this section to indicate where an enacting jurisdiction should review its respective statutory requirements for acknowledgments and the recording of documents and amend, if necessary for consistency, the terminology and substance of the bracketed language. Likewise, the bracketed language "This document prepared by:" at the conclusion of the Agent's certification form may be omitted or amended as necessary to conform with the jurisdiction's statutory requirements for acknowledgments or the recording of documents.]

Comment

This section provides an optional form that may be used by an agent to certify facts concerning a power of attorney. Although the form contains statements of fact about which persons commonly request certification, other factual statements may be added to the form for the purpose of providing an agent certification pursuant to Section 119.

ARTICLE 4. MISCELLANEOUS PROVISIONS

§401. Uniformity of Application and Construction.

In applying and construing this uniform act, consideration must be given to the need to promote uniformity of the law with respect to its subject matter among the states that enact it.

§402. Relation to electronic signatures in global and national commerce act.

This [act] modifies, limits, and supersedes the federal Electronic Signatures in Global and National Commerce Act,15 U.S.C. Section 7001 et seq., but does not modify, limit, or supersede Section 101(c) of that act, 15 U.S.C. Section 7001(c), or authorize electronic delivery of any of the notices described in Section 103(b) of that act, 15 U.S.C. Section 7003(b).

§403. Effect on existing powers of attorney.

Except as otherwise provided in this [act], on [the effective date of this [act]]:

(1) this [act] applies to a power of attorney created before, on, or after [the effective date of this [act]];

(2) this [act] applies to a judicial proceeding concerning a power of attorney commenced on or after [the effective date of this [act]];

(3) this [act] applies to a judicial proceeding concerning a power of attorney commenced before [the effective date of this [act]] unless the court finds that application of a provision of this [act] would substantially interfere with the effective conduct of the judicial proceeding or prejudice the rights of a party, in which case that provision does not apply and the superseded law applies; and

(4) an act done before [the effective date of this [act]] is not affected by this [act].

§404. Repeal.

The following are repealed:

(1) [Uniform Durable Power of Attorney Act]

(2) [Uniform Statutory Form Power of Attorney Act]

(3) [Article 5, Part 5 of the Uniform Probate Code]

§405. Effective date.

This [act] takes effect ________________.

PART VI

~

UNIFORM PRINCIPAL AND INCOME ACT (1997, REV. 2000)

Uniform Principal and Income Act (1997, Rev. 2000)

TABLE OF CONTENTS

UNIFORM PRINCIPAL AND INCOME ACT

Prefatory Note

This revision of the 1931 Uniform Principal and Income Act and the 1962 Revised Uniform Principal and Income Act has two purposes.

One purpose is to revise the 1931 and the 1962 Acts. Revision is needed to support the now widespread use of the revocable living trust as a will substitute, to change the rules in those Acts that experience has shown need to be changed, and to establish new rules to cover situations not provided for in the old Acts, including rules that apply to financial instruments invented since 1962.

The other purpose is to provide a means for implementing the transition to an investment regime based on principles embodied in the Uniform Prudent Investor Act, especially the principle of investing for total return rather than a certain level of "income" as traditionally perceived in terms of interest, dividends, and rents.

Revision of the 1931 and 1962 Acts

The prior Acts and this revision of those Acts deal with four questions affecting the rights of beneficiaries:

(1) How is income earned during the probate of an estate to be distributed to trusts and to persons who receive outright bequests of specific property, pecuniary gifts, and the residue?

(2) When an income interest in a trust begins (i.e., when a person who creates the trust dies or when she transfers property to a trust during life), what property is principal that will eventually go to the remainder beneficiaries and what is income?

(3) When an income interest ends, who gets the income that has been received but not distributed, or that is due but not yet collected, or that has accrued but is not yet due?

(4) After an income interest begins and before it ends, how should its receipts and disbursements be allocated to or between principal and income?

Changes in the traditional sections are of three types: new rules that deal with situations not covered by the prior Acts, clarification of provisions in the 1962 Act, and changes to rules in the prior Acts.

New rules. Issues addressed by some of the more significant new rules include:

(1) The application of the probate administration rules to revocable living trusts after the settlor's death and to other terminating trusts. Articles 2 and 3.

(2) The payment of interest or some other amount on the delayed payment of an outright pecuniary gift that is made pursuant to a trust agreement instead of a will when the agreement or state law does not provide for such a payment. Section 201(3).

(3) The allocation of net income from partnership interests acquired by the trustee other than from a decedent (the old Acts deal only with partnership interests acquired from a decedent). Section 401.

(4) An "unincorporated entity" concept has been introduced to deal with businesses operated by a trustee, including farming and livestock operations, and investment activities in rental real estate, natural resources, timber, and derivatives. Section 403.

(5) The allocation of receipts from discount obligations such as zero-coupon bonds. Section 406(b).

(6) The allocation of net income from harvesting and selling timber between principal and income. Section 412.

(7) The allocation between principal and income of receipts from derivatives, options, and asset-backed securities. Sections 414 and 415.

(8) Disbursements made because of environmental laws. Section 502(a)(7).

(9) Income tax obligations resulting from the ownership of S corporation stock and interests in partnerships. Section 505.

(10) The power to make adjustments between principal and income to correct inequities caused by tax elections or peculiarities in the way the fiduciary income tax rules apply. Section 506.

Clarifications and changes in existing rules. A number of matters provided for in the prior Acts have been changed or clarified in this revision, including the following:

(1) An income beneficiary's estate will be entitled to receive only net income actually received by a trust before the beneficiary's death and not items of accrued income. Section 303.

(2) Income from a partnership is based on actual distributions from the partnership, in the same manner as corporate distributions. Section 401.

(3) Distributions from corporations and partnerships that exceed 20 percent of the entity's gross assets will be principal whether or not intended by the entity to be a partial liquidation. Section 401(d)(2).

(4) Deferred compensation is dealt with in greater detail in a separate section. Section 409.

(5) The 1962 Act rule for "property subject to depletion," (patents, copyrights, royalties, and the like), which provides that a trustee may allocate up to 5 percent of the asset's inventory value to income and the balance to principal, has been replaced by a rule that allocates 90 percent of the amounts received to principal and the balance to income. Section 410.

(6) The percentage used to allocate amounts received from oil and gas has been changed—90 percent of those receipts are allocated to principal and the balance to income. Section 411.

(7) The unproductive property rule has been eliminated for trusts other than marital deduction trusts. Section 413.

(8) Charging depreciation against income is no longer mandatory, and is left to the discretion of the trustee. Section 503.

Coordination with the Uniform Prudent Investor Act

The law of trust investment has been modernized. See Uniform Prudent Investor Act (1994); Restatement (Third) of Trusts: Prudent Investor Rule (1992) (hereinafter Restatement of Trusts 3d: Prudent Investor Rule). Now it is time to update the principal and income allocation rules so the two bodies of doctrine can work well together. This revision deals conservatively with the tension between modern investment theory and traditional income allocation. The starting point is to use the traditional system. If prudent investing of all the assets in a trust viewed as a portfolio and traditional allocation effectuate the intent of the settlor, then nothing need be done. The Act, however, helps the trustee who has made a prudent, modern portfolio-based investment decision that has the initial effect of skewing return from all the assets under management, viewed as a portfolio, as between income and principal beneficiaries. The Act gives that trustee a power to reallocate the portfolio return suitably. To leave a trustee constrained by the traditional system would inhibit the trustee's ability to fully implement modern portfolio theory. . . .

UNIFORM PRINCIPAL AND INCOME ACT [ARTICLE] 1 DEFINITIONS AND FIDUCIARY DUTIES

§101. Short Title

This [Act] May Be Cited as the Uniform Principal and Income Act.

§102. Definitions

In this [Act]:

(1) "Accounting period" means a calendar year unless another 12_month period is selected by a fiduciary. The term includes a portion of a calendar year or other 12_month period that begins when an income interest begins or ends when an income interest ends.

(2) "Beneficiary" includes, in the case of a decedent's estate, an heir [, legatee,] and devisee and, in the case of a trust, an income beneficiary and a remainder beneficiary.

(3) "Fiduciary" means a personal representative or a trustee. The term includes an executor, administrator, successor personal representative, special administrator, and a person performing substantially the same function.

(4) "Income" means money or property that a fiduciary receives as current return from a principal asset. The term includes a portion of receipts from a sale, exchange, or liquidation of a principal asset, to the extent provided in [Article] 4.

(5) "Income beneficiary" means a person to whom net income of a trust is or may be payable.

(6) "Income interest" means the right of an income beneficiary to receive all or part of net income, whether the terms of the trust require it to be distributed or authorize it to be distributed in the trustee's discretion.

(7) "Mandatory income interest" means the right of an income beneficiary to receive net income that the terms of the trust require the fiduciary to distribute.

(8) "Net income" means the total receipts allocated to income during an accounting period minus the disbursements made from income during the period, plus or minus transfers under this [Act] to or from income during the period.

(9) "Person" means an individual, corporation, business trust, estate, trust, partnership, limited liability company, association, joint venture, government; governmental subdivision, agency, or instrumentality; public corporation, or any other legal or commercial entity.

(10) "Principal" means property held in trust for distribution to a remainder beneficiary when the trust terminates.

(11) "Remainder beneficiary" means a person entitled to receive principal when an income interest ends.

(12) "Terms of a trust" means the manifestation of the intent of a settlor or decedent with respect to the trust, expressed in a manner that admits of its proof in a judicial proceeding, whether by written or spoken words or by conduct.

(13) "Trustee" includes an original, additional, or successor trustee, whether or not appointed or confirmed by a court.

Comment

"Income beneficiary." The definitions of income beneficiary (Section 102(5)) and income interest (Section 102(6)) cover both mandatory and discretionary beneficiaries and interests. . . .

"Net income." The reference to "transfers under this Act to or from income" means transfers made under Sections 104(a), 412(b), 502(b), 503(b), 504(a), and 506. . . .

§103. Fiduciary Duties; General Principles

(a) In allocating receipts and disbursements to or between principal and income, and with respect to any matter within the scope of [Articles] 2 and 3, a fiduciary:

(1) shall administer a trust or estate in accordance with the terms of the trust or the will, even if there is a different provision in this [Act];

(2) may administer a trust or estate by the exercise of a discretionary power of administration given to the fiduciary by the terms of the trust or the will, even if the exercise of the power produces

a result different from a result required or permitted by this [Act];

(3) shall administer a trust or estate in accordance with this [Act] if the terms of the trust or the will do not contain a different provision or do not give the fiduciary a discretionary power of administration; and

(4) shall add a receipt or charge a disbursement to principal to the extent that the terms of the trust and this [Act] do not provide a rule for allocating the receipt or disbursement to or between principal and income.

(b) In exercising the power to adjust under Section 104(a) or a discretionary power of administration regarding a matter within the scope of this [Act], whether granted by the terms of a trust, a will, or this [Act], a fiduciary shall administer a trust or estate impartially, based on what is fair and reasonable to all of the beneficiaries, except to the extent that the terms of the trust or the will clearly manifest an intention that the fiduciary shall or may favor one or more of the beneficiaries. A determination in accordance with this [Act] is presumed to be fair and reasonable to all of the beneficiaries.

Comment

. . . **Fiduciary discretion.** The general rule is that if a discretionary power is conferred upon a trustee, the exercise of that power is not subject to control by a court except to prevent an abuse of discretion. Restatement (Second) of Trusts §187. The situations in which a court will control the exercise of a trustee's discretion are discussed in the comments to §187. See also id. §233 Comment *p*.

. . . **Duty of impartiality.** Whenever there are two or more beneficiaries, a trustee is under a duty to deal impartially with them. Restatement of Trusts 3d: Prudent Investor Rule §183 (1992). This rule applies whether the beneficiaries' interests in the trust are concurrent or successive. If the terms of the trust give the trustee discretion to favor one beneficiary over another, a court will not control the exercise of such discretion except to prevent the trustee from abusing it. Id. §183, Comment *a*. "The precise meaning of the trustee's duty of impartiality and the balancing of competing interests and objectives inevitably are matters of judgment and interpretation. Thus, the duty and balancing are affected by the purposes, terms, distribution requirements, and other circumstances of the trust, not only at the outset but as they may change from time to time." Id. §232, Comment *c*.

The terms of a trust may provide that the trustee, or an accountant engaged by the trustee, or a committee of persons who may be family members or business associates, shall have the power to determine what is income and what is principal. If the terms of a trust provide that this Act specifically or principal and income legislation in general does not apply to the trust but fail to provide a rule to deal with a matter provided for in this Act, the trustee has an implied grant of discretion to decide the question. Section 103(b) provides that the rule of impartiality applies in the exercise of such a discretionary power to the extent that the terms of the trust do not provide that one or more of the beneficiaries are to be favored. The fact that a person is named an income beneficiary or a remainder beneficiary is not by itself an indication of partiality for that beneficiary.

§104. Trustee's Power to Adjust

(a) A trustee may adjust between principal and income to the extent the trustee considers necessary if the trustee invests and manages trust assets as a prudent investor, the terms of the trust describe the amount that may or must be distributed to a beneficiary by referring to the trust's income, and the trustee determines, after applying the rules in Section 103(a), that the trustee is unable to comply with Section 103(b).

(b) In deciding whether and to what extent to exercise the power conferred by subsection (a), a trustee shall consider all factors relevant to the trust and its beneficiaries, including the following factors to the extent they are relevant:

(1) the nature, purpose, and expected duration of the trust;

(2) the intent of the settlor;

(3) the identity and circumstances of the beneficiaries;

(4) the needs for liquidity, regularity of income, and preservation and appreciation of capital;

(5) the assets held in the trust; the extent to which they consist of financial assets, interests in closely held enterprises, tangible and intangible personal property, or real property; the extent to which an asset is used by a beneficiary; and whether an asset was purchased by the trustee or received from the settlor;

(6) the net amount allocated to income under the other sections of this [Act] and the increase or decrease in the value of the principal assets, which the trustee may estimate as to assets for which market values are not readily available;

(7) whether and to what extent the terms of the trust give the trustee the power to invade principal or accumulate income or prohibit the trustee from invading principal or accumulating income, and the extent to which the trustee has exercised a power from time to time to invade principal or accumulate income;

(8) the actual and anticipated effect of economic conditions on principal and income and effects of inflation and deflation; and

(9) the anticipated tax consequences of an adjustment.

(c) A trustee may not make an adjustment:

(1) that diminishes the income interest in a trust that requires all of the income to be paid at least annually to a spouse and for which an estate tax or gift tax marital deduction would be allowed,

in whole or in part, if the trustee did not have the power to make the adjustment;

(2) that reduces the actuarial value of the income interest in a trust to which a person transfers property with the intent to qualify for a gift tax exclusion;

(3) that changes the amount payable to a beneficiary as a fixed annuity or a fixed fraction of the value of the trust assets;

(4) from any amount that is permanently set aside for charitable purposes under a will or the terms of a trust unless both income and principal are so set aside;

(5) if possessing or exercising the power to make an adjustment causes an individual to be treated as the owner of all or part of the trust for income tax purposes, and the individual would not be treated as the owner if the trustee did not possess the power to make an adjustment;

(6) if possessing or exercising the power to make an adjustment causes all or part of the trust assets to be included for estate tax purposes in the estate of an individual who has the power to remove a trustee or appoint a trustee, or both, and the assets would not be included in the estate of the individual if the trustee did not possess the power to make an adjustment;

(7) if the trustee is a beneficiary of the trust; or

(8) if the trustee is not a beneficiary, but the adjustment would benefit the trustee directly or indirectly.

(d) If subsection (c)(5), (6), (7), or (8) applies to a trustee and there is more than one trustee, a cotrustee to whom the provision does not apply may make the adjustment unless the exercise of the power by the remaining trustee or trustees is not permitted by the terms of the trust.

(e) A trustee may release the entire power conferred by subsection (a) or may release only the power to adjust from income to principal or the power to adjust from principal to income if the trustee is uncertain about whether possessing or exercising the power will cause a result described in subsection (c)(1) through (6) or (c)(8) or if the trustee determines that possessing or exercising the power will or may deprive the trust of a tax benefit or impose a tax burden not described in subsection (c). The release may be permanent or for a specified period, including a period measured by the life of an individual.

(f) Terms of a trust that limit the power of a trustee to make an adjustment between principal and income do not affect the application of this section unless it is clear from the terms of the trust that the terms are intended to deny the trustee the power of adjustment conferred by subsection (a).

Comment

Purpose and Scope of Provision. The purpose of Section 104 is to enable a trustee to select investments using the standards of a prudent investor without having to realize a particular portion of the portfolio's total return in the form of traditional trust accounting income such as interest, dividends, and rents. Section 104(a) authorizes a trustee to make adjustments between principal and income if three conditions are met: (1) the trustee must be managing the trust assets under the prudent investor rule; (2) the terms of the trust must express the income beneficiary's distribution rights in terms of the right to receive "income" in the sense of traditional trust accounting income; and (3) the trustee must determine, after applying the rules in Section 103(a), that he is unable to comply with Section 103(b). In deciding whether and to what extent to exercise the power to adjust, the trustee is required to consider the factors described in Section 104(b), but the trustee may not make an adjustment in circumstances described in Section 104(c).

Section 104 does not empower a trustee to increase or decrease the degree of beneficial enjoyment to which a beneficiary is entitled under the terms of the trust; rather, it authorizes the trustee to make adjustments between principal and income that may be necessary if the income component of a portfolio's total return is too small or too large because of investment decisions made by the trustee under the prudent investor rule. The paramount consideration in applying Section 104(a) is the requirement in Section 103(b) that "a fiduciary must administer a trust or estate impartially, based on what is fair and reasonable to all of the beneficiaries, except to the extent that the terms of the trust or the will clearly manifest an intention that the fiduciary shall or may favor one or more of the beneficiaries." The power to adjust is subject to control by the court to prevent an abuse of discretion. Restatement (Second) of Trusts §187 (1959). See also id. §§183, 232, 233, Comment *p* (1959).

Section 104 will be important for trusts that are irrevocable when a State adopts the prudent investor rule by statute or judicial approval of the rule in Restatement of Trusts 3d: Prudent Investor Rule. Wills and trust instruments executed after the rule is adopted can be drafted to describe a beneficiary's distribution rights in terms that do not depend upon the amount of trust accounting income, but to the extent that drafters of trust documents continue to describe an income beneficiary's distribution rights by referring to trust accounting income, Section 104 will be an important tool in trust administration.

Three conditions to the exercise of the power to adjust. The first of the three conditions that must be met before a trustee can exercise the power to adjust—that the trustee invest and manage trust assets as a prudent investor—is expressed in this Act by language derived from the Uniform Prudent Investor Act, but the condition will be met whether the prudent investor rule applies because the Uniform Act or other prudent investor legislation has been enacted, the prudent investor rule has been approved by the courts, or the terms of the trust require it. Even if a State's legislature or courts have not formally adopted the rule, the Restatement establishes the prudent investor rule as an authoritative interpretation of the common law prudent man rule, referring to the prudent investor rule as a "modest reformulation of the Harvard College dictum and the basic rule of prior Restatements." Restatement of Trusts 3d: Prudent Investor Rule, Introduction, at 5. As a result, there is a basis for concluding that the first condition is satisfied in virtually all States except those in which a trustee is permitted to invest only in assets set forth in a statutory "legal list."

The second condition will be met when the terms of the trust require all of the "income" to be distributed at regular intervals; or when the terms of the trust require a trustee to distribute all of the income, but permit the trustee to decide how much to distribute to each member of a class of beneficiaries; or when the terms of a trust provide that the beneficiary shall receive the greater of the trust accounting income and a fixed dollar amount (an annuity), or of trust accounting income and a fractional share of the value of the trust assets (a unitrust amount). If the trust authorizes the trustee in its discretion to distribute the trust's income to the beneficiary or to accumulate some or all of the income, the condition will be met because the terms of the trust do not permit the trustee to distribute more than the trust accounting income.

To meet the third condition, the trustee must first meet the requirements of Section 103(a), i.e., she must apply the terms of the trust, decide whether to exercise the discretionary powers given to the trustee under the terms of the trust, and must apply the provisions of the Act if the terms of the trust do not contain a different provision or give the trustee discretion. Second, the trustee must determine the extent to which the terms of the trust clearly manifest an intention by the settlor that the trustee may or must favor one or more of the beneficiaries. To the extent that the terms of the trust do not require partiality, the trustee must conclude that she is unable to comply with the duty to administer the trust impartially. To the extent that the terms of the trust do require or permit the trustee to favor the income beneficiary or the remainder beneficiary, the trustee must conclude that she is unable to achieve the degree of partiality required or permitted. If the trustee comes to either conclusion—that she is unable to administer the trust impartially or that she is unable to achieve the degree of partiality required or permitted—she may exercise the power to adjust under Section 104(a).

Impartiality and productivity of income. The duty of impartiality between income and remainder beneficiaries is linked to the trustee's duty to make the portfolio productive of trust accounting income whenever the distribution requirements are expressed in terms of distributing the trust's "income." The 1962 Act implies that the duty to produce income applies on an asset by asset basis because the right of an income beneficiary to receive "delayed income" from the sale proceeds of underproductive property under Section 12 of that Act arises if "any part of principal . . . has not produced an average net income of a least 1 percent per year of its inventory value for more than a year . . . ." Under the prudent investor rule, "[t]o whatever extent a requirement of income productivity exists, . . . the requirement applies not investment by investment but to the portfolio as a whole." Restatement of Trusts 3d: Prudent Investor Rule §227, Comment *i*, at 34. The power to adjust under Section 104(a) is also to be exercised by considering net income from the portfolio as a whole and not investment by investment. Section 413(b) of this Act eliminates the underproductive property rule in all cases other than trusts for which a marital deduction is allowed; the rule applies to a marital deduction trust if the trust's assets "consist substantially of property that does not provide the spouse with sufficient income from or use of the trust assets . . ."—in other words, the section applies by reference to the portfolio as a whole.

While the purpose of the power to adjust in Section 104(a) is to eliminate the need for a trustee who operates under the prudent investor rule to be concerned about the income component of the portfolio's total return, the trustee must still determine the extent to which a distribution must be made to an income beneficiary and the adequacy of the portfolio's liquidity as a whole to make that distribution.

For a discussion of investment considerations involving specific investments and techniques under the prudent investor rule, see Restatement of Trusts 3d: Prudent Investor Rule §227, Comments *k-p*.

Factors to consider in exercising the power to adjust. Section 104(b) requires a trustee to consider factors relevant to the trust and its beneficiaries in deciding whether and to what extent the power to adjust should be exercised. Section 2(c) of the Uniform Prudent Investor Act sets forth circumstances that a trustee is to consider in investing and managing trust assets. The circumstances in Section 2(c) of the Uniform Prudent Investor Act are the source of the factors in paragraphs (3) through (6) and (8) of Section 104(b) (modified where necessary to adapt them to the purposes of this Act) so that, to the extent possible, comparable factors will apply to investment decisions and decisions involving the power to adjust. If a trustee who is operating under the prudent investor rule decides that the portfolio should be composed of financial assets whose total return will result primarily from capital appreciation rather than dividends, interest, and rents, the trustee can decide at the same time the extent to which an adjustment from principal to income may be necessary under Section 104. On the other hand, if a trustee decides that the risk and return objectives for the trust are best achieved by a portfolio whose total return includes interest and dividend income that is sufficient to provide the income beneficiary with the beneficial interest to which the beneficiary is entitled under the terms of the trust, the trustee can decide that it is unnecessary to exercise the power to adjust.

Assets received from the settlor. Section 3 of the Uniform Prudent Investor Act provides that "[a] trustee shall diversify the investments of the trust unless the trustee reasonably determines that, because of special circumstances, the purposes of the trust are better served without diversifying." The special circumstances may include the wish to retain a family business, the benefit derived from deferring liquidation of the asset in order to defer payment of income taxes, or the anticipated capital appreciation from retaining an asset such as undeveloped real estate for a long period. To the extent the trustee retains assets received from the settlor because of special circumstances that overcome the duty to diversify, the trustee may take these circumstances into account in determining whether and to what extent the power to adjust should be exercised to change the results produced by other provisions of this Act that apply to the retained assets. See Section 104(b)(5); Uniform Prudent Investor Act §3, Comment, 7B U.L.A. 18, at 25-26 (Supp. 1997); Restatement of Trusts 3d: Prudent Investor Rule §229 and Comments *a-e*.

Limitations on the power to adjust. The purpose of subsections (c)(1) through (4) is to preserve tax benefits that may have been an important purpose for creating the trust. Subsections (c)(5), (6), and (8) deny the power to adjust in the circumstances described in those subsections in order to prevent adverse tax consequences, and subsection (c)(7) denies the power to adjust to any beneficiary, whether or not possession of the power may have adverse tax consequences.

Under subsection (c)(1), a trustee cannot make an adjustment that diminishes the income interest in a trust that requires all of the income to be paid at least annually to a spouse and for which an estate tax or gift tax marital deduction is allowed; but this subsection does not prevent the trustee from making an adjustment that increases the amount of income paid from a marital deduction trust to the spouse. Subsection (c)(1) applies to a trust that qualifies for the marital deduction because the spouse has a general power of appointment over the trust, but it applies to a qualified terminable interest property (QTIP) trust only if and to the extent that the fiduciary makes the election required to obtain the tax deduction. Subsection (c)(1) does not apply to a so-called "estate" trust. This type of trust qualifies for the marital deduction because the terms of the trust require the principal and undistributed income to be paid to the surviving spouse's estate when the spouse dies; it is not necessary for the terms of an estate trust to require the income to be distributed annually. Reg. §20.2056(c)_2(b)(1)(iii).

Subsection (c)(3) applies to annuity trusts and unitrusts with no charitable beneficiaries as well as to trusts with charitable income or remainder beneficiaries; its purpose is to make it clear that a beneficiary's right to receive a fixed annuity or a fixed fraction of the value of a trust's assets is not subject to adjustment under Section 104(a). Subsection (c)(3) does not apply to any additional amount to which the beneficiary may be entitled that is expressed in terms of a right to receive income from the trust. For example, if a beneficiary is to receive a fixed annuity or the trust's income, whichever is greater, subsection (c)(3) does not prevent a trustee from making an adjustment under Section 104(a) in determining the amount of the trust's income.

If subsection (c)(5), (6), (7), or (8), prevents a trustee from exercising the power to adjust, subsection (d) permits a cotrustee who is not subject to the provision to exercise the power unless the terms of the trust do not permit the cotrustee to do so.

Release of the power to adjust. Section 104(e) permits a trustee to release all or part of the power to adjust in circumstances in which the possession or exercise of the power might deprive the trust of a tax benefit or impose a tax burden. For example, if possessing the power would diminish the actuarial value of the income interest in a trust for which the income beneficiary's estate may be eligible to claim a credit for property previously taxed if the beneficiary dies within ten years after the death of the person creating the trust, the trustee is permitted under subsection (e) to release just the power to adjust from income to principal.

Trust terms that limit a power to adjust. Section 104(f) applies to trust provisions that limit a trustee's power to adjust. Since the power is intended to enable trustees to employ the prudent investor rule without being constrained by traditional principal and income rules, an instrument executed before the adoption of this Act whose terms describe the amount that may or must be distributed to a beneficiary by referring to the trust's income or that prohibit the invasion of principal or that prohibit equitable adjustments in general should not be construed as forbidding the use of the power to adjust under Section 104(a) if the need for adjustment arises because the trustee is operating under the prudent investor rule. Instruments containing such provisions that are executed after the adoption of this Act should specifically refer to the power to adjust if the settlor intends to forbid its use. See generally, Joel C. Dobris, Limits on the Doctrine of Equitable Adjustment in Sophisticated Postmortem Tax Planning, 66 Iowa L. Rev. 273 (1981).

Examples. The following examples illustrate the application of Section 104:

Example (1)—T is the successor trustee of a trust that provides income to A for life, remainder to B. T has received from the prior trustee a portfolio of financial assets invested 20 percent in stocks and 80 percent in bonds. Following the prudent investor rule, T determines that a strategy of investing the portfolio 50 percent in stocks and 50 percent in bonds has risk and return objectives that are reasonably suited to the trust, but T also determines that adopting this approach will cause the trust to receive a smaller amount of dividend and interest income. After considering the factors in Section 104(b), T may transfer cash from principal to income to the extent T considers it necessary to increase the amount distributed to the income beneficiary.

Example (2)—T is the trustee of a trust that requires the income to be paid to the settlor's son C for life, remainder to C's daughter D. In a period of very high inflation, T purchases bonds that pay double-digit interest and determines that a portion of the interest, which is allocated to income under Section 406 of this Act, is a return of capital. In consideration of the loss of value of principal due to inflation and other factors that T considers relevant, T may transfer part of the interest to principal.

Example (3)—T is the trustee of a trust that requires the income to be paid to the settlor's sister E for life, remainder to charity F. E is a retired schoolteacher who is single and has no children. E's income from her social security, pension, and savings exceeds the amount required to provide for her accustomed standard of living. The terms of the trust permit T to invade principal to provide for E's health and to support her in her accustomed manner of living, but do not otherwise indicate that T should favor E or F. Applying the prudent investor rule, T determines that the trust assets should be invested entirely in growth stocks that produce very little dividend income. Even though it is not necessary to invade principal to maintain E's accustomed standard of living, she is entitled to receive from the trust the degree of beneficial enjoyment normally accorded a person who is the sole income beneficiary of a trust, and T may transfer cash from principal to income to provide her with that degree of enjoyment.

Example (4)—T is the trustee of a trust that is governed by the law of State X. The trust became irrevocable before State X adopted the prudent investor rule. The terms of the trust require all of the income to be paid to G for life, remainder to H, and also give T the power to invade principal for the benefit of G for "dire emergencies only." The terms of the trust limit the aggregate amount that T can distribute to G from principal during G's life to 6 percent of the trust's value at its inception. The trust's portfolio is invested initially 50 percent in stocks and 50 percent in bonds, but after State X adopts the prudent investor rule T determines that, to achieve suitable risk and return objectives for the trust, the assets should be invested 90 percent in stocks and 10 percent in bonds. This change increases the total return from the portfolio and decreases the dividend and interest income. Thereafter, even though G does not experience a dire emergency, T may exercise the power to adjust under Section 104(a) to the extent that T determines that the adjustment is from only the capital appreciation resulting from the change in the portfolio's asset allocation. If T is unable to determine the extent to which capital appreciation resulted from the change in asset allocation or is unable to maintain adequate records to determine the extent to which principal distributions to G for dire emergencies do not exceed the 6 percent limitation, T may not exercise the power to adjust. See Joel C. Dobris, Limits on the Doctrine of Equitable Adjustment in Sophisticated Postmortem Tax Planning, 66 Iowa L. Rev. 273 (1981).

Example (5)—T is the trustee of a trust for the settlor's child. The trust owns a diversified portfolio of marketable financial assets with a value of $600,000, and is also the sole beneficiary of the settlor's IRA, which holds a diversified portfolio of marketable financial assets with a value of $900,000. The trust receives a distribution from the IRA that is the minimum amount required to be distributed under the Internal Revenue Code, and T allocates 10 percent of the distribution to income under Section 409(c) of this Act. The total return on the IRA's assets exceeds the amount distributed to the trust, and the value of the IRA at the end of the year is more than its value at the beginning of the year. Relevant factors that T may consider in determining whether to exercise the power to adjust and the extent to which an adjustment should be made to comply with Section 103(b) include the total return from all of the trust's assets, those owned directly as well as its interest in the IRA, the extent to which the trust will be subject to income tax on the portion of the IRA distribution that is allocated to principal, and the extent to which the income beneficiary will be subject to income tax on the amount that T distributes to the income beneficiary.

Example (6)—T is the trustee of a trust whose portfolio includes a large parcel of undeveloped real estate. T pays real property taxes on the undeveloped parcel from income each year pursuant to Section 501(3). After considering the return from the trust's portfolio as a whole and other relevant factors described in Section 104(b), T may exercise the power to adjust under Section 104(a) to transfer cash from principal to income in order to distribute to the income beneficiary an amount that T considers necessary to comply with Section 103(b).

Example (7)—T is the trustee of a trust whose portfolio includes an interest in a mutual fund that is sponsored by T. As the manager of the mutual fund, T charges the fund a management fee that reduces the amount available to distribute to the trust by $2,000. If the fee had been paid directly by the trust, one-half of the fee would have been paid from income under Section 501(1) and the other one-half would have been paid from principal under Section 502(a)(1). After considering the total return from the portfolio as a whole and other relevant factors described in Section 104(b), T may exercise its power to adjust under Section 104(a) by transferring $1,000, or half of the trust's proportionate share of the fee, from principal to income.

§105. Judicial Control of Discretionary Power

(a) The court may not order a fiduciary to change a decision to exercise or not to exercise a discretionary power conferred by this [Act] unless it determines that the decision was an abuse of the fiduciary's discretion. A fiduciary's decision is not an abuse of discretion merely because the court would have exercised the power in a different manner or would not have exercised the power.

(b) The decisions to which subsection (a) applies include:

(1) a decision under Section 104(a) as to whether and to what extent an amount should be transferred from principal to income or from income to principal.

(2) a decision regarding the factors that are relevant to the trust and its beneficiaries, the extent to which the factors are relevant, and the weight, if any, to be given to those factors, in deciding whether and to what extent to exercise the discretionary power conferred by Section 104(a).

(c) If the court determines that a fiduciary has abused the fiduciary's discretion, the court may place the income and remainder beneficiaries in the positions they would have occupied if the discretion had not been abused, according to the following rules:

(1) To the extent that the abuse of discretion has resulted in no distribution to a beneficiary or in a distribution that is too small, the court shall order the fiduciary to distribute from the trust to the beneficiary an amount that the court determines will restore the beneficiary, in whole or in part, to the beneficiary's appropriate position.

(2) To the extent that the abuse of discretion has resulted in a distribution to a beneficiary which is too large, the court shall place the beneficiaries, the trust, or both, in whole or in part, in their appropriate positions by ordering the fiduciary to withhold an amount from one or more future distributions to the beneficiary who received the distribution that was too large or ordering that beneficiary to return some or all of the distribution to the trust.

(3) To the extent that the court is unable, after applying paragraphs (1) and (2), to place the beneficiaries, the trust, or both, in the positions they would have occupied if the discretion had not been abused, the court may order the fiduciary to pay an appropriate amount from its own funds to one or more of the beneficiaries or the trust or both.

(d) Upon [petition] by the fiduciary, the court having jurisdiction over a trust or estate shall determine whether a proposed exercise or nonexercise by the fiduciary of a discretionary power conferred by this [Act] will result in an abuse of the fiduciary's discretion. If the petition describes the proposed exercise or nonexercise of the power and contains sufficient information to inform the beneficiaries of the reasons for the proposal, the facts upon which the fiduciary relies, and an explanation of how the income and remainder beneficiaries will be affected by the proposed exercise or nonexercise of the power, a beneficiary who challenges the proposed exercise or nonexercise has the burden of establishing that it will result in an abuse of discretion.

Comment

General. All of the discretionary powers in the 1997 Act are subject to the normal rules that govern a fiduciary's exercise of discretion. Section 105 codifies those rules for purposes of the Act so that they will be readily apparent and accessible to fiduciaries, beneficiaries, their counsel, and the courts if and when questions concerning such powers arise.

Section 105 also makes clear that the normal rules governing the exercise of a fiduciary's powers apply to the discretionary power to adjust conferred upon a trustee by Section 104(a). Discretionary provisions authorizing trustees to determine what is income and what is principal have been used in governing instruments for years; Section 2 of the 1931 Uniform Principal and Income Act recognized that practice by providing that "the person establishing the principal may himself direct the manner of ascertainment of income and principal . . . or grant discretion to the trustee or other person to do so. . . ." Section 103(a)(2) also recognizes the power of a settlor to grant such discretion to the trustee. Section 105 applies to a discretionary power granted by the terms of a trust or a will as well as the power to adjust in Section 104(a).

Power to adjust. The exercise of the power to adjust is governed by a trustee's duty of impartiality, which requires the trustee to strike an appropriate balance between the interests of the income and remainder beneficiaries. Section 103(b) expresses this duty by requiring the trustee to "administer a trust or estate impartially, based on what is fair and reasonable to all of the beneficiaries, except to the extent that the terms of the trust or the will clearly manifest an intention that the fiduciary shall or may favor one or more of the beneficiaries." Because this involves the exercise of judgment in circumstances rarely capable of perfect resolution, trustees are not expected to achieve perfection; they are, however, required to make conscious decisions in good faith and with proper motives.

In seeking the proper balance between the interests of the beneficiaries in matters involving principal and income, a trustee's traditional approach has been to determine the settlor's objectives from the terms of the trust, gather the information needed to ascertain the financial circumstances of the beneficiaries, determine the extent to which the settlor's objectives can be achieved with the resources available in the trust, and then allocate the trust's assets between stocks and fixed-income securities in a way that will produce a particular level or range of income for the income beneficiary. The key element in this process has been to determine the appropriate level or range of income for the income beneficiary, and that will continue to be the key element in deciding whether and to what extent to exercise the discretionary power conferred by Section 104(a). If it becomes necessary for a court to determine whether an abuse of the discretionary power to adjust between principal and income has occurred, the criteria should be the same as those that courts have used in the past to determine whether a trustee has abused its discretion in allocating the trust's assets between stocks and fixed-income securities.

A fiduciary has broad latitude in choosing the methods and criteria to use in deciding whether and to what extent to exercise the power to adjust in order to achieve impartiality between income beneficiaries and remainder beneficiaries or the degree of partiality for one or the other that is provided for by the terms of the trust or the will. For example, in deciding what the appropriate level or range of income should be for the income beneficiary and whether to exercise the power, a trustee may use the methods employed prior to the adoption of the 1997 Act in deciding how to allocate trust assets between stocks and fixed-income securities; or may consider the amount that would be distributed each year based on a percentage of the portfolio's value at the beginning or end of an accounting period, or the average portfolio value for several accounting periods, in a manner similar to a unitrust, and may select a percentage that the trustee believes is appropriate for this purpose and use the same percentage or different percentages in subsequent years. The trustee may also use hypothetical portfolios of marketable securities to determine an appropriate level or range of income within which a distribution might fall.

An adjustment may be made prospectively at the beginning of an accounting period, based on a projected return or range of returns for a trust's portfolio, or retrospectively after the fiduciary knows the total realized or unrealized return for the period; and instead of an annual adjustment, the trustee may distribute a fixed dollar amount for several years, in a manner similar to an annuity, and may change the fixed dollar amount periodically. No inference of abuse is to be drawn if a fiduciary uses different methods or criteria for the same trust from time to time, or uses different methods or criteria for different trusts for the same accounting period.

While a trustee must consider the portfolio as a whole in deciding whether and to what extent to exercise the power to adjust, a trustee may apply different criteria in considering the portion of the portfolio that is composed of marketable securities and the portion whose market value cannot be determined readily, and may take into account a beneficiary's use or possession of a trust asset.

Under the prudent investor rule, a trustee is to incur costs that are appropriate and reasonable in relation to the assets and the purposes of the trust, and the same consideration applies in determining whether and to what extent to exercise the power to adjust. In making investment decisions under the prudent investor rule, the trustee will have considered the purposes, terms, distribution requirements, and other circumstances of the trust for the purpose of adopting an overall investment strategy having risk and return objectives reasonably suited to the trust. A trustee is not required to duplicate that work for principal and income purposes, and in many cases the decision about whether and to what extent to exercise the power to adjust may be made at the same time as the investment decisions. To help achieve the objective of reasonable investment costs, a trustee may also adopt policies that apply to all trusts or to individual trusts or classes of trusts, based on their size or other criteria, stating whether and under what circumstances the power to adjust will be exercised and the method of making adjustments; no inference of abuse is to be drawn if a trustee adopts such policies.

General rule. The first sentence of Section 105(a) is from Restatement (Second) of Trusts §187 and Restatement (Third) of Trusts (Tentative Draft No. 2, 1999) §50(1). The second sentence of Section 105(a) derives from Comment e to §187 of the Second Restatement and Comment b to §50 of the Third Restatement.

The reference in Section 105(a) to a fiduciary's decision to exercise or not to exercise a discretionary power underscores a fundamental precept, which is that a fiduciary has a duty to make a conscious decision about exercising or not exercising a discretionary power. Comment b to §50 of the Third Restatement states:

> [A] court will intervene where the exercise of a power is left to the judgment of a trustee who improperly fails to exercise that judgment. Thus, even where a trustee has discretion whether or not to make any payments to a particular beneficiary, the court will interpose if the trustee, arbitrarily or without knowledge of or inquiry into relevant circumstances, fails to exercise the discretion.

Section 105(b) makes clear that the rule of subsection (a) applies not only to the power conferred by Section 104(a) but also to the evaluation process required by Section 104(b) in deciding whether and to what extent to exercise the power to adjust. Under Section 104(b), a trustee is to consider all of the factors that are relevant to the trust and its beneficiaries, including, to the extent the trustee determines they are relevant, the nine factors enumerated in Section 104(b). Section 104(b) derives from Section 2(c) of the Uniform Prudent Investor Act, which lists eight circumstances that a trustee shall consider, to the extent they are relevant, in investing and managing assets. The trustee's decisions about what factors are relevant for purposes of Section 104(b) and the weight to be accorded each of the relevant factors are part of the discretionary decision-making process. As such, these decisions are not subject to change for the purpose of changing the trustee's ultimate decision unless the court determines that there has been an abuse of discretion in determining the relevancy and weight of these factors.

Remedy. The exercise or nonexercise of a discretionary power under the Act normally affects the amount or timing of a distribution to the income or remainder beneficiaries. The primary remedy under Section 105(c) for abuse of discretion is the restoration of the beneficiaries and the trust to the positions they would have occupied if the abuse had not occurred. It draws on a basic principle of restitution that if a person pays money to someone who is not intended to receive it (and in a case to which this Act applies, not intended by the settlor to receive it in the absence of an abuse of discretion by the trustee), that person is entitled to restitution on the ground that the payee would be unjustly enriched if he or she were permitted to retain the payment. See Restatement of Restitution §22 (1937). The objective is to accomplish the restoration initially by making adjustments between the beneficiaries and the trust to the extent possible; to the extent that restoration is not possible by such adjustments, a court may order the trustee to pay an amount to one or more of the beneficiaries, the trust, or both the beneficiaries and the trust. If the court determines that it is not possible in the circumstances to restore them to the their appropriate positions, the court may provide other remedies appropriate to the circumstances. The approach of Section 105(c) is supported by Comment b to §50 of the Third Restatement of Trusts:

When judicial intervention is required, a court may direct the trustee to make or refrain from making certain payments; issue instructions to clarify the standards or guidelines applicable to the exercise of the power; or rescind the trustee's payment decisions, usually directing the trustee to recover amounts improperly distributed and holding the trustee liable for failure or inability to do so. .

. .

Advance determinations. Section 105(d) employs the familiar remedy of the trustee's petition to the court for instructions. It requires the court to determine, upon a petition by the fiduciary, whether a proposed exercise or nonexercise of a discretionary power by the fiduciary of a power conferred by the Act would be an abuse of discretion under the general rule of Section 105(a). If the petition contains the information prescribed in the second sentence of subsection (d), the proposed action or inaction is presumed not to result in an abuse, and a beneficiary who challenges the proposal must establish that it will.

Subsection (d) is intended to provide a fiduciary the opportunity to obtain an assurance of finality in a judicial proceeding before proceeding with a proposed exercise or nonexercise of a discretionary power. Its purpose is not, however, to have the court instruct the fiduciary how to exercise the discretion. A fiduciary may also obtain the consent of the beneficiaries to a proposed act or an omission to act, and a beneficiary cannot hold the fiduciary liable for that act or omission unless:

(a) the beneficiary was under an incapacity at the time of such consent or of such act or omission; or

(b) the beneficiary, when he gave his consent, did not know of his rights and of the material facts which the trustee knew or should have known and which the trustee did not reasonably believe that the beneficiary knew; or

(c) the consent of the beneficiary was induced by improper conduct of the trustee.

Restatement (Second) of Trusts §216.

If there are many beneficiaries, including some who are incapacitated or unascertained, the fiduciary may prefer the greater assurance of finality provided by a judicial proceeding that will bind all persons who have an interest in the trust.

[ARTICLE] 2

DECEDENT'S ESTATE OR TERMINATING INCOME INTEREST

§201. Determination and Distribution of Net Income

After a decedent dies, in the case of an estate, or after an income interest in a trust ends, the following rules apply:

(1) A fiduciary of an estate or of a terminating income interest shall determine the amount of net income and net principal receipts received from property specifically given to a beneficiary under the rules in [Articles] 3 through 5 which apply to trustees and the rules in paragraph (5). The fiduciary shall distribute the net income and net principal receipts to the beneficiary who is to receive the specific property.

(2) A fiduciary shall determine the remaining net income of a decedent's estate or a terminating income interest under the rules in [Articles] 3 through 5 which apply to trustees and by:

(A) including in net income all income from property used to discharge liabilities;

(B) paying from income or principal, in the fiduciary's discretion, fees of attorneys, accountants, and fiduciaries; court costs and other expenses of administration; and interest on death taxes, but the fiduciary may pay those expenses from income of property passing to a trust for which the fiduciary claims an estate tax marital or charitable deduction only to the extent that the payment of those expenses from income will not cause the reduction or loss of the deduction; and

(C) paying from principal all other disbursements made or incurred in connection with the settlement of a decedent's estate or the winding up of a terminating income interest, including debts, funeral expenses, disposition of remains, family allowances, and death taxes and related penalties that are apportioned to the estate or terminating income interest by the will, the terms of the trust, or applicable law.

(3) A fiduciary shall distribute to a beneficiary who receives a pecuniary amount outright the interest or any other amount provided by the will, the terms of the trust, or applicable law from net income determined under paragraph (2) or from principal to the extent that net income is insufficient. If a beneficiary is to receive a pecuniary amount outright from a trust after an income interest ends and no interest or other amount is provided for by the terms of the trust or applicable law, the fiduciary shall distribute the interest or other amount to which the beneficiary would be entitled under applicable law if the pecuniary amount were required to be paid under a will.

(4) A fiduciary shall distribute the net income remaining after distributions required by paragraph (3) in the manner described in Section 202 to all other beneficiaries, including a beneficiary who receives a pecuniary amount in trust, even if the beneficiary holds an unqualified power to withdraw assets from the trust or other presently exercisable general power of appointment over the trust.

(5) A fiduciary may not reduce principal or income receipts from property described in paragraph (1) because of a payment described in Section 501 or 502 to the extent that the will, the terms of the trust, or applicable law requires the fiduciary to make the payment from assets other than the property or to the extent that the fiduciary recovers or expects to recover the payment from a third party. The net income and principal receipts from the property are determined by including all of the amounts the fiduciary receives or pays with respect to the property, whether those amounts accrued or became due before, on, or after the date of a decedent's death or an income interest's terminating event, and by making a reasonable provision for amounts that the fiduciary believes the estate or terminating income interest may become obligated to pay after the property is distributed.

§202. Distribution to Residuary and Remainder Beneficiaries

(a) Each beneficiary described in Section 201(4) is entitled to receive a portion of the net income equal to the beneficiary's fractional interest in undistributed principal assets, using values as of the distribution date. If a fiduciary makes more than one distribution of assets to beneficiaries to whom this section applies, each beneficiary, including one who does not receive part of the distribution, is entitled, as of each distribution date, to the net income the fiduciary has received after the date of death or terminating event or earlier distribution date but has not distributed as of the current distribution date.

(b) In determining a beneficiary's share of net income, the following rules apply:

(1) The beneficiary is entitled to receive a portion of the net income equal to the beneficiary's fractional interest in the undistributed principal assets immediately before the distribution date, including assets that later may be sold to meet principal obligations.

(2) The beneficiary's fractional interest in the undistributed principal assets must be calculated without regard to property specifically given to a beneficiary and property required to pay pecuniary amounts not in trust.

(3) The beneficiary's fractional interest in the undistributed principal assets must be calculated on the basis of the aggregate value of those assets as of the distribution date without reducing the value by any unpaid principal obligation.

(4) The distribution date for purposes of this section may be the date as of which the fiduciary calculates the value of the assets if that date is reasonably near the date on which assets are actually distributed.

(c) If a fiduciary does not distribute all of the collected but undistributed net income to each person as of a distribution date, the fiduciary shall maintain appropriate records showing the interest of each beneficiary in that net income.

(d) A fiduciary may apply the rules in this section, to the extent that the fiduciary considers it appropriate, to net gain or loss realized after the date of death or terminating event or earlier distribution date from the disposition of a principal asset if this section applies to the income from the asset.

Comment

Relationship to prior Acts. Section 202 retains the concept in Section 5(b)(2) of the 1962 Act that the residuary legatees of estates are to receive net income earned during the period of administration on the basis of their proportionate interests in the undistributed assets when distributions are made. It changes the basis for determining their proportionate interests by using asset values as of a date reasonably near the time of distribution instead of inventory values; it extends the application of these rules to distributions from terminating trusts; and it extends these rules to gain or loss realized from the disposition of assets during administration, an omission in the 1962 Act that has been noted by several commentators. . . .

[ARTICLE] 3

APPORTIONMENT AT BEGINNING AND END OF INCOME INTEREST

§301. When Right to Income Begins and Ends

(a) An income beneficiary is entitled to net income from the date on which the income interest begins. An income interest begins on the date specified in the terms of the trust or, if no date is specified, on the date an asset becomes subject to a trust or successive income interest.

(b) An asset becomes subject to a trust:

(1) on the date it is transferred to the trust in the case of an asset that is transferred to a trust during the transferor's life;

(2) on the date of a testator's death in the case of an asset that becomes subject to a trust by reason of a will, even if there is an intervening period of administration of the testator's estate; or

(3) on the date of an individual's death in the case of an asset that is transferred to a fiduciary by a third party because of the individual's death.

(c) An asset becomes subject to a successive income interest on the day after the preceding income interest ends, as determined under subsection (d), even if there is an intervening period of administration to wind up the preceding income interest.

(d) An income interest ends on the day before an income beneficiary dies or another terminating event occurs, or on the last day of a period during which there is no beneficiary to whom a trustee may distribute income.

§302. Apportionment of Receipts and Disbursements When Decedent Dies or Income Interest Begins

(a) A trustee shall allocate an income receipt or disbursement other than one to which Section 201(1) applies to principal if its due date occurs before a decedent dies in the case of an estate or before an income interest begins in the case of a trust or successive income interest.

(b) A trustee shall allocate an income receipt or disbursement to income if its due date occurs on or after the date on which a decedent dies or an income interest begins and it is a periodic due date. An income receipt or disbursement must be treated as accruing from day to day if its due date is not periodic or it has no due date. The portion of the receipt or disbursement accruing before the date on which a decedent dies or an income interest begins must be allocated to principal and the balance must be allocated to income.

(c) An item of income or an obligation is due on the date the payer is required to make a payment. If a payment date is not stated, there is no due date for the purposes of this [Act]. Distributions to shareholders or other owners from an entity to which Section 401 applies are deemed to be due on the date fixed by the entity for determining who is entitled to receive the distribution or, if no date is fixed, on the declaration date for the distribution. A due date is periodic for receipts or disbursements that must be paid at regular intervals under a lease or an obligation to pay interest or if an entity customarily makes distributions at regular intervals.

§303. Apportionment When Income Interest Ends

(a) In this section, "undistributed income" means net income received before the date on which an income interest ends. The term does not include an item of income or expense that is due or accrued or net income that has been added or is required to be added to principal under the terms of the trust.

(b) When a mandatory income interest ends, the trustee shall pay to a mandatory income beneficiary who survives that date, or the estate of a deceased mandatory income beneficiary whose death causes the interest to end, the beneficiary's share of the undistributed income that is not disposed of under the terms of the trust unless the beneficiary has an unqualified power to revoke more than five percent of the trust immediately before the income interest ends. In the latter case, the undistributed income from the portion of the trust that may be revoked must be added to principal.

(c) When a trustee's obligation to pay a fixed annuity or a fixed fraction of the value of the trust's assets ends, the trustee shall prorate the final payment if and to the extent required by applicable law to accomplish a purpose of the trust or its settlor relating to income, gift, estate, or other tax requirements.

[ARTICLE] 4

ALLOCATION OF RECEIPTS DURING ADMINISTRATION OF TRUST

[PART 1 RECEIPTS FROM ENTITIES]

§401. Character of Receipts

(a) In this section, "entity" means a corporation, partnership, limited liability company, regulated investment company, real estate investment trust, common trust fund, or any other organization in which a trustee has an interest other than a trust or estate to which Section 402 applies, a business or activity to which Section 403 applies, or an asset-backed security to which Section 415 applies.

(b) Except as otherwise provided in this section, a trustee shall allocate to income money received from an entity.

(c) A trustee shall allocate the following receipts from an entity to principal:

(1) property other than money;

(2) money received in one distribution or a series of related distributions in exchange for part or all of a trust's interest in the entity;

(3) money received in total or partial liquidation of the entity; and

(4) money received from an entity that is a regulated investment company or a real estate investment trust if the money distributed is a capital gain dividend for federal income tax purposes.

(d) Money is received in partial liquidation:

(1) to the extent that the entity, at or near the time of a distribution, indicates that it is a distribution in partial liquidation; or

(2) if the total amount of money and property received in a distribution or series of related distributions is greater than 20 percent of the entity's gross assets, as shown by the entity's year-end financial statements immediately preceding the initial receipt.

(e) Money is not received in partial liquidation, nor may it be taken into account under subsection (d)(2), to the extent that it does not exceed the amount of income tax that a trustee or beneficiary must pay on taxable income of the entity that distributes the money.

(f) A trustee may rely upon a statement made by an entity about the source or character of a distribution if the statement is made at or near the time of distribution by the entity's board of directors or other person or group of persons authorized to exercise powers to pay money or transfer property comparable to those of a corporation's board of directors.

§402. Distribution from Trust or Estate

A trustee shall allocate to income an amount received as a distribution of income from a trust or an estate in which the trust has an interest other than a purchased interest, and shall allocate to principal an amount received as a distribution of principal from such a trust or estate. If a trustee purchases an interest in a trust that is an investment entity, or a decedent or donor transfers an interest in such a trust to a trustee, Section 401 or 415 applies to a receipt from the trust.

§403. Business and Other Activities Conducted by Trustee

(a) If a trustee who conducts a business or other activity determines that it is in the best interest of all the beneficiaries to account separately for the business or activity instead of accounting for it as part of the trust's general accounting records, the trustee may maintain separate accounting records for its transactions, whether or not its assets are segregated from other trust assets.

(b) A trustee who accounts separately for a business or other activity may determine the extent to which its net cash receipts must be retained for working capital, the acquisition or replacement of fixed assets, and other reasonably foreseeable needs of the business or activity, and the extent to which the remaining net cash receipts are accounted for as principal or income in the trust's general accounting records. If a trustee sells assets of the business or other activity, other than in the ordinary course of the business or activity, the trustee shall account for the net amount received as principal in the trust's general accounting records to the extent the trustee determines that the amount received is no longer required in the conduct of the business.

(c) Activities for which a trustee may maintain separate accounting records include:

(1) retail, manufacturing, service, and other traditional business activities;

(2) farming;

(3) raising and selling livestock and other animals;

(4) management of rental properties;

(5) extraction of minerals and other natural resources;

(6) timber operations; and

(7) activities to which Section 414 applies.

[PART 2 RECEIPTS NOT NORMALLY APPORTIONED]

§404. Principal Receipts

A trustee shall allocate to principal:

(1) to the extent not allocated to income under this [Act], assets received from a transferor during the transferor's lifetime, a decedent's estate, a trust with a terminating income interest, or a payer under a contract naming the trust or its trustee as beneficiary;

(2) money or other property received from the sale, exchange, liquidation, or change in form of a principal asset, including realized profit, subject to this [article];

(3) amounts recovered from third parties to reimburse the trust because of disbursements described in Section 502(a)(7) or for other reasons to the extent not based on the loss of income;

(4) proceeds of property taken by eminent domain, but a separate award made for the loss of income with respect to an accounting period during which a current income beneficiary had a mandatory income interest is income;

(5) net income received in an accounting period during which there is no beneficiary to whom a trustee may or must distribute income; and

(6) other receipts as provided in [Part 3].

§405. Rental Property

To the extent that a trustee accounts for receipts from rental property pursuant to this section, the trustee shall allocate to income an amount received as rent of real or personal property, including an amount received for cancellation or renewal of a lease. An amount received as a refundable deposit, including a security deposit or a deposit that is to be applied as rent for future periods, must be added to principal and held subject to the terms of the lease and is not available for distribution to a beneficiary until the trustee's contractual obligations have been satisfied with respect to that amount.

§406. Obligation to Pay Money

(a) An amount received as interest, whether determined at a fixed, variable, or floating rate, on an obligation to pay money to the trustee, including an amount received as consideration for prepaying principal, must be allocated to income without any provision for amortization of premium.

(b) A trustee shall allocate to principal an amount received from the sale, redemption, or other disposition of an obligation to pay money to the trustee more than one year after it is purchased or acquired by the trustee, including an obligation whose purchase price or value when it is acquired is less than its value at maturity. If the obligation matures within one year after it is purchased or acquired by the trustee, an amount received in excess of its purchase price or its value when acquired by the trust must be allocated to income.

(c) This section does not apply to an obligation to which Section 409, 410, 411, 412, 414, or 415 applies.

§407. Insurance Policies and Similar Contracts

(a) Except as otherwise provided in subsection (b), a trustee shall allocate to principal the proceeds of a life insurance policy or other contract in which the trust or its trustee is named as beneficiary, including a contract that insures the trust or its trustee against loss for damage to, destruction of, or loss of title to a trust asset. The trustee shall allocate dividends on an insurance policy to income if the premiums on the policy are paid from income, and to principal if the premiums are paid from principal.

(b) A trustee shall allocate to income proceeds of a contract that insures the trustee against loss of occupancy or other use by an income beneficiary, loss of income, or, subject to Section 403, loss of profits from a business.

(c) This section does not apply to a contract to which Section 409 applies.

[PART 3 RECEIPTS NORMALLY APPORTIONED]

§408. Insubstantial Allocations Not Required

If a trustee determines that an allocation between principal and income required by Section 409, 410, 411, 412, or 415 is insubstantial, the trustee may allocate the entire amount to principal unless one of the circumstances described in Section 104(c) applies to the allocation. This power may be exercised by a cotrustee in the circumstances described in Section 104(d) and may be released for the reasons and in the manner described in Section 104(e). An allocation is presumed to be insubstantial if:

(1) the amount of the allocation would increase or decrease net income in an accounting period, as determined before the allocation, by less than 10 percent; or

(2) the value of the asset producing the receipt for which the allocation would be made is less than 10 percent of the total value of the trust's assets at the beginning of the accounting period.

§409. Deferred Compensation, Annuities, and Similar Payments

(a) In this section, "payment" means a payment that a trustee may receive over a fixed number of years or during the life of one or more individuals because of services rendered or property transferred to the payer in exchange for future payments. The term includes a payment made in money or property from the payer's general assets or from a separate fund created by the payer, including a private or commercial annuity, an individual retirement account, and a pension, profit-sharing, stock-bonus, or stock-ownership plan.

(b) To the extent that a payment is characterized as interest or a dividend or a payment made in lieu of interest or a dividend, a trustee shall allocate it to income. The trustee shall allocate to principal the balance of the payment and any other payment received in the same accounting period that is not characterized as interest, a dividend, or an equivalent payment.

(c) If no part of a payment is characterized as interest, a dividend, or an equivalent payment, and all or part of the payment is required to be made, a trustee shall allocate to income 10 percent of the part that is required to be made during the accounting period and the balance to principal. If no part of a payment is required to be made or the payment received is the entire amount to which the trustee is entitled, the trustee shall allocate the entire payment to principal. For purposes of this subsection, a payment is not "required to be made" to the extent that it is made because the trustee exercises a right of withdrawal.

(d) If, to obtain an estate tax marital deduction for a trust, a trustee must allocate more of a payment to income than provided for by this section, the trustee shall allocate to income the additional amount necessary to obtain the marital deduction.

(e) This section does not apply to payments to which Section 410 applies.

§410. Liquidating Asset

(a) In this section, "liquidating asset" means an asset whose value will diminish or terminate because the asset is expected to produce receipts for a period of limited duration. The term includes a leasehold, patent, copyright, royalty right, and right to receive payments during a period of more than one year under an arrangement that does not provide for the payment of interest on the unpaid balance. The term does not include a payment subject to Section 409, resources subject to Section 411, timber subject to Section 412, an activity subject to Section 414, an asset subject to Section 415, or any asset for which the trustee establishes a reserve for depreciation under Section 503.

(b) A trustee shall allocate to income 10 percent of the receipts from a liquidating asset and the balance to principal.

§411. Minerals, Water, and Other Natural Resources

(a) To the extent that a trustee accounts for receipts from an interest in minerals or other natural resources pursuant to this section, the trustee shall allocate them as follows:

(1) If received as nominal delay rental or nominal annual rent on a lease, a receipt must be allocated to income.

(2) If received from a production payment, a receipt must be allocated to income if and to the extent that the agreement creating the production payment provides a factor for interest or its equivalent. The balance must be allocated to principal.

(3) If an amount received as a royalty, shut-in-well payment, take-or-pay payment, bonus, or delay rental is more than nominal, 90 percent must be allocated to principal and the balance to income.

(4) If an amount is received from a working interest or any other interest not provided for in paragraph (1), (2), or (3), 90 percent of the net amount received must be allocated to principal and the balance to income.

(b) An amount received on account of an interest in water that is renewable must be allocated to income. If the water is not renewable, 90 percent of the amount must be allocated to principal and the balance to income.

(c) This [Act] applies whether or not a decedent or donor was extracting minerals, water, or other natural resources before the interest became subject to the trust.

(d) If a trust owns an interest in minerals, water, or other natural resources on [the effective date of this [Act]], the trustee may allocate receipts from the interest as provided in this [Act] or in the manner used by the trustee before [the effective date of this [Act]]. If the trust acquires an interest in minerals, water, or other natural resources after [the effective date of this [Act]], the trustee shall allocate receipts from the interest as provided in this [Act].

§412. Timber

(a) To the extent that a trustee accounts for receipts from the sale of timber and related products pursuant to this section, the trustee shall allocate the net receipts:

(1) to income to the extent that the amount of timber removed from the land does not exceed the rate of growth of the timber during the accounting periods in which a beneficiary has a mandatory income interest;

(2) to principal to the extent that the amount of timber removed from the land exceeds the rate of growth of the timber or the net receipts are from the sale of standing timber;

(3) to or between income and principal if the net receipts are from the lease of timberland or from a contract to cut timber from land owned by a trust, by determining the amount of timber removed from the land under the lease or contract and applying the rules in paragraphs (1) and (2); or

(4) to principal to the extent that advance payments, bonuses, and other payments are not allocated pursuant to paragraph (1), (2), or (3).

(b) In determining net receipts to be allocated pursuant to subsection (a), a trustee shall deduct and transfer to principal a reasonable amount for depletion.

(c) This [Act] applies whether or not a decedent or transferor was harvesting timber from the property before it became subject to the trust.

(d) If a trust owns an interest in timberland on [the effective date of this [Act]], the trustee may allocate net receipts from the sale of timber and related products as provided in this [Act] or in the manner used by the trustee before [the effective date of this [Act]]. If the trust acquires an interest in timberland after [the effective date of this [Act]], the trustee shall allocate net receipts from the sale of timber and related products as provided in this [Act].

§413. Property Not Productive of Income

(a) If a marital deduction is allowed for all or part of a trust whose assets consist substantially of property that does not provide the spouse with sufficient income from or use of the trust assets, and if the amounts that the trustee transfers from principal to income under Section 104 and distributes to the spouse from principal pursuant to the terms of the trust are insufficient to provide the spouse with the beneficial enjoyment required to obtain the marital deduction, the spouse may require the trustee to make property productive of income, convert property within a reasonable time, or exercise the power conferred by Section 104(a). The trustee may decide which action or combination of actions to take.

(b) In cases not governed by subsection (a), proceeds from the sale or other disposition of an asset are principal without regard to the amount of income the asset produces during any accounting period.

§414. Derivatives and Options

(a) In this section, "derivative" means a contract or financial instrument or a combination of contracts and financial instruments which gives a trust the right or obligation to participate in some or all changes in the price of a tangible or intangible asset or group of assets, or changes in a rate, an index of prices or rates, or other market indicator for an asset or a group of assets.

(b) To the extent that a trustee does not account under Section 403 for transactions in derivatives, the trustee shall allocate to principal receipts from and disbursements made in connection with those transactions.

(c) If a trustee grants an option to buy property from the trust, whether or not the trust owns the property when the option is granted, grants an option that permits another person to sell property to the trust, or acquires an option to buy property for the trust or an option to sell an asset owned by the trust, and the trustee or other owner of the asset is required to deliver the asset if the option is exercised, an amount received for granting the option must be allocated to principal. An amount paid to acquire the option must be paid from principal. A gain or loss realized upon the exercise of an option, including an option granted to a settlor of the trust for services rendered, must be allocated to principal.

§415. Asset-Backed Securities

(a) In this section, "asset-backed security" means an asset whose value is based upon the right it gives the owner to receive distributions from the proceeds of financial assets that provide collateral for the security. The term includes an asset that gives the owner the right to receive from the collateral financial assets only the interest or other current return or only the proceeds other than interest or current return. The term does not include an asset to which Section 401 or 409 applies.

(b) If a trust receives a payment from interest or other current return and from other proceeds of the collateral financial assets, the trustee shall allocate to income the portion of the payment which the payer identifies as being from interest or other current return and shall allocate the balance of the payment to principal.

(c) If a trust receives one or more payments in exchange for the trust's entire interest in an asset-backed security in one accounting period, the trustee shall allocate the payments to principal. If a payment is one of a series of payments that will result in the liquidation of the trust's interest in the security over more than one accounting period, the trustee shall allocate 10 percent of the payment to income and the balance to principal.

Comment

Scope of section. Typical asset-backed securities include arrangements in which debt obligations such as real estate mortgages, credit card receivables, and auto loans are acquired by an investment trust and interests in the trust are sold to investors. The source for payments to an investor is the money received from principal and interest payments on the underlying debt. An asset-backed security includes an "interest only" or a "principal only" security that permits the investor to receive only the interest payments received from the bonds, mortgages, or other assets that are the collateral for the asset-backed security, or only the principal payments made on those collateral assets. An asset-backed security also includes a security that permits the investor to participate in either the capital appreciation of an underlying security or in the interest or dividend return from such a security, such as the "Primes" and "Scores" issued by Americus Trust. An asset-backed security does not include an interest in a corporation, partnership, or an investment trust described in the Comment to Section 402, whose assets consist significantly or entirely of investment assets. Receipts from an instrument that do not come within the scope of this section or any other section of the Act would be allocated entirely to principal under the rule in Section 103(a)(4), and the trustee may then consider whether and to what extent to exercise the power to adjust in Section 104, taking into account the return from the portfolio as whole and other relevant factors.

[ARTICLE] 5

ALLOCATION OF DISBURSEMENTS DURING ADMINISTRATION OF TRUST

§501. Disbursements from Income

A trustee shall make the following disbursements from income to the extent that they are not disbursements to which Section 201(2)(B) or (C) applies:

(1) one-half of the regular compensation of the trustee and of any person providing investment advisory or custodial services to the trustee;

(2) one-half of all expenses for accountings, judicial proceedings, or other matters that involve both the income and remainder interests;

(3) all of the other ordinary expenses incurred in connection with the administration, management, or preservation of trust property and the distribution of income, including interest, ordinary repairs, regularly recurring taxes assessed against principal, and expenses of a proceeding or other matter that concerns primarily the income interest; and

(4) recurring premiums on insurance covering the loss of a principal asset or the loss of income from or use of the asset.

Comment

Trustee fees. The regular compensation of a trustee or the trustee's agent includes compensation based on a percentage of either principal or income or both.

Insurance premiums. The reference in paragraph (4) to "recurring" premiums is intended to distinguish premiums paid annually for fire insurance from premiums on title insurance, each of which covers the loss of a principal asset. Title insurance premiums would be a principal disbursement under Section 502(a)(5).

Regularly recurring taxes. The reference to "regularly recurring taxes assessed against principal" includes all taxes regularly imposed on real property and tangible and intangible personal property.

§502. Disbursements from Principal

(a) A trustee shall make the following disbursements from principal:

(1) the remaining one-half of the disbursements described in Section 501(1) and (2);

(2) all of the trustee's compensation calculated on principal as a fee for acceptance, distribution, or termination, and disbursements made to prepare property for sale;

(3) payments on the principal of a trust debt;

(4) expenses of a proceeding that concerns primarily principal, including a proceeding to construe the trust or to protect the trust or its property;

(5) premiums paid on a policy of insurance not described in Section 501(4) of which the trust is the owner and beneficiary;

(6) estate, inheritance, and other transfer taxes, including penalties, apportioned to the trust; and

(7) disbursements related to environmental matters, including reclamation, assessing environmental conditions, remedying and removing environmental contamination, monitoring remedial activities and the release of substances, preventing future releases of substances, collecting amounts from persons liable or potentially liable for the costs of those activities, penalties imposed under environmental laws or regulations and other payments made to comply with those laws or regulations, statutory or common law claims by third parties, and defending claims based on environmental matters.

(b) If a principal asset is encumbered with an obligation that requires income from that asset to be paid directly to the creditor, the trustee shall transfer from principal to income an amount equal to the income paid to the creditor in reduction of the principal balance of the obligation.

§503. Transfers from Income to Principal for Depreciation

(a) In this section, "depreciation" means a reduction in value due to wear, tear, decay, corrosion, or gradual obsolescence of a fixed asset having a useful life of more than one year.

(b) A trustee may transfer to principal a reasonable amount of the net cash receipts from a principal asset that is subject to depreciation, but may not transfer any amount for depreciation:

(1) of that portion of real property used or available for use by a beneficiary as a residence or of tangible personal property held or made available for the personal use or enjoyment of a beneficiary;

(2) during the administration of a decedent's estate; or

(3) under this section if the trustee is accounting under Section 403 for the business or activity in which the asset is used.

(c) An amount transferred to principal need not be held as a separate fund.

Comment

Prior Acts. The 1931 Act has no provision for depreciation. Section 13(a)(2) of the 1962 Act provides that a charge shall be made against income for ". . . a reasonable allowance for depreciation on property subject to depreciation under generally accepted accounting principles . . . ." That provision has been resisted by many trustees, who do not provide for any depreciation for a variety of reasons. One reason relied upon is that a charge for depreciation is not needed to protect the remainder beneficiaries if the value of the land is increasing; another is that generally accepted accounting principles may not require depreciation to be taken if the property is not part of a business. The Drafting Committee concluded that the decision to provide for depreciation should be discretionary with the trustee. The power to transfer funds from income to principal that is granted by this section is a discretionary power of administration referred to in Section 103(b), and in exercising the power a trustee must comply with Section 103(b).

One purpose served by transferring cash from income to principal for depreciation is to provide funds to pay the principal of an indebtedness secured by the depreciable property. Section 504(b)(4) permits the trustee to transfer additional cash from income to principal for this purpose to the extent that the amount transferred from income to principal for depreciation is less than the amount of the principal payments.

§504. Transfers from Income to Reimburse Principal

(a) If a trustee makes or expects to make a principal disbursement described in this section, the trustee may transfer an appropriate amount from income to principal in one or more accounting periods to reimburse principal or to provide a reserve for future principal disbursements.

(b) Principal disbursements to which subsection (a) applies include the following, but only to the extent that the trustee has not been and does not expect to be reimbursed by a third party:

(1) an amount chargeable to income but paid from principal because it is unusually large, including extraordinary repairs;

(2) a capital improvement to a principal asset, whether in the form of changes to an existing asset or the construction of a new asset, including special assessments;

(3) disbursements made to prepare property for rental, including tenant allowances, leasehold improvements, and broker's commissions;

(4) periodic payments on an obligation secured by a principal asset to the extent that the amount transferred from income to principal for depreciation is less than the periodic payments; and

(5) disbursements described in Section 502(a)(7).

(c) If the asset whose ownership gives rise to the disbursements becomes subject to a successive income interest after an income interest ends, a trustee may continue to transfer amounts from income to principal as provided in subsection (a).

Comment

Prior Acts. The sources of Section 504 are Section 13(b) of the 1962 Act, which permits a trustee to "regularize distributions," if charges against income are unusually large, by using "reserves or other reasonable means" to withhold sums from income distributions; Section 13(c)(3) of the 1962 Act, which authorizes a trustee to establish an allowance for depreciation out of income if principal is used for extraordinary repairs, capital improvements, and special assessments; and Section 12(3) of the 1931 Act, which permits the trustee to spread income expenses of unusual amount "throughout a series of years." Section 504 contains a more detailed enumeration of the circumstances in which this authority may be used, and includes in subsection (b)(4) the express authority to use income to make principal payments on a mortgage if the depreciation charge against income is less than the principal payments on the mortgage.

§505. Income Taxes

(a) A tax required to be paid by a trustee based on receipts allocated to income must be paid from income.

(b) A tax required to be paid by a trustee based on receipts allocated to principal must be paid from principal, even if the tax is called an income tax by the taxing authority.

(c) A tax required to be paid by a trustee on the trust's share of an entity's taxable income must be paid proportionately:

(1) from income to the extent that receipts from the entity are allocated to income; and

(2) from principal to the extent that:

(A) receipts from the entity are allocated to principal; and

(B) the trust's share of the entity's taxable income exceeds the total receipts described in paragraphs (1) and (2)(A).

(d) For purposes of this section, receipts allocated to principal or income must be reduced by the amount distributed to a beneficiary from principal or income for which the trust receives a deduction in calculating the tax.

§506. Adjustments between Principal and Income Because of Taxes

(a) A fiduciary may make adjustments between principal and income to offset the shifting of economic interests or tax benefits between income beneficiaries and remainder beneficiaries which arise from:

(1) elections and decisions, other than those described in subsection (b), that the fiduciary makes from time to time regarding tax matters;

(2) an income tax or any other tax that is imposed upon the fiduciary or a beneficiary as a result of a transaction involving or a distribution from the estate or trust; or

(3) the ownership by an estate or trust of an interest in an entity whose taxable income, whether or not distributed, is includable in the taxable income of the estate, trust, or a beneficiary.

(b) If the amount of an estate tax marital deduction or charitable contribution deduction is reduced because a fiduciary deducts an amount paid from principal for income tax purposes instead of deducting it for estate tax purposes, and as a result estate taxes paid from principal are increased and income taxes paid by an estate, trust, or beneficiary are decreased, each estate, trust, or beneficiary that benefits from the decrease in income tax shall reimburse the principal from which the increase in estate tax is paid. The total reimbursement must equal the increase in the estate tax to the extent that the principal used to pay the increase would have qualified for a marital deduction or charitable contribution deduction but for the payment. The proportionate share of the reimbursement for each estate, trust, or beneficiary whose income taxes are reduced must be the same as its proportionate share of the total decrease in income tax. An estate or trust shall reimburse principal from income.

[ARTICLE] 6
MISCELLANEOUS PROVISIONS

§601. Uniformity of Application and Construction

In applying and construing this Uniform Act, consideration must be given to the need to promote uniformity of the law with respect to its subject matter among States that enact it.

§602. Severability Clause

If any provision of this [Act] or its application to any person or circumstance is held invalid, the invalidity does not affect other provisions or applications of this [Act] which can be given effect without the invalid provision or application, and to this end the provisions of this [Act] are severable.

§603. Repeal

The following acts and parts of acts are repealed:

(1) ....

(2) ....

(3) ....

§604. Effective Date

This [Act] takes effect on ....

§605. Application of [Act] to Existing Trusts and Estates

This [Act] applies to every trust or decedent's estate existing on [the effective date of this [Act]] except as otherwise expressly provided in the will or terms of the trust or in this [Act].

Part VII

~

Uniform Probate Code Article II (1990, As Amended)

UNIFORM PROBATE CODE ARTICLE II (1990, AS AMENDED)

PREFATORY NOTE

The Uniform Probate Code was promulgated in 1969. In 1990, Article II of the Code underwent significant revision. The 1990 revisions are the culmination of a systematic study of the Code conducted by the Joint Editorial Board for the Uniform Probate Code (JEB-UPC) and a special Drafting Committee to Revise Article II. The 1990 revisions concentrate on Article II, which is the article that covers the substantive law of intestate succession; spouse's elective share; omitted spouse and children; probate exemptions and allowances; execution and revocation of wills; will contracts; rules of construction; disclaimers; the effect of homicide and divorce on succession rights; and the rule against perpetuities and honorary trusts.

In the 20 or so years between the original promulgation of the Code and the 1990 revisions, several developments occurred that prompted the systematic round of review. Three themes were sounded: (1) the decline of formalism in favor of intent-serving policies; (2) the recognition that will substitutes and other inter-vivos transfers have so proliferated that they now constitute a major, if not the major, form of wealth transmission; (3) the advent of the multiple-marriage society, resulting in a significant fraction of the population being married more than once and having stepchildren and children by previous marriages and in the acceptance of a partnership or marital-sharing theory of marriage.

The 1990 revisions respond to these themes. The multiple-marriage society and the partnership/marital-sharing theory are reflected in the revised elective-share provisions of Part 2. As the General Comment to Part 2 explains, the revised elective share grants the surviving spouse a right of election that implements the partnership/marital-sharing theory by adjusting the elective share to the length of the marriage.

The children-of-previous-marriages and stepchildren phenomena are reflected most prominently in the revised rules on the spouse's share in intestacy.

The proliferation of will substitutes and other inter-vivos transfers is recognized, mainly, in measures tending to bring the law of probate and nonprobate transfers into greater unison. One aspect of this tendency is reflected in the restructuring of the rules of construction. Rules of construction are rules that supply presumptive meaning to dispositive and similar provisions of governing instruments. Part 6 of the pre-1990 Code contained several rules of construction that applied only to wills. Some of those rules of construction appropriately applied only to wills; provisions relating to lapse, testamentary exercise of a power of appointment, and ademption of a devise by satisfaction exemplify such rules of construction. Other rules of construction, however, properly apply to all governing instruments, not just wills; the provision relating to inclusion of adopted persons in class gift language exemplifies this type of rule of construction. The 1990 revisions divide pre-1990 Part 6 into two parts—Part 6, containing rules of construction for wills only; and Part 7, containing rules of construction for wills and other governing instruments. A few new rules of construction are also added.

In addition to separating the rules of construction into two parts, and adding new rules of construction, the revocation-upon-divorce provision (Section 2-804) is substantially revised so that divorce not only revokes devises, but also nonprobate beneficiary designations, in favor of the former spouse. Another feature of the 1990 revisions is a new section (Section 2-503) that brings the execution formalities for wills more into line with those for nonprobate transfers.

The 1990 Article II revisions also respond to other modern trends. During the period from 1969 to 1990, many developments occurred in the case law and statutory law. Also, many specific topics in probate, estate, and future-interests law were examined in the scholarly literature. The influence of many of these developments is seen in the 1990 revisions of Article II.

ARTICLE II

INTESTACY, WILLS, AND DONATIVE TRANSFERS (1990)

Part 1. Intestate Succession

Part 1. Intestate Succession

General Comment

The pre-1990 Code's basic pattern of intestate succession, contained in Part 1, was designed to provide suitable rules for the person of modest means who relies on the estate plan provided by law. The 1990 revisions are intended to further that purpose, by fine-tuning the various sections and bringing them into line with developing public policy.

The principal features of the 1990 revisions are:

1. So-called negative wills are authorized, under which the decedent who dies intestate, in whole or in part, can by will disinherit a particular heir.

2. A surviving spouse receives the whole of the intestate estate, if the decedent left no surviving descendants and no parents or if the decedent's surviving descendants are also descendants of the surviving spouse and the surviving spouse has no descendants who are not descendants of the decedent. The surviving spouse receives the first $200,000 plus three-fourths of the balance if the decedent left no surviving descendants but a surviving parent. The surviving spouse receives the first $150,000 plus one-half of the balance of the intestate estate, if the decedent's surviving descendants are also descendants of the surviving spouse but the surviving spouse has one or more other descendants. The surviving spouse receives the first $100,000 plus one-half of the balance of the intestate estate, if the decedent has one or more surviving descendants who are not descendants of the surviving spouse.

3. A system of representation called per-capita-at-each-generation is adopted as a means of more faithfully carrying out the underlying premise of the pre-1990 UPC system of representation. Under the per-capita-at-each-generation system, all grandchildren (whose parent has predeceased the intestate) receive equal shares.

4. Although only a modest revision of the section dealing with the status of adopted children and children born of unmarried parents is made at this time, the question is under continuing review and further revisions may be presented in the future.

5. The section on advancements is revised so that it applies to partially intestate estates as well as to wholly intestate estates.

§2-101. Intestate Estate

(a) Any part of a decedent's estate not effectively disposed of by will passes by intestate succession to the decedent's heirs as prescribed in this Code, except as modified by the decedent's will.

(b) A decedent by will may expressly exclude or limit the right of an individual or class to succeed to property of the decedent passing by intestate succession. If that individual or a member of that class survives the decedent, the share of the decedent's intestate estate to which that individual or class would have succeeded passes as if that individual or each member of that class had disclaimed his [or her] intestate share.

§2-102. Share of Spouse

The intestate share of a decedent's surviving spouse is:

(1) the entire intestate estate if:

(i) no descendant or parent of the decedent survives the decedent; or

(ii) all of the decendent's surviving descendants are also descendants of the surviving spouse and there is no other descendant of the surviving spouse who survives the decedent;

(2) the first [$200,000], plus three-fourths of any balance of the intestate estate, if no descendant of the decedent survives the decedent, but a parent of the decedent survivies the decedent;

(3) the first [$150,000], plus one-half of any balance of the intestate estate, if all of the decedent's surviving descendants are also descendants of the surviving spouse and the surviving spouse has one or more surviving descendants who are not descendants of the decedent;

(4) the first [$100,000] plus one-half of any balance of the intestate estate, if one or more of the decedent's surviving descendants are not descendants of the surviving spouse.

[ALTERNATIVE PROVISION FOR COMMUNITY PROPERTY STATES]

§ 2-102A. Share of Spouse

(a) The instestate share of a surviving spouse in separate property is:

(1) the entire intestate estate if:

(i) no descentant or parent of the decedent survives the decedent; or

(ii) all of the decedent's surviving descendants are also descendants of the surviving spouse and there is no other descendant of the surviving spouse who survives the decedent;

(2) The first [$200,000], plus three-fourths of any balance of the intestate estate, if no descendant of the decedent survivies the decedent, but a parent of the decedent survives the decedent;

(3) the first [$150,000], plus one-half of any balance of the intestate estate, if all of the decedent's surviving descendants are also descendants of the surviving spouse and the surviving spouse has one of more surviving descendant's who are not descendants of the decedent;

(4) the first [$100,000], plus one-half of any balance of the intestate estate, if one or more of the decedent's surviving descendants are not descendants of the surviving spouse.

(b) The one-half of community property belonging to the decendent passes to the [surviving spouse] as the intestate share.]

Comment

Purpose and Scope of Revisions. This section is revised to give the surviving spouse a larger share than the pre-1990 UPC. If the decedent leaves no surviving descendants and no surviving parent or if the decedent does leave surviving descendants but neither the decedent nor the surviving spouse has other descendants, the surviving spouse is entitled to all of the decedent's intestate estate.

If the decedent leaves no surviving descendants but does leave a surviving parent, the decedent's surviving spouse receives the first $200,000 plus three-fourths of the balance of the intestate estate.

If the decedent leaves surviving descendants and if the surviving spouse (but not the decedent) has other descendants, and thus the decedent's descendants are unlikely to be the *exclusive* beneficiaries of the surviving spouse's estate, the surviving spouse receives the first $150,000 plus one-half of the balance of the intestate estate. The purpose is to assure the decedent's own descendants of a share in the decedent's intestate estate when the estate exceeds $150,000.

If the decedent has other descendants, the surviving spouse receives $100,000 plus one-half of the balance. In this type of case, the decedent's descendants who are not descendants of the surviving spouse are not natural objects of the bounty of the surviving spouse.

Note that in all the cases where the surviving spouse receives a lump sum plus a fraction of the balance, the lump sums must be understood to be in addition to the probate exemptions and allowances to which the surviving spouse is entitled. . . .

Under the pre-1990 Code, the decedent's surviving spouse received the entire intestate estate only if there were neither surviving descendants nor parents. If there were surviving descendants, the descendants took one-half of the balance of the estate in excess of $50,000 (for example, $25,000 in a $100,000 estate). If there were no surviving descendants, but there was a surviving parent or parents, the parent or parents took that one-half of the balance in excess of $50,000. . .

§2-103. Share of Heirs Other Than Surviving Spouse

Any part of the intestate estate not passing to the decedent's surviving spouse under Section 2-102, or the entire intestate estate if there is no surviving spouse, passes in the following order to the individuals designated below who survive the decedent:

(1) to the decedent's descendants by representation;

(2) if there is no surviving descendant, to the decedent's parents equally if both survive, or to the surviving parent;

(3) if there is no surviving descendant or parent, to the decendant's of the decedent's parents or either of them by representation;

(4) if there is no surviving descendant, parent, or descendant of a parent, but the decedent is survivied by one or more grandparents or descendants of grandparents, half of the estate

passes to the decedent's paternal grandparents equally if both survive, or to the surviving paternal grandparent, or to the descendants of the decedent's paternal grandparents or either of them if both are deceased, the descendants taking by representation; and the other half passes to the decedent's maternal relatives in the same manner; but if there is no surviving grandparent or descendant of a grandparent on either the paternal or the materanl side, the entire estate passes to the decedent's relatives on the other side in the same manner as the half.

§2-104. Requirement That Heir Survive Decedent for 120 Hours

An individual who fails to survive the decedent by 120 hours is deemed to have predeceased the decedent for purposes of homestead allowance, exempt property, and intestate succession, and the decedent's heirs are determined accordingly. If it is not established by clear and convincing evidence that an individual who would otherwise be an heir survived the decedent by 120 hours, it is deemed that the individual failed to survive for the required period. This section is not to be applied if its application would result in a taking of intestate estate by the state under Section 2-105.

§2-105. No Taker

If there is no taker under the provisions of this Article, the intestate estate passes to the [state].

§2-106. Representation

(a) [Definitions.] In this section:

(1) "Deceased descendant," "deceased parent," or "deceased grandparent" means a descendant, parent, or grandparent who either predeceased the decedent or is deemed to have predeceased the decedent under Section 2-104.

(2) "Surviving descendant" means a descendant who neither predeceased the decedent nor is deemed to have predeceased the decedent under Section 2-104.

(b) [Decedent's Descendants.] If, under Section 2-103(1), a decedent's intestate estate or a part thereof passes "by representation" to the decedent's descendants, the estate or part thereof is divided into as many equal shares as there are (i) surviving descendants in the generation nearest to the decedent which contains one or more surviving descendants and (ii) deceased descendants in the same generation who left surviving descendants, if any. Each surviving descendant in the nearest generation is allocated one share. The remaining shares, if any, are combined and then divided in the same manner among the surviving descendants of the deceased descendants as if the surviving descendants who were allocated a share and their surviving descendants had predeceased the decedent.

(c) [Descendants of Parents or Grandparents.] If, under Section 2-103(3) or (4), a decedent's intestate estate or a part thereof passes "by representation" to the descendants of the decedent's deceased parents or either of them or to the descendants of the decedent's deceased paternal or maternal grandparents or either of them, the estate or part thereof is divided into as many equal shares as there are (i) surviving descendants in the generation nearest the deceased parents or either of them, or the deceased grandparents or either of them, that contains one or more surviving descendants and (ii) deceased descendants in the same generation who left surviving descendants, if any. Each surviving descendant in the nearest generation is allocated one share. The remaining shares, if any, are combined and then divided in the same manner among the surviving descendants of the deceased descendants as if the surviving descendants who were allocated a share and their surviving descendants had predeceased the decedent.

Comment

Purpose and Scope of Revisions. This section is revised to adopt the system of representation called per-capita-at-each-generation. The per-capita-at-each-generation system is more responsive to the underlying premise of the original UPC system, in that it always provides equal shares to those equally related; the pre-1990 UPC achieved this objective in most but not all cases. . . .

In addition, a recent survey of client preferences, conducted by Fellows of the American College of Trust and Estate Counsel, suggets that the per-capita-at-each-generation system of representation is preferred by most clients. See Young, "Meaning of 'Issue' and 'Descendants,'" 13 ACTEC Probate Notes 225 (1988). The survey results were striking: Of 761 responses, 541 (71%) chose the per-capita-at-each-generation system; 145 (19.1%) chose the per-stirpes system, and 70 (9.2%) chose the pre-1990 UPC system. . . .

§2-107. Kindred of Half Blood

Relatives of the half blood inherit the same share they would inherit if they were of the whole blood.

§2-108. Afterborn Heirs

An individual in gestation at a particular time is treated as living at that time if the individual lives 120 hours or more after birth.

§2-109. Advancements

(a) If an individual dies intestate as to all or a portion of his [or her] estate, property the decedent gave during the decedent's lifetime to an individual who, at the decedent's death, is an heir is treated as an advancement against the heir's intestate share only if (i) the decedent declared in a contemporaneous writing or the heir acknowledged in writing that the gift is an advancement or (ii) the decedent's contemporaneous writing or the heir's written acknowledgment otherwise indicates that the gift is to be taken into account in computing the division and distribution of the decedent's intestate estate.

(b) For purposes of subsection (a), property advanced is valued as of the time the heir came into possession or enjoyment of the property or as of the time of the decedent's death, whichever first occurs.

(c) If the recipient of the property fails to survive the decedent, the property is not taken into account in computing the division and distribution of the decedent's intestate estate, unless the decedent's contemporaneous writing provides otherwise.

§2-110. Debts to Decedent

A debt owed to a decedent is not charged against the intestate share of any individual except the debtor. If the debtor fails to survive the decedent, the debt is not taken into account in computing the intestate share of the debtor's descendants.

§2-111. Alienage

No individual is disqualified to take as an heir because the individual or an individual through whom he [or she] claims is or has been an alien.

§2-112. Dower and Curtesy Abolished

The estates of dower and curtesy are abolished.]

§2-113. Individuals Related to Decedent Through Two Lines

An individual who is related to the decedent through two lines of relationship is entitled to only a single share based on the relationship that would entitle the individual to the larger share.

§2-114. Parent and Child Relationship

(a) Except as provided in subsections (b) and (c), for purposes of intestate succession by, through, or from a person, an individual is the child of his [or her] natural parents, regardless of their marital status. The parent and child relationship may be established under [the Uniform Parentage Act] [applicable state law] [insert appropriate statutory reference].

(b) An adopted individual is the child of his [or her] adopting parent or parents and not of his [or her] natural parents, but adoption of a child by the spouse of either natural parent has no effect on (i) the relationship between the child and that natural parent or (ii) the right of the child or a descendant of the child to inherit from or through the other natural parent.

(c) Inheritance from or through a child by either natural parent or his [or her] kindred is precluded unless that natural parent has openly treated the child as his [or hers], and has not refused to support the child.

Part 2
Elective Share of Surviving Spouse

§ 2-201. Definitions

In this Part:

(1) As used in sections other than Section 2-205, "decedent's nonprobate transfers to others" means the amounts that are included in the augmented estate under Section 2-205.

(2) "Fractional interest in property held in joint tenancy with the right of survivorship," whether the fractional interest is unilaterally severable or not, means the fraction, the numerator of which is one and the denominator of which, if the decedent was a joint tenant, is one plus the number of joint tenants who survive the decedent and which, if the decedent was not a joint tenant, is the number of joint tenants.

(3) "Marriage," as it relates to a transfer by the decedent during marriage, means any marriage of the decedent to the decedent's surviving spouse.

(4) "Nonadverse party" means a person who does not have a substantial beneficial interest in the trust or other property arrangement that would be adversely affected by the exercise or nonexercise of the power that he [or she] possesses respecting the trust or other property arrangement. A person having a general power of appointment over property is deemed to have a beneficial interest in the property.

(5) "Power" or "power of appointment" includes a power to designate the beneficiary of a beneficiary designation.

(6) "Presently exercisable general power of appointment" means a power of appointment under which, at the time in question, the decedent, whether or not he [or she] then had the capacity to exercise the power, held a power to create a present or future

interest in himself [or herself], his [or her] creditors, his [or her] estate, or creditors of his [or her] estate, and includes a power to revoke or invade the principal of a trust or other property arrangement.

(7) "Probate estate" means property that would pass by intestate succession if the decedent died without a valid will.

(8) "Property" includes values subject to a beneficiary designation.

(9) "Right to income" includes a right to payments under a commercial or private annuity, an annuity trust, a unitrust, or a similar arrangement.

(10) "Transfer," as it relates to a transfer by or of the decedent, includes (A) an exercise or release of a presently exercisable general power of appointment held by the decedent, (B) a lapse at death of a presently exercisable general power of appointment held by the decedent, and (C) an exercise, release, or lapse of a general power of appointment that the decedent created in himself [or herself] and of a power described in Section 2-205(2)(ii) that the decedent conferred on a nonadverse party.

Comment

Pre-1990 Provision. The pre-1990 provisions granted the surviving spouse a one-third share of the augmented estate. The one-third fraction was largely a carry over from common-law dower, under which a surviving widow had a one-third interest for life in her deceased husband's life.

Purpose and Scope of Revisions. The revision of this section is the first step in the overall plan of implementing a partnership or marital-sharing theory of marriage, with a support theory back-up.

Subsection (a). Subsection (a) implements the partnership theory by increasing the maximum elective-share percentage of the augmented estate to fifty percent, but by phasing that ultimate entitlement in so that it does not reach the maximum fifty-percent level until the marriage has lasted at least 15 years. If the decedent and the surviving spouse were married to each other more than once, all periods of marriage to eachother are added together for purposes of subsection (a); periods between marriages are not counted.

Subsection (b). Subsection (b) implements the support theory of the elective share by providing a [$50,000] supplemental elective-share amount in case the surviving spouse's assets and other entitlements are below this figure. . . .

§2-202. Elective Share

(a) [Elective-Share Amount.] The surviving spouse of a decedent who dies domiciled in this State has a right of election, under the limitations and conditions stated in this Part, to take an elective-share amount equal to the value of the elective-share percentage of the augmented estate, determined by the length of time the spouse and the decedent were married to each other, in accordance with the following schedule:

If the decedent and the spouse were married to each other:	The elective-share percentage is:
Less than 1 year	Supplemental Amount Only.
1 year but less than 2 years	3% of the augmented estate.
2 years but less than 3 years	6% of the augmented estate.
3 years but less than 4 years	9% of the augmented estate.
4 years but less than 5 years	12% of the augmented estate.
5 years but less than 6 years	15% of the augmented estate.
6 years but less than 7 years	18% of the augmented estate.
7 years but less than 8 years	21% of the augmented estate.
8 years but less than 9 years	24% of the augmented estate.
9 years but less than 10 years	27% of the augmented estate.
10 years but less than 11 years	30% of the augmented estate.
11 years but less than 12 years	34% of the augmented estate.
12 years but less than 13 years	38% of the augmented estate.
13 years but less than 14 years	42% of the augmented estate.
14 years but less than 15 years	46% of the augmented estate.
15 years or more	50% of the augmented estate.

(b) [Supplemental Elective-Share Amount.] If the sum of the amounts described in Sections 2-207, 2-209(a)(1), and that part of the elective-share amount payable from the decedent's probate estate and nonprobate transfers to others under Section 2-209(b) and (c) is less than [$50,000], the surviving spouse is entitled to a supplemental elective-share amount equal to [$50,000], minus the sum of the amounts described in those sections. The supplemental elective-share amount is payable from the decedent's probate estate and from recipients of the decedent's nonprobate transfers to others in the order of priority set forth in Section 2-209(b) and (c).

(c) [Effect of Election on Statutory Benefits.] If the right of election is exercised by or on behalf of the surviving spouse, the surviving spouse's homestead allowance, exempt property, and family allowance, if any, are not charged against but are in addition to the elective-share and supplemental elective-share amounts.

(d) [Non-Domiciliary.] The right, if any, of the surviving spouse of a decedent who dies domiciled outside this State to take an elective share in property in this State is governed by the law of the decedent's domicile at death.

§2-203. Composition of the Augmented Estate

Subject to Section 2-208, the value of the augmented estate, to the extent provided in Sections 2-204, 2-205, 2-206, and 2-207, consists of the sum of the values of all property, whether real or personal; movable or immovable, tangible or intangible, wherever situated, that constitute the decedent's net probate estate, the decedent's nonprobate transfers to others, the decedent's nonprobate transfers to the surviving spouse, and the surviving spouse's property and nonprobate transfers to others.

§2-204. Decedent's Net Probate Estate

The value of the augmented estate includes the value of the decedent's probate estate, reduced by funeral and administration expenses, homestead allowance, family allowances, exempt property, and enforceable claims.

§2-205. Decedent's Nonprobate Transfers to Others

The value of the augmented estate includes the value of the decedent's nonprobate transfers to others, not included under Section 2-204, of any of the following types, in the amount provided respectively for each type of transfer:

(1) Property owned or owned in substance by the decedent immediately before death that passed outside probate at the decedent's death. Property included under this category consists of:

(i) Property over which the decedent alone, immediately before death, held a presently exercisable general power of appointment. The amount included is the value of the property subject to the power, to the extent the property passed at the decedent's death, by exercise, release, lapse, in default, or otherwise, to or for the benefit of any person other than the decedent's estate or surviving spouse.

(ii) The decedent's fractional interest in property held by the decedent in joint tenancy with the right of survivorship. The amount included is the value of the decedent's fractional interest, to the extent the fractional interest passed by right of survivorship at the decedent's death to a surviving joint tenant other than the decedent's surviving spouse.

(iii) The decedent's ownership interest in property or accounts held in POD, TOD, or co-ownership registration with the right of survivorship. The amount included is the value of the decedent's ownership interest, to the extent the decedent's ownership interest passed at the decedent's death to or for the benefit of any person other than the decedent's estate or surviving spouse.

(iv) Proceeds of insurance, including accidental death benefits, on the life of the decedent, if the decedent owned the insurance policy immediately before death or if and to the extent the decedent alone and immediately before death held a presently exercisable general power of appointment over the policy or its proceeds. The amount included is the value of the proceeds, to the extent they were payable at the decedent's death to or for the benefit of any person other than the decedent's estate or surviving spouse.

(2) Property transferred in any of the following forms by the decedent during marriage:

(i) Any irrevocable transfer in which the decedent retained the right to the possession or enjoyment of, or to the income from, the property if and to the extent the decedent's right terminated at or continued beyond the decedent's death. The amount included is the value of the fraction of the property to which the decedent's right related, to the extent the fraction of the property passed outside probate to or for the benefit of any person other than the decedent's estate or surviving spouse.

(ii) Any transfer in which the decedent created a power over income or property, exercisable by the decedent alone or in conjunction with any other person, or exercisable by a nonadverse party, to or for the benefit of the decedent, creditors of the decedent, the decedent's estate, or creditors of the decedent's estate. The amount included with respect to a power over property is the value of the property subject to the power, and the amount included with respect to a power over income is the value of the property that produces or produced the income, to the extent the power in either case was exercisable at the decedent's death to or for the benefit of any person other than the decedent's surviving spouse or to the extent the property passed at the decedent's death, by exercise, release, lapse, in default, or otherwise, to or for the benefit of any person other than the decedent's estate or surviving spouse. If the power is a power over both income and property and the preceding sentence produces different amounts, the amount included is the greater amount.

(3) Property that passed during marriage and during the two-year period next preceding the decedent's death as a result of a transfer by the decedent if the transfer was of any of the following types:

(i) Any property that passed as a result of the termination of a right or interest in, or power over, property that would have been included in the augmented estate under paragraph (1)(i), (ii), or (iii), or under paragraph (2), if the right, interest, or power had not terminated until the decedent's death. The amount included is the value of the property that would have been included under those paragraphs if the property were valued at the time the right, interest, or power terminated, and is included only to the extent the property passed upon termination to or for the benefit of any person other than the decedent or the decedent's estate, spouse, or surviving spouse. As used in this subparagraph, "termination," with respect to a right or interest in property, occurs when the right or interest terminated by the terms of the governing instrument or the decedent transferred or relinquished the right or interest, and, with respect to a power over property, occurs when the power terminated by exercise, release, lapse, default, or otherwise, but, with respect to a power described in paragraph (1)(i), "termination" occurs when the power terminated by exercise or release, but not otherwise.

(ii) Any transfer of or relating to an insurance policy on the life of the decedent if the proceeds would have been included in the augmented estate under paragraph (1)(iv) had the transfer not occurred. The amount included is the value of the insurance proceeds to the extent the proceeds were payable at the decedent's death to or for the benefit of any person other than the decedent's estate or surviving spouse.

(iii) Any transfer of property, to the extent not otherwise included in the augmented estate, made to or for the benefit of a person other than the decedent's surviving spouse. The amount included is the value of the transferred property to the extent the aggregate transfers to any one donee in either of the two years exceeded $10,000.

§2-206. Decedent's Nonprobate Transfers to the Surviving Spouse

Excluding property passing to the surviving spouse under the federal Social Security system, the value of the augmented estate includes the value of the decedent's nonprobate transfers to the decedent's surviving spouse, which consist of all property that passed outside probate at the decedent's death from the decedent to the surviving spouse by reason of the decedent's death, including:

(1) the decedent's fractional interest in property held as a joint tenant with the right of survivorship, to the extent that the decedent's fractional interest passed to the surviving spouse as surviving joint tenant,

(2) the decedent's ownership interest in property or accounts held in co-ownership registration with the right of survivorship, to the extent the decedent's ownership interest passed to the surviving spouse as surviving co-owner, and

(3) all other property that would have been included in the augmented estate under Section 2-205(1) or (2) had it passed to or for the benefit of a person other than the decedent's spouse, surviving spouse, the decedent, or the decedent's creditors, estate, or estate creditors.

§2-207. Surviving Spouse's Property and Nonprobate Transfers to Others

(a) [Included Property.] Except to the extent included in the augmented estate under Section 2-204 or 2-206, the value of the augmented estate includes the value of:

(1) property that was owned by the decedent's surviving spouse at the decedent's death, including:

(i) the surviving spouse's fractional interest in property held in joint tenancy with the right of survivorship,

(ii) the surviving spouse's ownership interest in property or accounts held in co-ownership registration with the right of survivorship, and

(iii) property that passed to the surviving spouse by reason of the decedent's death, but not including the spouse's right to homestead allowance, family allowance, exempt property, or payments under the federal Social Security system; and

(2) property that would have been included in the surviving spouse's nonprobate transfers to others, other than the spouse's fractional and ownership interests included under subsection (a)(1)(i) or (ii), had the spouse been the decedent.

(b) [Time of Valuation.] Property included under this section is valued at the decedent's death, taking the fact that the decedent predeceased the spouse into account, but, for purposes of subsection (a)(1)(i) and (ii), the values of the spouse's fractional and ownership interests are determined immediately before the decedent's death if the decedent was then a joint tenant or a co-owner of the property or accounts. For purposes of subsection (a)(2), proceeds of insurance that would have been included in the spouse's nonprobate transfers to others under Section 2-205(1)(iv) are not valued as if he [or she] were deceased.

(c) [Reduction for Enforceable Claims.] The value of property included under this section is reduced by enforceable claims against the surviving spouse.

§2-208. Exclusions, Valuation, and Overlapping Application

(a) [Exclusions.] The value of any property is excluded from the decedent's nonprobate transfers to others (i) to the extent the decedent received adequate and full consideration in money or money's worth for a transfer of the property or (ii) if the property was transferred with the written joinder of, or if the transfer was consented to in writing by, the surviving spouse.

(b) [Valuation.] The value of property:

(1) included in the augmented estate under Section 2-205, 2-206, or 2-207 is reduced in each category by enforceable claims against the included property; and

(2) includes the commuted value of any present or future interest and the commuted value of

amounts payable under any trust, life insurance settlement option, annuity contract, public or private pension, disability compensation, death benefit or retirement plan, or any similar arrangement, exclusive of the federal Social Security system.

(c) [Overlapping Application; No Double Inclusion.] In case of overlapping application to the same property of the paragraphs or subparagraphs of Section 2-205, 2-206, or 2-207, the property is included in the augmented estate under the provision yielding the greatest value, and under only one overlapping provision if they all yield the same value.

§ 2-209. Sources from Which Elective Share Payable

(a) [Elective-Share Amount Only.] In a proceeding for an elective share, the following are applied first to satisfy the elective-share amount and to reduce or eliminate any contributions due from the decedent's probate estate and recipients of the decedent's nonprobate transfers to others:

(1) amounts included in the augmented estate under Section 2-204 which pass or have passed to the surviving spouse by testate or intestate succession and amounts included in the augmented estate under Section 2-206; and

(2) amounts included in the augmented estate under Section 2-207 up to the applicable percentage thereof. For the purposes of this subsection, the "applicable percentage" is twice the elective-share percentage set forth in the schedule in Section 2-202(a) appropriate to the length of time the spouse and the decedent were married to each other.

(b) [Unsatisfied Balance of Elective-Share Amount; Supplemental Elective-Share Amount.] If, after the application of subsection (a), the elective-share amount is not fully satisfied or the surviving spouse is entitled to a supplemental elective-share amount, amounts included in the decedent's probate estate and in the decedent's nonprobate transfers to others, other than amounts included under Section 2-205(3)(i) or (iii), are applied first to satisfy the unsatisfied balance of the elective-share amount or the supplemental elective-share amount. The decedent's probate estate and that portion of the decedent's nonprobate transfers to others are so applied that liability for the unsatisfied balance of the elective-share amount or for the supplemental elective-share amount is equitably apportioned among the recipients of the decedent's probate estate and of that portion of the decedent's nonprobate transfers to others in proportion to the value of their interests therein.

(c) [Unsatisfied Balance of Elective-Share and Supplemental Elective-Share Amounts.] If, after the application of subsections (a) and (b), the elective-share or supplemental elective-share amount is not fully satisfied, the remaining portion of the decedent's nonprobate transfers to others is so applied that liability for the unsatisfied balance of the elective-share or supplemental elective-share amount is equitably apportioned among the recipients of the remaining portion of the decedent's nonprobate transfers to others in proportion to the value of their interests therein.

§2-210. Personal Liability of Recipients

(a) Only original recipients of the decedent's nonprobate transfers to others, and the donees of the recipients of the decedent's nonprobate transfers to others, to the extent the donees have the property or its proceeds, are liable to make a proportional contribution toward satisfaction of the surviving spouse's elective-share or supplemental elective-share amount. A person liable to make contribution may choose to give up the proportional part of the decedent's nonprobate transfers to him [or her] or to pay the value of the amount for which he [or she] is liable.

(b) If any section or part of any section of this Part is preempted by federal law with respect to a payment, an item of property, or any other benefit included in the decedent's nonprobate transfers to others, a person who, not for value, receives the payment, item of property, or any other benefit is obligated to return the payment, item of property, or benefit, or is personally liable for the amount of the payment or the value of that item of property or benefit, as provided in Section 2-209, to the person who would have been entitled to it were that section or part of that section not preempted.

§2-211. Proceeding for Elective Share; Time Limit

(a) Except as provided in subsection (b), the election must be made by filing in the court and mailing or delivering to the personal representative, if any, a petition for the elective share within nine months after the date of the decedent's death, or within six months after the probate of the decedent's will, whichever limitation later expires. The surviving spouse must give notice of the time and place set for hearing to persons interested in the estate and to the distributees and recipients of portions of the augmented estate whose interests will be adversely affected by the taking of the elective share. Except as provided in subsection (b), the decedent's nonprobate transfers to others are not included within the augmented estate for the purpose of computing the elective-share, if the petition is filed more than nine months after the decedent's death.

(b) Within nine months after the decedent's death, the surviving spouse may petition the court for an extension of time for making an election. If, within nine months after the decedent's death, the spouse gives notice of the petition to all persons interested in the decedent's nonprobate transfers to others, the court for cause shown by the surviving spouse may extend the time for election. If the court grants the spouse's petition for an extension, the decedent's nonprobate transfers to others are not excluded from the augmented estate for the purpose of computing the elective-share and supplemental elective-share amounts, if the spouse makes an election by filing in the court and mailing or delivering to the personal representative, if any, a petition for the elective share within the time allowed by the extension.

(c) The surviving spouse may withdraw his [or her] demand for an elective share at any time before entry of a final determination by the court.

(d) After notice and hearing, the court shall determine the elective-share and supplemental elective-share amounts, and shall order its payment from the assets of the augmented estate or by contribution as appears appropriate under Sections 2-209 and 2-210. If it appears that a fund or property included in the augmented estate has not come into the possession of the personal representative, or has been distributed by the personal representative, the court nevertheless shall fix the liability of any person who has any interest in the fund or property or who has possession thereof, whether as trustee or otherwise. The proceeding may be maintained against fewer than all persons against whom relief could be sought, but no person is subject to contribution in any greater amount than he [or she] would have been under Sections 2-209 and 2-210 had relief been secured against all persons subject to contribution.

(e) An order or judgment of the court may be enforced as necessary in suit for contribution or payment in other courts of this State or other jurisdictions.

§2-212. Right of Election Personal to Surviving Spouse; Incapacitated Surviving Spouse

(a) [Surviving Spouse Must Be Living at Time of Election.] The right of election may be exercised only by a surviving spouse who is living when the petition for the elective share is filed in the court under Section 2-211(a). If the election is not exercised by the surviving spouse personally, it may be exercised on the surviving spouse's behalf by his [or her] conservator, guardian, or agent under the authority of a power of attorney.

(b) [Incapacitated Surviving Spouse.] If the election is exercised on behalf of a surviving spouse who is an incapacitated person, that portion of the elective-share and supplemental elective-share amounts due from the decedent's probate estate and recipients of the decedent's nonprobate transfers to others under Section 2-209(b) and (c) must be placed in a custodial trust for the benefit of the surviving spouse under the provisions of the [Enacting state] Uniform Custodial Trust Act, except as modified below. For the purposes of this subsection, an election on behalf of a surviving spouse by an agent under a durable power of attorney is presumed to be on behalf of a surviving spouse who is an incapacitated person. For purposes of the custodial trust established by this subsection, (i) the electing guardian, conservator, or agent is the custodial trustee, (ii) the surviving spouse is the beneficiary, and (iii) the custodial trust is deemed to have been created by the decedent spouse by written transfer that takes effect at the decedent spouse's death and that directs the custodial trustee to administer the custodial trust as for an incapacitated beneficiary.

(c) [Custodial Trust.] For the purposes of subsection (b), the [Enacting state] Uniform Custodial Trust Act must be applied as if Section 6(b) thereof were repealed and Sections 2(e), 9(b), and 17(a) were amended to read as follows:

(1) Neither an incapacitated beneficiary nor anyone acting on behalf of an incapacitated beneficiary has a power to terminate the custodial trust; but if the beneficiary regains capacity, the beneficiary then acquires the power to terminate the custodial trust by delivering to the custodial trustee a writing signed by the beneficiary declaring the termination. If not previously terminated, the custodial trust terminates on the death of the beneficiary.

(2) If the beneficiary is incapacitated, the custodial trustee shall expend so much or all of the custodial trust property as the custodial trustee considers advisable for the use and benefit of the beneficiary and individuals who were supported by the beneficiary when the beneficiary became incapacitated, or who are legally entitled to support by the beneficiary. Expenditures may be made in the manner, when, and to the extent that the custodial trustee determines suitable and proper, without court order but with regard to other support, income, and property of the beneficiary [exclusive of] [and] benefits of medical or other forms of assistance from any state or federal government or governmental agency for which the beneficiary must qualify on the basis of need.

(3) Upon the beneficiary's death, the custodial trustee shall transfer the unexpended custodial trust property in the following order: (i) under the residuary clause, if any, of the will of the beneficiary's predeceased spouse against whom the elective share was taken, as if that predeceased spouse died immediately after the beneficiary; or (ii) to that predeceased spouse's heirs under Section 2-711 of [this State's] Uniform Probate Code.

[STATES THAT HAVE NOT ADOPTED THE UNIFORM CUSTODIAL TRUST ACT SHOULD ADOPT THE FOLLOWING ALTERNATIVE SUBSECTION (b) AND NOT ADOPT SUBSECTION (b) OR (c) ABOVE]

[(b) [Incapacitated Surviving Spouse.] If the election is exercised on behalf of a surviving spouse who is an incapacitated person, the court must set aside that portion of the elective-share and supplemental elective-share amounts due from the decedent's probate estate and recipients of the decedent's nonprobate transfers to others under Section 2-209(b) and (c) and must appoint a trustee to administer that property for the support of the surviving spouse. For the purposes of this subsection, an election on behalf of a surviving spouse by an agent under a durable power of attorney is presumed to be on behalf of a surviving spouse who is an incapacitated person. The trustee must administer the trust in accordance with the following terms and such additional terms as the court determines appropriate:

(1) Expenditures of income and principal may be made in the manner, when, and to the extent that the trustee determines suitable and proper for the surviving spouse's support, without court order but with regard to other support, income, and property of the surviving spouse [exclusive of] [and] benefits of medical or other forms of assistance from any state or federal government or governmental agency for which the surviving spouse must qualify on the basis of need.

(2) During the surviving spouse's incapacity, neither the surviving spouse nor anyone acting on behalf of the surviving spouse has a power to terminate the trust; but if the surviving spouse regains capacity, the surviving spouse then acquires the power to terminate the trust and acquire full ownership of the trust property free of trust, by delivering to the trustee a writing signed by the surviving spouse declaring the termination.

(3) Upon the surviving spouse's death, the trustee shall transfer the unexpended trust property in the following order: (i) under the residuary clause, if any, of the will of the predeceased spouse against whom the elective share was taken, as if that predeceased spouse died immediately after the surviving spouse; or (ii) to the predeceased spouse's heirs under Section 2-711.]

§2-213. Waiver of Right to Elect and of Other Rights

(a) The right of election of a surviving spouse and the rights of the surviving spouse to homestead allowance, exempt property, and family allowance, or any of them, may be waived, wholly or partially, before or after marriage, by a written contract, agreement, or waiver signed by the surviving spouse.

(b) A surviving spouse's waiver is not enforceable if the surviving spouse proves that:

(1) he [or she] did not execute the waiver voluntarily; or

(2) the waiver was unconscionable when it was executed and, before execution of the waiver, he [or she]:

(i) was not provided a fair and reasonable disclosure of the property or financial obligations of the decedent;

(ii) did not voluntarily and expressly waive, in writing, any right to disclosure of the property or financial obligations of the decedent beyond the disclosure provided; and

(iii) did not have, or reasonably could not have had, an adequate knowledge of the property or financial obligations of the decedent.

(c) An issue of unconscionability of a waiver is for decision by the court as a matter of law.

(d) Unless it provides to the contrary, a waiver of "all rights," or equivalent language, in the property or estate of a present or prospective spouse or a complete property settlement entered into after or in anticipation of separation or divorce is a waiver of all rights of elective share, homestead allowance, exempt property, and family allowance by each spouse in the property of the other and a renunciation by each of all benefits that would otherwise pass to him [or her] from the other by intestate succession or by virtue of any will executed before the waiver or property settlement.

§2-214. Protection of Payors and Other Third Parties

(a) Although under Section 2-205 a payment, item of property, or other benefit is included in the decedent's nonprobate transfers to others, a payor or other third party is not liable for having made a payment or transferred an item of property or other benefit to a beneficiary designated in a governing instrument, or for having taken any other action in good faith reliance on the validity of a governing instrument, upon request and satisfactory proof of the decedent's death, before the payor or other third party received written notice from the surviving spouse or spouse's representative of an intention to file a petition for the elective share or that a petition for the elective share has been filed. A payor or other third party is liable for payments made or other actions taken after the payor or other third party received written notice of an intention to file a petition for the elective share or that a petition for the elective share has been filed.

(b) A written notice of intention to file a petition for the elective share or that a petition for the elective share has been filed must be mailed to the payor's or other third party's main office or home by registered or certified mail, return receipt requested, or served upon the payor or other third party in the same manner as a summons in a civil action. Upon receipt of written notice of intention to file a petition for the elective share or that a petition for the elective share has been filed, a payor or other third party may pay any amount owed or transfer or deposit any item of property held by it to or with the court having jurisdiction of the probate proceedings relating to the decedent's estate, or if no proceedings have been commenced, to or with the court having jurisdiction of probate proceedings relating to decedents' estates located in the county of the decedent's residence. The court shall hold the funds or item of property, and, upon its determination under Section 2-211(d), shall order disbursement in accordance with the determination. If no petition is filed in the court within the specified time under Section 2-211(a) or, if filed, the demand for an elective share is withdrawn under Section 2-211(c), the court shall order disbursement to the designated beneficiary. Payments or transfers to the court or deposits made into court discharge the payor or other third party from all claims for amounts so paid or the value of property so transferred or deposited.

(c) Upon petition to the probate court by the beneficiary designated in a governing instrument, the court may order that all or part of the property be paid to the beneficiary in an amount and subject to conditions consistent with this Part.

Part 3
Spouse and Children Unprovided for in Wills

§2-301. Entitlement of Spouse; Premarital Will

(a) If a testator's surviving spouse married the testator after the testator executed his [or her] will, the surviving spouse is entitled to receive, as an intestate share, no less than the value of the share of the estate he [or she] would have received if the testator had died intestate as to that portion of the testator's estate, if any, that neither is devised to a child of the testator who was born before the testator married the surviving spouse and who is not a child of the surviving spouse nor is devised to a descendant of such a child or passes under Sections 2-603 or 2-604 to such a child or to a descendant of such a child, unless:

(1) it appears from the will or other evidence that the will was made in contemplation of the testator's marriage to the surviving spouse;

(2) the will expresses the intention that it is to be effective notwithstanding any subsequent marriage; or

(3) the testator provided for the spouse by transfer outside the will and the intent that the transfer be in lieu of a testamentary provision is shown by the testator's statements or is reasonably inferred from the amount of the transfer or other evidence.

(b) In satisfying the share provided by this section, devises made by the will to the testator's surviving spouse, if any, are applied first, and other devises, other than a devise to a child of the testator who was born before the testator married the surviving spouse and who is not a child of the surviving spouse or a devise or substitute gift under Section 2-603 or 2-604 to a descendant of such a child, abate as provided in Section 3-902.

As amended in 1993.

§ 2-302. Omitted Children

(a) Except as provided in subsection (b), if a testator fails to provide in his [or her] will for any of his [or her] children born or adopted after the execution of the will, the omitted after-born or after-adopted child receives a share in the estate as follows:

(1) If the testator had no child living when he [or she] executed the will, an omitted after-born or after-adopted child receives a share in the estate equal in value to that which the child would have received had the testator died intestate, unless the will devised all or substantially all of the estate to the other parent of the omitted child and that other parent survives the testator and is entitled to take under the will.

(2) If the testator had one or more children living when he [or she] executed the will, and the will devised property or an interest in property to one or more of the then-living children, an omitted after-born or after-adopted child is entitled to share in the testator's estate as follows:

(i) The portion of the testator's estate in which the omitted after-born or after-adopted child is entitled to share is limited to devises made to the testator's then-living children under the will.

(ii) The omitted after-born or after-adopted child is entitled to receive the share of the testator's estate, as limited in subparagraph (i), that the child would have received had the testator included all omitted after-born and after-adopted children with the children to whom devises were made under the will and had given an equal share of the estate to each child.

(iii) To the extent feasible, the interest granted an omitted after-born or after-adopted child under this section must be of the same character, whether equitable or legal, present or future, as that devised to the testator's then-living children under the will.

(iv) In satisfying a share provided by this paragraph, devises to the testator's children who were living when the will was executed abate ratably. In abating the devises of the then-living children, the court shall preserve to the maximum extent possible the character of the testamentary plan adopted by the testator.

(b) Neither subsection (a)(1) nor subsection (a)(2) applies if:

(1) it appears from the will that the omission was intentional; or

(2) the testator provided for the omitted after-born or after-adopted child by transfer outside the will and the intent that the transfer be in lieu of a testamentary provision is shown by the testator's statements or is reasonably inferred from the amount of the transfer or other evidence.

(c) If at the time of execution of the will the testator fails to provide in his [or her] will for a living child solely because he [or she] believes the child to be dead, the child is entitled to share in the estate as if the child were an omitted after-born or after-adopted child.

(d) In satisfying a share provided by subsection (a)(1), devises made by the will abate under Section 3-902.

As amended in 1991 and 1993.

Comment

This section provides for both the case where a child was born or adopted after the execution of the will and not foreseen at the time and thus not provided for in the will, and the rare case where a testator omits one of his or her children because of the mistaken belief that the child is dead.

Basic Purpose and Scope of Revisions. This section is substantially revised. The revisions have two basic objectives. The first basic objective is to provide that a will that devised, under trust or not, all or substantially all of the testator's estate to the other parent of the omitted child prevents an after-born or after-adopted child from taking an intestate share if none of the testator's children was living when he or she executed the will. (Under this rule, the other parent must survive the testator and be entitled to take under the will.)

Under the pre-1990 Code, such a will prevented the omitted child's entitlement only if the testator had one or more children living when he or she executed the will. The rationale for the revised rule is found in the empirical evidence . . . that suggests that even testators with children tend to devise their entire estates to their surviving spouses, especially in smaller estates. The testator's purpose is not to disinherit the children; rather, such a will evidences a purpose to trust the surviving parent to use the property for the benefit of the children, as appropriate. This attitude of trust of the surviving parent carries over to the case where none of the children have been born when the will is executed.

The second basic objective of the revisions is to provide that if the testator had children when he or she executed the will, and if the will made provision for one or more of the then-living children, an omitted after-born or after-adopted child does not take a full intestate share (which might be substantially larger or substantially smaller than given to the living children). Rather, the omitted after-born or after-adopted child participates on a pro rate basis in the property devised, under trust or not, to the then-living children. . . .

Part 4
Exempt Property and Allowances

General Comment

For decedents who die domiciled in this State, this part grants various allowances to the decedent's surviving spouse and certain children. The allowances have priority over unsecured creditors of the estate and persons to whom the estate may be devised by will. If there is a surviving spouse, all of the allowances described in this Part, which (as revised to adjust for inflation) total $25,000, plus whatever is allowed to the spouse for support during administration, normally pass to the spouse. If the surviving spouse and minor or dependent children live apart from one another, the minor or dependent children may receive some of the support allowance. If there is no surviving spouse, minor or dependent children become entitled to the homestead exemption of $15,000 and to support allowances. The exempt property section confers rights on the spouse, if any, or on all children, to $10,000 in certain chattels, or funds if the unencumbered value of chattels is below the $10,000 level. This provision is designed in part to relieve a personal representative of the duty to sell household chattels when there are children who will have them.

These family protection provisions supply the basis for the important small estate provisions of Article III, Part 12.

States adopting the Code may see fit to alter the dollar amounts suggested in these sections, or to vary the terms and conditions in other ways so as to accommodate existing traditions. Although creditors of estates would be aided somewhat if all family exemption provisions relating to probate estates were the same throughout the country, there is probably less need for uniformity of law regarding these provisions than for any of the other parts of this article. Still, it is quite important for all states to limit their homestead, support allowance and exempt property provisions, if any, so that they apply only to estates of decedents who were domiciliaries of the state.

Cross Reference. Notice that under Section 2-104 a spouse or child claiming under this Part must survive the decedent by 120 hours.

§2-401. Applicable Law

This Part applies to the estate of a decedent who dies domiciled in this State. Rights to homestead allowance, exempt property, and family allowance for a decedent who dies not domiciled in this State are governed by the law of the decedent's domicile at death.

§2-402. Homestead Allowance

A decedent's surviving spouse is entitled to a homestead allowance of [$15,000]. If there is no surviving spouse, each minor child and each dependent child of the decedent is entitled to a homestead allowance amounting to [$15,000] divided by the number of minor and dependent children of the decedent. The homestead allowance is exempt from and has priority over all claims against the estate. Homestead allowance is in addition to any share passing to the surviving spouse or minor or dependent child by the will of the decedent, unless otherwise provided, by intestate succession, or by way of elective share.

§2-402A. Constitutional Homestead

The value of any constitutional right of homestead in the family home received by a surviving spouse or child must be charged against the spouse or child's homestead allowance to the extent the family home is part of the decedent's estate or would have been but for the homestead provision of the constitution.]

§2-403. Exempt Property

In addition to the homestead allowance, the decedent's surviving spouse is entitled from the estate to a value, not exceeding $10,000 in excess of any security interests therein, in household furniture, automobiles, furnishings, appliances, and personal effects. If there is no surviving spouse, the decedent's children are entitled jointly to the same value. If encumbered chattels are selected and the value in excess of security interests, plus that of other exempt property, is less than $10,000, or if there is not $10,000 worth of exempt property in the estate, the spouse or children are entitled to other assets of the estate, if any, to the extent necessary to make up the $10,000 value. Rights to exempt property and assets needed to make up a deficiency of exempt property have priority over all claims against the estate, but the right to any assets to make up a deficiency of exempt property abates as necessary to permit earlier payment of homestead allowance and family allowance. These rights are in addition to any benefit or share passing to the surviving spouse or children by the decedent's will, unless otherwise provided, by intestate succession, or by way of elective share.

§2-404. Family Allowance

(a) In addition to the right to homestead allowance and exempt property, the decedent's surviving spouse and minor children whom the decedent was obligated to support and children who were in fact being supported by the decedent are entitled to a reasonable allowance in money out of the estate for their maintenance during the period of administration, which allowance may not continue for longer than one year if the estate is inadequate to discharge allowed claims. The allowance may be paid as a lump sum or in periodic installments. It is payable to the surviving spouse, if living, for the use of the surviving spouse and minor and dependent children; otherwise to the children, or persons having their care and custody. If a minor child or dependent child is not living with the surviving spouse, the allowance may be made partially to the child or his [or her] guardian or other person having the child's care and custody, and partially to the spouse, as their needs may appear. The family allowance is exempt from and has priority over all claims except the homestead allowance.

(b) The family allowance is not chargeable against any benefit or share passing to the surviving spouse or children by the will of the decedent, unless otherwise provided, by intestate succession or by way of elective share. The death of any person entitled to family allowance terminates the right to allowances not yet paid.

§2-405. Source, Determination, and Documentation

(a) If the estate is otherwise sufficient, property specifically devised may not be used to satisfy rights to homestead allowance or exempt property. Subject to this restriction, the surviving spouse, guardians of minor children, or children who are adults may select property of the estate as homestead allowance and exempt property. The personal representative may make those selections if the surviving spouse, the children, or the guardians of the minor children are unable or fail to do so within a reasonable time or there is no guardian of a minor child. The personal representative may execute an instrument or deed of distribution to establish the ownership of property taken as homestead allowance or exempt property. The personal representative may determine the family allowance in a lump sum not exceeding $18,000 or periodic installments not exceeding $1,500 per month for one year, and may disburse funds of the estate in payment of the family allowance and any part of the homestead allowance payable in cash. The personal representative or an interested person aggrieved by any selection, determination, payment, proposed payment, or failure to act under this section may petition the court for appropriate relief, which may include a family allowance other than that which the personal representative determined or could have determined.

(b) If the right to an elective share is exercised on behalf of a surviving spouse who is an incapacitated person, the personal representative may add any unexpended portions payable under the homestead allowance, exempt property, and family allowance to the trust established under Section 2-212(b).

As amended in 1993.

Part 5
Wills, Will Contracts, and Custody and Deposit of Wills

General Comment

Part 5 of Article II is retitled to reflect the fact that it now includes the provisions on will contracts (pre-1990 Section 2-701) and on custody and deposit of wills (pre-1990 Sections 2-901 and 2-902).

Part 5 deals with capacity and formalities for execution and revocation of wills. The basic intent of the pre-1990 sections was to validate wills whenever possible. To that end, the minimum age for making wills was lowered to eighteen, formalities for a written and attested will were reduced, holographic wills written and signed by the testator were authorized, choice of law as to validity of execution was broadened, and revocation by operation of law was limited to divorce or annulment. In addition, the statute also provided for an optional method of execution with acknowledgment before a public officer (the self-proved will).

These measures have been retained, and the purpose of validating wills whenever possible has been strengthened by the addition of a new section, Section 2-503, which allows a will to be upheld despite a harmless error in it execution.

§2-501. Who May Make Will

An individual 18 or more years of age who is of sound mind may make a will.

§2-502. Execution; Witnessed Wills; Holographic Wills

(a) Except as provided in subsection (b) and in Sections 2-503, 2-506, and 2-513, a will must be:

(1) in writing;

(2) signed by the testator or in the testator's name by some other individual in the testator's conscious presence and by the testator's direction; and

(3) signed by at least two individuals, each of whom signed within a reasonable time after he [or she] witnessed either the signing of the will as described in paragraph (2) or the testator's acknowledgment of that signature or acknowledgment of the will.

(b) A will that does not comply with subsection (a) is valid as a holographic will, whether or not witnessed, if the signature and material portions of the document are in the testator's handwriting.

(c) Intent that the document constitute the testator's will can be established by extrinsic evidence, including, for holographic wills, portions of the document that are not in the testator's handwriting.

§2-503. Writings Intended as Wills, etc.

Although a document or writing added upon a document was not executed in compliance with Section 2-502, the document or writing is treated as if it had been executed in compliance with that section if the proponent of the document or writing establishes by clear and convincing evidence that the decedent intended the document or writing to constitute (i) the decedent's will, (ii) a partial or complete revocation of the will, (iii) an addition to or an alteration of the will, or (iv) a partial or complete revival of his [or her] formerly revoked will or of a formerly revoked portion of the will.

Comment

Purpose of New Section. By way of dispensing power, this new section allows the probate court to excuse a harmless error in complying with the formal requirements for executing or revoking a will. The measure accords with legislation in force in the Canadian province of Manitoba and in several Australian jurisdictions. The Uniform Laws Conference of Canada approved a comparable measure for the Canadian Uniform Wills Act in 1987.

Legislation of this sort was enacted in the state of South Australia in 1975. The experience there has been closely studied by a variety of law reform commissions and in the scholarly literature. See, e.g., Law Reform Commission of British Columbia, Report on the Making and Revocation of Wills (1981); New South Wales Law Reform Commission Wills: Execution and Revocation (1986); Langbein, Excusing Harmless Errors in the Execution of Wills: A Report on Australia's Tranquil Revolution in Probate Law, 87 Colum. L. Rev. 1 (1987). A similar measure has been in effect in Israel since 1965 (see British Columbia Report, supra, at 44-46; Langbein, supra, at 48-51).

Consistent with the general trend of the revisions of the UPC, Section 2-503 unifies the law of probate and nonprobate transfers, extending to will formalities the harmless error principle that has long been applied to defective compliance with the formal requirements for nonprobate transfers. See, e.g., Annot., 19 A.L.R.2d 5 (1951) (life insurance beneficiary designation).

Evidence from South Australia suggests that the dispensing power will be applied mainly in two sorts of cases. See Langbein, *supra*, at 15-33. When the testator misunderstands the attestation requirements of Section 2-502(a) and englects to obtain one or both witnesses, new Section 2-503 permits the proponents of the will to prove that the defective execution did not result from irresolution or from circumstances suggesting duress or trickery—in other words, that the defect was harmless to the purpose of the formality. The measure reduces the tension between holographic wills and the two-witness requirement for attested wills under Section 2-502(a). Ordinarily, the testator who attempts to make an attested will but blunders will still have achieved a level of formality that compares favorably with that permitted for holographic wills under the Code.

The other recurrent class of case in which the dispensing power has been invoked in South Australia entails alterations to a previously executed will. Sometimes the testator adds a clause, that is, the testator attempts to interpolate a defectively executed codicil. More frequently, the amendment has the character of a revision—the testator crosses out former text and inserts replacement terms. Lay persons do not always understand that the execution and revocation requirements of Section 2-503 call for fresh execution in order to modify a will; rather, lay persons often think that the original execution has continuing effect.

By placing the burden of proof upon the proponent of a defective instrument, and by requiring the proponent to discharge that burden by clear and convincing evidence (which courts at the trial and appellate levels are urged to police with rigor), Section 2-503 imposes procedural standards appropriate to the seriousness of the issue. Experience in Israel and South Australia strongly supports the view that a dispensing power like Section 2-503 will not breed litigation. Indeed, as an Israeli judge reported to the British Law Reform Commission, the dispensing power "actually prevents a great deal of unnecessary litigation," because it eliminates disputes about technical lapses and limits the zone of dispute to the functional question of whether the instrument correctly expresses the testator's intent. British Columbia Report, *supra*, at 46.

The larger the departure from Section 2-502 formality, the harder it will be to satisfy the court that the instrument reflects the testator's intent. Whereas the South Australian and Israeli courts lightly excuse breaches of the attestation requirements, they have never excused noncompliance with the requirement that a will be in writing, and they have been extremely reluctant to excuse noncompliance with the signature requirement. See Langbein, *supra*, at 23-29, 49-50. The main circumstance in which the South Australian courts have excused signature errors has been in the recurrent class of cases in which two wills are prepared for simultaneous execution by two testators, typically husband and wife, and each mistakenly signs the will prepared for the other. E.g., Estate of Blakely, 32 S.A.S.R. 473 (1983). Recently, the New York Court of Appeals remedied such a case without aid of statute, simply on the ground "what has occurred is so obvious, and what was intended so clear." In re Snide, 52 N.Y.2d 193, 196, 418 N.E.2d 656, 657, 437 N.Y.S.2d 63, 64 (1981).

Section 2-503 means to retain the intent-serving benefits of Section 2-502 formality without inflicting intent-defeating outcomes in cases of harmless error.

Reference. The rule of this section is supported by the Restatement (Second) of Property (Donative Transfers) §33.1 comment g (as approved by the American Law Institute at the 1990 annual meeting).

§2-504. Self-Proved Will

(a) A will may be simultaneously executed, attested, and made self-proved, by acknowledgment thereof by the testator and affidavits of the witnesses, each made before an officer authorized to administer oaths under the laws of the state in which execution occurs and evidenced by the officer's certificate, under official seal, in substantially the following form:

> I, ______, the testator, sign my name to this instrument this ____ day of ______, and being first duly sworn, do hereby declare to the undersigned authority that I sign and execute this instrument as my will and that I sign it willingly (or willingly direct another to sign for me), that I execute it as my free and voluntary act for the purposes therein expressed, and that I am eighteen years of age or older, of sound mind, and under no constraint or undue influence.
>
> __________________
> Testator
>
> We, ______, ______, the witnesses, sign our names to this instrument, being first duly sworn, and do hereby declare to the undersigned authority that the testator signs and executes this instrument as [his] [her] will and that [he] [she] signs it willingly (or willingly directs another to sign for [him] [her]), and that each of us, in the presence and hearing of the testator, hereby signs this will as witness to the testator's signing, and that to the best of our knowledge the testator is eighteen years of age or older, of sound mind, and under no constraint or undue influence.
>
> __________________
> Witness
>
> __________________
> Witness
>
> The State of ______
> County of ______
> Subscribed, sworn to and acknowledged before me by ______, the testator, and subscribed and sworn to before me by ______, and ______, witness, this ____ day of ______.
>
> (Signed) ______________________
>
> ______________________
> (Official capacity of officer)

(b) An attested will may be made self-proved at any time after its execution by the acknowledgment thereof by the testator and the affidavits of the witnesses, each made before an officer authorized to administer oaths under the laws of the state in which the acknowledgment occurs and evidenced by the officer's certificate, under the official seal, attached or annexed to the will in substantially the following form:

> The State of ______
> County of ______
> We, ______, ______, and ______, the testator and the witnesses, respectively, whose names are signed to the attached or foregoing instrument, being first duly sworn, do hereby declare to the undersigned authority that the testator signed and executed the instrument as the testator's will and that [he] [she] had signed willingly (or willingly directed another to sign for [him] [her]), and that [he] [she] executed it as [his] [her] free and voluntary act for the purposes therein expressed, and that each of the witnesses, in the presence and hearing of the testator, signed the will as witness and that to the best of [his] [her] knowledge the testator was at that time eighteen years or age or older, of sound mind, and under no constraint or undue influence.
>
> __________________
> Testator

____
Witness
____
Witness
Subscribed, sworn to and acknowledged before me by ______, the testator, and subscribed and sworn to before me by ______, and ______, witnesses, this ____ of ______.
(Seal)
(Signed) ____________________
____
(Official capacity of officer)

(c) A signature affixed to a self-proving affidavit attached to a will is considered a signature affixed to the will, if necessary to prove the will's due execution.

Comment

A self-proved will may be admitted to probate as provided . . . without the testimony of any subscribing witness, but otherwise it is treated no differently from a will not self proved. . . .

A new subsection (c) is added to counteract an unfortunate judicial interpretation of similar self-proving will provisions in a few states, under which a signature on the self-proving affidavit has been held not to constitute a signature on the will, resulting in invalidity of the will in cases where the testator or witnesses got confused and only signed on the self-proving affidavit. . . .

§2-505. Who May Witness

(a) An individual generally competent to be a witness may act as a witness to a will.

(b) The signing of a will by an interested witness does not invalidate the will or any provision of it.

§2-506. Choice of Law as to Execution

A written will is valid if executed in compliance with Section 2-502 or 2-503 or if its execution complies with the law at the time of execution of the place where the will is executed, or of the law of the place where at the time of execution or at the time of death the testator is domiciled, has a place of abode, or is a national.

§2-507. Revocation by Writing or by Act

(a) A will or any part thereof is revoked:

(1) by executing a subsequent will that revokes the previous will or part expressly or by inconsistency; or

(2) by performing a revocatory act on the will, if the testator performed the act with the intent and for the purpose of revoking the will or part or if another individual performed the act in the testator's conscious presence and by the testator's direction. For purposes of this paragraph, "revocatory act on the will" includes burning , tearing, canceling, obliterating, or destroying the will or any part of it. A burning, tearing, or canceling is a "revocatory act on the will," whether or not the burn, tear, or cancellation touched any of the words on the will.

(b) If a subsequent will does not expressly revoke a previous will, the execution of the subsequent will wholly revokes the previous will by inconsistency if the testator intended the subsequent will to replace rather than supplement the previous will.

(c) The testator is presumed to have intended a subsequent will to replace rather than supplement a previous will if the subsequent will makes a complete disposition of the testator's estate. If this presumption arises and is not rebutted by clear and convincing evidence, the previous will is revoked; only the subsequent will is operative on the testator's death.

(d) The testator is presumed to have intended a subsequent will to supplement rather than replace a previous will if the subsequent will does not make a complete disposition of the testator's estate. If this presumption arises and is not rebutted by clear and convincing evidence, the subsequent will revokes the previous will only to the extent the subsequent will is inconsistent with the previous will; each will is fully operative on the testator's death to the extent they are not inconsistent.

§2-508. Revocation by Change of Circumstances

Except as provided in Sections 2-803 and 2-804, a change of circumstances does not revoke a will or any part of it.

§2-509. Revival of Revoked Will

(a) If a subsequent will that wholly revoked a previous will is thereafter revoked by a revocatory act under Section 2-507(a)(2), the previous will remains revoked unless it is revived. The previous will is revived if it is evident from the circumstances of the revocation of the subsequent will or from the testator's contemporary or subsequent declarations that the testator intended the previous will to take effect as executed.

(b) If a subsequent will that partly revoked a previous will is thereafter revoked by a revocatory act under Section 2-507(a)(2), a revoked part of the previous will is revived unless it is evident from the circumstances of the revocation of the subsequent will or from the testator's contemporary or subsequent declarations that the testator did not intend the revoked part to take effect as executed.

(c) If a subsequent will that revoked a previous will in whole or in part is thereafter revoked by another, later, will, the previous will remains revoked in whole or in part, unless it or its revoked part is revived. The previous will or its revoked part is revived to the extent it appears from the terms of the later will that the testator intended the previous will to take effect.

§2-510. Incorporation by Reference

A writing in existence when a will is executed may be incorporated by reference if the language of the will manifests this intent and describes the writing sufficiently to permit its identification.

§2-511. Testamentary Additions to Trusts

(a) A will may validly devise property to the trustee of a trust established or to be established (i) during the testator's lifetime by the testator, by the testator and some other person, or by some other person, including a funded or unfunded life insurance trust, although the settlor has reserved any or all rights of ownership of the insurance contracts, or (ii) at the testator's death by the testator's devise to the trustee, if the trust is identified in the testator's will and its terms are set forth in a written instrument, other than a will, executed before, concurrently with, or after the execution of the testator's will or in another individual's will if that other individual has predeceased the testator, regardless of the existence, size, or character of the corpus of the trust. The devise is not invalid because the trust is amendable or revocable, or because the trust was amended after the execution of the will or the testator's death.

(b) Unless the testator's will provides otherwise, property devised to a trust described in subsection (a) is not held under a testamentary trust of the testator, but it becomes a part of the trust to which it is devised, and must be administered and disposed of in accordance with the provisions of the governing instrument setting forth the terms of the trust, including any amendments thereto made before or after the testator's death.

(c) Unless the testator's will provides otherwise, a revocation or termination of the trust before the testator's death causes the devise to lapse.

§2-512. Events of Independent Significance

A will may dispose of property by reference to acts and events that have significance apart from their effect upon the dispositions made by the will, whether they occur before or after the execution of the will or before or after the testator's death. The execution or revocation of another individual's will is such an event.

§2-513. Separate Writing Identifying Devise of Certain Types of Tangible Personal Property

Whether or not the provisions relating to holographic wills apply, a will may refer to a written statement or list to dispose of items of tangible personal property not otherwise specifically disposed of by the will, other than money. To be admissible under this section as evidence of the intended disposition, the writing must be signed by the testator and must describe the items and the devisees with reasonable certainty. The [illegible] be referred to as one to be in existence [illegible] the testator's death; it may be prepa[illegible] after the execution of the will; it may be altered by the testator after its preparation; and it may be a writing that has no significance apart from its effect on the dispositions made by the will.

Comment

Purpose and Scope of Revision. As part of the broader policy of effectuating a testator's intent and of relaxing formalities of execution, this section permits a testator to refer in his or her will toa separate document disposing of tangible personalty other than money. . . .

The language "items of tangible personal property" does not require that the separate document specifically itemize each item of tangible personal property covered. The only requirement is that the document describe the items covered "with reasonable certainty." Consequently, a document referring to "all my tangible personal property other than money" or to "all my tangible personal property located in my office" or using similar catch-all type of language would normally be sufficient.

The separate document disposing of an item or items of personal property may be prepared after execution of the will, so would not come within Section 2-510 on incorporation by reference. It may even be altered from time to time. The only requirement is that the document be signed by the testator. . . . The signature requirement is designed to prevent mere drafts from becoming effective against the testator's wishes. An unsigned document could still be given effect under Section 2-503, however, if the proponent could carry the burden of proving by clear and convincing evidence that the testator intended the document to be effective.

The typical case covered by this section would be a list of personal effects and the persons whom the decedent desired to take specified items. . . .

§2-514. Contracts Concerning Succession

A contract to make a will or devise, or not to revoke a will or devise, or to die intestate, if executed after the effective date of this Article, may be established only by (i) provisions of a will stating material provisions of the contract, (ii) an express reference in a will to a contract and extrinsic evidence proving the terms of the contract, or (iii) a writing signed by the decedent evidencing the contract. The execution of a joint will or mutual wills does not create a presumption of a contract not to revoke the will or wills.

§2-515. Deposit of Will with Court in Testator's Lifetime

A will may be deposited by the testator or the testator's agent with any court for safekeeping, under rules of the court. The will must be sealed and kept confidential. During the testator's lifetime, a deposited will must be delivered only to the testator or to a person authorized in writing signed by the testator to receive the will. A conservator may be allowed to examine a deposited will of a protected testator under procedures designed to maintain the confidential character of the document to the extent possible, and to ensure that it will be resealed and kept on deposit after the examination. Upon being informed of the testator's death, the court shall notify any person designated to receive the will and deliver it to that person on request; or the court may deliver the will to the appropriate court.

§2-516. Duty of Custodian of Will; Liability

After the death of a testator and on request of an interested person, a person having custody of a will of the testator shall deliver it with reasonable promptness to a person able to secure its probate and if none is known, to an appropriate court. A person who wilfully fails to deliver a will is liable to any person aggrieved for any damages that may be sustained by the failure. A person who wilfully refuses or fails to deliver a will after being ordered by the court in a proceeding brought for the purpose of compelling delivery is subject to penalty for contempt of court.

§2-517. Penalty Clause for Contest

A provision in a will purporting to penalize an interested person for contesting the will or instituting other proceedings relating to the estate is unenforceable if probable cause exists for instituting proceedings.

Part 6

Rules of Construction Applicable Only to Wills

General Comment

Parts 6 and 7 address a variety of construction problems that commonly occur in wills, trusts, and other types of governing instruments. All of the "rules" set forth in these parts yield to a finding of a contrary intention and are therefore rebuttable presumptions.

The rules of construction set forth in Part 6 apply only to wills. The rules of construction set forth in Part 7 apply to wills and other governing instruments.

The sections in Part 6 deal with such problems as death before the testator (lapse), the inclusiveness of the will as to property of the testator, effect of failure of a gift in the will, change in form of securities specifically devised, ademption by reason of fire, sale and the like, exoneration, and exercise of a power of appointment by general language in the will.

§2-601. Scope

In the absence of a finding of a contrary intention, the rules of construction in this Part control the construction of a will.

§2-602. Will May Pass All Property and After-Acquired Property

A will may provide for the passage of all property the testator owns at death and all property acquired by the estate after the testator's death.

§2-603. Antilapse; Deceased Devisee; Class Gifts

(a) [Definitions.] In this section:

(1) "Alternative devise" means a devise that is expressly created by the will and, under the terms of the will, can take effect instead of another devise on the happening of one or more events, including survival of the testator or failure to survive the testator, whether an event is expressed in condition-precedent, condition-subsequent, or any other form. A residuary clause constitutes an alternative devise with respect to a nonresiduary devise only if the will specifically provides that, upon lapse or failure, the nonresiduary devise, or nonresiduary devises in general, pass under the residuary clause.

(2) "Class member" includes an individual who fails to survive the testator but who would have taken under a devise in the form of a class gift had he [or she] survived the testator.

(3) "Devise" includes an alternative devise, a devise in the form of a class gift, and an exercise of a power of appointment.

(4) "Devisee" includes (i) a class member if the devise is in the form of a class gift, (ii) an individual or class member who was deceased at the time the testator executed his [or her] will as well as an individual or class member who was then living but who failed to survive the testator, and (iii) an appointee under a power of appointment exercised by the testator's will.

(5) "Stepchild" means a child of the surviving, deceased, or former spouse of the testator or of the donor of a power of appointment, and not of the testator or donor.

(6) "Surviving devisee" or "surviving descendant" means a devisee or a descendant who

neither predeceased the testator nor is deemed to have predeceased the testator under Section 2-702.

(7) "Testator" includes the donee of a power of appointment if the power is exercised in the testator's will.

(b) [Substitute Gift.] If a devisee fails to survive the testator and is a grandparent, a descendant of a grandparent, or a stepchild of either the testator or the donor of a power of appointment exercised by the testator's will, the following apply:

(1) Except as provided in paragraph (4), if the devise is not in the form of a class gift and the deceased devisee leaves surviving descendants, a substitute gift is created in the devisee's surviving descendants. They take by representation the property to which the devisee would have been entitled had the devisee survived the testator.

(2) Except as provided in paragraph (4), if the devise is in the form of a class gift, other than a devise to "issue," "descendants," "heirs of the body," "heirs," "next of kin," "relatives," or "family," or a class described by language of similar import, a substitute gift is created in the surviving descendant's of any deceased devisee. The property to which the devisees would have been entitled had all of them survived the testator passes to the surviving devisees and the surviving descendants of the deceased devisees. Each surviving devisee takes the share to which he [or she] would have been entitled had the deceased devisees survived the testator. Each deceased devisee's surviving descendants who are substituted for the deceased devisee take by representation the share to which the deceased devisee would have been entitled had the deceased devisee survived the testator. For the purposes of this paragraph, "deceased devisee" means a class member who failed to survive the testator and left one or more surviving descendants.

(3) For the purposes of Section 2-601, words of survivorship, such as in a devise to an individual "if he survives me," or in a devise to "my surviving children," are not, in the absence of additional evidence, a sufficient indication of an intent contrary to the application of this section.

(4) If the will creates an alternative devise with respect to a devise for which a substitute gift is created by paragraph (1) or (2), the substitute gift is superseded by the alternative devise only if an expressly designated devisee of the alternative devise is entitled to take under the will.

(5) Unless the language creating a power of appointment expressly excludes the substitution of the descendants of an appointee for the appointee, a surviving descendant of a deceased appointee of a power of appointment can be substituted for the appointee under this section, whether or not the descendant is an object of the power.

(c) [More Than One Substitute Gift; Which One Takes.] If, under subsection (b), substitute gifts are created and not superseded with respect to more than one devise and the devises are alternative devises, one to the other, the determination of which of the substitute gifts takes effect is resolved as follows:

(1) Except as provided in paragraph (2), the devised property passes under the primary substitute gift.

(2) If there is a younger-generation devise, the devised property passes under the younger-generation substitute gift and not under the primary substitute gift.

(3) In this subsection:

(i) "Primary devise" means the devise that would have taken effect had all the deceased devisees of the alternative devises who left surviving descendants survived the testator.

(ii) "Primary substitute gift" means the substitute gift created with respect to the primary devise.

(iii) "Younger-generation devise" means a devise that (A) is to a descendant of a devisee of the primary devise, (B) is an alternative devise with respect to the primary devise, (C) is a devise for which a substitute gift is created, and (D) would have taken effect had all the deceased devisees who left surviving descendants survived the testator except the deceased devisee or devisees of the primary devise.

(iv) "Younger-generation substitute gift" means the substitute gift created with respect to the younger-generation devise.

As amended in 1991 and 1993.

§2-604. Failure of Testamentary Provision

(a) Except as provided in Section 2-603, a devise, other than a residuary devise, that fails for any reason becomes a part of the residue.

(b) Except as provided in Section 2-603, if the residue is devised to two or more persons, the share of a residuary devisee that fails for any reason passes to the other residuary devisee, or to other residuary devisees in proportion to the interest of each in the remaining part of the residue.

§2-605. Increase in Devised Securities; Accessions

(a) If a testator executes a will that devises securities and the testator then owned securities that meet the description in the will, the devise includes additional securities owned by the testator at death to the extent the additional securities were acquired by the testator after the will was executed as a result of the testator's ownership of the described securities and are securities of any of the following types:

(1) securities of the same organization acquired by reason of action initiated by the organization or any successor, related, or acquiring organization,

excluding any acquired by exercise of purchase options;

(2) securities of another organization acquired as a result of a merger, consolidation, reorganization, or other distribution by the organization or any successor, related, or acquiring organization; or

(3) securities of the same organization acquired as a result of a plan of reinvestment.

(b) Distributions in cash before death with respect to a described security are not part of the devise.

§2-606. Nonademption of Specific Devises; Unpaid Proceeds of Sale, Condemnation, or Insurance; Sale by Conservator or Agent

(a) A specific devisee has a right to the specifically devised property in the testator's estate at death and:

(1) any balance of the purchase price, together with any security agreement, owing from a purchaser to the testator at death by reason of sale of the property;

(2) any amount of a condemnation award for the taking of the property unpaid at death;

(3) any proceeds unpaid at death on fire or casualty insurance on or other recovery for injury to the property;

(4) property owned by the testator at death and acquired as a result of foreclosure, or obtained in lieu of foreclosure, of the security interest for a specifically devised obligation;

(5) real or tangible personal property owned by the testator at death which the testator acquired as a replacement for specifically devised real or tangible personal property; and

(6) unless the facts and circumstances indicate that ademption of the devise was intended by the testator or ademption of the devise is consistent with the testator's manifested plan of distribution, the value of the specifically devised property to the extent the specifically devised property is not in the testator's estate at death and its value or its replacement is not covered by paragraphs (1) through (5).

(b) If specifically devised property is sold or mortgaged by a conservator or by an agent acting within the authority of a durable power of attorney for an incapacitated principal, or if a condemnation award, insurance proceeds, or recovery for injury to the property are paid to a conservator or to an agent acting within the authority of a durable power of attorney for an incapacitated principal, the specific devisee has the right to a general pecuniary devise equal to the net sale price, the amount of the unpaid loan, the condemnation award, the insurance proceeds, or the recovery.

(c) The right of a specific devisee under subsection (b) is reduced by any right the devisee has under subsection (a).

(d) For the purposes of the references in subsection (b) to a conservator, subsection (b) does not apply if after the sale, mortgage, condemnation, casualty, or recovery, it was adjudicated that the testator's incapacity ceased and the testator survived the adjudication by one year.

(e) For the purposes of the references in subsection (b) to an agent acting within the authority of a durable power of attorney for an incapacitated principal, (i) "incapacitated principal" means a principal who is an incapacitated person, (ii) no adjudication of incapacity before death is necessary, and (iii) the acts of an agent within the authority of a durable power of attorney are presumed to be for an incapacitated principal.

§2-607. Nonexoneration

A specific devise passes subject to any mortgage interest existing at the date of death, without right of exoneration, regardless of a general directive in the will to pay debts.

§2-608. Exercise of Power of Appointment

In the absence of a requirement that a power of appointment be exercised by a reference, or by an express or specific reference, to the power, a general residuary clause in a will, or a will making general disposition of all of the testator's property, expresses an intention to exercise a power of appointment held by the testator only if (i) the power is a general power and the creating instrument does not contain a gift if the power is not exercised or (ii) the testator's will manifests an intention to include the property subject to the power.

§2-609. Ademption by Satisfaction

(a) Property a testator gave in his [or her] lifetime to a person is treated as a satisfaction of a devise in whole or in part, only if (i) the will provides for deduction of the gift, (ii) the testator declared in a contemporaneous writing that the gift is in satisfaction of the devise or that its value is to be deducted from the value of the devise, or (iii) the devisee acknowledged in writing that the gift is in satisfaction of the devise or that its value is to be deducted from the value of the devise.

(b) For purposes of partial satisfaction, property given during lifetime is valued as of the time the devisee came into possession or enjoyment of the property or at the testator's death, whichever occurs first.

(c) If the devisee fails to survive the testator, the gift is treated as a full or partial satisfaction of the devise, as appropriate, in applying Sections 2-603 and 2-604, unless the testator's contemporaneous writing provides otherwise.

Part 7

Rules of Construction Applicable to Wills and Other Governing Instruments

General Comment

Part 7 contains rules of construction applicable to wills and other governing instruments, such as deeds, trusts, appointments, beneficiary designations, and so on. Like the rules of construction in Part 6 (which apply only to wills), the rules of construction in this Part yield to a finding of a contrary intention.

Some of the sections in Part 7 are revisions of sections contained in Part 6 of the pre-1990 Code. Although these sections originally applied only to wills, their restricted scope was inappropriate.

Some of the sections in Part 7 are new, having been added to the Code as desirable means of carrying out common intention.

Application to Pre-Existing Governing Instruments. Under Section 8-101(b), for decedents dying after the effective date of enactment, the provisions of this Code apply to governing instruments executed prior to as well as on or after the effective date of enactment. The Joint Editorial Board for the Uniform Probate Code has issued a statement concerning the constitutionality under the Contracts Clause of this feature of the Code. The statement, titled "Joint Editorial Board Statement Regarding the Constitutionality of Changes in Default Rules as Applied to Pre-Existing Documents," can be found at 17 Am.C.Tr. & Est. Couns. Notes 184 (1991) or can be obtained from the headquarters office of the National Conference of Commissioners on Uniform State Laws, 676 N. St. Clair St., Suite 1700, Chicago, IL 60611, Phone 312/915-0195, FAX 312/915-0187.

Historical Note. This General Comment was revised in 1993. For the prior version, see 8 U.L.A. 137 (Supp.1992).

§2-701. Scope

In the absence of a finding of a contrary intention, the rules of construction in this Part control the construction of a governing instrument. The rules of construction in this Part apply to a governing instrument of any type, except as the application of a particular section is limited by its terms to a specific type or types of provision or governing instrument.

As amended in 1991.

§2-702. Requirement of Survival by 120 Hours

(a) [Requirement of Survival by 120 Hours Under Probate Code.] For the purposes of this Code, except as provided in subsection (d), an individual who is not established by clear and convincing evidence to have survived an event, including the death of another individual, by 120 hours is deemed to have predeceased the event.

(b) [Requirement of Survival by 120 Hours under Governing Instrument.] Except as provided in subsection (d), for purposes of a provision of a governing instrument that relates to an individual surviving an event, including the death of another individual, an individual who is not established by clear and convincing evidence to have survived the event by 120 hours is deemed to have predeceased the event.

(c) [Co-owners With Right of Survivorship; Requirement of Survival by 120 Hours.] Except as provided in subsection (d), if (i) it is not established by clear and convincing evidence that one of two co-owners with right of survivorship survived the other co-owner by 120 hours, one-half of the property passes as if one had survived by 120 hours and one-half as if the other had survived by 120 hours and (ii) there are more than two co-owners and it is not established by clear and convincing evidence that at least one of them survived the others by 120 hours, the property passes in the proportion that one bears to the whole number of co-owners. For the purposes of this subsection, "co-owners with right of survivorship" includes joint tenants, tenants by the entireties, and other co-owners of property or accounts held under circumstances that entitles one or more to the whole of the property or account on the death of the other or others.

(d) [Exceptions.] Survival by 120 hours is not required if:

(1) the governing instrument contains language dealing explicitly with simultaneous deaths or deaths in a common disaster and that language is operable under the facts of the case;

(2) the governing instrument expressly indicates that an individual is not required to survive an event, including the death of another individual, by any specified period or expressly requires the individual to survive the event by a specified period; but survival of the event or the

specified period must be established by clear and convincing evidence;

(3) the imposition of a 120-hour requirement of survival would cause a nonvested property interest or a power of appointment to fail to qualify for validity under Section 2-901(a)(1), (b)(1), or (c)(1) or to become invalid under Section 2-901(a)(2), (b)(2), or (c)(2); but survival must be established by clear and convincing evidence; or

(4) the application of a 120-hour requirement of survival to multiple governing instruments would result in an unintended failure or duplication of a disposition; but survival must be established by clear and convincing evidence.

(e) [Protection of Payors and Other Third Parties.]

(1) A payor or other third party is not liable for having made a payment or transferred an item of property or any other benefit to a beneficiary designated in a governing instrument who, under this section, is not entitled to the payment or item of property, or for having taken any other action in good faith reliance on the beneficiary's apparent entitlement under the terms of the governing instrument, before the payor or other third party received written notice of a claimed lack of entitlement under this section. A payor or other third party is liable for a payment made or other action taken after the payor or other third party received written notice of a claimed lack of entitlement under this section.

(2) Written notice of a claimed lack of entitlement under paragraph (1) must be mailed to the payor's or other third party's main office or home by registered or certified mail, return receipt requested, or served upon the payor or other third party in the same manner as a summons in a civil action. Upon receipt of written notice of a claimed lack of entitlement under this section, a payor or other third party may pay any amount owed or transfer or deposit any item of property held by it to or with the court having jurisdiction of the probate proceedings relating to the decedent's estate, or if no proceedings have been commenced, to or with the court having jurisdiction of probate proceedings relating to decedents' estates located in the county of the decedent's residence. The court shall hold the funds or item of property and, upon its determination under this section, shall order disbursement in accordance with the determination. Payments, transfers, or deposits made to or with the court discharge the payor or other third party from all claims for the value of amounts paid to or items of property transferred to or deposited with the court.

(f) [Protection of Bona Fide Purchasers; Personal Liability of Recipient.]

(1) A person who purchases property for value and without notice, or who receives a payment or other item of property in partial or full satisfaction of a legally enforceable obligation, is neither obligated under this section to return the payment, item of property, or benefit nor is liable under this section for the amount of the payment or the value of the item of property or benefit. But a person who, not for value, receives a payment, item of property, or any other benefit to which the person is not entitled under this section is obligated to return the payment, item of property, or benefit, or is personally liable for the amount of the payment or the value of the item of property or benefit, to the person who is entitled to it under this section.

(2) If this section or any part of this section is preempted by federal law with respect to a payment, an item of property, or any other benefit covered by this section, a person who, not for value, receives the payment, item of property, or any other benefit to which the person is not entitled under this section is obligated to return the payment, item of property, or benefit, or is personally liable for the amount of the payment or the value of the item of property or benefit, to the person who would have been entitled to it were this section or part of this section not preempted.

As amended in 1991 and 1993.

§2-703. Choice of Law as to Meaning and Effect of Governing Instrument

The meaning and legal effect of a governing instrument is determined by the local law of the state selected in the governing instrument, unless the application of that law is contrary to the provisions relating to the elective share described in Part 2, the provisions relating to exempt property and allowances described in Part 4, or any other public policy of this State otherwise applicable to the disposition.

As amended in 1991 and 1993.

§2-704. Power of Appointment; Meaning of Specific Reference Requirement

If a governing instrument creating a power of appointment expressly requires that the power be exercised by a reference, an express reference, or a specific reference, to the power or its source, it is presumed that the donor's intention, in requiring that the donee exercise the power by making reference to the particular power or to the creating instrument, was to prevent an inadvertent exercise of the power.

§2-705. Class Gifts Construed to Accord with Intestate Succession

(a) Adopted individuals and individuals born out of wedlock, and their respective descendants if appropriate to the class, are included in class gifts and other terms of relationship in accordance with the rules for intestate succession. Terms of relationship that do not differentiate relationships by blood from those by affinity, such as "uncles," "aunts," "nieces," or "nephews", are construed to exclude relatives by affinity. Terms of relationship that do not differentiate relationships by the half blood from those by the whole blood, such as "brothers," "sisters," "nieces," or "nephews", are construed to include both types of relationships.

(b) In addition to the requirements of subsection (a), in construing a dispositive provision of a transferor who is not the natural parent, an individual born to the natural parent is not considered the child of that parent unless the individual lived while a minor as a regular member of the household of that natural parent or of that parent's parent, brother, sister, spouse, or surviving spouse.

(c) In addition to the requirements of subsection (a), in construing a dispositive provision of a transferor who is not the adopting parent, an adopted individual is not considered the child of the adopting parent unless the adopted individual lived while a minor, either before or after the adoption, as a regular member of the household of the adopting parent.

As amended in 1991.

§2-706. Life Insurance; Retirement Plan; Account with POD Designation; Transfer-on-Death Registration; Deceased Beneficiary

(a) [Definitions.] In this section:

(1) "Alternative beneficiary designation" means a beneficiary designation that is expressly created by the governing instrument and, under the terms of the governing instrument, can take effect instead of another beneficiary designation on the happening of one or more events, including survival of the decedent or failure to survive the decedent, whether an event is expressed in condition-precedent, condition-subsequent, or any other form.

(2) "Beneficiary" means the beneficiary of a beneficiary designation under which the beneficiary must survive the decedent and includes (i) a class member if the beneficiary designation is in the form of a class gift and (ii) an individual or class member who was deceased at the time the beneficiary designation was executed as well as an individual or class member who was then living but who failed to survive the decedent, but excludes a joint tenant of a joint tenancy with the right of survivorship and a party to a joint and survivorship account.

(3) "Beneficiary designation" includes an alternative beneficiary designation and a beneficiary designation in the form of a class gift.

(4) "Class member" includes an individual who fails to survive the decedent but who would have taken under a beneficiary designation in the form of a class gift had he [or she] survived the decedent.

(5) "Stepchild" means a child of the decedent's surviving, deceased, or former spouse, and not of the decedent.

(6) "Surviving beneficiary" or "surviving descendant" means a beneficiary or a descendant who neither predeceased the decedent nor is deemed to have predeceased the decedent under Section 2-702.

(b) [Substitute Gift.] If a beneficiary fails to survive the decedent and is a grandparent, a descendant of a grandparent, or a stepchild of the decedent, the following apply:

(1) Except as provided in paragraph (4), if the beneficiary designation is not in the form of a class gift and the deceased beneficiary leaves surviving descendants, a substitute gift is created in the beneficiary's surviving descendants. They take by representation the property to which the beneficiary would have been entitled had the beneficiary survived the decedent.

(2) Except as provided in paragraph (4), if the beneficiary designation is in the form of a class gift, other than a beneficiary designation to "issue," "descendants," "heirs of the body," "heirs," "next of kin," "relatives," or "family," or a class described by language of similar import, a substitute gift is created in the surviving descendants of any deceased beneficiary. The property to which the beneficiaries would have been entitled had all of them survived the decedent passes to the surviving beneficiaries and the surviving descendants of the deceased beneficiaries. Each surviving beneficiary takes the share to which he [or she] would have been entitled had the deceased beneficiaries survived the decedent. Each deceased beneficiary's surviving descendants who are substituted for the deceased beneficiary take by representation the share to which the deceased beneficiary would have been entitled had the deceased beneficiary survived the decedent. For the purposes of this paragraph, "deceased beneficiary" means a class member who failed to survive the decedent and left one or more surviving descendants.

(3) For the purposes of Section 2-701, words of survivorship, such as in a beneficiary designation to an individual "if he survives me," or in a beneficiary designation to "my surviving children," are not, in the absence of additional evidence, a sufficient indication of an intent contrary to the application of this section.

(4) If a governing instrument creates an alternative beneficiary designation with respect to a beneficiary designation for which a substitute gift is created by paragraph (1) or (2), the substitute gift is superseded by the alternative beneficiary designation only if an expressly designated beneficiary of the alternative beneficiary designation is entitled to take.

(c) [More Than One Substitute Gift; Which One Takes.] If, under subsection (b), substitute gifts are created and not superseded with respect to more than one beneficiary designation and the beneficiary designations are alternative beneficiary designations, one to the other, the determination of which of the substitute gifts takes effect is resolved as follows:

(1) Except as provided in paragraph (2), the property passes under the primary substitute gift.

(2) If there is a younger-generation beneficiary designation, the property passes under the younger-generation substitute gift and not under the primary substitute gift.

(3) In this subsection:

(i) "Primary beneficiary designation" means the beneficiary designation that would have taken effect had all the deceased beneficiaries of the alternative beneficiary designations who left surviving descendants survived the decedent.

(ii) "Primary substitute gift" means the substitute gift created with respect to the primary beneficiary designation.

(iii) "Younger-generation beneficiary designation" means a beneficiary designation that (A) is to a descendant of a beneficiary of the primary beneficiary designation, (B) is an alternative beneficiary designation with respect to the primary beneficiary designation, (C) is a beneficiary designation for which a substitute gift is created, and (D) would have taken effect had all the deceased beneficiaries who left surviving descendants survived the decedent except the deceased beneficiary or beneficiaries of the primary beneficiary designation.

(iv) "Younger-generation substitute gift" means the substitute gift created with respect to the younger-generation beneficiary designation.

(d) [Protection of Payors.]

(1) A payor is protected from liability in making payments under the terms of the beneficiary designation until the payor has received written notice of a claim to a substitute gift under this section. Payment made before the receipt of written notice of a claim to a substitute gift under this section discharges the payor, but not the recipient, from all claims for the amounts paid. A payor is liable for a payment made after the payor has received written notice of the claim. A recipient is liable for a payment received, whether or not written notice of the claim is given.

(2) The written notice of the claim must be mailed to the payor's main office or home by registered or certified mail, return receipt requested, or served upon the payor in the same manner as a summons in a civil action. Upon receipt of written notice of the claim, a payor may pay any amount owed by it to the court having jurisdiction of the probate proceedings relating to the decedent's estate or, if no proceedings have been commenced, to the court having jurisdiction of probate proceedings relating to decedents' estates located in the county of the decedent's residence. The court shall hold the funds and, upon its determination under this section, shall order disbursement in accordance with the determination. Payment made to the court discharges the payor from all claims for the amounts paid.

(e) [Protection of Bona Fide Purchasers; Personal Liability of Recipient.]

(1) A person who purchases property for value and without notice, or who receives a payment or other item of property in partial or full satisfaction of a legally enforceable obligation, is neither obligated under this section to return the payment, item of property, or benefit nor is liable under this section for the amount of the payment or the value of the item of property or benefit. But a person who, not for value, receives a payment, item of property, or any other benefit to which the person is not entitled under this section is obligated to return the payment, item of property, or benefit, or is personally liable for the amount of the payment or the value of the item of property or benefit, to the person who is entitled to it under this section.

(2) If this section or any part of this section is preempted by federal law with respect to a payment, an item of property, or any other benefit covered by this section, a person who, not for value, receives the payment, item of property, or any other benefit to which the person is not entitled under this section is obligated to return the payment, item of property, or benefit, or is personally liable for the amount of the payment or the value of the item of property or benefit, to the person who would have been entitled to it were this section or part of this section not preempted.

As amended in 1993.

§2-707. Survivorship with Respect to Future Interests under Terms of Trust; Substitute Takers

(a) [Definitions.] In this section:

(1) "Alternative future interest" means an expressly created future interest that can take effect in possession or enjoyment instead of another future interest on the happening of one or more events, including survival of an event or failure to survive an event, whether an event is expressed in condition-precedent, condition-subsequent, or any other form. A residuary clause in a will does not create an alternative future interest with respect to a future interest created in a nonresiduary devise in the will, whether or not the will specifically provides that lapsed or failed devises are to pass under the residuary clause.

(2) "Beneficiary" means the beneficiary of a future interest and includes a class member if the future interest is in the form of a class gift.

(3) "Class member" includes an individual who fails to survive the distribution date but who

would have taken under a future interest in the form of a class gift had he [or she] survived the distribution date.

(4) "Distribution date," with respect to a future interest, means the time when the future interest is to take effect in possession or enjoyment. The distribution date need not occur at the beginning or end of a calendar day, but can occur at a time during the course of a day.

(5) "Future interest" includes an alternative future interest and a future interest in the form of a class gift.

(6) "Future interest under the terms of a trust" means a future interest that was created by a transfer creating a trust or to an existing trust or by an exercise of a power of appointment to an existing trust, directing the continuance of an existing trust, designating a beneficiary of an existing trust, or creating a trust.

(7) "Surviving beneficiary" or "surviving descendant" means a beneficiary or a descendant who neither predeceased the distribution date nor is deemed to have predeceased the distribution date under Section 2-702.

(b) [Survivorship Required; Substitute Gift.] A future interest under the terms of a trust is contingent on the beneficiary's surviving the distribution date. If a beneficiary of a future interest under the terms of a trust fails to survive the distribution date, the following apply:

(1) Except as provided in paragraph (4), if the future interest is not in the form of a class gift and the deceased beneficiary leaves surviving descendants, a substitute gift is created in the beneficiary's surviving descendants. They take by representation the property to which the beneficiary would have been entitled had the beneficiary survived the distribution date.

(2) Except as provided in paragraph (4), if the future interest is in the form of a class gift, other than a future interest to "issue," "descendants," "heirs of the body," "heirs," "next of kin," "relatives," or "family," or a class described by language of similar import, a substitute gift is created in the surviving descendants of any deceased beneficiary. The property to which the beneficiaries would have been entitled had all of them survived the distribution date passes to the surviving beneficiaries and the surviving descendants of the deceased beneficiaries. Each surviving beneficiary takes the share to which he [or she] would have been entitled had the deceased beneficiaries survived the distribution date. Each deceased beneficiary's surviving descendants who are substituted for the deceased beneficiary take by representation the share to which the deceased beneficiary would have been entitled had the deceased beneficiary survived the distribution date. For the purposes of this paragraph, "deceased beneficiary" means a class member who failed to survive the distribution date and left one or more surviving descendants.

(3) For the purposes of Section 2-701, words of survivorship attached to a future interest are not, in the absence of additional evidence, a sufficient indication of an intent contrary to the application of this section. Words of survivorship include words of survivorship that relate to the distribution date or to an earlier or an unspecified time, whether those words of survivorship are expressed in condition-precedent, condition-subsequent, or any other form.

(4) If a governing instrument creates an alternative future interest with respect to a future interest for which a substitute gift is created by paragraph (1) or (2), the substitute gift is superseded by the alternative future interest only if an expressly designated beneficiary of the alternative future interest is entitled to take in possession or enjoyment.

(c) [More Than One Substitute Gift; Which One Takes.] If, under subsection (b), substitute gifts are created and not superseded with respect to more than one future interest and the future interests are alternative future interests, one to the other, the determination of which of the substitute gifts takes effect is resolved as follows:

(1) Except as provided in paragraph (2), the property passes under the primary substitute gift.

(2) If there is a younger-generation future interest, the property passes under the younger-generation substitute gift and not under the primary substitute gift.

(3) In this subsection:

(i) "Primary future interest" means the future interest that would have taken effect had all the deceased beneficiaries of the alternative future interests who left surviving descendants survived the distribution date.

(ii) "Primary substitute gift" means the substitute gift created with respect to the primary future interest.

(iii) "Younger-generation future interest" means a future interest that (A) is to a descendant of a beneficiary of the primary future interest, (B) is an alternative future interest with respect to the primary future interest, (C) is a future interest for which a substitute gift is created, and (D) would have taken effect had all the deceased beneficiaries who left surviving descendants survived the distribution date except the deceased beneficiary or beneficiaries of the primary future interest.

(iv) "Younger-generation substitute gift" means the substitute gift created with respect to the younger-generation future interest.

(d) [If No Other Takers, Property Passes Under Residuary Clause or to Transferor's Heirs.] Except as provided in subsection (e), if, after the application of subsections (b) and (c), there is no surviving taker, the property passes in the following order:

(1) if the trust was created in a nonresiduary devise in the transferor's will or in a codicil to the transferor's will, the property passes under the residuary clause in the transferor's will; for purposes of this section, the residuary clause is treated as creating a future interest under the terms of a trust.

(2) if no taker is produced by the application of paragraph (1), the property passes to the transferor's heirs under Section 2-711.

(e) [If No Other Takers and If Future Interest Created by Exercise of Power of Appointment.] If, after the application of subsections (b) and (c), there is no surviving taker and if the future interest was created by the exercise of a power of appointment:

(1) the property passes under the donor's gift-in-default clause, if any, which clause is treated as creating a future interest under the terms of a trust; and

(2) if no taker is produced by the application of paragraph (1), the property passes as provided in subsection (d). For purposes of subsection (d), "transferor" means the donor if the power was a nongeneral power and means the donee if the power was a general power.

As amended in 1993.

§2-708. Class Gifts to "Descendants," "Issue," or "Heirs of the Body"; Form of Distribution if None Specified

If a class gift in favor of "descendants," "issue," or "heirs of the body" does not specify the manner in which the property is to be distributed among the class members, the property is distributed among the class members who are living when the interest is to take effect in possession or enjoyment, in such shares as they would receive, under the applicable law of intestate succession, if the designated ancestor had then died intestate owning the subject matter of the class gift.

§2-709. Representation; Per Capita at Each Generation; Per Stirpes

(a) [Definitions.] In this section:

(1) "Deceased child" or "deceased descendant" means a child or a descendant who either predeceased the distribution date or is deemed to have predeceased the distribution date under Section 2-702.

(2) "Distribution date," with respect to an interest, means the time when the interest is to take effect in possession or enjoyment. The distribution date need not occur at the beginning or end of a calendar day, but can occur at a time during the course of a day.

(3) "Surviving ancestor," "surviving child," or "surviving descendant" means an ancestor, a child, or a descendant who neither predeceased the distribution date nor is deemed to have predeceased the distribution date under Section 2-702.

(b) [Representation; Per Capita at Each Generation.] If an applicable statute or a governing instrument calls for property to be distributed "by representation" or "per capita at each generation," the property is divided into as many equal shares as there are (i) surviving descendants in the generation nearest to the designated ancestor which contains one or more surviving descendants (ii) and deceased descendants in the same generation who left surviving descendants, if any. Each surviving descendant in the nearest generation is allocated one share. The remaining shares, if any, are combined and then divided in the same manner among the surviving descendants of the deceased descendants as if the surviving descendants who were allocated a share and their surviving descendants had predeceased the distribution date.

(c) [Per Stirpes.] If a governing instrument calls for property to be distributed "per stripes," the property is divided into as many equal shares as there are (i) surviving children of the designated ancestor and (ii) deceased children who left surviving descendants. Each surviving child, if any, is allocated one share. The share of each deceased child with surviving descendants is divided in the same manner, with subdivision repeating at each succeeding generation until the property is fully allocated among surviving descendants.

(d) [Deceased Descendant With No Surviving Descendant Disregarded.] For the purposes of subsections (b) and (c), an individual who is deceased and left no surviving descendant is disregarded, and an individual who leaves a surviving ancestor who is a descendant of the designated ancestor is not entitled to a share.

As amended in 1993.

§2-710. Worthier-Title Doctrine Abolished

The doctrine of worthier title is abolished as a rule of law and as a rule of construction. Language in a governing instrument describing the beneficiaries of a disposition as the transferor's "heirs," "heirs at law," "next of kin," "distributees," "relatives," or "family," or language of similar import, does not create or presumptively create a reversionary interest in the transferor.

As amended in 1991.

§2-711. Interests in "Heirs" and Like

If an applicable statute or a governing instrument calls for a present or future distribution to or creates a present or future interest in a designated individual's "heirs," "heirs at law," "next of kin," "relatives," or "family," or language of similar import, the property passes to those persons, including the state, and in such shares as would

succeed to the designated individual's intestate estate under the intestate succession law of the designated individual's domicile if the designated individual died when the disposition is to take effect in possession or enjoyment. If the designated individual's surviving spouse is living but is remarried at the time the disposition is to take effect in possession or enjoyment, the surviving spouse is not an heir of the designated individual.
As amended in 1991 and 1993.

Part 8

General Provisions Concerning Probate and Nonprobate Transfers

General Comment

Part 8 contains four general provisions that cut across probate and nonprobate transfers. Section 2-801 incorporates portions of the Uniform Disclaimer of Property Interests Act; these portions replace portions of the narrower Uniform Disclaimer of Transfers By Will, Intestacy or Appointment Act, which had been incorporated into the pre-1990 Code. The broader disclaimer provisions are now appropriate, given the broadened scope of Article II in covering nonprobate as well as probate transfers.

Section 2-802 deals with the effect of divorce and separation on the right to elect against a will, exempt property and allowances, and an intestate share.

Section 2-803 spells out the legal consequence of intentional and felonious killing on the right of the killer to take as heir and under wills and revocable inter-vivos transfers, such as revocable trusts and life-insurance beneficiary designations.

Section 2-804 deals with the consequences of a divorce on the right of the former spouse (and relatives of the former spouse) to take under wills and revocable inter-vivos transfers, such as revocable trusts and life-insurance beneficiary designations.

Application to Pre-Existing Governing Instruments. Under Section 8-101(b), for decedents dying after the effective date of enactment, the provisions of this Code apply to governing instruments executed prior to as well as on or after the effective date of enactment. The Joint Editorial Board for the Uniform Probate Code has issued a statement concerning the constitutionality under the Contracts Clause of this feature of the Code. The statement, titled "Joint Editorial Board Statement Regarding the Constitutionality of Changes in Default Rules as Applied to Pre-Existing Documents," can be found at 17 Am.C.Tr. & Est.Couns. Notes 184 (1991) or can be obtained from the headquarters office of the National Conference of Commissioners on Uniform State Laws, 676 N. St. Clair St., Suite 1700, Chicago, IL 60611, Phone 312/915-0195, FAX 312/915-0187.

Historical Note. This General Comment was revised in 1993. For the prior version, see 8 U.L.A. 156 (Supp.1992).

§2-801. Disclaimer of Property Interests

(a) [Right to Disclaim Interest in Property.] A person, or the representative of a person, to whom an interest in or with respect to property or an interest therein devolves by whatever means may disclaim it in whole or in part by delivering or filing a written disclaimer under this section. The right to disclaim exists notwithstanding (i) any limitation on the interest of the disclaimant in the nature of a spendthrift provision or similar restriction or (ii) any restriction or limitation on the right to disclaim contained in the governing instrument. For purposes of this subsection, the "representative of a person" includes a personal representative of a decedent, a conservator of a disabled person, a guardian of a minor or incapacitated person, and an agent acting on behalf of the person within the authority of a power of attorney.

(b) [Time of Disclaimer.] The following rules govern the time when a disclaimer must be filed or delivered:

(1) If the property or interest has devolved to the disclaimant under a testamentary instrument or by the laws of intestacy, the disclaimer must be filed, if of a present interest, not later than [nine] months after the death of the deceased owner or deceased donee of a power of appointment and, if of a future interest, not later than [nine] months after the event determining that the taker of the property or interest is finally ascertained and his [or her] interest is indefeasibly vested. The disclaimer must be filed in the [probate] court of the county in which proceedings for the administration of the estate of the deceased owner or deceased donee of the power have been commenced. A copy of the disclaimer must be delivered in person or mailed by registered or certified mail, return receipt requested, to any personal representative or other fiduciary of the decedent or donee of the power.

(2) If a property or interest has devolved to the disclaimant under a nontestamentary instrument or contract, the disclaimer must be delivered or filed, if of a present interest, not later than [nine] months after the effective date of the nontestamentary instrument or contract and, if of a future interest, not later than [nine] months after the event determining that the taker of the property or interest is finally ascertained and his [or her] interest is indefeasibly vested. If the person entitled to disclaim does not know of the existence of the interest, the disclaimer must be delivered or filed not later than [nine] months

after the person learns of the existence of the interest. The effective date of a revocable instrument or contract is the date on which the maker no longer has power to revoke it or to transfer to himself [or herself] or another the entire legal and equitable ownership of the interest. The disclaimer or a copy thereof must be delivered in person or mailed by registered or certified mail, return receipt requested, to the person who has legal title to or possession of the interest disclaimed.

(3) A surviving joint tenant [or tenant by the entireties] may disclaim as a separate interest any property or interest therein devolving to him [or her] by right of survivorship. A surviving joint tenant [or tenant by the entireties] may disclaim the entire interest in any property or interest therein that is the subject of a joint tenancy [or tenancy by the entireties] devolving to him [or her], if the joint tenancy [or tenancy by the entireties] was created by act of a deceased joint tenant [or tenant by the entireties], the survivor did not join in creating the joint tenancy [or tenancy by the entireties], and has not accepted a benefit under it.

(4) If real property or an interest therein is disclaimed, a copy of the disclaimer may be recorded in the office of the [Recorder of Deeds] of the county in which the property or interest disclaimed is located.*

*If Torrens system is in effect, add provisions to comply with local law.

(c) [Form of Disclaimer.] The disclaimer must (i) describe the property or interest disclaimed, (ii) declare the disclaimer and extent thereof, and (iii) be signed by the disclaimant.

(d) [Effect of Disclaimer.] The effects of a disclaimer are:

(1) If property or an interest therein devolves to a disclaimant under a testamentary instrument, under a power of appointment exercised by a testamentary instrument, or under the laws of intestacy, and the decedent has not provided for another disposition of that interest, should it be disclaimed, or of disclaimed, or failed interests in general, the disclaimed interest devolves as if the disclaimant had predeceased the decedent, but if by law or under the testamentary instrument the descendants of the disclaimant would share in the disclaimed interest by representation or otherwise were the disclaimant to predecease the decedent, then the disclaimed interest passes by representation, or passes as directed by the governing instrument, to the descendants of the disclaimant who survive the decedent. A future interest that takes effect in possession or enjoyment after the termination of the estate or interest disclaimed takes effect as if the disclaimant had predeceased the decedent. A disclaimer relates back for all purposes to the date of death of the decedent.

(2) If property or an interest therein devolves to a disclaimant under a nontestamentary instrument or contract and the instrument or contract does not provide for another disposition of that interest, should it be disclaimed, or of disclaimed or failed interests in general, the disclaimed interest devolves as if the disclaimant has predeceased the effective date of the instrument or contract, but if by law or under the nontestamentary instrument or contract the descendants of the disclaimant would share in the disclaimed interest by representation or otherwise were the disclaimant to predecease the effective date of the instrument, then the disclaimed interest passes by representation, or passes as directed by the governing instrument, to the descendants of the disclaimant who survive the effective date of the instrument. A disclaimer relates back for all purposes to that date. A future interest that takes effect in possession or enjoyment at or after the termination of the disclaimed interest takes effect as if the disclaimant had died before the effective date of the instrument or contract that transferred the disclaimed interest.

(3) The disclaimer or the written waiver of the right to disclaim is binding upon the disclaimant or person waiving and all persons claiming through or under either of them.

(e) [Waiver and Bar.] The right to disclaim property or an interest therein is barred by (i) an assignment, conveyance, encumbrance, pledge, or transfer of the property or interest, or a contract therefor, (ii) a written waiver of the right to disclaim, (iii) an acceptance of the property or interest or a benefit under it or (iv) a sale of the property or interest under judicial sale made before the disclaimer is made.

(f) [Remedy Not Exclusive.] This section does not abridge the right of a person to waive, release, disclaim, or renounce property or an interest therein under any other statute.

(g) [Application.] An interest in property that exists on the effective date of this section as to which, if a present interest, the time for filing a disclaimer under this section has not expired or, if a future interest, the interest has not become indefeasibly vested or the taker finally ascertained, may be disclaimed within [nine] months after the effective date of this section.

As amended in 1993.

§2-802. Effect of Divorce, Annulment, and Decree of Separation

(a) An individual who is divorced from the decedent or whose marriage to the decedent has been annulled is not a surviving spouse unless, by virtue of a subsequent marriage, he [or she] is married to the decedent at the time of death. A decree of separation that does not terminate the status of husband and wife is not a divorce for purposes of this section.

(b) For purposes of Parts 1, 2, 3, and 4 of this Article, and of Section 3-203, a surviving spouse does not include:

(1) an individual who obtains or consents to a final decree or judgment of divorce from the decedent or an annulment of their marriage, which decree or judgment is not recognized as valid in this State, unless subsequently they participate in a marriage ceremony purporting to marry each to the other or live together as husband and wife;

(2) an individual who, following an invalid decree or judgment of divorce or annulment obtained by the decedent, participates in a marriage ceremony with a third individual; or

(3) an individual who was a party to a valid proceeding concluded by an order purporting to terminate all marital property rights.

§2-803. Effect of Homicide on Intestate Succession, Wills, Trusts, Joint Assets, Life Insurance, and Beneficiary Designations

(a) [Definitions.] In this section:

(1) "Disposition or appointment of property" includes a transfer of an item of property or any other benefit to a beneficiary designated in a governing instrument.

(2) "Governing instrument" means a governing instrument executed by the decedent.

(3) "Revocable," with respect to a disposition, appointment, provision, or nomination, means one under which the decedent, at the time of or immediately before death, was alone empowered, by law or under the governing instrument, to cancel the designation, in favor of the killer, whether or not the decedent was then empowered to designate himself [or herself] in place of his [or her] killer and whether or not the decedent then had capacity to exercise the power.

(b) [Forfeiture of Statutory Benefits.] An individual who feloniously and intentionally kills the decedent forfeits all benefits under this Article with respect to the decedent's estate, including an intestate share, an elective share, an omitted spouse's or child's share, a homestead allowance, exempt property, and a family allowance. If the decedent died intestate, the decedent's intestate estate passes as if the killer disclaimed his [or her] intestate share.

(c) [Revocation of Benefits Under Governing Instruments.] The felonious and intentional killing of the decedent:

(1) revokes any revocable (i) disposition or appointment of property made by the decedent to the killer in a governing instrument, (ii) provision in a governing instrument conferring a general or nongeneral power of appointment on the killer, and (iii) nomination of the killer in a governing instrument, nominating or appointing the killer to serve in any fiduciary or representative capacity, including a personal representative, executor, trustee, or agent; and

(2) severs the interests of the decedent and killer in property held by them at the time of the killing as joint tenants with the right of survivorship [or as community property with the right of survivorship], transforming the interests of the decedent and killer into tenancies in common.

(d) [Effect of Severance.] A severance under subsection (c)(2) does not affect any third-party interest in property acquired for value and in good faith reliance on an apparent title by survivorship in the killer unless a writing declaring the severance has been noted, registered, filed, or recorded in records appropriate to the kind and location of the property which are relied upon, in the ordinary course of transactions involving such property, as evidence of ownership.

(e) [Effect of Revocation.] Provisions of a governing instrument are given effect as if the killer disclaimed all provisions revoked by this section or, in the case of a revoked nomination in a fiduciary or representative capacity, as if the killer predeceased the decedent.

(f) [Wrongful Acquisition of Property.] A wrongful acquisition of property or interest by a killer not covered by this section must be treated in accordance with the principle that a killer cannot profit from his [or her] wrong.

(g) [Felonious and Intentional Killing; How Determined.] After all right to appeal has been exhausted, a judgment of conviction establishing criminal accountability for the felonious and intentional killing of the decedent conclusively establishes the convicted individual as the decedent's killer for purposes of this section. In the absence of a conviction, the court, upon the petition of an interested person, must determine whether, under the preponderance of evidence standard, the individual would be found criminally accountable for the felonious and intentional killing of the decedent. If the court determines that, under that standard, the individual would be found criminally accountable for the felonious and intentional killing of the decedent, the determination conclusively establishes that individual as the decedent's killer for purposes of this section.

(h) [Protection of Payors and Other Third Parties.]

(1) A payor or other third party is not liable for having made a payment or transferred an item of property or any other benefit to a beneficiary designated in a governing instrument affected by an intentional and felonious killing, or for having taken any other action in good faith reliance on the validity of the governing instrument, upon request and satisfactory proof of the decedent's death, before the payor or other third party received written notice of a claimed forfeiture or revocation under this section. A payor or other

third party is liable for a payment made or other action taken after the payor or other third party received written notice of a claimed forfeiture or revocation under this section.

(2) Written notice of a claimed forfeiture or revocation under paragraph (1) must be mailed to the payor's or other third party's main office or home by registered or certified mail, return receipt requested, or served upon the payor or other third party in the same manner as a summons in a civil action. Upon receipt of written notice of a claimed forfeiture or revocation under this section, a payor or other third party may pay any amount owed or transfer or deposit any item of property held by it to or with the court having jurisdiction of the probate proceedings relating to the decedent's estate, or if no proceedings have been commenced, to or with the court having jurisdiction of probate proceedings relating to decedents' estates located in the county of the decedent's residence. The court shall hold the funds or item of property and, upon its determination under this section, shall order disbursement in accordance with the determination. Payments, transfers, or deposits made to or with the court discharge the payor or other third party from all claims for the value of amounts paid to or items of property transferred to or deposited with the court.

(i) [Protection of Bona Fide Purchasers; Personal Liability of Recipient.]

(1) A person who purchases property for value and without notice, or who receives a payment or other item of property in partial or full satisfaction of a legally enforceable obligation, is neither obligated under this section to return the payment, item of property, or benefit nor is liable under this section for the amount of the payment or the value of the item of property or benefit. But a person who, not for value, receives a payment, item of property, or any other benefit to which the person is not entitled under this section is obligated to return the payment, item of property, or benefit, or is personally liable for the amount of the payment or the value of the item of property or benefit, to the person who is entitled to it under this section.

(2) If this section or any part of this section is preempted by federal law with respect to a payment, an item of property, or any other benefit covered by this section, a person who, not for value, receives the payment, item of property, or any other benefit to which the person is not entitled under this section is obligated to return the payment, item of property, or benefit, or is personally liable for the amount of the payment or the value of the item of property or benefit, to the person who would have been entitled to it were this section or part of this section not preempted.

As amended in 1993.

§2-804. Revocation of Probate and Nonprobate Transfers by Divorce; No Revocation by Other Changes of Circumstances

(a) [Definitions.] In this section:

(1) "Disposition or appointment of property" includes a transfer of an item of property or any other benefit to a beneficiary designated in a governing instrument.

(2) "Divorce or annulment" means any divorce or annulment, or any dissolution or declaration of invalidity of a marriage, that would exclude the spouse as a surviving spouse within the meaning of Section 2-802. A decree of separation that does not terminate the status of husband and wife is not a divorce for purposes of this section.

(3) "Divorced individual" includes an individual whose marriage has been annulled.

(4) "Governing instrument" means a governing instrument executed by the divorced individual before the divorce or annulment of his [or her] marriage to his [or her] former spouse.

(5) "Relative of the divorced individual's former spouse" means an individual who is related to the divorced individual's former spouse by blood, adoption, or affinity and who, after the divorce or annulment, is not related to the divorced individual by blood, adoption, or affinity.

(6) "Revocable," with respect to a disposition, appointment, provision, or nomination, means one under which the divorced individual, at the time of the divorce or annulment, was alone empowered, by law or under the governing instrument, to cancel the designation in favor of his [or her] former spouse or former spouse's relative, whether or not the divorced individual was then empowered to designate himself [or herself] in place of his [or her] former spouse or in place of his [or her] former spouse's relative and whether or not the divorced individual then had the capacity to exercise the power.

(b) [Revocation Upon Divorce.] Except as provided by the express terms of a governing instrument, a court order, or a contract relating to the division of the marital estate made between the divorced individuals before or after the marriage, divorce, or annulment, the divorce or annulment of a marriage:

(1) revokes any revocable (i) disposition or appointment of property made by a divorced individual to his [or her] former spouse in a governing instrument and any disposition or appointment created by law or in a governing instrument to a relative of the divorced individual's former spouse, (ii) provision in a governing instrument conferring a general or nongeneral power of appointment on the divorced individual's former spouse or on a relative of the divorced individual's former spouse, and (iii) nomination in a governing instrument, nominating a divorced individual's former spouse

or a relative of the divorced individual's former spouse to serve in any fiduciary or representative capacity, including a personal representative, executor, trustee, conservator, agent, or guardian; and

(2) severs the interests of the former spouses in property held by them at the time of the divorce or annulment as joint tenants with the right of survivorship [or as community property with the right of survivorship], transforming the interests of the former spouses into tenancies in common.

(c) [Effect of Severance.] A severance under subsection (b)(2) does not affect any third-party interest in property acquired for value and in good faith reliance on an apparent title by survivorship in the survivor of the former spouses unless a writing declaring the severance has been noted, registered, filed, or recorded in records appropriate to the kind and location of the property which are relied upon, in the ordinary course of transactions involving such property, as evidence of ownership.

(d) [Effect of Revocation.] Provisions of a governing instrument are given effect as if the former spouse and relatives of the former spouse disclaimed all provisions revoked by this section or, in the case of a revoked nomination in a fiduciary or representative capacity, as if the former spouse and relatives of the former spouse died immediately before the divorce or annulment.

(e) [Revival if Divorce Nullified.] Provisions revoked solely by this section are revived by the divorced individual's remarriage to the former spouse or by a nullification of the divorce or annulment.

(f) [No Revocation for Other Change of Circumstances.] No change of circumstances other than as described in this section and in Section 2-803 effects a revocation.

(g) [Protection of Payors and Other Third Parties.]

(1) A payor or other third party is not liable for having made a payment or transferred an item of property or any other benefit to a beneficiary designated in a governing instrument affected by a divorce, annulment, or remarriage, or for having taken any other action in good faith reliance on the validity of the governing instrument, before the payor or other third party received written notice of the divorce, annulment, or remarriage. A payor or other third party is liable for a payment made or other action taken after the payor or other third party received written notice of a claimed forfeiture or revocation under this section.

(2) Written notice of the divorce, annulment, or remarriage under subsection (g)(2) must be mailed to the payor's or other third party's main office or home by registered or certified mail, return receipt requested, or served upon the payor or other third party in the same manner as a summons in a civil action. Upon receipt of written notice of the divorce, annulment, or remarriage, a payor or other third party may pay any amount owed or transfer or deposit any item of property held by it to or with the court having jurisdiction of the probate proceedings relating to the decedent's estate or, if no proceedings have been commenced, to or with the court having jurisdiction of probate proceedings relating to decedents' estates located in the county of the decedent's residence. The court shall hold the funds or item of property and, upon its determination under this section, shall order disbursement or transfer in accordance with the determination. Payments, transfers, or deposits made to or with the court discharge the payor or other third party from all claims for the value of amounts paid to or items of property transferred to or deposited with the court.

(h) [Protection of Bona Fide Purchasers; Personal Liability of Recipient.]

(1) A person who purchases property from a former spouse, relative of a former spouse, or any other person for value and without notice, or who receives from a former spouse, relative of a former spouse, or any other person a payment or other item of property in partial or full satisfaction of a legally enforceable obligation, is neither obligated under this section to return the payment, item of property, or benefit nor is liable under this section for the amount of the payment or the value of the item of property or benefit. But a former spouse, relative of a former spouse, or other person who, not for value, received a payment, item of property, or any other benefit to which that person is not entitled under this section is obligated to return the payment, item of property, or benefit, or is personally liable for the amount of the payment or the value of the item of property or benefit, to the person who is entitled to it under this section.

(2) If this section or any part of this section is preempted by federal law with respect to a payment, an item of property, or any other benefit covered by this section, a former spouse, relative of the former spouse, or any other person who, not for value, received a payment, item of property, or any other benefit to which that person is not entitled under this section is obligated to return that payment, item of property, or benefit, or is personally liable for the amount of the payment or the value of the item of property or benefit, to the person who would have been entitled to it were this section or part of this section not preempted.

As amended in 1993.

Comment

Purpose and Scope of Revision. The revisions of this section, pre-1990 Section 2-508, intend to unify the law of probate and nonprobate transfers. As originally promulgated, pre-1990 Section 2-508 revoked a predivorce devise to the testator's former spouse. The revisions expand the section to cover "will substitutes" such as revocable inter-vivos trusts, life-insurance and retirement-plan beneficiary designations, transfer-on-death accounts, and other revocable dispositions to the former spouse that the divorced individual established before the divorce (or annulment). As revised, this section also effects a severance of the interests of the former spouses in property that they held at the time of the divorce (or annulment) as joint tenants with the right of survivorship; their co-ownership interests become tenancies in common.

As revised, this section is the most comprehensive provision of its kind, but many states have enacted piecemeal legislation tending in the same direction. . . . The courts have also come under increasing pressure to use statutory construction techniques to extend statutes like the pre-1990 version of Section 2-508 to various will substitutes. . . .

Part 9

Statutory Rule Against Perpetuities; Honorary Trusts

Adoption of Uniform Statutory Rule Against Perpetuities

Note that Part 9, Subpart 1, of Revised Article II has also been adopted as the free-standing Uniform Statutory Rule Against Perpetuities. See Volume 8B Uniform Laws Annotated, Master Edition or ULA Database on Westlaw.

SUBPART 1. STATUTORY RULE AGAINST PERPETUITIES

SUBPART 2. [HONORARY TRUSTS]

General Comment

Subpart 1 of this Part incorporates into the Code the Uniform Statutory Rule Against Perpetuities (USRAP or Uniform Statutory Rule) and Subpart 2 contains an optional section on honorary trusts and trusts for pets. Subpart 2 is under continuing review and, after appropriate study, might subsequently be revised to add provisions affecting certain types of commercial transactions respecting land, such as options in gross, that directly or indirectly restrain alienability.

In codifying Subparts 1 and 2, enacting states may deem it appropriate to locate them at some place other than in the probate code.

SUBPART 1. STATUTORY RULE AGAINST PERPETUITIES

General Comment

Simplified Wait-and-See / Deferred-Reformation Approach Adopted. The Uniform Statutory Rule reforms the common-law Rule Against Perpetuities (common-law Rule) by adding a simplified wait-and-see element and a deferred-reformation element.

Wait-and-see is a two-step strategy. Step One (Section 2-901(a)(1)) preserves the validating side of the common-law Rule. By satisfying the common-law Rule, a nonvested future interest in property is valid at the moment of its creation. Step Two (Section 2-901(a)(2)) is a salvage strategy for future interests that would have been invalid at common law. Rather than invalidating such interests at creation, wait-and-see allows a period of time, called the permissible vesting period, during which the nonvested interests are permitted to vest according to the trust's terms.

The traditional method of measuring the permissible vesting period has been by reference to lives in being at the creation of the interest (the measuring lives) plus 21 years. There are, however, various difficulties and costs associated with identifying and tracing a set of actual measuring lives to see which one is the survivor and when he or she dies. In addition, it has been documented that the use of actual measuring lives plus 21 years does not produce a period of time that self-adjusts to each disposition, extending dead-hand control no further than necessary in each case; rather, the use of actual measuring lives (plus 21 years) generates a permissible vesting period whose length almost always exceeds by some arbitrary margin the point of actual vesting in cases traditionally validated by the wait-and-see strategy. The actual-measuring-lives approach, therefore, performs a margin-of-safety function. Given this fact, and given the costs and difficulties associated with the actual-measuring-lives approach, the Uniform Statutory Rule forgoes the use of actual measuring lives and uses instead a permissible vesting period of a flat 90 years.

The philosophy behind the 90-year period is to fix a period of time that approximates the average period of time that would traditionally be allowed by the wait-and-see doctrine. The flat-period-of-years method was not used as a means of increasing permissible dead-hand control by lengthening the permissible vesting period beyond its traditional boundaries. In fact, the 90-year period falls substantially short of the absolute maximum period of time that could theoretically be achieved under the common-law Rule itself, by the so-called "twelve-healthy-babies ploy"-a ploy that would average out to a period of about 115 years,[1] 25 years or 27.8% longer than the 90 years allowed by USRAP. The fact that the traditional period roughly averages out to a longish-sounding 90 years is a reflection of a quite different

[1] Actuarially, the life expectancy of the longest living member of a group of twelve new-born babies is about 94 years; with the 21-year tack-on period, the "twelve-healthy-babies ploy" would produce, on average, a period of about 115 years (94 + 21).

phenomenon: the dramatic increase in longevity that society as a whole has experienced in the course of the twentieth century.

The framers of the Uniform Statutory Rule derived the 90-year period as follows. The first point recognized was that if actual measuring lives were to have been used, the length of the permissible vesting period would, in the normal course of events, be governed by the life of the youngest measuring life. The second point recognized was that no matter what method is used to identify the measuring lives, the youngest measuring life, in standard trusts, is likely to be the transferor's youngest descendant living when the trust was created.[2] The 90-year period was premised on these propositions. Using four hypothetical families deemed to be representative of actual families, the framers of the Uniform Statutory Rule determined that, on average, the transferor's youngest descendant in being at the transferor's death—assuming the transferor's death to occur between ages 60 and 90, which is when 73 percent of the population die—is about 6 years old. See Waggoner, "Perpetuities: A Progress Report on the Draft Uniform Statutory Rule Against Perpetuities," 20 U. Miami Inst. on Est. Plan. Ch. 7 at 7-17 (1986). The remaining life expectancy of a 6-year-old is about 69 years. The 69 years, plus the 21-year tack-on period, gives a permissible vesting period of 90 years.

Acceptance of the 90-year-period Approach under the Federal Generation-skipping Transfer Tax. Federal regulations, to be promulgated by the U.S. Treasury Department under the generation-skipping transfer tax, will accept the Uniform Statutory Rule's 90-year period as a valid approximation of the period that, on average, would be produced by lives in being plus 21 years. See Temp. Treas. Reg. § 26.2601-1(b)(1)(v)(B)(2) (as to be revised). When originally promulgated in 1988, this regulation was prepared without knowledge of the Uniform Statutory Rule Against Perpetuities, which had been promulgated in 1986; as first promulgated, the regulation only recognized a period measured by actual lives in being plus 21 years. After the 90-year approach of the Uniform Statutory Rule was brought to the attention of the U.S. Treasury Department, the Department issued a letter of intent to amend the regulation to treat the 90-year period as the equivalent of a lives-in-being-plus-21-years period. Letter from Michael J. Graetz, Deputy Assistant Secretary of the Treasury (Tax Policy), to Lawrence J. Bugge, President, National Conference of Commissioners on Uniform State Laws (Nov. 16, 1990). For further discussion of the coordination of the federal generation-skipping transfer tax with the Uniform Statutory Rule, see the Comment to Section 2-901(e), infra, and the Comment to Section 1(e) of the Uniform Statutory Rule Against Perpetuities.

The 90-year Period Will Seldom be Used Up. Nearly all trusts (or other property arrangements) will terminate by their own terms long before the 90-year permissible vesting period expires, leaving the permissible vesting period to extend unused (and ignored) into the future long after the contingencies have been resolved and the property distributed. In the unlikely event that the contingencies have not been resolved by the expiration of the permissible vesting period, Section 2-903 requires the disposition to be reformed by the court so that all contingencies are resolved within the permissible period.

In effect, wait-and-see with deferred reformation operates similarly to a traditional perpetuity saving clause, which grants a margin-of-safety period measured by the lives of the transferor's descendants in being at the creation of the trust or other property arrangement (plus 21 years).

No New Learning Required. The Uniform Statutory Rule does not require the practicing bar to learn a new and unfamiliar set of perpetuity principles. The effect of the Uniform Statutory Rule on the planning and drafting of documents for clients should be distinguished from the effect on the resolution of actual or potential perpetuity-violation cases. The former affects many more practicing lawyers than the latter.

With respect to the planning and drafting end of the practice, the Uniform Statutory Rule requires no modification of current practice and no new learning. *Lawyers can and should continue to use the same traditional perpetuity-saving/termination clause, using specified lives in being plus 21 years, they used before enactment.* Lawyers should not shift to a "later of" type clause that purports to operate upon the *later of* (A) 21 years after the death of the survivor of specified lives in being or (B) 90 years. As explained in more detail in the Comment to Section 2-901, such a clause is not effective. If such a "later of" clause is used in a trust that contains a violation of the common-law rule against perpetuities, Section 2-901(a), by itself, would render the clause ineffective, limit the maximum permissible vesting period to 90 years, and render the trust vulnerable to a reformation suit under Section 2-903. Section 2-901(e), however, saves documents using this type of clause from this fate. By limiting the effect of such clauses to the 21-year period following the death of the survivor of the specified lives, subsection (e) in effect transforms this type of clause into a traditional perpetuity-saving/termination clause, bringing the trust into compliance with the common-law rule against perpetuities and rendering it invulnerable to a reformation suit under Section 2-903.

Far fewer in number are those lawyers (and judges) who have an actual or potential perpetuity-violation case. An actual or potential perpetuity-violation case will arise very infrequently under the Uniform Statutory Rule. When such a case does arise, however, lawyers (or judges) involved in the case will find considerable guidance for its resolution in the detailed analysis contained in the commentary accompanying the Uniform Statutory Rule itself. In short, the detailed analysis in the commentary accompanying the Uniform Statutory Rule need not be part of the general learning required of lawyers in the drafting and planning of dispositive documents for their clients. The detailed analysis is supplied in the commentary for the assistance in the resolution of an actual violation. Only

[2] Under §2-707, the descendants of a beneficiary of a future interest are presumptively made substitute beneficiaries, almost certainly making those descendants in being at the creation of the interest measuring lives, were measuring lives to have been used.

then need that detailed analysis be consulted and, in such a case, it will prove extremely helpful.

General References. Fellows, "Testing Perpetuity Reforms: A Study of Perpetuity Cases 1984-89," 25 Real Prop. Prob. & Tr. J. 597 (1991) (testing the various types of perpetuity reform measures and concluding, on the basis of empirical evidence, that the Uniform Statutory Rule is the best opportunity offered to date for a uniform perpetuity law that efficiently and effectively achieves a fair balance between present and future property owners); Waggoner, "The Uniform Statutory Rule Against Perpetuities: Oregon Joins Up," 26 Willamette L. Rev. 259 (1990) (explaining the operation of the Uniform Statutory Rule); Waggoner, "The Uniform Statutory Rule Against Perpetuities: The Rationale of the 90-Year Waiting Period," 73 Cornell L. Rev. 157 (1988) (explaining the derivation of the 90-year period); Waggoner, "The Uniform Statutory Rule Against Perpetuities," 21 Real Prop., Prob. & Tr. J. 569 (1986) (explaining the theory and operation of the Uniform Statutory Rule).

§2-901. Statutory Rule Against Perpetuities

(a) [Validity of Nonvested Property Interest.] A nonvested property interest is invalid unless:

(1) when the interest is created, it is certain to vest or terminate no later than 21 years after the death of an individual then alive; or

(2) the interest either vests or terminates within 90 years after its creation.

(b) [Validity of General Power of Appointment Subject to a Condition Precedent.] A general power of appointment not presently exercisable because of a condition precedent is invalid unless:

(1) when the power is created, the condition precedent is certain to be satisfied or becomes impossible to satisfy no later than 21 years after the death of an individual then alive; or

(2) the condition precedent either is satisfied or becomes impossible to satisfy within 90 years after its creation.

(c) [Validity of Nongeneral or Testamentary Power of Appointment.] A nongeneral power of appointment or a general testamentary power of appointment is invalid unless:

(1) when the power is created, it is certain to be irrevocably exercised or otherwise to terminate no later than 21 years after the death of an individual then alive; or

(2) the power is irrevocably exercised or otherwise terminates within 90 years after its creation.

(d) [Possibility of Post-death Child Disregarded.] In determining whether a nonvested property interest or a power of appointment is valid under subsection (a)(1), (b)(1), or (c)(1), the possibility that a child will be born to an individual after the individual's death is disregarded.

(e) [Effect of Certain "Later-of" Type Language.] If, in measuring a period from the creation of a trust or other property arrangement, language in a governing instrument (i) seeks to disallow the vesting or termination of any interest or trust beyond, (ii) seeks to postpone the vesting or termination of any interest or trust until, or (iii) seeks to operate in effect in any similar fashion upon, the later of (A) the expiration of a period of time not exceeding 21 years after the death of the survivor of specified lives in being at the creation of the trust or other property arrangement or (B) the expiration of a period of time that exceeds or might exceed 21 years after the death of the survivor of lives in being at the creation of the trust or other property arrangement, that language is inoperative to the extent it produces a period of time that exceeds 21 years after the death of the survivor of the specified lives.

§2-902. When Nonvested Property Interest or Power of Appointment Created

(a) Except as provided in subsections (b) and (c) and in Section 2-905(a), the time of creation of a nonvested property interest or a power of appointment is determined under general principles of property law.

(b) For purposes of Subpart 1 of this Part, if there is a person who alone can exercise a power created by a governing instrument to become the unqualified beneficial owner of (i) a nonvested property interest or (ii) a property interest subject to a power of appointment described in Section 2-901(b) or (c), the nonvested property interest or power of appointment is created when the power to become the unqualified beneficial owner terminates. [For purposes of Subpart 1 of this Part, a joint power with respect to community property or to marital property under the Uniform Marital Property Act held by individuals married to each other is a power exercisable by one person alone.]

(c) For purposes of Subpart 1 of this Part, a nonvested property interest or a power of appointment arising from a transfer of property to a previously funded trust or other existing property arrangement is created when the nonvested property interest or power of appointment in the original contribution was created.

§2-903. Reformation

Upon the petition of an interested person, a court shall reform a disposition in the manner that most closely approximates the transferor's manifested plan of distribution and is within the 90 years allowed by Section 2-901(a)(2), 2-901(b)(2), or 2-901(c)(2) if:

(1) a nonvested property interest or a power of appointment becomes invalid under Section 2-901 (statutory rule against perpetuities);

(2) a class gift is not but might become invalid under Section 2-901 (statutory rule against perpetuities) and the time has arrived when the

share of any class member is to take effect in possession or enjoyment; or

(3) a nonvested property interest that is not validated by Section 2-901(a)(1) can vest but not within 90 years after its creation.

§2-904. Exclusions from Statutory Rule Against Perpetuities

Section 2-901 (statutory rule against perpetuities) does not apply to:

(1) a nonvested property interest or a power of appointment arising out of a nondonative transfer, except a nonvested property interest or a power of appointment arising out of (i) a premarital or postmarital agreement, (ii) a separation or divorce settlement, (iii) a spouse's election, (iv) a similar arrangement arising out of a prospective, existing, or previous marital relationship between the parties, (v) a contract to make or not to revoke a will or trust, (vi) a contract to exercise or not to exercise a power of appointment, (vii) a transfer in satisfaction of a duty of support, or (viii) a reciprocal transfer;

(2) a fiduciary's power relating to the administration or management of assets, including the power of a fiduciary to sell, lease, or mortgage property, and the power of a fiduciary to determine principal and income;

(3) a power to appoint a fiduciary;

(4) a discretionary power of a trustee to distribute principal before termination of a trust to a beneficiary having an indefeasibly vested interest in the income and principal;

(5) a nonvested property interest held by a charity, government, or governmental agency or subdivision, if the nonvested property interest is preceded by an interest held by another charity, government, or governmental agency or subdivision;

(6) a nonvested property interest in or a power of appointment with respect to a trust or other property arrangement forming part of a pension, profit-sharing, stock bonus, health, disability, death benefit, income deferral, or other current or deferred benefit plan for one or more employees, independent contractors, or their beneficiaries or spouses, to which contributions are made for the purpose of distributing to or for the benefit of the participants or their beneficiaries or spouses the property, income, or principal in the trust or other property arrangement, except a nonvested property interest or a power of appointment that is created by an election of a participant or a beneficiary or spouse; or

(7) a property interest, power of appointment, or arrangement that was not subject to the common-law rule against perpetuities or is excluded by another statute of this State.

§2-905. Prospective Application

(a) Except as extended by subsection (b), Subpart 1 of this Part applies to a nonvested property interest or a power of appointment that is created on or after the effective date of Subpart 1 of this Part. For purposes of this section, a nonvested property interest or a power of appointment created by the exercise of a power of appointment is created when the power is irrevocably exercised or when a revocable exercise becomes irrevocable.

(b) If a nonvested property interest or a power of appointment was created before the effective date of Subpart 1 of this Part and is determined in a judicial proceeding, commenced on or after the effective date of Subpart 1 of this Part, to violate this State's rule against perpetuities as that rule existed before the effective date of Subpart 1 of this Part, a court upon the petition of an interested person may reform the disposition in the manner that most closely approximates the transferor's manifested plan of distribution and is within the limits of the rule against perpetuities applicable when the nonvested property interest or power of appointment was created.

§2-906. [Supersession][Repeal]

Subpart 1 of this Part [supersedes the rule of the common law known as the rule against perpetuities][repeals (list statutes to be repealed)].

SUBPART 2. [HONORARY TRUSTS]

[Optional provision for validating and limiting the duration of so-called honorary trusts and trusts for pets.]

§2-907. Honorary Trusts; Trusts for Pets

(a) [Honorary Trust.] Subject to subsection (c), if (i) a trust is for a specific lawful noncharitable purpose or for lawful noncharitable purposes to be selected by the trustee and (ii) there is no definite or definitely ascertainable beneficiary designated, the trust may be performed by the trustee for [21] years but no longer, whether or not the terms of the trust contemplate a longer duration.

(b) [Trust for Pets.] Subject to this subsection and subsection (c), a trust for the care of a designated domestic or pet animal is valid. The trust terminates when no living animal is covered by the trust. A governing instrument must be liberally construed to bring the transfer within this subsection, to presume against the merely precatory or honorary nature of the disposition, and to carry out the general intent of the transferor. Extrinsic evidence is admissible in determining the transferor's intent.

(c) [Additional Provisions Applicable to Honorary Trusts and Trusts for Pets.] In addition to the provisions of subsection (a) or (b), a trust covered by either of those subsections is subject to the following provisions:

(1) Except as expressly provided otherwise in the trust instrument, no portion of the principal or income may be converted to the use of the trustee or to any use other than for the trust's purposes or for the benefit of a covered animal.

(2) Upon termination, the trustee shall transfer the unexpended trust property in the following order:

(i) as directed in the trust instrument;

(ii) if the trust was created in a nonresiduary clause in the transferor's will or in a codicil to the transferor's will, under the residuary clause in the transferor's will; and

(iii) if no taker is produced by the application of subparagraph (i) or (ii), to the transferor's heirs under Section 2-711.

(3) For the purposes of Section 2-707, the residuary clause is treated as creating a future interest under the terms of a trust.

(4) The intended use of the principal or income can be enforced by an individual designated for that purpose in the trust instrument or, if none, by an individual appointed by a court upon application to it by an individual.

(5) Except as ordered by the court or required by the trust instrument, no filing, report, registration, periodic accounting, separate maintenance of funds, appointment, or fee is required by reason of the existence of the fiduciary relationship of the trustee.

(6) A court may reduce the amount of the property transferred, if it determines that that amount substantially exceeds the amount required for the intended use. The amount of the reduction, if any, passes as unexpended trust property under subsection (c)(2).

(7) If no trustee is designated or no designated trustee is willing or able to serve, a court shall name a trustee. A court may order the transfer of the property to another trustee, if required to assure that the intended use is carried out and if no successor trustee is designated in the trust instrument or if no designated successor trustee agrees to serve or is able to serve. A court may also make such other orders and determinations as shall be advisable to carry out the intent of the transferor and the purpose of this section.]

As amended in 1993.

[Part 10, the Uniform International Wills Act, has been omitted.]

Part VIII

~

Uniform Prudent Investor Act (1994)

Uniform Prudent Investor Act (1994)

PREFATORY NOTE

Over the quarter century from the late 1960s the investment practices of fiduciaries experienced significant change. The Uniform Prudent Investor Act (UPIA) undertakes to update trust investment law in recognition of the alterations that have occurred in investment practice. These changes have occurred under the influence of a large and broadly accepted body of empirical and theoretical knowledge about the behavior of capital markets, often described as "modern portfolio theory."

This Act draws upon the revised standards for prudent trust investment promulgated by the American Law Institute in its Restatement (Third) of Trusts: Prudent Investor Rule (1992) [hereinafter Restatement of Trusts 3d: Prudent Investor Rule; also referred to as 1992 Restatement].

Objectives of the Act. UPIA makes five fundamental alterations in the former criteria for prudent investing. All are to be found in the Restatement of Trusts 3d: Prudent Investor Rule.

(1) The standard of prudence is applied to any investment as part of the total portfolio, rather than to individual investments. In the trust setting the term "portfolio" embraces all the trust's assets. UPIA §2(b).

(2) The tradeoff in all investing between risk and return is identified as the fiduciary's central consideration. UPIA §2(b).

(3) All categoric restrictions on types of investments have been abrogated; the trustee can invest in anything that plays an appropriate role in achieving the risk/return objectives of the trust and that meets the other requirements of prudent investing. UPIA §2(e).

(4) The long familiar requirement that fiduciaries diversify their investments has been integrated into the definition of prudent investing. UPIA §3.

(5) The much criticized former rule of trust law forbidding the trustee to delegate investment and management functions has been reversed. Delegation is now permitted, subject to safeguards. UPIA §9.

Literature. These changes in trust investment law have been presaged in an extensive body of practical and scholarly writing. See especially the discussion and reporter's notes by Edward C. Halbach, Jr., in Restatement of Trusts 3d: Prudent Investor Rule (1992); see also Edward C. Halbach, Jr., Trust Investment Law in the Third Restatement, 27 Real Property, Probate & Trust J. 407 (1992); Bevis Longstreth, Modern Investment Management and the Prudent Man Rule (1986); Jeffrey N. Gordon, The Puzzling Persistence of the Constrained Prudent Man Rule, 62 N.Y.U.L. Rev. 52 (1987); John H. Langbein & Richard A. Posner, The Revolution in Trust Investment Law, 62 A.B.A.J. 887 (1976); Note, The Regulation of Risky Investments, 83 Harvard L. Rev. 603 (1970). A succinct account of the main findings of modern portfolio theory, written for lawyers, is Jonathan R. Macey, An Introduction to Modern Financial Theory (1991) (American College of Trust & Estate Counsel Foundation). A leading introductory text on modern portfolio theory is R.A. Brealey, An Introduction to Risk and Return from Common Stocks (2d ed. 1983).

Legislation. Most states have legislation governing trust-investment law. This Act promotes uniformity of state law on the basis of the new consensus reflected in the Restatement of Trusts 3d: Prudent Investor Rule. Some states have already acted. California, Delaware, Georgia, Minnesota, Tennessee, and Washington revised their prudent investor legislation to emphasize the total-portfolio standard of care in advance of the 1992 Restatement. These statutes are extracted and discussed in Restatement of Trusts 3d: Prudent Investor Rule §227, reporter's note, at 60-66 (1992).

Drafters in Illinois in 1991 worked from the April 1990 "Proposed Final Draft" of the Restatement of Trusts 3d: Prudent Investor Rule and enacted legislation that is closely modeled on the new Restatement. 760 ILCS §5/5 (prudent investing); and §5/5.1 (delegation) (1992). As the Comments to this Uniform Prudent Investor Act reflect, the Act draws upon the Illinois statute in several sections. Virginia revised its prudent investor act in a similar vein in 1992. Virginia Code §26-45.1 (prudent investing) (1992). Florida revised its statute in 1993. Florida Laws, ch. 93-257, amending Florida Statutes §518.11 (prudent investing) and creating §518.112 (delegation). New York legislation drawing on the new Restatement and on a preliminary version of this Uniform Prudent Investor Act was enacted in 1994. N.Y. Assembly Bill 11683-B, Ch. 609 (1994), adding Estates, Powers and Trusts Law §11-2.3 (Prudent Investor Act).

Remedies. This Act does not undertake to address issues of remedy law or the computation of damages in trust matters. Remedies are the subject of a reasonably distinct body of doctrine. See generally Restatement (Second) of Trusts §§197-226A (1959) [hereinafter cited as Restatement of Trusts 2d; also referred to as 1959 Restatement].

Implications for charitable and pension trusts. This Act is centrally concerned with the investment responsibilities arising under the private gratuitous trust, which is the common vehicle for conditioned wealth transfer within the family. Nevertheless, the prudent investor rule also bears on charitable and pension trusts, among others. "In making investments of trust funds the trustee of a charitable trust is under a duty similar to that of the trustee of a private trust." Restatement of Trusts 2d §389 (1959). The Employee Retirement Income Security Act (ERISA), the federal regulatory scheme for pension trusts enacted in 1974, absorbs trust-investment law through the prudence standard of ERISA §404(a)(1)(B), 29 U.S.C. §1104(a). The Supreme Court has said: "ERISA's legislative history confirms that the Act's fiduciary responsibility provisions 'codif[y] and mak[e] applicable to [ERISA] fiduciaries certain principles developed in the evolution of the law of trusts.'" *Firestone Tire & Rubber Co. v. Bruch*, 489 U.S. 101, 110-11 (1989) (footnote omitted).

Other fiduciary relationships. The Uniform Prudent Investor Act regulates the investment responsibilities of trustees. Other fiduciaries—such as executors, conservators, and guardians of the property—sometimes have responsibilities over assets that are governed by the standards of prudent investment. It will often be appropriate for states to adapt the law governing investment by trustees under this Act to these other fiduciary regimes, taking account of such changed circumstances as the relatively short duration of most executorships and the intensity of court supervision of conservators and guardians in some jurisdictions. The present Act does not undertake to adjust trust-investment law to the special circumstances of the state schemes for administering decedents' estates or conducting the affairs of protected persons.

Although the Uniform Prudent Investor Act by its terms applies to trusts and not to charitable corporations, the standards of the Act can be expected to inform the investment responsibilities of directors and officers of charitable corporations. As the 1992 Restatement observes, "the duties of the members of the governing board of a charitable corporation are generally similar to the duties of the trustee of a charitable trust." Restatement of Trusts 3d: Prudent Investor Rule §379, Comment *b*, at 190 (1992). See also id. §389, Comment *b*, at 190-91 (absent contrary statute or other provision, prudent investor rule applies to investment of funds held for charitable corporations).

UNIFORM PRUDENT INVESTOR ACT

§1. Prudent Investor Rule

(a) Except as otherwise provided in subsection (b), a trustee who invests and manages trust assets owes a duty to the beneficiaries of the trust to comply with the prudent investor rule set forth in this [Act].

(b) The prudent investor rule, a default rule, may be expanded, restricted, eliminated, or otherwise altered by the provisions of a trust. A trustee is not liable to a beneficiary to the extent that the trustee acted in reasonable reliance on the provisions of the trust.

Comment

This section imposes the obligation of prudence in the conduct of investment functions and identifies further sections of the Act that specify the attributes of prudent conduct.

Origins. The prudence standard for trust investing traces back to *Harvard College v. Amory*, 26 Mass. (9 Pick.) 446 (1830). Trustees should "observe how men of prudence, discretion and intelligence manage their own affairs, not in regard to speculation, but in regard to the permanent disposition of their funds, considering the probable income, as well as the probable safety of the capital to be invested." Id. at 461.

Prior legislation. The Model Prudent Man Rule Statute (1942), sponsored by the American Bankers Association, undertook to codify the language of the *Amory* case. See Mayo A. Shattuck, The Development of the Prudent Man Rule for Fiduciary Investment in the United States in the Twentieth Century, 12 Ohio State L.J. 491, at 501 (1951); for the text of the model act, which inspired many state statutes, see id. at 508-09. Another prominent codification of the *Amory* standard is Uniform Probate Code §7-302 (1969), which provides that "the trustee shall observe the standards in dealing with the trust assets that would be observed by a prudent man dealing with the property of another . . . ."

. . . **Objective standard.** The concept of prudence in the judicial opinions and legislation is essentially relational or comparative. It resembles in this respect the "reasonable person" rule of tort law. A prudent trustee behaves as other trustees similarly situated would behave. The standard is, therefore, objective rather than subjective. Sections 2 through 9 of this Act identify the main factors that bear on prudent investment behavior.

Variation. Almost all of the rules of trust law are default rules, that is, rules that the settlor may alter or abrogate. Subsection (b) carries forward this traditional attribute of trust law. Traditional trust law also allows the beneficiaries of the trust to excuse its performance, when they are all capable and not misinformed. Restatement of Trusts 2d §216 (1959).

§2. Standard of Care; Portfolio Strategy; Risk and Return Objectives

(a) A trustee shall invest and manage trust assets as a prudent investor would, by considering the purposes, terms, distribution requirements, and other circumstances of the trust. In satisfying this standard, the trustee shall exercise reasonable care, skill, and caution.

(b) A trustee's investment and management decisions respecting individual assets must be evaluated not in isolation but in the context of the trust portfolio as a whole and as a part of an overall investment strategy having risk and return objectives reasonably suited to the trust.

(c) Among circumstances that a trustee shall consider in investing and managing trust assets are such of the following as are relevant to the trust or its beneficiaries:

(1) general economic conditions;

(2) the possible effect of inflation or deflation;

(3) the expected tax consequences of investment decisions or strategies;

(4) the role that each investment or course of action plays within the overall trust portfolio, which may include financial assets, interests in closely held enterprises, tangible and intangible personal property, and real property;

(5) the expected total return from income and the appreciation of capital;

(6) other resources of the beneficiaries;

(7) needs for liquidity, regularity of income, and preservation or appreciation of capital; and

(8) an asset's special relationship or special value, if any, to the purposes of the trust or to one or more of the beneficiaries.

(d) A trustee shall make a reasonable effort to verify facts relevant to the investment and management of trust assets.

(e) A trustee may invest in any kind of property or type of investment consistent with the standards of this [Act].

(f) A trustee who has special skills or expertise, or is named trustee in reliance upon the trustee's representation that the trustee has special skills or expertise, has a duty to use those special skills or expertise.

Comment

Section 2 is the heart of the Act. Subsections (a), (b), and (c) are patterned loosely on the language of the Restatement of Trusts 3d: Prudent Investor Rule §227 (1992), and on the 1991 Illinois statute, 760 §ILCS 5/5a (1992). Subsection (f) is derived from Uniform Probate Code §7-302 (1969).

Objective standard. Subsection (a) of this Act carries forward the relational and objective standard made familiar in the *Amory* case, in earlier prudent investor legislation, and in the Restatements. Early formulations of the prudent person rule were sometimes troubled by the effort to distinguish between the standard of a prudent person investing for another and investing on his or her own account. The language of subsection (a), by relating the trustee's duty to "the purposes, terms, distribution requirements, and other circumstances of the trust," should put such questions to rest. The standard is the standard of the prudent investor similarly situated.

Portfolio standard. Subsection (b) emphasizes the consolidated portfolio standard for evaluating investment decisions. An investment that might be imprudent standing alone can become prudent if undertaken in sensible relation to other trust assets, or to other nontrust assets. In the trust setting the term "portfolio" embraces the entire trust estate.

Risk and return. Subsection (b) also sounds the main theme of modern investment practice, sensitivity to the risk/return curve. See generally the works cited in the Prefatory Note to this Act, under "Literature." Returns correlate strongly with risk, but tolerance for risk varies greatly with the financial and other circumstances of the investor, or in the case of a trust, with the purposes of the trust and the relevant circumstances of the beneficiaries. A trust whose main purpose is to support an elderly widow of modest means will have a lower risk tolerance than a trust to accumulate for a young scion of great wealth.

Subsection (b) of this Act follows Restatement of Trusts 3d: Prudent Investor Rule §227(a), which provides that the standard of prudent investing "requires the exercise of reasonable care, skill, and caution, and is to be applied to investments not in isolation but in the context of the trust portfolio and as a part of an overall investment strategy, which should incorporate risk and return objectives reasonably suitable to the trust."

Factors affecting investment. Subsection (c) points to certain of the factors that commonly bear on risk/return preferences in fiduciary investing. This listing is nonexclusive. Tax considerations, such as preserving the stepped-up basis on death under Internal Revenue Code §1014 for low-basis assets, have traditionally been exceptionally important in estate planning for affluent persons. Under the present recognition rules of the federal income tax, taxable investors, including trust beneficiaries, are in general best served by an investment strategy that minimizes the taxation incident to portfolio turnover. See generally Robert H. Jeffrey & Robert D. Arnott, Is Your Alpha Big Enough to Cover Its Taxes?, Journal of Portfolio Management 15 (Spring 1993).

Another familiar example of how tax considerations bear upon trust investing: In a regime of pass-through taxation, it may be prudent for the trust to buy lower yielding tax-exempt securities for high-bracket taxpayers, whereas it would ordinarily be imprudent for the trustees of a charitable trust, whose income is tax exempt, to accept the lowered yields associated with tax-exempt securities.

When tax considerations affect beneficiaries differently, the trustee's duty of impartiality requires attention to the competing interests of each of them.

Subsection (c)(8), allowing the trustee to take into account any preferences of the beneficiaries respecting heirlooms or other prized assets, derives from the Illinois act, 760 ILCS §5/5(a)(4) (1992).

Duty to monitor. Subsections (a) through (d) apply both to investing and managing trust assets. "Managing" embraces monitoring, that is, the trustee's continuing responsibility for oversight of the suitability of investments already made as well as the trustee's decisions respecting new investments.

Duty to investigate. Subsection (d) carries forward the traditional responsibility of the fiduciary investor to examine information likely to bear importantly on the value or the security of an investment—for example, audit reports or records of title. E.g., *Estate of Collins*, 72 Cal. App. 3d 663, 139 Cal. Rptr. 644 (1977) (trustees lent on a junior mortgage on unimproved real estate, failed to have land appraised, and accepted an unaudited financial statement; held liable for losses).

Abrogating categoric restrictions. Subsection 2(e) clarifies that no particular kind of property or type of investment is inherently imprudent. Traditional trust law was encumbered with a variety of categoric exclusions, such as prohibitions on junior mortgages or new ventures. In some states legislation created so-called "legal lists" of approved trust investments. The universe of investment products changes incessantly. Investments that were at one time thought too risky, such as equities, or more recently, futures, are now used in fiduciary portfolios. By contrast, the investment that was at one time thought ideal for trusts, the long-term bond, has been discovered to import a level of risk and volatility—in this case, inflation risk—that had not been anticipated. Accordingly, section 2(e) of this Act follows Restatement of Trusts 3d: Prudent Investor Rule in abrogating categoric restrictions. The Restatement says: "Specific investments or techniques are not per se prudent or imprudent. The riskiness of a specific property, and thus the propriety of its inclusion in the trust estate, is not judged in the abstract but in terms of its anticipated effect on the particular trust's portfolio." Restatement of Trusts 3d: Prudent Investor Rule §227, Comment f, at 24 (1992). The premise of subsection 2(e) is that trust beneficiaries are better protected by the Act's emphasis on close attention to risk/return objectives as prescribed in subsection 2(b) than in attempts to identify categories of investment that are per se prudent or imprudent.

The Act impliedly disavows the emphasis in older law on avoiding "speculative" or "risky" investments. Low levels of risk may be appropriate in some trust settings but inappropriate in others. It is the trustee's task to invest at a risk level that is suitable to the purposes of the trust.

The abolition of categoric restrictions against types of investment in no way alters the trustee's conventional duty of loyalty, which is reiterated for the purposes of this Act in Section 5. For example, were the trustee to invest in a second mortgage on a piece of real property owned by the trustee, the investment would be wrongful on account of the trustee's breach of the duty to abstain from self-dealing, even though the investment would no longer automatically offend the former categoric restriction against fiduciary investments in junior mortgages.

Professional fiduciaries. The distinction taken in subsection (f) between amateur and professional trustees is familiar law. The prudent investor standard applies to a range of fiduciaries, from the most sophisticated professional investment management firms and corporate fiduciaries, to family members of minimal experience. Because the standard of prudence is relational, it follows that the standard for professional trustees is the standard of prudent professionals; for amateurs, it is the standard of prudent amateurs. Restatement of Trusts 2d §174 (1959) provides: "The trustee is under a duty to the beneficiary in administering the trust to exercise such care and skill as a man of ordinary prudence would exercise in dealing with his own property; and if the trustee has or procures his appointment as trustee by representing that he has greater skill than that of a man of ordinary prudence, he is under a duty to exercise such skill." Case law strongly supports the concept of the higher standard of care for the trustee representing itself to be expert or professional. See Annot., Standard of Care Required of Trustee Representing Itself to Have Expert Knowledge or Skill, 91 A.L.R. 3d 904 (1979) & 1992 Supp. at 48-49.

The Drafting Committee declined the suggestion that the Act should create an exception to the prudent investor rule (or to the diversification requirement of Section 3) in the case of smaller trusts. The Committee believes that subsections (b) and (c) of the Act emphasize factors that are sensitive to the traits of small trusts; and that subsection (f) adjusts helpfully for the distinction between professional and amateur trusteeship. Furthermore, it is always open to the settlor of a trust under Section 1(b) of the Act to reduce the trustee's standard of care if the settlor deems such a step appropriate. The official comments to the 1992 Restatement observe that pooled investments, such as mutual funds and bank common trust funds, are especially suitable for small trusts. Restatement of Trusts 3d: Prudent Investor Rule §227, Comments *h*, *m*, at 28, 51; reporter's note to Comment *g*, id. at 83.

Matters of proof. Although virtually all express trusts are created by written instrument, oral trusts are known, and accordingly, this Act presupposes no formal requirement that trust terms be in writing. When there is a written trust instrument, modern authority strongly favors allowing evidence extrinsic to the instrument to be consulted for the purpose of ascertaining the settlor's intent. See Uniform Probate Code §2-601 (1990), Comment; Restatement (Third) of Property: Donative Transfers (Preliminary Draft No. 2, ch. 11, Sept. 11, 1992).

§3. Diversification

A trustee shall diversify the investments of the trust unless the trustee reasonably determines that, because of special circumstances, the purposes of the trust are better served without diversifying.

Comment

The language of this section derives from Restatement of Trusts 2d §228 (1959). ERISA insists upon a comparable rule for pension trusts. ERISA

§404(a)(1)(C), 29 U.S.C. §1104(a)(1)(C). Case law overwhelmingly supports the duty to diversify. See Annot., Duty of Trustee to Diversify Investments, and Liability for Failure to Do So, 24 A.L.R. 3d 730 (1969) & 1992 Supp. at 78-79.

The 1992 Restatement of Trusts takes the significant step of integrating the diversification requirement into the concept of prudent investing. Section 227(b) of the 1992 Restatement treats diversification as one of the fundamental elements of prudent investing, replacing the separate section 228 of the Restatement of Trusts 2d. The message of the 1992 Restatement, carried forward in Section 3 of this Act, is that prudent investing ordinarily requires diversification.

Circumstances can, however, overcome the duty to diversify. For example, if a tax-sensitive trust owns an underdiversified block of low-basis securities, the tax costs of recognizing the gain may outweigh the advantages of diversifying the holding. The wish to retain a family business is another situation in which the purposes of the trust sometimes override the conventional duty to diversify.

Rationale for diversification. "Diversification reduces risk . . . [because] stock price movements are not uniform. They are imperfectly correlated. This means that if one holds a well diversified portfolio, the gains in one investment will cancel out the losses in another." Jonathan R. Macey, An Introduction to Modern Financial Theory 20 (American College of Trust and Estate Counsel Foundation, 1991). For example, during the Arab oil embargo of 1973, international oil stocks suffered declines, but the shares of domestic oil producers and coal companies benefitted. Holding a broad enough portfolio allowed the investor to set off, to some extent, the losses associated with the embargo.

Modern portfolio theory divides risk into the categories of "compensated" and "uncompensated" risk. The risk of owning shares in a mature and well-managed company in a settled industry is less than the risk of owning shares in a start-up high-technology venture. The investor requires a higher expected return to induce the investor to bear the greater risk of disappointment associated with the start-up firm. This is compensated risk—the firm pays the investor for bearing the risk. By contrast, nobody pays the investor for owning too few stocks. The investor who owned only international oils in 1973 was running a risk that could have been reduced by having configured the portfolio differently—to include investments in different industries. This is uncompensated risk—nobody pays the investor for owning shares in too few industries and too few companies. Risk that can be eliminated by adding different stocks (or bonds) is uncompensated risk. The object of diversification is to minimize this uncompensated risk of having too few investments. "As long as stock prices do not move exactly together, the risk of a diversified portfolio will be less than the average risk of the separate holdings." R.A. Brealey, An Introduction to Risk and Return from Common Stocks 103 (2d ed. 1983).

There is no automatic rule for identifying how much diversification is enough. The 1992 Restatement says: "Significant diversification advantages can be achieved with a small number of well-selected securities representing different industries . . . . Broader diversification is usually to be preferred in trust investing," and pooled investment vehicles "make thorough diversification practical for most trustees." Restatement of Trusts 3d: Prudent Investor Rule §227, General Note on Comments *e-h*, at 77 (1992). See also Macey, supra, at 23-24; Brealey, supra, at 111-13.

Diversifying by pooling. It is difficult for a small trust fund to diversify thoroughly by constructing its own portfolio of individually selected investments. Transaction costs such as the round-lot (100 share) trading economies make it relatively expensive for a small investor to assemble a broad enough portfolio to minimize uncompensated risk. For this reason, pooled investment vehicles have become the main mechanism for facilitating diversification for the investment needs of smaller trusts.

Most states have legislation authorizing common trust funds; see 3 Austin W. Scott & William F. Fratcher, The Law of Trusts §227.9, at 463-65 n.26 (4th ed. 1988) (collecting citations to state statutes). As of 1992, 35 states and the District of Columbia had enacted the Uniform Common Trust Fund Act (UCTFA) (1938), overcoming the rule against commingling trust assets and expressly enabling banks and trust companies to establish common trust funds. 7 Uniform Laws Ann. 1992 Supp. at 130 (schedule of adopting states). The Prefatory Note to the UCTFA explains: "The purposes of such a common or joint investment fund are to diversify the investment of the several trusts and thus spread the risk of loss, and to make it easy to invest any amount of trust funds quickly and with a small amount of trouble." 7 Uniform Laws Ann. 402 (1985).

Fiduciary investing in mutual funds. Trusts can also achieve diversification by investing in mutual funds. See Restatement of Trusts 3d: Prudent Investor Rule, §227, Comment *m*, at 99-100 (1992) (endorsing trust investment in mutual funds). ERISA §401(b)(1), 29 U.S.C. §1101(b)(1), expressly authorizes pension trusts to invest in mutual funds, identified as securities "issued by an investment company registered under the Investment Company Act of 1940 . . . ."

§4. Duties at Inception of Trusteeship

Within a reasonable time after accepting a trusteeship or receiving trust assets, a trustee shall review the trust assets and make and implement decisions concerning the retention and disposition of assets, in order to bring the trust portfolio into compliance with the purposes, terms, distribution requirements, and other circumstances of the trust, and with the requirements of this [Act].

Comment

Section 4, requiring the trustee to dispose of unsuitable assets within a reasonable time, is old law, codified in Restatement of Trusts 3d: Prudent Investor Rule §229 (1992), lightly revising Restatement of Trusts 2d §230 (1959). The duty extends as well to investments that were proper when purchased but subsequently become improper. Restatement of Trusts 2d §231 (1959). The same standards apply to successor trustees, see Restatement of Trusts 2d §196 (1959).

The question of what period of time is reasonable turns on the totality of factors affecting the asset and the trust. The 1959 Restatement took the view that "[o]rdinarily any time within a year is reasonable, but under some circumstances a year may be too long a time and under other circumstances a trustee is not liable although he fails to effect the conversion for more than a year." Restatement of Trusts 2d §230, comment *b* (1959). The 1992 Restatement retreated from this rule of thumb, saying, "No positive rule can be stated with respect to what constitutes a reasonable time for the sale or exchange of securities." Restatement of Trusts 3d: Prudent Investor Rule §229, comment *b* (1992).

The criteria and circumstances identified in Section 2 of this Act as bearing upon the prudence of decisions to invest and manage trust assets also pertain to the prudence of decisions to retain or dispose of inception assets under this section.

§5. Loyalty

A trustee shall invest and manage the trust assets solely in the interest of the beneficiaries.

Comment

The duty of loyalty is perhaps the most characteristic rule of trust law, requiring the trustee to act exclusively for the beneficiaries, as opposed to acting for the trustee's own interest or that of third parties. The language of Section 4 of this Act derives from Restatement of Trusts 3d: Prudent Investor Rule §170 (1992), which makes minute changes in Restatement of Trusts 2d §170 (1959).

The concept that the duty of prudence in trust administration, especially in investing and managing trust assets, entails adherence to the duty of loyalty is familiar. ERISA §404(a)(1)(B), 29 U.S.C. §1104(a)(1)(B), extracted in the Comment to Section 1 of this Act, effectively merges the requirements of prudence and loyalty. A fiduciary cannot be prudent in the conduct of investment functions if the fiduciary is sacrificing the interests of the beneficiaries.

The duty of loyalty is not limited to settings entailing self-dealing or conflict of interest in which the trustee would benefit personally from the trust. "The trustee is under a duty to the beneficiary in administering the trust not to be guided by the interest of any third person. Thus, it is improper for the trustee to sell trust property to a third person for the purpose of benefitting the third person rather than the trust." Restatement of Trusts 2d §170, comment *q*, at 371 (1959).

No form of so-called "social investing" is consistent with the duty of loyalty if the investment activity entails sacrificing the interests of trust beneficiaries—for example, by accepting below-market returns—in favor of the interests of the persons supposedly benefitted by pursuing the particular social cause. See, e.g., John H. Langbein & Richard Posner, Social Investing and the Law of Trusts, 79 Michigan L. Rev. 72, 96-97 (1980) (collecting authority). For pension trust assets, see generally Ian D. Lanoff, The Social Investment of Private Pension Plan Assets: May it Be Done Lawfully under ERISA?, 31 Labor L.J. 387 (1980). Commentators supporting social investing tend to concede the overriding force of the duty of loyalty. They argue instead that particular schemes of social investing may not result in below-market returns. See, e.g., Marcia O'Brien Hylton, "Socially Responsible" Investing: Doing Good Versus Doing Well in an Inefficient Market, 42 American U.L. Rev. 1 (1992). In 1994 the Department of Labor issued an Interpretive Bulletin reviewing its prior analysis of social investing questions and reiterating that pension trust fiduciaries may invest only in conformity with the prudence and loyalty standards of ERISA §§403-404. Interpretive Bulletin 94-1, 59 Fed. Regis. 32606 (Jun. 22, 1994), to be codified as 29 CFR §2509.94-1. The Bulletin reminds fiduciary investors that they are prohibited from "subordinat[ing] the interests of participants and beneficiaries in their retirement income to unrelated objectives."

§6. Impartiality

If a trust has two or more beneficiaries, the trustee shall act impartially in investing and managing the trust assets, taking into account any differing interests of the beneficiaries.

Comment

The duty of impartiality derives from the duty of loyalty. When the trustee owes duties to more than one beneficiary, loyalty requires the trustee to respect the interests of all the beneficiaries. Prudence in investing and administration requires the trustee to take account of the interests of all the beneficiaries for whom the trustee is acting, especially the conflicts between the interests of beneficiaries interested in income and those interested in principal.

The language of Section 6 derives from Restatement of Trusts 2d §183 (1959); see also id., §232. Multiple beneficiaries may be beneficiaries in succession (such as life and remainder interests) or beneficiaries with simultaneous interests (as when the income interest in a trust is being divided among several beneficiaries).

The trustee's duty of impartiality commonly affects the conduct of investment and management functions in the sphere of principal and income allocations. This Act prescribes no regime for allocating receipts and expenses. The details of such allocations are commonly handled under specialized legislation, such as the Revised Uniform Principal and Income Act (1962) (which is presently under study by the Uniform Law Commission with a view toward further revision).

§7. Investment Costs

In investing and managing trust assets, a trustee may only incur costs that are appropriate and reasonable in relation to the assets, the purposes of the trust, and the skills of the trustee.

§8. Reviewing Compliance

Compliance with the prudent investor rule is determined in light of the facts and circumstances existing at the time of a trustee's decision or action and not by hindsight.

Comment

This section derives from the 1991 Illinois act, 760 ILCS 5/5(a)(2) (1992), which draws upon Restatement of Trusts 3d: Prudent Investor Rule §227, comment *b*, at 11 (1992). Trustees are not insurers. Not every investment or management decision will turn out in the light of hindsight to have been successful. Hindsight is not the relevant standard. In the language of law and economics, the standard is ex ante, not ex post.

§9. Delegation of Investment and Management Functions

(a) A trustee may delegate investment and management functions that a prudent trustee of comparable skills could properly delegate under the circumstances. The trustee shall exercise reasonable care, skill, and caution in:

(1) selecting an agent;

(2) establishing the scope and terms of the delegation, consistent with the purposes and terms of the trust; and

(3) periodically reviewing the agent's actions in order to monitor the agent's performance and compliance with the terms of the delegation.

(b) In performing a delegated function, an agent owes a duty to the trust to exercise reasonable care to comply with the terms of the delegation.

(c) A trustee who complies with the requirements of subsection (a) is not liable to the beneficiaries or to the trust for the decisions or actions of the agent to whom the function was delegated.

(d) By accepting the delegation of a trust function from the trustee of a trust that is subject to the law of this State, an agent submits to the jurisdiction of the courts of this State.

Comment

This section of the Act reverses the much-criticized rule that forbad trustees to delegate investment and management functions. The language of this section is derived from Restatement of Trusts 3d: Prudent Investor Rule §171 (1992), discussed infra, and from the 1991 Illinois act, 760 ILCS §5/5.1(b), (c) (1992).

Former law. The former nondelegation rule survived into the 1959 Restatement: "The trustee is under a duty to the beneficiary not to delegate to others the doing of acts which the trustee can reasonably be required personally to perform." The rule put a premium on the frequently arbitrary task of distinguishing discretionary functions that were thought to be nondelegable from supposedly ministerial functions that the trustee was allowed to delegate. Restatement of Trusts 2d §171 (1959).

The Restatement of Trusts 2d admitted in a comment that "There is not a clear-cut line dividing the acts which a trustee can properly delegate from those which he cannot properly delegate." Instead, the comment directed attention to a list of factors that "may be of importance: (1) the amount of discretion involved; (2) the value and character of the property involved; (3) whether the property is principal or income; (4) the proximity or remoteness of the subject matter of the trust; (5) the character of the act as one involving professional skill or facilities possessed or not possessed by the trustee himself." Restatement of Trusts 2d §171, comment *d* (1959). The 1959 Restatement further said: "A trustee cannot properly delegate to another power to select investments." Restatement of Trusts 2d §171, comment *h* (1959). . . .

The modern trend to favor delegation. The trend of subsequent legislation, culminating in the Restatement of Trusts 3d: Prudent Investor Rule, has been strongly hostile to the nondelegation rule. See John H. Langbein, Reversing the Nondelegation Rule of Trust-Investment Law, 59 Missouri L. Rev. 105 (1994).

The delegation rule of the Uniform Trustee Powers Act. The Uniform Trustee Powers Act (1964) effectively abrogates the nondelegation rule. It authorizes trustees "to employ persons, including attorneys, auditors, investment advisors, or agents, even if they are associated with the trustee, to advise or assist the trustee in the performance of his administrative duties; to act without independent investigation upon their recommendations; and instead of acting personally, to employ one or more agents to perform any act of administration, whether or not discretionary . . . ." Uniform Trustee Powers Act §3(24), 7B Uniform Laws Ann. 743 (1985). The Act has been enacted in 16 states. . . .

The delegation rule of the 1992 Restatement. The Restatement of Trusts 3d: Prudent Investor Rule (1992) repeals the nondelegation rule of Restatement of Trusts 2d §171 (1959), extracted supra, and replaces it with substitute text that reads:

> §171. Duty with Respect to Delegation. A trustee has a duty personally to perform the responsibilities of trusteeship except as a prudent person might delegate those responsibilities to others. In deciding whether, to whom, and in what manner to delegate fiduciary authority in the administration of a trust, and thereafter in supervising agents, the trustee is under a duty to the beneficiaries to exercise fiduciary discretion and to act as a prudent person would act in similar circumstances.

Restatement of Trusts 3d: Prudent Investor Rule §171 (1992). The 1992 Restatement integrates this delegation standard into the prudent investor rule of section 227, providing that "the trustee must . . . act with prudence in deciding whether and how to delegate to others . . . ." Restatement of Trusts 3d: Prudent Investor Rule §227(c) (1992).

Protecting the beneficiary against unreasonable delegation. There is an intrinsic tension in trust law between granting trustees broad powers that facilitate flexible and efficient trust administration, on the one hand, and protecting trust beneficiaries from the misuse of such powers on the other hand. A broad set of trustees' powers, such as those found in most lawyer-drafted instruments and exemplified in the Uniform Trustees' Powers Act, permits the trustee to act vigorously and expeditiously to maximize the interests of the beneficiaries in a variety of transactions and administrative settings. Trust law relies upon the duties of loyalty and prudent administration, and upon procedural safeguards such as periodic accounting and the availability of judicial oversight, to prevent the misuse of these powers. Delegation, which is a species of trustee power, raises the same tension. If the trustee delegates effectively, the beneficiaries obtain the advantage of the agent's specialized investment skills or whatever other attributes induced the trustee to delegate. But if the trustee delegates to a knave or an incompetent, the delegation can work harm upon the beneficiaries.

Section 9 of the Uniform Prudent Investor Act is designed to strike the appropriate balance between the advantages and the hazards of delegation. Section 9 authorizes delegation under the limitations of subsections (a) and (b). Section 9(a) imposes duties of care, skill, and caution on the trustee in selecting the agent, in establishing the terms of the delegation, and in reviewing the agent's compliance.

The trustee's duties of care, skill, and caution in framing the terms of the delegation should protect the beneficiary against overbroad delegation. For example, a trustee could not prudently agree to an investment management agreement containing an exculpation clause that leaves the trust without recourse against reckless mismanagement. Leaving one's beneficiaries remediless against willful wrongdoing is inconsistent with the duty to use care and caution in formulating the terms of the delegation. This sense that it is imprudent to expose beneficiaries to broad exculpation clauses underlies both federal and state legislation restricting exculpation clauses, e.g., ERISA §§404(a)(1)(D), 410(a), 29 U.S.C. §§1104(a)(1)(D), 1110(a); New York Est. Powers Trusts Law §11-1.7 (McKinney 1967).

Although subsection (c) of the Act exonerates the trustee from personal responsibility for the agent's conduct when the delegation satisfies the standards of subsection 9(a), subsection 9(b) makes the agent responsible to the trust. The beneficiaries of the trust can, therefore, rely upon the trustee to enforce the terms of the delegation.

Costs. The duty to minimize costs that is articulated in Section 7 of this Act applies to delegation as well as to other aspects of fiduciary investing. In deciding whether to delegate, the trustee must balance the projected benefits against the likely costs. Similarly, in deciding how to delegate, the trustee must take costs into account. The trustee must be alert to protect the beneficiary from "double dipping." If, for example, the trustee's regular compensation schedule presupposes that the trustee will conduct the investment management function, it should ordinarily follow that the trustee will lower its fee when delegating the investment function to an outside manager.

§10. Language Invoking Standard of [Act]

The following terms or comparable language in the provisions of a trust, unless otherwise limited or modified, authorizes any investment or strategy permitted under this [Act]: "investments permissible by law for investment of trust funds," "legal investments," "authorized investments," "using the judgment and care under the circumstances then prevailing that persons of prudence, discretion, and intelligence exercise in the management of their own affairs, not in regard to speculation but in regard to the permanent disposition of their funds, considering the probable income as well as the probable safety of their capital," "prudent man rule," "prudent trustee rule," "prudent person rule," and "prudent investor rule."

§11. Application to Existing Trusts

This [Act] applies to trusts existing on and created after its effective date. As applied to trusts existing on its effective date, this [Act] governs only decisions or actions occurring after that date.

§12. Uniformity of Application and Construction

This [Act] shall be applied and construed to effectuate its general purpose to make uniform the law with respect to the subject of this [Act] among the States enacting it.

§13. Short Title

This [Act] may be cited as the "[Name of Enacting State] Uniform Prudent Investor Act."

§14. Severability

If any provision of this [Act] or its application to any person or circumstance is held invalid, the invalidity does not affect other provisions or applications of this [Act] which can be given effect without the invalid provision or application, and to this end the provisions of this [Act] are severable.

§15. Effective Date

This [Act] takes effect ________________.

§16. Repeals

The following acts and parts of acts are repealed:

(1)
(2)
(3)

PART IX

~

UNIFORM PRUDENT MANAGEMENT OF INSTITUTIONAL FUNDS ACT

(2006)

UNIFORM PRUDENT MANAGEMENT OF INSTITUTIONAL FUNDS ACT (2006)

TABLE OF CONTENTS

Prefatory Note

Reasons for Revision. The Uniform Prudent Management of Institutional Funds Act (UPMIFA) replaces the Uniform Management of Institutional Funds Act (UMIFA). The National Conference of Commissioners on Uniform State Laws approved UMIFA in 1972, and 47 jurisdictions have enacted the act. UMIFA provided guidance and authority to charitable organizations within its scope concerning the management and investment of funds held by those organizations, UMIFA provided endowment spending rules that did not depend on trust accounting principles of income and principal, and UMIFA permitted the release of restrictions on the use or management of funds under certain circumstances. The changes UMIFA made to the law permitted charitable organizations to use modern investment techniques such as total-return investing and to determine endowment fund spending based on spending rates rather than on determinations of "income" and "principal."

UMIFA was drafted almost 35 years ago, and portions of it are now out of date. The prudence standards in UMIFA have provided useful guidance, but prudence norms evolve over time. The new Act provides modern articulations of the prudence standards for the management and investment of charitable funds and for endowment spending. The Uniform Prudent Investor Act (UPIA), an Act promulgated in 1994 and already enacted in 43 jurisdictions, served as a model for many of the revisions. UPIA updates rules on investment decision making for trusts, including charitable trusts, and imposes additional duties on trustees for the protection of beneficiaries. UPMIFA applies these rules and duties to charities organized as nonprofit corporations. UPMIFA does not apply to trusts managed by corporate and other fiduciaries that are not charities, because UPIA provides management and investment standards for those trusts.

In applying principles based on UPIA to charities organized as nonprofit corporations, UPMIFA combines the approaches taken by UPIA and by the Revised Model Nonprofit Corporation Act (RMNCA). UPMIFA reflects the fact that standards for managing and investing institutional funds are and should be the same regardless of whether a charitable organization is organized as a trust, a nonprofit corporation, or some other entity. See Bevis Longstreth, Modern Investment Management and the Prudent Man Rule 7 (1986) (stating "[t]he modern paradigm of prudence applies to all fiduciaries who are subject to some version of the prudent man rule, whether under ERISA, the private foundation provisions of the Code, UMIFA, other state statutes, or the common law."); Harvey P. Dale, Nonprofit Directors and Officers - Duties and Liabilities for Investment Decisions, 1994 N.Y.U. Conf. Tax Plan. 501(c)(3) Org's. Ch. 4.

UPMIFA provides guidance and authority to charitable organizations concerning the management and investment of funds held by those organizations, and UPMIFA imposes additional duties on those who manage and invest charitable funds. These duties provide additional protections for charities and also protect the interests of donors who want to see their contributions used wisely.

UPMIFA modernizes the rules governing expenditures from endowment funds, both to provide stricter guidelines on spending from endowment funds and to give institutions the ability to cope more easily with fluctuations in the value of the endowment.

Finally, UPMIFA updates the provisions governing the release and modification of restrictions on charitable funds to permit more efficient management of these funds. These provisions derive from the approach taken in the Uniform Trust Code (UTC) for modifying charitable trusts. Like the UTC provisions, UPMIFA's modification rules preserve the historic position of the attorneys general in most states as the overseers of charities.

As under UMIFA, the new Act applies to charities organized as charitable trusts, as nonprofit corporations, or in some other manner, but the rules do not apply to funds managed by trustees that are not charities. Thus, the Act does not apply to trusts managed by corporate or individual trustees, but the Act does apply to trusts managed by charities.

Prudent Management and Investment. UMIFA applied the 1972 prudence standard to investment decision making. In contrast, UPMIFA will give charities updated and more useful guidance by incorporating language from UPIA, modified to fit the special needs of charities. The revised Act spells out more of the factors a charity should consider in making investment decisions, thereby imposing a modern, well accepted, prudence standard based on UPIA.

Among the expressly enumerated prudence factors in UPMIFA is "the preservation of the endowment fund," a standard not articulated in UMIFA.

In addition to identifying factors that a charity must consider in making management and investment decisions, UPMIFA requires a charity and those who manage and invest its funds to:

Give primary consideration to donor intent as expressed in a gift instrument,

Act in good faith, with the care an ordinarily prudent person would exercise,

Incur only reasonable costs in investing and managing charitable funds,

Make a reasonable effort to verify relevant facts,

Make decisions about each asset in the context of the portfolio of investments, as part of an overall investment strategy,

Diversify investments unless due to special circumstances, the purposes of the fund are better served without diversification,

Dispose of unsuitable assets, and

In general, develop an investment strategy appropriate for the fund and the charity.

UMIFA did not articulate these requirements. Thus, UPMIFA strengthens the rules governing management and investment decision making by charities and provides more guidance for those who manage and invest the funds.

Donor Intent with Respect to Endowments. UPMIFA improves the protection of donor intent with respect to expenditures from endowments. When a donor expresses intent clearly in a written gift instrument, the Act requires that the charity follow the donor's instructions. When a donor's intent is not so expressed, UPMIFA directs the charity to spend an amount that is prudent, consistent with the purposes of the fund, relevant economic factors, and the donor's intent that the fund continue in perpetuity. This approach allows the charity to give effect to donor intent, protect its endowment, assure generational equity, and use the endowment to support the purposes for which the endowment was created.

Retroactivity. Like UMIFA, UPIA, the Uniform Principal and Income Act of 1961, and the Uniform Principal and Income Act of 1997, UPMIFA applies retroactively to institutional funds created before and prospectively to institutional funds created after enactment of the statute....

Endowment Spending. UPMIFA improves the endowment spending rule by eliminating the concept of historic dollar value and providing better guidance regarding the operation of the prudence standard. Under UMIFA a charity can spend amounts above historic dollar value that the charity determines to be prudent. The Act directs the charity to focus on the purposes and needs of the charity rather than on the purposes and perpetual nature of the fund. Amounts below historic dollar value cannot be spent. The Drafting Committee concluded that this endowment spending rule created numerous problems and that restructuring the rule would benefit charities, their donors, and the public. The problems include:

1. Historic dollar value fixes valuation at a moment in time, and that moment is arbitrary. If a donor provides for a gift in the donor's will, the date of valuation for the gift will likely be the donor's date of death. (UMIFA left uncertain what the appropriate date for valuing a testamentary gift was.) The determination of historic dollar value can vary significantly depending upon when in the market cycle the donor dies. In addition, the fund may be below historic dollar value at the time the charity receives the gift if the value of the asset declines between the date of the donor's death and the date the asset is actually distributed to the charity from the estate.

2. After a fund has been in existence for a number of years, historic dollar value may become meaningless. Assuming reasonable long term investment success, the value of the typical fund will be well above historic dollar value, and historic dollar value will no longer represent the purchasing power of the original gift. Without better guidance on spending the increase in value of the fund, historic dollar value does not provide adequate protection for the fund. If a charity views the restriction on

spending simply as a direction to preserve historic dollar value, the charity may spend more than it should.

3. The Act does not provide clear answers to questions a charity faces when the value of an endowment fund drops below historic dollar value. A fund that is so encumbered is commonly called an "underwater" fund. Conflicting advice regarding whether an organization could spend from an underwater fund has led to difficulties for those managing charities. If a charity concluded that it could continue to spend trust accounting income until a fund regained its historic dollar value, the charity might invest for income rather than on a total-return basis. Thus, the historic dollar value rule can cause inappropriate distortions in investment policy and can ultimately lead to a decline in a fund's real value. If, instead, a charity with an underwater fund continues to invest for growth, the charity may be unable to spend anything from an underwater endowment fund for several years. The inability of a charity to spend anything from an endowment is likely to be contrary to donor intent, which is to provide current benefits to the charity.

The Drafting Committee concluded that providing clearly articulated guidance on the prudence rule for spending from an endowment fund, with emphasis on the permanent nature of the fund, would provide the best protection of the purchasing power of endowment funds.

Presumption of Imprudence. UPMIFA includes as an optional provision a presumption of imprudence if a charity spends more than seven percent of an endowment fund in any one year. The presumption is meant to protect against spending an endowment too quickly. Although the Drafting Committee believes that the prudence standard of UPMIFA provides appropriate and adequate protection for endowments, the Committee provided the option for states that want to include a mechanical guideline in the statute. A major drawback to any statutory percentage is that it is unresponsive to changes in the rate of inflation or deflation.

Modification of Restrictions on Charitable Funds. UPMIFA clarifies that the doctrines of cy pres and deviation apply to funds held by nonprofit corporations as well as to funds held by charitable trusts. Courts have applied trust law rules to nonprofit corporations in the past, but the Drafting Committee believed that statutory authority for applying these principles to nonprofit corporations would be helpful. UMIFA permitted release of restrictions but left the application of cy pres uncertain. Under UPMIFA, as under trust law, the court will determine whether and how to apply cy pres or deviation and the attorney general will receive notice and have the opportunity to participate in the proceeding. The one addition to existing law is that UPMIFA gives a charity the authority to modify a restriction on a fund that is both old and small. For these funds, the expense of a trip to court will often be prohibitive. By permitting a charity to make an appropriate modification, money is saved for the charitable purposes of the charity. Even with respect to small, old funds, however, the charity must notify the attorney general of the charity's intended action. Of course, if the attorney general has concerns, he or she can seek the agreement of the charity to change or abandon the modification, and if that fails, can commence a court action to enjoin it. Thus, in all types of modification the attorney general continues to be the protector both of the donor's intent and of the public's interest in charitable funds.

Other Organizational Law. For matters not governed by UPMIFA, a charitable organization will continue to be governed by rules applicable to charitable trusts, if it is organized as a trust, or rules applicable to nonprofit corporations, if it is organized as a nonprofit corporation.

Relation to Trust Law. Although UPMIFA applies a number of rules from trust law to institutions organized as nonprofit corporations, in two respects UPMIFA creates rules that do not exist under the common law applicable to trusts. The endowment spending rule of Section 4 and the provision for modifying a small, old fund in subsection (d) of Section 6 have no counterparts in the common law or the UTC. The Drafting Committee believes that these rules could be useful to charities organized as trusts, and the Committee recommends conforming amendments to the UTC and the Principal and Income Act to incorporate these changes into trust law.

§1. Short title.

This [act] may be cited as the Uniform Prudent Management of Institutional Funds Act.

§2. Definitions.

In this [act]:

(1) "Charitable purpose" means the relief of poverty, the advancement of education or religion, the promotion of health, the promotion of a governmental purpose, or any other purpose the achievement of which is beneficial to the community.

(2) "Endowment fund" means an institutional fund or part thereof that, under the terms of a gift instrument, is not wholly expendable by the institution on a current basis. The term does not include assets that an institution designates as an endowment fund for its own use.

(3) "Gift instrument" means a record or records, including an institutional solicitation, under which

property is granted to, transferred to, or held by an institution as an institutional fund.

(4) "Institution" means:

(A) a person, other than an individual, organized and operated exclusively for charitable purposes;

(B) a government or governmental subdivision, agency, or instrumentality, to the extent that it holds funds exclusively for a charitable purpose; and

(C) a trust that had both charitable and noncharitable interests, after all noncharitable interests have terminated.

(5) "Institutional fund" means a fund held by an institution exclusively for charitable purposes. The term does not include:

(A) program-related assets;

(B) a fund held for an institution by a trustee that is not an institution; or

(C) a fund in which a beneficiary that is not an institution has an interest, other than an interest that could arise upon violation or failure of the purposes of the fund.

(6) "Person" means an individual, corporation, business trust, estate, trust, partnership, limited liability company, association, joint venture, public corporation, government or governmental subdivision, agency, or instrumentality, or any other legal or commercial entity.

(7) "Program-related asset" means an asset held by an institution primarily to accomplish a charitable purpose of the institution and not primarily for investment.

(8) "Record" means information that is inscribed on a tangible medium or that is stored in an electronic or other medium and is retrievable in perceivable form.

§3. Standard of conduct in managing and investing institutional fund.

(a) Subject to the intent of a donor expressed in a gift instrument, an institution, in managing and investing an institutional fund, shall consider the charitable purposes of the institution and the purposes of the institutional fund.

(b) In addition to complying with the duty of loyalty imposed by law other than this [act], each person responsible for managing and investing an institutional fund shall manage and invest the fund in good faith and with the care an ordinarily prudent person in a like position would exercise under similar circumstances.

(c) In managing and investing an institutional fund, an institution:

(1) may incur only costs that are appropriate and reasonable in relation to the assets, the purposes of the institution, and the skills available to the institution; and

(2) shall make a reasonable effort to verify facts relevant to the management and investment of the fund.

(d) An institution may pool two or more institutional funds for purposes of management and investment.

(e) Except as otherwise provided by a gift instrument, the following rules apply:

(1) In managing and investing an institutional fund, the following factors, if relevant, must be considered:

(A) general economic conditions;

(B) the possible effect of inflation or deflation;

(C) the expected tax consequences, if any, of investment decisions or strategies;

(D) the role that each investment or course of action plays within the overall investment portfolio of the fund;

(E) the expected total return from income and the appreciation of investments;

(F) other resources of the institution;

(G) the needs of the institution and the fund to make distributions and to preserve capital; and

(H) an asset's special relationship or special value, if any, to the charitable purposes of the institution.

(2) Management and investment decisions about an individual asset must be made not in isolation but rather in the context of the institutional fund's portfolio of investments as a whole and as a part of an overall investment strategy having risk and return objectives reasonably suited to the fund and to the institution.

(3) Except as otherwise provided by law other than this [act], an institution may invest in any kind of property or type of investment consistent with this section.

(4) An institution shall diversify the investments of an institutional fund unless the institution reasonably determines that, because of special circumstances, the purposes of the fund are better served without diversification.

(5) Within a reasonable time after receiving property, an institution shall make and carry out decisions concerning the retention or disposition of the property or to rebalance a portfolio, in order to bring the institutional fund into compliance with the purposes, terms, and distribution requirements of the institution as necessary to meet other circumstances of the institution and the requirements of this [act].

(6) A person that has special skills or expertise, or is selected in reliance upon the person's representation that the person has special skills or expertise, has a duty to use those skills or that

expertise in managing and investing institutional funds.

§4. Appropriation for expenditure or accumulation of endowment fund; rules of construction.

(a) Subject to the intent of a donor expressed in the gift instrument [and to subsection (d)], an institution may appropriate for expenditure or accumulate so much of an endowment fund as the institution determines is prudent for the uses, benefits, purposes, and duration for which the endowment fund is established. Unless stated otherwise in the gift instrument, the assets in an endowment fund are donor-restricted assets until appropriated for expenditure by the institution. In making a determination to appropriate or accumulate, the institution shall act in good faith, with the care that an ordinarily prudent person in a like position would exercise under similar circumstances, and shall consider, if relevant, the following factors:

(1) the duration and preservation of the endowment fund;

(2) the purposes of the institution and the endowment fund;

(3) general economic conditions;

(4) the possible effect of inflation or deflation;

(5) the expected total return from income and the appreciation of investments;

(6) other resources of the institution; and

(7) the investment policy of the institution.

(b) To limit the authority to appropriate for expenditure or accumulate under subsection (a), a gift instrument must specifically state the limitation.

(c) Terms in a gift instrument designating a gift as an endowment, or a direction or authorization in the gift instrument to use only "income", "interest", "dividends", or "rents, issues, or profits", or "to preserve the principal intact", or words of similar import:

(1) create an endowment fund of permanent duration unless other language in the gift instrument limits the duration or purpose of the fund; and

(2) do not otherwise limit the authority to appropriate for expenditure or accumulate under subsection (a).

[(d) The appropriation for expenditure in any year of an amount greater than seven percent of the fair market value of an endowment fund, calculated on the basis of market values determined at least quarterly and averaged over a period of not less than three years immediately preceding the year in which the appropriation for expenditure was made, creates a rebuttable presumption of imprudence. For an endowment fund in existence for fewer than three years, the fair market value of the endowment fund must be calculated for the period the endowment fund has been in existence. This subsection does not:

(1) apply to an appropriation for expenditure permitted under law other than this [act] or by the gift instrument; or

(2) create a presumption of prudence for an appropriation for expenditure of an amount less than or equal to seven percent of the fair market value of the endowment fund.]

[§5. Delegation of management and investment functions.

(a) Subject to any specific limitation set forth in a gift instrument or in law other than this [act], an institution may delegate to an external agent the management and investment of an institutional fund to the extent that an institution could prudently delegate under the circumstances. An institution shall act in good faith, with the care that an ordinarily prudent person in a like position would exercise under similar circumstances, in:

(1) selecting an agent;

(2) establishing the scope and terms of the delegation, consistent with the purposes of the institution and the institutional fund; and

(3) periodically reviewing the agent's actions in order to monitor the agent's performance and compliance with the scope and terms of the delegation.

(b) In performing a delegated function, an agent owes a duty to the institution to exercise reasonable care to comply with the scope and terms of the delegation.

(c) An institution that complies with subsection (a) is not liable for the decisions or actions of an agent to which the function was delegated.

(d) By accepting delegation of a management or investment function from an institution that is subject to the laws of this state, an agent submits to the jurisdiction of the courts of this state in all proceedings arising from or related to the delegation or the performance of the delegated function.

(e) An institution may delegate management and investment functions to its committees, officers, or employees as authorized by law of this state other than this [act].]

§6. Release or modification of restrictions on management, investment, or purpose.

(a) If the donor consents in a record, an institution may release or modify, in whole or in part, a restriction contained in a gift instrument on the management, investment, or purpose of an institutional fund. A release or modification may not allow a fund to be used for a purpose other than a charitable purpose of the institution.

(b) The court, upon application of an institution, may modify a restriction contained in a gift instrument regarding the management or investment of an institutional fund if the restriction has become impracticable or wasteful, if it impairs the management or investment of the fund, or if, because of circumstances not anticipated by the donor, a modification of a restriction will further the purposes of the fund. The institution shall notify the [Attorney General] of the application, and the [Attorney General] must be given an opportunity to be heard. To the extent practicable, any modification must be made in accordance with the donor's probable intention.

(c) If a particular charitable purpose or a restriction contained in a gift instrument on the use of an institutional fund becomes unlawful, impracticable, impossible to achieve, or wasteful, the court, upon application of an institution, may modify the purpose of the fund or the restriction on the use of the fund in a manner consistent with the charitable purposes expressed in the gift instrument. The institution shall notify the [Attorney General] of the application, and the [Attorney General] must be given an opportunity to be heard.

(d) If an institution determines that a restriction contained in a gift instrument on the management, investment, or purpose of an institutional fund is unlawful, impracticable, impossible to achieve, or wasteful, the institution, [60 days] after notification to the [Attorney General], may release or modify the restriction, in whole or part, if:

(1) the institutional fund subject to the restriction has a total value of less than [$25,000];

(2) more than [20] years have elapsed since the fund was established; and

(3) the institution uses the property in a manner consistent with the charitable purposes expressed in the gift instrument.

§7. Reviewing compliance.

Compliance with this [act] is determined in light of the facts and circumstances existing at the time a decision is made or action is taken, and not by hindsight.

§8. Application to existing institutional funds.

This [act] applies to institutional funds existing on or established after [the effective date of this act]. As applied to institutional funds existing on [the effective date of this act] this [act] governs only decisions made or actions taken on or after that date.

§9. Relation to electronic signatures in global and national commerce act.

This [act] modifies, limits, and supersedes the Electronic Signatures in Global and National Commerce Act, 15 U.S.C. Section 7001 et seq., but does not modify, limit, or supersede Section 101 of that act, 15 U.S.C. Section 7001(a), or authorize electronic delivery of any of the notices described in Section 103 of that act, 15 U.S.C. Section 7003(b).

§10. Uniformity of application and construction.

In applying and construing this uniform act, consideration must be given to the need to promote uniformity of the law with respect to its subject matter among states that enact it.

§11. Effective date.

This [act] takes effect . . . .

§12. Repeal.

The following acts and parts of acts are repealed:

(a) [The Uniform Management of Institutional Funds Act]

PART X

~

UNIFORM TRUST CODE

UNIFORM TRUST CODE

Uniform Trust Code

PREFATORY NOTE

The Uniform Trust Code (2000) is the first national codification of the law of trusts. The primary stimulus to the Commissioners' drafting of the Uniform Trust Code is the greater use of trusts in recent years, both in family estate planning and in commercial transactions, both in the United States and internationally. This greater use of the trust, and consequent rise in the number of day-to-day questions involving trusts, has led to a recognition that the trust law in many States is thin. It has also led to a recognition that the existing Uniform Acts relating to trusts, while numerous, are fragmentary. The Uniform Trust Code will provide States with precise, comprehensive, and easily accessible guidance on trust law questions. On issues on which States diverge or on which the law is unclear or unknown, the Code will for the first time provide a uniform rule. The Code also contains a number of innovative provisions.

Default rule. Most of the Uniform Trust Code consists of default rules that apply only if the terms of the trust fail to address or insufficiently cover a particular issue. Pursuant to Section 105, a drafter is free to override a substantial majority of the Code's provisions. The exceptions are scheduled in Section 105(b).

Innovative provisions. Much of the Uniform Trust Code is a codification of the common law of trusts. But the Code does contain a number of innovative provisions. Among the more significant are specification of the rules of trust law that are not subject to override in the trust's terms (Section 105), the inclusion of a comprehensive article on representation of beneficiaries (Article 3), rules on trust modification and termination that will enhance flexibility (Sections 410-417), and the inclusion of an article collecting the special rules pertaining to revocable trusts (Article 6).

Models for drafting. While the Uniform Trust Code is the first comprehensive Uniform Act on the subject of trusts, comprehensive trust statutes are already in effect in several States. Notable examples include the statutes in California, Georgia, Indiana, Texas, and Washington, all of which were referred to in the drafting process. Most influential was the 1986 California statute, found at Division 9 of the California Probate Code (Sections 15000 et seq.), which was used by the Drafting Committee as its initial model.

Existing uniform laws on trust law subjects. Certain older Uniform Acts are incorporated into the Uniform Trust Code. Others, addressing more specialized topics, will continue to be available for enactment in free-standing form.

The following Uniform Acts are incorporated into or otherwise superseded by the Uniform Trust Code:

Uniform Probate Code Article VII—Originally approved in 1969, Article VII has been enacted in about 15 jurisdictions. Article VII, although titled "Trust Administration," is a modest statute, addressing only a limited number of topics. Except for its provisions on trust registration, Article VII is superseded by the Uniform Trust Code. Its provisions on jurisdiction are incorporated into Article 2 of the Code, and its provisions on trustee liability to persons other than beneficiaries are replaced by Section 1010.

Uniform Prudent Investor Act (1994) —This Act has been enacted in 35 jurisdictions. This Act, and variant forms enacted in a number of other States, has displaced the older "prudent man" standard, bringing trust law into line with modern investment practice. States that have enacted the Uniform Prudent Investor Act are encouraged to recodify it as part of their enactment of the Uniform Trust Code. A place for this is provided in Article 9.

Uniform Trustee Powers Act (1964)—This Act has been enacted in 16 States. The Act contains a list of specific trustee powers and deals with other selected issues, particularly relations of a trustee with persons other than beneficiaries. The Uniform Trustee Powers Act is outdated and is entirely superseded by the Uniform Trust Code, principally at Sections 815, 816, and 1012. States enacting the Uniform Trust Code should repeal their existing trustee powers legislation.

Uniform Trusts Act (1937)—This largely overlooked Act of similar name was enacted in only six States, none within the past several decades. Despite a title suggesting comprehensive coverage of its topic, this Act, like Article VII of the UPC, addresses only a limited number of topics. These include the duty of loyalty, the registration and voting of securities, and trustee liability to persons other than beneficiaries. States enacting the Uniform Trust Code should repeal this earlier namesake.

The following Uniform Acts are not affected by enactment of the Uniform Trust Code and do not need to be amended or repealed:

Uniform Common Trust Fund Act—Originally approved in 1938, this Act has been enacted in 34 jurisdictions. The Uniform Trust Code does not address the subject of common trust funds. In recent years, many banks have replaced their common trust funds with mutual funds that may also be available to non-trust customers. The Code addresses investment in mutual funds at Section 802(f).

Uniform Custodial Trust Act (1987)—This Act has been enacted in 14 jurisdictions. This Act allows standard trust provisions to be automatically incorporated into the terms of a trust simply by referring to the Act. This Act is not displaced by the Uniform Trust Code but complements it.

Uniform Management of Institutional Funds Act (1972)—This Act has been enacted in 47 jurisdictions. It governs the administration of endowment funds held by charitable, religious, and other eleemosynary institutions. The Uniform Management of Institutional Funds Act establishes a standard of prudence for use of appreciation on assets, provides specific authority for the making of investments, authorizes the delegation of this authority, and specifies a procedure, through either donor consent or court approval, for removing restrictions on the use of donated funds.

Uniform Principal and Income Act (1997)—The 1997 Uniform Principal and Income Act is a major revision of the widely enacted Uniform Act of the same name approved in 1962. Because this Act addresses issues with respect both to decedent's estates and trusts, a jurisdiction enacting the revised Uniform Principal and Income Act may wish to include it either as part of this Code or as part of its probate laws.

Uniform Probate Code—Originally approved in 1969, and enacted in close to complete form in about 20 States but influential in virtually all, the UPC overlaps with trust topics in several areas. One area of overlap, already mentioned, is UPC Article VII. Another area of overlap concerns representation of beneficiaries. UPC Section 1-403 provides principles of representation for achieving binding judicial settlements of matters involving both estates and trusts. The Uniform Trust Code refines these representation principles, and extends them to nonjudicial settlement agreements and to optional notices and consents. See Uniform Trust Code, Section 111 and Article 3. A final area of overlap between the UPC and trust law concerns rules of construction. The UPC, in Article II, Part 7, extends certain of the rules on the construction of wills to trusts and other nonprobate instruments. The Uniform Trust Code similarly extends to trusts the rules on the construction of wills. Unlike the UPC, however, the Trust Code does not prescribe the exact rules. Instead, Section 112 of the Uniform Trust Code is an optional provision applying to trusts whatever rules the enacting jurisdiction already has in place on the construction of wills.

Uniform Statutory Rule Against Perpetuities—Originally approved in 1986, this Act has been enacted in 27 jurisdictions. The Act reforms the durational limit on when property interests, including interests created under trusts, must vest or fail. The Uniform Trust Code does not limit the duration of trusts or alter the time when interests must otherwise vest, but leaves this issue to other state law. The Code may be enacted without change regardless of the status of the perpetuities law in the enacting jurisdiction.

Uniform Supervision of Trustees for Charitable Purposes Act (1954)—This Act, which has been enacted in four States, is limited to mechanisms for monitoring the actions of charitable trustees. Unlike the Uniform Trust Code, the Supervision of Trustees for Charitable Purposes Act does not address the substantive law of charitable trusts.

Uniform Testamentary Additions to Trusts Act—This Act is available in two versions: the 1960 Act, with 24 enactments; and the 1991 Act, with 20 enactments through 1999. As its name suggests, this Act validates pour-over devises to trusts. Because it validates provisions in wills, it is incorporated into the Uniform Probate Code, not into the Uniform Trust Code.

Role of Restatement of Trusts. The Restatement (Second) of Trusts was approved by the American Law Institute in 1957. Work on the Restatement Third began in the late 1980s. The portion of Restatement Third relating to the prudent investor rule and other investment topics was completed and approved in 1990. A tentative draft of the portion of Restatement Third relating to the rules on the creation and validity of trusts was approved in 1996, and the portion relating to the office of trustee, trust purposes, spendthrift provisions and the rights of creditors was approved in 1999. The Uniform Trust Code was drafted in close coordination with the writing of the Restatement Third.

OVERVIEW OF UNIFORM TRUST CODE

The Uniform Trust Code consists of 11 articles. The substance of the Code is focused in the first 10 articles; Article 11 is primarily an effective date provision.

Article 1—General Provisions and Definitions—In addition to definitions, this article addresses miscellaneous but important topics. The Uniform Trust Code is primarily default law. A settlor, subject to certain limitations, is free to draft trust terms departing from the provisions of this Code. The settlor, if minimum contacts are present, may in addition designate the trust's principal place of administration; the trustee, if certain standards are met, may transfer the principal place of administration to another State or country. To encourage nonjudicial resolution of disputes, the Uniform Trust Code provides more certainty for when such settlements are binding. While the Code does not prescribe the exact rules to be applied to the construction of trusts, it does extend to trusts whatever rules the enacting jurisdiction has on the construction of wills. The Uniform Trust Code, although comprehensive, does not legislate on every issue. Its provisions are supplemented by the common law of trusts and principles of equity.

Article 2—Judicial Proceedings—This article addresses selected issues involving judicial proceedings concerning trusts, particularly trusts having contacts with more than one State or country. The courts in the trust's principal place of administration have jurisdiction over both the trustee and the beneficiaries as to any matter relating to the trust. Optional provisions on subject-matter jurisdiction and venue are provided. The minimal coverage of this article was deliberate. The Drafting Committee concluded that most issues related to jurisdiction and procedure are not appropriate to a Trust Code, but are best left to other bodies of law.

Article 3—Representation—This article deals with the representation of beneficiaries and other interested persons, both by fiduciaries (personal representatives, guardians and conservators), and through what is known as virtual representation. The representation principles of the article apply to settlement of disputes, whether by a court or nonjudicially. They apply for the giving of required notices. They apply for the giving of consents to certain actions. The article also authorizes a court to appoint a representative if the court concludes that representation of a person might otherwise be inadequate. The court may appoint a representative to represent and approve a settlement on behalf of a minor, incapacitated, or unborn person or person whose identity or location is unknown and not reasonably ascertainable.

Article 4—Creation, Validity, Modification and Termination of Trust—This article specifies the requirements for creating, modifying and terminating trusts. Most of the requirements relating to creation of trusts (Sections 401 through 409) track traditional doctrine, including requirements of intent, capacity, property, and valid trust purpose. The Uniform Trust Code articulates a three-part classification system for trusts: noncharitable, charitable, and honorary. Noncharitable trusts, the most common type, require an ascertainable beneficiary and a valid purpose. Charitable trusts, on the other hand, by their very nature are created to benefit the public at large. The so-called honorary or purposes trust, although unenforceable at common law, is valid and enforceable under this Code despite the absence of an ascertainable beneficiary. The most common example is a trust for the care of an animal.

Sections 410 through 417 provide a series of interrelated rules on when a trust may be terminated or modified other than by its express terms. The overall objective of these sections is to enhance flexibility consistent with the principle that preserving the settlor's intent is paramount. Termination or modification may be allowed upon beneficiary consent if the court concludes that the trust or a particular provision no longer serves a material purpose or if the settlor concurs; by the court in response to unanticipated circumstances or to remedy ineffective administrative terms; or by the court or trustee if the trust is of insufficient size to justify continued administration under its existing terms. Trusts may be reformed to correct a mistake of law or fact, or modified to achieve the settlor's tax objectives. Trusts may be combined or divided. Charitable trusts may be modified or terminated under cy pres to better achieve the settlor's charitable purposes.

Article 5—Creditor's Claims; Spendthrift and Discretionary Trusts—This article addresses the validity of a spendthrift provision and other issues relating to the rights of creditors to reach the trust to collect a debt. To the extent a trust is protected by a spendthrift provision, a beneficiary's creditor may not reach the beneficiary's interest until distribution is made by the trustee. To the extent not protected by a spendthrift provision, a creditor can reach the beneficiary's interest, subject to the court's power to limit the award. Certain categories of claims are exempt from a spendthrift restriction, including certain governmental claims and claims for child support or alimony. Other issues addressed in this article include creditor claims against discretionary trusts; creditor claims against a settlor, whether the trust is revocable or irrevocable; and the rights of creditors when a trustee fails to make a required distribution within a reasonable time.

Article 6—Revocable Trusts—This short article deals with issues of significance not totally settled under current law. The basic policy of this article and of the Uniform Trust Code in general is to treat the revocable trust as the functional equivalent of a will. The article specifies a standard of capacity, provides that a trust is presumed revocable unless its terms provide otherwise, prescribes the procedure for revocation or amendment of a revocable trust, addresses the rights of beneficiaries during the settlor's lifetime, and provides a statute of limitations on contests.

Article 7—Office of Trustee—This article contains a series of default rules dealing with the office of trustee, all of which may be modified in the terms of the trust. Rules are provided on acceptance of office and bonding. The role of the cotrustee is addressed, including the extent that one cotrustee may delegate to another, and the extent to which one cotrustee can be held liable for actions of another trustee. Also covered are changes in trusteeship, including the circumstances when a vacancy must be filled, the procedure for resignation, the grounds for removal, and the process for appointing a successor trustee. Finally, standards are provided for trustee compensation and reimbursement for expenses.

Article 8—Duties and Powers of Trustee—This article states the fundamental duties of a trustee and enumerates the trustee's powers. The duties listed are not new, although some of the particulars have changed over the years. This article was drafted where possible to conform to the Uniform Prudent Investor Act. The Uniform Prudent Investor Act prescribes a trustee's responsibilities with respect to the management and investment of trust property. This article also addresses a trustee's duties regarding distributions to beneficiaries.

Article 9—Uniform Prudent Investor Act—This article provides a place for a jurisdiction to enact, reenact or codify its version of the Uniform Prudent Investor Act. States adopting the Uniform Trust Code which have previously enacted the Uniform Prudent Investor Act are encouraged to reenact their version of the Prudent Investor Act in this article.

Article 10—Liability of Trustees and Rights of Persons Dealing With Trustees—Sections 1001 through 1009 list the remedies for breach of trust, describe how money damages are to be determined, provide a statute of limitations on claims against a trustee, and specify other defenses, including consent of a beneficiary and recognition of and limitations on the effect of an exculpatory clause. Sections 1010 through 1013 address trustee relations with persons other than beneficiaries. The objective is to encourage third parties to engage in commercial transactions with trustees to the same extent as if the property were not held in trust.

Article 11—Miscellaneous Provisions—The Uniform Trust Code is intended to have the widest possible application, consistent with constitutional limitations. The Code applies not only to trusts created on or after the effective date, but also to trusts in existence on the date of enactment.

The Drafting Committee was assisted by numerous officially designated advisors and observers, representing an array of organizations. In addition to the American Bar Association advisors listed above, advisors and observers who attended a majority of the Drafting Committee meetings include Edward C. Halbach, Jr., Reporter, Restatement (Third) of Trust Law; Kent H. McMahan, American College of Trust and Estate Counsel; Alex Misheff,

American Bankers Association; and Lawrence W. Waggoner, Reporter, Restatement (Third) of Property: Wills and Other Donative Transfers. Significant input was also received from the Joint Editorial Board for Uniform Trusts and Estates Acts and the Committee on State Laws of the American College of Trust and Estate Counsel.

Uniform Trust Code

ARTICLE 1

GENERAL PROVISIONS AND DEFINITIONS

The Uniform Trust Code is primarily a default statute. Most of the Code's provisions can be overridden in the terms of the trust. The provisions not subject to override are scheduled in Section 105(b). These include the duty of a trustee to act in good faith and with regard to the purposes of the trust, public policy exceptions to enforcement of spendthrift provisions, the requirements for creating a trust, and the authority of the court to modify or terminate a trust on specified grounds.

The remainder of the article specifies the scope of the Code (Section 102), provides definitions (Section 103), and collects provisions of importance not amenable to codification elsewhere in the Uniform Trust Code. Sections 106 and 107 focus on the sources of law that will govern a trust. Section 106 clarifies that despite the Code's comprehensive scope, not all aspects of the law of trusts have been codified. The Uniform Trust Code is supplemented by the common law of trusts and principles of equity. Section 107 addresses selection of the jurisdiction or jurisdictions whose laws will govern the trust. A settlor, absent overriding public policy concerns, is free to select the law that will determine the meaning and effect of a trust's terms.

Changing a trust's principal place of administration is sometimes desirable, particularly to lower a trust's state income tax. Such transfers are authorized in Section 108. The trustee, following notice to the "qualified beneficiaries," defined in Section 103(12), may without approval of court transfer the principal place of administration to another State or country if a qualified beneficiary does not object and if the transfer is consistent with the trustee's duty to administer the trust at a place appropriate to its purposes, its administration, and the interests of the beneficiaries. The settlor, if minimum contacts are present, may also designate the trust's principal place of administration.

Sections 104 and 109 through 111 address procedural issues. Section 104 specifies when persons, particularly persons who work in organizations, are deemed to have acquired knowledge of a fact. Section 109 specifies the methods for giving notice and excludes from the Code's notice requirements persons whose identity or location is unknown and not reasonably ascertainable. Section 110 allows beneficiaries with remote interests to request notice of actions, such as notice of a trustee resignation, which are normally given only to the qualified beneficiaries.

Section 111 ratifies the use of nonjudicial settlement agreements. While the judicial settlement procedures may be used in all court proceedings relating to the trust, the nonjudicial settlement procedures will not always be available. The terms of the trust may direct that the procedures not be used, or settlors may negate or modify them by specifying their own methods for obtaining consents. Also, a nonjudicial settlement may include only terms and conditions a court could properly approve.

The Uniform Trust Code does not prescribe the rules of construction to be applied to trusts created under the Code. The Code instead recognizes that enacting jurisdictions are likely to take a diversity of approaches, just as they have with respect to the rules of construction applicable to wills. Section 112 accommodates this variation by providing that the State's specific rules on construction of wills, whatever they may be, also apply to the construction of trusts.

§101. Short Title

This [Act] may be cited as the Uniform Trust Code.

§102. Scope

This [Code] applies to express trusts, charitable or noncharitable, and trusts created pursuant to a statute, judgment, or decree that requires the trust to be administered in the manner of an express trust.

§103. Definitions

In this [Code]:

(1) "Action," with respect to an act of a trustee, includes a failure to act.

(2) "Beneficiary" means a person that:

(A) has a present or future beneficial interest in a trust, vested or contingent; or

(B) in a capacity other than that of trustee, holds a power of appointment over trust property.

(3) "Charitable trust" means a trust, or portion of a trust, created for a charitable purpose described in Section 405(a).

(4) "[Conservator]" means a person appointed by the court to administer the estate of a minor or adult individual.

(5) "Environmental law" means a federal, state, or local law, rule, regulation, or ordinance relating to protection of the environment.

(6) "[Guardian]" means a person appointed by the court [, a parent, or a spouse] to make decisions regarding the support, care, education, health, and welfare of a minor or adult individual. The term does not include a guardian ad litem.

(7) "Interests of the beneficiaries" means the beneficial interests provided in the terms of the trust.

(8) "Jurisdiction," with respect to a geographic area, includes a State or country.

(9) "Person" means an individual, corporation, business trust, estate, trust, partnership, limited liability company, association, joint venture, government; governmental subdivision, agency, or instrumentality; public corporation, or any other legal or commercial entity.

(10) "Power of withdrawal" means a presently exercisable general power of appointment other than a power exercisable only upon consent of the trustee or a person holding an adverse interest.

(11) "Property" means anything that may be the subject of ownership, whether real or personal, legal or equitable, or any interest therein.

(12) "Qualified beneficiary" means a beneficiary who, on the date the beneficiary's qualification is determined:

(A) is a distributee or permissible distributee of trust income or principal;

(B) would be a distributee or permissible distributee of trust income or principal if the interests of the distributees described in subparagraph (A) terminated on that date; or

(C)would be a distributee or permissible distributee of trust income or principal if the trust terminated on that date.

(13) "Revocable," as applied to a trust, means revocable by the settlor without the consent of the trustee or a person holding an adverse interest.

(14) "Settlor" means a person, including a testator, who creates, or contributes property to, a trust. If more than one person creates or contributes property to a trust, each person is a settlor of the portion of the trust property attributable to that person's contribution except to the extent another person has the power to revoke or withdraw that portion.

(15) "Spendthrift provision" means a term of a trust which restrains both voluntary and involuntary transfer of a beneficiary's interest.

(16) "State" means a State of the United States, the District of Columbia, Puerto Rico, the United States Virgin Islands, or any territory or insular possession subject to the jurisdiction of the United States. The term includes an Indian tribe or band recognized by federal law or formally acknowledged by a State.

(17) "Terms of a trust" means the manifestation of the settlor's intent regarding a trust's provisions as expressed in the trust instrument or as may be established by other evidence that would be admissible in a judicial proceeding.

(18) "Trust instrument" means an instrument executed by the settlor that contains terms of the trust, including any amendments thereto.

(19) "Trustee" includes an original, additional, and successor trustee, and a cotrustee.

Comment

. . . "Terms of a trust" (paragraph (17)) is a defined term used frequently in the Uniform Trust Code. While the wording of a written trust instrument is almost always the most important determinant of a trust's terms, the definition is not so limited. Oral statements, the situation of the beneficiaries, the purposes of the trust, the circumstances under which the trust is to be administered, and, to the extent the settlor was otherwise silent, rules of construction, all may have a bearing on determining a trust's meaning. See Restatement (Third) of Trusts Section 4 cmt. a (Tentative Draft No. 1, approved 1996); Restatement (Second) of Trusts Section 4 cmt. a (1959). If a trust established by order of court is to be administered as an express trust, the terms of the trust are determined from the court order as interpreted in light of the general rules governing interpretation of judgments. See Restatement (Third) of Trusts Section 4 cmt. f (Tentative Draft No. 1, approved 1996).

A manifestation of a settlor's intention does not constitute evidence of a trust's terms if it would be inadmissible in a judicial proceeding in which the trust's terms are in question. See Restatement (Third) of Trusts Section 4 cmt. b (Tentative Draft No. 1, approved 1996); Restatement (Second) of Trusts Section 4 cmt. b (1959). See also Restatement (Third) Property: Donative Transfers Sections 10.2, 11.1-11.3 (Tentative Draft No. 1, approved 1995). For example, in many states a trust of real property is unenforceable unless evidenced by a writing, although Section 407 of this Code does not so require, leaving this issue to be covered by separate statute if the enacting jurisdiction so elects. Evidence otherwise relevant to determining the terms of a trust may also be excluded under other principles of law, such as the parol evidence rule. . . .

§104. Knowledge

(a) Subject to subsection (b), a person has knowledge of a fact if the person:

(1) has actual knowledge of it;

(2) has received a notice or notification of it; or

(3) from all the facts and circumstances known to the person at the time in question, has reason to know it.

(b) An organization that conducts activities through employees has notice or knowledge of a fact involving a trust only from the time the information was received by an employee having responsibility to act for the trust, or would have been brought to the employee's attention if the organization had exercised reasonable diligence. An organization exercises reasonable diligence if it maintains reasonable routines for communicating significant information to the employee having responsibility to act for the trust and there is reasonable compliance with the routines. Reasonable diligence does not require an employee of the organization to communicate information unless the communication is part of the individual's regular duties or the individual knows a matter involving the trust would be materially affected by the information.

§105. Default and Mandatory Rules

(a) Except as otherwise provided in the terms of the trust, this [Code] governs the duties and powers of a trustee, relations among trustees, and the rights and interests of a beneficiary.

(b) The terms of a trust prevail over any provision of this [Code] except:

(1) the requirements for creating a trust;

(2) the duty of a trustee to act in good faith and in accordance with the purposes of the trust;

(3) the requirement that a trust and its terms be for the benefit of its beneficiaries, and that the trust have a purpose that is lawful, not contrary to public policy, and possible to achieve;

(4) the power of the court to modify or terminate a trust under Sections 410 through 416;

(5) the effect of a spendthrift provision and the rights of certain creditors and assignees to reach a trust as provided in [Article] 5;

(6) the power of the court under Section 702 to require, dispense with, or modify or terminate a bond;

(7) the power of the court under Section 708(b) to adjust a trustee's compensation specified in the terms of the trust which is unreasonably low or high;

(8) except for a qualified beneficiary who has not attained 25 years of age, the duty under Section 813(b)(2) and (3) to notify qualified beneficiaries of an irrevocable trust who have attained 25 years of age of the existence of the trust, of the identity of the trustee, and of their right to request trustee's reports;

(9) the duty under Section 813(a) to respond to the request of a beneficiary of an irrevocable trust for trustee's reports and other information reasonably related to the administration of a trust;

(10) the effect of an exculpatory term under Section 1008;

(11) the rights under Sections 1010 through 1013 of a person other than a trustee or beneficiary;

(12) periods of limitation for commencing a judicial proceeding; [and]

(13) the power of the court to take such action and exercise such jurisdiction as may be necessary in the interests of justice [; and

(14) the subject-matter jurisdiction of the court and venue for commencing a proceeding as provided in Sections 203 and 204].

Comment

Subsection (a) emphasizes that the Uniform Trust Code is primarily a default statute. While this Code provides numerous procedural rules on which a settlor may wish to rely, the settlor is generally free to override these rules and to prescribe the conditions under which the trust is to be administered. With only limited exceptions, the duties and powers of a trustee, relations among trustees, and the rights and interests of a beneficiary are as specified in the terms of the trust.

Subsection (b) lists the items not subject to override in the terms of the trust. . . .

The terms of a trust may not deny a court authority to take such action as necessary in the interests of justice, including requiring that a trustee furnish bond. Subsection (b)(6), (13). . . .

Section 813 imposes a general obligation to keep the beneficiaries informed as well as several specific notice requirements. Subsections (b)(8) and (b)(9) specify limits on the settlor's ability to waive these information requirements. With respect to beneficiaries age 25 or older, a settlor may dispense with all of the requirements of Section 813 except for the duties to inform the beneficiaries of the existence of the trust, of the identity of the trustee, and to provide a beneficiary upon request with such reports as the trustee may have prepared. Among the specific requirements that a settlor may waive include the duty to provide a beneficiary upon request with a copy of the trust instrument (Section 813(b)(1)), and the requirement that the trustee provide annual reports to the qualified beneficiaries (Section 813(c)). The furnishing of a copy of the entire trust instrument and preparation of annual reports may be required in a particular case, however, if such information is requested by a beneficiary and is reasonably related to the trust's administration.

Responding to the desire of some settlors that younger beneficiaries not know of the trust's bounty until they have reached an age of maturity and self-sufficiency, subsection (b)(8) allows a settlor to provide that the trustee need not even inform beneficiaries under age 25 of the existence of the trust. However, pursuant to subsection (b)(9), if the younger beneficiary learns of the trust and requests information, the trustee must respond. More generally, subsection (b)(9) prohibits a settlor from overriding the right provided to a beneficiary in Section 813(a) to request from the trustee of an irrevocable trust copies of trustee reports and other information reasonably related to the trust's administration. . . .

Waiver by a settlor of the trustee's duty to keep the beneficiaries informed of the trust's administration does not otherwise affect the trustee's duties. The trustee remains accountable to the beneficiaries for the trustee's actions.

Neither subsection (b)(8) nor (b)(9) apply to revocable trusts. The settlor of a revocable trust may waive all reporting to the beneficiaries, even in the event the settlor loses capacity. If the settlor is silent about the subject, reporting to the beneficiaries will be required upon the settlor's loss of capacity. See Section 603.

In conformity with traditional doctrine, the Uniform Trust Code limits the ability of a settlor to exculpate a trustee from liability for breach of trust. The limits are specified in Section 1008. Subsection (b)(10) of this section provides a cross-reference. . . .

§106. Common Law of Trusts; Principles of Equity

The common law of trusts and principles of equity supplement this [Code], except to the extent modified by this [Code] or another statute of this State.

§107. Governing Law

The meaning and effect of the terms of a trust are determined by:

(1) the law of the jurisdiction designated in the terms unless the designation of that jurisdiction's law is contrary to a strong public policy of the jurisdiction having the most significant relationship to the matter at issue; or

(2) in the absence of a controlling designation in the terms of the trust, the law of the jurisdiction having the most significant relationship to the matter at issue.

§108. Principal Place of Administration

(a) Without precluding other means for establishing a sufficient connection with the designated jurisdiction, terms of a trust designating the principal place of administration are valid and controlling if:

(1) a trustee's principal place of business is located in or a trustee is a resident of the designated jurisdiction; or

(2) all or part of the administration occurs in the designated jurisdiction.

(b) A trustee is under a continuing duty to administer the trust at a place appropriate to its purposes, its administration, and the interests of the beneficiaries. © Without precluding the right of the court to order, approve, or disapprove a transfer, the trustee, in furtherance of the duty prescribed by subsection (b), may transfer the trust's principal place of administration to another State or to a jurisdiction outside of the United States.

(d) The trustee shall notify the qualified beneficiaries of a proposed transfer of a trust's principal place of administration not less than 60 days before initiating the transfer. The notice of proposed transfer must include:

(1) the name of the jurisdiction to which the principal place of administration is to be transferred;

(2) the address and telephone number at the new location at which the trustee can be contacted;

(3) an explanation of the reasons for the proposed transfer;

(4) the date on which the proposed transfer is anticipated to occur; and

(5) the date, not less than 60 days after the giving of the notice, by which the qualified beneficiary must notify the trustee of an objection to the proposed transfer.

(e) The authority of a trustee under this section to transfer a trust's principal place of administration terminates if a qualified beneficiary notifies the trustee of an objection to the proposed transfer on or before the date specified in the notice.

(f) In connection with a transfer of the trust's principal place of administration, the trustee may transfer some or all of the trust property to a successor trustee designated in the terms of the trust or appointed pursuant to Section 704.

§109. Methods and Waiver of Notice

(a) Notice to a person under this [Code] or the sending of a document to a person under this [Code] must be accomplished in a manner reasonably suitable under the circumstances and likely to result in receipt of the notice or document. Permissible methods of notice or for sending a document include first-class mail, personal delivery, delivery to the person's last known place of residence or place of business, or a properly directed electronic message.

(b) Notice otherwise required under this [Code] or a document otherwise required to be sent under this [Code] need not be provided to a person whose identity or location is unknown to and not reasonably ascertainable by the trustee.

(c) Notice under this [Code] or the sending of a document under this [Code] may be waived by the person to be notified or sent the document.

(d) Notice of a judicial proceeding must be given as provided in the applicable rules of civil procedure.

§110. Others Treated as Qualified Beneficiaries

(a) Whenever notice to qualified beneficiaries of a trust is required under this [Code] , the trustee must also give notice to any other beneficiary who has sent the trustee a request for notice.

(b) A charitable organization expressly designated to receive distributions under the terms of a charitable trust or a person appointed to enforce a trust created for the care of an animal or another noncharitable purpose as provided in Section 408 or 409 has the rights of a qualified beneficiary under this [Code].

(c) The [attorney general of this State] has the rights of a qualified beneficiary with respect to a charitable trust having its principal place of administration in this State.

§111. Nonjudicial Settlement Agreements

(a) For purposes of this section, "interested persons" means persons whose consent would be required in order to achieve a binding settlement were the settlement to be approved by the court.

(b) Except as otherwise provided in subsection (c), interested persons may enter into a binding nonjudicial settlement agreement with respect to any matter involving a trust.

(c) A nonjudicial settlement agreement is valid only to the extent it does not violate a material purpose of the trust and includes terms and conditions that could be properly approved by the court under this [Code] or other applicable law.

(d) Matters that may be resolved by a nonjudicial settlement agreement include:

(1) the interpretation or construction of the terms of the trust;

(2) the approval of a trustee's report or accounting;

(3) direction to a trustee to refrain from performing a particular act or the grant to a trustee of any necessary or desirable power;

(4) the resignation or appointment of a trustee and the determination of a trustee's compensation;

(5) transfer of a trust's principal place of administration; and

(6) liability of a trustee for an action relating to the trust.

(e) Any interested person may request the court to approve a nonjudicial settlement agreement, to determine whether the representation as provided in [Article] 3 was adequate, and to determine whether the agreement contains terms and conditions the court could have properly approved.

Comment

While the Uniform Trust Code recognizes that a court may intervene in the administration of a trust to the extent its jurisdiction is invoked by interested persons or otherwise provided by law (see Section 201(a)), resolution of disputes by nonjudicial means is encouraged. This section facilitates the making of such agreements by giving them the same effect as if approved by the court. To achieve such certainty, however, subsection (c) requires that the nonjudicial settlement must contain terms and conditions that a court could properly approve. Under this section, a nonjudicial settlement cannot be used to produce a result not authorized by law, such as to terminate a trust in an impermissible manner.

Trusts ordinarily have beneficiaries who are minors, incapacitated, unborn or unascertained. Because such beneficiaries cannot signify their consent to an agreement, binding settlements can ordinarily be achieved only through the application of doctrines such as virtual representation or appointment of a guardian ad litem, doctrines traditionally available only in the case of judicial settlements. The effect of this section and the Uniform Trust Code more generally is to allow for such binding representation even if the agreement is not submitted for approval to a court. For the rules on representation, including appointments of representatives by the court to approve particular settlements, see Article 3 . . . .

§112. Rules of Construction

The rules of construction that apply in this State to the interpretation of and disposition of property by will also apply as appropriate to the interpretation of the terms of a trust and the disposition of the trust property.]

Comment

This section is patterned after Restatement (Third) of Trusts Section 25(2) and comment e (Tentative Draft No. 1, approved 1996), although this section, unlike the Restatement, also applies to irrevocable trusts. The revocable trust is used primarily as a will substitute, with its key provision being the determination of the persons to receive the trust property upon the settlor's death. Given this functional equivalence between the revocable trust and a will, the rules for interpreting the disposition of property at death should be the same whether the individual has chosen a will or revocable trust as the individual's primary estate planning instrument. Over the years, the legislatures of the States and the courts have developed a series of rules of construction reflecting the legislative or judicial understanding of how the average testator would wish to dispose of property in cases where the will is silent or insufficiently clear. Few legislatures have yet to extend these rules of construction to revocable trusts, and even fewer to irrevocable trusts, although a number of courts have done so as a matter of judicial construction. See Restatement (Third) of Trusts Section 25, Reporter's Notes to cmt. d and e (Tentative Draft No. 1, approved 1996). . . .

§201. Role of Court in Administration of Trust

(a) The court may intervene in the administration of a trust to the extent its jurisdiction is invoked by an interested person or as provided by law.

(b) A trust is not subject to continuing judicial supervision unless ordered by the court.

(c) A judicial proceeding involving a trust may relate to any matter involving the trust's administration, including a request for instructions and an action to declare rights.

§202. Jurisdiction over Trustee and Beneficiary

(a) By accepting the trusteeship of a trust having its principal place of administration in this State or by moving the principal place of administration to this State, the trustee submits personally to the jurisdiction of the courts of this State regarding any matter involving the trust.

(b) With respect to their interests in the trust, the beneficiaries of a trust having its principal place of administration in this State are subject to the jurisdiction of the courts of this State regarding any matter involving the trust. By accepting a distribution from such a trust, the recipient submits personally to the jurisdiction of the courts of this State regarding any matter involving the trust.

(c) This section does not preclude other methods of obtaining jurisdiction over a trustee, beneficiary, or other person receiving property from the trust.

§203. Subject-Matter Jurisdiction

(a) The [designate] court has exclusive jurisdiction of proceedings in this State brought by a trustee or beneficiary concerning the administration of a trust.

(b) The [designate] court has concurrent jurisdiction with other courts of this State of other proceedings involving a trust.]

§204. Venue

(a) Except as otherwise provided in subsection (b), venue for a judicial proceeding involving a trust is in the [county] of this State in which the trust's principal place of administration is or will be located and, if the trust is created by will and the estate is not yet closed, in the [county] in which the decedent's estate is being administered.

(b) If a trust has no trustee, venue for a judicial proceeding for the appointment of a trustee is in a [county] of this State in which a beneficiary resides, in a [county] in which any trust property is located, and if the trust is created by will, in the [county] in which the decedent's estate was or is being administered.]

§301. Representation: Basic Effect

(a) Notice to a person who may represent and bind another person under this [article] has the same effect as if notice were given directly to the other person.

(b) The consent of a person who may represent and bind another person under this [article] is binding on the person represented unless the person represented objects to the representation before the consent would otherwise have become effective.

(c) Except as otherwise provided in Sections 411 and 602, a person who under this [article] may represent a settlor who lacks capacity may receive notice and give a binding consent on the settlor's behalf.

§302. Representation by Holder of General Testamentary Power of Appointment

To the extent there is no conflict of interest between the holder of a general testamentary power of appointment and the persons represented with respect to the particular question or dispute, the holder may represent and bind persons whose interests, as permissible appointees, takers in default, or otherwise, are subject to the power.

Comment

This section specifies the circumstances under which a holder of a general testamentary power of appointment may receive notices on behalf of and otherwise represent and bind persons whose interests are subject to the power, whether as permissible appointees, takers in default, or otherwise. Such representation is allowed except to the extent there is a conflict of interest with respect to the particular matter or dispute. Typically, the holder of a general testamentary power of appointment is also a life income beneficiary of the trust, oftentimes of a trust intended to qualify for the federal estate tax marital deduction. See I.R.C. Section 2056(b)(5). Without the exception for conflict of interest, the holder of the power could act in a way that could enhance the holder's income interests to the detriment of the appointees or takers in default, whoever they may be.

§303. Representation by Fiduciaries and Parents

To the extent there is no conflict of interest between the representative and the person represented or among those being represented with respect to a particular question or dispute:

(1) a [conservator] may represent and bind the estate that the [conservator] controls;

(2) a [guardian] may represent and bind the ward if a [conservator] of the ward's estate has not been appointed;

(3) an agent having authority to act with respect to the particular question or dispute may represent and bind the principal;

(4) a trustee may represent and bind the beneficiaries of the trust;

(5) a personal representative of a decedent's estate may represent and bind persons interested in the estate; and

(6) a parent may represent and bind the parent's minor or unborn child if a [conservator] or [guardian] for the child has not been appointed.

§304. Representation by Person Having Substantially Identical Interest

Unless otherwise represented, a minor, incapacitated, or unborn individual, or a person whose identity or location is unknown and not reasonably ascertainable, may be represented by and bound by another having a substantially identical interest with respect to the particular question or dispute, but only to the extent there is no conflict of interest between the representative and the person represented.

§305. Appointment of Representative

(a) If the court determines that an interest is not represented under this [article], or that the otherwise available representation might be inadequate, the court may appoint a [representative] to receive notice, give consent, and otherwise represent, bind, and act on behalf of a minor, incapacitated, or unborn individual, or a person whose identity or location is unknown. A [representative] may be appointed to represent several persons or interests.

(b) A [representative] may act on behalf of the individual represented with respect to any matter arising under this [Code], whether or not a judicial proceeding concerning the trust is pending.

(c) In making decisions, a [representative] may consider general benefit accruing to the living members of the individual's family.

ARTICLE 4

CREATION, VALIDITY, MODIFICATION, AND TERMINATION OF TRUST

§401. Methods of Creating Trust

A trust may be created by:

(1) transfer of property to another person as trustee during the settlor's lifetime or by will or other disposition taking effect upon the settlor's death;

(2) declaration by the owner of property that the owner holds identifiable property as trustee; or

(3) exercise of a power of appointment in favor of a trustee.

Comment

. . . The methods specified in this section are not exclusive. Section 102 recognizes that trusts can also be created by special statute or court order. See also Restatement (Third) of Trusts Section 1 cmt. a (Tentative Draft No. 1, approved 1996); Unif. Probate Code Section 2-212 (elective share of incapacitated surviving spouse to be held in trust on terms specified in statute); Unif. Probate Code Section 5-411(a)(4) (conservator may create trust with court approval); Restatement (Second) of Trusts Section 17 cmt. i (1959) (trusts created by statutory right to bring wrongful death action).

A trust can also be created by a promise that creates enforceable rights in a person who immediately or later holds these rights as trustee. See Restatement (Third) of Trusts Section 10(e) (Tentative Draft No. 1, approved 1996). A trust thus created is valid notwithstanding that the trustee may resign or die before the promise is fulfilled. Unless expressly made personal, the promise can be enforced by a successor trustee. For examples of trusts created by means of promises enforceable by the trustee, see Restatement (Third) of Trusts Section 10 cmt. g (Tentative Draft No. 1, approved 1996); Restatement (Second) of Trusts Sections 14 cmt. h, 26 cmt. n (1959).

A trust created by self-declaration is best created by reregistering each of the assets that comprise the trust into the settlor's name as trustee. However, such reregistration is not necessary to create the trust. . . .

§402. Requirements for Creation

(a) A trust is created only if:

(1) the settlor has capacity to create a trust;

(2) the settlor indicates an intention to create the trust;

(3) the trust has a definite beneficiary or is:

(A) a charitable trust;

(B) a trust for the care of an animal, as provided in Section 408; or

(C) a trust for a noncharitable purpose, as provided in Section 409;

(4) the trustee has duties to perform; and

(5) the same person is not the sole trustee and sole beneficiary.

(b) A beneficiary is definite if the beneficiary can be ascertained now or in the future, subject to any applicable rule against perpetuities.

(c) A power in a trustee to select a beneficiary from an indefinite class is valid. If the power is not exercised within a reasonable time, the power fails and the property subject to the power passes to the persons who would have taken the property had the power not been conferred.

§403. Trusts Created in other Jurisdictions

A trust not created by will is validly created if its creation complies with the law of the jurisdiction in which the trust instrument was executed, or the law of the jurisdiction in which, at the time of creation:

(1) the settlor was domiciled, had a place of abode, or was a national;

(2) a trustee was domiciled or had a place of business; or

(3) any trust property was located.

§404. Trust Purposes

A trust may be created only to the extent its purposes are lawful, not contrary to public policy, and possible to achieve. A trust and its terms must be for the benefit of its beneficiaries.

§405. Charitable Purposes; Enforcement

(a) A charitable trust may be created for the relief of poverty, the advancement of education or religion, the promotion of health, governmental or municipal purposes, or other purposes the achievement of which is beneficial to the community.

(b) If the terms of a charitable trust do not indicate a particular charitable purpose or beneficiary, the court may select one or more charitable purposes or beneficiaries. The selection must be consistent with the settlor's intention to the extent it can be ascertained.

(c) The settlor of a charitable trust, among others, may maintain a proceeding to enforce the trust.

§406. Creation of Trust Induced by Fraud, Duress, or Undue Influence

A trust is void to the extent its creation was induced by fraud, duress, or undue influence.

§407. Evidence of Oral Trust

Except as required by a statute other than this [Code], a trust need not be evidenced by a trust instrument, but the creation of an oral trust and its terms may be established only by clear and convincing evidence.

§408. Trust for Care of Animal

(a) A trust may be created to provide for the care of an animal alive during the settlor's lifetime. The trust terminates upon the death of the animal or, if the trust was created to provide for the care of more than one animal alive during the settlor's lifetime, upon the death of the last surviving animal.

(b) A trust authorized by this section may be enforced by a person appointed in the terms of the trust or, if no person is so appointed, by a person appointed by the court. A person having an interest in the welfare of the animal may request the court to appoint a person to enforce the trust or to remove a person appointed.

(c) Property of a trust authorized by this section may be applied only to its intended use, except to the extent the court determines that the value of the trust property exceeds the amount required for the intended use. Except as otherwise provided in the terms of the trust, property not required for the intended use must be distributed to the settlor, if then living, otherwise to the settlor's successors in interest.

§409. Noncharitable Trust without Ascertainable Beneficiary

Except as otherwise provided in Section 408 or by another statute, the following rules apply:

(1) A trust may be created for a noncharitable purpose without a definite or definitely ascertainable beneficiary or for a noncharitable but otherwise valid purpose to be selected by the trustee. The trust may not be enforced for more than [21] years.

(2) A trust authorized by this section may be enforced by a person appointed in the terms of the trust or, if no person is so appointed, by a person appointed by the court.

(3) Property of a trust authorized by this section may be applied only to its intended use, except to the extent the court determines that the value of the trust property exceeds the amount required for the intended use. Except as otherwise provided in the terms of the trust, property not required for the intended use must be distributed to the settlor, if then living, otherwise to the settlor's successors in interest.

§410. Modification or Termination of Trust; Proceedings for Approval or Disapproval

(a) In addition to the methods of termination prescribed by Sections 411 through 414, a trust terminates to the extent the trust is revoked or expires pursuant to its terms, no purpose of the trust remains to be achieved, or the purposes of the trust have become unlawful, contrary to public policy, or impossible to achieve.

(b) A proceeding to approve or disapprove a proposed modification or termination under Sections 411 through 416, or trust combination or division under Section 417, may be commenced by a trustee or beneficiary, and a proceeding to approve or disapprove a proposed modification or termination under Section 411 may be commenced by the settlor. The settlor of a charitable trust may maintain a proceeding to modify the trust under Section 413.

§411. Modification or Termination of Noncharitable Irrevocable Trust by Consent

(a) A noncharitable irrevocable trust may be modified or terminated upon consent of the settlor and all beneficiaries, even if the modification or termination is inconsistent with a material purpose of the trust. A settlor's power to consent to a trust's modification or termination may be exercised by an agent under a power of attorney only to the extent expressly authorized by the power of attorney or the terms of the trust; by the settlor's [conservator] with the approval of the court supervising the [conservatorship] if an agent is not so authorized; or by the settlor's [guardian] with the approval of the court supervising the [guardianship] if an agent is not so authorized and a conservator has not been appointed.

(b) A noncharitable irrevocable trust may be terminated upon consent of all of the beneficiaries if the court concludes that continuance of the trust is not necessary to achieve any material purpose of the trust. A noncharitable irrevocable trust may be modified upon consent of all of the beneficiaries if the court concludes that modification is not inconsistent with a material purpose of the trust.

(c) A spendthrift provision in the terms of the trust is not presumed to constitute a material purpose of the trust.

(d) Upon termination of a trust under subsection (a) or (b), the trustee shall distribute the trust property as agreed by the beneficiaries.

(e) If not all of the beneficiaries consent to a proposed modification or termination of the trust under subsection (a) or (b), the modification or termination may be approved by the court if the court is satisfied that:

(1) if all of the beneficiaries had consented, the trust could have been modified or terminated under this section; and

(2) the interests of a beneficiary who does not consent will be adequately protected.

Comment

. . . The provisions of Article 3 on representation, virtual representation, and the appointment and approval of representatives appointed by the court apply to the determination of whether all beneficiaries have signified consent under this section. The authority to consent on behalf of another person, however, does not include authority to consent over the other person's objection. See Section 301(b). Regarding the persons who may consent on behalf of a beneficiary, see Sections 302 through 305. A consent given by a representative is invalid to the extent there is a conflict of interest between the representative and the person represented. Given this limitation, virtual representation of a beneficiary's interest by another beneficiary pursuant to Section 304 will rarely be available in a trust termination case, although it should be routinely available in cases involving trust modification, such as a grant to the trustee of additional powers. If virtual or other form of representation is unavailable, Section 305 of the Code permits the court to appoint a representative who may give the necessary consent to the proposed modification or termination on behalf of the minor, incapacitated, unborn, or unascertained beneficiary. The ability to use virtual and other forms of representation to consent on a beneficiary's behalf to a trust termination or modification has not traditionally been part of the law, although there are some notable exceptions. Compare Restatement (Second) Section 337(1) (1959) (beneficiary must not be under incapacity), with Hatch v. Riggs National Bank, 361 F.2d 559 (D.C. Cir. 1966) (guardian ad litem authorized to consent on beneficiary's behalf). . . .

§412. Modification or Termination because of Unanticipated Circumstances or Inability to Administer Trust Effectively

(a) The court may modify the administrative or dispositive terms of a trust or terminate the trust if, because of circumstances not anticipated by the settlor, modification or termination will further the purposes of the trust. To the extent practicable, the modification must be made in accordance with the settlor's probable intention.

(b) The court may modify the administrative terms of a trust if continuation of the trust on its existing terms would be impracticable or wasteful or impair the trust's administration.

(c) Upon termination of a trust under this section, the trustee shall distribute the trust property in a manner consistent with the purposes of the trust.

Comment

This section broadens the court's ability to apply equitable deviation to terminate or modify a trust. Subsection (a) allows a court to modify the dispositive provisions of the trust as well as its administrative terms. For example, modification of the dispositive provisions to increase support of a beneficiary might be appropriate if the beneficiary has become unable to provide for support due to poor health or serious injury. Subsection (a) is similar to Restatement (Third) of Trusts Section 66(1) (Tentative Draft No. 3, approved 2001), except that this section, unlike the Restatement, does not impose a duty on the trustee to petition the court if the trustee is aware of circumstances justifying judicial modification. The purpose of the "equitable deviation" authorized by subsection (a) is not to disregard the settlor's intent but to modify inopportune details to effectuate better the settlor's broader purposes. Among other things, equitable deviation may be used to modify administrative or dispositive terms due to the failure to anticipate economic change or the incapacity of a beneficiary. For numerous illustrations, see Restatement (Third) of Trusts Section 66 cmt. b (Tentative Draft No. 3, approved 2001). While it is necessary that there be circumstances not anticipated by the settlor before the court may grant relief under subsection (a), the circumstances may have been in existence when the trust was created. . . .

Subsection (b) broadens the court's ability to modify the administrative terms of a trust. . . . Subsections (a) and (b) are not mutually exclusive. Many situations justifying modification of administrative terms under subsection (a) will also justify modification under subsection (b). Subsection (b) is also an application of the requirement in Section 404 that a trust and its terms must be for the benefit of its beneficiaries. See also Restatement (Third) of Trusts Section 27(2) & cmt. b (Tentative Draft No. 2, approved 1999). Although the settlor is granted considerable latitude in defining the purposes of the trust, the principle that a trust have a purpose which is for the benefit of its beneficiaries precludes unreasonable restrictions on the use of trust property. An owner's freedom to be capricious about the use of the owner's own property ends when the property is impressed with a trust for the benefit of others. See Restatement (Second) of Trusts Section 124 cmt. g (1959). Thus, attempts to impose unreasonable restrictions on the use of trust property will fail. See Restatement (Third) of Trusts Section 27 Reporter's Notes to cmt. b (Tentative Draft No. 2, approved 1999). Subsection (b), unlike subsection (a), does not have a direct precedent in the common law, but various states have insisted on such a measure by statute. See, e.g., Mo. Rev. Stat. Section456.590.1. . . .

§413. Cy Pres

(a) Except as otherwise provided in subsection (b), if a particular charitable purpose becomes unlawful, impracticable, impossible to achieve, or wasteful:

(1) the trust does not fail, in whole or in part;

(2) the trust property does not revert to the settlor or the settlor's successors in interest; and

(3) the court may apply cy pres to modify or terminate the trust by directing that the trust property be applied or distributed, in whole or in part, in a manner consistent with the settlor's charitable purposes.

(b) A provision in the terms of a charitable trust that would result in distribution of the trust property to a noncharitable beneficiary prevails over the power of the court under subsection (a) to apply cy pres to modify or terminate the trust only if, when the provision takes effect:

(1) the trust property is to revert to the settlor and the settlor is still living; or

(2) fewer than 21 years have elapsed since the date of the trust's creation.

Comment

Subsection (a) codifies the court's inherent authority to apply cy pres. The power may be applied to modify an administrative or dispositive term. The court may order the trust terminated and distributed to other charitable entities. Partial termination may also be ordered if the trust property is more than sufficient to satisfy the trust's current purposes. Subsection (a), which is similar to Restatement (Third) of Trusts Section 67 (Tentative Draft No. 3, approved 2001), modifies the doctrine of cy pres by presuming that the settlor had a general charitable intent when a particular charitable purpose becomes impossible or impracticable to achieve. Traditional doctrine did not supply that presumption, leaving it to the courts to determine whether the settlor had a general charitable intent. If such an intent is found, the trust property is applied to other charitable purposes. If not, the charitable trust fails. See Restatement (Second) of Trusts Section 399 (1959). In the great majority of cases the settlor would prefer that the property be used for other charitable purposes. Courts are usually able to find a general charitable purpose to which to apply the property, no matter how vaguely such purpose may have been expressed by the settlor. . . .

§414. Modification or Termination of Uneconomic Trust

(a) After notice to the qualified beneficiaries, the trustee of a trust consisting of trust property having a total value less than [$50,000] may terminate the trust if the trustee concludes that the value of the trust property is insufficient to justify the cost of administration.

(b) The court may modify or terminate a trust or remove the trustee and appoint a different trustee if it determines that the value of the trust property is insufficient to justify the cost of administration.

(c) Upon termination of a trust under this section, the trustee shall distribute the trust property in a manner consistent with the purposes of the trust.

(d) This section does not apply to an easement for conservation or preservation.

§415. Reformation to Correct Mistakes

The court may reform the terms of a trust, even if unambiguous, to conform the terms to the settlor's intention if it is proved by clear and convincing evidence that both the settlor's intent and the terms of the trust were affected by a mistake of fact or law, whether in expression or inducement.

§416. Modification to Achieve Settlor's Tax Objectives

To achieve the settlor's tax objectives, the court may modify the terms of a trust in a manner that is not contrary to the settlor's probable intention. The court may provide that the modification has retroactive effect.

§417. Combination and Division of Trusts

After notice to the qualified beneficiaries, a trustee may combine two or more trusts into a single trust or divide a trust into two or more separate trusts, if the result does not impair rights of any beneficiary or adversely affect achievement of the purposes of the trust.

ARTICLE 5

CREDITOR'S CLAIMS; SPENDTHRIFT AND DISCRETIONARY TRUSTS

§501. Rights of Beneficiary's Creditor or Assignee

To the extent a beneficiary's interest is not protected by a spendthrift provision, the court may authorize a creditor or assignee of the beneficiary to reach the beneficiary's interest by attachment of present or future distributions to or for the benefit of the beneficiary or other means. The court may limit the award to such relief as is appropriate under the circumstances.

§502. Spendthrift Provision

(a) A spendthrift provision is valid only if it restrains both voluntary and involuntary transfer of a beneficiary's interest.

(b) A term of a trust providing that the interest of a beneficiary is held subject to a "spendthrift trust," or words of similar import, is sufficient to restrain both voluntary and involuntary transfer of the beneficiary's interest.

(c) A beneficiary may not transfer an interest in a trust in violation of a valid spendthrift provision and, except as otherwise provided in this [article], a creditor or assignee of the beneficiary may not reach the interest or a distribution by the trustee before its receipt by the beneficiary.

§503. Exceptions to Spendthrift Provision

(a) In this section, "child" includes any person for whom an order or judgment for child support has been entered in this or another State.

(b) Even if a trust contains a spendthrift provision, a beneficiary's child, spouse, or former spouse who has a judgment or court order against the beneficiary for support or maintenance, or a judgment creditor who has provided services for the protection of a beneficiary's interest in the trust, may obtain from a court an order attaching present or future distributions to or for the benefit of the beneficiary.

(c) A spendthrift provision is unenforceable against a claim of this State or the United States to the extent a statute of this State or federal law so provides.

§504. Discretionary Trusts; Effect of Standard

(a) In this section, "child" includes any person for whom an order or judgment for child support has been entered in this or another State.

(b) Except as otherwise provided in subsection (c), whether or not a trust contains a spendthrift provision, a creditor of a beneficiary may not compel a distribution that is subject to the trustee's discretion, even if:

(1) the discretion is expressed in the form of a standard of distribution; or

(2) the trustee has abused the discretion.

(c) To the extent a trustee has not complied with a standard of distribution or has abused a discretion:

(1) a distribution may be ordered by the court to satisfy a judgment or court order against the beneficiary for support or maintenance of the beneficiary's child, spouse, or former spouse; and

(2) the court shall direct the trustee to pay to the child, spouse, or former spouse such amount as is equitable under the circumstances but not more than the amount the trustee would have been required to distribute to or for the benefit of the beneficiary had the trustee complied with the standard or not abused the discretion.

(d) This section does not limit the right of a beneficiary to maintain a judicial proceeding against a trustee for an abuse of discretion or failure to comply with a standard for distribution.

§505. Creditor's Claim Against Settlor

(a) Whether or not the terms of a trust contain a spendthrift provision, the following rules apply:

(1) During the lifetime of the settlor, the property of a revocable trust is subject to claims of the settlor's creditors.

(2) With respect to an irrevocable trust, a creditor or assignee of the settlor may reach the maximum amount that can be distributed to or for the settlor's benefit. If a trust has more than one settlor, the amount the creditor or assignee of a particular settlor may reach may not exceed the settlor's interest in the portion of the trust attributable to that settlor's contribution.

(3) After the death of a settlor, and subject to the settlor's right to direct the source from which liabilities will be paid, the property of a trust that was revocable at the settlor's death is subject to claims of the settlor's creditors, costs of administration of the settlor's estate, the expenses of the settlor's funeral and disposal of remains, and [statutory allowances] to a surviving spouse and children to the extent the settlor's probate estate is inadequate to satisfy those claims, costs, expenses, and [allowances].

(b) For purposes of this section:

(1) during the period the power may be exercised, the holder of a power of withdrawal is treated in the same manner as the settlor of a revocable trust to the extent of the property subject to the power; and

(2) upon the lapse, release, or waiver of the power, the holder is treated as the settlor of the trust only to the extent the value of the property affected by the lapse, release, or waiver exceeds the greater of the amount specified in Section 2041(b)(2) or 2514(e) of the Internal Revenue Code of 1986, or Section 2503(b) of the Internal Revenue Code of 1986, in each case as in effect on [the effective date of this [Code]] [, or as later amended].

§506. Overdue Distribution

Whether or not a trust contains a spendthrift provision, a creditor or assignee of a beneficiary may reach a mandatory distribution of income or principal, including a distribution upon termination of the trust, if the trustee has not made the distribution to the beneficiary within a reasonable time after the designated distribution date.

§507. Personal Obligations of Trustee

Trust property is not subject to personal obligations of the trustee, even if the trustee becomes insolvent or bankrupt.

ARTICLE 6

REVOCABLE TRUSTS

§601. Capacity of Settlor of Revocable Trust

The capacity required to create, amend, revoke, or add property to a revocable trust, or to direct the actions of the trustee of a revocable trust, is the same as that required to make a will.

§602. Revocation or Amendment of Revocable Trust

(a) Unless the terms of a trust expressly provide that the trust is irrevocable, the settlor may revoke or amend the trust. This subsection does not apply to a trust created under an instrument executed before [the effective date of this [Code]].

(b) If a revocable trust is created or funded by more than one settlor:

(1) to the extent the trust consists of community property, the trust may be revoked by either spouse acting alone but may be amended only by joint action of both spouses; and

(2) to the extent the trust consists of property other than community property, each settlor may revoke or amend the trust with regard to the portion of the trust property attributable to that settlor's contribution; and

(3) upon the revocation or amendment of the trust by fewer than all of the settlers, the trustee

shall promptly notify the other settlers of the revocation or amendment.

(c) The settlor may revoke or amend a revocable trust:

(1) by substantial compliance with a method provided in the terms of the trust; or

(2) if the terms of the trust do not provide a method or the method provided in the terms is not expressly made exclusive, by:

(A) a later will or codicil that expressly refers to the trust or specifically devises property that would otherwise have passed according to the terms of the trust; or

(B) any other method manifesting clear and convincing evidence of the settlor's intent.

(d) Upon revocation of a revocable trust, the trustee shall deliver the trust property as the settlor directs.

(e) A settlor's powers with respect to revocation, amendment, or distribution of trust property may be exercised by an agent under a power of attorney only to the extent expressly authorized by the terms of the trust or the power.

(f) A [conservator] of the settlor or, if no [conservator] has been appointed, a [guardian] of the settlor may exercise a settlor's powers with respect to revocation, amendment, or distribution of trust property only with the approval of the court supervising the [conservatorship] or [guardianship].

(g) A trustee who does not know that a trust has been revoked or amended is not liable to the settlor or settlor's successors in interest for distributions made and other actions taken on the assumption that the trust had not been amended or revoked.

Comment

. . . Revocation or amendment by will is mentioned in subsection (c) not to encourage the practice but to make clear that it is not precluded by omission. See Restatement (Third) of Property: Will and Other Donative Transfers Section 7.2 cmt. e (Tentative Draft No. 3, approved 2001), which validates revocation or amendment of will substitutes by later will. Situations do arise, particularly in death-bed cases, where revocation by will may be the only practicable method. In such cases, a will, a solemn document executed with a high level of formality, may be the most reliable method for expressing intent. A revocation in a will ordinarily becomes effective only upon probate of the will following the testator's death. For the cases, see Restatement (Third) of Trusts Section 63 Reporter's Notes to cmt. h-i (Tentative Draft No. 3, approved 2001).

A residuary clause in a will disposing of the estate differently than the trust is alone insufficient to revoke or amend a trust. The provision in the will must either be express or the will must dispose of specific assets contrary to the terms of the trust. The substantial body of law on revocation of Totten trusts by will offers helpful guidance. The authority is collected in William H. Danne, Jr., Revocation of Tentative ("Totten") Trust of Savings Bank Account by Inter Vivos Declaration or Will, 46 A.L.R. 3d 487 (1972).

Subsection (c) does not require that a trustee concur in the revocation or amendment of a trust. Such a concurrence would be necessary only if required by the terms of the trust. If the trustee concludes that an amendment unacceptably changes the trustee's duties, the trustee may resign as provided in Section 705. . . .

A settlor's power to revoke is not terminated by the settlor's incapacity. The power to revoke may instead be exercised by an agent under a power of attorney as authorized in subsection (e), by a conservator or guardian as authorized in subsection (f), or by the settlor personally if the settlor regains capacity.

Subsection (e), which is similar to Restatement (Third) of Trusts Section 63 cmt. l (Tentative Draft No. 3, approved 2001), authorizes an agent under a power of attorney to revoke or modify a revocable trust only to the extent the terms of the trust or power of attorney expressly so permit. An express provision is required because most settlors usually intend that the revocable trust, and not the power of attorney, to function as the settlor's principal property management device. The power of attorney is usually intended as a backup for assets not transferred to the revocable trust or to address specific topics, such as the power to sign tax returns or apply for government benefits, which may be beyond the authority of a trustee or are not customarily granted to a trustee.

Subsection (f) addresses the authority of a conservator or guardian to revoke or amend a revocable trust. Under the Uniform Trust Code, a "conservator" is appointed by the court to manage the ward's party, a "guardian" to make decisions with respect to the ward's personal affairs. See Section 103. Consequently, subsection (f) authorizes a guardian to exercise a settlor's power to revoke or amend a trust only if a conservator has not been appointed.

Many state conservatorship statutes authorize a conservator to exercise the settlor's power of revocation with the prior approval of the court supervising the conservatorship. See, e.g., Unif. Probate Code Section 411(a)(4). Subsection (f) ratifies this practice. Under the Code, a conservator may exercise a settlor's power of revocation, amendment, or right to withdraw trust property upon approval of the court supervising the conservatorship. Because a settlor often creates a revocable trust for the very purpose of avoiding conservatorship, this power should be exercised by the court reluctantly. Settlors concerned about revocation by a conservator may wish to deny a conservator a power to revoke. However, while such a provision in the terms of the trust is entitled to considerable weight, the court may override the restriction if it concludes that the action is necessary in the interests of justice. See Section 105(b)(13). . . .

§603. Settlor's Powers; Powers of Withdrawal

(a) While a trust is revocable and the settlor has capacity to revoke the trust, rights of the beneficiaries are subject to the control of, and the duties of the trustee are owed exclusively to, the settlor.

(b) If a revocable trust has more than one settlor, the duties of the trustee are owed to all of the settlors having capacity to revoke the trust.

(c) During the period the power may be exercised, the holder of a power of withdrawal has the rights of a settlor of a revocable trust under this section to the extent of the property subject to the power.

Comment

This section has the effect of postponing enforcement of the rights of the beneficiaries of a revocable trust until the death or incapacity of the settlor or other person holding the power to revoke the trust. This section thus recognizes that the settlor of a revocable trust is in control of the trust and should have the right to enforce the trust.

Pursuant to this section, the duty under Section 813 to inform and report to beneficiaries is owed to the settlor of a revocable trust as long as the settlor has capacity. . . .

If the settlor loses capacity, subsection (a) no longer applies, with the consequence that the rights of the beneficiaries are no longer subject to the settlor's control. The beneficiaries are entitled to request information concerning the trust and the trustee must provide the beneficiaries with annual trustee reports and whatever other information may be required under Section 813. However, because this section may be freely overridden in the terms of the trust, a settlor is free to deny the beneficiaries these rights, even to the point of directing the trustee not to inform them of the existence of the trust. . . .

Subsection (c) makes clear that a holder of a power of withdrawal has the same powers over the trust as the settlor of a revocable trust. Equal treatment is warranted due to the holder's equivalent power to control the trust. For the definition of power of withdrawal, see Section 103(10).

2001 Amendment. By a 2001 amendment, former subsection (b) was deleted. Former subsection (b) provided: "While a trust is revocable and the settlor does not have capacity to revoke the trust, rights of the beneficiaries are held by the beneficiaries." No substantive change was intended by this amendment. Former subsection (b) was superfluous. Rights of the beneficiaries are always held by the beneficiaries unless taken away by some other provision. Subsection (a) grants these rights to the settlor of a revocable trust while the settlor has capacity. Upon a settlor's loss of capacity, these rights are held by the beneficiaries with or without former subsection (b).

§604. Limitation on Action Contesting Validity of Revocable Trust; Distribution of Trust Property

(a) A person may commence a judicial proceeding to contest the validity of a trust that was revocable at the settlor's death within the earlier of:

(1) [three] years after the settlor's death; or

(2) [120] days after the trustee sent the person a copy of the trust instrument and a notice informing the person of the trust's existence, of the trustee's name and address, and of the time allowed for commencing a proceeding.

(b) Upon the death of the settlor of a trust that was revocable at the settlor's death, the trustee may proceed to distribute the trust property in accordance with the terms of the trust. The trustee is not subject to liability for doing so unless:

(1) the trustee knows of a pending judicial proceeding contesting the validity of the trust; or

(2) a potential contestant has notified the trustee of a possible judicial proceeding to contest the trust and a judicial proceeding is commenced within 60 days after the contestant sent the notification.

(c) A beneficiary of a trust that is determined to have been invalid is liable to return any distribution received.

ARTICLE 7

OFFICE OF TRUSTEE

§701. Accepting or Declining Trusteeship

(a) Except as otherwise provided in subsection (c), a person designated as trustee accepts the trusteeship:

(1) by substantially complying with a method of acceptance provided in the terms of the trust; or

(2) if the terms of the trust do not provide a method or the method provided in the terms is not expressly made exclusive, by accepting delivery of the trust property, exercising powers or performing duties as trustee, or otherwise indicating acceptance of the trusteeship.

(b) A person designated as trustee who has not yet accepted the trusteeship may reject the trusteeship. A designated trustee who does not accept the trusteeship within a reasonable time after knowing of the designation is deemed to have rejected the trusteeship.

(c) A person designated as trustee, without accepting the trusteeship, may:

(1) act to preserve the trust property if, within a reasonable time after acting, the person sends a rejection of the trusteeship to the settlor or, if the settlor is dead or lacks capacity, to a qualified beneficiary; and

(2) inspect or investigate trust property to determine potential liability under environmental or other law or for any other purpose.

§702. Trustee's Bond

(a) A trustee shall give bond to secure performance of the trustee's duties only if the court finds that a bond is needed to protect the interests of the beneficiaries or is required by the terms of the trust and the court has not dispensed with the requirement.

(b) The court may specify the amount of a bond, its liabilities, and whether sureties are necessary. The court may modify or terminate a bond at any time.

[(c) A regulated financial-service institution qualified to do trust business in this State need not give bond, even if required by the terms of the trust.]

§703. Cotrustees

(a) Cotrustees who are unable to reach a unanimous decision may act by majority decision.

(b) If a vacancy occurs in a cotrusteeship, the remaining cotrustees may act for the trust.

(c) A cotrustee must participate in the performance of a trustee's function unless the cotrustee is unavailable to perform the function because of absence, illness, disqualification under other law, or other temporary incapacity or the cotrustee has properly delegated the performance of the function to another trustee.

(d) If a cotrustee is unavailable to perform duties because of absence, illness, disqualification under other law, or other temporary incapacity, and prompt action is necessary to achieve the purposes of the trust or to avoid injury to the trust property, the remaining cotrustee or a majority of the remaining cotrustees may act for the trust.

(e) A trustee may not delegate to a cotrustee the performance of a function the settlor reasonably expected the trustees to perform jointly. Unless a delegation was irrevocable, a trustee may revoke a delegation previously made.

(f) Except as otherwise provided in subsection (g), a trustee who does not join in an action of another trustee is not liable for the action.

(g) Each trustee shall exercise reasonable care to:

(1) prevent a cotrustee from committing a serious breach of trust; and

(2) compel a cotrustee to redress a serious breach of trust.

(h) A dissenting trustee who joins in an action at the direction of the majority of the trustees and who notified any cotrustee of the dissent at or before the time of the action is not liable for the action unless the action is a serious breach of trust.

§704. Vacancy in Trusteeship; Appointment of Successor

(a) A vacancy in a trusteeship occurs if:

(1) a person designated as trustee rejects the trusteeship;

(2) a person designated as trustee cannot be identified or does not exist;

(3) a trustee resigns;

(4) a trustee is disqualified or removed;

(5) a trustee dies; or

(6) a [guardian] or [conservator] is appointed for an individual serving as trustee.

(b) If one or more cotrustees remain in office, a vacancy in a trusteeship need not be filled. A vacancy in a trusteeship must be filled if the trust has no remaining trustee.

(c) A vacancy in a trusteeship of a noncharitable trust that is required to be filled must be filled in the following order of priority:

(1) by a person designated in the terms of the trust to act as successor trustee;

(2) by a person appointed by unanimous agreement of the qualified beneficiaries; or

(3) by a person appointed by the court.

(d) A vacancy in a trusteeship of a charitable trust that is required to be filled must be filled in the following order of priority:

(1) by a person designated in the terms of the trust to act as successor trustee;

(2) by a person selected by the charitable organizations expressly designated to receive distributions under the terms of the trust if the [attorney general] concurs in the selection; or

(3) by a person appointed by the court.

(e) Whether or not a vacancy in a trusteeship exists or is required to be filled, the court may appoint an additional trustee or special fiduciary whenever the court considers the appointment necessary for the administration of the trust.

§705. Resignation of Trustee

(a) A trustee may resign:

(1) upon at least 30 days' notice to the qualified beneficiaries, the settlor, if living, and all cotrustees; or

(2) with the approval of the court.

(b) In approving a resignation, the court may issue orders and impose conditions reasonably necessary for the protection of the trust property.

(c) Any liability of a resigning trustee or of any sureties on the trustee's bond for acts or omissions of the trustee is not discharged or affected by the trustee's resignation.

§706. Removal of Trustee

(a) The settlor, a cotrustee, or a beneficiary may request the court to remove a trustee, or a trustee may be removed by the court on its own initiative.

(b) The court may remove a trustee if:

(1) the trustee has committed a serious breach of trust;

(2) lack of cooperation among cotrustees substantially impairs the administration of the trust;

(3) because of unfitness, unwillingness, or persistent failure of the trustee to administer the trust effectively, the court determines that removal of the trustee best serves the interests of the beneficiaries; or

(4) there has been a substantial change of circumstances or removal is requested by all of the qualified beneficiaries, the court finds that removal of the trustee best serves the interests of all of the beneficiaries and is not inconsistent with a material purpose of the trust, and a suitable cotrustee or successor trustee is available.

(c) Pending a final decision on a request to remove a trustee, or in lieu of or in addition to removing a trustee, the court may order such appropriate relief under Section 1001(b) as may be necessary to protect the trust property or the interests of the beneficiaries.

§707. Delivery of Property by Former Trustee

(a) Unless a cotrustee remains in office or the court otherwise orders, and until the trust property is delivered to a successor trustee or other person entitled to it, a trustee who has resigned or been removed has the duties of a trustee and the powers necessary to protect the trust property.

(b) A trustee who has resigned or been removed shall proceed expeditiously to deliver the trust property within the trustee's possession to the cotrustee, successor trustee, or other person entitled to it.

§708. Compensation of Trustee

(a) If the terms of a trust do not specify the trustee's compensation, a trustee is entitled to compensation that is reasonable under the circumstances.

(b) If the terms of a trust specify the trustee's compensation, the trustee is entitled to be compensated as specified, but the court may allow more or less compensation if:

(1) the duties of the trustee are substantially different from those contemplated when the trust was created; or

(2) the compensation specified by the terms of the trust would be unreasonably low or high.

§709. Reimbursement of Expenses

(a) A trustee is entitled to be reimbursed out of the trust property, with interest as appropriate, for:

(1) expenses that were properly incurred in the administration of the trust; and

(2) to the extent necessary to prevent unjust enrichment of the trust, expenses that were not properly incurred in the administration of the trust.

(b) An advance by the trustee of money for the protection of the trust gives rise to a lien against trust property to secure reimbursement with reasonable interest.

ARTICLE 8

DUTIES AND POWERS OF TRUSTEE

§801. Duty to Administer Trust

Upon acceptance of a trusteeship, the trustee shall administer the trust in good faith, in accordance with its terms and purposes and the interests of the beneficiaries, and in accordance with this [Code].

§802. Duty of Loyalty

(a) A trustee shall administer the trust solely in the interests of the beneficiaries.

(b) Subject to the rights of persons dealing with or assisting the trustee as provided in Section 1012, a sale, encumbrance, or other transaction involving the investment or management of trust property entered into by the trustee for the trustee's own personal account or which is otherwise affected by a conflict between the trustee's fiduciary and personal interests is voidable by a beneficiary affected by the transaction unless:

(1) the transaction was authorized by the terms of the trust;

(2) the transaction was approved by the court;

(3) the beneficiary did not commence a judicial proceeding within the time allowed by Section 1005;

(4) the beneficiary consented to the trustee's conduct, ratified the transaction, or released the trustee in compliance with Section 1009; or

(5) the transaction involves a contract entered into or claim acquired by the trustee before the person became or contemplated becoming trustee.

(c) A sale, encumbrance, or other transaction involving the investment or management of trust property is presumed to be affected by a conflict between personal and fiduciary interests if it is entered into by the trustee with:

(1) the trustee's spouse;

(2) the trustee's descendants, siblings, parents, or their spouses;

(3) an agent or attorney of the trustee; or

(4) a corporation or other person or enterprise in which the trustee, or a person that owns a significant interest in the trustee, has an interest that might affect the trustee's best judgment.

(d) A transaction between a trustee and a beneficiary that does not concern trust property but that occurs during the existence of the trust or while the trustee retains significant influence over the beneficiary and from which the trustee obtains an advantage is voidable by the beneficiary unless the trustee establishes that the transaction was fair to the beneficiary.

(e) A transaction not concerning trust property in which the trustee engages in the trustee's individual capacity involves a conflict between personal and fiduciary interests if the transaction concerns an opportunity properly belonging to the trust.

(f) An investment by a trustee in securities of an investment company or investment trust to which the trustee, or its affiliate, provides services in a capacity other than as trustee is not presumed to be affected by a conflict between personal and fiduciary interests if the investment complies with the prudent investor rule of [Article] 9. In addition to its compensation for acting as trustee, the trustee may be compensated by the investment company or investment trust for providing those services out of fees charged to the trust. If the trustee receives compensation from the investment company or investment trust for providing investment advisory or investment management services, the trustee at least annually shall notify the persons entitled under Section 813 to receive a copy of the trustee's annual report of the rate and method by which the compensation was determined.

(g) In voting shares of stock or in exercising powers of control over similar interests in other forms of enterprise, the trustee shall act in the best interests of the beneficiaries. If the trust is the sole owner of a corporation or other form of enterprise, the trustee shall elect or appoint directors or other managers who will manage the corporation or enterprise in the best interests of the beneficiaries.

(h) This section does not preclude the following transactions, if fair to the beneficiaries:

(1) an agreement between a trustee and a beneficiary relating to the appointment or compensation of the trustee;

(2) payment of reasonable compensation to the trustee;

(3) a transaction between a trust and another trust, decedent's estate, or [conservatorship] of which the trustee is a fiduciary or in which a beneficiary has an interest;

(4) a deposit of trust money in a regulated financial-service institution operated by the trustee; or

(5) an advance by the trustee of money for the protection of the trust.

(I) The court may appoint a special fiduciary to make a decision with respect to any proposed transaction that might violate this section if entered into by the trustee.

Comment

. . . Subsection (f) attempts to retain the advantages of mutual funds while at the same time making clear that such investments are subject to traditional fiduciary responsibilities. Nearly all of the States have enacted statutes authorizing trustees to invest in funds from which the trustee might derive additional compensation. Portions of subsection (f) are based on these statutes. Subsection (f) makes clear that such dual investment-fee arrangements are not automatically presumed to involve a conflict between the trustee's personal and fiduciary interests, but subsection (f) does not otherwise waive or lessen a trustee's fiduciary obligations. The trustee, in deciding whether to invest in a mutual fund, must not place its own interests ahead of those of the beneficiaries. The investment decision must also comply with the enacting jurisdiction's prudent investor rule. To obtain the protection afforded by subsection (f), the trustee must disclose at least annually to the beneficiaries entitled to receive a copy of the trustee's annual report the rate and method by which the additional compensation was determined. Furthermore, the selection of a mutual fund, and the resulting delegation of certain of the trustee's functions, may be taken into account under Section 708 in setting the trustee's regular compensation. See also Uniform Prudent Investor Act Sections 7 and 9 and Comments; Restatement (Third) of Trusts: Prudent Investor Rule Section 227 cmt. m (1992). . . .

§803. Impartiality

If a trust has two or more beneficiaries, the trustee shall act impartially in investing, managing, and distributing the trust property, giving due regard to the beneficiaries' respective interests.

Comment

. . . This section is identical to Section 6 of the Uniform Prudent Investor Act, except that this section also applies to all aspects of trust administration and to decisions by a trustee with respect to distributions. The Prudent Investor Act is limited to duties with respect to the investment and management of trust property. The differing beneficial interests for which the trustee must act impartially include those of the current beneficiaries versus those of beneficiaries holding interests in the remainder; and among those currently eligible to receive distributions. In fulfilling the duty to act impartially, the trustee should be particularly sensitive to allocation of receipts and disbursements between income and principal and should consider, in an appropriate case, a reallocation of income to the principal account and vice versa, if allowable under local law. For an example of such authority, see Uniform Principal and Income Act Section 104 (1997).

The duty to act impartially does not mean that the trustee must treat the beneficiaries equally. Rather, the trustee must treat the beneficiaries equitably in light of the purposes and terms of the trust. . . .

§804. Prudent Administration

A trustee shall administer the trust as a prudent person would, by considering the purposes, terms, distributional requirements, and other circumstances of the trust. In satisfying this standard, the trustee shall exercise reasonable care, skill, and caution.

§805. Costs of Administration

In administering a trust, the trustee may incur only costs that are reasonable in relation to the trust property, the purposes of the trust, and the skills of the trustee.

§806. Trustee's Skills

A trustee who has special skills or expertise, or is named trustee in reliance upon the trustee's representation that the trustee has special skills or expertise, shall use those special skills or expertise.

§807. Delegation by Trustee

(a) A trustee may delegate duties and powers that a prudent trustee of comparable skills could properly delegate under the circumstances. The trustee shall exercise reasonable care, skill, and caution in:

(1) selecting an agent;

(2) establishing the scope and terms of the delegation, consistent with the purposes and terms of the trust; and

(3) periodically reviewing the agent's actions in order to monitor the agent's performance and compliance with the terms of the delegation.

(b) In performing a delegated function, an agent owes a duty to the trust to exercise reasonable care to comply with the terms of the delegation.

(c) A trustee who complies with subsection (a) is not liable to the beneficiaries or to the trust for an action of the agent to whom the function was delegated.

(d) By accepting a delegation of powers or duties from the trustee of a trust that is subject to the law of this State, an agent submits to the jurisdiction of the courts of this State.

Comment

. . . This section encourages and protects the trustee in making delegations appropriate to the facts and circumstances of the particular trust. Whether a particular function is delegable is based on whether it is a function that a prudent trustee might delegate under similar circumstances. For example, delegating some administrative and reporting duties might be prudent for a family trustee but unnecessary for a corporate trustee.

This section applies only to delegation to agents, not to delegation to a cotrustee. For the provision regulating delegation to a cotrustee, see Section 703(e). . . .

§808. Powers to Direct

(a) While a trust is revocable, the trustee may follow a direction of the settlor that is contrary to the terms of the trust.

(b) If the terms of a trust confer upon a person other than the settlor of a revocable trust power to direct certain actions of the trustee, the trustee shall act in accordance with an exercise of the power unless the attempted exercise is manifestly contrary to the terms of the trust or the trustee knows the attempted exercise would constitute a serious breach of a fiduciary duty that the person holding the power owes to the beneficiaries of the trust.

(c) The terms of a trust may confer upon a trustee or other person a power to direct the modification or termination of the trust.

(d) A person, other than a beneficiary, who holds a power to direct is presumptively a fiduciary who, as such, is required to act in good faith with regard to the purposes of the trust and the interests of the beneficiaries. The holder of a power to direct is liable for any loss that results from breach of a fiduciary duty.

§809. Control and Protection of Trust Property

A trustee shall take reasonable steps to take control of and protect the trust property.

§810. Recordkeeping and Identification of Trust Property

(a) A trustee shall keep adequate records of the administration of the trust.

(b) A trustee shall keep trust property separate from the trustee's own property.

(c) Except as otherwise provided in subsection (d), a trustee shall cause the trust property to be designated so that the interest of the trust, to the extent feasible, appears in records maintained by a party other than a trustee or beneficiary.

(d) If the trustee maintains records clearly indicating the respective interests, a trustee may invest as a whole the property of two or more separate trusts.

§811. Enforcement and Defense of Claims

A trustee shall take reasonable steps to enforce claims of the trust and to defend claims against the trust.

§812. Collecting Trust Property

A trustee shall take reasonable steps to compel a former trustee or other person to deliver trust property to the trustee, and to redress a breach of trust known to the trustee to have been committed by a former trustee.

§813. Duty to Inform and Report

(a) A trustee shall keep the qualified beneficiaries of the trust reasonably informed about the administration of the trust and of the material facts necessary for them to protect their interests. Unless unreasonable under the circumstances, a trustee shall promptly respond to a beneficiary's request for information related to the administration of the trust.

(b) A trustee:

(1) upon request of a beneficiary, shall promptly furnish to the beneficiary a copy of the trust instrument;

(2) within 60 days after accepting a trusteeship, shall notify the qualified beneficiaries of the acceptance and of the trustee's name, address, and telephone number;

(3) within 60 days after the date the trustee acquires knowledge of the creation of an irrevocable trust, or the date the trustee acquires knowledge that a formerly revocable trust has become irrevocable, whether by the death of the settlor or otherwise, shall notify the qualified beneficiaries of the trust's existence, of the identity of the settlor or settlors, of the right to request a copy of the trust instrument, and of the right to a trustee's report as provided in subsection (c); and

(4) shall notify the qualified beneficiaries in advance of any change in the method or rate of the trustee's compensation.

(c) A trustee shall send to the distributees or permissible distributees of trust income or principal, and to other qualified or nonqualified beneficiaries who request it, at least annually and at the termination of the trust, a report of the trust property, liabilities, receipts, and disbursements, including the source and amount of the trustee's compensation, a listing of the trust assets and, if feasible, their respective market values. Upon a vacancy in a trusteeship, unless a cotrustee remains in office, a report must be sent to the qualified beneficiaries by the former trustee. A personal representative, [conservator], or [guardian] may send the qualified beneficiaries a report on behalf of a deceased or incapacitated trustee.

(d) A beneficiary may waive the right to a trustee's report or other information otherwise required to be furnished under this section. A beneficiary, with respect to future reports and other information, may withdraw a waiver previously given.

Comment

. . . The trustee is under a duty to communicate to a qualified beneficiary information about the administration of the trust that is reasonably necessary to enable the beneficiary to enforce the beneficiary's rights and to prevent or redress a breach of trust. See Restatement (Second) of Trusts Section 173 cmt. c (1959). Ordinarily, the trustee is not under a duty to furnish information to a beneficiary in the absence of a specific request for the information. See Restatement (Second) of Trusts Section 173 cmt. d (1959). Thus, the duty articulated in subsection (a) is ordinarily satisfied by providing the beneficiary with a copy of the annual report mandated by subsection (c). However, special circumstances may require that the trustee provide additional information. For example, if the trustee is dealing with the beneficiary on the trustee's own account, the trustee must communicate material facts relating to the transaction that the trustee knows or should know. See Restatement (Second) of Trusts Section 173 cmt. d (1959). Furthermore, to enable the beneficiaries to take action to protect their interests, the trustee may be required to provide advance notice of transactions involving real estate, closely-held business interests, and other assets that are difficult to value or to replace. See In re Green Charitable Trust, 431 N.W. 2d 492 (Mich. Ct. App. 1988); Allard v. Pacific National Bank, 663 P.2d 104 (Wash. 1983). The trustee is justified in not providing such advance disclosure if disclosure is forbidden by other law, as under federal securities laws, or if disclosure would be seriously detrimental to the interests of the beneficiaries, for example, when disclosure would cause the loss of the only serious buyer.

Subsection (a) provides a different standard if a beneficiary, whether qualified or not, makes a request for information. In that event, the trustee must promptly comply with the beneficiary's request unless unreasonable under the circumstances. Further supporting the principle that a beneficiary should be allowed to make an independent assessment of what information is relevant to protecting the beneficiary's interest, subsection (b)(1) requires the trustee on request to furnish a beneficiary with a complete copy of the trust instrument and not merely with those portions the trustee deems relevant to the beneficiary's interest. For a case reaching the same result, see Fletcher v. Fletcher, 480 S.E. 2d 488 (Va. Ct. App. 1997). Subsection (b)(1) is contrary to Section 7-303(b) of the Uniform Probate Code, which provides that "[u]pon reasonable request, the trustee shall provide the beneficiary with a copy of the terms of the trust which describe or affect his interest. . . ."

The drafters of this Code decided to leave open for further consideration by the courts the extent to which a trustee may claim attorney-client privilege against a beneficiary seeking discovery of attorney-client communications between the trustee and the trustee's attorney. The courts are split because of the important values that are in tension on this question. . . .

The Uniform Trust Code employs the term "report" instead of "accounting" in order to negate any inference that the report must be prepared in any particular format or with a high degree of formality. The reporting requirement might even be satisfied by providing the beneficiaries with copies of the trust's income tax returns and monthly brokerage account statements if the information on those returns and statements is complete and sufficiently clear. The key factor is not the format chosen but whether the report provides the beneficiaries with the information necessary to protect their interests. For model account forms, together with practical advice on how to prepare reports, see Robert Whitman, Fiduciary Accounting Guide (2d ed. 1998). . .

§814. Discretionary Powers; Tax Savings

(a) Notwithstanding the breadth of discretion granted to a trustee in the terms of the trust, including the use of such terms as "absolute", "sole", or "uncontrolled", the trustee shall exercise a discretionary power in good faith and in accordance with the terms and purposes of the trust and the interests of the beneficiaries.

(b) Subject to subsection (d), and unless the terms of the trust expressly indicate that a rule in this subsection does not apply:

(1) a person other than a settlor who is a beneficiary and trustee of a trust that confers on the trustee a power to make discretionary distributions to or for the trustee's personal benefit may exercise the power only in accordance with an ascertainable standard relating to the trustee's individual health, education, support, or maintenance within the meaning of Section 2041(b)(1)(A) or 2514(c)(1) of the Internal Revenue Code of 1986, as in effect on [the effective date of this [Code]] [, or as later amended]; and

(2) a trustee may not exercise a power to make discretionary distributions to satisfy a legal obligation of support that the trustee personally owes another person.

(c) A power whose exercise is limited or prohibited by subsection (b) may be exercised by a majority of the remaining trustees whose exercise of the power is not so limited or prohibited. If the power of all trustees is so limited or prohibited, the court may appoint a special fiduciary with authority to exercise the power.

(d) Subsection (b) does not apply to:

(1) a power held by the settlor's spouse who is the trustee of a trust for which a marital deduction, as defined in Section 2056(b)(5) or 2523(e) of the Internal Revenue Code of 1986, as in effect on [the effective date of this [Code]] [, or as later amended], was previously allowed;

(2) any trust during any period that the trust may be revoked or amended by its settlor; or

(3) a trust if contributions to the trust qualify for the annual exclusion under Section 2503(c) of the Internal Revenue Code of 1986, as in effect on [the effective date of this [Code]] [, or as later amended].

Comment

Despite the breadth of discretion purportedly granted by the wording of a trust, no grant of discretion to a trustee, whether with respect to management or distribution, is ever absolute. A grant of discretion establishes a range within which the trustee may act. The greater the grant of discretion, the broader the range. Pursuant to subsection (a), a trustee's action must always be in good faith, with regard to the purposes of the trust, and in accordance with the trustee's other duties, including the obligation to exercise reasonable skill, care, and caution. See Sections 801 (duty to administer trust) and 804 (duty to act with prudence). The standard stated in subsection (a) applies only to powers which are to be exercised in a fiduciary as opposed to a nonfiduciary capacity. Regarding the standards for exercising discretion and construing particular language of discretion, see Restatement (Third) of Trusts Section 50 (Tentative Draft No. 2, approved 1999); Restatement (Second) of Trusts Section 187 (1959). See also Edward C. Halbach, Jr., Problems of Discretion in Discretionary Trusts, 61 Colum. L. Rev. 1425 (1961). An abuse by the trustee of the discretion granted in the terms of the trust is a breach of trust that can result in surcharge. See Section 1001(b) (remedies for breach of trust).

Subsections (b) through (d) rewrite the terms of a trust that might otherwise result in adverse estate and gift tax consequences to a beneficiary-trustee. This Code does not generally address the subject of tax curative provisions. These are provisions that automatically rewrite the terms of trusts that might otherwise fail to qualify for probable intended tax benefits. . . .

§815. General Powers of Trustee

(a) A trustee, without authorization by the court, may exercise:

(1) powers conferred by the terms of the trust; or

(2) except as limited by the terms of the trust:

(A) all powers over the trust property which an unmarried competent owner has over individually owned property;

(B) any other powers appropriate to achieve the proper investment, management, and distribution of the trust property; and

(C) any other powers conferred by this [Code].

(b) The exercise of a power is subject to the fiduciary duties prescribed by this [article].

Comment

This section is intended to grant trustees the broadest possible powers, but to be exercised always in accordance with the duties of the trustee and any limitations stated in the terms of the trust. This broad authority is denoted by granting the trustee the powers of an unmarried competent owner of individually owned property, unlimited by restrictions that might be placed on it by marriage, disability, or cotenancy.

The powers conferred elsewhere in this Code that are subsumed under this section include all of the specific powers listed in Section 816 as well as other powers described elsewhere in this Code. See Sections 108(c) (transfer of principal place of administration), 414(a) (termination of uneconomic trust with value less than $50,000), 417 (combination and division of trusts), 703(e) (delegation to cotrustee), 802(h) (exception to duty of loyalty), 807 (delegation to agent of powers and duties), 810(d) (joint investments), and Article 9 (Uniform Prudent Investor Act). The powers conferred by this Code may be exercised without court approval. If court approval of the exercise of a power is desired, a petition for court approval should be filed.

A power differs from a duty. A duty imposes an obligation or a mandatory prohibition. A power, on the other hand, is a discretion, the exercise of which is not obligatory. The existence of a power, however created or granted, does not speak to the question of whether it is prudent under the circumstances to exercise the power.

§816. Specific Powers of Trustee

Without limiting the authority conferred by Section 815, a trustee may:

(1) collect trust property and accept or reject additions to the trust property from a settlor or any other person;

(2) acquire or sell property, for cash or on credit, at public or private sale;

(3) exchange, partition, or otherwise change the character of trust property;

(4) deposit trust money in an account in a regulated financial-service institution;

(5) borrow money, with or without security, and mortgage or pledge trust property for a period within or extending beyond the duration of the trust;

(6) with respect to an interest in a proprietorship, partnership, limited liability company, business trust, corporation, or other form of business or enterprise, continue the business or other enterprise

and take any action that may be taken by shareholders, members, or property owners, including merging, dissolving, or otherwise changing the form of business organization or contributing additional capital;

(7) with respect to stocks or other securities, exercise the rights of an absolute owner, including the right to:

(A) vote, or give proxies to vote, with or without power of substitution, or enter into or continue a voting trust agreement;

(B) hold a security in the name of a nominee or in other form without disclosure of the trust so that title may pass by delivery;

(C) pay calls, assessments, and other sums chargeable or accruing against the securities, and sell or exercise stock subscription or conversion rights; and

(D) deposit the securities with a depositary or other regulated financial-service institution;

(8) with respect to an interest in real property, construct, or make ordinary or extraordinary repairs to, alterations to, or improvements in, buildings or other structures, demolish improvements, raze existing or erect new party walls or buildings, subdivide or develop land, dedicate land to public use or grant public or private easements, and make or vacate plats and adjust boundaries;

(9) enter into a lease for any purpose as lessor or lessee, including a lease or other arrangement for exploration and removal of natural resources, with or without the option to purchase or renew, for a period within or extending beyond the duration of the trust;

(10) grant an option involving a sale, lease, or other disposition of trust property or acquire an option for the acquisition of property, including an option exercisable beyond the duration of the trust, and exercise an option so acquired;

(11) insure the property of the trust against damage or loss and insure the trustee, the trustee's agents, and beneficiaries against liability arising from the administration of the trust;

(12) abandon or decline to administer property of no value or of insufficient value to justify its collection or continued administration;

(13) with respect to possible liability for violation of environmental law:

(A) inspect or investigate property the trustee holds or has been asked to hold, or property owned or operated by an organization in which the trustee holds or has been asked to hold an interest, for the purpose of determining the application of environmental law with respect to the property;

(B) take action to prevent, abate, or otherwise remedy any actual or potential violation of any environmental law affecting property held directly or indirectly by the trustee, whether taken before or after the assertion of a claim or the initiation of governmental enforcement;

(C) decline to accept property into trust or disclaim any power with respect to property that is or may be burdened with liability for violation of environmental law;

(D) compromise claims against the trust which may be asserted for an alleged violation of environmental law; and

(E) pay the expense of any inspection, review, abatement, or remedial action to comply with environmental law;

(14) pay or contest any claim, settle a claim by or against the trust, and release, in whole or in part, a claim belonging to the trust;

(15) pay taxes, assessments, compensation of the trustee and of employees and agents of the trust, and other expenses incurred in the administration of the trust;

(16) exercise elections with respect to federal, state, and local taxes;

(17) select a mode of payment under any employee benefit or retirement plan, annuity, or life insurance payable to the trustee, exercise rights thereunder, including exercise of the right to indemnification for expenses and against liabilities, and take appropriate action to collect the proceeds;

(18) make loans out of trust property, including loans to a beneficiary on terms and conditions the trustee considers to be fair and reasonable under the circumstances, and the trustee has a lien on future distributions for repayment of those loans;

(19) pledge trust property to guarantee loans made by others to the beneficiary;

(20) appoint a trustee to act in another jurisdiction with respect to trust property located in the other jurisdiction, confer upon the appointed trustee all of the powers and duties of the appointing trustee, require that the appointed trustee furnish security, and remove any trustee so appointed;

(21) pay an amount distributable to a beneficiary who is under a legal disability or who the trustee reasonably believes is incapacitated, by paying it directly to the beneficiary or applying it for the beneficiary's benefit, or by:

(A) paying it to the beneficiary's [conservator] or, if the beneficiary does not have a [conservator], the beneficiary's [guardian];

(B) paying it to the beneficiary's custodian under [the Uniform Transfers to Minors Act] or custodial trustee under [the Uniform Custodial Trust Act], and, for that purpose, creating a custodianship or custodial trust;

(C) if the trustee does not know of a [conservator], [guardian], custodian, or custodial trustee, paying it to an adult relative or other person having legal or physical care or custody of the beneficiary, to be expended on the beneficiary's behalf; or

(D) managing it as a separate fund on the beneficiary's behalf, subject to the beneficiary's continuing right to withdraw the distribution;

(22) on distribution of trust property or the division or termination of a trust, make distributions in divided or undivided interests, allocate particular assets in proportionate or disproportionate shares, value the trust property for those purposes, and adjust for resulting differences in valuation;

(23) resolve a dispute concerning the interpretation of the trust or its administration by mediation, arbitration, or other procedure for alternative dispute resolution;

(24) prosecute or defend an action, claim, or judicial proceeding in any jurisdiction to protect trust property and the trustee in the performance of the trustee's duties;

(25) sign and deliver contracts and other instruments that are useful to achieve or facilitate the exercise of the trustee's powers; and

(26) on termination of the trust, exercise the powers appropriate to wind up the administration of the trust and distribute the trust property to the persons entitled to it.

§817. Distribution Upon Termination

(a) Upon termination or partial termination of a trust, the trustee may send to the beneficiaries a proposal for distribution. The right of any beneficiary to object to the proposed distribution terminates if the beneficiary does not notify the trustee of an objection within 30 days after the proposal was sent but only if the proposal informed the beneficiary of the right to object and of the time allowed for objection.

(b) Upon the occurrence of an event terminating or partially terminating a trust, the trustee shall proceed expeditiously to distribute the trust property to the persons entitled to it, subject to the right of the trustee to retain a reasonable reserve for the payment of debts, expenses, and taxes.

(c) A release by a beneficiary of a trustee from liability for breach of trust is invalid to the extent:

(1) it was induced by improper conduct of the trustee; or

(2) the beneficiary, at the time of the release, did not know of the beneficiary's rights or of the material facts relating to the breach.

ARTICLE 9

UNIFORM PRUDENT INVESTOR ACT

[The Uniform Prudent Investor Act is included as Part VI of this Code.]

General Comment

Because of the widespread adoption of the Uniform Prudent Investor Act, no effort has been made to disassemble and integrate the Uniform Prudent Investor Act into the Uniform Trust Code. States adopting the Uniform Trust Code that have previously enacted the Prudent Investor Act are encouraged to reenact their version of the Prudent Investor Act as Article 9 of the Uniform Trust Code. Reenacting the Uniform Prudent Investor Act as a unit will preserve uniformity with States that have enacted the Uniform Prudent Investor Act in free-standing form.

The Uniform Prudent Investor Act prescribes a series of duties relevant to the investment and management of trust property. The Uniform Trust Code, Article 8 contains duties and powers of a trustee relevant to the investment, administration, and distribution of trust property. There is therefore significant overlap between Article 8 and the Prudent Investor Act. Where the Uniform Prudent Investor Act and Uniform Trust Code are duplicative, enacting jurisdictions are encouraged to enact the Uniform Prudent Investor Act in this article but without the provisions already addressed in Article 8 of the Uniform Trust Code. The duplicative provisions of the Uniform Prudent Investor Act and Article 8 of this Code are as follows:

Prudent Investor Act Article 8
Special skills 2(f) 806
Loyalty 5 802
Impartiality 6 803
Investment costs 7 805
Delegation 9 807

Deleting these duplicative provisions leaves the following sections of the Uniform Prudent Investor Act for enactment in this article:

Section 1 Prudent Investor Rule
Section 2 (a)-(e) Standard of Care; Portfolio Strategy; Risk and
Return Objectives
Section 3 Diversification
Section 4 Duties at Inception of Trusteeship
Section 8 Reviewing Compliance
Section 10 Language Invoking Standard of [Act]

ARTICLE 10

LIABILITY OF TRUSTEES AND RIGHTS OF PERSONS DEALING WITH TRUSTEE

§1001. Remedies for Breach of Trust

(a) A violation by a trustee of a duty the trustee owes to a beneficiary is a breach of trust.

(b) To remedy a breach of trust that has occurred or may occur, the court may:

(1) compel the trustee to perform the trustee's duties;

(2) enjoin the trustee from committing a breach of trust;

(3) compel the trustee to redress a breach of trust by paying money, restoring property, or other means;

(4) order a trustee to account;

(5) appoint a special fiduciary to take possession of the trust property and administer the trust;

(6) suspend the trustee;

(7) remove the trustee as provided in Section 706;

(8) reduce or deny compensation to the trustee;

(9) subject to Section 1012, void an act of the trustee, impose a lien or a constructive trust on trust property, or trace trust property wrongfully disposed of and recover the property or its proceeds; or

(10) order any other appropriate relief.

§1002. Damages for Breach of Trust

(a) A trustee who commits a breach of trust is liable to the beneficiaries affected for the greater of:

(1) the amount required to restore the value of the trust property and trust distributions to what they would have been had the breach not occurred; or

(2) the profit the trustee made by reason of the breach.

(b) Except as otherwise provided in this subsection, if more than one trustee is liable to the beneficiaries for a breach of trust, a trustee is entitled to contribution from the other trustee or trustees. A trustee is not entitled to contribution if the trustee was substantially more at fault than another trustee or if the trustee committed the breach of trust in bad faith or with reckless indifference to the purposes of the trust or the interests of the beneficiaries. A trustee who received a benefit from the breach of trust is not entitled to contribution from another trustee to the extent of the benefit received.

Comment

Subsection (a) is based on Restatement (Third) of Trusts: Prudent Investor Rule Section 205 (1992). If a trustee commits a breach of trust, the beneficiaries may either affirm the transaction or, if a loss has occurred, hold the trustee liable for the amount necessary to compensate fully for the consequences of the breach. This may include recovery of lost income, capital gain, or appreciation that would have resulted from proper administration. Even if a loss has not occurred, the trustee may not benefit from the improper action and is accountable for any profit the trustee made by reason of the breach.

For extensive commentary on the determination of damages, traditionally known as trustee surcharge, with numerous specific applications, see Restatement (Third) of Trusts: Prudent Investor Rule Sections 205-213 (1992). For the use of benchmark portfolios to determine damages, see Restatement (Third) of Trusts: Prudent Investor Rule Reporter's Notes to Sections 205 and 208-211 (1992). On the authority of a court of equity to reduce or excuse damages for breach of trust, see Restatement (Second) of Trusts Section 205 cmt. g (1959). . . .

§1003. Damages in Absence of Breach

(a) A trustee is accountable to an affected beneficiary for any profit made by the trustee arising from the administration of the trust, even absent a breach of trust.

(b) Absent a breach of trust, a trustee is not liable to a beneficiary for a loss or depreciation in the value of trust property or for not having made a profit.

§1004. Attorney's Fees and Costs

In a judicial proceeding involving the administration of a trust, the court, as justice and equity may require, may award costs and expenses, including reasonable attorney's fees, to any party, to be paid by another party or from the trust that is the subject of the controversy.

§1005. Limitation of Action Against Trustee

(a) A beneficiary may not commence a proceeding against a trustee for breach of trust more than one year after the date the beneficiary or a representative of the beneficiary was sent a report that adequately disclosed the existence of a potential claim for breach of trust and informed the beneficiary of the time allowed for commencing a proceeding.

(b) A report adequately discloses the existence of a potential claim for breach of trust if it provides sufficient information so that the beneficiary or representative knows of the potential claim or should have inquired into its existence.

(c) If subsection (a) does not apply, a judicial proceeding by a beneficiary against a trustee for breach of trust must be commenced within five years after the first to occur of:

(1) the removal, resignation, or death of the trustee;

(2) the termination of the beneficiary's interest in the trust; or

(3) the termination of the trust.

§1006. Reliance on Trust Instrument

A trustee who acts in reasonable reliance on the terms of the trust as expressed in the trust instrument is not liable to a beneficiary for a breach of trust to the extent the breach resulted from the reliance.

Comment

It sometimes happens that the intended terms of the trust differ from the apparent meaning of the trust instrument. This can occur because the court, in determining the terms of the trust, is allowed to consider evidence extrinsic to the trust instrument. See Section 103(17) (definition of "terms of a trust"). Furthermore, if a trust is reformed on account of mistake of fact or law, as authorized by Section 415, provisions of a trust instrument can be deleted or contradicted and provisions not in the trust instrument may be added. The concept of the "terms of a trust," both as defined in this Code and as used in the doctrine of reformation, is intended to effectuate the principle that a trust should be administered and distributed in accordance with the settlor's intent. However, a trustee should also be able to administer a trust with some dispatch and without concern that a reasonable reliance on the terms of the trust instrument is misplaced. This section protects a trustee who so relies on a trust instrument but only to the extent the breach of trust resulted from such reliance. This section is similar to Section 1(b) of the Uniform Prudent Investor Act, which protects a trustee from liability to the extent that the trustee acted in reasonable reliance on the provisions of the trust. . . .

§1007. Event Affecting Administration or Distribution

If the happening of an event, including marriage, divorce, performance of educational requirements, or death, affects the administration or distribution of a trust, a trustee who has exercised reasonable care to ascertain the happening of the event is not liable for a loss resulting from the trustee's lack of knowledge.

§1008. Exculpation of Trustee

(a) A term of a trust relieving a trustee of liability for breach of trust is unenforceable to the extent that it:

(1) relieves the trustee of liability for breach of trust committed in bad faith or with reckless indifference to the purposes of the trust or the interests of the beneficiaries; or

(2) was inserted as the result of an abuse by the trustee of a fiduciary or confidential relationship to the settlor.

(b) An exculpatory term drafted or caused to be drafted by the trustee is invalid as an abuse of a fiduciary or confidential relationship unless the trustee proves that the exculpatory term is fair under the circumstances and that its existence and contents were adequately communicated to the settlor.

§1009. Beneficiary's Consent, Release, or Ratification

A trustee is not liable to a beneficiary for breach of trust if the beneficiary, consented to the conduct constituting the breach, released the trustee from liability for the breach, or ratified the transaction constituting the breach, unless:

(1) the consent, release, or ratification of the beneficiary was induced by improper conduct of the trustee; or

(2) at the time of the consent, release, or ratification, the beneficiary did not know of the beneficiary's rights or of the material facts relating to the breach.

§1010. Limitation on Personal Liability of Trustee

(a) Except as otherwise provided in the contract, a trustee is not personally liable on a contract properly entered into in the trustee's fiduciary capacity in the course of administering the trust if the trustee in the contract disclosed the fiduciary capacity.

(b) A trustee is personally liable for torts committed in the course of administering a trust, or for obligations arising from ownership or control of trust property, including liability for violation of environmental law, only if the trustee is personally at fault.

(c) A claim based on a contract entered into by a trustee in the trustee's fiduciary capacity, on an obligation arising from ownership or control of trust property, or on a tort committed in the course of administering a trust, may be asserted in a judicial proceeding against the trustee in the trustee's fiduciary capacity, whether or not the trustee is personally liable for the claim.

§1011. Interest as General Partner

(a) Except as otherwise provided in subsection (c) or unless personal liability is imposed in the contract, a trustee who holds an interest as a general partner in a general or limited partnership is not personally liable on a contract entered into by the partnership after the trust's acquisition of the interest if the fiduciary capacity was disclosed in the contract or in a statement previously filed pursuant to the [Uniform Partnership Act or Uniform Limited Partnership Act].

(b) Except as otherwise provided in subsection (c), a trustee who holds an interest as a general partner is not personally liable for torts committed by the partnership or for obligations arising from ownership or control of the interest unless the trustee is personally at fault.

(c) The immunity provided by this section does not apply if an interest in the partnership is held by the trustee in a capacity other than that of trustee or is held by the trustee's spouse or one or more of the trustee's descendants, siblings, or parents, or the spouse of any of them.

(d) If the trustee of a revocable trust holds an interest as a general partner, the settlor is personally liable for contracts and other obligations of the partnership as if the settlor were a general partner.]

§1012. Protection of Personal Dealing with Trustee

(a) A person other than a beneficiary who in good faith assists a trustee, or who in good faith and for value deals with a trustee, without knowledge that the trustee is exceeding or improperly exercising the trustee's powers is protected from liability as if the trustee properly exercised the power.

(b) A person other than a beneficiary who in good faith deals with a trustee is not required to inquire into the extent of the trustee's powers or the propriety of their exercise.

(c) A person who in good faith delivers assets to a trustee need not ensure their proper application.

(d) A person other than a beneficiary who in good faith assists a former trustee, or who in good faith and for value deals with a former trustee, without knowledge that the trusteeship has terminated is protected from liability as if the former trustee were still trustee.

(e) Comparable protective provisions of other laws relating to commercial transactions or transfer of securities by fiduciaries prevail over the protection provided by this section.

§1013. Certification of Trust

(a) Instead of furnishing a copy of the trust instrument to a person other than a beneficiary, the trustee may furnish to the person a certification of trust containing the following information:

(1) that the trust exists and the date the trust instrument was executed;

(2) the identity of the settlor;

(3) the identity and address of the currently acting trustee;

(4) the powers of the trustee;

(5) the revocability or irrevocability of the trust and the identity of any person holding a power to revoke the trust;

(6) the authority of cotrustees to sign or otherwise authenticate and whether all or less than all are required in order to exercise powers of the trustee;

(7) the trust's taxpayer identification number; and

(8) the manner of taking title to trust property.

(b) A certification of trust may be signed or otherwise authenticated by any trustee.

(c) A certification of trust must state that the trust has not been revoked, modified, or amended in any manner that would cause the representations contained in the certification of trust to be incorrect.

(d) A certification of trust need not contain the dispositive terms of a trust.

(e) A recipient of a certification of trust may require the trustee to furnish copies of those excerpts from the original trust instrument and later amendments which designate the trustee and confer upon the trustee the power to act in pending transaction.

(f) A person who acts in reliance upon a certification of trust without knowledge that the representations contained therein are incorrect is not liable to any person for so acting and may assume without inquiry the existence of the facts contained in the certification. Knowledge of the terms of the trust may not be inferred solely from the fact that a copy of all or part of the trust instrument is held by the person relying upon the certification.

(g) A person who in good faith enters into a transaction in reliance upon a certification of trust may enforce the transaction against the trust property as if the representations contained in the certification were correct.

(h) A person making a demand for the trust instrument in addition to a certification of trust or excerpts is liable for damages if the court determines that the person did not act in good faith in demanding the trust instrument.

(i) This section does not limit the right of a person to obtain a copy of the trust instrument in a judicial proceeding concerning the trust.

ARTICLE 11

MISCELLANEOUS PROVISIONS

§1101. Uniformity of Application and Construction

In applying and construing this Uniform Act, consideration must be given to the need to promote uniformity of the law with respect to its subject matter among States that enact it.

§1102. Electronic Records and Signatures

The provisions of this [Code] governing the legal effect, validity, or enforceability of electronic records or electronic signatures, and of contracts formed or performed with the use of such records or signatures, conform to the requirements of Section 102 of the Electronic Signatures in Global and National Commerce Act (15 U.S.C. Section 7002) and supersede, modify, and limit the requirements of the Electronic Signatures in Global and National Commerce Act.

§1103. Severability Clause

If any provision of this [Code] or its application to any person or circumstances is held invalid, the invalidity does not affect other provisions or application of this [Code] which can be given effect without the invalid provision or application, and to this end the provisions of this [Code] are severable.

§1104. Effective Date

This [Code] takes effect on ________________.

§1105. Repeals

The following Acts are repealed:

(1) Uniform Trustee Powers Act;

(2) Uniform Probate Code, Article VII;

(3) Uniform Trusts Act (1937); and

(4) Uniform Prudent Investor Act.

§1106. Application to Existing Relationships

(a) Except as otherwise provided in this [Code], on [the effective date of this [Code]]:

(1) this [Code] applies to all trusts created before, on, or after [its effective date];

(2) this [Code] applies to all judicial proceedings concerning trusts commenced on or after [its effective date];

(3) this [Code] applies to judicial proceedings concerning trusts commenced before [its effective date] unless the court finds that application of a particular provision of this [Code] would substantially interfere with the effective conduct of the judicial proceedings or prejudice the rights of the parties, in which case the particular provision of this [Code] does not apply and the superseded law applies;

(4) any rule of construction or presumption provided in this [Code] applies to trust instruments executed before [the effective date of the [Code]] unless there is a clear indication of a contrary intent in the terms of the trust; and

(5) an act done before [the effective date of the [Code]] is not affected by this [Code].

(b) If a right is acquired, extinguished, or barred upon the expiration of a prescribed period that has commenced to run under any other statute before [the effective date of the [Code]], that statute continues to apply to the right even if it has been repealed or superseded.

Glossary

This glossary gives definitions for key terms and concepts used in this Florida Probate Code and Related Provisions: Student Edition.

Abatement: The process by which the decedent's estate is reduced (after payment of creditors' claims and other debts) to provide for the payment of all the bequests under the will or to provide for the share of an omitted child or spouse. State statutes specify an order of abatement that sets forth the priority by which certain testamentary gifts will be reduced.

Accelerate (i.e., accelerate a remainder): A situation that results in a future interest becoming possessory. Common events that trigger acceleration of a remainder are disclaimer and the application of a slayer (or unworthy heir) statute.

Acknowledgment (of a will): A situation in which a testator confirms to witnesses that a document is his or her will or that the signature on the will is that of the testator. Many states do not require that the testator actually sign in the witnesses' presence but merely that the testator "acknowledge" his or her will or his or her signature. Acknowledgment generally arises if the testator has signed the will prior to the attestation by witnesses.

Active trust: A trust in which the trustee has affirmative duties to perform in managing the trust property for the benefit of the beneficiaries. An active trust may be distinguished from a passive trust in which the trustee's only responsibility is to hold title to the property. Because a passive trust is not a valid trust, the beneficiary is entitled to the property.

Acts of independent significance: A doctrine that permits a court to admit extrinsic evidence (i.e., evidence outside the will) in order to determine certain beneficiaries and certain property that passes under the testator's will. Reference to events of independent significance allows the testator to make testamentary dispositions based on the occurrence or nonoccurrence of specified acts or facts.

Ademption: A situation that arises when a specific gift that was the subject of an at-death transfer is not found in the transferor's estate at death, causing the testamentary gift to fail. If property is adeemed, the distributee's rights are extinguished, i.e., the distributee has no right to other estate property.

Ademption by extinction: A form of ademption that occurs if the subject of the testamentary gift was destroyed during the decedent's lifetime.

Ademption by satisfaction: A form of ademption that occurs if the decedent made an inter vivos gift of the property that was the subject of the testamentary bequest.

Administration: The process of collecting the decedent's assets, making an inventory and appraisal of the property, paying creditors' claims and other debts, and distributing the remaining property to the heirs or beneficiaries.

Administrator: The personal representative who administers the estate of a decedent who dies intestate (without a will); formerly the term "administratrix" referred to a female in this position but in modern usage, the term "administrator" refers to persons of either gender.

Administrator c.t.a.* (cum testamento annexo)*: The personal representative who administers an estate of a decedent who left a will that failed to name an executor or that named an executor who does not wish to serve, is incapacitated, or predeceased the decedent.

Administrator d.b.n.* (de bonis non)*: A successor personal representative, i.e., the personal representative who administers estate assets that are not administered, for example, if the appointed representative was not able to complete his or her administration.

Administrator pendente lite: A personal representative who is appointed while litigation is pending.

Adoption: A process which creates legal rights and responsibilities in the adoptive parent(s) and, generally, terminates legal rights and responsibilities in the biological parent(s).

Adult adoption: The process by which one adult adopts another adult; persons may be motivated to resort to adult adoption to create a legally recognized familial relationship for the establishment of inheritance rights and/or decisionmaking in the event of incapacity.

Advance directive: An instrument that conveys the individual's wishes for medical treatment upon incapacity; a "living will" is a form of advance directive.

Advancement: An inter vivos gift of real or personal property that anticipates the recipient's inheritance, i.e., is subtracted from the recipient's share of the decedent's estate.

Affinity: The presence of a relationship based upon marriage, distinguishable from *consanguinity*, which is a relationship based upon blood.

Alienage (inheritance laws based on): Laws that limit the right of a nonresident to inherit property; states increasingly are abolishing such limitations.

Ambiguity: An uncertainty in a testamentary document as to the meaning of a provision that often raises the issue of the admissibility of extrinsic evidence; an ambiguity may be "patent" (i.e., one that appears on the face of a will) or "latent" (one that becomes apparent in attempting to apply the will provision to a particular person or property).

Ambulatory: The characteristic of a testamentary document that enables it to be revised or revoked until the testator's death and that enables it to operate on all property owned by the testator at death.

American Law Institute (ALI): An organization of prominent judges, lawyers, and law professors that aims to promote clarification of the law and to improve its administration; also drafters of the *Restatements of the Law* and the *Principles of the Law of Family Dissolution*.

Ancestor: A person who is related to the decedent in an ascending line (such as a parent), compared to a descendant who is related to the decedent in a descending line (such as a child).

Ancillary administration: A probate proceeding in a jurisdiction where the decedent's property is located that is a jurisdiction other than the testator's domicile (the probate proceeding in the latter jurisdiction is termed *domiciliary administration*).

Animus revocandi: The requisite intent to revoke a will; a valid revocation requires the requisite intent and a legally sufficient act.

Annuity: A contract purchased by a party from an insurance company that obligates the company to make payments for a guaranteed interest rate to a beneficiary.

Ante-Mortem Probate: A method of proving the validity of a will prior to the death of the testator by having the testator physically present for observation and examination.

Antenuptial agreement: A contract (also called a *prenuptial* or *premarital* agreement) that is executed by prospective spouses and that determines the parties' property rights in the event of death or dissolution.

Anticontest clause: A testamentary provision that limits the beneficiary's ability to contest the will by causing a forfeiture of that beneficiary's interest.

Anti-lapse statute: A statute that provides, in the event that a devisee predeceases the testator, for a substitute taker (i.e., the issue of the predeceased devisee).

Appraisal (also appraisement): One of the primary tasks of a personal representative that involves a determination of the estate assets and their value; also the personal representative must file a document called an *inventory and appraisal*, i.e., a public record of all assets that are owned by the decedent as of the date of death and that are subject to probate administration.

Ascendants: Ancestors (also termed "lineal ascendants"); persons who are related to the intestate in an ascending line (such as the decedent's parents or grandparents).

Assignment of an expectancy: The transfer by a potential heir that assigns his or her expected interest in the decedent's estate to someone other than the intestate for consideration; an assignment of an expectancy is not binding on the assignor's issue. *See also* Release (of an expectancy).

Attest: To witness, as of a will.

Attestation: The procedure of signing a will by witnesses.

Attestation clause: A testamentary provision in which the witnesses recite the events of the will execution and other facts (e.g., the testator is of sound mind and not operating under duress); the presence of an attestation clause creates a presumption of due execution.

Attested will: A will that has been signed by witnesses (also referred to as a *formal* will or *formally executed will*), distinguished from a *holographic* will that requires no witnesses.

Attesting witnesses: The persons who witness a will; almost all states today require that a will be signed by two witnesses.

Augmented estate: The elective share of the surviving spouse (as conceptualized by the drafters of the Uniform Probate Code) that includes certain of the decedent's inter vivos nonprobate transfers in order to protect the surviving spouse from disinheritance (i.e., in such a case, the probate estate is "augmented" or increased by certain qualifying inter vivos transfers).

Bank account trust: A special type of savings account that functions as a form of will substitute, enabling the depositor to use the funds during his or her lifetime but to pay the balance to a designated beneficiary upon the death of the depositor, also called a *Totten trust, savings bank trust*, or *tentative trust.*

Beneficial interest: The property owned by a beneficiary of a trust.

Beneficiary: A person who inherits property by a will; also the person who has equitable title to a trust.

Bequeath: The historical term for the act of making a testamentary gift of personal property; modern usage interprets the term more broadly to include real and personal property.

Bequest: The historical term for a testamentary gift of personal property; modern usage interprets the term more broadly to include real and personal property.

Blockbuster will: A will that attempts to control the disposition of nonprobate assets (such as life insurance proceeds, joint tenancy property), i.e., a will that enables the testator to change the conditions and provisions of will substitutes through the use of testamentary instruments.

Bona fide purchaser rule: A doctrine that protects a person who has purchased property in good faith in cases in which the property has been transferred to him or her improperly.

Bond: An obligation to pay money upon the occurrence of some event.

Breach of trust: The performance of an unauthorized act by a fiduciary; a violation of a duty imposed by law or the trust provisions.

Cancellation: A method of revocation of a will by physical act, such as by writing the word "canceled" across the face of the will or by putting an X through a testamentary provision.

Canon law system for counting degrees of kinship: A method of determining degrees of consanguinity for those who qualify as next of kin of an intestate; the process involves counting the steps (generations) from the decedent to the nearest common ancestor and then down to the claimant. Instead of adding these two sums (as in the civil law system), the relevant degree of kinship involved in the calculation is the larger of the two lines of kinship. Specifically, the claimant with the smallest degree count takes the intestate estate. This method is also called the common law system for counting degrees of kinship.

Canons of Descent: Rules developed at common law that established the distributive pattern of real property; according to the Canons of Descent, only the eldest male inherited (termed *primogeniture*) and female children shared equally (as *coparceners*).

Cestui que trust: The historical term for a beneficiary of a trust (derived from Norman French).

Charitable trust: A trust for a charitable purpose, such as the relief of poverty, the advancement of education or religion, the promotion of health, etc.

Civil law system for counting degrees of kinship: A method of determining degrees of consanguinity for those who qualify as next of kin of an intestate; the process involves counting the steps from the decedent to the nearest common ancestor and then down to the claimant. (*Common ancestor* means the ancestor who is shared by the decedent and claimant.) The total is the total number of steps (a step is a generation).

Claflin doctrine: A rule for modification or termination of a trust (based on *Claflin v. Claflin*, 20 N.E. 454 (Mass. 1889)), which requires that all the beneficiaries have the requisite capacity, all consent, and also that the modification/termination will not defeat a material purpose of the trust.

Class gift: A disposition to a group of persons who share a common characteristic (such as "children," "nephews and nieces") in which each member of the class takes an equal share.

Closing of a class: A rule that applies to class gifts that determines the time within which a person must be born to be included in the class, i.e., after a class "closes," persons born after that date cannot share in the class gift.

Co-administrator: A person who serves as administrator with another administrator or administrators.

Codicil: A testamentary document that amends a will and must be executed with the requisite statutory formalities.

Co-executor: A person who serves as executor with another executor or executors.

Collateral relative: A person who is related to the decedent in neither an ascending nor descending line but who is related to the decedent *through* a common ancestor; for example, a sister or brother is related to the decedent through common parents whereas an aunt or uncle is related to the decedent through common grandparents.

Commingling: The mixing of assets of a fiduciary with his or her personal assets without properly identifying the assets; a violation of the duty to earmark or segregate is a breach of trust.

Common law: The body of law based on the English legal system as developed by judicial decisions.

Community property: A marital property regime based on a partnership model in which each spouse is the respective owner of an undivided half interest in all property that was acquired during the marriage.

Competent witness (to a will): A witness who is able to give testimony to establish the validity of a will.

Concurrent ownership: A form of joint ownership of property (i.e., joint tenancy, tenancy by the entireties, tenancy in common).

Conditional will: A will whose effectiveness is conditional upon an event, such as death from a particular cause; if the condition does not occur, then the will is not effective.

Confidential relationship: A personal relationship in which one person reposes considerable trust in another and depends on the latter's advice (including, but not limited to, a relationship such as attorney-client; priest-penitent, etc.); the existence of a confidential relationship may raise a presumption of undue influence in the execution of the will.

Conflict of laws: The determination of which state law will be applied by a court to resolve a dispute.

Consanguinity: The presence of a blood relationship between persons. Degrees of consanguinity determine the takers of an intestate's estate (*degrees* refers to the number of steps or generations between the decedent and the claimant). For example, the decedent's parents are related to the decedent in the first degree of consanguinity, and the decedent's grandparents are related to the decedent in the second degree of consanguinity.

Conscious presence test: The requirement that a witness must sign the will within the testator's hearing, knowledge, and understanding.

Conservator: A person appointed by a court to manage the estate of an incompetent. Note that in California, a person who is appointed to manage the property of a minor is referred to as a *guardian* rather than a conservator.

Construction: The process of assigning a legal consequence to a testamentary provision when the testator's intent cannot be ascertained; distinguished from *interpretation,* which is the process of determining the testator's intent, usually by reliance on the language of the will and/or extrinsic evidence.

Constructive trust: A trust created by operation of law (rather than by the express intent of a settlor); an equitable remedy imposed by a court to prevent unjust enrichment, i.e., to prevent a wrongdoer from enjoying an interest in property that was obtained by his or her wrongful act.

Contestant (of a will): A person who attempts to prove that a will is invalid; distinguished from a *proponent* of a will who advocates probate of a will and who attempts to prove that the will is validly executed.

Contingent remainder: A future interest that may not necessarily take effect; distinguished from vested remainder.

Contractual will: A will that is subject to a contract.

Corpus: The principal of a trust (also referred to as the trust *res*).

Co-trustee: A person who serves as a trustee with another trustee or trustees.

Court trust: A testamentary trust that is subject to the continuing jurisdiction of the probate court.

Creditor: A person to whom the decedent owes money or other obligation; the personal representative of the decedent must give notice to creditors notifying them of the death of the decedent and the opportunity to present their claims.

Curtesy: The husband's right at common law to his deceased wife's real property.

Custodian: A fiduciary who manages property for a minor under the Uniform Transfer to Minors Act.

Cy pres (regarding charitable trusts): The doctrine that permits modification of a charitable trust; derived from the Norman French term *si près*, meaning "as near."

Dead hand control: The decedent's post-mortem attempts, by way of testamentary restrictions, to control a beneficiary's enjoyment of the decedent's wealth.

Decedent: A person who is deceased.

Declaration of trust: A method of trust creation by means of a present "declaration" of the trust by the property owner.

Delusion. See *Insane delusion*.

Demonstrative gift: A testamentary gift, typically of money, that is payable from a particular source but if that source is insufficient, then the gift is payable from the general assets of the estate.

Dependent relative revocation: A doctrine that disregards the revocation of a will that was based on a mistaken belief.

Derangement: Mental aberration or delusion that affects testamentary capacity.

Descendant: A person who is related to the decedent in a descending line (such as a child), compared to an *ascendant* who is related to the decedent in an ascending line (such as a parent); another term for descendant is *issue*.

Descent: The historical term for succession to real property; distinguished from the succession to personal property by *distribution*.

Descent and distribution: At common law, the passage of real property to an intestate's heirs and the passage of personal property to the intestate's next of kin; modern law treats both types of property (real and personal) similarly.

Devise: The historical term for the testamentary disposition of real property; according to modern usage, the term refers to a testamentary disposition of both real and personal property.

Devisee: The historical term for a person who inherited real property under a will; in modern usage, the beneficiary of real or personal property.

Disclaimer: A recipient's refusal or renunciation of a gift or inheritance.

Discretionary trust: A trust in which the trustee has discretion to withhold payment of income and/or principal from the beneficiary.

Dispensing power: The authorization by which probate courts excuse harmless errors, i.e., disregard formal statutory requirements if the courts are satisfied that the testamentary document embodies the intent of the testator.

Dissolution: Modern term for divorce, i.e., the legal termination of marriage.

Distribution: The historical term for the succession to personal property; distinguished from the succession of real property by *descent*.

Doctrine of Worthier Title: A doctrine that converts a remainder or executory interest in the transferor's descendants to a reversion in the transferor.

Domicile: A legal concept that is required for the assertion of jurisdiction in such legal matters as marriage, divorce, custody, adoption, probate, etc.; the place where one intends to live permanently (distinguishable from "residence" where a person lives temporarily).

Domiciliary jurisdiction: A probate proceeding in the jurisdiction in which the decedent is domiciled at the date of death.

Donee: The recipient of a gift or power of appointment.

Donor: A person who gives a gift without receiving consideration.

Double inheritance provision: A statutory provision that prevents a person from taking two shares via intestate succession.

Dower: The provision for the widow at common law, consisting of her entitlement to a life estate in one-third of any real property of which the husband was seised during the marriage and that provided protection against the husband's inter vivos transfers and testamentary dispositions.

Dry trust: A trust (also called a *passive trust*) that confers no active duties on the trustee.

Duplicate wills: An executed duplicate original will.

Durable power: A power of attorney that remains effective upon the grantor's incompetency or disability; a mechanism to permit an agent to make health care decisions for an incompetent.

Duress: The use or threat of violence to the testator (or the testator's family) that induces the testator to execute or revoke a testamentary document.

Duty of loyalty: The trustee's duty of impartiality that prohibits the trustee from favoring his or her own interests, requiring that the trustee remain objective when dealing with the interests of the trust beneficiaries.

Duty to diversify: The trustee's duty to spread the trust property among different investments.

Duty to segregate and earmark: The duty of a trustee to separate trust property from the trustee's own property and to identify the assets of the trust as trust property rather than the trustee's property.

Earmark: The process of identifying the assets of a trust as trust property.

Election: A doctrine that permits a surviving spouse to refuse the decedent's testamentary scheme and to "elect" instead to take his or her statutorily specified share; also a doctrine that permits the surviving spouse to retain any of his or her property that was the subject of the decedent's testamentary gift to a third party.

Elective share: The share specified by statute that enables a surviving spouse to reject the decedent's testamentary plan in favor of a designated share of the decedent's estate; a modern doctrine that replaces the common law doctrines of dower and curtesy.

Equitable adoption: A judicially created equitable remedy that enables a child to inherit from a deceased parent's intestate estate in cases in which a foster parent or stepparent agreed to adopt the child but the adoption was never finalized; sometimes referred to as *virtual adoption.*

Equitable title: The beneficiary's interest in a trust; distinguished from the trustee's interest or legal title.

Equivocation: A description that accurately applies to more than one asset or person and that creates an ambiguity in the interpretation of a term in a will or trust.

ERISA: The acronym for the Employee Retirement Income Security Act, i.e., the federal law that governs retirement benefits.

Escheat: The process of distributing the decedent's assets to the state in cases in which the decedent does not have heirs that are statutorily specified as "next of kin."

Escrow: A deposit (of writing, money, or other property) by a grantor with a third party until the performance of a condition upon which the property is to be delivered to a grantee.

Exculpatory clause: An express provision in a trust instrument by which the settlor alters the usual rules regarding trust investments (e.g., expanding the types of permissible investments) or the applicable standard of care; such clauses will not excuse bad faith.

Executor: The personal representative of the estate of a testate decedent; formerly the term *executrix* referred to a female in this position but in modern usage, the term *executor* refers to persons of either gender.

Exempt personal property: The right of the surviving spouse and minor children to retain certain personal property free from the claims of the decedent's creditors.

Exoneration: The doctrine that provides that the beneficiary of encumbered specific gifts takes free from liens; at common law, exoneration was presumed; today many states and the UPC reverse the presumption and provide for exoneration only if required by the will.

Exordium: An introductory provision in a will that specifies the place of a testator's residence and generally includes an express revocation of all prior wills and codicils.

Expectancy: The interest that a potential heir anticipates receiving from a potential decedent.

Express trust: A trust that is created based on the expressed intent of a settlor distinguished from trusts created by operation of law (i.e., resulting or constructive trusts); express trusts may be either private express trusts or charitable trusts.

Extrinsic evidence: Evidence that is "extrinsic" or outside of (i.e., not on the face of) a testamentary document; rules govern the admissibility of extrinsic evidence to determine the intent of the testator.

Facts of independent significance. *See Independent significance.*

Family allowance: An allowance for the support of the surviving spouse and minor children (sometimes including adult dependent children) for a statutorily designated period of time.

Family consent statute: A statute that facilitates health care decisions in the absence of an advance directive by the ill or incompetent person.

Fertile octogenarian: The presumption that a person is able to have children as long as she or he is alive.

Fiduciary: A person who is entrusted with handling property for another person, such as a personal representative (executor, administrator), trustee, guardian, conservator.

Fiduciary relationship: The relationship that arises between parties requiring a high standard of care when one person places trust in another.

Forced share: The doctrine that enables a surviving spouse to take a certain portion of the decedent's estate if the decedent disinherits the spouse or fails to bequeath the survivor a minimum amount; also called the *elective share*.

Fraud: An intentional misrepresentation that is intended to induce reliance or a promise made without intent to perform.

Fraud in the execution (of a will): Fraud that deceives the testator as to the identity of the instrument or its contents; also called *fraud in the factum*.

Fraud in the inducement (of a will): Fraud that deceives the testator as to some fact that causes the testator to make a will (or will provision) contrary to what the testator would have done if the testator had known the truth.

Fraudulent conveyance: A transfer that is subject to attack by creditors.

Funded trust: An inter vivos trust that holds property which has been transferred to it; distinguished from an *unfunded trust*.

Future interest: An interest in property that does not envisage present possession or enjoyment but rather provides for future enjoyment; examples include a remainder, executory interest, reversion.

General power of appointment: A power regarding the disposition of property that is exercisable in favor of the decedent, the decedent's estate, or his or her creditors.

General devise: A testamentary gift that is payable out of the general estate rather than from particular assets.

Gift: A voluntary transfer, without consideration, that requires donative intent and delivery.

Gift causa mortis: A doctrine that pertains to contemplation-at-death transfers; applicable to a donor who is in fear of imminent death; similar to other gifts (in terms of the requisites of donative intent, delivery, and acceptance) but conditional and revocable.

Grantor: A person who creates an inter vivos trust (also termed a *settlor* or *trustor*).

Guardian: The representative of a minor and/or incompetent (depending on the jurisdiction); guardianship encompasses the dual roles of guardian of the person (a person who makes medical decisions, for example) and guardian of the estate (a person who makes financial decisions).

Guardian ad litem: The judicially appointed representative of a minor or an incompetent (not necessarily an attorney).

Half-blood: A person (such as a half-sister or half-brother) who shares only one common ancestor with the decedent. Most states, as well as the UPC, treat half-bloods as equivalent to relatives of the whole blood for inheritance purposes.

Heir: The historical term for a person who succeeds to the real property of a decedent who dies intestate; according to modern usage, a person who takes either real or personal property by intestate succession.

Holographic will: A handwritten will, valid in some jurisdictions.

Homestead exemption: The protection for the residence used by the decedent's family that exempts it from the claims of the decedent's creditors.

Honorary trust: A trust with no ascertainable human beneficiary in which the trustee has only a moral, but not legal, obligation (e.g., a trust for an animal or the care of a grave).

Hotchpot: The process of equalization by which advancements (inter vivos gifts) are charged against the recipient's ultimate share of the intestate estate.

Illegitimate child. See *Nonmarital child.*

Illusory trust: An invalid trust generally created by a testator to defeat the rights of the surviving spouse.

Incorporation by reference: A doctrine that applies when a testamentary instrument refers to an extrinsic writing in an effort to give the latter testamentary significance; requirements include: (1) the testator must have intended to incorporate the extrinsic writing into the will, (2) the extrinsic writing must be in existence when the testator executed the will, (3) the will must describe sufficiently the extrinsic writing, and (4) the writing must conform to the description in the will.

Independent significance (acts or facts of): A doctrine that allows the testator to make testamentary dispositions based on the occurrence of specified acts or facts that have significance other than to pass property at death (e.g., a bequest of $10,000 "to the person who is my housekeeper at my death").

Insane delusion: A testator must have mental capacity when making a will. The will will be invalid if the testator manifests mental derangement that leads to the disposition of the testator's property differently than had the testator been of sound mind. According to case law, an insane delusion is "the conception of a disordered mind which imagines facts to exist of which there is no evidence and the belief in which is adhered to against all evidence and argument to the contrary, and which cannot be accounted for on any reasonable hypothesis. One cannot be said to act under an insane delusion if his condition of mind results from a belief or inference, however irrational and unfounded, drawn from facts which are shown to exist." In re Nigro's Estate, 52 Cal. Rptr. 128 (Cal. Ct. App. 1966).

Insolvent (estate): An estate in which the liabilities exceed the assets.

Insurance trust: A trust created by a settlor to hold and manage the proceeds of life insurance.

Integration: The process of establishing which writings were intended by the testator to be part of his or her will; the doctrine requires that the testator intended the separate writings to be part of the will and that the separate writings must have been present at the time of execution.

Interested witness: A witness to a will who takes a pecuniary interest under the testator's will.

Interpretation: The process of ascertaining the intent of the parties from the instrument itself; distinguished from the process of *construction* which assigns a legal consequence to the words used by the testator unless extrinsic evidence shows a contrary intention.

In terrorem: A testamentary provision that disinherits any beneficiary who contests a will in an attempt to deter a contest, also sometimes termed an *anticontest clause.*

Inter vivos trust: A trust that is established during the settlor's lifetime as distinguished from a testamentary trust created by a will; also termed a *living trust*.

Intestacy: The state of dying without a will.

Intestate: A decedent who dies without a valid will.

Intestate succession: The manner of distributing a decedent's property if he or she dies without a will.

Inventory and appraisement: A document filed with the court that includes an inventory or list of estate assets and also that determines the value of the assets in the estate.

In vitro fertilization: The process by which an egg from a donor is fertilized and implanted into a woman who will bear the child.

Irrevocable trust: A trust in which the settlor permanently cedes control of the trust property.

Issue: Descendants, including children, grandchildren, and others (of all degrees) in the descending linc.

Joint tenancy: A form of concurrent ownership of a nonprobate asset by which each owner enjoys an undivided interest in the property, generally including the feature of a right of survivorship such that the surviving joint tenant(s) succeeds to ownership of the property.

Joint will: A single document that is the will of two or more persons and which is probated on the death of each of the testators.

Lapse: The failure of a testamentary gift to a beneficiary who predeceases the testator; at common law, a lapsed gift was a testamentary gift that fails because the devisee predeceased the testator by dying after execution of the will but before the death of the testator as distinguished from a *void gift* that fails because the devisee predeceased the testator by dying before execution of the will; in modern usage, both situations qualify as *lapse*.

Latent ambiguity: An ambiguity that is apparent in attempting to apply the will provision(s) to a particular person or property, distinguished from a *patent ambiguity* that is apparent on the face of the will. Under the traditional rule, courts admit extrinsic evidence to resolve a latent ambiguity but not a patent ambiguity.

Legacy: A testamentary gift of personal property, usually a sum of money.

Legatee: The historical term for a person who inherits personal property under a will.

Letters of administration: The document that authorizes a personal representative (an administrator) to administer an intestate estate.

Letters testamentary: The document that authorizes a personal representative (an executor) to administer a testate estate.

Life insurance: A contract (and nonprobate asset) in which a policy owner (the insured) pays premiums to an insurance company (the insurer) that agrees to pay a death benefit (proceeds) to a beneficiary upon the death of the insured.

Lineal: An ancestor or descendant who is related to the decedent by consanguinity (and today includes adoptees).

Living trust: Another term for an inter vivos trust.

Living will: A document that includes written instructions regarding health care (i.e., end-of-life decisions) in the event of an individual's becoming incapacitated.

Lost or destroyed will statute: A statute that provides for the probate of a will that is lost or cannot be found at the death of the testator.

Loyalty. See *Duty of loyalty*.

Marital property: Property that is acquired by a husband and wife during the marriage.

Merger: The combination of legal and equitable title that results in termination of the trust.

Mistake in the execution (of a will): A mistake regarding the identity or contents of an instrument that prevents the testator from having the requisite testamentary intent; also called *mistake in the factum*.

Mistake in the inducement (of a will): A mistake that leads the testator to make a will based on some erroneous fact.

Mistake in the revocation (of a will). *See Dependent relative revocation.*

Model Code of Professional Responsibility: The rules (together with the Model Rules of Professional Conduct) promulgated by the American Bar Association that govern the conduct of lawyers.

Model Probate Code (MPC): Model legislation that preceded the Uniform Probate Code.

Model Rules of Professional Conduct: The rules (together with the Model Code of Professional Responsibility) promulgated by the American Bar Association that govern the conduct of lawyers.

Mortmain restriction: A limitation on a testamentary gift to charity that requires the testator (for the gift to be valid) to survive by a certain period of time after executing the will.

Mutual wills: Separate testamentary documents executed by two persons (usually husband and wife) that contain reciprocal or mirror provisions, sometimes referred to as *reciprocal wills.*

Negative beneficiary: A beneficiary who has been disinherited by the decedent's will.

Negative will: A will or will provision that states the testator's intention to disinherit a potential heir.

Next of kin: The persons who take the estate of a decedent who dies intestate.

No contest provision: A provision in a will providing that a beneficiary who contests the will will lose some or all of the benefits under the will; also called an *in terrorem* or *forfeiture clause.*

Nonclaim statute: A statute that provides for the filing of claims of the creditors of a decedent; creditors must file within a statutorily designated period or be forever barred.

Noncourt trust: A trust (such as an inter vivos trust) that is not subject to the continuing jurisdiction of a court but must be brought to the court's attention, distinguished from a court trust (such as a testamentary trust) that is subject to the continuing jurisdiction of a probate court.

Nongeneral power of appointment: A power of appointment regarding the disposition of property that may not be exercised in favor of the powerholder, the powerholder's estate, or powerholder's creditors, as distinguished from a general power of appointment that may be exercised in favor of the foregoing persons; also termed a *limited* or *special power of appointment.*

Nonmarital child: The modern term for a child who is born out of wedlock, formerly termed an illegitimate child.

Nonprobate asset: An asset that passes outside of the decedent's estate (i.e., other than by intestate or testate succession); examples include joint tenancies with rights of survivorship, life insurance, retirement plans, payable-on-death accounts, etc.

Nonresident alien: A person who is not a citizen or resident of the United States.

Nuncupative: An oral will that is declared by a testator during a last illness, before witnesses, and later reduced to writing by a person who was present at the declaration.

Oral trust: A trust that is established by parol (instead of by a writing); oral trusts of real property violate the Statute of Frauds.

Orphan's court: A court with probate jurisdiction in some states (e.g., Pennsylvania).

Parentelic: A system of determining inheritance rights of the next of kin of an intestate that dispenses with counting degrees of kinship and, instead, distributes the estate to the grandparents and their descendants (and if none, to the great-grandparents and their descendants).

Partial intestacy: The situation that arises when a decedent fails to dispose of the entire estate by a valid testamentary instrument; the remainder of the decedent's property passes intestate.

Partial revocation: The testator's revocation of only part of his or her will; the doctrine is not recognized by all jurisdictions (in which case, the will is still effective).

Partition: A judicial proceeding that separates the interests of co-owners of property.

Passive trust: A trust in which the trustee has no active duties and therefore is invalid, also termed a *dry trust.*

Patent ambiguity: An ambiguity that is apparent on the face of the document, as distinguished from a *latent ambiguity* which is only apparent in attempting to apply the will provision(s) to a particular person or property. Under the traditional rule, courts admit extrinsic evidence to resolve a latent ambiguity but not a patent ambiguity.

Payable-on-death (POD) account: An account that is created by means of a contract between the depositor and the financial institution; the balance of which passes outside of probate; also one of the forms of multiple-party accounts.

Pendente lite: During the litigation.

Per capita (distribution): A method of distribution that divides the estate in equal shares among persons who are equally related to the decedent; the applicable method if all of the decedent's children survive the decedent.

Per capita at each generation: The method of estate distribution (followed by the new Uniform Probate Code) of an intestate decedent by representation among descendants in which the division of the estate starts *per capita with representation* (the first division of the estate is at the generation with any living takers); the property is distributed into as many equal shares as there are living members of that generation and deceased members who leave issue then living; however, the shares of deceased members who leave issue then living are combined and then distributed among persons per capita at the next generation among descendants who are either alive or left issue living (and the process repeats until the estate is distributed).

Per capita with representation: The method of distribution of an intestate estate among descendants in which the first division of the estate is at the generation with any living descendants; the property then is divided into as many equal shares as there are living members of that generation and deceased members of that generation who leave issue then living; the share of each deceased member of that generation who leaves issue then living is then divided in the same manner among his or her then living issue.

Personal property set-aside: The personal property of a decedent that is specified by statute and that passes by law to the decedent's surviving spouse and/or children.

Personal representative: The fiduciary who is either an executor or administrator and who performs the tasks of probate administration.

Per stirpes: Literally, by root or stocks; a method of distribution of an intestate estate by representation among descendants, in which a descendant takes the share of his or her predeceased ancestor (the particular version depends on the jurisdiction).

Plain-meaning rule: The doctrine that provides that terms should be given their literal meaning.

Posthumous heir: An heir who was conceived while the intestate was alive but born after the intestate's death. At common law and according to the Uniform Probate Code, posthumous heirs inherit as if they had been born during the decedent's lifetime.

Postnuptial agreement: A contract that is executed by the spouses during the marriage (in contrast to an *antenuptial agreement* that is executed by prospective spouses) that determines the parties' property rights in the event of death or dissolution.

Pour-over will (or will provision): A provision in a will that makes a gift of probate assets to an existing inter vivos trust. Use of this common estate planning measure enables a testator to devise property to a trust even though the trust has been altered subsequently after the execution of the will.

Pour-over trust: The inter vivos trust that receives the probate assets from a pour-over will.

Power: The authority that is conferred (by an instrument or implied by law) on a fiduciary to act.

Power of appointment: The authority conferred upon a person (termed a *donee*) to direct the passage of property; powers may be exercised by will or inter vivos.

Power of attorney: The authority that is conferred by one person (termed a *principal*) upon another person (termed an *attorney in fact*) to perform an act for the principal (who is not necessarily an attorney); a form of agency relationship.

Powerholder: The holder of a power of appointment, also termed the *donee of a power of appointment.*

Precatory language: Directions in an instrument that merely request that an act be performed but that do not impose any legal obligation.

Predeceased: A person who dies before another person (i.e., before the decedent).

Prenuptial agreement. *See Antenuptial agreement.*

Pretermitted heir: A child or other heir who has been unintentionally omitted from the decedent's will.

Pretermitted heir statute: A statute that protects those persons (generally, children) who have been unintentionally omitted from a decedent's will (e.g., a child who was born after the testator executed the will).

Primogeniture: The English rule by which the eldest male descendant inherited real property; abolished by Parliament in the Administration of Estates Act in 1925.

Probate: The process of proving the validity of a will and administering an estate (testate or intestate); also the appropriate court that undertakes these tasks.

Probate asset: An asset that passes by intestate or testate succession.

Probate avoidance: The process of avoiding probate (with its cost and delay) by the use of will substitutes and nonprobate property.

Probate estate: The estate that is subject to administration by a court.

Probate homestead: The real property of a decedent that is selected by a court and set aside for the protection of the surviving spouse and children from attachment by creditors.

Proponent (of a will): A person who is in favor of probating a will and who attempts to prove that the will is validly executed; distinguished from a *contestant* of a will who attempts to prove that the will is invalid.

Pro rata: Proportionately, as in the term *pro rata abatement* in which all the shares of the beneficiaries in a given class are reduced equally.

Proxy: A third party who executes a will (by signing in the testator's presence and at the testator's direction) or revokes a will on behalf of a testator who generally is unable to perform the act.

Prudent person doctrine: Rules that specify a fiduciary's standard of care.

Publication: A statement by a testator to witnesses that a given document is his or her will.

Purchase money resulting trust: A trust created by operation of law that arises when one person purchases property that is titled in the name of another; the titleholder is presumed to hold the property on resulting trust.

Putative spouse: A person who, although not legally married, is treated as a legal spouse for some purposes (i.e., intestate succession) provided that the person has a good faith belief in the validity of the marriage (such as cases in which the partner has not been validly divorced from a former spouse).

Quasi-community property: Property that is treated (i.e., on dissolution or death) as if it were community property because it was acquired by the domiciliary of a community property state while that person was living in a separate property state (i.e., before moving to the community property jurisdiction).

Reciprocity statute: A statute governing the right of a nonresident heir to inherit property from the decedent, providing that the heir may inherit if the law of his or her domicile permits a citizen of our country to inherit from the decedent.

Reformation: The remedial process of correcting a written instrument to conform to the maker's intention.

Release (of an expectancy): The process by which a potential heir releases a potential interest in the decedent's estate to the decedent (prior to the decedent's death) and that enables the heir to receive an early distribution of the owner's property.

Remainder: A type of future interest; a *vested remainder* gives the donee the right to obtain possession of property upon the termination of the preceding estate; a *contingent remainder* permits a donee to obtain possession of the property only if a certain condition (the condition precedent) is satisfied.

Renunciation: The process of declining a testamentary gift or a share of an intestate's estate (also termed *disclaimer*).

Republication: The process of validating an invalid will.

Republication by codicil: A doctrine that updates a will by means of a subsequent codicil; the valid codicil republishes the will (i.e., enabling the will to "speak again" as of the date of the codicil).

Res: The corpus or principal of a trust.

Residuary disposition (residue): A gift of the property that remains in the estate after the payment of debts and the distribution of devises.

Restatements of the Law: Works produced by the American Law Institute that explain current law of a given subject matter.

Resulting trust: A trust created by operation of law that is implied from the circumstances to carry out the parties' intentions; such a trust arises when an express trust fails or provides an incomplete disposition of the trust property, or in the situation of a purchase money resulting trust. *See Purchase money resulting trust.*

Revival: The doctrine that applies upon the revocation of a revoking instrument in order to bring to testamentary life ("revive") a prior will.

Revocable trust: A trust created by a settlor in which the settlor retains the power to revoke and modify the trust.

Revocation (of a will) by operation of law: The revocation of a will when certain circumstances (e.g., divorce) have changed such that it is presumed that the testator would have wished his or her will (or some of its provisions) to be revoked.

Revocation (of a will) by physical act: The revocation of a will by a legally designated method, such as cancellation, obliteration, burning, tearing, or other means of destruction.

Revocation (of a will) by subsequent instrument: The revocation of a prior will (expressly or impliedly) by a subsequent testamentary document.

Right of representation: The heirs take "by right of representation" when they take the share that a predeceased relative would have taken had the aforementioned relative survived.

Rule Against Perpetuities: The statutory formulation that restricts dead hand control involving property; the relevant time period within which an interest must vest depends on the jurisdiction.

Satisfaction: The failure of a testamentary gift because the testator has transferred the property to the beneficiary after the execution of the will and prior to the decedent's death; a doctrine that is analogous to the concept of *advancement* applicable in intestate succession. See also *Ademption by satisfaction.*

Savings bank trust. See *Totten trust.*

Secret trust: A will that makes an absolute gift (i.e., is silent about the existence of a trust) but extrinsic evidence reveals that the beneficiary of the gift was supposed to hold that property in trust for the person indicated by the testator; in such a situation, the court may impose a constructive trust for the person indicated.

Self-proving will: A witnessed will that includes a notarized affidavit in which the testator and witnesses affirm under oath that all the statutory requirements have been fulfilled; a self-proved will facilitates probate by enabling the will to be admitted without the necessity of testimony by subscribing witnesses.

Semi-secret trust: A will that contains a gift in trust but without designation of the terms of the trust; in such a situation, most courts hold that the trust fails and that the property should be distributed via resulting trust.

Settlor: The person who creates a trust, also termed a *trustor* or *grantor*.

Severance: The method by which a joint tenancy is terminated and converted into a tenancy in common.

Simultaneous death statute: Legislation that provides for the distribution of estates when the decedent and the beneficiary both die in the same accident or disaster.

Slayer disqualification: State statutes that prohibit a murderer from inheriting property of the victim.

Soldier's and sailor's will: Wills that are permitted by some states for military personnel and mariners and that dispense with some of the formal requirements (e.g., writing, attestation).

Solemn form probate: Probate administration that is commenced after giving notice to interested persons, also termed *formal probate*; distinguished from common form (or informal) probate that permits probate without the need for notice to interested persons and that begins with an ex parte proceeding.

Specific devise: A gift of a particular item of personal property or parcel of real property.

Spendthrift trust (or clause): A trust (or trust provision) that protects the beneficiary from the claims of creditors by restraining the beneficiary's ability to transfer (voluntarily or involuntarily) the trust property.

Statute of Charitable Uses: Legislation (enacted by Parliament in 1601) that included a list of recognized charitable purposes in its Preamble and also provided a method of enforcement of charitable trusts.

Statute of Distribution: Legislation (enacted by Parliament in 1670) that established the distributive pattern of intestate succession for personal property.

Statute of Frauds: Legislation (enacted by Parliament in 1677) that required a writing for transfers of real property, including testamentary dispositions of real property, and also imposed requirements on testamentary disposition of personal property (but not a writing).

Statute of Uses: Legislation (enacted by Parliament in 1535) that "executed" uses, i.e., transformed equitable estates into legal estates.

Statute of Wills: Legislation (enacted by Parliament in 1540) that created the power to devise real property that was owned by the testator at the time the will was executed.

Statutory fees: Fees that are specified by statute to be paid to a personal representative and attorney for an estate.

Statutory will: A fill-in-the-blank will form that is authorized by state statute.

Stepparent relationship: A relationship that arises when a child's biological parent remarries; generally, only a stepchild who is *adopted* by the new spouse may inherit from or through the stepparent.

Stranger-to-the-adoption rule: A doctrine that treats adopted children as biological children for intestate succession regarding the estates of only their adoptive parent(s) but not that of the estate of any other person who was a nonparty to the adoption (hence, a "stranger to the adoption").

Subscribing witness: A person who signs his or her name to a will to attest to its validity.

Subscription: The requirement that the signatures of witnesses to a will must be located at the end of the document.

Substantial compliance: A doctrine advocated by Professor John Langbein in an influential law review article in 1975, in which he proposed liberalization of the formal requirements for will execution by means of the application of the contract doctrine of substantial compliance to the law of wills; according to this doctrine, fatally defective wills should still be admitted to probate if the will proponent could prove that the functions of the will formalities were satisfied.

Supernumerary: An additional, nonessential, attesting witness; the presence of a supernumerary witness may serve to validate a will in cases in which an essential witness takes a pecuniary benefit under the will.

Super-will. See *Blockbuster will.*

Support trust: A trust containing a provision that restricts the use of trust income, principal, or both to the beneficiary's support (i.e., food, clothing, medical care, and educational expenses).

Surcharge: A remedy to redress a breach of trust by holding the fiduciary personally liable for any resulting loss.

Surplusage approach: The view that permits the probate of a holographic will by disregarding "surplusage," i.e., certain nonessential nonholographic material.

Surrogate's court: The court having probate jurisdiction in some jurisdictions (e.g., New York).

Tentative trust. *See Totten trust.*

Testament: The historical term, derived from Latin, for a will.

Testamentary trust: A trust that is created by the decedent's will, distinguished from an *inter vivos trust* that is created by the settlor during the settlor's lifetime.

Testate succession: The manner of distributing a decedent's property if she or he dies with a will.

Testator: A person who has died, leaving a will. Formerly, a man was termed a *testator,* whereas a woman was termed a *testatrix.* Modern usage refers to persons of either gender as a testator.

Totten trust: A savings account trust (in the form of "X, in trust for Y"), derived from the case of In re Totten (71 N.E. 748 (N.Y. 1904)), in which a surviving beneficiary (or beneficiaries) succeed to the balance in the account upon the death of the depositor; also known as a *tentative trust.*

Tracing: A procedure that permits a trust beneficiary to recover the misappropriated trust property (or its proceeds) from the trustee or a third party unless the property is in the hands of a bona fide purchaser.

Trust: A relationship regarding property in which a person or persons (a trustee or trustees) hold(s) legal title to the trust property and is subject to a fiduciary obligation to manage it on behalf of a beneficiary (or beneficiaries) who hold(s) equitable title.

Trust corpus: The trust property, sometimes termed the *trust res* or *principal* of a trust.

Trustee: The fiduciary who holds legal title to the trust property and administers the trust.

Trustor: The creator of a trust, also called a *settlor* or *grantor.*

Trust res: The trust property, sometimes referred to as the *trust corpus* or *principal* of a trust.

Undue influence: Grounds for invalidating a will when the document is the result of an action that subverts the will of the testator and replaces the will of the testator with that of the person exerting the unfair persuasion.

Unfunded trust. See *Funded trust.*

Universal succession: The manner in which heirs to an intestate estate assume all liabilities for the decedent's taxes, debts, creditor's claims, and distributions to other heirs entitled to property.

Unworthy heir statutes: State statutes that preclude certain "unworthy" persons from inheriting by intestate succession.

Use: The precursor of the modern trust; method of property ownership in which a property owner would convey property to another to hold "for the use" of a beneficiary.

Virtual adoption. See *Equitable adoption.*

Virtual representation: The doctrine by which unrepresented beneficiaries may be bound by a decision of those persons who have substantially identical interests.

Void gift: At common law, a testamentary gift that fails because the devisee predeceased the testator by dying before execution of the will, in contrast to a *lapsed gift* that fails because the devisee predeceased the testator by dying after execution of the will but before the death of the testator; in modern usage, both situations qualify as *lapse.*

Wait-and-see doctrine: An approach under the Rule of Perpetuities that measures the validity of interests not by what might happen, but what in fact actually occurs.

Ward: A person for whom a guardian has been appointed.

Waste: Acts that adversely affect the value of the (trust) property.

Will: A testamentary instrument.

Will contest: A proceeding that is brought by an individual (contestant) seeking to have a will declared invalid (e.g., on grounds of capacity, undue influence, or lack of due execution).

Will contract: An agreement to make or revoke a will, to devise certain property, or to die intestate, or not to contest a will.

Will substitute: A nonprobate form of transmission of property ownership that avoids the need for a will by means of a document that is not formally executed according to states' wills legislation; common will substitutes include inter vivos trusts, joint tenancies with the right of survivorship, and multiple-party accounts.

Wills Act: Legislation (enacted by Parliament in 1837) that prescribed the requirements for testamentary disposition of real and personal property.

Wills legislation: State statutes that prescribe the formalities for executing a will.

Worthier Title. See *Doctrine of Worthier Title.*

TABLE OF CASES

TABLE OF STATUTES

References are to page numbers in this work

INDEX

Abbreviations

FLA. BAR RULE	Florida Bar Rule
FLA. CONST.	Florida Constitution
FLA. PROBATE RULES	Florida Probate Rules
FLA. RULES CIV. PROC.	Florida Rules of Civil Proceedings
FLA. STAT.	Florida Statutes
IRC	Internal Revenue Code
TREAS. REG.	Treasury Regulations
UNIF. ANAT. GIFT ACT	Uniform Anatomical Gift Act
UNIF. ELECTRONIC TRANS. ACT	Uniform Electronic Transactions Act
UNIF. POWER OF ATTORNEY ACT	Uniform Power of Attorney Act
UNIF. PRINCIPLE & INCOME ACT	Uniform Principle and Income Act
UNIF. PRUDENT INVESTOR ACT	Uniform Prudent Investor Act
UNIF. PRUDENT MNGMT. OF FUNDS ACT	Uniform Prudent Management of Institutional Funds Act
UNIF. TRUST CODE	Uniform Trust Code
UNIF. PROBATE CODE	Uniform Probate Code
US CODE	United States Code

References are to code sections, rules, and pages. Page references are in *italics*.

ABA MODEL RULES
conflicts of interest, *84–85*; FLA. BAR RULE 4–1.8, *85*

ABANDONED PROPERTY. *See* **ESCHEAT**

ABANDONMENT
of child, RESTATEMENT (THIRD) OF PROPERTY §2.5, *33*, *409*
of spouse, *33*

ABATEMENT, *341*
order of, *341*; FLA. STAT. §733.805, *343*
personal representative's payment from trust for insufficiency, FLA. STAT. §733.607, *343–344*
pretermitted child, *341*; FLA. STAT. §732.302, *342*
pretermitted spouse, *341*; FLA. STAT. §732.301, *342*
priority of administration expenses, FLA. STAT. §733.707, *344*
sources from which to satisfy spouse's elective share, *341*; FLA. STAT. §732.2075, *342–343*

ABUSE. *See also* **ADULT PROTECTIVE SERVICES ACT**
defined, FLA. STAT. §415.102, *356–357*
false reporting, FLA. STAT. §415.102, *357*
hotline, FLA. STAT. §415.103, *359*
unworthy heir statutes, *33–34*

ACKNOWLEDGMENT OF WILLS. *See* **WILLS**

ACTIVE TRUSTS, RESTATEMENT (THIRD) OF TRUSTS §6, *171*, *425*

ADEMPTION DOCTRINE, *339–340*; UNIF. PROBATE CODE §2–606, *544*
Ademption by Satisfaction, *35*, *341*; FLA. STAT. §732.609, *36*, *341*; UNIF. PROBATE CODE §2–609, *544*
exceptions, FLA. STAT. §732.606, *340*
securities, changes in, *340*; FLA. STAT. §732.605, *340*

ADMINISTRATION. *See also* **PERSONAL REPRESENTATIVES' POWERS AND DUTIES**
beneficiaries, determining, FLA. STAT. §733.105, *264–265*
contest of will, *278–279*
  adjudication before issuance of letters, FLA. STAT. §733.2123, *279*
  adversary proceedings, FLA. PROBATE RULES 5.025, *280–281*
  burden of proof, FLA. PROBATE RULES 5.275, *280*; FLA. STAT. §733.107, *279*
  effect of fraud, duress, mistake, and undue influence, FLA. STAT. §732.5165, *280–281*
  filing of objections, FLA. PROBATE RULES 5.240, *279*; FLA. STAT. §733.212, *280*
  penalty clause, FLA. STAT. §732.517, *279*
defined, *3*
establishment of death, FLA. PROBATE RULES 5.205, *275*; FLA. STAT. §731.103, *274*
filing of objections, FLA. PROBATE RULES 5.240, *269–270*; FLA. STAT. §733.212, *263*, *271*
jurisdiction, *6*; FLA. CONST. Art. 5, §§5(b), 20c, *7*; FLA. STAT. §26.012, *6*, *263*; FLA. STAT. §733.101, *7*
missing persons, FLA. STAT. §733.209, *275*

successor agents, *479*; UNIF. POWER OF ATTORNEY ACT §111, *483*
termination, *479*; UNIF. POWER OF ATTORNEY ACT §110, *482–483*
title, Unif. Power of Attorney Act §101, *480*
validity of power of attorney, *479*; UNIF. POWER OF ATTORNEY ACT §106, *482*
when power of attorney effective, *479*; UNIF. POWER OF ATTORNEY ACT §109, *482*
miscellaneous provisions
effect on existing power of attorney, UNIF. POWER OF ATTORNEY ACT §403, *498*
effective date, Unif. Power of Attorney Act §405, *498*
relation to Electronic Signatures in Global and National Commerce Act, UNIF. POWER OF ATTORNEY ACT §402, *498*
repeal, Unif. Power of Attorney, 404, *498*
uniformity of application and construction, UNIF. POWER OF ATTORNEY ACT §401, *498*
overview, 374, 479–480
statutory forms
agent's certification, UNIF. POWER OF ATTORNEY ACT §302, *497–498*
power of attorney, *480*; UNIF. POWER OF ATTORNEY ACT §301, *493–497*

UNIFORM PRINCIPAL AND INCOME ACT (1997, REV. 2000). *See also* **FLORIDA UNIFORM PRINCIPLE AND INCOME ACT (UPAIA)**
allocation of disbursements
adjustments for taxes, UNIF. PRINCIPAL & INCOME ACT §506, *519*
depreciation, transfers from income to principal for, UNIF. PRINCIPAL & INCOME ACT §503, *518*
from income, Unif. Principal & Income Act §501,*517*
income taxes, Unif. Principal & Income Act §505,*519*
from principal, UNIF. PRINCIPAL & INCOME ACT §502,*517–518*
reimbursements, transfers from income to principal, UNIF. PRINCIPAL & INCOME ACT §504,*518–519*
allocation of receipts
annuities and similar payments, UNIF. PRINCIPAL & INCOME ACT §409,*515*
asset-backed securities, UNIF. PRINCIPAL & INCOME ACT §415, *517*
business and other activities conducted by trustee, UNIF. PRINCIPAL & INCOME ACT §403,*514*
character of receipts, UNIF. PRINCIPAL & INCOME ACT §401, *513–514*
deferred compensation, UNIF. PRINCIPAL & INCOME ACT §409,*515*
derivatives and options, UNIF. PRINCIPAL & INCOME ACT §414,*516–517*
distribution from trust or estate, UNIF. PRINCIPAL & INCOME ACT §402, *514*
insubstantial allocations, UNIF. PRINCIPAL & INCOME ACT §408,*515*
insurance policies and similar contracts, UNIF. PRINCIPAL & INCOME ACT §407, *515*
liquidating asset, UNIF. PRINCIPAL & INCOME ACT §410,*515*
minerals, water, and other natural resources, UNIF. PRINCIPAL & INCOME ACT §411,*515–516*
obligation to pay money, UNIF. PRINCIPAL & INCOME ACT §406,*514–515*
principal receipts, UNIF. PRINCIPAL & INCOME ACT §404,*514*
property not productive of income, UNIF. PRINCIPAL & INCOME ACT §413,*516*
rental property, Unif. Principal & Income Act §405,*514*
timber, Unif. Principal & Income Act §412, *516*
application and construction, uniformity of, UNIF. PRINCIPAL & INCOME ACT §601,*519*
application to existing trusts and estates, provisions for, UNIF. PRINCIPAL & INCOME ACT §605,*520*
apportionment
when decedent dies or income interest begins, UNIF. PRINCIPAL & INCOME ACT §302,*513*
when income interest ends, UNIF. PRINCIPAL & INCOME ACT §303,*513*
when right to income begins and ends, UNIF. PRINCIPAL & INCOME ACT §301,*512–513*
decedent's estate
distribution to residuary and remainder beneficiaries, UNIF. PRINCIPAL & INCOME ACT §202,*512*
net income, determination and distribution of, UNIF. PRINCIPAL & INCOME ACT §201, *511–512*
definitions, UNIF. PRINCIPAL & INCOME ACT §102,*503*
effective date provision, UNIF. PRINCIPAL & INCOME ACT §604,*520*
fiduciary duties, UNIF. PRINCIPAL & INCOME ACT §103, *503–504*
general principles, UNIF. PRINCIPAL & INCOME ACT §103, *503–504*
purpose of revision, *501–502*
repeal provisions, UNIF. PRINCIPAL & INCOME ACT §603,*519*
revisions to, *502*
severability clause, UNIF. PRINCIPAL & INCOME ACT §602,*519*
taxes
adjustments for, Unif. Principal & Income Act §506, *519*
allocation, Unif. Principal & Income Act §505,*519*
title, UNIF. PRINCIPAL & INCOME ACT §101,*503*
trustees
discretionary power, judicial control of, UNIF. PRINCIPAL & INCOME ACT §105, *508–511*
power to adjust between principal and income, UNIF. PRINCIPAL & INCOME ACT §104, *504–508*
Uniform Prudent Investor Act, coordination with, *503*

UNIFORM PROBATE CODE (UPC)
abatement, 341
acknowledgment of wills, *79*
allowances and exemptions
applicable law, UNIF. PROBATE CODE §2–401, *536*
constitutional homestead, UNIF. PROBATE CODE §2–402A, *537*
exempt property, UNIF. PROBATE CODE §2–403, *537*